# Current Biography Yearbook 2013

H. W. Wilson

A Division of EBSCO Information Services

Ipswich, Massachusetts

**GREY HOUSE PUBLISHING**

SEVENTY-FOURTH ANNUAL CUMULATION—2013

International Standard Serial No. 0084-9499

International Standard Book No. 978-0-8242-1210-0

Library of Congress Catalog Card No. 40-27432

*Current Biography Yearbook*, 2013, published by Grey House Publishing, Inc., Amenia, NY, under exclusive license from EBSCO Information Services, Inc.

PRINTED IN THE UNITED STATES OF AMERICA

# CONTENTS

# LIST OF BIOGRAPHICAL SKETCHES

# LIST OF OBITUARIES

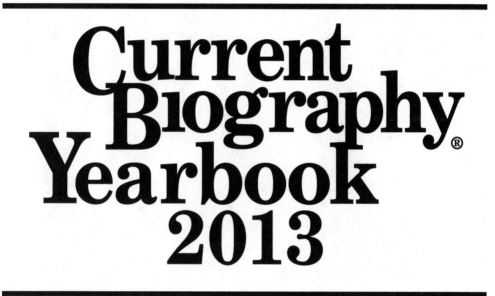

# Current Biography® Yearbook 2013

# Current Biography Yearbook 2013

## Lynsey Addario

**Born:** November 13, 1973
**Occupation:** Photojournalist

Photojournalist and war correspondent Lynsey Addario has dedicated her life to documenting the lives of both civilians and soldiers in some of the most dangerous regions of the world. Her coverage of humanitarian crises has taken her to over forty countries, including Afghanistan, Iraq, Libya, the Congo, the Darfur region of Sudan, Sierra Leone, India, and Haiti. In Afghanistan, Addario photographed both the Taliban and American sides of the conflict, as well as Afghani women fighting for the right to be educated. In the Democratic Republic of the Congo, she interviewed and photographed women who had been raped as a weapon of war. In Haiti, after the devastating January 2010 earthquake, she focused on orphans who had been given up by parents who could no longer care for them. These and other powerful photo essays, published mainly by the *New York Times*, *National Geographic*, and *TIME*, have earned Addario a MacArthur fellowship, the Pulitzer Prize, and numerous other honors.

Despite being held captive twice—for one day in Iraq in April 2004 and for six days in Libya in March 2011, during which she was sexually assaulted—Addario has not let these and other scares prevent her from continuing to do her job. "This is what I cover," she told Lauren Wolfe for the Committee to Protect Journalists (4 Apr. 2011). "I cover conflict."

### EARLY LIFE AND EDUCATION

Lynsey Addario was born to two hairdressers on November 13, 1973, in Norwalk, Connecticut. She was given her first camera at the age of thirteen and received darkroom training from a family friend during high school. After graduating from high school in 1991, Addario attended the University of Wisconsin at Madison, where she majored in international relations and Italian. During her junior year abroad in Italy, she began to photograph in earnest. Addario earned her bachelor's degree in 1995.

The following year, Addario moved to Buenos Aires, Argentina, with the intention of learning to speak Spanish. While there, she decided

Courtesy of the John D. & Catherine T. MacArthur Foundation

to try out photographing for a newspaper, even though she had no prior training in professional photography. After repeated requests to the *Buenos Aires Herald*, they gave her a job. "I basically pushed and pushed, till finally they got so annoyed with me, they gave me an opportunity," Addario told Abigail Pesta for *Marie Claire* (6 June 2011). That opportunity was to capture photographs of Madonna while she was filming *Evita* (1996); Addario succeeded by "talking my way on to the set," she told Pesta. After that, the *Herald* continued to give Addario assignments, and she learned how to be a photographer on the job. In addition, Addario decided to cover the effects of the Argentinean Dirty War, a period of military dictatorship from 1976 to 1983. Thus began her career as a photographer of human rights conflicts.

### FROM CUBA TO INDIA

Addario moved to New York in 1997, where she freelanced regularly for the Associated Press for three years under the guidance of a mentor.

When not freelancing, Addario worked on several international assignments that she gave to herself. Her main focus was Cuba. She first traveled to Havana in 1997 to document the influence of capitalism on younger Cubans, who had grown up under a Communist regime. She returned in 1998 for Pope John Paul II's visit to Cuba, and then went back each year through 2002 in order to fully document life under the rule of communism. "I've always been interested in the rest of the world," she told Pesta. "I'm incredibly focused. . . . I'm so driven that nothing else can stand in my way."

In January 2000, Addario decided that she could make it on her own as a freelance photographer and moved to New Delhi, India. During the eight months that she was based there, she photographed for the Associated Press as well as for such newspapers as the *Boston Globe*, the *Houston Chronicle*, and the *Christian Science Monitor*. In addition to news about India, Addario's projects covered Nepal, Pakistan, and Afghanistan under the rule of the Taliban. Most of her time was dedicated to covering the lives of women: women living under Taliban rule, female burn victims in Pakistan, and the lives of women along the Ganges River in India.

### VENTURING INTO AFGHANISTAN

A suggestion by Addario's landlord in New Delhi prompted her first trip to Afghanistan. He told her, "You really should try and make a trip to Afghanistan because that's where you're going to see women oppressed," Addario recalled to Joe Castaldo for *Canadian Business* (1 Mar. 2012). "When I read about women living under the Taliban, I really wanted to travel there and see for myself," Addario told Pesta. "Is it that bad? What is the situation?" Photography was illegal in Afghanistan at the time. Although Addario was scared that she might be stopped by the Taliban, she brought her camera there anyway.

Under the protection of the United Nations and a landmine organization for her first week in Afghanistan, in May of 2000, Addario was able to take photographs by sneaking around quickly. After that first week, she was partnered with a Taliban minder who followed her around. By Islamic law, he could not follow her into homes with women present, so she took advantage of this opportunity to document the lives of families living under Taliban rule.

During Addario's second trip to Afghanistan—she has been there many times—she got in trouble for breaking the photography ban. In Kabul, men from the Vice and Virtue Ministry, whose job was to stop people from committing illegal acts, saw her camera and demanded that she give them her film. "I managed to switch the film out and hide the roll that I had been using in my bra, and give them an empty roll," she told

Castaldo. "That was pretty scary, and I ended up moving right after that."

Mexico City was Addario's base of operations from April 2001 to January 2003, where she photographed mainly for the *New York Times*, covering human rights issues, immigration, and other social topics in Latin America. After the terrorist attacks of September 11, 2001, Addario spent a significant amount of time in South Asia so that she could cover the war in Afghanistan. Afghani women were her main focus, particularly their fight for education after the fall of the Taliban.

### WAR AND CAPTURE IN IRAQ

Addario's next move was to Istanbul, Turkey, in January 2003. She spent about seven months traveling in northern and central Iraq to cover the war for several magazines as well as for the *New York Times*. Addario's *Times* coverage continued into 2005.

On April 7, 2004, Addario and reporter Jeffrey Gettleman were driving outside of Baghdad when they were surrounded by Iraqi insurgents. The insurgents took their driver and translator. They then started to take Gettleman captive, and did not seem to know what to do with Addario. They were "confused by the sight of a woman dressed like a Muslim who didn't speak Arabic amidst the chaos," Addario wrote for *Digital Journalist* (May 2004). In an effort to help Gettleman, Addario "stood up, in full attire, and rubbed my index fingers together, symbolizing the union of a man and a woman, and said, 'that is my husband, I am not leaving him,'" she wrote. "Family ties are strong in the Arab world, and I figured the insurgents were less likely to kill a foreigner if he was with a woman, than alone."

Gettleman told the insurgents that they were journalists who wanted to document civilian deaths. After confirming Gettleman and Addario's press identification cards and viewing their photographs, the insurgents decided to let them go. Their capture lasted less than a day. "There were a few hours where it was unclear what our fate would be because our car had been surrounded by gunmen," Addario told Castaldo. "When I first called my father after, he said, 'Please come home.' And that's the first time he had said anything like that. I remember realizing at that point that it is a very selfish career. As selfless as it is to dedicate your life to trying to reveal these injustices and to document history, it is also selfish because you put your loved ones through a lot."

### DARFUR, SIERRA LEONE, AND THE CONGO

While covering the war in Iraq and after, Addario continued to pursue projects related to humanitarian crises. She photographed stories about Turkey, Lebanon, Libya, South Africa, and the Congo, among other places. To document the conflict in Darfur, she first traveled to the war-torn area in 2004, where she visited displaced civilians and rebel groups; burned-out, abandoned villages; and Sudanese refugee camps in Chad. She would cover Darfur for six years. Continuing her focus on women's issues, Addario compiled a project documenting the high rate of maternal mortality in Sierra Leone; the project, "Maternal Mortality in Sierra Leon: The Story of Mama," follows the story of one woman who died after giving birth to twins. "Maternal Mortality" was published in *TIME* magazine, along with an article by Alice Park, on June 14, 2010.

Addario began covering the conflict in the Democratic Republic of Congo in 2006. She returned in 2007 and then in 2008 with a grant from the Columbia College of Chicago to document how rape has been used as a weapon of war. Her photographs became part of a traveling exhibition called "Congo Women," which raises funds to help Congolese women receive surgery to repair physical damage caused by rape. "As a photojournalist, I felt there was very little I could do for the women in the DRC but record their stories, and hope there would be some way to change the pattern in the future through awareness," Addario wrote for the website *Women Under Siege* (7 Feb. 2012). "I was surprised by how many women agreed to speak openly about their traumatic experiences with the mere hope that it might help others avoid rape and seek treatment for physical injuries in the future."

## DOCUMENTING "TALIBANISTAN"
Addario's documentation of the lives of Afghani women, a photo essay titled "Veiled Rebellion," was published by *National Geographic* in December 2010. She covered both sides of the war in Afghanistan for *New York Times Magazine*: "Battle Company Is Out There" (24 Feb. 2008), written by Elizabeth Rubin, is an inside look at the lives of American soldiers; "Talibanistan," which accompanies Dexter Filkins's story "Right at the Edge" (5 Sept. 2008), follows members of the Taliban along the Afghani-Pakistani border. The story won Filkins and Addario a 2009 Pulitzer Prize for international reporting. Addario's photo essay on Iraq toward the end of the war, "Baghdad: After the Storm," created with journalist Brian Turner, was published in *National Geographic* in July 2011.

Given the Taliban's restrictions on women, Addario would not have been able to take some of her photographs for "Talibanistan" if she had not been with Filkins. He convinced a Taliban commander to allow a fully veiled Addario into a meeting by naming her his wife and stating that he did not want to leave her alone in a hotel. Eventually, Filkins was granted permission to have his "wife" take photographs. "I was terrified," Addario told Amy Bedik for *PopPhoto. com* (3 Feb. 2010). "There is a fine line when

photographing in these delicate, dangerous situations—I always try not to look too professional (it probably helped that I was shooting through my veil at this point!). I really calculate my shots and shoot sparingly."

## ORPHANS IN HAITI
Addario has also made children the focus of much of her work. "I try to do women's stories when I can," Addario wrote in a piece for the *Lens*, a New York Times blog (30 Mar. 2011). "But I don't want to be pigeonholed as just a women's photographer, because my interest is in covering the whole story—and human rights abuses and humanitarian issues." When the January 12, 2010, earthquake hit Haiti, Addario was living in India, but she traveled to Haiti in February. "I started thinking about how I could tell the story of what's happening in Haiti from a different perspective," she told James Estrin for the *Lens* (10 Mar. 2010). "And I realized that a lot of what I was seeing was from the outside. It was bodies, rubble, street scenes. I wasn't seeing full stories."

The story that Addario and *Times* correspondent Ginger Thompson found when they arrived in Haiti was that many parents were abandoning their children because they could no longer provide for them. Thompson wrote about the problems with orphanages in Haiti in a piece titled "Bleak Portrait of Haiti Orphanages Raises Fears" (6 Feb. 2010), which is accompanied by Addario's photographs. In a slideshow titled "Even Orphanages Spawn Orphans in Haiti," compiled by Estrin (10 Mar. 2010), Addario's photographs document the birth of a child at a relief camp. "I am looking for something different in each story," Addario told David McKay Wilson for *On Wisconsin*, the University of Wisconsin–Madison alumni magazine (June 2011), "but generally, I am trying to convey the reality on the ground, raw emotion, whatever elements make up the particular story I am shooting."

## CAPTURE IN LIBYA
In addition to being robbed and kidnapped in Iraq in 2004, Addario has had other scares during her travels. On May 9, 2009, she ended up in a car accident while traveling to Islamabad, the capital of Pakistan, after visiting a refugee camp. Addario broke her collarbone; the journalist with her, Teru Kuwayama for *Newsweek*, was also injured; and their driver was killed. Despite the time it took to heal from the injury, Addario went through with her wedding that July to Paul de Bendern, a journalist for the news service Reuters, whom she had met in Turkey. "I imagine I'll look pretty funny as a bride in the next six weeks," she wrote to her colleagues at the *New York Times*, according to David W. Dunlap for the *Lens* (18 May 2009). "But hey, it's character building."

While on assignment in Libya in March 2011, covering the insurrection against dictator Colonel Muammar Qaddafi, Addario and three other correspondents spent six days in captivity. The four—Addario, photographer Tyler Hicks, reporter and videographer Stephen Farrell, and *New York Times* Beirut bureau chief Anthony Shadid—were captured by Libyan forces loyal to Qaddafi on March 15, 2011, in the eastern rebel-controlled part of the country. They were detained for being in the country without visas. "They entered the country illegally and when the army, when they liberated the city of Ajdabiya from the terrorists and they found her [Addario], they arrest her because you know, foreigners in this place," Qaddafi's son Seif al-Islam al-Qaddafi told Christiane Amanpour in an *ABC News* interview on March 18, as reported by David D. Kirkpatrick for the *New York Times* (18 Mar. 2011). After the *Times* announced that their four correspondents were missing, Qaddafi government officials promised to locate and release them.

### BEING HELD CAPTIVE
The four *Times* journalists had decided that the fighting had gotten too dangerous for them to continue reporting; they were nearing Libya's border to Egypt when their driver, Mohamed Shaglouf, accidentally drove to a checkpoint held by Qaddafi's forces. As they were pulled from the car, rebels began firing. The four journalists ran, but after they took cover behind a small building, they were once again detained by Qaddafi's men. They would have been shot and killed if not for one of the soldiers, who recognized them as American. Shaglouf was missing by that point, and presumed dead.

For the next forty-eight hours, the journalists were tied up and driven toward Tripoli, beaten, and threatened with death. Addario was also sexually assaulted. "There was a lot of groping," Addario recalled in a telephone interview after their release, as reported by Jeremy W. Peters for the *New York Times* (21 Mar. 2011). "Every man who came in contact with us basically felt every inch of my body short of what was under my clothes." The third day, they were forced onto an airplane to Tripoli where they were placed in the custody of Libyan defense officials. From that point, the journalists were well-treated and were allowed to call home. They still had to wait three days, however, while negotiations were made for their release, which occurred on March 21.

### A FEMALE CORRESPONDENT ABROAD
Addario, Shadid, Hicks, and Farrell wrote of their capture in Libya for the *New York Times* on March 22, 2011, in a piece titled "Four *Times* Journalists Held Captive in Libya Faced Days of Brutality." In response to comments that asked how the newspaper could allow a woman to go to a war zone, Addario wrote in defense of her job for the *Lens* (30 Mar. 2011). "To me, that's grossly offensive. This is my life, and I make my own decisions. If a woman wants to be a war photographer, she should. It's important. Women offer a different perspective." She added, "I have always been offered the utmost hospitality and protection and shelter in the Muslim world. . . . My translators and drivers have put their lives before mine. It's very important for people to recognize that these qualities do exist."

In August 2011, at six months pregnant, Addario traveled to the Horn of Africa to cover the drought there. This meant venturing into Somalia, "one of the most dangerous places on the planet," as she told Castaldo. "I thought, 'Am I really an idiot? Am I really going to go to Somalia?' And then I thought . . . 'I really can't tell the story adequately without going to Somalia.' And so I went."

### AWARD-WINNING PHOTOGRAPHY
Addario is the recipient of numerous awards and honors in addition to her Pulitzer Prize, most notably a 2009 MacArthur fellowship. The fellowship granted Addario $100,000 annually for five years for her "powerful images," which "are visual testimony to the most pressing conflicts and humanitarian crises of the twenty-first century," according to the MacArthur Foundation website (26 Jan. 2009). Addario's earlier honors include the 2008 Getty Images Grant for editorial photography for what would become six years of work in Darfur; being named a Columbia College of Chicago fellow for documenting sexual assault in the Democratic Republic of Congo; and the Infinity Award for young photographer of the year in 2002, from the International Center of Photography; among other honors.

Addario is married to Paul de Bendern, a journalist for Reuters. The couple have a son, born on December 28, 2011, and are based in London.

### SUGGESTED READING
Estrin, James. "Women Shooting on the Front Lines." *New York Times*. New York Times Co., 28 Jan. 2013. Web. 7 Feb. 2013.

Pesta, Abigail. "From the Front Lines of Libya." *Marie Claire*. Hearst Communications, 6 June 2011. Web. 7 Feb. 2013.

Shadid, Anthony, Lynsey Addario, Stephen Farrell, and Tyler Hicks. "Four *Times* Journalists Held Captive in Libya Faced Days of Brutality." *New York Times*. New York Times Co., 22 Mar. 2011. Web. 7 Feb. 2013.

Wolfe, Lauren. "Q&A: NYT's Lynsey Addario on Libya Sexual Assault." *CPJ*. Committee to Protect Journalists, 4 Apr. 2011. Web. 7 Feb. 2013.

—Julia Gilstein

---

# Ayad Akhtar

**Born:** October 28, 1970
**Occupation:** Actor and writer

© Nina Subin

As the American-born son of Muslim immigrants from Pakistan, Ayad Akhtar developed an acute sensitivity to the complexities of faith, ethnicity, and identity from an early age. Though he was never a particularly devout follower of Islam, his experiences growing up in the faith and living with the challenges of being a Muslim in the United States inspired in Akhtar a strong creative spirit that eventually propelled him to a successful career as a novelist, playwright, and actor. Religion and identity have been the dominant themes of his works, many of which have earned him high critical praise and widespread recognition.

Although he regularly attended mosque as a child, Akhtar slowly drifted away from Islam as he grew into adulthood, by which time he found himself coming to embrace writing and artistic creativity as his personal passion. In his collegiate years, Akhtar pursued theater and directing degrees and took a serious interest in acting. Around that same time, he began to realize that shying away from his ethnic and religious heritage was, in fact, inhibiting his creative abilities. When Akhtar finally came to terms with his background, his creative floodgates were opened, and he embarked on a quickly blossoming career in the arts. As he told Elena Ferrarin in an interview for *Brown Alumni Magazine* (16 Apr. 2013), "It was about my own personal development, about accepting certain parts of myself that I was aware of—or in flight from. My turning to really see where I came from coincided with a burst of creativity that allowed me to give form, shape, and voice to a community that I have known all my life."

In a matter of just a few years, Akhtar took the helm of several creative projects that were all thematically based on the realities of being a Muslim in the United States and, to some degree, his own experiences with those challenges. After creating and starring in *The War Within*, a 2005 film about the sudden radicalization of a Muslim American everyman, Akhtar went on to tackle a number of other projects, including writing *American Dervish*, his first novel. His most notable accomplishment, however, came with the 2012 debut of his play *Disgraced*. The play, centered on a dinner party conversation in which one man's Islamic background becomes a heated topic, was a critical success, earning Akhtar the 2013 Pulitzer Prize for drama and cementing his reputation as a highly regarded creative visionary.

## EARLY LIFE AND EDUCATION
Akhtar was born on October 28, 1970, in New York City and was raised in Milwaukee, Wisconsin. His mother and father, a radiologist and cardiologist, respectively, were both Pakistani-born immigrants who had immigrated to the United States in the 1960s. While his family lived a largely secular lifestyle, they maintained intimate ties to both their Pakistani traditions and Islamic roots. As a youngster, Akhtar regularly joined his parents in attending services at a local mosque on Milwaukee's south side.

On his path to adulthood, Akhtar moved further and further away from his ethnic and religious heritage, essentially distancing himself from his past identity. As he told Alexandra Alter for the *Wall Street Journal* (6 Jan. 2012), he experienced "the death of a childlike relationship with faith." Simultaneously, Akhtar was nurturing his growing interest in artistic creativity that led him to embrace literature and drama and to pursue a career in the arts. After graduating from Brookfield Central High School in 1988, Akhtar attended Brown University, where he earned a degree in theater in 1993. He later enrolled in Columbia University's graduate film program, where he completed a degree in directing. He also took up an avid interest in acting, spending time in between his enrollment at Brown and Columbia to study the craft under the tutelage of renowned theatrical innovator Jerzy Grotowski in Italy. Akhtar also dabbled in writing, working on an eventually abandoned novel, about a poet who works as a database researcher at Goldman Sachs, and trying his hand at writing short scripts and screenplays.

Despite his efforts, Akhtar felt he was missing some crucial element that would allow him to fully tap into his creative reserves and produce the type of meaningful, quality work that he expected of himself. As he made the transition from his late twenties to his early thirties, Akhtar came to a realization that fundamentally altered both his creative direction and his life. The crucial element he was missing was the very thing he had been pushing away for most of his adult years: his heritage. In an interview with Stephen Moss for the London *Guardian* (7 May 2013), Akhtar explained that this discovery marked a major turning point in his life, both personally and creatively. "In my early 30s, I started to realize I was avoiding something on a personal level, but also as a writer. I was in denial about who I was, and was trying to be someone who I was not," Akhtar said. "All I did metaphorically was to turn and look over my shoulder at what I was running away from. And at that moment there was an explosion of creativity." In finally embracing his ethnic and religious background as a source of inspiration, Akhtar suddenly had a focus for his creativity that instantly afforded him some much-needed direction and set him on the artistic journey that would earn him the 2013 Pulitzer Prize for drama.

## AKHTAR AS ACTOR

Following his life-changing moment of self-discovery, Akhtar made his first major foray into the arts with the 2005 film *The War Within*, a project he had first envisioned with the help of fellow Columbia students Tom Glynn and Joseph Castelo. In addition to writing the film with Glynn and Castelo, Akhtar opted to take on the task of playing the lead role, that of would-be terrorist Hassan. In the film, Hassan is a Pakistani man involved in a terrorist plot to bomb Grand Central Station in New York City. When he moves in with an old friend who lives nearby in order to facilitate his plan, the aspiring terrorist experiences a crisis that leaves him conflicted on whether or not to proceed with his dangerous scheme. Speaking about *The War Within* in an interview with Annie Wagner for the *Stranger* (13 Oct. 2005), Akhtar said the film sought to explore the causes of terrorism in a deeper, more profound way than is typically the case. "We

were trying to get underneath the level of political discourse that has become pretty stale about a lot of these topics," Akhtar said. "And to identify the root human cause of people going out and blowing themselves up in some giant statement of protest and murder. . . . Who is giving voice to the oppressed? It's no longer Franz Fanon. It's now the bomb." For their work on the film, Akhtar, Glynn, and Castelo were nominated for an Independent Spirit Award for best screenplay.

After the release of *The War Within*, Akhtar struggled for a time to find roles he felt were complex and compelling enough to satisfy his interests as an actor. His search for a more substantive part than those he was typically offered eventually landed him a place in the cast of *Too Big to Fail*, an HBO-produced film about the 2008 financial crisis that first aired in May 2011. Akhtar was cast as Neel Kashkari, the then special assistant to US Treasury Secretary Henry Paulson. In this performance, Akhtar portrayed Kashkari as he devised the Troubled Asset Relief Program (TARP), which was used to help bail out failing banks. In an interview for the *Journal Sentinel*'s *Tap Milwaukee* website, when asked by Duane Dudekwhy playing the part of Kashkari was of interest to him (19 May 2011), Akhtar cited the personal impact the financial crisis had on him. "When the financial crisis hit, the money dropped out of the independent film market like you couldn't believe," Akhtar said. "Nobody had money to put into anything. And that directly affected me."

## *AMERICAN DERVISH*

Having found some success as a filmmaker and actor, Akhtar turned his attention to the written word. In 2012 he made his debut as an author with the publication of *American Dervish*. With this novel, Akhtar again turned to the Muslim American experience and, indeed, some of his own personal experiences to construct a story that highlights the struggles of a young man who is simultaneously dealing with an unexpected religious awakening and an improbable romantic interest.

The plot of *American Dervish* follows Hayat Shah, a Muslim American teenager living in a Milwaukee suburb in the 1980s, a setup that closely mirrors Akhtar's own adolescence. Initially, Hayat is a typical American teen not particularly invested in religion, despite his family's faith. His world is irrevocably changed, however, when Mina, a close friend of Hayat's mother, arrives from Pakistan hoping to escape a bad marriage. Mina is a devoutly faithful Muslim and a beautiful young woman with whom Hayat is immediately smitten. Enraptured by Mina's beauty and intelligence, Hayat quickly finds himself drawn into her deep sense of spirituality and begins to embrace Islam in a way he never had before. At the same time, however, just as his feelings for Mina reach their apex, Hayat is crushed to learn that she has taken up with another man. Hurt and confused, Hayat interprets Mina's actions as a betrayal and contemplates a response that could have serious implications for everyone involved.

For Akhtar, *American Dervish* represented an important opportunity to show readers that Muslim Americans such as himself are, in many ways, not altogether different from other Americans. *American Dervish*, as Akhtar pointed out in an interview with Dudek (11 Jan. 2012), was, in fact, an American story, not just a Muslim story. "I wanted to tell a story about faith that was universal," Akhtar said. "It's called *American Dervish* because it's not just about Islam, it's about the American experience [and] the tradition, rupture and renewal at the heart of every generation of Americans." He also told Dudek that he wrote *American Dervish* to illustrate that Muslims share a key quality with people of other faiths: doubt. "I think there's a perception that Muslims have no doubt, which is why they'll blow themselves up, because they believe so strongly," Akhtar said. "And I wanted people to know that grappling with doubt is a universal [quality]." Reviewing the novel for the *New York Times* (4 Jan. 2012), critic Adam Langer praised *American Dervish*, writing, "What distinguishes Mr. Akhtar's novel is its generosity and its willingness to embrace the contradictions of its memorably idiosyncratic characters and the society they inhabit."

## TAKING THE STAGE

On the heels of *American Dervish*'s release, Akhtar focused his creative energies in yet another direction, this time writing two plays that both hit theater stages in 2012. As with his other noted works, the plays contain strong religious themes and illustrate many of the issues Muslim Americans face. In addition, both plays, *Disgraced* and *The Invisible Hand*, received critical praise and helped establish Akhtar as a renowned playwright.

*The Invisible Hand*, which premiered at the Repertory Theatre of St. Louis in March 2012, is a dark tale about an affluent investment banker who gets kidnapped by Islamic militants and must rely on his wits and a willingness to do whatever is necessary to survive. Through the play, Akhtar explores the moral ambiguity of humankind's survival instincts and the potential consequences of the questionable choices individuals make in extreme circumstances.

Though *The Invisible Hand* was generally well received by critics, *Disgraced* proved to be Akhtar's true stage success. *Disgraced* premiered at the American Theater Company in Chicago in January 2012. Set in present-day New York, the play focuses on Amir Kapoor, a corporate lawyer and Muslim Pakistani American who has found great success in both his professional and personal life. While Amir has done well for himself, his place in life has come at a great cost, specifically as it relates to his identity as a Muslim. During a dinner party he and his wife are hosting at their apartment, an innocent conversation devolves into a heated spat in which Amir's crisis of identity comes boiling to the surface and threatens to destroy everything for which he has worked.

With *Disgraced*, Akhtar set out to create a story infused with the essence of classic tragedy that would be relatable to and resonant with modern audiences, as he told Mark Kennedy in an interview for the Associated Press (15 Apr. 2013). "I really wanted to write a play that was going to have a legitimately tragic dimension for a contemporary audience," Akhtar said. "I wanted the play to have immediacy and aliveness of engagement that harkened back to a tragic form but a mass form, something that would have audiences gasping." In accomplishing this goal, Akhtar crafted a play that impressed critics and theatergoers alike and garnered the 2013 Pulitzer Prize for drama.

## PERSONAL LIFE

Akhtar lives in the New York City neighborhood of Harlem. In addition to building a successful career for himself, Akhtar has committed himself to helping others looking to pursue a life in the arts. Since 1999, he has taught acting classes to help aspiring actors hone their skills and prepare for a career on the stage or screen. His method, based on the concept of film naturalism and the importance of a film-oriented approach, places emphasis on the need for actors to be in control of their own work and be capable of evaluating and modifying their own performances without the help of directors or producers. As part of his program, Akhtar also encourages his students to embrace the Sufi, Kabbalah, and Vedic spiritual traditions as a means of enhancing their acting techniques through a deeper connection to the inner self.

When he is not busy working with up-and-coming actors, Akhtar continues to move forward in his own career. His newest play, *The Who & The What*, is set to premiere in February 2014 at the La Jolla Playhouse in San Diego, California. The drama follows a young Muslim woman as she writes a book on the Prophet Muhammad and encounters strong resistance from her father and sister when they learn what she is planning to say about Islam's most sacred figure. Akhtar is also writing a second novel, which will illustrate the cultural challenges faced by a Pakistani American artist who resides in Vienna. His goal with this novel, as he told Alter, is to "explore modern young Western-born Muslims living in a highly politicized anti-Islamic environment."

Though Akhtar continues to excel in many areas of his career, the role that is most important to him remains that of storyteller, as he told Ferrarin. "I think of myself as a dramatic storyteller," Akhtar said. "Giving literary form, dramatic form, to the lives that I am in contact with, metaphorically and actually, is really the best artistic endowment."

## SUGGESTED READING

Alter, Alexandra. "'Dervish' Whirls into Publishing World." *Wall Street Journal*. Dow Jones, 6 Jan. 2012. Web. 5 June 2013.

Dudek, Duane. "Akhtar Finds New Opportunities in Fiction, HBO." *Tap Milwaukee*. Journal Sentinel, 19 May 2011. Web. 5 June 2013.

Dudek, Duane. "'American Dervish' a Tale of Struggle and Faith." *Tap Milwaukee*. Journal Sentinel, 11 Jan. 2012. Web. 5 June 2013.

Ferrarin, Elena. "Ayad Akhtar '93 Wins Drama Pulitzer." *Brown Alumni Magazine*. Brown Alumni Mag., 16 Apr. 2013. Web. 5 June 2013.

Kennedy, Mark. "Ayad Akhtar's 'Shocked' by Pulitzer Prize Win." *AP*. Associated P, 15 Apr. 2013. Web. 5 June 2013.

Moss, Stephen. "Pulitzer Playwright Ayad Akhtar: 'I Was in Denial.'" *Guardian*. Guardian News and Media, 7 May 2013. Web. 5 June 2013.

Wagner, Annie. "Annie Wagner Talks to Ayad Akhtar and Tom Glynn." *Stranger*. Index Newspapers, 13 Oct. 2005. Web. 5 June 2013.

## SELECTED WORKS

*The War Within*, 2005; *Too Big to Fail*, 2011; *American Dervish*, 2012; *Disgraced*, 2012; *The Invisible Hand*, 2012

—*Jack Lasky*

---

# Will Allen

**Born:** February 8, 1949
**Occupation:** Retired basketball player and urban farmer

The son of sharecroppers whose ancestors had been enslaved, Will Allen initially wanted nothing to do with farming, but he has since become known as a pioneer in the field of urban agriculture. "The desire to farm hid inside me," Allen explained in his book, *The Good Food Revolution* (2012). "It hid in my feet. They wanted the moist earth beneath them. It hid in my hands. They wanted to be callused and rough and caked with soil. It hid in my heart. I missed the rhythms of agriculture." Allen began farming on land that once belonged to his wife's family, and after walking away from a corporate job, he founded an urban agriculture organization that became

Associated Press

known as Growing Power. By 2012, Growing Power's three city acres of urban farm in Milwaukee, Wisconsin, housed thousand of plants and produced forty tons of vegetables annually.

Allen's goal has always been to bring fresh, healthy food into urban areas. He explained to Van Jones for *Time* magazine (29 Apr. 2010), "Everybody, regardless of their economic means, should have access to the same healthy, safe, affordable food that is grown naturally." Allen has also noted that food grown locally not only is fresh and healthy but also benefits the environment by not being shipped long distances, thus using less fossil fuel.

Growing Power's work has expanded to include fish farming, vermiculture, and composting. The organization offers weekend workshops on food-growing techniques. Growing Power has also partnered with Heifer International and has gained the attention of various foundations: Allen was awarded a Ford Foundation grant in 2005, a MacArthur Foundation "genius" grant in 2008, and grants from the Kellogg Foundation in 2009 and 2012. Allen received an honorary doctor of agriculture degree in 2012 from the University of Wisconsin–Milwaukee, also delivering the commencement address that year.

## EARLY LIFE AND EDUCATION

Will Allen was born on February 8, 1949, to parents living in a small African American community outside Washington, DC. His mother wanted to become a teacher but instead worked as a domestic servant. Although Allen's father, a sharecropper and construction laborer, was illiterate, he was successful as a farmer and was ultimately able to save enough money to buy an eight-acre farm of his own. He sold extra produce to southern African Americans who had come north looking for work and missed the fresh produce they were used to eating.

By the seventh grade, Allen stood six feet tall. His older brother Joe had introduced him to basketball, and for an entire summer one year,

Allen worked at the American University swimming pool and played pickup basketball with college students in the school's gym after work. Allen wrote in his book that basketball changed his life. "Once I began to play this game, I wanted nothing else in life. I had found a physical language that was my own, and the sport spoke through me. The long and strong body that for years I had seen as a liability was suddenly an asset."

## BASKETBALL CAREER

As a high school freshman, Allen made the varsity basketball team and became the first player to be named one of the top ten high school players in Washington, DC, for three consecutive years. He became the starting center of the varsity team his sophomore year, scoring 349 points in twenty games. His successes attracted the attention of college basketball scouts and prompted over one hundred scholarship offers. Allen entered the University of Miami in 1967 and became the first African American member of the university's basketball team, the Miami Hurricanes.

Allen was drafted to the National Basketball Association (NBA) team the Baltimore Bullets in April 1971. He did not make the final cut, however, and was picked up by the Miami Floridians, an American Basketball Association (ABA) team. After the Floridians disbanded in 1972, Allen played for several Belgian teams in the European league.

Allen renewed his interest in natural farming while in Belgium, where he began gardening and raising chickens. Realizing that his body was suffering from playing basketball on the concrete floors in Europe, Allen retired from the game in 1977 and returned to the United States with his wife, Cyndy, and their three children.

## CORPORATE LIFE

Allen had no real prospects or direction after returning from Europe, but Cyndy's family owned several properties in Wisconsin, and they lived on the second story of a restaurant Cyndy's family owned and operated. Allen first worked as a teacher's aide in a local high school and later opened a disco in the restaurant, at times serving as the disc jockey in the basement, where he set up a jazz club. Allen recalled in *Good Food Revolution*, "The business was successful, but I became disillusioned with the disco lifestyle. I didn't like having to break up fights, or arriving home on Sunday mornings at 3 a.m. with my clothes saturated in cigarette smoke."

Allen took a position as district manager of six local Kentucky Fried Chicken (KFC) restaurants and went on to win several sales awards. "It was just a job," he told Elizabeth Royte for the *New York Times* (1 July 2009). "I was aware

it wasn't the greatest food, but I also knew that people didn't have a lot of choice about where to eat: there were no sit-down restaurants in that part of the city." At the same time that Allen was improving KFC's profitability and winning awards, he was also farming. He often rose before dawn to get in several hours of agricultural work before checking on his stores.

Allen's next career change came in 1987, when he joined the consumer goods company Procter & Gamble as a sales representative for paper goods. In 1993, he moved into analyzing sales histories of Procter & Gamble products sold in grocery stores and won six sales awards in one year. His true joy, however, was in working on the farm.

## FONDY FARMERS MARKET

While in Belgium, Allen toured the countryside and delighted in the gardens and the creative use of space he saw there. When he returned to the United States, he built a garden behind his in-laws' restaurant and began growing his own food. When his mother-in-law offered Allen and his wife fifty acres of land, Allen expanded his efforts and soon began selling surplus produce at the Fondy Farmers Market in downtown Milwaukee, Wisconsin. Allen also became an advocate for local farmers of Hmong descent, who initially faced resistance from the predominantly white growers.

When Milwaukee's city government threatened to cease financial backing of the Fondy Farmers Market as a cost-cutting measure, Allen's fundraising and organizational skills made him a natural leader. Farmers wanted to prevent privatization, which would save the city thousands of dollars per year but would also increase the rent for each stall. Rather than simply rally the neighborhood in support of the market, Allen suggested that the farmers form a cooperative and run the market themselves. The city agreed to lease the land for one dollar per year. Allen was elected the first president of the Fondy Farmers Market Co-op. Additional farmers joined the co-op, which in turn reduced stall rental fees.

## OF WORMS AND WASTE

When Procter & Gamble closed its local office in 1992 as part of a restructuring move, Allen began commuting a few days a week to Oak Brook, Illinois, which was a two-hour drive. Disliking life in the corporate world and wanting to do more than sell paper products, Allen decided to take a chance and begin his true life's work. Allen cashed in his retirement savings and bought a greenhouse on two acres of land in one of Milwaukee's "food deserts," neighborhoods in which there are convenience stores and fast-food restaurants but no grocery stores. Not coincidentally, the property was also only half a mile from the city's largest public housing project.

At first Allen worked alone, teaching anyone in the neighborhood who wanted to learn, particularly young people. In 1995 he worked with a local YWCA youth program, members of which helped him with harvesting the crops. The young people set up a table at the Fondy Farmers Market and split the proceeds. A newspaper article about the project led to calls from school administrators and teachers interested in partnering with Allen to create gardens of their own. Sensing an opportunity to expand his vision, Allen formed the Farm-City Link, using the greenhouses as a living laboratory and classroom.

In 1996, Heifer International, a nonprofit organization committed to ending world hunger and poverty, received a W. K. Kellogg Foundation grant to begin working in urban agriculture. Implementing urban agriculture programs proved difficult, however, as the organization focuses on livestock, and most urban areas do not allow residents to keep animals such as goats or chickens. A solution was developed after the US Department of Agriculture classified worms as livestock. Allen was approached to partner with Heifer because of his work with at-risk youth and his experience in urban agriculture and composting, which was a perfect fit with vermiculture—composting with the help of worms.

Warned that worms would not survive the harsh Wisconsin winters, Allen studied red wiggler worms for five years to determine their food and habitat preferences. By 2009, six million tons of food waste that would otherwise have gone to landfills was generating over one hundred thousand pounds of compost every four months, three quarters of which he sold. Allen has referred to the fertile soil created with the help of worms as black gold.

Aquaponics, growing plants in water, is another element of Allen's partnership with Heifer International, as is fish farming. Fish such as tilapia and perch are raised in tanks. The water from the tanks is recycled to the plants, which act as filters, and then returned to the fish tanks.

## GROWING POWER

Shortly before community organizer Hope Finkelstein toured Allen's facility in 1998, she dreamed of an organization that would unite all of the area growers. She even had a name for it: Growing Power. Finkelstein had begun organizing local small farmers in nearby Madison, and her desire to expand the fledgling group coincided with Allen's desire to expand the Farm-City Link program. Allen became a board member and later codirector of the organization, and his greenhouses became the physical site for Growing Power. Finkelstein handled the planning, strategizing, and grant writing from her home. When Finkelstein and her husband moved to Alaska in 2000, Allen's daughter Erika took over those tasks.

Although Allen has successfully raised money by selling produce and holding seminars, Growing Power still relies on money from grants and foundations. Allen has pointed out that urban farming is not unique in that regard; indeed, large-scale agribusiness is subsidized with government funds and price supports. Volunteer labor is also crucial to the organization, and Growing Power is further committed to hiring workers whose opportunities would otherwise be limited. Along with hiring local young people, Allen has offered jobs to workers with visual impairments. He explained to Royte, "I was cutting sprouts in the dark one night, and I realized you don't need sight to do this." Allen grows sprouts for his market baskets, which sell in the neighboring areas, and for local high-end restaurants that are committed to the model of fresh, local, and organically grown food.

Over the years, Allen has expanded the organization's operations while achieving energy-efficient solutions along the way. When he needed bees to pollinate crops, he then added honey to his product line. Goats "mow" grassy areas, and the body heat of chickens allows him to grow spinach even in winter. "My intention in time is to build a facility that is entirely off the grid and that uses only the power of the sun, the earth, and decaying waste to grow food. I'm not there yet, but I believe I can make it happen," Allen wrote in his book.

## REVERSING A TREND

Allen is aware of the high incidences in the United States of diabetes, heart disease, and obesity, particularly among African Americans. He traces this to the inaccessibility of fresh, healthy food. "We've got to change the system so everyone has safe, equitable access to healthy food," Allen told Royte.

In addition to his market baskets, which Allen sells in neighborhoods that lack sources of wholesome food, Allen also contracts with local schools to provide fresh, healthy food. Allen explained to Linda Sechrist for *Natural Awakenings* magazine (June 2012), "Until we have a new model for a local and regional food system, and view nutrient-dense food as medicine we can take three times a day to improve our health, we can't have the kind of healthy community that people are longing for."

Allen is also committed to helping African Americans overcome the stigma of farming, which many still associate with slavery and sharecropping. He hopes to encourage more small-farm operations, particularly among African Americans, and he believes that everyone can grow food, even in container gardens.

## PERSONAL LIFE

After two years of dating, Allen married University of Miami classmate Cyndy Bussler in 1969, on his twentieth birthday. Cyndy's parents initially objected to the interracial marriage, fearing their daughter would face a difficult life filled with racism and discrimination. However, they came to accept the marriage and ultimately contributed greatly to Allen's career in agriculture.

Allen was diagnosed with thyroid cancer in his late twenties and developed a tumor in his salivary gland a decade later. After several successful surgeries at the time of both diagnoses, Allen was deemed cancer-free, but the surgery to remove the mass in his salivary gland left him with problems moving the right side of his mouth.

The Allens have two daughters and one son. Their eldest child, Erika, serves as director of Growing Power's Chicago satellite office.

### SUGGESTED READING

Allen, Will. "Growing Power: Milwaukee's Urban Farm." *Edible Estates: Attack on the Front Lawn*. Ed. Fritz Haeg. New York: Metropolis, 2010. 2028–35. Print.

Allen, Will, and Charles Wilson. *Growing Power: Growing Healthy Food, People, and Communities*. New York: Gotham, 2012. Print.

Jones, Van. "Will Allen." *Time 100*. Time, 29 Apr. 2010. Web. 15 July 2013.

Royte, Elizabeth. "Street Farmer." *New York Times*. New York Times, 1 July 2009. Web. 15 July 2013.

Sechrist, Linda. "Inspiring Communities to Build Sustainable Food Systems: An Interview with Growing Power Founder Will Allen." *Natural Milwaukee*. Natural Awakenings, June 2012. Web. 15 July 2013.

—*Judy Johnson*

---

# Sophia Amoruso

**Born:** April 20, 1984
**Occupation:** Founder and CEO of Nasty Gal

Sophia Amoruso is the founder and CEO of the online women's clothing company Nasty Gal. Amoruso began the venture in 2006, when she started selling vintage clothing on the auction and shopping website eBay at age twenty-two. The company—named after a 1975 album by Miles Davis's funk-singing ex-wife, Betty Davis—has been a cash cow for Amoruso, a community-college dropout who has accumulated an estimated net worth of $250 million since the company's inception. Cashing in early on the marketing potential of social media sites such as MySpace, Facebook, Twitter, and Instagram, Amoruso has built her small company into a thriving business with little to no help from traditional advertising outlets.

Associated Press

Additionally, as Victoria Barret wrote for *Forbes* magazine (28 June 2012), "Amoruso has bucked fashion trends not so much with the styles she sells (which can be found elsewhere, often at lower prices) but in the machine she's built to sell them." Nasty Gal offers only limited runs of each piece it sells; while most clothing companies are forced to mark down about one-third of all styles, Amoruso is able to sell a staggering 93 percent of all Nasty Gal items at full price.

Amoruso has cultivated a vast network of loyal Nasty Gal shoppers, predominantly young women in their twenties. According to Barret, more than half of Nasty Gal's sales come from just 20 percent of the site's customers. When Amoruso launched her company on eBay, she curated the outfits and photographed the models (usually her friends) herself. That spirit has not changed. Amoruso continues to stock the online boutique with clothing she herself would wear—she even designed a line of clothing for Nasty Gal in 2012. The frequently updated blog and "lookbook" on the company's website contribute to the feeling that girls are not buying clothes from a brand, but are shopping from Amoruso's own closet. According to Barret, the company strives to "get dressed" with its customers every day with its frequent posts on social networking sites. With a new magazine, *Super Nasty*, and more than $100 million in annual sales, the hard-working Amoruso can say that Nasty Gal has experienced consistent growth from her first sale on eBay to the present day. "It's been very charmed, but I'm not willing to rest on my laurels," she told Nicole Perlroth for the *New York Times* (25 Mar. 2013). "It's only going to get harder to keep building from here."

## EARLY LIFE AND EDUCATION

Amoruso was born on April 20, 1984, in San Diego and grew up in Sacramento, California. She is the only child of Greek American parents. "I've never seen someone work for a salary," she told Barret for *Forbes*, referring to her family's entrepreneurialism; her father sold mortgage loans and her mother sold houses, but both lost their jobs when Amoruso was ten. It was a difficult time for the family, and Amoruso's parents took her out of her Catholic school to save money. But Amoruso was developing her own business acumen. At the age of nine, she ran lemonade and craft stands on her street and bought her first book about startup companies. She delivered newspapers with her father and worked at a Subway sandwich shop as a teenager. According to Barret, Amoruso adopted her father's workaday mantra: "Show up. Don't stop moving. Sweep the floors even when they don't ask you to."

Amoruso's parents divorced when she was a senior in high school. She moved in with a group of friends and worked a number of jobs—at two photo labs, a record store, and a shoe store to name a few—while taking classes at a San Francisco community college. By the age of twenty-two, she had changed jobs ten times. Amoruso dropped out of school and moved in with her step-aunt. To make money, she checked student IDs at a local art school. She considered studying photography, but she did not want to take on the debt. "I was always someone who always thought I could do better, but I just didn't know how," she told Richard Nieva for *Pando Daily*, a Silicon Valley online news site (31 Jan. 2013). She was at a standstill.

While surfing the social networking site MySpace at her job, Amoruso saw that she was receiving a number of friend requests from eBay sellers hawking vintage wares. Amoruso had loved vintage clothing since childhood. Her grandfather had owned a motel in West Sacramento and she loved to scavenge the so-called junk room for treasures from the 1960s and 1970s. As an adult, she often wore vintage pieces and posted photographs she had taken herself on her MySpace profile.

## BEGINNINGS ON EBAY

In 2006, Amoruso decided to sell a few of her own pieces on eBay, as well as a few pieces she had found at Goodwill thrift stores. She studied the methods of other sellers and, after selling her first items, developed a simple motto. "My philosophy," she told Barret, "is that you sell things for more than you bought them." She once bought a Chanel jacket for eight dollars at a Salvation Army thrift store and sold it for more than one thousand dollars. Soon, she quit her job to scour flea markets, Goodwill outlets, and even other eBay sellers for goods. Explaining to Barret how she purchased items off of eBay only to resell them on the same site for nearly five times the original asking price, she quipped, "You have to prove it is worth more." She searched Google for misspellings of designer names such as Yves Saint Laurent, trying to root out sellers who did not know the real worth of their product. An eBay seller's marketing capabilities are limited, and Amoruso obsessed over the few things she could control. She styled and photographed the clothes herself. She used her friends as models and her aunt's garage door as a backdrop, carefully devising each pose and fold of fabric. Initially, she was making about twenty-five sales each week.

She posted her best shots on her MySpace page to get feedback from her growing fan base and sent out automated friend requests to people with similar tastes, quickly amassing tens of thousands of online followers. Her efforts to siphon customers off of eBay to her MySpace page did not go over well with other sellers, and in 2008, she was kicked off the site after being flagged repeatedly by her competitors. By that time, she had accrued more than thirty thousand friends on MySpace as well as $115,000 in sales with a net profit of $20,000. She had moved out of her step-aunt's house and was running her small business from a studio in Benicia, outside of San Francisco. A few weeks after her break with eBay she launched a new website with the support of her MySpace friends, who turned out to be an invaluable asset for her growing business. Style websites and editors heard of her through word-of-mouth and her popularity grew, though through it all, she pointed out to Nieva, "I was just a girl in a room with a keyboard and a MySpace profile."

## NASTY GAL VINTAGE

Amoruso named her business Nasty Gal after the 1975 Betty Davis album of the same name. Amoruso considers the provocative 1970s funk singer the embodiment of the Nasty Gal aesthetic. She told Andrea Chang for the *Los Angeles Times* (26 Aug. 2012) that Davis is "the patron saint of badass women." But of course, the woman who best embodies the Nasty Gal aesthetic is Amoruso. The company continues to take its style cues from its founder, whose edgy and offbeat outfits—leather jackets with fringe down to the knee or leggings with sheer side panels from ankle to waist—have found a large and unexpected following of fashionistas. Still, the leap from eBay into the wilds of the Internet was a far one for Amoruso. It was the beginning of the recession, and she was up against more competitors with bigger names. Not to mention, Amoruso was only one person, although she used "we" in all of her business communications to suggest a larger operation. "[That's] the beauty of the Web," she told Barret. "You can pretend to be anything you want. But people figure out pretty quick if you don't live up to it."

Her website was called Nasty Gal Vintage. The domain NastyGal.com belonged to a pornography site, an association which still causes the company some grief, but Amoruso is unfazed. "If [the name is] a big shock when you hear it," she told Chang, "you're probably not our customer anyway." The company has since bought out the NastyGal.com domain.

Amoruso doubled down on her social media presence long before other companies were even speaking in such terms. She created a Facebook profile and a Twitter account. Accounts on Instagram, Pinterest, and Tumblr followed. Social networking continues to make up for the majority of Nasty Gal's advertising; Amoruso makes sure that all of Nasty Gal's sites are updated several times daily. The business continued to grow, but Amoruso was looking to expand out of the vintage market. There were high returns on vintage items like the Chanel jacket, but it took a tremendous amount of work to market one-of-a-kind items.

## A CYBER HOME FOR A TECH OUTSIDER

Amoruso was featured on the fashion blog WhoWhatWear.com in 2008 and, shortly afterward, got a call from talk show host Kelly Ripa's stylist for an item that had already sold. It was clear that Nasty Gal had reached a new level of exposure, and Amoruso decided to hire her first employee. She chose a woman named Christina Ferrucci who, according to Barret, is still one of Nasty Gal's top buyers. Ferrucci was the first person to respond to Amoruso's ad on the classifieds website Craigslist. Together, the two women began looking for non-vintage items to complement Nasty Gal's stock. They found a number of unusual pieces from Korean vendors in the Los Angeles Fashion District. The items were so popular that Amoruso was making the six-hour drive to Los Angeles every other week. After several months, Amoruso and Ferrucci decided to visit fashion trade shows in the hopes of landing more recognizable brands. They met with representatives from the shoemaker Sam Edelman, who turned down their offer to carry the brand on their site. An hour later, Amoruso returned to the Edelman representatives with her iPhone. She showed them the sleek Nasty Gal homepage and told them (as quoted by Barret), "We'll make your brand cooler." The reps accepted the deal.

In 2009, Nasty Gal raked in $1.1 million in sales. In 2010, that figure jumped to $6.5 million, and in 2011 it was $28 million. Nasty Gal was officially the fastest-growing retailer on the Internet, posting a whopping 500 percent

revenue increase each year in the first five years of its existence. In early 2011, Amoruso and Nasty Gal moved to Los Angeles to be closer to the company's vendors. She leased an office space downtown near Pershing Square where her chic employees (70 percent of whom are women) mix with the straight-laced lawyer types that populate the area.

In early 2012, Amoruso met with Silicon Valley investor Index Ventures. She had been contacted by venture capitalists before, but their pitches were less than desirable. "They would say, 'We want to invest in a woman-owned business—it's part of our investment thesis,'" she told Perlroth. With her business rapidly growing, she certainly did not need the money. "I don't think they got it," she added. "[It was] this bunch of guys sitting around saying, 'Oh, yeah, let's start a Web site and put Kim Kardashian's face on it,'" she said, referring to ShoeDazzle, a venture that garnered a lot of investments yet failed to gain serious traction. But after a website snafu on Black Friday in 2011, Amoruso knew she could use some help. Index, a firm that had invested in companies such as Facebook, Dropbox, Etsy, and the online clothing store ASOS, saw the enormous potential of Nasty Gal. "The demand and obsession that girls have for Nasty Gal turned out to be true and growing," Danny Rimmer of Index told Donna Fenn for the online business magazine *Inc.* (28 May 2013). "There's no reason why [the company] shouldn't be as big as ASOS one day." The firm initially invested $9 million into the company, but in August 2012, put in an additional $40 million.

## CONTINUED GROWTH

Amoruso understood that one of her company's greatest assets was its connection to customers, so she oversaw the creation of a Nasty Gal blog, where staffers post about everything from makeup to personal vacations. In 2013, with the help of Index's investment, Amoruso expanded that effort to a full magazine called *Super Nasty* that comes free with each order. The first issue featured photography by Terry Richardson and an article written by author Lesley Arfin, who is also a staff writer for the award-winning HBO show *Girls*.

In the spring of 2012, Nasty Gal debuted a line of clothing designed by Amoruso herself. She called the line "Weird Science." It featured the same rock-and-roll aesthetic that Nasty Gal is known for but, as Diana Tsui wrote for *New York Magazine* (28 Aug. 2012), "with a techno twist." Amoruso attributed the neon color palette to a photograph she saw of tangled network cables and wires. About 70 percent of the collection was manufactured in Los Angeles. "We're exploring the fact that we've been online all this time, but now we actually get to make things for our customers," she told Tsui. "We are transitioning from a retailer to a full-fledged brand," Amoruso explained in an interview for *Entrepreneur* magazine (18 Dec. 2012).

As of 2013, Nasty Gal has a 7,500-square-foot warehouse in Emeryville, California, and a 500,000-square-foot fulfillment center in Shepherdsville, Kentucky. Amoruso manages more than 280 employees, many of whom she lured from companies like Urban Outfitter, Zappos, Juicy Couture, and Gap. In early 2013, rumors swirled that Amoruso had been approached by retailer Urban Outfitters about a potential acquisition; however, as Amoruso told Sasha Bronner for the *Huffington Post* (26 Mar. 2013), "While it's always flattering to get phone calls, we're committed to what we're building here and at this point Nasty Gal is not for sale."

## PERSONAL LIFE

Amoruso lives in the Los Feliz neighborhood of Los Angeles with her boyfriend. Her business has made her a multimillionaire, though she has allowed herself few extravagant purchases. Among her splurges, according to Chang, are a white Porsche (paid for in cash) and a pair of Christian Louboutin heels.

## SELECTED READING

Barret, Victoria. "Nasty Gal's Sophia Amoruso: Fashion's New Phenom." *Forbes*. Forbes.com, 28 June 2012. Web. 2 July 2013.

Chang, Andrea. "Nasty Gal Clothing Company—As Red-Hot as Its Founder's Lipstick." *Los Angeles Times*. Los Angeles Times, 26 Aug. 2012. Web. 2 July 2013.

Fenn, Donna. "Unselfconsciously Sexy Style." *Inc.* Mansueto Ventures, 28 May 2013. Web. 2 July 2013.

Nieva, Richard. "Sophia Amoruso Reflects on Success: 'I Wouldn't Have Done Any of This.'" *PandoDaily*. PandoDaily, 31 Jan. 2013. Web. 2 July 2013.

Perlroth, Nicole. "Naughty in Name Only." *New York Times* 25 Mar. 2013, New York ed.: B1. Print.

Tsui, Diana. "Tastemaker: Nasty Gal's Sophia Amoruso Is Building an Indie Fashion Empire." *New York Magazine*. New York Media, 28 Aug. 2012. Web. 2 July 2013.

—*Molly Hagan*

# José Andrés

**Born:** July 14, 1969
**Occupation:** Chef and author

From the time he first set foot in the United States, José Andrés was determined to make an impact on the American dining scene. Steeped in the culinary traditions of his native Spain, Andrés set out to introduce American eaters to Spanish ingredients, dishes, and styles of cooking and eating. Since his move across the Atlantic, Andrés has established himself as one of the most accomplished chefs in the United States as well as one of the nation's most respected experts on Spanish cuisine.

To say that Andrés is known only for his traditional dishes would hardly be accurate, however. In fact, he is equally recognized as one of the most innovative modernist chefs in the Western world, thanks to his mastery of the cutting-edge, science-based culinary techniques of molecular gastronomy. Renowned for his use of the science of food to create futuristic dishes, Andrés has built himself an almost unparalleled reputation in the realm of avant-garde dining. He has also distinguished himself as a highly successful restaurateur. As president of the restaurant management company ThinkFoodGroup, he oversees restaurants throughout the United States, including Jaleo and Café Atlántico in Washington, DC; The Bazaar by José Andrés in Beverly Hills, California; and China Poblano in Las Vegas, Nevada. In recognition of his work, Andrés was honored with the 2011 James Beard Award for outstanding chef.

Keenly aware of the toll hunger takes on many Americans, Andrés is an active philanthropist, supporting charitable efforts to feed the hungry in some of the United States' poorest neighborhoods. Over the course of his career, he has worked closely with DC Central Kitchen, a Washington-area organization that provides meals for low-income and homeless individuals, both as a volunteer and as a celebrity fund-raiser. He has also been a supporter of First Lady Michelle Obama's campaign to encourage healthier eating habits throughout the country. With his culinary finesse, respect for Spanish tradition, pioneering of innovative cooking techniques, and commitment to food-related philanthropy, Andrés has positioned himself as one of the top professional chefs in the United States and, indeed, the world.

## EARLY LIFE AND EDUCATION

Andrés was born on July 14, 1969, in Mieres, a coal-mining town in the mountains of northern Spain. Food was a prominent part of Andrés's life from his childhood. His parents prepared most of the family's meals at home, and as a result, Andrés was exposed to traditional Spanish cuisine and cooking techniques from a very early age. With his parents' encouragement, he began experimenting in the kitchen himself, helping his mother with her baking by the time he was eight years old and making paella with his father at twelve.

The many days Andrés spent helping his father prepare paella for as many as sixty people

Jose Andres

Andrés's association with Neichel led him to an apprenticeship at the restaurant elBulli under chef Ferran Adrià, himself a former protégé of Neichel, in 1988. Since that time, Andrés has cited Adrià as his most important mentor and the person most responsible for molding him into the chef he eventually became. By the time his schooling and apprenticeship with Adrià were completed, Andrés was ready to start making a name for himself in the culinary world.

### EARLY CAREER IN THE UNITED STATES

After completing his education, Andrés briefly served in the Spanish navy, during which time he made his first trip to the United States. Upon receiving his discharge from the military, Andrés found work in various restaurants in New York, California, and Puerto Rico. His big break came when restaurateurs Rob Wilder and Roberto Alvarez, owners of the Proximo restaurant group, hired him to oversee their newest venture, Jaleo, in 1993.

Located in Washington, DC, Jaleo specialized in the tapas, or small plate, style of dining that was popular in Spain. The venue was an overwhelming success and made Andrés's name synonymous with the suddenly trendy Spanish dishes. Though he was quick to point out that tapas had arrived in the Americas hundreds of years before he had, Andrés acknowledged in an interview with the blog of the competitive cooking program *The Taste* (11 Mar. 2013) that the way he, Wilder, and Alvarez presented the concept likely had more than a little to do with its booming popularity. "Imagine a table of four people with sixteen tapas on the table," Andrés said. "It's like a rainbow of flavors, dishes, and textures. It's the coolest way to eat."

Impressed with how quickly he had made Jaleo a success, Wilder and Alvarez next tasked Andrés with taking over Café Atlántico, a Proximo restaurant that was in dire need of a face-lift. After revitalizing Café Atlántico's menu, Andrés and his partners at Proximo (which was renamed ThinkFoodGroup after the departure of Alvarez in 2006) opened additional Jaleo locations in Maryland and Virginia. A third location opened in Las Vegas in 2010. Having established his reputation as one of the United States' leading Spanish chefs, Andrés next expanded into other cuisines with the opening of the Mediterranean-themed Zaytinya in 2002 and the Mexican-themed Oyamel in 2004, proving that his skills were not confined to the cuisine with which he was most familiar.

### FROM THE KITCHEN TO THE TELEVISION STUDIO

Though his culinary star was clearly rising thanks to his efforts in the kitchen, Andrés soon began to think about applying his skills to a different medium. Offered the chance to host his own cooking show on the Spanish television network

sparked a serious interest in cooking in the young man and taught him the importance of paying attention to all the details of preparing a meal, no matter how big or small. Andrés was responsible for gathering wood and tending to the fire to make sure it stayed lit, though he desperately wanted to be more involved in the actual cooking process. "One day I got very upset, and he told me to go away," Andrés said in a June 2011 interview with *Wine Spectator*'s Harvey Steiman. "Later he came to me and said, 'Don't you see, without the fire I can't cook? You have the most important job.'"

Equally important to his growing fascination with food and cooking was the availability of high-quality ingredients in nearby markets. "The markets in Spain are astonishing," Andrés told the website *JustLuxe* (Feb. 2012). "It's amazing, every town has so many, with fresh fruits, vegetables, and fish. The goodness of the earth is all around those markets and it's very astonishing to see."

Inspired by his family's culinary traditions and the bountiful ingredients that surrounded him, Andrés persuaded his parents to allow him to leave high school at the age of fifteen to pursue his dream of becoming a professional chef. He immediately enrolled in a culinary program in Barcelona, though he spent little time in the classroom, instead preferring to learn by experience. While in Barcelona, he found his first cooking job at a restaurant in the city's convention center. There, he focused mainly on foreign cuisines rather than on traditional Spanish fare. Before long, his quickly blossoming skills earned him a spot at Neichel, a Barcelona restaurant operated by French chef Jean-Louis Neichel.

Televisión Española, Andrés jumped at the opportunity to share his love of food and cooking with the masses in his native country. *Vamos a cocinar* (Let's cook) premiered in 2005 and became a tremendous success, prompting the now famous Andrés to consider returning to Spain permanently. Though he was eventually drawn back to his restaurant ventures in the United States, *Vamos a cocinar* would not be Andrés's only foray into television.

Andrés set his sights on American television in 2008, starring in the Public Broadcasting Service (PBS) series *José Made in Spain*. Throughout the course of the twenty-six-part series, Andrés visited each of Spain's unique regions, highlighted the special dishes for which each region is known, and demonstrated how viewers could re-create these dishes in their own homes. In a 2007 press release announcing the show's premiere, Andrés explained why the concept of *José Made in Spain* was so important to him. "People have come to know Spanish food through tapas and paella and with great wines like Rioja, but they don't know where it all comes from or how easy it is to enjoy at home," Andrés said. "I have wanted to bring the best of my country to America and now with this series on public television, I am realizing my dream."

In addition to his own shows, Andrés has made numerous appearances on other television programs, including late-night talk shows such as *The Late Show with David Letterman* and *Conan* and food-themed shows such as *Unique Eats*, *Top Chef*, and *Iron Chef America*. Seeking to promote Spanish cuisine among home cooks as well as restaurant goers, he has published the cookbooks *Tapas: A Taste of Spain in America* (2005) and *Made in Spain: Spanish Dishes for the American Kitchen* (2008), both cowritten with journalist Richard Wolffe.

## MOLECULAR GASTRONOMY
Although it was his skill with and devotion to traditional Spanish cuisine that made him famous, Andrés has never been reluctant to experiment with even the most avant-garde cooking techniques. From his earliest days as a chef, he was interested in pushing the boundaries of food preparation and bringing the most advanced, futuristic culinary practices into his kitchen. In particular, Andrés has been one of the United States' leading advocates of molecular gastronomy, a science-driven approach to cooking.

Pioneered by scientists Nicholas Kurti and Hervé This in the 1980s and popularized by such renowned chefs as Andrés's mentor Ferran Adrià, molecular gastronomy is a culinary philosophy based on the science of food and taste. Practitioners of molecular gastronomy typically use the laws of these sciences to create unique, intensely flavorful dishes in unusual ways. One of Andrés's most famous molecular

gastronomy–inspired dishes, for example, is a deconstructed New England clam chowder that consists of clam spheres, littleneck clams encased in a gel-like mixture of clam juice and other ingredients, placed on top of a concoction of onion puree, potato foam, chive oil, and bacon cream.

Andrés has incorporated his love for molecular gastronomy into virtually all of his restaurant endeavors, but nowhere more so than at minibar by José Andrés, his Washington, DC, establishment that opened in 2003. His cutting-edge cooking techniques are also on display at The Bazaar by José Andrés, a Las Vegas restaurant opened in 2008. Such unusual culinary techniques are not just a fad or an interesting distraction for Andrés, however. In an addendum to *The James Beard Foundation's Best of the Best* (2012), he explained that molecular gastronomy has had an important influence on his entire career. "Ninety-five percent of my brain is on my avant-garde cooking," Andrés said. "It all trickles down from there. Technically, this is what gives me the fire to keep on being a chef."

## PHILOSOPHY AND PHILANTHROPY
For Andrés, cooking boils down to giving something of oneself to others. He incorporates this deep-seated belief into the philosophies of his restaurants and even into his menus; at é by José Andrés in Las Vegas, for instance, every meal begins with canapés that diners eat with their hands. "I make food and I hand it to you," Andrés told Steiman. "I want to surprise you, to entertain you, and I want you to like it. It's me for you." This philosophy has not only served as the underlying foundation of Andrés's culinary business ventures but also been the main inspiration for his numerous philanthropic efforts.

Andrés was first moved to realize the important correlation between food and helping others when he paid a visit to the Ivory Coast, in West Africa, during his tour of duty with the Spanish navy. Witnessing the extreme poverty there left the future celebrity chef with a lasting impression of the pain of hunger and a drive to do something about it. Almost as soon as he arrived in Washington, DC, in 1993, Andrés began volunteering with local charities committed to ending hunger. After first working with Share Our Strength, which focuses on childhood hunger, he found his way to DC Central Kitchen, an organization that uses leftover food from area restaurants to provide meals for the city's hungry residents. For Andrés, DC Central Kitchen offers chefs the opportunity to help the city's residents while improving the efficiency of their own businesses. "Food waste is the essence of business—don't waste food and your business is going to be more successful," Andrés told James Eppard for *Montgomery Magazine* (Mar./Apr.

2013). "The same for a city. If you are making sure that you don't waste food, at the very least you will have no hungry people."

Andrés's philanthropy has not been limited to Washington, DC, or even to the United States. In 2010 he traveled to Haiti following the disastrous January 12 earthquake that left much of the country in ruins. He brought with him a solar cooking device that he had recently been testing and taught the locals how to prepare meals without relying on dangerous, smoke-producing stoves. Andrés has continued his clean-cooking campaign in the years following the earthquake and in 2011 founded World Central Kitchen, an organization devoted to developing and promoting sustainable solutions to the problem of hunger.

With three children of his own, Andrés is keenly aware of the issues surrounding childhood obesity across the United States. Wanting to take a more active role in promoting healthy eating habits, he has lent his outspoken support to First Lady Michelle Obama's antiobesity campaign, in part by demonstrating healthy cooking techniques in an educational video. He also strengthened his commitment to progressive food education by designing his own course, The World on a Plate: How Food Shapes Civilization, at George Washington University. Held in the winter and spring of 2013, the course illustrated for students how food and eating affect virtually every aspect of society.

Through these and other philanthropic endeavors, Andrés has demonstrated that food is much more than his profession—it is his philosophy and his very way of life. Food, according to the chef, is not about providing for oneself but about serving others. "In the end we are all one," Andrés told Eppard. "We're only as good as the people next to us. And if we are all believing that we are supporting each other, chances are things are going to be better."

## SUGGESTED READING

Eppard, James. "The World on His Plate." *Montgomery Magazine*. Insight Media, Mar./Apr. 2013. Web. 16 Apr. 2013.

"Getting to Know José Andrés." *The Taste*. American Broadcasting Company, 11 Mar. 2013. Web. 16 Apr. 2013.

"Meet the Chef: José Andrés." *JustLuxe*. LuxeMont, Feb. 2012. Web. 16 Apr. 2013.

Steiman, Harvey. "Tales of José Andrés." *Wine Spectator*. Wine Spectator, 30 June 2011. PDF File.

Wohl, Kit. "2011: José Andrés: Chapter Twenty-Two." *The James Beard Foundation's Best of the Best*. James Beard Foundation, 2012. PDF File.

—Jack Lasky

# Erin Andrews

**Born:** May 4, 1978
**Occupation:** Journalist and television personality

With her long blond hair and voluptuous figure, the five-foot-ten sportscaster Erin Andrews has normally stood out amid the sweat, dirt, and grit of the playing field. Though her striking appearance has drawn much attention, Andrews has proved to be more than just another pretty face. Known for her "obsession with studying football scores, stats and minutiae," as Chris Greenberg noted for the *Huffington Post* (16 Sept. 2011), she has won the respect of colleagues, coaches, and athletes alike with her vast sports acumen and for her unparalleled work ethic and dedication to her craft. A graduate of the University of Florida, Andrews worked for a series of television stations in Florida and Georgia before landing her dream job, as a sideline reporter for sports network ESPN, in 2004. During the following eight years, she emerged as one of the network's most popular and ubiquitous personalities, while achieving goddess-like status among college football fans and on the Internet. She reported from the sidelines for college football and college basketball games and also provided coverage for National Hockey League (NHL) and Major League Baseball (MLB) telecasts and other special events.

Andrews's enormous popularity came with drawbacks, however; for example, in the summer of 2009, she was the victim of a traumatizing stalking episode that received national media attention. Afterward, her popularity only increased; she made an appearance on *The Oprah Winfrey Show* to discuss the incident, participated as a contestant on the tenth installment of the popular ABC show *Dancing with the Stars*, and became a contributor to that network's news program *Good Morning America*. In 2012, after spending the previous two years working on ESPN's flagship Saturday-morning college football program *College GameDay*, Andrew signed a multiyear contract with Fox Sports, where she began hosting a college football primetime show and contributing to network coverage of MLB and National Football League (NFL) games and other sporting events.

## EARLY LIFE AND EDUCATION

Erin Jill Andrews was born in Lewiston, Maine, May 4, 1978, to Stephen Andrews, a broadcast journalist, and Paula Andrews, a teacher. She has a sister, Kendra, who is four years her junior. When Andrews was a child, she moved with her family to Tampa, Florida, where her father worked as an investigative reporter for the NBC-affiliated station WFLA-TV.

Andrew developed an early passion for sports from her father, an avid sports fan who rooted

Mitch Stringer/CSM/Landov

for the Boston Celtics and Red Sox and the Green Bay Packers. Andrews, who danced from a young age but never played sports, became captivated as a girl by the Celtics' hall of fame forward Larry Bird, who represented "everything about me growing up, and me loving sports," as she noted to Greenberg. She has also recalled coming home from school on Monday nights eager to watch *Monday Night Football*, which sparked her interest in broadcasting. "I would always love to see what the sideline reporter was doing that night," she said, as quoted by James Andrew Miller and Tom Shales in their book *Those Guys Have All the Fun: Inside the World of ESPN* (2011). "I would sit there and critique them when I was younger, and it made me really, really want to be a part of it."

Andrews attended Bloomingdale High School, in Valrico, Florida, where she participated in student government and cheerleading. She also excelled academically as a member of the National Honor Society. By the time Andrews entered her junior year of high school, she was set on becoming a sideline reporter for ESPN. Andrews, who drew inspiration from her father, a six-time Emmy Award winner, as well as from such current and former ESPN female sportscasters as Hannah Storm, Suzy Kolber, Melissa Stark, and Lesley Visser, practiced her broadcasting skills by conducting mock interviews with friends and writing detailed questionnaires. "People signed my yearbook 'Hope to see you on ESPN' and

stuff like that," she recalled to Greenberg. "It was just always something I knew I was going to do."

After graduating from Bloomingdale High in 1997, Andrews enrolled at the University of Florida (UF) in Gainesville. She chose the school not only because of its nationally recognized sports teams but also for its prestigious journalism program. During her sophomore through senior years, Andrews, who would camp out for ESPN's *College GameDay* when it visited the UF campus, was a member of the school's dance squad, the Dazzlers, which performed at home games for multiple sports teams. She was also a member of the Gamma Iota chapter of the Zeta Tau Alpha sorority.

While attending UF, Andrews interned at her father's television station, WFLA-TV, in Tampa, where she learned many of the ins and outs of television sports reporting. One of her mentors during this time included the ESPN *SportsCenter* anchor Sage Steele, who was then working for another Tampa affiliate. Steele "took me under her wing," Andrews recalled to Rafi Kohan for *GQ* (29 Dec. 2010). "When I was interning, other women were not as instructive to me and I understand people are always worrying about their jobs and stuff, but I vowed I would never turn my back on someone who I could tell was eager." She received a BA degree in telecommunications from Florida in 2000.

## EARLY BROADCAST CAREER

Upon graduating from college, Andrews landed her first broadcasting job at Fox Sports Florida South, where she worked as a freelance reporter. Then, in 2001, she was hired as a sideline reporter for the Orlando-based Sunshine Network (now Sun Sports), where she covered her hometown hockey team, the NHL's Tampa Bay Lightning. Noting her lack of hockey knowledge at the time, Andrews told AOL's now-defunct sports website *FanHouse* (14 Oct. 2010) that "the night before I got the job I was reading 'Hockey For Dummies,'" in an effort to get a crash-course education on the sport.

In 2002, Andrews left the Sunshine Network to join Turner Sports, a division of Turner Broadcasting System (TBS), which is headquartered in Atlanta, Georgia. She signed a two-year deal to work as a reporter and studio host for the network. During that time she received her first national exposure, providing coverage of MLB's Atlanta Braves and local college football teams for TBS and covering Atlanta's NBA and NHL teams, the Hawks and Thrashers, for Turner Sports South. Meanwhile, she dedicated herself to becoming a student of the sports she covered. Andrews's fervent drive and determination, as well as her impressive understanding and knowledge of sports eventually caught the attention of ESPN, and in May 2004, the network hired her to work as a reporter for their annual NHL playoff coverage. Andrews, whose contract with Turner Sports was not renewed, auditioned for ESPN by covering a Tampa Bay Lightning game. "She knew all the players and all their stories and they knew her so she really impressed everyone at ESPN," her father told Walt Belcher for the *Tampa Tribune* (27 May 2008).

## ESPN SIREN

At ESPN, Andrews enjoyed a meteoric rise. After covering the 2004 Stanley Cup playoffs, which culminated with the Lightning defeating the Calgary Flames in the finals to win their first-ever title, she signed a multiyear deal with the network. That fall she joined ESPN's *College Football Saturdays* broadcast team as a sideline reporter and also started reporting from the sidelines of Big Ten college basketball games, as part of the network program *Saturday Primetime*. In 2005, she also began reporting for Thursday-night college football and MLB games; soon afterward she started reporting events such as the College World Series, Great Outdoor Games, and Scripps National Spelling Bee.

Over the following several years, Andrews became an ESPN fixture and one of the most widely recognizable sideline reporters in the country. With her magnetic personality and approachable charm, she developed strong contacts among coaches and athletes and instantly won their respect as a first-rate interviewer. Meanwhile, her well-manicured appearance and good looks garnered the obsessive adoration of college male sports fans all over the country. Andrews replaced "the old Farrah Fawcett poster as reigning campus sex symbol," as noted by Miller and Shales, while becoming "TV sports' first It Girl," according to Michael Hiestand for *USA Today* (16 Apr. 2008). Thanks to the emergence of the sports blogosphere, Andrews, who routinely had her name chanted at the games she covered, became an Internet phenomenon, even earning the nickname "Erin Pageviews" for the amount of instant hits her name would yield on such sites as YouTube. Her popularity was such that she was voted "America's Sexiest Sportscaster" in online polls conducted by the popular men's magazine *Playboy* in both 2007 and 2008.

## STALKING INCIDENT

One of the pitfalls of celebrity reared its ugly head in the summer of 2009, when Andrews was secretly videotaped in the nude through a hotel room peephole by an Illinois-based insurance executive named Michael David Barrett. Portions of the video were leaked to the Internet and quickly went viral, while news outlets such as the *New York Post* published still images taken from the video. Mortified and worried that the incident would jeopardize her career, Andrews immediately hired an attorney to help

prevent the video from further proliferating; she then assisted FBI agents in tracking down Barrett, who was eventually caught and arrested in October 2009. In March of the following year, Barrett, who admitted to videotaping Andrews in the nude on two separate occasions in hotels in Nashville, Tennessee, and Milwaukee, Wisconsin, was sentenced to two and a half years in prison for stalking.

Upon release of the video, Andrews became the unwitting victim of a torrent of media criticism that included allegations that she leaked the video herself for publicity and judgments of her questionable wardrobe choices and provocative magazine shoots. For example, one of Andrews's peers, the veteran *USA Today* sports columnist Christine Brennan, accused her of bringing the incident upon herself by "playing to the frat house" with her zany "shtick," thus "encouraging the complete nut case to drill a hole in your room," as quoted by Miller and Shales. Despite such criticism, Andrews returned to work quickly after the incident upon receiving calls of encouragement and support from her ESPN colleagues and some of the most renowned college coaches in the country, including Urban Meyer, Mack Brown, John Calipari, Roy Williams, and Les Miles. "That was a really gratifying moment for me, just seeing all the support, and the reason why they were calling was because they respected my work," Andrews said, as quoted by Miller and Shales. However, she acknowledged to Abigail Pesta, in an interview with *Marie Claire* (13 July 2011), "Being a woman in a male-dominated industry, you are so afraid of people thinking you are weak. It's creepy that you're a crime victim and you don't want people to think you're weak [by not returning to work]."

In the wake of the incident, Andrews, who also received numerous letters from other victims of stalking and video-voyeurism, appeared on *The Oprah Winfrey Show* to discuss her traumatizing experience. She also became an advocate for strengthening laws against stalkers. In 2010, she traveled to Washington, DC, to lobby for tougher antistalking legislation and also filed a negligence lawsuit against the hotels in which her privacy was invaded. "The laws are so outdated, and technology has just gotten better and crazier and faster," she told Pesta. "The laws need to be strengthened—they're a joke. Hopefully, we can get something done. I've brought attention to the crime. Now let's fix it."

## *DANCING WITH THE STARS* AND BEYOND

Prior to the surfacing of Barrett's peephole video, Andrews agreed to appear as a contestant on the tenth season of ABC's dance competition show *Dancing with the Stars*, which premiered in March 2010. Teaming with the professional Ukrainian dancer Maksim Chmerkovskiy, she placed third out of the eleven celebrity contestants. Andrews's appearance on the show helped broaden her popularity beyond the sports world as well as open up new entertainment opportunities. Nonetheless, during the airing of the show, Andrews found herself in the middle of another media dustup when television personality Elisabeth Hasselbeck, then a cohost on the ABC daytime talk show *The View*, mocked her scantily-clad dance attire in light of her stalking situation. "That was basically throwing stalking in the face of every victim," Andrews told Pesta, "and laughing about it." Soon afterward Hasselbeck issued a public apology to Andrews for her comments.

During the summer of 2010, Andrews agreed to terms on a new two-year contract with ESPN. Her role expanded to include hosting the first hour of an expanded *College GameDay* program on ESPNU and joining the ESPN *College GameDay* broadcast team as a contributing reporter, which she described to Hiestand for *USA Today* (3 Sept. 2010) as "a pinch-yourself moment." She also began serving as a correspondent for ABC's long-running news program *Good Morning America*.

On July 1, 2012, after passing on an offer to extend her contract with ESPN, Andrews joined Fox Sports, as part of that network's push into college football. At Fox, with whom she signed a multiyear deal, Andrews began cohosting a new thirty-minute primetime college football pregame show, with former NFL players Eddie George and Joey Harrington. She also became a contributor to Fox's MLB and NFL coverage, working as a features and sideline reporter for the programs *MLB on Fox* and *Fox NFL Sunday*. By 2013, she had covered other major sporting events for the network that included the MLB All-Star Game, the National League Championship Series and World Series, the National Football Conference playoffs, and NASCAR's Daytona 500.

### PERSONAL LIFE
Andrews lives in both New York City and Los Angeles. She has been romantically linked to the NHL hockey player Jarret Stoll, who was a member of the 2012 Stanley Cup–winning Los Angeles Kings. She has appeared in television commercials for the daily probiotic supplement TruBiotics and has made guest spots on such television programs as *The Rachael Ray Show*, *Jimmy Kimmel Live!*, and *The Tonight Show with Jay Leno*. She also had a cameo appearance in the Adam Sandler comedy *That's My Boy* (2012). She has been involved in charitable causes and has participated in the Make-A-Wish Foundation, Kraft Foods' Huddle to Fight Hunger campaign, and the Girls Night Out initiative, which helps raise funds for the Tragedy Assistance Program for Survivors program. She has also raised prostate cancer awareness through the social media initiative AbolishCancer. Her father battled and beat the disease in 2009.

### SUGGESTED READING
Andrews, Erin. Interview by Chris Greenberg. "Erin Andrews Interview: ESPN Sideline Reporter Talks Larry Bird, Role Models and Female Sports Fans." *Huffington Post*. TheHuffingtonPost.com, 16 Sept. 2011. Web. 13 June 2013.

Andrews, Erin. Interview by Rafi Kohan. "Thirty Minutes in Football Heaven with Erin Andrews." *GQ*. Condé Nast, 29 Dec. 2010. Web. 13 June 2013.

"Erin Andrews Opens Up about Career, Family, Dancing and the Law." *AolNews*. AOL News, 14 Oct. 2010. Web. 13 June 2013.

Hiestand, Michael. "Erin Moves Up with the Big Boys." *USA Today* 3 Sept. 2010: Sports 03c. Print.

Jenkins, Sally. "Andrews Was Victimized, But She's No Victim." *Washington Post* 4 Sept. 2009: D03. Print.

Miller, James Andrew, and Tom Shales. *Those Guys Have All the Fun: Inside the World of ESPN*. New York: Little, 2011. Print.

—*Chris Cullen*

---

# Aziz Ansari

**Born:** February 23, 1983
**Occupation:** Actor, writer, and comedian

Aziz Ansari began his career in comedy as a freshman at New York University (NYU) in 2000. Now twenty-nine years old, Ansari has become a star not only in stand-up, but also in television, film, and beyond. As an Indian American, Ansari is one of several twenty-first-century performers of South Asian descent to enter the mainstream without playing stereotypical characters. Working his way through small venues and eventually joining the renowned Upright Citizens Brigade Theatre, Ansari cocreated the sketch comedy Human Giant, an act that later put him on television and led to his most notable role yet on the television series *Parks and Recreation*.

In a *New Yorker* profile of Ansari, his friend and creative collaborator Jason Woliner said, "From the beginning I think Aziz had this fully formed persona—he knew who he was, and had this confidence, or swagger, that people really could latch on to" (1 Nov. 2010). This persona has made Ansari a multiplatform mainstream star known for his drive and enthusiasm. His seemingly ubiquitous presence in popular culture—from his Twitter feed and blog, to his semi-serious Food Club, to an appearance in a Jay-Z and Kanye West music video, to meeting

FilmMagic

and campaigning for President Barack Obama, to filming an instructional video on napping— Ansari has remained humble as his success has continued to grow.

## CHILDHOOD AND EDUCATION

Aziz Ismail Ansari was born on February 23, 1983, in Columbia, South Carolina, to Tamil Indian immigrants. His father, Shoukath, is a gastroenterologist and his mother, Fatima, works in a medical office. Though his parents are Muslim, Ansari himself is an atheist. Ansari was raised in Bennettsville, South Carolina, with his parents and his younger brother, Aniz. Bennettsville was a small town, but Ansari notes that he did not face much discrimination growing up there. "You read that I was the only minority in school, you envision this little brown boy sitting in a corner by himself," he told *Rolling Stone*'s Gavin Edwards (8 July 2010). "It wasn't like that."

Ansari attended Marlboro Academy and eventually the South Carolina Governor's School for Science and Mathematics (GSSM), where he spent his final two years of high school before graduating in 2000. "Going to the school helped me grow in a myriad of ways," he told Susan Cohen for the *Charleston City Paper* (1 Feb. 2012). "To meet so many kids from different backgrounds with different ideas and interests, it really influenced me." At GSSM Ansari played tennis and performed well academically, despite having a reputation as somewhat of a class clown. He did research on immunology but told Cohen, "It was fun and I learned a lot, but I realized biology wasn't for me."

In 2000 Ansari began his freshman year at NYU, where he enrolled in the Stern School of Business to study marketing. He recognized early on he did not want to pursue a corporate career and considered transferring to the Tisch School of the Arts. "I wasn't really aware of the whole finance culture, like I didn't know *anything* about Goldman Sachs and that stuff," he told Renée Alfuso for the Spring 2012 issue of *NYU Alumni Magazine*, "so it was all kind of foreign to me." Nonetheless, Ansari stayed the course, graduating in 2004.

## STAND-UP COMEDY AND *HUMAN GIANT*

Ansari began performing stand-up in 2001 when he was a college freshman, passing out flyers in Times Square in exchange for five-minute performance slots at comedy clubs. Speaking about these early shows, Ansari told the *Los Angeles Times'* Deborah Vankin, "The joke-writing ability wasn't there yet, but I was really comfortable on stage" (11 Sept. 2012). He added, "I never had any aspirations of putting out big specials or being an actor. It was more like: 'Lemme just keep writing good jokes.' I started going to open mikes . . . I've never taken a long break from stand-up since." He performed at open-mike nights throughout college and began doing evening-long sets.

At the age of twenty-two, Ansari was noticed by Matt Besser, one of the founding members of the Upright Citizens Brigade (UCB), an improvisational comedy group. In June 2005 Ansari created and began hosting UCB's Monday night show *Crash Test*—a popular alt stand-up showcase for new talent. *Crash Test* won the 2006 Jury Award for Live Performance at the US Comedy Arts Festival; Ansari was named best stand-up with fellow comedian Mitch Fatel.

During his time with *Crash Test*, Ansari began performing with friends Paul Scheer and Rob Huebel, and the trio began conceptualizing short film sketches. Calling themselves the Human Giant, Ansari, Scheer, and Huebel—along with director Jason Woliner—wrote and starred in a series of online shorts. The videos were also shown at venues like Channel 101, a monthly short-film festival. The energetic and offbeat Human Giant videos gained an online audience and eventually caught the attention of an executive at MTV, who offered the group a television pilot. In an interview with the *A.V. Club*, Ansari told Amelie Gillette about getting picked up by MTV: "They were also really psyched about what we had done, and were just ready to go ahead and shoot this. It wasn't like, 'Okay, so we'll develop this for a year. You guys can write a script.' They're like, 'No, we really want you guys to do this'" (8 May 2007). *Human Giant* premiered on April 5, 2007, and combined the group's sketches into a variety show. Notable sketches include "Shutterbugs" and "Illusionators."

Writing and starring in the *Human Giant* television program was more involved and exhausting than Ansari and his partners anticipated. Ansari played bizarre characters ranging from a children's talent agent, to a police officer who pursues criminals by hot-air balloon, to a magician with low self-esteem. They worked together for up to twenty hours a day, doing everything from pitching jokes to planning the costumes and props for the skits. The show aired on MTV for two full seasons, ending in April 2008. The stars opted out of pursuing a third season, instead choosing to focus on other aspects of their careers. With the end of the show, Ansari moved across the country to Los Angeles.

## EARLY FILM AND TELEVISION APPEARANCES

During his years with UCB, *Crash Test*, and Human Giant, Ansari picked up roles in popular television series and feature films. In 2007 he appeared on the HBO series *Flight of the Conchords*, starring Bret McKenzie and Jemaine Clement. Ansari played Sinjay, a racist fruit seller who refuses to sell produce to New Zealanders. In 2009 Ansari appeared in recurring roles on the shows *Reno 911* and *Scrubs*. In the mockumentary show *Reno 911*, Ansari played an insurance representative in three episodes of the comedy's final season. In *Scrubs* Ansari portrayed Ed Dhandapani, a slacker doctor known for creating catchphrases; the character was written out of the show after four episodes so that Ansari could pursue other television work. On Ansari's comic timing and improvisational skills, *Scrubs* star Zach Braff told the *Wall Street Journal*'s Ellen Gamerman: "With Aziz, you really get a sense that he's just coming up with this crazy, random stuff off the top of his mind" (27 Mar. 2009).

In 2006 and 2008 Ansari appeared in two motion picture comedies—*School for Scoundrels* and *The Rocker*—in which he made small appearances. Neither film received particularly positive reviews, and Ansari's parts were incidental. In 2009, however, he appeared in three comedies featuring major stars and in which he had more substantial roles. *I Love You, Man* stars Paul Rudd and Jason Segal, with Ansari playing a friend of Rudd's character. In *Observe and Report* Ansari plays an Arab shopkeeper who is confronted by the main character, a security guard played by Seth Rogan. The most important of Ansari's 2009 film appearances was *Funny People*, a movie written, directed, and produced by Judd Apatow and starring Adam Sandler and Seth Rogan.

In *Funny People* Ansari plays Randy Springs—an abrasive and offensive, but very popular, comedian—who became the breakout character of the film. Randy (or "Raaaaaaaandy" with eight *a*'s, as the character insists it should be) is, according to the *New Yorker*'s Kalefa Sanneh, "a salacious hip-hop comedian who is secure in his belief that profanity has rendered punch lines obsolete" (1 Nov. 2010). She adds: "Even though Randy was supposed to represent everything that was wrong with stand-up comedy, something about him—his cracked confidence, perhaps, or his salty joy—made him the film's most enduring character." After the release of *Funny People*, Randy's popularity among audiences (and even among the people involved with the film, notably Rogan and Apatow) led to the creation of a website for Randy. Apatow also paid Ansari to appear in a three-part Randy documentary that follows the fictional comedian. Years after the movie Ansari is still hailed by fans with the cry "Raaaaaaaandy!" in the character's trademark sing-song voice.

## *PARKS AND RECREATION*

In the summer of 2008, Ansari was cast in an NBC television program that was being billed as a possible spinoff of the hit comedy *The Office*. He was the first member of the cast to be hired, describing his excitement to Gamerman saying: "[The creators] could've told me the premise is that you and Vin Diesel run a day-care center together and at night you fight crime, and it's shot like 'The Office,' documentary-style, I'd be like, 'I'm doing that show.'" (27 Mar. 2009). Ansari was soon joined by the show's star, *Saturday Night Live* actor Amy Poehler. Poehler knew of Ansari from her work as an original member of the Upright Citizens Brigade. Michael Schur, the show's cocreator, told David Itzkoff for the *New York Times* that Ansari "defies categorization," adding that "he's really sarcastic but also kind of lovable" and that "there's so much going on with him that we felt it would be funny just to have him and Amy Poehler in the same room" (3 June 2010).

The show abandoned the notion of tying its plots or characters to *The Office* and became *Parks and Recreation*—a mockumentary-style comedy about a parks department in a fictional Indiana town. *Parks and Recreation* premiered on April 9, 2009, and stars Poehler and Ansari, along with actors Rashida Jones, Nick Offerman, and Aubrey Plaza, who attended NYU at the same time as Ansari; the show's cast later added actors Adam Scott and Rob Lowe. Ansari plays Tom Haverford, an unmotivated mid-level government employee obsessed with fashion and popular culture. His character is vain and cocky, with business skills that cannot match his bragging and lofty goals. Haverford is known for having a lot of swagger with seemingly little substance but occasionally shows signs of growth and maturity in his relationships with his colleagues.

Like Ansari, Haverford is an Indian American born in South Carolina. Said Gavin Edwards of Ansari's character: "Much of Ansari's freshness comes from the way he plays with notions of race and representation—by essentially not acknowledging it, making the audience grapple with the inherent humor of this awkward Indian kid doing nothing to conform to any kind of racial stereotypes. In *Parks and Recreation*, the basic joke about his character is that he's named Tom Haverford and identifies with hip-hop more than his own ethnic background" (8 July 2010). The show also allows Ansari to utilize his improvisational skills, which often yield some of its funniest lines. Indeed, Ansari is often credited as a scene-stealer, with Haverford emerging as one of the show's breakout characters. With its fifth season airing in 2012 and 2013, *Parks and Recreation* is one of television's most critically acclaimed series.

## STAND-UP SPECIALS

During breaks between filming *Parks and Recreation*, Ansari continued to write and perform stand-up. In 2008 and 2009 Ansari embarked on his Glow in the Dark tour—a name taken from the concert tour of Kanye West, a performer Ansari admires while also gently mocking him in his comedy. Ansari's routines from the Glow in the Dark tour led to his debut album: *Intimate Moments for a Sensual Evening*. The *Intimate Moments for a Sensual Evening* special aired on Comedy Central on January 19, 2010. The special was well received by critics and comedians alike (including Judd Apatow and Patton Oswalt) and covered a broad range of topics ranging from bedsheets, Craigslist, Kanye West, and Ansari's younger cousin Harris. The show also featured the return of Randy Springs when Ansari performed ten minutes of jokes in character.

In the summer of 2010, Ansari hosted the MTV Movie Awards before embarking on a new comedy tour. The Dangerously Delicious tour included a performance at the Bonnaroo Music Festival and a sold-out show at Carnegie Hall. In the summer of 2012, Ansari self-released the *Dangerously Delicious* special on his website with little fanfare, allowing users to download it for five dollars. The no-frills release was modeled after a similar comedy special from Louis CK, a comedian whom Ansari admires. Ansari explained his reasoning to critic Alan Sepinwall for the website *HitFix*: "I think it's great to be able to get something directly from an artist, where it's his vision, not edited, not censored. It's exactly what I wanted it to be" (20 Mar. 2012). *Dangerously Delicious* features bits about communication with women, rappers 50 Cent and Jay-Z, and the Internet. Shortly after *Dangerously Delicious* went online, Ansari began a new tour—Buried Alive!—which will include all new material.

## FILM CAREER

Between his two major tours, Ansari costarred in the film *30 Minutes or Less* (2011) with Jesse Eisenberg and comedians Danny McBride and Nick Swardson. Ansari utilized his improv background in playing the character Chet, a teacher who becomes caught in a ransom and bank-robbery plot with his friend, played by Eisenberg. "This is the first time I've been in a movie the whole time," he told Amy Kaufman for the *Los Angeles Times* (1 May 2011). "I hope people are up for it. I hope they're not like, 'Oh, what? He's in the movie for longer than five minutes? No! I can only take him in small doses!' That would be bad for my career." Ansari also made small appearances in the films *Get Him to the Greek* (2010) and *Ice Age: Continental Drift* (2012).

Off screen, he has been working on a three-film writing deal with Judd Apatow and Universal Pictures. Ansari and Jason Woliner—who has directed episodes of *Parks and Recreation* in addition to his work with *Human Giant*—had three comedy pitches picked up, all of which feature scripts that star Ansari. One film, tentatively titled *Let's Do This*, is about two traveling motivational speakers. Another, called *Space Men*, features a disgraced astronaut who must return to the moon to clear his name. The final is rumored to be a spinoff of *Funny People* that could potentially feature Randy Springs.

## PERSONAL LIFE

Between his regular work on television, his stand-up tours, his film career (as both an actor and a writer), and other projects and appearances, Ansari has kept very busy and is rarely idle. Generally quiet about his personal life, Ansari's latest tour addresses his life at twenty-nine. In an interview with *Pitchfork*, he told Carrie Battan, "On my new tour, I talk about three things: babies, marriage, and how hard it is to find someone. . . . This tour is driven mostly by fear: I'm 29 now, am I really ready to get married and have a kid? I don't think so. So it's about coming to the realization that a lot of people I know are doing that right now and how it's scary to me" (22 July 2012). Despite his fears, Ansari is known as a high-energy, fearless performer. He has a reputation as a hard worker, and he explained his work ethic to *Time* (14 Feb. 2011) using a quote from actor and comedian Steve Martin: "Be undeniably good." Ansari added: "It's about working hard, being patient and holding yourself up to such a high standard that when you reach it, people will have to take notice."

Ansari is also a popular presence online and in social media. His Twitter account and blog—*Aziz is Bored*—have millions of followers. He uses them to share his interest in topics such as popular culture and films, comedy, music, and charities, as well as his often humorous observations about them. Vankin described him in the *Los Angeles Times*, saying: "His sensibility is hip yet inclusive, pointed but not mean. And he's become something of a 'Where's Waldo' of the digital zeitgeist, riffing on and appearing in pop-cultural currents gone viral" (11 Sept. 2012). Ansari is also noted for his interest in musicians such as R. Kelly, Kanye West, and Jay-Z, as well as his admiration of President Barack Obama and comic icons including Chris Rock, Louis CK, and Larry David. Known as a food enthusiast, Ansari frequently writes about food online and is often eating during interviews. His unofficial food club (called, naturally, "Food Club") consists of him and his friends eating at restaurants and bestowing them with plaques if they are deemed worthy.

Ansari's Indian ethnicity is also an important part of his life and career, though he is uninterested in playing characters that are racially stereotyped. Like his fellow young writer-performers Mindy Kaling and Danny Pudi, Ansari has become part of a wave of Indian and South Asian Americans in mainstream entertainment. Ansari's career has shown no signs of slowing down, and with his upcoming film and comedy projects, it is likely that his star will continue to rise. Asked by a *Time* reader about a fallback career, however, Ansari joked, "I would probably sell knives on the Home Shopping Network. No, make that swords. I can brag about the craftsmanship. Should be fine" (14 Feb. 2011).

© Ramin Talaie/Corbis

### SUGGESTED READING

Gamerman, Ellen. "The Rise of the Likeable Jerk." *Wall Street Journal* 27 Mar. 2009: W4. Print.

Itzkoff, Dave. "Feeding the Comedy Beast without Serving Leftovers." *New York Times* 4 June 2010: C1. Print.

Sanneh, Kelefa. "Funny Person." *New Yorker* 1 Nov. 2010: 60–70. Print.

Vankin, Deborah. "Aziz Ansari, Wired to Joke." *Los Angeles Times.* Los Angeles Times, 11 Sept. 2012. Web. 13 Dec. 2012.

Weiner, Jonah. "Comedy's New Wave." *Rolling Stone* 15 Sept. 2011: 3–12. Print.

—*Kehley Coviello*

## Michael Arad

**Born:** July 21, 1969
**Occupation:** Architect; designer of the National September 11 Memorial

In 2004, Israeli American architect Michael Arad's design for the National September 11 Memorial (originally known as the World Trade Center Memorial) in New York City was selected from over 5,200 entries in an international contest sponsored by the Lower Manhattan Development Corporation (LMDC). Entries were judged by a panel of thirteen jurors that included Maya Lin, the famous architect and visionary behind the Vietnam War Memorial in Washington, DC. Lin was an outspoken advocate for Arad's design, titled *Reflecting Absence*. The plan featured two reflecting pools in the footprints of the towers, representing space that cannot be filled. Aspects of Arad's winning design evolved during the extended planning period, but his core vision—of the dichotomy of life and death represented by two voids within a larger gathering space—has remained.

Arad's design was peaceful and reflective, but the planning and construction of the memorial were not. Handfuls of invested parties, each with its own agenda, descended on the site as soon as the planning process began in 2004. By 2006, the memorial's price tag, which had been estimated somewhat arbitrarily at about $300 million, had ballooned to over $1 billion. No one was happy, least of all Arad, who felt that the city was trying to bully him off of his own project. A thirty-four-year-old unknown when his design was selected, Arad was unprepared for the bureaucratic tug-of-war that followed his selection, and his responses to the increasing pressure at times alienated colleagues and other involved parties. "I think it was because he was young," Peter Walker, a landscape architect who worked alongside Arad on the memorial, told

Ted Loos for the *New York Times* (1 Sept. 2011). "If he couldn't get somebody to do it the way he wanted it done, he couldn't see that there was an alternative." Arad agreed, telling Loos, "I was very apprehensive about any changes to the design. Whether I wanted to or not, I learned that you can accept some changes to its form without compromising its intent. But it's a leap of faith that I didn't want to make initially—to put it mildly." While the adjacent museum remains incomplete, the memorial opened to the public on September 11, 2011, the ten-year anniversary of the terrorist attacks.

## EARLY LIFE AND EDUCATION
Michael Arad was born to Rivka and Moshe Arad in London, England, on July 21, 1969. His father was the Israeli ambassador to Mexico from 1983 to 1987 and to the United States from 1987 to 1990. By the time Arad graduated from high school, he had lived in Mexico City, Jerusalem, New York City, and Washington, DC. He attended Dartmouth College but left school to serve in the Israeli military (a requirement for all Israeli citizens), serving with the Golani Brigade during the first intifada in the late 1980s. He returned to Dartmouth and graduated with a bachelor's degree in government studies in 1991.

Adar discovered his love of architecture while taking various elective courses in studio art and art history at Dartmouth. After spending a year snowboarding in Colorado with his soon-to-be wife, Melanie Fitzpatrick, Arad enrolled in Georgia Tech's College of Architecture in 1995. He told Nancy A. Ruhling for the American-Israeli Cooperative Enterprise's (AICE) *Jewish Virtual Library* that he was intimidated by the difficulty of doing meaningful work. "I entered the field with hesitation because I wasn't sure if I could do what I hoped to do," he said. He earned his master's degree in 1999 and moved to New York City the same year.

## BECOMING A NEW YORKER
Arad began his architectural career at Kohn Pedersen Fox Associates in Manhattan. One of his first projects was designing the top twenty floors of a skyscraper in Hong Kong. He also worked on the design team for Espirito Santo Plaza, a skyscraper in Miami, Florida, that won the 2001 New York American Institute of Architects Award. He spent three years with the firm before joining the design department of the New York City Housing Authority after being impressed by a new police station in his neighborhood. Tired of building skyscrapers, Arad assisted in the design of two police stations in the city. In 2003, he went on paternity leave after the birth of his first child, Nathaniel. The time off gave Arad the opportunity to work on a project that he had been turning over in his mind since the terrorist attacks on September 11, 2001.

Arad was a two-year resident of the city in 2001, living in the East Village. He had lived there for some time as a teenager too, but he still felt like an outsider. On the morning of the attacks, Arad was at home and saw the second plane hit the South Tower from his rooftop. He was unable to reach his wife, who was working as a tax attorney several blocks from the Twin Towers, so he rode downtown on his bike to find her. He found her as she was being evacuated from her office building on Broad Street, and the two headed east. They narrowly missed the cloud of dust and smoke that engulfed her building minutes later as the first tower collapsed, and they saw the second tower fall when they reached the Williamsburg Bridge.

A few days later, unable to sleep, Arad rode his bike through the deserted downtown neighborhoods in the middle of the night and came upon an impromptu vigil at Washington Square Park. It was a strange yet profound moment for Arad. "I think people came there the same way that I did, alone or maybe with one other friend, but people stood there together," he told *Habitus* magazine (9 Sept. 2011). "And when I walked up to that fountain, that circular fountain, I joined that circle of people and I didn't feel alone anymore. I don't think I understood the significance of that moment, but in many ways it was a very transformative moment for me: I felt that I became a New Yorker, realizing that this is my home."

## THE SEEDS OF A DESIGN
The sense of community Arad felt that night in Washington Square Park would serve as the impetus for his design commemorating the attack. He found inspiration in seemingly random things, such as when the pastry shop next door to his apartment set a cake in the window with an image of the Twin Towers and the phrase "We will never forget" etched in frosting. He was taken aback by the gesture at first but came to appreciate it as time went on. He compared his own architectural sketches to the cake; he was finding solace through his own personal mode of expression. Arad told *Habitus*, "I was trying to find a way to make sense, to acknowledge what we had seen, what we had suffered. I spent close to a year on what was a very personal and very cathartic exercise of exploring these ideas."

Arad kept returning to the image of water falling into a void, the physical manifestation of what he described to *Habitus* as the "sense that the fabric of space had somehow been torn open." He built a miniature fountain, envisioning a memorial located not at the former site of the towers but on the Hudson River. A year later, the Lower Manhattan Development Corporation (LMDC), an organization jointly founded by the city and state of New York to oversee the rebuilding of lower Manhattan after September 11, announced an international competition to design a memorial to be built where the towers once stood. Arad decided to reformat his Hudson River idea for the contest and enlisted several of his friends, including architects Bruno Caballé, Lihi Gerstner, and Eric Howeler, to help him flesh out the design. They began working two weeks before the competition's deadline in June 2003.

### REFLECTING ABSENCE

Arad's design featured immense reflecting pools slightly south of the Twin Tower footprints; the sunken pools were each an acre in size. The waterfalls that fed the square pools began just below ground level and tumbled down into the thirty-foot abyss. The powerful simplicity of the design was attractive to some of the jurors, particularly Lin, though Arad also had other advocates. Among the cavernous skyscrapers of lower Manhattan and the proposed Freedom Tower (now called World Trade Center One) directly adjacent to the memorial site, the pools were a visceral reminder of the enormity of the loss suffered on September 11. The names of those who died in the attacks as well as the six people who died in the 1993 bombing attack at the World Trade Center were to be inscribed on parapets surrounding the pools in an underground gallery. Arad's design also called for a flat area surrounding the pools that would serve as a city gathering space.

The LMDC received 5,201 submissions from professional and amateur architects in sixty-three countries. A thirteen-member jury of architects, politicians, artists, and family members of victims sifted through every single entry and in November 2003 narrowed the field down to eight finalists. As a finalist, Arad received $100,000 from the LMDC to revise his design, which many of the jurors thought was too barren and observers in the media criticized as "stark" and "cold." Doug Allen, Arad's former professor from Georgia Tech with whom he was in contact during the process, attested to the intense pressure the criticism added to Arad's difficult task. "His world has changed," Allen told Kimberly Link-Wills for the Georgia Tech magazine *Tech Topics* (2004).

To revise the design for the plaza around the reflecting pools, Arad worked with renowned landscape architect Peter Walker. Walker designed bands of pathways around the pools, softened by groves of sycamore, locust, and linden trees. The addition of Walker to Arad's team—the two share credit for the design, a stipulation at which Arad initially balked—gave Arad, who was still considered a novice, an air of legitimacy. The veteran Walker had worked on Millennium Park for the Sydney Olympics, among a number of high-profile projects. Arad and Walker's design made the cut when the jury whittled

the pool down to three finalists, though it still did not enjoy overwhelming public support. In early 2004, around the time Arad was informed that the design had been selected as the winner, the *New York Times* referred to his design as the "dark horse" of the three finalists, according to Allen.

### TOO MANY COOKS

Arad and Walker's design was publicly unveiled on January 14, 2004. Despite earlier hostilities, the public largely embraced the plan and celebrated the success of the unknown Arad. At the same time, tensions developed between Arad and the LMDC. Arad hired a lawyer and aggressively lobbied the LMDC for a contract that clearly defined his role as the lead architect of the memorial and identified Walker as his subcontractor. Among other things, Arad also asked the corporation to fund a new firm that he would call Arad Architects. The LMDC was willing to meet some of Arad's conditions but hesitated when it came to calling him the lead architect. Within months, rumors of Arad's unpleasant behavior began to surface, including stories that he had threatened the LMDC with taking his grievances public. Sources said that Arad was unwilling to compromise in the face of multiple changes to his design that were suggested immediately after the unveiling.

One problem with Arad's design was that it deviated significantly from the master plan for the sixteen-acre site developed by the famous architect Daniel Libeskind, which included the 1,776-foot Freedom Tower, a cultural center, and a museum. Libeskind was hired before the competition was announced, and the LMDC stipulated that the submitted designs should fit Libeskind's master plan—though they simultaneously encouraged applicants to ignore it. The inconsistencies between the two plans caused disputes between Arad and Libeskind as well as serious problems for the project as a whole.

"Imagine that you're trying to cook a meal," Allen told Link-Wills of Arad's situation, "and you have twenty people yelling at you at full volume every five seconds what ingredients ought to be in it. You can't concentrate on the task at hand because there are all these distractions. And the ante is pretty high already." The ante to which Allen referred was the diverse coalition of groups to which Arad was expected to answer. Arad's main client was technically the LMDC; however, he also had to consider the PATH (Port Authority Trans-Hudson) train tracks below the site and answer to the Port Authority of New York and New Jersey, the owner of the bulk of the site. The LMDC hired three additional architecture firms to work on different aspects of the memorial, and former New York governor George Pataki, former New York City mayor Rudy Giuliani, and succeeding mayor

Michael Bloomberg were politically invested in the project. Arad also had to consider the needs of developer Larry Silverstein, who owns most of the World Trade Center complex, having purchased a ninety-nine-year lease weeks before the attacks. Finally, and perhaps most importantly, Arad had to answer to several coalitions of family members of the victims and several more coalitions of lower Manhattan residents.

### ROAD TO COMPLETION
By 2005, it seemed as though the plans for the memorial were falling to pieces. In the spring of 2006, a profile of Arad in *New York* magazine and several articles in the *New York Times* reported a sense of futility from insiders and outsiders alike. But things began to change later that year. After battling for months, Arad made a huge concession to those pushing for changes to his original design. He had planned for the memorial to feature underground galleries where visitors would see the names of the victims with the falling water behind them. Amid cost and security concerns, however, Arad was forced to eliminate the underground space altogether and have the names surround the pools above ground instead. Arad was devastated, as he had seen the chambers as an integral part of his vision. But in his defeat, he won a number of allies, including Bloomberg. In 2006, Bloomberg became chair of the memorial foundation, which took over the reins on the project from the LMDC. Bloomberg became an advocate for the battle-tested Arad, who in turn felt less defensive in negotiations because the mayor believed in his ultimate vision.

The memorial opened to the public on the ten-year anniversary of the attacks, on September 11, 2011. Arad had made some more concessions, but he had also declared a few victories. The names surrounding the pools are arranged, Arad has said, according to "meaningful adjacencies." This means that the names of the victims not only align with where they worked in the towers, if they did, but also are placed in groupings of friends, family members, and other important relationships. With Bloomberg's support, Arad and his team were able to ask family members for requests regarding name placement; they received 1,200 such requests and were able to honor every single one. "There are incredibly sad stories that are now embedded in the very fabric of this memorial design," Arad told *Habitus*. "These relationships, to the naked eye, are invisible: it looks like a random array of names, but in fact there are constellations of adjacencies."

### PERSONAL LIFE
Arad and his wife, Melanie Fitzpatrick, a corporate lawyer, met as students at Dartmouth and married in Boston, Massachusetts, on February 25, 2001. They have three young children: Nathaniel, Ariel, and Dani. Arad and his family live in New York City.

### SUGGESTED READING
Arad, Michael. "A Conversation with Michael Arad." *Habitus*. Habitus, 9 Sept. 2011. Web. 31 July 2013.

Hagan, Joe. "The Breaking of Michael Arad." *New York*. New York Media, May 2006. Web. 31 July 2013.

Link-Wills, Kimberly. "'His World Has Changed': Arad Gains International Fame with World Trade Center Memorial." *Tech Topics* Spring 2004: 25–26. Print.

Loos, Ted. "Architect and 9/11 Memorial Both Evolved over the Years." *New York Times*. New York Times, 1 Sept. 2011. Web. 31 July 2013.

Ruhling, Nancy A. "Michael Arad (1969– )." *Jewish Virtual Library*. American-Israeli Cooperative Enterprise, n.d. Web. 31 July 2013.

—*Molly Hagan*

---

# Fred Armisen
**Born:** December 4, 1966
**Occupation:** Comedian and actor

*Saturday Night Live* (*SNL*) veteran Fred Armisen is a comedian and actor best known as the cocreator and star, with Carrie Brownstein, of the Independent Film Channel's (IFC) hit show *Portlandia*. Armisen, who left the cast of *SNL* at the end of the 2013 season, is a master of impersonations. His arsenal of real-life personages is diverse and includes US president Barack Obama, former New York governor David Paterson, television host Larry King, Iranian president Mahmoud Ahmadinejad, former Apple chief executive Steve Jobs, and actor Tony Danza. Armisen, who also wrote for the show, created a number of popular recurring characters as well, including the Venezuelan nightclub comedian Fericito; Garth, one half of the perpetually unprepared singing duo Garth and Kat, with Kristin Wiig; and Nicholas Fehn, the political comedian who reads newspaper headlines on the show's "Weekend Update." Armisen ended his eleven-year stint on the legendary sketch program to devote more time to *Portlandia*. He did not make a formal announcement, though his departure had been rumored for some time. In his last sketch as a cast member, Armisen reprised his character Ian Rubbish in a sing-along with surprise guests Brownstein, his *Portlandia* costar, and musicians Kim Gordon and Aimee Mann, among others. He told Elise Czajkowski for the comedy website *Splitsider* (28 June 2013) that the farewell sketch was "a love letter to all the music I grew up with, and also to my friends and to *SNL* and

© Kurt Krieger/Corbis

to Lorne [Michaels] and to the cast. There was a lot of emotion attached to it, but it was a very positive emotion."

Armisen teamed up with Brownstein in 2010 to create the sketch show *Portlandia*, which premiered on IFC in 2011. A send-up of Brownstein's hometown, Portland, Oregon, the satirical sketch show neatly walks the line between playful parody and mockery. For Armisen and Brownstein, all aspects of the liberal, eco-friendly city are fair game. *Portlandia* is a heightened portrayal of hipsters, locavores, dumpster divers, music nerds, DIY-ers, and twenty-first-century artisans. In one sketch, the two start a business with the tagline "We can pickle that!" and brine everything in sight. *Portlandia* quickly became IFC's most popular show, drawing 1.1 million viewers for its season-three premiere.

## EARLY LIFE

Fred Armisen was born on December 4, 1966, in Hattiesburg, Mississippi. He spent a part of two years of his childhood in Rio de Janeiro, Brazil, before moving to Valley Stream in Long Island, New York. His mother is originally from Venezuela and his father is of German-Japanese descent. Growing up, Armisen was a voracious music fan. He loved the Clash and other rock bands, but he was also a fan of the enigmatic pop star Prince, whom he would later portray on *SNL*. "I do it because I wanna meet him some day," Armisen half-joked to Amelie Gillette for the *A.V. Club* (11 Jan. 2006). Armisen jumped into the music scene after dropping out of the

School of Visual Arts in Manhattan. He started a band with Damon Locks, whom he had met in an art history class in 1987. Locks has attested to Armisen's sense of humor, but he never thought he would end up in comedy. Armisen had hoped to work in television in some capacity, but oddly, life as a comedian never crossed his mind.

Throughout the 1990s, Armisen was a drummer in the Chicago-based rock group Trenchmouth. He was known for playing the drums standing up. "He didn't want to be the typical drummer," Locks, Trenchmouth's former lead singer, told Dave Itzkoff for the *New York Times* (30 Sept. 2005). "He didn't want the drums to be a background element, and he didn't want to be a background element." After Locks was admitted to the School of the Art Institute of Chicago, Armisen joined him in the city in 1988. In an interview with Christopher Borrelli for the *Chicago Tribune* (11 Jan. 2012), bandmate Wayne Montana described Trenchmouth as "post-hardcore, pre-emo." Trenchmouth played house parties and bowling alleys and eventually signed with Skene! Records in Minneapolis. When he was not performing with the band, Armisen worked at a music venue called Lounge Ax where he stamped hands and answered phones. Armisen continued to work in music after the band broke up in 1996. He was a fill-in drummer for other bands, headed a salsa band called Armisen y Su Mensaje de Caracas, and worked for one year as a drummer for the Chicago Blue Man Group. He took a couple of improvisation classes at Second City in Chicago but found he did not like it.

## "FRED ARMISEN'S GUIDE TO MUSIC AND SXSW"

After a few years, Armisen was fed up with the music scene and decided to have a little fun at its expense. He created a videotape while attending the 1998 South by Southwest (SXSW) music conference in Austin, Texas—a festival that consists of small-scale concerts and panels run by industry bigwigs. Armisen explained the genesis of his idea for the video to Borrelli, saying, "I don't know if I was still frustrated about Trenchmouth, but I saw that they had these seminars on, like, *how to make it in the biz*. And I thought, 'You can't have a seminar on something like that!' So I tried all this man-on-the-street stuff and did this video." The tape shows Armisen crashing various panel discussions in different disguises. In one tape, according to Itzkoff, Armisen asks former record executive Gary Gersh and influential music critic David Fricke to kiss.

The compiled tape was titled "Fred Armisen's Guide to Music and SXSW" and became a highly sought-after bootleg for fans and musicians alike. Jeff Tweedy, the lead singer of the band Wilco, called the tape "genius on a lot of levels." In an interview with Itzkoff, Tweedy explained, "It's poking fun at a lot of people who don't get teased a whole lot. The indie rock community and all the people outside of the mainstream think of themselves as the good guys, but they're just as easily lampooned as anybody else." Armisen admits that the comedy on the tape has a harder edge than the stuff he does now, particularly on *Portlandia*, where he and Brownstein are careful not to mock the city's residents too harshly. Armisen told Gillette of the video, "I think at the time, too, I was just highly not-succeeding at music. . . . Getting that camera was a little bit of an act of anger."

Despite the tone, the twenty-minute video landed him his first gig as an actor. He was hired to produce a series of comedy shorts for HBO Zone called *Fred*. Armisen moved from Chicago to Los Angeles in January 2000 and honed his comedy skills at the Largo club. He appeared on the HBO music series *Reverb* in 1999, *Late Night with Conan O'Brien* in 2000, and Comedy Central's *Premium Blend* in 2001. He hired an agent and was doing stand-up and a short-lived sketch show called *Next!* with comedian Bob Odenkirk when he got the call from the producers at *SNL*.

### SATURDAY NIGHT LIVE

Armisen was invited to audition for *Saturday Night Live* in the summer of 2002 and won a spot as a featured cast member. He was made a full cast member at the start of the 2004 season. In addition to his duties as a performer, Armisen also wrote for the show. *SNL* airs nearly every Saturday night during the regular season and bases much of it comedy on current events, making the show's already grueling schedule all the more challenging, though the process is fairly collaborative. According to Armisen, writers and performers meet with Lorne Michaels, the show's longtime producer, each Monday and then write, day and night, through Wednesday morning. (Armisen told Czajkowski that he has fond memories of watching the sun come up from behind a computer screen in his *SNL* office.) On Wednesday afternoon, the performers read all of the scripts out loud. They choose which sketches will make the show—the criteria is strictly "funny"—and rehearse right up until show time on Saturday night, undertaking a steady stream of rewrites and improvisation along the way. "*Saturday Night Live* is like this 24-hour day job," Armisen told Robin Finn for the *New York Times* (7 May 2011). "You almost feel doing these sketches, bringing them to life, it's like having a baby every week."

Armisen quickly became known for his extensive repertoire of spot-on impersonations, showcasing his uncanny ability to imitate anyone from oddball celebrities to steely dictators. His characters are eccentric yet familiar; in so many words and actions, they illustrate what the audience already knew but could never quite

put a finger on, such as the overwhelming self-importance of alternative culture or the ability of close friends to both praise and eviscerate each other to total strangers in a single breath. (The latter is a reference to Armisen and Vanessa Bayer's *SNL* bit in which they play the so-called best friends of famous dictators.)

One of Armisen's most famous characters on the show was a Venezuelan bandleader named Fericito. The character was Armisen's homage to Tito Puente, the late Latin bandleader whose act Armisen comically described to Itzkoff as "here comes a joke. Here's the joke. I just told a joke!" Fericito also gave Armisen one of his early catchphrases on the show: "I am jus' kidding!" (So the audience understood that he "just told a joke," of course.) Armisen's formidable talent and, in some instances, his ambiguous ethnicity, allowed him to play everyone from Barack Obama to Libyan dictator Muammar Gaddafi to comedian Joy Behar. Unlike some of *SNL*'s more familiar faces through the years, Armisen never let his real-life personality peek through whatever character he was playing. He dove into each sketch with the focus of a dramatic character actor. Amos Barshad, a writer for the online magazine *Grantland*, shared an opinion not far from that of many *SNL* fans when he wrote of Armisen's departure (16 May 2013): "Fred Armisen was one of the greatest utility men in the history of the show."

Armisen left the show during its thirty-eighth season, along with Seth Meyers (who was also the show's head writer), Bill Hader, and Jason Sudeikis. He did not formally announce his retirement before his last show but in his final sketch he reprised his British punk rocker, Ian Rubbish. In a star-studded medley, Armisen sang the song's meaning-laden last lyrics: "It's been all right / I've had a lovely night with you."

### PORTLANDIA

*Portlandia* debuted on IFC in January 2011, but the seeds of the project had begun to take root shortly after Armisen met Carrie Brownstein in 2003 at an *SNL* after-party. Like Armisen, Brownstein began her performance career as a musician, playing guitar for the indie band Sleater-Kinney. (She is currently a member of the critically acclaimed power-pop band Wild Flag.) The two friends began making Internet videos poking fun at hipster culture under the name ThunderAnt in 2005. One of their first bits featured two self-serious feminist bookstore employees. The characters, Toni and Candace, are now regulars on *Portlandia*. In 2010, after gaining the support of Lorne Michaels and his studio Broadway Video, Armisen and Brownstein combined their various sketches into one show and shot a pilot of *Portlandia* for the small cable network IFC. Portland seemed an obvious choice for the show's setting—Brownstein lives there—and the two comedians were attracted to the city's urban yet upbeat, small-town vibe. Reviewing the show in an article for the *New Yorker* (2 Jan. 2012), Margaret Talbot wrote how the show looks at Portland through a "honeyed, fantastical aura."

Indeed, everything in Armisen and Brownstein's version of the city is heightened; for instance, a long wait for a weekend brunch is presented as an odyssey through a postapocalyptic landscape. "In general, things in a place like Portland are really great, so little concerns become ridiculous," Brownstein told Talbot. "There are a lot of people here who can afford—financially but also psychologically—to be really, really concerned about buying local, for instance. It becomes mock epic." Armisen and Brownstein appear in every sketch (there are a handful in each half-hour episode) and play a number of recurring characters, outfitted in different wigs and costumes. There are Peter and Nance, the cripplingly conscientious couple who travel to a local farm in the middle of their meal at a restaurant to make sure their chicken is free range and has "a lot of friends." There are also Kath and Dave, who are real outdoorsy types, though they know nothing about the outdoors, and tough guy Lance and his girlfriend, the sweetly feminine Lisa, for whom Brownstein and Armisen swap genders to portray.

The show has also hosted many celebrity guests (Jim Gaffigan, Roseanne Barr, Chloë Sevigny, and folksinger Sarah McLachlan, to name a few) and also casts Portland residents. Real-life Portland mayor Sam Adams appeared in an episode as the assistant to actor Kyle MacLachlan's Portlandia mayor. The show boasts a number of Portland and indie music inside-jokes, but its wide appeal is evidence that Armisen and Brownstein have successfully captured a larger cultural shift.

*Portlandia*, which has become a favorite of audiences and critics alike, sets itself apart from other sketch shows for its moments of emotional honesty amid the jokes. And although the show is presented as a collection of random sketches, all of the characters and storylines in *Portlandia* find points of intersection, lending a satisfyingly expansive quality to the show as a whole. *Portlandia* won a Peabody Award in 2012.

## PERSONAL LIFE

Armisen was married to English singer Sally Timms from 1998 to 2004. He married Elisabeth Moss, an actor best known for her role as Peggy Olson on the AMC television show *Mad Men*, in October 2009. The couple separated eight months later in June 2010; their divorce was finalized in May 2011. Armisen and Brownstein, who text each other every night before they go to sleep, have both said in interviews that they have trouble with romantic relationships, but they are candid about their friendship. "Carrie and I are more romantic than any other romantic relationship I've ever had—that sense of anticipation about seeing the other person, the secret bond," he told Talbot. Armisen lives on the Upper West Side in New York City.

## SUGGESTED READING

Armisen, Fred. Interview by Amelie Gillette. *A.V. Club*. Onion, 11 Jan. 2006. Web. 13 Aug. 2013.

Barshad, Amos. "The *SNL* Star-Hemorrhage Continues." *Grantland*. ESPN Internet Ventures, 16 May 2013. Web. 13 Aug. 2013.

Borrelli, Christopher. "Fred Armisen: The Chicago Years." *Chicago Tribune*. Tribune Newspaper, 11 Jan. 2012. Web. 13 Aug. 2013.

Czajkowski, Elise. "Talking to Fred Armisen about 'SNL,' 'Portlandia,' and Being Part of a Comedy Collective." *Splitsider*. Splitsider, 28 June 2013. Web. 13 Aug. 2013.

Finn, Robin. "First Things First: Feed the Fish." *New York Times*. New York Times Co., 7 May 2011. Web. 13 Aug. 2013.

Itzkoff, Dave. "Eccentric on 'S.N.L.' Is 'Jus' Keeeeding!'." *New York Times*. New York Times Co., 30 Sept. 2005. Web. 13 Aug. 2013.

Talbot, Margaret. "Stumptown Girl." *New Yorker*. Condé Nast, 2 Jan. 2012. Web. 13 Aug. 2013.

—*Molly Hagan*

# Luciana Aymar

**Born:** August 10, 1977
**Occupation:** Field hockey player

When compiling a list of the greatest Argentine athletes, the five-foot-ten, 128-pound Luciana Aymar ranks near the top, a remarkable feat considering her chosen sport is not tennis, soccer, or basketball, but field hockey, a sport that traditionally has been at best on the fringes of mainstream popularity. In fact, Aymar has raised the profile of both the sport in her native country and her national team on the international stage, guiding Las Leonas ("the Lionesses"), as the group is affectionately known, to four Olympic medals, two World Cup golds, and a string of International Hockey Federation Champions trophies. Though not yet a household name in the United States—especially when compared to such Argentine sports compatriots as soccer star Diego Maradona, NBA basketball player Manu Ginobili, and tennis champion Gabriela Sabatini—Aymar is known in the international field hockey community for her graceful but aggressive tactics on the field, her team leadership, and a physical beauty that has led to a modeling

Juan Mabromata/AFP/Getty Images

## EARLY LIFE AND EDUCATION

Born on August 10, 1977, in Rosario, Argentina, the largest city in the north-central province of Santa Fe, Aymar was raised in an athletic family. She played numerous sports as a child, including tennis and swimming, and began playing field hockey when she was either six or seven. She and her sister Cintia, with whom she played professionally for a brief period in 2003 for Barcelona's Real Polo Club, competed for the Fisherton Club as children, relocating to the more prestigious Jockey Club de Rosario when Aymar was thirteen. By this point, Aymar was already a determined athlete, dedicating her free time to the rigors of training. When asked in 2012 by the *New Zealand Herald* how she became such a dominant player, she replied, "It's simple . . . when I young I spent a lot of time—I mean a lot—by myself with the stick" (5 Feb. 2012).

The family's move to the Jockey Club de Rosario earned the sisters attention from the Argentine national team, and in 1994, at seventeen years old, Aymar began making the 186-mile journey by bus to Buenos Aires, waking at 3 a.m., to train with the junior national team twice a week. In 1996 Aymar was promoted to the senior national team, touring with the squad in Great Britain as it prepared for the 1996 Summer Olympics in Atlanta. During the tour Aymar earned her first minutes with the team, substituting for Maria Paula Castelli during an exhibition game. Despite her introduction to senior-level competition, Aymar did not make the Olympic team. However, she was soon to become the most dominant player not only on her team but also in the world.

## STINT IN EUROPE AND THE 1998 WORLD CUP

Aymar continued to log commuter miles between Rosario and Buenos Aires, and as an amateur athlete in Argentina during difficult economic times, she was not compensated for her contribution to the national team. She received no money for travel or lodging, though she stayed steadfast in her dedication to her team. Because the Argentina Hockey Confederation was either unable or unwilling to provide financial compensation, Aymar was forced to forgo her collegiate studies in business administration. Nonetheless, in 1998, she and the national team earned international attention for their play at the World Cup, held in Utrecht, the Netherlands, at which they finished in fourth place, losing 3–2 to the German team in the third-place match. The 1998 World Cup is generally agreed to be the tournament at which the Argentine team began its ascension into the top tier of female hockey teams, joining perennial favorites Australia and the Netherlands.

After the tournament, and given the fact that she was essentially paying to play for the national team, Aymar decided to take an offer

career and acting aspirations. Her place among her country's sports greats and her status as a pop-culture phenomenon in Argentina were confirmed when she was selected by the Argentine Olympic Committee to be the flag bearer at the Opening Ceremony of the 2012 Summer Olympics in London, beating out several well-known Argentine athletes, including basketball player Luis Scola, for the honor.

Though the thirty-five-year-old Aymar, who acquired the nickname La Maga ("the Magician") for her ball-handling trickery and artistic and innovative dribbling technique, was unable to lead her team to a gold medal in the 2012 Olympics as she had hoped, she has become the face of the burgeoning modern female athlete: beautiful, strong, and independent, with a marketable image. "I feel like a female athlete should be able to be seen differently. . . . I began to open doors and break stereotypes. I can be an athlete, but one also can be allowed to be pretty, charismatic, and attractive," she told Vicente L. Panetta for the Associated Press (17 July 2012). She has garnered endorsements from numerous companies, including Nike, and plans to eventually transition from athletics to acting. "Being an actress is a desire I have had since childhood, delayed by hockey," she explained to *Gente* magazine in a September 2010 interview (qtd. in *Argentina Independent* 22 Oct. 2012). She has become not only a sex symbol but also a role model to hockey-playing youth of Argentina, often hosting school clinics to promote her sport.

to play professionally in Europe, doing so with Rot Weiss Koln, a German team. She was accompanied by Ayelén Stepnik, her commuting companion from Rosario and a member of the Argentine national team at two Olympics. The two friends spent six months in Germany, where Rot Weiss Koln subsidized their lodging and expenses. During her stay, Aymar was a key component of the Koln team's German championship in 1998 and it European Cup championship in 1999.

At the end of Aymar's six-month stay in Germany, several teams from both Germany and the Netherlands approached her to continue playing in Europe. Though she was tempted by the opportunity to continue playing at the highest professional level, she felt an obligation to the Argentine team and decided to rejoin Las Leonas for international play, helping the team to a gold medal at the 1999 Pan American Games in Winnipeg, Canada, besting the American team in the final match, 5–2.

## THE BEST IN THE GAME

The 2000 Summer Olympics in Sydney represented a turning point in the Aymar's career and the fortunes of Las Leonas, a moniker the team adopted for the Sydney Games, feeling it symbolized their fighting spirit and affixing a patch of a caricatured lioness to their jerseys. (Incidentally, another of Aymar's nicknames is Lucha, a diminutive for Luciana but also roughly translates as "the fighter.") The team earned the silver medal, losing 3–1 in the final match to the host-nation Australian team, led by superstar Alyson Annan. Also in 2000 Aymar was named the Champion's trophy player of the tournament for the first of six times, though the team finished fourth for the second consecutive year.

In 2001 Aymar won the first of her record seven World Hockey Player of the Year awards, leading her team to its first Champions Trophy and defeating the defending-champion Dutch team in a tightly contested 3–2 match. Beginning in 2001, in the Champions Trophy competition, Las Leonas have won five gold medals (2001, 2008, 2009, 2010, 2012), three silver medals (2002, 2007, 2011), and one bronze (2004), with Aymar at the heart of the action in each tournament; she was named the player of the tournament in 2000, 2001, 2005, 2008, 2010, and 2012.

With each victory and award, Aymar has elevated the profile of field hockey, especially in her country, establishing a tradition of excellence that is unmatched in the sport. Both Australia and the Netherlands have won six Champions Trophies, one more than the Argentine team, but most agree that it is Aymar and Las Leonas that have heightened the world's awareness of the sport. Aymar told the *New Zealand Herald*, "When I started nobody knew about hockey. . . .

Then we started to win tournaments and everybody started following it. That's what I am most proud of" (5 Feb. 2012). Despite her personal success and that of her team, an Olympic gold medal eluded the Argentineans; the team had to settle for bronze in 2004 in Athens and 2008 in Beijing, losing to the Netherlands in the semifinal round of each tournament.

## "LA MARADONA DEL HOCKEY"

Without question the most famous (and infamous) athlete to hail from Argentina is soccer star Diego Maradona. A midfielder known for his masterful ball-handling ability and mercurial personality, Maradona may be best known as the leader of the Argentine team that won the 1986 World Cup Final, during which he scored perhaps the most controversial goal of the tournament's history, known euphemistically as the "Hand of God." One of Aymar's numerous nicknames is La Maradona del Hockey ("the Maradona of Hockey"), a sobriquet with she seems comfortable, as it draws a comparison between their similar styles as ball-handling midfielders and symbols of their respective national clubs. "He was an idol with incredible talent. . . . But the other thing with Diego was that he played from the heart and was able to transmit that. It's an honour they talk about him and I," Aymar told the *New Zealand Herald* (5 Feb. 2012).

The juxtaposition of Maradona and Aymar provides an astute comparison, especially for sports fans familiar with the former's style of play but less so with the world of women's field hockey. Like many elite athletes, including Maradona, Aymar often controls a game at will, outrunning and outmaneuvering her opponents. Stacey Michelsen, a midfielder with New Zealand's national field hockey team, known as the Black Sticks, told the *New Zealand Herald*, "It's incredible. . . . Sometimes you know what she is going to do but you still can't stop her; you just have to limit the damage" (5 Feb. 2012). Though Michelsen indicates otherwise, Aymar is often unpredictable in how she attacks an opponent's defense, especially when she employs the skills that have garnered her the nickname La Maga: weaving through opponents, stopping and spinning on a dime, her stick steadying the inert ball, or firing a pass to a teammate positioned in front of the goal.

The comparison with Maradona was perhaps best exemplified by a goal Aymar scored against the Chinese national team on September 4, 2010, in the sixtieth minute of a World Cup tournament game played before her hometown crowd in Rosario, Argentina. The video of the goal-scoring sequence quickly became an Internet phenomenon once it was uploaded to YouTube, garnering praise from some—perhaps hyperbolically—as the finest goal ever scored in the history of field hockey. Regardless of where it ranks historically, the goal is a snapshot of Aymar's strengths as a hockey player. She began with the ball on the left side of the pitch in her team's territory and quickly surveyed both the defenders and teammates in front of her. In a flash, she headed diagonally toward the middle of the field, duped a defender, angled quickly to the left, zigzagged to the right past another defender, and zipped through an opening, her head up and her back arched, tricking a third defender and dodging a fourth as she entered the scoring area. With three Chinese defenders in the general vicinity, she shot from the left side of the goal, angling the attempt past a sliding goalkeeper. The Argentine team won the game, 2–0, and eventually earned the tournament's gold medal, besting the Dutch team 3–1 in the final match. Scoring five goals, Aymar was named the tournament's top player, as the catalyst for her team's success.

## 2012 OLYMPICS DISAPPOINTMENT AND THOUGHTS OF RETIREMENT

"I picture winning the gold medal," a candid Aymar told Panetta for the Associated Press before the 2012 Olympics. "I'm thinking only of the gold medal I am missing. I think of it when I wake up at 7 and go to the train, and when I'm resting and eating" (17 July 2012). Aymar's obsession with winning the gold medal stems from the frustration and disappointment she and her teammates experienced following previous Olympic performances, for which they had won two bronze medals and one silver but had lost in either the semifinal or final rounds. Before the 2012 Olympics, Aymar stated publically that she would retire after the London Games, a decision that seemed natural given her age and her desire to pursue acting and modeling.

In her interview with Panetta, Aymar seemed emphatic and unwavering about her retirement, discussing with him her post–athletic career plans and stating, "London will present a series of different emotions. . . . There is the sadness of knowing this is my last tournament." Furthermore, speaking with Andy Smith for *PUSH Hockey*, she seemed to reiterate resignation to the transition from star athlete to ordinary citizen, determined to enjoy her last appearance on the international hockey stage. "I try to put myself in the shoes of a 20-year-old player like it was my first Olympics, enjoying every moment. . . . I'm not worrying about anything, I'm going to really enjoy the 20 days I've got here" (25 July 2012). However, at the conclusion of the Olympics, Aymar's future seemed less certain.

As expected Las Leonas advanced to the gold-medal round of the tournament; they faced the Dutch team, their archrival and defending Olympic gold medalists, who had defeated the Argentine team in the semifinals of the 2008 Beijing Games. Despite her effort and despite it

being her thirty-fifth birthday, Aymar was unable to rally her team to victory, as the Dutch scored first in the fortieth minute, puncturing a tight, defensive match, and added a second goal later in the contest. As time expired, a visibly disappointed and exhausted Aymar, crouched with her elbows resting on her thighs, watched as the victorious Dutch team circled into a celebratory huddle. What Aymar had assumed would be her celebratory swan song had turned into another bitter loss and prompted a subsequent period of soul searching. "It's going to be extremely difficult not to find me in the pitch again because I do love this sport. . . . Physically I think I could continue, and my teammates do try to convince me to continue. . . . Right now the most important thing for me is to rest physically and mentally and after that I may consider whether I want to continue playing," she explained to Reuters (11 Aug. 2012). The certainty of her retirement had given way to doubt fueled by her competitive spirit.

## PERSONAL LIFE AND FUTURE ENDEAVORS

As 2012 ended Aymar had yet to make a decision about her return to field hockey, leaving open the possibility that she would join her national team for the 2014 World Cup, to be played in the Netherlands. Regardless of the direction her athletic career might take, Aymar will continue to pursue modeling. Given her public image, however, there seems to be one line that she will not cross. Approached by *Playboy* to appear nude in its periodical, she turned down the offer, realizing that, despite her physical attractiveness, she had an obligation to the youth that revered her as a role model: "The money [*Playboy*] offered me was fine, but I said no because I care for my image," as quoted by *Argentina English* (3 Mar. 2011). However, she has been less concerned about modeling in swimsuits and of taking advantage of her apparent sex appeal.

Beyond modeling, Aymar has aspirations of acting and has been inspired by her fiancé, Michel Gurfi, a professional soccer player who has also garnered fame as a soap-opera actor in Mexico, Colombia, and his native Argentina. Aymar has made numerous appearances on talk shows, and though she employed a therapist early in her hockey career to help with the anxiety and stress of being in the limelight, she seems comfortable in front of a television audience. Her transition from elite athlete to actor would seem to be a natural one, as she has lived under the watchful eye of sports fans, especially those in Argentina, for nearly two decades.

From her days commuting to Buenos Aires for training with the Argentine national field hockey team to her role as Argentina's flag bearer in the 2012 Summer Olympics, a position weighted with the symbolism of her importance to her people, Aymar has journeyed from single-minded dedication and obscurity to international athlete and Argentine celebrity, raising the profile of her sport and that of her national team along the way. As her retirement approaches, Aymar has accomplished that which only the most transcendent athletes are able to—dominate their chosen sport to the point that they alter and heighten its perception on the world stage, much as someone like Tony Hawk did for an alternative sport like skateboarding or Serena Williams has for an established sport like tennis.

### SUGGESTED READING

"Aymar Backtracks on Retirement after Missing Gold." *World News Australia*. Reuters, 11 Aug. 2012. Web. 13 Dec. 2012.

Breidthardt, Annika. "Hockey: Rosario's Other Famous Export, Rosario Eyes Gold." *Reuters US Edition*. Reuters,17 July 2012. Web. 13 Dec. 2012.

"Hockey: Aymar the Magician, Hockey's Goddess." *New Zealand Herald*. APN Holdings NZ Limited, 5 Feb. 2012. Web. 13 Dec. 2012.

"Lion Queen Aymar Bows Out in Style." *Argentina Independent*. Argentina Independent, 22 Oct. 2012. Web. 13 Dec. 2012.

Orrison, Wendy Cobb. "Luciana Aymar." *Great Athletes: Olympic Sports*. Pasadena: Salem, 2010. 37. Print.

Panetta, Vicente L. "Argentina's Other 'Maradona' Chasing Gold Medal." AP English Worldstream, 17 July 2012. Web. 13 Dec. 2012.

Smith, Andy. "Luciana Aymar Feels Like She Is Twenty Again." *PUSH Hockey*. PUSHHockey, 25 July 2012. Web. 13 Dec. 2012.

—*Christopher Rager*

© David Emm/ActionPlus/Corbis

# Victoria Azarenka

**Born:** July 31, 1989
**Occupation:** Tennis player

With her victory in the finals of the 2012 Australian Open, Victoria Azarenka captured her first Grand Slam championship and claimed the world number-one spot in the Women's Tennis Association (WTA) singles rankings, becoming the first Belarusian tennis player to achieve that position. The victory marked one of the many high points of Azarenka's breakout 2012 season, which saw her collect five additional singles titles, notch a twenty-six-match winning streak, break the WTA prize money record for a single season, and capture two medals in her Olympic debut at the 2012 Summer Games in London, England.

Prior to the 2012 season, Azarenka, who turned professional in 2003, had only reached one Grand Slam semifinal and had been known more for her guttural on-court shrieks and emotional outbursts than for her top-notch tennis game. Despite enjoying a steady ascent up the WTA singles rankings in the first seven years of her career, Azarenka often self-destructed in matches against elite opponents; in early 2011, after a series of poor performances, she considered quitting the sport altogether. Receiving inspirational advice from her grandmother, she returned to tennis after a brief hiatus and seemed to possess a newfound maturity, confidence, and passion for the game.

Azarenka defended her Australian Open title in 2013 to win her second career Grand Slam and is believed by many to have only scratched the surface of her full potential. According to Christopher Clarey, writing for the *New York Times* (28 Jan. 2012), she "has the strokes and . . . the stage presence to make a long-range impact [on the game]." Commenting on her transformation, Azarenka told Joanne Gerstner for espnW (24 May 2012), "Things are never perfect, so I never get too high about things, or get too down. . . . I have learned how to better handle things as they come."

### EARLY LIFE

Victoria Azarenka was born on July 31, 1989, to Fedor and Alla Azarenka in Minsk, Belarus, which is part of the former Soviet Union. Azarenka's family gave her the nickname Vika early on, and she and her older brother Max were raised in an apartment that the family shared with Azarenka's grandparents. Azarenka's father worked two jobs to make ends meet, and her mother worked long hours at Minsk's National

Tennis Center. Her grandmother taught kindergarten at a local school.

Azarenka was first introduced to tennis at the age of seven when she began accompanying her mother to the tennis center. While her mother worked, Azarenka would hit balls against a wall to keep herself occupied. Eventually, she started playing on real courts after a coach at the club spotted her and suggested she join one of his group lessons where she quickly developed a knack for the sport. Soon she was hitting upwards of a thousand balls and spending as many as ten hours a day at the club. "A year after I started playing tennis, I just got so into it," she recalled to Olivia Glinka for *Yahoo! Sports* (18 Mar. 2013). "That's all I wanted to do, so I decided that if I want to do it, I have to do it right and have to become a professional."

## TURNING PROFESSIONAL

Azarenka's athletic talent was evident from the time she first picked up a racket, but the inadequate facilities in Belarus forced her to train in other countries. Azarenka turned professional in 2003 when she was fourteen and made her debut on the International Tennis Federation (ITF) junior circuit, a precursor to the WTA Tour. That same year she also received financial assistance from a sponsor to train at a tennis academy in Marbella, Spain. Azarenka grew frustrated with the coaching and lack of quality competition there, however, and she left after nine months. Kristin Haider-Maurer, a former professional tennis player, remembered Azarenka as a "complete beast who didn't surrender a single ball, extremely ambitious, tenacious," as she told Stefan Wagner for the *Red Bulletin* (June 2013).

After returning to Minsk, Azarenka caught the attention of Russian professional hockey player Nikolai Khabibulin, who was then the goaltender for the National Hockey League's (NHL) Tampa Bay Lightning, and his Belarusian wife, Victoria, a former junior tennis player. Recognizing Azarenka's potential and drive, they offered to sponsor her and pay for her training in the United States. "In Russia, not many people have money and the opportunity to be athletes," Azarenka explained to Greg Garber for ESPN (3 Apr. 2009). "Nik understands this and gave me this opportunity. He just wanted to give me that and see what I could do with it."

During the summer of 2005, Azarenka left Belarus to live with the Khabibulins in Scottsdale, Arizona, where she began training with António Van Grichen, a former Portuguese Davis Cup player. At the time, Azarenka ranked 220 on the WTA singles rankings. However, by the end of the 2005 season, Azarenka had won one singles title and one doubles title on the ITF circuit and had played her first two WTA main draws, and she had improved her world ranking to 136. She also finished the season as the number one ranked junior women's tennis player in the world after winning the Australian Open and US Open junior singles titles, becoming the first Belarusian to achieve that feat.

## RISE UP THE WTA RANKINGS

In 2006 Azarenka made her singles debut at all four WTA Grand Slam tournaments, losing in the first round at the Australian Open, French Open, and Wimbledon Championships and reaching the third round at the US Open. She also reached the singles semifinals and won the women's doubles title with her partner Tatiana Poutchek at the Tashkent Open, in Tashkent, Uzbekistan. She ended the year ranked at ninety-two, marking the first time in her career that she was in the top hundred of the WTA singles rankings.

Azarenka continued to build on her success in 2007, particularly in mixed doubles competition. She partnered with her fellow countryman Max Mirnyi to win the title at the US Open. The duo also reached the finals of the Australian Open. In singles competition, Azarenka achieved runner-up finishes, the first of her career, at the Estoril Open in Oeiras, Portugal, and at the Tashkent Open. She reached the quarterfinals at WTA tournaments held in Los Angeles, California; Luxembourg; and Moscow, Russia. She improved on her performances in Grand Slams, reaching the fourth round at the US Open and third round at the Australian Open and Wimbledon. Azarenka finished the season at thirty and thirty-two on the WTA singles and WTA doubles rankings, respectively. Despite these improvements, Azarenka tended to let her emotions take hold during pivotal junctures of matches, leading some observers to question her maturity and mental toughness.

Prior to the 2008 season, Azarenka worked with the legendary strength and conditioning coach Pat Etcheberry. Although she was dogged by injuries throughout the season, she earned her first top-twenty finishes in both singles and doubles, with season-ending rankings of fifteen and twelve, respectively. Azarenka's best all-around performance came at the 2008 French Open, where she reached the fourth round in women's singles before losing to Svetlana Kuznetsova, 6–2, 6–3. Azarenka paired with Bob Bryan to claim her second career Grand Slam mixed doubles title. Nonetheless, Azarenka's emotional fragility once again came under intense scrutiny after she broke down in tears during her fourth-round loss to Kuznetsova and after faltering in the finals of two more singles tournaments, the Mondial Australian Women's Hardcourts and the Prague Open in the Czech Republic.

## FIRST WTA SINGLES TITLES

In Azarenka's first event of the 2009 season, the Brisbane International in Australia, she recorded a straight-set defeat (6–3, 6–1) against Marion Bartoli of France to claim her first WTA title. "After that, the next final I played," she told an interviewer for tennis.com (26 July 2009), "I was completely different." Azarenka followed up that victory with a strong performance at the 2009 Australian Open where she advanced to the fourth round after taking the first set against Serena Williams, who was then ranked number two in the world. Azarenka was forced to retire from the match in the middle of the second set due to heat exhaustion. Less than a month later, she rebounded to win her second career singles title at the 2009 Cellular South Cup, in Memphis, Tennessee. Azarenka and Caroline Wozniacki then won the doubles title at the same tournament.

Later in 2009, Azarenka won her third career singles title at the Sony Ericsson Open in Key Biscayne, Florida, beating Serena Williams. Shortly after this victory, Greg Garber wrote, "Azarenka's got the chops to beat anyone . . . she can really bang the ball from the baseline [and] when she flattens it out, her shots can be breathtaking." Azarenka also recorded her best performances in a Grand Slam when she reached the quarterfinals at both the 2009 French Open and the 2009 Wimbledon Championships. At the latter tournament during her fourth round match against Nadia Petrova, Azarenka again reinforced her reputation as a hothead after arguing with an umpire over a disputed call. At the year-end 2009 WTA Tour Championships in Doha, Qatar, Azarenka threw another temper tantrum during a loss to Wozniacki in which she hit a ball into the stands and smashed two of her rackets in frustration. Azarenka finished the season in seventh place on the WTA singles rankings, cracking the top ten for the first time in her career. Around this time, she parted ways with Van Grichen and began working with French coach Sam Sumyk.

## TRANSFORMATION INTO ELITE PLAYER

In 2010, Azarenka won singles tournaments at the Bank of the West Classic in Stanford, California, and the Kremlin Cup in Moscow. She also advanced to the quarterfinals of the 2010 Australian Open but was defeated by Serena Williams. Azarenka's performances in the year's other Grand Slams continued to disappoint: she lost in the first round of the French Open to unseeded Gisela Dulko, fell in the third round at Wimbledon to Petra Kvitova, and was forced to withdraw from her second-round match at the US Open due to dizziness and blurred vision. Her performance at the year-end 2010 WTA championships in Qatar was also lackluster because she failed to reach the semifinals after dropping her first two round-robin matches. Azarenka's year-end singles ranking subsequently dropped three spots to number ten.

During the start of the 2011 season, Azarenka lost to Li Na of China in the fourth round of the Australian Open and then lost in the finals of the women's doubles event when she and her partner, Maria Kirilenko, were defeated by Gisela Dulko and Flavia Pennetta, 2–6, 7–5, 6–1. Next, Azarenka was ousted in the third round of the 2011 Dubai Tennis Championships, and she then suffered a first-round loss to Daniela Hantuchova at the 2011 Qatar Ladies Open in Doha.

Frustrated with her play and "too intense for her own good," as Stephen Tignor noted for *Tennis* (June 2012), Azarenka contemplated quitting the game until her grandmother intervened with sage advice. "She told me not to quit, to work hard, and see what will happen," Azarenka recalled in her interview with Gerstner. "Give it a year or so, and if it is not working, I can always come home. She changed the perspective of my life."

After a brief hiatus, Azarenka returned to the court rejuvenated and with a more positive mindset and composed demeanor that paid immediate dividends. In the 2011 Sony Ericsson Open in Florida, Azarenka defeated Maria Sharapova in straight sets to claim her second career title at the event. She then won the 2011 Andalucia Tennis Experience in Marbella, Spain, defeating Irina-Camelia Begu. Later that year, Azarenka advanced to her first Grand Slam semifinal at the 2011 Wimbledon Championships, where she was defeated by Petra Kvitova. After notching another victory at the 2011 BGL Luxembourg Open and advancing to the finals of the 2011 WTA championships, Azarenka rose to number three on the WTA rankings and became the first Belarusian to crack the top five in tennis rankings.

## FIRST GRAND SLAM TITLES AND TOP WORLD RANKING

Azarenka firmly established herself among the women's tennis elite in 2012. After defeating Li Na in the finals of the 2012 Apia International Sydney in Australia and winning her first title of the season, she entered the 2012 Australian Open as the number-three seed; she defeated Agnieszka Radwańska and Kim Clijsters in the quarter and semifinal rounds to become the first Belarusian player since Natasha Zvereva in 1988 to advance to a Grand Slam final. In the finals, Azarenka defeated Maria Sharapova, formerly ranked world number one and a multiple Grand Slam winner, in straight sets to become the first Belarusian player to win a Grand Slam title. Christopher Clarey described Azarenka's performance as "a one-woman demonstration of power, depth and . . . poise" and that she "countered Sharapova's increasingly desperate returns and ground strokes with big, on-target hitting."

With her Apia International and Australian Open victories, Azarenka was propelled to the number one world ranking, which she held for nineteen consecutive weeks. During this time Azarenka also won singles tournaments in the Qatar Total Open and the BNP Paribas Open, and she reached the finals of the Porsche Tennis Grand Prix in Stuttgart, Germany, and the Mutua Madrid Open in Spain.

Azarenka then reclaimed the top spot after she reached the semifinals at Wimbledon, where she lost to Serena Williams for the sixth straight time. Azarenka then competed at the 2012 Olympic Games in London and won a bronze medal in women's singles and a gold medal in mixed doubles with partner Max Mirnyi; both were the first Olympic medals in tennis for Belarus.

Azarenka again went against Williams in the women's singles final of the US Open, but she lost in a hotly contested three-set battle. Azarenka claimed her sixth and final singles title of the year at the Generali Ladies Linz in Austria, and she closed out the season with a semifinal finish at WTA championships in Istanbul, Turkey. During the 2012 season, Azarenka earned $7.9 million in prize money, which set a WTA record for most prize money in a single season.

At the 2013 Australian Open, Azarenka successfully defended her title by defeating Li Na in three sets to claim her second career Grand Slam title. She also successfully defended her title at the Qatar Total Open after defeating Williams for only the second time of her career. However, one week after that victory, Azarenka relinquished the top spot in the WTA world rankings to Williams, after holding the spot for thirty-two consecutive weeks.

**PERSONAL LIFE**

Azarenka lives and trains in Monte Carlo, Monaco. She has been romantically linked to Stefan Gordy, an American musician, DJ, and rapper who goes by the stage name Redfoo; he is best known for being part of the Los Angeles–based electronic dance music duo LMFAO. Azarenka is fluent in Belarusian, Russian, and English, and she also speaks some French. She has sponsorship deals with Nike sportswear, Wilson sports equipment, the energy drink Red Bull, and the credit card company American Express.

**SUGGESTED READING**

Clarey, Christopher. "Azarenka Sweeps Past Sharapova to Her First Grand Slam Crown." *New York Times*. New York Times, 28 Jan. 2012. Web. 2 Aug. 2013.
Garber, Greg. "How the Goalie Helped the Tennis Star." *Espn Tennis*. ESPN Internet Ventures, 3 Apr. 2009. Web. 2 Aug. 2013.
Gerstner, Joanne C. "Victoria Azarenka Is Centered on Court." *EspnW*. ESPN Internet Ventures, 24 May 2012. Web. 2 Aug. 2013.
Rothenberg, Benjamin. "No. 1 with a Sound and Style All Her Own." *New York Times*. New York Times, 6 Sept. 2012. Web. 2 Aug. 2013.
Tignor, Stephen. "Beautiful Mind." *Tennis* June 2012: 24–30. Print.
"Victoria Azarenka: The Story So Far." *Tennis*. Tennis.com, 26 July 2009. Web. 2 Aug. 2013.
Wagner, Stefan. "Red Bulletin: War and Peace." *RedBull*. Red Bull, 1 June 2013. Web. 2 Aug. 2013.

—*Chris Cullen*

# Joyce Banda

**Born:** April 12, 1950
**Occupation:** President of Malawi

In April 2012, Joyce Banda became president of Malawi. She is the country's first female president and the second woman to become an African head of state. During her prior eight-year career in public service, she served as Malawi's foreign minister and its first female vice president. A skilled politician, Banda successfully negotiated Malawi's tumultuous political culture and fractures within the Democratic Progressive Party (DPP) in order to remain an influential government figure. She left the DPP in 2010 to found the People's Party. Prior to becoming president, Banda was at odds with her predecessor, President Bingu wa Mutharika. When Mutharika died on April 5, 2012, after suffering a heart attack, a tense two-day power transition ensued.

The government of Malawi faces significant economic challenges. In the decades following its independence from the United Kingdom in July 1964, the country has struggled to achieve lasting economic growth. In 2011, Malawi ranked 171 out of 187 countries listed on the United Nations Development Programme (UNDP) Human Development Index, which measures health, education, and living standards. Relations between Malawi and foreign donors, including the United States, Britain, Germany, and the European Union soured in the later years of the Mutharika administration. Western countries were critical of Mutharika's use of police force to put down antigovernment protests and his efforts to stifle the work of human rights activists and journalists. The West also frowned upon Mutharika's open cooperation with Sudan's Omar al-Bashir and Zimbabwe's Robert Mugabe, whom they consider violent despots. In 2011, Western nations and international aid groups moved to suspend aid to Malawi in response to Mutharika's policies. As president, Banda is tasked with mending the country's relationships with international aid regimes.

AFP/Getty Images

## EARLY LIFE AND EDUCATION

Banda was born Joyce Hilda Mtila on April 12, 1950, in Malemia, a village in southeastern Malawi. At the time, the Zomba region in which Malemia was located was a part of the British protectorate known as Nyasaland. Banda's father, a well-known musician, led the national police brass band. Banda was fourteen years old when Malawi declared independence from Britain on July 6, 1964. After completing her primary education, Banda began her career as a secretary. She later successfully applied for enrollment to Columbus University, a distance education institution in the United States, where she earned a bachelor's degree in early childhood education.

Banda had three children with her first husband, Roy Kachale, whom she married in 1972. The couple separated in 1981. Banda later admitted that the marriage was abusive. "Most African women are taught to endure abusive marriages," she told the BBC (10 Apr. 2012), "They say endurance means a good wife, but most women endure abusive relationships because they are not empowered economically. They depend on their husbands." After her separation, Banda started several small businesses, including a clothing company and a bakery. "I made up my mind that that was never going to happen to me again," Banda told David Smith for the *Guardian* (29 Apr. 2012), "I made a brave step to walk out in a society when you didn't walk out of an abusive marriage."

Banda married her second husband, Richard Banda, in 1981. She has spoken frankly about how her husband's position as a high court judge aided her success in business. "I moved from zero to hero," she explained to Smith. "I was running the largest business owned by a woman in Malawi. But [my husband's] fingerprint was all

over. If I wanted training, he paid. If I wanted a loan, he paid. Because of his status in society everything was easy for me, so I had succeeded, but I had succeeded because I was privileged."

Inspired by her personal experiences with domestic abuse and sexism, Banda founded the National Association of Business Women (NABW), a women's empowerment program that transformed her into a nationally known gender equality advocate. "I began to think about those that were not able to walk out of an abusive marriage," Banda told Smith, "or maybe those that did not know where to go, that were single, or widows. I was thinking what it was I could do to reach out to them."

## ADVOCACY WORK

Banda's success with the NABW led to the establishment of two other organizations in which served as founder and executive; the Young Women's Leaders Network (YWLN), and the Joyce Banda Foundation (JBF). All three organizations aim to improve the lives of women in Malawi, via education and health initiatives and business training. "We know that early marriage, early pregnancy, and early death of young women are connected to how long they stay in school," Banda told *Al Arabiya* (7 Apr. 2012).

The JBF was founded in 1997, in part by the prize money Banda was awarded in conjunction with the Africa Prize for Leadership for the Sustainable End of Hunger. Banda and Mozambique President Joaquim Chissano were co-recipients of the award. The JBF focuses on agricultural development, building water and sanitation systems, and providing education. In addition, the organization provides childcare for orphaned children in Malawi. JFB has opened a school for orphans in Malawi that services two hundred students. The group's thirty orphan care centers assist approximately five thousand orphans, most aged three to five years old. Many of the orphans are HIV positive and many suffer from malnutrition.

Malawi's Youth Movement for Development was founded in August 2010 under the auspices of the JBF. It works to increase the involvement of young people in Malawi in community development initiatives. The JBF also oversees the Market Women's Activities in Development, which helps provide health counseling and helps coordinate business strategies among women entrepreneurs.

## POLITICAL CAREER

In 1971, Malawi's first president, Hastings Banda (no relation to Joyce Banda or her husband) declared himself president for life. One-party rule was maintained in Malawi until May 1994, when the country held its first multiparty election. The election brought President Bakili Muluzi to power. In 1999, Banda ran successfully for a seat on the Malawian parliament as a member of Muluzi's United Democratic Front (UDF). In addition to serving as minister for Gender and Community Services, Banda continued to act as a champion of gender equality and as an advocate for children. As a member of parliament, Banda designed Malawi's National Platform for Action on Orphans and Vulnerable Children. She also led the Zero Tolerance Campaign against Child Abuse.

Banda was reelected to parliament in 2004. That same year, Mutharika was elected president, representing the UDF. In February 2005, Mutharika founded the DPP. President Mutharika named Banda as foreign minister in 2006. As Malawi's foreign minister, Banda worked to negotiate closer economic ties with China, including a $6 billion aid package. As a consequence, Malawi ended forty-two years of diplomatic ties with Taiwan.

In 2009, Mutharika selected Banda as his vice presidential running mate. The Mutharika-Banda ticket, representing the DPP, was elected. However, the political goodwill between Banda and Mutharika did not last. In December 2010, Mutharika fired Banda from her role as DPP vice president, and also fired DPP deputy president Khumbo Kachali. Although Banda was constitutionally allowed to maintain her role as vice president of Malawi, the firing caused a national political crisis. The DPP announced that Banda and Kachali had been fired from the DPP as a result of "anti-party activities." DPP publicity secretary Hetherwick Ntaba reported allegations that Banda and Kachali were working to form a new political party. Banda's supporters maintained that she was fired so that Mutharika's brother, Peter Mutharika, could run as the DPP's presidential candidate in 2014. Prior to her removal from the DPP, Banda had rejected endorsing Mutharika's brother for president.

Despite Mutharika's attempts to marginalize her, Banda persevered. In 2011, she founded the People's Party. President Mutharika's decision to fire her from the DPP caused many Malawians and political officials to end their allegiance to the DPP and support the People's Party. In the meantime, Banda began preparations for a presidential campaign.

President Mutharika was flown to a hospital in South Africa after suffering cardiac arrest on the morning of April 5, 2012. Initial news reports stated that Mutharika was in critical condition, and Banda made a public statement wishing him a quick recovery. "I was getting into the car when somebody called me and said the president had collapsed," Banda told the *Guardian* (17 Dec. 2012). News of Mutharika's poor health prompted fears of a governmental crisis in Malawi. The country's constitution stipulated that as vice president, Banda should take over the role as head of state in the event of the president's death, but it was unclear how the president's supporters would react. The army was deployed to Banda's residence following threats of violence. Following news of Mutharika's death, it was reported that DPP loyalists were moving to name speaker of parliament Henry Chimunthu Banda (no relation to Banda or her husband) to the office of president. Banda told the *Guardian* (17 Dec. 2012) that after hearing confirmation of Mutharika's death on the BBC, she "heard that the cabinet was meeting at Capital Hill, choosing another president. In 48 hours, they tried to take over the government and sideline me—and by that, sideline the constitution. In that 48 hours, I fought for my rights."

In order to ensure her immediate and legal transition to the office of president, Banda turned to the army. Efforts by members of the DPP to retain the presidency ended when the country's army commanders, including its chief General Henry Odillo, announced their support of Banda and the country's constitutional stipulations regarding the transfer of power. As the *Guardian* (17 Dec. 2012) later reported, Banda expressed thanks for the support received following Mutharika's death. "I will be forever thankful to the Malawians and the international community, and my professional army and [General Odillo] who said, 'No, we will follow the constitution.' That's why I'm here." Banda assumed office as president on April 7, 2012.

**PRESIDENT OF MALAWI**

President Banda has implemented a range of economic and social reforms in Malawi. Some economic analysts have been critical of her decision to devalue the county's currency, which they say has led to price increases. After appointing twenty-three cabinet ministers and nine deputy ministers, Banda reached out to numerous foreign officials, including Britain's Parliamentary undersecretary of state Henry Bellingham and American secretary of state Hillary Clinton. Soon after taking office, she announced that Malawi would not host the June 2012 summit of the African Union (AU). Previously, Mutharika had agreed to host the summit, and to the condition that the government of Malawi not serve Sudan's Bashir with a warrant from the International Criminal Court. The June 2012 AU summit took place in Ethiopia.

President Banda has moved to decrease government spending, opting to sell the jet and a fleet of luxury vehicles employed by her predecessor. In May 2012, she announced her intention to overturn Malawi's ban on gays and lesbians. Banda has also expressed her desire to renegotiate how Malawian resources are sold to foreign buyers, particularly China. As she told the *Guardian* (17 Dec. 2012), "I want Malawians, in twenty years, to look back, when we have depleted our resources, and say, 'We had oil, but we benefited. Our country became a better place.'"

Upon taking office, Banda spoke candidly about her position as Malawi's first female head of state. Describing the burden of leading Malawi's development efforts as "heavy" she said, "I am able to carry it. Why? Because I'm an African woman. An African woman carries heavy loads anyway. That's how we are trained. We are brought up [learning] that nothing is unbearable. I use that [training] now, positively" (*Guardian* 17 Dec. 2012). As she continues to work to open Malawi to the international community and grow its economy, Banda faces significant challenges related to inflation, health, hunger, and education. Her term as president expires in 2014.

## AWARDS AND ACCOLADES
Over the course of her career, Banda has received numerous accolades for her leadership and advocacy work. In 2012, she was awarded the Martin Luther King Drum Major Award. She ranked number 71 on *Forbes* magazine's 2012 list of the most powerful women in the world. That same year, the magazine ranked her as the most powerful woman in Africa.

## SUGGESTED READING
"In Mourning, Malawi Swears In a New President." *New York Times*. New York Times Co., 7 Apr. 2012. Web. 17 Feb. 2013.

Lamble, Lucy, Nick Francis, and Marc Francis. "Joyce Banda: 'I Want Malawians to Say Our Country Became a Better Place.'" *Guardian*. Guardian News and Media, 17 Dec. 2012. Web. 19 Feb. 2013.

McCracken, John. *A History of Malawi*. Woodbridge: Currey, 2012. Print.

Smith, David. "Malawi's Joyce Banda Puts Women's Rights at Centre of New Presidency." *Guardian*. Guardian News and Media, 29 Apr. 2012. Web. 21 Feb. 2013.

—*Josh Pritchard*

# Sam Beam

**Born:** July 26, 1974
**Occupation:** Singer-songwriter

Profiles of Sam Beam, a musician who performs under the name Iron & Wine, almost all touch upon a handful of the same tropes: Beam's luxuriantly bushy beard; his devotion to his wife and children; his early career as a film studies professor; the lo-fi recordings he made in his bedroom; and his artistic similarities to both Leonard Cohen and the late Nick Drake. Where these profiles risk being predictable, they are saved by the

FilmMagic

genuine delight and enthusiasm that even the most seasoned music journalists seem to feel upon hearing Beam's work. Calling him "the ultimate folk hero and the anti-rock star," Christian Schaeffer wrote for the *Riverfront Times* (22 Oct. 2003), "[Beam's music] is potent, ear-catching stuff." In a piece for the *News Journal* (31 Jan. 2003), Chris Fitz poetically opined, "It's the soundtrack to lonely interstate jaunts, post-dinner porch-sitting, night swimming and Sunday afternoon apathy all collected in one beautifully rendered package."

Beam's music is most often categorized as folk, and while he has stressed that he wants to change and evolve with each album, he has not disavowed that label. "Folk music has got a bad rap since the '60s—it was cardigans and crusty hippies," he told Chris Coomey for the *New Times* (25 Mar. 2004). "What it is [really], is the people's music. Rock is folk music. Religious music is folk music. I have no problem being stuck in that category." However it is categorized, most listeners agree that Beam's work is transformative. "While music on the whole is becoming one big glossy Wal-Mart rack," Melissa Perkins wrote for the *Daily Mississippian* (10 Mar. 2005), "Iron & Wine is like a hidden treasure blooming forth from a new kind of fresh and leafy Americana."

## EARLY YEARS AND EDUCATION
Samuel Beam was born on July 26, 1974, in Columbia, South Carolina. His father worked for the state office of land management and his mother

taught school. His grandfather owned a farm where Beam spent a great deal of time as a child.

Beam's parents loved music, particularly the songs of Carole King and Fleetwood Mac—artists who provided the soundtrack to Beam's youth. At the age of fifteen, he got his first guitar. He harbored few musical ambitions, however, focusing instead on a future career in art or film. He was often sequestered in his bedroom, sketching and drawing, and he also made amateur movies. (One of his childhood friends was Jeter Rhodes, who went on to some success as a film director and editor.)

Beam attended Virginia Commonwealth University, in Richmond, where he studied graphic design, photography, and painting. After earning his bachelor's degree, he entered Florida State University, earning a master's degree in cinema. Because of his background in film studies and visual arts, music critics often seize upon the idea that Beam's songs are more narratively complex than most, and they point to such song titles as "Bird Stealing Bread" and "Muddy Hymnal," which evoke, to some, the titles of photographs. He concurs that his filmmaking and artwork have influenced his music. "I've definitely adopted a lot of the stuff I learned, but the songs are not scripts," Beam told Fiona Sturges for the London *Independent* (25 Feb. 2005). "Screenwriting is a discipline where you learn to describe an action rather than explain it. Everything is on a visual basis. You have to see what characters are dealing with. I would say it brings about a very visual writing style."

### EARLY CAREER

Armed with his master's degree, Beam found occasional production work on movies and television commercials. He was, for example, a lighting technician on the Mel Gibson film *The Patriot* (2000), although the job was so minor that he was not given an on-screen credit. The experience, he has said, was a terrible one, and he feels particularly bad about working on the film without having been part of a union. Beam subsequently moved to Miami and—at that point married and in need of a steadier source of income—took jobs teaching cinematography at the University of Miami and at Miami International University of Art and Design.

As a creative outlet and form of recreation, he wrote songs, which he recorded in his bedroom using a basic four-track recorder he had picked up. He assumed that he would occasionally trade the tapes, on which he played the guitar and banjo, with a few friends and that music would remain a hobby. He was correct in those assumptions until a friend—Ben Bridwell, a fellow musician who was then playing in a band called Carissa's Weird—passed a tape along to Mike McGonigal. McGonigal was publishing a small but influential culture magazine called

*Yeti*, based in Seattle. Seeking to compile a promotional album to give away, he included two of Beam's songs.

That tape made its way to executives at Sub Pop Records, the iconic Seattle-based label credited with discovering the band Nirvana and popularizing the genre of music known as grunge. Beam was surprised but intrigued when he heard from Jonathan Poneman, the head of the well-known record company. "I always had a mistrust of the entertainment industry, and in particular the music industry, and I've never been particularly ambitious," he explained to Fiona Sturges. "But as someone who has a guitar and likes to play music, you always think, 'Wouldn't it be fun to make a living out of this?' It's like the impossible dream."

Beam agreed to send Poneman several of his songs, and out of the roughly two-dozen tracks, eleven were chosen to comprise Beam's debut album, including the Appalachian-influenced "The Rooster Moans," the gospel-tinged "Southern Anthem," and the tribute to a mother's love "Upward Over the Mountain."

### MUSICAL LAUNCH

Beam decided to call himself Iron & Wine, a phrase he had seen years before while browsing in a country store attached to a gas station in Georgia. He had spied a dusty bottle of a dietary supplement called Beef, Iron, and Wine, and although the thought of swallowing any of the concoction made him shudder, he liked the strong, poetic sound of the name.

Iron & Wine's first album, *The Creek Drank the Cradle*, was released in the fall of 2002 and became an immediate critical sensation. "The hushed ghostly quality of *The Creek Drank the Cradle* . . . give it a timeless feel. It could be a lost Alan Lomax field recording from the '30s or '40s," Curtis Ross wrote for the *Tampa Tribune* (17 Jan. 2003), referring to the great folklorist and musicologist who recorded thousands of tracks for the Archive of American Folk Song at the Library of Congress during those decades. "There's an inherent quality with recording at home," Beam told Ross. "I picked up on the sound and sort of ran with it. I really like [those Lomax field] recordings. They're pretty magical."

Calling *The Creek Drank the Cradle* "a stunning debut and one of the best records of 2002," Tim Sendra wrote for the *All Music Guide*, "Beam isn't interested in rocking out or obscuring the beauty that bursts from within his simple songs; he embraces it and lets his sadness twist in the wind for all to see." These sentiments were echoed by critics from major publications across the country.

### SUBSEQUENT RECORDINGS

Iron & Wine next released *The Sea and the Rhythm* (2003), a five-track EP that consisted of songs recorded at the same time as the full-length debut album: "Beneath the Balcony," "The Night Descending," "Jesus the Mexican Boy," "Someday the Waves," and the title song. Like *The Creek Drank the Cradle*, the EP was praised for its literate lyrics and pure harmonies, and critics considered it a satisfying offering during the wait for another full-length recording.

That wait was mercifully short; in March of the following year, Iron & Wine released the album *Our Endless Numbered Days*, which featured vocals by Beam's sister, Sarah. Although this time he had worked in a recording studio, rather than in his bedroom, most critics agreed that little authenticity had been lost. "Luckily all the technology in the world can't affect Beam's voice, which still sounds like it comes right from his lips into your ear as if he were an angel perched on your shoulder," Tim Sendra wrote for the *All Music Guide*. Many listeners had particular praise for "Naked as We Came," a plaintive meditation on the death of a beloved, and "Cinder and Smoke," which features an arrangement for bass and banjo.

The year 2005 saw the release of two EPs: the six-track *Woman King* and *In the Reins*, a collaboration with the Tex-Mex indie rock band Calexico. Of the first effort, Andrew Dansby wrote for the *Houston Chronicle* (13 Feb. 2005), "There's no fat here, just some of the most consistently gorgeous, literate, thoughtful and progressive pop music that you'll hear this year. Of course, 'pop' here is used as the broadest catchall: *Woman King* is as edgy as any rock 'n' roll, mournful as any country music, basic as the best blues and as vibrantly detailed and lyrical as good short fiction."

*In the Reins* was received just as positively, even though some were surprised that Beam had joined forces with another band. "On paper it seems like the most bizarre pairing imaginable, the spooky, understated Iron & Wine with Calexico, the Tucson, Arizona, Morricone-by-way-of-mariachi powerhouse combo," a reviewer wrote for the *Sensible Sound* (Sept. 2006). "But spin *In the Reins*, the bands' collaborative release . . . , and the picture snaps into place like an Escher drawing—disorienting at first, but possessed of its own skewed and lovely logic." Most pointed to the track "A History of Lovers," with its glitzy horn section and compelling beat, as proof that Beam was expanding his horizons considerably.

## CHANGING SOUND

When *The Shepherd's Dog* (2007) was released, Beam's continued evolution was evident. A quantum leap away from the lo-fi solo recordings Beam had made in his bedroom, *The Shepherd's Dog* features several backing musicians on accordions, organ, vibraphone, and harmonica, among other instruments. "Nothing too strange in the everything-goes world of indie rock circa 2007, but for

Iron & Wine, it's a widescreen revelation," Tim Sendra opined. "Perhaps working with Calexico . . . inspired Beam to use all the colors in the paint box. Maybe it's a natural progression. Either way it leads to an inspiringly lush album, full of imaginative and rich arrangements."

Iron & Wine's most recent album, *Kiss Each Other Clean* (2011), was recorded for Warner Brothers, making it Beam's first major-label release. Exhibiting such diverse influences as 1970s pop, African beats, and R&B, the album garnered mainly positive reviews, and most critics expressed relief that Beam seemed to be remaining true to his stated musical goals despite the jump to Warner. "At this point, I'm just trying to keep myself surprised," he explained to John Schacht for *Creative Loafing* (19 Apr. 2011). "It's harder to do [now], so I play with a lot of other people who are better than me." Beam also pointed out to journalists who questioned him that Warner had long owned a substantial stake in Sub Pop, and that the massive label was home to such respected artists as the Flaming Lips and Jack White.

## LIVE PERFORMANCES AND LICENSING

Beam and his backing musicians now frequently play to sold-out venues filled with reverential fans. His earlier, cult-like following has swelled as his songs are used with increasing regularity on soundtracks. Among the big-screen films with which he has been involved are *Garden State* (2004), an indie picture that featured his cover of "Such Great Heights," a song by the Postal Service, and the blockbuster vampire movie *Twilight* (2008), to which he contributed "Flightless Bird, American Mouth."

Iron & Wine is also a favorite with those seeking background music for television shows, and his songs have been heard on programs including *The O.C.*, *Six Feet Under*, *Grey's Anatomy*, *Friday Night Lights*, and *House M.D.* He has also been featured in commercials, much to the dismay of the purists in his fan base. He has explained, however, that since giving up his teaching jobs to record and tour full-time, he cannot afford to avoid licensing his songs when approached to do so.

## PERSONAL LIFE

Much of the reason for Beam's financial concern is his large family. He and his wife, Kim, have five daughters. When he does phone interviews, they can frequently be heard clamoring for his attention in the background. Beam has quipped that when asked to go out to party while on tour, he always declines, because touring provides the only chance he has to get a full night's sleep.

Kim is a midwife by profession and she gave birth to each of their daughters at home. Beam has told journalists that, although he is far from a political activist, it is important to him that all women have the opportunity to use a midwife, and he plays benefit concerts for the Midwives Alliance of North America.

While the family lived in Florida for several years, they recently moved to Dripping Springs, Texas, about an hour outside of Austin. They have extended family in the area, and Kim is licensed to practice midwifery there. Beam has built a recording studio on the property.

Reporters are sometimes told by Warner Brothers publicists to avoid asking Beam about his beard because it has already been written about exhaustively. Some are able to resist, while others still make mention of it. (He is most often deemed to look like a "mountain man" or a "Civil War general.") Whether or not they are fixated on his facial hair, almost every journalist who has interviewed Beam has commented on his humility, affability, and dedication to family life.

## SUGGESTED READING

Coomey, Chris. "Rivers of Song." *New Times*. New Times BPD, 25 Mar. 2004. Web. 3 Aug. 2012.

Dansby, Andrew. "Woman King, Divinely Right." *Houston Chronicle* 13 Feb. 2005: Z04.

Fitz, Chris. "It's a Party, So Show Up Late and Wear Your Jammies." *News Journal* [Wilmington] 31 Jan. 2003: Z20. Print.

Gross, Joe. "The Man Behind Iron & Wine." *Austin American-Statesman* 27 Sept. 2007: T18.

Leahy, Andrew. "Iron & Wine, 'Jezebel.'" *American Songwriter*. American Songwriter, 9 Apr. 2012. Web. 3 Aug. 2012.

Perkins, Melissa. "Iron & Wine EP Provides Needed Relief to Scene." *Daily Mississippian*. University of Mississippi, 10 Mar. 2005. Web. 3 Aug. 2012.

Ross, Curtis. "Iron & Wine Has Timeless Quality." *Tampa Tribune* 17 Jan. 2003: F20.

Schacht, John. "Iron & Wine Shows Growth Through Experimentation." *Creative Loafing*. Creative Loafing, 19 Apr. 2011. Web. 3 Aug. 2012.

Schaeffer, Christian. "Punk-Folking-Rock!" *Riverfront Times*. Riverfront Times, 22 Oct. 2003. Web. 3 Aug. 2012.

Sturges, Fiona. "Gentleman Sam." *Independent* [London] 25 Feb. 2005: F18.

—*Mari Rich*

# Rob Bell

**Born:** 1970
**Occupation:** Author and pastor

Variously called "hipster," "heretic," "poser," and "provocateur," and likened to the well-known evangelist Billy Graham, entrepreneur Steve Jobs, and his childhood hero, late-night comedian David Letterman, Rob Bell isn't a

EPA/Justin Lane /Landov

run-of-the-mill evangelical preacher. Founder of a Michigan megachurch, the tall, bespectacled, black-clad minister drew a great deal of controversy—as well as renown—for his take on the afterlife in the 2011 book *Love Wins: A Book about Heaven, Hell, and the Fate of Every Person Who Ever Lived*.

In an age when most American Christians believe in the Second Coming, even if not in their own lifetimes, and the majority, including over half of evangelical Protestants, believe non-Christians can go to heaven, the debate about heaven and hell may seem a moot issue. Yet curiosity about the afterlife continues to inspire books on heaven, and a hunger for spirituality remains, despite the declining church membership of recent decades. Bell specifically seeks to attract the younger generation of Americans, for whom he says Christianity "is no longer relevant. It doesn't fit. It's outdated. . . . It's not that there isn't any truth in it or that all the people before them were misguided or missed the point. It's just that every generation has to ask the difficult questions of what it means to be a Christian here and now, in this place at this time," as quoted by Debra Bendis in *Christian Century* (24 Mar. 2009). Bell's open questioning of traditional evangelical theology and his view of God as inclusive make him especially appealing to the millennial and Generation X audiences he targets, and especially threatening to evangelical leaders who fear a dilution of the faith and decline in church participation similar to that seen in more liberal "mainline" denominations.

## CHILDHOOD AND EDUCATION

Robert Holmes Bell Jr. was born in 1970 to Robert Holmes Bell Sr., later appointed a US district court judge by President Ronald Reagan, and Helen Bell, an English professor. The Bells had met at Wheaton College, a prominent evangelical Christian college in suburban Illinois. They raised their three children, Rob, Ruth, and Jonathan, in Okemos, Michigan, in what many in the evangelical community would term a "good Christian home." As a child, Bell played soccer, read works by the famed novelist and Christian apologist C. S. Lewis, and attended church regularly on Sundays and Wednesdays. At age ten he prayed to "invite Jesus into his heart," an act he fondly recalls and one that is central to salvation, according to evangelical Christian thought.

After high school, Bell studied psychology at his parents' alma mater, earning his bachelor's degree from Wheaton in 1992. During his second year there he and his friends formed the alternative rock band Ton Bundle, with Bell singing. (In fact, Bell had aspired to a musical career until a case of viral meningitis unexpectedly put an end to those ambitions.) At Wheaton, Bell also met and befriended his future wife, Kristen.

## EARLY MINISTRY

Bell delivered his first sermon barefoot at a Wisconsin summer camp at the tender age of twenty-one. Working as a water-ski instructor, Bell was called upon to fill in for the preacher. It was to be a watershed moment in Bell's life, prompting him to seek formal ministerial training at Fuller Theological Seminary in Pasadena, California, that autumn. He recalled to Kelefa Sanneh for the *New Yorker* (26 Nov. 2012), "I just wanted to preach. . . . I was totally single-minded." Focused on preaching as he was, Bell was not always comfortable at Fuller. He chafed at the preaching style taught at the school, finding it dull and uninspiring, and he was less interested in biblical studies and interpretation at that point.

He seemed to hit his stride after graduation when he served as a youth minister in Southern California. On a trip home to Michigan, Bell met Rev. Ed Dobson of Calvary Church in Grand Rapids. Dobson (no relation to James Dobson, founder of the conservative Focus on the Family organization) saw a great deal of promise in the young pastor and soon invited him to join Calvary's staff, an offer Bell readily accepted. At Calvary, Bell gained experience (and fans) serving the younger generation by leading Saturday young adult–oriented worship services.

## MARS HILL

Critical of what he sees as the failures of Christianity to meet the true needs of humanity today, Bell set out to create a different kind of church experience. As he told Bendis, "The church has spent extraordinary energy focused on things that feel like gnats. They are not the weightier matters of the law." So in 1998, the twenty-eight-year old Bell left Calvary to establish his own nondenominational church, Mars Hill Bible Church, which opened in February 1999. Hundreds of Calvary worshippers followed him, helping form his new parish. In true megachurch style, the church began in a loaned building space and then moved into a former suburban shopping mall in Grandville, Michigan, where it has been situated since 2000. So immensely popular was Mars Hill that Bell told Bendis, "We've been swamped and have played catchup from day one." In fact, at its peak, attendance at Mars Hill reached around eleven thousand.

Seeking to further distinguish his church from others and emphasize its community feel, Bell eschewed many of the usual trappings, including even a choir and pulpit. Congregants were encouraged to wear what they liked and to sing and hear one another singing, as opposed to simply listening to a stage performance as in other megachurches. While praise-and-worship music abounded, Christian indie rock music could be heard there as well. Social justice and community outreach were other cornerstones upon which Bell founded Mars Hill. Speaking of its enormous growth and the difficulties of caring for so many, Bell explained to Bendis, "We believe that every person is a priest with a particular ministry. . . . We assume the body [of the church] will take care of itself and that the staff's job is to enlist and empower and encourage." This notion takes on how the church is often seen versus how Bell believes it should be. Eric Marrapodi, writing for the *CNN* Religion blog (19 Mar. 2011), quoted Bell as saying, "Rarely do you hear people say, 'Oh yeah, those [Christians] are the people who never stop talking about love. Oh a Christian church—that's where you go if [you] feel beaten down and kicked and someone has their boot on your neck. You go there because it's a place of healing and a place of love.'"

## CRISIS OF FAITH

Around the turn of the millennium, Bell developed an interest in what is often termed "liberal theology," taking to studying biblical history and interpretation, especially as it related to the New Testament and first-century Christianity. As a result of his readings—among them works by Anglican bishop N. T. Wright—Bell began to have serious doubts about the inerrancy of the Bible and entertain questions about the doctrine he had been raised with and was then preaching. In an April 2009 interview, Bell described his newfound faith to *Christianity Today* editor Mark Galli as "militant mysticism," elaborating, "I'm really absolutely sure of some things that I don't quite know."

Bell's changing spiritual direction led to some fairly radical changes at Mars Hill as well. In 2003, Bell decided to include women in the then all-male church leadership, a move that cost the congregation about two thousand of its more conservative members who believed that women should not be allowed to lead the church. Three years later, around another thousand disaffected members left in response to Bell's "The New Exodus" sermons calling for more involvement in social justice issues. In 2008, he decided to reduce the number of sermons he delivered to twenty per year, perhaps in part to accommodate his media activities and touring schedule. (That year alone he had gone on a twenty-two-city tour entitled The Gods Aren't Angry.)

The straw that broke the camel's back was the outraged response to *Love Wins* in the spring of 2011. Outsiders called on Mars Hill congregants to account for the theological issues presented in Bell's book and to defend their membership at Bell's church. In the aftermath, another thousand members left. That September, Bell announced his resignation and, in December, gave his farewell sermon, leaving his co-pastor of two years, Shane Hipps, to lead the church in his absence. Mars Hill named Bell its "pastor emeritus," a title usually reserved for retired clergy. In 2012, the church found a replacement in Kent Dobson, the son of Bell's former mentor.

## SPREADING THE WORD

In keeping with his desire to reach people where they are, Bell has written a handful of books and created numerous films. His is a highly anecdotal, stream-of-consciousness, and plain-spoken style that eschews the chapter-and-verse recitation and sophisticated technical vocabulary common among evangelists and theologians. Known for paraphrasing and occasionally truncating quotations, Bell has been accused of selective quotation, a claim to which he responds, "'You're just picking the verses you like'? I think everybody is," as quoted by Sanneh for the *New Yorker*.

Between 2001 and 2009, the nasally voiced preacher released the highly popular NOOMA videos, a series of twenty-four short films, named after the Greek word *pneuma*, meaning "spirit." Each moody-feeling short was twelve minutes in length and delivered in monologue format. Church Bible study groups frequently turned to them as conversation starters, and as of March 2011 some two million copies of the NOOMA DVDs had been sold worldwide, with viewers from some eighty countries.

Bell has also released a number of other videos, including *The Gods Aren't Angry* (2008), *Drops like Stars* (2010), and *Poets Prophets & Preachers* (2009). His only feature-length film, *Everything Is Spiritual* (2007), ranked among the best-selling Christian DVDs in the United Kingdom in 2008.

In 2005, Bell published his best-selling debut book, *Velvet Elvis: Repainting the Christian Faith*, which was aimed at reintroducing Christianity to those who might have been put off by it in the past. *Publishers Weekly* praised its accessibility to non-Christians and Gen X readers. Its success led to *Sex God: Exploring the Endless Connections between Sexuality and Spirituality* (2007), in which Bell uses close analyses of biblical passages to talk about the relationship between human physical love and God. Together, his first two books sold nearly 600,000 copies by 2008. Bell's newfound emphasis on social justice is evident in *Jesus Wants to Save Christians: A Manifesto for the Church in Exile* (2008), a book he cowrote with Don Golden on global wealth inequality and how to be a Christian within that reality. His 2009 *Drops like Stars: A Few Thoughts on Creativity and Suffering*, the shortest of his works to date, was panned by reviewers for being overly anecdotal.

## HEAVEN AND HELL, HERE AND NOW

Bell's 2011 book *Love Wins* has by far garnered the most attention, positive and negative, of all his works. Inspired by the troubling question, "Gandhi's in hell?" Bell began an earnest exploration of the possibilities for the afterlife and specifically how much can be known about humanity's fate after death. The result was *Love Wins*, in which Bell argues that God deeply desires for everyone to be saved and leaves open the possibility that all may be reconciled to God in the end. He also questions the separation between the here-and-now life and the afterlife, as well as the eternal nature of hell.

In his 2009 interview with Mark Galli for *Christianity Today*, Bell indicated his disdain for what he terms "evacuation theology," which centralizes the afterlife. "The evacuation theology that says, 'figure out the ticket, say the right prayer, get the right formula, and then we'll go somewhere else' is lethal to Jesus, who endlessly speaks of the renewal of all things." Bell focuses on the "here-and-now" aspects of Jesus' preaching, as opposed to atonement theology. He explained to Marrapodi, "In the Jewish context in which [Jesus] lived and moved, you didn't have that articulated belief system about when you die. It was very rooted in this life— dirt and wine and banquets, family and fishing. . . . This world is our home, this world that God loves, that God is redeeming—so that's the starting point." Suggesting that heaven and hell are conditions humans create on earth, Bell says, "He [Jesus] speaks of it [heaven] as sort of a real place and yet it's always heaven and earth becoming one. As opposed to how do we get there, his interest is how do we bring there here?" as Lillian Kwon reported in the *Christian Post* (15 Mar. 2011).

## BACKLASH

Bell's stance led many conservative Christians to deride him as a heretic and a universalist (someone who believes everyone, regardless of faith, will go to heaven). A few weeks prior to its scheduled release date, blogger Justin Taylor instigated an online debate based on promos for the book. Twitter and Facebook erupted in response, much of it critical. Among his critics were Baptist minister John Piper of Minneapolis, North Park University theology professor Scot McKnight, and Southern Baptist Theological Seminary president R. Albert Mohler Jr. In the midst of the heated discussion, *Christianity Today*'s Galli called for calmer, more open debate of the issues Bell raises. When *Love Wins* came out on March 15, two weeks earlier than scheduled, a number of Christian bookstores refused to carry the book. Nonetheless it soon became a *New York Times* and *Publishers Weekly* nonfiction best seller.

Critics noted the book's lack of substantiating evidence and its "elliptical style" and "sometimes obscure discussion," as Erik Eckholm called it in his March 4, 2011, *New York Times* review. By that summer, more than a handful of rebuttals to *Love Wins* were in print, among them one by Galli. All this is part of what Bell sees as an ongoing tradition of debate within the church. As he explained to Marrapodi, "No one has the last word other than God. I am taking part in a discussion that's been going on for thousands of years. Everyone can play a part in that discussion."

A number of Bell's critics hold that divine wrath and the punishment of hell are an integral part of the concept of free will—that is, if God truly gives human beings choice, humans must be able to choose separation from God in hell, and everyone being saved would nullify that choice. However, Bell himself could be seen as a separationist, someone who believes that those who are in hell choose to be there, rather than a universalist or an annihilationist (someone who believes existence ceases at death). In *Love Wins*, Bell claims that "God gives us what we want, and if that's hell, we can have it. We have that kind of freedom, that kind of choice. We are that free." Emphasizing that all discussion of the afterlife involves speculation, Bell expresses comfort with paradox, particularly with respect to God being both loving and just.

Other critics fear that without an eternal hell in the afterlife, people would not be motivated to live a Christian life now. Asked about this concern, Bell responded, "We can choose the way of compassion, of forgiveness, of generosity or we can choose other paths and those have real consequences in the world," according to Kwon's report of a book tour event in mid-March 2011.

## AFTER *LOVE WINS*

After resigning from Mars Hill in late 2011, Bell and his wife, Kristen, moved to Orange County, California, with their sons Preston and Trace and daughter Violet. There he has sought "the divine in the daily," surfing and discovering clothes in colors other than black. As he explained to Bendis a few years earlier, "If you can't find God in the peanut butter and jelly sandwiches and the dinner with beloved friends from across the street, then I don't know if God will be found on the mountaintop. If I lose the sense of wonder about today and this afternoon and this evening, then there's no point in spouting off about how to fix things."

But Bell has by no means been idle since leaving Mars Hill. In 2012, he published *The Rob Bell Reader*, a free e-book containing segments from all his previous written works, and he led a two-day retreat in Laguna Beach. Partnering with *LOST* producer Carlton Cuse, Bell set his sights on a new medium: television. The ABC network purportedly bought the rights to their drama *Stronger*, but as no pilot has been shot, Cuse and Bell have been working on a possible talk show. Bell's latest book, *What We Talk about When We Talk about God*, is set to come out in 2013.

## SUGGESTED READING

Bell, Rob. "The Giant Story." Interview by Mark Galli. *Christianity Today* Apr. 2009: 34–36. Print.

Bendis, Debra. "Bell's Appeal." *Christian Century* 24 Mar. 2009: 22. Print.

Marrapodi, Eric. "Rob Bell Punches Back against Claims of Heresy." *Cable News Network*. CNN, 19 Mar. 2011. Web. 19 Dec. 2012.

Meacham, Jon. "Pastor Rob Bell: What If Hell Doesn't Exist?" *Time*. Time, 14 Apr. 2011. Web. 19 Dec. 2012.

Sanneh, Kelefa. "The Hell-Raiser." *New Yorker* 26 Nov. 2012: 56–65. Print.

Wellman, James K. *Rob Bell and a New American Christianity*. Nashville: Abingdon, 2012. Print.

—*Céleste Codington-Lacerte*

# Michelle Bernstein

**Born:** ca. 1969
**Occupation:** Chef and entrepreneur

Michelle Bernstein has distinguished herself as "one of the rare cooks who can seamlessly and judiciously weave together culinary traditions from around the world—Latin America to Asia to the Mediterranean—and create vibrant, memorable dishes," according to Diana Abu-Jaber for *Oprah Magazine* (Mar. 2009). A native of Miami, Florida, Bernstein has been widely

© Martin Roe ./Retna Ltd./Corbis

credited with reinventing that city's dining scene with her globally inspired Latin cuisine, which draws influence from her Argentine Jewish background. An alumnus of the prestigious College of Culinary Arts at the North Miami campus of Johnson & Wales University, she trained under such famed chefs as Mark Militello, Jean-Louis Palladin, and Eric Ripert before coming to the attention of the food cognoscenti in 2000, when she became executive chef of Azul at Miami's Mandarin Oriental hotel. The restaurant was one of the first in Miami to earn the AAA Five Diamond Award, the most prestigious honor in the hospitality industry, and helped catapult Bernstein into the national culinary spotlight, leading to a cohosting stint on the now defunct Food Network program *The Melting Pot*.

In 2004 Bernstein left Azul and, in 2005, opened her first restaurant, Michy's, a modern bistro in Miami's Upper East Side neighborhood, with her husband and business partner David Martinez. Michy's quickly became a Miami hotspot and was recognized as one of the best restaurants in America by *Gourmet* magazine. The success of Michy's allowed Bernstein, who was named the best chef in the South by the James Beard Foundation in 2008, to pursue other culinary ventures. In 2008 she and Martinez opened Senora Martinez, a tapas restaurant in Miami's Design District, which enjoyed critical and commercial success before closing in 2012. Their latest restaurant concept, Crumb on Parchment, a breakfast-and-lunch café in the Design District, debuted in 2011.

In addition to her restaurant projects, Bernstein has worked as a consulting chef for other restaurants as well as for such companies as Delta Airlines and Lean Cuisine; released a line of signature cookware; published a cookbook; and appeared on numerous television shows, including as a contestant on the Food Network's *Iron Chef America* (2005), judge on Bravo's *Top Chef* (2007–13), and host of the South Florida edition of PBS's *Check, Please!* (2008–). While being grateful for the many career opportunities her culinary success has afforded her, Bernstein explained to Susan Josephs for *Jewish Woman Magazine*, "For me, the greatest satisfaction comes from watching people eat my food and seeing that they're happy."

## EARLY LIFE AND EDUCATION

Michelle Bernstein was born in 1969 in Miami, Florida. Her mother, born Martha Cohan, is of Argentine Jewish ancestry; her father, who hails from Minnesota, has Italian Jewish roots. She has an older sister, Nicolette. Bernstein grew up in Miami Shores, a suburb north of Miami, but spent her childhood summers in her mother's homeland of Argentina. She has called her mother her greatest culinary influence and has credited her with exposing her to different food cultures early on. In an interview with the quarterly literary magazine *Oxford American* (9 Mar. 2010), Bernstein said that she "was always in the kitchen with my mom [as a child]" and that there "were always dishes that had touches of all cultures." She reportedly made her first roast chicken at the age of four; by age nine, "when most of her peers were playing with Easy-Bake Ovens, [she] was begging for an escargot set," as Amy Keller noted for *Florida Trend* (Dec. 2008).

Before setting plans of a culinary career in motion, however, Bernstein had aspirations of becoming a professional ballerina. She developed a love of dance from the time she was three, and was admitted into her first dance class after a Russian ballet teacher spotted her dancing in the lobby of a building where one of her sister's dance classes was taking place. Throughout her youth and adolescence Bernstein received training in classical and contemporary dance; after graduating from North Miami Senior High School (at age sixteen, according to one source), she won a scholarship to study with the Alvin Ailey American Dance Theater, a prestigious modern dance company based in New York.

Not long after arriving in New York, Bernstein, despite having promising talent, became disenchanted with the hypercompetitive and ultraskinny world of professional dance. "I wanted to eat," she told Keller, admitting that she "thought about food all the time" and "went to sleep with cookbooks" during her time with Alvin Ailey. After returning home to Florida, Bernstein studied nutrition for a time at Emory and Georgia State universities in Atlanta. It was during one of her college breaks, however, that she rediscovered her passion for cooking. Unsure about her professional future, Bernstein, on the suggestion of her mother, visited the North Miami campus of Johnson & Wales University's (JWU) College of Culinary Arts, which had recently opened near her parents' home. "I got these weird butterflies in my stomach and felt like I had to do this," she recalled to Mary Constantine for the *Knoxville News Sentinel* (12 May 2011). "I went in and signed up just like that." She graduated with honors from JWU in 1994.

## EARLY RESTAURANT CAREER

While attending JWU, Bernstein began working in restaurants. Despite developing serviceable culinary skills from years of cooking with her mother in the family kitchen, she was "one of the very people who didn't even know how to hold a knife properly" when she entered culinary school, as she told Constantine. Bernstein gained her first formal cooking experience in 1992, when she started working as a prep cook at Janjo's restaurant in Miami's Coconut Grove neighborhood, where she trained under chef Jan Jorgensen.

Bernstein next received training at Mark's Place, a highly regarded North Miami Beach restaurant founded by James Beard Award–winning chef Mark Militello. She spent a year and a half working at the restaurant's pizza and salad station before being promoted to line cook. After her stint at Mark's Place, Bernstein worked as a fishmonger at famed French chef Jean-Louis Palladin's eponymous restaurant at the Watergate Hotel in Washington, DC. In her interview with Amy Keller, she recalled Palladin, a notoriously temperamental chef who died of lung cancer in 2001, handling mistakes with "humiliating scoldings and the occasional pot thrown her way." Bernstein next worked as a sous chef at several acclaimed New York restaurants, one of which included Le Bernardin, where she worked under Palladin protégé Eric Ripert. In the late 1990s she returned to Florida to become an executive chef, first at the Red Fish Grill, a seafood establishment in Coral Gables, and then at Tantra, a restaurant and club in Miami Beach.

Bernstein remained at Tantra, which opened to acclaim, for only a brief time before leaving to become executive chef and a partner in the Strand, another restaurant located in Miami Beach. Despite being granted the freedom to experiment more with her own style of cooking, her stint with the restaurant lasted only ten months, during which she worked grueling twenty-hour days and dropped to eighty-five pounds.

## RISE TO NATIONAL PROMINENCE

Bernstein's culinary fortunes changed in December 2000, when she became the executive chef of Azul, an upscale, fine-dining restaurant at the Mandarin Oriental hotel, located on scenic Brickell Key Drive in Miami. She was selected to helm the restaurant after a nationwide search of more than a hundred candidates. Featuring innovative dishes characterized by multicultural influences and locally sourced ingredients, the opulent 120-seat Azul, which was designed by Tony Chi, immediately won rave reviews from critics. Most notably, *Esquire* magazine food critic John Mariani chose it as the best new restaurant in America in 2001. In his *Esquire* review (Dec. 2001), Mariani called Azul "a summation of everything twenty-first-century gastronomy can be at its best," and made note of Bernstein's "amalgam of Floridian, Caribbean, French, and Asian flavors." With Azul, Bernstein explained to Keller, "I wanted to define fine food and fine dining in this city, and I wanted to take it by storm."

The year 2001 also saw Bernstein make her television debut as a cohost of the Food Network program *The Melting Pot*, a gig she landed after a fortuitous encounter with the celebrity chef Bobby Flay at Azul. On the show, which she hosted for two years, she introduced home cooks to her contemporary Latin-based cuisine, dubbed "Nuevo Latin cuisine." Bernstein held her executive chef role at Azul for about five years, during which the restaurant earned the rare and highly coveted five-diamond rating from AAA. It was also during this time that she met her future husband and business partner, David Martinez, who served as Azul's assistant manager. Martinez, Bernstein told Kristen Doyle, "gave me the courage and inspired me to stand alone . . . to break out from under the names I was working for and to make a name for myself." The couple opened their first restaurant, MB, at the Fiesta Americana Grand Aqua hotel in Cancun, Mexico, in 2004.

## MICHY'S

While the rigorous standards of excellence at Azul catered to her perfectionist streak, Bernstein has said that she grew "sick of watching people that hadn't dressed up for the evening get turned away from the dining room," as she explained to Mary Constantine. "This is my town, and you don't tell people that live here that you can't come in because you aren't dressed properly." With that idea in mind, Bernstein resolved to open a reasonably priced neighborhood restaurant with a hip, yet down-to-earth, atmosphere. In 2005, after they both left Azul, she and her husband opened what would become their flagship restaurant, Michy's (Bernstein's childhood nickname), in Miami's once-seedy but now trendy Upper East Side neighborhood. "I just wanted to cook for the people of Miami, so we took a leap of faith, and we did it," Bernstein said to Constantine.

Featuring a vibrant dining room designed by Bernstein's sister Nicolette, the fifty-seat

Michy's opened to wide acclaim and quickly developed a reputation as one of Miami's best restaurants. *Gourmet* magazine listed Michy's as one of the top fifty restaurants in America and *Food & Wine* magazine named it the country's best new restaurant of 2006. In an article for the latter publication (June 2006), Jennifer Rubell called Michy's "the Miami version of those mom-and-pop Michelin one-stars in the French countryside," and wrote that its food "draws on all of Bernstein's heritage, history and interests, and then weaves those influences seamlessly into a bright, refined, multicultural cuisine." Michy's features an eclectic range of starters, entrees, and desserts, and also offers a family-style tasting menu. Nearly all of Michy's offerings are available in both half and full portions. On the restaurant's website, Bernstein described her dishes as "luxurious comfort food."

## TELEVISION AND OTHER WORK

As Bernstein was getting Michy's off the ground, she helped increase her national profile when she appeared on the popular Food Network cooking show *Iron Chef America* in 2005. On the show, which features world-class guest chefs battling resident "Iron Chefs" in a one-hour cooking competition revolving around a secret ingredient, she defeated Bobby Flay by a convincing margin. That victory and Michy's success led to Bernstein becoming involved in other culinary ventures and projects.

In 2006 Bernstein became a consulting chef for Delta Airlines, for whom she began developing Business Elite and First Class meals. That same year she partnered with the restaurateur Jeffrey Chodorow to work as a consulting chef for his Social restaurant chain. Bernstein's Miami tapas restaurant, Senora Martinez, opened in the city's Design District in 2008. Like Michy's, Senora Martinez became an immediate culinary hotspot and was recognized as one of the best new restaurants in America by *Esquire* magazine. Later in 2008 Bernstein was named best chef in the South during the James Beard Foundation's annual awards ceremony, the so-called Oscars of the food world.

Bernstein's first cookbook, *Cuisine à Latina: Fresh Tastes and a World of Flavors from Michy's Miami Kitchen*, was published by Houghton Mifflin Harcourt in November 2008. Cowritten with Andrew Friedman, the book features easy-to-follow recipes that highlight Bernstein's modern interpretation of Latin cuisine. In writing the book, Bernstein told Patricia Letakis in an undated article for *Florida Travel + Life* magazine, "I wanted to make sure that anyone who wasn't a professional could do my recipes and the outcome would be just as good."

Bernstein began serving as the host of the Emmy Award–nominated PBS weekly restaurant review program, *Check, Please! South Florida*, in 2008. She has served as a guest judge on Bravo's Emmy- and James Beard Award–winning cooking competition series *Top Chef*, and made regular guest appearances on other television shows, including *The Today Show* and *The Martha Stewart Show*.

In the fall of 2009, Bernstein and her husband opened another restaurant, called Michelle Bernstein's at the Omphoy, at the Omphoy Ocean Resort in Palm Beach, Florida. The following year Bernstein launched her own line of cookware, called michelleB Forged Aluminum, on the Home Shopping Network (HSN). Then, in 2011, she and her husband debuted their latest restaurant endeavor, Crumb on Parchment, a café in the Design District that serves casual breakfast and lunch fare.

The year 2012 was one of change for Bernstein. She and Martinez closed Senora Martinez and ended their partnership with the Omphoy Ocean Resort, but found new opportunities as well. The couple opened a second Crumb on Parchment location at the swank Webster hotel on South Beach. Bernstein also became a consulting chef for the Lean Cuisine brand of frozen foods and started writing a blog about baby food for NBC Latino.

Bernstein's latest television project is a reality television show, *Michy*, which premiered in August 2013 on Chello Latin America's Casa Club TV channel.

## COMMUNITY INITIATIVES

Bernstein has been active in the local community and helped establish the Miami chapter of Common Threads, an after-school program dedicated to teaching underprivileged youths about nutrition and different food cultures through cooking. She has also partnered with the Miami-Dade County public school system on an initiative to improve the quality of cafeteria food around the country. She told Kristen Doyle, "I love that I have the opportunity to share what food can do to bring people together with others."

## PERSONAL LIFE

Bernstein and Martinez married in 2005. They live in the Belle Meade neighborhood of Miami, located on the city's Upper East Side, with their adopted son, Zachary Gray Martinez, who was born in 2011.

## SUGGESTED READING

Abu-Jaber, Diana. "Miami Alfresco." *Oprah Magazine* Mar. 2009: 174–79. Print.

Bernstein, Michelle. "Interview with Michelle Bernstein." *Oxford American*. Oxford American, 9 Mar. 2010. Web. 2 Sept. 2013.

Bernstein, Michelle. "South Florida's Best and Brightest." *Aventura Business Monthly*. Aventura Business Monthly, 1 May 2011. Web. 2 Sept. 2013.

Constantine, Mary. "One-time Ballerina Finds Great Success in Switch to Culinary Career." *Knoxville News Sentinel*. Scripps Interactive Newspapers Group, 12 May 2011. Web. 18 Sept. 2013.

Keller, Amy. "Michelle Bernstein's Pressure Cooker." *Florida Trend*. Trend Magazines, 1 Dec. 2008. Web. 18 Sept. 2013.

Letakis, Patricia. "Meet Florida's Culinary Darling." *Florida Travel + Life*. Florida Travel + Life, 2013. Web. 2 Sept. 2013.

Shatzman, Marci. "Chef Michelle Bernstein Shares Food and Advice." *Sun-Sentinel*. Sun Sentinel, 13 Mar. 2013. Web. 2 Sept. 2013.

—*Chris Cullen*

Francis Specker/Landov

# Gina Bianchini

**Born:** 1972
**Occupation:** Entrepreneur

For nearly two decades, Gina Bianchini has worked tirelessly on a variety of social networking and investment ventures. She is the chief executive officer (CEO) of Mightybell, a social networking platform that brings specific skills and small-group discussions together, and the former CEO of Ning. She is also a cofounder (with Sheryl Sandberg, Rachel Thomas, and Debi Hemmeter) of LeanIn.org, which aims to connect and empower women in business. Bianchini helped to provide the networking technology that powers LeanIn.org and forms the network among its members.

A successful entrepreneur and business leader, Bianchini is one of the professional networking site LinkedIn's Influencers, industry professionals chosen to submit articles and video for members. In 2013, she was one of more than one hundred entrepreneurs and innovators whom the United Nations commissioned to discuss opportunities to expand the global talent pool in STEM—science, technology, engineering, and mathematics. Dubbed UnGrounded, the ten-hour brainstorming session generated creative solutions to meet the need for better-trained employees in these fields. The day after the session, four projects that the group wanted to back were presented to the United Nations' International Telecommunication Union.

## EARLY LIFE AND EDUCATION

Bianchini was born in 1972 and grew up in Cupertino, California, in the area known as Silicon Valley. Her father was a high school history teacher and coached wrestling, and her mother was a homemaker who held several odd jobs to help make ends meet. Bianchini was a young competitive walker and demonstrated her entrepreneurial spirit early; by the age of nine, she was breeding lop rabbits and placing classified ads in the local newspaper to sell them locally. When Bianchini was only eleven, her father was killed by a drunk driver. She told Dean Takahashi for *Venture Beat* (22 Oct. 2012) that such difficult life experiences proved to be valuable lessons for her. "It's not about what happens to you," she explained. "It's what do you do next. How do you bounce back from failure? Try to stay focused on the things I can control and look at life as a series of small moments that I have some control over."

As a child and adolescent, Bianchini was always involved in a variety of activities, ranging from debate to peer counseling. She was named an All-American field hockey player at Lynbrook High School. Although she lost her bid to be elected vice president of her class, as a high school junior Bianchini worked as a page in congressman Norman Mineta's office. In high school, she worked as a waitress at a Hobee's Restaurant. She held several jobs while earning a bachelor's degree in political science at Stanford University, including working as a mountain-biking park ranger, selling advertising for the *Stanford Daily*, and working in the admissions office. She was also named Regional All-American in field hockey while at Stanford.

## HARMONIC COMMUNICATIONS

After graduating from Stanford University in 1994, Bianchini began work as an analyst in the high-technology group of Goldman Sachs's San Francisco office. As the Internet became increasingly important, she took on a heightened level of responsibility in the company. Through her work on an initial public offering for the CKS Group, she received an invitation from CKS's chief executive, Mark Kvamme, to serve as their acquisitions manager. She worked there for more than two years before returning to Stanford to earn a master's degree in business administration, teaching a spinning class two nights a week to help pay her way. While she was still working on her degree, she and Kvamme founded Harmonic Communications, a software company focused on tracking and measuring advertising. Upon graduating in 2000, Bianchini took on the role of president of the company before transitioning to the position of chief marketing officer. Like many technology companies, Harmonic Communications fared poorly during the dot-com crash of the early 2000s, and it was ultimately acquired by the Japanese advertising agency Dentsu in 2003.

## NING
Bianchini cofounded Ning (which means "peace" in Mandarin) in 2004 with Marc Andreessen, who had made a fortune developing and then selling the computer services company Netscape and had sat on the board of Harmonic Communications. Andreessen invested $15 million of start-up money into Ning, and they spent a year building the architecture for the online platform before launching in 2005. Ning is an online platform that enables its users to build personalized social networks. The networks are based on topics, permitting targeted advertising using Google's AdSense. By 2008, Ning had accrued members in more than 176 countries, with about 40 percent of the total number coming from outside the United States. The platform was quickly made available in several languages other than English, including Dutch, Japanese, and Spanish. Within four years, more than half a million networks had been founded through it, including networks established by companies as a way to connect directly with their customers; for example, General Motors created a network for owners of Saturn vehicles in order to share information about the brand and connect with its customers.

Ning particularly appealed to companies and other organizations because it eliminated the need for in-house dedicated personnel to build and host the technology for a social network. Using a service such as Ning removed both the time and the cost of developing an internal network. "When your currency is ideas, people become emotionally attached," Bianchini told Adam Penenberg for Fast Company (May 2008). "Then you become a public utility like Blogger, YouTube, or Facebook."

In addition to companies, Ning hosted networks devoted to a wide range of interests and causes. Bianchini told Daisy Wademan Dowling for the New York Times (28 Dec. 2008), "I set aside time each day to look at new social networks on Ning, and I'm constantly inspired. Recently at a conference, one of the participants told me that he and his wife were starting a site for parents of terminally ill children. Enabling those types of connections reminds me why we do what we do."

Bianchini stepped down as the chief executive of Ning in March 2010 to join the Andreessen Horowitz venture capital firm as executive in residence. Ning was sold in 2011 to Glam Media for a reported $150 million.

## FINDING FUNDING
One of the difficulties in business, especially for women, is obtaining venture capital to fund a start-up. Because of the success of Ning, Bianchini did not have this problem when beginning her next endeavor. She explained to Nadine Heintz for Inc. magazine (Dec. 2012), "When you've created something millions of people used, people are more willing to take a bet on you." For her next start-up, a social networking platform called Mightybell, Bianchini raised $3.6 million from three sources, First Round Capital, Floodgate, and Greylock.

In March 2013, Bianchini, who is herself an investor in tech start-ups created and led by women, spoke to a group of businesswomen who had gathered at the headquarters of the social networking site Facebook. Jon Swartz reported for USA Today (5 Nov. 2012) that Bianchini told the group, "There's energy and excitement at the early-stage investment level for women partners and women entrepreneurs. All of this is against a backdrop, however, where an increasing amount of venture capital is being consolidated in the hands of roughly six firms, three of which have zero women partners and no real movement to recruit them." Putting her ideas into practice, in 2011 Bianchini provided venture capital for Levo League, a website devoted to young women in business that provides mentoring advice and an online support network.

## MIGHTYBELL
For her next venture, Bianchini founded Mightybell, a social networking platform that enables groups to organize and collaborate online. At the time of its launch in 2011, Mightybell allowed its users to create and share step-by-step guidelines to teach a skill or accomplish a goal. It soon evolved into something more collaborative, adding discussion and scheduling features that facilitate group projects and initiatives. As Bianchini, who serves as chief executive of Mightybell, told Quentin Hardy for the New York Times (15 Apr. 2013), "This is a way for people to create their

own branches of groups. What if an influencer, or a brand, or an organization, could go from having passive followers to an active army? It's like nothing that's been offered before." The site hosts videos, image sharing, discussion rooms, and chat features. Bianchini likens it to a chat room with features that allow for more collaboration. "We're thinking of how to scale intimacy and create deeper interactions for groups of people around projects, themes, content and more," Bianchini explained to Leena Rao for *TechCrunch* (16 Sept. 2012).

Mightybell still offers guides with step-by-step instructions for ventures as serious as writing a business plan or as frivolous as planning a weekend getaway. These how-to sites are located in a separate section called "Steps." Members can create and market their own guides, with 25 percent of revenues from those guides going to Mightybell for hosting the site and providing the software. After an initial free period, Mightybell began offering a premium service that included online stores, communication management, and data analytics.

The social network has evolved to incorporate the concept of Lean In circles, networking and support groups based on the approach developed by Sheryl Sandberg, chief operating officer of Facebook, in the 2013 book *Lean In: Women, Work, and the Will to Lead*. These circles are small groups that promote encouragement and support as well as mutual learning and skill building among their members. Bianchini told *USA Today* (11 Mar. 2013) that Mightybell "provides an easy way for groups to meet, post, and chat in private spaces while still staying connected to new materials and resources from Lean In."

## LEANIN.ORG

As a child, Bianchini learned the value of group support after the tragic death of her father. In her profile on LeanIn.org, she explained how her brother, sister, and cousins formed a tight-knit family group that offered both benefits and drawbacks. Their loyalty to one another was unquestioned, though they did disagree among themselves frequently. In addition, after her father's death, members of the community created a protective network for Bianchini and her two siblings. She noted that her work for the Lean In campaign arose from her own desire to become better at team building and strengthen her skills in entrepreneurship.

The Lean In campaign is designed to offer practical training in skills and also seeks to provide mentorship opportunities, support, and encouragement. LeanIn.com was tested with multiple focus groups over several months; as a result, the concepts of online education and real-world discussion merged. The site offers a community network as well as Lean In education, which includes educational materials from Stanford University, and Lean In circles, which

are small groups of users who meet periodically for discussion and networking.

Discussing Lean In circles, Rachel Thomas, the president of LeanIn.org, told Hardy, "We think of them as book clubs with a purpose. People can name and personalize their groups. We hope people will try an action, share the results, and continue to meet more often." Although most of the initial interest in Lean In circles came from within the United States, groups from such countries as Germany, Canada, and China have also expressed interest.

Speaking to Hardy, Bianchini contrasted Ning with LeanIn.org, saying, "Ning had 'the empty group problem.' People form a group, but after a while they may not have any idea what to do." In contrast, LeanIn.org aims to offer new material for participants to react to and increase group engagement. "No one has done networks like this," she continued. "It's been done in the real world, and it is how the Web itself was built, but it hasn't been done for groups."

## PERSONAL LIFE

Bianchini told Robert L. Mitchell for *Computerworld* (10 Nov. 2008) that blogging was her favorite technology. "I think blogging in all of its current and future iterations is a true breakthrough. Any opportunity for so many new voices to express themselves and to be heard is truly profound." She also cited reading as her favorite pastime, stating that books offered a lifetime of learning.

Bianchini lives in Palo Alto, California, with husband John Alstrom. Regarding the quest for a work-life balance, she told Sarah Tomlinson for *Ladies Who Launch* (20 Aug. 2008), "My strategy has been to really reduce and edit my life in such a way that I maximize the amount of time that I work and don't feel guilty about it." Part of that strategy involves creating a weekly review in which she writes down the lessons of the previous week and goals for the following week.

## SUGGESTED READING

Bianchini, Gina. "The Benefits of a Network." *New York Times* 28 Dec. 2008, New York ed.: BU9. Print.

Bianchini, Gina. "Ning Co-Founder Makes the Connection." Interview by Jennifer Frazier. *Success*. CMS, Sept. 2010. Web. 8 Aug. 2013.

Hardy, Quentin. "'Lean In' Software Goes Corporate." *New York Times*. New York Times, 15 Apr. 2013. Web. 8 Aug. 2013.

Pack, Thomas. "A Million Social Networks Not Enough? Start Your Own." *Information Today*. Information Today, Dec. 2009. Web. 8 Aug. 2013.

Penenberg, Adam L. "Ning's Infinite Ambition." *Fast Company*. Mansueto Ventures, 1 May 2008. Web. 7 Aug. 2013.

—*Judy Johnson*

# Michael Ian Black

**Born:** August 12, 1971
**Occupation:** Comedian, actor, writer, and director

In an article for *Daily Variety* (19 Apr. 2007), entertainment writer Steven Zeitchik called comedian Michael Ian Black a "pop culture gadfly." Indeed, Black is perhaps best known for his humorous comments on the media, celebrities, and fads of various decades in the popular VH1 series that began with *I Love the '80s* in 2002 and culminated with *I Love the New Millennium* in 2008. His career, however, has extended far beyond pop culture commentary. Firmly grounded in stand-up and sketch comedy, Black has been featured in several television shows, including *The State, Ed, Viva Variety,* and *Stella.* He has also published children's books and essay collections and wrote the screenplays for the 2006 film *Wedding Daze*, which he directed, and the 2007 film *Run, Fatboy, Run.*

Black has almost two million followers on Twitter, where he is known for his snarky material and biting wit. Although he has accrued a long list of credits, he remains largely a cult celebrity. "Being at my level of fame is not very fun because people often recognize me, but don't know why they recognize me, and then they make a big show of telling me they know me, but do not know who I am," he explained in a post on his website (28 Oct. 2007). "It's kind of a contradictory statement: 'I know you but I have no idea who you are.'" Nevertheless, Black has enjoyed a wide-ranging career in entertainment. He told Scott King for *Chicago Now* (3 Nov. 2011), "I've been fortunate to do a lot of different things. When one gets tiresome, I've been able to sort of switch to another one."

## EARLY LIFE

Born Michael Ian Schwartz on August 12, 1971, Black changed his name when he began to work in show business in order to avoid confusion with an established actor named Michael Schwartz. (The change required only a simple translation, as *schwartz* means "black" in Yiddish.) The second of three children, he was raised in Hillsborough Township, New Jersey, where his family moved from Chicago when he was a toddler. His parents, Jill and Robert, divorced when he was about four years old. His mother, who ran a stationery store, became an ardent feminist and came out as a lesbian following her divorce. Growing up, Black lived with her and her female partner. He quipped to Eric Spitznagel for *Esquire* (15 Feb. 2012), "I was only five, but I had a clear sense of the way her entire worldview had shifted, and instinctively understood that her relationship to men as a species had altered. I was now in enemy territory." He admitted, however, that he was "pretty sure she wouldn't ever phrase it that way."

© Todd Selby/Corbis

Black's father, an executive at AT&T, later began taking graduate classes at Rutgers University. One night, when Black was twelve years old, the police found his father's car pulled over to the side of the road with Robert inside, suffering from a terrible head wound. Although the details were never made clear, police concluded that Black's father had been the victim of a random attack. After being rushed to the hospital and undergoing emergency brain surgery, he appeared to be on the mend. However, he contracted an infection shortly after returning home and was given the wrong medication by doctors. Black's father died soon thereafter. "My dad was not good with younger kids, but we were getting to an age where he was really starting to relate to us and be able to communicate with us," Black told Terry Gross for the National Public Radio (NPR) program *All Things Considered* (15 July 2009). "And to lose him then was . . . something you never really recover from."

Black has described himself as an exceptionally awkward and sensitive child who was prone to bursting into tears. He felt constant anxiety about his sister, who has Down syndrome. The money from the malpractice lawsuit mounted after the death of Black's father was used to establish a trust fund for her.

## EDUCATION

As a teenager, Black developed an interest in comedy and acting. He began taking weekend acting lessons from the legendary acting teacher Sanford Meisner and in the summers attended Stagedoor Manor, a well-known performing arts camp located in Loch Sheldrake, a town in upstate New York. "I was not well regarded at home. At Stagedoor, I felt like I found my people," he recalled to Mickey Rapkin for *GQ* (3 June 2010). "At Stagedoor I was popular. I was somebody in a way that I never was at home. Ever. And my dreams felt valid there in a way they didn't at home." His work at Stagedoor earned Black his first agent, a gruff-talking, chain-smoking woman named Shirley Grant, who sent him on auditions for commercials and pilots. Memorably, he tried out for the title role in the hit sitcom *Doogie Howser, M.D.*, a part that ultimately went to Neil Patrick Harris.

Black attended the Tisch School of the Arts at New York University (NYU). Not long after his junior year started, he was offered a job performing as Rafael, one of the Teenage Mutant Ninja Turtles, at promotional events. The four crime-fighting turtles—each named after a Renaissance painter—were at the height of their popularity in the late 1980s and early 1990s. The animated show dominated the Saturday-morning lineup, and their images could be found on a wide array of toys, lunchboxes, and other products. "When that opportunity presents itself, one doesn't say, "Oh, no thank you, I don't want to be a Teenage Mutant Ninja Turtle," Black joked to Ophira Eisenberg for the NPR program *Ask Me Another* (19 Apr. 2013). "You seize that by the shell and you run."

Black dropped out of NYU to travel the country as the character, making promotional appearances at malls and other venues. He never returned to school. He has recalled that his turtle costume weighed almost one hundred pounds and was rarely cleaned.

## THE STATE

While at NYU, Black was part of a sketch-comedy troupe that came to be known as The State, which performed on campus and at small venues around the city. In 1992, the group produced a show for MTV titled *You Wrote It, You Watch It*, which involved interviewing people on the street, asking them for funny stories from their own lives, and then reenacting the stories. "We served as our own cast and crew, and were given a video camera, three lights, a one-room office, and a $50 per week prop budget," the group's website explains. The following year, MTV began airing *The State*, a sketch-comedy show featuring the members of the group. The program ultimately ran on MTV until 1995, when the young comics agreed to approach CBS.

CBS signed the troupe for a series of specials and discussed the possibility of airing a regular program meant to compete with NBC's juggernaut *Saturday Night Live* the following fall. *Saturday Night Live* had been a major comedic influence on Black, who greatly admired original cast member John Belushi for his no-holds-barred humor and gonzo persona. However, the network's plans never came to fruition. After the

troupe's Halloween special garnered an exceptionally low audience share, CBS's programming chief canceled a planned New Year's Eve special and terminated the network's relationship with the comedy group.

Despite their experience with CBS, the group remained close, and its members continued to perform together in various configurations. "*The State*, for me, is like someone who went to a big football school. They will always identify themselves as an alumni of that school," Black told Sean McManus for *Philadelphia Weekly* (9 Mar. 2011). "As in college, I formed some of the closest relationships during that time. Those people will continue to be my lifelong friends. For all of us, it's an origin place. It's where we started. I think that's where we've gone back to time and time again. We work with each other all the time."

## TELEVISION SHOWS

Black and his fellow cast members from *The State* next developed a show called *Viva Variety*, which began airing in 1997 on Comedy Central. The premise of the short-lived program was that a European variety show featuring such acts as the world's only fiddle-playing contortionist and Scotland's premier regurgitation expert was trying to gain a foothold in the United States. Black played Johnny Blue Jeans, a would-be lothario with an Elvis-inspired pompadour who served as a sidekick to the hosts. Black has explained to journalists that he envisioned Johnny as a European latchkey child who was exposed to hundreds of hours of American television and who desperately loves every bit of American culture, no matter how cheesy or campy.

From 2000 to 2004, Black appeared in *Ed*, an hour-long show about a lawyer (played by Tom Cavanagh) who returns to his small hometown and buys a bowling alley. Black portrayed a bowling alley employee who continually hatches various harebrained schemes in order to make money. In 2004, he guest hosted the *Late Late Show* on CBS and vied for the spot of permanent host, a job that ultimately went to Craig Ferguson.

In 2005, Black starred in Comedy Central's *Stella*, which also featured Michael Showalter and David Wain, former cast members of *The State*. The three adapted their stage show for the television series, mainly by removing some of the most blatantly sexual and scatological material. In 2009, Black and Showalter created *Michael and Michael Have Issues*, which starred the pair as hosts of their own fictitious sketch show. Black has joked about how short lived most of his television projects have been. In one of his stand-up routines he said, "You guys may know me from such shows as *Canceled, Comedy Central Presents: No Longer on the Air*, and my sitcom, *Two and a Half Episodes*."

Black's most enduring television work has been the sardonically nostalgic VH1 series *I Love the . . .*, which skewers the pop culture sensibilities of various decades. "Black's bone-dry delivery was the funniest thing about [the series]," Simon Peter Groebner wrote for the Minneapolis *Star Tribune* (15 Nov. 2007). Black has also made guest appearances in such series as *Reno 911!*, *Reaper*, *Backwash*, and *Robot Chicken*. In 2012, Black began appearing in the web series *Burning Love*, a parody of reality dating shows.

## FILMS

In 2001, Black appeared in the movie *Wet Hot American Summer*, directed by David Wain and written by Wain and Michael Showalter. The film, set in 1981, depicts the hijinks that occur on the last day of camp. Although it was dismissed by critics, A. O. Scott wrote for the *New York Times* (27 July 2001), "If you have reached that stage of life when the opportunities for short-sheeting your counselor's bed or sneaking a frog into someone else's underwear are not as plentiful as they once were, then this sloppy comedy may be a pleasant reminder of days gone by."

Black wrote and directed *Wedding Daze* (2006), which stars Isla Fisher and Jason Biggs as two strangers who decide to get married on a whim, and wrote the screenplay for the 2007 comedy *Run, Fatboy, Run*, about an out-of-shape man who tries to win back the love of his life by running a marathon. In 2012, Black had a small role as an accountant in the comedy *This Is 40*, directed by Judd Apatow.

## BOOKS

Black has found consistent success as an author. In 2008, he published *My Custom Van: And 50 Other Mind-Blowing Essays That Will Blow Your Mind All Over Your Face*, which includes pieces titled "What I Would Be Thinking If I Were Billy Joel Driving to a Holiday Party Where I Knew There Was Going to Be a Piano" and "I No Longer Love You, Magic Unicorn." In a review for the *Buffalo News* (20 July 2008), Christopher Schobert wrote, "Kudos to Michael Ian Black for bringing his raised-middle-finger wit to the page, and making it work."

For *You're Not Doing It Right: Tales of Marriage, Sex, Death, and Other Humiliations*, published in 2012, Black drew from his own life, writing about his childhood, his sometimes-rocky marriage, and parenthood. "Black is carving out his own unique niche as an author, landing comfortably between Tina Fey and Augusten Burroughs along the comedy memoir spectrum," Chris Keech wrote for *Booklist* (1 Jan. 2012).

Also in 2012, Black collaborated with Meghan McCain, the daughter of Senator John McCain, to write *America, You Sexy Bitch: A Love Letter to Freedom*, in which they chronicle their cross-country speaking tour. "Along the way, they visit such cultural touchstones as Graceland and Branson, party in Las Vegas and New Orleans, pretend to be Mormon in Salt Lake City (only for a second), and go to a mosque in Dearborn, Michigan," the book jacket states. "But mostly Meghan McCain and Michael Ian Black talk to each other: about their differences, their similarities, and how American politics has gotten so divided."

Black also writes frequently for the literary journal *McSweeney's* and has authored a number of gently humorous children's books, including *The Purple Kangaroo* (2009), *Chicken Cheeks* (2009), *A Pig Parade Is a Terrible Idea* (2010), and *I'm Bored* (2012).

## OTHER PROJECTS

In addition to his film and television appearances, Black often deploys his dry, absurdist humor in commercials. Among the best known of these is an advertisement for Sierra Mist soda in which he plays a hapless traveler whose beverage is confiscated by airport security.

In the late 1990s, Black began performing as a sock puppet in advertisements for Pets.com. The ad campaign was noteworthy in part because during Black's tenure the company initiated copyright infringement litigation against Robert Smigel, a comedian known for performing the hand puppet character Triumph the Insult Comic Dog. Notably, Smigel had been performing as Triumph for several years before the introduction of the Pets.com campaign featuring Black. The company's lawsuit against Smigel ended when Pets.com went out of business in 2000.

Fans on Twitter can follow Black to read his unique take on the news, fellow celebrities, and other topics. On July 4, 2013, in reference to recent revelations about data gathering by the National Security Administration, he tweeted, "Happy Fourth of July. May your emails be gathered and your drones fly forever free!" Black also participates in Witstream, a curated comedy news ticker available via the web or mobile devices.

## PERSONAL LIFE

Black has been married since 1998 to Martha Hagen, a stylist whom he met early in his career. They have two children: Elijah, born in 2001, and Ruth, born in 2003. They live in Redding, Connecticut. "I wonder if, like me, there are people who occasionally experience the curious, disembodying sensation of not recognizing their present life as their own," Black wrote in *You're Not Doing It Right*. "It is a feeling I can only describe as the opposite of déjà vu."

## SUGGESTED READING

Coyle, Jake. "Michael Ian Black on Middle Age." *Chicago Sun-Times*. Sun-Times Media, 27 Mar. 2012. Web. 10 July 2013.

McManus, Sean. "Re-Introducing the 'Very Famous' Michael Ian Black." *Philadelphia Weekly*. Philadelphia Weekly, 9 Mar. 2011. Web. 10 July 2013.

Rapkin, Mickey. "Michael Ian Black's Theater Camp Confessions!" *GQ*. Condé Nast, 3 June 2010. Web. 10 July 2013.

Schawbel, Dan. "Michael Ian Black on His Career, Expedia and Social Media." *Forbes*. Forbes.com, 12 Apr. 2012. Web. 10 July 2013.

Spitznagel, Eric. "The State of Michael Ian Black." *Esquire*. Hearst Communications, 15 Feb. 2012. Web. 10 July 2013.

**SELECTED WORKS**
*The State*, 1993–95; *Viva Variety*, 1997; *Ed*, 2000–2004; *Stella*, 2005

—*Mari Rich*

# The Black Keys
**Music group**

**DAN AUERBACH**
**Born:** May 14, 1979
**Occupation:** Guitarist and vocalist

**PATRICK CARNEY**
**Born:** April 15, 1980
**Occupation:** Drummer

When Dan Auerbach and Patrick Carney, members of the two-man rock band the Black Keys, began playing music together at their Ohio high school, they were embarking on a career that would not only one day sell out Madison Square Garden in fifteen minutes, but one that would also win them three Grammy Awards and a formidable reputation, both creatively and commercially. Since their 2002 debut, the Black Keys have released six additional albums and pursued numerous side-projects and musical collaborations. The band's 2011 release, *El Camino*, debuted at number two on Billboard's Top 200.

Noted for their blues-rock sound and emphasis on the guitar and drums, Auerbach and Carney have also toyed with psychedelic sounds, rhythm and blues, and rap, as well as experimental equipment and recording spaces. "We love the way records sound when they just sound good," Carney told Ken Micallef of *Electronic Musician* (Jan. 2012), adding, "We're a heavily influenced band, song to song and instrument to instrument. We try to reference as many different things as possible."

Getty Images

## EARLY LIFE

Daniel Quine Auerbach was born in Akron, Ohio, on May 14, 1979. His parents, Mary and Jim Auerbach, were both interested in music and influenced their son from an early age. "Ever since I was a kid, family reunions, they'd play and sing together in a circle, do two- and three-part harmonies," Auerbach told Brian Hiatt for *Rolling Stone* (18 Jan. 2012). "Playing old spiritual songs, bluegrass songs, blues songs, folk songs, a lot of Stanley Brothers tunes, a lot of Bill Monroe songs, which are basically blues songs sung by white people." In addition to the family's penchant for folk and blues music, Auerbach notably attended a Grateful Dead concert with his father at the age of fifteen.

At Akron's Firestone High School Auerbach was captain of the soccer team and began learning guitar. In 1997, when Auerbach was seventeen years old, his brother Geoff encouraged him to hang out with the brother of one of his friends. Geoff's friend, Michael Carney, lived around the corner from the Auerbach family, where sixteen-year-old Patrick Carney had been learning to play the drums.

Patrick J. Carney was born on April 15, 1980, to parents Mary and Jim. Jim Carney played music from bands like the Rolling Stones, the Beatles, and Jimmy Hendrix for his son, instilling in him an interest in classic and indie rock music. After his parents divorced, eight-year-old Carney began spending time at his father's new house—located in the same neighborhood as the Auerbachs. When Carney was a teenager he was often picked on as an outcast, an identity he embraced in high school. "I was trying to pretend I was eccentric just to get a rise out of other people," he told Hiatt. Carney initially played the guitar, but switched his focus to the drums simply by being the only one of his friends and bandmates to own a set.

The pair admits that, without music, they would not have become friends. But with their guitar, drum kit, and space provided in Jim Carney's basement they clicked right away. "It was immediate, we could immediately make something," Auerbach explained to Hiatt. "His drumming was so all over the place, but because I listened to lots of blues that was all over the place, lots of fingerpicked stuff where time signatures would stretch, I could follow him immediately."

After high school Carney briefly attended the Art Institute of Pittsburgh before transferring to the University of Akron, from which he and Auerbach both dropped out before graduating. Driven in part by boredom and frustrated at living with their parents, Auerbach and Carney officially formed the Black Keys in 2001.

## DEBUT AND EARLY CAREER SUCCESS
The band's first album, *The Big Come-Up*, was released on Alive Records on May 14, 2002. *The Big Come-Up* included the song "I'll Be Your Man," which gained popularity after being used in the television series *Hung* and *Rescue Me*. The funk and blues-inspired debut—produced by Carney in his basement—was a critical and commercial success, garnering interest from the record label Fat Possum. The Black Keys signed with Fat Possum for their 2003 follow-up *Thickfreakness*.

Loud and energetic, *Thickfreakness* expanded on the musicality and low-fidelity sound developed in *The Big Come-Up*. Of the sound of the album, Auerbach noted to Davis Inman for *American Songwriter*: "That record we cut in one day, in one straight session." The second album also cemented the band's comparisons to the White Stripes, a rock duo featuring Jack and Meg White. Their similar make-up and sounds established both groups as leaders in the garage rock revival of the early 2000s, but also set the groundwork for conflict as both became more successful.

*Thickfreakness* was followed by the 2003 *The Split Parts Seven/The Black Keys EP*, a split recording with the band the Split Parts Seven. Another EP—*The Moan*—was released in 2004. It was during this period that the Black Keys lost thousands of dollars during a European tour. Confronted with conflicting feelings about commercial success and the ever-present fear of being broke, Auerbach and Carney ultimately decided to license their music. Shortly after, the song "Set You Free" appeared in commercials for Nissan cars. Reflecting on the decision in 2011, Auerbach told NPR's *Fresh Air* "It's helped us immensely. . . . we'd never had a real song regularly played on rock radio. We didn't have that support, and getting these songs in commercials was almost like having your song on the radio."

## RUBBER FACTORY AND MAGIC POTION
In 2004 the Black Keys embarked on an increasingly busy period of recordings and performances. After the release of *Moan* they appeared at music festivals including South by Southwest, Coachella, and Bonnaroo; during this time they were also recording their next album. To make *Rubber Factory*, Auerbach and Carney were forced to leave the basement and seek new studio space, this time in an old tire-manufacturing factory in Akron. The album met with positive reviews as critics praised the band's strengthened songwriting and unvarnished sound. According to David Browne for *Entertainment Weekly*, "*Rubber Factory* is indeed a lo-fi version of classic-rock boogie—done by utterly earnest indie-rock nerds, and done the right way." He added that the album was "shockingly well-done."

Between their third and fourth albums the Black Keys recorded their first live video album—*Live*—in 2005, as well as *Chulahoma: The Songs of Junior Kimbrough*, a tribute to blues musician Junior Kimbrough, in 2006. With the release of *Chulahoma*, Auerbach and Carney fulfilled their contract with Fat Possum and signed with Nonesuch Records, a record label owned by Warner Music Group. Like their decision to license their songs, the switch from an independent label raised eyebrows among some fans.

To record their fourth studio album, *Magic Potion*, the Black Keys returned to Carney's basement. *Magic Potion* not only marked the band's first album after signing with Nonesuch, but it was also their first to feature all original material. "We had an idea for this record," Carney told Malcolm Abram for the *Akron Beacon Journal* (17 Sept. 2006). "We wanted to simplify, condense and focus more, because *Rubber Factory* was more all over the place and this is more just a rock 'n' roll album. I think it's much more subtle the way the songs fit together." Though *Magic Potion* did not meet with the same praise as previous albums, listeners still responded positively to the band's mainstays: Auerbach's voice, powerful guitar riffs, and crashing drums. With this latest record also came the duo's biggest tour, in which they sold out European shows and opened for Pearl Jam.

## COLLABORATIONS AND SIDE PROJECTS
In July 2007 Carney married girlfriend Denise Grollmus. Auerbach was by this time married to wife Stephanie Gonis and expecting their first child, Sadie Little Auerbach, who was born that fall.

Later in 2007 Auerbach and Carney began a series of recording sessions intended to be part of a duet album with musician Ike Turner. The album was the project of producer Danger Mouse (Brian Burton) who previously worked with performers including Gorillaz and Beck. Turner died before the project was complete and the Black Keys were left with enough music—recorded in a real studio this time—to make their next album, *Attack & Release*. In describing the experience to *Rolling Stone*'s Austin Scaggs, Danger Mouse said: "I love them. They have such a dirty, heavy sound, and they're the kind of people I probably would've hung out with in school" (17 Apr. 2008). In April 2008, *Attack & Release* debuted at number fourteen on the Billboard 200 and would eventually appear on *Rolling Stone*'s list of the hundred best albums of the year.

Problems arose in the band in 2008 and 2009 due to tension between Carney's wife and Auerbach, who told Hiatt: "I really hated her from the start and didn't want anything to do with her" (19 Jan. 2012). As marital problems persisted, Carney eventually got a divorce. During this time Auerbach wrote and recorded his first solo effort *Keep It Hid* without Carney's knowledge, which increased tensions between them. When Auerbach went on tour Carney formed the band Drummer with four other Ohio drummers: Greg Boyd, Stephen Clements, John Finley, and Jamie Stillman.

Auerbach and Carney reconciled later in 2009 and embarked on a collaborative hip-hop/rock album, *BlakRoc*. Working with producer Damon Dash, the Black Keys' project included Mos Def, RZA, Ludacris, and Ol' Dirty Bastard. The collective project was generally considered a success, with *Esquire*'s Scott Frampton noting that "fusing hip-hop and rock isn't the goal but a starting place. The rappers make it great, stepping up their game to flow with Auerbach and Carney's bluesy swing" (21 Dec. 2009).

### BROTHERS

After *BlakRoc* the Black Keys returned to their blues roots where they created what would be their most successful project—critically and commercially—yet. The cover of the 2010 release simply states: "This is an album by The Black Keys. The name of this album is *Brothers*." On the album's name, Auerbach told Josh Eells for *Rolling Stone*, "Pat and I have spent more time together than with anybody in our families. We understand each other better than anybody on Earth. We love each other, we get on each other's nerves, we piss each other off. But like brothers, we know it's all OK." *Brothers* sold over 73,000 copies in its first week and debuted at number three on the Billboard Top 200 and at number two on Billboard Current Albums Chart. It also produced several hit singles, including the Danger Mouse–produced "Tighten Up."

*USA Today*'s Jerry Shriver said: "There's not one ounce of bull or excess on this tough, taut outing from the Akron, Ohio, blues-rock duo. The album's generous 15 songs succinctly plumb the genre's familiar themes of despair, heartache, violence and lust—but they avoid cliches like the plague" (18 May 2010). *Entertainment Weekly*'s Leah Greenblatt reviewed *Brothers* positively, saying "Six albums in, the Akron, Ohio, duo's backwoods-Zeppelin shuck remains paramount, but there's a new kind of shrewdness, too: real songwriting, and real hooks, beneath all that mondo riffage" (21 May 2010).

Later in 2010, *Brothers* went platinum and was second in *Rolling Stone*'s list of the year's best albums with a review calling it "their best record yet" and "rock minimalism pushed to the max." After a January performance on *Saturday Night Live* the Black Keys readied themselves for the Fifty-third Grammy Awards, held February 13, 2011. At the ceremony Black Keys won Grammy Awards for best alternative music album and best rock performance by a duo or group with vocal. Michael Carney, Patrick's brother, won best recording package for *Brothers*.

Drained from a year of promoting *Brothers*, the Black Keys canceled tour dates in Australia, New Zealand, and Europe. "We realized we could tour for two straight years, but at the end of the two years we'd have to deal with making a 'comeback record,'" Carney told Jillian Maps for *Billboard* (14 Jan. 2012). "We just wanted to make another record. We didn't want to have to prove ourselves again." The Black Keys headed to Easy Eye Studios—Auerbach's studio in Nashville, Tennessee—and spent forty days recording what would be their seventh album, *El Camino*. This would be the first album not recorded in Akron.

### EL CAMINO

*El Camino* was released by Nonesuch Records on December 6, 2011. The Black Keys were once again joined by producer Danger Mouse and together they created fast-paced, more up-tempo sounds that many saw as a departure from *Brothers*. Alan Light for the *New York Times* called *El Camino* "the most urgent and irresistible music they have ever made; the album's 11 songs are fast, punchy and loaded with hooks, with traces of glitter-rock stomp, girl-group melodies and surf guitar" (1 Dec. 2011). The bandmates attribute the faster sound to the pressure of the increased attention on the band. Carney told Light: "I had to be forced into adapting to the idea that the Black Keys were no longer an underdog but now were expected to be a great band." He also added "But with music, I think maintaining the status quo is when you kind of give up."

Auerbach and Carney decided to stream five songs from *El Camino* on their website before the official release date, including lead single "Lonely Girls." The band made headlines when they chose not to put the album on online music services like Spotify, Rhapsody, and Rdio, noting that they relied on record sales for income. *El Camino* debuted at number two on the Billboard

Top 200 and sold over 200,000 copies in its first week; "Lonely Boys" eventually peaked at number one on *Billboard*'s rock and alternative charts.

In the success of *El Camino*'s release the Black Keys returned to *Saturday Night Live* and made other appearances on programs such as *The Late Show with David Letterman* and *The Colbert Report*. Despite its December release, the album also made it onto many best-of lists for the end of the year, including the best albums lists for *Time* and *Rolling Stone* magazines. Album sales were strong, but the band was also surprised at the ticket sales for the tour; the Black Keys sold out at Madison Square Garden in fifteen minutes and added a second performance night at the arena to accommodate their fans. "Do you see my brains coming out of my ears?" Auerbach asked Hiatt upon learning of the Garden show (19 Jan. 2012). "It's not supposed to happen to bands like us. It's really not. It's crazy."

## 2012 AND BEYOND
The Black Keys appeared on the cover of the January 19, 2012, issue of *Rolling Stone*; the accompanying profile article became well known after Carney's pointed comments about the band Nickelback: "Rock & roll is dying because people became OK with Nickelback being the biggest band in the world. So they became OK with the idea that the biggest rock band in the world is always going to be s—," also referring to the band as "horrendous." Carney later apologized for the remarks.

The *El Camino* tour carried Auerbach and Carney through the spring and summer of 2012 and included headlining performances at music festivals like Coachella and Lollapalooza. The arena tour performances were recorded and the Black Keys returned to the studio in July 2012.

During this time, the duo continued to license their songs for commercial use, with their music appearing in ads for product including Subaru, Playstation, Sony, American Express, and Victoria's Secret. The band was notably the most-licensed band on Warner Music Group's roster in 2010, reportedly being approached nearly every day for material. In May 2012 Auerbach and Carney sued the companies Home Depot and Pizza Hut for copyright infringement, alleging that the businesses had used music from *El Camino* without consent.

On September 15, 2012, Carney married girlfriend Emily Ward at a ceremony in the backyard of their Nashville home. In addition to touring, recording, and spending time with their families, each member of the duo made time to work as producers on side projects. Auerbach worked with iconic blues and jazz musician Dr. John (Mac Rebennack) to produce the singer's 2012 album *Locked Down*. Whereas Auerbach collaborated with a classic musician, Carney produced the album *The Sheepdogs* for the up-and-coming Canadian rock band the Sheepdogs. The Black Keys hope to release a new album of their own in 2013. Meanwhile, a successful 2012 culminated in five Grammy nominations on December 5, including album of the year and record of the year. Auerbach also received a nod as producer of the year, which includes his work on the Keys' *El Camino*.

## SUGGESTED READING
Eells, Josh. "Two Against Nature." *Rolling Stone* 27 May 2010: 48–80. Print.
Mapes, Jillian. "Tightened Up." *Billboard* 14 Jan. 2012: 18–24. Print.
Micallef, Ken. "The Black Keys: On *El Camino*, Dan Auerbach and Patrick Carney Take a Minimalist Recording for a Bluesy, '60s Style 'Hi-fi' Sound." *Electronic Musician* 28.1 (2012): 18–26. Print.

—*Kehley Coviello*

---

# Sara Blakely
**Born:** February 21, 1971
**Occupation:** Founder of Spanx

Sara Blakely, founder of the Atlanta-based apparel company Spanx, was forty-one years old when she made headlines in 2012 as the world's youngest female self-made billionaire. She was on the cover of *Forbes* magazine's March 2012 issue on world billionaires, in which she was ranked the 416th richest person in the United States and 1153rd richest person in the world. In April 2012, she made *Time* magazine's annual list of the world's most influential people, the Time 100.

Whenever she hears that she is on the *Forbes* list, Blakely remembers her early career selling office equipment. "I can't hear that I am on that list without laughing. . . . I can't help but think of the days when my job was to cold call people in Clearwater [Florida] to try and sell them fax machines and how many of them said 'No, no, no,'" she said in a phone interview with Robert Trigaux for the *Tampa Bay Times* (8 Mar. 2012). Her sense of humor, intelligence, and persistence served her well as she turned her initial $5,000 investment into a billion-dollar company between 1998 and 2012. As her husband, the musician and entrepreneur Jesse Itzler, was quoted by Zoe Wood in the *Observer* as saying, "Sara is 50 percent Lucille Ball, 50 percent Einstein" (10 Mar. 2012).

One of Blakely's earliest fans was Oprah Winfrey, who listed Blakely's first Spanx product, a pair of footless panty hose, as one of her

Getty Images for Time

Favorite Things in 2000. Since then, Spanx has enjoyed phenomenal and growing success. As of March 2012, Spanx, which is still solely owned by Blakely, had sales of $350 million and sold more than two hundred products. In Hollywood, stars such as Gwyneth Paltrow, Octavia Spencer, and Emily Blunt all admit to wearing Spanx for red-carpet appearances. And it is not just women who have come to rely on Spanx when they want to look their best. After learning that men were ordering her women's bodywear for themselves, Blakely developed Manx, a line that includes body-shaping T-shirts and underwear for men.

## EARLY LIFE

Sara Blakely was born in Clearwater, Florida, on February 21, 1971, to Ellen Ford, an artist, and John Blakely, an attorney who focused on personal-injury cases. Blakely has a brother, Ford, who is also an entrepreneur. According to Clare O'Connor for *Forbes* (7 Mar. 2012), Blakely "always had a knack for hucksterism. . . . She'd set up a haunted house at Halloween and charge her neighbors admission. . . . Or, tearing a page from Tom Sawyer, she'd trick her friends into doing her chores by turning [weed pulling] into a competition." Popular and smart, Blakely was both a cheerleader and a champion debater.

Blakely's father was influential in her development as an entrepreneurial risk taker. At the family dinner table, he would ask Sara and Ford what they failed at that day. In an interview by Diane Sawyer for ABC's *World News*, Blakely recounted that she would say, "I tried out for this sport and I was horrible!" to which her father would respond, "Way to go!" and give her a high five. "It just completely reset my definition of failure. So for my brother and me, failure is not trying" (9 Mar. 2012).

When Blakely was sixteen years old, she experienced multiple tragedies. Her parents divorced, she witnessed her best friend get struck and killed by a car, and her two prom dates also died. Blakely found some comfort in listening to her father's Wayne Dyer motivational tapes. She was so impressed with them that she asked the principal at Clearwater High School to include them as part of the curriculum. She reported to O'Connor that her friends were less impressed with the tapes. "People used to fight over who had to ride home with me at night after a party," says Blakely. "No one wanted to be in my car— they'd be, like, 'No! She's going to make us listen to that motivational crap!'"

## EARLY CAREER AND COLLEGE

Blakely retained her entrepreneurial streak after graduating from high school. In 1990, she began her first business venture, an unofficial club for kids at the Clearwater Beach Hilton. Charging eight dollars per child, Blakely watched the kids at the hotel while their parents tanned. She was unlicensed, inexperienced, and uninsured, but she escaped the hotel's notice for three summers before being caught out by the general manager when she attempted to give him a sales pitch for her club.

Blakely attended Florida State University, where she was a Delta Delta Delta sorority member. After graduating in 1993 with a degree in communications, Blakely aspired to become a lawyer like her father, but she failed the LSAT twice and did not get into law school. Her fallback was to apply for work at Disney World, where she auditioned to play the part of Goofy but reportedly was not tall enough. She stayed on at the resort as a ride greeter, but as she told Zoe Wood for the *Observer*, it was not exactly a glamorous position: "I would see friends I hadn't seen for a while and I'd be wearing these big Mickey Mouse ears with my name on. . . . They'd say, 'Sara, is that you?' And I'd reply, 'Yes, now get on the ride.'"

After working at Disney, Blakely was hired by Danka Business Systems, an office equipment supplier that has since become part of Ricoh Company. She worked there for seven years, selling photocopiers and fax machines by cold calling customers and making door-to-door sales calls. Although the experience was "humbling," as Blakely told Trigaux, it gave her a chance to refine the sales skills and persistence that would be essential to starting Spanx and fostering its extraordinary growth. "I was given four ZIP codes in Clearwater and a cubicle and told to sell $20,000 worth of fax machines a month," she said. Later, she was transferred to Atlanta, Georgia, where she would found Spanx and make her home.

## VISIBLE PANTY LINES AND $5,000

By 1998, Blakely had moved up the Danka sales ranks to become national sales manager. She traveled to conduct sales trainings and often moonlighted as a stand-up comic. One evening, Blakely found herself trying to find the right underpants to wear under a pair of white slacks. Discouraged, she took a pair of scissors and cut the feet off a pair of panty hose. The altered hose eliminated her visible panty lines in the short term, but the lack of viable underwear options inspired Blakely to come up with a solution. She decided to invest her life savings—all five thousand dollars—to find one.

Blakely faced considerable obstacles in her quest for the perfect underwear. She had never taken a business class, she had zero experience in the apparel industry, and she had no other financing besides her own savings. What she did have, according to Suzanne Ridgway for the Los Angeles–based website Working World, was "her unfailing belief in the product, . . . her sales savvy, and her willingness to go out and sell the product."

Working out of her Atlanta apartment, Blakely did much of the early work herself in order to save money. After conducting her own patent research and reading a textbook on patenting products, she wrote a patent and designed packaging for "Footless Body-Shaping Pantyhose." But when she called manufacturers, no one was interested in helping her make her product. Finally, one manufacturer returned her call. According to Ridgway, his two daughters had persuaded him that Blakely's footless hose was not a "crazy idea" but one that actually had potential.

After Blakely found someone willing to take a chance on her, it took her and the hosiery mill a year to create a prototype that met her standards for comfort. With the prototype ready, Blakely secured a ten-minute meeting with a buyer at Neiman Marcus, part of which was conducted in the ladies' room so Blakely could personally demonstrate the effectiveness of her product. By the end of the pitch, she came away with an order for three thousand pairs of hose. In an article for the UK *Daily Mail* by Victoria Wellman, Neiman Marcus CEO Karen Katz notes Blakely's "character and charm" during the pitch: "Sara's effort was to solve an age-old problem for women in a modern way. . . . We were smitten from the beginning" (8 Mar. 2012).

Blakely continued to be her own best spokesmodel, "regularly strip[ping] down to her smalls in the boardroom"—and on QVC—"to road-test the latest 'magic' bra and pant prototypes," according to Wood. On the Spanx website, Blakely claims that for the first three years of the company's existence, she wore the same outfit: white pants and a black T-shirt with "Spanx" ironed onto it. As Blakely explained to Wood, "I had no money to advertise, so I was the promotion."

## BUSINESS GROWS AFTER BLAKELY'S OPRAH MOMENT

Blakely found further validation of her idea when she tuned in to the *Oprah Winfrey Show* one day after work. When Winfrey lifted her pant leg and showed her television audience that she cuts the feet off of her panty hose, Blakely said she flipped out. "OK, I'm not crazy," she told Ridgway. "This is a sign. I called all the hosiery mills and told them I believe in this. . . . I just saw Oprah do this. So, I took a week off work and drove around to all the mills." When Blakely had her prototype, business name, and packaging ready, she sent Winfrey a sample in a gift basket as a thank-you for the much-needed inspiration. A short time later, Blakely got the call that would change everything: Winfrey had selected Spanx Footless Body-Shaping Pantyhose as one of her "Favorite Things" of 2000 and wanted to feature it on her show.

After the show aired, Spanx began getting press attention in magazines and on television as well as a number of fans among the rich and famous, including Gwyneth Paltrow and Beyoncé Knowles. The company did not even have a website at the time, yet "business exploded," according to Wellman. First-year sales in 2000 reached $4 million, followed by $10 million in 2001. The success allowed Blakely to move operations from her apartment in Atlanta to an office in Decatur, Georgia. She started to design more products and in 2002 hired Laurie Ann Goldman as CEO to help manage the business.

## TELEVISION APPEARANCES AND PHILANTHROPY

Blakely was a contestant on daredevil billionaire Richard Branson's reality television series *The Rebel Billionaire: Branson's Quest for the Best*, which aired on the Fox network for one season starting in November 2005. Branson put the "young rebels" through a series of hair-raising tasks as they vied for the chance to become president of Branson's company, Virgin Worldwide. Blakely and another contestant, having failed to walk a plank between two hot-air balloons, were made to scramble up the side of one of the balloons to join Branson at the top for a tea party.

At the end of *Rebel Billionaire* in 2005, Blakely had lost the top spot but was first runner-up and received $750,000 from Branson for the Sara Blakely Foundation, which she launched in 2006. Blakely started the philanthropic organization in 2006 as a way to empower young women around the world. In a video on the Spanx company website, Blakely explains the philosophical underpinnings of her philanthropy: "At Spanx, we not only shape women's bodies and rears; believe it or not, we're trying to help shape women's lives."

In early 2007, Winfrey asked Blakely to return to her show for a "How'd You Do That" segment. According to Chary Southmayd for the *Belleair Bee* (8 Feb. 2007), after Winfrey thanked Blakely for "shaping up the rear ends of women around the world," Blakely had a surprise thank-you of her own: a one-million-dollar donation to Winfrey's Leadership Academy for Girls in South Africa. "Oprah was speechless," Southmayd wrote. "Both of them had tears in their eyes."

In mid-2007, Blakely appeared as a judge on the second and last season of the ABC series *American Inventor*, along with George Foreman, Pat Croce, and Peter Jones. When asked by Joseph Hudak for TVGuide.com whether being an inventor herself made her more judgmental or compassionate toward the contestants on the show, Blakely said, "A little bit of both. Because I didn't have the money when I started, I have a real sense of what it's going to take. That makes me a little bit harsher. But I find myself being lenient and wanting to say yes" (18 July 2007).

## BUSINESS EXPANDS

During the 2000s, Spanx introduced over two hundred garments in several categories, including bras (notably Bra-llelujah!), swimwear, activewear, and slimming apparel. In 2006, Blakely partnered with Target to launch her AS-SETS line of leggings, tights, swimwear, bras, camisoles, and other shapewear. Another line of shapewear, Haute Contour, was launched by the company in 2009.

Once Spanx realized that male Hollywood agents were ordering extra-large sizes for themselves, the company developed a line for men, Manx. Carried by online retailer Zappos.com and Nordstrom, Manx includes undershirts and underwear and comes in two "power levels," or levels of compression: medium and "hard core." As of March 2012 the company was sending out nine different catalogs to six million shoppers annually and was being sold by more than 11,500 boutiques, department stores, and online retailers.

On November 2, 2012, Blakely opened her first Spanx retail store at Tysons Corner, an upscale mall in McLean, Virginia. The stand-alone store follows the success of a pop-up store that Blakely opened inside a New York City Bloomingdale's in 2011. In late 2012, Blakely expects to open another two stores, one in the Plaza at King of Prussia in King of Prussia, Pennsylvania, and the other in Westfield Garden State Plaza in Paramus, New Jersey.

## PERSONAL LIFE

Blakely is a frequent traveler, and due to her high-profile television appearances, she is often recognized by her customers. In an interview by Mia Rodriguez-Lopez for QVC.com, Blakely described one such encounter: "I was in the airport and this woman recognized me. As she was running by she yelled, 'Spanx and wheels on luggage: two of the greatest inventions in the past

fifty years!" Sometimes her customers are so enthusiastic they flash their Spanx at Blakely—and her husband, former rapper and entrepreneur Jesse Itzler, a.k.a Jesse Jaymes. "Women flash me their Spanx all the time! My husband gets the biggest kick out of it!"

Blakely married Itzler in 2008 in a lavish ceremony at the Gasparilla Inn and Club in Boca Grande, Florida. Celebrities such as Matt Damon and his wife, Luciana, cheered when Olivia Newton-John surprised wedding guests with a live performance. Blakely and Itzler have a son, Lazer Blake Itzler, who was born in 2009. They split their time between Atlanta, Georgia, and an apartment in Central Park West, Manhattan.

With both spouses running their businesses from different locations, they have a team of what Lea Goldman, reporting for *Marie Claire*, called "a team of minders: personal assistants, drivers, chefs, a 24-hour nanny on call, and 'house managers' who ensure that, at any given time, there's Diet Coke in the fridge, gas in the tanks, and clean sheets on the bed" (20 Mar. 2011). Yet despite their hectic schedules, the couple have a deal that they both must be home for dinner every night, no matter where home is at the time. As Blakely told Goldman, "We don't have the luxury of time. We spend more because of how we live, but it's important to be with our family and friends."

## SUGGESTED READING

O'Connor, Clare. "Undercover Billionaire: Sara Blakely Joins the Rich List Thanks to Spanx." *Forbes*. Forbes.com, 7 Mar. 2012. Web. 13 Nov. 2012.

---. "Watch Out, Victoria's Secret: Spanx Billionaire Sara Blakely Opens First Retail Store." *Forbes*. Forbes.com, 1 Nov. 2012. Web. 8 Nov. 2012.

Southmayd, Chary. "All Thanks to Spanx: Hometown Girl Makes American Dream Come True." *Tampa Bay Newspapers*. Tampa Bay Newspapers, 8 Feb. 2007. Web. 16 Nov. 2012.

Wood, Zoe. "Sara Blakely: A Woman with a Great Grasp of Figures." *Observer*. Guardian News and Media, 10 Mar. 2012. Web. 14 Nov. 2012.

—Lisa Phillips

# Jeremy Bloom

**Born:** April 2, 1982
**Occupation:** Former Olympian and entrepreneur

At age fifteen, Jeremy Bloom became the youngest male athlete ever to join the United States Ski Team. By nineteen, Bloom ranked as the top moguls skier in the world. Today, he is a

Associated Press

firm, which he cofounded in 2010. At the 2011 American Business Award ceremonies, Integrate was named New Company of the Year. That same year, *Forbes* named Bloom to its annual list of "30 under 30" business people to watch.

## EARLY LIFE AND EDUCATION

Jeremy Bloom was born on April 2, 1982, in Fort Collins, Colorado, and grew up in nearby Loveland, Colorado. His father, Larry, is a psychology professor at Colorado State University and his mother, Char, is a skiing instructor. Bloom has two older siblings, Molly and Jordan, who are five and three years his senior, respectively. As a young man, Bloom wanted an Olympic gold medal and an NFL Super Bowl ring, telling John Harris for the *Wall Street Journal* (29 July 2008), "My goal was to ski in the Olympics and play in the NFL since I was eight years old." His mother told Tim Layden for *Sports Illustrated* (14 Nov. 2005), "He would draw pictures when he was young, one day a skier with a medal around his neck, the next day a football player. I guess he was trying to tell us something." When he was three years old, his grandfather, Jerry Bloom, taught him to ski, motivating him by tossing miniature candy bars down the slopes. Bloom's parents separated when he was a high school freshman and later divorced.

As Bloom explained to a reporter for *People* magazine (30 Jan. 2006), his father "was insane as far as skiing. We'd be in line waiting for the lifts to open. We would not leave until the sun went down." It was no surprise that, by the age of three, young Bloom was flying down the runs, a red Superman cape billowing behind him. At age five, Bloom entered his first skiing competition, at the Small World Cup. The Blooms purchased a condo at Colorado's Keystone ski area, staying there on the weekends. As Bloom told Layden, "If it was snowing, we skied. If it was cold, we skied. This was not about sipping hot chocolate and waiting for après-ski. It was great family time. And I loved going fast."

In addition to skiing, Bloom took karate lessons as a child, earning a first-degree black belt at the age of twelve. He also competed in track-and-field events as a student at Loveland High School, helping his team win two consecutive class 5A state championship titles in his junior and senior years. Bloom was also the star receiver of his school's football team, breaking three school records in the 2000 state playoffs with nine receptions for 204 yards and four touchdowns. Bloom was offered a full scholarship to play football at the University of Colorado, where he enrolled as an undergraduate.

## SPORTS CHAMPION

Bloom became a member of the US Ski Team in eighth grade, the youngest male athlete ever to be on the team. By seventeen, he was a national

three-time World Champion and eleven-time World Cup gold medalist in freestyle moguls skiing. Although Olympic gold eluded him in both 2002 and 2006, he was inducted into the Ski and Snowboard Hall of Fame in April 2013. The Philadelphia Eagles drafted him to the National Football League (NFL) in 2006 and the Pittsburgh Steelers signed him in 2007; however, due to injuries and a growing interest in business, he never played in a professional football game during the regular season. He returned to the world of skiing in 2008, but was unmoved by it and ended his skiing career in 2009. "I remember being in a starting gate at a World Cup and feeling, 'What am I doing here?'" he told John Meyer for the *Denver Post* (12 Apr. 2013). "I was so inspired about Wish of a Lifetime and starting the next chapter of my life. I recognized that and I said, 'This is just not in me anymore.'" Bloom considers his chief accomplishment to be the 2008 founding of his nonprofit, Wish of a Lifetime, which grants wishes to senior citizens. "The foundation is the most important thing I've done in my life and what I am most proud of," he told *Denver Business Journal* (16 Mar. 2012), which named Bloom to its list of "40 under 40" in 2012. "I love my grandparents, and I wanted to do more for the greatest generation. This is the most important thing I've done because it is unlocking the ability for people to live out their lifelong dreams." However, Bloom's major success has come through his entrepreneurial endeavor with Integrate, an advertising technology champion. At nineteen he was a world champion and Olympian, but finished a disappointing ninth in the moguls at Salt Lake's 2002 Winter Olympics. At the University of Colorado, he became a football receiver and was named All-American during his freshmen and sophomore years.

The National Collegiate Athletic Association refused to allow him to play during his last two years of college due to a rule that college athletes could not accept endorsements. Because Bloom had accepted a fee for a professional endorsement of skiing equipment, he was no longer classed as an amateur, even in football. Although Bloom challenged the law, appearing before a congressional panel to argue that the rules needed to be changed in light of multisport athletes, he lost after two years of court battles. Thereafter he concentrated on preparing for the upcoming Olympics, winning six consecutive victories at the FIS Freestyle Skiing World Cup in 2005, a world record, before the 2006 Winter Games.

As Jonny Moseley, the US gold medalist at the 1998 Olympics, told Layden for *Sports Illustrated*, "Jeremy used to be great, and now he's just dominant. He's always had the skill, and he's an amazing competitor, and now he's reached the point where he can just make magic happen." However, the magic eluded Bloom when he raced the freestyle mogul course in Torino, Italy, at the 2006 Winter Olympics. He placed only sixth, with no medal. Three days later, he attended the NFL tryouts in Indianapolis, fueling himself with the frustration of his loss in Italy. Although only five feet nine inches tall, Bloom was very fast; his time for the forty-yard dash was 4.3 seconds. He was angling for a position as wide receiver kick returner. He felt that, because of the limits placed on him during college, football was unfinished business. Bloom explained his drive to Juliet Macur for the *New York Times* (7 Feb. 2006), "Everyone always said: 'You can't play football. You're too small. You're not good enough,' but I proved them wrong. But then football was gone, and that challenge was gone. It was the worst feeling you can imagine." Drafted by the Philadelphia Eagles in the fifth round, he injured a hamstring in training camp and was sidelined for the season.

These two apparent defeats led him to consider what life after sports would look like. "My biggest fear was that I was going to be worthless to society after athletics," he told John Patrick Pullen for *Entrepreneur* magazine (Mar. 2013). "It kept me up at night." As an injured member of the reserve team, Bloom took advantage of a program designed to help professional athletes develop careers to sustain them after their sports careers ended. He earned a degree in real estate and financial entrepreneurship at the prestigious Wharton School at the University of Pennsylvania in 2006.

In 2007, he signed with the Pittsburgh Steelers, but was cut the following summer at training camp after he was sidelined by another injury. In 2008, he returned to the World Cup circuit. However, the lure of skiing no longer held. He found himself more interested in his classes at Wharton than in the slopes. "I noticed a big shift in my life," he told Pullen. "I found myself more interested in reading stories about entrepreneurs like Larry Page and Sergey Brin than in working out."

## WISH OF A LIFETIME

Inspired by two of his grandparents—maternal grandmother, Donna Wheeler, who lived with the Blooms when Jeremy was young, and paternal grandfather, Jerry Bloom, who was not only a World War II veteran but also Bloom's first ski instructor—Bloom established the charitable foundation Wish of a Lifetime in 2008. He utilized the skills he had gained at Wharton and modeled the charity on the Make-a-Wish Foundation for terminally ill children. Bloom supplied the first $25,000 in funding himself. In its first five years, the foundation raised $2.2 million to grant wishes.

The organization places a focus on the members of what has been called "the greatest generation," particularly those of low income. As Bloom told Meyer, "I just felt like the oldest people in our country were sometimes forgotten and sometimes put in a place where we couldn't see them, sometimes thought of as in the way in a very fast-moving, youth-oriented society." From a modest four wishes its first year, by 2013 the foundation had granted wishes for more than five hundred people in forty-five states. The average age of recipients is eighty-five. Wishes range from being as simple as arranging a meeting for family members who live at a distance, to as complex as getting four Tuskegee Airmen back to the Alabama field where they had trained for service in World War II. As Bloom stated on the foundation's website, "WOL Foundation is built on the premise that senior citizens should be respected, honored and aided in our society. They have given a lifetime of service, wisdom and most of all love to their community and families." In a 2012 poll of WOL wish recipients, more than 93 percent of respondents reported improvement in their overall level of happiness and their quality of life since having their wishes granted.

## INTEGRATE

After finishing his degree program at Wharton, Bloom established a startup called MDInfo with technology entrepreneur Hart Cunningham. The website, which offers information in multiple languages, was designed to assist people looking for medical information, including clinical trials. "As we were running healthcare offers through MDInfo, we had the idea to get further distribution on those offers, so we created the Integrate exchange," he told Dan Primack for *Fortune* (14 Dec. 2010). "It was originally just MDInfo, but we watched it scale into 34 verticals." Realizing that they needed to cross platforms, they determined to build the technology themselves. Eventually, based on the success of the exchange, Bloom and Cunningham established Integrate as a separate company.

Integrate provides analysis for performance-based advertisements. It allows a company to select various platforms—for example, online advertising and television commercials—and then to monitor and compare the ad campaigns' effectiveness in real time. Integrate has partnered with more than seven thousand radio stations and more than eight thousand magazines and newspapers, as well as both regional and national television aggregates. Billboards and Yellow Pages are also part of the company's reach. In 2011, Integrate was named the best new company of the year at the American Business Awards. The following year, Integrate was the silver winner for company growth at the Golden Bridge Awards.

With offices in Boston, New York, Denver, San Francisco, and Scottsdale, Integrate has hired more than 150 employees as of 2013. In two rounds of funding, the company gained more than $15.3 million within twenty-three months. In 2012 alone, Integrate raised $11 million from three capital investment sources in order to grow the company. "We've grown the business 800% top line since we took the Series A," Bloom told Lizette Chapman for the *Wall Street Journal* (21 Mar. 2012). Among the company's 2,500 digital media and traditional clients are such household names as Hewlett-Packard and Dell. "It takes the guesswork out of, 'Where should I spend my ad dollars?'" Bloom explained to Meyer. "I think we have a really big opportunity. If we win the game we're playing, we're going to win really big and have a chance to change how media is purchased."

## COMPLEMENTARY COFOUNDERS

While not exactly yin and yang, Bloom and Cunningham bring differing skills to Integrate. As president, Bloom is in charge of business development and sales, representing the public face of the company. As the company's chair, Cunningham is in charge of the technical structure of Integrate and its daily operations. Both men emphasize that Bloom's name recognition and sports background are less helpful than many assume. As Cunningham told Pullen for *Entrepreneur*, "Ironically a lot of the people who do take a meeting with us because of his background, they're not the ones who end up doing business with us. It's actually helped a little bit less than you would think."

Sometimes, Bloom's sports background has even been a drawback. However, some advantages remain. For example, Seth Levine, the managing director of the Foundry Group, one of Integrate's principal investors, credits Bloom's sports background for some important life lessons. As he told Pullen, "He's one of the most coachable people I've ever worked with. Despite being the best in the world, he's used to asking people for coaching, accepting that coaching, thinking about it and acting on it." Levine's respect for Bloom and Cunningham led to his company's $6.75 million investment in Integrate. Bloom's competitiveness and determination have driven the success of Integrate. "When you're ultra-competitive, like most professional athletes or most CEOs, you're setting goals on this treadmill that never ends," Bloom explained to Pullen. "You're never able to truly achieve this greatness that you think exists, because it doesn't—there's always more."

## PERSONAL LIFE

Bloom's self-described "next chapter" after his sports career included various jobs. He dabbled in modeling, working for Tommy Hilfiger, Abercrombie & Fitch, and Under Armour, as well as being featured in advertising spreads for Equinox gyms. He was a subject of and narrator for *Higher Ground*, Warren Miller's 2005 documentary about skiing and snowboarding. He also appeared on a celebrity dating show, *The Choice*, in 2012 and has done on-air sports analysis for ESPN and NBC.

Bloom has dated several women, notably actresses Cameran Eubanks of MTV's *The Real World* and Jessica Lowndes of *90210*, but the latter relationship ended in 2013 under the strain of a bicoastal romance following Bloom's move to New York City. Bloom remains unmarried. However, after relocating to Manhattan, he began organizing monthly get-togethers for former Olympians who met at the 2002 Winter Games. The focus is on some physical activity, such as beach volleyball or rock climbing, followed by a meal together.

## SUGGESTED READING

Ellin, Abby. "Life After the Games for Five Former Olympians." *New York Times* 19 June 2012, New York ed.: B16+. Print.

Layden, Tim. "Full Bloom." *Sports Illustrated* 14 Nov. 2005: 64–72. Print.

Meyer, John. "Jeremy Bloom: From Skiing Moguls to Business Mogul." *Denver Post*. Denver Post, 12 Apr. 2013. Web. 17 May 2013.

Pullen, John Patrick. "The Next Mogul." *Entrepreneur*. Entrepreneur Media, 19 Mar. 2013. Web. 17 May 2013.

Rosen, Karen. "Jeremy Bloom's Foundation Sets Out to Grant Wishes." *New York Times* 26 Apr. 2009, New York ed.: SP7. Print.

—*Judy Johnson*

# Joe Bonamassa

**Born:** May 8, 1977
**Occupation:** Blues and rock musician

Incorporating the mystical bombast of Jimmy Page, the precision of Eric Clapton, and the deftness and delicacy of Mark Knopfler, Joe Bonamassa is a blues guitar god for the twenty-first century. Just thirty-five years old, he has been playing professionally for more than twenty years—a fourth generation musical prodigy that has finally begun to surface near the mainstream. From his earliest days sitting in with Danny Gatton and opening for B. B. King to his collaborations with classic rock icons, Bonamassa is a true student of the blues who has been able to incorporate his influences (and their influences) into a cohesive style dubbed "modern blues" that marks him as the progeny of a long line of American and British blues musicians. Furthermore, he has stripped away the artifice often inherent in the entertainment business, forging a blue-collar ethic that has allowed him to maintain a steady and ambitious touring and recording schedule.

## EARLY LIFE AND EDUCATION

Born in New Hartford, New York, a suburb of Utica, Bonamassa exhibited an early aptitude for music, and his father—the owner of a guitar shop and an accomplished, though not famous, musician in his own right—gave him his first guitar when he was four years old. Bonamassa's life has included little else since that moment. In grade school, he emulated Stevie Ray Vaughn and Jimi Hendrix, learning some of their solos precisely; he also spent free time with his parents listening to their extensive collection of albums, primarily those from generation of British blues musicians who came of age in the late 1960s and early 1970s. "I was always drawn to the British blues guys because it's what my dad listened to," Bonamassa explained in a May 8, 2012, interview with Michael Rampa for *American Songwriter*. "He would play records for me growing up and I always gravitated towards those '60s British guys . . . Clapton, Page, [Jeff] Beck, and Rory Gallagher (who is Irish) . . . that's just where I feel at home."

Thus, Bonamassa learned about the American folk music of the blues via the British progenitors who set the template for the classic rock genre. Though, as an adult artist, Bonamassa would cover the songs of and pay homage to foundational American bluesmen such as Robert Johnson, John Lee Hooker, Elmore James, Albert Collins, and B. B. King, his introduction to the American art form was secondhand, as he gravitated toward the heavy riffing and experimentation of such bands as the Yardbirds, Cream, and Jethro Tull—influences that are readily apparent

Wirelmage

on all of his albums and in the personnel he employs as his backing band.

Bonamassa's big break—while attending a blues festival in his home state—was a combination of luck, timing, and an uncharacteristic courage and confidence for an eleven-year-old. One of the bands was searching for someone to replace their truant guitarist, and Bonamassa took the opportunity to showcase his skills. "My dad asked me if I wanted to go have some fun. I was an adventurous 11-year old, so I went up there and played. The crowd liked it, partly because I was a little kid playing, but I did pretty good," he told Matt Blackett for *Guitar Player* magazine (Apr. 2009). The show's promoter introduced Bonamassa to legendary harmonica player James Cotton, once a member of Muddy Waters's band, whom he joined onstage. He told Blackett: "That year I got to sit in with Duke Robillard, Albert Collins, Clarence "Gatemouth" Brown. A year later, I'm on stage with B. B. King and Buddy Guy and John Lee Hooker. What a year!"

In fact, King was enamored by the playing of the prepubescent Bonamassa, stating, "This kid's potential is unbelievable. He hasn't even begun to scratch the surface. He's one of a kind" (qtd. in the biography section of Bonamassa's website). However, it was Gatton—a guitarist with a singular style that incorporated numerous American genres such as jazz, rockabilly, country, and the blues—who mentored Bonamassa. Gatton let Bonamassa sit in with his band whenever it was in the New York area and opened the boy's mind to the multifarious interpretations of blues-based music, educating him on the history of rock and roll, and teaching him jazz chords and the rockabilly sensibility. "Here I am, a 13-year old kid sitting in Danny Gatton's Winnebago and suddenly my life went from mono to stereo," he told Blackett. Sadly, Gatton committed suicide only a few years after the two met, but he left an indelible mark on Bonamassa's broad-minded approach to the guitar, casting him in the role as a torchbearer for an American traditional music.

## FROM PRODIGY TO SOLO ARTIST

"As far as me being a prodigy," Bonamassa explained to Blackett, "I listen back now to myself when I was a kid, and I think I was on the line between being a prodigy and just being good for my age. There were times when I was really good and I excelled and there were times when I was pretty bad." Being labeled a prodigy can either embolden a performer or hamper a career, as the person strives to live up to the expectations of mentors and fans. As Bonamassa would come to realize, his early start was both a blessing and a curse, providing him with the support and connections necessary to become a professional musician, but also burdening him with the task of becoming a unique presence in rock apart from the influence of predecessors.

In 1994, Bonamassa, still a teenager, joined with the sons of three famous musicians to form the band Bloodline. Besides Bonamassa, the group consisted of Erin Davis (Miles Davis); Berry Oakley Jr. (Berry Oakley, the late bassist for the Allman Brothers Band); and Waylon Krieger (Robby Krieger of the Doors). The band produced only one album, and Bonamassa went on to play with numerous rock luminaries during the remainder of the 1990s.

Finally, in 2000, at twenty-three years old, Bonamassa released his debut album, *A New Day Yesterday*, a title taken from a Jethro Tull song. Paying homage to his classic rock forebears would be something he would repeat on forthcoming albums, and *A New Day Yesterday* includes covers of songs by Jethro Tull, Free, Rory Gallagher, and Al Kooper. The record was produced by Tom Dowd, a legendary producer who worked with a who's who of rock, jazz, and R & B legends. Though Bonamassa's first album is a fan favorite, he has ambivalent feelings about it, specifically about working with Dowd. He "was like a father to me and really set the tone for the rest of my career. My biggest regret was that I didn't have the skills at the time that were worthy of working with a guy like him. When I listen to it . . . I hear a kid who was still trying to find himself and his sound," Bonamassa told Blackett.

In 2002, Bonamassa recorded his second album, *So, It's Like That*. It is his only album to contain all original material, and it shot to the number one on the Billboard Top Blues Album chart. Bonamassa's next two albums, 2003's *Blues Deluxe* and 2004's *Had to Cry Today* (named for a song on the only album by Blind Faith, a rock supergroup that included Clapton and Steve Winwood), were both produced by Bob Held. The former album featured a bevy of blues covers, as Bonamassa interpreted the work of James, Collins, B. B. King, and Freddie King, showcasing his wide-ranging knowledge of the blues and rock artists who preceded him.

## A MODERN BLUES PARTNERSHIP

In 2006, Bonamassa began collaborating with producer Kevin Shirley—who has worked with such hard rock luminaries as Iron Maiden, Rush, Aerosmith, and the Black Crowes—an indication that Bonamassa desired to increasingly incorporate more of the classic rock influence of his musical heroes and expand his range from primarily a blues artist. His partnership with Shirley has been a fruitful one, as the two have worked together on six studio albums to date, all of which assimilate a broad range of styles and genres into the blues base. On his relationship with Shirley, Bonamassa told Blackett: "Kevin deserves most of the credit on these albums. He's the guy who spearheads the vision, takes me out of my comfort zone, and forces me to play different stuff." For example, *You & Me* (2006) features a cover of Led Zeppelin's "Tea for One," a blues-based ballad, but also a piece titled "Django," named for the seminal French Gypsy guitar player Django Reinhardt, whose song "Vous et Moi" provides the inspiration for the album's title.

*Sloe Gin*, Bonamassa's 2007 album, highlights his growth as both a songwriter and an interpreter of others' material; it was his first album to crack the Billboard Top 200, peaking at 184. The follow-up, *The Ballad of John Henry* (2009), nearly broke into the Billboard Top 100 and again streaked to the top of the blues chart; the album features some his most thematically diverse material, specifically the title track, a take on the American folk hero. In an April 23, 2009, review of the album, the *Guardian*'s Alfred Hickling sees the Bonamassa's reference to John Henry as emblematic of his career: "It is . . . a conscious attempt to acknowledge his place in the continuum. Henry . . . has been celebrated by everyone from Leadbelly to Johnny Cash, and there is something Henry-ish about Bonamassa's steady ascent." 2009 was also the year that Bonamassa performed a sold-out show at London's Royal Albert Hall featuring a guest appearance from Clapton—a moment commemorated on the 2010 live album and DVD *Live from the Royal Albert Hall* and one that emblematized Bonamassa's ascension to his status as the guitar "god" of his generation. Interestingly, though Bonamassa has found success in his native country, it is in England, the home of so many of his musical idols, that he has been embraced as the torchbearer for Clapton, Page, Beck, and others of their generation.

In 2010, the year that *Black Rock*—an album recorded in Greece that features Bonamassa's experimentation with instruments such as the bouzouki, a hard-rocking title track, and a collaboration with B. B. King—cracked the Billboard Top 40, Bonamassa seemed philosophical about his career path in an interview with Guitar Center: "Ten years ago I realized I had a monumental task that lay before me," he recalled. "Many people told my manager and me that it [being a blues musician] was a lost cause. . . . But we just wouldn't take no for an answer. . . . If you want success enough and you're hungry enough for it, it can happen, but nobody is going to hand it to you on a silver platter."

## BLACK COUNTRY COMMUNION

In 2010, Bonamassa indulged his penchant for hard rock by joining Black Country Communion, a quartet of rock veterans that also includes drummer Jason Bonham, son of the late Led Zeppelin drummer John Bonham; bassist and lead singer Glenn Hughes, formerly of Trapeze and Deep Purple; and Derek Sherinian, once a member of Dream Theater. Black Country Communion (or BCC as they are sometimes known) developed into a successful side project for Bonamassa, allowing him not only to be part of a collective but also to use a more basic approach than he does on solo projects. In an October 12, 2010, interview for the heavy metal website *Rush on Rock*, Bonamassa told Simon Rushworth: "With BCC I could play a rock style that I do dabble with and flirt with from time to time but wouldn't work on my solo albums. I brought out the Marshall [amplifier] and just shredded for awhile." A noted guitar and tech geek, Bonamassa sets aside his custom-made and specialized guitar equipment for BCC, and by exclusively using a Marshall amplifier aligned himself with the many other hard-rock guitarists, such as the Who's Pete Townshend, AC/DC's Angus Young, and Led Zeppelin's Page, who swear by the amp for its heavy and powerful sound.

Black Country Communion's first album, *Black Country*, went to number one on the UK Rock Album chart and garnered reviews as the finest hard-rock album of the year. Hughes and Bonamassa were the primary songwriters on an album that offers an unabashed take on the oft-maligned genre. The band followed up its debut album in 2011 with *2*, again topping the UK Rock Album chart. To promote the album, the band toured Europe, which provided footage for a DVD, *Live over Europe*, released in October 2011.

Despite the band's success and its recording of a third album, *Afterglow* (2012), tensions began to develop between Hughes, who wanted to commit more time to touring with the BCC, and Bonamassa, who has always maintained that his concert schedule as a solo artist was his priority. "You could set your watch to my tours in 2000, and you can set your watch to my tours in 2012," Bonamassa told Damian Fanelli for *Guitar World* (25 Oct. 2012). He continued that, when someone (referring to Hughes) "calls you out . . . in hopes that it will bully you into a situation, well, don't take my kindness as weakness." At the end of 2012, Bonamassa continued involvement with BCC was undetermined, a mixture of disappointment with his bandmate and his solo obligations for 2013.

## PERSONAL LIFE

In addition to his time in Black Country Communion, Bonamassa collaborated with singer-songwriter Beth Hart on the 2011 album *Don't Explain*. In the same year he also released his ninth studio album, *Dust Bowl*, which garnered some of the best reviews of his career and included appearance by Vince Gill and John Hiatt, adding a tinge of country music to the growing eclecticism of his modern blues. In 2012, he released *Driving towards the Daylight*, which features Aerosmith's rhythm guitarist Brad Whitford and showcases his expanding abilities as a songwriter. On May 7, 2012, *Blues Rock Review* singled out the title track as evidence of Bonamassa's progression: "Bonamassa has joked at live performances about never writing a 'hit' song, but if he were to, 'Driving towards the Daylight' has as good a shot as any."

Bonamassa has been candid about the fact that playing guitar is his only sustaining interest in life, going so far as to call it an "addiction" in several interviews. He is not married and does not plan to have children, stating somewhat frivolously that his guitars are his "children," especially those that he and Gibson Guitars designed specifically for a Joe Bonamassa product line. "I have a couple hundred guitars, but I'm so proud of these Gibson Inspired by Joe Bonamassa Les Pauls that I primarily used them on the whole record. I don't plan on breeding, and these goldtops are like my children," he explained to Blackett. Bonamassa is as comfortable playing the guitar as he is discussing the technical configuration of his equipment.

As a musician who feels indebted to those players who preceded him, especially those that mentored him in his adolescence, Bonamassa feels an obligation to guide the next generation of guitar players. He created the nonprofit organization Keeping the Blues Alive for just such a purpose, and he often selects young musicians to open for him on the road. "When we go on tour and pick the opening acts, I try to get young kids. I think that's the greatest thing because if there's not a new generation of kids playing the music, there won't be a new generation of fans" (*Guitar Player*). A live album and DVD entitled *An Acoustic Evening at the Vienna Opera House* (2013) highlights Bonamassa's versatility and his commitment to paying homage to the blues and advancing the genre in the twenty-first century.

## SUGGESTED READING

Carney, Jennifer. "Joe Bonamassa: The TVD Interview." *Vinyl District*. Mom & Pop Shop Media, 24 Oct. 2012. Web. 14 Feb. 2013.

Rampa, Michael. "Who's Been Talkin'? A Q&A with Joe Bonamassa." *American Songwriter*. American Songwriter, 8 May 2012. Web. 14 Feb. 2013.

Ross, Brian. "Joe Bonamassa: The Best Living Guitarist You've Never Heard of . . . " *Huffington Post*. AOL-HuffPost Entertainment, 11 Dec. 2010. Web. 14 Feb. 2013.

Rushworth, Simon. "Exclusive—Joe Bonamassa Interview." *Rush on Rock*. Rush on Rock, 12 Oct. 2010. Web. 14 Feb. 2013.

Whitaker, Sterling. "Joe Bonamassa on Black Country Communion's Future: 'Never Say Never.'" *Ultimate Classic Rock*. Ultimate Classic Rock, 31 Oct. 2012. Web. 14 Feb. 2013.

## SELECTED WORKS

*A New Day Yesterday*, 2001; *So, It's Like That*, 2002; *Had to Cry Today*, 2004; *Sloe Gin*, 2007; *Black Country* (with Black Country Communion), 2010; *Black Rock*, 2010; *Dust Bowl*, 2011; *Don't Explain* (with Beth Hart), 2011; *Driving towards the Daylight*, 2012; *An Acoustic Evening at the Vienna Opera House*, 2013

—*Christopher Rager*

# Ian Bremmer

**Born:** November 12, 1969
**Occupation:** Political scientist, author, entrepreneur

Ian Bremmer's life story proves that it is possible to find a niche and make a fortune. In 1998—with just $25,000 in start-up capital—he formed Eurasia Group, a consulting firm that employs leading political science experts to provide risk assessments of various nations for corporate, financial, and political clients. Prior to launching Eurasia Group, Bremmer had no business experience. Today, the firm has offices in three major cities and is considered an industry leader. Bremmer has parlayed his own political science background and experience into a successful career as a television analyst and author. He has penned several bestselling books, including *The J Curve: A New Way to Understand Why Nations*

© Marc Bryan-Brown

*Rise and Fall* (2006), *The End of the Free Market: Who Wins the War Between States and Corporations?* (2010), and *Every Nation for Itself: Winners and Losers in a G-Zero World* (2012). Bremmer has also written for numerous leading newspapers, magazines, and websites.

When asked in an interview with the Armenian General Benevolent Union (1 Dec. 2012) what advice he would give to young political scientists and businesspeople, Bremmer answered: "I think it's necessary to have a wider, more global understanding of countries, their politics, and their economies, and how they all impact one another and the rest of the world."

## EARLY LIFE AND EDUCATION

Ian Bremmer was born in Baltimore, Maryland, on November 12, 1969. His father is of German descent and his mother is of Armenian descent. His parents—who were childhood sweethearts—eloped when they were very young but put off having children for some time because of the frequent relocating required by his father's career as a military officer. After being stationed at various postings throughout his father's twenty-two years in the military, including a stint in Ecuador, the Bremmer family settled in Baltimore in the late 1960s. After Ian's father died when he was four years old, his mother decided to move to Chelsea, Massachusetts, where members of her family resided.

Bremmer grew up in public housing in Boston, Massachusetts. A gifted student, he skipped several grades at his local Catholic school and graduated from high school at age fifteen. Before the age of sixteen, he received an undergraduate scholarship to Tulane University, in New Orleans, Louisiana. On the advice of his teachers, he took courses in chemical engineering. "I disliked it immensely," he recalled to Lori Janjigian for *Yerevan* magazine (Fall 2010). "The early courses required far too much memorization of formulas, and I didn't find the subject matter interesting." Later, Bremmer became a political science major. The coursework better suited his passion for current events and world affairs. He completed his bachelor's at Tulane as an honors student in international relations, graduating magna cum laude in 1989. Bremmer continued his education at Stanford University in California, where he earned a master's degree in political science in 1991 and a PhD in 1994.

## EARLY CAREER AND FIRST BOOKS

At Stanford, Bremmer coedited *Soviet Nationalities Problems* (1990) with historian Norman M. Naimark. The focus of the book is a conference held in March 1989 that focused on the politics and economics of independent states emerging from the Soviet Union, which split into fifteen separate countries in December 1991. In 1993, with Ray Taras, Bremmer coedited *Nations and Politics in the Soviet Successor-States*. A revised version of the book was republished under the new title *New States, New Politics: Building the Post-Soviet Nations* in 1997.

At age twenty-five, Bremmer became the youngest national fellow at the Hoover Institution, a conservative public policy think tank at Stanford. He has also served in research and faculty positions at Columbia University, the East-West Institute, the Lawrence Livermore National Laboratory, and the World Policy Institute.

After working several years in academia, Bremmer decided to see if he could use his education and experience in political science in the private sector. As he explained in his interview with the Armenian General Benevolent Union, "I met with various people in the finance industry [in New York City] who thought what I did was very interesting, but they all said that they don't normally hire political scientists. After about a year of being frustrated, I went back to the same people, and asked them if I were to start a company, would they come on as my client—and they almost all said yes. So I ended up starting my own business because there was a space where I felt I could use my background and experiences and create something that would be valuable to others."

With a list of potential clients and $25,000 of his own money in hand, Bremmer formed Eurasia Group in 1998, a consulting firm dedicated to assessing global and national political risks for corporate, financial, and government clients interested in doing business in specific countries. Today, Eurasia Group is the world's leading global risk index firm, employing more than 150 people in offices located in New York City, London, and Washington, DC.

As the Eurasia Group's profile grew, Bremmer found himself in demand as a commentator for various media outlets, including National Public Radio, CNN, CNBC, and the Fox News Channel. He also began writing articles on politics and economics for leading publications such as the *Wall Street Journal, Washington Post, New York Times, Newsweek, Harvard Business Review*, and *Foreign Affairs*. Bremmer is a regular contributor to Reuters.com, the *Financial Times*, and *Foreign Policy*.

## THE J CURVE

Much of Bremmer's success as an author stems from the 2006 publication of his book *The J Curve: A New Way to Understand Why Nations Rise and Fall*. The book presents Bremmer's theory on the political and economic stability of countries in the international state system. He employs a J-shaped curve moving from left to right to demonstrate how closed dictatorships like North Korea or Cuba are more stable than more open countries like China, Russia, and India at the bottom part of the curve. Yet, according to Bremmer, none of these countries are as stable as open democracies like the United Kingdom and the United States, which are found at the top of the curve. Bremmer's J curve demonstrates that different countries are stable for different reasons. He argues that countries like North Korea risk their stability when they seek to become more open and involved in the world economy—with no guarantee that its regime would remain in power at the end of a transition period. According to Bremmer, it is easier for autocratic regimes to tighten control over their populations and isolate their nations in order to maintain stability, rather than risk their survival by transitioning to a more secure system of open market democracy. He also notes that the transition from a closed political economy to a more open political economy requires that long-term policy initiatives be maintained over several decades. Bremmer maintains that the benefits of being open and stable in the international system are many. For example, nations like the United States are able to withstand contested presidential elections and economic emergencies without any major systemic breakdowns in order, while authoritarian states such as North Korea contend with mass starvation and depend on international aid.

*The J Curve* proved to be both a critical and popular success. In the *Telegraph* (30 Sept. 2006), Damian Thompson called the book "the intellectual accessory of the moment." A reviewer for the *Economist* (31 Aug. 2006) noted "the world has seemed a riskier place of late. Mr Bremmer's analyses of China, Russia and Iran, in particular—each of which he places on the authoritarian left side of the J curve—convincingly make the case that it is going to get riskier."

### THE END OF THE FREE MARKET

In his 2010 book, *The End of the Free Market*, Bremmer argues that the greatest modern danger to the free-market capitalist system is the emergence in recent decades of what he terms "state capitalism"—in which a national government, and not a variety of private companies, serves as a nation's major economic player. According to Bremmer, state-run economies such as a China, Russia, and Saudi Arabia are a danger to the free-market economies of the European Union, the United States, and Japan because such nations unduly influence the global economy for their own self-interests. Particularly distressing for Bremmer is the fact that state capitalist countries control three-quarters of the world's crude-oil reserves. Moreover, he fears their influence on emerging market economies like India and Brazil. Bremmer wants free-market economies like the United States to counter the influence of state capitalism by working to achieve equal access to emerging markets.

*The End of the Free Market* saw somewhat more mixed reviews than *The J Curve*. In the *New York Times* (5 June 2010), Devin Leonard called it a "well-crafted, thought-provoking book about the rise of state-controlled economies and the challenges they pose to American companies—and, ultimately, to the United States itself." In the *Wall Street Journal* (19 May 2010), Matthew Reese declared: "Mr. Bremmer himself celebrates markets—for raising global living standards—but his book is supposed to be about 'the end of the free market,' so state capitalism is going to prevail, right? Apparently not. State capitalism, he says, has limited appeal to the masses (since it was created to 'maximize political leverage and state profits'); and its philosophy is zero-sum—seeking gains for some at the expense of others. Let us hope that Mr. Bremmer's ultimate prediction is more accurate than his book's title."

### EVERY NATION FOR ITSELF AND OTHER WORKS

Bremmer published his third book, *Every Nation for Itself: Winners and Losers in a G-Zero World*, in 2012. In it, he argues that no single nation or alliance of nations can provide the leadership required to face the world's most serious challenges: nuclear proliferation, economic stagnation, and the need for environmental protection and conservation. At no other time in recent history, Bremmer argues, has the world been so filled with self-interested nations that have proved so incapable of developing meaningful alliances aimed at solving global problems. He notes that the members of existing alliances—economic organizations like the Group of Twenty and political institutions like the United Nations Security—have been unable to agree on common social, political, and economic values in the interest of global progress. Bremmer calls this state "G-Zero."

Nevertheless, Bremmer concludes his book by asserting that the current state of global affairs is not permanent. Alexander Heffner summarizes Bremmer's theory in a review for *USA Today* (15 May 2012), "Nature is protean, and so are countries," he writes, leaving "two possible outcomes: a further fragmentation of power within economically weak nations or a protracted Cold War 2.0 between the U.S and China." Evan Osnos for the *New Yorker* (17 May 2012) notes that Bremmer "has little choice but to strenuously reject the declinist label, even as he is describing a 'world without leaders.' His final, prescriptive chapter pays homage to America's advantages—mainly, military might and democratic, entrepreneurial values—but his more persuasive point is simply that power is relative: if the world descends into a barroom brawl, the United States will still be the largest, strongest drunk in the joint."

Bremmer is the coauthor of *The Fat Tail: The Power of Political Knowledge for Strategic Investing* (2009), with Preston Keat, and the coeditor of the e-book *What's Next: Essays on Geopolitics that Matter* (2012), with Douglas Rediker. He also edited *Managing Strategic Surprise: Lessons from Risk Management and Risk Assessment* with Paul Bracken and David Gordon in 2008. In 2007, Bremmer was named a Young Global Leader at the World Economic Forum. He lives in New York and Washington, DC.

### SUGGESTED READING

Heffner, Alexander. "Bremmer's 'Every Nation for Itself' Explains G-Zero World." *USA Today*. USA Today, 15 May 2012. Web. 26 Apr. 2013.

Janjigian, Lori A. "Ian Bremmer Weighing Political Risks." *Yerevan*. Yerevan, Fall 2010. Web. 29 Apr. 2013.

Leonard, Devin. "A War for Hearts and Minds, Economically Speaking." *New York Times*. New York Times Co., 5 June 2010. Web. 26 Apr. 2013.

Osnos, Evan. "Is the End of American Dominance the Same as American Decline?" *New Yorker*. New Yorker, 17 May 2012. Web. 26 Apr. 2013.

Reese, Matthew. "Politicians As Plutocrats." *Wall Street Journal*. Wall Street Journal, 19 May 2010. Web. 26 Apr. 2013.

"The Geometry of Geopolitics." *Economist*. Economist, 31 Aug. 2006. Web. 26 Apr. 2013.

Thompson, Damian. "Here's How the World Works." *Telegraph*. Telegraph, 30 Sept. 2006. Web. 25 Apr. 2013.

## SELECTED WORKS
*Soviet Nationalities Problems*, 1990; *Nations and Politics in the Soviet Successor-States*, 1993; *New States, New Politics: Building the Post-Soviet Nations*, 1997; *The J Curve: A New Way to Understand Why Nations Rise and Fall*, 2006; *The End of the Free Market: Who Wins the War Between States and Corporations?*, 2010; *Every Nation for Itself: Winners and Losers in a G-Zero World*, 2012

—Christopher Mari

# Brian Burke
**Born:** June 30, 1955
**Occupation:** Hockey executive

NHLI via Getty Images

Although he began his career in professional hockey as a player in the minor leagues, Brian Burke is best known for his work off the rink. After graduating from Harvard Law School and working for several years as an agent overseeing contract negotiations, Burke focused his talents in the field of hockey management, working with teams on the east and west coasts of both the United States and Canada. As general manager of the Vancouver Canucks and the Anaheim Ducks, Burke helped to rejuvenate struggling teams, even leading the Ducks to a Stanley Cup victory in 2007. Burke encountered significant public scrutiny after signing on as president and general manager of the Toronto Maple Leafs, one of the oldest and most high-profile teams in the National Hockey League (NHL), in 2008. In his role as the general manager, Burke worked hard to reclaim the Maple Leafs' status as a championship-winning franchise, but the Stanley Cup remained out of reach. Team ownership decided to replace Burke in early 2013, just weeks before the scheduled beginning of the hockey season. Although the decision took him by surprise, Burke remained optimistic about his future in the NHL. "I don't think I'm done from a hockey perspective," Burke explained in a press conference (12 Jan. 2013). "I am definitely in the job market, no question."

## EARLY LIFE AND EDUCATION
Brian Burke was born in Providence, Rhode Island, on June 30, 1955. He was the fourth of ten children born to Bill Burke, an appliance salesman, and Joan Burke. The family moved frequently, ultimately settling in Edina, Minnesota, when Burke was twelve.

Burke was determined to play hockey, the sport of choice in his new hometown. "I didn't have any equipment, I didn't know how to play, but I went down to the neighborhood rink in the middle of a team practice and asked the

coach if I could play," he told Mary Rogan for *GQ* (Jan. 2011). "The first game I played, I could hardly stand up." He learned quickly, advancing through the recreational leagues and eventually playing varsity hockey for Edina West High School.

After graduating from high school, Burke enrolled in Rhode Island's Providence College and joined the school's Division I hockey team. Under coach Lou Lamoriello, who would go on to become general manager of the New Jersey Devils as well as the 1998 US Olympic hockey team, Burke improved as a player and developed the work ethic and leadership skills that would shape his career off the rink. "I went to Providence a boy and came out a man," Burke told John McGourty for NHL.com (21 Oct. 2008). "Lou Lamoriello was the biggest influence in my life, other than my dad." Burke graduated from Providence in 1977 with a bachelor's degree in history.

## EARLY CAREER
Although Harvard Law School offered Burke admission, he chose instead to pursue a career in hockey. He was drafted by the Philadelphia Flyers, an NHL team, and joined their American Hockey League (AHL) affiliate, the Springfield Indians. He played for the Indians in several games during the 1976–77 season, and when the Flyers ended their affiliation with the Indians and established a new farm team, the Maine Mariners, the following season, Burke moved to Maine. The Mariners had a successful season and advanced to the AHL playoffs, ultimately winning the Calder Cup.

Despite the success of the Mariners, Burke felt that his own skill as a hockey player had reached its limit. He consulted with the Flyers' general manager, Keith Allen, who encouraged Burke to enroll in law school and confirmed what he already suspected—he would likely not make it as a professional hockey player. "It's a kick in the butt for an athlete to be told that by his boss, but Keith was brutally honest and gave me very sound advice," Burke admitted to McGourty. "It was the right decision."

Burke left the Mariners in 1978 and enrolled in Harvard Law. After graduating in 1981, he practiced sports law for several years in Massachusetts, serving as an agent for professional hockey players and gaining expertise in navigating contract negotiations. His work prepared him well for a career in hockey management, which requires a deep knowledge of the game as well as an understanding of the negotiation strategies key to developing strong teams, and in 1987, Burke moved to Canada to take the position of assistant general manager of the Vancouver Canucks.

As assistant general manager, Burke helped take the Canucks to the playoffs three times before stepping down from the position in 1992 to join the Hartford Whalers as general manager for the 1992–93 season. He left the Whalers at the beginning of the following season to take the position of senior vice president and director of hockey operations for the NHL. In that role, Burke was responsible for overseeing the creation of collective bargaining agreements and managing disciplinary action such as player suspensions and fines. While Burke argued that a certain amount of physical violence was necessary to the game, he made a point of cracking down on attacks with hockey sticks as well as blows to the head and other particularly brutal attacks. "I like physical hockey," he explained to E. M. Swift for *Sports Illustrated* (11 Oct. 1993), "but not cheap shots and not stickwork. And we are going to nail repeat offenders." True to his word, Burke meted out tough discipline throughout his tenure in the league office, suspending and fining numerous players for crossing the line.

## CANUCKS AND DUCKS

Burke stepped down from his position with the NHL in 1998 and returned to the Canucks, becoming president and general manager of the team. The Canucks had not made it to the playoffs during the previous two seasons and had never won the Stanley Cup, and as general manager, Burke was tasked with improving the team's chances and overall performance. He began by hiring a new coach, Marc Crawford, who would remain with the team through 2006. Burke also focused on making a number of key trades that brought talented players such as twins Daniel and Henrik Sedin to Vancouver. Another of Burke's trades allowed for the formation of a trio

of offensive players that became known by fans as the West Coast Express and dominated the rink during the 2002–3 season.

Under Burke's leadership, the Canucks advanced to the playoffs four times and won the team's first Northwest Division title in 2004, though the franchise was unable to capture the Stanley Cup. The number of points scored per year increased dramatically during his tenure, and Burke also worked to increase ticket sales and seek out additional sources of revenue. Despite these efforts, Burke's contract was not renewed when it expired after the 2003–4 season.

The 2004–5 NHL season was canceled due to an extended salary dispute between league management and the NHL Players' Association (NHLPA). Burke returned to hockey the following season, this time as general manager of the Mighty Ducks of Anaheim (the team's owners changed the team's name to the Anaheim Ducks in 2006). The Ducks' fifth general manager since the team's founding in 1993, Burke was again tasked with rebuilding a struggling franchise. He hired coach Randy Carlyle, whose aggressive yet structured style of coaching meshed well with Burke's own approach. "You have to start with a guy who shares your philosophy," Burke explained to Scott Burnside for *ESPN.com* (29 May 2007).

Working with Carlyle and the other members of the Ducks' management, Burke assembled a team that proved to have the right mix of skills. In 2007, the Ducks won the Pacific Division and the Western Conference and proceeded to the Stanley Cup Final, ultimately defeating the Ottawa Senators, four games to one. Late the following year, Burke declined to extend his contract with the Ducks, choosing instead to look for a new position on the East Coast so that he could spend more time with his family there.

## TORONTO MAPLE LEAFS AND THE VANCOUVER OLYMPICS

In November of 2008, the Toronto Maple Leafs announced that Burke had signed a six-year contract to serve as president and general manager of the team, one of the oldest franchises in the NHL. In a press conference on November 29, 2008, Burke described the team as "the center of the hockey universe" and the position of general manager as "one of the most important jobs in hockey." "It's a dream job," he explained.

As in Anaheim and Vancouver, Burke was faced with a struggling team. The Maple Leafs had not been to the playoffs since 2004 and had not won the Stanley Cup since 1967. Emphasizing an aggressive style of play, intelligent use of funds, and engagement with the Toronto community, Burke set out to combat what he termed "Maple Leaf complacency." He explained to *Toronto Life* (28 Oct. 2010), "It's a notion that if you play in Toronto, so long as you play OK, that's good enough. You make big money, there are twenty reporters waiting to talk to you when you come off the ice, you're adored. Mediocrity is not good enough for me."

While managing the Maple Leafs, Burke also served as general manager of the US Olympic hockey team that would compete in the 2010 Winter Olympics in Vancouver. Burke assembled a team consisting of players from more than fifteen different NHL franchises; only one player, Phil Kessel, played for Toronto. The US team prevailed throughout much of the tournament, defeating Finland in the semifinals, but ultimately claimed the silver medal while Canada took the gold. Although his players did not leave Vancouver as Olympic champions, Burke was proud of their accomplishment. "For a team to go in and excel like we did and not lose a game until the last game of the tournament, in overtime, and to come that close was an indication and a validation of the young men we took," he told Harry Thompson for *USA Hockey* magazine (Aug. 2010).

Burke's efforts with the Maple Leafs, however, did not prove to be as successful. The number of points scored each season changed minimally during his tenure, and the team was unable to make it to the playoffs during any season. In March of 2012, Burke hired former colleague Randy Carlyle—who by then had been fired from the Ducks and had played for the Maple Leafs for two seasons in the 1970s—to replace Leafs coach Ron Wilson. Burke hoped the change would allow the team to duplicate the Ducks' success.

### CONTROVERSIAL LEADERSHIP

In a talk delivered at the University of Toronto's Rotman School of Management on January 25, 2012, Burke likened his style of leadership to that of Apple founder Steve Jobs, which he described as ruthless. "Has there ever been a great business leader in this country, or a great politician, who wasn't ruthless when he needed to be?" he asked the audience. "The answer is no. It's an element you need to be successful in any field." Still, Burke acknowledged that there is a downside to this style of leadership. "I've done more good things for my players over time than I have ruthless things, but I will do what's necessary to make our team better," he said. "If that's hard on a family, I'm still going to do it. . . . It's a lonely side of the business."

Throughout his career, Burke generated controversy with his brusque persona and tendency to speak his mind. But while Burke has admitted that what he refers to as his "brand" may be off-putting to some, he has no intention of pretending to be someone else. "The people that hired me hired Brian Burke," he explained to the press (AP 12 Jan. 2013). "I'm not going to change how I do things. That's not possible." As general

manager of the Maple Leafs, a particularly high-profile team, Burke also became the focus of scrutiny for some of his management decisions, particularly his controversial decision to trade a second-round draft pick and two first-round picks for Kessel, a player whose performance was deemed by some fans and commentators to be disappointing.

On January 9, 2013, less than two weeks before the anticipated beginning of the NHL season and just days after the tentative end of a several-month labor dispute between the NHL and the NHLPA, the owners of the Maple Leafs announced their decision to replace Burke as president and general manager, handing off the position to Leafs executive Dave Nonis, who had previously replaced Burke as general manager of the Canucks. Although Burke acknowledged that his public persona and the team's inability to make it to the playoffs likely contributed to his firing, he admitted that the event still took him by surprise. "Sometimes when you get fired . . . you see the vultures circling and you understand it's coming," he explained in a press conference (AP 12 Jan. 2013) three days later. "This one here was like a two-by-four upside the head to me." Though Burke was set to stay with the Maple Leafs as a senior advisor until his contract expired in late 2014, he told the press that he hopes to continue to work as a general manager in the NHL and would gladly take a new position "tomorrow."

### PERSONAL LIFE

Burke lives in Toronto with his wife, CTV news anchor Jennifer Burke, with whom he has two daughters. He and his first wife, Kelly, divorced in 1995; they had two sons and two daughters together.

Burke is a prominent supporter of GLBT causes, particularly those focused on ending discrimination and homophobia in sports. In 2009, Burke's son Brendan, a college hockey student manager who had come out as gay to his family two years before, publically came out in an effort to call attention to the presence of GLBT individuals in sports and seek an end to the casual homophobia prevalent in locker rooms and sports facilities. "There are gay men in professional hockey," Burke told John Buccigross for *ESPN.com* (2 Dec. 2009). "We would be fools to think otherwise. And it's sad that they feel the need to conceal this." He added, "I wish this burden would fall on someone else's shoulders, not Brendan's. Pioneers are often misunderstood and mistrusted. But since he wishes to blaze this trail, I stand beside him with an axe!"

Brendan died in a car accident in early 2010. In the years since, Burke has remained devoted to GLBT activism, marching in the Toronto gay pride parade and serving as an active member of Parents, Families, and Friends of Lesbians and

Gays (PFLAG). He is a member of the advisory board for the You Can Play Project, an organization cofounded by his son Patrick and dedicated to ending homophobia in sports. For his work with GLBT causes, Burke received the Ally Award from the Toronto chapter of PFLAG in 2012. Burke is also a supporter of a variety of other causes and in January 2013 received a Canadian Forces Medallion for Distinguished Service in recognition of his support of Canadian service members during his tenure with the Maple Leafs.

## SUGGESTED READING

Buccigross, John. "We Love You, This Won't Change Anything." *ESPN.com*. ESPN, 2 Dec. 2009. Web. 16 Jan. 2013.

Frei, Terry. "Multifaceted Mogul Burke Kingpin of NHL Contrasts." *Denver Post*. Denver Post, 6 June 2007. Web. 16 Jan. 2013.

Johnston, Chris. "Brian Burke Fired: Former Toronto Maple Leafs GM Says Farewell." *Huffington Post Canada*. HPMG News, 12 Jan. 2013. Web. 16 Jan. 2013.

McGourty, John. "Getting By with Some Help from His Friends." *NHL.com*. National Hockey League, 21 Oct. 2008. Web. 16 Jan. 2013.

Rogan, Mary. "Out on the Ice." *GQ* Jan. 2011: 80–99. Print.

—*Joy Crelin*

# Sam Calagione

**Born:** May 22, 1969
**Occupation:** Brewer and founder of Dogfish Head Craft Brewery

Sam Calagione started making beer in his New York City apartment after college. When the sour-cherry ale he made was a success with friends, he decided to start his own craft-brewing business. In 1995, he founded the Dogfish Head Craft Brewery, which has since become one of the fastest-growing and most beloved craft breweries in the United States.

Calagione is fond of saying, "Nature makes wine. Brewers make beer." And he does his best to live up to the sentiment, creating beers with such unique ingredients as chicory, coffee, honey, and saffron, among others. Since about 2005, Calagione and his business have been receiving a great deal of media attention. He has been profiled in many major publications, and he was featured on the Discovery Channel reality show Brew Masters in 2010. The following year, he published his third book, *Brewing Up a Business: Adventures in Beer from the Founder of Dogfish Head Craft Brewery*, and collaborated with two other craft brewers and restaurateur

Getty Images for The New Yorker

Mario Batali to open La Birreria, a rooftop brewery and restaurant atop Eataly, the Italian food extravaganza, in New York City's Flatiron District.

## EARLY YEARS

Sam Calagione was born on May 22, 1969. He grew up as a middle child in Greenfield, Massachusetts. According to a profile by Burkhard Bilger for the *New Yorker* (24 Nov. 2008), Calagione is "the heir to a long line of winemakers." Bilger continued, "His father and his uncle used to drive to Worcester to meet the trains that brought grapes from California. When they got home, and the juice had been stomped out in the basement, Sam would help bottle it."

Calagione attended the Northfield Mount Hermon preparatory school, where he played football. An intelligent student, Calagione also liked to have fun, and often got into trouble for it. During his junior year in high school, he was reprimanded for persuading adults to buy him beer and then selling it to fellow students at a profit. In his senior year, only months before graduation, Calagione was expelled from high school for numerous violations, including flipping a truck on school property and breaking into a skating rink to play hockey naked.

## STARTING OUT

Despite not having a high school diploma, Calagione attended Muhlenberg College in Allentown, Pennsylvania, where he studied English. In 1992, after receiving his bachelor's degree, he moved to New York City. He continued to take writing classes at Columbia University and worked as a waiter to earn some money.

Calagione had never tasted craft beer until working at the restaurant. Once he did, it inspired him to try making his own beer. He approached the matter both practically and academically, spending a good deal of time at the library researching beer and at home brewing his own sour-cherry ale. Even then, Calagione was ahead of the curve; he was aware that craft breweries mostly made traditional types of beer, such as pilsner and pale ale, and he wanted to do something different.

In 1992, in his New York City apartment, Calagione threw a party where the featured drink was his sour-cherry pale ale. The brew was such a hit that he immediately decided to start his own craft-brewing business. According to the Brewers Association website, an American craft brewer is a "small, independent and traditional" brewer that makes "6 million barrels of beer or less" per year and is "less than 25% . . . owned or controlled by an alcoholic beverage industry member who is not themselves a craft brewer."

## DOGFISH HEAD IS BORN

In 1995 Calagione opened Dogfish Head Brewings and Eats, a restaurant and pub in Rehoboth Beach, Delaware. To start the business, he took out a bank loan and borrowed money from his father and several acquaintances. After signing the lease to the property, Calagione learned that in Delaware it was illegal for a pub to bottle beer and sell it outside the establishment. He took immediate action: He and his lawyer petitioned the state government to change the law, and six months later the governor signed the bill.

Although the tavern was a great success, Bilger writes, the beer "took a little longer." Calagione had been making beer largely by improvisation, experimenting with different herbs, fruits, and spices, but this method was not sustainable on a large scale. In the early days of the pub, he had only three fifteen-gallon kegs, meaning that he had to brew beer several times a day—a significantly bigger operation than he was used to. But Calagione learned, and because he still made relatively small batches, he could still experiment. In addition, the profits from the restaurant supported his brewing operation and allowed it to expand. During the company's first year, Calagione brewed only about two hundred barrels.

Aside from his determination and hard work, Calagione had another advantage: his ability to promote Dogfish Head in creative ways. He was just as willing to experiment in the marketing of his company as he was in the making of his beer. His first big publicity stunt took place in 1997, the same year that Dogfish Head separated the beer-packaging operation from the restaurant. Calagione built an eighteen-foot rowing boat, put some new Dogfish Head beer in it, and rowed it for hours across the Delaware River to New Jersey. Although a mishap with press releases meant that only a handful of fans greeted Calagione when he arrived, the stunt was not for

naught; executives at a Levi Strauss & Co. brand heard about it and asked him to pose for an ad campaign featuring young entrepreneurs. The ad appeared in such magazines and *GQ* and *Sports Illustrated* and brought Calagione and his company more recognition than they had ever had before.

At the time of the stunt, Dogfish Head was making an annual profit of about $90,000, Calagione told Melanie Wells for *Forbes* magazine (1 Nov. 1999). Two years later, at the time of the interview, he expected the company to make approximately $800,000 for the year—nearly a tenfold increase. "Once I thought I was at a disadvantage because I was an English major in college and I was trying to start a small business," Calagione told Bob Townsend for the *Atlanta Journal-Constitution* (17 Feb. 2011), reflecting on his unusual marketing campaign. "But I learned that at the heart of any entrepreneurial endeavor is the element of storytelling. Let's face it, there's no greater example of a work of fiction than a business plan. Then you spend your time turning it into nonfiction and making it all come true." By 1999, the company was making five brands of beer year round and distributing them in close to a dozen states.

According to Bilger, 1999 was a pivotal year for the company, as it was the year Calagione developed a new method of brewing. He got his inspiration while watching a cooking show on television. "The chef, who was making a soup, was saying that several grindings of pepper, added to the pot at different points, would give the dish more flavor than a single dose added at the beginning," wrote Bilger. Soon, Calagione had devised a contraption that would pour "a steady stream of hops" into the kettle during the brewing process, rather than adding them all at once. That experiment led to the creation of the 60 Minute IPA, one of Dogfish Head's most beloved year-round beers.

## DOGFISH HEAD GROWS

In 2000, Dogfish Head Craft Brewery received the Domestic Beer of the Year award from the *Malt Advocate*, a magazine for beer and whiskey connoisseurs. At the time, the company was brewing about 4,500 barrels a year, a significant increase from its first year, though still small compared to a major company. According to the Dogfish Head website, in the summer of 2002, the company had outgrown its distributing brewery, so it moved its operations to a 100,000-square-foot space in nearby Milton, Delaware.

At that time, Dogfish Head was putting out about 10,000 barrels a year; by 2005, it was up to 21,000 barrels a year, and the beer was being distributed not only in the United States but also in the United Kingdom, Canada, and Puerto Rico. Calagione was receiving more and more attention in the press as the years went by. In a profile of the brewery for the *Washington Post* (18 Nov. 2005), Fritz Hahn wrote, "In the increasingly crowded world of microbrews, Delaware's Dogfish Head Brewery has made its mark by embracing the unconventional, eschewing crowd-pleasing lagers to produce some of the most esoteric beers around."

**THE BEER**

The Dogfish Head beers that are generally available to the public come in three categories: the year-round, the rare, and the seasonal. There are also beers that result from collaborations between Dogfish Head and other small breweries, as well as brewpub exclusives, such as Ardent IPA, which are available for purchase only at the Rehoboth Beach brewpub.

There are eight different kinds of year-round beer, including 60 Minute IPA, Indian Brown Ale, Raison D'Etre, and Midas Touch. The 60 Minute IPA is so called because it is boiled for sixty minutes. The Indian Brown Ale, a cross between India pale ale, American brown ale, and Scotch ale, is a brown beer with a hint of caramel. Raison D'Etre, one of the favorites of craft-beer enthusiasts, is a mahogany-colored Belgian-style brown ale with sugar and raisin flavors.

Midas Touch, which is part of the company's Ancient Ales series, was born out of a collaboration between Calagione and Patrick McGovern, a beer enthusiast and a biomolecular archaeologist at the University of Pennsylvania Museum of Archaeology and Anthropology. The ingredients for this beer are based on McGovern's analysis of the residue found in 2,700-year-old drinking vessels that were excavated from the tomb popularly believed to have belonged to the Phrygian king Midas; the name refers to the mythical King Midas, who was said to turn everything he touched into gold. The ingredients of Midas Touch include honey, muscat grapes, barley, and saffron.

The Dogfish Head seasonal brews include Punkin Ale, Aprihop, and Chicory Stout. The last, available only during the winter, is a dark beer flavored with Mexican coffee, roasted chicory, St. John's wort, and licorice root. Punkin Ale is brewed with pumpkin, brown sugar, and various spices. Aprihop, available only during the spring months, is a well-hopped beer made with apricots.

There are more than twenty varieties of occasional rarities, including 120 Minute IPA, Black & Blue, Hellhound on My Ale, and Bitches Brew. The 120 Minute IPA is between 15 and 20 percent alcohol by volume (ABV); beer is generally around 5 percent ABV, but many Dogfish Head beers exceed 7 percent. It is made in the same way as the 60 Minute IPA, but boiled and hopped for twice as long. Black & Blue, a Belgian-style ale made with blackberries and blueberries, also has a high alcohol

content—10 percent ABV. Bitches Brew and Hellhound on My Ale were made in collaboration with the Sony Legacy music record label to commemorate music greats. Bitches Brew, released in honor of the forty-year anniversary of the Miles Davis album of the same name, is a dark beer made with honey and gesho root, the latter of which is used to brew Ethiopian mead and beer. Hellhound on My Ale, a tribute to the great bluesman Robert Johnson, is a very hoppy ale full of citrusy flavors, accentuated by the addition of lemon and lemon peel.

One of the best examples of how far Calagione is willing to go to create new flavors begins with John Gasparine, a businessman who owns a flooring company. When Gasparine was in Paraguay in 2006, he came across a kind of wood called *palo santo* (holy wood), which is extremely hard and heavy. Gasparine found the wood to be unusually aromatic, so he contacted Calagione with the idea of using it to make beer barrels. Intrigued, Calagione sent Gasparine back to Paraguay to procure enough wood for a 9,000-gallon barrel, which he used to make his Palo Santo Marron beer. Bilger described the beer as having "hints of tobacco and molasses in it, black cherries and dark chocolate, all interlaced with the wood's spicy resin. It tasted like some ancient elixir that the Inca might have made."

**BOOKS AND TELEVISION**

Calagione's love of beer has spilled over into several related projects. He is the author of several books on beer, the first of which, *Extreme Brewing: An Enthusiast's Guide to Brewing Craft Beer at Home* (2006), is a how-to guide for aspiring home brewers. Calagione also cowrote the book *He Said Beer, She Said Wine: Impassioned Food Pairings to Debate and Enjoy; From Burgers to Brie and Beyond* (2008) with wine expert Marnie Old. *Brewing Up a Business: Adventures in Beer from the Founder of Dogfish Head Craft Brewery* (2011) is part autobiography, part how-to guide for the beer-business entrepreneur.

In November and December 2010, Calagione was featured in the Discovery Channel television series *Brew Masters*, which was produced by the same team behind *Anthony Bourdain: No Reservations*. The show took Calagione around the world in search of unique ideas and ingredients for beer, while also offering an inside look at his beer-making practices. Speaking to Bob Townsend for the *Atlanta Journal-Constitution* (17 Feb. 2011), Calagione said, "The best thing I think the show does is demystify the craft brewing process and the craft brewing community. And maybe it gives people who aren't beer geeks but just getting into better beer the confidence to go outside their comfort zone and explore. It was pretty neat because in this age of scanner data, you could see that when the show aired, the demand for craft beer went up."

## LA BIRRERIA

In 2010 Dogfish Head announced that it was collaborating with craft brewers Baladin and Del Borgo as well as restaurateur Mario Batali to open La Birreria, a rooftop restaurant and brewery atop Eataly, an Italian food extravaganza with five restaurants and a multivendor marketplace, all under one roof in New York City's Flatiron District. La Birreria became Eataly's sixth restaurant when it opened its doors in June 2011. The restaurant offers unfiltered, unpasteurized house brewed cask ales on tap, serves hearty fare, and has a retractable roof that is opened as weather permits.

Calagione lives in Lewes, Delaware, with his wife, Mariah, who is vice president of Dogfish Head. They have two children, Sammy and Grier.

## SUGGESTED READING

Bilger, Burkhard. "A Better Brew: The Rise of Extreme Beer." *New Yorker* 24 Nov. 2008: 88+. Print.

Eels, Josh. "Reality TV Pours Itself a Cold One." *New York Times* 21 Nov. 2010, Arts and Leisure sec.: 15. Print.

Hahn, Fritz. "Dogfish, Making Headway in Gaithersburg." *Washington Post* 18 Nov. 2005, Weekend sec.: 5. Print.

Huang, Patricia. "Chateau Dogfish: How to Sell a \$9 Bottle of Beer." *Forbes* 28 Feb. 2005: 57–59. Print.

Townsend, Bob. "Brewer Has New Venture, TV Show." *Atlanta-Journal Constitution* 17 Feb. 2011, Food and Drink sec.: 1F. Print.

—*Dmitry Kiper*

---

# Bruce Campbell

**Born:** June 22, 1958
**Occupation:** Actor, writer, producer

"I'm not interested in playing the straightforward square-jawed type. I never was," versatile veteran actor Bruce Campbell told Joe Rhodes for the *New York Times* (12 Sept. 2008). "I'd be doing soap operas and hourlong dramas right now if I was really into that. But I was always looking for stuff that was more off-kilter." Over thirty years ago, Campbell burst onto the scene playing the lead in the 1981 cult horror classic *The Evil Dead*, as well as its two sequels. Since then he has eschewed traditional leading-man roles in favor of playing a wide range of colorful characters on the big and small screens. These roles include a bounty hunter in the FOX sitcom *The Adventures of Brisco County Jr.*; a charming thief in the hit syndicated series *Hercules: The Legendary Journeys* (1995–99) and *Xena: Warrior*

WireImage

*Princess* (1996–99); a creepy plastic surgeon in the action film *Escape from L.A.* (1996); a wrongfully accused police officer in the horror film *Maniac Cop* (1988); and the legendary Elvis Presley in *Bubba Ho-Tep* (2002). Most recently, Campbell has been a small-screen fixture, as a fun-loving, skirt-chasing former Navy SEAL in the long-running USA network drama *Burn Notice*.

## EARLY LIFE AND EDUCATION

Bruce Lorne Campbell was born on June 22, 1958, in Royal Oak, Michigan, and grew up in nearby Birmingham. His mother, Joanne (Pickens) Campbell, was a homemaker and his father, Charlie Newton Campbell, worked in the advertising field as a traveling billboard inspector. He also has two older siblings, Don and Michael.

Campbell developed a love of acting at the age of eight, when he first saw his father perform with the Detroit-based troupe Saint Dunstan's Theatre Guild of Cranbrook. "I went to see my dad in a play . . . he was in *Brigadoon* and I thought, wow, my dad is acting so weird!" Campbell told Jordan Morris for the *Sound of Young America* (22 Aug. 2011). "He's dancing with chicks that are not my mom, what is happening? What's going on here? And the audience is clapping and laughing. I had just seen a different part of my dad, and I liked that part."

When Campbell was fourteen, he followed in his father's footsteps, appearing as the title character in a local production of the musical *The King and I*. He went on to perform in community theater productions of *South Pacific* and *Sweet Bird of Youth*. Campbell also spent his free time making amateur stop-animation films with a neighborhood friend, who was a photographer.

While attending Wylie E. Groves High School, in Beverly Hills, Michigan, Campbell played soccer for a year before quitting the team to join the drama class. There, he became good friends with Sam Raimi, although the two had already crossed paths at West Maple Junior High School. "I met Sam . . . very briefly while I was with a friend of his—and he was dressed as Sherlock Holmes, playing with dolls. I thought he was a creepy weirdo, and I avoided him, officially, until drama class in high school, in 1975," Campbell revealed to Ken P. in a December 18, 2002, interview for *IGN*. Soon after, the two of them, along with several of their high school buddies, were collaborating on homemade Super 8 millimeter films; they made about fifty films altogether.

## ACTING CAREER AND COLLABORATIONS WITH RAIMI

During the summer of 1976, after graduating from high school, Campbell volunteered at Cherry County Playhouse, a professional theater company in Traverse City, Michigan. As an intern, he worked extensively behind the scenes, creating sets for some of the productions while also serving as the assistant manager and running errands. That fall, Campbell studied drama at Western Michigan University, in Kalamazoo, but he dropped out after only six months to launch an acting career. He subsequently worked in Detroit as a production assistant for commercials and as a filmmaking instructor at a vocational center.

In 1978, Campbell joined forces with Raimi, then a disenchanted Michigan State University (MSU) student, and Robert Tapert, a fellow MSU classmate, to produce *Within the Woods*, a half-hour, Super 8 horror movie that was based on a short story written by Raimi. "We were very familiar with *Texas Chainsaw Massacre* and *Halloween*, and none of those movies had anybody—no name actors were in any of those movies," Campbell said in his conversation with Morris. "We knew that we could get away with that. Horror movies you don't need fancy cars and clothes. [A] lot of times they're in one location, we had a cabin. So that made it cheaper."

The trio presented *Within the Woods* to prospective investors, including several of Campbell's family members, and eventually managed to raise $350,000 to turn their short film into a full-length feature movie. In August 1979 they founded Renaissance Pictures to produce the film, which they renamed *Book of the Dead*. Shot over a two-year period (from 1979 to 1981) in Detroit and Tennessee, *Book of the Dead* revolves around five MSU students spending their spring break vacation in an isolated cabin. During the weekend getaway, they find a mysterious book and an audiotape containing incantations that unleash gruesome spirits and demons.

Campbell performed double duty on the low-budget thriller, which served as Raimi's directorial debut. In addition to starring in the film as Ashley "Ash" J. Williams—the reluctant protagonist who initially cowers in fear before eventually gaining the courage to kill and eviscerate his friends who have been possessed by the evil spirits—Campbell shared coexecutive producer credits with Raimi and Tapert.

In December 1981, two months after *Book of the Dead* premiered in Detroit, Campbell, Raimi, and Tapert were still struggling to get their film distributed in the United States. They screened the film for people in the industry, including veteran producer Irvin Shapiro, who agreed to help them land a foreign distribution deal. (Shapiro had previously arranged similar transactions for George Romero's 1968 horror classic *Night of the Living Dead* and Martin Scorsese's 1973 crime drama *Mean Streets*.)

Not only did Shapiro rename the movie *The Evil Dead*, he also made the fateful decision to have it screened at the 1982 Cannes Film Festival. *The Evil Dead* garnered attention, particularly after legendary suspense writer Stephen King, one of the festival's attendees, hailed it as "the most ferociously original horror film of the year," in his review for the November 1982 issue of *Twilight Zone* magazine.

### *THE EVIL DEAD* BRINGS CULT SUCCESS

Buoyed by King's endorsement, which was included in the film's poster, *The Evil Dead* found distributors. In February 1983, the British distribution company Palace Pictures simultaneously released a censored version of the movie in London cinemas and an uncut version on VHS and Betamax in the United Kingdom. With the help of a massive promotional campaign, the latter version quickly eclipsed the 1980 big-screen adaptation of King's 1977 novel *The Shining* to become the best-selling video in England. Its notoriety in the United Kingdom led to a US distribution deal with New Line Cinema.

In late April 1983, *The Evil Dead* made its American debut in New York City before premiering in Los Angeles in May. The film's violence and sexual content earned an X rating from the Motion Picture Association of America (MPAA), designating it off-limits to children under the age of seventeen. When the movie was released across Europe and Asia a year later, it was banned in several countries. Despite the controversy, *The Evil Dead* managed to find an audience and grossed $2.4 million domestically and more than $29 million worldwide.

In a bit of a role reversal, Raimi starred in *Thou Shalt Not Kill . . . Except* (1985), a low-budget, independent thriller cowritten by Campbell, who also served as the supervising sound editor. It was adapted from the Super 8 millimeter short *Stryker's War*, which starred Campbell as a wounded and troubled Vietnam veteran who returns home only to find himself back into battle, when he must rescue his girlfriend, the victim of a kidnapping by a cult leader (Raimi) and his followers. Although the film was not a box-office hit, it became a minor cult classic and was released on DVD nearly three decades later.

Also in 1985, Campbell partnered with Raimi for the film noir comedy *Crimewave* (1985), which Raimi directed and on which Campbell served as coproducer, along with Tapert. Campbell also had a minor role as gangster Renaldo "The Heel." However, *Crimewave* proved to be a vastly different filmmaking experience than their previous, more successful collaboration. "It was the complete antithesis of *Evil Dead*, in every respect. *Evil Dead* was successful, we had total creative control, it was low budget," Campbell said to Ken P. "*Crimewave* cost too much money, it was our first experience with unions, and we had problems with actors. The film was recut, it was retitled, it didn't make any money—it was . . . eye-opening, dealing with the studio sort of world, and we realized it just sucked."

After the failure of *Crimewave*, the trio decided to make the sequel to their 1981 cult classic. When financing negotiations with *Crimewave*'s distributor, Embassy Pictures, stalled, Stephen King came to their rescue once again, convincing producer Dino De Laurentiis to bankroll the movie, which was filmed in Wadesboro, North Carolina, with a budget of $3.5 million—ten times more than the original. Campbell reprised the role of Ash, this time depicting him as a braver character.

Released in March 1987, *Evil Dead 2: Dead by Dawn* adopted a more over-the-top gory and tongue-in-cheek style than its predecessor. Campbell earned critical praise for his physical comedy and his self-deprecating humor regarding his movie-star looks. The movie proved to be popular with US audiences, grossing more than $5.9 million domestically.

## CEMENTING HIS STATUS AS KING OF B MOVIES

Following the success of both *Evil Dead* films, Campbell moved to Los Angeles to focus exclusively on his acting career. He was determined to carve out a career on his own merit, away from Raimi and Tapert. Campbell had an auspicious beginning, acing his first audition and landing a guest-starring part in the November 5, 1987, episode of the nighttime CBS soap opera *Knots Landing*—an experience that he did not initially enjoy. "It was so impersonal, and so fast. . . . and the director—who never even spoke to me during the course of shooting, for four or five days . . . would just sort of point and say, 'You're sitting over there,'" he revealed in his conversation with Ken P. "It really was a factory."

Consequently, Campbell decided to concentrate on big-screen roles instead. Over the next six years, he found consistent work, mostly in low-budget independent films. After playing Jack Forrest, a wrongly accused policeman, in William Lustig's *Maniac Cop*, Campbell costarred as vampire Robert Van Helsing in the 1989 quirky comedy *Sundown: The Vampire in Retreat* and as a police officer in Josh Becker's horror film *Intruder* (1989). He briefly appeared in the short-lived NBC television soap opera *Generations* (1989), in the recurring role of Alan Stuart, before returning to the big screen in the sci-fi flick *Moontrap* (1989), in which he played astronaut Ray Tanner, who does battle against an alien invasion. Next came an uncredited appearance in the horror film *The Dead Next Door* (1989), which Raimi produced.

A year later, Campbell reprised his role in *Maniac Cop 2* and then reunited with Raimi for the big-budget action thriller *Darkman* (1990). For the latter film, Campbell, Raimi's original choice to play the lead, had a brief cameo but mostly performed sound editing in postproduction—a stint that only reinforced his negative view of the Hollywood studio system. "I noticed him progressing again as a filmmaker, but I realized that he was entering into a world of s——, because the studios were all over him," he told Ken P. "He had to recut that film, and it was a mess. . . . It was like *Crimewave* again."

Campbell reteamed with Becker in *Lunatics: A Love Story* (1991), an offbeat romantic comedy in which he costarred and served as coproducer. In 1992, came appearances in a series of low-budget horror movies, including *Waxwork II: Lost in Time*, *Eddie Presley*, and *Mindwarp*. For his next project, Campbell reunited with Raimi and De Laurentiis for *Army of Darkness* (1992), the big-budget final installment in the *Evil Dead* trilogy. Once again, Campbell served as coproducer and resumed the role of Ash, who is propelled into a time vortex and ends up in a medieval setting, where he continues to do battle with demons (known as "deadites"), including an evil version of himself. *Army of Darkness* encountered interference from the coproducers—executives at Universal Studios, who encouraged Raimi to shoot a new ending and to cut the film from ninety-six minutes down to eighty-one minutes.

Released in 1993, *Army of Darkness* adopted more of an action-adventure feel and a slapstick tone like its predecessor, but it failed to win over the critics. However, the film still managed to outperform the previous two *Evil Dead* movies, with a domestic gross of more than $11.5 million, while also amassing more than $21.5 million worldwide.

## GRAVITATING TOWARD THE SMALL SCREEN

By the time that *Army of Darkness* made its debut in American cinemas, Campbell had already started work on his next project: the Western/science-fiction television series *The Adventures of Brisco County Jr.* Despite his earlier reservations about working in television, Campbell instantly gravitated toward the script. "I thought it was a very unique idea, he was a Harvard educated lawyer as well as a cowboy," Campbell told Andrew Orillion for *Slant Magazine* (8 June 2010). "I also liked all the modern day references. It was old fashioned and new fashioned at the same time."

Campbell was eventually cast in the lead role after an impressive first audition, during which he performed an impromptu backflip in the middle of a fight scene. "After seeing that, it was impossible to not imagine Brisco could be anyone but Bruce," Carlton Cuse, the show's head writer, said to Orillion. The show, about a lawyer-turned-bounty-hunter assigned to hunt down a band of criminals and their leader, premiered on the FOX network in August 1993. Despite the mixed reaction, the series, which aired Fridays, enjoyed a loyal following, but it was ultimately canceled in May 1994 due to low ratings. During *Brisco*'s run, Campbell had a small but memorable role, opposite Tim Robbins and Paul Newman, in the Coen brothers' comedy *The Hudsucker Proxy* (1994). A year later Campbell costarred with Laura Linney in the big-screen adaptation of Michael Crichton's book *Congo*; however, his scenes in *The Quick and the Dead* (1995), Raimi's spaghetti Western tribute, ended up on the cutting-room floor.

In the latter half of the 1990s Campbell landed guest-starring roles in a number of high-profile television programs. In addition to playing villainous Bill Church Jr. in the ABC adventure series *Lois and Clark: The New Adventures of Superman*, he portrayed a lieutenant in the CBS supernatural drama *American Gothic*, as well as a ruthless firefighter in the NBC crime show *Homicide: Life on the Street*. He also made appearances on two sci-fi series: *Timecop*, a small-screen adaptation of the 1994 film, and the FOX cult drama *The X-Files*.

Campbell returned to episodic television as Autolycus, a recurring character on *Hercules: The Legendary Journeys* and its sister show *Xena: Warrior Princess*, both produced by Tapert. The following year he joined the cast of Ellen DeGeneres's ABC sitcom, *Ellen*, in a recurring capacity. Campbell's other television credits included leading roles in several made-for-television movies, most notably *Tornado!* (1996), *Missing Links* (1997), and *In the Line of Duty: Blaze of Glory* (1997).

## A WEEKLY TELEVISION FIXTURE

Since 2000, Campbell has remained a fixture on the small screen. After starring in the short-lived swashbuckling drama *Jack of All Trades* (2000), which he also coproduced, Campbell made guest appearances in the Showtime comedy series *Beggars and Choosers* (2001) and the CW network's supernatural drama *Charmed* (2002). In 2006, he accepted the role of Sam Axe, a washed-up former Navy SEAL, on the USA network drama *Burn Notice*, currently in its sixth season. "I said yes to what it was *not*," he told Matt Richenthal for TVFanatic.com (7 July 2011). "It's not a cop show, although there is life and death situation. It's not a legal show, though you are dealing with issues . . . I was attracted to the premise and the flawed characters."

Campbell continues to make big-screen appearances. In 2002, he won multiple acting prizes, including a US Comedy Arts Festival Award, for his performance in *Bubba Ho-Tep*, as an aging Elvis Presley living in a nursing home. He also collaborated with Raimi on *Spider-Man* (2002) and its sequels, in 2004 and 2007, respectively. Campbell made his feature-film directorial debut in *Man with the Screaming Brain* (2005); two years later he spoofed himself in *My Name Is Bruce* (2007). He costarred opposite James Franco and Mila Kunis in both the independent film *Tar* (2012) and *Oz the Great and Powerful* (2013).

## PERSONAL LIFE

Since 1991, Campbell has been married to costume designer Ida Gearon; the couple lives outside Medford, Oregon. He also has two children, Rebecca and Andy, with former wife Christine Deveau. He is the author of the 2002 best-selling memoir *If Chins Could Kill: Confessions of a B Movie Actor* and the novel *Make Love! The Bruce Campbell Way* (2005).

## SUGGESTED READING

Frost, Caroline. "Bruce Campbell: From *Evil Dead* to *Burn Notice*—Season 4 and Onwards." *Huffington Post*. TheHuffingtonPost.com, 21 Dec. 2011. Web. 15 Mar. 2013.

McIntyre, Gina. "Bruce Campbell's Spoof Hits Home in Several Ways." *Los Angeles Times*. Los Angeles Times, 19 Dec. 2008. Web. 15 Mar. 2013.

Morris, Jordan. "Bruce Campbell, Producer, Writer and B-Movie Icon." *Maximum Fun*. Maximum Fun, 22 Aug. 2011. Web. 15 Mar. 2013.

Orillion, Andrew. "A Fistful of Geek: A Look Back at The Adventures of Brisco County Jr." *Slant Magazine*. Slant Magazine, 8 June 2010. Web. 15 Mar. 2013.

P., Ken. "An Interview with Bruce Campbell: The *Evil Dead*, *Brisco County*, and *Xena* Actor Discusses His Career." *IGN*. IGN Entertainment, 18 Dec. 2002. Web. 15 Mar. 2013.

Rhodes, Joe. "Bruce Campbell's Prime-Time Moment." *New York Times*. New York Times, 12 Sept. 2008. Web. 15 Mar. 2013.

Thill, Scott. "Shut Up and Act." *Salon*. Salon Media Group, 14 July 2005. Web. 15 Mar. 2013.

## SELECTED WORKS

### Books
*If Chins Could Kill: Confessions of a B Movie Actor*, 2002; *Make Love! The Bruce Campbell Way*, 2005

### Films
*The Evil Dead*, 1981; *Evil Dead II: Dead by Dawn*, 1987; *Maniac Cop*, 1988; *Lunatics: A Love Story*, 1991; *Army of Darkness*, 1992; *The Hudsucker Proxy*, 1994; *Congo*, 1995; *Escape from L.A.*, 1996; *In the Line of Duty: Blaze of Glory*, 1997; *Spider-Man*, 2002; *Burn Notice: The Fall of Sam Axe*, 2011; *Oz the Great and Powerful*, 2013

### Television Shows
*Knots Landing*, 1987; *Generations*, 1989; *The Adventures of Brisco County Jr.*, 1993–94; *Lois and Clark: The New Adventures of Superman*, 1995; *Homicide: Life on the Street*, 1996; *Ellen*, 1996–97; *Hercules: The Legendary Journeys*, 1995–99; *Xena: Warrior Princess*, 1996–99; *Burn Notice*, 2007–; *1600 Penn*, 2013

—Bertha Muteba

© Derek Storm /Retna Ltd./Corbis

# Eric Carle

**Born:** June 25, 1929
**Occupation:** Children's book author and illustrator

Eric Carle is one of the most beloved figures in children's literature. Since illustrating his first picture book—*Brown Bear, Brown Bear, What Do You See?*—in 1967, he has published some seventy volumes, which have collectively sold more than 110 million copies, and has won numerous awards from such groups as the Association of Booksellers for Children, the American Booksellers Association, and the American Library Association. He receives an estimated ten thousand fan letters from children each year.

Among his most popular and enduring books is *The Very Hungry Caterpillar*, originally published in 1969, which has been translated into dozens of languages. The story of a caterpillar that eats his way through an astonishing variety of food on his journey to become a butterfly, the book is illustrated in Carle's signature style, which involves vibrantly colored tissue-paper collages.

In an introduction to *The Art of Eric Carle* (1996), a book published that explores Carle's legacy, critic and historian Leonard S. Marcus praised him as "maker of children's books of radiant tenderness, poetic insight, and rare graphic distinction." Marcus continued, "Carle's gentle incisive illustrations are an open invitation to readers to make more pictures of their own, and to regard his books not only as finished works but as challenging, playful points of departure. It is an invitation that children throughout the world have taken to heart."

## EARLY YEARS
Carle was born on June 25, 1929, in Syracuse, New York. His parents, Erich and Johanna, were immigrants from Germany. An artistically minded young man, Carle's father had been forced by his own father, a customs official in Stuttgart, to enter civil service. Unhappy, he had come to the United States in 1925, at the age of twenty-one, and found a job spray-painting washing machines at a manufacturing company. While the work was not exactly artistic, he was happy to be settling into his adopted country and earning a steady income.

Carle's parents had begun courting before his father left Stuttgart, and Erich continued to woo Johanna from the United States, sending illustrated letters on a regular basis. Finally, in 1927, unable to speak a single word of English, she joined him in New York, where she found a job with a wealthy family as a maid. The couple married in 1928, and thirteen months later Carle was born.

By all accounts, Carle was a bright and inquisitive child who loved exploring nature. He had inherited his father's talent for drawing, and his kindergarten teacher called his mother to the school one day to explain that she should be encouraging this ability at home. Although Johanna had what some observers have characterized as a Teutonic sense of discipline and restraint, she took the advice seriously and provided Carle with a generous supply of paints, crayons, and papers.

## MOVE TO GERMANY

Johanna eventually became homesick, and when Carle was six years old, his parents returned with him to Germany. They settled in Stuttgart, in a multistory building filled with members of their extended family. Initially, Carle's new classmates called him "Amerikaner." It was not a derogatory appellation; they admired the United States and its culture, and Carle was sometimes asked to sing American tunes for their entertainment. While Carle enjoyed making new friends and exploring his new neighborhood, other aspects of the move to Germany were problematic. The educational system in Stuttgart was much stricter than the one in Syracuse, and Carle was horrified to discover that making an error in class—no matter how small—could result in being struck on the palms with a thin bamboo rod. He began to hate school and repeatedly asked his parents when they would be returning to the United States. When he realized that they had no intention of doing so, he began dreaming of becoming a bridge builder when he grew up. He would construct a massive bridge from Stuttgart to Syracuse, he planned, and he would then walk across it, taking his beloved maternal grandmother, to whom he had grown exceedingly close, with him.

While he never came to like school, Carle was happy. He spent long hours visiting his grandparents and his many aunts and uncles, and he took particular delight in vacationing on the farms owned by members of his extended family or their friends; he had retained his love of nature and spent much of his time learning to milk the cows, watching bees swarm around their hives, and gathering eggs from the chickens.

## LIFE DURING WORLD WAR II

World War II, however, intruded on Carle's tranquil life. Carle recalls a family vacation in 1939 being interrupted by news on the radio that Adolf Hitler had invaded Poland. His father was immediately drafted and was later wounded near Stalingrad. Stuttgart was a major target of the Allies, and a large portion of the city was eventually flattened by bombs, leaving many of Carle's aunts and uncles homeless.

Carle's school was damaged but still operating sporadically, and, infused with a young boy's excitement about war, Carle began drawing tanks and fighter planes in art class. One day, Herr Kraus, his art teacher, prohibited by state regulation from teaching anything but realism, secretly showed him a set of reproductions by Pablo Picasso, Henri Matisse, and other artists who had been deemed "degenerate" by the German authorities. He advised Carle to always remember their joyfully free style. "At first I was upset," Carle recalled to Debbie Elliott for the National Public Radio program *All Things Considered* (15 July 2007). "I thought this man was crazy because I had never seen anything like this . . . I was shocked and attracted to it at the same time." Carle now counts those artists as some of his greatest influences.

In 1943, the students at Carle's school were evacuated to the countryside for safety. Carle was sent to live with a family on the outskirts of the Black Forest, where he remained until age fifteen. He was subsequently conscripted to work alongside prisoners of war and German men too old to fight, digging trenches near the Rhine River on what was known as the Siegfried Line. Slightly wounded in an air attack that killed several of the people standing near him, he spent several days in the hospital before returning home.

When the war ended, in 1945, Carle's father was missing in action. After a year, the family received word that he was in a Russian prison camp; he would not return home until 1947— eight long years after first being drafted—ill with malaria and weighing only eighty pounds.

Meanwhile, Carle found a job as a file clerk with the Denazification Department of the US Military Government, which was charged with ridding German society of any traces of National Socialist Party ideology. There, Carle rapidly relearned how to speak English, having lost the ability to do so during the years he spent growing up in Germany. After a few months, he applied to the highly competitive Akademie der bildenden Künste (academy of visual arts), realizing that graphic arts might provide a viable career option for him. Although he was only sixteen— two years younger than the minimum required age—he was accepted, and for the next three semesters, he toiled as an apprentice in the typesetting department, working under Professor Ernst Schneidler.

Carle remained at the academy for four years. During his final year he was commissioned to create a series of posters for the US Information Center; he has told interviewers that he remains proud of the distinctive, stylish work he produced for the organization.

## ART CAREER

Immediately after graduating, Carle found work as an art director in the promotional department of a fashion magazine. In May 1952, after amassing a professional portfolio and saving some money, he returned to the United States, and, landing in New York, he set out to find a job. At the suggestion of an acquaintance, he went to see the annual New York Art Directors Show, and while there, he secured an interview with Leo Lionni, the art director for *Fortune* magazine.

It was a fortuitous meeting. While Lionni was not able to offer him a job at *Fortune*, he hired the young artist to help him with occasional freelance work. Additionally, Lionni introduced him to George Krikorian, an art director at the *New York Times*. Krikorian gave Carle a full-time spot for what for him was the princely sum of eighty-five dollars a week.

Carle's elation was short-lived, however. Just a few months after securing work, with the Korean War ongoing, Carle received a draft notice ordering him to report for basic training at Fort Dix in New Jersey. He was sent to Germany to serve with the Seventh United States Army in Stuttgart. He received permission to sleep at his family's home each evening, rather than remain in the barracks.

Discharged in 1954, he returned to New York and resumed his old job at the newspaper. In 1956, he accepted a higher paying job as the art director for an advertising agency whose main clients were pharmaceutical companies. Soon, however, he became disenchanted with corporate life, and he quit his job in order to freelance from home. Among his early clients was a small educational publisher, and while the few books he illustrated for them in the mid-1960s are now considered collector's items, Carle found the work drab and uninspired.

One day, however, he was approached by Bill Martin Jr., an educator who had written a simple children's book called *Brown Bear, Brown Bear, What Do You See?*, which he needed illustrated. Martin had been inspired to contact Carle after seeing an ad he had created featuring a lobster rendered with torn bits of tissue paper. "Now the large sheets of paper, the colorful paints and fat brushes of my [American kindergarten] came to my mind," Carle wrote in an essay in *The Art of Eric Carle*. "I was set on fire! It was possible, after all, to do something special, something that would show a child the joy to be found in books."

## CHILDREN'S BOOKS

After *Brown Bear, Brown Bear, What Do You See?* was published in 1967, Carle knew he might have found a niche. While delivering cookbook illustrations to an editor named Ann Beneduce, who later became an influential figure in children's publishing, he discussed some of his ideas with her. With her encouragement, he prepared a wordless counting book, *1, 2, 3 to the Zoo* (1968), which featured riotously colored animals. Carle has also credited the famed children's author Ezra Jack Keats, to whom he was introduced by a mutual friend, with convincing him that it was possible to make a living in children's literature, if one were careful with the contracts, advances, and royalties that make up the business side of the endeavor.

The following year *The Very Hungry Caterpillar*, which he both wrote and illustrated, was released. Beneduce, who had suggested that the protagonist be a caterpillar (Carle had originally envisioned a worm) explained in *The Art of Eric Carle*: "In this book, many of the things we now think of as characteristic of his work appeared: his warm grasp of subject matter, presenting an abstract or general idea through a particular story and an individual character; his deep empathy with nature (i.e. animals, plants, and insects) as well as his interest in natural processes and events; his eagerness to share with children the joy of learning; his innovative approach to bookmaking, using die-cut holes and different sized pages to make his points clearer and more dramatic; and, of course, his dazzling art and effects."

*The Very Hungry Caterpillar* has received universal acclaim and is often listed among the best children's books ever published. "*The Very Hungry Caterpillar* is only 32 pages and 224 words long, but there is a reason one remembers it so vividly: the bulging salami, the lurid watermelon, the caterpillar itself, with its humpbacked body and impudent expression," Emma Brockes wrote for the London *Guardian* (13 Mar. 2009). "He has so few words to play with that every one must count, and so it does. When the caterpillar turns into a butterfly it's a joyful moment, but there's also a lurch; something is lost. How many books for the under-fives have subtext?"

Attempting to explain his popularity, Carle told Carol Lawson for the *New York Times* (14 Apr. 1994), "The success of my books is not in the characters or the words or the colors, but in the simple, simple feelings. . . . I remember that as a child, I always felt I would never grow up and be big and articulate and intelligent. 'Caterpillar' is a book of hope: you, too, can grow up and grow wings."

Carle maintained a close friendship and professional relationship with Martin until the latter's death in 2004. In addition to *Brown Bear, Brown Bear, What Do You See?*, they collaborated on *Polar Bear, Polar Bear, What Do You Hear?* (1991) and *Panda Bear, Panda Bear, What Do You See?* (2003).

## COLLAGE ART

Carle initially used store-bought tissue paper, which came in about fifty shades, to create his art. He cut or tore the paper into various shapes and then pasted them on rigid boards with rubber cement to create his designs. He later found that painting on the tissue paper added more variety and texture.

Eventually, however, he discovered that the works made of painted tissue tended to fade and that the rubber cement discolored the material and came loose. As a result, he began working with higher quality archival paper, and he chose only white, which he then painted himself.

Visitors to Carle's studio frequently comment on the beauty of the painted tissue paper, which Carle prepares in batches and stores flat, in carefully organized files. He also replaced rubber cement with wallpaper paste, which he found solved the problems of discoloration and deterioration.

Certain colors pose particular challenges. While Carle finds it easy to create various shades of green—from the cheerful hue of the snake in *The Greedy Python* (1985) to the muddy brownish green inspired by wartime camouflage—he has only a handful of yellows in his repertoire. (Still, he has told journalists that it is one of his favorite colors, and a beaming yellow sun can often be found somewhere in his books.) Carle frequently gives workshops to show others how to make tissue-paper collages, and teachers around the world now plan lessons based on the technique.

In 2002, Carle and his wife founded the Eric Carle Museum of Picture Book Art, in Amherst, Massachusetts. Its website explains that it is "the only full-scale museum of its kind in the United States, . . . [which] collects, preserves, presents, and celebrates picture books and picture book illustrations from around the world." It houses a collection of more than ten thousand illustrations, three art galleries, an art studio, a theater, and extensive libraries of both scholarly books and picture books.

## PERSONAL LIFE

In 1954, shortly before his discharge from the US Army, Carle married nineteen-year-old Dorothea Wohlenberg, the sister of a former coworker. She returned with him to the United States when his tour of duty was over, and they settled in the New York City borough of Queens before moving to the bucolic village of Irvington-on-Hudson, in upstate New York. They had a daughter, Cirsten, and a son, Rolf, before divorcing.

In 1973, Carle married Barbara (Bobbie) Morrison, a special education teacher, and the following year they moved to Massachusetts, where they lived for decades. In about 2006, tired of northeastern winters, they moved to Key Largo, Florida, to a home overlooking the ocean.

Many observers have posited an inverse link between Carle's childhood during World War II, with its attendant deprivations, and his color-drenched, joyful artwork. He agrees that there is some causative relationship and has told journalists that if he had grown up in a safer, more relaxed era, he might be "pumping gas" for a living.

## SUGGESTED READING

Bernstein, Fred. "At Home with Eric Carle: Hungry Caterpillar in the Florida Keys." *New York Times.* New York Times, 13 Dec. 2007. Web. 1 July 2013.

Brockes, Emma. "This One's Got Legs." *Guardian.* Guardian News and Media, 13 Mar. 2009. Web. 1 July 2013.

Elliott, Debbie. "Eric Carle's Colorful World of Children's Books." *All Things Considered.* Natl. Public Radio, 15 July 2007. Web. 1 July 2013. Radio.

Lawson, Carol. "In the Studio with: Eric Carle; For Children, Very Simple Stories with Very Vibrant Art." *New York Times.* New York Times, 14 Apr. 1994. Web. 1 July 2013.

## SELECTED WORKS

*Brown Bear, Brown Bear, What Do You See,* 1967; *The Very Hungry Caterpillar,* 1969; *Pancakes, Pancakes!,* 1970; *Do You Want to Be My Friend?,* 1971; *The Mixed-Up Chameleon,* 1975; *The Grouchy Ladybug,* 1977; *The Very Busy Spider,* 1984; *Papa, Please Get the Moon for Me,* 1986; *The Very Quiet Cricket,* 1990; *Polar Bear, Polar Bear, What Do You Hear?,* 1991; *Draw Me a Star,* 1992; *The Very Lonely Firefly,* 1995; *From Head to Toe,* 1997; *Does a Kangaroo Have a Mother, Too?,* 2000; *"Slowly, Slowly, Slowly," Said the Sloth,* 2002; *Panda Bear, Panda Bear, What Do You See?,* 2003; *Mister Seahorse,* 2004; *The Artist Who Painted a Blue Horse,* 2011

—Mari Rich

# Magnus Carlsen

**Born:** November 30, 1990
**Occupation:** Professional chess player

The Norwegian chess grandmaster Magnus Carlsen has earned the title "the Mozart of chess"—first conferred upon him by the renowned Czech American chess player and columnist Lubomir Kavalek—for his effortless talents and triumphs in the "royal game." Known for his prodigious memory and his unconventional and intuitive playing style, Carlsen has earned numerous distinctions since bursting onto the international chess scene as a young teenager in the early twenty-first century. In 2004, at just thirteen years of age, he became one of the youngest grandmasters in the history of chess, and by 2010, at age nineteen, he had become the youngest player ever to top the world chess rankings. Carlsen further made history in 2012, when he broke the record for the world's highest rating by the World Chess Federation (also known as the FIDE, or Fédération internationale des échecs). Garry Kasparov, arguably the greatest chess player of all time, and the man whose rating record Carlsen surpassed, told Eben Harrell for *Time* (11 Jan. 2010) that Carlsen, whom

EPA/Toussaint Kluiters /Landov

he has coached and mentored, has a "deep intuitive sense no computer can teach" and "a natural feel for where to place the pieces."

Carlsen, who has achieved a level of celebrity rarely seen in his sport, will try to add to his legacy in November 2013, when he is scheduled to challenge the Indian chess grandmaster and reigning world champion Viswanathan Anand at the sport's most prestigious tournament, the World Chess Championship, in Chennai, India. Anand told D. T. Max for the *New Yorker* (21 Mar. 2011) that Carlsen is "capable of being many different players. He can be tactical. He can be positional. He can be many things." Meanwhile, Kasparov added to Harrell, "Before he is done . . . [he] will have changed our ancient game considerably."

### EARLY LIFE

The second of four children, Carlsen was born Sven Magnus Øen Carlsen on November 30, 1990, in Tønsberg, Norway, to parents who were both engineers. His father, Henrik, was a respectable tournament-level chess player who was well known in Norway for organizing chess events. The game of chess is far from a national pastime in Norway, unlike in countries like Russia, but Henrik Carlsen nonetheless tried to teach the game to his young children, who, in addition to Magnus, include daughters Ellen, Ingrid, and Signe. Magnus initially showed little interest in chess and instead directed his energy toward other activities.

By all accounts, Carlsen's extraordinary intellectual gifts were apparent from the time he was a toddler. At the age of two he displayed "prodigious problem-solving and memory skills," as Stephen Moss noted for the London

*Guardian* (10 Mar. 2013), reportedly being able to complete fifty-piece jigsaw puzzles, as well as recite the names of every automobile brand. At four he was building sprawling cities out of Lego blocks and soon afterward he was memorizing facts about every country in the world. As a boy, Carlsen demonstrated a preternatural ability to focus single-mindedly on a task until he mastered it, but if "you had told him to do something that he wasn't motivated to do, he wouldn't do it," his father explained to Moss.

Carlsen mustered the motivation to play chess only after his sister, Ellen, who is a year older, started playing. Driven by a desire to beat her, he learned the basic rules of the game, which he found to be "just a richer and more complicated game than any other," as he told D. T. Max. Carlsen soon beat his sister, prompting her to quit, and immersed himself in chess, studying for two to three hours a day and devouring his father's wealth of literature about the game. He played in his first tournament at the age of eight, and by nine, he was good enough to beat his father, who promptly arranged for him to further develop his skills under the tutelage of chess instructor Torbjørn Ringdal Hansen, an FIDE-ranked international master (IM) and former Norwegian junior champion.

### TRAINING AND SCHOOLING

Carlsen, who was also involved in soccer, skiing, and ski-jumping as a youth, began studying several hours a week with Hansen, who taught him some of the finer points of the game, such as strategic board positions and moves. Hansen was immediately struck by his pupil's exceptional memory and the ease with which he grasped the complexities of the game. "It didn't take long before it got more and more difficult for me to win," Hansen recalled to D. T. Max. Carlsen studied with Hansen for roughly a year, during which he participated in numerous tournaments, mostly against adults whom he routinely beat.

In 2001, after surpassing Hansen, Carlsen began training with grandmaster Simen Agdestein, a former Norwegian chess champion who also played on Norway's national soccer team. Acting more as a guide than a teacher, Agdestein worked mostly on honing Carlsen's discipline while meeting with him several times a month to analyze various tournament and computer games he played in. According to Agdestein, Carlsen, who is part of a generation of players who have received much of their chess training and skills from powerfully advanced computer programs, played in more than seven thousand online games during the four years that Agdestein trained him. Carlsen has for the most part sought out human opponents to play online, but has not entirely been averse to computer chess preparation and instruction; he is not swayed by the traditionalist argument that technology is obliterating the mystique of live chess.

During his time training with Agdestein, Carlsen continued to attend school and participate in other activities like soccer. School and schoolwork in general, however, always took a backseat to Carlsen's chess endeavors. For instance, "If there was an interesting tournament," he explained to Stephen Moss, "I thought there was no reason to go to school instead." In 2003, when he was twelve, Carlsen was pulled out of school for a year to travel with his family around Europe, which helped expand his horizons while simultaneously allowing him to compete in high-level chess tournaments that had largely not been available to him in Norway. By then, he had already reached international master status (the FIDE rank just below grandmaster) and was competing in 150 tournament games a year. Carlsen attended the Norwegian College of Elite Sport, an exclusive secondary school for elite athletes, but left without graduating in 2009 after reportedly losing interest in high school. "We didn't want him to do it," his father told Sarah Lyall for the *New York Times* (8 Apr. 2013), "but he was capable of making his own decisions."

## CHESS GRANDMASTER

By 2004, Carlsen's chess prowess had proved too much for Agdestein, who relinquished his teaching duties after realizing he could no longer take his pupil to a higher level of play. That year, Carlsen, then just thirteen, firmly established himself in the world of chess after a series of exceptional performances at several world-class chess tournaments. At the January 2004 Corus International Tournament (now the Tata Steel Chess Tournament), a prestigious annual event held in the small Dutch town of Wijk aan Zee, he was the winner in his group, losing only one game and achieving the highest rating of all players. Carlsen received the most attention for his play in the deciding game of the tournament, against the Dutch grandmaster Sipke Ernst, in which he made a quick succession of brilliant, unanticipated moves. Carlsen's performance at this tournament led the Czech American grandmaster Lubomir Kavalek, then a chess columnist for the *Washington Post*, to hail him as "the Mozart of chess." Meanwhile, Evgeni Bebchuk, the former head of the Russian Chess Federation, said of the performance, as quoted in the book *Fighting Chess with Magnus Carlsen* (2012) by Adrian Mikhalchishin and Oleg Stetsko, "As a person closely acquainted with the play of all the great grandmasters, I can confidently say that in the history of chess no one has played like this at the age of 13."

Carlsen followed up his performance in Wijk aan Zee with an even more impressive display at the March 2004 Reykjavik Open in Iceland, when he matched wits against two of the most storied chess players in history. First, he defeated Russian former world champion Anatoly Karpov in a game of "blitz chess," in which each player has no more than fifteen minutes to make all of his or her moves. Then, on the day after, he squared off for the first time against Garry Kasparov, Karpov's former longtime adversary and at the time the top-ranked player in the world. In the first of their two games of "rapid chess," another variation of the game in which each player can have anywhere from fifteen to sixty minutes to make all of his or her moves, Carlsen pushed Kasparov to a draw. Carlsen was then quickly defeated by Kasparov in the second game, but he nonetheless made a lasting impression on the Russian legend, who immediately entertained the possibility of training him.

One month after the Reykjavik tournament, at the 2004 Dubai Open Chess Championship in the United Arab Emirates, Carlsen earned a high enough rating to be officially designated a grandmaster by the FIDE. At thirteen years, four months, and twenty-seven days, he became the youngest grandmaster in the world and the second-youngest grandmaster in chess history; he now holds the distinction of being the third-youngest grandmaster in history after India's Parimarjan Negi surpassed his mark by just five days in 2006. Carlsen's history-making achievement earned him an invite to the 2004 FIDE World Chess Championship, held in Tripoli, Libya, where he lost in the first round to Armenian player and current grandmaster Levon Aronian. That loss notwithstanding, Carlsen was the youngest player ever to participate in the tournament. Meanwhile, his status as a chess prodigy helped him land a sponsorship deal with Microsoft, and he quickly received offers from world-renowned chess instructors who wanted to train him.

## RISE TO THE CHESS ELITE

After becoming a grandmaster, Carlsen enjoyed a rapid climb to the top of the world chess rankings. By age fifteen, he was already a full-time chess professional and traveling upwards of 150 days a year; from 2004 to 2008, he moved up nearly 700 places in the official FIDE rating list to a ranking of number six. During this time, Carlsen distinguished himself at a number of highly regarded tournaments, most of which he attended with his father, who began overseeing his career. Among these tournaments was the 2005 Chess World Cup in Khanty-Mansiysk, Russia, where he beat some of the world's top chess players en route to a tenth-place finish, to earn qualification for the 2007 FIDE World Chess Candidates Tournament. (The Candidates is a periodically held tournament that determines who will face the incumbent world champion in a match for the FIDE world chess title.)

In 2006 Carlsen tied for first place with the grandmaster and former Russian champion Alexander Motylevat at the Corus "B" Tournament in Wijk aan Zee, and later that year, he won his first Norwegian title after defeating his former teacher, Simen Agdestein, at the Norwegian Chess Championship in Oslo. Then, in 2007, after performing poorly in his debut playing in the top "A" group at that year's Wijk aan Zee tournament, he placed second at the prestigious Linares International Chess Tournament, in Linares, Spain, behind India's Viswanathan Anand, who would go on to claim the 2007 World Chess Championship. Carlsen was eliminated from that year's championship after being defeated by Levon Aronian in the first round of the Candidates Tournament, but subsequently shared first place with Aronian at the 2008 Corus "A" Group Tournament in Wijk aan Zee. He then finished second at the 2008 Linares tournament, again behind Anand, before adding victories at the Grand Prix and Aerosvit chess tournaments, in Baku, Azerbaijan, and Foros, Ukraine, respectively.

During the years of his meteoric rise, Carlsen continued to hone his chess skills through independent study, as well as through additional training with the Danish grandmaster Peter Heine Nielsen, who helped him expand his opening repertoire. Unlike many chess players, who try to quickly dismantle their opponents at the beginning stages of a match with extensive, carefully planned opening moves, Carlsen is known to approach his matches without having any clear-cut plan in mind, using a wide variety of openings and styles and favoring protracted positional battles that wear down his opponents. He explained to Mark Lewis for the Associated Press (6 May 2013) that his goal "is to make sure I get a playable position [in the opening] and then the main battle is going to happen in the middle game and the later game." Carlsen's prowess in the endgame, the point of the game when only a few pieces are left on the board, has been referred to as the "Carlsen effect," a phrase first coined by the British grandmaster Jon Speelman. As noted by Malcolm Pein for the London *Telegraph* (11 Mar. 2013), Speelman explained in *New in Chess* magazine that "[Carlsen] plays on forever, calmly, methodically and, perhaps most importantly of all, without fear: calculating superbly, with very few outright mistakes and a good proportion of the 'very best' moves. This makes him a monster and makes many opponents wilt." Carlsen can reportedly calculate anywhere from fifteen to twenty moves ahead and effortlessly play multiple games at a time while blindfolded.

## WORLD NUMBER ONE

Carlsen made it apparent that he wanted to take his chess game to an even greater level in 2009, when he began training under Garry Kasparov, who had retired from serious competitive chess in 2005 and led previous unsuccessful efforts to train him. Under Kasparov, Carlsen further expanded his opening repertoire and received guidance on how to prepare for opponents. The union paid immediate dividends, and Carlsen enjoyed the finest year of his career to date, winning four major tournaments and finishing no worse than fifth in seven others. The last of those four wins came at the inaugural December 2009 London Chess Classic, which was held at the Olympia Conference Centre in the West Kensington area of London. The tournament featured eight of the world's top grandmasters and was considered the most competitive chess tournament to be held in London in a quarter century. Less than one month after winning the tournament, on January 1, 2010, Carlsen reached the number one spot in the FIDE world rankings list. At nineteen years and thirty-two days, he became the youngest top-ranked chess player in history, breaking the record previously held by Russia's Vladimir Kramnik. He also became the first number one from a Western country since the late great American world chess champion Bobby Fischer, who held the top spot for a period of fifty-four months in the early 1970s.

After reaching the top spot, Carlsen "won nearly every event" he competed in, "bullying the opposition with a combination of strategic mastery . . . [and] superior physical endurance," Malcolm Pein noted. It was around this time, however, that he parted ways with Kasparov, whose strong personality proved too much for Carlsen's own. Carlsen said to D. T. Max about Kasparov, who also commanded an annual salary of several hundred thousand dollars a year, "I felt like every day I just had to build up my energy to be able to face him." Difficult professional decisions notwithstanding, Carlsen won a total of six major tournaments in 2010, closing out the year with another win at the London Chess Classic, but opted to skip out on the 2011 Candidates Tournament due to differences over its playing format. As a result, he did not compete for the world title at the 2012 World Chess Championship in Moscow, Russia, which Viswanathan Anand won for his third title defense.

Despite his absence from the game's most prestigious tournament, in 2012 Carlsen would achieve the highest FIDE Elo rating in history. (Created in 1960 by the Hungarian-born physics professor and master-level chess player Arpad Elo, the Elo rating system is the official FIDE method for measuring a player's skills.) With his win at that year's London Chess Classic, Carlsen increased his overall Elo rating to 2861, breaking his former teacher Garry Kasparov's record of 2851, which had stood since 1999 and been considered the most coveted record in chess. In the process he officially became rated the strongest chess player of all time.

In February 2013, after winning the Tata Steel Chess Tournament in Wijk aan Zee, Carlsen reached a peak Elo rating of 2872. The following month he played in the 2013 Candidates Tournament in London, which he won after defeating the former Russian world champion Vladimir Kramnik in a tiebreak. In November 2013, Carlsen will square off against Anand at the World Chess Championship, to be held in Chennai, India, in a match to determine the next world chess champion.

In addition to his high-profile status in the chess world, Carlsen has crossed over into mainstream popular culture as the face of twenty-first century chess. Sarah Lyall wrote, "Chess has its superstars, but on a wider stage, there is no one like Carlsen. . . . Not since the days of Fischer, Kasparov and Karpov has a player managed to move so deftly beyond the world of chess into the world at large." Unlike most chess players, Carlsen has a full-time manager and has secured lucrative sponsorship deals worth upwards of a million dollars per year. He has also modeled clothes for the Dutch fashion house G-Star RAW, made guest appearances on such television programs as CBS's *60 Minutes* and Comedy Central's *The Colbert Report*, and conducted chess exhibitions all over the world in efforts to broaden the appeal of the game beyond its esoteric realm. Carlsen is regarded as an icon in his native Norway and was named one of the world's one hundred most influential people by *Time* magazine in 2013.

## PERSONAL LIFE

D. T. Max described Carlsen as having a "baby face that is quickly solidifying into that of a young man" and "the same loose sandy locks as [the pop star] Justin Bieber." Carlsen lives in an apartment in his parents' house in Baerum, an affluent suburb of Oslo. He spends most of the year traveling but enjoys playing video games, online poker, watching sports, and working out in his spare time. Carlsen has had little time for dating due to his peripatetic lifestyle, but has not ruled out the possibility of settling down one day. He explained to Stephen Moss, "It's hard to sustain relationships when I'm travelling all the time, so most of my flings, if you would call them that, have been fairly short-lived. Perhaps as I get older I will find something stable and long-lasting."

## SUGGESTED READING

Harrell, Eben. "A Bold Opening for Chess Player Magnus Carlsen." *Time*. Time, 11 Jan. 2010. Web. 29 Apr. 2013.

Lyall, Sarah. "Shrewd Marketing Moves for Top-Ranked Chess Player." *New York Times*. New York Times, 8 Apr. 2013. Web. 29 Apr. 2013.

"Magnus Carlsen." *Magnuscarlsen.com*. Magnus Carlsen, 2012. Web. 29 Apr. 2013.

Max, D. T. "The Prince's Gambit." *New Yorker*. Conde Nast, 21 Mar. 2011. Web. 29 Apr. 2013.

Mikhalchishin, Adrian, and Oleg Stetsko. *Fighting Chess with Magnus Carlsen*. Zurich: Edition Olms, 2012. Print.

Moss, Stephen. "Chess Prodigy Magnus Carlsen Enters Endgame for World Title." *Guardian*. Guardian News and Media, 10 Mar. 2013. Web. 29 Apr. 2013.

Pein, Malcolm. "Norwegian Chess Prodigy Magnus Carlsen Sets Sights on Right to Play for World Championship." *Telegraph*. Telegraph Media Group, 11 Mar. 2013. Web. 29 Apr. 2013.

—*Chris Cullen*

# Majora Carter

**Born:** October 27, 1966
**Occupation:** Urban revitalization strategist

In 2006, when Majora Carter took the stage at the California-based TED conference, an annual invitation-only gathering of innovative thinkers and influential public figures, she was wearing a T-shirt exhorting the audience to "Green the Ghetto." She explained that she was fighting for environmental justice because "no community should be saddled with more environmental burdens and less environmental benefits than any other." She asserted that many minority or low-income communities, including her native South Bronx, were suffering from just that fate. "Unfortunately, race and class are extremely reliable indicators of where one might find the good stuff, like parks and trees, and the bad stuff, like power plants and waste facilities." Explaining the motivation behind her push for environmental justice, Carter said "economic degradation begets environmental degradation, which begets social degradation."

Carter is the founder of the nonprofit group Sustainable South Bronx (SSBx), whose accomplishments include spearheading the $3 million Hunts Point Riverside Park, a green oasis bordering the Bronx River on what had once been a desolate garbage-choked site, and the creation of the Bronx Environmental Stewardship Training (BEST) program, which educates local residents in such skills as green construction and waterway restoration. Now head of the for-profit Majora Carter Group, she works as a private consultant in order to help other community groups, businesses, and city governments attain similar results.

## EARLY LIFE

Majora Carter was born on October 27, 1966, in the New York City borough of the Bronx.

© James Leynse/Corbis

when teachers or fellow students referred disparagingly to the South Bronx. "The common perception was that only pimps, [drug] pushers, and prostitutes came from the South Bronx," she told Doyle.

Carter graduated from high school in 1984 and left for Middletown, Connecticut, where she attended Wesleyan University, which had been founded in the 1830s as a Methodist liberal-arts school. Explaining why she had chosen the more suburban setting of Connecticut, she told Laine Bergeson for the magazine *Experience L!fe* (Oct. 2008), "I didn't want to be associated with a place that had the stigma of being the poster child for urban blight." Carter graduated from Wesleyan in 1988 with a bachelor's degree in film studies.

## RETURNING TO THE BRONX

Following graduation, Carter moved back to the South Bronx to live with her parents in order to afford graduate school. Having been away from her old neighborhood for years, Carter—who ultimately earned her master of fine arts degree in 1997 from New York University—was uncomfortable; she walked to and from the subway briskly, not taking the time to reacquaint herself with her surroundings, and she stayed in Manhattan as late as possible before returning to her childhood home.

That changed when she met one of the people who had started the POINT Community Development Corporation, a youth organization devoted to the arts that was right down the block from her parents' house. She was shocked. She walked by the building on a regular basis but had never noticed it, so intent was she to get to the subway and leave the neighborhood behind. A visual artist and poet, she decided to become involved, and she began to organize various public art projects under the auspices of the group, including the first-ever South Bronx-based film festival and an initiative called "Street Trees," in which participants installed sculptures made of scrap metal and found objects on blocks devoid of greenery. Carter started to think seriously about settling down in her old neighborhood permanently.

## BECOMING AN ENVIRONMENTAL ACTIVIST

While she was volunteering at the POINT, Carter became distressed by New York mayor Rudolph Giuliani's plans to build a new waste transfer station in Hunts Point. With no rigorous environmental review and no input from the community, the mayor had seemingly decided to shut down Fresh Kills, a major landfill on Staten Island, and relocate a portion of the operations to the South Bronx, which was already handling some 40 percent of the city's commercial waste and was home to a sewage sludge pelletizing plant, a sewage treatment plant, and four power

Her father was the son of a freed slave and was a Pullman porter who later worked as a janitor in a juvenile detention facility. He and Carter's mother hailed from the Deep South but moved to a South Bronx neighborhood known as Hunts Point in the 1940s, becoming one of the few black families in the white, working-class area. That changed as more African American residents moved in, and Caucasian families decamped to suburban areas in a phenomenon commonly referred to as "white flight."

Carter is the youngest of ten children. By the time she was attending Head Start, a federal program for pre-school children from low-income families, Hunts Point had become a hotbed of crime, pollution, and poverty. "I watched half of the buildings in my neighborhood burn down," she told Andrea Doyle for *Convene* magazine (Dec. 2006). "My brother Lenny fought in Vietnam only to come home and be gunned down a few blocks from our home. I grew up with a crack house across the street."

## HIGH SCHOOL AND COLLEGE

Carter, who attended local primary schools, won admission to the Bronx High School of Science, one of the most competitive public high schools in the New York City system. The school, located in the northern section of the Bronx, boasts numerous Nobel laureates as alumni. While Carter appreciated the academic opportunities and more peaceful milieu, she was bothered plants. Some 60,000 trash trucks passed through the area every week, emitting toxic diesel fumes.

Carter had previously shown little interest in the environment. She frequently quips to journalists that growing up, she thought the word *environment* did not apply to her own urban ecosystem: When she visited extended family in the suburbs of New Jersey, their backyards and gardens constituted an "environment," not the grimy streets of Hunts Point. Still, her interest—and ire—were piqued by the news of Giuliani's machinations. "I began to realize that if we're not actively meeting the environmental needs of our community, then all the art in the world isn't gonna help," she told Amanda Griscom Little for *Grist* (29 Sept. 2006).

Carter began by staging street protests, sometimes marching while wearing garbage bags festooned with old aluminum cans. She later characterized such efforts as "cute" and eventually decided that in order to be taken seriously by those in positions of power, she needed to be involved in a more substantive way. She organized boat trips along the Bronx River (the only freshwater river in the entire city) and mobilized tours of the waste treatment plants and other facilities that were polluting the neighborhood. Giuliani's plans were ultimately quashed.

## SUSTAINABLE SOUTH BRONX
In 2001 Carter founded Sustainable South Bronx "not as a moral crusade, but as an economic-development group that was about planning our future, not just reacting to the environmental blight," she told Little. "I wanted to give our community permission to dream, to plan for healthy air, healthy jobs, healthy children, and safe streets."

Winning a seed grant of $10,000 from a city-run agency called the Partnership for Parks, Carter was charged with trying to revitalize a section of the Bronx River waterfront. She remembers thinking that the administrators were well-meaning but somewhat naïve. How, she wondered, could a section of the waterfront be revitalized when access to the river was blocked by industrial facilities and illegal dumping grounds?

Then, one day Carter was walking her dog Xena who began pulling Carter through a debris-strewn lot at the dead end of gritty Lafayette Avenue that Carter assumed would lead to one dismal eyesore or another. When she reached the end of the lot, however, she was in for a surprise. "I was totally amazed—there I was standing on waterfront property completely unobstructed by highways, warehouses, and factories," she told Little. "Within weeks I'd dashed out the first proposal to convert this area into a waterfront park." Over the course of the next five years, Carter saw the $10,000 in seed money increase to more than $3 million as word of her mission

spread among city officials and she became adept at navigating New York's political maze.

In the meantime, volunteers cleaned up the site and it became an unofficial meeting spot for various groups, including a nonprofit called Rocking the Boat, an environmental education initiative that teaches urban teens to build and operate wooden boats. Rocking the Boat had previously been launching their crafts at a park almost thirty minutes away from the nearest subway station.

New York City Parks Department landscape architects also got to work, and soon trees were planted to block the surrounding industrial facilities from sight. An amphitheater with carved stone seats was constructed, and a whimsical nautical-themed play area with fountains was erected near a graveled beach leading down to the river.

## HUNTS POINT RIVERSIDE PARK
In mid-2007, Hunts Point Riverside Park, the first waterfront park in the South Bronx in six decades, was opened to the public. Carter's favorite feature of the project was a group of bushes that attracted swarms of monarch butterflies. "If you had lived through the fires and the abandonment and the drugs and the death, you would have as hard a time as I do believing there would be butterflies here," she told Linda McIntyre for *Landscape Architecture* (Dec. 2007).

Carter has pointed out that the park is much more than a mere recreational area and has the potential to have an enormous impact on the health of those living in Hunts Point. "As a black person in America, I am twice as likely as a white person to live in an area where air pollution poses the greatest risk to my health; I am five times more likely to live within walking distance from a power plant or chemical facility, which I do," she wrote for the Summer 2006 issue of *Race, Poverty and the Environment*. "These land-use decisions create the hostile conditions that lead to problems like obesity, diabetes, and asthma. Why would someone leave their home to go for a brisk walk in a toxic neighborhood?" The editors of *Prevention* magazine agreed, dubbing her a Health Hero in 2007.

The Hunts Point Riverside Park was just the first step in the burgeoning Bronx greenway movement, a push to construct an ambitious network of waterfront and on-street routes connecting the borough's parks. When it is completed, the greenway, which will be accessible to bikes and pedestrians, is expected to encompass 1.5 miles of waterfront, 8.5 miles of new green streets, and almost 12 acres of new waterfront open space.

## OTHER ENVIRONMENTALLY BASED PROJECTS
In 2003 Carter and Sustainable South Bronx initiated a program called Bronx Environmental

Stewardship Training (BEST) in order to teach Hunts Point residents, including many ex-convicts, about environmentally based careers. Participants, the vast majority of whom had been living on public assistance, learned about green construction, urban forestry, park maintenance, and brownfield remediation, among other topics. (The term *brownfield* refers to a site contaminated with hazardous substances or pollutants.) Within two years over one hundred people had graduated from the program; most were placed in jobs, although a small percentage elected to continue their studies in college. The program was funded in part by the Clinton Global Initiative, which was founded by former President Bill Clinton.

Some of the BEST participants helped install a new 3,000-square foot roof on the historic American Banknote Company Building that houses SSBx's office. Called the South Bronx Green and Cool Roofs Demonstration Project, it was the first roof of its kind in the city. (Later, Carter installed a green roof on her own brownstone, which became the first private home in the city with that feature.) To construct a green roof, wildflowers and greens are planted to replace the tar-based materials generally used on the city's housing stock. The plants reduce heat in the summer, provide insulation in the winter, improve air quality, and divert storm water that can cause sewer overflow. Although such roofs are more expensive to install, they last longer than conventional roofs and can pay for themselves through energy savings.

### PRIVATE CONSULTING AND MEDIA WORK
In 2006, Carter brought her environmental awareness to a worldwide virtual audience with the seminar titled "Greening the Ghetto," which was one of the first six publicly released video conferences that launched the popular TED.com website. Since then, Carter, an engaging and lively speaker known for her infectious smile and thick dreadlocks, has also enjoyed frequent stints as a radio host and media commentator. Her projects have included HBO's *The Black List*, American Public Media's *Market Place*, and PRX's *This I Believe* series. She has also hosted segments on urban sustainability for the Science Channel and has appeared on *The Green*, which aired on Robert Redford's Sundance Channel. In 2008 Carter began hosting the Peabody Award–winning public-radio program *The Promised Land*, which profiles innovative thinkers who are changing their communities.

In 2008 Carter left SSBx to found a private, for-profit consulting firm, the Majora Carter Group. Her mission is to apply the lessons she learned in Hunts Point to other locales. "There are South Bronxes in every part of the world," she told Juleyka Lantigua for *Giant Magazine* (July 2009). "They look different, but share poverty, environmentally borne health problems and a similar degree of hopelessness for poor residents." The group advises clients on how to encourage community engagement, create green jobs, and define a communications strategy.

Among the high-profile organizations with which Carter has collaborated is Brad Pitt's Make It Right Foundation, which is endeavoring to revitalize New Orleans's Lower Ninth Ward destroyed by Hurricane Katrina. In 2012, grocery-delivery service FreshDirect hired Carter's consulting firm to help with its controversial plan to place a massive distribution facility in the South Bronx, subsidized by $130 million in public funds. Many South Bronx residents and activist groups such as South Bronx Unite felt the noxious fumes from the delivery trucks would further pollute the air in a neighborhood where asthma rates are six times the national average. It was hoped that Carter's influence and reputation in the Bronx would ease the company's transition to the area.

### AWARDS AND HONORS
In 2005 Carter won a John D. and Catherine T. MacArthur Foundation Fellowship, commonly referred to as a "genius grant," for "profoundly transforming the quality of life for South Bronx residents," as the award citation noted. The prestigious fellowship included a $500,000 stipend. "She is probably the only person to receive an award from John Podesta's [liberal] Center for American Progress, and a Liberty Medal for Lifetime Achievement from [conservative] Rupert Murdoch's *New York Post*," her official American Public Media bio jokes.

Among her many other accolades are former Bronx borough president Adolfo Carrión Jr.'s Bronx Super Hero title (2000), an Open Society Institute New York City Community Fellowship (2001), a NYC Council/Women's History Month Pacesetter Award (2002), a United States Department of Energy Clean Cities Award (2003), a National Audubon Society Rachel Carson Award (2007), a New York State Women of Excellence Award (2007), the Eleanor Roosevelt Val-Kill Medal (2008), an honorary doctoral degree from the City University of New York (2009), the Grey Panthers' Award for Environmental Justice (2010), the Brooklyn Botanic Gardens Better Earth Award (2011), and the Italy's Parchi Monumentali Bardini e Peyron Foundation Monito del Giardino Award (2012).

### PERSONAL LIFE
On October 7, 2006, Carter married James Burling Chase, a filmmaker who served as her communications director at Sustainable South Bronx. He serves in the same capacity at the Majora Carter Group. Although the Hunts Point Riverside Park was not yet fully completed at the time, their wedding ceremony was held there.

In late 2012, Carter's dog, Xena, died of kidney failure. Carter credits her late pet with discovering the site for the park that helped direct the course of her career.

Although she is now running a private firm instead of a nonprofit, Carter's mission remains the same. "People [in places like the South Bronx] aren't going to install solar panels on their roofs or drive a Prius, but they can demand institutional change and decent business practices," she once told Karen Breslau for *Newsweek* (24 Dec. 2006).

## SUGGESTED READING

Aston, Adam. "Majora Carter: Greener Neighborhoods, Sustainable Jobs." *BusinessWeek.* Bloomberg LP, 27 Oct. 2008. Web. 26 Feb. 2013.

Bergeson, Laine. "An Artful Activist." *Experience L!fe.* Lifetime Fitness, Oct. 2008. Web. 9 Mar. 2013.

Carter, Majora. "Green Is the New Black." *Race, Poverty, the Environment.* Urban Habitat, 2006. Web. 9 Mar. 2013.

Clowney, David, and Patricia Mosto, eds. *Earthcare: An Anthology in Enviornmental Ethics.* Lanham: Rowman, 2009. 319–21. Print.

Doyle, Andrea. "Not Your Ordinary Environmental Leader." *Convene* Dec. 2006: 78–83. Print.

Holloway, Marguerite. "The Green Power Broker." *New York Times.* New York Times Co., 12 Dec. 2008. Web. 11 Mar. 2013.

McIntyre, Linda. "Parks Come to the Point." *Landscape Architecture.* American Society of Landscape Architects, Dec. 2007. Web. 9 Mar. 2013.

Piperato, Susan. "Green the Ghetto." *Yoga + Joyful Living* Mar./Apr. 2008: 48. Print.

Royte, Elizabeth. "A Bronx Tale." *Elle* May 2006: 223. Print.

Waldman, Amy. "A Dreamer, Working for Beauty in the South Bronx." *New York Times.* New York Times Co., 15 Aug. 2001. Web. 26 Feb. 2013.

—*Mari Rich*

# Neko Case

**Born:** September 8, 1970
**Occupation:** Singer-songwriter

Neko Case is a Grammy Award–nominated singer-songwriter who has achieved success as a solo artist with her unique blend of folk-tinged rock and alternative-country styles. A member of the Canadian pop band the New Pornographers, Case has also teamed up with Canadian singer Carolyn Mark—as the Corn Sisters, they recorded the raucous *The Other Women* in

Jordan Strauss/Invision/AP

2000. Other collaborators have included the alt-country band, the Sadies, who appear on Case's live record *The Tigers Have Spoken* (2004), and Garth Hudson of the Band, who plays piano, organ, and accordion on several tracks of Case's record *Fox Confessor Brings the Flood* (2006).

As for Case herself, she has been compared to Patsy Cline, the patron saint of country singers; rock-and-roll singer Stevie Nicks; and, strangely and frequently, the filmmaker David Lynch. Case's strong voice is classic country, but her writing influences are anything but. Reappearing images—knives, predatory animals, tornadoes, and dark fairy tales—baffle and then transfix listeners. As Tom Moon, for the National Public Radio (NPR) program *All Things Considered* (7 Apr. 2006), put it, Case "uses [her] voice as a lure to bring listeners inside her surreal, fantastical songs, where the normal becomes grotesque in the blink of an eye."

After a rough adolescence, Case got her start in music as a stand-in drummer in a punk band. She eventually worked her way to the microphone and struck a record deal with the indie label Mint Records to record her first album. Her six studio albums to date have been critically successful, and for an indie musician who has turned down several major record deals, she fares well commercially too. This can be attributed in part to her dual career with the New Pornographers, but the primary cause of Case's success seems to be the talent and unique sound of the artist herself. Case has honed her sound over the years, developing a musical style that is completely her own. She has said that of any label that has been applied to her, she prefers the made-up term "country noir."

## EARLY LIFE AND EDUCATION

Case was born in Alexandria, Virginia, on September 8, 1970, though she spent her childhood living all over the Northwest. She considers Spanaway, a suburb of Tacoma, Washington, her hometown. Her parents, both Ukrainian immigrants, were very young when she was born, and they divorced when Case was only five or six years old. After that, Case divided her time between her father, an unhappy man who abused drugs and alcohol, and her mother and stepfather. The family as a whole was very poor. "Government-issue American cheese was a treat," Case told Daniel Menaker for the *New York Times* (15 Feb. 2009). She spent a lot of time with her grandparents, Mary Ann and Clyde Windon, and even dedicated her first album to them. Mary Ann listened to country records while Case was growing up but confessed to a reporter that prior to the release of Case's first album, she did not know her granddaughter could sing.

By the time Case was a teenager, she had drifted away from her parents. She lived in the basement of a friend's family's house, and at the age of fifteen, she left Tacoma for good. She spent some time absorbing the Northwest punk scene that was then in its heyday. After completing her GED, Case managed to borrow enough money to attend the Emily Carr Institute of Art and Design in Vancouver, British Columbia, where she studied photography, sculpture, and printmaking. "I was a mad kid," she told Menaker, but it was her anger that convinced her that she needed to pursue something in her life. "I was sick of being poor. I was sick of being a girl. I felt completely unimportant, I didn't matter to the world, and I was just going to get love any way I could."

## EARLY CAREER AND SOLO DEBUT

Case began her musical career as a drummer for several Tacoma and Vancouver punk bands, including the Propanes, the Del Logs, Cub, and Maow. She began singing with Maow but eventually left to perform with the group Neko Case and Her Boyfriends—a band featuring members of other indie bands such as Zumpano, the Softies, and Shadowy Men on a Shadowy Planet. The musicians in Her Boyfriends were ever changing and also included, at one time or another, members of Super Friendz, Untamed Youths, and Model Rockets. "I don't know if I ever realized I was a good singer," she told David Bauder for the Associated Press (30 May 2006) of her first experience singing for a crowd in Toledo, Ohio, in 1993. "I just realized that I wanted to sing."

Although Case was introduced to country artists such as George Jones and Loretta Lynn during her childhood, her first solo album, 1997's *The Virginian*, won her more comparisons to Patsy Cline and rockabilly star Wanda Jackson. Case's transition from punk to a traditional country sound was the result of a number of diverse influences, including Lynn, the Everly Brothers, the Louvin Brothers duo, and Sheila E., who worked with Prince. "I didn't think anyone would notice it," Case told George Lang for the *Daily Oklahoman* (26 Jan. 2001) of her album released through Mint Records in Vancouver. "I just wanted to make a recording, and I had never done it before. I like all kinds of music—there isn't just one thing, and I picked songs that I really felt passionate about." The record contains both original songs and covers, including Lynn's "Somebody Led Me Away" and the Everly Brothers' "Bowling Green."

### FURNACE ROOM LULLABY

Case's next record, *Furnace Room Lullaby* (2000), was a stark departure from her first album—a risk she would not have been able to take with a major label. The record showcased, for the first time, Case's more gothic side; she sings, for example, about murdering boyfriends and disposing of their dismembered remains in a large basement furnace. *Furnace Room Lullaby* was produced by Darryl Neudorf of Mint Records, a small company formed in the early 1990s, and features appearances by the Sadies and Canadian singer-songwriter Ron Sexsmith. While recording the album, Case learned to play the tenor guitar; she now boasts a formidable collection of the instrument.

The album was the first taste of mainstream success for both Case and Mint. It was reviewed by major publications such as *Rolling Stone*, *Spin*, and *TIME*. The *New York Times* included it in its list of the ten best albums of the year. Despite the positive critical reception of both *The Virginian* and *Furnace Room Lullaby*—as well as the overwhelming country influence on both records—the country music industry did not take an interest in Case. She has even been banned for life from the industry's mecca, the Grand Ole Opry in Nashville, Tennessee. In 2002 she performed at an outdoor stage at the Opry, where it was so hot that she removed her shirt and played the rest of the set in her bra. "I wasn't trying to be sexy or rebellious," she told Neva Chonin for *Rolling Stone* (31 Oct. 2002). "I was just getting heatstroke up there." Case reportedly tried to make amends but was unsuccessful, and if anything, the incident helped cement her reputation and credibility as an outsider.

## QUEEN OF COUNTRY NOIR

In 2001, Case self-released an extended play (EP) called *Canadian Amp*—a tribute, she told the *Fretboard Journal* in 2006, to the vintage Garnet tube amp. The album features covers of songs originally performed by Hank Williams and Neil Young, among others; indie musician

Andrew Bird plays violin on the record. By her third studio release, *Blacklisted* (2002), Case was living and recording in Chicago. (She insists the title of the album has nothing to do with Nashville or the Opry.) Sasha Frere-Jones, the music critic for the *New Yorker* (16 Mar. 2009), described the album—in the larger sense of Case's career—as "her last and best iteration of the countrified middle ground." Frere-Jones contends that *Blacklisted* marks Case's shift from country-style music (twangy waltzes and mid-century Nashville ballads) to something else entirely—something Case might call "country noir." After *Blacklisted*, Case's verses became longer and more complex; she used traditional country hallmarks such as reverb and the waltz time signature, but to a different, fuller, and, as Kaulkin said, more cinematic effect.

In 2004 Case released a live album with the Sadies and Kelly Hogan titled *The Tigers Have Spoken*. The record mostly features covers, including versions of "Rated X" by Lynn, "Loretta" by the Nervous Eaters, "Soulful Shade of Blue" by Buffy Sainte-Marie, and "Train from Kansas City" by the Shangri-Las. Case recorded the album over several nights at shows in Chicago and Toronto.

Case released *Fox Confessor Brings the Flood* in 2006. The title of the album refers to a mythical creature from dark Eastern European fairy tales, and the content is satisfyingly strange. The record features a number of musicians and singers in Case's circle, including the Sadies, Joey Burns of Calexico, Howe Gelb of Giant Sand, Rachel Flotard of Visqueen, Hogan, and Garth Hudson of the legendary group the Band. More atmospheric than her previous records, the album was recorded over two years. Case said the extra time was beneficial to the work as a whole, and Frere-Jones seemed to agree. "[The record] is in some ways the first Neko Case album," he wrote. *Fox Confessor* sold about two hundred thousand copies in the United States.

Case's most recent studio release, *Middle Cyclone*, debuted at number three on the Billboard chart in March 2009. It was the highest debut for an indie record that year. Though it was inspired by a dream in which she befriended a tornado, the record is anything but whimsical. To make it, Case shut herself away on her hundred-acre farm in Vermont, recording the entire album in her barn. Among other instruments, Case stocked the makeshift studio with eight pianos that she acquired for free through the Internet—of the eight, she has admitted that only six were tunable. The pianos appear most prominently on the track "Don't Forget Me," a Harry Nilsson cover. The album's other cover song, keeping with the environmental theme of the title, is "Never Turn Your Back on Mother Earth," by the 1970s band Sparks. "The foundations of Case's music are still—somewhere down there, almost subterranean—country and indie rock," Menaker wrote of *Middle Cyclone*, "but for some time now her melodies have been growing more complex, the instrumentations more varied and ambitious, the modulations more surprising, the lyrics more imagistic." The album was nominated for two Grammy Awards: best contemporary folk album and best recording package.

## THE NEW PORNOGRAPHERS

Case met the members of the pop band the New Pornographers in Vancouver around the time she began recording her own music in 1997. The two endeavors could not be more different for Case. Singing with the band, Case told Kate McCaffrey for the *Pittsburgh Post-Gazette* (30 July 2006), is "like being in spinning class for hours or going to rock 'n' roll Six Flags." Despite the differences between her musical projects, she added, "I honestly can't imagine one without the other."

In addition to Case, the New Pornographers is made up of A. C. Newman, Dan Bejar, Blaine Thurier, John Collins, Todd Fancey, Kurt Dahle, and Kathryn Calder. Of the band members, most, like Case, have their own solo projects. Rob Mitchum, for the online music magazine *Pitchfork* (21 Aug. 2005), called the New Pornographers not "so much a band as a Davis Cup team of Canada's finest indie singer-songwriters." When they record an album, the band sends Case the songs in advance and she meets them in the studio, usually for only three or four days of recording. To date, the New Pornographers have released five studio albums: *Mass Romantic* (2000), *Electric Version* (2003), *Twin Cinema* (2005), *Challengers* (2007), and *Together* (2010). Mitchum called *Mass Romantic* a pop classic and deemed *Twin Cinema* the group's most satisfying offering, writing, "Whether it's weaving in opaque, double-meaning lyrics or sneaking a horn part way deep in the mix, the compositions on *Twin Cinema* are immediate yet multilayered. They'd be great in their own right, but by comparison to the plagiaristic, close-minded, infinitely repeating world of power pop, it's all the more special an accomplishment."

## PERSONAL LIFE

Case is a vocal proponent of abortion rights and the humane treatment of animals. At one time, she adopted three rescued greyhounds from the Tucson Greyhound Park racetrack. Though she spends much of the year on tour, she spends much of her remaining time at her farm in Vermont.

In the spring of 2013 Case was working on her next album, tentatively titled *The Worse Things Get, the Harder I Fight. The Harder I Fight, the More I Love You.* NPR aired several segments chronicling Case's process of making the record.

## SELECTED RECORDINGS

*The Virginian* (with Her Boyfriends), 1997; *Furnace Room Lullaby* (with Her Boyfriends), 2000; *Canadian Amp*, 2001; *Blacklisted*, 2002; *The Tigers Have Spoken* (with the Sadies), 2004; *Fox Confessor Brings the Flood*, 2006; *Middle Cyclone*, 2009

## SUGGESTED READING

Chonin, Neva. "Country Lust." *Rolling Stone* 31 Oct. 2002: 44. Print.

Frere-Jones, Sasha. "The Winds: Neko Case Is the Horn Section." *New Yorker*. Condé Nast, 16 Mar. 2009. Web. 11 Apr. 2013.

Lang, George. "Movin' On Neko Case Changes Scenes." *NewsOK*. NewsOK.com, 26 Jan. 2001. Web. 9 Apr. 2013.

Menaker, Daniel. "Wild Thing." *New York Times*. New York Times, 15 Feb. 2009. Web. 8 Apr. 2013.

Moon, Tom. "Neko Case Continues to Shift on 'Fox Confessor.'" Narr. Melissa Block and Tom Moon. *All Things Considered*. Natl. Public Radio, 7 Apr. 2006. Web. 9 Apr. 2013. Transcript.

—*Molly Hagan*

# Julián Castro

**Born:** September 16, 1974
**Occupation:** Politician and mayor of San Antonio, Texas

When Julián Castro was first elected mayor of San Antonio, Texas—the seventh-largest city in the United States—in 2009 at the age of thirty-four, he became the youngest mayor of a major US city. In 2012, he became the first person of Hispanic descent to deliver the keynote address at the Democratic National Convention (DNC). The distinction solidified Castro's status as a rising star in US politics. Many drew comparisons between Castro and Barack Obama, who, as a virtually unknown senator, gave the rousing keynote address that launched his national career in 2004. But as Zev Chafets pointed out in his profile of Castro for the *New York Times* (9 May 2010), Castro was much younger than Obama when he gave his address—at thirty-five, Castro's age when he spoke at the 2012 DNC, Obama was just entering the Illinois State Senate. Despite his relative youth, Castro is not new to politics. He and his identical twin brother, Joaquín, began attending political rallies with their mother, a Chicana activist in the 1970s, when they could barely walk. Joaquín, a rising star in his own right, is now a US representative for Texas's Twentieth Congressional District.

Associated Press

Castro's work has won the admiration of his constituents and other lawmakers, but inevitably, as the grandson of a Mexican immigrant, he represents something much larger. He and his brother, and their mother before them, grew up in near poverty on San Antonio's West Side. Both Castro brothers attended Stanford University and Harvard Law School but returned to their hometown after graduation. Castro even began fundraising for his city council campaign on the Harvard campus in Cambridge, Massachusetts.

His rise to prominence has coincided with the escalation of tensions in the southwestern United States over immigration policies. Those policies, and others affecting the country's growing Latino population, took center stage during the 2012 presidential election. The Republican Party supported stricter immigration laws and a harsh rhetoric regarding undocumented immigrants that alienated a large number of voters. Unsurprisingly, as a voting bloc, Latinos overwhelmingly favored President Obama and the Democratic Party. As both parties grapple with a lack of diversity that does not accurately reflect the country's shifting demographics, many Democrats are hoping that voters will rally around the young and talented Castro, who, by all accounts, has been put on the fast track to national success.

"To be honest, I can see a path to Washington for Julián," his brother told Chafets. "That path leads through the governor's mansion in Austin. A Democrat who can win the governorship of Texas would automatically be under consideration for a spot on the national ticket." A few years ago, Joaquín's speculation would have sounded ludicrous. Texas has long been a Republican stronghold, but as the demographics of the state are changing, so are its politics. Castro could be the candidate to turn Texas blue, or rather, purple. After his keynote there was a movement drafting him to run in the 2014 gubernatorial election, but Castro announced in early 2013 that he will seek a third term as mayor, noting that he hopes to serve a total of four two-year terms. He is careful not to sacrifice public trust for personal ambition. "There's a push-and-pull here," he told Chafets. In San Antonio, "nobody likes people with big heads."

## EARLY LIFE AND EDUCATION

Castro was born on September 16, 1974, and raised on San Antonio's West Side. He is one minute older than his identical twin brother, Joaquín. The boys were raised by their single mother, Chicana activist Maria del Rosario "Rosie" Castro, who introduced them to politics at an early age. Castro's mother was a leader of the civil-rights organization La Raza Unida (RUP), which campaigned for better housing, improved working conditions, and increased educational opportunities for Mexican Americans.

Rosie's mother, Victoria, came to San Antonio from Mexico as an orphan when she was only six years old. Growing up in the impoverished West Side community, Rosie tended to the dogs of a local white family while her mother cleaned houses. Early on, she became aware of the disparities between the city's white residents and its Hispanic residents. Rosie, who earned a master's degree, ran unsuccessfully for city council in 1971, but she is best known as a community organizer and leader and remains an inspirational figure in the community. When Castro and his brother were only toddlers, their mother took them to rallies and events. "Growing up, when we would get dragged to these events, I didn't want to be there," Castro told a reporter for Reuters (4 Sept. 2012). "Over time, as we got older, I developed a real appreciation of the importance of being involved in the democratic process."

The boys grew up in near poverty. They shared a room with each other until they were seventeen—adding fuel to their early sibling rivalry—and sometimes shared with their grandmother as well. The night before the boys were born, Victoria won three hundred dollars in a cooking contest—she made menudo, a Mexican tripe stew. The family used the money to pay Rosie's hospital bill the next day. Rosie and Castro's father, Jesse Guzman, had met through community activism and never married. The couple separated when the boys were eight. Guzman is now a retired teacher, while Rosie works as a student affairs administrator at Palo Alto College in San Antonio.

Castro and his brother attended Jefferson High School, where they played on the tennis team. They both skipped the tenth grade and graduated in 1992, after only three years of high school. Castro was ninth in their graduating class, while Joaquín ranked twenty-seventh. The brothers were inseparable, but they were also notoriously competitive with each other, to the frustration of their mother. Still, they opted to attend the same college, choosing to enroll in Stanford University because the school offered to admit both of them.

## STANFORD AND HARVARD LAW

As a freshman at Stanford University in California, Castro wrote an essay for a professor that was titled "Politics . . . Maybe." It was written in response to a question the professor had posed to Castro's class, Cecilia Ballí wrote for *Texas Monthly* (Oct. 2002): "Do people ever make assumptions about what you'll do after college? How do you feel when they do?" Castro, of course, had grown up the son of a local hero, but he associated politics with dull meetings, speakers, and events that seemed to effect change at a glacial pace. Family friends expected him to enter the same world. "'So, what are you going to do after you finish school?' my mother's friend asks me. 'Uhh. . . .' Can he see my eyes float along the carpet?" the eighteen-year-old Castro wrote, as quoted by Ballí. "Maria del Rosario Castro has never held a political office. However, today, years later, I read the newspapers, and I see that more Valdezes are sitting on school boards, that a greater number of Garcias are now doctors, lawyers, engineers and, of course, teachers." He closed the essay by answering his mother's friend: "Maybe politics." Castro's professor was so impressed by his essay that she arranged for its publication in the textbook *Writing for Change* (1994).

Castro and his brother took an urban politics class with political scientist Luis Fraga. Fraga, who is also of Mexican descent, hails from Corpus Christi, Texas. He became a mentor to the two young men. "They have always been equally able and equally confident in a low-income neighborhood as in a corporate boardroom," Fraga told Reuters of the pair. Leaving their San Antonio home helped them to understand new ways to improve it. The brothers experienced their first political campaign at Stanford, running for student senate during their junior year. They won, both accruing the same number of votes. Castro majored in communications and political science and worked as a White House intern during the summer of 1994. He graduated from Stanford in 1996.

Castro and his brother enrolled in Harvard Law School in 1997. He had been accepted to Yale University, but Joaquín had not, so their choice was clear. Castro joined the school's Hispanic organization, La Alianza, and served on the Law School Council, but his sights were set on his hometown. During school breaks, he returned to San Antonio to meet with city leaders. He hung a map of District 7 in San Antonio on the wall of his room; he had his eye on the city council seat that had eluded his mother in 1971. Castro announced his candidacy for the position during his final year of law school and held his first fundraiser in Cambridge, raising about two thousand dollars. He graduated from Harvard Law in 2000 and was elected to the San Antonio

City Council in 2001, capturing 59 percent of the vote and defeating five other candidates.

## SAN ANTONIO POLITICS

At twenty-six years old, Castro was the youngest council member in San Antonio history. "When Julián was installed, it was just such an incredible thing to be there because for years we had been struggling to be there," his mother told Ballí. "There was so much hurt associated with being on the outside. And I don't mean personal hurt, but a whole group of people had been on the outside—the educational, social, political, economic outside." Castro displayed traits in common with his populist mother, particularly during a debate pertaining to the construction of a golf resort called PGA Village on the city's outer edge, but set himself apart by displaying a quieter demeanor, gaining a reputation for moderation.

The PGA Village debate showcased all of these aspects of Castro's personality. The council was voting to decide whether to create a special tax district for the proposed luxury resort. A vote yes meant that the developer, Lumbermen's Investment Company, would rake in an estimated $52 million at the expense of the city by collecting all property and sales taxes from the district over the next fifteen years. Supporters of the project hoped that the resort would boost employment and tourism. Castro was against the project, but most of the council members, including the mayor, supported the proposal. Still, Castro had his say, methodically stating his case against the project amid high emotions on both sides.

As a lawyer for the prestigious firm Akin Gump Strauss Hauer & Feld, Castro had been asked to abstain from voting on the issue. The firm had drafted the proposed contract, and his vote would be a conflict of interest. Because of his strong feelings on the issue, Castro decided to quit the job to cast his ballot. (He had kept his job at the law firm after winning the city council election because council members were paid only twenty dollars per meeting.) Only one council member voted with Castro against the project, but the debate continued. After Castro's presentation, community activists collected nearly seventy thousand signatures to call a referendum on the issue, eventually prompting the project backers to withdraw their proposal rather than face a citywide vote.

## MAYORAL CAMPAIGNS

Castro's work against the PGA Village earned him a number of fervent supporters, though few of them were from the business community. Regardless, Castro decided to run for mayor in 2005. The previous mayor, Ed Garza, had fulfilled his term limit of two two-year terms (the limit was increased to four two-year terms in 2008) but was also spectacularly unpopular. Garza was also in his early thirties, and his blundering tenure spawned a suggestion that crippled Castro's campaign. "San Antonio needs a grown-up for mayor" was the whisper around town, Jan Jarboe Russell reported for *Texas Monthly* (Dec. 2004).

To make matters worse, Castro was involved in his own minor scandal. Facetiously referred to as "twin-gate," the scandal occurred when Castro made plans to attend the city's annual River Parade but at the last minute did not attend. Joaquín attended the parade but did not correct the announcer who introduced him to the crowd as his brother. The brothers insisted it was a mix-up—Joaquín had planned to attend the event with his brother, and Castro forgot to tell city officials that he would not be there. Some thought the incident was funny, but others thought it was a deceptive and immature prank. Whatever the case, the residents of San Antonio did not immediately forget the incident.

Castro placed first in the runoff election, but was ultimately bested by seventy-year-old former judge Phil Hardberger. This defeat did not discourage Castro, who spent the following years forging friendships with San Antonio business leaders while strengthening his relationship with his working-class base. In 2009, following Hardberger's retirement, Castro ran for mayor again and won in the first round of balloting. He was reelected in 2011 with almost 82 percent of the vote.

## MAYOR

Castro's initiatives as mayor have included an ambitious prekindergarten program and a nonprofit organization that pairs inner-city students with local business leaders and professionals. Such programs address the education gap between the city's Hispanic and non-Hispanic citizens, but Castro has also worked hard to shake the "barrio candidate" label. (*Barrio* means "neighborhood" in Spanish.) So far, his efforts have been successful, a success for which he credits a new generation of bridge builders connecting the diverse communities of San Antonio.

When Castro's mother was running for office in the 1970s, the RUP was chipping away at a political structure that solely installed white candidates promoting the issues of white citizens. Rosie and others like her worked tirelessly for a voice in local government. In turn, they improved race relations in the city and witnessed an increasing number of Mexican Americans working white-collar jobs. Castro is fully aware that he owes his career to that work and believes tremendous progress has been made. "The American dream is not a sprint, or even a marathon, but a relay," Castro said in his DNC keynote address. "Our families don't always cross the finish line in the span of one generation, but each generation passes on to the next the fruits of their labor."

The generational divide between the Castro brothers and their mother is apparent, however. Castro does not speak fluent Spanish, and his approach to politics and social justice is different from that of many of his predecessors. Antonio Gonzalez, of the William C. Velasquez Institute, told Nia-Malika Henderson for the *Washington Post* (1 Aug. 2012), "[Castro] has taken the traditional Latino civil rights agenda, and rather than cast it aside, he's had a modern interpretation of the Latino worldview. He isn't post-racial. He gets the inclusion narrative of an immigrant community, and he doesn't cast race aside. But he broadens the issues to include environment and the economy and the growth of business."

## PERSONAL LIFE

Castro met Erica Lira, a teacher and teaching consultant, one summer when he was home from law school. They dated, mostly long-distance, for eight years and married in 2007. They have a young daughter named Carina, who was born on March 14, 2009, shortly before Castro was elected mayor. Carina stole the show during her father's keynote address at the DNC—the then three-year-old was mesmerized at seeing herself on the Jumbotron.

## SUGGESTED READING

Ballí, Cecilia. "Twins Peak." *Texas Monthly*. Texas Monthly, Oct. 2002. Web. 10 Apr. 2013.

Chafets, Zev. "The Post-Hispanic Hispanic Politician." *New York Times Magazine* 9 May 2010: MM38. Print.

Cornish, Audie. "Julian Castro Brings Post-Racial Politics to DNC." *All Things Considered*. Natl. Public Radio, 4 Sept. 2012. Web. 11 Apr. 2013.

Henderson, Nia-Malika. "Latino Democrat Bound for Spotlight." *Washington Post* 1 Aug. 2012, suburban ed.: A04. Print.

"San Antonio Mayor in Spotlight at Democratic Convention." *Reuters*. Thomson Reuters, 4 Sept. 2012. Web. 11 Apr. 2013.

—*Molly Hagan*

# Tamika Catchings

**Born:** July 21, 1979
**Occupation:** Professional basketball player

Tamika Catchings, a forward for the Indiana Fever of the Women's National Basketball Association (WNBA), is one of the most decorated female basketball players of all time. Known for her energetic and hard-nosed style of play, Catchings emerged in the early 2000s as one of

Anthony Nesmith/CSM/Landov

the most versatile players in the WNBA, standing out for her prowess on both offense and defense. "Catch is a multidimensional player," Lin Dunn, head coach of the Fever, told Cliff Brunt for the Associated Press (14 Sept. 2011). Dunn added, "She gets assists, she gets steals, she gets rebounds, she scores, and she defends like nobody else in the league." Aside from her all-around basketball skills, Catchings stands out from her peers and most athletes in general in one major respect: she was born with moderately severe hearing loss in both ears. Since her youth, Catchings has relied on a steadfast work ethic to compensate for her hearing loss, which has caused her to have a slight speech impediment.

Catchings had an illustrious four-year career at the University of Tennessee before being selected by the Fever with the third overall pick of the 2001 WNBA draft. She missed the entire 2001 season with a knee injury but returned in 2002 to win Rookie of the Year honors after leading the Fever to its first playoff appearance. Catchings quickly became the leader and face of the Fever franchise, playing a major role in the team and clinching eight consecutive playoff berths from 2005 to 2012. She has been selected as an All-Star eight times, won an unprecedented five Defensive Player of the Year Awards, and was named the WNBA's Most Valuable Player (MVP) in 2011, the same year she became the league's all-time steals leader. In 2012 Catchings added a WNBA title to her already impressive resume when she helped the Fever overcome the Minnesota Lynx in the WNBA Finals. The Lynx forward Maya Moore, the number-one overall pick of the 2011 WNBA draft, described Catchings as "one of those players you want to model yourself after," as quoted by Mechelle Voepel for *espnW* (21 Oct. 2012). "She has a view of the bigger picture of the sport," Moore explained. "She's never just thinking about herself."

In addition to her WNBA career, Catchings has played for professional teams in South Korea, Russia, Poland, Turkey, and China. She has also served as a member of the US women's basketball team, helping the team capture gold medals at the 2004, 2008, and 2012 Olympic Games.

## EARLY LIFE

Tamika Devonne Catchings was born on July 21, 1979, in Stratford, New Jersey, to Harvey and Wanda Catchings. She has two brothers, Kenyon and Bryce, and two sisters, Tauja and Chrystie. Her father is a former professional basketball player who spent eleven seasons in the National Basketball Association (NBA), from 1974 to 1985. Harvey Catchings played center and power forward for the Philadelphia 76ers, New Jersey Nets, Milwaukee Bucks, and Los Angeles Clippers before spending the last season of his career in a professional Italian league.

Catchings moved frequently as a child because of her father's profession, but she was raised mostly in the Chicago suburb of Deerfield, Illinois. She was introduced to sports early on through her father. Beginning when Catchings was about six years old, her father would run her and her siblings through basketball drills in the family driveway. Catchings's father also allowed her and her siblings to accompany him to weekly pickup games at a local gym. "They all enjoyed playing," he said of his children to Mark Adams for the *New York Times Magazine* (25 May 2003), "but Mika is like an addict."

## DIFFERENT BUT NOT DEFEATED

For Catchings, sports provided her with an outlet to overcome adversity. She was three years old when her parents first noticed that there was something wrong with her hearing. Diagnosed with binaural hearing loss, in which hearing ability is fairly reduced in both ears, Catchings, who cannot hear certain pitches, sounds, and tones, began wearing hearing aids and receiving speech therapy to correct the problem. She was nonetheless tormented on a daily basis by her classmates for the bulky hearing aids she wore and the accompanying speech impediment that came with her condition. To win her classmates' acceptance, Catchings resolved to dedicate herself to becoming the best athlete she could be. "On the playing field, I knew that if I practiced and got really good, that no one could make fun of me for any of my disabilities," she explained in an interview with Brianna Cook for *The Everygirl* (25 Mar. 2013).

While Catchings played other sports growing up, including soccer, volleyball, and track and field, it was at basketball that she demonstrated the most proficiency, and by the time she reached the seventh grade, she was already determined to become a professional basketball player. By then, Catchings had stopped wearing hearing aids and attending speech therapy classes altogether out of a desire "to be normal for a little while," as she told Melody K. Hoffman for *Jet* (23 Aug. 2010). She began focusing on reading lips and facial expressions to compensate for her lack of full hearing.

Catchings spent her freshman and sophomore years at Adlai E. Stevenson High School in Lincolnshire, Illinois, where she played on the basketball team with her sister Tauja, who is twenty-one months older. As a sophomore Catchings teamed up with her sister, then a junior, to lead Stevenson to the 1995 Illinois Class 2A title. That same year she was named Illinois Miss Basketball, becoming the first underclassman in state history to receive the honor.

After her sophomore year, Catchings moved with her mother, who by that time had divorced her father, to the city of Duncansville, a suburb of Dallas, Texas. She closed out her high school career at Duncanville High School, where she enjoyed further basketball success. As a senior she led Duncanville High to the 1997 Texas Class 5A title and took home the coveted Naismith Prep Player of the Year Award.

Catchings was recruited by nearly every major college basketball program in the country, but she chose to attend the University of Tennessee in Knoxville so she could play for legendary women's basketball coach Pat Summitt, the college basketball coach with the most wins in NCAA history. "I wanted a coach who would push me," she explained to Kelli Anderson for *Sports Illustrated* (23 Nov. 1998).

Upon arriving in Knoxville, Catchings instantly won over Summitt, a famously intense and demanding coach, and the rest of the Tennessee coaching staff with her dogged work ethic. In spite of that work ethic, Summitt immediately picked up on Catchings's hearing impairment and convinced her to start wearing hearing aids again so she could realize her full potential on the basketball court and in life. "She said that I could inspire kids with what I had been able to accomplish and could still accomplish, despite the torment I had been through because of my disability," Catchings wrote in an article for the *Huffington Post* (13 Nov. 2012). "I have tried to live by that mantra ever since."

## NCAA BASKETBALL STAR

Under the guidance of Summitt, Catchings emerged as one of the best female college basketball players in the nation. She was named Freshman of the Year by the Southeastern Conference

(SEC) in 1998, after she helped lead the Lady Volunteers to a perfect 39–0 record and a third consecutive NCAA national championship. She then received the Naismith National Player of the Year Award as a junior in 2000, when she led the Lady Vols in points (15.7), rebounds (7.9), and steals (2.5) per game and guided them to an NCAA Tournament runner-up finish. Despite having her senior season cut short by a devastating right knee injury, Catchings was named a Kodak All-American all four years of her college career, becoming one of only a handful of players in women's basketball history to earn the honor four times. She was also a First Team All-SEC selection her freshman through junior seasons.

Catchings finished her career at the University of Tennessee as the school's second all-time leader in steals (311) and blocked shots (140) and third all-time leader in points (2,113) and rebounds (1,004). She graduated with honors a semester early from Tennessee in December 2000, with a bachelor's degree in sports management and a minor in business. She went on to earn a master's degree in sports studies from Tennessee in May 2005.

## INDIANA FEVER

Many considered Catchings to be a potential number-one WNBA draft pick before she suffered her knee injury. Her arrival to the WNBA, whose inaugural season was in 1997, was nonetheless highly anticipated. The Indiana Fever, who had debuted as a WNBA franchise in 2000, a year in which they won only nine games and suffered twenty-three losses, considered Catchings a potential cornerstone player that they could build their franchise around and, as a result, selected her third overall in the 2001 WNBA draft.

After sitting out the entire 2001 WNBA season while rehabbing her knee injury, which required two surgeries, Catchings returned in 2002 to make her long-awaited WNBA debut. Shortly after the 2002 WNBA season began, she expressed her lofty goals to Will Allison for the *Indianapolis Monthly* (June 2002): "I want to be one of the best players—if not the best player— in women's basketball." Catchings did, in fact, waste little time proving herself to the league. She earned Rookie of the Year honors after leading the Fever in points (18.6), rebounds (8.6), assists (3.7), steals (2.94), and blocks (1.34) per game. She also finished second in the voting for the league's Most Valuable Player (MVP) and Defensive Player of the Year Awards and became the first Fever player to earn an All-NBA First Team selection as well as be named a starter for the WNBA All-Star Game. Bolstered by Catchings's all-around play, the Fever enjoyed a six-game improvement from the previous year, going 16–16 and advancing to the playoffs for the first time in franchise history.

In the fall of 2002, after the conclusion of the WNBA season—which typically runs from May until September, with each of the league's twelve teams playing a thirty-four-game schedule—Catchings played on the US women's basketball team in the World Championships in China, helping them win a gold medal. That winter she joined the Woori Bank Hansae of the Women's Korean Basketball League (WKBL), the top women's basketball league in South Korea, leading the team to the regular-season title and earning All-Star Game MVP honors.

## FROM THE WNBA TO THE OLYMPIC GAMES

By the start of the 2003 season, Catchings was already being heralded as the WNBA's "next big thing." Around this time, the Hall of Famer and women's basketball pioneer Nancy Lieberman told Adams, "Catchings is the now and the future of the game. I've played and coached against the best players in the world, and no one has played like she does."

That season Catchings again finished as the runner-up for the WNBA's MVP and Defensive Player of the Year Awards after averaging 19.7 points per game and 2.1 steals per game, good for third and second in the league, respectively. She was also an All-WNBA First Team selection and was named an All-Star starter for the second consecutive year. In 2004 Catchings earned an All-WNBA Second Team selection after finishing among the WNBA's top five leaders in points (16.7), rebounds (7.3), and steals (2.0) per game. That summer she joined the US women's basketball team for the Summer Olympic Games, held in Athens, Greece, helping the team bring home their third straight Olympic gold medal.

Catchings led the Fever back to the playoffs during the 2005 season, which began a string of eight consecutive playoff appearances for the team. That season she led the league in steals per game (2.6), made her third career All-Star team, and was named the WNBA Defensive Player of the Year. Also in 2005 she became the fastest player in WNBA history to reach two thousand career points and earned the first of eight consecutive WNBA All-Defensive First Team selections. By then, Catchings had added an effective long range jump shot to her already well-rounded game. "When she came from Tennessee, she wasn't going to shoot often from any more than about six feet out," Fever coach Lin Dunn explained to Voepel, adding, "She got to where she was comfortable from eight feet, and then ten feet, then twelve feet, then sixteen feet."

In 2006 Catchings was named Defensive Player of the Year for the second straight year. She was also the leading vote-getter for that year's All-Star Game, at which she was honored as a member of the WNBA All-Decade Team.

Catchings was enjoying a career year during the 2007 season, until a foot injury forced her to miss the last thirteen regular-season games. She nonetheless finished with personal-best numbers in rebounds (9.0), assists (4.7), and steals (3.1) per game, leading the league in the latter category for the third straight year. Catchings battled injuries for most of the 2008 season but returned to health in time for the 2008 Olympic Games, which were held in Beijing, China. In eight Olympic contests, she led the United States with fourteen steals, helping them easily defeat Australia, 92–65, to win their fourth straight gold medal.

## LEAGUE MVP

Over the next four seasons, Catchings solidified her status as one of the best WNBA players of all time, as the Fever emerged as perennial title contenders. In 2009 she teamed up with guard/forward and fellow superstar Katie Douglas to lead the Fever to a conference-best 22–12 record and a runner-up finish in the WNBA Finals; in a closely contested best-of-five series, the Fever lost to the Phoenix Mercury, three games to two.

Catchings won the Defensive Player of the Year Award that year and again in 2010, making league history as the first player to win the award four times. In 2011 Catchings won her first MVP Award, after being the runner-up for the award the previous two seasons, and became the first WNBA player in history to amass at least five thousand points, two thousand rebounds, and one thousand assists. She also surpassed Ticha Penicheiro, a guard who played most of her career with the Sacramento Monarchs, as the league's all-time steals leader and earned her seventh career All-Star selection. At the 2011 WNBA All-Star Game, she was honored as one of the top fifteen players in league history. The Fever, meanwhile, made their fourth Eastern Conference Finals appearance in seven seasons, losing to the Atlanta Dream, two games to one, in a best-of-three series.

After getting off to a mediocre start in the 2012 season, with a 10–7 record, the Fever went on to win twelve of their last seventeen games and entered the playoffs with the second-best record in the Eastern Conference. Catchings, who won her fifth Defensive Player of the Year Award that season—in which she also began serving as president of the WNBA Players Association—helped the Fever defeat the Atlanta Dream and Connecticut Sun in the Eastern Conference semifinals and finals, respectively, before facing the defending WNBA champion Minnesota Lynx in the WNBA Finals. Despite entering the series as a heavy underdog, and being without number-two scorer Katie Douglas, the Fever, led by Catchings, defeated the Lynx in four games to win their first ever WNBA championship. Catchings was named Finals MVP after averaging 22.3 points, 6.0 rebounds, 3.5 assists, 2.0 steals, and 2.3 blocks per game in the series. "The journey we've been on—it's a dream come true," Catchings said in the wake of the Fever's championship run, according to Voepel. "More than anything, playing here [in Indianapolis] has given me the chance to let my light shine."

In August 2012, approximately two months before winning her first WNBA title, Catchings won a third gold medal while playing for the US women's basketball team at the 2012 Olympic Games, in London, England. She is one of only eight players to have won an NCAA title, an Olympic gold medal, a world championship, and a WNBA championship. Despite entering the 2013 season, her twelfth in the WNBA, as one of the oldest players in the league—at age thirty-three—Catchings continued to serve as the Fever's offensive and defensive anchor. She was named to her eighth career All-Star team after entering that season's midpoint, averaging more than seventeen points, nearly seven rebounds, and three steals per game.

## CHARITABLE WORK AND PERSONAL LIFE

Catchings, who lives in Indianapolis, has been widely known for her many charitable and community-service activities; she has created a model of excellence on and off the field in the tradition of other Indiana sports icons such as Peyton Manning and Reggie Miller. In 2004 Catchings established the Catch the Stars Foundation, which works to help disadvantaged youths in the Indianapolis area. The foundation has a college scholarship program for Indianapolis high school scholar-athletes, runs basketball and fitness clinics around the country, and regularly donates tickets to Fever games, among other activities.

Catchings serves as an ambassador for the WNBA's "Dribble to Stop Diabetes" campaign and has won the WNBA Cares Community Assist Award on eight occasions, in addition to receiving numerous other honors and awards. The Los Angeles Sparks forward Candace Parker, who played with Catchings on the 2008 and 2012 US women's Olympic teams, told Graham Hays for *espnW* (27 July 2013), "She's a great leader, and she leads by example more so than words."

## SUGGESTED READING

Adams, Mark. "Elevated." *New York Times Magazine* 25 May 2003: 26. Print.

Anderson, Kelli. "Now Hear This." *Sports Illustrated* 23 Nov. 1998: 144. Print.

Catchings, Tamika. "How I Overcame Disability to Become a National Champion." *HuffingtonPost.com*. TheHuffingtonPost.com, 13 Nov. 2012. Web. 20 Aug. 2013.

Hays, Graham, "Catchings an Oldie But Goodie." *espnW.com*. ESPN Internet Ventures, 27 July 2013. Web. 20 Aug. 2013.

Voepel, Mechelle. "Tamika Catchings Wins Elusive Title." *espnW.com*. ESPN Internet Ventures, 21 Oct. 2012. Web. 20 Aug. 2013.

—*Chris Cullen*

# Juju Chang

**Born:** September 17, 1965
**Occupation:** Television journalist

Starting out as a desk assistant and rising to the position of correspondent on ABC's late-night news program *Nightline*, Juju Chang has worked for ABC News for more than twenty-five years, serving in a wide variety of roles. "Juju has really paid her dues. She's done everything that you could do from the entry level and touched all the bases all the way up," her husband, Neal Shapiro, said in a segment for *Good Morning America*, "Getting to Know Juju Chang" (5 Jan. 2010). Her insightful coverage and dedication to the news have contributed to her meteoric rise to one of the most prominent positions in the news media.

Chang began her atypical career trajectory as a network assistant for ABC and worked as a hybrid, filing stories for affiliate stations, before returning to the network as an on-air reporter. She contributed stories to the prime-time news magazine *20/20* and anchored the early-morning program *Good Morning America* before moving into her role as special correspondent and fill-in anchor on *Nightline*. She has received an Emmy Award for outstanding live team coverage of a breaking news story as well as two Gracie Awards for stories she contributed to ABC's *20/20* and PBS's *NOW*.

## EARLY LIFE

Juju Chang was born Hyunju Chang in Seoul, South Korea, on September 17, 1965. When she was four years old, Chang immigrated to the United States with her parents, Okyong and Palki Chang, and her two older sisters, Hailey and Yonni. Chang's younger sister, Mimi, and her brother, Jae, would be born in the United States. The Chang family settled in Sunnyvale, California, in the center of Silicon Valley. Her parents worked at the Friendship Inn in Sunnyvale, eventually becoming owners of the small hotel. "We were one of the first Korean American families in the Bay Area," Chang told Jinah Kim for *KoreAm* (13 Dec. 2010). "My father worked very long hours to be successful. Our whole family got involved. . . . We cleaned hotel rooms and changed sheets and towels."

In an interview with ABC News for the segment "Getting to Know Juju Chang," Chang's former schoolteachers remembered her as an

© Ron Sachs/Corbis

excellent student and an extremely bright and insightful young girl. Growing up, Chang became a devoted fan of the television show *Star Trek*, and in "Getting to Know Juju Chang," her sisters recalled having to step between Chang and the television in order to break her focus when she was watching the show. Chang participated in a wide variety of extracurricular activities as a child. At age ten, she was ranked among the fastest nine- to ten-year-old swimmers in the United States for the hundred-meter breaststroke. Her swim coach, Bill Thompson, had a penchant for giving nicknames to his athletes, and he coined the name Juju after the announcers at swim competitions repeatedly had difficulty pronouncing Chang's name. "The announcers would go 'Susie Smith! Anne Reynolds!' And then they'd get to my name and there'd be, like, silence. And they'd butcher my name. So my coach said this isn't right. We're gonna call you . . . Juju! Those were the days before anyone had heard of Hyundai cars," Chang explained to Kim. The nickname would stick with Chang for the rest of her life.

## EDUCATION AND EARLY CAREER

In 1983, Chang graduated from Adrian Wilcox High School and then enrolled in Stanford University. "I thought I was going to be an engineer and work at Hewlett-Packard or something like that. I mean, Apple was born in a garage not too far from where I grew up. But then I got to Stanford and basically flunked calculus," she told

Kim. However, she excelled in her introduction to political science class, earning the highest grade in the course. Her mother encouraged her to pursue broadcast journalism, citing the many speech contests Chang had won in high school. In her interview with Kim, Chang explained, "I felt even more compelled when my mom said to me, 'Oh, you could be like Connie Chung. She's Asian, she talks a lot.'" Chang majored in political science and communications, earning the Edwin Cotrell Political Science Prize. She graduated from Stanford with honors in 1987.

After graduation, Chang began working for ABC News as a desk assistant, or "the gofer," as she referred to the position years later at the symposium TV News in Transition, hosted on April 6, 2006, at the Massachusetts Institute of Technology. In her first role in the news industry, Chang was responsible for making copies, fetching coffee, and organizing the telexes coming in overnight from ABC's international bureaus. Early in her career with ABC she met future husband Neal Shapiro, who worked as a producer for the network. In 1988, she traveled to South Korea to help cover the Olympic Games in Seoul for ABC News.

Chang progressed from her position as desk assistant to the roles of researcher, producer, and off-air reporter. As a reporter, she covered the 1992 presidential campaign and the Gulf War, among other stories. As one of the few women in the office, she sometimes felt pigeonholed into covering the "girl stories" or puff pieces but was committed to covering each story as thoroughly and objectively as possible, as she recalled at the MIT symposium. Chang helped to produce the news report "American Agenda: Women's Health Week," which, along with four other outstanding reports, earned ABC News a 1995 Alfred I. du-Pont-Columbia University Award for excellence in broadcast news.

### ON-AIR DEBUT
In 1995, Chang transitioned to her first on-air position, becoming a correspondent for KGO-TV in San Francisco, a local affiliate of ABC News. "It was really a sink-or-swim situation because I had been at the network for six or seven years in a variety of roles, and so I felt like I had the skills to do the actual reporting," she told Kim. As a producer, Chang had honed all the skills needed by an on-air reporter—researching stories, interviewing subjects, writing stories—but she had never acquired any on-air experience. Recognizing Chang's potential, ABC News offered her an on-air position at KGO to see how she would fare as a correspondent. At the MIT symposium, Chang described this opportunity as a "trial by fire." Chang excelled in San Francisco, one of the largest news markets in the country.

Late in 1995, Chang married Shapiro, who had proposed earlier that year. A fellow *Star Trek*

fan, Shapiro prepared a short video starring actor William Shatner, who portrayed Captain Kirk in the original series. In the short film, "A Day in the Life of William Shatner," Shatner faces the camera and says, "My ship's sensors indicate that you are a very lucky man, that you have found a beautiful, intelligent, funny, and patient woman. . . . Set your phaser on stun and fire when ready." Shapiro played the video for Chang after taking her out to dinner and then proposed. The couple married on December 2, 1995, at the 200 Fifth Club in New York. Chang converted to Judaism upon her marriage to Shapiro.

In 1996, Chang transferred to Washington, DC, where she worked as a "hybrid," filing network pieces for local ABC affiliate stations while covering Capitol Hill, the Supreme Court, and the 1996 presidential election. In 1998, having gained several years of on-air experience, Chang asked ABC to consider her for an anchoring position. The network arranged for Chang to anchor the early-morning broadcasts of *World News Now* and *World News This Morning* alongside a "young, unknown guy by the name of Anderson Cooper," as she recalled at the MIT symposium.

### MOTHERHOOD
In 2000, upon discovering she was pregnant with her first child, Chang left her position as anchor and began working part-time, filing stories for the television news magazine *20/20* on ABC. Speaking at the 2011 Social Good Summit, Chang recalled thinking she would spend her maternity leave reading. Instead she found herself fully focused on her children. "I sort of stepped away from my career a little bit for the first time, really, in my life," she added. Her first son, Jared, was born in 2000, and sons Travis and Mason were born in 2003 and 2007, respectively. In her interview with Kim, Chang confessed, "When the babies started coming, I had a real existential crisis. I said to myself 'Who am I? What am I doing? What do I want to spend my time doing?' And I have never done anything half-a—— in my life." Despite her commitment to her sons and her part-time status at the network, Chang continued to earn recognition for her work, receiving a Gracie Award from the Alliance for Women in Media for her coverage of a story on gender parity in the sciences. Chang also hosted a PBS series called *The Art of Women's Health*, which went on to win a FREDDIE Award from the International Health and Medical Media Awards. She earned a second Gracie Award for a story on judicial activism that aired on the PBS newsmagazine *NOW*. In 2008, Chang shared an Emmy Award with her ABC News coworkers for their live coverage of the 2007 California wildfires, "California Burning."

Chang told Kim that motherhood has shifted the focus of her career. "The nature of the stories I wanted to cover changed," she explained. "So instead of chasing hurricanes and presidential elections, I did more of the magazine-type stories—everything you would sit on a psychiatrist's couch and discuss, I did. But it was because they were human stories, and that allowed me to explore the stories in my own life. . . . I ended up being able to do really cool stories and also have a home life." Chang also started the video blog *Juju Juggles*, in which she discussed motherhood and maintaining a balance between work and family life.

### GOOD MORNING AMERICA

In December 2009, Chang joined ABC's program *Good Morning America* as a news anchor, replacing former anchor Chris Cuomo. In this role, Chang became the first Korean American journalist to hold a major role in a morning news show. It was difficult for Chang to adjust to the breakneck pace at *Good Morning America*, which often left her jetlagged and sleep deprived. She woke every day at 4:45 in the morning, having gone to bed the night before at the same time as her young boys. "I usually roll out of bed with wet hair and sweat pants and go to the studio where there's a dressing room full of clothing that are all prematched because I'm really very fashion challenged," she told Kim.

As news anchor for *Good Morning America*, Chang traveled to Haiti following the earthquake that devastated the country in January 2010. While in Haiti, she met a young girl who had been pulled from the rubble after being trapped for five days. "She'd had a nail puncture her thigh, but it was healing nicely. I met her a week after she'd been pulled from the rubble, and she had yet to receive any medical attention. She complained of a headache. I gave her my ibuprofen," Chang wrote in a blog post for the Women's Conference website (18 Oct. 2010). In response to the disaster, Chang organized a team of more than sixty ABC News colleagues to compete in the Housatonic Valley Sprint Triathlon. Through their efforts, "Team Juju" raised more than $50,000 for the UNICEF relief fund for children in Haiti.

In March 2011, Chang announced she was leaving *Good Morning America* to serve as a special correspondent and fill-in anchor for *Nightline*. In a memo released by ABC News president Ben Sherwood on March 29, he described Chang as one of the "most talented and versatile" members of the ABC team and cited the transfer as an opportunity for Chang to "contribute even more of the in-depth and insightful journalism that has always been her hallmark."

### PERSONAL LIFE

Chang lives on the Upper West Side of New York City with Shapiro and their three sons, Jared, Travis, and Mason. Chang is active in the Council on Foreign Relations and is a founding board member of the Korean American Community Foundation. She also hosts *Moms Get Real*, an online-only show for ABC News NOW in which mothers share advice, personal confessions, and support.

### SUGGESTED READING

Chang, Juju, and Neal Shapiro. "TV News in Transition." Interview by Stuart Brotman. *MIT World*. Massachusetts Institute of Technology, 6 Apr. 2006. Web. 19 Feb. 2013.

Finn, Robin. "Family First, Baseball a Close Second." *New York Times* 31 Oct. 2010, New York ed.: MB2. Print.

"Getting to Know Juju Chang." *ABC News*. ABC, 5 Jan. 2010. Web. 19 Feb. 2013.

Kim, Jinah. "Up Close and Personal with Juju." *KoreAm*. KoreAm Journal, 13 Dec. 2010. Web. 19 Feb. 2013.

—*Mary Woodbury*

# Tom Colicchio

**Born:** August 15, 1962
**Occupation:** Celebrity chef and television personality

Among television viewers Tom Colicchio is perhaps best known as a key member of the panel of judges that determines which contestants will be told to pack their knives and go each week on the competitive reality program *Top Chef*. Since 2006 Colicchio has appeared in ten seasons of the Bravo series, which in 2010 won the Emmy Award for outstanding reality-competition program. But to foodies, gourmets, and others familiar with the American culinary scene, Colicchio is much more than a television chef.

A self-taught cook, Colicchio rose from humble beginnings in the snack bars and burger joints of New Jersey to become one of New York's high-profile chefs and restaurateurs. As cofounder of Gramercy Tavern and the owner and chef of Craft, Colicchio received several prestigious awards from the James Beard Foundation, which recognizes outstanding chefs, restaurants, and cookbooks each year. During Colicchio's tenure as chef, both Gramercy Tavern and Craft earned three-star (excellent) ratings from the *New York Times*.

Despite his recognition by both culinary peers and restaurant critics, Colicchio's style of food has been characterized by many as approachable and unpretentious. His menus feature such delicacies as white truffles and wagyu beef, but he is no slave to culinary trends. Colicchio has dubbed truffle oil "overrated," and he told Frank Bruni for the *New York Times* blog *Diner's Journal* (10 Aug. 2007), "I don't want to

WireImage

see micro-greens in my kitchen." Asked to describe his cooking philosophy, he told Edward Lewine for the *New York Times Magazine* (29 Apr. 2009), "Buy the best you can find or afford and don't overmanipulate it. If I cook a scallop, the best praise you can give me is that it tastes like a scallop." Through the design of his menus and the individual dishes he serves in his restaurants, Colicchio calls attention to both the quality of the ingredients and the skill with which they were prepared.

## EARLY LIFE

Thomas Patrick Colicchio was born August 15, 1962, in Elizabeth, New Jersey, the second of three sons. His father, Thomas, owned a barbershop before taking a position as a correctional officer, and his mother, Beverly, was a homemaker who later worked in the Elizabeth High School cafeteria.

Like many chefs Colicchio developed a love of food and cooking early in life. Sunday dinners of pasta and meat sauce, known in his house as macaroni and gravy, and holiday meals of fish and beet salad made a deep impression on him. While Colicchio was never interested in specializing in Italian cooking, his early meals shaped his outlook toward food and cooking as a whole. He told Judith Weinraub for the oral history project *Voices from the Food Revolution* (19 Apr. 2011), "I, like a lot of other Italian American chefs from my generation, . . . stayed away from Italian food." But, he added, the food served at his restaurant Craft, which is typically considered an American restaurant, shares the "spirit" of Italian cuisine.

Colicchio began cooking seriously at the age of thirteen, teaching himself with the help of books such as *La Technique*, an illustrated

guide by renowned French chef Jacques Pépin. His father encouraged him to pursue his love of cooking professionally. Colicchio explained to Weinraub, "He instilled in us, 'Find something that you like to do and do it. Don't worry about money. Just find something that you love. You'll probably be good at it.'"

## EARLY CAREER

Colicchio worked at a vegetable stand run by an uncle at a local market before taking his first cooking position at a snack bar, where he cooked hamburgers and grilled cheese sandwiches. A position as a busboy in a local seafood restaurant transitioned into a prep cook job shortly after Colicchio graduated from high school. Despite his family's concerns Colicchio decided to forgo college and pursue a cooking career instead. "I certainly had no idea what it would turn into," he told Weinraub. "That wasn't the point. The point was I love food."

Colicchio worked in a number of restaurants in New Jersey before moving to New York, which would become the setting for much of his career. He traveled to France for several months and completed a *stage*, or unpaid apprenticeship, at a restaurant in the Gascony region. Upon his return to New York, he took a position as a cook at the restaurant Rakel, owned by noted chef Thomas Keller. He soon moved up to the position of sous chef. He worked at the restaurant Mondrian for a time before returning to France to work for chef Michel Bras. After his time in France, he returned to Mondrian, this time in the role of head chef. The restaurant received critical praise during his tenure, including a three-star review from the *New York Times*. Colicchio was named one of the United States' top ten best new chefs by *Food and Wine* in 1991.

## GRAMERCY TAVERN

While at Mondrian Colicchio became friends with Danny Meyer, a restaurateur and owner of the Union Square Café. When Mondrian closed in 1992, Colicchio and Meyer began to consider the possibility of opening a restaurant together. "We talked about doing a restaurant that was about American food, but something that's more polished," Colicchio told Weinraub. "What American food was, we wanted to push it a little further."

In 1994 Colicchio and Meyer opened Gramercy Tavern, a 160-seat restaurant in Manhattan's Gramercy neighborhood. Although some critics found that the new restaurant did not yet fully meet their expectations, its potential to become one of the best in the city was obvious to many. In her first review of Gramercy Tavern, published in the *New York Times* on October 14, 1991, shortly after the restaurant opened, critic Ruth Reichl likened eating there to "drinking a great wine when it is still in the barrel." When she returned less than two years later, the restaurant and Colicchio had hit their stride. "He [Colicchio] seems to be trying to extract the essence of each ingredient," Reichl wrote in her February 2, 1996, three-star review of the restaurant, "and he is fearless in following through."

Colicchio's tenure at Gramercy Tavern garnered him significant attention from critics as well as fellow chefs. He received nine James Beard Award nominations and won the awards for best chef in New York and outstanding service in 2000 and 2001, respectively.

## CRAFT

While at Gramercy Tavern Colicchio began to consider the idea of opening a restaurant on his own. When he learned that an appropriate space was available, he leapt at the opportunity to establish a restaurant that reflected his culinary sensibilities and ideas about service and atmosphere. The resulting restaurant, Craft, opened in 2001 a block away from Gramercy Tavern. "The name came about because to me this was about the craft of cooking, not so much the artistry of cooking," Colicchio told Weinraub. "It was about just really focusing on those individual ingredients."

In order to call attention to the quality of specific ingredients, Colicchio designed a menu that allowed diners to choose the main protein, the manner in which it was cooked, the sauce or seasoning, and the side dishes separately rather than as a preassembled meal. He later simplified the process, offering diners a variety of main dishes and side dishes to be ordered à la carte. He focused on relatively simple preparations, allowing the flavors of the ingredients to take center stage.

Craft was an immediate success, earning a three-star review from the *New York Times* shortly after opening and receiving the James Beard Award for best new restaurant in 2002. In 2005 the restaurant was awarded a star rating by the prestigious Michelin restaurant guide. For his work at Craft, Colicchio received the James Beard Award for outstanding chef in 2010. The restaurant's success led Colicchio to begin expanding, opening Craftsteak, a steakhouse based on the Craft model, in Las Vegas, Nevada, in 2002.

## EXPANSION

Colicchio continued to be involved in the operations of Gramercy Tavern until 2006, when he left to focus on further expanding his Craft restaurant group, both within New York and outside of the city. He opened Craft locations in Dallas, Los Angeles, and Atlanta, as well as a Craftsteak at the Foxwoods casino in Connecticut. In addition, Colicchio opened a number of restaurants that served less expensive meals. "I took my cue from clothing designers by hitting three different price points, but always with the idea that quality would be the driver," he told Lisa Fickenscher for *Crain's New York Business* (23–29 May 2005).

Beginning in 2002 Colicchio opened Craftbar locations in New York, Los Angeles, and Atlanta. Billed by Craft Restaurants as the "casual sibling" of Craft, Craftbar offered Colicchio's style of meals at a lower price than the flagship restaurant. In 2003 Colicchio cofounded 'wichcraft, a chain of sandwich shops using artisan breads and ingredients from small farms. The chain eventually opened more than ten locations in New York as well as locations in San Francisco and Las Vegas.

Like any business endeavor the expansion of the Craft brand was not always successful. The Atlanta Craft and Craftbar closed in early 2011, while the Dallas Craft location closed the following year. The flagship restaurant has nevertheless continued to experience both financial and critical success. Craft New York earned a second three-star review from the *New York Times* in 2011, ten years after the first. Reviewer Sam Sifton lauded it, saying it was "as magical and delicious as it was when it opened, and it is all the more exciting for that" (6 Sept. 2011). When asked how he keeps his restaurant relevant, Colicchio replied that he and his colleagues focus on constant improvement. "We don't try to make it the same; we try to make it better," he told Beth Landman for the *New York* magazine blog *Grub Street* (31 Aug. 2012). "We are always pushing it, and if there is something that doesn't work, it stops."

In addition to the restaurants that fall under his Craft brand, Colicchio has opened the restaurant Colicchio and Sons in the Chelsea neighborhood of Manhattan as well as the restaurant at the Topping Rose House, a luxury hotel on Long Island that Colicchio also operates. He also partnered with chef Sisha Ortúzar, a cofounder of 'wichcraft, to open the New York restaurant Riverpark in 2010.

Colicchio has admitted to interviewers that he is unable to cook as regularly as he would like and that he misses it. However, he is adamant that this is due not to the scope of his restaurant business or his media endeavors but to his job description. "It's not the fact that I have this far-flung restaurant empire that keeps me from cooking," he explained to Pete Wells for *Diner's Journal* (30 Sept. 2008). "It's the fact that I'm a chef that keeps me from the stove." In 2008, seeking to reconnect with the hands-on cooking that played such a key role in his early career, Colicchio launched the now-defunct "Tom: Tuesday Dinner," a twice-monthly event in Craft's private dining room during which diners ate a fixed-price meal prepared by Colicchio himself.

## TOP CHEF

As Colicchio gained significant notice for his successful restaurants, he attracted the attention of Magical Elves Production, a television production company that had previously produced the competitive reality program *Project Runway*. The company's representatives approached Colicchio, asking him to appear as a judge in a similar program then in development, this one about cooking. Colicchio was initially reluctant and expressed concerns about the nature of reality television. "I'm not an actor and I'm not there to deliver some witty one-liners and sort of knock the chefs down," he told Weinraub. "I wanted it to be a serious food show, I want the chefs to be high-caliber chefs and I wanted the conversation to be about the food." Despite his concerns, Colicchio agreed to become a judge, and *Top Chef* premiered on the television network Bravo in March 2006.

As a member of *Top Chef*'s panel of judges, the makeup of which varies from season to season, Colicchio is responsible for evaluating the quality of the food created by contestants in a number of inventive challenges. Through their deliberations, the judges determine which contestant or contestants are eliminated from the competition each week. In keeping with his belief that the show should focus on high-quality food and cooking rather than behind-the-scenes drama or the personalities of the contestants, Colicchio can be a tough critic, and some of his decisions as judge have generated controversy among both contestants and viewers of the show. However, while a number of television chefs have become more famous for their explosive conduct in the kitchen than for their culinary expertise, Colicchio takes a more measured approach. "I know from personal experience, if a chef yelled at me in a kitchen, the first thing I'd want to do is hit them with a pot," he told Sarah Hepola for *Salon* (9 June 2008). Colicchio added that he has continued to correspond with and advise several contestants after their time on *Top Chef* ended. "I'd like to see all the chefs do well," he explained to Hepola.

### CELEBRITY CHEF

Colicchio has written several cookbooks, including *Think like a Chef* (2000), which won a James Beard Award, and *'wichcraft* (2009). He has contributed introductions to such books as *Top Chef: The Cookbook* (2008), *James Beard's American Cookery* (2010), and *The Oxford Companion to Beer* (2011) and has written numerous magazine articles on topics ranging from cooking fresh-caught fish to sourcing local ingredients.

While Colicchio's status as one of the most well-known chefs in the United States has proved beneficial to his restaurants, he has also sought to use his position to promote causes he supports. He is an avid proponent of efforts to improve school lunch programs, particularly in low-income areas, and provide children with more nutritious, balanced meals. In 2010 Colicchio testified before the Education and Labor Committee of the US House of Representatives,

expressing his support for the proposed Improving Nutrition for America's Children Act.

Colicchio has also sought to call attention to the issue of hunger among Americans in general, serving as an executive producer for the documentary *A Place at the Table*, which chronicles the experiences of several American families from different areas and backgrounds who struggle with hunger. Directed by Kristi Jacobson and Colicchio's wife, Lori Silverbush, the film premiered at the 2012 Sundance Film Festival, where it was nominated for the Grand Jury Prize. The film is scheduled for theatrical release in March 2013. "This is the work that, looking forward, I will be most proud of," Colicchio told Pamela Parseghian for *Nation's Restaurant News* (16 May 2011).

### PERSONAL LIFE

Colicchio married Silverbush, whom he met while she was working at Gramercy Tavern, on September 15, 2001. The couple have two young sons, Luka and Mateo. Colicchio's son from a previous relationship, Dante, is a college student.

When not filming *Top Chef* on location in cities throughout the United States, Colicchio splits his time between New York City and Long Island. In his free time Colicchio enjoys fishing, boxing, and playing guitar.

### SUGGESTED READING

Colicchio, Tom. "Tom Colicchio Interview 1." Interview by Judith Weinraub. *Voices from the Food Revolution*. Fales Lib., 19 Apr. 2011. Web. 17 Dec. 2012.

---. "Tom Colicchio Interview 2." Interview by Judith Weinraub. *Voices from the Food Revolution*. Fales Lib., 12 May 2011. Web. 17 Dec. 2012.

Fickenscher, Lisa. "Crafting an Empire." *Crain's New York Business* 23–29 May 2005: 3+. Print.

Hepola, Sarah. "*Top Chef*'s Top Dog." *Salon*. Salon, 9 June 2008. Web. 17 Dec. 2012.

Landman, Beth. "Tom Colicchio on His New Hamptons Inn, the End of Craft's Expansion, and Finding a Way to Retire." *Grub Street*. New York Media, 31 Aug. 2012. Web. 17 Dec. 2012.

—Joy Crelin

# Ted Cruz

**Born:** December 22, 1970
**Occupation:** Politician

Prior to his election to the US Senate in 2012, Texas Republican Ted Cruz had already been recognized as an influential leader who, Republicans hoped, could unite the party around its

© Ron Sachs/Corbis

conservative base. A former debate champion who had memorized the Constitution as a teenager, Cruz established a strong right-leaning record as policy advisor for presidential candidate George W. Bush in 2000, as a private practice attorney, and as Texas's state solicitor. Cruz told supporters that his decision to run came from the fact that there were so few members of Congress arguing effectively for conservative principles of low taxes, constitutional originalism, and traditional social values. During the Senate campaign, he drew comparisons to Florida Representative Marco Rubio for his youth, impressive oratory abilities, and Hispanic background as a Cuban American. Still, many observers were surprised when, after collecting national endorsements from Tea Party leaders, Cruz handily won the Republican nomination over lieutenant governor David Dewhurst, who was by far the better-funded, more established candidate. Cruz told Kate Zernike for the *New York Times* (18 Nov. 2011): "If you really believe that we're fighting to save our country, how many people are effectively making the argument?" Since taking office, Cruz has turned heads with his outspoken attacks on the legislative agenda of reelected President Barack Obama and Democrats in Congress. Those attacks have rankled many Democrats but heartened conservatives who see Cruz as the future of their party.

## EARLY LIFE

Rafael Edward Cruz was born in Calgary, Alberta. Cruz's father, also named Rafael, was born in Cuba but had left in 1957 in the midst of the Cuban revolution led by Fidel Castro to overthrow the tyrannical dictator Fulgencio Batista. Rafael Cruz had fought on the side of rebel forces until being captured, imprisoned, and tortured at age eighteen. He eventually managed to leave Cuba on a student visa and immigrate to Austin, Texas. With very little money and speaking little English, he took low paying jobs—such as washing dishes for fifty cents an hour—to work his way through the University of Texas, where he earned a degree in mathematics. During that time, he met his wife, Eleanor, who is of Italian descent and was raised in Delaware. She was also studying mathematics but at Rice University in Houston. Rafael Cruz founded a small business processing seismic data for the oil industry and moved to Canada in the 1960s to take advantage of the region's oil boom.

The Cruz family returned to the United States—settling in Houston—when Ted Cruz was four years old. Because of his experience living under an oppressive government, Cruz's father instilled in his son the importance of freedom. Cruz has often told audiences, as quoted by Zernike, "When I was a kid, my father would always say, 'When we faced oppression in Cuba, I had a place to flee to. If we lose our freedom here, where do we go?'"

## EDUCATION

Cruz expressed an early interest in conservative politics—as well as a skill in public debate. In high school he took part in speech contests sponsored by the Free Enterprise Institute, a nonprofit educational institution devoted to promoting conservative ideals. He traveled to civic groups around the state delivering memorized twenty-minute speeches by thinkers such as the nineteenth-century French political theorist Frederic Bastiat, Nobel Prize–winning economist Friedrich Hayak, and Austrian libertarian Ludwig von Mises. As one of the Freedom Institute's "Constitutional Corroborators," Cruz would also spend hours debating constitutional issues before audiences and reciting the text of the Constitution, having memorized it using a mnemonic device.

Cruz attended Princeton University, where he studied public policy. During his time there, Cruz won the 1992 US National Debate Championship and the North American Debate Championship. Cruz's thesis advisor, Professor Robert P. George, told Erick Eckholm for the *New York Times* (2 Aug. 2012) that he recalled Cruz as "intellectually and morally serious." George further noted, "I'd have predicted that he would be a professor, not a politician." Cruz wrote his senior thesis on the separation of powers, arguing that the Ninth and Tenth Amendments supported the idea that powers not enumerated in the Constitution, are not possessed by the federal government.

After graduating from Princeton, Cruz attended Harvard Law School. There he founded the *Latino Law Review* and excelled as an actor, starring in Harvard's production of Arthur Miller's *The Crucible* during his first year. According to his fellow law students, Cruz's fierce intelligence was obvious to everyone. However, as Frank Bruni noted in an article for the *New York Times* (17 Feb. 2013), not all of Cruz's colleagues remember him fondly. Bruni quoted classmates who dubbed him "arrogant, sour and self-serving." Cruz graduated from Harvard magna cum laude in 1995.

## EARLY CAREER IN DC

In his first year after law school, Cruz served as a law clerk for J. Michael Littig, a judge serving on the Fourth Circuit Court of Appeals. Beginning in the summer of 1996, Cruz clerked for Chief Supreme Court Justice William Rehnquist, becoming the justice's first clerk of Hispanic descent. After Cruz's clerkship was over, he entered private practice with the small DC-based firm Cooper, Carvin & Rosenthal. During his two-year tenure there, Cruz assisted in a number of high-profile cases, including one in which Ohio representative John Boehner sued Washington representative Jim McDermott, a Democrat, for violating the Electronic Communications Privacy Act by leaking the contents of one of Boehner's cell phone conversations to reporters. (The case was not resolved until 2008, when McDermott was ordered to pay Boehner more than $1 million.)

At an event in Washington, DC, in June 1999, Cruz met Joshua B. Bolten, the campaign policy director for George W. Bush. At that time Bush was the governor of Texas and had recently announced his candidacy for president. Impressed with Cruz's intelligence and drive, Bolten offered him a job with Bush's campaign. Cruz became a domestic policy advisor. After Bush was elected in November 2000, Cruz briefly served as associate deputy attorney general within the Justice Department. For two years he also served as director of policy planning at the Federal Trade Commission (FTC). He led the Office of Police Planning, which provides advice on cases with complex legal issues and was also chair of the FTC's State Action Task Force, Noerr-Pennington Task Force, and Internet Task Force.

## TEXAS SOLICITOR GENERAL

In January 2003, Cruz left the FTC to become Texas state solicitor general (a post equivalent to assistant attorney general) under Texas's attorney general, Greg Abbott. During his five-year tenure there, Cruz championed traditionally conservative causes, submitting more than eighty briefs to the US Supreme Court and arguing more than forty cases, including nine before the Supreme Court. In one of his most notable cases, *Van Orden v. Perry* (2005), he argued that displaying the Ten Commandments on a monument at the Texas State Capitol in Austin did not violate the establishment clause of the First Amendment. The Supreme Court ruled 5–4 in favor of Cruz's team, which also included Paul D. Clement, then the interim US solicitor general. In the 2008 case *Medellin v. Texas*, Cruz defended Texas's right to refuse to comply with an International Court of Justice ruling in a Texas murder case involving a Mexican national. Cruz also worked on several cases in which he defended the pledge of allegiance against claims that its inclusion of the words "under God" violated the First Amendment. Other cases he worked involved protecting an individual's right to bear arms and the right of Texas to redraw its congressional map to make it easier to elect Republicans there. In 2008, Cruz returned to private practice, heading the Supreme Court practice of the global law firm Morgan Lewis (today known as Morgan Lewis & Bockius).

## US SENATE RACE CAMPAIGN

Cruz declared that he was running for US Senate on January 19, 2011, during a blogger conference call. His announcement came shortly after Republican Kay Bailey Hutchison, the US senator from Texas since 1993, announced she would not seek reelection in 2012. Cruz, the first candidate to enter the race for the Republican Senate primary, was soon joined in the race by several others, most notably David Dewhurst, a rancher and businessman—as well as the sitting lieutenant governor under Rick Perry. Touting himself as the conservative candidate who would fill "the weeping, screaming void of effective, free-market champions," as he noted to Zernike, Cruz garnered support from the Republican Party's right wing, which praised his fiscal views, his family story, and his oratory skills. Republicans were also attracted to his Hispanic heritage—which many hoped would draw more Texas Hispanics to the Republican Party. In an editorial for the *Washington Post* (16 June 2011), George Will called Cruz's candidacy "as good as it gets" and praised his positions on immigration and other issues. "Regarding immigration, Cruz, 40, demands secure borders and opposes amnesty for illegal immigrants but echoes Ronald Reagan's praise of legal immigrants as 'Americans by choice,' people who are 'crazy enough' to risk everything in the fundamentally entrepreneurial act of immigrating," Will noted. "He believes Hispanics are—by reasons of faith, industriousness and patriotism—natural Republicans."

Dewhurst was widely considered the favorite from the beginning of the campaign because of his name recognition and the early support he received from Perry and others in state government. Cruz, however, ran an aggressive, high-profile campaign that won him endorsements from a number of national Republican leaders such as Mike Lee of Utah, Rand Paul of Kentucky, Patrick J. Toomey of Pennsylvania, and Jim DeMint of South Carolina. He also received endorsements from the conservative groups Club for Growth PAC and Freedom-Works PAC, the conservative radio show host Mark Levin, and members of the powerful grassroots Tea Party organization. As Cruz came to be seen as a champion of the right, Dewhurst was faulted for some of the more moderate positions he had taken as lieutenant governor, including his support of a payroll tax increase and his failure to support certain measures backed by the Tea Party in areas of immigration and national security. Erick Erickson, the editor of RedState.com, dubbed Dewhurst "DewCrist," a reference to former Florida governor Charlie Crist, who ran for US Senate in 2010, but was deemed insufficiently conservative and ultimately lost the seat to Marco Rubio.

**REPUBLICAN PRIMARY AND RUNOFF ELECTION**
In the May 29, 2012, Republican primary, Cruz finished in second place, with about 34 percent of the vote. Dewhurst earned about 45 percent, and the rest of the votes were divided among the other seven candidates. Observers were surprised that Dewhurst had failed to win a majority of the vote. "This is an incredible, unbelievable night, and this is a testament to every single one of you," Cruz said, as quoted by Manny Fernandez for the *New York Times* (30 May 2012). "Nobody in the state thought we could do it, and together, we did." Because no candidate won a majority of votes, a runoff election was held on July 31, 2012. In the weeks prior to the runoff, Cruz continued to attract high-profile endorsements from influential conservatives such as Sarah Palin and Rick Santorum. He criticized all aspects of Dewhurst's record and characterized his supporters as lobbyists and "everyone who makes their living keeping the government gravy train going," as quoted by Aman Batheja for the *New York Times* (3 Aug. 2012). Cruz also benefited from the success of the grassroots coalition he built throughout the state. Whereas Dewhurst contributed $10 million of his own money into his campaign, Cruz's funds consisted mainly of small donations. The average contribution to Cruz's campaign was $167, compared to an average donation of $1,653 to Dewhurst's campaign.

**US SENATE VICTORY**
Though the press portrayed the race as quite close, Cruz managed to defeat Dewhurst handily by almost 14 percentage points in the July 31, 2012, contest. His victory shocked the GOP establishment and seemed to symbolize the renewed energy in the Republican Party's conservative wing. Cruz was tapped to deliver a prime time speech at the Republican National Convention, held in Tampa, Florida, on the weekend of August 27 to August 30, where Mitt Romney and Paul Ryan officially received presidential and vice presidential nominations by party delegates. "What is happening is a great awakening," Cruz said in his August 27 speech, as quoted on the Texas GOP Vote website. "A national movement of 'We the People,' fueled by what unites us—a love of liberty, a belief in the unlimited potential of free men and women." In the November general election, Cruz easily defeated Democratic nominee and former Texas state representative Paul Sadler, with 56.6 percent of the vote. His win was not a surprise in the consistently Republican state.

In an election that saw more Democratic victories than Republican ones—Democratic president Barack Obama was reelected, and Democrats gained seats in both houses of Congress, kept their Senate majority, and successfully passed laws legalizing gay marriage in three states—Cruz's victory was viewed as a small triumph for conservatives. After the surprise retirement of Senator Jim DeMint, a prominent leader of the Tea Party, in November 2012, Cruz was also considered a potential leader of the movement.

**AN OUTSPOKEN FRESHMAN IN THE SENATE**
Unlike many senators who refrain from taking on controversial issues in their first few years in the Senate while they learn the institution's procedures and collect allies, Cruz has been notably outspoken since taking office. On January 3, the day he was confirmed to his Senate seat, an opinion piece he wrote ran in the *Washington Post*, in which he criticized Republicans for failing to stand up to criticism by Democrats in the 2012 campaign and defended the "opportunity conservatism" of the right. Shortly after taking office, he criticized his own party for brokering a tax deal with Democrats that averted the fiscal cliff—simultaneous tax increases and spending cuts— and stated that he would not have voted for the act.

Over the next two months, negotiations between party leaders began over how to create a deficit reduction law. As the March 1 deadline approached, rather than make efforts to help party leaders reach a compromise, Cruz, along with several other conservative Republicans, expressed the controversial view that a sequester—automatic across-the-board cuts to federal spending, the consequence of failing to act by March 1—might be an acceptable option to restore "fiscal sanity" on the federal budget. "I think the last time we saw a shutdown, the fact that Republicans were willing to stand together—on fiscally conservative principles—ended up producing a result that was responsible and that benefited the country and that ultimately produced enormous economic growth," Cruz said, referring to shut down of the federal government in the 1990s under President Bill Clinton, as quoted by Stephen Dinan and Tom Howell for the *Washington Times* (7 Jan. 2013). Congress ultimately failed to agree on legislation to prevent the sequester, and on March 1, the government began reducing its spending by about $85 billion.

## HAGEL CONFIRMATION HEARING

Cruz garnered significant attention in February for his pointed questioning of former Republican senator Chuck Hagel during his Senate confirmation hearing to become secretary of defense in the Obama administration. Though many Republicans, including Arizona senator John McCain, asked pointed questions about Hagel's foreign policy views and credentials, Cruz's questioning was particularly aggressive. He criticized Hagel for statements he had made during an Al-Jazeera interview in which he seemed to acknowledge that the United States had lost credibility in the world and demanded that he release five years' worth of financial information (rather than the standard two years' worth). In making the latter request, Cruz implied that Hagel was trying to hide some sinister financial contributions. "We do not know, for example, if he received compensation for giving paid speeches at extreme or radical groups," Cruz stated before the Senate Armed Services Committee prior to its vote, as quoted by Ruth Marcus for the *Washington Post* (15 Feb. 2013). "It is at a minimum relevant to know if that $200,000 that he deposited in his bank account came directly from Saudi Arabia, came directly from North Korea." Senators from both parties viewed Cruz's insinuations as disrespectful. Missouri's Democratic senator Clair McCaskill compared his behavior to the 1950s-era red scare, noting, "In this country we had a terrible experience with innuendo and inference when Joe McCarthy hung out in the United States Senate, and I just think we have to be more careful." Hagel was ultimately confirmed to his cabinet post, 58–41.

## OTHER SENATE WORK

Cruz has also been vocal about several other issues in Congress. Taking steps to keep the promise he made during his Senate campaign to "repeal every last syllable of Obamacare," Cruz filed a bill in late January to repeal the 2010 Patient Protection and Affordable Care Act, though he has acknowledged it has little chance of passing the Democratic Senate. He has fiercely opposed the efforts of Obama and other Democrats to create new gun control legislation, in the wake of several recent mass shootings. While questioning California Senator Diane Feinstein about a bill she sponsored to ban assault weapons during a Senate hearing, Cruz took what many have considered a patronizing tone when he explained the content of the Second Amendment of the Constitution and asked whether she thought Congress had the right to place similar such limits on other rights, such as speech or assembly. Before responding to Cruz's question, Feinstein replied, "I'm not a sixth grader. . . . Thank you for the lecture."

Cruz is currently a member of the Senate Committee on Armed Services; the Committee on the Judiciary; the Committee on Commerce, Science and Transportation; the Committee on Rules and Administration; and the Special Committee on Aging. He was voted by Republicans to be the National Republican Senatorial Committee's vice chairman for grassroots outreach, an impressive position for a freshman senator. In March he was a keynote speaker at the Conservative Political Action Conference (CPAC), a meeting of the most conservative members of congressional Republicans.

Aligned with the Tea Party, Cruz was at the forefront of a failed congressional strategy in the fall of 2013 to defund the Affordable Care Act, or Obamacare. His efforts, which included the fourth-longest speech in Senate history, were highly criticized among members of the senator's own party.

## PERSONAL LIFE

Cruz met his wife, the former Heidi Nelson, while they were both working on George W. Bush's 2000 campaign. She is a Harvard Business School graduate who currently works as a vice president of Goldman Sachs. They have two daughters, Caroline and Catherine, and reside in Houston.

## SUGGESTED READING

Batheja, Aman. "Sadler Reminds Texas Who He Was." *New York Times*. 3 Aug. 2012: A27. Print.

Bruni, Frank. "The G.O.P.'s Nasty Newcomer." *New York Times* 17 Feb. 2013: SR3. Print.

Eckholm, Erick. "A Republican Voice with Tea Party Mantle and Intellectual Heft." *New York Times* 2 Aug. 2012: A11. Print.

Fernandez, Manny. "Texas Runoff Set in G.O.P. Race for Senate." *New York Times*. 30 May 2012: A15. Print.

Marcus, Ruth. "Cruz Stoops to Conquer." *Washington Post* 15 Feb. 2013: A19. Print.

Will, George F. "A Candidacy as Good as It Gets." *Washington Post*. 16 June 2011: A23. Print.

Zernike, Kate. "New Face in Texas with a Familiar Story." *New York Times* 18 Nov. 2011: A8. Print.

*—Margaret Roush Mead*

# Alain de Botton

**Born:** December 20, 1969
**Occupation:** Writer, television presenter, and entrepreneur

Alain de Botton, who has written several novels and a dozen or so works of nonfiction, is one of the most divisive authors working today. During the first part of his career, when he was primarily writing fiction, he received critical acclaim from major publications both in the United Kingdom (where he resides) and in the United States. He also garnered a broad readership that loved his intellectual takes on modern relationships.

Since switching to writing nonfiction exclusively in 1997, with the publication of *How Proust Can Change Your Life*, de Botton has sought to use philosophy, literature, architecture, and other aspects of high culture to help average readers better understand aspects of modern society. While many of these books have been celebrated by book critics for demonstrating philosophy's relevance to everyday life, others have been derided for being little more than philosophy highlights repackaged as self-help books for middle-class readers wanting to seem more intellectual.

De Botton branched into entrepreneurship in 2008 with the establishment of the School of Life, which seeks to give its students the tools they need to live better, more productive, and happier lives. The following year, he established Living Architecture. The program enables individuals to rent vacation homes designed by some of the world's best architects. De Botton cofounded these outreach efforts out of a singular fear, as he told Lynn Barber for the London *Observer* (21 Mar. 2009): "I'm often struck by the fear that books don't do very much. I think they're the most important things in the world, but I also think . . . could one get the message across in another way[?] . . . And that's where the entrepreneurship comes in—how can you spread ideas? What I want to do is make a difference."

## EARLY LIFE

Alain de Botton was born on December 20, 1969, in Zurich, Switzerland, the son of Egyptian-born banker, financier, and art collector Gilbert de Botton and the former Jacqueline Burgauer. Although de Botton grew up in a Jewish family, Gilbert de Botton was an atheist who discouraged any religious observances in Alain and his older sister Miel, now a neuroscientist living in France. "I was brought up in a very atheistic Jewish family," he said in an interview with the *Sydney Morning Herald* (14 Jan. 2012). "My father was like [fellow atheist author] Richard Dawkins's [father]—very fiercely anti-religion."

© Colin McPherson/Corbis

to head Rothschild Bank, but in 1983 he left the bank to establish Global Asset Management, an organization that offered wealth management and investment services to institutions, corporations, and private individuals. The elder de Botton founded the firm with just one million British pounds; when he sold it to UBS in 1999, it was worth an estimated 420 million British pounds. Upon their father's death in 2000, de Botton and his sister were left with a large trust fund, worth hundreds of millions of US dollars (reports vary as to its actual size). The author has denied ever using the money and claims to have lived off of his own income since completing his formal education.

De Botton, who describes his childhood as being financially stable but emotionally insecure, has called his father a "cruel tyrant" in numerous interviews. Continually under intense pressure because he was responsible for so many people's fortunes, Gilbert de Botton would frequently get angry, throw things, break objects around the house, and belittle the accomplishments of his children, particularly his son. In an interview with Robert Chalmers for the London *Independent* (25 Mar. 2012), Alain de Botton tried to explain the source of his father's anger: "His parents divorced when he was very young. His mother [Yolande Harmer] was a very spirited woman; a Zionist spy living in Alexandria. She left my grandfather just after the birth of my father. He was then rejected by his father. So he grew up in this very uncertain atmosphere. She was a single parent; they were Jews living in Egypt. There were times when he was looked after by the neighbors because his mother was in prison. So the fact that the guy was able to have a successful life was extraordinary. But the idea that he would ever be 'Dad'—no."

## A PRESTIGIOUS EDUCATION
Because the elder de Botton had been raised in Egypt while that nation was a British protectorate, he held the British educational system in particularly high regard. When Alain turned eight, he was sent to board at the Dragon School in Oxford, England, despite being both painfully shy and knowing little English at the time. "It was miserable," de Botton recalled to Barber. "I was foreign and Jewish, with a funny name, and was very small and hated sport, a real problem at an English prep school. So the way to get round it was to become the school joker, which I did quite effectively—I was always fooling around to make the people who would otherwise dump me in the loo laugh."

Following the Dragon School, de Botton attended the Harrow School in London, one of the most prestigious schools in the world for boys. He then went on to the equally prestigious University of Cambridge, where he earned degrees in history and philosophy. During his time at both Harrow and Cambridge, de Botton felt lonely and isolated and had difficulty making friends and dating girls. He was also self-conscious of the fact that he began losing his hair at age twenty. He found a greater bond at the library, among the great writers and philosophers, than he did with anyone his own age. At Cambridge, he began working on a doctorate but stopped before completing it because he had discovered something in his devotion to reading that became far more important to him: a love of writing.

## EARLY CAREER IN FICTION
De Botton had not dreamed of a writing career; in fact, he became a devoted reader pretty late in his adolescence. "I was a very un-literary child," he recalled in a New York Times interview (24 Jan. 2013), "which might reassure parents with kids who don't read. Lego [the popular line of construction toys] was my thing, as well as practical books like 'See inside a Nuclear Power Station.' It wasn't till early adolescence that I saw the point of books and then it was the old stalwart, The Catcher in the Rye, that got me going. By sixteen, I was lost—often in the philosophy aisles, in a moody and melodramatic state."

The first book de Botton wrote is a semiautobiographical novel, Essays in Love (titled On Love in the United States), which was published in 1993 when he was just twenty-three years old. The book mixes the traditional styles of fiction with nonfiction as it intimately analyzes the ways its characters fall in and out of love. It received

rave reviews on both sides of the Atlantic and has sold more than two million copies worldwide since its initial publication. Twenty years after its debut, Essays in Love remains a favorite for many readers, including journalist Lynn Barber, who called it "brilliantly original" during her 2009 interview with its author.

De Botton followed this novel with two others, The Romantic Movement: Sex, Shopping, and the Novel, published in 1994, and Kiss & Tell, published in 1995. Both novels, like their predecessor, are semiautobiographical in nature and focus on intelligent people falling in and out of love. Although The Romantic Movement received a stellar review by noted American author John Updike in the New Yorker and Kiss & Tell tallied excellent reviews in such diverse publications as the Washington Post Book World, the New Yorker, the San Francisco Chronicle, and Vogue, de Botton has said in interviews that he now prefers to forget these two novels and does not list them on his CV on his official website.

## A TURN TO NONFICTION
A shift to nonfiction, with the publication of How Proust Can Change Your Life in 1997, is what de Botton believes enabled him to reach a worldwide audience. In this unusual self-help book, the author details the ways in which French author Marcel Proust's great early–twentieth century seven-volume novel À la recherche du temps perdu—commonly translated as Remembrance of Things Past or In Search of Lost Time, the translation de Botton prefers—could help make someone a better person. De Botton uses Proust's masterpiece to inspire self-improvement in his readers, in everything from learning how to be a better friend to being happy in love, and even how to "suffer successfully." Among the book's many enthusiastic fans was Frank Gannon, who wrote for the New York Times (15 June 1997): "For Americans mired in a culture in which 'self-help' is an adjective, a noun, and too often an emetic, Mr. de Botton's book, a self-help manual for the intelligent person, is a welcome departure from the usual bellyaching. . . . 'How Proust Can Change Your Life' is witty, funny, and tonic—and it provides ample justification for all the college courses that make Proust required reading."

De Botton followed this book's success with The Consolations of Philosophy, published in 2000, which he considers to be something of a companion to How Proust Can Change Your Life. In it, as the title suggests, the author looks to many of the greatest philosophers of all time, from Arthur Schopenhauer to Immanuel Kant to Friedrich Nietzsche, to see how they addressed life's humble problems and everyday concerns. The result is another unusual self-help book, again bringing high culture to the masses in a digestible manner.

The author believes that the success of these nonfiction works is due to his own need to think through his personal problems via philosophy. As de Botton told Barber: "Yes, [my writing] is self-therapy. And if other people find value in it, it's precisely on that basis. So I'm the opposite of an academic who comes at knowledge from a desire to find out exactly what [ancient Greek philosopher] Plato thought. My view is: OK, let's find out what Plato thought because he might make a difference to me, to you, he might tell us something that is of use."

## PHILOSOPHICAL RUMINATIONS

Since the success of these two volumes, de Botton has worked exclusively as a nonfiction author. In each subsequent book he has published since the start of the twenty-first century, he focuses on a specific topic and ruminates on its meaning in a philosophical manner, much like the way earlier philosophers thought about the issues and challenges of their own times.

Some of the subjects de Botton has written about include the psychology of travel in *The Art of Travel* (2002); the stresses we endure wondering if other people judge us to be successes or failures in *Status Anxiety* (2004); and why we consider certain structures ugly or beautiful in *The Architecture of Happiness* (2006). Later works include *The Pleasures and Sorrows of Work* (2009), which analyzes various types of workplaces and reflects on the significance of work itself; *A Week at the Airport* (2009), a diary of de Botton's experiences as London Heathrow Airport's first writer-in-residence; *Religion for Atheists* (2012), a book that suggests committed atheists like himself should cull from religion various practices and communal ideas that might make society more livable; and *How to Think More about Sex* (2012), which, as the title suggests, implores people to not only think about sex more often but also with more consideration and intelligence.

## CRITICAL BACKLASH

De Botton's digestible and highly readable examinations on these subjects have garnered him legions of fans and have helped him sell millions of copies of his books around the world. But they have also often produced a vitriolic critical response. In a review of the television documentary version of *The Art of Travel* (in which de Botton was featured) for the *Guardian* (31 Dec. 2004), Charlie Brooker calls the author "a slapheaded, ruby-lipped pop philosopher who's forged a lucrative career stating the bleeding obvious . . . if you pick up one of his books and read it cover to cover, you'll come away with less insight into the human condition than if you'd worked your way through a copy of *Mr. Tickle* instead."

Other books have also not faired favorably in critical circles. Reviewing *The Pleasures and Sorrows of Work* for the *New York Times* (28 June 2009), Caleb Crain states: "Everyone has a price in theory; a worker is someone who has agreed to a number. He is exposed as someone under constraint, like a prisoner in a stockade. To mock him for being less than perfectly free in his thoughts and actions is easy. Unfortunately, the British essayist Alain de Botton indulges in this kind of mockery in his new book." Reviewing *Religion for Atheists* in the *Guardian* (12 Jan. 2012), Terry Eagleton wrote, "What the book does, in short, is hijack other people's beliefs, empty them of content and redeploy them in the name of moral order, social consensus, and aesthetic pleasure. It is an astonishingly impudent enterprise. It is also strikingly unoriginal."

## LIVING ARCHITECTURE AND THE SCHOOL OF LIFE

In his defense, de Botton has argued that his work has found an avid readership among those who are interested in better understanding the modern world through the prism of literature or philosophy, but who may not have had access to it previously. He told Chalmers that he prefers to be remembered as "somebody who has made a few stabs at trying to bring elite culture into the wider world." One of these efforts is the nonprofit Living Architecture program, which he cofounded in 2009. The program offers patrons the opportunity to rent vacation homes around the United Kingdom designed by some of the most critically acclaimed architects working today.

The author has also sought to broaden his outreach through his School of Life, founded in 2008. Based out of a storefront in London, the school teaches its students how to live better and more wisely, as well as giving them philanthropic principles to live by. The school has drawn numerous writers, editors, and thinkers to serve as guest lecturers, despite the school itself frequently being ridiculed in the British media. Of both these efforts de Botton told Chalmers, "I think I have grown impatient with just being a writer. I like working with people. I believe change can only come through collaboration." He added, "What interests me is guidance. I have a therapeutic view of literature. And that vision, which has been expressed in fifteen books, can also be expressed in other ways."

## PERSONAL LIFE

De Botton has said that he struggled for a number of years to find personal happiness and that he only grew as a person after undergoing two years of psychotherapy in his early thirties. In these sessions he learned that there is no such thing as the perfect relationship, occupation, or life. This revelation has allowed him to not only live more fully each day, but ultimately to find a wife and have children.

De Botton met his wife in 2001, through mutual friends. When someone asked him to describe his ideal girlfriend, he did so in remarkable detail: she must be a doctor's daughter who grew up outside of London, have received a Christian education, and have some involvement in either science or business. The next weekend, one of his friends introduced him to Charlotte Neser, a businesswoman with this very same background. The couple married in 2003, soon after they first met; they have two sons, Samuel and Saul. Charlotte de Botton manages the commercial, financial, and legal aspects of Seneca Productions, a documentary television production company. Alain de Botton, a broadcaster for Seneca, has presented several series based on his work.

## SUGGESTED READING

"Alain de Botton: By the Book." *New York Times* 27 Jan. 2013: BR8. Print.

Barber, Lynn. "Office Affairs." *Observer*. Guardian News, 21 Mar. 2009. Web. 15 July 2013.

Chalmers, Robert. "Alain de Botton: 'My Father Was Physically Quite Violent . . . He Would Destroy the House." *Independent*. Independent, 25 Mar. 2012. Web. 15 July 2013.

Clark-Flory, Tracy. "Think More about Sex!" Rev. of *How to Think More about Sex*, by Alain de Botton. *Salon*. Salon Media, 22 Dec. 2012. Web. 15 July 2013.

Eagleton, Terry. "*Religion for Atheists* by Alain de Botton—Review." Rev. of *Religion for Atheists*, by Alain de Botton. *Guardian*. Guardian News, 12 Jan. 2012. Web. 15 July 2013.

"Interview: Alain de Botton." *Sydney Morning Herald*. Sydney Morning Herald, 14 Jan. 2012. Web. 15 July 2013.

## SELECTED WORKS

*Essays in Love* (US title: *On Love*), 1993; *How Proust Can Change Your Life: Not a Novel*, 1997; *The Consolations of Philosophy*, 2000; *The Art of Travel*, 2002; *The Architecture of Happiness*, 2006; *The Pleasures and Sorrows of Work*, 2009; *How to Think More about Sex*, 2012; *Religion for Atheists: A Non-Believer's Guide to the Uses of Religion*, 2012

—*Christopher Mari*

---

# Giada De Laurentiis

**Born:** August 22, 1970
**Occupation:** Celebrity chef

Despite having a famous grandfather in legendary movie producer Dino De Laurentiis, Giada De Laurentiis never intended to become a celebrity. "I was very shy as a young girl. I had no

© RD/ Thomas/Retna Ltd./Corbis

interest in the movie industry at all," she told Daniel Lindley for *Coastal Elegance and Wealth* (20 Feb. 2006). "I ended up going into cooking because that's where my passion was. Never in a million years would I have thought I would be where I am today, in front of a camera."

De Laurentiis has become a fixture on the Food Network channel, where she has hosted several shows since her 2003 debut, including *Everyday Italian*, *Behind the Bash*, *Weekend Getaways*, and *Giada at Home*. She also has six cookbooks to her credit: *Everyday Italian: 125 Simple and Delicious Recipes* (2005); *Giada's Family Dinners* (2006); *Everyday Pasta* (2007); *Giada's Kitchen: New Italian Favorites* (2008); *Giada at Home: Family Recipes from Italy and California* (2010); and *Weeknights with Giada: Quick and Simple Recipes to Revamp Dinner* (2012).

## EARLY LIFE AND EDUCATION

Giada Pamela De Laurentiis was born to Veronica De Laurentiis and Alex De Benedetti in Rome, Italy, on August 22, 1970. She is the oldest of four children; in addition to her sister, Eloisa, she has two brothers, Dino and Igor. De Laurentiis hails from a creative family. Both of her parents, as well as her grandmother, Silvana Mangano, are actors. Her maternal grandfather is the late film producer Dino De Laurentiis, whose film credits include Federico Fellini's *La Strada*, Roger Vadim's *Barbarella*, and a 1976 remake of *King Kong*.

## A PASSION FOR COOKING

De Laurentiis began cooking when she was five years old. At the age of seven, she moved with her family to New York City and shared a Central Park apartment with her grandfather. After her parents divorced a year later, De Laurentiis, along with her mother and siblings, followed her grandfather to Los Angeles. At the time, she was struggling to adapt to her new culture. "I had a very tough childhood," De Laurentiis recalled to Lori Berger in a *Redbook* interview (Feb. 2011). "I came here from Italy and didn't speak a word of English, so the kids at school tormented me." She found solace at home, often spending time in the kitchen, where she inherited her family's passion for cooking. "I learned tradition from my grandfather, who grew up selling pasta in Naples; simplicity from my mom, who had four kids and had to get dinner on the table fast every night; and creativity from my aunt. " De Laurentiis said in an interview for *Shape* (Dec. 2009).

De Laurentiis knew that cooking was her calling by her early teens, after spending lots of her time at the Los Angeles branch of DDL Foodshow, her grandfather's newly launched restaurant and gourmet food store. (He also opened another one in New York City.) "I was twelve, and I would go there after school. I just fell in love with the whole scene," she told Alice Parker for *Time* (2 June 2006). "I loved being in the kitchen, watching the customers come in and talk about what they liked and didn't like. [My grandfather] had to close the stores after two years, but for me, they left an imprint."

## PURSUING A CAREER AS A CHEF

After graduating from Marymount High School, De Laurentiis put her culinary dreams on hold and attended college at the urging of her family. "My parents felt that it was necessary for me to go . . . because I couldn't know at that age what I would want to be doing with the rest of my life," De Laurentiis told Lindley. Despite studying social anthropology at the University of California, Los Angeles (UCLA) and earning her bachelor's degree in 1996, she remained undeterred, subsequently enrolling at Le Cordon Bleu, a prestigious cooking school in Paris, France.

In a final attempt to change De Laurentiis's mind, her family encouraged her to work behind the scenes on one of her grandfather's films. The summer she spent on the film set before heading off to culinary school only reinforced her decision. "I hated it. Nothing about it made me want to get up and work—except for the catering truck. It was interesting for me to see how they did so much from such a little truck," she told Lindley.

Following her stint at Le Cordon Bleu, where she trained as a cuisine and pastry chef, De Laurentiis returned to Los Angeles. She honed her cooking skills while toiling away in the kitchens

of some of the city's best restaurants, including the Ritz-Carlton Fine Dining Room, in Marina del Rey, and Wolfgang Puck's Spago, in Beverly Hills. However, the low pay and long hours prompted De Laurentiis to become a personal chef and to launch her own catering company, GDL Foods, in 1998. Among her first clients was the director Ron Howard; she served as his personal chef for a year.

## THE FOOD NETWORK

De Laurentiis earned additional income by styling food for print publications. Her work appeared in *Martha Stewart Living* and in *Food & Wine*. Her big break came after helping on a Thanksgiving-themed food photo shoot for *Food & Wine*, when someone at the magazine contacted her regarding a story idea. "They wanted to do a lunch with my family, and it happened to coincide with the year my grandfather was honored with a Lifetime Achievement award at the Oscars," she told Park. "And they said I could style my own food—that was the hook for me."

The article, which appeared in the February 2002 edition of *Food & Wine*, featured photos of De Laurentiis and her relatives seated around a table, eating traditional Italian dishes that she prepared. After the issue came out, the piece raised her profile considerably. "Well, an executive at the Food Network found the article and read the recipes, and called me up saying he was looking to do an Italian cooking show and asked if I had experience," she told Jen Murphy in an online interview for *Food & Wine* (Feb. 2002). "He said he had seen my recipes and seen me but didn't know how I'd be on camera, so he asked me to put together a demo."

Despite initially rejecting the offer, De Laurentiis changed her mind nine months later. "It took me six months to make that tape! I was like, I can't do it, I can't talk to a camera, I'm too shy," she confided to Park. With her brother Dino's help, she submitted a tape of herself, preparing her mother's baked pasta with béchamel sauce. De Laurentiis was subsequently offered the opportunity to host her own cooking show.

## BECOMING A CULINARY SENSATION

*Everyday Italian* debuted on the Food Network on September 15, 2003. Unlike the other shows airing on the channel, the half-hour series, which featured De Laurentiis making quick and healthy classic Italian dishes alongside family and friends, was shot in a rented home in California, rather than in the network's New York City studio. "I thought it was going to be hard enough for me to be on TV, and if I didn't have the support of my family, then I didn't think I could do it," she said to Park. "Plus, I don't have the personality to do a studio show."

De Laurentiis's lack of on-camera experience, coupled with her good looks and sex appeal, made her the target of critics, who maintained that she was not a real chef, but an actor or model hired by the show's producers. She subsequently took measures to improve her onscreen performance. "My brother would follow me around with a TV camera and make me talk—make me go through every single thing I was doing. Whatever it was—picking up dry cleaning, anything—he would follow me around," she told April Lisante in an interview for the *Philadelphia Daily News* (30 Oct. 2008).

Despite the criticism, *Everyday Italian* proved to be an immediate hit with viewers—and the Food Network eventually ordered a second season of the show. Her success, however, was tinged with sadness, when her younger brother, Dino, passed away from melanoma at the age of thirty-one. "It was such a shock to have someone die that fast, that young. I realized at that point that life is so fragile, you have to make the most of it," she told Janice Kaplan in a *Ladies' Home Journal* interview.

## CAPITALIZING ON HER SUCCESS

In 2005, De Laurentiis published the book *Everyday Italian: 125 Simple and Delicious Recipes*, a collection of her family recipes. The book peaked at number five on the *New York Times* best-seller list. De Laurentiis's increasing success also led to other opportunities. In October 2005, De Laurentiis assumed hosting duties for a second Food Network program, *Behind the Bash*, in which she gave viewers a firsthand, behind-the-scenes look at the catering involved for some of the largest weddings and events in the United States, such as the Grammy Awards.

In 2006, De Laurentiis published her second cookbook, *Giada's Family Dinner*, which reached the top spot of the *New York Times* best-seller list. That same year, she served as a correspondent for NBC's *Today Show* during its coverage of the Olympic Games in Torino, Italy. Her work with NBC led to a contributing correspondent role on the morning program. Other small screen credits included an appearance on the cooking challenge show *Iron Chef America*. In November 2006, De Laurentiis and fellow Food Network chef Bobby Flay unsuccessfully competed against two other chefs from the channel, Mario Batali and Rachael Ray.

In January 2007, De Laurentiis started hosting her third Food Network series, *Giada's Weekend Getaways*, in which she visited popular food destinations in cities across America, including Seattle, San Francisco, and South Beach. In 2007, De Laurentiis published her third cookbook, *Everyday Pasta*, which debuted at number two on the *New York Times* best-seller list. The two-part special *Giada in Paradise*, which aired in June 2007 on the Food Network, followed De Laurentiis as she visited two exotic locales: Capri, Italy, and Santorini, Greece. De Laurentiis

was also among the presenters at the inaugural Food Network Awards in 2007 and served as a guest judge during the third season of the competition reality show *The Next Food Network Star*.

## ADDITIONAL ACCOLADES

De Laurentiis and her show *Everyday Italian* were big winners at the 2008 Daytime Emmy Awards, held in June at the Kodak Theater in Los Angeles. Not only did the series capture the prize for outstanding lifestyle program, but De Laurentiis was also named outstanding lifestyle host. When De Laurentiis's fourth cookbook, *Giada's Kitchen: New Italian Favorites*, was released in September 2008, it reached second on the *New York Times* best-seller list. A month later, she began hosting yet another Food Network program: *Giada at Home*, a lifestyle show that displays her in the kitchen, preparing dishes for her family and friends and planning special events. Despite the show's title, the program is set in a rented home in Malibu, California, not De Laurentiis's house.

De Laurentiis added another Daytime Emmy to her collection in 2009, when *Giada at Home* claimed the award for outstanding directing in a lifestyle/culinary program. *Giada at Home* also earned a nod in the category of outstanding culinary program. In March 2010, her fifth cookbook (named after this show) debuted at number one on the *New York Times* best-seller list. *Giada at Home* earned another four Daytime Emmy nominations in 2010, winning for outstanding directing in a lifestyle or culinary program, as well as outstanding culinary program. In June 2010, De Laurentiis returned to *The Next Food Network Star* as a mentor to the finalists.

*Weeknights with Giada: Quick and Simple Recipes to Revamp Dinner*, De Laurentiis's sixth cookbook, was published in March 2012. "I wrote the book because of my need to manage time and still make mealtime fun, interesting, and yummy for me and my family," Laurentiis told Jane Ammeson in a interview for *the Times of Northwest Indiana* (28 Mar. 2012). "It has forced me to be more creative. So that is the focus of this new book—dishes that taste great and come together quickly." She was among the nominees at the 2012 Daytime Emmys, where *Giada at Home* garnered nominations for outstanding lifestyle/culinary host; outstanding culinary program; outstanding directing in a lifestyle/culinary program; outstanding achievement in multiple camera editing; and outstanding achievement in single-camera photography (film or electronic). That same year, De Laurentiis was also inducted in the Culinary Hall of Fame. In March 2013, she announced plans to publish a four-book series for young children.

Since 2010, De Laurentiis has teamed up with Target stores to launch her own line of food items and cookware. She is also a spokesperson for Pyrex Glassware and for Barilla pasta, the world's largest manufacturer and producer of pasta.

De Laurentiis has been married to clothing designer Todd Thompson since 2003. The couple has a daughter named Jade and lives in a home overlooking the Santa Monica Mountains.

## SUGGESTED READING

Dunn, Jancee. "Giada's Recipe for the Good Life." *Redbook*. Hearst Corporation, n.d. Web. 12 Mar. 2013.

Haldeman, Peter. "High Design for a Chef." *Architectural Digest* Dec. 2008: 160–65. Print.

"Giada De Laurentiis' Recipe for a Happy Life." *Shape*. Weider Publications, n.d. Web. 12 Mar. 2013.

Kalogerakis, George. "Let's Do Lunch." *Food & Wine*. American Express Publishing, Feb. 2002. Web. 12 Mar. 2013.

Kaplan, Janice. "Giada De Laurentiis: The Sweet Life." *Ladies Home Journal*. Meredith Corporation, n.d. Web. 12 Mar. 2013.

Lindley, Daniel. "Behind the Woman Behind the Bash." *Coastal Elegance & Wealth*. Scripps Southwest Florida Group, 20 Feb. 2006. Web. 12 Mar. 2013.

Lisante, April. "Once-Shy Giada De Laurentiis Savors the Spotlight." *Philadelphia Daily News*. Philadelphia Media Network, 30 Oct. 2008. Web. 12 Mar. 2013.

Park, Alice. "Get to Know Giada." *Time*. Time, 2 June 2006. Web. 12 Mar. 2013.

Spencer, Amy. "The Sizzler: Giada De Laurentiis." *New York Post*. News Corporation, 28 Sept. 2008. Web. 12 Mar. 2013.

## SELECTED WORKS

*Everyday Italian: 125 Simple and Delicious Recipes*, 2005; *Giada's Family Dinners*, 2006; *Everyday Pasta*, 2007; *Giada's Kitchen*, 2008; *Giada at Home: Family Recipes from Italy and California*, 2010; *Weeknights with Giada: Quick and Simple Recipes to Revamp Dinner*, 2012.

—Bertha Muteba

# R. A. Dickey

**Born:** October 29, 1974
**Occupation:** Baseball player

According to Tyler Kepner for the *New York Times* (8 July 2010), Toronto Blue Jays pitcher R. A. Dickey "embodies the power of an ever-hopeful outlook." The only active knuckleball pitcher in Major League Baseball (MLB), Dickey has endured a tumultuous career path that strongly

Fred Thornhill/Reuters/Landov

parallels that of his signature knuckleball, "a pitch that dips and dives and dances and usually travels slower than the speed of interstate traffic" as L. Jon Wertheim noted for *Sports Illustrated* (2 Apr. 2012). Selected eighteenth overall by the Texas Rangers in the 1996 MLB Draft, Dickey was discovered to have a rare physical defect shortly before signing with the team. He spent ten years trying to make it in the major leagues as a conventional pitcher before being forced to reinvent himself as a knuckleball pitcher during the 2005 season. He spent the next four seasons trying to perfect the pitch while bouncing around with various major and minor-league organizations.

In 2010, following a succession of short-lived stints with the Milwaukee Brewers, Seattle Mariners, and Minnesota Twins, Dickey rejuvenated his career as a member of the New York Mets, where he emerged as a reliable—and at times dominant—front-of-the-rotation starter. Dickey took the baseball world by storm in 2012, when he became the first knuckleballer in history to win the Cy Young Award, after leading the majors and National League (NL) in a number of pitching categories. During the 2013 off-season, Dickey signed a two-year contract with the Toronto Blue Jays.

## EARLY LIFE

Robert Allen "R. A." Dickey was born on October 29, 1974, in Nashville, Tennessee. He has a younger sister named Jane. His father, Harry Lee Dickey, worked as a heavy equipment operator and moonlighted as a night watchman at the Davidson County Juvenile Delinquent Center. His mother, Leslie Bowers, worked as a receptionist. Dickey's parents divorced when he was about five years old.

Dickey grew up wearing hand-me-down clothes and ate with silverware that his family scrounged from a local restaurant. "Money was always an issue," he recalled in his 2012 memoir *Wherever I Wind Up*, written with the New York *Daily News* sportswriter Wayne Coffey. "I won't tell you that I grew up hungry, but every day was a battle to get by." Dickey was often left to fend for himself while his single mother was out working. As a result, he sought out extracurricular activities to alleviate boredom. Among those activities were playing and watching sports.

Dickey's favorite sport growing up was baseball. He regularly attended Nashville Sounds games when the team was the New York Yankees' top triple-A affiliate. Dickey went to many games with his father, a former standout pitcher who had received tryouts with several MLB teams. Dickey fondly remembers being signed out of school early by his father, who would make up phony excuses for him so the two could play catch. He also frequently played catch with his mother, who was a star softball player.

## HIGH SCHOOL AND COLLEGE BASEBALL

Dickey attended St. Edward Elementary and Wright Middle School in Nashville, before he was awarded a scholarship, at age thirteen, to the prestigious Montgomery Bell Academy (MBA), which "probably saved my life," as he told George Vecsey for the *New York Times* (14 Sept. 2010). At MBA, Dickey became a three-sport star in football, basketball, and baseball. As an eighth-grader, he began pitching and playing shortstop for the varsity baseball squad. By the time he was a sophomore, major-league scouts were attending his games.

During his senior year, Dickey posted a 15–3 record with 218 strikeouts, helping to lead MBA to a state championship. Dickey's strikeout total for the season was the highest in the country. After being named Tennessee Player of the Year and earning All-American honors, he was selected by the Detroit Tigers in the tenth round of the 1993 MLB Draft. He also received scholarship offers from several National Collegiate Athletic Association (NCAA) Division II and Division III schools to play football and basketball. Dickey, however, decided to forgo those opportunities, instead accepting a scholarship to play baseball at the University of Tennessee (UT) in Knoxville.

Dickey pitched for three seasons at UT, during which he set school records for wins (thirty-eight) and innings pitched (434) while posting a solid 3.40 ERA. By the time he entered his junior season, his fastball was consistently clocked in the mid-nineties, thanks to an intense weight-lifting regimen that added more than thirty pounds of muscle to his body. He earned All-America honors for the third consecutive year and was named an Academic All-American.

## TEXAS RANGER AND MEDICAL MARVEL

Dickey's pitching prowess at UT drew the attention of several major-league teams. In June 1996, he was selected by the Texas Rangers in the first round of that year's MLB Draft. Meanwhile, he joined Team USA that summer and pitched at the Summer Olympic Games in Atlanta, Georgia. As part of the run-up to the Olympics, Dickey appeared on the cover of *Baseball America* along with other members of Team USA's starting rotation. The United States lost to Japan in the semifinals in Atlanta, but defeated Nicaragua in the bronze-medal game.

After returning home from the Olympics, Dickey was offered an $810,000 signing bonus by the Rangers. That offer, however, was quickly rescinded when the Rangers' head trainer, Danny Wheat, looked at Dickey's *Baseball America* cover photograph and spotted an abnormality in his right elbow, which was bent at an unusual angle. The discovery forced Dickey to undergo a series of tests, which revealed that he had no ulnar collateral ligament (UCL), the primary stabilizer of the elbow.

Though Dickey's extremely rare condition remained asymptomatic, the Rangers worried that it might eventually lead to UCL reconstruction (more popularly known as Tommy John surgery, named after the former major-league pitcher who was the first to have it performed). The club immediately lowered their offer to $75,000. Devastated and unsure of his baseball future, Dickey accepted the offer, instead of returning to Tennessee to complete his degree in English literature. He likened the experience to "winning the lottery and then losing the ticket," as he told Alan Schwarz for *Baseball America* (28 May 2003). "Doctors look at me and say I shouldn't be able to turn a doorknob without feeling pain . . . . It's a miracle," he added.

## MINOR LEAGUE CAREER

In the fall of 1996, Dickey pitched for the Rangers in the Florida Instructional League (FIL), before being assigned to the organization's single-A affiliate in Port Charlotte, Florida. He made only six starts for the club before having his season cut short by a bone spur in his pitching elbow, which required him to undergo arthroscopic surgery.

Upon returning to the Charlotte Rangers in 1998, Dickey was designated as the team's closer, a role in which he flourished. That year he recorded thirty-eight saves in fifty-seven appearances and was named to the FSL All-Star team. Dickey was then promoted to the Rangers' double-A affiliate in Tulsa, Oklahoma, where he spent most of the 1999 season, alternating his time between closer and starter. He finished that year with the organization's top minor-league team, the Triple-A Oklahoma City Red-Hawks, pitching twenty-three innings in six appearances.

Dickey remained with the RedHawks for the entire 2000 season, posting an 8–9 record with a 4.49 ERA as a starter and reliever. The following year, the RedHawks made him a full-time starter and he went 11–7 with a 3.75 ERA. Dickey also saw the first big league action of his career in 2001. On April 22, he made his major-league debut in a relief appearance against the Oakland Athletics. Dickey appeared in three more games for the Rangers that year, but after allowing thirteen hits and nine runs in eleven innings, the team relegated him back to the RedHawks.

Despite a lackluster 2002 campaign with the RedHawks, in which he gave up 176 hits in 154 innings, Dickey spent most of the 2003 and 2004 seasons with the Rangers. He was inconsistent as a spot starter and long-reliever, posting a combined 5.35 ERA in sixty-three games. He earned a spot on the Rangers' opening day roster to begin the 2005 season, but was soon jettisoned to the RedHawks after posting a dismal 8.10 ERA in five relief appearances.

## LEARNING THE KNUCKLEBALL

Dickey reached a crossroads in his career in mid-April 2005, when Rangers manager Buck Showalter and the team's pitching coach Orel Hershiser propositioned him with the idea of becoming a full-time knuckleball pitcher. Convinced the knuckleball would offer him the best chance for a job in the big leagues, Dickey agreed to adopt the pitch and began learning how to throw it in earnest.

Dickey's initial experiences with the knuckleball were humbling. In July 2005 he was with the RedHawks when he had his first start as a professional knuckleball pitcher, during which he gave up fourteen hits and twelve runs in less than six innings. Dickey again struggled in several subsequent outings, but improved enough to earn a call-up to the Rangers that September, and a spot on the team's opening day roster the following spring. However, in his first start of the 2006 season, Dickey gave up six home runs in less than four innings against the Detroit Tigers, tying the modern-day record for most home runs given up in a single game. One day later, he was optioned back to the RedHawks, and two weeks after that, he was officially taken off the Rangers forty-man roster. With the RedHawks, he continued his struggles, finishing with a 9–8 record and a 4.92 ERA, while suffering with shoulder problems.

Over the next three seasons, Dickey would split his time between Triple-A and the major leagues, as he tried to refine his knuckleball. In 2007, he signed a minor-league contract with the Milwaukee Brewers and spent the entire season with their triple-A affiliate in Nashville, Tennessee. Dickey pitched very well, leading the team and the Pacific Coast League (PCL) with thirteen wins and earning PCL Pitcher of the Year honors.

## JOURNEYMAN PITCHER

Following the 2007 season, Dickey turned down an offer to pitch in Korea to sign a minor-league deal with the Minnesota Twins. He remained with the team for only a week before being claimed by the Seattle Mariners in the annual Rule 5 draft, which prevents talent-heavy teams from stockpiling major-league-caliber players in their minor-league systems. At thirty-four years old, Dickey became the oldest player ever taken in the Rule 5 draft. He went on to appear in thirty-two games with the Mariners during the 2008 season, in which he went 5–8 with a 5.21 ERA, while alternating between starter and reliever. That year, despite continuing to enjoy steady progress and more consistency with his knuckleball, Dickey achieved another dubious distinction when he tied the MLB record for most wild pitches in an inning, with four, during an August game against the Minnesota Twins.

Dickey rejoined the Twins during the 2009 season, when the team picked him up as a free agent. After making the Twins' opening day roster, he pitched almost exclusively out of the bullpen for the club, posting a 4.62 ERA in thirty-five appearances. After enduring a rough patch during the second half of the season, he was assigned to the Twins triple-A affiliate in Rochester, New York.

During his conversion to a knuckleball pitcher, Dickey worked at various times with three of the most celebrated knuckleball pitchers in baseball history; Charlie Hough, Tim Wakefield, and Hall of Famer Phil Niekro. He has credited Hough with teaching him the proper grip and delivery, Wakefield with shaping his release and follow-through, and Niekro with building up his confidence to trust and embrace the pitch. "I used what they gave me and infused the pitch with my own personality," he explained to Sheinin. Unlike his predecessors, Dickey is unique in the fact that his knuckleball is thrown at a much higher velocity, often clocking in at eighty-one to eighty-two miles per hour, as opposed to the mid-to-low-sixties. The speed of his knuckler allows him to have better command and control of the notoriously temperamental pitch, which, when thrown properly, can suddenly drop in any direction as it approaches home plate.

## UNPRECEDENTED RUN OF SUCCESS

Dickey's mastery of the knuckleball came full circle in 2010. After becoming a free agent for the fourth consecutive year, he signed a minor-league deal with the New York Mets. That spring, he was invited to the Mets' annual spring training camp, but after being the first player cut, he was sent to the organization's triple-A affiliate, the Buffalo Bisons, in Rochester, New York. Undaunted, Dickey went 4–2 with a 2.23 ERA in eight starts for the club. One of his more noteworthy starts for the Bisons came on April 29, 2010, against the Durham Bulls, when he missed a perfect game by only one out. Dickey was called-up to the Mets during the second month of the season.

As a member of the Mets starting rotation during the 2010 season, Dickey enjoyed his first sustained run of success against major-league batters. He finished the season with an 11–9 record and a 2.84 ERA, which was seventh-best in the NL. More remarkably, he only walked forty-two batters in 174 innings, and his walk-per-nine-inning rate of 2.2 was the third-best in the NL. The highlight of Dickey's season came on August 13, when he pitched a one-hitter against the Philadelphia Phillies, the thirty-fifth in Mets history. Dickey attributed his breakthrough success to the fact that he started throwing knuckleballs eighty-five percent of the time, as opposed to sixty-five percent of the time when he first started throwing the pitch. This allowed him to experiment more with varying the speed of his knuckleball by as much as thirty miles per hour, while opening up chances to mix in his mid-eighties fastball, which kept hitters off balance. "He's got both dimensions . . . a hard one and a soft one," Orel Hershiser told Tyler Kepner, in another article for the *New York Times* (16 June 2012).

In January 2011, the Mets expressed their faith in Dickey by signing him to a two-year contract worth $7.8 million. Dickey pitched well again during the 2011 season, leading the Mets with a 3.28 ERA and twenty-two quality starts (pitching at least six innings and allowing no more than three runs), despite finishing with a record of 8–11.

## MAKING HISTORY

Years of hard work, dedication, and perseverance crystallized for Dickey in 2012, when he posted arguably the greatest season by a knuckleball pitcher in MLB history. After going 3–1 with a 4.45 ERA in the month of April, Dickey embarked on a dominant stretch of pitching. He went undefeated in May and then was named the NL Pitcher of the Month for June after going 5–0 with 0.93 ERA. He earned fifty-five strikeouts in forty-eight and one-third innings. In back-to-back starts against the Tampa Bay Rays and Baltimore Orioles, on June 13 and June 18, respectively, Dickey pitched consecutive complete-game one-hitters, becoming only the tenth pitcher in baseball history to accomplish such a feat and the first since 1988. Between May

27 and June 24, he set a Mets record of forty-four and two-thirds innings without allowing an earned run. He entered the 2012 midseason break with a major-league-best 12–1 record and a stellar 2.40 ERA and was named to his first All-Star team.

Dickey cooled off during the second half of the season but still finished with dominant numbers, going 20–6 with a 2.73 ERA. He finished first in the majors in quality starts (27) and led the NL in strikeouts (230), innings pitched (233.2), complete games (5), and shutouts (3), while finishing second in the league in both wins and ERA. He became only the sixth Mets pitcher in history to reach twenty wins and the first since Frank Viola in 1990. In November, Dickey was named the winner of the 2012 NL Cy Young Award, becoming the first knuckleballer and only third Met to receive the honor.

## TORONTO BLUE JAYS

While Dickey expressed his desire to remain with the Mets, the financially strapped organization chose not to extend his contract, instead trading him to the Toronto Blue Jays in exchange for several minor-league prospects in December 2012. That month, Dickey made the trade official when he reached a two-year contract extension with the Blue Jays worth $25 million.

Entering the 2013 season, first-year manager John Gibbons named Dickey the team's opening day starter. On April 2, Dickey lost his debut for the club, giving up six hits and three earned runs against the Cleveland Indians. By the 2013 season midpoint, Dickey had struggled to reclaim the magic of the previous year, despite showing flashes of his brilliance in a June game against the Tampa Bay Rays, in which he recorded a two-hit complete-game shutout.

## PERSONAL LIFE

One of baseball's most cerebral and introspective players, Dickey is widely known for his love of his books and writing. In March 2012, he published the memoir *Wherever I Wind Up: My Quest for Truth, Authenticity, and the Perfect Knuckleball*. The book chronicles Dickey's journey from conventional pitcher to knuckleballer and reveals details of the traumatic and emotionally scarring sex abuse he suffered as an eight-year-old child. It also sheds light on how therapy helped him overcome his demons and become a better husband and father. *Wherever I Wind Up* became a best seller and received unanimous critical acclaim, with Wertheim proclaiming that it "might be the finest piece of nonfiction baseball writing since [fellow knuckleballer Jim Bouton's] *Ball Four*." With that success, Dickey secured a deal to publish three children's books. The first, an adaptation of his memoir entitled *Throwing Strikes: My Quest for Truth and the Perfect Knuckleball*, was published in March 2013.

Dickey has also won attention for his intrepid charitable activities. In January 2012, he climbed Mount Kilimanjaro in Tanzania as part of efforts to raise awareness of international human sex trafficking and to benefit the foundation Bombay Teen Challenge. The following winter he traveled to Mumbai, India, on behalf of the same cause.

Dickey married his girlfriend from middle school, Anne Bartholomew, in 1997. The couple lives in Nashville with their four children, daughters Mary and Lila, and sons Eli and Van.

**SUGGESTED READING**

Kepner, Tyler. "Otherworldly Pitch Meets Its Jedi Master." *New York Times*. New York Times Co., 16 June 2012. Web. 17 June 2013.

McGrath, Ben. "Oddball: Is R. A. Dickey Too Good to Be True?" *New Yorker* 6 May 2013: 52. Print.

Schwarz, Alan. "Rangers' Dickey Defies Odds as Often as Possible." *Baseball America*. GrindMedia, 28 May 2003. Web. 17 June 2013.

Sheinin, Dave. "Mets Knuckleballer R. A. Dickey Has Straightened Out His Life and Crooked-Out His Pitches." *Washington Post*. Washington Post, 6 June 2012. Web. 17 June. 2013.

Vescey, George. "Dickey Is at Home, in Any House." *New York Times*. New York Times Co., 14 Sept. 2010. Web. 17 June 2013.

Wertheim, Jon L. "Much More to R. A. Dickey Than the Knuckleball." *SI.com*. Time Inc., 2 Apr. 2012. Web. 17 June 2013.

—*Chris Cullen*

# Peter Dinklage

**Born:** June 11, 1969
**Occupation:** Actor

Peter Dinklage is perhaps best known for his role as Tyrion Lannister, or "the Imp," in HBO's *Game of Thrones*, a fantasy series based on George R. R. Martin's Song of Ice and Fire novels. Dan Kois, writing for the *New York Times Magazine* (11 Sept. 2011), called his performance "one of the richest on television." One of the most popular characters in both the novels and the HBO series, underdog Tyrion gets not only some of the best lines but also the support of readers and viewers alike. With more than four million viewers each week, the show has achieved what *Rolling Stone*'s Brian Hiatt (24 May 2012) called "an improbable level of mainstream success." For his portrayal of Tyrion, Dinklage won a Primetime Emmy Award (2011) and a Golden Globe Award (2012).

At just under four and a half feet in height, Dinklage struggled early in his career to find

FilmMagic

nonexploitative roles for actors his size, a struggle that he wishes more actors with dwarfism would undertake. "I just feel like it's the responsibility of people my size to persevere a bit more about what they do. Because it will just perpetuate itself if you agree to do these things," he said to Hiatt. "I don't know. I just can't do it. I have to play a person. I can't play an adjective. Or adverb? Are they adverbs or adjectives?"

Despite gaining a reputation for turning down such parts, he eventually managed to find roles that he could be proud of and that paid well. Dinklage has worked steadily as an actor since the late 1990s. He has appeared on stage as Richard III; on television in *30 Rock* (2009), *Nip/Tuck* (2006), and *Threshold* (2005–6), among other series; and in over thirty movies, including *The Station Agent* (2003), *Elf* (2003), and *Death at a Funeral* (UK version 2007, US version 2010).

**EARLY LIFE AND EDUCATION**

Dinklage was born in Morristown, New Jersey, and grew up in nearby Mendham Township. His father, John, sold insurance, and his mother, Diane, taught music at an elementary school. His older brother, Jonathan, is now a professional violinist. Perhaps not surprisingly, the household embraced the arts, especially music. Dinklage recalled to Hiatt that when he was about six or seven years old, he and his older brother would stage shows in the basement of their parents' house for an audience of their elderly neighbors: "We'd do a puppet *Quadrophenia*, set up little drum kits with tuna-fish cans and do a whole show and sell tickets for a bottle cap or whatever. We'd put the stereo speakers facedown on the floor upstairs, so it would come through the ceiling. We were basically the Little Rascals of New Jersey."

Dinklage and his brother were not the only rascals living under his parents' roof, however. "It was like a zoo in my house. We had a lot of pets," he told Eric Spitznagel for *Vanity Fair* (20 Jan. 2011). "My family had a habit of collecting creatures that didn't always want to be pets. The first animal I can remember was a Lab named Zoe. Before that, there was a parrot, but I don't remember his name because I was an infant. The parrot only loved me, which was very strange. He wouldn't let anybody get near me. He'd attack anybody that even came close."

Dinklage, who is now four feet five, began to notice that he was different from other children when he was about five years old. His legs were bowed, which made it hard for him to walk. He was diagnosed with achondroplasia, a genetic condition that causes dwarfism. "My proportions are askew," Dinklage explained to Dinitia Smith for the *New York Times* (2 Oct. 2003). "The cartilage doesn't develop right. It's lack of pituitary." To prevent complications from the condition and straighten his legs, Dinklage underwent painful surgeries while he was still young and had to wear leg casts separated by a bar. He recalled to Smith that his father "would carry [him] around with the bars like a suitcase."

Dinklage's condition was rarely mentioned by his parents, who, according to Hiatt, "never moved anything from the high shelves in their house, just expected him to get on with it, to climb up for what he wanted, and that's what he's always done." School was a different story. "Being the size I am, adolescence [was] tricky," Dinklage said to Smith. Dinklage felt especially out of place at Morristown's Delbarton School, an all-boys Catholic high school that focused on sports. He told Hiatt, "I was a sullen kid who smoked cigarettes and wore black every day, and I went to a school that was lacrosse players and Izods." Yet Dinklage found his place in the school's drama club, led by English teacher Matthew Dougherty. When Dinklage was a junior, Dougherty cast him in an Irish melodrama, *Sharon's Grave*, which had a part written for someone with dwarfism—the first such role that Dinklage would take. According to Smith, Dinklage relished playing a physically challenged man "who rides around on the back of his dim-witted brother, hurling bile." The experience made Dinklage realize that roles written for people his size were out there and that they were not "just Gilbert and Sullivan" (*Rolling Stone* 24 May 2012).

## BENNINGTON COLLEGE

With Dougherty's help, Dinklage applied to and was accepted by Vermont's Bennington College, where he matriculated after graduating from Delbarton in 1987. In a commencement speech that he delivered at Bennington (1 June 2012), Dinklage recalled his first visit to the college as a prospective student. "I was a kid from New Jersey who went to an all-boys Catholic high school. I was four-foot-something. I mumbled when I spoke. I wore a sort of woman's black velvet cape, black tights, combat boots, and a scowl. But here at Bennington, I was home." Dinklage majored in drama and took part in several plays, including those by Anton Chekhov, Maxim Gorky, and John Guare. Between classes and productions, he "smoked too much pot, stayed up too late[, and] listened to a lot of Pixies and Dinosaur Jr." (*Rolling Stone* 24 May 2012). "It was a debauched, crazy school," he said to Smith. "I loved it. Three girls to every guy—it was very free." He also had untreated panic attacks, but these eventually went away on their own.

While at Bennington, Dinklage met a group of friends with whom he would remain close, both personally and professionally, long after graduation. "There are not shinier, more important people out there," he told Bennington's graduating class of 2012. "Your fellow students, your friends, sitting around you, are as good as it gets."

## WILLIAMSBURG, BROOKLYN

Dinklage graduated from Bennington in 1991 and set out for New York City to seek his fortune as an actor—a daunting prospect considering that he did not have "cash, a credit card, a bank account, or an apartment" and had to pay his own way. "My parents didn't have much money, but they struggled to send me to the best schools," he explained in his commencement address. "And one of the most important things they did for me . . . is that once I graduated, I was on my own. Financially, it was my turn."

After a period of couch surfing, Dinklage moved to the Williamsburg section of Brooklyn—long before it became gentrified—with his friend and Bennington classmate Ian Bell. Living in an abandoned warehouse without heat, the two friends started a theater group and held readings and parties. "We wanted to be like Steppenwolf"—the Chicago-based resident ensemble theater company started in the mid-1970s by Gary Sinise, Jeff Perry, and Terry Kinney—Dinklage explained to Smith. Though the friends charged admission to the parties to help cover rent, Dinklage took a series of jobs to support the theater company and his dream of becoming a professional actor. "I dusted pianos at a piano store on Ludlow Street for five months," he told the Bennington class of 2012.

"I worked on the property of a Shakespeare scholar for a year pulling weeds and removing bees' nests. . . . I helped hang paintings at galleries, paintings that inspired you to think, 'I could do that.'"

When Dinklage and Bell found themselves locked out of their apartment one day after not being able to pay the rent, the dream of running their own theater company collapsed, though the two remained friends. Bell moved to Seattle, and Dinklage took a full-time data entry job processing applications for Professional Examination Services—a job he would hold for six years. "I hated that job and I clung to that job," Dinklage said in his speech at Bennington. The job did enable him to afford his own industrial loft in Williamsburg; however, "in 1993," Dinklage told the new graduates, "'industrial loft' meant 'not legal to live there.'" It had hot water but was unheated, had mushrooms growing in the shower, and was located near a plant that made chemicals for putting out chemical fires.

When not working his day job, Dinklage found occasional work as an actor, sometimes in off-Broadway plays written by best friend and Bennington classmate Jonathan Marc Sherman. Dinklage found that the roles that paid well for dwarves—elves, especially in November, or leprechauns—were exploitative and based on stereotypes, and he refused to take them. Sherman told Kois for the *New York Times* (29 Mar. 2012) that as hard as it might have been to turn down paying gigs, Dinklage was able to stay true to himself with the support of his friends. "If they'd offered me those elf roles, I would've taken them in a second," he added.

## FILM DEBUT: *LIVING IN OBLIVION*

Dinklage made his silver screen debut in the 1995 independent comedy *Living in Oblivion*, directed by Tom DiCillo. The film stars Steve Buscemi as a luckless director on the set of a chaotic indie film production. In the film, Dinklage portrays a dwarf named Tito who becomes irate when he finds out he has been hired to appear in the production's dream sequence. Tito is anything but cute or magical as he vents his spleen at Buscemi's director: "Have you ever had a dream with a dwarf in it? . . . You can take this dwarf sequence and shove it up your a——" (*New York Times* 29 Mar. 2012; *Vanity Fair* 20 Jan. 2011).

Although the film increased his name recognition, he was still unable to find an agent, a setback he attributes to his refusal to take roles that he deemed exploitative. "I just wasn't a type that agents were looking for," he told Hiatt. "I was too specific. They didn't have the imagination to send me on auditions for things that weren't written for a dwarf. They would only see ads at Christmastime, and if I didn't want to do those, what business would I bring them?"

## QUITS DAY JOB: *IMPERFECT LOVE* AND *13 MOONS*

In the late 1990s, Dinklage decided to commit himself more fully to his acting career. "When I was twenty-nine, I told myself the next acting job I get, no matter what it pays, I will from now on, for better or worse, be a working actor," he told Bennington graduates in 2012. He quit his job at Professional Examination Services; in addition to no longer having a job, he also gave up his Internet access. But the decision paid off—albeit not very much at first. "I got a low-paying theater job in a play called *Imperfect Love* [2000], which led to a film called *13 Moons* [2002] with the same writer, which led to other roles, which led to other roles, and I've worked as an actor ever since. But I didn't know that would happen. At twenty-nine, walking away from data processing, I was terrified."

Whatever terror Dinklage felt when he left his day job was not apparent when he started working on *13 Moons*. Alexandre Rockwell, who directed and cowrote the film with Brandon Cole, writer and director of *Imperfect Love*, described to Kois for the *New York Times* what it was like to meet Dinklage for the first time. "You might come in with some luggage about Peter's physicality," Rockwell said. "Right away he cuts right through that. You're thinking, He's a dwarf, he's a dwarf, but Peter comes shining through as a personality beyond any kind of diminutive-size issue."

## THE STATION AGENT

Dinklage met writer and director Tom McCarthy during the production of McCarthy's off-off-Broadway play *The Killing Act* (1995), about circus showman P. T. Barnum. McCarthy was looking to cast the part of Tom Thumb, one of Barnum's hit attractions, and, as he put it, "searched the New York theatre community for a little person and all roads led to Peter Dinklage" (*Landmark Theatres* 2004). When McCarthy ran into Dinklage in New York about five years later, he noticed the unwanted attention passersby paid to Dinklage because of his size. The observation inspired McCarthy, who was in the middle of writing a new screenplay, to create a lead character based on Dinklage. Dinklage would not only star in the film (along with Patricia Clarkson and Bobby Cannavale) but also give McCarthy vital feedback as he developed the script. The result was *The Station Agent*, a film about a loner with dwarfism named Fin McBride who inherits a small train depot in rural New Jersey.

*The Station Agent* was a success at the Sundance Film Festival, where it won the Audience Award for best feature as well as the Waldo Salt Screenwriting Award. McCarthy sold the film there, as well. According to *Vanity Fair*'s Eric Spitznagel, the film was the first to feature someone with dwarfism as the protagonist "and, no less substantially, the first movie to deal with the subject of dwarfism with anything approaching dignity." The film was a breakthrough project for both McCarthy and Dinklage, and it went on to earn further awards; several film societies and festivals nominated Dinklage for his performance in the lead role. Beyond the acclaim, Dinklage found the project satisfying for the very reasons that led him to pursue acting in New York in the first place: "I'd been in great films before, but I'd never been involved in something from the early stages," Dinklage told Kois for the *New York Times*. "It's the way I wanted to work. Like Steppenwolf—loyal to the ensemble." Dinklage found that part of being loyal to the ensemble was learning to contain his charm—a charm that had served him well. "When people are infected by my charm, they don't see my size," he said to Smith. According to Smith, McCarthy told Dinklage to drop the "Dinklage charm" to play Fin, an introvert. "I tend to be a big flirt—I like to make people laugh," Dinklage said. "[McCarthy] said I had to get rid of all that stuff. It was hard doing scenes with Bobby Cannavale because I would break up laughing."

## THE CHRONICLES OF NARNIA: PRINCE CASPIAN

Despite Dinklage's success in *The Station Agent*, few lead roles came his way in the several years that followed. During that time, and despite his usual refusal to play such parts, he accepted the role of the dwarf Trumpkin—a magical, long-bearded creature with pointy shoes—in *The Chronicles of Narnia: Prince Caspian* (2008). The film was shot over a seven-month period in Eastern Europe and New Zealand. The beard was physically uncomfortable, but Dinklage seems to have come to terms with what his younger self might have seen as a moral compromise. Addressing his "twentysomething self" during his interview with Hiatt, Dinklage said, "'Go enjoy your mac-and-cheese again for dinner. Look under your oven—oh, yeah, that is a rat. I'm jet-setting first class, man. I'll see you later.' That's what I would say to that snob."

## GAME OF THRONES

Unlike *Prince Caspian*'s Trumpkin, *Game of Thrones*' Tyrion Lannister is "all too human" (*Rolling Stone* 24 May 2012). "That's what I like about that show, he does have a sexual appetite," Dinklage said to Hiatt. "You never see one of those Narnian creatures with that. Those scenes are fun! We get so much flak for it, but what's wrong? I just find it to be so sad, people get in such an uproar about breasts, but not chopping people's heads off."

When Dinklage first heard that *Game of Thrones* was based on a series of fantasy novels, he was understandably cautious. "Dwarves

in these genres always have this look. My guard was up. Not even my guard—my metal fence, my barbed wire was up. Even *Lord of the Rings* had dwarf-tossing jokes in it," he told Kois for the *New York Times*. The creators of the HBO series, David Benioff and D. B. Weiss, assured him that Tyrion was "a real human being."

Benioff and Weiss felt that Dinklage was the one actor who could play Tyrion. George R. R. Martin, the author of the series on which *Game of Thrones* is based, said to Hiatt, "If he hadn't accepted the part, oh, boy." Benioff called Tyrion one of the great characters not just in fantasy literature but in literature, period. He's "a brilliant, caustic, horny, drunken, self-flagellating mess of a man. And there was only one choice to play him" (*Rolling Stone* 24 May 2012). Furthermore, on a show that is notorious for killing off its lead characters, Tyrion appears to be one of the survivors. Dinklage signed a contract for six seasons, and the show itself has just begun its third.

Dinklage was satisfied with Benioff and Weiss's treatment of Tyrion as a character and accepted the relatively lengthy contract. As he told *All Things Considered*'s Audie Cornish during a 2012 interview, while Tyrion tells the jokes, he is not one himself; although Tyrion's size and features are part of the role, they alone do not define the character. "It would be stupid if he weren't addressed as an 'imp' in this world, given the surroundings," he said to Cornish. "It does address the size issue but it doesn't knock you over the head with it. Because you don't really need to."

Playing a complicated character such as Tyrion has affected not only Dinklage's career but also his psyche. "Maybe it's had an effect on me," he said to Hiatt. "It's kind of sad when you play a character that's much better than you are. . . . I guess people who played super-heroes have suffered from that all the time—if you can't fly, what good are you?" At fan conventions and other show-related events, Dinklage finds himself acting the part of Tyrion even though he is off-screen. The fans are "somewhat expecting Tyrion, you know?" he said to Kois for the *New York Times*. "He's a great character to hide behind. He's a large personality." As Dinklage explained to Hiatt, Tyrion is a "much more arrogant version" of himself.

In January 2012, Dinklage accepted the Golden Globe Award for best supporting television actor for his role as Tyrion. After accepting his award and giving his thanks, he said, "I want to mention a gentleman I've been thinking about, in England. His name is Martin Henderson. Google him." In October 2011, Henderson, who is four feet two, was attacked by an unknown assailant who picked Henderson up and threw him. Although Henderson survived, he was partially paralyzed. "Dwarves are still the butt of jokes," Dinklage told Kois. "It's one of the last bastions of acceptable prejudice. Not just by people who've had too much to drink in England and want to throw a person. But by media, everything."

## UPCOMING RELEASES AND PROJECTS
In addition to his work on *Game of Thrones*, Dinklage has been involved in several upcoming film projects, including *Knights of Badassdom*, *A Case of You*, *Rememory*, and *The Angriest Man in Brooklyn*. He will star in *My Dinner with Hervé*, a film about the life of Hervé Villechaize, the French Filipino actor famous for playing Tattoo on the television series *Fantasy Island* and who committed suicide in 1993. Dinklage had worked for years on the screenplay for the film with his friend Sacha Gervasi, the journalist who had interviewed Villechaize right before his death.

On February 13, 2013, director Bryan Singer announced on Twitter that Dinklage had officially joined the cast of *X-Men: Days of Future Past*, although he did not specify what part Dinklage would play. *Days of Future Past* is due to start filming in mid-2013 and is scheduled for release on July 18, 2014.

Dinklage has been married to theater director Erica Schmidt since April 2005. During breaks from *Game of Thrones* and other projects, Dinklage and Schmidt collaborate on theater projects. They live in upstate New York with their daughter, born in December 2011, and dog, Kevin.

## SUGGESTED READING
Dinklage, Peter. Interview by Audie Cornish. *All Things Considered*. Natl. Public Radio. NPR, 21 May 2012. Web. 21 Feb. 2013. Transcript.

Hiatt, Brian. "Peter Dinklage: Master of the Game." *Rolling Stone*. Rolling Stone, 24 May 2012. Web. 14 Feb. 2013.

Kois, Dan. "Peter Dinklage Was Smart to Say No." *New York Times*. New York Times, 29 Mar. 2012. Web. 21 Feb. 2013.

Smith, Dinitia. "Dark, Handsome, and Short; Star of a Sundance Hit Is Ready for an Encore." *New York Times*. New York Times, 2 Oct. 2003. Web. 21 Feb. 2013.

Spitznagel, Eric. "Peter Dinklage's Porn Name Is, Not Surprisingly, Peter Dinklage." *Vanity Fair*. Condé Nast, 20 Jan. 2011. Web. 21 Feb. 2013.

## SELECTED WORKS
*Living in Oblivion*, 1995; *13 Moons*, 2002; *The Station Agent*, 2003; *Elf*, 2003; *The Chronicles of Narnia: Prince Caspian*, 2008; *Game of Thrones*, 2011–

—*Lisa Phillips*

# Emma Donoghue
**Born:** October 24, 1969
**Occupation:** Playwright, author

A prolific writer by her early thirties, Irish author Emma Donoghue is known and respected in literary circles and by audiences as a novelist, short-story writer, playwright, screenwriter, literary historian, and editor of anthologies. Her first novel, *Stir-Fry* (1994), was published when Donoghue was only twenty-three years old and a student at University College Dublin. *Stir-Fry* initiated two decades of creative output, with works addressing subjects ranging from Ireland to women's sexuality. Donoghue, a lesbian, is a transnational writer with a distinct voice known for addressing—and transgressing—geographical and sexual boundaries.

The writer's career shows no sign of slowing down or stopping, as she continues to create new works across multiple genres to much critical acclaim. "I'm highly promiscuous in my writing," Donoghue told Stacia Bensyl in an interview for the *Irish Studies Review* (Apr. 2000). She added, "I'll sometimes have about five things on the go at once. But I see it more like tending a garden. I find this a very useful image in that you can be bringing one thing to the point of harvesting while you're planting another."

## CHILDHOOD AND EARLY LIFE
Donoghue was born in Dublin, Ireland, on October 24, 1969, the youngest of eight children born to Frances and Denis Donoghue. Frances Donoghue was a secondary-school English teacher who encouraged her children to read. Denis Donoghue is a renowned literary critic considered to be a leading scholar of Irish literature; a widely published writer, he worked as a professor in Dublin during Donoghue's childhood before eventually taking a position at New York University, where he continues to teach in 2012. With two parents who frequently discussed literature and named their daughter after Jane Austen's famous protagonist, Donoghue was immersed in an environment that, she told Bensyl, "made me think English was a perfectly credible thing to be obsessed with your whole life."

Donoghue first traveled to North America at the age of nine, when her father took a yearlong position at New York University. "I had this one dazzling year in the US," she told Sarah Crown for the *Guardian*, "and it opened my eyes. Ireland was terribly homogenous and old-fashioned at the time, so New York blew me away" (19 Oct. 2012). She added, "It made me more confident, more aware of a wider world. And of course as soon as I realised I was gay, I told myself 'I want a wider world!'" As a teenager back in Ireland, where she attended Catholic convent school, Donoghue decided that she wanted

Getty Images

to be a writer when she fourteen years old; she told the website AfterEllen.com that this was "absolutely simultaneous to discovering I was a lesbian" (12 Jan. 2008).

## UNIVERSITY COLLEGE DUBLIN AND THE UNIVERSITY OF CAMBRIDGE

In the late 1980s Donoghue attended University College Dublin, where she studied English and French. "What I found liberating about university were the aspects of university life that anyone has ever found liberating. . . . I could wear what I liked, nobody was watching, there were no nuns keeping an eye on me," she explained to Bensyl. "I loved the fact that I would just bury myself in the library and work away on my own. By the second year I was skipping most of my lectures because I didn't find them particularly inspiring on the average." Donoghue began writing *Stir-Fry* during her first year at the university and met her literary agent, Caroline Davidson, when she was twenty-one. In 1990 Donoghue graduated with a first-class honors BA at the age of twenty-three, the same age at which Davidson got her a two-novel contract with the publisher Penguin.

After University College Dublin, Donoghue pursued her PhD at the University of Cambridge in England. There, she wrote her thesis on the friendship between men and women in mid-eighteenth-century fiction. "It bought me time, basically," Donoghue said of her PhD to Linda Richards for *January Magazine* (Nov. 2000). "It bought me three years before I started my career where instead of having to get a real job I was able to be a grad student and write novels and plays. So it was crucial for buying me that head space."

## FIRST PUBLICATIONS

*Stir-Fry* is a coming-of-age story about a teenage girl who learns that her new roommates are a lesbian couple. The novel addresses issues of identity and burgeoning sexuality while also examining female friendships. Readers, notably lesbian readers, were surprised at the frankness of *Stir-Fry*'s subject matter in Catholic Ireland. *Stir-Fry* was a Lambda Literary Award finalist in 1994.

Donoghue's autobiographical second novel was 1995's *Hood*, which the author has said is closest to her own experiences as a teenager. *Hood* is the story of a lesbian couple who met in convent school and the period of bereavement that follows thirteen years later when one of them is killed in a car crash. The novel won the 1997 American Library Association's (ALA) Gay and Lesbian Book Award (now the Stonewall Book Award). The *New York Times'* Catherine Lockerbie called the book "utterly charming" and added that "Ms. Donoghue displays her confidence by avoiding the grandiose and showy, and dipping into the ordinary with control and the occasional sustaining descriptive flashes of a born writer" (24 Mar. 1996).

In 1997 Donoghue published *Kissing the Witch: Old Tales in New Skins*, a collection of thirteen reimagined fairy tales. "That was fun because it helped me get away from contemporary naturalism and try out a different style," she told Richards. *Kissing the Witch* was nominated for a James Tiptree Award and, though originally intended for adults, named an ALA Popular Paperback for Young Adults.

## DRAMA AND NONFICTION

In the mid-1990s, while she was garnering critical acclaim for her novels and short stories, Donoghue was also working on theater pieces for the stage and radio. Her 1993 play *I Know My Heart* was performed by Glasshouse Productions in Dublin and was inspired by Regency-period diaries. The year 1993 also saw the publication of Donoghue's survey *Passions between Women: British Lesbian Culture, 1668–1801*, written at the same time that Donoghue was working on her PhD. *Kirkus* called the work "an impressive piece of scholarship" (15 Mar. 1995).

In 1996 Donoghue wrote the stage play *Ladies and Gentlemen*, about vaudeville actors, and the radio play *Trespasses*, about a witch trial. After the publication of *Kissing the Witch*, Donoghue released *We Are Michael Field* (1998), a biography of writers Katherine Bradley and Edith Cooper, who wrote under the pen name Michael Field. On writing the biography, Donoghue told Bensyl that the challenge was "making a text that a reader who's never heard of them will be interested in reading. It's quite different from writing the biography of someone who's already famous. You do have to think of it almost like a novel."

## THREE WORKS OF HISTORICAL FICTION

*Slammerkin*, a best-selling historical novel, was published in 2000. The book was based on a murder that took place in 1763 and is about a young prostitute. "I remember saying to my partner, 'No one's ever going to buy this book. It's horribly grim—why would anyone want to read it?' And I remember my agent saying to me (this was mid-1990s), 'Oh, Emma, historical fiction is really hard to sell,' " Donoghue wrote in the *Writer Magazine*. "The book *was* hard to sell, and the publisher I was with at the time . . . turned it down. Yet it ended up being published by other publishers and doing extremely well" (6 Dec. 2004; ellipsis in orig.). The novel did so well, in fact, that it was a finalist for the 2001 Irish Times Irish Literature Prize for fiction and was named a notable book by *Publishers Weekly* and the *New York Times*, among other accolades.

Donoghue followed *Slammerkin* with *The Woman Who Gave Birth to Rabbits*, a collection of short stories published in 2002. These tales, set in England and Ireland and based on historical events and folklore, earned the author a place as a finalist for the 2003 Stonewall Book Award. Barbara Love, writing for *Library Journal*, wrote, "Each portrait is so strikingly original and so utterly convincing that readers will be hard pressed to believe the story could have happened any other way" (15 May 2002).

For her third work in this series of consecutive historical fiction, Donoghue wrote *Life Mask*. This novel was published in 2004, just before the birth of Donoghue and partner Chris Roulston's first child, their son, Fin. The story is set in late eighteenth-century England and features a love triangle between historic figures actress Eliza Farren, sculptor Anne Damer, and politician Edward Smith-Stanley. "In *Life Mask*, I'm writing about the same things I wrote about in *Passions between Women*," she told Charlotte Abbott for *Publishers Weekly*. "I started with something relatively close to my own experience, and then began telling stories farther and farther from my experience. Now, I'm coming back to that early subject matter with a broader and more mature vision of what's going on" (4 Oct. 2004). *Life Mask* was a 2005 finalist for the Lambda Literary Award for lesbian fiction, the Ferro-Grumley Award for LGBT fiction, and the Stonewall Book Award.

## TOUCHY SUBJECTS, LANDING, AND THE SEALED LETTER

In 2006 Donoghue published *Touchy Subjects*, a collection of short stories that was longlisted for the Frank O'Connor International Short Story Award that year. The collection featured the story "Pluck," about a man who is fixated by a hair growing out of his girlfriend's chin; this story was the basis for Donoghue's script for the 2002 short film *Pluck*, directed by Neasa Hardiman and produced by Vanessa Finlow.

Following the success of *Life Mask* and the birth of her son, Donoghue returned to writing contemporary novels with 2007's *Landing*, a love story with autobiographical elements related to Donoghue and Roulston's transatlantic relationship. This story of two women, one in Ireland and the other in the Canadian town of Ireland, Ontario, examines love and distance and is considered a romantic comedy. *Landing* won the 2008 Golden Crown Literary Society's award for dramatic/general fiction. It is also Donoghue's first work to feature her new Canadian home, where she and Roulston welcomed their daughter, Una, in July 2007.

In 2008 Donoghue returned to the genre of historical fiction. *The Sealed Letter* joins previous works *Slammerkin* and *Life Mask* in examining class in British history. Set in the nineteenth century, *The Sealed Letter* is based on the infamous 1864 divorce of Admiral Henry (Harry) Codrington and his wife, Helen, and focuses on Helen's relationship with women's-rights activist Emily Faithfull. Susann Cokal wrote in the *New York Times* that "the plot is psychologically informed, fast paced and eminently readable," adding that "Donoghue's sympathy for all three of her central characters emerges through intimate narration and lifts the novel out of the tabloid muck" (12 Oct. 2008). The novel was a joint winter of the Lambda Literary Award for lesbian fiction and was longlisted for the Orange Prize and the Giller Prize. On paperback-fiction charts it reached number one in Ireland and number seven in England.

## ROOM

Donoghue's novel *Room*, her most critically and commercially successful work, appeared in 2010. *Room* is written from the perspective of a five-year-old named Jack who was born and raised in a single room with his mother; it becomes clear to the reader that Jack and his mother are being held captive by an abusive kidnapper and rapist. Throughout the story Jack slowly learns about the world outside of the room, and he is eventually able to escape and join it. The book was inspired by the case of Josef Fritzl, an Austrian man who imprisoned his daughter in a basement for over twenty years. "From the Fritzl case I took only the basic notion of an imprisoned woman raising her rapist's child as happily as possible: an extraordinary act of motherhood," Donoghue told Tom Ue in an interview for *Journal of Gender Studies* (Mar. 2012). It was for this "extraordinary act of motherhood" that critics praised the book's depiction of the love between a parent and child.

*Room* was an international best seller and received many accolades, including the Hughes & Hughes Irish Novel of the Year award, the Rogers

Writers' Trust Fiction Prize for best Canadian fiction, a Commonwealth Writers' Prize for best book from Canada or the Caribbean, and an ALA Alex Award. It was included on best-books lists by the *New Yorker*, National Public Radio (NPR), the *New York Times*, and the *Washington Post*. *Room* was also shortlisted for various prizes, including the Orange Prize for Fiction, the Galaxy National Book Award for international author of the year, and—most notably—the Man Booker Prize. "It's not the done thing to show pleasure at being caught up in the Man Booker Prize whirlwind, whether by being longlisted, or shortlisted, or (heaven forfend) by having one's life disrupted by winning the thing," Donoghue wrote in an article for *New Statesman*. "Well, call me a wide-eyed 40-year-old ingénue, but I'm enjoying every minute" (11 Oct. 2010).

**2012 AND ONWARD**

Donoghue followed the success of *Room* with *Astray*, a collection of short stories published in the fall of 2012. The fourteen stories span four hundred years and feature travels both literal and spiritual. An editor's choice book for the *New York Times*, the work was praised for the voices of its many characters. "Donoghue slips into various periods with a costumer's agility," Heller McAlpin wrote for the *Washington Post*. "But what is most impressive about these stories is her ability to plumb historical footnotes for timeless emotional resonance and reanimate 'real people who left traces in the historical record'" (29 Oct. 2012).

In 2012 Donoghue also finished her fourth full-length play, *The Talk of the Town*, following 2005's *Don't Die Wondering* and a 2000 stage version of *Kissing the Witch*. Donoghue's next work is expected to be another work of historical fiction: a novel about an unsolved murder in mid-nineteenth-century San Francisco. Always tending her "garden," Donoghue plans to continue writing, though she does not think she will top the success of *Room*, which she sees as her career peak. "You cannot predict literary success," she told Crown; "the only way you can possibly aim for it is to do your thing and do it well."

In 1998 Donoghue moved to Ontario, Canada, to be with her partner, women's-studies professor Chris Roulston, whom she met while working on her PhD. She became a Canadian citizen in 2004. The couple have two children, a son and a daughter.

**SUGGESTED READING**

Bensyl, Stacia. "Swings and Roundabouts: An Interview with Emma Donoghue." *Irish Studies Review* 8.1 (2000): 73–81. Print.
Crown, Sarah. "Emma Donoghue: The Books Interview." *Guardian*. Guardian News and Media, 19 Oct. 2012. Web. 15 Nov. 2012.
Donoghue, Emma. "How I Write: Emma Donoghue." *Writer Magazine*. Madavor Media, 6 Dec. 2004. Web. 15 Nov. 2012.
---. "I've Caught the Booker Bug." *New Statesman* 11 Oct. 2010: 8. Print.
---. "Voices Heard on the Page." *Wall Street Journal*. Dow Jones, 26 Oct. 2012. Web. 15 Nov. 2012.
Ue, Tom. "An Extraordinary Act of Motherhood: A Conversation with Emma Donoghue." *Journal of Gender Studies* 21.1 (2012): 101–6. Print.

—*Kehley Coviello*

---

# Jean Dujardin

**Born:** June 19, 1972
**Occupation:** Actor and comedian

French actor Jean Dujardin was virtually unknown to American audiences until his breakthrough role in the art house film *The Artist* (2011). His portrayal of a silent movie star not only earned him critical acclaim, but also won him best actor at the 2012 Academy Awards. With his Oscar victory, he became the first Frenchman ever to be so honored.

Dujardin is already a household name in his native country, where he first garnered attention in the popular 1990s television sitcom *Un gars, une fille* (One guy, one girl). He also made his mark on the big screen with starring roles in the cult hit *Brice de Nice* (2005) and the commercially successful comedy *OSS 117: Le Caire, nid d'espions* (OSS 117: Cairo, Nest of Spies, 2006) and its sequel, *OSS 117: Rio ne répond plus* (OSS 117: Lost in Rio, 2009). Since winning his Academy Award, Dujardin has starred in two French films, *Les infidèles* (The Players, 2012) and *Möbius* (2013). Despite his newfound success, the actor has no Hollywood aspirations. "I'm very happy with what I have. If a wonderful project comes my way, I'll do it," he told Kee Chang for *Anthem Magazine* (25 Nov. 2011). "I care most about interesting directors and characters to play. To make a film and cinema is a different thing. I want to make cinema."

**EARLY LIFE**

The youngest of four boys, Jean Edmond Dujardin was born on June 19, 1972, in the residential and industrial suburb of Rueil-Malmaison, located west of Paris, France. He and his brothers grew up in the neighboring suburb of Plaisir, in the rural Yvelines department. As a child Dujardin, whose parents managed a construction firm, was shy but had a very active imagination. "I passed my time daydreaming. They called me 'Jean *de la lune*' (Jean of the moon) because I

Mike Blake/Reuters/Landov

didn't concentrate, I didn't listen," he told Stephen Galloway and Rebecca Leffler for the *Hollywood Reporter* (7 Feb. 2012). "I was just in my own world."

From an early age Dujardin dreamed of becoming a comic book illustrator. "I spoke very little as a child, so everything I saw I put on paper," he told Chloe Malle in an interview for *Vogue* (23 Nov. 2011). "I loved telling stories on the page." Subsequent to finishing high school, he briefly worked as a glazier and locksmith before performing mandatory military service in 1994. During the ten months Dujardin served in an infantry unit in northern France, he took the opportunity to explore his creative side. Military service is "surely the only place where you see all of society," he explained to Tracy McNicoll for the *Daily Beast* (13 Nov. 2011). "It was very cold. I wrote, with a headlamp in my bed, characters I'd seen in the afternoon."

## SKETCH COMEDY

By the end of his military service, Dujardin had penned a one-man show inspired by the various people he encountered during his ten-month stint. While working as a locksmith's apprentice, he approached a bar owner in Paris with a surprising request. "I had written 11 characters, and I asked to perform them," he told Galloway and Leffler. He soon debuted his comedy sketch, which he subsequently performed in the basements of other Parisian bars and cabarets, including Le Carré Blanc. While performing there, Dujardin befriended fellow comedians Bruno Salomone, Eric Collado, Sonia Mathieu, Luc Antoni, Emmanuel Joucia, and Eric Massot. They joined forces to form the comedy group La Bande du Carré Blanc.

Dujardin made his television debut in 1996, performing sketch comedy with his troupe on several episodes of the popular French talent competition show *Graînes de star* (Star Seeds) between 1997 and 1998. One of his more memorable characters was Brice de Nice, a blond, thirty-something wannabe surfer who dresses only in yellow, watches the surfing movie *Point Break*, and spends his time partying on the French Riviera. (Dujardin had created the character of Brice during his stand-up days.) La Bande du Carré Blanc quickly caught the attention of the television host Patrick Sébastien; in 1997 they performed their sketch comedy act on three of his shows: *Fiesta, Le plus grand cabaret du monde* (The biggest cabaret in the world), and *Étonnant et drôle* (Astonishing and funny). That same year the group also recorded the single "Nous Ç Nous," their parody of the '90s boy bands, and released an accompanying video. Following the song's popularity, La Bande du Carré Blanc decided to rename itself after their new hit single. In 1998 Dujardin performed sketches alongside fellow troupe member Salomone on the television comedy *Farce attaque* (Farce attack), hosted by Laurent Baffie.

## THE SMALL AND BIG SCREENS

Dujardin's big break came in 1999, when he was cast opposite Alexandra Lamy in the television sitcom *Un gars, une fille*. This French adaptation of a similarly titled show from Quebec showcases the witty banter between a thirty-something couple, while also offering viewers a glimpse into the humdrum events in their daily lives, such as going to the supermarket or preparing a meal. (The series also spawned other adaptations, including an American version, *Love Bites*.) However, unlike the original series, whose episodes were half an hour long, its French counterpart adopted a much shorter format, airing vignettes between five and seven minutes long, usually right before the eight o'clock evening news on the television channel France 2. The pairing of Dujardin and Lamy proved vastly popular with French audiences; *Un gars, une fille*, which aired five days a week, attracted nearly five million viewers per day at the series' peak in 2000. In addition to his starring role, Dujardin penned several episodes of the show.

Dujardin also began to pursue a career on the big screen. Following a small part in the 2002 short *À l'abri des regards indiscrets* (Away from prying eyes), he made his feature film debut that same year in the comedy *Ah! Si j'étais riche* (If I Were a Rich Man). In 2003 *Un gars, une fille* came to an end after five seasons, just as his big-screen career was starting to take off. His film credits included the 2003 comedies *Toutes les filles sont folles* (All Girls Are Crazy), in which he played a police commissioner, and *Les clefs de bagnole* (The Car Keys), which was written, produced, and directed by Baffie and in which Dujardin had a cameo appearance. Dujardin also portrayed a fugitive in another comedy, *Bienvenue chez les Rozes* (*Welcome to the Roses*).

After appearing in the 2004 comedic short *Rien de grave* (*Nothing Serious*), Dujardin starred in his first big-screen drama: director Nicolas Boukhrief's heist film *Le convoyeur* (*Cash Truck*, 2004), in which Dujardin played the villain. He followed that up with supporting roles, as a best man experiencing his own marital problems in the ensemble comedy *Mariages!* (2004) and as a cowboy in the Western spoof *Les Dalton* (*Lucky Luke and the Daltons*, 2004), a movie adaptation based on the popular Belgian comic-strip character of the same name.

## LEADING MAN

In 2005 Dujardin brought the character of Brice to the big screen in the James Huth comedy *Brice de Nice*, which he also cowrote and in which he costarred opposite Lamy. Dujardin recorded two tracks for the film's soundtrack, "Yellow" and "Le casse de Brice." *Brice de Nice* was a box-office hit, selling over 1.3 million tickets in its opening week and going on to become the highest-grossing French film of the year. Dujardin also landed the romantic lead in *L'amour aux trousses* (Love by the heels, 2005), in which he played a police officer involved in an affair with his partner's wife. In *Il ne faut jurer . . . de rien!* (*Never Say . . . Never*, 2005), he played the dissolute man whose uncle wants to marry him off.

Dujardin subsequently embarked on a fruitful collaboration with Michel Hazanavicius, a cowriter on *Lucky Luke and the Daltons*. In 2006 Dujardin took on the role of a secret agent, opposite Hazanavicius's longtime partner, Bérénice Bejo, in *OSS 117: Cairo, Nest of Spies*, which was referred to as the French *Austin Powers*. The 1950s-era parody almost was not made due to its highly controversial script, which focused on political intrigue and terrorism in the Middle East—subject matter that many feared would alienate France's Muslim population. Dujardin "went looking for a director, and they all turned him down," Hazanavicius told David D'Arcy for the *San Francisco Chronicle* (9 May 2010). "I accepted because I found it wildly funny. Then I met Jean and we realized that we had the same eagerness to make the same film."

Dujardin's performance as bungling spy Hubert Bonisseur de la Bath earned him a best actor nomination at the César Awards, France's equivalent to the Academy Awards. He also garnered critical praise in the United States, where the film was released in 2008. "Dujardin is somehow able to play his clueless hero as a few degrees above the doofus level, mixing in a little suave charm and then effortlessly drifting into charmingly crafted comments that are bold insults," *Chicago Sun-Times* film critic Roger Ebert concluded in his June 25, 2008, review. Equally complimentary was William Arnold for the *Seattle Post-Intelligencer* (8 May 2008), who wrote, "The real joy here is the performance of Jean Dujardin, who, besides being very funny as the Gallic Maxwell Smart, is also enormously charismatic and is made to look uncannily . . . like the young Sean Connery of 'Dr. No' and 'Goldfinger.'" The film went on to earn $21.6 million worldwide.

## MORE DRAMATIC PARTS

Over the next several years, Dujardin continued to pursue comedy while also tackling more dramatic parts. In 2007 he played a police captain investigating the murder of his daughter in the Frank Mancuso crime thriller *Contre-enquête* (*Counter Investigation*). Dujardin returned to the small screen, as a recently separated attorney who becomes involved with a free spirit (Lamy) in *Deux sur la balançoire* (the 2007 romantic drama based on the William Gibson play *Two for the Seesaw*). After reuniting with Lamy and Salomone in the comedy *Cherche fiancé tous frais payés* (Seeking fiancé all expenses paid, 2007), Dujardin starred in the drama *99 francs* (2007), as a successful advertising executive who becomes disillusioned by his profession.

In 2008 Dujardin stepped behind the camera and directed forty episodes of the television sitcom *Palizzi*. He also portrayed the title character in the heist drama *Ca$h* and costarred opposite the legendary Jean-Paul Belmondo in Francis Huster's *Un homme et son chien* (A man and his dog). In 2009 Dujardin reunited with Huth for the Western *Lucky Luke*, in which he played the titular character. That same year he reteamed with Hazanavicius for *OSS 117: Lost in Rio*, earning mixed reviews for his starring role in the sequel to the 2006 film. "Jean Dujardin pulls off a charming, Peter Sellers–esque performance as he bumbles his way through retro cloak-and-dagger intrigue, displaying his character's uncanny ability to insult anyone . . . who's not 100% Gallic, male and a diehard Charles de Gaulle fanatic," Jordan Mintzer wrote for *Variety* (15 Apr. 2009).

Dujardin continued to seek out serious roles in 2010. In addition to playing an alcoholic writer stricken with brain cancer in the black comedy *Le bruit des glaçons* (*The Clink of Ice*), he portrayed a hard-partying drug addict who suffers a near-fatal accident in the comedic drama in *Les petits mouchoirs* (*Little White Lies* in English). Dujardin played against type for his role as family man Marc, who embarks on an affair with his childhood sweetheart, in the thriller *Un balcon sur la mer* (known as *A View of Love* in English).

## THE ARTIST

Dujardin collaborated again with Hazanavicius for his next project—a black-and-white silent film set in the 1920s era. (The film was shot in color and then changed to black and white during postproduction.) Although Dujardin was Hazanavicius's first choice to play the charismatic George Valentin, a popular silent film star who becomes despondent when his career is threatened by the advent of talking pictures, the actor almost turned down the role. "I hesitated, and I even said no. I had some angst about it," Dujardin told Donna Freydkin for *USA Today* (25 Jan. 2012). "I felt like I'd be more of an explorer than an actor because I didn't really know, I didn't understand it. I didn't want to do Charlie Chaplin."

Dujardin prepared himself for the Los Angeles film shoot by immersing himself in numerous black-and-white silent movie classics, studying the movements of Douglas Fairbanks and Gene Kelly. Dujardin also drew inspiration from the Italian actor Vittorio Gassman. "I realized that dialogues were a burden," he told Maia de la Baume for the *New York Times* (18 Nov. 2011). "What I could say with my body I didn't need to express it by talking." The actor also reread the script about fifty times to gain more insight into his character and sported a pencil-thin mustache modeled after Clark Gable's.

For about six months Dujardin and the female lead, Bejo, underwent intensive tap dance training with choreographer Fabien Ruiz for the movie's closing dance sequence. Prior to filming Dujardin also bonded with another costar, a Jack Russell terrier named Uggie, who spent several days training at home with him.

## BEST ACTOR AWARDS

Dujardin's hard work paid off. *The Artist* debuted in mid-May at the 2011 Cannes Film Festival, where Dujardin was named best actor. In October the film premiered in France; a month later it opened in limited release in the United States, where it was well received. In a review for the *New York Observer* (22 Nov. 2011), Rex Reed singled out Dujardin as "an unconventional leading man with the Gallic charm and insouciant charisma of a young Maurice Chevalier." Mick LaSalle was equally effusive. "In Dujardin's performance we discover something extraordinary and lovely, the first truly great silent film performance in about 80 years," he wrote for the *San Francisco Chronicle* (2 Dec. 2011).

For his effort Dujardin was named best actor at several notable awards shows, including the British Academy Film (BAFTA) Awards, the Screen Actors Guild (SAG) Awards, the Independent Spirit Awards, the Golden Globe Awards, and the London Film Critics' Circle, as well as a nomination at the César Awards. He made history by becoming the first Frenchman to win best actor at the Academy Awards, where *The Artist* became the second silent picture ever to win best picture.

## FEATURE FILM DIRECTORIAL DEBUT

Dujardin returned to his French comedy roots with his next movie, *Les infidèles* (*The Players*), a compilation of six adultery-themed vignettes. In addition to starring in the film, which was released in February 2012, Dujardin served as its cowriter, codirector, and coproducer. He came under scrutiny for the movie's racy posters, one of which showed Dujardin holding a woman's legs in the air. The billboards were quickly pulled so as not to hinder Dujardin's chances of winning an Oscar. That same year he also appeared in an episode of television series *Saturday Night Live*.

In 2013 Dujardin created the sketch comedy series *Le débarquement* (The landing) with director Gilles Lellouche. On the big screen he starred in the romantic thriller *Möbius*, in which he played a spy in pursuit of a ruthless money launderer. Dujardin has two upcoming American films: *The Wolf of Wall Street*, starring Leonardo DiCaprio, and *The Monuments Men*, starring George Clooney and Matt Damon. He has reportedly reunited with former Nous Ç Nous members Bruno Salomone, Eric Massot, and Eric Collado, as well as Lamy and her sister Audrey, in the upcoming French comedy *Le petit joueur* (The little player).

Dujardin, who has two sons from his first marriage, lives in France with his second wife, Alexandra Lamy, and stepdaughter. The couple divide their time between Paris and the French countryside.

## SUGGESTED READING

De la Baume, Maia. "French Twist: A Comic Does Nuance." *New York Times*. New York Times, 18 Nov. 2011. Web. 11 Aug. 2013.

Dujardin, Jean. "Q & A with Jean Dujardin." Interview by Kee Chang. *Anthem Magazine*. Anthem, 25 Nov. 2011. Web. 11 Aug. 2013.

Ebert, Roger. "OSS 117: Cairo, Nest of Spies." Rev. of *OSS 117: Cairo, Nest of Spies*, dir. Michel Hazanavicius. *RogerEbert.com*. Ebert Digital, 26 June 2008. Web. 11 Aug. 2013.

Freydkin, Donna. "The Artist Star Jean Dujardin Finds His Voice in the USA." *USA Today*. Gannett, 25 Jan. 2012. Web. 11 Aug. 2013.

Galloway, Stephen, and Rebecca Leffler. "The Artist's Jean Dujardin Is a Star, But Will He Be Welcomed into Hollywood?" *Hollywood Reporter*. Prometheus Global Media, 7 Feb. 2012. Web. 11 Aug. 2013.

Malle, Chloe. "Jean Dujardin: Quiet Force." *Vogue*. Condé Nast, 23 Nov. 2011. Web. 11 Aug. 2013.

McNicoll, Tracy. "A Silent Film Makes Noise." Rev. of *The Artist*, dir. Michel Hazanavicius. *Daily Beast*. Newsweek Daily Beast, 13 Nov. 2011. Web. 11 Aug. 2013.

## SELECTED WORKS

*Un gars, une fille*, 1998–2003; *Brice de Nice*, 2005; *OSS 117: Le Caire, nid d'espions* (*OSS 117: Cairo, Nest of Spies*), 2006; *Ca$h*, 2008; *OSS 117: Rio ne répond plus* (*OSS 117: Lost in Rio*), 2009; *Lucky Luke*, 2009; *Les petits mouchoirs* (*Little White Lies*), 2010; *The Artist*, 2011; *Les infidèles* (*The Players*), 2012; *Möbius*, 2013

—Bertha Muteba

---

# Paul Epworth

**Born:** July 25, 1974
**Occupation:** Music producer

Paul Epworth is an award-winning songwriter and record producer who has worked with a number of artists including, perhaps most famously, the British pop and retro-soul singer Adele. Epworth's collaboration with Adele, which has yielded the megahit "Rolling in the Deep" from the album *21* and the Academy Award–winning James Bond theme "Skyfall," among others songs, began in 2011. In 2012, the duo garnered six Grammy Awards including record of the year and song of the year for "Rolling in the Deep," and album of the year for *21*, for which Epworth also won producer of the year.

A former frontman for the rock band Lomax, Epworth got his start as a producer in the mid-1990s; he gained prominence in that role after producing the Futureheads' debut album in 2004. The eponymous album and Bloc Party's *Silent Alarm* (2005), also an Epworth production, became iconic albums that heralded the postpunk revival in Britain in the early 2000s. Since then, Epworth's output has been prolific. He has worked with the pagan pop outfit Florence and the Machine (stylized Florence + The Machine), R & B singer and rapper Cee-Lo Green, the American indie band Foster the People, and R & B singer/songwriter John Legend. Epworth has sought collaborations varied in genre and influence—in late 2012 he even began collaborating with ex-Beatle Paul McCartney on a solo album—and bristles at the notion of a "signature sound." "Some producers get stuck in the idea that they have a sound, like it's a badge of their identity, when the badge of their work should be about how exciting it is rather than how it sounds," he told Stuart Clarke for *Music Week* (6 Sept. 2008). "I hope to be the guy that can help someone realize their vision and help them sound unique as an artist, otherwise why would you want to make lots of records that sound the same?"

Record producers fulfill a unique role in the studio, and not every producer performs

Jayne Kamin-Oncea/UPI/Landov

the same tasks. Some are project managers, others are music or vocal technicians, and still others provide a creative influence. Epworth's strengths—songwriting and aesthetic vision—make him a particularly hands-on shepherd if a collaborator is willing. "Between being a performer on the records, being a cowriter who contributes a chorus or a hook, someone who contributes an aesthetic or acts as a foil for people to bounce off, or someone who just finds interesting sounds—I could be any one or all of those things at any one time," he told Adam Woods for *Music Week* (20 Mar. 2010).

## EARLY LIFE AND INFLUENCES

Epworth was born in Bishop's Stortford in Hertfordshire, England, on July 25, 1974. His father is an electrical engineer responsible for designing optical fibers and his mother is a nurse. His younger sister, Mary Epworth, is a folk singer and songwriter who has gained attention in her own right. Growing up, Epworth was influenced by the musical tastes of his parents; his father favored artists like Bob Dylan and Yes, while his mother was more partial to Marvin Gaye, Otis Redding, and the African group Ladysmith Black Mambazo. Epworth began playing the guitar as a teenager. His own musical tastes, though varied, centered on the postpunk sounds of the early 1980s. Bands like Joy Division and Gang of Four would provide a strong palette for the postpunk revival Epworth would help define in 2004 and 2005.

Epworth also fell in love with American electro music and hip-hop acts like Public Enemy and the Beastie Boys—though the latter inspired him to lead "a hood ornament–stealing racket," which, according to Piers Martin for the online magazine *XLR8R* (19 Mar. 2007), earned him a criminal record. At the age of eighteen, Epworth enrolled in a basic sound engineering course at Islington Music Workshop. He worked in a demo studio for two years and in 1995 began his first job as a runner at Associated Independent Recording (AIR) Studios, owned by famed Beatles producer George Martin, in Hampstead, London. At the time, the British recording industry was booming thanks to Britpop, characterized by bands like Oasis and Blur. Epworth, whose petty tasks at the time included making tea for artists, was even a part of the drug-addled production of the 1997 Oasis album *Be Here Now*. He also worked with Michael Jackson and the Fugees and learned a number of recording tricks from Bruce Botnick, an American engineer who had worked with the Doors and the Beach Boys.

In the late 1990s, Epworth became a studio assistant at Strongroom in London's Shoreditch district, and in 2000 he became the first soundman of 93 Feet East, a club on Brick Lane. The well-known record producer Tommy D—who has worked with artists like Kanye West and Jay-Z—used to specifically request Epworth when he recorded at Strongroom. "You know there are people, at whatever level, who just love what they do? I knew from the first time I worked with him that he had this enthusiasm, this eagerness," D told Woods of Epworth. "And he made really good tea."

## CREATIVE SIDE PROJECTS

In 2002, Epworth became the singer and guitarist of an indie rock band called Lomax, which he described to Craig McLean for the London *Evening Standard* (1 Feb. 2013) as "very, very loud." Epworth also wrote songs for the band, which produced several singles and one record, *A Symbol of Modern Living* (2003), before breaking up in 2004. Despite Epworth's self-deprecating attitude, Lomax's lone album is considered by some, including the London *Times*, to be an underappreciated gem.

Around the same time, Epworth began disc jockeying and crafting remixes under the names Phones (for all-digital mixes), Echo Channel (for live and analog mixes), and Epic Man. In fact, it was a combination of the Lomax record and a Phones remix of Shaznay Lewis's "Never Felt Like This Before" that won him the job on the Futureheads' debut album. "With my remixes I work very conceptually," he told Gareth Dobson for the music website *Drowned in Sound* (14 Jan. 2005), "and can usually hear the track in my head before I open the laptop." Epworth often employs a similar quasi-mystical approach in the studio; he told Steve Jelbert for the London

*Times* (15 Apr. 2005) that he "sees" sound in texture and color.

Epworth continued his various side gigs, with the exception of Lomax, after taking on a full-time workload as a producer. He has estimated that during the early and mid-2000s, he was making an average of about one hundred tracks a year among all of his separate projects.

## FUTUREHEADS, BLOC PARTY, AND THE HEIGHT OF THE POSTPUNK REVIVAL

In 2003, Epworth toured as a live soundman with LCD Soundsystem and the Rapture, and in 2004, he was hired to produce the Futureheads' self-titled debut album. He actually "inherited" the job, according to Woods, from Gang of Four producer Andy Gill, who produced several tracks before the band sought out Epworth. "It was the first time I knew I had to deliver something to a standard, but it was also the first time I had actually had the tools to compete with other producers," he told Woods. Epworth had been a fan of the band since their formation in 2000. After four years, pressure to produce a stellar debut, matching reports of their much-hyped live shows, was high. In the studio, Epworth and the band worked together, drawing on unusual source material—including the band's talent for a cappella and the techniques of avant-garde composer Steve Reich—to create an entirely new sound. Barry Hyde, the band's frontman, later described Epworth the producer as possessing "a unique attitude that people . . . find terrifying and, after a while, kind of inspirational," he told Jelbert.

After its release in July 2004, the album was praised for its pop influences as well as its well-turned nod to the band's postpunk forbearers. Sam Ubi, for the influential online music magazine *Pitchfork* (29 July 2004), wrote that the Futureheads' vocals were the album's "uncontested centerpiece . . . evoking a decidedly Anglo brattiness, but the band's angular guitar/drum interplay provides an equally impressive framework, summoning a Gang of Four more interested in delivering sparkling melody."

In 2005, Epworth produced *Silent Alarm*, the debut album of another postpunk indie band called Bloc Party. The album was recorded in Denmark over a span of twenty-eight days. Fusing postpunk and dance beats, *Silent Alarm* became an iconic album of the era; taken alongside his work a year earlier with the Futureheads, Epworth is credited with forging a new direction in British alternative music. Subsequent collaborations—Maximo Park's *A Certain Trigger* (2005), the Rakes' *Capture/Release* (2005), and the Rapture's *Pieces of the People We Love* (2006)—solidified his status. In 2008, Epworth produced the album *Beautiful Future* with the veteran indie rock band Primal Scream.

## A TURN TOWARD POP

In a somewhat surprising turn, Epworth began working with the British singer/songwriter and musician Kate Nash in 2007. Nash, who was only a teenager at the time, rose to industry fame after posting demos of her finely wrought and lyrically complex songs on the social networking site MySpace. After meeting Epworth, the two penned what would become Nash's first two singles, "Foundations" and "Pumpkin Soup." The work earned her a record contract, and "Foundations," a delightfully incongruous pop song about a crumbling relationship, reached the number two slot on the UK Singles Chart. "I had always been a songwriter—that is how I got into making music," Epworth told Woods, "but Kate was the first person I was able to write with." Their successful partnership culminated in Nash's debut album *Made of Bricks* (2007), which reached number one on the charts.

In 2009, Epworth teamed up with Florence Welch, the powerhouse singer behind the goth-tinged indie band Florence and the Machine. "With Flo, we had this crazy idea of making pagan R & B," Epworth told Woods. "The great thing about her is, she is up for trying absolutely anything. We went out and sampled fireworks and crows—all these crazy field recordings and found sounds." For Welch's debut album *Lungs* (2009), Epworth cowrote and produced the songs "Rabbit Heart (Raise It Up)," "Howl," and "Blinding." He also produced the exuberant Welch-penned "Cosmic Love." The rock and pop–influenced album, which can be described as both ethereal and bombastic, made Florence and the Machine an international sensation. Epworth also produced and cowrote Welch's second album *Ceremonials* (2011), honing the expansive sound that has made Welch famous.

In 2011, Epworth produced several tracks on the debut album of the Los Angeles–based indie trio Foster the People. The album, called *Torches*, includes the hit single "Pumped Up Kicks" and features some of Epworth's writing. As with his other collaborations around that time, Epworth's interest in Foster the People shows his movement toward more American acts, and a more American sound. In 2010, Epworth surprised fans again by collaborating on *The Lady Killer*, the third solo album of CeeLo Green, one half of the duo Gnarls Barkley. The album showcases Green's classic soul roots, even on the Epworth-produced cover "No One's Gonna Love You," which was originally released by the indie rock band Band of Horses. Epworth also worked with R & B superstar John Legend on a song called "Who Did That to You?" which appeared on the *Django Unchained* soundtrack (2013). Epworth began next to work on several tracks for Paul McCartney's sixteenth solo album, set for release in late 2013.

## "ROLLING IN THE DEEP"

"The greatest pop records are forward-thinking, exciting; they change music, but it doesn't mean they are painful to listen to," Epworth told Woods. "Pop has that power to be simultaneously creative and yet pleasing to everybody." He counts the Ronettes' 1963 Motown classic "Be My Baby" and Beyonce's 2003 "Crazy in Love" as pop game changers, and some critics have suggested that the Epworth-produced "Rolling in the Deep"—which James McKinley Jr. for the *New York Times* (10 Feb. 2012) called "one of the biggest crossover hits of the last quarter century"—might carry the same weight.

In 2009, British soul singer Adele was hot off her best-selling album *19* (2008) and looking to begin recording her highly anticipated follow-up, *21*. (The numbers denote her age at the time of the recording.) In October, Adele met with Epworth for a songwriting session. She was distracted at the time, nursing the fresh wounds of a bad breakup. Explaining the situation to Epworth, she teared up again but decided to channel her hurt into a new riff she was working on—it would turn out to be the opening lines of "Rolling in the Deep," including the words "there's a fire," that set the song in motion. "I said wow, and I just grabbed a guitar and quickly tried to figure out what the key was," Epworth told McKinley. "We wrote the core of the song—her verses and the chords—in under fifteen minutes. And the rest of it was structured over two hours."

The song sprung from Adele's raw emotion, and Epworth made the wise decision to use her original demo, the one she recorded that day, on the album. He told McKinley that he believed that the hair-raising power of her first takes would be nearly impossible to recreate.

A slew of awards and global sales numbers proved Epworth right. The song, and the award-winning album it appeared on, made Adele a beloved star the world over. In 2012, she and Epworth continued their collaboration to write and produce a song called "Skyfall" for the James Bond movie of the same name. They recorded the vocal and piano tracks in Epworth's small studio and then wrapped up the track with a full orchestra at Abbey Road Studios (London). In 2013, "Skyfall" became the first James Bond theme to win best original song at the Academy Awards.

Epworth is married to makeup artist Danielle Epworth. The two have a daughter named Vivienne and live in Brondesbury Park in London. Epworth has been working on a solo album since 2008.

## SUGGESTED READING

Clarke, Stuart. "Epworth's on the Button." *Music Week* 6 Sept. 2008: 8. Print.

Dobson, Gareth. "'I Just Wish We Could Un-Imagine Keane . . .'" *Drowned in Sound*. DrownedinSound.com, 14 Jan. 2005. Web. 11 June 2013.

Jelbert, Steve. "The Man Who Sees Hits." *Times* [London]. Times Newspapers, 15 Apr. 2005. Web. 11 June 2013.

Martin, Piers. "Paul Epworth: Totally Epic." *XLR8R*. Spin Media, 19 Mar. 2007. Web. 11 June 2013.

McKinley, James C., Jr. "Hot Tracks, the Collaborative Method." *New York Times* 10 Feb. 2012: C1. Print.

McLean, Craig. "The Spin Doctor: The Man Adele and Florence Turn to When They Want a Hit." *Evening Standard* [London]. Evening Standard, 1 Feb. 2013. Web. 11 June 2013.

Woods, Adam. "Worthy Contender." *Music Week* 20 Mar. 2010: 16–21. Print.

## SELECTED WORKS

*The Futureheads* (with the Futureheads), 2004; *Silent Alarm* (with Bloc Party), 2005; *Pieces of the People We Love* (with the Rapture), 2006; *Made of Bricks* (with Kate Nash), 2007; *Intimacy* (with Bloc Party), 2009; *Lungs* (with Florence and the Machine), 2009; *The Lady Killer* (with CeeLo Green), 2010; *Torches* (with Foster the People), 2011; *Ceremonials* (with Florence and the Machine), 2011; *21* (with Adele), 2011

—*Molly Hagan*

# Samuel Eto'o

**Born:** March 10, 1981
**Occupation:** Soccer player

In the summer of 2011, Cameroonian soccer star Samuel Eto'o signed with the Russian team Anzhi Makhachkala, reportedly making him the highest-paid player in soccer (known in Europe as "football"). He joined the Russian squad after five years with Spain's FC Barcelona, which he helped lead to prestigious UEFA (Union of European Football Associations) Champions League titles in 2006 and 2009; Spanish league championships in 2005, 2006, and 2009; and a 2009 win at Spain's oldest annual soccer competition, the Copa del Rey. By winning three major trophies in 2009, Barcelona achieved a "treble" and became the first Spanish soccer team to achieve such a feat.

The following year, Eto'o moved to Italy to play for Inter Milan. His first year with the team brought the country their first-ever treble. The honor also made Eto'o the first player to achieve the treble in consecutive seasons. Eto'o

Richard Heathcote/Getty Images for Puma

is a member of the Cameroonian national team that won the gold medal at the 2000 Summer Olympics.

## EARLY LIFE AND AMATEUR CAREER

Samuel Eto'o Fils was born on March 10, 1981, in Nkon, a town in the west African nation of Cameroon. He grew up in the capital city of Douala with his parents and five brothers and sisters. After his father was laid off from his job as an accountant, his mother worked as a street vendor, selling fish that she would purchase at the nearby port.

Eto'o developed a love of soccer at a young age, after he attended a soccer game that featured legendary player and fellow Cameroonian Roger Milla. "I was lucky enough to have seen him play a great match when I was only six," Eto'o said in an interview for *AskMen.com*. "At the end of the match, Milla threw his shirt to the fans and I was very lucky to catch it. Ever since then, I was fascinated by football."

Eto'o grew up playing the sport on the streets with other neighborhood children, using makeshift soccer balls made of tightly wrapped plastic bags bound with tape. At the age of twelve, he was admitted to l'Ecole de Football des Brasseries du Cameroun, a sports academy in Douala where he started honing his soccer skills. In his early teens, he also attended the Kadji Sports Academy and played for UCB Douala, a second-division club.

When Eto'o was fifteen, he made his first international appearance as a member of Cameroon's national under-sixteen squad. While competing at a tournament, Eto'o captured the attention of Jose Pirri, a former player and scout for Real Madrid, a professional soccer team based in Spain and one of Europe's top clubs.

## REAL MADRID

In February 1997, fifteen-year-old Eto'o signed a contract with Real Madrid and traveled from Cameroon to join his new team. Since Eto'o was a minor, he was initially assigned to Real Madrid's reserve squad in Segunda (Real Madrid B), the third-highest level of the Spanish league. (The reserve squad usually consists of rising youth players and first-team squad players.)

As a foreign-born player, however, Eto'o was not allowed to play in the Segunda División B. As a result, Real Madrid B loaned him out to Club Deportivo Leganés, a team in the Segunda División. Eto'o scored three goals in twenty-eight appearances during the 1997–98 season. In June 1998, he represented his native country in the FIFA World Cup. Although Cameroon failed to advance past the first round, the seventeen-year-old, who made his lone appearance as a substitute, was the youngest player in the tournament.

Eto'o saw no action in 1999 when he joined Reial Club Deportiu (RCD) Espanyol de Barcelona, on loan from Real Madrid. He recalled his season-long stint with the team as a very challenging experience. "The coach, Miguel Brindisi, never played me and I felt depressed there and couldn't wait to return to Madrid," he told Dan Brennan for *Sports Illustrated* (6 Jan. 2010). His wish came true the following season, however, when Eto'o left Espanyol and played briefly for Real Club Deportivo (RCD) Mallorca, which had also secured his services on loan. (Mallorca is a first-division team in La Liga, Spain's top professional soccer league.)

## NATIONAL AND INTERNATIONAL LEVELS

In late January 2000, Eto'o rejoined the national team at the African Cup of Nations. After making it past the first round of the tournament, Cameroon defeated Algeria in the quarterfinals to reach the semifinals, where Eto'o and his teammates registered a three-goal shutout against Tunisia. Cameroon defeated Nigeria in a penalty shoot-out to capture the championship. Eto'o scored four goals during the tournament, and in September of that year, the Cameroon national squad (also known as the Indomitable Lions) received an Olympic gold medal—the country's first—during the Summer Games in Sydney, Australia, with a penalty-kick shootout victory over Spain. Eto'o finished third in the voting for the African Player of the Year award.

In July 2001, during the summer transfer window (the period from July 1 to August 31 when players are traded between teams), Eto'o left Real Madrid and signed with RCD Mallorca for $6.3 million—then a club record. During his first season with the squad, he made thirty

appearances, twenty-three starts, and scored six goals. RCD Mallorca finished the regular season with a record of eleven wins, ten draws, and seventeen losses; the team competed in the UEFA Cup, where it was eliminated in the third round. For the second straight year, Eto'o placed third in the African Player of the Year voting.

In January 2002, Eto'o and his Cameroon national teammates successfully defended their African Cup of Nations title. Another penalty-kick shootout win, this time against Senegal, earned the team their second consecutive World Cup berth, but the team failed to make it past the first round. Eto'o then returned to Mallorca for the 2002–03 season. He amassed fourteen goals in twenty-nine starts, while his team posted a regular-season record of fourteen wins, ten draws, and fourteen losses. Eto'o also scored two of his team's three goals to help Mallorca win the prestigious Copa del Rey trophy, which is an annual contest between Spanish soccer clubs. Also in 2003, Eto'o finally captured the African Player of the Year prize.

Eto'o performed solidly for Mallorca in 2003–04, scoring seventeen goals in thirty-one starts. The team's regular season ended with fifteen wins, six draws, and seventeen losses. The team also reached the fourth round of the UEFA Cup. For the second consecutive year, Eto'o was named African Player of the Year.

## FC BARCELONA

In August 2004, Eto'o signed with first-division rival FC Barcelona for a reported €24 million, which was then the equivalent of over $30 million. He made headlines in November during a match in Madrid against fellow Spanish team Getafe Club de Fútbol when opposing fans hurled racist insults at him every time he made contact with the ball. Eto'o reacted in frustration by kicking the ball into the stands where the chants were loudest. He was also the subject of racism while playing against another Spanish team, Real Zaragoza, in February 2005. Eto'o almost walked off the field as a result of the fans' racist remarks; following Barcelona's victory, Eto'o taunted the spectators in return. Only two of the abusive fans were identified, and they were given five-month sporting events bans. The Royal Spanish Football Federation, the governing body of soccer in Spain, received criticism for levying a modest fine of €600 on Real Zaragoza for their fans' behavior.

Despite these difficulties, Eto'o had a breakthrough performance in his debut season with FC Barcelona. He started in thirty-seven games and scored twenty-four goals—the second-best scorer in the league—and helped his new team edge out his former club to clinch the La Liga (the Spanish soccer league) title. Eto'o drew ire for repeatedly chanting the phrase "Madrid, bastards, hail the champion" during on-the-field celebrations—an act that earned him a federation fine of €12,000. Eto'o, whose team also reached the first round of the UEFA Champions League, issued a public apology to his former team and their fans. In June 2005, Eto'o won his third African Player of the Year award and signed a contract extension reportedly worth €5.5 million.

The following season, Eto'o was the league's high scorer, with twenty-six goals in thirty-five starts. His effort helped Barcelona capture their second straight La Liga championship. In the UEFA Champions League tournament, Barcelona defeated Chelsea (England) in the first round and then shut out Benfica (Portugal) and Milan (Italy) in the quarterfinals and semifinals, respectively, before edging out Arsenal (England) in the final match by a score of two to one.

Eto'o, who scored six times during the entire tournament, including the game-tying goal, won the UEFA Best Forward of the Year prize. As the top scorer in the league, he was also awarded the Pichichi trophy. He scored his first hat trick (three goals in one game) during a game against the Greek team Panathinaikos F.C. Additionally, Eto'o was the third-highest vote-getter for the 2005 FIFA World Player of the Year honors behind teammate Ronaldinho Gaúcho and Chelsea's Frank Lampard.

His impressive season was also marked by an incident that occurred in late February 2005, during a game against Real Zaragoza in their home stadium. A visibly upset Eto'o threatened to walk off Zaragoza's field after being subjected to racist verbal taunts by their fans. Although several fans were identified, fined, and banned from attending sporting events for five months, Eto'o remarked that the punishment was too light and suggested the stadium be closed for a year.

Eto'o also experienced disappointment while playing for the Cameroon national squad. In addition to not qualifying for the 2006 World Cup, Team Cameroon suffered a loss in the quarterfinals of the African Cup of Nations. The Ivory Coast won the penalty kick shootout to advance to the semifinals. Despite missing the decisive game-tying penalty kick, Eto'o led the tournament's scorers with five goals.

## ADVERSITY AND MILESTONES

Eto'o was injured at the start of the 2006–07 season when he tore the meniscus in his right knee during a game against the German team Werder Bremen. After undergoing surgery, Eto'o was sidelined for four months and began training again in mid-January 2007. He returned a month later and found himself in the midst of controversy when manager Frank Rijkaard accused him of refusing to enter a game as a substitute. Eto'o refuted Rijkaard's claim, saying he had declined to play because he was not properly warmed up. Ronaldinho labeled his teammate's actions as selfish, a claim that Eto'o promptly denied. A few days later the teammates had apparently resolved their differences and were photographed embracing during a training session.

Eto'o suffered a minor setback in late August when he aggravated his meniscus while playing in an exhibition game against FC Internazionale Milano. By early December he had returned to the field. Despite his injuries, Eto'o managed to score eleven goals in seventeen starts. With twenty-two victories, ten draws, and six losses, Barcelona finished second. The team was unable to successfully defend its title, losing to Liverpool in the first round of the UEFA Champions League.

In 2007–08, Eto'o started in eighteen games and scored sixteen goals. He also registered his second career hat trick during a four-run victory over Spain's Levante Unión Deportiva. Barcelona placed third in the league, with nineteen wins, ten draws, and nine losses. Eto'o and his teammates reached the semifinals of the UEFA Champions League.

As a member of the Cameroonian national team, Eto'o was the leading scorer at the 2008 African Cup of Nations, where his team lost to Egypt in the finals. However, his season was not without controversy. He made headlines in June 2008 for headbutting Cameroonian journalist Philippe Boney during an altercation between local reporters and Team Cameroon players following a pregame press conference. Eto'o apologized to Boney, who also sustained a broken arm, and offered to cover his medical costs.

In 2009, FC Barcelona clinched the La Liga title—its first since 2006—after amassing a record of twenty-seven wins, six draws, and five losses. Eto'o and his teammates were also winners of the Copa del Rey and the UEFA Champions League tournament, making them the first Spanish club to capture a treble. Eto'o achieved several individual milestones. During a game against Spain's Unión Deportiva Almeria, he registered the fastest hat trick in FC Barcelona history, notching three goals in only twenty-three minutes. His first four-goal game came against Real Valladolid Club de Fútbol. Eto'o ended the season as the league's second-leading scorer, with thirty goals.

## FC INTERNAZIONALE MILANO

In July 2009, Eto'o joined Italian club Internazionale Milano (also known as Inter Milan) as part of a transfer agreement between the Italian club and FC Barcelona, who received Zlatan Ibrahimovic and €46 million in exchange. (Also included in the deal was Aleksandr Hleb, who was loaned to Inter Milan for one season.) Eto'o denied any animosity toward his former coach Pep Guardiola, who actively encouraged the transfer and with whom he had shared a rocky relationship. During his five years with Barcelona, Eto'o scored 108 goals in 145 appearances to become one of the club's all-time leading scorers.

Two months after signing a five-year contract with his new club, Eto'o took legal action, claiming that FC Barcelona owed him €3 million. Eto'o referred to a Spanish Players Union rule stating that a player can claim fifteen percent of his transfer fee; Barcelona responded that the rule only applied to transfers between Spanish clubs. (The case remained in litigation until early April 2012, when Eto'o dropped his lawsuit.)

Eto'o enjoyed a memorable first season with Inter Milan. He scored twelve goals in thirty-two games and helped lead his team to the Series A title, also known as the "Scudetto." Eto'o and his teammates also defeated rival Italian club Associazione Sportiva (AS) Roma to win the Coppa Italia. At the UEFA Champions League, he scored the lone goal in the first-round match against Chelsea FC that allowed his team to advance to the quarterfinals.

After defeating CSKA Moscow, Eto'o and his teammates edged out FC Barcelona to reach the Champions League final. With its two-goal shutout victory over Bayern Munich, Inter Milan became the first Italian club to win the treble. Eto'o also earned the distinction of being the only player to accomplish a treble in consecutive seasons. Inter Milan also competed in the 2009 Supercoppa Italiana but suffered a loss to Società Sportiva Lazio.

In 2010–11, Eto'o improved upon the previous season's performance. He amassed a team-high twenty-one goals in thirty-five appearances for Inter Milan, who finished second to A.C. Milan for the Serie A title. Eto'o and his teammates also earned runner-up status at the 2010 UEFA Super Cup, which was won by Atlético Madrid.

In the summer of 2010, Inter Milan and Roma faced off again, this time in the Supercoppa Italiana, an annual preseason soccer competition. Eto'o scored two goals to propel his team to victory. At the FIFA World Cup, newly appointed captain Eto'o and his Cameroonian teammates failed to make it past the first round, although Eto'o scored a goal in a first-round match against Denmark. Later that year, Inter Milan reached the finals of the FIFA World Club Cup, where Eto'o scored one of three goals to help his team clinch and successfully defend the title. Eto'o also made history by becoming the first person to earn four African Player of the Year honors.

## ANZHI MAKHACHKALA

In August 2011, Eto'o was transferred to the Russian club Anzhi Makhachkala. He subsequently signed a three-year contract, reportedly worth €30 million, to become the world's highest-paid player. "It's not every day you have the chance of taking part in something so grandiose,

of transforming an unknown club into a European force. Battling the odds and making history is what drives me and Anzhi offered me all of that," Eto'o told Kevin Palmer for *ESPN FC* (22 Jan. 2012). His decision to join Anzhi was surprising, since Russian fans have been known to target dark-skinned players. Although Eto'o claims that he has not been subjected to racial abuse since he started playing for Anzhi, a rival fan targeted his teammate Roberto Carlos, who is Brazilian, during a game against FC Krylia Sovetov Samara.

In November 2011, Team Cameroon defeated Morocco to capture the LG Cup Africa. However, a month after the LG Cup victory, Cameroon's football federation imposed a fifteen-game suspension on Eto'o and his teammates for boycotting an exhibition game against Algeria. They decided to sit out as protest over unpaid bonuses from the LG Cup win. Also in November, Eto'o was nominated for the Golden Ball trophy, given to the world's best soccer player.

In April 2012, the Italian newspaper *Corriere dello Sport* reported that Eto'o was unhappy with the conditions of the fields in the Russian Premier League and planned to request a transfer back to his former club Inter Milan. His representative, Peppino Tirri, has refuted the claim. Three months later, Eto'o was charged with four counts of tax evasion for allegedly failing to report income earned while playing for Barcelona from 2006 to 2009. Although Eto'o has denied the charges, if convicted he faces a potential sentence of up to five years prison for each count and a fine of up to €21 million.

Eto'o is sponsored by such companies as Puma, a German shoe and sportswear company, and US car manufacturer Ford Motor Company. He has established Fundesport Academy, a sports foundation that promotes education, cooperation, and child development among Cameroon's youths by using soccer as a social integration tool. Eto'o married in July 2007, and he and his wife, Georgette, have three children.

## SUGGESTED READING

Badenhausen, Kurt. "Soccer's Samuel Eto'o Scores Record New Contract." *Forbes*. Forbes. com, 21 Aug. 2011. Web. 11 Sept. 2012.

Brennan, Dan. "Q&A with Cameroon Hero Eto'o." *SI.com*. Turner Broadcasting System, 6 Jan. 2010. Web. 11 Sept. 2012.

Cary, Tom. "Spain Told to Get Tough on Racism." *Telegraph*. Telegraph Media Group, 3 Mar. 2006. Web. 12 Sept. 2012.

Clegg, Jonathan, and Allan Cullison. "Sports Has a New Salary King." *Wall Street Journal*. Dow Jones, 24 Aug. 2011. Web. 11 Sept. 2012.

McRae, Donald. "World Cup 2010: Samuel Eto'o on His Incredible Journey." *Guardian*. Guardian News and Media, 7 June 2010. Web. 11 Sept. 2012.

Palmer, Kevin. "Eto'o Committed to Anzhi Project." *ESPN FC*. ESPN Internet Ventures, 22 Jan. 2012. Web. 17 Sept. 2012.

"Samuel Eto'o." *AskMen*. IGN Entertainment, 1996–2012. Web. 21 Sept. 2012.

—*Bertha Muteba*

Courtesy of Gregory Euclide

# Gregory Euclide

**Born:** February 11, 1974
**Occupation:** Artist

Gregory Euclide started out making paintings and drawings with an intense focus on the theme of nature. By 2008 he had developed the style for which he is now known—three-dimensional scenes of nature, for which he uses such diverse ingredients as acrylic paint, paper, pencil, moss, dirt, foam, fern, and grass. His works have been exhibited in galleries and museums across the country, such as the David B. Smith Gallery in Denver, Colorado, and the Museum of Arts and Design in New York City. His work will be featured in current and upcoming solo shows at the Martha Otero Gallery in Los Angeles through May 16, 2013; the StolenSpace Gallery in London, United Kingdom, from November 8 to December 1, 2013; and, at the Art Center of Saint Peter in Saint Peter, Minnesota, starting on December 7, 2013. He is also participating in several group exhibits both in the United States and abroad, and will be part of performances this year in Minnesota and Belgium. Photographic reproductions of his work have appeared in two art books, *Badlands: New Horizons in Landscape* (2008) and *Otherworldly: Optical Delusions and Small Realities* (2011).

What likely brought Euclide the greatest notice—particularly outside the art world—was his creation of an album cover for indie-rock musician Bon Iver. The album cover of *Bon Iver, Bon Iver* (2011) was seen by many people who otherwise might not have seen Euclide's work. "The crowd that is interested in actively seeking out visual art is very small compared to the amount of people who listen to or know about a musician like Bon Iver," Euclide told *Current Biography* in an e-mail interview, the source for all quotes for this article unless otherwise noted. "Being 'better known' is never really an end to my production, but it is a really wonderful by-product of this collaboration. Art is communication, and of course I want to have a dialog with the largest amount of people possible."

## EARLY LIFE

Gregory Euclide was born in Milwaukee, Wisconsin, on February 11, 1974. Euclide and his brother, Brian, grew up in Cedarburg, Wisconsin. Euclide's father, Bill, was an art teacher, and his mother, Sandy, worked as a landscape gardener. From an early age, art and nature were very important to Euclide. Growing up in a rural area had a profound effect on him as a child. "I spent a lot of time in the fields and tree lines between the farm fields," he recalled. "I am very thankful that there were areas by our house that could not be farmed. Those areas were rich with plant life and wildlife and they seemed to have no owner. . . . As a child I walked wherever I wanted to, mostly through fields and forests. I gained a real appreciation for observation." Yet this environment also proved isolating, especially for a child. "It forced me to be creative," Euclide said. His parents were very supportive, buying him art supplies for his birthday and for Christmas. "They allowed me to be unique without making me feel self-conscious," he said.

While in junior high school, he played a lot of sports (basketball, tennis, soccer, as well as skateboarding) and he was very much into music—collecting tapes, CDs, and records; he also played in bands. Euclide was raised Catholic, but "if it did anything," it was to make him "question the cultural conventions." It made him wonder about the human need to believe in what he came to see as fantastical stories. Although the stories interest him, he says that he "firmly [rejects] any organized religion."

During his high school years, Euclide began to focus more on making art. According to his own account, Euclide was "decent" at art. His teachers liked his work. He won awards. And even back then, he did a fair amount of experimentation. A teacher taught him to use a technique of layering washes of linseed oil and pigment, which produced a watercolor effect. He was also fascinated by surrealists such as Salvador Dalí, René Magritte, and Yves Tanguy. Throughout high school, he continued to paint using oils—he would spend every lunch period in the art room—and experiment in art, for example by making his own frames and adding dimensions to the surface. "I would do this," he recalled, "through the addition of extra wood to build the canvas up or by pulling the canvas back into the frame through the use of fishing line and fishing hooks. I have no idea where I got the idea to do such things. I just know that we did not really know what 'art' was, so we did not know the conventional limitations to it. It felt like we were being experimental in the most honest sense of the word. We were just exploring possibilities and making objects."

## COLLEGE AND BEYOND

After graduating from Cedarburg High School in 1992, Euclide enrolled at the University of Wisconsin, Oshkosh, where he pursued both a bachelor of fine arts degree and a bachelor of arts in education. While in college, his understanding of art broadened. He became interested in the artists Egon Schiele, Gustav Klimt, Alphonse Mucha, and Vincent van Gogh. "In college I always wanted to paint the air around the still lives as much as the still life," said Euclide. "I think when I started seeing van Gogh and how he was treating the sky and air with his brush strokes, I had a mixed reaction. First, it was pure excitement; someone else had acknowledged the invisible. Secondly, there was this feeling that someone had already done it." Although Euclide did not use as much paint as van Gogh did, he did use many layers. Also in college, he abandoned oils and switched to acrylics, because breathing in the oil paint fumes while painting made him feel ill. Euclide received his bachelor's degrees in 1997.

After college, he started reading more about various art movements, about the ideas and philosophies behind them, and about the implementation of those ideas. He became interested in the symbolists, a late nineteenth-century art and poetry movement, and art nouveau, a movement in art, decoration, and architecture that followed and blossomed in the very early twentieth century. "Once I started reading art history, I began to understand and appreciate all of the different types of art," Euclide recalled. "It was no longer important for me to like them; I simply wanted to understand them." Euclide also became interested in the yet more radical twentieth-century multidisciplinary modern art movements Fluxus and Arte Povera. What Euclide found most appealing was their originality, their efforts to make unique art.

## GRADUATE SCHOOL

After graduating from college, Euclide started teaching art at a high school in Minnesota and continued to make art. He began to exhibit his work, both in group and solo shows, in 2005, at first in Minnesota, and then in galleries in New York, San Francisco, Miami, and other cities across the country. His pieces were primarily works on paper, although he was also starting to use paper not only as a surface but also as a medium. But he wanted to advance his artistic practice—to "explore what was possible with the surface."

In 2006 Euclide enrolled in the MFA program at the Minneapolis College of Art and Design in Minnesota. During those two years, he learned a lot from his mentor, the sculptor and 3-D shop director Don Myhre—a "wonderful asset," said Euclide, "in that he exposed me to tools, processes, and ways of thinking that I had not had access to before." Because Euclide's art was so focused on the surface, a sculptor was the perfect mentor. He even learned processes like foundry work and welding. "If I dreamed up a form, Don knew how to arrive at it," Euclide recalled. "I am very intuitive in the studio and so it took great patience to undergo these often-slow processes involved in sculpting. I gained a grain of discipline and scratched the surface of how I might use that." By 2008, Euclide was manipulating the surface of his works. Each painting consisted of two or three sheets of paper. He not only painted the representations of land, he treated the surface like a landscape; into the folds of the paper, he would pour pools of blue paint. He would then add artifacts from the land and his surroundings—such as moss, dirt, and Styrofoam—in order to contrast it with what was realistically painted. "Adding material from the land was a way for me to introduce another mode of representation," Euclide explained. He received his MFA degree from the Minneapolis College of Art and Design in 2008.

## BON IVER

By 2009, Euclide was exhibiting his work at various galleries in Minnesota, as well as California, Colorado, Florida, Illinois, New York, and Ohio. Euclide went on to have a lasting relationship with one of the galleries, Denver's David B. Smith Gallery. One day Euclide received an e-mail from Justin Vernon, a singer-songwriter who goes by the stage name Bon Iver. Bon Iver's debut album, *For Emma, Forever Ago* (2007) made waves in the indie-rock world, primarily because of Vernon's sensitive singing and stripped-down instrumentation. The album was also recorded in a cabin in Wisconsin, which added an aura of mystery to the whole project. So when Vernon e-mailed Euclide, he asked if he would like to make a cover for Bon Iver's second album. Euclide gave an enthusiastic yes. "I was extremely excited," he recalled. Euclide, even as far back as high school, never wanted to use his art to sell any product—or anything he didn't believe in. But because he was such a fan of Bon Iver's first album, he had no qualms about making an album cover for *Bon Iver, Bon Iver* (2011). The cover, with various influences, including Japanese art, features a solitary house in the woods, in nature, surrounded by trees and lakes. "I was very pleased with the way we executed the album cover," said Euclide. "The way the art was presented like art . . . you can see the edge of the painting. That means a lot to me. It was not a graphic for an album cover, it was an album cover with a photograph of a painting on it." In part, the popularity of Bon Iver and the album helped to make the name Gregory Euclide known to more people.

## AWARDS, TEACHING, AND CHARITY

Euclide has been the recipient of various awards, fellowships, and grants, including the Prairie Lakes Regional Arts Council Emerging Artist Grant, 2012; Jerome Foundation Fellowship for Emerging Artists, 2011–12; Open Studios, Museum of Arts and Design, in New York City, 2011; Minnesota State Arts Board Artist Initiative Grant, 2008; third place Jurors' Award from the Duluth Art Institute, 58th Arrowhead Biennial, in Duluth, Minnesota, 2008; the Hungarian Multicultural Center, International Artist-in-Residency Program, 2008; a Merit Award from the Northwest Art Center, Paperworks Competition, in Minot, North Dakota, 2007; the Minneapolis College of Art and Design Trustee Scholarship, 2006; the Minnesota State Arts Board Artist Initiative Grant, 2005; and the Blacklock Nature Sanctuary Fellowship/Residency, 2005.

Euclide has taught art at various high schools, museums, and colleges. From 1997 to 2000, he served as an art instructor at the Kingsland High School, in Spring Valley, Minnesota; and starting in 2001, he took on a job as an art instructor at Prior Lake High School, in Prior Lake, Minnesota, a position he still held as of 2012. In 2008, he served as an art instructor at the Frye Art Museum, in Seattle, Washington. In 2009, he was a visiting instructor in art at the Carleton College, in Northfield, Minnesota; and the following year he served as a visiting artist at the University of Arizona, in Tucson.

When asked to comment on the state of art in the United States, Euclide replied: "I teach nine months out of the year, so I feel I can comment on this question best by saying that my foreign exchange students are always amazing at art. Whether they are from Japan, Russia, Mongolia, or Germany—it doesn't matter. They simply know how to observe better than my American students do. They have the ability to focus and notice differences. It could be the type of student that reaches out for study abroad . . . or it could be that their cultures are different. I think it is a mix of both with an emphasis on the latter."

As part of his deal with Bon Iver, it was agreed that there would be five hundred high-quality reproductions of the album cover put up for sale. The David B. Smith Gallery produced the prints, and part of the proceeds went to charity, most notably Connecting Kids, in Mankato, Minnesota, which provides funds for children to get involved in youth development programs.

Euclide resides in Le Sueur, Minnesota, which he says is a "beautiful place to live."

## SUGGESTED READING

Euclide, Gregory. *Gregory Euclide*. Gregory Euclide, n. d. Web. 17 Sept. 2012.
"Gregory Euclide." *David B. Smith Gallery*. David B. Smith Gallery, 2012. Web. 17 Sept. 2012.
Hasse Goebel, Leanne. "Gregory Euclide." *Art Ltd*. Lifescapes, Mar. 2010. Web. 17 Sept. 2012.
Owen, Sarah. "Terra Incognita, Gregory Euclide." *New York Times Style Magazine*. New York Times, 4 Mar. 2011. Web. 17 Sept. 2012.

—*Dmitry Kiper*

# Chris Evans

**Born:** June 13, 1981
**Occupation:** Actor

Chris Evans is no stranger to playing a superhero on the big screen. After first achieving box-office success portraying Johnny Storm, the Human Torch, in *Fantastic Four* (2005) and its 2007 follow-up, *Fantastic Four: Rise of the Silver Surfer*, Evans starred in *Push* (2009) as Nick Gant, a man with telekinetic powers who finds himself at odds with a government organization intent on creating an army of psychic soldiers. He was then catapulted into Hollywood superstardom with his portrayal of the titular Marvel Comics superhero in *Captain America: The First Avenger* (2011), a role he reprised the following year in *The Avengers* (2012).

However, Evans is not afraid of being typecast. "You might say these characters are in a familiar wheelhouse for me," he told Bob Thompson for the *National Post* (22 July 2011). "But I'm OK with that, simply because I'm interested in making good movies."

## EARLY LIFE

Christopher Robert Evans was born to Lisa Marie Evans, sister of politician Michael Capuano, and G. Robert Evans III on June 13, 1981, in Framingham, Massachusetts. When he was eleven years old, he and his three siblings—two sisters and a brother—moved with their parents to nearby Sudbury, where his father worked as a dentist. His mother was a dancer who later became artistic director for the Concord Youth Theatre, a community children's theater in Concord, Massachusetts.

Throughout his childhood, Evans, whose mother introduced him to classic and Oscar-winning movies, gradually developed a passion for the cinema. "I fell deeper in love with movies

Christine Chew/UPI/Landov

because I liked the way a film could make you feel," he told Cindy Pearlman for the Toledo Blade (29 Apr. 2012). "One movie could change your entire outlook, but it had to be the right movie. I don't know many other art forms that can change your entire outlook."

Evans was bitten by the performing bug at an early age, often putting on puppet shows and plays in the basement of the family home. He decided to try his hand at acting after seeing his older sister, Carly, perform with the Concord Youth Theatre. "Her play would end, and she'd get flowers and candy, and it just seemed like such a good time. She was having a ball and hanging out with her acting friends—it just looked awesome," Evans revealed to Jessica Gardner for Backstage magazine (21 Sept. 2011).

Evans soon followed in his sister's footsteps and joined the Concord Youth Theatre. The two acted together in his first production with the troupe, and he and his siblings all went on to perform in numerous shows. "Each of us must have done at least fifteen to twenty shows there," he recalled to Gardner. While attending Lincoln-Sudbury Regional High School, Evans appeared in several plays, including a production of William Shakespeare's The Winter's Tale. He also spent his summers at acting camp in Boston. "Camp was where I learned how to be comfortable onstage," he told Alexandra Cheney for the Wall Street Journal (5 Oct. 2011).

## BREAKING IN

During his junior year, Evans became determined to pursue a professional acting career. He persuaded his parents to allow him to take acting classes that summer at the renowned Lee Strasberg Theatre and Film Institute in New York City. He also served as an intern for Bonnie Finnegan, a high-profile casting agent whose credits include the Michael J. Fox television show Spin City. "By the end of the summer I'd become friendly with two or three agents," he told Judy Abel for the Boston Globe (17 July 2011). He continued, "I asked three different agents to give me five minutes of their time for an audition and one of them said, 'Yeah, let's do this.'"

After landing an agent, Evans returned to Sudbury to complete his senior year of high school. Following his early graduation in January 1999, the seventeen-year-old relocated to New York, where he resumed his internship at Finnegan's casting office and subsequently began auditioning for television roles. Evans flew to Los Angeles, California, to try out for the drama Get Real, opposite Anne Hathaway. Although he was not cast in that pilot, he made his weekly television debut in another Fox series, Opposite Sex, in which he costarred as Cary Baston, one of three teenage boys attending a former all-girls high school. The series aired in 2000 and was canceled after only eight episodes.

Next came a guest-starring turn in The Fugitive (2000–2001), the CBS remake of the 1960s series and the 1993 Harrison Ford thriller. In the episode Evans plays a sheriff's son who seeks vengeance on the title character, who is masquerading as a liquor-store owner, when he refuses to sell him and his friends alcohol. Also in 2000, he made his feature-film debut in the low-budget family drama The Newcomers.

## GRADUATION TO LEADING MAN

After appearing in a 2001 episode of the acclaimed Fox high school drama Boston Public (2000–2004), Evans landed his first leading-man role in Not Another Teen Movie (2001), a parody of the teenage romantic comedies of the 1980s and 1990s. He stars as a popular high school athlete who bets his classmates that he can transform an ugly duckling, played by Chyler Leigh, into prom queen.

In 2002 Evans had a supporting role in a failed pilot for Eastwick, the small-screen adaptation of the 1984 John Updike novel The Witches of Eastwick and the 1987 film of the same name. Following appearances in the short film The Paper Boy (2003) and the short-lived Jerry Bruckheimer series Skin (2003), he costarred opposite Scarlett Johansson in another high school comedy, The Perfect Score (2004), in which he plays Kyle, a college-bound senior who schemes with classmates to break into a testing center and steal the answers to the upcoming SAT exam.

Evans graduated to more adult roles with his next film, the suspense drama *Cellular* (2004), in which he plays Ryan, an unwitting man who receives a random cell phone call from a woman who claims to have been kidnapped (Kim Basinger). Despite the film receiving mixed reviews, his performance garnered notice from critics. In a review for *Entertainment Weekly* (8 Sept. 2004), Owen Gleiberman remarked, "Chris Evans is blithely likable despite a few faux-Cruise mannerisms," while Wesley Morris wrote for the *Boston Globe* (10 Sept. 2004), "Evans is part of the movie's fun. . . . As Ryan continues to be surprised by his own ingenuity, his likability grows."

## BOX-OFFICE SUCCESS

Following a serious role in the 2005 thriller *Fierce People*, Evans tackled more lighthearted fare later that year in *Fantastic Four*, the big-screen adaptation inspired by the Marvel Comics superheroes of the same name. Although the film met with mostly negative reviews, some critics enjoyed his portrayal of Johnny Storm, also known as the Human Torch, a cocky astronaut whose exposure to cosmic rays gives him the ability to burst into flames. In a review for *USA Today* (7 July 2005), Claudia Puig remarked, "[Michael] Chiklis [as the Thing] and Evans are fine in roles that don't call for much beyond comic-book simplicity, though Evans gets most of the laughs."

The film ultimately earned more than $330 million worldwide. The same year, Evans lent his voice to the character in a *Fantastic Four* video game. Next came a starring role as a drug addict in the gritty independent drama *London*, which premiered in 2005 and had a limited US release a year later. In 2007 Evans reprised the role of the Human Torch in *Fantastic Four: Rise of the Silver Surfer*, which grossed a respectable $289 million at the box office despite critical panning.

Evans again played an astronaut in Danny Boyle's science-fiction thriller *Sunshine* (2007), in which a crew embarks on a space mission to revive the dying sun and thus save Earth. To prepare for this ensemble film, which costarred Cillian Murphy, Michelle Yeoh, and Rose Byrne, Evans met with astronaut Daniel W. Bursch, who had once co-held the record for longest spaceflight by an American. At the director's suggestion, the cast lived together in dorm rooms to simulate the pressures of living in a confined space with other people. They also attended lectures, took scuba-diving lessons, and flew in a zero-gravity plane to experience weightlessness. Also in 2007, Evans reunited with Johansson in the film version of Emma McLaughlin and Nicola Kraus's 2002 novel *The Nanny Diaries* and voiced characters in the computer-animated films *TMNT* and *Battle for Terra*.

Over the next two years, Evans had leading roles in a string of little-seen movies, including the crime drama *Street Kings* (2008); the independent drama *The Loss of a Teardrop Diamond* (2008), based on Tennessee Williams's 1957 screenplay; and the 2009 science-fiction thriller *Push*. He also voiced several characters in a third-season episode of the animated television series *Robot Chicken*, which aired on the Cartoon Network's Adult Swim channel in 2008.

## BREAKING OUT

Following appearances in the ensemble action comedies *The Losers* (2010) and *Scott Pilgrim vs. the World* (2010), Evans achieved world-wide fame and attention as the title character in *Captain America: The First Avenger*, another big-screen adaptation of a Marvel Comics superhero. However, Evans almost turned down the role of Steve Rogers, a scrawny, sickly US Army enlistee who volunteers for a top-secret scientific experiment that transforms him into the World War II–era superhero.

Although Evans was the first choice of director Joe Johnston and Marvel Studios president Kevin Feige, the actor rejected the part several times and never even auditioned. "I got a call and they said they want me to audition, and I said, 'Great!' And then I thought about it and I said, 'No thanks,'" he told Josh Horowitz for MTV News (14 July 2011), as reported by Terri Schwartz. "And then they called back and they said, 'Well, they want you to test' . . . and again I just said, 'I think I'm good. This isn't really what I'm looking for.'"

One factor affecting his decision was the daunting nine-picture commitment, which was eventually scaled back to six movies. Explaining his hesitation to Dave Itzkoff for the *New York Times* (8 July 2011), Evans asked, "In a few years what if I don't want to act anymore? What if I just want to—I don't know—do something else?" He later admitted, "The reason I kept saying no is because I was scared." However, after meeting with Johnston and Feige, Evans finally agreed to star in three *Captain America* movies and appear as the same character in three *Avengers* films. Released in July 2011, *Captain America: The First Avenger* was a critical and commercial success, earning more than $368 million worldwide and catapulting Evans into Hollywood superstardom. He also provided the superhero's voice for the 2011 video game *Captain America: Super Soldier*.

Also in 2011, Evans gave another critically acclaimed performance in the gritty drama *Puncture*, which tells the real-life story of the late Michael David Weiss, a drug-addicted attorney who is drawn into the case of an ER nurse who contracted HIV from an accidental needle stick. "The picture benefits from its performances, notably Evans's roguish appeal as a guy simultaneously driven and destructive," Robert Abele wrote in a review for the *Los Angeles Times* (23 Sept. 2011). "His superhero torso might not immediately scream 'user,' but his eyes and body language do, and they give this underdog saga a memorably churning sense of self-inflicted danger." Equally complimentary was Rex Reed, who wrote for the *New York Observer* (21 Sept. 2011), "Chris Evans is as dynamic in the small scenes as he is in the crashing melodramatic ones." Evans switched gears for his next film, appearing opposite Anna Faris in the romantic comedy *What's Your Number?* (2011).

### RETURNING TO HIS SUPERHERO ROOTS

Evans reprised the role of Captain America the following year in director Joss Whedon's *The Avengers*, which is based on the titular Marvel Comics superhero team. The ensemble cast also features Robert Downey Jr. as Tony Stark (Iron Man), Mark Ruffalo as Bruce Banner (the Hulk), and Chris Hemsworth as Thor. Evans was again reunited with Johansson, who took on the role of Natasha Romanoff (Black Widow). The film, which premiered in early April 2012, set several box-office records. Not only did *The Avengers* record the biggest opening weekend in North America, it also became the fastest film to earn $1 billion and the third-highest-grossing film in history.

For the criminal biopic *The Iceman* (2012), Evans played against type, sporting long hair and a shaggy beard for his portrayal of Robert Pronge, the protégé of professional contract killer Richard Kuklinski (Michael Shannon). Evans took over for James Franco, who dropped out of the movie.

Films scheduled to premiere in 2013 include director Bong Joon-ho's apocalyptic thriller *Snowpiercer*, which costars Tilda Swinton and Jamie Bell, and the comedy *A Many Splintered Thing*. In 2014, Evans will star in the thriller *The Ten O'Clock People*, based on a short story by Stephen King, and *Captain America: The Winter Soldier*, the sequel to his 2011 blockbuster hit. The follow-up to *The Avengers* is scheduled for release in the summer of 2015.

### PERSONAL LIFE

Evans, a practicing Buddhist, is a spokesman for Gucci's Guilty fragrance line. He splits his time between Los Angeles and Boston and is reportedly involved with actress Minka Kelly, whom he briefly dated in 2007.

Evans's younger brother, Scott, is a professional actor as well, best known for his regular role on the soap opera *One Life to Live* from 2008 to 2010. His sister Carly is a high school English and drama teacher, and his other sister, Shanna, has taught classes at the Concord Youth Theatre, where their mother still works. In early 2013, the theater found a permanent home for

the first time since 2005, aided by a $60,000 donation from Evans.

### SUGGESTED READING

Abel, Judy. "All-American Hero." *Boston Globe*. New York Times Co., 17 July 2011. Web. 13 June 2013.

Abele, Robert. "Movie Review: *Puncture*, dir. Adam Kassen and Mark Kassen." *The Los Angeles Times*. Los Angeles Times, 23 Sept. 2011. Web. 8 June 2013.

Cheney, Alexandra. "My First Job: Chris Evans." *Wall Street Journal*. Dow Jones, 5 Oct. 2011. Web. 13 June 2013.

Itzkoff, Dave. "Star-Spangled and Searching His Own Psyche." *New York Times*. New York Times, 8 July 2011. Web. 13 June 2013.

Pearlman, Cindy. "Chris Evans: Hard Work Pays Off for This Superhero." *Blade* [Toledo]. Blade, 29 Apr. 2012. Web. 13 June 2013.

Schwartz, Terri. " Chris Evans Reveals He Said 'No Thanks' to 'Captain America.'" *MTV*. Viacom, 14 July 2011. Web. 13 June 2013.

Thompson, Bob. "Captain America's Chris Evans on Being a Wimpy Kid." *National Post*. National Post, 22 July 2011. Web. 13 June 2013.

### SELECTED WORKS

*Not Another Teen Movie*, 2001; *Cellular*, 2004; *Fantastic Four*, 2005; *London*, 2005; *Sunshine*, 2007; *Fantastic Four: Rise of the Silver Surfer*, 2007; *Push*, 2009; *Captain America: The First Avenger*, 2011; *The Avengers*, 2012; *The Iceman*, 2012

—Bertha Muteba

# Justine Ezarik

**Born:** March 20, 1984
**Occupation:** Internet personality and lifecaster

Justine Ezarik, more commonly known by the name of her Internet persona, iJustine, is an Internet celebrity of lifecasting and YouTube fame. The freelance web and graphic designer and video editor is a popular video blogger, or "vlogger." Ezarik first began vlogging her day-to-day antics on her website *Tasty Blog Snack* in 2006. As her posts grew in popularity, Justin Kan of Justin.tv asked her to become a lifecaster—in other words, to broadcast a constant Internet video stream of her life. The six months of 2007 that Ezarik spent broadcasting her life, for nearly twenty-four hours a day and seven days a week, boosted Ezarik's Internet fame even more. After those initial six months, Ezarik toned down her lifecasting to only a few hours per week, ceasing altogether in 2009.

Getty Images for Activision

Although Ezarik was a popular lifecaster, it was an edited one-minute video that would rocket her to international fame. In August 2007, Ezarik posted online a video about her first iPhone bill—all three hundred pages of it, sent in the mail. The video quickly went viral, landing Ezarik's name in newspapers and on television networks worldwide.

In addition to Ezarik's website, *iJustine*—the central hub for all of her social media accounts and vlogs, Ezarik hosts five channels on You-Tube, which have received hundreds of millions of views. Ezarik's videos range from everyday comedic antics, to music video spoofs, to reviews of video games and tech products.

## EARLY LIFE AND EDUCATION

Justine Ezarik was born on March 20, 1984, to Michelle and Steve Ezarik, a physical education teacher and a coal miner. The eldest of three sisters, Ezarik grew up in Scenery Hill, Pennsylvania. Her interest in creating videos began at an early age. "I started making videos in the sixth grade, and as technology changed, I just became more interested," she told Kim Lyons for the *Pittsburgh Tribune-Review* (16 Aug. 2007). "Now I just don't leave my computer," she added.

After finishing high school in 2002, Ezarik attended the Pittsburgh Technical Institute, graduating two years later. She worked as a graphic designer and video editor for several jobs and then in 2006 started her own freelance web design business in the Pittsburgh area.

## *TASTY BLOG SNACK* AND OTHER EARLY VIDEO VENTURES

The video editor began making her mark on the screen in 2006, when she entered the Yahoo! Talent Show. Ezarik became one of five finalists in December 2006 and had to compete in three

online video challenges; she earned second place in the competition. She then became an extra for *The Kill Point*, a Spike TV television show filmed in May 2007, for which she played a photojournalist covering a Pittsburgh bank robbery. Ezarik would later cover the show's premiere party in July 2007, during her stint as a lifecaster. In January 2007, Ezarik became a cohost and panel member on *MacBreak* and its spinoff, *MacBreak Weekly*, two video podcast series that discuss Apple products.

Ezarik ran an increasingly popular blog called *Tasty Blog Snack* from 2006 to 2010, where she posted many short, often comedic videos hosted by websites like Revver, Jumpcut, and YouTube. She and her friend, roommate, and business partner Desiree Cramer also created short comedic videos for a web show called *Mommy Pack My Lunch* in early 2007. Ezarik's website, *iJustine*—the jumping-off point for all of her video blogs and social media accounts—was founded in January 2007.

## JUSTIN.TV

On April 18, 2007, Ezarik made her first appearance on Justin.tv, filling in for the website's usual lifecaster, Justin Kan. Justin.tv had begun as a broadcast of the life of Internet entrepreneur Justin Kan a month earlier. Kan, who popularized the term "lifecasting," became famous for his baseball cap–camera equipment, which continuously streamed his life to a laptop in a backpack—and from there online—for much of 2007.

Kan had met Ezarik in January 2007 at the Macworld Expo in San Francisco. "He was wearing a camera strapped to his head, and I was like, 'What is that?'" Ezarik told Emily Gould for the *MIT Technology Review* (20 Oct. 2008). She asked Kan if she could try out his camera, and they discussed lifecasting. Although Kan did not yet have his lifecast continuously streaming live on Justin.tv at the time, he was already experimenting with the practice. After Kan's lifecast did go live, a number of his viewers encouraged him to find a guest lifecaster. Having watched Ezarik's vlogs, Kan knew that she would make a great one. "She's a natural star," he told Jessica Guynn for the *San Francisco Chronicle* (29 May 2007), describing her as "his perfect match, name and all." Ezarik, already a viewer of Justin. tv, agreed to join the website.

Ezarik's first appearance on Justin.tv was a one-day trial run. She filled in for Kan, who had to attend a private meeting with venture capitalists in San Francisco. Ezarik kept viewers entertained by shopping at an Apple store and at Old Navy, dancing with a street performer, having lunch with James Hong of HotorNot.com, and attending the Web 2.0 Expo with the use of Kan's visitor badge. This was followed by dinner with Kan and then going out to party. "It was a lot of fun," Ezarik told Guynn. "I got a great response."

## IJUSTINE.TV
Ezarik began lifecasting regularly on May 29, 2007, as a beta tester for Justin.tv. Being a beta tester meant volunteering to broadcast her life for nearly twenty-four hours a day, seven days a week, before Justin.tv opened its platform to a select group of lifecasters and eventually to the public. Kan and his three website partners planned to host a new lifecast each week for eight weeks during the summer; Ezarik was the first of these. Justin.tv opened to the public in October 2007, and thanks to lifecasters like Ezarik, the platform quickly built up thousands of accounts.

Unlike Kan, Ezarik would not stream every moment of every day online for the continuous six-month period she agreed to lifecast for; she left the camera behind for private moments. Still, as she told Guynn before embarking on this venture, "I am going to try as much as I can to do 24/7." That would include video footage of Ezarik working at her freelance business. "If people want to watch me edit video and make Web sites, that's fine," she told Guynn. "Desiree [Cramer] and I together are always up for crazy adventures," she told Asher Moses for the *Sydney Morning Herald* (31 May 2007). "But our real work does have to come first which can make for boring 'TV.'"

Nevertheless, Ezarik's lifecast on her Justin.tv channel, iJustine.tv, made her one of the most popular lifecasters on the web. Ezarik created the name "iJustine" in 2002, shortly after Apple released its second-generation iPod. At the time, she wanted to create an Internet user name. Since "Justine" was already taken on most websites, Ezarik decided to place an "i" in front of her name because of her love for Apple products—and the name has stuck since then.

## MOVING ON FROM LIFECASTING
Ezarik would tone down her lifecasting to only a few hours per week by April 2008. One reason for this was the intrusive nature of the practice. While being on camera all the time did not generally bother Ezarik, it did interfere with the lives of those she cared about. Her friends were sometimes even mocked by viewers. "Someone e-mailed and was like, 'We're going to have to vote [a friend] off your show," she told Gould, referencing one instance. "And I was like, 'Actually, it's not a show; actually, this is just my life.'" As for all the attention Ezarik herself was receiving as an Internet star: "I don't hate it," she told Gould. "What I like the most about everything is the community of people I've brought together. When I was lifecasting, I was a way for people to connect. It wasn't even about me. I was sitting there doing nothing, and people were having

conversations about politics and their life. And it was kind of cool to see that."

No longer having to worry about lifecasting meant more time for Ezarik to focus on her freelance business—which also benefited from her move to Los Angeles, California, later in 2008. "There are so many more projects [here]," she told Gould. "It's a lot easier having someone else shoot and edit for you." In April 2009, Ezarik stopped lifecasting altogether on Justin.tv. Given her increasing popularity online, she no longer needed Justin.tv as a platform for her video antics.

## THE 300-PAGE IPHONE BILL
On August 13, 2007, Ezarik released a one-minute video about her first iPhone bill. The video, which was posted on *Tasty Blog Snack* and hosted on a number of video websites such as YouTube and Revver, quickly went viral. Ezarik, an avid fan of Apple products, had covered the release of the first iPhone at the Mall of America in Bloomington, Minnesota, in June 2007, as part of her lifecast. She also bought the iPhone as soon as it was released. When she received her first bill from AT&T—three hundred pages, delivered in a box because it was so hefty——she decided to create a video about it. For her, the problem was not that the bill charged $275; the problem was its number of pages.

The edited video, titled "IPHONE BILL," features Ezarik sitting in a café and flipping through page after page of her bill, as the video's speed runs faster and faster. It ends with the note, "Use e-billing. Save a forest." Ezarik was not the only customer to receive such a detailed, hefty bill, but her video helped bring attention to the problem. Ten days after the video was released, it had been viewed more than three million times and had received coverage by news sources worldwide. Ezarik had also been interviewed by these news sources as a sort of unofficial spokesperson for paperless billing. "If they're sending this to everyone who sends a lot of text messages, and uses their iPhone extensively, this is a lot of waste," Ezarik stated in a television interview, as quoted by Gregg Keizer for *PCWorld* (16 Aug. 2007). Ezarik estimated during the interview that she was sending more than 30,000 text messages per month.

## "IPHONE BILL" AFTERMATH
As for AT&T, spokesperson Mark Siegel told Keizer that customers do have the option to receive a summary bill or can choose paperless billing, also called e-billing, so that they can view their bills online. Nevertheless, as a result of Ezarik's video and other customer complaints about the size of their bills, AT&T began sending summarized bills as their default from September 2007 onward.

By the end of the year, Ezarik's iPhone video had been viewed more than eight million times and had earned Ezarik a reported $5,000 payout from Revver. Being in the international spotlight gave Ezarik such a popularity boost that when she released a video about wanting to order a cheeseburger in August 2008, for example, it received more than 600,000 views by the end of its first week online.

## HOSTING AND ADVERTISING

Although she has achieved fame online, Ezarik has also wanted to become famous on television or in film. She credits her vlogging and lifecasting experience with building her acting skills. "I had to be 'on' at all times," she told Gould, referring to her lifecasting. "It was kind of like a résumé-building experience. I mean, I wasn't acting, but I kind of was." Whether edited or not, Ezarik has controlled every aspect of how she appears on video. "I feel like iJustine has become sort of like this character," she told Gould. "It's not like I don't drink or go out and do stuff, but I won't drink on camera, and if I swear I'll bleep it out. I really try to keep it clean."

The years 2008 and 2009 saw Ezarik's acting career begin to form. In October 2008, she hosted *The PluggedIn* 5, an online, twice weekly Plugged In lifestyle and music program. She then became a spokesperson for AT&T online. Ezarik and blogger Karen Nguyen teamed up to star in *Lost in America* in November 2008, an online advertising campaign for AT&T mobile phones that features Ezarik and Nguyen "getting lost" in various locations across the United States. They use their AT&T phones to learn about where they are and to solve problems caused by being lost. The first eleven episodes released received only 31,000 views, a very low number by advertising standards, and the ad campaign was dropped.

In addition to her AT&T gig, Ezarik was hired to do commercials for a national television advertising campaign for Mozy, an online backup and recovery system. She hosted online pre-shows for MTV award broadcasts and was a guest host for web series such as *The Station* and *Totally Sketch* in 2009. Ezarik also appeared on an episode of *The Price is Right* in 2009, where she won $37,905 worth of prizes.

## ANNOYING ORANGE

Characters other than iJustine began to fill Ezarik's acting résumé from 2009 onward. Her television guest appearances have included such shows as *Law & Order: Special Victims Unit* (2009), *Criminal Minds* (2010), and *The Vampire Diaries* (2012). She has also appeared in web series such as *Video Game High School*, *The Guild*, and *MyMusic* (all in 2012).

Ezarik has been a series regular on *The High Fructose Adventures of Annoying Orange*, as the voice of Passion Fruit. The animated series, created by and starring Dane Boedigheimer, is about an orange that sits on a kitchen counter, continuously cracking jokes and taunting whatever other food item gets placed nearby. Passion Fruit is an exception, however, as Annoying Orange is in love with her. The show, which was created in October 2009 and first aired on YouTube, became highly popular with children; as of April 2010, it had been viewed more than 108 million times.

Ben Huh, the founder of Cheezburger Network, explained to Geoffrey A. Fowler for the *Wall Street Journal* (26 Apr. 2010) that the reason for Boedigheimer's success in such a short amount of time is because "the Internet today is like TV was in the 1950s—it's a new technology that changes the way we view culture." Huh described the show to Fowler as "almost like watching a car wreck." Nevertheless, he added, "The awfulness of the orange is what brings the enjoyment." By allowing advertisements on their YouTube channels, people like Boedigheimer can earn more than half of the ad revenue accrued by YouTube, making thousands of dollars per month. "When Dane puts up a [YouTube] show on Friday, by Monday it has a million and a half views," Boedigheimer's manager told Fowler. "Any cable network would take those numbers." One soon did: the Cartoon Network picked up *Annoying Orange* for television, where it first aired in August 2012.

## IJUSTINE AS A BRAND

Like Boedigheimer, Ezarik earns money for her vlogging through advertising revenue. To encourage people to watch her videos and to increase and maintain her popularity, Ezarik has learned the benefits of creating a brand. Spread across a website, a blog, multiple YouTube channels, a Twitter account, a mySpace account, a Facebook page, and other social media accounts, iJustine has become more than just a character. Ezarik even sells iJustine merchandise on her website, ranging from logo T-shirts to branded iPhone cases. The vlogger, who freely endorses Apple and other tech products in her videos, also earns money through conference appearances and promotional events.

According to Gould, Ezarik describes herself as a "Mac user, blogger, Internet lover and new-media connoisseur." Her *iJustine* website calls her an "avid video gamer and tech obsessed individual." Ezarik's technology and vlogging obsessions eventually led her to build up five channels on YouTube: iJustine, her main channel; iJustine's Daily Vlogs—also called iJustine's iPhone channel, this channel consists of unedited videos posted directly from Ezarik's phone; iJustine Gaming; iJ's Reviews, of supposedly anything; and iJ's 2nd Channel, or "otherjustine," which hosts miscellaneous videos and outtakes from her other channels.

Ezarik's fan base consists mainly of teenagers, as she has determined by her fan e-mail. By the beginning of 2013, her main YouTube channel was home to more than 560 videos and had more than 1,345,000 subscribers; the videos on her various YouTube channels have received more than 366 million views combined. In 2010, Ezarik's iJustine persona was nominated for the Streamy Awards for best vlogger and for the Teen Choice Awards for web star. She won the Webby Awards People's Voice award for best web personality or host in 2011.

Ezarik lives in the Los Angeles area, where she has continued to vlog, act, edit videos, and do web design.

## SUGGESTED READING

Fowler, Geoffrey A. "Now Playing on a Computer Near You: A Fruit with an Obnoxious Streak." *Wall Street Journal*. Dow Jones, 26 Apr. 2010. Web. 15 Jan. 2013.

Gould, Emily. "iTube: Why 23,201 People Care that Justine Ezarik Just Ate a Cookie." *MIT Technology Rev.* MIT Technology Rev., 20 Oct. 2008. Web. 15 Jan. 2013.

Guynn, Jessica. "Can't Get Enough Justin? You Can Watch Justine." *San Francisco Chronicle*. Hearst Communications, 29 May 2007. Web. 15 Jan. 2013.

Keizer, Gregg. "A 300-Page iPhone Bill?" *PC-World*. IDG Consumer & SMB, 16 Aug. 2007. Web. 15 Jan. 2013.

Stross, Randall. "A Site Andy Warhol Would Relish." *New York Times*. New York Times Co., 14 Oct. 2007. Web. 15 Jan. 2013.

## SELECTED WORKS

### Internet

*Mommy Pack My Lunch*, 2007; iJustine.tv, 2007–9; *Tasty Blog Snack*, 2006–10; iJustine (YouTube.com), 2006–; *iJustine* (ijustine.com), 2007–.

### Television

*Annoying Orange*, 2012.

—*Julia Gilstein*

# Paloma Faith

**Born:** July 21, 1985
**Occupation:** Actor and singer

Pop music fans in Great Britain agree: if any singer will likely add to their nation's recent infatuation with the retro-soul sound, it is Paloma Faith, the singer and actor who has combined

John Stillwell/PA Photos/Landov

a theatrical cabaret image with a heartbreaking voice of marked singularity. After first gaining a reputation around London as a premiere stage act, she was signed by a talent scout for Epic Records. Since her debut album, *Do You Want the Truth or Something Beautiful?*, was released in 2009, Faith has impressed music fans and critics alike with her showmanship, retro styles, and ability to emulate such classic singers from the 1940s and 1950s as Billie Holiday and Etta James with a modern twist. When she first appeared on the music scene, she was often compared to the late Amy Winehouse, one of Britain's premiere vocalists of the early 2000s. But since Winehouse's untimely death in July 2011, Faith has emerged from her contemporary's long shadow by demonstrating that there is much more to her than mere imitation or flamboyance. Both of her studio albums have been certified double platinum in the United Kingdom, and she now seeks to broaden her appeal to not only the rest of Europe but America as well. "I am ambitious," Faith noted to David Smyth for an interview published in the *London Evening Standard* (11 May 2012). "I'd like to do as well as I can possibly do on every level—internationally and everything. But I'm not one of those people who's willing to do whatever it takes, gouging out a few eyes in the process."

## CHILDHOOD AND EDUCATION

The only child of a Spanish father and English mother, Paloma Faith Blomfield was born on July 21, 1985, in Hackney, a part of northeast

London, England. Her parents separated when she was two and divorced when she was four. She grew to love jazz and good food through her father, whom she saw mostly on weekends. From her mother, a primary school special education teacher who raised Faith on her own, she received piano lessons and a dedication to dance. "My mum wanted me to be everything she wasn't," Faith told Charlotte Philby for the *Independent* (30 Jan. 2010). "She put great value on things that people take for granted, like being able to swim and dance and drive, the things she couldn't do and felt inadequate [about] because she couldn't do them." Although Faith gave up the piano at age thirteen—a decision she grew to regret— dance continued to be a central part of her life through college.

In several interviews, Faith has described her time at her state-run secondary school, Islington Green, as being very rough. She tried her best to fit in at a place where the police were often called in to break up violent confrontations. (After decades of problems, the school was closed in 2008.) She was, however, an excellent student—that is, once she began to focus. In an interview with Teddy Jamieson published in the *Herald* (21 Sept. 2009), she recalled, "I was a bit of a daydreamer. . . . I found it really hard to learn to read and numbers to this day give me anxiety. I used to memorize books and pretend I was reading them. I think I read my first book aged ten, which is quite late, and then what happened was I went from the bottom of the class to the top. I became a grade A student."

## DANCE AND THEATER

Being such an outstanding student enabled Faith to enroll at the Northern School of Contemporary Dance in Leeds, where she earned her bachelor of professional arts degree in contemporary dance. But her experience at the school did not convince her to try to pursue a career as a dancer, in large part because being a performer made her very self-conscious and a bit vain. "I became overly sensitive about my body. I'm naturally curvy and that's not encouraged in dance; if you bulk up easily or whatever they're not very nice," she told Charlotte Philby. "Like with everything, if you don't fit in perfectly, if you're not thin and blonde, then they're not nice to you."

Faith did, however, continue her education at Central St. Martins College of Arts and Design in London, where she studied theater and obtained a master's degree in theater design and direction. Although she loved her time there and believes it helped further her creativity, she ultimately did not find work in the theater. Music beckoned, despite her never having had a single singing lesson.

## EARLY CAREER

During her student years, Faith worked a wide variety of odd jobs: She posed as a life-drawing model, sold ice cream from a van, played a ghost on a ghost train, boiled chickens, served as a magician's assistant, and modeled Agent Provocateur 's clothing at its shop in London's Soho neighborhood. She also worked at a pub throughout college. It was there she first took to the stage as a singer, when the pub's manager asked her to be the singer in his band, which they quickly named Paloma and the Penetrators. "They asked me to be in it without even knowing whether I could sing. My first gig I was so nervous my voice was wobbly and I was out of tune," she recalled to Teddy Jamieson. What her band mates did like about her, however, was her eclectic style that recalled the fashions of a previous era and her strong passion for such classic torch singers as Billie Holiday, Frank Sinatra, Ella Fitzgerald, and Etta James.

Faith was spotted performing at a cabaret show by an artists and repertoire (A & R) scout from Epic Records who liked the show and felt she compared favorably to Amy Winehouse, the highly regarded British singer-songwriter who was a rising star with her soulful singing. He asked Faith to come and sing for the head of the label (without the rest of the band), and she readily agreed. During her audition a few days later, however, she became irate when her future boss spent more time texting on his cell phone than listening to her. When she asked him to stop and he refused, she told him she would rather sing in pubs for the rest of her life than sign with him. Then she walked out. "I didn't care about the money at that point," she explained to Philby. "I was broke but I was working lots, doing cabaret and performance art and feeling really creative. I felt like my life was exciting and it was all down to me."

Nine months later the same man called her again, claiming he had not seen any act as outstanding as hers had been. When he offered her a contract with Epic, she signed.

## DO YOU WANT THE TRUTH OR SOMETHING BEAUTIFUL?

On her first album, *Do You Want the Truth or Something Beautiful?*, released in 2009, a number of critics remarked on her vocal resemblance to Winehouse, in large part because of their throaty singing and throwback style of soul music with a twenty-first-century twist. Many critics and fans in Britain believed Faith to be the best of the torch singers who had followed in Winehouse's wake. Faith's debut album produced two top 20 singles in the United Kingdom, "Stone Cold Sober" and "New York." As for the record itself, it was certified double platinum, selling more than five hundred thousand copies in her native country, and was a hit in several European countries.

*Do You Want the Truth or Something Beautiful?* also received generally good reviews from many music critics. Writing for the *Independent* (25 Sept. 2009), Andy Gill called it an "impressive debut album" and added that "she may not have the authentic edgy spirit of Amy [Winehouse], but her simulation is delivered with both barrels blazing." Reviewing the album for BBC Music (16 Sept. 2009), Mike Diver had less to complain about, noting, "Faith's voice is the first element of these sumptuous arrangements to strike, its idiosyncratic ticks and sharp inflections separating her from the pack . . . Faith's sentiments are never in doubt." Diver concluded, "Perhaps she's playing up, acting out the role of a superlative pop-soul singer—but whether the lines are predetermined or not, one can't find much fault with Paloma Faith's performance here."

### FALL TO GRACE
Faith's sophomore effort, *Fall to Grace*, released in 2012, was eagerly awaited by her growing fanbase, which lifted it all the way to number 2 on the British album charts. Much of this double-platinum record's success was due to the power of Faith's debut single, "Picking Up the Pieces," which peaked at number 8 on the Hot Dance Club Play chart. The record produced three more singles—"30 Minute Love Affair," "Never Tear Us Apart," and "Just Be." None has been as successful as "Picking Up the Pieces," but they have nevertheless helped to cement Faith's place in British pop music as a performer who is much more than simply an imitator of Winehouse or Adele. Many music fans and critics were taken not only the record's production values, but also with the distinctiveness of Faith's choked-up and deep voice, which, like Billie Holiday's, is not traditionally beautiful but can be powerfully moving and sensual.

Nick Levine, reviewing the album for BBC Music (18 May 2012), cheered: "None of the sumptuous production would matter if Faith hadn't delivered some decent tunes. . . . The quality slips towards the finish, but not enough to spoil a supremely accomplished sophomore album. *Fall to Grace* is proof that pop doesn't need to be grey and restrained to feel grown-up." In the *New York Daily News* (11 Dec. 2012), Jim Farber was somewhat more restrained in his praise, noting, "For all the rawness of both Faith's words and voice, the production on the album can be dense and overworked. . . . She probably feels she needs all that color to balance out the darkness of the rest. But she needn't be so self-conscious. Faith's talent is its own reward, found in a voice whose brutishness carries its own beauty."

### BRANCHING OUT
In addition to her musical career, Paloma Faith has also worked periodically as an actor, both on British television and in film. Her big-screen performances have included parts in *St. Trinian's* (2007), a comedic remake starring Talulah Riley and Rupert Everett; *The Imaginarium of Doctor Parnassus* (2009), director Terry Gilliam's imaginative tale of a traveling sideshow, starring Christopher Plummer and Heath Ledger; and *Dread* (2009), a psychological thriller about the things people fear. But Faith's main focus is on touring to promote her music, both in the United Kingdom and abroad. She has been particularly inspired to win over fans in America, thanks to her experience performing with Prince during the two-day New Power Generation (NPG) Music and Arts Festival in Copenhagen, Denmark. She released her second album in the United States in late 2012 and embarked on a cross-country tour following the release of the first single "Picking Up the Pieces." She explained to Stacy Anderson for *Rolling Stone* (10 Aug. 2012), "I've succeeded beyond my expectations in the UK, but every time you climb to the top of the ladder, you see a new ladder. I feel like America is my new ladder."

She also remains keen to distinguish herself from contemporary singers she admires, both through her outsized stage presence and on her records. When asked about press comparisons with British singers like Adele or Winehouse, both of whom have thus far outsold her, Faith told David Smyth, "I don't feel in competition with anyone. Real talent shines through regardless of how many others there are around you. People love brilliant songs and love great voices. I think there's room for everyone."

### PERSONAL LIFE
Unlike Winehouse, who was known for her self-destructive behavior and died of accidental alcohol poisoning, Paloma Faith admits to no vices, stating she does not drink to excess or abuse drugs but will smoke a cigarette on occasion. Her lack of addictions is due in large part to experiences she had growing up. While she does not discuss her childhood in great detail and will not even reveal her parents' names to interviewers, she did tell Hermione Eyre for the London *ES Magazine* (22 Oct. 2009): "I saw a lot of the effects of addiction, growing up. All I can say is that I don't want to destroy my emotional life and I think if you get hooked that is inevitable. You end up lonely and desensitized."

She is also, unlike many music stars, a relatively frugal homebody who is very interested in settling down and having children. By September 2012 she had saved enough money to fulfill her oft-mentioned dream of buying her own permanent home. In several interviews she has claimed to have never had a one-night stand and has described herself as "a serial monogamist." That said, she also believes that no matter her domestic arrangements, she will still be performing in fifty years. She told Eyre, "We all get old, but I always say the skinny, pretty girls will be screwed. . . . They will be old with no personality and I will be fat wearing my leopard-print coat, having a laugh with all the pervy old men."

## SUGGESTED READING

Anderson, Stacy. "British Pop Star Paloma Faith on Conquering America, 'Dating' Tom Waits." *Rolling Stone*. Rolling Stone, 10 Aug. 2012. Web. 7 June 2013.

Diver, Mike. "Paloma Faith *Do You Want the Truth Or Something Beautiful?* Review." *BBC Music*. BBC News, 16 Sept. 2009. Web. 7 June 2013.

Eyre, Hermione. "The Lives and Loves of Paloma Faith." *ES Magazine*. London Evening Standard, 22 Oct. 2009. Web. 7 June 2013.

Farber, Jim. "CD Review: 'Fall to Grace' by Paloma Faith." *New York Daily News*. NYDailyNews.com, 11 Dec. 2012. Web. 7 June 2013.

Jamieson, Teddy. "Paloma Faith: Style Icon, Singer, Actress." *Herald*. Herald Scotland, 21 Sept. 2009. Web. 7 May 2013.

Philby, Charlotte. "Paloma Faith: From Burlesque Performer to Music's Next Big Thing." *Independent*. Independent, 30 Jan. 2010. Web. 7 May 2013.

Smyth, David. "Interview: Paloma Faith on Men, Marilyn and House Prices." *London Evening Standard*. London Evening Standard, 11 May 2012. Web. 7 May 2013.

—*Christopher Mari*

---

# Mick Fanning

**Born:** June 13, 1981
**Occupation:** Professional surfer

Nicknamed White Lightning by his peers for his platinum-blond hair and ability to surf with flawless precision at breakneck speeds, the Australian-born Mick Fanning has established himself as one of the top competitive surfers in the world. Arguably the most successful and innovative Australian male surfer of his generation, Fanning has been known to ride waves "with a speed and creativity unmatched in the surfing world," renowned surf writer Tim Baker wrote in his book *High Surf: The World's Most Inspiring Surfers* (2007). "He's got an agility and a quickness that some of the other competitors don't have," five-time world surfing champion Mark Richards told Tommy Conlon for the *Irish Independent* (3 Dec. 2007).

Fanning made his debut on the Association of Surfing Professionals (ASP) World Championship Tour—the highest level of competitive surfing—in 2002, finishing fifth in the world

Sergio Moraes/Reuters/Landov

and earning ASP Rookie of the Year honors. Since then, Fanning has won two ASP world titles (2007 and 2009), amassed fifteen professional victories, and earned millions of dollars in prize money and endorsement deals. He has also finished the ASP world tour in all but two of his eleven years on the professional circuit. Fanning, who has overcome a career-threatening injury as well as personal tragedy in his rise to surfing superstardom, told Baker for *High Surf*, "Surfing has taught me how to deal with life's situations. . . . If I didn't surf or have a close relationship with the ocean I don't know what I would be doing. Maybe I would be out of control but [the] ocean and surfing has kept me relaxed and content with all aspects of my life."

## EARLY LIFE

The youngest of five children, Michael Eugene Fanning was born on June 13, 1981, in Penrith, a suburb of Sydney, in the state of New South Wales in Australia. His father, John Fanning, a contractor, hails from the town of Malin Head, the most northerly point of mainland Ireland; his mother, Elizabeth Osborne, a former nurse, is of Anglo-Irish descent and grew up in the town of Warwickshire, near Birmingham, England. The couple, who had met at an Irish church dance hall in Birmingham, immigrated to Australia in search of a better life in 1971. They settled in Perth, the capital of the state of Western Australia, and spent a year there before moving across the continent to the western suburbs of Sydney, Australia's largest and most populous city, for better work opportunities.

Fanning's parents separated when he was two years old, largely because of his father's various work commitments, which routinely kept him away from home. As a result, Mick and his four older siblings—sister Rachel and brothers Peter, Edward, and Sean—were raised by their mother, who struggled to make ends meet. When Fanning was four, his mother, wanting her children to have a paternal influence in their lives, sent him and his siblings to live with their father in Coffs Harbour, a coastal city in New South

Wales located about 350 miles north of Sydney. That arrangement proved to be overwhelming for Fanning's father, who continued to work long hours, and only lasted two years. However, it was in Coffs Harbour, known for its beaches and surf breaks (formations such as rocks or coral reefs that cause the ocean to form waves suitable for surfing), that Fanning first developed his love of the ocean.

After leaving Coffs Harbour, Fanning and his brothers Edward and Sean returned to their mother's home in Sydney's western suburbs for the next several years, while their two eldest siblings, Rachel and Peter, attended college. During this time Osborne nurtured her younger sons' growing desire to surf by driving them to beaches up and down the coast on weekends. When Fanning was eight, his mother took a job as a mental health administrator on New South Wales's north coast, at which point she moved the family to the beach town of Ballina. In Fanning's 2009 memoir, *Surf for Your Life*, cowritten with Baker, his mother called surfing "the best thing that's ever happened to [her] family." She added, "I had no money and five children. Surfing was great for me. If you got them a board and a pair of board shorts, that was all they needed. The best thing I could do was get a nice house near to the beach." In Ballina, Fanning honed his surfing skills by riding small waves that formed under a nearby bridge.

## A "COOLY KID" IS BORN

In 1993 Fanning and his family moved north again, settling in the coastal town of Tweed Heads. It was in Tweed Heads, located on the New South Wales-Queensland border and adjacent to the town of Coolangatta, where Fanning's surfing career took off. He started surfing competitively on the junior circuit at the age of twelve, after he and his brother Sean, also a gifted surfer, were offered sponsorship deals with the California-based surf wear company Quiksilver.

By all accounts, when he was first starting out, Fanning's surfing was awkward and erratic. However, after befriending fellow Tweed Heads–Coolangatta natives Dean Morrison and Joel Parkinson—then both dominant forces on the Australian junior surfing circuit—he began to take his surfing to the next level. "When I was a kid those guys used to smoke me all the time," Fanning recalled to Nick Smart for the Molendinar, Australia, *Gold Coast Bulletin* (8 Nov. 2007). "I was always trying to be better than those guys." Practicing daily at such world-renowned surf breaks as Currumbin, Palm Beach, Kirra, Snapper Rocks, and Duranbah, Fanning developed what would become his signature lightning-fast surfing style.

Along with Morrison and Parkinson, Fanning emerged as a standout on the junior surfing circuit, and the trio became known collectively as the "Cooly Kids," as they lived and surfed in and around Coolangatta. Fanning, Morrison, and Parkinson drew comparisons to another Gold Coast trio: 1970s Australian surf icons Wayne "Rabbit" Bartholomew, Peter Townend, and Michael Peterson, who were known as the original Cooly Kids. Bartholomew remembered Fanning as a "little ball of energy." He told Conlon, "He always had this real dynamic about him. When he was young he was out of control with his surfing. He wasn't scared, he was going for big stuff."

## GROUNDED BY TRAGEDY

By the age of sixteen, Fanning was distinguishing himself in surfing competitions around the world. He took third place in the juniors division of the Australian National Titles in 1997, and he soon signed a lucrative contract with the Australian surf wear company Rip Curl. Fanning attended Palm Beach Currumbin State High School, in the Gold Coast suburb of Currumbin. While the school's sports excellence program in surfing accommodated Fanning's wave-riding needs, he ultimately left school to focus on his surfing career.

Fanning continued his upward career trajectory until August 14, 1998, when his brother Sean and close friend Joel Green were killed in a car accident. Fanning, who shared an extremely strong bond with Sean, just three years his senior, was left heartbroken. "They were so close," their mother told Will Swanton for the Sydney *Sun-Herald* (2 Mar. 2008). "We called them 'the little ones.' They did everything together." Fanning found out about his brother's death while walking home from a party the two had attended earlier in the night. Friends stopped him before he reached the nearby accident scene, and after being taken home, Fanning was charged with the difficult task of breaking the news to his entire family.

In an interview with Huw J. Williams for the Red Bull website (12 Aug. 2009), Fanning, who had dreamed of surfing with his brother on the ASP World Tour, described Sean as an "amazing surfer" and recalled pushing himself "to reach his level." A memorial surf competition honoring Sean Fanning and Joel Green has been held at Snapper Rocks every year since the 1998 accident, and Fanning has since had his brother's name tattooed on the inside of his left arm.

## SOLACE IN SURFING

Following his brother's death, Fanning resolved to dedicate himself fully to surfing, and he soon returned to competition with a newfound appreciation for life. He recalled in *Surf for Your Life*, "I began thinking about what I wanted: I want to be a pro surfer, and that's what I'm going to do." The highlight of Fanning's junior career came in

1999, when he won the Pro Junior title at Narrabeen in northern Sydney. Fanning followed this victory with another just a week later at the Jetty Surf Pro Junior at Bells Beach in Victoria, Australia. Also that year he won a specialty surfing event, the Konica Super Skins, which was held at Sandon Point in Wollongong, on the south coast of New South Wales. The event featured some of the world's top surfers and offered a significant cash prize.

In 2000 Fanning joined the ASP World Qualifying Series (WQS). Affectionately referred to in surfing circles as "the Grind," the ASP WQS consists of approximately forty-five events per season, with each event being rated on a prize-based star system ranging from one to six stars. Surfers with the highest amount of prize winnings and ratings points by the end of the season qualify for the ASP World Tour, in which the world's top thirty-four surfers compete in ten events per season. In his first season on the ASP WQS circuit, Fanning performed solidly, winning the Mark Richards Newcastle City Pro in Newcastle, Australia, a four-star event, and narrowly missing out on qualifying for the ASP World Tour. He returned in 2001 to win a six-star event at Margaret River in western Australia. That victory helped Fanning earn a wildcard invitation to the Rip Curl Pro at Bells Beach, the world's longest-running professional surfing tournament. He won the event and finished the 2001 ASP WQS season in first place, automatically earning entry into the 2002 ASP World Tour. At the 2001 Surfer Poll Awards, an annual event honoring surfing's top competitors, Fanning received the award for breakthrough performer of the year.

## RISE TO THE ASP WORLD TOUR

Despite entering his rookie campaign with modest expectations, Fanning quickly established himself among the surfing elite, winning his first tour event as a professional at the 2002 Billabong Pro in Jeffreys Bay, South Africa. He went on to make the finals of two more events—at Saquarema in Brazil and Pipeline in Hawaii, respectively—and finished the 2002 ASP World Tour season ranked fifth. At the end of the season, Fanning was named ASP Rookie of the Year.

As Fanning's career began to accelerate, his mother quit her job to become his full-time manager. In this role, she handles his accounting, oversees all of his business endeavors, and negotiates with his sponsors, which include Rip Curl, the Austrian energy drink maker Red Bull, the California-based surf brand Reef, and the Utah-based headphone company Skullcandy, among others. Despite initially being underestimated in the surf industry because of her status as a woman and inexperience as a sports manager, Osborne, who by choice receives less compensation than what is standard for sports managers, has earned praise for her keen negotiating skills and has been credited with helping her son become one of the wealthiest surfers in the world, with annual earnings estimated to be in the millions. Osborne's work is especially important considering the relatively short length of most professional surfers' careers. "You've got ten years to increase their wealth," she explained to Conlon, "so that when they leave the professional surfing circuit they have something to fall back on."

## CAREER-THREATENING INJURY

After rising to number four in the ASP World Tour rankings in 2003, Fanning entered the 2004 season as one of the favorites to win that year's championship. By that time, however, the grueling nature of the tour had begun to take its toll. In an interview with *Surfer* magazine (22 July 2010), Fanning recalled, "I don't think I'd been home for a month in five years. I'd have ten days or maximum three weeks. Everything just got to be so stressful." In the summer of 2004, after starting the season off with a string of lackluster performances, Fanning agreed to go on a Rip Curl–sponsored boat trip to Indonesia in an effort to recharge his batteries. The trip took an unfortunate turn, however, when a freak wipeout tore Fanning's left hamstring completely off his pelvic bone, immediately ending his season and putting his surfing career in jeopardy.

Because of the isolated location of the Indonesian surf spot, Fanning was forced to take a ten-hour boat ride and three plane trips to get back to Australia. After undergoing a procedure to reattach his hamstring, Fanning was ordered to stay out of the water for six months, during which he underwent a long and arduous rehabilitation process. Under the direction of his chiropractor, he began an all-encompassing training program called Corrective Holistic Exercise Kinesiology (CHEK), which focuses on core strength and flexibility as well as nutrition and psychology. The program helped speed up his recovery process and he was able to start surfing again by the end of the year. Seeking to avoid further injuries and improve his physical fitness, Fanning, who also has the spine condition scoliosis, has since integrated CHEK as well as yoga and breath enhancement training into his daily regimen.

## COMEBACK AND ASP WORLD TITLES

In 2005, Fanning reclaimed his spot on the ASP World Tour as an injury wildcard. Concerns about his postinjury performance were quickly put to rest when he won the first event of the season, the Quiksilver Pro at Snapper Rocks, in front of thousands of hometown fans. Later that season Fanning added another win at the Rip Curl Pro Search at Reunion Island, off the eastern coast of Africa, and posted a runner-up finish at the Rip Curl Pipeline Masters in Oahu, Hawaii. He finished the season in third place.

In 2006 Fanning finished third for the second consecutive year, after reaching the quarterfinals or better in half of the season's events and collecting two more ASP tour victories—his second career Billabong Pro in Jeffreys Bay and the Nova Schin Festival in Imbituba, Brazil. The following year, Fanning posted one of the most dominant seasons in competitive surfing history, winning three events (the Quiksilver Pro at Snapper Rocks; the Quiksilver Pro in Hossegor, France; and the Hang Loose Pro in Santa Catarina, Brazil) and accumulating one runner-up finish and three third-place finishes. Fanning's phenomenal season culminated in November of that year, when he clinched his first career ASP World Tour title with his victory at the Hang Loose Santa Catarina Pro, edging out perennial ASP world champion Kelly Slater and fellow Australian Taj Burrow. Fanning became the first Australian to win a men's world surfing title since Mark Occhilupo in 1999; he also became only the second non-American to capture the title over a fifteen-year span. His victory, which he dedicated to his brother Sean, solidified his status as one of the world's best surfers. It also led many observers to tout him as a likely heir to Slater, who had won eight of the previous fifteen ASP World Tour titles and holds the record for most ASP Tour titles with eleven.

After finishing a disappointing eighth in the rankings during the 2008 season, in which he faltered under increased media attention and was hampered by injuries, Fanning returned to surfing glory in 2009 when he won his second ASP world title. That year he won three events (the Hurley Pro at Trestles, in California; the Quiksilver Pro in Seignosse, France; and the Rip Curl Pro Search in Peniche, Portugal) en route to the title, which he claimed after narrowly beating out childhood friend Parkinson. During the 2010–12 ASP World Tour seasons, Fanning remained one of the most consistent surfers on the tour. Despite an injury-plagued 2011 campaign in which he ranked eleventh, he finished third in the championship tour in both 2010 and 2012. Fanning claimed his fifteenth professional victory at the Billabong Pro Tahiti in French Polynesia in August 2012.

### PERSONAL LIFE

Fanning lives in Tweed Heads with his wife, model Karissa Dalton, whom he married in March 2008. In 2009 Fanning published the memoir *Surf for Your Life*, which chronicles his journey to the top of the surfing world. He has appeared in numerous surf documentaries, including *Fanning the Fire* (2002), *Mick, Myself and Eugene* (2005), *Down the Barrel* (2007), and *Going Vertical: The Shortboard Revolution* (2010). He has also been involved in philanthropic work, which has included serving as an ambassador for both the Christian advocacy organization World Vision and the National Breast Cancer Foundation.

### SUGGESTED READING

Conlon, Tommy. "White Lightning." *Independent*. ie. Independent News and Media, 30 Dec. 2007. Web. 16 Apr. 2013.

"Mick Fanning." *Mickfanning.com.au*. Mick Fanning, 2012. Web. 16 Apr. 2013.

Swanton, Will. "Secret World of a Champion." *Sydney Morning Herald*. Sydney Morning Herald, 2 Mar. 2008. Web. 16 Apr. 2013.

"The Surfer Interview: Mick Fanning." *Surfer*. GrindMedia, 22 July 2010. Web. 16 Apr. 2013.

Williams, Huw J. "Hero's Hero: Mick Fanning." *Red Bull*. Red Bull, 12 Aug. 2009. Web. 16 Apr. 2013.

—*Chris Cullen*

# Susan Feniger

**Born:** ca. 1953
**Occupation:** Chef and restaurateur

Celebrity chef Susan Feniger has made her career introducing American consumers to authentic home-style food from the backstreets of far-flung places around the globe. Classically trained in the French tradition, Feniger has traveled a long way, physically and culinarily, from her early years in the highly competitive and male-dominated industry. Food, for Feniger, is a means of exploring the world and getting to know other cultures. As she told Nicole Campoy in an interview for *Fodor's* travel magazine, "Through food, you open up a world that is so informative and exciting and truly opens the hearts of people who live there. You learn so much about a culture through their food" (15 Aug. 2012). In particular, street food—fast food made home-style at roadside stands in cities and towns the world over—has the power to unite complete strangers. Discussing its appeal with Megan Rowe for *Restaurant Hospitality* magazine, Feniger explains, "If it's great food, you don't care if it's fancy. You end up forming great relationships with people. You find out about cultures in a way you don't get when you eat in a fancy restaurant" (Oct. 2012).

In a collaboration with fellow chef Mary Sue Milliken lasting over three decades, Feniger has run more than a half dozen restaurants, authored nearly as many cookbooks, and taken the airwaves and small screen by storm. One of the few top female chefs in the United States and an open lesbian, Feniger seeks not only to broaden American palates but also to transform the industry itself.

## EARLY LIFE AND EDUCATION

Born in the early 1950s to a family of Russian Jewish extraction, Susan Feniger credits her mother's cooking for visitors as an important early influence. She recalled to Joleen Oshiro for the *Honolulu Star-Advertiser*, "My mom loved things really well seasoned. I think my taste for strong flavors came from her in a big way" (29 Aug. 2012).

Experiences in Feniger's adolescence took her far from her hometown of Toledo, Ohio, where she worked in her father's flower shop as a child and in Smith's Cafeteria as a teen. At age fifteen, while attending Ottawa Hills High School, she had the opportunity to do a home-stay in the Netherlands, an experience that gave her a first taste of "exotic" cuisine. A couple years later, Feniger lived for a time on Kibbutz Ruhama in Israel's Negev Desert. Speaking to Ed Morita in an interview for the Hawai'i Food and Wine Festival, she said of this time, "We had no money and were camping on beaches and going around by bus and eating street food in Israel."

After high-school graduation, Feniger enrolled first at Goddard College in Plainville, Vermont, and then at Pitzer College in Claremont, California, graduating from the latter in 1976. At the suggestion of a Pitzer cafeteria chef, Feniger decided to pursue formal culinary studies. She went on to receive training in traditional French cuisine—and its attendant kitchen hierarchy—from the highly prestigious Culinary Institute of America in Hyde Park, New York.

## FRENCH CHEFS

In 1978, Feniger landed her first real cooking gig at Le Perroquet, a high-end restaurant in Chicago, where she met fellow chef Mary Sue Milliken, with whom she would develop a strong bond of friendship. Surrounded by men, both women, and Feniger especially, endured verbal abuse and high demands from head chef Jovan Treboyevic. Refusing to be cowed by the pressure, Feniger and Milliken ultimately proved themselves to him and were even left in charge on a few occasions when Treboyevic was absent.

Looking for new adventures, both set off for kitchens in France, Milliken in Paris and Feniger at L'Oasis on the French Riviera. There, Feniger once again found herself trying to prove her worth in a male-dominated kitchen and sometimes taking on physical tasks that she could not handle alone. After her stint in France, Feniger returned to Southern California and reunited with Milliken at Wolfgang Puck's Ma Maison in Los Angeles. Not long after, the two decided it was time to stop working for men and venture out on their own.

## CHANGE OF SCENE, CHANGE OF CUISINE

Two bottles of wine and a rainbow sealed the business partnership between Feniger and Milliken in 1981, and the City Cafe on Los Angeles's Melrose Avenue was born. The tiny restaurant boasted only eleven tables with seating for thirty-nine. Its cooking equipment consisted of a twenty-four-inch square prep table, a hot plate, and a hibachi grill in the alley outside. But diverse food offerings made it a success, and it was not long before Feniger and Milliken were opening another eatery, the CITY Restaurant, in 1985.

Feniger often cites a 1984 trip she took to visit a friend in India as the major turning point in her culinary career. There, she became enchanted with new flavors, methods, and tools, and especially with the messy homemade dishes that she encountered in a small village. The stark contrast to the French cuisine Feniger had been taught was an epiphany. She told Rowe that this first trip to India was "such an incredible experience for me in terms of flavors that one had never tasted, the cotton materials, the pots and pans, walking through a market seeing all the spices and colors." She waxed lyrical about the trip to Campoy: "This opened my eyes to a whole new world, one I fell in love with and have been ever since. It was soulful, romantic, inspirational, and shaped who I am in the food world in a huge way."

Yet Feniger and Milliken are undoubtedly best known for their chain of Mexican restaurants, which debuted when the City Cafe transformed into the Los Angeles flagship Border Grill in 1985. Its bold décor of brightly colored patterns and modern artwork combined with the chefs' authentic but little-known dishes made the Border Grill a hit. By 1990, the original location was too small, and the cooking duo moved to a location in Santa Monica near the Third Street Promenade. Mandalay Bay Hotel and Casino approached Feniger and Milliken about adding a Border Grill in Las Vegas, which they did in 1999. In a 2007 *Restaurant Business* article by Sam Smith, Feniger called this one of their best business decisions, as the Las Vegas location attracts a much larger volume of customers than their ones in Southern California. More recently, the Border Grill branched out to serve the needs of on-the-go eaters, launching the Border Grill Truck, a mobile dining room that roams the Los Angeles area, and Border Grill Stop, a kiosk located at a city bus stop for the breakfast and lunchtime convenience of hungry office workers.

In the midst of this expansion, Feniger and Milliken launched Ciudad in downtown Los Angeles in 1991. Unlike Border Grill, which focuses exclusively on Mexican fare, the menu of Ciudad drew from cuisines all over Latin America, from Cuba to Brazil. Ciudad closed after eleven years in operation, and the owners chose to replace it with a Border Grill. CITY Restaurant closed in 1994, after a nine-year run.

## GOING STREET

Thanks to her globe-trotting, Feniger is very passionate about street food from all corners of the world. Her curiosity is a big part of that passion. As she explained to Rowe, "When you are eating at a stand or visiting a market stand where someone is making a fantastic dish, you can see how they make it. Are they cooking on a hot griddle or fire? Do they sear something? Are they putting mayo or acid on it? . . . There's something very authentic about this experience that I love." When asked about the potential growth of street food in the United States, Feniger replied, "I think there are great things that can happen without needing a truck . . . more and more we've embraced global cuisine—way more so than twenty years ago. And maybe all the excitement about the trucks is changing opinions."

In 2009, Feniger decided to return to the multiculturalism that drove City Cafe and Ciudad. Establishing the restaurant Street with Kajsa Alger, Feniger drew once again on India for inspiration, spending two weeks there. With help from Alger and from Liz Lachman, her longtime partner, Feniger then developed an eclectic menu of street food that now changes on a quarterly basis. "We don't want to be all-India or all-Vietnam . . . We want to pull from Eastern Europe, southeast Asia, the southern United States," she told Jennifer Exley for the *Hollywood Reporter* (17 July 2012). Prodding customers to test their comfort zones is a kind of calling for the adventurous Feniger, who explained to Exley, "You always try to push people

a little bit so they expand their horizons but you also don't want to do something that's going to scare them."

Opening a restaurant on her own was not without its challenges. In the early weeks after Street opened, Feniger sweated it out for hours in front of the wood stove, which she jokingly referred to as "a quick diet," according to an *Advocate* profile of her in 2010. Furthermore, the restaurant's focus on street food garnered criticism from some quarters for bringing common or "lowbrow" food into a high-end market with correspondingly higher prices, Exley reports. Nonetheless, Street has taken off and is generally regarded as a success.

## BRINGING STREET FOOD HOME

Throughout their joint career, Feniger and Milliken have authored a number of cookbooks, which often represent a particular phase in their cuisine. In 1989, the famed cooking duo published *City Cuisine*, following the success of City Cafe and CITY Restaurant. During the mid-1990s, paralleling the expansion of the Border Grill franchise and the establishment of Ciudad, the two penned several cookbooks on Mexican cuisine, including *Mesa Mexicana* in 1994, *Cantina* in 1996, and finally *Cooking with Too Hot Tamales* in 1997, on which they collaborated with Helene Siegel. They reprised this theme for *Mexican Cooking for Dummies*, published in 2011 as part of the For Dummies series of how-to books.

Three years after the debut of Street, Feniger, Alger, and Lachman produced *Susan Feniger's Street Food: Irresistibly Crispy, Creamy, Crunchy, Spicy, Sticky, Sweet Recipes* (2012). Like Street itself, the cookbook represents a new chapter in Feniger's career and focuses on menu items from the eponymous restaurant. Unlike Milliken and Feniger's earlier cookbooks, *Street Food* features color photographs throughout, an addition that Feniger admitted to Morita she was "really excited about." Describing the book's other novel features to Rowe, Feniger highlighted the user-friendliness of the recipes, which "allow the user to produce these very interesting dishes without being forced to find exotic ingredients," and added, "Also, instead of a glossary, we provided little pictures of all these ingredients so if you walk into a market and no one speaks English, someone can help you." As she explained to Exley, "A recipe is a road map. . . . If you don't have [a particular] ingredient you don't have to freak out and not do the dish. It's meant to be fun and creative."

## MEDIA VENTURES

In 1993, Julia Child invited Feniger and Milliken to appear on her television show *Cooking with Master Chefs*. This television debut led to other television appearances and even a couple of series of their own. Between 1995 and 1999, the two hosted the Food Network series *Too Hot Tamales*—from which they derive their nickname, the Two Hot Tamales—as well as its sequel, *Tamales World Tour*. Feniger later competed in reality cooking-contest shows *Iron Chef America* in 2005 and *Top Chef Masters* from 2010 to 2012, winning the latter in season two.

Feniger and Milliken hosted the weekly California public radio program *Good Food* from 1995 until 1998, when Evan Kleiman took over as host. Recalling their experiences on air, Feniger told Gary Baum for the *Hollywood Reporter*, "We really felt as though we'd made it when [Ana Gasteyer and Molly Shannon] spoofed us [on *Saturday Night Live*]. It felt like such a huge honor. It makes you feel, like, 'Wow, I didn't know our life was so exciting'" (1 Dec. 2011).

In November 2011, the ABC network and former Disney executive Michael Eisner announced that plans are in the works for a single-camera sitcom based loosely on Feniger and Milliken's early careers and collaboration, set in the 1980s. *Working Together*, the project's provisional title, shares its name with Eisner's 2010 book in which he profiles the cooking duo. Eisner, screenwriter and producer Jeff Greenstein, and executive producers Noel Bright and Steve Cohen have all signed on to the project. The sitcom's screenwriter has been in consultation with Feniger and Millikan, who will also be executive producers, to ensure that the actors appear authentic in the kitchen. As of late 2012, the show has yet to air.

Despite her heavy media presence and full schedule, Feniger continues to find time to teach culinary arts and cooks at the Border Grill Santa Monica whenever she can and the need arises. She still prefers making food above all else.

## A SIDE OF PROGRESSIVE POLITICS

Gender and sexuality perhaps unavoidably bring politics into business for a lesbian celebrity chef. The gender gap in the high-end culinary business has been an ongoing issue throughout Feniger's career, not only in terms of tense emotional dynamics in the kitchen but also in numerical terms. When Feniger and Milliken got their start in the early 1980s, the only well-known female chef in the United States was Julia Child, who is famed for bringing French cuisine to the American palate. Feniger told Oshiro that in the beginning, her primary aim "was to learn everything about food, from pastries to butchering to filleting fish, to being on the line, dishwasher," and said that she "was barely aware that being a woman made any difference," though the gender-related biases Feniger faced as a young chef seemingly belie this assertion.

Even today, a chef's gender seems to matter, a fact Feniger more readily admits when discussing the money side of the industry. In

2010, women still made up less than 11 percent of executive chefs and the average salary of a female executive chef was $59,474, compared to $76,410 for men in the same job, according to *StarChefs* magazine. Discussing the ongoing disparity with Sunnivie Brydum for the *Advocate*, Feniger stated, "You see a lot more men out there funded for [restaurant] expansion and growth than you do women" (Oct. 2012).

In addition to establishing a successful female-female business partnership and working to support other female chefs, Feniger has become an open advocate for gay people in the kitchen as well as in the community. She realized her own sexual orientation in the late 1970s and was initially reluctant to come out publicly due to cultural perceptions of homosexuality at that time. But times have changed, and as she told Brydum, she now sees it as her duty to speak up, "to give my opinion about who I am and . . . to talk about it whenever I can, because I think it's important to make strong statements." She concluded, "If you can make one person be a little bit more aware and open, that's a big step."

## SUSTAINING BODIES, SUSTAINING THE ENVIRONMENT

In light of the California Global Warming Solutions Act passing in 2006, Feniger and Milliken provided energy-cost data on the Border Grill to analysts for *Catalyst*, a Union of Concerned Scientists publication, in spring 2010. The findings showed that over the next ten years, the Border Grill's energy costs might rise about three cents per twenty dollars spent—what the owners deemed "a minuscule increase" that, "even if noticed, would not cause our customers any heartburn." They added, "We're worried about a Too Hot Future. Our customers are just as worried as we are, and would be more than willing to pay an extra three cents to help avoid the most catastrophic impacts of global warming."

That worry about the environment has translated into a number of choices regarding sustainability, from buying directly from producers at farmer's markets to switching to organic produce, despite the cost factor. Feniger and Milliken have also removed Chilean sea bass and swordfish from menus in response to what they consider unsustainable fishing practices. Feniger even played a founding role in Chefs Collaborative, a nonprofit organization dedicated to sourcing foods grown in sustainable ways and to educating the culinary industry and the general consumer. Together with the Whole Foods grocery chain, Feniger and Milliken developed the Border Girls line of ready-to-eat meals based on entrees offered in their Border Grill restaurants. In 2007, they formed a similar partnership with Sodexho Alliance, now Sodexo, catering company to provide on-the-run meals. Part of the chefs' stated aim in striking the deal was to encourage Sodexo "to think about sustainability and hormone-free" and "help them effect change in their company," which they foresee "will have a big effect on the whole food industry," as Molly Gise reported in the June 2007 issue of *Nation's Restaurant News*.

## PERSONAL LIFE

Feniger and her domestic partner, filmmaker Liz Lachman, reside in Brentwood, California. The couple have been together for seventeen years, not in spite of but because of the grueling schedule both keep, according to Lachman. On a typical day, Feniger and Lachman are up before 7 a.m., eating dinner around 9 or 10 p.m. after the restaurants close, and finally crawling into bed after 1 a.m. Speaking to T. A. Gilmartin for *Lesbian News* about Feniger's long hours and frequent travel, Lachman said, "She's got a schedule that most people wouldn't put up with. . . . For me it's great. I don't mind that she's gone all the time. We're compatible" (July 2005).

That compatibility was something Feniger ultimately did not find with her former highschool sweetheart and husband of eight years, architect Josh Schweitzer. Feniger and Schweitzer divorced in the late 1970s after Feniger decided to pursue an interest in a woman. She was subsequently instrumental in matching Milliken and Schweitzer, who married in 1984, and all three remain close friends.

In addition to traveling, writing new recipes, managing restaurants, and appearing in various media outlets, Feniger contributes to philanthropic ventures. She has long been active in her community, serving on the boards of the Los Angeles Gay and Lesbian Center and the Los Angeles Sports and Entertainment Commission. Sometimes work and charity overlap, as in 1988, when she helped establish the Cool Comedy–Hot Cuisine annual fundraising dinner to benefit the Scleroderma Research Foundation, or in April 2011, when she participated in the Evening of Food and Fotos dinner to raise money for Foundation Rwanda, an organization that helps educate children of rape victims from the Rwandan genocide.

## SUGGESTED READING

Brydum, Sunnivie. "Queers in the Kitchen." *Advocate* Oct. 2012: 39–43. Print.

Campoy, Nicole. "Susan Feniger on Eating (and Crossing the Street) in Southeast Asia." *Fodor's Travel Intelligence*. Fodor's Travel, 15 Aug. 2012. Web. 19 Nov. 2012.

Exley, Jennifer. "Celebrity Chef Susan Feniger Dishes on Her New Street Food Book." *Hollywood Reporter*. Hollywood Reporter, 17 July 2012. Web. 19 Nov. 2012.

Morita, Ed. "Know Your Chef: Susan Feniger of Street." *Hawai'i Food and Wine Festival*. Hawai'i Food and Wine Festival, n.d. Web. 19 Nov. 2012.

Rowe, Megan. "Streetwise, Savvy." *Restaurant Hospitality* Oct. 2012: 46–47. Print.

## SELECTED WORKS

*City Cuisine* (with Mary Sue Milliken), 1989; *Mesa Mexicana* (with Mary Sue Milliken and Helene Siegel), 1994; *Cantina* (with Mary Sue Milliken), 1996; *Susan Feniger's Street Food* (with Kajsa Alger and Liz Lachman), 2012

—*Céleste Codington-Lacerte*

---

# Alex Filippenko

**Born:** July 25, 1958
**Occupation:** Astrophysicist and professor

Alex Filippenko is considered one of the world's foremost authorities in the field of astronomy. An observational astronomer who makes frequent use of the Hubble Space Telescope, the Keck ten-meter telescopes, and the Lick three-meter telescope, Filippenko's primary areas of research include black holes, active galaxies, gamma-ray bursts, supernovae, and observational cosmology. He is credited with spearheading the Katzman Automatic Imaging Telescope (KAIT), which is considered one of the world's most successful automated search engines for nearby supernovae, or exploding stars. In the decade following KAIT's implementation, the robotic telescope discovered approximately 40 percent of all nearby supernovae detected worldwide. To date, KAIT has been credited with finding and imaging about one thousand supernovae.

Filippenko has also garnered national recognition for his popular Introduction to General Astronomy course at the University of California (UC), Berkeley, where he has been a faculty member since 1986. His ability to clarify difficult concepts in engaging and humorous ways has been a hit with students. Every Halloween he dons an all-black outfit in class to masquerade as a black hole and demonstrates the quantum mechanical evaporation of black holes by tossing students astronomy-themed candy, such as Starburst, Milky Way, and Eclipse gum. Students of UC Berkeley have voted Filippenko the best professor on campus a record-setting nine times. For his efforts, Filippenko earned the Carnegie/CASE National Professor of the Year Award (2006) for doctoral and research institutions and the Richard H. Emmons Award for undergraduate teaching (2010). He has also been featured in about one hundred science television shows, including about forty episodes of *The*

Michael Kleinfeld/UPI/Landov

*Universe*, a documentary series that airs on the History Channel and H2.

## CHILDHOOD AND EDUCATION

Alexei Vladimir Filippenko was born to Alexandra K. and Vladimir I. Filippenko on July 25, 1958, in Oakland, California. At the time of Filippenko's birth, his mother was attending library school and his father was pursuing a graduate degree in mathematics at UC Berkeley. When Filippenko was six years old, he moved with his parents and his brother, Ivan, to Santa Barbara and then to Goleta one year later. Growing up, he attended several schools, including Laguna Blanca School, Fairview Elementary School, and Goleta Valley Junior High School.

Filippenko had an interest in science from an early age. "In the first grade, I played with magnets and was intrigued by how they would attract or repel each other. . . . What was this very real but invisible force?" he said in an interview for the Mars Millennium Project 2030, a national arts, sciences, and technology education initiative. In the second grade—after one of the officials at Filippenko's primary school dismissed his fascination with magnets as strange—his parents transferred him to another school, where his growing interest in science was nurtured.

Filippenko thrived at his new school. "At the new school, there was a teacher who sent me to the library to make an electromagnet. Then there was Mr. Goodrich, a middle schoolteacher who let me explore chemistry," he told Lou Fancher

in an interview for the *San Jose Mercury News* (17 Jan. 2013). However, chemistry was not the only subject that fascinated Filippenko. In 1972, as a freshman at Dos Pueblos High School, he took up astronomy as a hobby after checking out the stars for the first time with a telescope that his parents had bought him as a Christmas gift. Filippenko was intrigued by the third object that he observed through the eyepiece. "To my utter amazement, I saw a small disk surrounded by exquisite rings—I was looking at Saturn! The sight nearly knocked my socks off," he said in an interview for the Mars Millennium Project. "From then on, the thrill of scientific discovery was permanently etched in my mind." In an interview with Patricia Yollin for the *San Francisco Gate* (1 Nov. 2007), Filippenko recalled this moment, saying, "It illustrated to me the addictive thrill you'd get during discovery. If I could get such a rush from finding an object that was well known, how much better would it be to find something for the first time in the existence of humanity?"

## SHIFT FROM CHEMISTRY TO PHYSICS

In 1975, after graduating a year early from high school, Filippenko attended the College of Creative Studies (CCS) at the University of California, Santa Barbara (UCSB). As a high school senior, Filippenko had won the CCS "Prize Exam" in chemistry. Although he had initially planned to pursue chemistry at UCSB, Filippenko switched his major to physics at the end of his freshman year after taking an introductory course in astronomy taught by Professor Stanton J. Peale, his mentor. "I realized that I was really most interested in the physical aspects of chemistry, and especially in physics," he revealed in an interview for *Inside Physics* (Fall 2007), the annual newsletter for the UCSB physics department.

Filippenko was equally fascinated by the large, research-oriented university's progressive teaching methods, which fostered his independent thinking and honed his analytical skills. "The College taught me early to have an open, inquiring, and creative mind, but at the same time one that is logical and critical. . . . We had to figure everything out for ourselves, as though no one had previously worked on this," he wrote for the CCS Alumni website. "We were also forced to solve problems on a blackboard, in front of two demanding professors who would not tolerate sloppy or incomplete solutions. Though initially very nerve-racking, this experience taught me how to think quickly on my feet, and to defend my methods with solid arguments." At UCSB, with the encouragement of Professor Peale, Filippenko also had two rare yearlong opportunities to teach a small seminar on introductory astronomy.

Filippenko spent two summers, in 1977 and 1978, at the University of California's Lick Observatory near San Jose, California, where he worked as a guide. While there, he was able to examine the RR Lyrae stars found in Messier 15 (a globular cluster located in the constellation Pegasus) with the observatory's twelve-inch refracting telescope.

## ASTRONOMY AT CALTECH

After earning his bachelor's degree in physics in 1979 and receiving UCSB's Nordsieck Award for the most outstanding graduate in physics, Filippenko enrolled at the California Institute of Technology (Caltech) on a Fannie and John Hertz Foundation fellowship. He pursued doctoral studies in astronomy under the supervision of Professor Wallace L. W. Sargent. While at Caltech, Filippenko frequently visited the Mount Wilson Observatory near Pasadena, California; the Palomar Observatory in San Diego County; and Las Campanas Observatory in northern Chile. The research that Filippenko compiled during his two summers at the Lick Observatory served as the basis for his first published paper in 1981.

For his thesis project, Filippenko made a noteworthy discovery upon examining the nuclei of various kinds of galaxies to figure out their physical conditions. "I found that many nearby, apparently normal-looking galaxies exhibit low-level activity of the kind seen much more strongly in the distant, luminous quasars," he told *Current Biography*. "This activity is probably produced by the swallowing of matter by an enormous black hole in the very center of each galaxy."

In May 1984, after obtaining his doctorate degree in astronomy from Caltech, Filippenko became a Miller Fellow for basic science research at UC Berkeley, where he continued the research that he first started at Caltech and launched other projects, as well. In February 1985, Filippenko and Sargent spent several nights at the Palomar Observatory, studying the centers of nearby galaxies. Using the five-meter Hale Telescope, the two were able to detect a bright light near the center of a spiral galaxy named NGC 4618. They determined that the source of this light was coming from a supernova, the catastrophic explosion of a massive star.

However, Filippenko and Sargent also believed that this supernova differed significantly from normal Type I or Type II, the two recognized classes of supernovae. Their findings, which identified a new subclass of supernovae, were published in the August 1, 1985, issue of *Nature*.

## SUPERNOVA SEARCH

In 1986 Filippenko was offered a faculty position at UC Berkeley as an assistant professor of astronomy. He was promoted to associate professor in 1988. A year later, Filippenko began supervising a group of astronomers and engineers responsible for the development of the thirty-inch Katzman Automatic Imaging Telescope (KAIT) at Lick Observatory, a fully robotic telescope that automates the search for supernovae and other celestial anomalies. "If you want to monitor an exploding star you often have to plead with colleagues for a small amount of time each night, sometimes at telescopes all around the world," he explained in a press release from the University of California, Berkeley (21 Oct. 1996). "So I embarked on a project to build an automated, dedicated telescope that could be used for a variety of projects: searching for supernovas, monitoring known variable stars, supernovas and novas, looking at quasars and active galaxies, and very importantly, homing in on targets of opportunity." Part of the funding for this project came from a 1989 Presidential Young Investigator Award that Filippenko had received from the National Science Foundation, as well as a substantial donation from the Sylvia and Jim Katzman Foundation.

KAIT's separate charge-couple device (CCD) imaging system for a guide star enables the telescope to remain fixed on one area of sky without the need for manual readjustments. As a prototype for KAIT, in the early 1990s Filippenko modified an existing twenty-inch telescope at UC Berkeley's Leuschner Observatory; it was known as the Berkeley Automatic Imaging Telescope (BAIT).

KAIT's main project is the Lick Observatory Supernova Search (LOSS), initiated in 1996. In 1997 Filippenko recruited Weidong Li, founder of the Beijing Astronomical Observatory Supernova Survey (BAOSS), to oversee telescope operations for KAIT. (The previous year the BAOSS had located six supernovae, including SN 1996W, the first supernova to be discovered by Chinese astronomers since the year 1054). Over the next several years, KAIT went on to become the world's most successful detector of relatively nearby supernovae. By the end of 1998, the telescope had uncovered twenty new supernovae, and the next year that number had doubled. There were thirty-eight supernova discoveries in 2000, the year that Filippenko was awarded a Guggenheim Fellowship. An additional sixty-eight supernovae were identified in 2001; that number increased to eighty-two in 2002 and ninety-five in 2003.

## THE EXPANSION OF THE UNIVERSE

As a member of the Supernova Cosmology Project and subsequently the High-Z Supernova Search Team, Filippenko helped make a landmark discovery in 1998 after an extensive search of distant Type Ia supernovae. (The Supernova Cosmology Project and the High-Z Supernova Search Team were two international teams of astronomers monitoring Type Ia supernovae to determine the history of the expansion of the universe from the present day to nine billion years in the past.)

After analyzing the distances and the recession speeds of Type Ia supernovae, the two teams discovered that the universe is expanding faster now than it was a few billion years ago, instead of more slowly as had been anticipated. The distance of each supernova is calculated by measuring its apparent brightness, and the speed is calculated by figuring out the redshift, or how much their color is shifted toward longer wavelengths of light due to the stretching of space. Filippenko used the Keck 10-meter telescopes in Hawaii to obtain the spectra from which the redshifts were determined, and which revealed whether the faint supernova candidates were indeed Type Ia supernovae. This means that the universe is expanding at an accelerating rate—and that about two-thirds of the universe's mass/energy content consists of strange "dark energy" or "vacuum energy." This landmark discovery was recognized by *Science* magazine as the "Top Science Breakthrough of 1998," and the two teams received the 2007 Gruber Cosmology Prize. Moreover, the team leaders and Adam Riess (Filippenko's postdoctoral scholar in the mid-to-late 1990s when this research was being conducted) were honored with the 2011 Nobel Prize in Physics for discovering the accelerating expansion of the universe.

By 2003 KAIT was also being used to search for the afterglow from gamma-ray bursts (GRBs), which are regarded as the most powerful and mysterious explosions in the universe since the Big Bang. (Gamma-ray bursts last only a few milliseconds to a few hundred seconds, making them difficult to gauge their distance, location, or cause.) Astronomers believe that GRBs are predominantly caused by the collapse of a massive star (about thirty times the sun's mass), whose matter is then drawn into a black hole. A jet of high-energy particles is released, which produces an afterglow that is briefly visible by gamma-ray and x-ray telescopes in Earth orbit.

At a January 2003 meeting of the American Astronomical Society (AAS), Filippenko announced that KAIT had automatically captured real-time photographs of the fading afterglow from a gamma-ray burst that occurred on December 11, 2002 (GRB 021211). These unprecedented images were taken less than 2 minutes (108 seconds) after the 2.5-second GRB was initially detected by the High Energy Transient Explorer (HETE-2) satellite. KAIT was able to record over 2.5 hours of exposures before dawn, more than any other robotic telescope. "For the first time, we have really good data showing the early-time afterglow from a gamma-ray burst and the transition to late-time decline," Filippenko said in a UC Berkeley press release (9 Jan. 2003).

The afterglow lasted only two-and-a-half hours, leading Filippenko to conclude that it may provide some insight into the mysterious dark GRBs, which give off gamma rays with little or no visible light. He also suggested that gas and dust could be obscuring the afterglow, making it more difficult to observe.

## NEW KINDS OF SUPERNOVAE

Filippenko once again garnered attention in 2006 following his team's study of the supernova SN 2006aj. At the time, smaller, less luminous supernovae were not known to be associated with GRBs; it was thought that a massive star collapsing to a black hole was a requirement for the creation of a GRB. However, the detection of GRB 060218 (the X-ray flash and corresponding weak GRB associated with SN 2006aj) provided strong evidence that GRBs are associated with different types of supernovae. Filippenko and his colleagues, including fellow astronomers from Italy's Trieste Observatory and the Kavli Institute for Theoretical Physics at UC Santa Barbara, determined that this exploding star originally possessed a mass twenty times the size of the sun—the lower limit for supernovae to form black holes. Filippenko concluded that when a star this size explodes, it can result in weaker GRBs characterized by flashes of high-energy X-rays rather than the more intense GRBs associated with larger stars. "Because massive stars are hard to form, there may be many more supernovae like this producing X-ray flashes than explosions of very massive stars to produce gamma-ray bursts," he told Ker Than for Space.com (30 Aug. 2006).

In November 2009, Filippenko and one of his postdoctoral scholars at UC Berkeley reported that a seven-year-old supernova (SN 2002bj), initially discovered by KAIT in 2002, had been mistakenly designated as a Type II supernova. Upon examining images taken before and after the discovery, they were unable to find any trace of the supernova after twenty-seven days, leading them to conclude that SN 2002bj had brightened and dimmed into obscurity far more rapidly than typical supernovae. (Most supernovae brighten and dim over a three-to-four-month period.) The rapid drop in brightness and its faintness seemed to support the theory that this explosion was caused by two white dwarfs, including one composed of helium that is slowly being drawn to its companion by gravity. "We think this may well be a new physical explosion mechanism, not just a minor variation of ones already known," Filippenko said, as quoted by *Science Daily* (6 Nov. 2009).

In December 2009 Filippenko confirmed the existence of another unusual supernova: SN 2007bi, whose exceptional luminosity was one hundred times greater than a typical supernova. Based on observations conducted over an eighteen-month period, he concluded that SN 2007bi was a pair-instability supernova, released from a star that was about 140 times the sun's size, a mass rarely found in the universe. Since then Filippenko has also confirmed the existence of a calcium-rich supernova (SN 2005E) that he believes is a new class of supernova altogether.

Filippenko's groundbreaking research has made him one of the most widely cited astronomers in the world. In 2009, Filippenko was elected to the prestigious National Academy of Sciences in recognition of his distinguished research contributions to the field of astronomy.

With Jay M. Pasachoff, Filippenko coauthored the introductory astronomy textbook *The Cosmos: Astronomy in the New Millennium*, which won the 2001 Texty Excellence Award for the best new textbook in the physical sciences. He has recorded five richly illustrated video courses on astronomy with The Great Courses. He has also given more than seven hundred public lectures on astronomy. In 2004, Filippenko was awarded the Carl Sagan Prize for Science Popularization.

## PERSONAL LIFE

Since 1986, Filippenko has been a professor of astronomy at UC Berkeley, where he has also served as the Richard and Rhoda Goldman Distinguished Professor in the Physical Sciences since 2009. Filippenko lives in Piedmont, California, with his wife, Noelle, and four children. During his free time he enjoys world travel, tennis, hiking, and skiing, as well as observing total solar eclipses.

## SUGGESTED READING

"Alex Filippenko." Mars Millennium Project 2030. *Mars Millennium Project 2030*, n.d. Web. 12 June 2013.

Fancher, Lou. "Piedmont: Astronomy Professor Traces His Career to Boyhood." *San Jose Mercury News*. Media News Group, 17 Jan. 2013. Web. 12 June 2013.

"Rapid Supernova Could Be New Class of Exploding Star." *Science Daily*. Science Daily, 6 Nov. 2009. Web. 12 June 2013.

Sanders, Robert. "Robotic Telescope Catches Early Afterglow of Gamma-Ray Burst." *UC Berkeley News*. UC Regents, 9 Jan. 2003. Web. 12 June 2013.

"Science Watch; New Kind of Supernova." *New York Times*. New York Times, 27 Aug. 1985. Web. 12 June 2013.

Than, Ker. "Strange Exploding Star Unlocks Supernova Secrets." *Space*. TechMediaNetwork. com, 30 Aug. 2006. Web. 12 June 2013.

Yollin, Patricia. "Professor Uses Performances to Hook Students on Astronomy." *San Francisco Gate*. Hearst Communications, 1 Nov. 2007. Web. 12 June 2013.

—Bertha Muteba

# Gillian Flynn

**Born:** 1971
**Occupation:** Author, former film and television critic for *Entertainment Weekly*

Gillian Flynn has always loved to read and has always loved to be scared. As a little girl she was drawn to the dark and sometimes violent stories of the Brothers Grimm, and as she grew, she read Agatha Christie mysteries and watched scary movies with her father. It was her wholesome and happy family and Midwestern upbringing, Flynn believes, that allowed her to explore the shadowy and often sinister worlds and characters she creates in her highly acclaimed and best-selling novels.

Flynn's stories revolve around damaged and disturbed female protagonists. As she explained in her essay "I Was Not a Nice Little Girl," posted on her personal website Gillian-Flynn (2012), "Libraries are filled with stories on generations of brutal men. . . . I wanted to write about the violence of women. . . . Isn't it time to acknowledge the ugly side [of women]?"

The 1948 black-and-white photo by Frederick Sommer titled *Livia* is Flynn's favorite. It is of a young girl who epitomizes innocence and youthful beauty: blond, braided hair and hands folded across a white, eyelet summer dress. Flynn is drawn to the girl with her intelligent eyes, stubborn lips, and mischievous face. But, as Flynn describes in her essay, the little girl's face is also "perhaps malevolent [and] . . . a reminder that girls—and women—can be bad."

## EARLY LIFE AND EDUCATION

Gillian Flynn was born in Kansas City, Missouri, to Matt and Judith Flynn, who were professors at Metropolitan Community College. Although now retired, Flynn's mother taught reading and her father taught theater, speech, and film; much of Gillian's childhood was therefore spent surrounded by books and movies. With interests that included feeding stunned ants to spiders and playing with her cousins as the lead role in the make-believe game "Mean Aunt Rosie," Flynn was not, by her own admission, "a nice little girl." She was, however, very shy, which in turn fed her love for reading and also helped to develop her writing skills: "Writing came naturally to me," Flynn explained to Steve Paul for the *Kansas City Star* (6 Nov. 2012), "because I didn't have to talk." As a youngster, Flynn's parents took her to see such potentially age-inappropriate

Getty Images

## ENTERTAINMENT REPORTER

After graduate school, it soon became apparent to Flynn that she was not suited for crime reporting: "I wasn't assertive enough or didn't have enough guts, absolutely not cut out for that kind of thing," she told Phillip Butta for *North by Northwestern* (25 Jan. 2011). Flynn then moved to New York City to try to break into the magazine business. At first she worked in restaurants waiting on tables, but soon she was offered a position as a full-time writer for the pop-culture magazine, *Entertainment Weekly* (*EW*). For the next ten years, Flynn divided her time between New York and Los Angeles as *EW*'s film and television critic, a job that combined her writing ability with her love of film, television, and books. For Flynn, this was a dream job: "I got paid to watch TV and movies and read books and then write about them," she told Sarah Norris for *Nashville Scene* (11 Oct. 2012). Flynn also travelled the world visiting film sets and interviewing A-list actors and favorite directors (like Peter Jackson) and spending hours talking about new films, popular television series, and favorite writers such as J. R. R. Tolkien. "What more could a pop-culture nerd wish for?" Flynn asked Norris.

Despite loving everything about her job, she could not stop thinking about an idea she had for a novel. It was always in the back of her mind, and over a period of years she kept thinking about the story and its protagonist. Flynn told Mike Thomas for the *Chicago Sun-Times* (17 July 2012) that eventually she decided to write the book simply to "see if I could" and also because, as she explained in a 2007 interview with Chris High, "it was time to let [the story and the main character] out and see what happened."

Flynn began to write in what spare time she had—on weekends, at night, and during downtimes while travelling. She knew she wanted to write about a woman and the woman's toxic relationship with her mother, but very little else was taking shape and Flynn felt she was not getting very far with her story. Although she was not intending to write a mystery novel, as she explained to Noah Charney for the *Daily Beast* (21 Nov. 2012), after she stayed up all night one night reading Dennis Lehane's *Mystic River*, she had an epiphany: "The next morning  I went into work bleary-eyed and happy and thought, That's how I do it. I tie my story to a mystery. And so I did." Flynn described to Butta another "aha! moment": She was on assignment for *EW* in New Orleans in order to write about the upcoming film *Runaway Jury* with Gene Hackman and Dustin Hoffman. She was in her hotel room and on the phone bringing her *EW* editor up to date on the story and the interviews she had conducted that day. Distracted, she began doodling in pen on her leg and suddenly realized that the protagonist in her novel did the same thing but

films as *The Elephant Man, The Great Santini,* and *Alien,* and at home she and her dad watched film classics such as Alfred Hitchcock's *Psycho,* but, as Flynn made clear to Steve Paul, her dad would talk with her about the films and explain "what worked and what didn't" and in doing to, he "helped [Flynn] develop [her] critical eye."

Flynn has always been interested in fantasy and "dark" literature and explained to Paul that she grew up "loving to be scared." When she was eight years old, Flynn wrote a story called "To the Outhouse," which Paul describes as "a raw . . . middle ground between . . . Laura Ingalls Wilder's 'Little House' stories and the brutal reality of unexpurgated Brothers Grimm." Flynn states on her website that the Brothers Grimm fairy tales were early favorites, and Agatha Christie mysteries and Tolkien were teenage passions.

Following high school, Flynn attended the University of Kansas and graduated in 1993 with degrees in journalism and English. Afterward, she moved to Los Angeles and worked for the next two years as a writer for a human resources trade magazine. She then moved to Chicago and attended the Medill School of Journalism at Northwestern University with the intention of becoming a crime reporter. While at Northwestern, Flynn spent a semester in Washington, DC, and worked for a short time as a freelance writer for *US News and World Report*. She earned her master's degree in journalism from Northwestern in 1997.

in a different form: "I looked down and thought, 'Well, that's what Camille does.' She carves words into her skin."

## SHARP OBJECTS

*Sharp Objects* is a dark story whose female protagonist is a Chicago crime reporter. Camille Preaker struggles with self-mutilation to release a painful past, and she uses alcohol to self-medicate and calm herself. There are other sides to Camille, as Flynn described to Chris High in 2007. Flynn explained that Camille has "a wry sense of humor . . . and is very self-aware and buoyant. I completely adore her."

Although Flynn had once hoped to be a crime reporter like her protagonist, she insists that there is very little similarity between Camille and herself. They share a sense of humor and a hope that people will act in a sensible way, but the comparison ends there for Flynn who said in her 2007 interview with Chris High, "I'm lucky that I really like my family and job, which is probably why I was able to write such a dark book." Flynn further explained to Butta that as she was writing *Sharp Objects*, she was careful to avoid using any pop-culture references in order to "keep the two worlds [reporting for *Entertainment Weekly* and novel writing] separate so my voice from one didn't leak over into the other."

Published in 2006 to high acclaim and huge sales, *Sharp Objects* quickly became a New York Times Best Seller, and readers, critics, and established authors alike praised its storyline and Flynn's writing style. (Most who have read the book are surprised, however, that it is a debut novel and wasn't written by a seasoned and long-published writer.) *Sharp Objects* was an Edgar Award finalist and was the winner of two of Great Britain's Dagger Awards, which was especially notable as it is the first book to win more than one Dagger Award in the same year.

Flynn posted on her website a blurb American horror and suspense writer Stephen King wrote the book's back cover in which he said, "I haven't read such a relentlessly creepy family saga . . . [in] thirty years," calling it "an admirably nasty piece of work elevated by sharp writing and sharper insights." King's comments, Flynn remarked to High, was "a fairly amazing thing" for her because she's been a fan of King's since she was a child.

## DARK PLACES AND GONE GIRL

In December of 2008, Flynn was laid off from *Entertainment Weekly*. Although the decision was not unexpected, Flynn struggled with what her next life-move would be, lamenting to Steve Paul that she didn't know "how to do anything but write." Within a few months, however, her second novel was published and Random House had contracted with her for a third project. Flynn soon adjusted to life as a full-time novelist.

*Dark Places*, Flynn's second book, is reminiscent of *Sharp Objects* in what Sarah Norris for *Nashville Scene* describes as containing a theme "of murder, deception and long-buried secrets," but the first draft of the book was very different from the finished product. As Flynn explained to Paul, after *Sharp Objects* she didn't want to write another book about a "dark, troubled female," and instead created the protagonist Libby Day as a "goodie two-shoes . . . who could've been an aerobics instructor." Flynn's husband Brett Nolan convinced her to start the book over after he read what she had written thus far. According to Paul, Nolan told Flynn that he didn't like the main character because she wasn't believable, and Flynn learned the hard lesson that as a writer, "you have to write the book you need to write . . . not the one you think you should write." *Dark Places* became a New York Times Best Seller and won a spot on several "best book" lists, including Publisher's Weekly Best Book of 2009.

*Gone Girl*, published in 2012, continues Flynn's theme of what Steve Paul refers to as "dark psychology," but rather than focusing on a single female protagonist, *Gone Girl* explores the murky side of a married couple. As Flynn told Stephan Lee for *Entertainment Weekly* (26 June 2012), she wanted to explore what happens "when you willingly yoke yourself to someone for life, what happens when it starts going wrong." The plot revolves around the downward spiral of Nick and Amy's marriage, Amy's disappearance, and Nick being named as the prime suspect. Flynn weaves in details about the couple's past by using entries from Amy's diary.

Despite the book becoming another New York Times Best Seller for Flynn, it has been criticized by many for its unexpected ending. Flynn has received e-mails and letters from fans who slam her for writing the ending as she did. The reactions also confuse Flynn slightly, but as she explained to Lee for *Entertainment Weekly* (4 Dec. 2012), "I wanted to end it in a way that feels real. . . . It's fine with me if people don't like the ending. . . . If you're still thinking about the book and have your opinions on it, I think it's a great thing."

## WRITING STYLE

Shortly after the birth of her son in 2010, Flynn decided she needed a space in her home with minimal distractions where she could concentrate on writing. Her husband created a space for her in their basement and then gave her an arcade-style Ms. Pac-Man/Galaga duel video-game console as a birthday gift.

Flynn described her morning writing routine to Charney as beginning with drinking half a pot of coffee before going to her basement office and then promising herself that after she finishes a particular scene she can take a break—which usually involves "a game or eight of Galaga." Her desk is wobbly (and "held together with gum and string") and above the desk is a movie poster for *Lord of the Rings*, which is signed by the director Peter Jackson with the message, "To Gillian, a genuine nerd!"

When asked by Sarah Norris why she was so drawn to writing crime fiction, Flynn replied that it was not the genre as such that fascinates her as much as it is the individuals who occupied the genre. Flynn explained that these people were her "heroes" and that she has a "deep affinity for losers, misfits, fools and people who can't get out of their own way." Crime novels, Flynn elaborated, allow her to look at the subject matter that interests her most: "envy, needfulness, infamy, rage, poverty, broken hearts." And, despite giving up her dream in the mid-1990s to be a crime reporter, Flynn is still, over a decade later, fascinated by the side of crime reporting that, as she related to the *Hollywood Reporter*'s Kimberly Nordyke (30 Nov. 2012), allowed a person to look at "bursts of violence, where they come from and how they unite people together." Writing crime novels allows Flynn to combine this interest "in turning over a rock and seeing what's underneath" with her love for literature and her talent for writing.

Flynn doesn't write using an outline, nor does she pay particular attention to the plot of the novel as she writes, believing it to be, as she clarified to Charney, "the least intriguing part [of the book]." Instead, she works on themes, characters, or events in the book that are interesting to her at that moment, and for every novel that is published, Flynn explained to Charney, she has probably written enough words to fill two books. At the revision stage, there are "lots of deleted scenes as I try to figure out what it is I'm really interested in, what it is I'm actually writing."

Given the subject matter of her books, Flynn is often asked how she manages to keep the macabre from seeping into her personal life. She explained to *EW*'s Lee (26 June 2012) that she always tries to "keep the crazy downstairs" and spends the last ten minutes of her workday listening to upbeat music. She elaborated to Chris High in a 2012 interview that she also watches the "Moses Supposes" dance routine with Gene Kelly and Donald O'Connor in the 1952 film *Singin' in the Rain*: "You can't help but be happy after that."

## FILM ADAPTATIONS AND FUTURE PROJECTS

All three of Flynn's novels have been optioned by Hollywood to be made into major motion pictures. Flynn explained to Nordyke that she believes her books are attractive to Hollywood executives because "they are murder-mysteries, but with character—strong character-led story lines." Flynn also believes that as more women become powerful and influential in the industry,

they are able to successfully pressure studios to cast them as Flynn's "very strong female [lead] characters" or take on projects themselves.

Actor and producer Reese Witherspoon, for instance, has bought the rights to the film version of *Gone Girl*. As Witherspoon told *International Business Times* (29 Dec. 2012), "Two years ago, I really decided I wanted to get back into finding projects to produce that had great female characters in them, and this is one of the first that came up." Her company will not only produce the project, but Witherspoon is slated to star in the film as well. Flynn is currently writing the screenplay and is finding that the years spent watching and discussing movies with her film professor father and her ten years as a film critic with *EW* are immensely helpful.

Flynn is looking forward to *Gone Girl* making it to movie theaters if for no other reason than to take her father to the film's premiere. As she told Nordyke, "Growing up, all my dad and I did on our father-daughter dates was go to the movies. I'd love to return the favor and take him to the premiere."

*Dark Places* is currently in production. French director Gilles Paquet-Brenner adapted the novel to the screen and is directing the film. It stars Amy Adams in the lead role of Libby Day. Although the film rights to *Sharp Objects* were also sold, its progress has stalled. Jason Blum has been chosen as the producer, but the film's executives are still searching for the right director.

Flynn has signed an additional two-book deal with Crown Publishing, which has slated her next book for publication in 2015. She has also signed with Delacorte Press to write her first young adult novel. The release dates for her fifth novel and her young adult novel have not been announced.

## PERSONAL LIFE

Flynn met her husband Brett Nolan during her postgraduate days at Northwestern. Nolan was studying law and is now a lawyer practicing in Chicago, Illinois, where he and Flynn live. Flynn gave birth to their first child in 2010 (a boy they named Flynn Nolan). The family also share their home with Roy, whom Gillian described to Bob Minzesheimer for *USA Today* (7 May 2009) as a "giant cat [who] loves to sit on my lap when I'm writing [and is] a real doorstopper."

## SELECTED READING

Charney, Noah. Gillian Flynn: How I Write." *Daily Beast*. The Newsweek/Daily Beast Co., 21 Nov. 2012. Web. 15 Jan. 2013.

High, Chris. "Interview with Gillian Flynn." *Chris High*. n.pub., 2007, 2009, 2012. Web. 15 Jan. 2013.

Lee, Stephen. "Gone Girl author Gillian Flynn Talks Murder, Marriage, and Con Games."

*EW's Shelf Life.* Entertainment Weekly, 26 June 2012. Web. 17 Jan. 2013.

Norris, Sarah. "Gillian Flynn, Author of the Number One Best-Seller *Gone Girl* Talks about Its Toxic Marriage and Its Bright Big-Screen Future." *Nashville Scene.* City Press, 11 Oct. 2012. Web. 15 Jan. 2013.

Thomas, Mike. "*Gone Girl* Puts Chicago Author Gillian Flynn in the Thriller Elite." *Chicago Sun-Times.* Sun-Times Media, 16 July 2012. Web. 15 Jan. 2013.

**SELECTED WORKS**
*Sharp Objects,* 2006; *Dark Places,* 2009; *Gone Girl,* 2012

—*Robin Hogan*

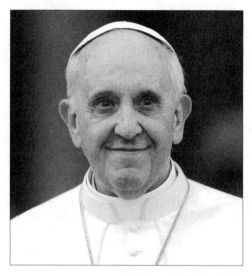

EPA/Alessandro Di Meo/Landov

# Francis

**Born:** December 17, 1936
**Occupation:** Pope of the Roman Catholic Church

Francis—the 266th pope in the Roman Catholic Church's two-thousand-year history—is a pontiff of many firsts. He is the first non-European pope in more than a millennium and the first to hail from Latin America, one of the church's growth regions. He is also the first pope in six hundred years to replace a still-living pope and the first to be a member of the Society of Jesus, considered one of the most independent and powerful religious orders in the Catholic Church. Perhaps most significantly, he is also the first pontiff to take the name Francis as his papal name and did so to honor Francis of Assisi, one of the most beloved saints in church history because of his devotion to the poor, the sick, and the forsaken.

The 2013 election of Pope Francis caught many Vatican observers off guard, but perhaps more surprising is how quickly so many of the Catholic faithful have embraced their new spiritual leader, who has become admired for his captivating acts of humility. "His election may have taken many of us by surprise, including me," remarked Archbishop Vincent Nichols of Westminster, England, according to Kevin Clarke for *America Magazine* (1 Apr. 2013). "But the more we learn about him, the more it becomes clear that the election of Pope Francis is an inspired one and that his papacy will be inspiring."

**EARLY LIFE AND EDUCATION**
Pope Francis was born Jorge Mario Bergoglio in Buenos Aires, Argentina, on December 17, 1936. His parents, Mario and Regina Sivori Bergoglio, were Italian immigrants who worked as an accountant and a homemaker, respectively.

According to published accounts, young Bergoglio was a dedicated student with a passion for such subjects as science, psychology, and literature. In fact, he studied chemistry at the University of Buenos Aires before deciding, at the relatively late age of twenty-one, to enter the novitiate of the Society of Jesus in March 1958. The previous year part of his right lung was surgically removed following a severe case of pneumonia.

Bergoglio's decision to become a Jesuit priest upset his mother but thrilled his father. The Society of Jesus has long been considered one of the most significant religious orders in the Roman Catholic Church. Founded in 1540 by Ignatius of Loyola, a former Spanish soldier turned priest, the Society of Jesus is well regarded for its missionary work as well as its devotion to education, intellectual research, cultural development, and ministry to the underprivileged. Jesuits are known for their vows of poverty, independence, passion for social justice, and willingness to go anywhere at a moment's notice at the pope's behest. For these attributes of service and sacrifice, as well as their founder's previous vocation as a soldier, Jesuits are sometimes nicknamed God's Soldiers.

During his time as a novice, Bergoglio studied the humanities in Chile and in 1963 returned to Argentina, where he earned his degree in philosophy from the Colegio Máximo de San José Centro Loyola in San Miguel. He taught literature and psychology for a time, first at the Colegio Inmaculada Concepción in Santa Fé from 1964 to 1965 and then at the Colegio del Salvatore in Buenos Aires in 1966. He returned to his studies in 1967, eventually earning a degree in theology from the Colegio de San José in 1970.

## RAPID RISE

Archbishop Ramón José Castellano ordained Bergoglio a priest on December 13, 1969, just four days before his thirty-third birthday. He took his final vows with the Jesuits on April 22, 1973, following some additional training in Spain. After serving in a number of positions, including theology professor and novice master, he was appointed the Jesuit provincial for Argentina—a major position for someone so recently ordained—in July 1973.

For the next six years Bergoglio supervised all of his order's activities in Argentina. His appointment came at a crucial time for both Argentina and the Catholic Church, which was struggling with how best to deal with the military dictatorship that controlled the nation from 1976 to 1983. During the so-called Dirty War, in which the country's military leadership repressed communists and other left-wing political groups, thousands of people disappeared or were summarily killed. Among the missing and the dead were numerous priests and other clergy who had worked against the dictatorship.

## A JESUIT IN ARGENTINA'S DIRTY WAR

Although individual priests and other clergy members resisted the junta, church leaders in Argentina, including Bergoglio, were charged with either aiding the military or not doing all they could to help their own members. As Jesuit provincial, Bergoglio was accused by opponents of the dictatorship, including a number of Catholic clergy, of turning a blind eye to numerous events, most infamously the kidnapping of two Jesuit priests, Orlando Yorio and Francisco Jalics, who were taken on May 23, 1976, and tortured for five months by the junta. Critics claimed Bergoglio had essentially handed them over to the Argentine military after he refused to sanction the work they were doing in the slums around Buenos Aires, where they had ministered.

Bergoglio has long denied the allegations that he colluded with the military in that matter or any other. It is a denial that is supported by human rights activist Adolfo Perez Esquivel, who was imprisoned and tortured by the junta. He told BBC News (20 Mar. 2013), "There were some bishops who were in collusion with the military, but Bergoglio is not one of them." After decades of silence on the matter, Father Jalics, following Bergoglio's election to the papacy, issued an online statement also denying the accusation. "I myself was once inclined to believe that we were the victims of a denunciation," Jalics stated, as quoted by Jonathan Watts in the *Guardian* (20 Mar. 2013). "[But] after numerous conversations, it became clear to me that this suspicion was unfounded. It is therefore wrong to assert that our capture took place at the initiative of Father Bergoglio. . . . The fact is: Orlando Yorio and I were not denounced by Father Bergoglio."

During the Dirty War, it was extremely dangerous even for church leaders such as Bergoglio to confront the dictatorship. Despite this, Bergoglio went covertly to Argentine dictator Jorge Rafael Videla and Admiral Emilio Eduardo Massera to plead for Jalics and Yorio's release. He also reportedly hid and protected people sought by the dictatorship for their antigovernment views. Later, as cardinal, he also began the process leading toward the beatification and canonization of several clergy members who lost their lives confronting the military dictatorship.

## BISHOP AND CARDINAL

After his tenure as Jesuit provincial, Bergoglio returned to the rectorship of the Colegio de San José and served as a parish priest in San Miguel for six years, from 1980 to 1986. Following this work, he completed his doctorate in Germany and then returned to Argentina to serve as a spiritual director and confessor. On May 20, 1992, he was appointed bishop of Auca and auxiliary of Buenos Aires. Five years later, on June 3, 1997, he was appointed coadjutor archbishop of Buenos Aires. Bergoglio succeeded Antonio Quarracino as archbishop on February 28, 1998. On February 21, 2001, Pope John Paul II named him a cardinal, one of the senior ecclesiastical officials of the Roman Catholic Church. Collectively, the College of Cardinals helps to administer the worldwide church and elect a new pope.

Despite rising to positions of leadership in the church hierarchy, Bergoglio remained close to the people of Buenos Aires. He continued to take public transportation, lived in a simple apartment in the archdiocese, and was frequently found ministering to residents of Villa 21–24, an expansive slum in which roughly forty-five thousand inhabits live in abject poverty. "He is adored by everyone here, I would say you'd find a photo of him in 60 percent of the homes in 21–24," Father Juan Isasmendi remarked to Sam Jones, Uki Goni, and Jonathan Watts for the *Guardian* (15 Mar. 2013). "He is a true man of God, he baptized so many children, he gave communion himself to thousands here. He is authentically religious, a true pastor, he was a father to so many people here and a father to us priests."

## MINISTRY

As both bishop and cardinal, Bergoglio was an outspoken advocate of the poor, the sick, and those shunted to the outskirts of society. He also condemned political corruption and any abuse of governmental authority. During the 2001 economic crisis that rocked Argentina and forced President Fernando de la Rua to resign his office, Bergoglio spoke out against the brutal tactics the police employed during the civil unrest.

That same year he visited HIV/AIDS patients at Muñiz Hospital in Buenos Aires and asked the staff for a jar of water. He then washed and kissed the patients' feet, as Jesus did to his disciples before the feast of the Passover to demonstrate to them that a master must serve those who follow him. Bergoglio told reporters at the time that he did this because "society forgets the sick and the poor," as quoted by Emily Schmall and Larry Rohter in the *New York Times* (13 Mar. 2013).

In 2007, Bergoglio again stressed the need to help the poor during a meeting of Latin American bishops. "We live in the most unequal part of the world, which has grown the most yet reduced misery the least," he said at the time, as quoted by John L. Allen Jr. in the *National Catholic Reporter* (3 Mar. 2013). "The unjust distribution of goods persists, creating a situation of social sin that cries out to Heaven and limits the possibilities of a fuller life for so many of our brothers." He has also been unafraid to critique his fellow members of the clergy. In September 2012, for example, he lambasted priests who refused the children of unmarried mothers the rite of baptism—a Christian rite that, by church law, is granted to anyone who freely desires it. According to Schmall and Rohter, Bergoglio denounced the priests' "hypocrisy," stating, "They are the ones who separate the people of God from salvation."

Bergoglio's tenure as cardinal was not without controversy, however. In keeping with the Catholic Church's traditional teachings against abortion and same-sex marriages, he led public protests against the Argentine government's efforts to liberalize the country's abortion laws and legalize same-sex marriages and adoptions. In 2010, he reportedly expressed a willingness to accept same-sex civil unions—granting most of legal rights of marriage to gay couples without that title—as a compromise. Despite Bergoglio's opposition, same-sex marriage became legal in Argentina that year.

## ELECTION TO THE PAPACY

On February 11, 2013, Pope Benedict XVI, who had succeeded to the papacy upon Pope John Paul II's death in 2005, announced that because of his advanced age and deteriorating health, he would retire as pontiff by the end of the month. Benedict's retirement astounded many observers, as the office of pope has traditionally been held for life. (The last pope to retire was Pope Gregory XII in 1415; the last to do so willingly was Pope Celestine V in 1294.)

On March 12, the College of Cardinals gathered in the Sistine Chapel at the Vatican to elect Benedict's successor. Many Vatican observers expected that the new pontiff would be someone younger or possibly from one of the church's growth regions in Africa or Latin America, but no one could say with certainty. Papal conclaves are held in absolute secrecy, and all notes and ballots taken are burned in the chimney of the Sistine Chapel. White smoke emerging from the chimney indicates that the cardinals have elected a new pope; black smoke signals that no majority has been reached. After the fifth ballot was held on March 13, white smoke billowed from the chimney. Shortly thereafter it was announced that seventy-six-year-old Bergoglio had been elected pope and had taken Francis as his papal name.

After emerging onto the balcony of Saint Peter's Basilica, Pope Francis asked the crowd gathered in the square below to pray for him as well as for his predecessor, the now-retired Benedict, before giving them his first papal blessing. Observers commented on this act of humility as well as the fact that Francis appeared wearing the same iron cross around his neck he had worn as cardinal and a simple white cassock.

## EARLY PAPACY

In the days following his election, it became clear that Francis sought to be a different kind of pope than his predecessors. The public learned, for example, that he took the name Francis to honor Francis of Assisi, a thirteenth-century Italian saint who gave up a life of privilege to devote himself to helping the poor and needy. One of the most highly regarded saints in church history, Francis is admired even in secular circles for his protection of animals and the environment as well as his efforts to end the Crusades by peaceful means. The new pope explained that he was inspired to take Francis as his name because a fellow cardinal reminded him, upon his election, not to forget the poor. "How I would like a church that is poor and that is for the poor," he told a gathering of over five thousand reporters, according to Clarke.

Since becoming the spiritual leader of the world's 1.2 billion Catholics, Francis has maintained the humble lifestyle that had been a hallmark of his ecclesiastic life. The day after being named pope, he returned to the hotel where he had stayed during the conclave to pay for his hotel bill in person. He has shunned the traditional platform popes have used in the past to greet the other archbishops and has decided to live in a simple hotel suite instead of the palatial apartment popes have lived in for more than one hundred years. During Easter week—the holiest week of the Christian calendar, during which the faithful believe Jesus Christ died and rose from the dead—he washed and kissed the feet of twelve people as Jesus did, but unlike previous pontiffs, he washed the feet not of priests but of twelve juvenile prisoners at the Casal del Marmo Penitentiary Institute for Minors. Two of the minors were women and one a Muslim—the first time a pope has included members of either group in this Easter week tradition. During his first Easter Sunday as pontiff, Francis thrilled a crowd of people in Saint Peter's Square by happily accepting a gift of a team jersey for his favorite soccer team, San Lorenzo, from an onlooker and by holding and kissing a physically disabled boy brought to him from the throng.

## REORIENTING THE CHURCH
Observers believe that Francis has been making warm and humble gestures to help bring the Catholic Church out of the cloak of clerical privilege its members have enjoyed inside the Vatican. Francis said as much in a speech to fellow cardinals just prior to attending the conclave that elected him pope, according to Cardinal Jaime Ortega of Havana, Cuba. "The church is called on to emerge from itself and move toward the peripheries, not only geographic but also existential (ones): those of sin, suffering, injustice, ignorance and religious abstention, thought and all misery," the future pontiff reportedly said at the meeting, as quoted by Andrea Rodriguez in an article for the Associated Press (26 Mar. 2013). "When the church does not emerge from itself to evangelize, it becomes self-referential and therefore becomes sick. . . . The evils that, over time, occur in ecclesiastical institutions have their root in self-referentiality, a kind of theological narcissism."

One of the major issues confronting Pope Francis in the early days of his papacy is how to restore trust among the faithful, who have grown weary during a string of scandals, including reported corruption among high officials in the Vatican as well as the infamous sex abuse scandal in which numerous local dioceses around the world covered up the sexual abuse of minors by clergy members, sometimes for decades. In early April 2013, Francis addressed the lingering scandal head on, saying that the church must "act decisively" to find and punish abusers "for the church and its credibility," according to Corky Siemaszko for the *New York Daily News* (5 Apr. 2013).

Prior to his election, Pope Francis authored several books in his native Spanish pertaining to both religious and social issues. One of these books, *On Heaven and Earth: Pope Francis on Faith, Family, and the Church in the Twenty-First Century*, is a series of interfaith dialogues on religion and reason cowritten with Rabbi Abraham Skorka; it was translated into English in 2013. For many this text offers a glimpse into the religious, social, economic, and political beliefs that will likely guide the new pontiff in the years to come.

## SUGGESTED READING
"Biography of the Holy Father Francis." *L'Osservatore Romano*. Libreria Editrice Vaticana, 2013. Web. 3 May 2013.

Clarke, Kevin. "Silence and Service: Pope Francis Captivates Catholics Worldwide." *America Magazine*. America Magazine, 1 Apr. 2013. Web. 3 May 2013.
Hewitt, Gavin. "Profile: Pope Francis." *BBC News*. BBC, 20 Mar. 2013. Web. 3 May 2013.
Jones, Sam, et al. "Pope Francis: A Man of Humility, or Harsh and Unbending?" *Guardian* 15 Mar. 2013: 14. Print.
McGregor, Jena. "Pope Francis and a Holy, Humble Break from Tradition." *Washington Post*. Washington Post, 29 Mar. 2013. Web. 3 May 2013.
Rodriguez, Andrea. "Cuba Cleric: Francis Criticized Church at Conclave." *Associated Press*. Associated Press, 26 Mar. 2013. Web. 3 May 2013.
Schmall, Emily, and Larry Rohter. "A Conservative with a Common Touch." *New York Times* 14 Mar. 2013: A1. Print.
Watts, Jonathan. "Pope Francis Did Not Denounce Me to Argentinian Junta, Says Priest." *Guardian* 20 Mar. 2013: 23. Print.

—*Christopher Mari*

# Bethenny Frankel
**Born:** November 4, 1970
**Occupation:** Television personality and entrepreneur

Going from completely broke in 2007 to multimillionaire entrepreneur and reality television star in 2012, Bethenny Frankel epitomizes the culture of self-made celebrity in the twenty-first century. Known for her canny ability to simultaneously promote her brand and her image, Frankel has utilized cameras to make both herself and her products household names. Frankel has thousands of ardent fans who follow the Skinnygirl lifestyle from the mogul's self-help books, workout videos, cosmetics, clothing, and—most famously—her liquor brand. With her reputation for candor and her comfort with being "famous for being famous," audiences respect her openness about her personal and professional lives, even when she is frank about her self-promotion.

In 2013—after the end of both her high-profile marriage and her successful series *Bethenny Ever After*, as well as the lucrative sale of Skinnygirl's liquor brand—Frankel is poised to move her empire in a new direction, starting with the daytime talk show *Bethenny*. Reflecting on the many directions her career has taken, Frankel wrote in her 2011 book *A Place of Yes*: "Changing course is not the same thing as giving up. When you hit a brick wall, you have to go in a different direction. You walk away for a while until your head clears and you make a new strategy.

Wirelmage

Don't torture yourself running into a wall over and over again. Think about turning the wheel just a little, to change direction. It might not take all that much of a shift to turn toward the next big thing."

## EARLY LIFE AND EDUCATION

Bethenny Frankel was born on Long Island in Port Washington, New York, on November 4, 1970, to parents Bernadette Birk and Robert J. Frankel. Robert Frankel was a successful and award-winning race horse trainer. Frankel was four years old when her father left the family and her parents were subsequently divorced. Her mother married John Parisella, another horse trainer, one year later. Frankel told *People* magazine's Liz McNeil (19 July 2010) that she saw very little of Robert Frankel as a child, describing Parisella as "the only father I've ever known."

From the ages of five to fifteen Frankel, her mother, and her stepfather moved at least seven times and she attended numerous schools. This instability contributed to a tumultuous childhood. "There was a lot of destruction: alcohol abuse, eating disorders and violent fights," she told McNeil, calling her mother "extremely volatile." Often spending time at racetracks, Frankel was drinking and gambling by the time she was a teenager. Around the age of thirteen Frankel also developed issues with food and began obsessively dieting—though she has maintained that she has never had an eating disorder—sparking a lifelong focus on food and eating.

In 1988 Frankel graduated from the Pine Crest School in Fort Lauderdale, Florida. She attended college at Boston University before transferring to New York University (NYU), from which she graduated in 1992 with a degree in communications and psychology. Immediately after leaving NYU, Frankel traveled to California to pursue an acting career in Los Angeles.

## EARLY ACTING AND ENTREPRENEURIAL CAREER

In 1992 Frankel began a series of miscellaneous jobs in both entertainment and business. She briefly worked as an assistant to fashion designer Kathy Hilton and occasionally babysat her daughters, socialites Paris and Nicky Hilton. She also worked as a personal assistant to television and film producer Jerry Bruckheimer and his wife, Linda. During this period Frankel also tried her hand at acting, appearing in several small films. In 1993 she was in the short film *Soiree Sans Hors D'oeuvres*. She followed that with *Hollywood Hills 90028* (1994) and *Wish Me Luck* (1995). Other miscellaneous work includes her time as a production assistant on the television series *Saved by the Bell*; she also did event planning for Merv Griffin Productions and worked for the Broadway Video distribution company. In 1996 she decided to move her life in a different direction. "When I turned twenty-six, I decided enough was enough. I hadn't 'made it,' and my time was up," she wrote in *A Place of Yes*, adding, "My acting career wasn't going to happen."

Moving away from the entertainment industry, but using her experience in the field, Frankel's first business venture was In Any Event—a party planning company that produced celebrity events. In Any Event proved to be unsuccessful and soon closed. She next started the company Princess Pashmina. Realizing the popular, but expensive, cashmere scarves she liked were available more cheaply in India, Frankel began buying the trendy accessories directly from Bombay (now Mumbai). She sold the pashminas online, at parties, at trade shows, and even at IKEA stores. The market for pashminas eventually froze, however, and as the scarves became easier and less expensive to purchase Frankel closed Princess Pashmina. "You have to build on what works, in a rational way," she explained in *A Place of Yes*. "But I didn't know that during Princess Pashmina. I was too excited by my quick success, and too big for my britches."

In the late 1990s Frankel left California to attend culinary school at the National Gourmet Institute for Health and Culinary Arts in New York City. She graduated from the school in 2001 and began to pursue a career focused on natural and healthy food. Realizing that she had a talent for making healthy food taste good, Frankel started BethennyBakes, a cookie company, in 2003. With her popular low-fat and vegan cookies, Frankel wanted her baked goods to be a recognizable brand like Famous Amos or Mrs. Fields. Instead, it was Frankel herself who became the recognizable brand.

## THE APPRENTICE AND THE REAL HOUSEWIVES OF NEW YORK

In 2005 Frankel was cast in the competitive reality television series *The Apprentice: Martha Stewart*, a spinoff of the series hosted by Donald Trump. "I was on *The Apprentice: Martha Stewart* because I wanted to be her successor," Frankel told *NY Report*'s Daria Meoli (1 Apr. 2011). "In my mind, I believed Martha Stewart would be wise enough to recognize that I could democratize health the way she had democratized style and she would pass me the reins. That could sound crazy, because I was just a competitor on *The Apprentice,* but that's the way you're supposed to dream and plan—big." The series focused on business areas related to entertaining, dining, design, style, and media; the sixteen contestants were in fields including interior design, event planning, marketing, and public relations. The competitors were divided into teams to participate in challenges—ranging from selling flowers, to creating a salad dressing, to holding a circus event—and were eliminated one at a time. Frankel was ultimately the competition's runner-up, losing to winner Dawna Stone.

Her strong showing worked to her advantage, though, and Frankel was able to use her new fame to enhance her business and brand. Frankel got an endorsement deal with the food brand Pepperidge Farms, working as a spokesperson for their products, hosting events for the company's natural foods line, and even creating recipes. The exposure also led to a deal with *Health* magazine and Frankel began writing a monthly column for the publication.

In 2008 Frankel was approached to join a candid reality show about women living in Manhattan. *The Real Housewives of New York City* was a spinoff of the popular Bravo network show *The Real Housewives of Orange County* and featured Frankel along with Jill Zarin, LuAnn de Lesseps, Alex McCord, and Ramona Singer. *The Real Housewives of New York City* premiered on March 4, 2008. Frankel appeared on the show for three seasons. "It's really not that easy to get on TV," Frankel told Meghan Casserly for *Forbes* (18 May 2011). She added: "I decided just to make it what I wanted it to be. To keep the focus on my brand and to just be me. It was the best decision I'd ever made."

On the show Frankel was known for her sarcasm, candor, brassy attitude, and occasionally combative behavior, as well as her status as the only unmarried cast member—the only "housewife" who was not, in fact, a wife at the time. The show followed its affluent stars as they moved between their homes, social events, and, in some cases, jobs. With their dramatic and often antagonistic personalities, the show's subjects became popular and Frankel was catapulted to the national spotlight. She attributed her complicated childhood for helping her cope with her costars, telling McNeil: "I was able to have some perspective on all the drama."

## SKINNYGIRL

With the success of *The Real Housewives of New York City* Frankel began to leverage her fame and expand her brand in other areas. In 2008 she published *Naturally Thin: Unleash Your Skinnygirl and Free Yourself from a Lifetime of Dieting.* The self-help book featured ten rules for dieters related to things like moderation and portion control (such as sharing food and taking small bites); the book also included recipes and lifestyle tips, encouraging self-control in eating as opposed to dieting. The book became a New York Times Best Seller.

Frankel's next project was a follow-up publication entitled *The Skinnygirl Dish: Easy Recipes for Your Naturally Thin Life* (2009). The book discussed Frankel's cooking philosophy, shared recipes, and offered tips for planning parties and menus. The book—which is not intended to be solely a cookbook— also included a chart of food substitutions for healthier cooking. Like *Naturally Thin, The Skinnygirl Dish* was criticized by some for prioritizing being skinny over being healthy; the books also encourage skipping meals and gives examples of meal plans that offer below the recommended daily requirement for calories.

Frankel's other big 2009 project was the launch of the Skinnygirl brand, starting with Frankel's Skinnygirl Margarita, a low-calorie, ready-to-drink alcoholic beverage. The idea for the project was conceived while Frankel was filming *The Real Housewives of New York City* and she partnered with David Kanbar—formerly of SKYY Vodka—to develop and promote the product. She told Meoli, "The minute I said the words 'skinnygirl margarita' on *The Real Housewives,* I knew it was going to be a successful cocktail." Frankel went on, adding "I remember thinking that this is something women are going to want." Though the margarita mix was marketed as having all-natural ingredients, it contained the preservative sodium benzoate and was pulled from the shelves of Whole Foods stores in 2011.

In addition to her self-help publications, Frankel forayed into fitness in 2010 with the release of her exercise DVD *Body by Bethenny.* Assisted by professional trainer Kristin McGee, Frankel's exercise video featured forty minutes of yoga, ten minutes of strength training, and a bonus cooking segment. A recipe booklet is also included with the purchase of the DVD. Following the success of the DVD and her books Frankel announced in 2010 that she would not be participating in the fourth season of *The Real Housewives of New York City,* having been a fixture in the first three.

## THE *BETHENNY* SHOWS

On June 10, 2010, Frankel's new reality series *Bethenny Getting Married?* debuted on Bravo and was the network's highest rated premiere. The first season of the series followed Frankel as she planned her wedding with fiancé Jason Hoppy, a sales executive she had met while filming *The Real Housewives of New York City*. Describing Hoppy to *People*'s McNeil, Frankel said "He's my anchor. I fell in love with a regular guy with a regular salary. He taught me that being taken care of was emotional and not financial." The season included Frankel's bridal shower, wedding, honeymoon, and the birth of her daughter.

For the second season the show changed its title from *Bethenny Getting Married?* to *Bethenny Ever After*. The season premiered on February 28, 2011, and featured events like Frankel's fortieth birthday and her appearance on the competitive reality series *Skating with the Stars*. An ABC show hosted by Vernon Kay, *Skating with the Stars* featured celebrities learning figure skating routines with professional partners. Frankel, along with partner Ethan Burgess, was the competition's runner-up.

In its third and final season, *Bethenny Ever After* featured products from Frankel's Skinnygirl line—which she told Meoli was "practically a cast member"—the remodeling of her apartment, and her sometimes difficult marriage. The season also included a boating incident off the coast of Nantucket when the Coast Guard reportedly had to be called. Frankel was on a boat with her husband, their marriage counselor, and her film crew when the GPS allegedly malfunctioned and the vessel went off course. The show was accused of manufacturing the rescue, however, to create drama and increase ratings. The season finale—which was also the series finale—aired on May 28, 2012.

## DIVERSIFYING

In December of 2011 Frankel published her third book, *A Place of Yes: 10 Rules for Getting Everything You Want Out of Life*. Another self-help book, *A Place of Yes* discussed Frankel's life and business, emphasizing her goals and how she overcame obstacles. Frankel included rules about truth, accountability, and success. This book notably included information about Frankel's early life and entrepreneurial ventures. In addition to the new book, Frankel released a follow-up to the *Body by Bethenny* DVD in 2011. *Bethenny's Skinnygirl Workout* consisted of three yoga workouts of varying lengths as well as a bonus stretching segment and a recipe booklet.

"You have to watch the road and pay attention to the signs," she told Dario Meoli for *NY Report*. "To be successful, you might have to change lanes and focus on something else; take a different road" (1 Apr. 2011). Following the success of her Skinnygirl Margarita, Frankel expanded her product line down a different road. Skinnygirl Beauty—a cosmetics and skincare line—was released in March of 2012. It included face lotions, cleansers, and simple makeup, emphasizing no-frills packaging. In May 2012 her Skinnygirl Smoothers 'n' Shapers was made available online and in retail stores; it included a marketing campaign that featured real women instead of models—including Frankel's hair stylist and personal assistant. Other Skinnygirl products range from ponytail holders to wine and vodka.

With her new brands and best-selling books—which by 2012 included the novel *Skinnydipping*, a slightly fictionalized version of her life that she wrote in installments on her Black-Berry phone—Frankel prepared to return to television. In 2012 Frankel filmed a test run of a syndicated daytime talk show called *Bethenny*. A typical talk show, *Bethenny* features cooking instructions, guest stars, and lifestyle segments. The program, produced by Fox, is set to premiere the fall of 2013.

## PERSONAL LIFE

In 1996 Frankel was briefly married to Peter Sussman; their marriage lasted for eight months. In the years between her first and second marriages Frankel dated off and on and has indicated in interviews that she broke off two additional engagements. She met Jason Hoppy at a nightclub in November of 2008 and the couple became engaged eleven months later. While planning their wedding, Bethenny discovered that she was pregnant. The couple was married in a well-publicized ceremony at the Four Seasons restaurant in Manhattan on March 28, 2010, when Frankel was seven months into her pregnancy. The couple's daughter, Bryn Casey Hoppy, was born on May 8, 2010. The first years of Frankel and Hoppy's married life were filmed for *Bethenny Ever After*. In February of 2012 Frankel disclosed to the media that she had suffered a miscarriage, but the tragedy was not mentioned on the show. At the end of 2012, after much speculation, Frankel announced that she and Hoppy were separating; she filed for divorce in January 2013.

In her life while the cameras are not rolling Frankel practices what she preaches in both her cooking and eating habit and in her active lifestyle. In addition to yoga, Frankel enjoys snowboarding and rollerblading. At the age of thirty-eight she had plastic surgery and underwent a breast lift; she has also admitted to trying Botox, but also that she does not like the injections. In discussing her balance between work and life, however, she told *NY Report*'s Daria Meoli (1 Apr. 2011): "I don't have balance in my life. I'm a workaholic and I think about work all the time. I just pray for seven hours of sleep and then I can do anything. I don't have much of a life aside from work and family." Following up, Meoli asked Frankel if there was anything about her life that she would change, to which Frankel responded: "No, I don't believe in regret; no way."

## SUGGESTED READING

Casserly, Meghan. "Can Bethenny Crack a Billion?" *Forbes*. Forbes.com, 18 May 2011. Web. 14 Jan. 2013.

Frankel, Bethenny. *A Place of Yes: 10 Rules for Getting Everything You Want Out of Life*. New York: Touchstone, 2011. Print.

McNeil, Liz. "Love Saved My Life." *People* 19 July 2010: 60–65. Print.

Pressler, Jessica. "76 Minutes With . . . Bethenny Frankel." *New York* 30 Jan. 2012: 14. Print.

Rosman, Katherine. "As Seen on TV: Brand Bethenny." *Wall Street Journal* 24 Nov., 2010: D1–3. Print.

—*Kehley Coviello*

# Martin Freeman

**Born:** September 8, 1971
**Occupation:** Actor

© Nancy Kaszerman/ZUMA Press/Corbis

Martin Freeman is an award-winning English film and television actor who is best known for his roles as Tim Canterbury in the Ricky Gervais–helmed comedy series *The Office* (2001–3), John Watson in the hit BBC drama series *Sherlock* (2010–), and Bilbo Baggins in the *Hobbit* trilogy of films (2012–14). Though he detests the term, a reporter for the Edinburgh *Scotsman* (27 Nov. 2009) aptly described Freeman as "British drama's most versatile Everyman." Steven Moffat, creator and cowriter of *Sherlock*, took his praise a step further, telling Brian Viner for the London *Independent* (30 Nov. 2012), "Martin finds a sort of poetry in the ordinary man."

Freeman was twenty-nine years old when he earned his big break on *The Office*, and he has spent much of his career since trying to cast off his likeable character's shadow—though it was exactly the qualities he exhibited as Tim that won him his largest role to date, in *The Hobbit*. Freeman played much darker roles before his star turn and subsequent typecasting as the "good guy" became a frustrating obstacle. Perhaps one reason for his eagerness to play a different type of role is the fact that his own personality is so different from that of the "everyman" he plays so well. Freeman, who lost his father at a young age, has told journalists that the loss became more acute as he got older, and he partly attributes his surprisingly dark outlook to this early encounter with death. In interviews, he comes across as intense and contemplative; he laments the world's ills—such as in his interview with Rebecca Hardy

for the *Daily Mail* (20 Nov. 2009), in which he castigated people for caring more about the television show *The X Factor* than homelessness—and becomes defensive when asked about his well-publicized Roman Catholicism.

But Freeman, who has enjoyed a steady stream of gigs since *The Office* ended in 2003, has acknowledged that he has little room to complain. He told Tom Huddleston for *Time Out* magazine (Dec. 2012) that he enjoys finding the subtleties of characters, such as Bilbo Baggins, who are not always as nice as they first appear. "[Bilbo] becomes more rounded as the tale goes on: he finds his bravery and he finds his rage," Freeman explained. "Life kicks him up the arse. I suppose until life does that to any of us, we don't really know ourselves. You're not fully you until life has booted you in the behind."

## EARLY LIFE AND EDUCATION

Martin John Christopher Freeman was born on September 8, 1971, in Aldershot, Hampshire, England. He is the youngest of five children. After his parents separated when he was very young, he lived with his father, Geoffrey, a former naval officer, until Geoffrey died of a heart attack when Freeman was ten. After his father's death, Freeman was raised by his mother, Philomena, and his stepfather, James. Unlike his more artistic siblings—his brother Tim was a singer in the British pop group Frazier Chorus—the young Freeman was more interested in sports. Despite suffering from chronic asthma and Legg-Calvé-Perthes disease, an illness that affected his hip, he played on the

British national squash squad from ages nine to fourteen.

It was while attending Salesian School, a Catholic secondary school in Surrey, that Freeman cultivated an interest in theater. He joined the Youth Action Theatre group in Teddington, a suburb of London, when he was fifteen. When he was seventeen, he acted in a performance of the Don Taylor historical drama *The Roses of Eyam*, about Britain's Great Plague of 1666, and something clicked. "It was the first time I got a lot of really positive feedback for my acting—the first time I had real confidence in myself," he told Hardy. He added, "Acting, for me, feels like an absolute expression—a really necessary one. It would be a lie if I said it's just a job. It's a lot more than that. Vocation doesn't even seem to cover it."

Freeman studied performing arts at Brooklands College in Surrey and then attended the prestigious Central School of Speech and Drama in London, though he left the latter early to work at the Royal National Theatre. In 1997, he made his acting debut with a guest appearance in the long-running British crime drama *The Bill*. His first feature film was the drama *The Low Down* (2000), and he also appeared in Sacha Baron Cohen's film *Ali G Indahouse* (2002). In 2001, he guest starred in several episodes of the comedy *World of Pub* and played a drug-abusing footballer who rapes a nurse in the television movie *Men Only*. Despite the horrifying nature of the latter role, Freeman has fond memories of the film, as he met his longtime partner, Amanda Abbington, on the set. During that period of his career, Freeman made numerous appearances in popular television shows and short films, though most of his roles were very small. That trend was forever changed when he landed the role of Tim Canterbury in *The Office*.

### THE OFFICE

*The Office* is a television show created by comedians Ricky Gervais and Stephen Merchant. In an interview with Mike Sacks for the 2009 book *And Here's the Kicker: Conversations with 21 Top Humor Writers on Their Craft*, Merchant said that the idea for the show came about in 1997, when he and Gervais were working for a radio station. To amuse Merchant at work, Gervais sometimes played a character who would later become the show's defining figure, general manager David Brent. The character was empty headed, well meaning yet inadvertently offensive, and full of cringe-inducing misconceptions and terrible ideas. In other words, Merchant told Sacks, the character "was kind of an observation of the types of people we had both worked with in the past." When Merchant was asked to make a training film for the BBC, he asked Gervais to play his office-worker character. They shot the film documentary style because it was faster and cheaper. The finished product was so popular at the BBC that *The Office*, a mockumentary about the employees of a paper company and their ridiculous boss, was born.

After shooting and then scrapping a slick pilot in 2001, Gervais and Merchant realized that they needed to return to the low production values and, more importantly, the inherent drama of true documentary-style filmmaking. Improvised dialogue, organic silences, and meaningful glances seemingly caught on camera by accident became the show's trademark. When asked to choose a favorite scene from the show's three short seasons, Merchant pointed to a scene from the end of season 2, in which Freeman, as the affable and lovelorn Tim, unhooks the microphone attached to him by the unseen film crew to talk to the object of his affection, Dawn, behind the closed doors of the meeting room. Viewers can see them, but they cannot hear them. "You couldn't do that in any other television show because it would just feel kind of mannered," Merchant told Sacks. He added, "And nothing we could have written would have been half as powerful as what the viewers imagined those two characters said." Though *The Office* is a comedy, moments such as that one gave it its heart.

After the show's premiere in 2001, millions of viewers tuned in to watch David Brent offend his employees and ended up rooting for Tim and receptionist Dawn, played by Lucy Davis, to get together. The romantic saga, which Merchant has called practically Victorian in its subtlety, was largely improvised by Freeman and Davis, and it was captivating. The level of excitement about Tim and Dawn's story line was almost as surprising as the level of excitement about *The Office* as a whole. No one involved with the show ever imagined that it would achieve the level of success that it did, least of all Freeman, who had to move out of his London home after fans began showing up on his doorstep in the middle of the night. The show ended after two seasons by design, but the cast filmed two Christmas specials that aired in 2003 and attracted over twelve million viewers. The *Office* franchise went on to be reimagined in a number of different countries, including the United States, whose version stars Steve Carell and features John Krasinski as Jim, the American take on Freeman's Tim.

### THE *HOBBIT* TRILOGY

Among the many fans of *The Office* was the Academy Award–winning film director Peter Jackson, the man behind the wildly successful 2001–3 adaptations of J. R. R. Tolkien's *Lord of the Rings* series. Jackson was preparing to adapt Tolkien's novel *The Hobbit*, the predecessor of *The Lord of the Rings*, into a second trilogy and wanted Freeman to play the lead character, Bilbo Baggins. Freeman agreed to play the role, but a series of obstacles nearly prevented him. The start date for shooting was postponed for financial reasons, and then, after two years of planning, director Guillermo del Toro left the project. Jackson took over as director but abandoned most of del Toro's preproduction work and started the planning process over again. By the time Jackson and the film studio were ready to shoot, Freeman was unavailable.

"When he wasn't available I really panicked," Jackson told John Hiscock for the *Telegraph* (10 Dec. 2012). Jackson wanted to shoot the trilogy back-to-back, on the same schedule as he had shot the *Lord of the Rings* films, which meant that Freeman needed to be available for one long eighteen-month stretch. However, he had already signed on to film the second season of the wildly popular British television show *Sherlock*, and the conflict was nonnegotiable. Another director might have found a new star, but Jackson was so determined to have Freeman that he rearranged the entire production schedule to accommodate him. "It was a very rare thing to do, but I was very glad we did because without Martin there'd have been no *Hobbit*," Jackson told Hiscock.

The first film in the trilogy, *The Hobbit: An Unexpected Journey*, was released in 2012. In his review of the film for the *New Yorker* (17 Dec. 2012), Anthony Lane criticized Jackson's decision to spread the narrative out over the course of three films but praised Freeman's performance, writing that he was "a snug fit in the difficult role of Bilbo" and "an excellent foil" to Ian McKellen's character, the wizard Gandalf.

## DR. WATSON AND OTHER ROLES

In 2003, Freeman appeared in the popular romantic comedy *Love Actually*. The movie features a number of intertwining stories, and Freeman plays a body double for a film actor with an explicit sex scene who works up the courage to ask his scene partner, played by Joanna Page, out on a date. Screenwriter Richard Curtis reportedly wrote the part specifically for Freeman. In 2005, Freeman starred in *The Hitchhiker's Guide to the Galaxy*, based on the popular 1979 science fiction book by Douglas Adams. As would later happen with *The Hobbit*, Freeman had the difficult task of pleasing the numerous devoted fans of the original novel, but he was not fazed. In one interview with talk-show host Jonathan Ross, as quoted by Viner, Freeman said of the latter, "It's a script, it's not the Qur'an."

Freeman's other major project is *Sherlock*, the BBC television adaptation of Arthur Conan Doyle's Sherlock Holmes stories. Benedict Cumberbatch stars as the title character, while Freeman plays the famous detective's equally famous sidekick, Dr. John Watson, a role for which he was nominated for an Emmy Award in 2012. The hugely successful show cuts closer to Doyle's vision than previous adaptations, despite the fact that it is set in present-day England. In the original stories, for instance, Watson is a veteran of the Second Anglo-Afghan War; in *Sherlock*, he is again a veteran of war in Afghanistan—the conflict that began in 2001. British actor Nigel Bruce was famous for playing Watson in the 1930s and 1940s, but he played the character, Viner explained, "as something of a buffoon," an interpretation that "greatly offended Holmes purists." Rather than serving as the butt of the joke, Freeman's Watson "lends a moral framework to Sherlock, who's more interested in the chase than in what's right or wrong," Freeman told Andrew Duncan for *Reader's Digest* (Aug. 2010).

Freeman appeared in the action comedy *Hot Fuzz* in 2007. The movie, an affectionate parody of the buddy-cop movie genre, was written by Edgar Wright and Simon Pegg, the team behind the zombie comedy *Shaun of the Dead* (2004), in which Freeman also makes a cameo appearance. In 2013, he had a main role in the duo's third film together, *The World's End*, about a pub crawl that turns into a battle to prevent the apocalypse. The three films make up what Wright, Pegg, and Pegg's costar Nick Frost refer to as the Cornetto trilogy.

## PERSONAL LIFE

Freeman is an ardent music fan as well as a student of classic British films. He is known for having a short temper and swearing frequently, personality traits for which he is unapologetic. He told Emma Jones for the *Independent* (5 July 2013), "If someone had a pint with me, they'd find out pretty quickly I'm not so nice, I'm not Tim from *The Office*, although a lot of people still think I am. I have absolutely no problem telling someone to f——k off."

Freeman met his partner, the English actor Amanda Abbington, on the set of *Men Only* in 2000. They are not married, though they often refer to each other as husband and wife. Freeman and Abbington have two children named Joe and Grace. They live in Hertfordshire, England.

## SUGGESTED READING

Duncan, Andrew. "Dr. Watson, I Presume?" *Reader's Digest UK* Aug. 2010: 36–41. Print.

Hardy, Rebecca. "'People Care More about *X Factor* than Homelessness': The *Office* Star Martin Freeman on the Things that Tick Him Off." *Daily Mail*. Associated Newspapers, 20 Nov. 2009. Web. 16 Sept. 2013.

Hiscock, John. "*The Hobbit*: The Vital Role of Martin Freeman." *Telegraph*. Telegraph Media Group, 10 Dec. 2012. Web. 16 Sept. 2013.

Jones, Emma. "'Don't Turn on the People That I Love': A Stern Martin Freeman Reveals He Is More Bilbo Baggins Than Tim from *The Office*." *Independent*. Independent.co.uk, 5 July 2013. Web. 16 Sept. 2013.

Viner, Brian. "Martin Freeman: No Ordinary Bilbo Baggins." *Independent*. Independent. co.uk, 30 Nov. 2012. Web. 16 Sept. 2013.

**SELECTED WORKS**
*The Office*, 2001–3; *Love Actually*, 2003; *The Hitchhiker's Guide to the Galaxy*, 2005; *Hot Fuzz*, 2007; *Sherlock*, 2010– ; *The Hobbit: An Unexpected Journey*, 2012; *The World's End*, 2013; *The Hobbit: The Desolation of Smaug*, 2013; *The Hobbit: There and Back Again*, 2014

—*Molly Hagan*

Andrew Harnik/The Washington Times /Landov

# Tulsi Gabbard

**Born:** April 12, 1981
**Occupation:** Politician

In 2012, Tulsi Gabbard was elected to represent Hawaii's Second Congressional District in the United States House of Representatives. A member of the Democratic Party, she is one of the first female combat veterans to serve in Congress as well as the first Hindu politician elected to the House. Having grown up in a multifaith household—her mother is Hindu and her father is Roman Catholic—Gabbard told Mark Oppenheimer for the *New York Times* (9 Nov. 2012), "I am a Hindu in the mold of the most famous Hindu, Mahatma Gandhi, who is my hero and role model."

Born in American Samoa and raised in Hawaii, Gabbard won her first election at the age of twenty-one, when she became the youngest person in history to be elected to the Hawaii state senate and the youngest woman to be elected to any state legislature. Gabbard's status as a rising star within her political party was cemented when she was invited to speak at the Democratic National Convention (DNC) in Charlotte, North Carolina, in 2012.

A veteran of the Iraq War, Gabbard was deployed twice, serving in Iraq and Kuwait. She earned a number of awards and recognitions during her career in the military. As a congressional representative, Gabbard serves on the Committee on Homeland Security and the Subcommittee on Borders and Maritime Security. She also serves on the Committee on Foreign Affairs and the Subcommittee on Asia and the Pacific.

## EARLY LIFE AND EDUCATION
Gabbard was born in Leloaloa, American Samoa, on April 12, 1981. She is the fourth of five children, all of whom have Hindi names; her siblings are Bhakti, Jai, Aryan, and Vrindavan. Gabbard's mother, Carol Porter Gabbard, is Caucasian, and her father, Mike Gabbard, is part Samoan and part Caucasian. Carol is a former Hawaii Board of Education member, and Mike is a Hawaii state senator. The family moved to Hawaii when Gabbard was two years old. Gabbard was homeschooled through elementary and high school and spent her spare time working at her family's small business, Hawaiian Toffee Treasures. She later studied international business at the Hawaii Pacific University, earning a degree in 2009.

Gabbard was raised in a very conservative home. Her father was a Republican politician and prominent antigay activist who in the 1990s proposed an amendment to the state constitution that would ban same-sex marriage. He was president of the nonprofit group Stop Promoting Homosexuality America and hosted a radio program called *Let's Talk Straight Hawaii*. Mike Gabbard still holds public office as a state senator. Inspired in part by his daughter, he became a member of the Democratic Party in 2007. However, he remains a staunch social conservative.

During her early life, Gabbard shared many of her father's political views, but her views changed after she spent time overseas as a member of the military. As Gabbard told Adrienne LaFrance for the *Honolulu Civil Beat* (17 Jan. 2012), she became a supporter of reproductive rights and of gay rights after "living and working in oppressive countries" and witnessing governmental attempts to control morality firsthand. "It really caused me to take a look at myself," said Gabbard, "and the way we're doing things here at home, locally, and nationally." Gabbard's "gradual metamorphosis" toward a more progressive political philosophy, as she describes it in her interview with LaFrance, was significant enough for her to win the support of the reproductive rights group Emily's List in her 2012 congressional campaign.

## EARLY CAREER
Growing up, Gabbard never aspired to be a politician. She described herself to B. J. Reyes for

the *Honolulu Star-Advertiser* (2 Jan. 2013) as a "very shy and introverted kid." At nineteen, she founded an environmental group with her father called the Healthy Hawaii Coalition (HHC). Gabbard served as the group's vice president, helping to promote its mission of water conservation and encouraging physical activity among Hawaiian youth. Gabbard helped to develop an environmental education curriculum with HHC that has been presented at over fifty public and private schools.

At the age of twenty-one, inspired by her passion for the environment and feeling a call to public service following the terrorist attacks of September 11, 2001, Gabbard decided to run for the Hawaii state legislature. Given her youth and inexperience, many people did not take her candidacy seriously. "So many people wrote me off, told me I was crazy to even try, or told me I would 'fail,'" she told Claudia Chan in an interview for Chan's website (25 Mar. 2013). Gabbard, who had no experience in public speaking or debating, felt sick the first time she had to address a large crowd of people. However, she told Chan that her conviction about what she was doing gave her the confidence to step outside of her comfort zone and learn how to campaign. In 2002, Gabbard won her seat representing Hawaii's Forty-Second District in West Oahu. The election made her the youngest person ever elected to the Hawaiian state legislature and the youngest woman elected to a state legislature in the country's history.

## MILITARY SERVICE
"In 2003, I felt the need to do more with my life and to do more in the way of service," Gabbard told Stephanie Gaskell for *Politico* (11 Dec. 2012). "I remember sitting in my office watching the Saddam Hussein statue topple [in Baghdad, Iraq]. That was shortly before I enlisted [in the Hawaii National Guard]." In May 2003, while serving her first term as a state representative, Gabbard entered basic training at Fort Jackson, South Carolina, where she graduated at the top of her class. She went on to complete advanced training in medical logistics in Texas, where she was a Distinguished Honor Graduate. In 2004, Gabbard's unit was deployed to Iraq for one-year tour of duty. Because of her deployment, she chose not to run for reelection to the state senate.

Gabbard served in Iraq with the Hawaii National Guard's Twenty-Ninth Brigade Combat Team from 2004 to 2006. Stationed fifty miles north of Baghdad at Area Anaconda, Gabbard served as a specialist in a medical company. As part of her job, she reviewed lists of casualties of Hawaiian service members and made sure that the soldiers received proper care. Due to the nature of her work, Gabbard told Jon Letman for the online magazine *Truthout* (5 Nov. 2012),

she was confronted with "the tremendous cost of war" every day. Gabbard—whose first sight in Iraq was a sign posted on the gates of her base that read cryptically, "Is Today the Day?"—relied on her Hindu faith and meditation to find solace amid the violence and death of war. At the end of her first tour, Gabbard was awarded a Meritorious Service Medal.

When Gabbard returned from her tour, she served as a legislative aide to Hawaiian senator Daniel K. Akaka in Washington, DC. At the same time, she attended and graduated from the Accelerated Officer Candidate School at the Alabama Military Academy in 2007. She was the first woman in the school's history to finish as the Distinguished Honor Graduate. In 2009, while still working for Akaka, Gabbard deployed with her National Guard unit as a platoon leader and second lieutenant to assist in the effort to provide antiterrorism training to the Kuwaiti National Guard.

She was the first woman ever to set foot on the particular Kuwaiti military base where her unit was assigned. "I was expected to train men who had never seen a woman on the base before, never mind a woman in military uniform in a position of authority telling them what to do," she told Aziz Haniffa for *India Abroad* (2 Nov. 2012). When she was introduced, many of the men ignored her and refused to shake her hand, but Gabbard persevered. At the end of her deployment, the Kuwaiti military presented her with an award in appreciation for her service, the first such honor given to a woman. Gabbard was commissioned as a captain in Hawaii's National Guard in 2011.

## PRIMARY UPSET
After Gabbard returned to Hawaii from Kuwait in 2010, she ran successfully for a seat on the Honolulu City Council. In that office, Gabbard served as chair of the Safety, Economic Development, and Government Affairs Committee and as vice chairperson of the Budget Committee. Before the end of her first term on the city council, the retirement of Senator Akaka led Gabbard to begin considering a run for congressional office. Former congressional representative Mazie Hirono announced her intention to run for Akaka's open Senate seat, and in turn, Gabbard began campaigning for Hirono's vacated seat in the House. Hirono won her bid, becoming the first Asian American woman elected to the US Senate. Gabbard's move to replace Hirono attracted some criticism, but she was determined to bring her experiences as a veteran to a larger legislative body.

From the beginning of Gabbard's campaign, the odds were against her. Among her five opponents in the Democratic Party primary was former Honolulu mayor Mufi Hanneman, a popular and familiar public figure with many more years of experience in politics than Gabbard. At the outset, Hanneman was the clear frontrunner. In February 2012, in a poll sponsored by the *Honolulu Star-Advertiser* and *Hawaii News Now*, Gabbard trailed Hanneman by forty-five percentage points. The race tightened throughout the summer, as Gabbard garnered support and nearly $500,000 worth of funding from progressive groups such as the Sierra Club Independent Action, the VoteVets.Org Action Fund, and Women Vote!, an offshoot of Emily's List. Hanneman criticized Gabbard for introducing mainland special interest groups into the race and reportedly loaned his own campaign $150,000 to counter Gabbard's successful fundraising efforts. By July, Hanneman's lead had dwindled to ten percentage points.

The result of primary voting on August 11, 2012, surprised many people, including Hanneman. After votes from Hawaii's twenty-seven voting districts had been tallied, Gabbard had bested Hanneman in all but one. It was an overwhelming victory for the thirty-year-old candidate.

## CONGRESSIONAL CAMPAIGN AND THE NATIONAL STAGE

In September 2012, as a candidate in Hawaii's congressional election, Gabbard was invited by House minority leader Nancy Pelosi to speak at the DNC in Charlotte, North Carolina. She spoke on the opening day of the convention, along with seven other female speakers. Gabbard spent her time at the podium talking about a subject close to her heart. "The sacrifices made by our troops and military families are immeasurable," she said. "These days it's often women in uniform—moms, wives, even grandmothers—who deploy and leave their families behind." Although Gabbard's moment in the national spotlight was brief, her inspiring words led the website *Politico* to name her one of five Democratic politicians to watch in Charlotte.

After Gabbard's stunning upset in the Democratic primary and her speech at the DNC, she was widely considered a favorite in her general election race against Republican Party challenger David Kawika Crowley. As a candidate, Gabbard pledged to work against partisan gridlock in the House. Her campaign supporters included environmentalist groups, veterans, and progressive women's organizations. Gabbard was also embraced by many in the Hindu and Indian American community. According to Deepti Hajela for the Associated Press (14 Jan. 2013), there are 1.79 million Hindus in the United States, the vast majority of whom are of Indian decent. "Hinduism encompasses a range of beliefs and practices, and there is no formal conversion practice," Hajela wrote. "That acceptance of plurality in the faith, that Hindus come

in many forms, would make it 'hypocritical' for Indian Hindus to look askance at Gabbard for not sharing their ethnicity."

During her campaign, a number of prominent Indian Americans outside of Hawaii held fundraisers for Gabbard. After she won her congressional race against Crowley—earning over 80 percent of the total vote—she became a member of the India Caucus in the House. As a new congresswoman, Gabbard took her oath of office using her personal copy of the Bhagavad Gita, a Hindu scripture.

## PERSONAL LIFE

Gabbard and former husband Eduardo Tamayo divorced in 2006, after Gabbard's deployment to Iraq. In accordance with her Hindu beliefs, which she fully embraced as a teenager, Gabbard is a vegetarian and always carries her *japa mala*, or prayer beads. She is a follower of the principles of karma yoga, which, she told Kim Geiger for the *Los Angeles Times* (5 Sept. 2012), is based on "dedicating one's life to the service of others." When not in Washington, Gabbard lives in Honolulu, where she practices yoga and meditates every day.

## SUGGESTED READING

Chan, Claudia. "Interview: Tulsi Gabbard." *ClaudiaChan.com*. SHE Global Media, 25 Mar. 2013. Web. 3 May 2013.

Gaskell, Stephanie. "Military Service Helped Define Hawaii's Tulsi Gabbard." *Politico*. Politico, 11 Dec. 2012. Web. 1 May 2013.

Geiger, Kim. "Iraq Veteran Would Be First Hindu in Congress." *Los Angeles Times*. Los Angeles Times, 5 Sept. 2012. Web. 2 May 2013.

Hajela, Deepti. "American Hindus Finally Have Member of Faith in Congress." *Associated Press*. Associated Press, 14 Jan. 2013. Web. 1 May 2013.

Haniffa, Aziz. "Tulsi Gabbard." *India Abroad*. Rediff, 2 Nov. 2012. Web. 1 May 2013.

LaFrance, Adrienne. "Tulsi Gabbard's Leftward Journey." *Honolulu Civil Beat*. Peer News, 17 Jan. 2012. Web. 2 May 2013.

Letman, Jon. "The Cost of War: An Interview with Hawaii Congressional Candidate and Veteran Tulsi Gabbard." *Truthout*. Truthout, 5 Nov. 2012. Web. 1 May 2013.

Oppenheimer, Mark. "Politicians Who Reject Labels Based on Religion." *New York Times*. New York Times, 9 Nov. 2012. Web. 1 May 2013.

Reyes, B. J. "Focus on Service Propelled Gabbard." *Honolulu Star-Advertiser*. Star Advertiser, 2 Jan. 2013. Web. 1 May 2013.

*—Molly Hagan*

# Sara Ganim

**Born:** 1987 or 1988
**Occupation:** Journalist

Sara Ganim is the Pulitzer Prize–winning journalist who reported the 2011 Pennsylvania State University (Penn State) sexual abuse scandal involving a revered former football coach and the young boys he mentored. Sixty-eight-year-old Jerry Sandusky—a retired assistant coach of the Penn State University football team—was sentenced to thirty to sixty years in prison for his crimes, which included forty-five counts of rape and sexual assault, in 2012. The case was explosive in the small Pennsylvania town where football is akin to a religion and a respected member of the community was accused of abusing the young boys he met through his own charity for troubled youth. Ganim, who investigated the case for nearly two years before breaking the story in the Harrisburg *Patriot-News*, knows better than anyone the difficulty of exposing such a crime. Determined ambivalence pervaded the Penn State academic and athletic hierarchy, the executives at Sandusky's charity the Second Mile, and the local authorities at every turn. "There were so many missed opportunities [to stop Sandusky] that it's a little outrageous," Ganim told Mallory Jean Tenore for the nonprofit Poynter Institute for journalism (2 Aug. 2012). "He was very open in the community. Other coaches, other parents, were seeing this activity and were blinded by it. They would testify at trial that they thought for a second that [his behavior with children] was strange and then would decide it really wasn't because of who he was and would move on. . . . Common sense went out the window an abnormal amount of times."

At the time, Ganim was working the crime beat for the small-circulation *Patriot-News*, where she once wrote an article about a woman who reported her friend to the police after the friend refused to return a $150 crock pot. She stumbled upon the first thread of the Sandusky case after receiving an offhand tip from a source. Her old-style reporting—knocking on doors and cultivating deep sources—have won her comparisons to the legendary *Washington Post* duo, Bob Woodward and Carl Bernstein, who exposed the Watergate scandal in the 1970s. Her dedication to the story and meticulous investigation skills impressed many of her colleagues—making it all the more remarkable that she was only twenty-four years old at the time the story broke.

Ganim won the Pulitzer Prize for local reporting for her work on the Jerry Sandusky case in 2012. She is one of the youngest recipients of the prize. (The youngest recipient was twenty-two.) Ganim also received the George Polk Award and the Sidney Award for socially conscious journalism. In 2012, she won the

John C. Whitehead/The Patriot-News/Landov

Distinguished Writing Award for Local Accountability Reporting from the American Society of News Editors, and in 2011, she won the Scripps Howard Award for Community Journalism. Newsweek even put her on their list of "150 Fearless Women in the World."

## LIFE AND EDUCATION

Ganim was born in Detroit in 1987 or 1988. She attended elementary school in Michigan before moving with her family to Fort Lauderdale, Florida. A natural reporter from an early age, Ganim told Jon Friedman of the *Wall Street Journal*'s website *MarketWatch* (14 Nov. 2011), "I was always the kid who asked the inappropriate question and would get yelled at." She attended Archbishop Edward A. McCarthy High School in Fort Lauderdale, where she founded the school's journalism club, and taught her classmates how to write, edit, and lay out a newspaper. She was editor-in-chief of the school paper, the *Maverick Post*, now known as the *AMP*, and graduated in 2005.

Ganim began writing for the South Florida *Sun Sentinel* as a "Next Generation" intern when she was fifteen. She continued to write for the paper after her high school graduation as a "College View" intern.

Ganim enrolled at Penn State University in State College, Pennsylvania, in 2005. She studied journalism and wrote for the school's independently run student newspaper, the *Daily Collegian*. One summer—she had promised her father that she would graduate in three years and was taking summer classes—she was the only staff member willing to attend daily briefings at the police station. The crime beat turned out to be a good fit for Ganim who quickly excelled in her new role. "Crime reporting can be technical or touching," she told Friedman. "You can really do a lot of good. I'm usually covering people on the worst days of their lives. I can write about DUI crash victims and maybe help to bring about changes in laws or in rules about medical assistance."

Ganim also served as an adjunct professor at Penn State and reported for WZWW Radio State College. She graduated in 2008.

## CENTRE-DAILY TIMES

Ganim began writing for the State College *Centre Daily Times*, where she covered the courts and crime beat, while she was still a student in 2007. She worked part-time on the night crime desk, a grueling position she held for eighteen months in addition to her schoolwork. For her job, and indeed throughout her time working on the local crime beat for the *Patriot-News*, she kept a police scanner on her bedside table. She would wake up periodically throughout the night to check for news. Ganim became focused on creating a source base in Centre County to better serve the paper's twenty-four thousand readers. She cultivated sources like an old-fashioned gumshoe: "I tend to look for known associates, neighbors, hang out in coffee shops, talk to school principals, school secretaries. People who gossip a lot in communities tend to be [good sources]," she told Tenore. She looked to her sources for tips that might lead to stories, adding, "90 percent of the tips that we get aren't true; they're crazy. But you never know what 10 percent are true unless you look at all 100."

It was one such tip that set her on the trail to the biggest story of her nascent career. At the end of every conversation with a source, Ganim asks some variation of the question, "Is there anything else I should know?" After one late night chat about another story she was working on, a source told her about a boy who had come to the police accusing Jerry Sandusky of sexual abuse. Six weeks later, her source retracted the tip.

Ganim was not familiar with Sandusky. He had retired from his job as the assistant coach of the Penn State football team in 1999, long before she became a student. She wrote his name on a sticky note to remind herself to research him online the next day. When she searched his name, the website of his charity, the Second Mile, came up on the screen. Sandusky founded the nonprofit group, which runs camp programs for children from disadvantaged backgrounds, in 1977. After his retirement, Sandusky devoted most of his time to the management of Second Mile, which was honored by President George H. W. Bush as one of his "thousand points of light" in 1990.

## UNCOVERING THE JERRY SANDUSKY SCANDAL

Ganim did a little more Internet digging and found some strange commentary on the Penn State message boards, usually reserved for conversations about football among fans and alumni, regarding rumors about the former coach's relationships with young boys. In August 2009, while researching another story, Ganim attended a golf tournament hosted by the Second Mile. Sandusky was not there. When Ganim asked why Sandusky was not at his own event, she got two different answers. (Sandusky retired his position with Second Mile a month later.) Intrigued, Ganim began knocking on doors, asking State College residents and those familiar with him and the school if they knew anything strange about Sandusky.

At the time Sandusky was in good standing within the community; the town and the university relied on and revered the Penn State football team. There was even an ice-cream flavor called Sandusky Blitz. Penn State's Nittany Lions are a big ten football team, raking in millions of dollars of revenue to the benefit of the school and, by extension, the surrounding area. But more than money, the football team was a source of local and alumni pride, lending prestige to the Penn State name. At the time of Ganim's investigation, the Nittany Lions were led by Joe Paterno, who was once the winningest coach in college football history. Paterno, who died in January 2012, had coached the team for an astounding forty-five years and was often affectionately referred to by his nickname "JoePa." During his tenure, Sandusky was Paterno's defensive coach and right-hand man. He coached a number of future National Football League (NFL) players and helped solidify the team's reputation as "Linebacker U."

This is all to say that Ganim's questions about Sandusky were largely unwelcome in the community. "Some people closed their doors in my face, and others definitely did not tell me the truth," Ganim told Brody. A few people even invited her into their homes and deliberately misinformed her to throw her off the case. "But many were relieved—they were done keeping the story bottled up inside." After a number of dead ends, Ganim identified two of Sandusky's victims and found out that Sandusky was the subject of a grand jury investigation for allegedly abusing a local high school student in 2009. (In Pennsylvania, such proceedings are confidential.) The boy, Ganim soon learned, was not the first victim to come forward, though he was the first victim to spur major action on the part of the authorities. For this reason, he is known as Victim One.

## BREAKING THE STORY AT THE *PATRIOT-NEWS*

Ganim left her job at the *Centre Daily Times* to take a position at the Harrisburg *Patriot-News* in January 2011. She had spent the previous year nailing down the hard facts of the case and, in March 2011, she sat down to write her first story about Sandusky. The original 1,300-word article, which relied heavily on information from five anonymous sources, ran on the front page of the *Patriot-News*. The article was thorough and damning, though many angry readers accused the paper of printing gossip.

The article centered on Sandusky's grand jury investigation, which at the time had already been going on for eighteen months. Ganim listed Paterno, athletic director Tim Curley, and retired university vice president and treasurer Gary Schultz as among those called to testify. She also reported that the boy in question, Victim One, had suffered abuse at the hands of Sandusky over a period of four years. She quoted Jack Raykovitz, the executive director of Second Mile, as saying that while he was aware of rumors regarding Sandusky's behavior, he was not aware of any investigation. She also quoted an anonymous Second Mile board member who said in her March 31, 2011 article: "We all know there's an investigation going on."

Ganim also uncovered an allegation against Sandusky from 1998. This case was particularly interesting to Ganim because the victim's mother, who was told by her son that he had taken a shower with Sandusky, immediately alerted the local police. As a part of that investigation, the victim's mother confronted Sandusky in her home with police listening to their conversation in the next room. (Ganim later found out that during that conversation, Sandusky admitted his indiscretion.) No charges against Sandusky were ever filed regarding that case.

Ganim continued to report on the Sandusky scandal through the spring, summer, and fall of 2011. The story only gained national attention in early November when Sandusky was indicted and placed under arrest.

## MOVING THE STORY FORWARD

After she broke the news, Ganim consistently remained one step ahead of every other major news network, not to mention her veteran peers, as the saga unfolded. Ganim has told a number of reporters that her journalistic motto is: "Move the story forward." And the story moved quickly. She told Tenore that often, even the *Patriot-News* website could not keep up. "Our website has a three-minute delay from when you post [a story] to when you go live, which does not seem that long, but when things are breaking every 15 minutes, three minutes is a really long time," she said. So, she began breaking updates on the social networking website Twitter. On this point, which is part of a larger debate about

social media within the journalism community, Ganim has been fairly vocal. "Social media is a really great tool when you're breaking a story," she told Tenore, "but it's not that great of a tool when you're investigating a story."

Ganim tried to address every unanswered question and approach the case from every angle. Indeed, some of her best work regarding the testimony of former graduate assistant Mike McQueary, the many missed opportunities to investigate Sandusky going back to 1995, and the stories of the mothers of Victim One and Victim Six, resulted from these two premises. On December 11, 2011, Ganim published an article regarding the story of McQueary, who testified that he witnessed Sandusky raping a young boy in the shower in the university football building in 2001. The story's chain of callous mismanagement is emblematic of the Sandusky scandal as a whole. McQueary did not stop the rape, but relayed the story to his father who passed the story, which grew less accurate with each telling until it reached up the Penn State chain of command to university president Graham Spanier. This chain also included Paterno, whose only action was to place an unenforceable ban on Sandusky forbidding him from bringing children from Second Mile into the Penn State football building. Spanier signed off the ban.

According to another Ganim report (this one on November 11, 2011), there were at least five missed opportunities to pursue an investigation of Sandusky before 2009. This first of these, in 1995, involved Sandusky's adopted son, Matt.

But one of Ganim's most famous articles was published on November 7, 2011, several days after the Sandusky story made national news. "In the first two days after Sandusky was charged, everyone else was focused on Penn State, and we abandoned the gaggle, went out on a limb and spent time with the mothers of two victims, telling a story that could have easily been lost in the hysteria," Ganim wrote in a letter nominating one of her editors for a journalism award, as quoted by the *Providence Journal* (13 Oct. 2012). Ganim as well as her editor realized, she wrote, "that this was a story about a crime, not about sports." She was the first journalist to talk to the mothers.

## THE FALLOUT

In several interviews about her role in the story, Ganim has admitted that she did not foresee the widespread fallout of the scandal outside of Sandusky's eventual conviction. The university forced the resignation of Spanier, the school's president, and fired Paterno, the school's long-time coach. The latter decision spawned student riots across campus, highlighting the cognitive dissonance (between empathy for the victims and sympathy for a local hero) that colored the punishments that followed. Curley and Schultz, the athletic director and former vice president and treasurer respectively, were later charged with perjury and failure to report a crime. The National Collegiate Athletic Association (NCAA) imposed several sanctions on the football team including $60 million in fines and the removal of 112 wins from the team's record between 1998 and 2011. The vacated wins also meant that Paterno forfeited his title as the winningest coach in college football history. Ganim reported that the vacated wins begin in the 1998 season because it was the year in which reports of Sandusky's crimes were first brought to Paterno's attention.

Ganim was even subpoenaed to take the stand in the Sandusky trial, regarding a text message she sent to a victim's mother. She refused to testify, telling the presiding judge that she was willing to go to jail to protect her sources. The subpoena was later withdrawn.

After the national media picked up the Sandusky story, Ganim became the go-to State College correspondent for major news networks including CNN. She joined the network as a correspondent based out of Atlanta, Georgia, in November 2012.

## SUGGESTED READING

Brody, Liz. "Meet the Woman Who Exposed Jerry Sandusky." *Glamour*. Condé Nast, 16 Apr. 2012. Web. 5 June 2013.

Friedman, Jon. "Ganim: Star Reporter on Penn State Scandal." *Market Watch*. MarketWatch, 14 Nov. 2011. Web. 5 June 2013.

Ganim, Sara. "Jerry Sandusky, Former Penn State Football Staffer, Subject of Grand Jury Investigation." *Patriot-News*. PA Media Group, 31 Mar. 2011. Web. 5 June 2013.

Tenore, Mallory Jean. "Pulitzer Winner Sara Ganim Explains How She Develops Sources, Gets Them to Open Up." *Poynter*. Poynter Inst., 2 Aug. 2012. Web. 5 June 2013.

—*Molly Hagan*

# Masha Gessen

**Born:** January 13, 1967
**Occupation:** Journalist and author

Masha Gessen is a Russian American journalist and author. She is a regular contributor to the *New York Times*, *Slate*, and the *New Republic*. She has also written for *Vanity Fair* and the *Guardian* and has served as deputy editor of *Bolshoi Gorod*, formerly Moscow's largest independent weekly. Gessen has written a number of nonfiction books that draw on aspects of her life, including the memoir *Ester and Ruzya: How My Grandmothers Survived Hitler's War and Stalin's*

© Colin McPherson/Corbis

*Peace* (2004), in which she recounts her grandmothers' tales of survival amid war, persecution, and totalitarianism. Gessen has also written a biography of Russian president Vladimir Putin, *The Man without a Face: The Unlikely Rise of Vladimir Putin* (2012). As Gabriel Sanders wrote for the *Jewish Daily Forward* (10 Dec. 2004), "Gessen has proved herself an able chronicler not only of the Russian present, but the Russian past as well."

Gessen immigrated to the United States with her family when she was fourteen, after facing years of anti-Semitism and oppression in Russia. She returned to her birth country in 1996. However, in 2013 she began making plans to leave the country again after facing persecution under Russia's discriminatory laws against gays and lesbians.

## EARLY LIFE AND CAREER

Masha Gessen was born Maria Alexandrovna Gessen on January 13, 1967, in Moscow, USSR. Her late mother, Yolochka, was a translator and literary critic, and her father, Sasha, is a computer scientist. Her younger brother, Keith (originally named Kostya) Gessen, is a well-known journalist and writer; he is the author of the novel *All the Sad Young Literary Men* (2008) and one of the founding coeditors of the literary and political magazine *n+1*.

Gessen had a fraught relationship with her parents, particularly her mother, which she describes more fully in her book *Blood Matters* (2008). She has many memories of her early years in the USSR, with especially vivid ones of the day she left the country for what would be more than a decade. Gessen was fourteen years old in 1981, when she and her family left to seek a better life in the United States. Prior to their departure and during the wave of anti-Semitism in the USSR in the 1970s, the Gessens had spent years as Jewish refuseniks, citizens who were repeatedly denied permission to emigrate.

Gessen struggled to adjust to her new life in Boston, Massachusetts. Although she passed her written tests in school, she failed her first year of high school because her spoken English was so bad. She was able to turn her academic career around, however, and after graduation attended the prestigious Cooper Union College in New York City, where she initially studied architecture. Gessen later switched her focus to journalism.

During the early 1990s, Gessen divided her time between New York, Boston, and San Francisco and worked on a number of stories about the human immunodeficiency virus (HIV) and the devastation of the acquired immunodeficiency syndrome (AIDS) epidemic, particularly in the gay community. She was keenly interested in topics involving math and science (she would later write a book about a famous Russian mathematician) and therefore enjoyed working the medical beat and spending time reading medical books. This proved to be good training, she told Viv Groskop for the *Guardian* (4 July 2008), for her later book about genetics and helped her develop skills that "she now considers [to have] saved her life."

In 1991, Gessen made her first trip back to Moscow on assignment. For the next several years she traveled between the United States and Russia as a foreign correspondent, and in 1996, she decided to return to her birth country for good.

## RETURN TO MOSCOW

Gessen's return to Moscow coincided with the dawn of Russia's postcommunist era and democratization, which was seen especially in the creation of a number of independent news organizations. Gessen was a founding staff member and chief correspondent of the weekly newspaper *Itogi*, and she later became a bureau reporter for *US News and World Moscow*. She also served as the deputy editor in chief of *Bolshoi Gorod* from 2004 to 2005. She continued reporting on HIV and AIDS and also reported from war-torn Chechnya, but when she reunited with her two grandmothers, Ester and Ruzya, in 1996, she began to write a book about their very different lives in the postwar Soviet Union.

In an article for the *Jewish Daily Forward*, Sanders described *Ester and Ruzya: How My Grandmothers Survived Hitler's War and Stalin's Peace* (2004) as a book "composed at once with a journalist's skepticism, a scholar's rigor, and a grandchild's devotion." Ester Gessen, Gessen's paternal grandmother, was born to a family of wealthy Zionists in Poland. During World War II, she fled to Siberia and defied pressure from the secret police to become a government informant. Later, as a young single mother with an infant son, she sought a desk job with the early KGB, only to be turned down because of her poor eyesight. Ruzya Solodovnik, Gessen's maternal grandmother, was born in the Pale of Settlement (a region of czarist Russia in which Jewish Russians were granted permanent residence) and moved to Moscow as a young girl. Ruzya's husband was killed during the war, and she became a government censor to provide for her daughter. Gessen's book offers no easy answers, but it succeeds in teasing out the complexities of her grandmothers' choices and shows, as Katha Pollitt wrote for the *New York Times* (6 Mar. 2005), how they were able to "preserve their individuality and their humanity" in a "deeply repressive" society.

## BLOOD MATTERS

The same year *Ester and Ruzya* was published, genetic testing revealed that Gessen had an 87 percent risk of developing breast cancer and a 40 to 50 percent chance of developing ovarian cancer. Gessen's mother had died of cancer at the age of forty-nine, and Gessen was thirty-seven at the time of the testing. The news shook her to her core; she felt healthy, yet she felt sick. "I got used to the idea that I had cancer," she wrote in *Blood Matters: From Inherited Illness to Designer Babies, How the World and I Found Ourselves in the Future of the Gene* (2008), her book about genetic testing and the diagnosis of inherited diseases. She explained to Groskop, "I imagined surgery, chemotherapy, and radiation. . . . I had to return to trying to make my impossible choice: live and wait for the cancer to come or start carving up a body that felt utterly healthy."

Gessen ultimately decided to have a preventive mastectomy in 2005. She began writing a series of articles about her decision for the online magazine *Slate*, and her research for the series led her to ponder the future of genetics. *Blood Matters* is a book about Gessen's own experience but is also much broader: she writes about hundreds of people living with genetic disorders and makes predictions about genetic advancements. Groskop pointed out that due in part to her medical research experience, "one of Gessen's talents as a reporter [is that] she renders complicated concepts accessible and easy to digest." Jennifer Senior, in her *New York Times* review (11 May 2008) of the book, concluded that "the enduring memory one takes away [from *Blood Matters*] is Gessen's intelligence and wit as she's staring down the barrel of a gun."

## THE MAN WITHOUT A FACE

Gessen's biography *The Man without a Face: The Unlikely Rise of Vladimir Putin* (2012) paints a grim picture of Russia's president and the country's political climate during his presidency. Her task was a difficult one because, according to Gessen, Putin was able to write his own personal history when he became a prominent figure in 1999. "When he spoke to his first and only official biographers in the early 2000s," Gessen told Dave Davies in an interview for National Public Radio (1 Mar. 2012), "he mostly concentrated on describing his street fights and on portraying himself as somebody who is aggressive, vengeful, and has a lot of trouble controlling his temper." In the book, Gessen writes that Putin's father was a member of the secret police during World War II, and she believes that he continued to work for the early KGB after the war. Like his father, Putin rose through the ranks of the KGB and served in East Germany before the fall of the Berlin Wall in 1989. He remained in the force after returning to the Soviet Union, though he also served in the Leningrad City Council. He was totally unknown to the public until President Boris Yeltsin appointed him prime minister in 1999.

Prior to her book's publication, the two Russian weeklies at which Gessen had worked—*Itogi* and *Bolshoi Gorod*—were closed. In the article "All Politics Is Economic," which Gessen wrote for the *New York Times* (15 Apr. 2013), she described the various ways in which the Russian government works to stifle the country's flagging free press, citing publications that have fired prominent journalists to "prove their loyalty to the Kremlin" and the pressure put on advertisers to drop publications that write about politics in any capacity. "Each closure, firing, or investor pullout has been presented as an economic decision," she wrote. "But every time, the same debate has flared up: how political are these economic decisions?" The state's tactics have become more overt and more frightening, Gessen noted. "What I argue in the book," she told Davies, "is that Putin has created a system in which people who run afoul of the government also fall outside of the protection of the law and know that they are living with a constant threat to their lives."

### OTHER WORK

In 2009, Gessen wrote a biography of Russian mathematician Grigori Perelman. *Perfect Rigor: A Genius and the Mathematical Breakthrough of the Century* describes Perelman as a reclusive genius who came to international attention in 2002 when he proved the Poincaré conjecture, one of the most elusive and unproven theories in topology. In 1904 a French mathematician named Henri Poincaré made the conjecture, which may be used in part to describe the shape of the universe, and in 2000, the Clay Mathematics Institute offered a $1 million prize to the person who solved it. Perelman's proof was a breakthrough in modern mathematics, but the mathematician himself behaved erratically after his success. He

resigned from his teaching position, ceased communication with all but a few close colleagues, and turned down the most prestigious award in mathematics, the Field's Medal.

Gessen independently uncovered Perelman's coming-of-age as a mathematical prodigy and a champion of Russian competitive mathematics in the 1970s. She has speculated that Perelman might have Asperger syndrome and observed that his disillusion with the math world might stem from an inability to play, as Jascha Hoffman for the *New York Times* (13 Dec. 2009) put it, "by anyone's rules but his own." Hoffman criticized the book for lacking a lucid explanation of Perelman's work but praised Gessen's investigation, writing that she had succeeded in creating "something rare: an accessible book about an unreachable man."

It was announced in 2013 that Gessen would write a book about Tamerlan and Dzhokhar Tsarnaev, the two brothers suspected of carrying out the Boston Marathon bombing. Gessen has several ties to the story, among them her years spent covering the violence in the brothers' native Chechnya and her years living in Boston.

### FLEEING RUSSIA AGAIN

In 2012, in St. Petersburg, Russia's second-largest city, a law was passed that banned all "homosexual propaganda." The offense was a baffling one, and in an article for the *Guardian* (10 Aug. 2013), Gessen wrote that she found the phrase funny when she first heard it. But the effects of the abrupt legal embrace of social conservatism have been chilling for Russian citizens such as Gessen, whose girlfriend was pregnant with the family's third child at the time. Gessen feared that the ambiguous law could be used to separate her from her children. Still, she did not decide to leave Russia right away, instead launching the pink-triangle campaign, which aimed to educate citizens about the law's implications. She appeared on television and testified at a hearing with other human rights activists, later writing in the *Guardian*, "Though I have always been publicly out, I had never done what I did then—talked about my family and asked to be seen as a lesbian rather than a journalist first."

In 2013, a prominent legislator began referring publicly to Gessen and what he called her "perverted family." Worried, Gessen contacted an adoption lawyer—her oldest child is adopted—to ask if social services might try to take the boy away from her. By way of response, the lawyer advised her to leave the country. That summer, she was beaten and detained in front of Parliament with twenty-five other protesters. "I realized that in all my interactions, including professional ones, I no longer felt I was perceived as a journalist first," she wrote. "I am now a person with a pink triangle." Like her parents before her, Gessen and her family began to make plans to move to the United States.

## PERSONAL LIFE

Gessen has three children. She adopted her son, Vova, from an HIV orphanage in St. Petersburg in 2000 after meeting him during her extensive reportage on the virus. Gessen also has a daughter named Yael, whom she conceived from a donor. Gessen raises her children with her ex-girlfriend, a photographer named Svenya, though the two are no longer together. Gessen also has a child with her current partner, a geographer named Dasha.

## SUGGESTED READING

Gessen, Masha. "All Politics Is Economic." *New York Times*. New York Times, 15 Apr. 2013. Web. 17 Sept. 2013.

Gessen, Masha. "As a Gay Parent I Must Flee Russia or Lose My Children." *Guardian*. Guardian News and Media, 10 Aug. 2013. Web. 17 Sept. 2013.

Groskop, Viv. "Masha's Choice." *Guardian*. Guardian News and Media, 4 July 2008. Web. 17 Sept. 2013.

Sanders, Gabriel. "Author Tells the Tale of Her Grandmothers' Survival." *Jewish Daily Forward*. Forward Association, 10 Dec. 2004. Web. 17 Sept. 2013.

Senior, Jennifer. "Chronicle of a Death Foretold." *New York Times*. New York Times, 11 May 2008. Web. 17 Sept. 2013.

## SELECTED WORKS

*Dead Again: The Russian Intelligentsia after Communism*, 1997; *Ester and Ruzya: How My Grandmothers Survived Hitler's War and Stalin's Peace*, 2004; *Perfect Rigor: A Genius and the Mathematical Breakthrough of the Century*, 2009; *The Man without a Face: The Unlikely Rise of Vladimir Putin*, 2012

—Molly Hagan

# Kirsten Gillibrand

**Born:** December 9, 1966
**Occupation:** US politician

Democratic Party politician Kirsten Gillibrand began her career in Congress as the representative for New York's Twentieth District, an upstate region that is significantly more rural and conservative than New York City and the areas surrounding it. As such, Gillibrand often butted heads with more liberal members of her party, who disagreed with her tough stance against illegal immigration and her opposition

Landov

to gay marriage. They also found her 100 percent approval rating from the National Rifle Association (NRA) highly unusual for a member of the Democratic Party.

Since being appointed in 2009 to fill the Senate seat that was vacated by Hillary Clinton, Gillibrand—who was elected to a full six-year term in 2012—has changed her approach to some issues. She has declared her support for gay marriage, assuring Latinos and Asians that she supports a path to citizenship for illegal immigrants, and expressed a willingness to reconsider her position on gun control. "Now I represent all of New York, and I have to represent all New Yorkers," she said in one speech, as quoted by Stephen Rodrick in *New York* magazine (7 June 2009).

## EARLY YEARS

Kirsten Elizabeth Rutnik Gillibrand was born on December 9, 1966 in Albany, New York. Her parents, Douglas Paul Rutnik and Polly Edwina Noonan, were both attorneys. Gillibrand's mother was one of only three women in her law school class. She took her criminal law final exam in a hospital bed, a day after giving birth to Gillibrand's older brother, Doug. Early in their careers, the couple founded an Albany-based law firm, Rutnik and Rutnik. The couple divorced in the 1980s.

In addition to her brother Doug, Gillibrand has a younger sister, Erin. The siblings grew up on Albany's Noonan Lane, a quiet street named in honor of their maternal grandparents, who owned the first home on the block. Several other members of the Gillibrand extended family have also lived on Noonan Lane.

## FAMILY TIES TO STATE POLITICS

In addition to his work as an attorney, Gillibrand's father served as a Republican Party lobbyist. His insider status and close ties to such GOP figures as Joe Bruno, Governor George Pataki, and Al D'Amato were later pilloried in the press by his daughter's opponents—particularly when a 2009 federal probe revealed that former New York State Senate leader Bruno had engaged in a questionable real estate deal that involved Gillibrand's father. (Bruno was later indicted on charges of corruption.) The press also widely reported on the divorced Rutnik's romantic relationship with a woman who worked as a senior gubernatorial aide to Pataki.

The Gillibrand family has long-established political ties in the state of New York. Gillibrand's maternal grandmother, Dorothea "Polly" Noonan, was the founder of the Albany Democratic Women's Club and a key member of Albany Mayor Erastus Corning II's political machine. Corning, who was referred to as "mayor for life," served in office from 1942 until his death in 1983, and Polly Noonan was often at his side. Because his own wife disliked attending political functions, she frequently hosted events and traveled with him, causing rampant speculation that the two were involved romantically. (The fact that Corning left Noonan's children a sizeable bequest upon his death fueled that conjecture.)

Whatever their personal relationship, Noonan worked tirelessly on behalf of Corning and Albany's Democratic Party. Gillibrand has said that her grandmother was a pivotal role model for her. "What I admired so much was her passion," Gillibrand said in a campaign speech, as quoted by Michael Powell and Raymond Hernandez for the *New York Times* (23 Jan. 2009). "I thought, 'Someday I may serve, someday I may be part of this.'" Gillibrand has recalled helping her grandmother by stuffing envelopes or applying bumper stickers—sometimes pasting the stickers directly over those of opponents on neighborhood cars. Noonan died in 2003, at the age of eighty-seven.

## EDUCATION

Gillibrand, who went by the nickname Tina as a child, attended the Academy of Holy Names, a Catholic elementary school in Albany. She went to high school in Troy, New York, at the prestigious, all-women's Emma Willard School, where she gained a reputation as a tenacious and tireless student. "I was a big nerd. I wasn't the smartest, but I'd put in tons of hours," she recalled to Rodrick. She was an equally resolute athlete, routinely trouncing opponents on the tennis court. The school stressed the importance of studying abroad as a means of expanding one's worldview and Gillibrand spent one semester in France.

After graduating from high school in 1984, Gillibrand enrolled at Dartmouth in Hanover, New Hampshire. She chose the college—the smallest of the Ivy League schools—because the students there struck her as more down-to-earth and outdoorsy than those at other campuses. As a student at Dartmouth, Gillibrand majored in Asian studies. "Learning Chinese doesn't have a lot to do with talent or skill," Gillibrand explained to Rodrick. "It is about putting in the hours doing rote memorization. And I knew I was good at that."

At Dartmouth, Gillibrand became a member of the Kappa Kappa Gamma sorority and played squash. She was skilled enough at the sport to be named a captain of the varsity team during her senior year. During semester breaks, she traveled extensively, often accompanied by her mother. Gillibrand visited China after American exchange students were allowed to travel there. She later went to India, where she met the Dalai Lama, who had fled the Chinese occupation of Tibet in the late 1950s. The experience led Gillibrand to become deeply involved with the issue of Tibetan autonomy, and upon her return to Dartmouth, she gave an enthusiastic talk on the topic, dressed in Tibetan garb. She also wrote her senior thesis on Tibet, entitled "The History of Tibetan Resistance to the Chinese Occupation of Tibet 1950–1988." Since college, Gillibrand has maintained her Chinese-language abilities, and during one of her campaigns, conducted an interview with a journalist entirely in Mandarin.

Gillibrand—who interned in the office of Senator Al D'Amato—graduated from Dartmouth, magna cum laude, in 1988. Despite her undisputed fondness for her alma mater and the friends she made there, she has been criticized in the press about her use of alumni lists for political fundraising purposes.

After Dartmouth, Gillibrand enrolled in law school at the University of California, Los Angeles. After interning with the United Nations Crime Prevention branch in Vienna, Austria, she earned her law degree in 1991.

## A CAREER IN LAW

After passing the bar exam, Gillibrand took a job at Davis Polk & Wardwell, an international law firm headquartered in New York City. The following year, she won a coveted clerkship with US Court of Appeals Judge Roger Miner. Miner was a Republican appointee, and many observers have asserted that Gillibrand—who was not at the top of her law-school class—received the clerkship because of her family connections to D'Amato.

After her clerkship, Gillibrand returned to Davis Polk & Wardwell, where she worked for almost a decade. Among her high profile clients was the tobacco company Philip Morris.

Although she has been censured in some quarters for working with the conglomerate, she has told journalists that she does not regret doing so, because proceeds from those efforts allowed her to take on several pro bono cases for battered women, tenant groups, and other disadvantaged clients.

According to most accounts, Gillibrand began considering a political career as a young woman. Her mother has told journalists that as a young law associate she spoke of one day running for office. In the late 1990s, she reportedly approached a Dartmouth friend who had found a job at the White House to ask for advice and contacts. One Democratic insider quoted by Rodrick said, "She has a single-mindedness about where she wants to go," and then added, "She wouldn't throw her mother under a train, but she'd run you over with a train if you got in her way."

In 1999, Gillibrand met Secretary of Housing and Urban Development (HUD) Andrew Cuomo at a fundraiser. Cuomo, a Democrat, offered her the post of HUD's special counsel. Gillibrand served in this role until 2000, when she returned to private practice for Boies, Schiller & Flexner, a firm known for its involvement in such high-profile actions as the Justice Department's antitrust prosecution of Microsoft and the US Supreme Court case regarding the 2000 presidential election.

During this period, Gillibrand also partook in fundraising efforts for various New York Democrats, including Eliot Spitzer and Hillary Clinton, whom she had met in the mid-1990s.

## ENTRY INTO POLITICS

In 2002, Gillibrand told the partners at Boies, Schiller & Flexner that she was thinking of competing for a political office and requested a transfer from New York City to the firm's Albany outpost, a move that allowed her to establish residency in Hudson, a town in the state's Twentieth Congressional District. (The district is bordered by Lake Placid to the north and includes parts of the Adirondacks, Catskills, and Hudson Valley.)

Gillibrand had initially considered a run for the city council or state assembly, but she knew competition for those seats in a city like New York could be fierce. She reasoned that a spot in the House of Representatives would allow her to be involved in federal issues. She believed that as a moderate Democrat she might have a chance of winning in a place like New York's Twentieth District. While registered Republicans outnumbered Democrats by an almost two-to-one margin in the region, Gilibrand's Democratic Party colleagues Clinton and Spitzer had made reasonable inroads there in the early 2000s.

In 2006, Gillibrand left her job as a lawyer to run for a seat in the lower house of Congress, representing the Twentieth District. As her candidacy gained momentum, her campaign funds exceeded $2 million, thanks to her experience in political fundraising and ability to mobilize contacts. "Because I did fund-raising and organizing in New York for ten years before I ever ran for office, I developed so many great relationships with all the people that care about elective politics. From the public servants to the donors to the community organizers," she told Jason Horowitz for the *New York Observer* (28 Jan. 2009). "These were all the relationships I called upon when I decided to run. When I did my first poll I asked Hillary Clinton to review it. I asked Andrew Cuomo to review it. I asked Eliot Spitzer to review it. These are all people that I had worked with helping them to get elected, working on their causes."

Her opponent in the race was Republican Party incumbent John E. Sweeney. With many of his constituents telling pollsters that they had started to perceive Sweeney as a Washington insider, they were receptive to Gillibrand's folksy manner and centrist message. A 2006 report from the Citizens for Responsibility and Ethics in Washington listing Sweeney as one of the twenty most corrupt members of Congress also cast a pall on his reelection effort. Then, just a week before the election, a police report was leaked to newspapers that detailed a 2005 incident in which state troopers had responded to a 911 call from Sweeney's wife—who claimed that he was choking and manhandling her. Following media reports related to the incident, it was rumored that someone in Gillibrand's campaign had arranged for the leak.

## HOUSE OF REPRESENTATIVES

With Sweeney being tarred as politically corrupt and abusive toward his spouse, Gillibrand won the November 7, 2006, election by a margin of six percent. She was sworn in on January 4, 2007. Her tenure got off to what the *New York Times* (20 Feb. 2007) called a "frenetic start." In the first of a series of articles tracing Gillibrand's experiences as a freshman representative, Raymond Hernandez wrote, "When Kirsten Gillibrand was elected to Congress this past November in a tide of Democratic victories, she soon learned that her campaigning was not over. This political novice found herself in a precarious position: a Democrat trying to represent an overwhelmingly Republican district extending into the state's North Country, a onetime Manhattan lawyer in a place of factory and mill workers, dairy farmers, and retired military veterans. Now, even as the congratulatory letters continue to trickle in, she often looks like a candidate who is still on the run. Ms. Gillibrand spends virtually every free moment scurrying back from Washington to her district to attend town hall gatherings, meet-and-greets at local malls, and—yes, already—a fund-raiser."

During her first term, Gillibrand was given assignments on the House Agriculture and Armed Services Committees, and she joined the Blue Dog Democrats—a fiscally and socially conservative group whose members often stray from the party line. Somewhat surprisingly for a freshman representative, she was also placed on the House Democratic Steering Committee, which sets legislative policy for House Democrats. In an unprecedented move, Gillibrand immediately began publishing what she called her "Sunlight Report," which makes public her personal financial information as well as all her meetings and earmark requests.

As a freshman in Congress, Gillibrand quickly earned both admiration and enmity for her political views. She took a hard line against illegal immigration and was one of only a handful of Democrats to vote against the Troubled Asset Relief Program (TARP), the program that arranged for the government bailout of the financial sector. Gillibrand's vote against TARP put her in direct opposition to Democratic House Speaker Nancy Pelosi. Additionally, Gillibrand was the only New York representative to vote for the May 2007 funding bill for the Iraq War. She also voted in favor of limiting information sharing on gun buyers between the Bureau of Alcohol, Tobacco, Firearms, and Explosives and the Federal Bureau of Investigation, a measure that helped earn her a 100 percent approval rating from the NRA.

In her 2008 race for reelection, Gillibrand faced Republican Sandy Treadwell, a wealthy executive who outspent her by a wide margin. Although Treadwell's campaign was largely self-financed, Gillibrand raised more money from outside sources than any other freshman representative running for reelection in 2008. Despite the disparity in campaign funds between the two candidates, Gillibrand defeated Treadwell to retain her Congressional seat, earning 62 percent of the vote.

## US SENATE

When it was announced in 2008 that Hillary Clinton would be assuming the office of Secretary of State in the administration of President Barack Obama, New York Governor David Paterson was charged with filling her vacant Senate seat. Along with Gillibrand, contenders included Paterson Westchester representative Nita Lowey, Manhattan representative Carolyn Maloney, and Randi Weingarten, president of the United Federation of Teachers. The prospects for all four women seemed dim when Caroline Kennedy, daughter of President John F. Kennedy, was rumored to be a candidate.

After Kennedy removed herself from contention at the last moment, Gillibrand emerged as the strong front-runner. Paterson, not wanting to anger his gay constituents, asked her if she

would consider reversing her position against gay marriage. Once Gillibrand had done so—reaching out by phone to the leaders of the nonprofit group Empire State Pride Agenda—the matter was settled. On January 23, 2009, Paterson appointed Gillibrand to fill Clinton's Senate seat. She was sworn in on January 27.

Although Gillibrand was criticized by some of her constituents for moving to the left on certain matters, she easily won a special 2010 election to retain her seat, and with that victory, became the youngest elected member of the Senate, at age forty-three. In 2012, she defeated Republican Party challenger Wendy Long, also a Dartmouth alumna, garnering a resounding 72 percent of the vote. Gillibrand sits on the Senate Committees on Agriculture, Nutrition, and Forestry; the Senate Armed Services Committee; the Special Committee on Aging; and the Committee on Environment and Public Works. Her six-year term expires in January 2019.

## PERSONAL LIFE

Gillibrand has been married to her husband, Jonathan Gillibrand, since 2001. The couple met in 1999, when Jonathan, a British-born financier, was in graduate school at Columbia University. The couple's first child, Theo, was born in 2003. Gillibrand became pregnant with their second child, Henry, shortly after she was elected to the House of Representatives. On May 14, 2008, she spent the entire day on the floor of the House, going into labor that evening. Her fellow representatives gave her a standing ovation when the news of Henry's birth the following day was announced.

Gillibrand has said that her status as a working mother gives her keen insight into the issues facing her constituents. She regularly writes for the website MomsRising, a grassroots organization that promotes family-friendly government policies. Gillibrand's columns have included, "As a Mother and a Lawmaker, Watching a Child Go Hungry Is Something I Just Will Not Stand For," "It's Time for Congress to Act on the Paycheck Fairness Act," and "The Right Priorities for Our Working Families."

Journalists often comment on Gillibrand's physical appearance, describing her as petite, blonde, and well dressed. Although she has commented that male politicians are not subjected to similar scrutiny, she takes such reporting in stride. She also ignores oft-repeated comments that she reminds her political colleagues and reporters of Tracy Flick, the annoyingly ambitious student-government candidate portrayed by Reese Witherspoon in the 1999 film *Election*. She once said, as quoted by Jonathan Van Meter for *Vogue* (October 2010), "I'm [just] going to try to wear people down by being a good senator and a good person."

## SUGGESTED READING

Barrett, Wayne. "Is Gillibrand Too Republican to Replace Clinton?" *Village Voice*. Voice Media Group, 22 Jan. 2009. Web. 12 July 2013.

Hernandez, Raymond. "Frenetic Start in Congress for One Democrat, Class of '06." *New York Times*. New York Times Co., 20 Feb. 2007. Web. 12 July 2013.

Horowitz, Jason. "Kirsten Gillibrand, Like Chuck Schumer with Connections." *New York Observer*. New York Observer, 28 Jan. 2009. Web. 12 July 2013.

Pickert, Kate. "2 Minute Bio: N.Y. Senator Kirsten Gillibrand." *Time*. Time, 23 Jan. 2009. Web. 12 July 2013.

Powell, Michael, and Raymond Hernandez. "Senate Choice: Folksy Centrist Born to Politics." *New York Times*. New York Times Co., 23 Jan. 2009. Web. 12 July 2013.

Rodrick, Stephen. "The Reintroduction of Kirsten Gillibrand." *New York*. New York Media, 7 June 2009. Web. 12 July 2013.

Van Meter, Jonathan. "In Hillary's Footsteps: Kirsten Gillibrand." *Vogue*. Condé Nast, Oct. 2010. Web. 12 July 2013.

—*Mari Rich*

Getty Images for Extra

# Ellie Goulding

**Born:** December 30, 1986
**Occupation:** Singer-songwriter

A self-taught folk performer at fifteen, British singer-songwriter Ellie Goulding never imagined that within ten years she would be an international pop superstar holding her own in the new wave of electronic dance music. After trading her acoustic guitar for synthesizers and remixers, the young singer began writing and recording songs in collaboration with young DJs and producers, seeking them out after discovering her passion for electronica as a university student. Goulding's rise to fame on both sides of the Atlantic is attributed to both her savvy for creating infectious dance tracks and her natural talent as a singer whose voice shines above the heavily layered music that accompanies it. While much music in her genre is primarily created on computers and mixing boards, Goulding is front and center in her sound.

Goulding grew up in the rural county of Herefordshire, near the Welsh border. As a songwriter she has drawn heavily from her difficult childhood and family life. Although her parents' divorce and her family's struggles with money left a mark on the singer, they did not deter her from attending the University of Kent, which proved to be the start of her path toward stardom. Not long after signing with Polydor Records, Goulding was at the top of the BBC's Sound of 2010 poll, which cited her as a cutting-edge performer with the potential to be great. In time, the poll proved to be prescient, as mere potential evolved into success. By 2013 Goulding had released two full-length studio albums that climbed to the top of the charts, performed at the White House and at the wedding of Prince William, and sold out concerts around the world. In a May 25, 2011, interview with *Glamour* magazine Goulding described her newfound fame to Jenn Selby, saying, "You have to change, you have to adapt, you have to be efficient, you have to do whatever you can to deal with the situation, which is not much sleep, missing meals, not being able to do things you want." She added, "If I became the biggest star in the world, that would be a bonus really. But it's not something I aspire to be. I'm quite happy really."

## CHILDHOOD AND EDUCATION

Elena Jane Goulding, known as Ellie, was born on December 30, 1986, in the Lyonshall parish near Hereford, England. Goulding was the second of three children born to Tracey and Arthur Goulding. Her parents divorced when she was five years old; Arthur disappeared from his children's lives, and Tracey eventually remarried. Goulding has been outspoken about her dislike of her stepfather and the difficulty of her childhood but has also noted that despite not being privileged, her upbringing made her ambitious and gave her the edge she is now known for.

Goulding's interest in music began at an early age. She began learning the clarinet at nine and taught herself how to play the guitar as a teenager, inspired by musicians such as Joni Mitchell. Goulding attended a local primary school before enrolling in Lady Hawkins' School in the town of Kingston, near the Welsh border. The proximity to Wales had an effect on young Goulding, and she has called the country her spiritual home. As a student at Lady Hawkins' School, she was interested in music and drama and performed in a stage version of *The Wizard of Oz*.

After leaving secondary school Goulding matriculated at the University of Kent, where she pursued a degree in drama. She spent two years studying at Kent before leaving to focus on her music. "I'd entered a university talent contest and was spotted by some people in the audience," she told the BBC (17 Nov. 2009). "People on the university's drama board were very supportive, telling me they couldn't stop a student who wanted to perform." She had been discovered by Jamie Lillywhite, who would go on to become her manager. With help from Lillywhite—as well as music manager Sarah Stennett—Goulding moved to London in 2007 to begin a career in music.

## EARLY CAREER

With Lillywhite as her manager and A&R (artists and repertoire), Goulding began to settle into life in London and write songs. While she had typically performed acoustically, Goulding began exploring electronic and dance music as she developed her sound. Using social media websites such as Myspace, she shared her music and started to acquire fans. During this period she was introduced to songwriter and producer Starsmith (Finlay Dow-Smith). Goulding and Starsmith immediately hit it off and began what would be a long-term artistic collaboration and friendship. With the help of Lillywhite and Starsmith, Goulding was signed to Polydor Records in July of 2009. "All the press we've had is through word of mouth and the love we've been getting on Myspace is amazing," she told Paul Ferguson for the *Herefordshire Times* (4 Sept. 2009). She added, "I feel really grateful to have so much attention because in the beginning I really did doubt myself, as I'm sure a lot of artists do."

Goulding's first single, "Under the Sheets," was produced by Starsmith and released on the independent label Neon Gold Records rather than the more commercial Polydor label. The song was released online in November 2009 and reached number fifty-three on the UK Singles Chart. Goulding was invited to perform "Under the Sheets" on the music television show *Later . . . with Jools Holland*, which raised her profile and boosted sales of her music. She subsequently released other songs digitally, including "Guns and Horses" and "Wish I Stayed," while working on her first full-length album.

In the meantime, the extended play (EP) *An Introduction to Ellie Goulding* was released digitally in December. The young singer closed out 2009 by supporting electropop singer Little Boots on her tour and winning a place at the top of the BBC's Sound of 2010, a list of rising stars compiled by critics and industry experts. In discussing Goulding as an emerging artist, the BBC called her a combination of singers Kate Bush, Björk, and Stevie Nicks.

## *LIGHTS*

Goulding's first full-length studio album, *Lights*, debuted on February 26, 2010. The culmination of several years of recording and collaborating with producers including Frankmusik (Vincent James Turner) and Starsmith, the album features Goulding's trademark sound, which combines her background in folk and indie music with her love of electropop and her strong soprano voice. Describing her music to *USA Today*'s Korina Lopez (20 May 2011), Goulding said, "I don't believe in rules or boundaries." She continued, "A beautiful song is a beautiful song. I often start writing a folk song, but then if it becomes electronica, then that's what the song was meant to be."

Much of *Lights* was recorded at Starsmith's house, where they shared ideas for the songs. When asked what her songs are about by BBC music reporter Ian Youngs (7 Jan. 2010), Goulding answered, "Everything—I sing often about love and heartbreak, not just my own but other peoples' stories. I'm fascinated by tales." Working with producer Frankmusik was also meaningful to Goulding; she credits his music for helping inspire her transition to electronic music. On working together, Goulding told Youngs, "It was like my songs had come alive. He made me realise that they could be something much more exciting and much more sparkly and pretty."

The album debuted on British charts at number one and, though dropping in the following week, remained a strong presence with the help of songs such as "Under the Sheets," the lead single, as well as "Starry Eyed" and "The Writer." Some critics praised Goulding's blend of vocals with synth and bass rhythms, with many terming her style "folktronica." Others were more wary of her style and called *Lights* middle-of-the-road and commercial. Most agreed, however, the Goulding showed a great deal of promise. On February 16, 2010, Goulding received the Critics' Choice BRIT Award, a prize given each year to a breakthrough performer; recent winners of the award include Adele and Florence and the Machine. "Well, this is mental," Goulding noted in her acceptance speech before going on to thank her label as well as Starsmith, Lillywhite, and Stennett.

In the spring and fall of 2010 Goulding began touring and performing at festivals to promote the album and also supported acts such as the band Passion Pit. That summer she also released two EPs: *Run into the Light*, which features remixed tracks, and *iTunes Festival: London 2010*, which features songs performed live. In November of 2010 she released *Bright Lights*, a reissue of *Lights* featuring seven new songs, including the single "Lights." The most successful of these new tracks was "Your Song," a cover of Elton John's classic 1970 ballad that reached number two on the UK Singles Chart. *Lights* was released in the United States in March 2011 and included three songs from the *Bright Lights* version.

## RISING STAR AND COMMERCIAL SUCCESS

With the singles from *Bright Lights* continuing to chart in the United Kingdom, Goulding spent 2011 performing and working on her second album. In February of that year she was nominated for the BRIT Awards' best British female and best British breakthrough act prizes but left empty handed. Later that month Goulding embarked on a tour of the United States and Canada, where *Lights* had recently been released. Overseas, Goulding performed at American festivals including Lollapalooza and Coachella and appeared on television programs such as *Jimmy Kimmel Live* and the *Ellen DeGeneres Show*. She was the musical guest for the seven hundredth episode of *Saturday Night Live*, which aired on May 7 and was hosted by Tina Fey. She also performed in Oslo, Norway, at the Nobel Peace Prize Concert on December 11, 2011, shortly after performing at the White House's tree lighting ceremony earlier in the month.

Perhaps most notably, Goulding was invited to perform at the wedding reception of Prince William and Catherine, the Duchess of Cambridge (Kate Middleton), on April 29, 2011. She was the only live singer at the reception and sang "Your Song" for the royal couple's first dance. She told *Vanity Fair*'s Lisa Robinson (Nov. 2012) that the wedding was "one of the best nights of [her] entire life." She continued, "[The royal couple] were very hospitable and welcoming to me, my band, and my crew. We must have done a good job, because everyone was very eager to meet us and hang with us."

Somehow finding time in her relentless schedule, Goulding also toured with pop singer Katy Perry and electronic musician Skrillex (Sonny Moore). Skrillex invited Goulding to sing on his *Bangarang* EP and join him on tours of North and South America. *Bangarang* won three Grammy Awards in 2013, including the awards for best dance recording and best dance/electronica album.

It was during this period that the single "Lights" slowly found success in the United States, over a year after its release. "Lights" jumped to number twenty-one on the Billboard Top 200 list on July 21, 2012, and reached number two in August. Remarkably, the single peaked two months before Goulding's next album, *Halcyon*, was set for release and one day before the new record's first single debuted. "To have a hit song in the US is extremely difficult for a British artist," she told Jason Lipshutz for *Billboard* (9 Aug. 2012). "I think it's kind of a triumph. I have to feel that in a positive way. I'm just hoping that it will kind of die down a bit so I can introduce my next song, my next adventure." On the timing of the song's much-delayed popularity, she told Lipshutz, "It's definitely weird and not necessarily a good thing, but I guess you can't moan about it."

### HALCYON

On October 5, 2012, Goulding released her second studio album with Polydor, *Halcyon*. Recorded in Herefordshire in collaboration with producers such as Madeon (Hugo Leclercq), Justin Parker, and Starsmith as well as performers Calvin Harris (Adam Wiles) and Tinie Tempah (Patrick Chukwuemeka Okogwu), the album features Goulding's signature synthesizers, pop hooks, and dance beats as well as the occasional folk-influenced ballad. "I've watched and learnt from DJs and remixers and paid way more attention to how I want my voice to sound. Before, as long as it was loud and in tune it was fine," she told Neil McCormick for the *Telegraph* (11 Dec. 2012). "I've discovered the difference made by various microphones and effects, so each track has a different vocal sound, my voice is woven into everything and it's above everything. I'm obsessed with this album."

Goulding's lyrics have been generalized as somewhat dark but honest, and she has acknowledged that several songs are about her conflicted feelings about the father who left her family. Discussing Arthur Goulding with McCormick, Goulding said, "It's been a constant area of confusion and fascination for me. I don't understand what happened. I don't know if he has heard this album, or my last album. I don't know if he knows anything about me. It has been the source of a lot of my writing. It's in everything I do. It's probably the reason why I do it." The singer has noted that the works of singer Patti Smith and writer Haruki Murakami as well as a recent breakup also influenced the mood of the album.

*Halcyon* debuted in the number-two spot on the UK Albums chart and at number nine on the US Billboard 200. The first single, "Anything Could Happen," reached number five on the UK Singles chart and, after ten weeks, reached number forty-seven on the US Billboard Hot 100 singles chart. "Figure 8" followed as the second single in December 2012. In addition to promoting album sales and downloads, Goulding's Halcyon Days tour sold out venues in Europe and North America. Goulding began 2013 with a full plate, already planning to tour with singer Bruno Mars when Halcyon Days ends in May.

## PERSONAL LIFE

Goulding and her recording and performing collaborator Skrillex dated in 2011 and 2012 but broke up around the time of *Halcyon*'s release. She has also been romantically linked to DJ Greg James, who inspired some of the songs on her sophomore album, and is currently dating British actor Jeremy Irvine.

When she is not performing, writing, or recording, Goulding continues to play the guitar and has added the drums to her repertoire. She also enjoys reading and has cited Murakami as a favorite author. In an interview with Zach Baron for the *New York Times* (12 Oct. 2012), Goulding noted that Murakami is an avid runner—a trait that the two share. Goulding runs every day and is occasionally joined by her fans, who have been known to wait outside hotels where the singer is staying to join her while she exercises. "I figured that the best way to interact with fans, that isn't weird or awkward, is by going out running with them," she told Baron, adding, "I don't like the idea of being better than anyone, so I liked that we were all in the same sweaty mess." She has run half marathons and plans to run a marathon. For the 2011 Run to the Beat half marathon in London, Goulding partnered the Nike sportswear company; she led group runs with fans and let people track her training progress online. Goulding and Nike also produced a short film, *Music Runs Ellie* (2011), which combines footage of her training and her performances.

Goulding has noted that she is still learning and growing, both musically and personally. She told Lipshutz, "The experience I've had and the people I've met over the past few years—I think I'm less naive and I'm less inexperienced." Going on, she added, "Just learning about sound, about mixing and about the difference between something sounding amazing and not very good. I would always love writing pop songs on my guitar because I love pop music, but also I've become really passionate about the way things end up, and the way things will end up on stage."

## SUGGESTED READING

Baron, Zach. "Ellie Goulding on Her New Album, 'Halcyon,' and More." *New York Times*. New York Times, 12 Oct. 2012. Web. 21 Feb. 2013.

Ferguson, Paul. "Herefordshire Singer, Ellie Goulding, Signs Recording Deal with Polydor." *Herefordshire Times*. Newsquest (Midlands South), 4 Sept. 2009. Web. 21 Feb. 2013.

Lipshutz, Jason. "Ellie Goulding on 'Lights' Explosion and Why Skrillex Isn't on Her New Album." *Billboard*. Billboard, 9 Aug. 2012. Web. 21 Feb. 2013.

McCormick, Neil. "Ellie Goulding Interview: 'I Do Have a Dark Side.'" *Telegraph*. Telegraph Media Group, 11 Dec. 2012. Web. 21 Feb. 2013.

Youngs, Ian. "BBC Sound of 2010: Ellie Goulding." *BBC*. BBC, 7 Jan. 2010. Web. 21 Feb. 2013.

## SELECTED WORKS

*An Introduction to Ellie Goulding* EP, 2009; Lights, 2010; *iTunes Festival: London 2010* EP, 2010; *Run into the Light* EP, 2010; *Halcyon*, 2012

—*Kehley Coviello*

# Brittney Griner

**Born:** October 18, 1990
**Occupation:** Basketball star and student at Baylor University

When six-feet-eight center Brittney Griner, the Associated Press 2012 player of the year for women's college basketball, slam dunked the basketball in a game against Jacksonville State during her freshman season at Baylor University, she became only the seventh female player to do so in a regular-season NCAA game—the first was University of West Virginia center Georgeann Wells, in 1984, though because no video or photographic evidence of her achievement surfaced until twenty-five years later, many refused to believe what those in attendance had seen. In 2006, Candace Parker, the six-feet-four University of Tennessee star who has gone on to become one of the premier players in the WNBA for the Los Angeles Sparks, was the first to slam the ball twice in a single game, doing so in the NCAA tournament, no less, against Army. On January 2, 2010, Griner joined Parker as the only players to dunk the ball twice in a game.

In a blow-out victory over Texas State, during which Baylor embarrassed its opponents 99–18, Griner exhibited her versatility, slamming the ball off a pass and then, later, posting up her defender on the right side of the basket, spinning away, and dunking the ball with one hand, in a move more reminiscent of her male counterparts in the NBA than her female colleagues at the collegiate and professional levels. The first slam dunk was visually electrifying—Baylor guard Kelli Griffin stole the ball, raced down the left side of the court, and passed the ball to guard Melissa Jones, who shoveled it to a trailing

Wirelmage

Griner in the middle of the lane; Griner leaped from the lower edge of the key and delivered an emphatic two-handed slam that caused the crowd to erupt in a mixture of amazement and incredulity. Though it came fourteen games into the season, for many, Griner's two-handed dunk represented a paradigm shift in women's basketball. After the game, Texas State coach Suzanne Fox said of Griner, "There's not anyone, especially in our Southland league, comparable to Brittney Griner. There's not, in very many places in the country (a player) comparable to her" (qtd. by Associated Press, 2 Jan. 2010).

### EARLY LIFE AND EDUCATION

Born in Houston, Texas, on October 18, 1990, Griner is the youngest of four siblings, the children of Raymond, a retired deputy sheriff, and Sandra, a cosmetologist. Given the heights of her parents—her father is the taller of the two at six feet one—and other family members, few could have guessed when Griner was born that she would eventually grow to six feet eight, though by high school, she was six feet three, towering over her classmates, as she does now over nearly every opponent she faces on the court.

Basketball was not a priority for Griner as a child; nonetheless, her height factored into the attention she received from coaches. She played organized soccer and volleyball, and is both a natural athlete and a risk taker. Discussing her adventurous proclivities, she told Elena Bergeron for *ESPN The Magazine*, "My mom caught me rollerblading holding on to the back of a car, and she almost had a fit. I was a climber—climb on trees, jump onto the house. . . . I was extreme" (29 Nov. 2012). Despite her height and athletic abilities, Griner did not seriously consider playing basketball until the coach at Nimitz High School, Debbie Jackson, approached her after

volleyball practice in the fall of 2005, her freshman year.

Griner joined the basketball team, first appearing on the junior varsity squad before being promoted to varsity, adapting quickly to her role as the team leader in a sport she was just learning. "She's like a sponge that just keeps absorbing," Jackson said, reflecting back to Griner's freshman season several years later (qtd. by Jeff Fedotin in RivalsHigh). By the following season, she was garnering national attention for both her size—she wore a men's size 16 tennis shoe when she was fifteen years old—and her burgeoning basketball abilities, and was already being recruited by top-tier university basketball programs. Griner had become a celebrity before she turned sixteen.

By her senior season in high school, Griner was considered by most to be the top female basketball prospect in the United States and, despite being recruited by women's basketball stalwarts University of Tennessee and University of Connecticut, committed to playing collegiately at nearby Baylor University in Waco, Texas. At this point, Griner's reputation preceded her, largely as the result of the millions of views that the videos of her slam dunks received on YouTube.

Griner averaged nearly two slam dunks a game during her high school career, and her abilities even caught the attention of NBA superstar Shaquille O'Neal, who visited with Griner in Houston as a member of the Phoenix Suns, before a game against the Rockets. Griner guided her team to the state championship game in her senior season, and despite the fact that the Nimitz High Cougars lost the game, Griner was already a local legend, based solely on her high school career. In fact, on May 7, 2009, Houston mayor Bill White commemorated Brittney Griner Day in the city.

### BUILDING A CHAMPION AT BAYLOR

In a prophetic statement during Griner's senior year at Nimitz High School, Coach Debbie Jackson told Fedotin that Griner "will change the face of women's basketball. . . . There's no doubt in my mind that she will be one of the top notch collegiate players, and it won't take long for her to do that." While many fans marveled at her dunking ability in her first season at Baylor, Griner proved that she possessed all-around basketball skills, with a repertoire that included hook and jump shots, passing and rebounding abilities, and, perhaps most important, a knack for shot-blocking that earned comparisons to all-time NBA greats such as Wilt Chamberlain and Kareem Abdul-Jabbar. In fact, shot blocking is the aspect of her game of which she has become most proud. "'Ooh, the blocks,'" she said to L. Jon Wertheim for *Sports Illustrated* (28 Mar. 2011) during her sophomore season, "I like those more than dunks. Blocks are the ultimate. Dunks are maybe more hype." In her first season, she led the league and set an NCAA single-season record with 223 blocks; furthermore, her 40 blocks in the NCAA tournament that year set another record, and she made 14 in one game, another record, in a second-round game against Georgetown. Baylor lost, 70–50, in the semi-final game against Connecticut, the eventual tournament champion. The team finished with a 27–10 record, and many predicted that Baylor would compete for the national championship in Griner's sophomore season.

Baylor improved its record to 34–3 the following season but lost in the quarterfinals of the NCAA tournament, a disappointment to many fans who believed Baylor could build on the previous season's finish. Nonetheless, Griner was Women's Basketball Coaches Association defensive player of the year, ranking first in blocks again, with 170. She also finished fourth in points-per-game with 23 and recorded a triple double (double digit totals in three statistical categories), giving her four during her two-year career. Most remarkably, Griner's triple doubles generally came in an unusual way: While most players who earn triple doubles do so in the categories of points, rebounds, and assists, Griner earned hers with blocks instead of assists, a type of triple double that is almost never tallied. Also in her sophomore year, she vastly improved her free-throw shooting, which had been one of her few weaknesses, elevating her percentage from .684 to .777, at one point making twenty-six consecutively.

## NATIONAL CHAMPIONSHIP AND PLAYER OF THE YEAR HONORS

Near the conclusion of her freshman season, Griner was suspended for two games, one by the NCAA and one by her coach Kim Mulky, for an incident in which she landed a right-handed punch that broke the nose of Texas Tech's Jordan Barncastle after the two players had maneuvered for position and Barncastle knocked Griner to the floor. The altercation belied Griner's usual affable demeanor and on-court self-control, and demonstrated that, though her talents were unquestioned, she had progress yet to make. The event can be credited to frustration stemming from Barncastle's antagonism, a playing style that seemed so foreign to Griner, a player whose talents often allowed her to dictate the pacing and circumstances of a contest. However, by her junior year, the bad taste from the episode had all but dissipated, and she had matured into the all-around player many scouts, coaches, and fans had always envisioned that she would become.

On the court Griner was joined by sophomore guard Odyssey Sims and junior forward Destiny Williams. Together, the three players helped comprise one of the most talented squads in women's college basketball. Expectations were high, but few understood at the time how magical 2011–12 would become. During the regular season, Baylor beat Tennessee, UCLA, Notre Dame, and Connecticut, all perennial contenders. Griner earned praised from around the league, as Baylor defeated one opponent after another. Oklahoma State's head coach Jim Littell, whose team Baylor crushed 71–44 in January, has said, "I don't think there's any limit on how good she is. When you have somebody like that, she's not only special but she makes everybody around her special" (qtd. in Griner42.com). As the season progressed and Baylor continued to manhandle opponents, Griner staked her claim to the moniker of greatest female college basketball player ever.

During her junior season, Griner improved her free-throw percentage to .800, averaged a career-high 23.2 points a game, and again led the league in blocked shots, with 206—in fact, she not only blocked more shots than any other individual player, she blocked more than any other *team*. Beginning in the quarterfinals of the NCAA tournament, Griner lead undefeated Baylor past a trifecta of elite college teams, besting Tennessee, Stanford, and, in the final game, top-ranked Notre Dame, the latter by the lopsided score of 80–61. The victory was the culmination of a 40–0 season, and Baylor became the first women's college basketball team to win forty games in one year. Griner was the player of the tournament, and, perhaps most important, the NCAA honored her with the Wade Trophy as the player of the year, an award she accepted with a wide grin, basking in the accomplishments of her junior season.

## PERSONAL LIFE, SENIOR SEASON, AND THE FUTURE

Hardworking on the court, Griner has always remained active off it, participating in many on-campus events and becoming a visible presence around Waco. "She just enjoys life," Coach Mulkey told Brice Cherry for the *Waco Tribune* (22 Dec. 2011). "She loves basketball and takes it serious, but there's a side of Brittney that's just loveable." Her favorite pastime is skateboarding, racing on her longboard between classes and even riding ramps and other obstacles, an activity for which she blames the broken arm she suffered during the summer of 2012, between her junior and senior years. Some wondered, however, if she would return for a senior season at all, given her team's championship and her on-court dominance. In fact, she was one of twenty-one players, and the only one in college, who were slated to be members of the US national basketball team at the 2012 Summer Olympics in London, England; she turned down the opportunity in order to take summer classes to progress toward graduation in spring 2013.

Addressing her return to Baylor, she stated, "I'm staying. I made a commitment. I said I was coming here, and I'm going to stay here until my time is up" (qtd. by ESPN.com News Services, 2012 Mar. 31). Her declaration was welcome news not only to her coach and teammates but also to her classmates, who have grown accustomed to her student involvement. She has donned face paint at Baylor football games, signs autographs and poses for photographs, and, on her first day at the school, introduced herself to everyone in all of her classes. "Brittney is a sweetheart," Mulky explains. "She just wants to be hugged and loved and hang around kids" (*Waco Tribune*, 22 Dec. 2011).

Fully recovered from her non-basketball-related injury, Griner began her senior season hoping to help her team repeat as champions and realizing that her postcollegiate career loomed, a career that fans are eager to follow. In all likelihood, she will be the first pick in the 2013 WNBA draft by the Phoenix Mercury. Despite her accolades and future prospects, she has remained philosophical about her place in the game: "Everyone tells me I'm changing the game, I'm a pioneer . . . But nah, I'm just adding on. Maybe I'm doing something . . . someone before me couldn't do. But I'm pretty sure that in the future there will be a post player who can do things I can't," she told Wertheim for *Sports Illustrated* (28 Mar. 2011).

In November 2012, Baylor suffered an early-season loss to Stanford at the Rainbow Wahine Classic in Hawaii, assuring that the team would not repeat its undefeated season of 2011–12, though Griner has continued to be the player for which no opposing team can adequately prepare. Elena Delle Donne, the University of Delaware's star player, discussing her admiration for Griner, illustrates what sets the latter apart: "You watch other teams, and their whole mindset is 'How can we shut down Brittney?' And going into games with that mindset, they still don't. It's awesome to watch something like that. She's changed women's basketball" (qtd. by Graham Hays in *ESPN: Outside the Lines*, 5 Dec. 2012). Fans and pundits alike have compared Griner to Lew Alcindor (who became known as Kareem Abdul-Jabbar), and this is perhaps the most apt analogy. While at UCLA (and later in the NBA), Alcindor redefined the center position, inventing his own shot (the sky hook) to circumvent the ban on the slam dunk (implemented primarily to curtail his dominance); though it is unlikely that any sort of rule change will occur because of Griner's abilities, her height and skill have altered the landscape of women's college basketball. Some players, including NBA center Dwight Howard, have stated openly that Griner could be the first woman to play in the NBA, and, while it is unlikely that she will make such a career move, the plausibility of the scenario demonstrates the level to which she transcends her competition.

## SUGGESTED READING

Anderson, Kelli. "Game Changer." *Sports Illustrated*. Time Warner, 21 Dec. 2009. Web. 10 Jan. 2013.

Cherry, Brice. "Off the Court with Brittney Griner." *Waco Tribune*. Wacotrib, 22 Dec. 2011. Web. 10 Jan. 2013.

Griner, Brittney. Interview by Elena Bergeron. "Laying Down Her Road: Baylor Center Brittney Griner's Game Is Going to Get Even Better." *ESPN The Magazine*. ESPN.com, 29 Nov. 2012. Web. 10 Jan. 2013.

Hawkins Stephen. "Baylor's Brittney Griner Focused on Senior Season." *The Grio*. NBC News, 15 Oct. 2012. Web. 10 Jan. 2013.

Hays, Graham. "Comfort Zone: Three to See." *ESPN: Outside the Lines*. ESPN.com, 5 Dec. 2012. Web. 10 Jan. 2013.

Justice, Richard. "Justice: Baylor Star Griner Is Difficult to Miss." *Houston Chronicle*. Hearst Communications, 28 Mar. 2011. Web. 10 Jan. 2013.

Krider, Dave. "Houston Rocket: Nimitz 6-6 Sophomore Brittney Griner Is Taking Off. *Sports Illustrated*. Time Warner, 16 Jan. 2007. Web. 10 Jan. 2013.

Wertheim, L. Jon. "Towering Power." *Sports Illustrated*. Time Warner, 28 Mar. 2011. Web. 10 Jan. 2013.

—*Christopher Rager*

# John Grotzinger

**Born:** ca. 1957
**Occupation:** Geologist

In an October 26, 2012, guest column for the *New York Times*, John Grotzinger, the chief scientist in charge of the Mars rover *Curiosity*, reported that based on the vehicle's analysis of smooth, flat rocks found on the surface, it was apparent that they had achieved their shape through the action of flowing water—to be precise, water that was "anywhere from ankle to hip-deep and flowed at about 3 feet per second." To be leading a team of hundreds of scientists examining a dry riverbed 180 million miles away on the surface of Mars, using the most cutting-edge scientific equipment available, borne on the most sophisticated vehicle ever created, is the culmination of about thirty years in the field for geologist Grotzinger, of the California Institute of Technology (CalTech). His globetrotting field studies have taken him from Siberia to Oman in search of insights into the conditions that allowed the earliest forms of life to evolve

Getty Images

on Earth. Now, he is applying those insights on Mars, both to discover if Mars once supported life, and to benefit the study of Earth as well. In an earlier *Times* column (3 Aug. 2012), he wrote, "The earliest history of Mars is better preserved than it is on Earth, and so we have a chance to gain insight into the development of our own planet through studying Mars."

## EARLY LIFE AND EDUCATION
John P. Grotzinger grew up in the small community of Huntingdon Valley, Pennsylvania, just north of Philadelphia, where he attended the William Penn Charter School. He received a bachelor of science degree in geoscience from Hobart College in upstate New York in 1979, a master's in geology from the University of Montana in 1981, and a PhD in geology from Virginia Polytechnic Institute in 1985. He was a postdoctoral fellow at Columbia University's Lamont-Doherty Earth Observatory from 1985 to 1986. Also in the 1980s, he was involved in regional mapping for the Geological Survey of Canada.

## MASSACHUSETTS INSTITUTE OF TECHNOLOGY
In 1988, Grotzinger joined the Department of Earth, Atmospheric, and Planetary Sciences at the Massachusetts Institute of Technology (MIT), where he taught and conducted research until 2005. Grotzinger's research interests have included sedimentology (the study of sediments and how they are deposited) and the related field of stratigraphy (the study of rock layers)—both key disciplines in studying the history of Earth. In particular, his work has focused on the interactions of Earth's surface environments and the forms of life on it, an interdisciplinary field

known as geobiology. His extensive studies of the chemical development of the early oceans and atmosphere and the environmental context of early animal evolution have thus contributed significantly to the field of paleontology.

An important strand of Grotzinger's career has had to do with trying to understand the Cambrian explosion—the relatively short period of time some 530 million years ago over which a huge number of complex species—the ancestors of all life on Earth today—suddenly evolved in the oceans after three billion years of life consisting of little more than single-celled organisms. In other words, Grotzinger is concerned with piecing together the environmental conditions under which life can evolve.

The issue of the Cambrian explosion—what preceded it and how it came about—has taken Grotzinger and his colleagues on expeditions to Canada, Siberia, Namibia, and Oman. Some of his richest research has come from rocks and fossils extracted from three miles beneath oil fields in Oman (Grotzinger has also worked with the oil and gas industry as a consultant on frontier oil exploration in the Middle East). By studying carbon isotopes in different rock layers, Grotzinger has worked to reconstruct the conditions of the primordial oceans that once covered Oman and other parts of Earth. He is among those who have contributed greatly to the idea that the Cambrian explosion was preceded by a rise in oxygen in Earth's oceans, a precondition for the evolution of multicellular organisms. "The presence of oxygen on Earth is the best indicator of life," Grotzinger told *Engineering & Science*, a CalTech publication, in 2007. "But it wasn't always that way. The history of oxygen begins about two and a half billion years ago and occurs in a series of steps."

Grotzinger's research indicates that originally, the ocean waters did not circulate the way they do today, and so any atmospheric oxygen that accumulated at the surface stayed near the surface, leaving the depths too oxygen-deprived to support complex life. "The ocean today is pretty well mixed and thus oxidized at all layers, but the ocean before the Cambrian period must have been very different," Grotzinger told *Engineering & Science*. Evidence shows that just before the Cambrian explosion, there was an uptick in oxygen in the deep ocean, indicating circulation between the layers, followed by a flourishing of marine life.

Because of his extensive experience with geobiology, sedimentology, and the conditions favorable for the evolution of life, Grotzinger was invited in 2003 to be part of the team of scientists working on NASA's Mars Exploration Rover (MER) mission, which landed two rovers, *Spirit* and *Opportunity*, on the red planet in early 2004. The MER mission is run by NASA's Jet Propulsion Laboratory in Pasadena, California. The Jet

Propulsion Laboratory is managed on NASA's behalf by nearby CalTech, and in 2005, Grotzinger accepted a faculty position in the school's Division of Geological and Planetary Sciences.

## MARS EXPLORATION ROVERS

NASA's Mars missions all follow an overarching strategy dubbed "Follow the Water." Although there are no signs of surface water or life on Mars, there have long been indications, in surface formations observed by orbiting spacecraft, that there was water there at some time in the past. This has raised the question whether there may have once been even simple microbial forms of life there. As Grotzinger states on his CalTech web page: "A long-standing goal of Mars environmental studies has been to understand the role of water throughout its geologic history. The presence of water is a strong indicator of potential habitability as well as of formerly different climatic conditions. Prior to studies by the Mars Exploration Rovers, most studies of water-related processes had been based on analysis of geomorphic attributes. However, we can now examine the record of past surface processes, including the role of water, through sedimentologic studies of the stratigraphic record of Mars."

Grotzinger's job on the MER team was long-term mission planning—in other words, getting the most bang for NASA's buck out of the mission. "I have to prevent day-to-day curiosity from interfering with the set of long-term scientific objectives," he told Denise Brehm for *MIT News* (28 Jan. 2004). For each rock the rover stops to analyze, he said, there might be a rock right next to it that looks interesting also. But, he said, "If you were to analyze it, that would take three to four days, and that might detract from achieving a longer-term goal. You have to weigh the tradeoffs of short- versus long-term objectives. Investing a lot of time in certain rocks may not lead to an understanding of water. So in leading that group, I'm constantly making sure that there aren't things off in the distance we can see that we should target to get information on the water issue."

*Spirit* and *Opportunity* left Earth in June and July, respectively, of 2003, and arrived safely on opposite sides of Mars in January 2004. By early March, Grotzinger was able to announce in a press conference several pieces of geologic evidence indicating the one-time presence of water, the most compelling being the presence of the mineral jarosite in a rock sample analyzed by *Opportunity*. "The only way to get that mineral is to precipitate it in the presence of water," Grotzinger told Brehm (3 Mar. 2004). Grotzinger and the rest of the team eventually concluded that large parts of Mars had once been covered with a flowing saltwater sea.

Working on a Mars mission meant working on Mars time—a bit of a challenge, said Grotzinger, because a Martian day, called a sol, is 39 minutes longer than an Earth day. "The first three weeks were not so easy," he told Brehm (28 Jan. 2004). "I was going to work at 10 o'clock at night and coming out at 10 o'clock in the morning. Then I'd eat breakfast and go to bed at noon. That schedule advances 39 minutes every day."

The two solar-powered MER vehicles were originally planned to be functional for ninety days, but ended up lasting far longer: *Spirit* was in operation until March 2010, and *Opportunity* is still active. Meanwhile, in 2007, Grotzinger joined another Mars project, the team operating the HiRISE camera aboard the Mars Reconnaissance Orbiter, circling the planet since 2006. The HiRISE (High Resolution Imaging Science Experiment) has enabled views of the surface of Mars at unprecedented resolution, allowing minute observation of geomorphic features over large areas.

## MARS SCIENCE LABORATORY

Unquestionably, Grotzinger's highest-profile role yet has been his appointment as project scientist (chief scientist) of NASA's latest mission to Mars, the Mars Science Laboratory, which landed the largest rover to date, the nearly 2,000-pound *Curiosity*, in the planet's Gale Crater on August 6, 2012 (August 5 Pacific time). This time, Grotzinger heads a team of more than four hundred scientists and is in charge of directing *Curiosity's* planned two-year mission. Shortly after the rover landed, he confided to Eric Hand for *Nature* (14 Aug. 2012) about the pressures of the job: "I feel the burden of two-and-a-half billion dollars," he said. "I feel the burden of the future of Mars exploration." In his column for the *New York Times* (3 Aug. 2012), he wrote: "Imagine buying a $2.5 billion car with a 10,000-page owner's manual; one that you don't just have to read but you must also write, because it's the first and only one that will ever be made."

*Curiosity* is exploring the interior of Gale Crater, moving toward the foothills of Aeolis Mons, the 18,000-foot mountain in the middle of the crater, dubbed more familiarly "Mount Sharp" by the NASA team. Once again, as with the *Spirit* and *Opportunity* mission, Grotzinger must strike a balance between careful examination of each study site and keeping the mission moving. Wrote Hand: "Colleagues say that, in his geological field studies on Earth, Grotzinger balances both tendencies, displaying an exuberant fitness that carries him across wide terrain even as he keeps an eye on the minutiae of mineralogy and texture."

Grotzinger's current job brings together both scientific and managerial skill, as Hand wrote: "Having an eye for detail and a gift for stratigraphic field work will certainly help Grotzinger to decode Mount Sharp and the millions of years of history that its layers represent. But he faces sociological challenges as well as scientific ones," meaning he does not have the final say over mission plans, but must work as part of a team. "As project scientist, he heads an executive committee that is made up of a representative from NASA headquarters and the principal investigators for the ten instruments." Raymond Arvidson, who worked with Grotzinger on the *Spirit* and *Opportunity* mission, told Hand he thinks Grotzinger is up to the job: "John's working the crowd. He really understands that in order to get buy-in, you have to establish trust."

Grotzinger has also learned something about being more in the media spotlight since heading the closely watched *Curiosity* mission. In November, he inadvertently set off widespread speculation with a comment about *Curiosity's* analysis of a Martian soil sample: "This data is going to be one for the history books. It's looking really good," he told Joe Palca of National Public Radio (20 Nov. 2012). After days of media speculation that the team might have found evidence of life, Grotzinger clarified that he had simply been referring to the amount and quality of data that the rover was sending back to Earth. "I think certainly what I've learned from this is that you have to be careful about what you say and even more careful about how you say it," Grotzinger told Kenneth Chang for the *New York Times* (3 Dec. 2012). "We're doing science at the speed of science. We live in a world that's sort of at the pace of Instagrams."

In his August 3, 2012, *Times* column, Grotzinger commented further on the significance of the geological study of Mars for the study of Earth's own development: "Everyone working on this mission is ready to take this trip back in geologic time to try to understand what secrets are preserved in Mount Sharp, what vistas we may reconstruct of times when Mars was so different from today, and if it ever had environments where microbes might have thrived. . . . The extraordinary perspective that *Curiosity* will provide may some day allow us to understand why a planet that initially may have not been so different from our own began its inexorable decline while ours blossomed and flourished. And in doing so it tells us something about ourselves and where our deepest roots may lie."

## SUGGESTED READING

Brehm, Denise. "It's Time to Rock and Rove for MIT's Grotzinger." *MIT News Office*. MIT, 28 Jan. 2004. Web. 21 Feb. 2013.

"Just Breathe." *Engineering & Science* 70.1 (2007): 4–5. Print.

Goho, Alexandra M. "Evolution's Missing Link." *MIT Technology Review*. MIT, 1 Mar. 2003. Web. 21 Feb. 2013.

Grotzinger, John. "Boldly Opening a New Window onto Mars." *New York Times*. New York Times Co., 3 Aug. 2012. Web. 21 Feb. 2013.

Hand, Eric. "Mars Scientists Await Feast of Data." *Nature*. Nature, 14 Aug. 2012. Web. 21 Feb. 2013.

—*Adam Groff*

---

# Gabrielle Hamilton

**Occupation:** Chef and author

James Beard award–winning chef and restaurant owner Gabrielle Hamilton did not always have high culinary aspirations though she began working in restaurants at the age of twelve. "This is kind of surreal because I still really identify as a dishwasher," she told a crowd in Minneapolis, as quoted by Kara Buckner for *City Pages* (1 Feb. 2012). Hamilton, who lives in New York City, was in the city promoting her memoir *Blood, Bones and Butter: The Inadvertent Education of a Reluctant Chef* (2011). The book debuted at number two on the New York Times Best Sellers list in 2011. In a world populated by celebrity chefs and Food Network stars, Hamilton is an anomaly. Before the publication of her book, her single national claim to fame was beating star chef Bobby Flay on the competitive *Iron Chef* television show in 2008. (Hamilton loves to tell the story about her subsequent screen test, an audition with the network to become an Iron Chef herself. She was asked why she wanted to be the next Iron Chef and, after a moment's thought, she replied that she did not really know, took off her microphone and left the set.)

But in addition to owning a small bistro in New York City's East Village called Prune, Hamilton has a master's degree in fiction writing from the University of Michigan. From this angle, Hamilton's book is less about celebrity—she is not interested in expanding her brand, if she has one, she says, or even in opening a second restaurant in New York—and more an iteration of the dual pursuits of her life. After struggling for years to choose one path or the other, Hamilton has settled into the hectic life of a chef and writer. Her writing has been published in the *New York Times*, the *New Yorker*, *GQ*, *Saveur*, *Bon Appetit*, and *Food & Wine*; her essays have been anthologized in seven editions of the annual collection *Best Food Writing*. Her kitchen accolades are just as impressive: in 2011, Hamilton was named best chef in New York City by the James Beard Foundation.

Hamilton says that both professions, while demanding, are necessary to the balance of her life. She cannot choose one she likes best, but the self-described "anti-foodie" told Buckner: "I'm a good cook, and I like to write. But I guess I value writing more than cooking. I have never

WireImage

whole lamb and chill chugs of wine and bottles of root beer in the nearby river. The night before the big day, they would sleep beside the fire pit in the backyard.

But the proverbial party ended abruptly when Hamilton was eleven and her parents divorced. "I felt as if I had fallen asleep by the lamb pit one night," she writes in her article "The Lamb Roast" in the *New Yorker* (17 Jan. 2011), "and woken up the next morning to the debris of a brilliant party, a bare cupboard, and an empty house."

Her description of the event is not entirely metaphorical. She writes that one summer, as the divorce was being finalized, her parents left her and her seventeen-year-old brother Simon to fend for themselves at the mill for weeks at a time. (Her mother had moved to Vermont. Her father was trying to find work in New York.) In her anguish, Hamilton rebelled. She experimented with cocaine, shoplifted, ran with an older crowd—much older than her thirteen years—and, perhaps incongruously beside her reckless ways, lied about her age to work as a dishwasher in a restaurant. As if something out of fiction, the restaurant was called Mother's.

## MOVE TO NEW YORK

At sixteen, Hamilton graduated early from an alternative high school called Solebury School in Solebury, Pennsylvania, and moved to the Hell's Kitchen neighborhood of New York City with her sister. She continued to work in restaurants, waiting tables and dishwashing, but she also continued her teenage fling with crime. At one point she stole a car and, with the help of her well-connected brother Todd, she managed to escape jail time, though she was advised to leave the state. She enrolled at Hampshire College for a time, and at nineteen, she traveled to Europe.

With only $1,200 to her name, Hamilton made her way across the continent. The experience had a profound influence on her views on food and eating. Due to her lack of funds, she depended on the generosity of people she did not know. The depth of her gratitude for their hospitality, she has said, has influenced the way she views customers in her own restaurant. Combined with the hunger she often felt while traveling—and in New York, where she was so poor that she used to steal ketchup packets from McDonald's—Hamilton also found new meaning in the term "satisfying meal." Regarding Prune, Hamilton told Lauren Salkeld for *Epicurious* in 2011: "When I opened the restaurant I wanted to bring that into it—that food you want when you're hungry. I don't eat for entertainment, and I don't eat to have my mind blown. I still eat for total pleasure and satisfaction on a gustatory level, so I wanted a restaurant that would really satisfy you when you arrived with appetite. You know, delicious food that you want to actually eat again and again."

been moved to tears by a meal, but I have definitely been moved by words on a page. Those moments when you're alone with a book that alters your freaking life and makes you feel accompanied. Those are the most powerful moments for me."

## EARLY LIFE

Hamilton was born in New Hope, Pennsylvania, a small town located on the bank of the Delaware River. She is the youngest of five children; her siblings include a sister, Melissa, and brothers, Simon, Todd, and Jeffrey. Her mother, Madeleine Artieres, is from France and a former ballet dancer with the Metropolitan Opera. Her father, Jim Hamilton, was a scenic designer who worked on sets for the Ringling Bros. and Barnum & Bailey Circus and on Broadway. He currently owns a restaurant himself called Hamilton's Grill Room in Lambertville, New Jersey.

In her memoir, Hamilton refracts the most important moments of her life through the prism of food. She began to look at the world in this way while growing up with bohemian parents in a converted silk mill in New Hope. In the opening chapter of her book, Hamilton describes her family's annual lamb roast. Between her mother's love of food and cooking—Hamilton credits Artieres with teaching her how to eat—and her father's ability to set a scene, the Hamiltons had reputations as generous hosts who threw fantastic parties. Though the lamb roast was a simple affair by Hamilton standards, the guest list often contained as many as two hundred names. Hamilton and her siblings would help prepare the

Hamilton returned to New York and worked catering jobs through her twenties, which she describes in stomach-turning detail in her memoir. When she turned thirty she realized that she had never actually chosen a life in the food business, and that bothered her. She told Buckner: "I started to realize that I was about to live the wrong life, and I didn't feel like I'd ever made a choice. . . . And it didn't seem like there was much more time left to get a whole new plan going, so I pulled the car off the side of the road, so to speak, and applied to graduate school." Hamilton was accepted into the graduate program in fiction writing at the University of Michigan and moved to Ann Arbor in 1995.

## UNIVERSITY OF MICHIGAN

Though Hamilton had come to Ann Arbor to escape her life in the kitchen, she immediately took a part-time job cooking to support herself. She worked for a catering company, just as she had in New York, but this experience was different. She met a woman named Misty Callies, "the tired, taciturn, slightly beaten chef" of the no-frills catering enterprise, Hamilton wrote in an essay for *Food & Wine* (July 2005). Callies seemed deflated at work but, as Hamilton quickly found out, flourished at home at her farmhouse where she made simple, rustic dishes that transported Hamilton back to the cooking of her childhood. "At Misty's house," she wrote, "and by her example, I relearned how to cook for myself, purely for pleasure and not for commercial consideration."

Hamilton was less enchanted by her classmates in the writing program, and found herself looking forward to the end of class and her return to the kitchen. In 1996, Callies left the catering company to open a restaurant called Zanzibar. Hamilton went with her. The endeavor did not go as Callies has planned, but Hamilton saw firsthand the daily struggles and triumphs of running a restaurant.

Hamilton received her MFA in 1999 and returned to New York City. She began writing a novel, but felt stalled. She was living in the East Village and spending a fair amount of time in her apartment staring at a blank page—the other half of the time, of course, she was working as an interim chef at a catering company.

## PRUNE

One day in New York, a neighbor showed her an abandoned storefront in their neighborhood. According to Hamilton, who tells the story in visceral detail in her memoir, the former bistro had gone bankrupt two years before. "It looked like the restaurant had desperately done business right up until 12:01 a.m., when the city marshal came and padlocked the place, leaving the coolers full of lamb shanks, dairy, and crème brûlées," she describes in *Blood, Bones and Butter*. There were still dirty dishes in the sink and cigarette butts in the ashtray. Despite the years of rot and infestation Hamilton was charmed. It was as if she had seen her future in the ruins. She continues: "I knew exactly what and how to cook in that kind of space, I knew exactly what kind of fork we should have, I knew right away how the menu should read and how it would look handwritten, and I knew immediately, even, what to call it."

The space on First Avenue became Prune—an American bistro named for Hamilton's childhood nickname. (According to her father, when she did not like something, she puckered her face like a prune.) Prune opened in October 1999. Hamilton hoped it would be an unpretentious neighborhood joint—a place where East Villagers would like to eat. But word of her simple and satisfying entrees spread. Dishes like the fried sweetbreads (like her mom used to make them) and whole grilled branzino fish began attracting other chefs looking for a good meal after their shift. "The food is not restauranty," Hamilton explained to Susan Sprague for the *Times of Trenton* (3 Apr. 2011).

Prune has garnered a number of awards over the years and has been featured on a slew of "Best of" lists—particularly for its superior weekend brunch. The brunch offerings, which include a decadent Monte Cristo, an inspired "Youth Hostel" breakfast spread, and no less than twelve variations on the Bloody Mary, are well known in the city. When the restaurant critic Frank Bruni dined there one weekend, he spotted Chelsea Clinton hovering over a pancake in the corner. The food continues to get consistently high marks from critics and patrons, though a common complaint is the restaurant's size. Hamilton squeezes thirty seats into the space, which according to Bruni, might be a few too many. He likened the effect—and the physical dining experience at Prune—to a game of Twister. But in many respects, the restaurant is as quirky as its chef. In a profile of Hamilton, *New York Times* writer Jeff Gordinier quoted Suzanne Goin (1 Mar. 2011), a chef and restaurateur from Los Angeles: "What I love about Prune is how absolutely personal it is. It is the personification of Gabrielle—Gabrielle between four walls, from the décor to the servers to the food itself."

## *BLOOD, BONES AND BUTTER*

Prune's growing popularity—even after over a decade of service—has lent her some national cachet. She was nominated for best chef in New York City by the James Beard Foundation in 2009 and 2010, and won the category in 2011.

Hamilton believed that Prune would be the end of her writing career. She has said that she saw it as the product of her final choice between her two competing paths. But just six weeks after the restaurant opened, she wrote her first essay for the *New Yorker*. She continues to write for publications like the *New York Times*, to which she has contributed numerous essays and recipes. In 2011, she published a memoir called *Blood, Bones and Butter: The Inadvertent Education of a Reluctant Chef*. Before the book's release it was generating the kind of buzz most writers only dream about. Anthony Bourdain, the famously outspoken (and critical) chef and writer, declared in his review that he was "choked with envy" over Hamilton's feat. Italian chef Mario Batali took his praise even further, writing that after reading her memoir, he wanted to burn his own books and apply for a job as a dishwasher at Prune so that he might learn "at the feet of my new queen." Bourdain and Batali were perhaps a bit hyperbolic in their endorsements, but the heart of their response to the book is important. It is notable that *New York Times* book critic Michiko Kakutani compared Hamilton's writing to Mary Karr and Andre Aciman. Hamilton had effectively upped the ante on the ubiquitous and obligatory chef memoir; she made it literary.

"While her roasted marrowbones may be great, her prose is virtuoso," Jennifer Reese wrote in her review for NPR (2 Mar. 2011). "Hamilton moves easily from rich metaphor to dark humor, from dreamy abstraction to the vivid and precise descriptions of anything from a maggot-infested rat to a plate of beautiful ravioli." By all accounts, intoxicating images are at the book's core. It follows the story of Hamilton's life, yet many reviewers point to odd gaps in her narrative. Her estrangement from her mother and her sexuality—Hamilton dated women all her life until, after the opening of Prune, she abruptly married and began a family with a man—are presented without context or satisfying explanation. And she has won both praise and criticism for her honest and often brutal portraits of her family members. *Blood, Bones and Butter* won the James Beard Foundation's award for Writing and Literature in 2012.

## PERSONAL LIFE

Hamilton was married to an Italian doctor named Michele Fuortes for over a decade. The last days of their marriage are captured in her memoir. The two are finalizing their divorce. She has written extensively about Fuortes's mother, Alda, whom the couple would visit at her summer home in Apulia, Italy. The elderly woman did not speak English, and the two women bonded through a mutual appreciation of cooking and food. Hamilton lives in a small Manhattan apartment with her two young sons, Marco and Leone.

## SUGGESTED READING

Buckner, Kara. "Gabrielle Hamilton tells the stories behind the stories of *Blood, Bones and Butter*." *City Pages* (Minneapolis). City Pages, 1–2 Feb. 2012. Web. 6 Mar. 2013.

Gordinier, Jeff. "A Chef's Life, With Scars and All." *New York Times*. New York Times Co., 1 Mar. 2011. Web. 5 Mar. 2013.

Hamilton, Gabrielle. "A Mentor Named Misty." *Food & Wine*. American Express Publishing, 1 July 2005. Web. 6 Mar. 2013.

Reese, Jennifer. "Take 'Blood, Bones & Butter,' Add Poignancy and Wit." *NPR*. NPR, 2 Mar. 2011. Web. 8 Mar. 2013.

Salkeld, Lauren. "A Q&A with Chef Gabrielle Hamilton." *Epicurious*. Condé Nast, 2011. Web. 6 Mar. 2013.

Sprague, Susan. "With a successful restaurant and best-selling memoir, Gabrielle Hamilton carries on legacy begun in Lambertville." *Times of Trenton*. New Jersey On-Line, 3 Apr. 2011. Web. 8 Mar. 2013.

—*Molly Hagan*

# Jon Hamm

**Born:** March 10, 1971
**Occupation:** Actor

For some viewers of the AMC drama *Mad Men*, it can be difficult to separate actor Jon Hamm from his most well-known character, Don Draper. As a struggling actor who seemed mature beyond his years at a time when many actors his age were still playing high school students, Hamm spent his twenties and early thirties working in Los Angeles restaurants and auditioning for small parts in television shows, with little success. Though he eventually earned recurring roles in several shows and small parts in such films as *Kissing Jessica Stein* (2001) and *We Were Soldiers* (2002), he remained largely unknown prior to securing the lead role in *Mad Men*. Hamm's portrayal of the stoic yet troubled Draper made him a household name and garnered him Emmy nominations, and he became known as much for the character's iconic suits and charismatic persona as for his own personality and acting ability.

Indeed, Hamm and Draper share some similarities; both are midwesterners who lost their parents early in life, and Hamm has acknowledged that his background in some ways influences his performance. But the similarities end there. Unlike Draper, Hamm is more comfortable in jeans and a baseball cap than a suit, and he eschews the smoking and womanizing for which the character is known (though he does, like Draper, enjoy a good bourbon). He also has a comedic side, which he has gleefully displayed in television guest appearances on *Saturday Night Live* (*SNL*) and *30 Rock* and

WireImage

in films such as *Bridesmaids* (2011) and *Friends with Kids* (2011). "I love being around comedy people and listening and laughing," Hamm told Eric Spitznagel for *Playboy* (13 Mar. 2012). "It's therapeutic."

## EARLY LIFE AND EDUCATION
Jonathan Daniel Hamm was born on March 10, 1971, in Saint Louis, Missouri. His mother, Deborah, worked as a secretary, while his father, Daniel, worked in the automobile and advertising businesses after the decline of his family's trucking company. Hamm's parents divorced when he was two. Following the divorce, Hamm lived primarily with his mother, whom he credits with giving him the confidence to succeed in both his life and his career. "She impressed upon me that achievement is something to be lauded and to work toward," Hamm told *Redbook* (May 2012). "She told me that I could accomplish anything I wanted, and that really stuck with me."

When Hamm was ten, his mother died of cancer. Hamm moved in with his father and grandmother, with whom he had a somewhat troubled relationship. A trust left to him by his mother enabled him to attend the John Burroughs School, a private preparatory school in Saint Louis. While in high school, Hamm played sports and was active in the school's theater program, building upon an interest in acting that had begun when he was cast as Winnie the Pooh in a first-grade play. A schoolmate introduced Hamm to future actor Paul Rudd, who was then a student at the University of Kansas. The two would remain close friends and later appear together in various films and comedy specials.

Following graduation Hamm enrolled in the University of Texas to study English. However, he left the university in 1991 after his father died of complications related to diabetes. Hamm struggled with depression during that period but was determined to continue his education. "I was in bad shape," he told Polly Vernon for the *Sydney Morning Herald* (9 Oct. 2011). "I knew I had to get back in school and back in some kind of structured environment."

Choosing to stay in his home state, Hamm enrolled in the University of Missouri to complete his degree. Although Hamm majored in English, he soon developed a name for himself in the university's theater department, ultimately performing in nearly fifteen plays and earning a theater scholarship. He graduated from the University of Missouri with a bachelor's degree in 1993.

## EARLY CAREER
After graduating, Hamm taught drama at the John Burroughs School for a year before deciding that he needed to pursue acting. He explained to Noel Murray for the *A.V. Club* (11 Aug. 2009), "I had a little bit of money saved, and my car sort of ran, so I was like, 'You know what, I'm gonna try it before I get any older and I lose any momentum I have.'" In late 1995 Hamm loaded everything he owned into his car and drove from Saint Louis to Los Angeles, where he stayed with relatives until moving into a house in the neighborhood of Silver Lake with a number of other aspiring actors. He found an agent relatively quickly, but Hamm's mature appearance made it difficult for him to get work. "It was just bad timing," he told Spitznagel for *Playboy* (13 Mar. 2012). "I was out of sync with what the market was looking for."

For several years Hamm struggled to find acting jobs and, like many actors before him, worked as a waiter and bartender to pay the bills. His agent eventually dropped him, and the car in which he had driven to Los Angeles was impounded by the city after amassing parking tickets Hamm could not pay. However, Hamm remained optimistic. "You don't chuck it all in and pitch a car westward and go to LA without thinking some day, down the line, ideally, it'll work out positively," he told Vernon.

By the late 1990s Hamm began to be cast in single-episode roles in television shows such as *Ally McBeal*. In 2000 he made his first appearance in the NBC drama *Providence*. Although his character was originally intended to appear in only one episode, the role became a recurring one, and Hamm ultimately returned for seventeen more episodes. He took on another recurring role in 2002, this time in the Lifetime police drama *The Division*. Hamm went on to appear in several episodes of the shows *What about Brian* and *The Unit* and guest star in *CSI: Miami* and *Numb3rs*.

Hamm also obtained a few film roles, beginning with a small part in 2000's *Space Cowboys*, directed by Clint Eastwood. In the independent romantic comedy *Kissing Jessica Stein*, Hamm played a role he had originated in the Off-Broadway run of the play *Lipschtick*, on which the film was based. Both the play and its film adaptation were cowritten by Hamm's long-time girlfriend, Jennifer Westfeldt, who was also its star. Hamm went on to appear in the 2002 war film *We Were Soldiers* and Westfeldt's *Ira & Abby* in 2006.

## MAD MEN

Hamm's big break came when he auditioned for the lead role of Don Draper in *Mad Men*, a television drama set in a 1960s advertising agency. Although he did not expect to be cast—"I thought they'd go with one of the five guys who look like me but are movie stars," he noted in the magazine *Interview* (Aug. 2008)— his audition impressed the show's creator, Matthew Weiner. "He looked like an old-fashioned leading man, like William Holden or Gregory Peck," Weiner told Brett Martin for *GQ* (Dec. 2008). "But he wasn't just a football player in a suit. You could see that he was intelligent. He was vulnerable. He was an adult." After seeing Hamm audition, Weiner reportedly told the casting director, "That man was not raised by his parents." As Weiner discerned early on, that element of Hamm's past would serve to create an emotional connection between the actor and the character, who was similarly orphaned at a young age.

*Mad Men* premiered on the cable network AMC in July of 2007. The first original scripted series developed by the network, which was previously known for airing classic films, *Mad Men* has received significant critical acclaim over the course of its five seasons. Many critics have focused on Hamm's performance as the mysterious Draper, whose veneer of charismatic ultramasculinity hides a secret past and a deeply troubled psyche. "Don is an incredibly damaged human being, had a terrible childhood," Hamm told *Time* magazine (2 Aug. 2010). "What he has accomplished, he has accomplished through the strength of his own will and his own ambition. I think that's what resonates throughout the show. It's a constant striving to be better."

Hamm's portrayal of the character has been informed by aspects of his own life, from the deaths of his parents to his relationship with and understanding of his father. "I remember the first time I was in costume: I was sitting in my dressing room, running lines in the mirror, and I thought: Oh, my God! I look just like my father," he told Martin. "Here's this guy that looks like he's got the whole package, but there's nothing inside but sadness." In recognition of his performance as Draper, Hamm has been awarded the Golden Globe for best performance by an actor in a dramatic television series, in addition to being nominated for several Emmy Awards. The show as a whole has won numerous awards, including four Emmy Awards for outstanding drama series and two Golden Globe awards for best drama.

## BEYOND DON DRAPER

In addition to proving that basic cable networks could produce compelling, successful dramas and rekindling interest in the aesthetic of the early 1960s, the success of *Mad Men* had a significant effect on the careers of its cast members, most notably Hamm. Once unable to find work, Hamm, now greatly in demand, has taken the opportunity to expand his repertoire, appearing in the disaster movie *The Day the Earth Stood Still* (2008) and *Howl* (2010), a historical film based on the events surrounding the publication of poet Allen Ginsberg's controversial work.

Hamm has noted that he works hard to avoid one of the pitfalls of playing an iconic character such as Draper: typecasting. "After the first and second seasons of *Mad Men* I got sent about forty scripts that were all set in the sixties, or had me playing advertising guys," he told Xan Brooks for the *Guardian* (9 Sept. 2010). Consequently Hamm has sought out films that allow him to play characters who are, like his FBI agent character in the 2010 crime drama *The Town*, "opposite to Don Draper in terms of [their] moral certainty." He added to *Time*, "It may be hard for other people . . . to see me and not see Don. But the challenge of being an actor is being able to create another persona and portray that accurately."

## WALKING ON THE FUNNY SIDE

Hamm's comedic roles may be particularly surprising to viewers familiar only with Hamm's serious portrayal of Draper. He was twice nominated for the Emmy Award for outstanding guest actor in a comedy series for his recurring role as Drew Baird, the absurdly handsome love interest of protagonist Liz Lemon in the NBC comedy *30 Rock*, and he has also appeared on *Saturday Night Live* as both a host and a special guest. He went on to appear in the Academy Award–nominated comedy film *Bridesmaids*, which featured several *SNL* alumni, and played alongside Westfeldt in *Friends with Kids* (2011), which she wrote and directed.

In response to fans and critics who have asked whether he prefers comedic or dramatic roles, Hamm has explained that he enjoys both and does not feel that he has to choose one or the other. "They're both fun. Believe it or not, it is actually fun to do the hard, emotional, dramatic stuff," he told *Time*. "It's part of why I like being an actor." Hamm has also noted that he especially enjoys British comedy, citing comedians such as

Sacha Baron Cohen and Eddie Izzard as particular favorites. "I'm a little bit of a comedy nerd," he told Stephen Armstrong for the *Sunday Times* (2 Dec. 2012).

Hamm leapt at the opportunity to produce and costar in the 2012 miniseries *A Young Doctor's Notebook*, a British dark comedy in which Hamm plays the older self of a young doctor played by *Harry Potter* star Daniel Radcliffe. "I get a lot of scripts, and you have to be really careful about what you pick," he explained to Armstrong. "But *SNL*, *30 Rock*, this [*A Young Doctor's Notebook*]? You take that opportunity as soon as it comes up."

## FUTURE PLANS

Although AMC had not yet announced a premiere date for the sixth season of *Mad Men* by the end of 2012, the season, which began filming earlier that year, is expected to air sometime in 2013. According to AMC's *Mad Men* blog, the season will include at least one episode directed by Hamm, who previously directed the fifth-season episode "Tea Leaves." Hamm signed a three-year contract with AMC in mid-2011, ensuring that Draper will remain part of the show for the foreseeable future.

In addition to his commitment to *Mad Men*, Hamm has signed on to appear in several upcoming films, including the HBO comedy *Clear History* and the sports drama *Million Dollar Arm*. Although Hamm's work in film has led some to ask whether he plans to leave television behind after *Mad Men* ends, he rejects the idea that he must choose between the two mediums. "I would happily work in television my whole life," Hamm told Maureen Ryan for the *Huffington Post* (13 Mar. 2012). "I think the distinction of small-screen stars and big-screen stars is gone. I've had an awesome time working on movies. . . . It's a completely different thing and I love it, but it's not fundamentally different from television." He added to Spitznagel for *Playboy* (13 Mar. 2012), "All I care about is working with people I enjoy being around."

## PERSONAL LIFE

Hamm has been in a relationship with actor, writer, and producer Westfeldt since 1998. The two own the production company Points West Pictures, which coproduced *Friends with Kids*. Hamm and Westfeldt live in the Los Feliz neighborhood of Los Angeles with their dog, Cora. They also own a home on New York's Upper West Side.

A sports lover, Hamm is a dedicated fan of the Saint Louis Cardinals and enjoys playing golf and tennis. He is also an avid reader and particularly enjoys novels by modern writers such as Michael Chabon and Jonathan Franzen as well as nonfiction works about scientific topics. "Reading isn't as easy to do as turning on a

television or getting on the Internet or twittering or whatever else you have to do in this modern society," he told Mamie Healey for *O* magazine (Aug. 2009), "but it's way more rewarding."

## SUGGESTED READING

Hamm, Jon. "Jon Hamm: The Playboy Interview." Interview by Eric Spitznagel. *Playboy*. Playboy, 13 Mar. 2012. Web. 9 Jan. 2013.

Handy, Bruce. "Don and Betty's Paradise Lost." *Vanity Fair* Sept. 2009: 268–339. Print.

Konigsberg, Eric. "A Fine Madness." *Rolling Stone* 16 Sept. 2010: 43–49. Print.

Martin, Brett. "Breakout: Jon Hamm" *GQ*. Condé Nast, Dec. 2008. Web. 9 Jan. 2013.

Stein, Joel. "Hard Sell." *Best Life* Sept. 2008: 138–61. Print.

—*Joy Crelin*

# Bryce Harper

**Born:** October 16, 1992
**Occupation:** Baseball player with the Washington Nationals

"I want to be the best," Bryce Harper told Bob Parasiliti for the *Herald-Mail* (4 Apr. 2011). "I want to be perfect in every aspect of the game." From amateur baseball to Major League Baseball (MLB), Harper has excelled at every level of the sport he has played, often besting much older and more experienced competition. His prodigious talent earned him the cover of *Sports Illustrated* in 2009, with a headline reading "Baseball's Chosen One." The excitement surrounding Harper during his teenage years raised questions about whether he would be able to live up to the hype. Since making his major league debut, Harper has defied his detractors. In 2012, he earned the National League (NL) Rookie of the Year Award while helping lead the Washington Nationals to their first postseason appearance since 1933.

## EARLY LIFE AND EDUCATION

The youngest of three children, Bryce Aron Max Harper was born on October 16, 1992, to Sheri (Brooks) and Ron Harper in Las Vegas, Nevada. He also has two older siblings, Caroline and Bryan. Harper, whose mother works as a paralegal and whose father is a retired ironworker, first developed an interest in baseball at age three, when he began playing little league. When he was nine years old, Harper began being invited to play for various travel teams. In organized youth baseball, travel teams compete in tournaments featuring the best young players in the country. Between the ages of nine and fifteen, Harper competed in games nationwide, with

Getty Images

travel teams covering the cost of flights, hotels, and rental vehicles. Commenting on the experience of being a player for hire at such a young age, Harper told Tom Verducci for *Sports Illustrated* (8 June 2009), "I would not take anything back. Everything about it was great. I got to go places, meet people, play baseball against older kids and better competition. I had a great time." Harper's father accompanied him to as many as 130 games a year—the equivalent of three weekends every month. During his amateur career, Harper played on teams based in California, Arizona, Oklahoma, and Nevada.

## ASCENT THROUGH THE TRAVEL BALL RANKS

As a member of the San Diego Stars' baseball academy, Harper reached the final game of the 2003 National American Tournament of Champions (NATC), held at Cooperstown Dreams Park in Milford, New York. The NATC is a national invitational youth baseball tournament comprised of two divisions: ten-and-under and twelve-and-under. During his performance in the 2003 NATC, Harper set a Cooperstown Dreams Park record by hitting ten home runs and commanded the championship game from the pitcher's mound, allowing just two hits while earning eleven strikeouts. He also had two hits, a run batted in (RBI), and a run scored, helping his ten-and-under squad win the game by a score of 7–1.

In 2004, Harper joined the Southern California Redwings of the United States Specialty Sports Association (USSSA). The USSSA organizes national baseball tournaments in various

age groups. Over the course of several years, Harper played for a variety of teams and competed in year-round tournaments as a USSSA player. As he grew older and more experienced, he began demonstrating his power hitting ability. During a 2004 USSSA tournament in Alabama, Harper had twelve hits in twelve at-bats, including eleven home runs.

## AT LAS VEGAS HIGH SCHOOL

In 2007, Harper enrolled at Las Vegas High School, where he assumed catching duties for the team's varsity pitching staff, which included his older brother Bryan, then a senior. During their first and only season together (2007–8), the brothers helped the Las Vegas High School Wildcats amass a record thirty-one victories while finishing fourth place in statewide rankings. Harper ended his freshman season with a .599 batting average, eleven home runs, sixty-seven RBIs, and thirty-six stolen bases in thirty-eight games. During the season, Harper hit a home run that became infamous in Las Vegas high school baseball lore. Traveling an estimated 570 feet, the ball rocketed over the outfield fence, some trees, past a sidewalk, over five lanes of traffic on South Hollywood Boulevard, and over another sidewalk before finally coming to rest in some vacant scrubland.

Harper had an equally successful sophomore season. In addition to compiling a .626 batting average, he notched fourteen home runs, fifty-five RBIs, twenty-two doubles, nine triples, seventy-six runs, and thirty-six stolen bases in 115 at-bats. Harper, who ended the season with a twenty-two game hitting streak, was named High School Player of the Year by *Baseball America*, becoming the first underclassman in the magazine's history to achieve this feat.

Harper's impressive sophomore season with the Wildcats was punctuated by another legendary home run. At the Third Annual International High School Power Showcase, held in January 2009 at Tropicana Stadium in St. Petersburg, Florida, the sixteen-year-old hit a baseball 502 feet—then the longest home run in the stadium's history. "I didn't hit it with the wood [bat], I hit it with aluminum," Harper recalled to David Picker for ESPN.com (12 Aug. 2009). "But when I hit the back of the dome, I was like, 'Wow, did that really just happen?'" Harper's home run at Tropicana Field helped to increase his national recognition dramatically. He then graced the cover of the June 8, 2009, edition of *Sports Illustrated*.

As an amateur baseball player, Harper also competed internationally, representing the United States as a member of the gold medal–winning junior national team that defeated Cuba at the 2008 Pan Am Junior Championships in Mexico. Harper was named the tournament's most valuable player after batting .571 in eight games with four home runs, six doubles, and sixteen RBIs. He also had six stolen bases.

## COLLEGE AND THE MLB DRAFT

In June 2009, upon completing his sophomore year in high school, Harper announced that he was leaving Las Vegas High School and enrolling in junior college in order to become eligible for the 2010 MLB Draft. After passing the General Educational Development (GED) test in December, Harper was accepted to the College of Southern Nevada (CSN), a Clark County junior college renowned for its outstanding Division I baseball program. He signed a letter of intent with CSN, agreeing to attend the school for one year. Harper was reunited with his brother Bryan at CSN, who had transferred from California State University.

In his first season with the College of Southern Nevada Coyotes, Harper started sixty-six games and batted .443 while striking out only forty-three times in 228 at-bats. He also scored ninety-eight runs and amassed ninety-eight RBIs, twenty-three doubles, and four triples. With his thirty-one home runs, Harper shattered the school's previous single-season record of twelve. Harper's hitting helped lead the Coyotes to a first place record of fifty-two wins and sixteen losses, earning the team the Scenic West Athletic Conference (SWAC) regular season conference title. After the Coyotes captured the SWAC championship, Harper was awarded SWAC Player of the Year honors.

The Coyotes next claimed the NJCAA Western District Championship to advance to the National Junior College (JUCO) World Series tournament. Despite getting off to a strong start, the team lost to San Jacinto College–North by a score of ten to eight. Harper was ejected from the tournament's final game after he questioned a strikeout call made by the home plate umpire by drawing a line in the sand to indicate that he thought the pitch was outside the strike zone. A video of the exchange between Harper and the umpire was posted on YouTube. The ejection resulted in an automatic one-game suspension. Harper's suspension was extended to two games due to another ejection he had received earlier in the season for taunting the opposing team.

Following his ejection, Harper apologized to his teammates and sent his coach, Tim Chambers, an apology via text message. For many scouts and sportswriters, who were already critical of Harper for his heavy use of eye black and his batting ritual, which involved putting the bat on the ground in front of home plate and wiping dirt into his bare hands, the incident only served to reinforce Harper's reputation as a prima donna. "Certainly, he shouldn't have done that," Chambers told Bob Nightengale for *USA Today* (6 June 2010). "But I also thought his maturity showed up when something that

dramatic happened on a stage like this. When he got tossed, he didn't respond."

Harper's amateur career ended after the JUCO World Series. In the off-season, he received the Golden Spikes Award, which is given annually to the best amateur baseball player in the United States. Following the ejection incident, some scouts questioned Harper's attitude, which resulted in speculation as to whether he would remain the top pick in the upcoming MLB draft.

## FIRST OVERALL PICK BY THE WASHINGTON NATIONALS

These doubts were put to rest on June 7, when the Washington Nationals selected Harper first overall in the 2010 MLB Draft. At seventeen years old, Harper became the third youngest player and the fifth catcher in MLB history to be drafted first overall. On August 16, Harper signed a five-year contract with the Nationals worth $9.9 million. The contract included a $6.25 million signing bonus. After signing Harper, the Nationals announced plans to move him to right field in order to boost his long-term offensive potential and preserve his health.

Instead of being assigned to the Gulf Coast League (GCL) Nationals, the team's Rookie Level affiliate in Viera, Florida, Harper spent his first professional season playing for the Florida Instructional League (FIL), where he received training on how to play the outfield. The FIL, an off-season professional baseball league for rookie prospects and veteran players who are recovering from injuries, plays its games in September and October. Harper thrived in his new surroundings, posting a .319 batting average with four doubles and a triple. He also led his team with four home runs, twelve RBIs, and seven walks.

Harper's progress in the instructional league convinced the Washington Nationals to promote him to the six-team Arizona Fall League (AFL), which is comprised of elite MLB prospects. At age eighteen, Harper's promotion to the AFL's Scottsdale Scorpions made him the second-youngest player in league history. He was only eligible to play twice a week while spending the rest of his time working out and developing his fundamental skills. Despite limited playing time, Harper hit .343 while knocking in a home run and seven RBIs in thirty-five plate appearances. His efforts helped the team capture the 2010 AFL Championship in late November.

## MINOR LEAGUE DEBUT

In February 2011, Harper arrived at the Nationals' spring training camp in Viera, Florida, determined to make the club's major league roster by Opening Day. He was the center of attention during batting practice and autograph-seeking fans regularly ambushed him. Despite compiling a .389 batting average in thirteen spring training games, Harper was sent down to the Hagerstown

Suns, Washington's Class-A affiliate in the South Atlantic League (SAL). Harper made his minor league debut in April 2011, earning two hits in four at-bats.

After getting off to a slow start in 2011, Harper visited the team's eye doctor, who informed him that his vision could be improved by wearing contact lenses. After being fitted for lenses, Harper noticed an immediate difference. "It was like I was seeing in HD," he told Dave Sheinin for the *Washington Post* (12 May 2011). On May 9, he earned SAL player-of-the-week honors after notching twelve hits in twenty-four at-bats, including four doubles, four RBIs, and one home run. Harper hit .471 over the course of an eighteen-game hitting streak.

Critics again questioned Harper's attitude and maturity in early June 2011. After breaking open a scoreless game by hitting a sixth-inning home run against Greensboro Grasshoppers pitcher Zach Neal, Harper stood at the plate for a few seconds, coolly tossed his bat, and watched his home run reach the outfield seats before beginning to round the bases. When Neal expressed disapproval with Harper, Harper responded by blowing him a kiss when he reached home plate. Neal retaliated by brushing Harper off the plate with a fastball in his next at-bat.

Harper was criticized after the incident for his perceived arrogance, recklessness, and lack of baseball etiquette. "The GM's office in Washington should slow down the player-development plans to promote Harper to Double-A—not because of talent but because of immaturity issues. A player's maturity is just as important as his talent, something the player must understand," former Washington Nationals General Manager Jim Bowden wrote for *ESPN.com* (7 June 2011). "Like Barry Bonds in his prime, Harper needs to learn now that his response to taunting or comments from opposing players must be made with his bat, not with gestures."

Later in June 2011, Harper was among seven Hagerstown players selected to compete in the SAL All-Star Game. He was named to the MLB All-Star Futures Game, an annual exhibition game featuring MLB prospects from around the world that takes place during All-Star weekend.

## MAJOR LEAGUE DEBUT

On July 4, 2011, Harper was assigned to play for the Harrisburg Senators, the Washington Nationals' Double-A affiliate in the Eastern League (EL). The eighteen-year-old had a memorable midseason debut, playing left field in front of a record crowd of nearly eighty-one hundred people at Metro Park in Harrisburg, Pennsylvania. In his first game in the EL, Harper had two hits, a walk, and scored a run. He again garnered negative headlines on August 11 when he was ejected for questioning a strikeout call. Harper's season was cut short a week later, when

he suffered a hamstring strain during the eighth inning of a game against the Akron Aeros at Canal Park in Ohio. Harper finished his Double-A debut with a .254 batting average, three home runs, and twelve RBIs.

In March 2012, after notching only eight hits in twenty-eight at-bats, two doubles, and no RBIs during spring training, Harper was sent down to the Syracuse Chiefs, the Nationals' Triple-A affiliate in the International League. On April 28, 2012, he was called up to replace injured Nationals third baseman Ryan Zimmerman on the club's major league roster. Harper made his highly anticipated major league debut a day later at Dodgers Stadium. He played left field and had a double, along with a game-tying sacrifice fly for the Nationals, who suffered a one-run loss. Harper made news on May 6 when Philadelphia Phillies pitcher Cole Hamels intentionally drilled him in the small of the back in his first plate appearance of the game. Harper got his revenge by stealing home after a pick-off throw to first base. Hamels's action earned him a five-game suspension.

Five days later, Harper was in the headlines again, after a bat that he threw against a dugout wall bounced back and struck him just above his left eye, requiring ten stitches. The incident was forgotten on May 14, when Harper belted his first major league home run during an 8–5 win against the San Diego Padres. Harper became the youngest player in the history of the major leagues to hit a home run. He was named National League Rookie of the Month for May after he batted .271 with four home runs, ten RBIs, and twenty-one runs scored. He found himself the center of attention in mid-June for his reply to a reporter, who asked Harper, a nondrinker, if he would commemorate a home run he hit against the Toronto Blue Jays by having a beer. Harper responded, "That's a clown question, bro." The quote gained popularity in the media and became a catch phrase. It was subsequently trademarked by Harper, who sold T-shirts bearing the phrase and donated a portion of the proceeds to charity.

Although Harper was not a first ballot selection to the 2012 All-Star Game, the rookie outfielder was added to the National League team following an injury to Miami Marlins outfielder Giancarlo Stanton. He had a strikeout and a walk for the triumphant National League squad. On August 29, Harper achieved two more personal milestones during a victory against the Marlins: his first two-run home run and his first major league ejection, which came in the ninth inning after he threw his helmet into the ground. The next month he made history again, becoming the second teenage player in MLB history (behind Tony Conigliaro) to hit twenty home runs in a season. Harper ended September on a high note, winning another Rookie of the Month prize after hitting .330 with seven home runs and twenty-six runs scored.

Harper's prowess at the plate helped the Washington Nationals capture the NL East division title, with their major league leading ninety-eight wins and sixty-four losses. It was the team's first division title since 1933. The Nationals advanced to the National League Division Series (NLDS), where the St. Louis Cardinals defeated them in five games. Harper struggled in the postseason, managing only three hits in twenty-three at-bats. However, he attained another milestone by becoming the second-youngest player (behind Andruw Jones) to hit a home run in the postseason. In November, Harper capped off a remarkable season, when he was named the second-youngest NL Rookie of the Year in MLB history, behind former New York Mets pitcher Dwight Gooden. Harper was also voted to the 2012 Topps All-Star Rookie Team.

Despite his youth, Harper has become one of the most popular players in baseball. His presence on the Washington Nationals has helped make the team a competitor following several seasons of relative obscurity. In February 2013 Harper reported to the Nationals' spring training camp in tremendous physical shape. He reportedly added nearly twenty pounds of muscle during the off-season. He then got off to an auspicious start to the 2013 season when he belted two home runs in his first two at-bats, becoming the youngest MLB player to hit two home runs in his team's first game of the season. His natural talent and dedication to the game will likely make him one of baseball's most widely recognized superstars for years to come.

## PERSONAL LIFE

Harper, who is not married, spends his off-season time in Las Vegas. He is a member of the Church of Jesus Christ of Latter-day Saints. Harper has made regular appearances at Washington Nationals charity events and is a spokesperson for the nutritional supplement company MusclePharm. His brother Bryan is a minor league pitcher in the Nationals organization.

## SUGGESTED READING

Bowden, Jim. "Immaturity Could Hold Bryce Harper Back." *ESPN.com*. ESPN Internet Ventures, 7 June 2011. Web. 20 Mar. 2013.

Parasiliti, Bob. "Harper Is Modern, Old-Time Baseball Player." *Herald-Mail*. Schurz Communications, 4 Apr. 2011. Web. 20 Mar. 2013.

Picker, David. "Prodigy Harper Handles the Pressure." *ESPN.com*. ESPN Internet Ventures, 12 Aug. 2009. Web. 20 Mar. 2013.

Nightengale, Bob. "Likely Top MLB Draft Pick Has Growing Up to Do." *USA Today*. Gannett, 7 June 2010. Web. 20 Mar. 2013.

—*Bertha Muteba*

# Jonathan Harris

**Born:** August 27, 1979
**Occupation:** Internet artist

Jonathan Harris is an unusual type of artist. Instead of working with traditional materials such as paint, wood, or stone, he uses his gifts as a computer programmer to bring a fresh perspective to human relationships. His work transforms the way people look at a wide array of subjects, ranging from blogging to whale hunting to pornography, and allows for a better understanding of how humans relate to technology and the world at large. In many ways, he approaches his work the way an anthropologist might, sifting through bits of data, both online and off, to find patterns—and perhaps meaning—in human interactions.

Harris's graceful and intriguing websites, boldly structured interactive films, and commissioned projects have earned him high praise from art critics, and his work has been displayed in major art galleries and museums the world over. In recent years, he has established a new website, Cowbird, which is devoted to more meaningful and more interactive storytelling than might be had on other social media websites. Harris has also begun to explore the complications involved with data collection in *Data Will Help Us* (2013), a project commissioned by the *New York Times*. "All data is the outcome of something that happened in the world, and it leaves a trace behind. And you can use that trace as a building block to make something bigger," Harris told Conrad Walters for the *Sydney Morning Herald* (4 June 2013). He added, "I see the Internet as becoming a collective nervous system that we all take part in. In a way, [my] projects are about individual people, but they're much more projects about the human collective."

## EARLY LIFE AND EDUCATION

Born in Shelburne, Vermont, on August 27, 1979, Jonathan Harris grew up painting and sketching. Throughout his childhood and adolescence, he demonstrated little interest in applying his creativity to computers; in fact, he did not do any computer coding at all until 1999, when, as an undergraduate at Princeton University, he created a webpage for a computer course. Harris went on to major in computer science, studying under Brian Kernighan, the Canadian computer scientist who aided in the development of the computer operating system Unix at Bell Laboratories. While at Princeton, he also studied photography with noted American photographer Emmet Gowin.

In 2001, Harris helped found Princeton's *Troubadour* magazine, along with fellow student Dan Hafetz. The first issue was published in January 2002. Harris and Hafetz established

© Oriel Ferrer

*Troubadour* in order to counteract some of the xenophobia they feared was developing in the wake of the terrorist attacks of September 11, 2001. The magazine used personal travel stories, photography, literature, and artwork to foster debate among Princeton students about the role of the United States in the post–September 11 world.

In an interview with Emily Spivack for *PopTech* (19 Apr. 2011), Harris said that he was originally an oil painter and sketcher. This changed in 2003, when he was robbed at gunpoint in Costa Rica; among the items stolen was a sketchbook containing nearly a year's worth of work. "At that point, I turned to the Web, and since then, all my work has always been part of the network," he told Spivack.

## EARLY WORK

Harris's computer-coded art found almost immediate success upon his graduation from Princeton. One of his earliest digital works, *Information Maps* (2003), was commissioned by Princeton's International Networks Archive (INA). The project employs maps of the world that are based on transactions between nations rather than geography.

Harris's work has been described as simple but thought provoking and elegant but accessible, and his early website *Wordcount*, which debuted in 2004, displays many of these attributes. The site is an interactive list of the 86,800 most popular words in the English language, determined by data collected from the British National Corpus. Users are able to search the list by either typing in a word to find its ranking or looking up a specific ranking and finding out which word falls there. As all the words are strung together as if in one long sentence and ranked in order of commonness, intriguing strings of words often appear, including "microsoft acquire salary

tremendous," "conservative reduce vote," and "hushed caledonian jerk embraces innocently polyester," according to Thomas Pack for *Information Today* (June 2007).

Another notable Harris website from 2004, called 10x10, scans major Internet news feeds such as Reuters, BBC News, and CNN.com on an hourly basis and posts the top hundred words and images in a grid. At a glance, users can see which words and images are most significant at the moment; they can also see the extremes of news coverage when, for example, words and images connected to pop culture are posted alongside those connected to war or disease.

Reviewing these and other early websites, Pack wrote, "Harris's work might be the most effective use of the Web to date as an artistic medium. Some of his projects might even be the most effective conceptual art to date in any medium. This is not meant to belittle the aesthetic appeal of his sites—which is considerable—but their greatest accomplishment is the unique way in which they let you explore and experience the human condition."

In July 2004, Harris began a residency at Fabrica, a communications research center in Treviso, Italy, that is part of the Benetton Group. Though he had a one-year contract, he left early, in February 2005, in order to pursue other work.

## COMING INTO PROMINENCE

Harris became widely known as an artist when he and fellow artist and computer scientist Sep Kamvar developed the website *We Feel Fine* (2006), which demonstrates the full range of human emotions by searching blogs every ten minutes for the words "I am feeling" or "I feel" and capturing sentences that incorporate those phrases on the site. By clicking on a sentence, a user can link to the original blog or explore other blogs with similar feelings. Daniel Nye Griffiths described *We Feel Fine* in *Forbes* (9 Aug. 2012) as "a project intended to capture and taxonomize the emotional state of the Internet, by scraping blogs for emotional expressions. By adjusting its various sliders, visitors could find out how many people in a particular place, at a particular time, of a particular age, felt good, or bad, or happy, or joyous or—often—bored." In 2009, the duo published a book version of their website, *We Feel Fine: An Almanac of Human Emotion.*

Two similar projects, also developed by Harris and Kamvar, are *Lovelines* (2006), which sifts through blogs to cull expressions of love or hate, and the interactive installation *I Want You to Want Me* (2008), which allowed visitors to the Museum of Modern Art (MoMA) in New York City to explore various Internet dating sites through a touch screen. Harris also designed *Time Capsule*, a project that was commissioned by Yahoo! to make what Harris's website calls "a digital fingerprint of the human world in 2006."

Released in ten languages and open online for thirty days in 2006, the project asked individuals how they were thinking or feeling about ten universal themes, including love, faith, and anger. People were allowed to respond via text, video, still images, sounds, or drawings.

Harris's projects from 2007 include *Universe*, which creates new constellations based on news items culled from twenty thousand international news sources, and *The Whale Hunt*, for which Harris traveled to Alaska to participate in a traditional whale hunt with an Iñupiat family. In seven days, he shot 3,214 photographs at five-minute intervals, which can be viewed by users in a variety of ways on the website, thereby allowing each individual to create his or her own narrative. A writer for *Creativity* (19 Feb. 2008) called *The Whale Hunt* "an exceedingly elegant version of the standard narrative slideshow."

## COWBIRD

In 2009, on Harris's thirtieth birthday, he began documenting his life by taking one photo and writing one short story a day. This project, titled *Today*, debuted in 2010 after continuing for 440 consecutive days. It also helped to inspire Cowbird, a website devoted to storytelling that he founded in 2011. Unlike Facebook and Twitter, social media sites that provide users with the ability to connect with friends and relatives briefly and quickly, Cowbird seeks to provide its users with more thoughtful and longer-lasting storytelling "by combining the traits of a cow (slow, steady, grounded) with the traits of a bird (fast, free, efficient) to create a new kind of storytelling environment, which is both efficient and deep," Harris told Griffiths.

Unlike posts to Facebook, Twitter, and traditional blogs, the stories uploaded to Cowbird are interconnected, thereby allowing users to read or share stories they may not have previously thought to look for. Also unlike the major social media sites, Cowbird originally took membership requests from prospective users, though it has since begun allowing open registration. In just its first three months of operation, from December 2011 to February 2012, more than seven thousand users from around the world created over 7,600 stories using words, pictures, and audio, each describing some important aspect of their lives or significant world events. As of August 2012, Cowbird had roughly sixteen thousand users, with each user having contributed an average of two stories. Some stories use a great deal of text, while others rely more on pictures and sounds.

Harris believes that further compression of communication is becoming impossible and that Cowbird enables individuals to keep and maintain what his website calls "a public library of human experience" that will be of lasting value. "Telling stories on Cowbird asks a little more of you than dashing off tweets from a cellphone, but we think it gives back a lot more, too," Harris told Jennifer Preston for the *New York Times* (19 Feb. 2012). "It's soul food, not fast food."

## RECENT PROJECTS

One of Harris's notable recent projects is *I Love Your Work* (2013), a documentary about nine women who make lesbian pornography. An interactive film comprising 2,202 ten-second video clips, it was designed to break down the stereotypes surrounding the women who make these films by showing them as everyday people living ordinary lives. Harris filmed each of these women every five minutes for ten seconds and captured whatever they happened to be doing at that moment. The documentary can only be accessed by ten viewers per day. After paying ten dollars for access, viewers have twenty-four hours in which they can watch approximately six hours of footage in a variety of ways. "With the ten viewers, I wanted to create an artificial scarcity around something that's not at all scarce," Harris explained to Azadeh Ensha for *T* magazine (16 May 2013). "And this is also the first time I've charged for something, because generally people expect Web content and 'porn' to be free, and I think it'd be a great thing to develop a culture where people pay for good digital content. And this project is a push in that direction."

Another recent work is *Data Will Help Us*, commissioned by the *New York Times* and published on June 20, 2013. In this self-described "brief manifesto," Harris questions the development of "Big Data," the term used to describe the online accumulation of massive amounts of information and statistics to help analyze everything from the buying habits of shoppers and the interests of the moviegoing public to the actions of terrorists. Harris believes this type of data collection is changing our lives in profound ways. He wrote on his personal website, "Data has become a kind of ubiquitous modern salve that now gets applied to almost any kind of ailment. . . . The rise of Big Data is poised to transform our world in fundamental ways comparable to the impact of the Internet. Like any new technology, Big Data contains the potential for both good and bad, and it's largely up to us to decide how we'll use it."

## "A LOVE FOR YOUR MATERIALS"

Although almost all of Harris's art is web based, he does not begin work online. Rather, he works out his ideas offline and then, once he believes he has an accurate sense of what he wants to do, begins coding. In his profile for *Creativity* magazine, he described working with code as "like working with anything—paints, wood, or being a car mechanic." He explained, "You have to develop a love for your materials. . . . I look at a lot of my early work now and it seems incredibly primitive and really crude, largely because I was trying to learn the materials. Now it's second nature. When I lie in bed at night falling asleep, I can see exactly how something is going to behave on screen and how it's going to be controlled. It's just a matter of executing."

Harris's work has been exhibited in museums around the world, including the Museum of Modern Art and the Pace Gallery in New York City, the Centre Pompidou in Paris, the Victoria and Albert Museum in London, the Garage Center for Contemporary Culture in Moscow, and the CAFA (China Central Academy of Fine Arts) Art Museum in Beijing. He has also received numerous awards for his work. He codesigned the state quarter for Vermont, was awarded a Fabrica fellowship in 2005, and has been nominated for numerous Webby Awards, winning two in 2005 and another one in 2008. Also in 2008, *Print* magazine named him as one of twenty most promising new visual artists, and *Creativity* magazine profiled him as one of its top fifty artists of the year. In 2009, he was one of the World Economic Forum's Young Global Leaders of the year. He has lectured at Google, Princeton University, Stanford University, and the 2007 TED conference in Monterey, California.

Harris lived in Brooklyn for several years before moving to Pacifica, California. In between, he spent time in Iceland and the Pacific Northwest. He returned to Brooklyn in January 2013.

### SUGGESTED READING

Ensha, Azadeh. "Site to Be Seen: The PG Lives of X-Rated Stars." *T Magazine*. New York Times, 16 May 2013. Web. 13 Aug. 2013.

Griffiths, Daniel Nye. "Cowbird: Facebook Stories' Launch Recalls an Artistic Storytelling Project." *Forbes*. Forbes.com, 9 Aug. 2012. Web. 13 Aug. 2013.

Harris, Jonathan. "6 Questions with . . . Jonathan Harris." Interview by Emily Spivack. *PopTech*. PopTech, 19 Apr. 2011. Web. 13 Aug. 2013.

"Jonathan Harris." *Creativity*. Crain Communications, 19 Feb. 2008. Web. 13 Aug. 2013.

Pack, Thomas. "Innovative Interfaces." *Information Today* June 2007: 34–35. Print.

Preston, Jennifer. "Pull Up a Mouse and Stay a While." *New York Times*. New York Times, 19 Feb. 2012. Web. 13 Aug. 2013.

### SELECTED WORKS

*Information Maps*, 2003; *Wordcount*, 2004; *10x10*, 2004; *Time Capsule*, 2006; *We Feel Fine* (with Sep Kamvar), 2006; *The Whale Hunt*, 2007; *I Want You to Want Me* (with Sep Kamvar), 2008; *Today*, 2010; *I Love Your Work*, 2013; *Data Will Help Us*, 2013

—*Christopher Mari*

# Heidi Heitkamp

**Born:** October 30, 1955
**Occupation:** Politician

Heidi Heitkamp is a United States senator from North Dakota. She served as the state's tax commissioner and attorney general before winning a seat in the Senate in 2012. Heitkamp was one of five women elected to the Senate that year, bringing the number of women in the upper chamber to a historic high of twenty. She ran unsuccessfully for governor in 2000, the same year that she was diagnosed with breast cancer. Heitkamp, who was raised in a working-class small town, has been a lifelong Democrat in a conservative state. North Dakota has been a reliable red state in presidential elections since 1968, but its citizens sent only Democrats to Congress from the early 1980s until 2010, when Republican and then-governor John Hoeven earned a seat in the Senate. The sparsely populated state has only one seat in the House.

Despite her party affiliation, Heitkamp has been known to break with fellow Democrats on some issues, including gun control and the Keystone XL pipeline. A former lawyer for the US Environmental Protection Agency (EPA), Heitkamp is a vocal supporter of a proposed expansion of the Keystone pipeline that would transport crude oil from Alberta, Canada to refineries on the Gulf Coast of Texas (an existing branch of the pipeline flows through North Dakota, but the proposed expansion would not). President Barack Obama initially came down on the side of environmentalist groups like the Sierra Club who opposed the project when he deferred his decision on the expansion in 2011. Heitkamp criticized the move, saying in a 2012 campaign ad, as quoted by Paige Lavender for the *Huffington Post* (12 June 2013), that the expansion would "create jobs while also contributing to our energy independence." Heitkamp's position on the pipeline could be attributed to the thriving oil industry in North Dakota, thanks to which the state's unemployment rate was less than 3 percent in 2012, the lowest in the country.

Her friction with the Obama administration and other Democrats has highlighted the difficulties of being a red-state Democrat in a polarized political climate. Heitkamp's popularity in North Dakota won her the Senate seat in 2012 by the thinnest of margins—it was one of only two Senate races that Nate Silver, the statistical wunderkind for the *New York Times*, predicted incorrectly. Maintaining that popularity while in Washington, amid pressures from her party, is expected to be a challenge for the North Dakotan.

### EARLY LIFE AND POLITICAL CAREER

Mary Kathryn "Heidi" Heitkamp was born on October 30, 1955, in Breckenridge, Minnesota.

Joshua Roberts/Reuters /Landov

She has six brothers and sisters. Her younger brother Joel Heitkamp is a talk show host on Fargo's KFGO Radio and a former North Dakota state senator. Heitkamp's mother, Doreen, worked as a school cook and custodian. Her father, Raymond, who died from skin cancer in 1982, was a seasonal construction worker. Heitkamp grew up in Mantador, a very, very small town in North Dakota near the Minnesota border. In her first Senate speech on April 23, 2013, Heitkamp told lawmakers, "My family was one-tenth the population of that town." Raymond Heitkamp, a World War II veteran, built a local Veterans of Foreign Wars (VFW) chapter and a ballpark for Mantador. "He was someone who really believed in community and believed when Mrs. Poster needed her sidewalk shoveled so she could go to work, that was our job," she said of her father, who instilled in her a sense of responsibility for one's neighbor. Her grandmother, who grew up during the administration of President Franklin D. Roosevelt, credited the progressive Democrat for getting the family through the Great Depression. "That was a lasting memory," she told Chuck McCutcheon for the *National Journal* (7 Nov. 2012) of her affiliation with the Democrats, "that this was a party that would help others when they needed a little help."

Heitkamp began working as a babysitter at the age of thirteen. Throughout high school she worked as a waitress and as part of a highway construction crew. She earned a bachelor's degree in political science from the University of North Dakota in 1977, and a law degree from Lewis and Clark Law School in Portland, Oregon, with a focus on the environment, in 1980. During law school, Heitkamp worked for the Northwest Environmental Defense Center and the Natural Resources Law Institute. After graduation, she spent two years as an attorney for the EPA. According to the nonprofit Council for a Livable World, Heitkamp left her post in 1981 after the election of President Ronald Reagan, and was hired as a North Dakota assistant attorney general. She worked for Attorney General Robert Wefald, a Republican.

At twenty-eight, Heitkamp ran her first political campaign, a race for state auditor against incumbent Robert W. Patterson in 1984. She lost. In 1985, Heitkamp began working as an attorney in the North Dakota Tax Department under Kent Conrad, who became an inspiration to her in her own political career. When Conrad ran for US Senate in 1986, Heitkamp replaced him as state tax commissioner. With Conrad's encouragement, she ran to keep the office two years later and won with 66 percent of the vote.

## ATTORNEY GENERAL, 1993–2000

Heitkamp successfully ran for North Dakota Attorney General in 1992 when incumbent Democrat Nicholas Spaeth stepped down to run for governor. She told Matt Bunk for the Bismarck-Mandan *Great Plains Examiner* (30 Jan. 2012) a story that compelled her to seek that office: She had once tried to help a woman seek a divorce from an abusive husband. The husband ended up shooting the woman and killing her daughter. "And I just remember thinking what could I have done differently. How could the people she had asked for help, how could we have changed this outcome. And it really made me want to begin to expose this for what it was. At the time, domestic violence was considered a public health problem not a criminal justice problem," she told Bunk. Heitkamp spoke with a number of law enforcement officials about the case, one of whom told her that men would always hit their wives and, as Heitkamp paraphrased, "there's nothing you can do to change it." But Heitkamp held a very different philosophy regarding domestic violence and governments in general. "I'm not going to give up my belief that [the world] can change," she told Bunk. "If we don't think we can change governments for the better by getting good people involved, then we're done."

Heitkamp won her first term in 1992 and second term in 1996 with over 60 percent of the vote. During her tenure, she led state lawsuits against leading tobacco companies. Her efforts culminated in a national settlement, which she helped negotiate, in 1998. North Dakota received $866 million in the settlement. In 2008, Heitkamp led a campaign to devote more of the state's settlement money, approximately $9 million a year, to antismoking campaigns. The measure passed as a ballot referendum. Heitkamp also spearheaded efforts to improve North Dakota's juvenile justice system and the anti–domestic violence system;

and she successfully sued the administration of President Bill Clinton over a number of land disputes within the state. In 2012, during her Senate campaign, former president Clinton spoke at a rally for her. He praised her bipartisan efforts and her willingness to go up against her own party, telling the crowd, as quoted by North Dakota's *Williston Herald* (30 Oct. 2012), "She sued me and beat me and won."

## GUBERNATORIAL RACE AND BREAST CANCER DIAGNOSIS

Heitkamp entered the North Dakota gubernatorial race in 2000. Her opponent was Republican John Hoeven, the president of the Bank of North Dakota. During Hoeven's tenure as bank president, Heitkamp worked on a commission that supervised the state-run bank. Throughout the campaign, poll numbers for Heitkamp and Hoeven remained close. But in mid-September, less than two months before Election Day, Heitkamp, who was forty-four, detected a lump in her right breast. She went to the doctor, and after a mammogram yielded inconclusive results, underwent a "blind biopsy," which revealed cancer cells in her lymph nodes. She was diagnosed with stage 3 breast cancer. Within a week of the diagnosis, Heitkamp's doctors performed a modified radical mastectomy of her right breast.

Heitkamp announced her diagnosis on September 20, and assured voters that she planned to stay in the race, though she would need to undergo cancer treatments including chemotherapy. "The one thing I know for sure is that all the reasons I had for getting into this race . . . are as valid today as they were a year ago," Heitkamp told supporters, as quoted by Chuck Haga for the Minneapolis *Star Tribune* (25 Sept. 2000). She cut back on her campaign efforts, however, often sending her running mate Aaron Krauter to events in her place. Despite an outpouring of support and a surge in her poll numbers after the announcement, Heitkamp lost the race to Hoeven, garnering only 130,000 votes to his 159,000. Sympathy for Heitkamp's condition certainly had an effect on the race, though the unscientific consensus in North Dakota seems to be that it was merely one factor among many that contributed to her ultimate defeat.

## CAMPAIGN FOR US SENATE

From 2001 to 2012, Heitkamp returned to her work as an attorney and became a director of the Dakota Gasification Company, which operates the Great Plains Synfuels Plant in Beulah, North Dakota, a producer of synthetic natural gas from coal. There was strong support for Heitkamp to run for the US Senate in 2010 against her former adversary Hoeven, who had served two terms as governor. Heitkamp's brother Joel even told Sean J. Miller for the Washington blog the *Hill* (7 Jan. 2010) that his sister was "very

interested" in serving the state, but ultimately, Heitkamp decided that it was the wrong time. After much speculation, in November 2011 she announced her intention to run in 2012.

The circumstances surrounding her decision were serendipitous. Her old political mentor Kent Conrad was retiring from his career in the Senate—a career that had begun when he left his position as the state's tax commissioner to campaign and passed on his title to Heitkamp. Heitkamp ran unopposed in the Democratic Senate primary. In the general election she faced Republican Rick Berg, a wealthy real estate developer and Tea Party supporter who was serving his first term as the state's lone representative in the House. Berg had the clout of the national Republican Party behind him in a presidential election year in which most North Dakotans would cast a vote for Republican presidential candidate Mitt Romney. Additionally, if Berg flipped Conrad's seat from Democrat to Republican, it would significantly increase the odds of a Republican majority in the Senate.

The race was extremely competitive, with each candidate drawing on his or her own pool of resources. Berg had more cash on hand than the Heitkamp team, but Heitkamp had former President Clinton, who stumped for her in October and even appeared in one of her ads. And unlike Berg, Heitkamp reveled in the more personal aspects of campaigning. "I love listening to what people care about and their ideas," she told Bunk. "There's so much wisdom out there. Those kinds of campaigns lead to a much more engaged and educated public official. So that's how I love to campaign." North Dakota has a population of about 680,000, and, according to Gail Collins of the *New York Times* (28 July 2012), most voters expect nothing less than to have personally met each candidate. Heitkamp became the darling of the state, while Berg came off as distant and unpersonable. Still, the race was considered a toss-up until Election Day, and Heitkamp ultimately won by fewer than 3,000 votes. It was the closest Senate race of 2012.

## RED STATE DEMOCRAT

Heitkamp was sworn into office in January 2013. Her duty to her largely Republican constituents is reflected in her moderate outlook. She favors a constitutional amendment that would require a balanced federal budget, with some exceptions to that stipulation, but opposes any cuts to Social Security and Medicare. She supports the construction of the Keystone XL pipeline, as well as other measures in regard to the environment that are opposed by most Democrats. "I think 'Drill, Baby Drill' is the way we need to do it," Heitkamp said, citing former Alaska governor Sarah Palin's famous line in her first debate with Berg, as quoted by David Catanese for *Politico* (5 Sept. 2012). "This is an area where

I have vehemently disagreed with the [Obama] administration. They've walked away from coal. They're hostile to oil."

When lawmakers of both parties called for stricter gun control laws after the December 2012 shooting at Sandy Hook Elementary School, Heitkamp maintained her opposition to such measures. In an interview with George Stephanopoulos for the television program *This Week* on January 6, 2013, Heitkamp said that proposals like universal background checks were "way, way in the extreme of what I think is necessary or even should be talked about." In April 2013, she voted against an amendment that would impose stricter gun control legislation. Her vote prompted former Obama White House chief of staff and secretary of commerce Bill Daley, who had donated money to Heitkamp's campaign, to write a scathing opinion piece about her for the *Washington Post* (19 Apr. 2013). The article began with the line: "I want my money back."

Heitkamp serves on five committees in the Senate: the Agriculture, Nutrition and Forestry Committee; the Homeland Security and Government Affairs Committee; the Small Business and Entrepreneurship Committee; the Indian Affairs Committee; and the Banking, Housing and Urban Affairs Committee.

Heitkamp is married to Dr. Darwin Lange, a family practice doctor. They live in Mandan, North Dakota and have two grown children, Ali and Nathan.

## SUGGESTED READING

Bunk, Matt. "In Focus with Heidi Heitkamp." *Great Plains Examiner* [Bismarck, ND]. Great Plains Examiner, 30 Jan. 2012. Web. 2 July 2013.

Catanese, David. "North Dakota Democrat Takes Palin Approach on Energy." *Politico*. Politico, 5 Sept. 2012. Web. 3 July 2013.

"Clinton Touts Heitkamp." *Williston Herald* [ND]. Williston Herald, 30 Oct. 2012. Web. 3 Jul. 2013.

Haga, Chuck. "Raising Campaign Spirits in ND; Supporters Rally for Ailing Gubernatorial Candidate." *Star Tribune* [Minneapolis]. Star Tribune, 25 Sept. 2000. Web. 30 June 2013.

Heitkamp, Heidi. "In First Senate Speech, Heitkamp Discusses Her Roots, Desire to Get Things Done." *Heidi Heitkamp*. Heitkamp. senate.gov, 23 Apr. 2013. Web. 28 June 2013.

Lavender, Paige. "Heidi Heitkamp: Keystone Pipeline Is 'the Kim Kardashian of Energy.'" *Huffington Post*. TheHuffingtonPost.com, 12 June 2013. Web. 30 June 2013.

McCutcheon, Chuck. "North Dakota, Senate: Heidi Heitkamp (D)." *National Journal*. National Journal Group, 7 Nov. 2012. Web. 3 July 2013.

—*Molly Hagan*

# Chris Hemsworth

**Born:** August 11, 1983
**Occupation:** Actor

Best known for his role as the Norse god turned superhero Thor in the Marvel Studios films *Thor* (2011) and *The Avengers* (2012), Australian actor Chris Hemsworth seems to have achieved international fame nearly overnight. In truth, Hemsworth's ascent to superhero-dom took several years and was hindered by studio bankruptcy and delayed releases. After more than three years on the hit Australian series *Home and Away*, Hemsworth, the middle sibling in a trio of actor brothers, moved to Los Angeles, California, to pursue a film career. He gained notice for his brief performance as doomed Starfleet officer George Kirk in 2009's *Star Trek* and was cast in major roles in the horror film *The Cabin in the Woods* as well as the remake of the 1980s action film *Red Dawn*; however, delays in releasing the latter two films kept Hemsworth out of the spotlight.

After gaining the attention of *Cabin in the Woods* cowriter and future *Avengers* writer and director Joss Whedon, who recommended him to *Thor* director Kenneth Branagh, Hemsworth was cast in the role that would make him a household name among superhero fans worldwide and grant him entrance into the expansive cinematic universe of Marvel's interconnected superhero films. Again working with Whedon, Hemsworth reprised his role as Thor in *The Avengers*, lending his imposing presence to the ensemble cast. "Chris Hemsworth is a god," Whedon told the *Manila Bulletin* (8 Mar. 2012). "This is a man who just makes other men stop going to the gym. It's not fair. He's very centered in the way he approaches a scene and the way he is in life." In addition to signing on for a third Marvel film, *Thor: The Dark World*, Hemsworth appeared in 2012's *Snow White and the Huntsman* and secured roles in a number of high-profile projects, including the Ron Howard–directed racing biopic *Rush*.

Despite his international fame and star billings alongside such Academy Award–winning actors as Anthony Hopkins, Natalie Portman, and Charlize Theron, Hemsworth remains aware of his humble roots. "I've been so fortunate," Hemsworth told Brantley Bardin for *InStyle* (May 2012). "People I've watched for years and wanted to work with—all of a sudden, I'm right among them."

## EARLY LIFE AND EDUCATION

The second of three sons, Chris Hemsworth was born in Melbourne, Australia, to Craig and Leonie Hemsworth. His mother is a teacher, and his father works in social services. All three of the Hemsworth children are actors. Luke, the eldest, became known for his roles on Australian

WireImage

television series such as the long-running soap opera *Neighbours* before leaving the industry to start his own flooring business, while Liam began his career on Australian television before gaining international fame in 2012 for his role as Gale Hawthorne in *The Hunger Games*.

When Hemsworth was young, he and his family moved to Bulman, a rural community in the Northern Territory. There, he and his brothers had an active and at times rambunctious childhood. "My brothers and I had dirt bikes and a variety of weapons we'd build or our grandpa would give us—knives, air rifles and other things our parents didn't know about," he told Ceri Davidon for the *Sunday Telegraph* (10 Apr. 2011). "We also built rope swings and flying foxes. I don't know how we survived."

Hemsworth has commented that his experience among the aboriginal community in the Northern Territory shaped his outlook. "I feel very fortunate to have lived in such a beautiful part of the world, with wonderful people, and to have an understanding of their situation," he told Davidon. His family later moved back to Melbourne and then to Phillip Island. Hemsworth attended Heathmont College, a secondary school in a suburb of Melbourne.

## EARLY CAREER

As a child, Hemsworth did not always want to be an actor. "I wanted to be something different every week," he told Davidon. "I'd go from wanting to be a professional footballer to a lawyer or a police officer. Then, one day, I thought, I can be an actor and pretend to be all those things—that solved the problem." Like his brother Luke before him, Hemsworth began his acting career with small roles in Australian television series. He described the extent of his brief appearance on *Neighbours*, in which Luke had previously played a recurring character, to Jeff Dawson for

the *Sunday Times* (20 May 2012): "The local mechanic shop had been robbed. I walked in and said, 'What's going on? Did you call the police?'" He also appeared in shows such as *Guinevere Jones* and *Fergus McPhail*, among others.

His next opportunity came when he was cast as the troubled Kim Hyde in the daily soap opera *Home and Away*. The series, which focuses on the lives of the residents of the fictional community of Summer Bay, has served as a sort of training ground for Australian actors since its premiere in 1987. In addition to Hemsworth, notable actors who appeared on *Home and Away* early in their careers include Heath Ledger, Ryan Kwanten, and Naomi Watts.

Working on the show "felt like high school," Hemsworth told Davidon. "You're thrown into a tight environment with people and some days you love them, some days you don't. The show ends up feeding into your real life in a very melodramatic way." Hemsworth ultimately appeared in nearly 150 episodes of *Home and Away* between 2004 and 2007. In 2006, while still a cast member, Hemsworth competed in the fifth season of the Australian version of *Dancing with the Stars*; he finished in fifth place.

## INTERNATIONAL CAREER

After moving to Los Angeles to pursue a career in film, Hemsworth appeared in 2009's *Star Trek* in the short-lived but pivotal role of George Kirk, whose act of self-sacrifice shapes the journey of his son, James Tiberius Kirk, in the reimagined take on the long-running franchise. Hemsworth also appeared in the films *A Perfect Getaway* (2009) and *Ca$h* (2010). After this, however, he had difficulty finding work. "You build up a thick skin in this industry," Hemsworth told Davidon. "There are doors being closed more often than opened. I once had a period of about eight months when I didn't have much work. It reached the stage where I wanted to pack it in and just come home." He persevered, however, working as a babysitter for his manager's children to pay the bills.

In 2009, Hemsworth filmed *Red Dawn*, a remake of the 1984 film of the same name, and *The Cabin in the Woods*, a horror film satirizing trends within the genre. However, the release of both films was delayed by the studio's financial difficulties. In late 2010, MGM filed for chapter 11 bankruptcy protection, leaving the fate of the two films uncertain. Despite this delay, Hemsworth's work on *The Cabin in the Woods* proved to have an immediate and significant impact on his career. The film's cowriter, Joss Whedon, recommended Hemsworth to British director Kenneth Branagh, who was slated to direct *Thor*, a superhero film based on the Marvel Comics character of the same name. "I received a completely unsolicited call from Joss Whedon during the casting process,"

Branagh told Joshua Neuman for the magazine *Flaunt*. "We were having a hard time casting the male lead, and he told me that Chris was immensely charming and a very good actor. It was an extremely unusual call for him to make and extremely heartfelt."

## THOR

When he auditioned for the role of *Thor's* titular hero, Hemsworth found himself competing against a number of actors, including his own younger brother. The audition process was only the first of several challenges Hemsworth had to face in his transformation into the superhero. To play the physically imposing Thor, Hemsworth, who is six feet three, embarked on a strenuous training regimen that included lifting weights and eating very large quantities of high-protein food. "It wasn't until *Thor* that I started lifting weights," he told Lara Rosenbaum for *Men's Health* (May 2011). "It was all pretty new to me." Hemsworth's hard work paid off; by the time *Thor* began filming, he had gained twenty pounds of muscle.

Physical training was not the only preparation Hemsworth had to undertake prior to suiting up as Thor. In order to play the beloved comic-book hero, he had to be introduced to the character's extensive history, which began with the publication of *Journey into Mystery* 83 in 1962 and continued through comics titles such as *Thor* and *The Mighty Thor*. "I knew about the character, but I never read the comics as a kid," Hemsworth told William Van Meter for *Interview* (May 2011). "Getting involved in the film was my introduction to it. Then I was inundated with many copies of *Thor* comics—the guys at Marvel gave me a stack. I also read a lot of books on Norse mythology."

Released in the spring of 2011, *Thor* proved to be a hit with audiences. "I think there is a very human story in the center of it, about father and son and brother and brother," Hemsworth told Van Meter. As Hemsworth's first starring role, the character of Thor introduced Hemsworth to moviegoers worldwide. Perhaps more significantly, the role granted him entry into a wider cinematic universe of interconnected superhero films that Marvel Studios had begun to assemble with the 2008 release of *Iron Man* and the subsequent releases of *The Incredible Hulk* (2008) and *Iron Man 2* (2010). These efforts to build a cohesive universe populated by superheroes, gods, aliens, and covert agencies would culminate in the release of *The Avengers* in 2012.

## THE AVENGERS

Hemsworth resumed his role as Thor in *The Avengers*, written and directed by Whedon and focusing on the superhero team of the same name. As one of the founding members of the team in the original comics, Thor plays a key role in *The Avengers*. The film and *Thor* share a villain, Thor's vengeful brother Loki, and *The Avengers* builds upon the extraterrestrial elements featured in the earlier film. Unlike *Thor*, however, *The Avengers* features an ensemble cast made up of the stars of the previous films as well as some new additions. Hemsworth has commented that the experience of making *The Avengers* was very different from that of making *Thor*. "It ends up being a back-and-forth ball game between seven or eight people, instead of a two-hander, which is very intimate," he told Anthony Breznican for *Entertainment Weekly* (7 Oct. 2011). "You don't want to drop the ball for the rest of the team."

For Hemsworth, this collaborative spirit was evident within the film itself. The characters all "put aside their individual interests and objectives," he told Breznican for *Entertainment Weekly* (4 May 2012). "The first half of the film is about them trying to fulfill their own goals, and that doesn't work out too well. They end up destroying things—and each other. Any community or family can't be defined by an individual. It's by the actions of the group."

In 2011, Hemsworth learned that he would play his role again in *Thor: The Dark World*. The film began shooting in the fall of 2012 and is scheduled for release late in the following year.

## OTHER PROJECTS

After a long delay, *The Cabin in the Woods* premiered in early 2012, and *Red Dawn* was released later that year. Hemsworth admitted to being nervous about audience response to his early performances. "Selfishly, I look back each week and think, oh, jeez, I knew nothing last week and now I get it," he told David Germain for the Canadian Press news agency (27 Apr. 2012). "So to go back three years, I sort of cringe at the thought of what I did then as opposed to now." Despite his concerns, *The Cabin in the Woods,* in particular, was successful at the box office and received praise from critics such as Roger Ebert.

In 2012, Hemsworth also appeared in *Snow White and the Huntsman*, a reimagining of the classic fairy tale. Although he was initially reluctant to take on the fantastical role of the huntsman, he changed his mind after meeting with director Rupert Sanders. "I . . . just kind of fell in love with what he had in mind," Hemsworth told Dawson. "The idea was to make it different, much dirtier, rougher." In response to the success of the film, the studio announced plans for a sequel, though casting details remained unclear.

Though undoubtedly rooted in the real world, Hemsworth's next major role was nonetheless larger than life. Hemsworth was cast as British Formula 1 racer James Hunt in the biographical film *Rush*, directed by Ron Howard, which focuses on Hunt's rivalry with Austrian racer Niki Lauda and its culmination in the 1976 World Championship. Hemsworth has commented that the real-life Hunt, who died in 1993, intrigues him. "He's kind of fascinating, quite contradictory," he told Dawson. "On the one hand there's this arrogant, brash, hot-tempered person, but there was a gentle side to him." The film finished filming in mid-2012 and is scheduled for release in September 2013.

## PERSONAL LIFE

Hemsworth lives in Los Angeles with his wife, Spanish actor Elsa Pataky. Their daughter, India Rose, was born in the spring of 2012. The experience of being a father has delighted Hemsworth. "Despite everything that is going on with work, it all paled into the background as soon as I had a baby," he told Lisa Marks and Jonathon Moran for the Sydney *Sunday Telegraph* (17 June 2012). "She has taken up all of my attention in the best way." While the family resides in the United States, Hemsworth has said that he hopes to raise his daughter as a proud Australian, and Pataky has reportedly chosen to speak to the baby only in her native Spanish. Hemsworth approves of this but has admitted that his own Spanish could use some work. "I better get with the program," he joked to Bardin. "The baby won't know what I'm saying and vice versa!"

In his free time, Hemsworth enjoys surfing, an activity he has loved since childhood. "Our whole family surfs," Hemsworth told Bardin. "Holiday destinations tend to be centered around the ocean." Hemsworth's brother Liam moved to the United States in 2009, and in 2012, Luke announced his intention to return to acting and move to Los Angeles. "We're all very close," Hemsworth told Bardin. "Having a family member here to bounce ideas around with and get a perspective you trust is hugely beneficial."

## SUGGESTED READING

Bardin, Brantley. "Man of Style: Chris Hemsworth." *InStyle* May 2012: 172–74. Print.
Breznican, Anthony. "First Look at the Avengers Dream Team." *Entertainment Weekly* 7 Oct. 2011: 34–40. Print.
Hemsworth, Chris, and Ceri Davidon. "In My Own Words: 'My Life Is More Complicated Now.'" [Sydney] *Sunday Telegraph* 10 April 2011: 21. Print.
Neuman, Joshua. "God of Waves." *Flaunt*. Flaunt, n.d. Web. 12 Nov. 2012.
Van Meter, William. "Chris Hemsworth." *Interview* May 2011: 98–103. Print.

—*Joy Crelin*

# Jennifer Higdon

**Born:** December 31, 1962
**Occupation:** Classical composer

Jennifer Higdon is a Pulitzer Prize– and Grammy Award–winning composer of contemporary classical music. Higdon, who taught herself to play the flute as a teenager, has been both celebrated and criticized for her large and various body of work, which has been described as both serious and accessible. "You don't need a PhD to understand my pieces," Higdon told Kevin Berger for the *Los Angeles Times* (25 Mar. 2012). "I work hard on making sure they communicate to everybody." Her work is performed several hundred times each year; the piece "blue cathedral," which she wrote after her brother's death, has been performed more than four hundred times since its premiere in 2000. Higdon has composed works for numerous performing groups, including the Chicago Symphony, the Indianapolis Symphony, and the Tokyo String Quartet.

Higdon's work, which has also been described as neoromantic, is at times inspired by American folk music as well as by her personal life and observations. The frenetic flute solo "rapid.fire," for instance, was written to express the relentless violence of the inner city. Higdon told Teresa Annas for the *Virginian-Pilot* (29 Oct. 2010) that the act of writing "blue cathedral" as a memorial to her brother was "cathartic" and identified the universal experience of loss as one of the reasons for the piece's popularity with audiences. "I think you try to write something that's true, that's heartfelt, and I think the audience will respond," she told Frank J. Oteri for the web magazine *New Music Box* (1 Sept. 2007). Higdon's *Percussion Concerto* won the Grammy Award for best contemporary classical composition in 2009. The following year, she won the Pulitzer Prize in music for her *Violin Concerto*. Higdon has also received awards from the Guggenheim Foundation, the American Society of Composers, Authors, and Publishers (ASCAP), and the American Academy of Arts and Letters. She is the Milton L. Rock Chair in Composition Studies at the Curtis Institute of Music in Philadelphia, Pennsylvania.

## EARLY LIFE AND EDUCATION

Higdon was born on December 31, 1962, in Brooklyn, New York. She and her younger brother, Andrew, spent their early years in Atlanta, Georgia. Higdon describes her parents, Kenny and Judy, both artists, as hippies who introduced her to avant-garde films and art. She rebelled against the disjointed nature of the experimental art she saw as a child, which included a show in which an artist covered himself in rubber cement for a performance involving fan-blown

AP Photo

feathers but passed out from the fumes before his piece began. "I remember thinking, 'What are these adults doing? This is what they call art?' I actually thought that at a young age," she told Oteri. "I actually might have gotten all the need for heavy experimenting out of my system by the time I was nine from attending so many things like this."

When Higdon was eleven, her family moved to rural Tennessee. She grew up listening to reggae and folk singers such as Bob Dylan and Peter, Paul and Mary. Her parents did not introduce her to classical music, though there were always instruments in the house. At fifteen, while attending Heritage High School in Maryville, Tennessee, Higdon discovered a flute in the family attic, taught herself to play, and joined the school marching band. She excelled at the instrument and decided to pursue a major in flute performance at Bowling Green State University in Ohio. There, she met Robert Spano, who later became the music director of the Atlanta Symphony Orchestra and one of Higdon's frequent collaborators. At the urging of flute professor Judith Bentley, Higdon composed her first piece, "Night Creatures," at the age of twenty-one. Higdon finished her flute studies but continued to compose music compulsively. "I had no choice, quite honestly, which I think is something most composers experience," she told Oteri. "You do it because you absolutely have to."

Higdon next attended the Curtis Institute of Music in Philadelphia, where she studied under Pulitzer Prize–winning composer Ned Rorem.

After earning an artist's diploma in 1988, she enrolled in the University of Pennsylvania to obtain her MA and PhD in music, studying with the Pulitzer Prize–winning composer George Crumb. Crumb, who is known for experimenting with unusual musical techniques, inspired Higdon to incorporate experimental flourishes into the more traditional structures of her own work; the beginning of the orchestral piece *Violin Concerto*, for instance, features the sound of knitting needles.

## BREAKTHROUGH

Higdon began receiving commissions in 1994, the same year she joined the faculty at the Curtis Institute. In 1998, she was commissioned to write a long piece for the Philadelphia Orchestra. It took her more than a year to determine the right structure for the work, in part because she typically favors fast tempos and had to readjust her mind-set for a longer piece. Shortly before the piece, *Concerto for Orchestra*, was scheduled to premiere in 2002, Higdon learned that the Philadelphia Orchestra planned to debut it during the prestigious American Symphony Orchestra League Conference. When she heard the news, Higdon recalled to Oteri, she nearly fainted. The annual conference was attended by nearly every orchestra programmer in the country; in other words, a premiere at the conference could make or break a young composer's career.

Higdon was proud of the fact that she was able to sustain herself on music alone, and she was afraid that a poor showing at the conference would disrupt her steady flow of commissions. "I realized everything in my life was coming down to thirty minutes," she told Oteri. The day of the premiere, the orchestra opened a rehearsal of the piece to the public. After the rehearsal was over, all four scheduled performances sold out within minutes. *Concerto for Orchestra* was met with acclaim from both audiences and critics. In a front-page review in the *Philadelphia Inquirer*, music critic David Patrick Stearns wrote (13 June 2002), "*Concerto for Orchestra* has shamelessly ecstatic climaxes, scintillating interplay among instruments, and an orchestration that delivers wave after heart-stopping wave of intoxicating color."

The piece is comprised of five movements and totals thirty-five minutes in length. In her program notes, Higdon revealed that she wrote the concerto "from the inside out," meaning that the third movement, in which each principal player has a solo, was written first. The second movement serves to highlight the sound of the Philadelphia Orchestra's string section, and the fourth movement is an exploration of rhythm and percussion. Higdon introduces the violins in the fifth movement and increases the tempo. The first movement, which Higdon wrote last, opens with chimes and is made up of what Higdon describes as "small chamber moments, in recognition of the fact that it takes many individuals to make the whole of the orchestra."

## INSPIRATION

Higdon's work has been compared to and performed alongside the work of the twentieth-century American composer Aaron Copland. Like Copland, Higdon is inspired by various genres of American folk music, including Appalachian dance music and bluegrass and Tennessee mountain music. Her work further mirrors that of mid-twentieth-century composers in that it is evocative and often melodic, characteristics that fell out of favor during contemporary classical music's more experimental phase. But Higdon seeks to combine the best of both worlds. Her work is accessible and emotionally frank—words that collaborators have also used to describe Higdon's personality—yet at times incredibly challenging.

In 1998, Higdon's brother, Andrew, died of metastatic melanoma at the age of thirty-three. Higdon, who was very close to her brother, wrote the piece "blue cathedral" in his memory, later noting in interviews that the piece's title was inspired in part by Andrew's middle name, Blue. The thirteen-minute orchestral piece features a duet between a flute, Higdon's instrument, and a clarinet, the instrument that Andrew once played. The piece is intensely emotional. When asked how it made her feel, Higdon told Annas, "It's like being swallowed by a wave." The piece premiered at a 2000 concert commemorating the Curtis Institute of Music's seventy-fifth anniversary.

Another one of Higdon's orchestral works, *City Scape*, was commissioned by and premiered with the Atlanta Symphony Orchestra in 2002; Spano conducted the performance. The thirty-minute piece is an ode to the city of Atlanta, where Higdon spent her early childhood. *City Scape* consists of three movements that can be performed individually. The first movement describes the bustling skyline; the second, titled "river sings a song to trees," captures the flow of water in the city parks; and the third, titled "Peachtree Street" after the city's main street, evokes Atlanta's roadways and intersections. Several reviews of the piece praised its internal momentum. "The first movement, 'SkyLine,' bolts from the gate and moves forward with jaunty, propulsive optimism. Even when the mood grows calm, there's a sense of motion, an unstoppable pulse—an anticipation that something grand is about to happen," one reviewer wrote for the *Atlanta Journal-Constitution* (10 Nov. 2002).

## COMMISSIONS AND COLLABORATIONS

Many of Higdon's most well-known pieces were commissioned by particular orchestras or created specifically for individual musicians or groups. She wrote her popular *Concerto 4-3* for a classically trained garage band of former students called Time for Three. Another orchestral piece, *Dooryard Bloom*, was commissioned by the Brooklyn Philharmonic and inspired by the poetry of Walt Whitman. Written for the Scottish solo percussionist Colin Currie, who favors the marimba, Higdon's twenty-three-minute *Percussion Concerto* premiered in 2005. The piece was designed to highlight the multitude of percussion instruments and virtuosity of Currie. On several occasions, performances of the piece elicited standing ovations for both the composer and the percussionist. *Percussion Concerto* won the Grammy Award for best contemporary classical composition in 2009.

Higdon has also written a number of chamber pieces for individual instruments, including many for the flute. She wrote the six-minute piece "running the edgE" for flutists Claudia Anderson and Jill Felber, who make up the duo ZAWA!. The piece, for two flutes and a piano, showcases the duo's formidable technique. Higdon paired up with Jennifer Koh, a violinist and former student of the Curtis Institute, for the twenty-minute violin and piano piece *String Poetic*. The particularly agile work became popular with both performers and audiences. Higdon also wrote a longer orchestral piece for Koh, *The Singing Rooms*, which premiered in 2007 with the Philadelphia Orchestra. The piece incorporates a chorus, an element that Higdon rarely uses, as well as lyrics based on a group of poems by Jeanne Minahan McGinn, a faculty member at the Curtis Institute.

Higdon's 2010 Pulitzer Prize–winning *Violin Concerto*, written for violin soloist and former Curtis student Hilary Hahn, premiered with the Indianapolis Symphony Orchestra in February 2009. The thirty-three-minute, three-movement concerto is a celebration of Hahn's instrument, the violin, and the commonalities between the composer and the soloist. The first movement is titled "1726," the street address of the Curtis Institute. In her program notes for the piece, Higdon explained that she was interested in exploring the theme of journeys, both musical and personal. The second movement, "Chaconni," features a dialogue between the orchestra and the soloist tailored to Hahn's individual tone, and the third movement, "Fly Forward," showcases Hahn's gifts in its speediness. Allan Kozinn for the *New York Times* (16 Feb. 2011) noted, "[*Violin Concerto*] fits Ms. Hahn's interpretive personality perfectly, drawing on both her pinpoint precision in fast, intricate passages and the singing tone she typically produces in slow, long-lined music."

In addition to Spano, Higdon frequently works with the conductor Marin Alsop, who is the music director of the Baltimore Symphony

Orchestra. The two have developed several pieces together. Higdon has likened her work to that of a playwright: although she typically completes a piece prior to beginning rehearsals, she acknowledges that the conductor and orchestra or solo performer must make a piece their own to bring it to life. Since winning the Grammy and the Pulitzer for her inventive, collaborative work, Higdon has continued to collaborate and expand the boundaries of her compositions. Her first opera, based on the Civil War novel *Cold Mountain* and composed in collaboration with librettist Gene Scheer, is scheduled to premiere with the Santa Fe Opera in 2015.

## PERSONAL LIFE

Unlike many composers, Higdon self-publishes all of her work. Originally, she chose to self-publish because larger companies were not interested in her material. As her career progressed, Higdon saw how expensive it was for musicians to acquire new work and realized the importance of a direct connection between performers and composers. As a self-published composer, Higdon is able to control not only who buys her pieces and for how much money but also which pieces are available to musicians. The name of Higdon's music publishing company, Lawdon Press, combines Higdon's last name and that of her longtime partner, Cheryl Lawson. Lawson, whom Higdon met in high school, manages the publication and sale of Higdon's work from their home in Philadelphia.

## SUGGESTED READING

Annas, Teresa. "VSO to Perform Work of Top American Composer (Who Has a Local Connection)." *PilotOnline*. Virginian-Pilot, 29 Oct. 2010. Web. 13 Aug. 2012.

Berger, Kevin. "Composer Jennifer Higdon Pursues Friendly Music." *Los Angeles Times*. Los Angeles Times, 25 Mar. 2012. Web. 12 Aug. 2012.

Kozinn, Allan. "Sound That's Lush and Slow, Speedy and Precise." *New York Times*. New York Times, 16 Feb. 2011. Web. 15 Aug. 2012.

Oteri, Frank J. "Jennifer Higdon: Down to Earth." *New Music Box*. New Music USA, 1 Sept. 2007. Web. 12 Aug. 2012.

## SELECTED COMPOSITIONS

"rapid.fire," 1992; "running the edgE," 1996; "blue cathedral," 1999; *City Scape*, 2002; *Concerto for Orchestra*, 2002; *Dooryard Bloom*, 2004; *Percussion Concerto*, 2005; *String Poetic*, 2006; *Concerto 4-3*, 2007; *The Singing Rooms*, 2007; *Violin Concerto*, 2008

—*Molly Hagan*

# Damien Hirst

**Born:** June 7, 1965
**Occupation:** Artist, entrepreneur, and art collector

While people may not agree as to whether Turner Prize–winning Damien Hirst is the best artist to emerge in the last twenty-five years, he is undoubtedly the wealthiest. Hirst has raked in more cash for his works—which most famously include a tiger shark submerged in formaldehyde and suspended in a glass case—than any other living artist. His net worth, an estimated $400 million, has become an integral part of his artistic statement.

Since the 1980s, Hirst, who was once the leader of a rabble-rousing movement known as the Young British Artists, has explored bold-faced themes of life and death in his work. Later in his career, however, wealth, particularly the money-making mechanisms of the commercialized art world, became just as alluring to him. "The art market is to Mr. Hirst as popular culture is to artists like Jeff Koons: his main content," Roberta Smith wrote for the *New York Times* (20 Sept. 2008).

Hirst's industrial approach to art—according to Richard Lacayo for *TIME* magazine (15 Sept. 2008), he employs a "small army" of assistants to reproduce en masse his most famous pieces—and his relationships with art dealers and auctioneers amount in themselves to a kind of performance art. In 2008, Hirst was the first artist to bypass gallery owners and dealers, taking a whopping 223 new pieces directly to auction at Sotheby's in London. Regarding his own work, Hirst is unabashedly both serious and superficial. He told a reporter for *Harper's Bazaar* (Apr. 2012), "In my lifetime, art meets business; artists become businessmen—nothing you can do about it."

## EARLY LIFE AND EDUCATION

Damien Steven David Brennan was born in Bristol, England, on June 7, 1965. He was raised in a working-class family in the industrial city of Leeds. His mother, Mary Brennan, married a car salesman named William Hirst in 1966. He adopted Damien in 1967, and Damien Brennan became Damien Hirst. Hirst has a younger brother named Bradley and a younger sister named Gabrielle. Their parents divorced when Hirst was twelve. Soon after, Brennan told her son that the elder Hirst was not his biological father. Several family members have attributed Hirst's teenage rebellion to this revelation. As a teen, he was arrested three times for shoplifting.

As a child, Hirst was fascinated by the macabre, particularly images of wounds and dismemberment. At sixteen, he began making regular visits to the anatomy department of the Leeds

PA Photos/Landov

Medical School, where he drew pictures of cadavers. Hirst was influenced by the artist Francis Bacon, and he eagerly copied the style of Bacon's graphic paintings. He has admitted that his Bacon interpretations are not very good, but as Lacayo has pointed out, Hirst and Bacon share a sensibility as well as a "key motif: tortured figures writhing within a bright, clinical space." Bacon, who died in 1992, depicted figures. Hirst, in the most literal sense, depicts animals—such as his decaying tiger shark, with jaws open and ready to bite.

Hirst attended Allerton Grange High School in Leeds. He applied to the prestigious Central St. Martin's School of Art and Design in London but failed to get in. In 1984, he moved to London and worked in construction before he was accepted by the fashionable Goldsmiths College at the University of London in 1986. There he met Charles Saatchi, an enterprising former advertising executive and art collector who opened his own gallery. Hirst studied fine art at Goldsmiths until 1989, but his first brush with fame occurred during his second year at the school.

### FREEZE EXHIBITION

In 1988, Hirst conceived and curated a group exhibition called *Freeze*. He gained sponsorship from the London Docklands Development Corporation and secured the empty Port of London Authority Building in Surrey Docks as a space. Hirst prepared the building, painting walls and

installing lights, while working part-time at the Anthony d'Offay Gallery. *Freeze* featured the work of sixteen artists, many of whom were Hirst's classmates at Goldsmiths, alongside his own. Hirst installed three pieces over the course of the exhibition: *Boxes*, a sculpture of cardboard boxes painted with gloss, and *Edge* and *Row*, two nearly identical spot paintings that Hirst applied directly to the wall.

Hirst began his spot painting series in 1986. The simplest and most iconic of them, such as the ones on display in *Freeze*, feature perfectly formed dots of varying colors—the colors do not repeat in any given piece—arranged on a grid against a white background. Of the spot paintings, Hirst told the late Gordon Burn for the book *On the Way to Work*, which the two men cowrote in 2001, "It was just a way of pinning down the joy of color."

The enterprising Hirst also secured enough funds to create a professional exhibition catalogue, which he distributed to galleries throughout London during the summer of 1988. The catalogue generated a significant amount of publicity by the time *Freeze* opened in August. The exhibition drew notable art-world figures such as the Royal Academy of Art's Norman Rosenthal, the Tate Modern's Sir Nicholas Serota, and Saatchi, who immediately took to Hirst and fellow *Freeze* artist Sarah Lucas, among others. *Freeze*, which New York University museum studies director Bruce Altshuler cites in *Biennials and Beyond* (2013) as one of the best art exhibitions of the period from 1962 to 2002, is considered the launching pad for a group of artists who came to be known as the Young British Artists, or the YBAs (YBA art is also called Britart). "The YBAs combined conceptual-art savvy with a will to bedazzle and provoke the widest possible audience," Peter Schjeldahl wrote for the *New Yorker* (23 Jan. 2012). "Their keynote was elegantly crafted effrontery."

### YOUNG BRITISH ARTISTS

Saatchi was the earliest champion of Hirst and the YBAs, who delighted in shocking the public with their vulgar subject matter. In 1990, Saatchi sponsored a warehouse show called *Modern Medicine*. It featured a print of one of Hirst's *Medicine Cabinets* installations. The twelve-piece series of pill bottles and objects arranged in medicine cabinets served as Hirst's thesis at Goldsmiths in 1989. Each piece of the series is titled after a track on the British punk band the Sex Pistols' only studio album, *Never Mind the Bollocks* (1977).

The success of *Modern Medicine* spawned another exhibition, *Gambler*, that same year. The exhibition featured Hirst's famous sculpture/installation *A Thousand Years*. The piece is composed of a decaying cow's head on one side of a split vitrine. On the other side of a glass partition with four holes, flies are hatched in an incubator. Over the course of whichever exhibition displays *A Thousand Years*, dead flies (killed by zapper) accumulate on the cow's head, which is doused in fake blood. Hirst later told *Burn* that he had set out to create a "life cycle in a box."

*Sensation*, Saatchi's most famous exhibition of YBA work, appeared at London's Royal Academy in 1997. The exhibition attempted to redefine the movement that had begun with *Freeze*, featuring Hirst's *A Thousand Years* alongside work by Mat Collishaw (*Bullet Hole*) and Marcus Harvey (*Myra*), among others. True to its name, the exhibition caused quite a sensation in London, where the gallery drew a record thirty thousand visitors and *Myra*, a portrait of a child murderer painted with children's fingerprints, spurred public outrage. The exhibition moved to the Brooklyn Museum in 1999, prompting New York City mayor Rudolph Giuliani to demand the removal of Chris Ofili's elephant dung–spattered painting *The Holy Virgin Mary*.

## NATURAL HISTORY SERIES

In 1991, Saatchi commissioned Hirst to create a piece that the artist titled *The Physical Impossibility of Death in the Mind of Someone Living*. The pickled fourteen-foot tiger shark, with jaws agape, became one of Hirst's most iconic pieces. It was exhibited at the Saatchi Gallery in London as a part of Saatchi's *Young British Artists I* exhibition in 1992. On Hirst's personal website, the catalogue entry for the piece reads: "By isolating the shark from its natural habitat, with the formaldehyde providing the illusion of life, the work explores our greatest fears, and the difficulty involved in adequately trying to express them." Saatchi bought the piece in 1991; in 2005, he sold it to an American hedge-fund manager for $12 million. The price tag raised quite a few eyebrows at the time. Indeed, economist Don Thompson published a critical book about money and the contemporary art world titled *The $12 Million Stuffed Shark* in 2010.

*The Physical Impossibility* is a part of Hirst's *Natural History* series, which he began in 1991. Hirst intended the series, he wrote on his website, to resemble a "zoo of dead animals." The series includes the 1994 piece *Away from the Flock*, which features a bisected lamb—literally a lamb cut in half. Each side of the animal is preserved in formaldehyde in a separate vitrine. "The lamb makes you think about all sorts of issues: life, death, the afterlife. The way we treat animals," Hirst told Fiametta Rocco for the London *Independent* (8 May 1994). Responding to criticisms of the piece, he added, "Either it ended up as dog food or in my art." The series also includes the 1993 piece *Mother and Child, Divided*, which earned Hirst the prestigious Turner Prize in 1995, when he was only thirty years old. The piece features a cow and calf, both bisected, with their separate sides preserved in vitrines filled with formaldehyde. As with *Away from the Flock*, the animals' organs, cut neatly down the center, are visible and intact.

In 1994, Simon Wilson of the Tate told Rocco that he was frustrated by viewers who were disgusted by Hirst's works with animals. The sensation surrounding the subject, he said, "has obscured the real seriousness of [Hirst's] art," which Wilson believes represents "a theme that is central to the tradition of Western art, which is about ephemerality and human existence on this earth."

## FOR THE LOVE OF GOD

In 2007, Hirst unveiled a sculpture called *For the Love of God*, a platinum-cast human skull layered with exactly 8,601 diamonds and features real human teeth. It was first presented at London's White Cube Gallery as a part of the *Beyond Belief* exhibition. The much-hyped piece signified a change of subject matter for Hirst. "His true medium is no longer flies or sharks or spots," Blake Gopnik wrote for *Newsweek* (2 Apr. 2012). "His medium is the tabloid press, and the auction market, and his collectors, and his art's peculiar reception." *For the Love of God* reportedly sold for more than $70 million, though it was later revealed to have been bought by a small group of investors—one of whom was Hirst.

## BEAUTIFUL INSIDE MY HEAD FOREVER

In 2008, Hirst became the first artist to bypass gallery owners and art dealers, bringing his work to auction at Sotheby's straight from the studio. (It is standard procedure for gallery owners to charge a 50 percent commission. Owners and art dealers then bring the works to auction.) Hirst had previously worked with Sotheby's, the legendary London auction house, in 2004, when he auctioned off the entire contents of a Notting Hill restaurant called Pharmacy, a venture he had opened in 1999. But Hirst's 2008 auction, which he titled *Beautiful Inside My Head Forever*, was much, much larger. Among the 223 works on the auction block were *The Golden Calf*, which includes the largest piece of gold plating ever attached to a glass case; *Togetherness*, in which cows' heads, preserved in formaldehyde, balance a beach ball on their noses; and a number of spin paintings, which Hirst and his assistants create by dripping paint onto a spinning canvas. Though many considered the auction a risk, it surpassed even the best expectations, bringing in a staggering $200.7 million for Hirst and Sotheby's.

Hirst has said that he is democratizing art by selling his work to the highest bidder, eschewing the pretentions of gallery owners who tend to look for the "right" buyer. "I hate the way when you walk into a gallery and say you want to buy a Damien Hirst they say: 'Who are you?' I much prefer to be in a shop where you can just go in and buy it," he told Lacayo. But while Hirst instructs his assistants to churn out hundreds of his signature spot paintings and spin paintings—and once delighted in a charity auction in which buyers had to guess whether a painting was a genuine Hirst or the work of local children—his critics claim that he "represents a particularly offensive form of cultural heresy," William Langley wrote for the London *Telegraph* (13 Sept. 2008), "one founded upon the notion that anything is art if the artist says it is."

## RETROSPECTIVES
In 2012, the Tate Modern in London exhibited a major retrospective of seventy-three Hirst works. Drawing in nearly half a million visitors, it was the most popular exhibition in the gallery's history. Among the pieces on display were *For the Love of God*; *A Thousand Years*; *Mother and Child, Divided*; and *In and Out of Love*, a two-room installation in which butterfly pupae hatch from white paintings and dead butterflies are pressed onto colorfully painted canvasses. Hirst, who first displayed the work in 1991, was taken to task in the newspapers for killing over nine thousand butterflies over the course of the retrospective.

After reaching a financial high watermark in 2008, Hirst began to suffer sluggish sales of his work. Poorly received still life paintings and a surplus of inventory at his "factory" have hurt the value of his work, leading Stephen Marche of *Esquire* (7 Jan. 2013) to write, "If you own a Hirst, sell now." The decrease in value is especially detrimental to the artist, Marche suggests, because Hirst's work, by Hirst's own construction, is worth only what buyers are willing to pay for it. In other words, the art is *about* how much it costs; Hirst's art, as demonstrated so perfectly in the decadence of his jewel-encrusted skull, is a celebration of money, and it has become an emblem of status for the superrich. It came as no surprise to critics then that his fall from favor with buyers coincided with a global economic crisis. His historic auction was held on September 15, 2008—the very day Lehman Brothers collapsed.

In late 2012, Hirst parted ways with his art dealer of seventeen years, Larry Gagosian, who is himself one of the wealthiest and most influential names in the art world. The split came after the two engineered a major retrospective of Hirst's spot paintings in 2012. *Damien Hirst: The Complete Spot Paintings, 1986–2011* featured 331 of Hirst's spot paintings mounted across all eleven of Gagosian's international galleries. In a review of the New York portion of the show for the *New York Times* (13 Jan. 2012), Smith stated that there are over 1,500 spot paintings in existence. Hirst has stated that he makes the paintings with the intention that they look like the work of a machine, yet Smith wrote that one of the most interesting things about them is their variation. It is clear that they are the work of many different hands. "In some works the colors are routine and vapid; in others they really sing, forming rhythms in spite of the fact that they never repeat," Smith wrote. Alternately "exhilarating" and "oppressive," the paintings could easily be a description of the artist's entire body of work.

## PERSONAL LIFE
Throughout the late 1980s and 1990s, Hirst was known as the consummate party boy, but he gave up drinking and drugs in 2002. Hirst was romantically involved with California fashion designer Maia Norman for nineteen years. The couple had three sons together before ending their relationship in 2012. Hirst lives in Devon, Gloucestershire, and London.

## SUGGESTED READING
*Damien Hirst*. Bureau for Visual Affairs, n.d. Web. 11 June 2013.
Gopnik, Blake. "A Brand Called Damien Hirst." *Newsweek* 2 Apr. 2012: 66–70. Print.
Lacayo, Richard. "Damien Hirst: Bad Boy Makes Good." *TIME* 15 Sept. 2008: 32–38. Print.
Rocco, Fiametta. "Profile: Damien Hirst: Lambs to Laughter." *Independent*. Independent, 8 May 1994. Web. 11 June 2013.
Smith, Roberta. "After the Roar of the Crowd, an Auction Post-Mortem." *New York Times* 20 Sept. 2008: B7. Print.
Smith, Roberta. "Hirst, Globally Dotting His 'I.'" *New York Times* 13 Jan. 2012: C25. Print.

## SELECTED WORKS
*Boxes*, 1988; *Medicine Cabinets*, 1989; *A Thousand Years*, 1990; *In and Out of Love*, 1991; *The Physical Impossibility of Death in the Mind of Someone Living*, 1991; *Mother and Child, Divided*, 1993; *Away from the Flock*, 1994; *For the Love of God*, 2007; *The Golden Calf*, 2008; *Damien Hirst: The Complete Spot Paintings, 1986–2011*, 2012

—Molly Hagan

# François Hollande
**Born:** August 12, 1954
**Occupation:** President of France

François Hollande was sworn into office as the president of France on May 15, 2012, after defeating incumbent president Nicolas Sarkozy. Hollande's election was viewed as an expression of public disgust over austerity measures being

Getty Images

initiated throughout the European Union (EU). As a result of cuts, many people in Europe had lost their jobs and pensions. During his campaign, Hollande promised to reduce the deficit to 3 percent by 2013 through a series of reforms that included both cuts and stimulus spending. After taking office as president, he pledged to balance the budget by the end of his first five-year term in 2017.

After a long career working behind the scenes, Hollande rose to the top of his party's ticket after front-runner, Dominique Strauss-Kahn, the former director of the International Monetary Fund, was charged with sexually assaulting a hotel maid in New York City. The charges were later dropped, but with the salacious details of the alleged encounter made public—and a separate charge of sexual assault awaiting him in France—Strauss-Kahn's political viability was destroyed. Hollande, who was dubbed "Mr. Normal" for his relatively banal private life, was viewed as a refreshing contrast to colleagues Strauss-Kahn and Sarkozy. Although Sarkozy had never faced any criminal charges, his public divorce and subsequent marriage to supermodel and singer Carla Bruni while in office did not do his public image any favors.

In an election that was seen as a referendum on Sarkozy, Hollande went out of his way to distinguish himself from his competitor. Where Sarkozy was seen as the "president of the rich," Hollande rode to work on a scooter and proposed a 75 percent tax rate on citizens who made more than €1 million, (approximately US$1.24 million) a year. "I like people, not money," he told Ruadhán Mac Cormaic for the Irish Times (21 Apr. 2012). Sarkozy, a member of the conservative Union for a Popular Movement party, sought to appeal to the hard right with anti-immigration policies and anti-Muslim rhetoric. Hollande presented himself as a moderate liberal and took care to reach out to political centrists. In

contrast to Sarkozy, who is known to be hard and brutally defensive in debates, Hollande was mellow, preferring to disarm opponents with subtle humor.

The emphasis of the 2013 election on personality seemed incongruous at such an important moment in France's history, when it faced major economic challenges domestically and within the EU. However, it was indicative of the two paths faced by French citizens in deciding how to restore France's position on the world stage.

## EARLY LIFE AND EDUCATION

François Gérard Georges Hollande was born on August 12, 1954, in Rouen, the historic capital of Normandy, in northern France. His father, Georges Gustave Hollande, was a doctor and his mother, Nicole Frédérique Marguerite Tribert, was a social worker. Hollande was raised in a middle-class Catholic home. Hollande's father was a political conservative. He ran for local office on a far-right ticket in 1959. In terms of his own political views, Hollande took after his mother, who was more progressive. She ran for a National Assembly seat on the Socialist ticket in 2008, a year before her death.

In 1968, when Hollande was thirteen years old, his father abruptly moved the family to Neuilly, outside of Paris. Hollande's father threw away the contents of his childhood bedroom and sent his older, rebellious brother to a strict Catholic boarding school. Hollande, who rarely talks about his relationship with his authoritarian father, was not as rebellious as his brother growing up. As he noted at a campaign rally, as quoted by Angelique Chrisafis in the London Guardian (18 Apr. 2012), "The [political] left wasn't my heritage, I chose it."

As a teenager, Hollande traveled across Europe with friends, listening to American rock music. In 1974, he spent a summer in the United States as a student, where he learned about American politics and culture.

Hollande was interested in public service from a young age. His mother once told a reporter that he had professed his desire to become president as a child. "Hollande is a career politician who, from his first teenage candidacy as a classroom rep and then student union leader, was interested in elections and how to win them," Chrisafis wrote. He worked his way through France's public school system and went on to earn a law degree. Hollande briefly attended the International Business School of Paris (École des Hautes Études Commerciales de Paris) before studying at the Paris Institute of Political Studies (Institut d'Études Politiques de Paris) and the prestigious National School of Administration (École nationale d'administration, or ENA). The ENA is considered the premiere training ground for the French political and business elite. Hollande's graduating class of 1980 included several future government ministers, ambassadors, and CEOs, as well as a woman named Ségolène Royal. Royal, who is also a politician, was Hollande's partner, co-parent, and political adversary for nearly thirty years.

## EARLY PARTY CAREER

In 1974, Hollande served as chairman of the support committee for François Mitterrand, who was then a Socialist Party presidential candidate. Mitterrand lost the 1974 election to Valéry Giscard d'Estaing of the Independent Republicans party. Hollande joined the Socialist party in 1979 and became an aide and advisor to President Mitterrand after he was elected in 1981. He drew comparisons to Mitterrand during his own presidential campaign in 2012. "Often people told me, 'Oh la la, François Mitterrand, what charisma, what a president!' But before he became president, they used to call him badly dressed, old, archaic, he knows nothing about the economy," Hollande told Steven Erlanger for the *New York Times* (13 Apr. 2012). Mitterrand's election fundamentally changed Hollande. As president, he described to Erlanger, "you are invested, you incarnate France—that changes everything."

The same year that Mitterrand became president, the twenty-six-year-old Hollande ran against seasoned conservative Jacques Chirac to represent the rural Corrèze region in southern France. Mitterrand had advised Hollande to build his political power by winning the support of rural areas, specifically Chirac's own Corrèze. Hollande lost the election to Chirac, who later served two terms as president. However, he famously won supporters after turning one of Chirac's remarks against him. Upon seeing Holland for the first time, Chirac, an old rival of Mitterrand, reportedly said, "They sent me an opponent no more well known than President Mitterrand's Labrador." Political commentator, Helene Jouan, told John Laurenson of the *BBC News* (14 Apr. 2012) that several days later, Hollande invited himself to one of Chirac's meetings. Raising his hand, he introduced himself as President Mitterrand's Labrador. Hollande's jibe "got him talked about," according to Jouan, "as a politician, he had come into existence."

## MEMBER OF PARLIAMENT

Although it took him seven years, Hollande finally became the member of Parliament (MP) of Corrèze in 1988, serving the region in the National Assembly until 2002. Despite its small size, representing Corrèze was no easy task for Hollande. Chirac had initiated a number of infrastructure projects that had sent the region into debt. Hollande proved himself up to the task, becoming a popular representative and successfully managing Corrèze's budget.

He later served as mayor of Tulle, the capital of Corrèze, from 2001 to 2008. Hollande and his conservative predecessor remain local heroes in the region. As Tulle journalist Alain Albinet told Kim Willsher of the London *Guardian* (21 Apr. 2012), the people of Corrèze expect their MPs to represent their concerns. "Because it is quite an isolated and poor region, people tend to feel forgotten," he explained. He added "with Hollande, the unspoken deal was they would support him and he would put down roots here, he would represent them and raise their concerns. Because he stayed, because he remained constant to Corrèze, the local people slowly accepted him and became loyal to him." According to Albinet, Hollande learned how to become a politician in Corrèze.

## SOCIALIST PRIMARY ELECTION

Hollande was named leader and secretary general of the Socialist Party in 1997, succeeding Lionel Jospin. He remained in this post until 2008. It was a difficult time for the party, which had not presented a winning candidate for the presidency since Mitterrand. Hollande was a quiet leader, who thrived behind the scenes, but he remained largely unknown in national politics. In 2007, Hollande faced his partner, Royal, in the Socialist primary for the presidential election. After she defeated him in the primary, Hollande supported her candidacy. General elections in France are held in rounds. A number of parties run candidates in the first round of the election. In the absence of a majority, the two candidates with the most votes qualify for a runoff election, or second round. Royal came in second in the first round of the 2007 election, qualifying for the second round where she was soundly beaten by Sarkozy.

Hours after Royal's defeat, she and Hollande revealed that they were separating after a thirty-year partnership. The French public is significantly less interested in the personal lives of its politicians than the American public. Nonetheless, during Royal's campaign, it was clear to many that the couple was merely putting on a good face for the cameras. Hollande had been seeing another woman, journalist Valérie Trierweiler, for some time before his separation with Royal.

According to some political analysts, Hollande began planning his 2012 presidential campaign as early as 2009, burnishing his persona in order to project a presidential image. Once known for being overweight, he went on a diet; he also replaced his previously sloppy attire with tailor-made suits. Hollande boned up on foreign policy during this period as well. On March 31, 2011, he returned to his loyal constituency in Corrèze to announce his intention to run in the Socialist Party presidential primary. After years of unglamorous work shaking hands in small towns and negotiating in party boardrooms, Hollande's time had come. "To be elected, it's necessary to have been beaten; to be loved, it's necessary to have suffered," he told Erlanger. "The scars, the blows, the fact that nothing has been given to you—people appreciate it."

## PRESIDENTIAL CAMPAIGN

In 2012, Hollande and Royal faced off in the Socialist Party presidential primary for a second time. Royal did not hold back her criticism of Hollande, but he succeeded in defeating her. Hollande faced political rival Martine Aubry in a runoff election. Aubry is best known for initiating France's thirty-five hour workweek in the 1990s. The second leg of the primary campaign was tumultuous, but after Hollande won the primary by a comfortable margin, Aubry subsequently threw her support behind him. The challenge, Socialist Party officials knew, would be facing Sarkozy in the general election.

Hollande and the far-right Front National candidate Marine Le Pen were viewed as Sarkozy's most serious challengers in France's 2012 presidential contest. Presidential campaigning began in earnest in February. Candidates temporarily suspended their campaigns in March after a shooting at a schoolhouse in Toulouse. As expected, the result of the first round of voting on April 22, 2012, favored Hollande and Sarkozy. As a candidate, Hollande was generally well liked, but not particularly dynamic. Hollande's reputation as "Mr. Normal" was reinterpreted by some voters as "Mr. Bland." His well-organized, if unexciting, campaign was compared to the 2012 presidential campaign of Republican Party candidate Mitt Romney in the United States. Like Romney, Hollande did not so much inspire a following of voters as gain a following of voters who had fallen out of love with his opponent. In fact, Sarkozy's popularity had fallen so far in the months leading up to the final vote that Hollande picked up the endorsement of Chirac.

Yet Hollande was not content simply to play Sarkozy's foil. "I must demonstrate I'm closer to people—a simpler, calmer presence, yet someone who can also make decisions and obtain promised results," Hollande told Bruce Crumley for *TIME* (13 Apr. 2012). "That's what voters are electing the president to do: make decisions—often hard, critical decisions—and get things done. Simply not being Nicolas Sarkozy won't be enough to win the election." Hollande introduced several proposals, including the renegotiation of an EU treaty that imposed strict rules on debt that was signed by Sarkozy in December 2011. He also promised to accelerate the withdrawal of French troops from Afghanistan and hire as many as sixty thousand new teachers. Hollande's most controversial proposal was a higher tax rate for France's wealthiest citizens. His proposal of a whopping 75 percent tax rate was, not surprisingly, very unpopular with wealthy citizens. Under threat of the tax, a number of French millionaires, including actor Gerard Depardieu, made very public plans to leave the country. After his election, Hollande defended the tax, noting that part of being French and loving France involves serving the country, however difficult it might be at the time.

## ELECTION AND EARLY PRESIDENCY

During the final stretch of campaigning before the May 6 election, Sarkozy's approval ratings hovered at a dismal 30 percent. Still, the election result was close, with Hollande receiving 51.9 percent of the vote to Sarkozy's 48.1 percent. Hollande was sworn into office as the president of France on May 15, 2012. Hollande is the first Socialist Party candidate to be elected to the presidency since Mitterrand, who served from 1981 to 1995.

Despite the triumph of his victory, Hollande's first hundred days as president were rocky. His inability to implement many of the reforms he had promised during his campaign caused his approval ratings to drop nearly as low as Sarkozy's in the last days of the campaign.

France continues to face significant economic issues, including a sizable deficit and high unemployment. As the second largest economy in the EU, France also faces challenges related to ending economic stagnation in Greece and Spain. Despite Sarkozy's international successes, notably his support for the overthrow of Libyan dictator Muammar Gaddafi, his domestic policies and support for austerity—large budget cuts aimed at forcibly reducing the deficit—did not sit well with voters.

Nevertheless, confidence in President Hollande soared after he chose to send the French military into Mali to turn back Islamist militants who had taken over large swaths of the country. The decision to take military action in Mali, a former colony of France, established Hollande as a firm, decisive commander in chief. In response to the French action in Mali, Hollande was awarded the Félix Houphouët-Boigny Peace Prize from the United Nations in 2013.

## PERSONAL LIFE

Although Hollande and Ségolène Royal never married, they endured a very public separation after Royal lost her 2007 presidential bid to Sarkozy. They were in a relationship from 1978 to 2007 and had four children: Thomas, Clémence, Julien, and Flora. Hollande has remained in a relationship with Valérie Trierweiler since his separation with Royal. Trierweiler's turbulent relationship with Royal caused some episodes of embarrassment for the Hollande administration.

Journalist Marie-Eve Malouines published a biography of Hollande entitled *François Hollande: The Strength of Mister Nice*, in 2012.

## SUGGESTED READING

Chrisafis, Angelique. "François Hollande: from marshmallow man to Sarkozy's nemesis?" *Guardian*. Guardian News and Media, 18 Apr. 2012. Web. 12 Mar. 2013.

Crumley, Bruce. "French Toast: How Sarkozy Found Himself on the Verge of Presidential Defeat." *TIME*. Time, 2 Apr. 2012. Web. 11 Mar. 2013.

Crumley, Bruce. "TIME Interviews French Presidential Front-Runner François Hollande." *TIME*. Time, 13 Apr. 2012. Web. 11 Mar. 2013.

Erlanger, Steven. "The Soft Middle of François Hollande." *New York Times*. New York Times, 13 Apr. 2012. Web. 12 Mar. 2013.

Mac Cormaic, Ruadhán. "We all know Sarko, but who's the other guy?" *Irish Times*. Irish Times, 21 Apr. 2012. Web. 11 Mar. 2013.

—*Molly Hagan*

# Khaled Hosseini

**Born:** March 4, 1965
**Occupation:** Author

© Elena Seibert

Khaled Hosseini, a former doctor, burst onto the literary scene in 2003 with his novel *The Kite Runner*, which remained on the *New York Times* best-seller list for more than four years and had sold a reported eighteen million copies worldwide by 2008. The book, about two Afghan boys whose friendship is shattered by a terrible betrayal, was widely credited with introducing American readers to a more nuanced view of that country than typically available on the nightly news. "I wanted to write about Afghanistan before the Soviet war because that is largely a forgotten period in modern Afghan history," Hosseini told Razeshta Sethna in an interview for Pakistan's *Newsline* magazine (2 Nov. 2003). "For many people in the west, Afghanistan is synonymous with the Soviet war and the Taliban. I wanted to remind people that Afghans had managed to live in peaceful anonymity for decades, that the history of the Afghans in the twentieth century has been largely pacific and harmonious."

As many critics have pointed out, however, the book's success is not due solely to its historical relevance and evocative setting. In an oft-echoed sentiment, Hosseini told Edward Guthmann for the *San Francisco Chronicle* (14 Mar. 2005), "Because its themes of friendship, betrayal, guilt, redemption and the uneasy love between fathers and sons are universal themes, and not specifically Afghan . . . the book has been able to reach across cultural, racial, religious and gender gaps to resonate with readers of varying backgrounds."

## EARLY YEARS

Hosseini was born on March 4, 1965, in Kabul, Afghanistan, a landlocked Islamic country bordered by Pakistan to the south and east, Iran to the west, and Tajikistan, Uzbekistan, and Turkmenistan to the north. The eldest of five children, Hosseini has one sister and three brothers. He also has "enumerable cousins and second cousins and whatnot and people that I consider cousins, who are not really actually related to me at all," he told an interviewer for the Academy of Achievement (3 July 2008). "The whole concept of family in Kabul is very loose, so I just had a very extended rich social life."

The household was an intellectual one. His mother was a high school teacher and vice principal who taught courses in history and Farsi, a language spoken predominately in Iran and parts of Afghanistan. (In Afghanistan, Farsi is also referred to as Dari. Both of Hosseini's parents hailed from Herat—a Dari-speaking area of the country—and while that was the language most often used in their home, Hosseini also learned Pashto, which had been the national language of Afghanistan by royal decree since 1936 and was a required part of his school's curriculum.) Consequently Hosseini was exposed at an early age to classic Persian poetry and literature. At a small bookstore in Kabul, he discovered Western novels translated into Farsi, and he became entranced by *Twenty-Thousand Leagues under the Sea*, *Treasure Island*, and other such classics. He began trying his hand at writing his own short stories, and while he loved the process, he did not consider a possible future as a professional writer until much later in life.

## POLITICAL UPHEAVAL

In 1973, when Hosseini was a child, Afghanistan's king, Zahir Shah—who had ruled since the early 1930s and had instituted a constitutional monarchy in the 1960s—was overthrown in a bloodless coup by his own cousin. "I actually remember the night that the king was overthrown," Hosseini told the Academy of Achievement. "I was in Kabul, my parents were at the hospital where my mother was giving birth to my youngest brother that night, and we heard the gunshots, and we heard the tanks rolling in and all of the rumbling. . . . We woke up to a whole new country."

In 1976 Hosseini's father, a diplomat, was assigned by the Afghan foreign ministry to a post in Paris, and the entire family relocated with him. During their stay in France, Afghanistan's political situation was plunged into chaos. In the spring of 1978, the centrist government was overthrown in a coup by left-wing military officers. The new government, which quashed any democratic opposition, forged close ties with the Soviet Union. The social reforms that were instituted were highly unpopular with Muslim Afghans, and insurgencies sprang up among several Islamic groups known collectively as the mujahideen. In an attempt to quell the uprisings—as well as the infighting that was going on among various government factions—the Soviets invaded Afghanistan in December 1979, sending in an estimated eighty thousand troops by mid-1980.

The Soviet-Afghan War quickly reached a stalemate; thousands of Soviet troops controlled the cities and larger towns, while the mujahideen roamed the countryside. Soviet troops tried to discourage their civilian support by bombing rural areas, sparking a massive wave of refugees fleeing to Pakistan and Iran.

## A MOVE TO THE UNITED STATES

Hosseini's family members, unable to return to their native country, were granted asylum in the United States, and in 1980 they left Paris for San Jose, California. The adjustment was difficult. His parents, used to having responsible, well-paying jobs, were initially forced to accept public assistance in order to feed their five children—a turn of events they found mortifying. They were dismayed as well by news filtering to them from Afghanistan. Several friends and acquaintances had been killed or imprisoned by the Soviets. An uncle of Hosseini's future wife, a popular Afghan entertainer who spoke out publicly against the Communists, subsequently disappeared; the family is still unsure of his fate. Until later in the decade, when increasing numbers of Afghans began settling in the area, the family also battled loneliness and cultural isolation.

Hosseini's parents found work in various jobs, his father as a driving instructor and later a city employee and his mother first as a waitress and later a beautician. He and his siblings quickly settled into American schools. Within two years Hosseini had learned English, and he recalls being deeply affected by reading *The Grapes of Wrath* in high school in 1983. "John Steinbeck's book was the first book I read in English where I had an 'Aha!' moment," he recalled in a 2004 interview for Barnes and Noble's Meet the Writers series. "For some reason, I identified with the disenfranchised farm workers in that novel—I suppose in one sense, they reminded me of my own country's traumatized people."

Earning his high school diploma in 1984, Hosseini entered Santa Clara University, where he completed a bachelor's degree in biology in 1988. In 1993 he graduated from the School of Medicine at the University of California at San Diego.

Following his residency at Cedars-Sinai Medical Center in Los Angeles, Hosseini became an internist first in Southern California and a few years later at a Kaiser Permanente facility in Silicon Valley. He entered into what has been described by some journalists as a "semi-arranged" marriage to Roya, then a law student. Speaking to Guthmann for the *San Francisco Chronicle*, Hosseini described their courtship as "fairly traditional" and said they married shortly after meeting. Roya is variously referred to in the press as a fellow Afghan immigrant and sometimes as a native-born American.

## BECOMING A WRITER

Despite his demanding job, Hosseini had never lost the urge to write, and he began penning short stories—mainly thrillers or tales of horror—in his spare time. A handful of these were published in small, experimental magazines, but he accumulated mainly rejection notices.

One day, while watching the news, Hosseini learned that the extremist Taliban regime then ruling Afghanistan had outlawed flying kites (a pastime known as *gudiparan bazi*) on the grounds that it was un-Islamic. (Subsequent bans have been put in place in other countries because people are often injured while kite fighting, an activity that involves trying to cut the string of an opponent's kite with your own.) He was inspired to write a short story about two kite-flying friends, and Roya, impressed, encouraged him to expand the piece.

Hosseini began waking before dawn every day so that he could write from 5 a.m. to 8 a.m., before leaving to treat patients. Within fifteen months he had produced a draft of *The Kite Runner*. "Two-thirds of the way through the manuscript, [the terrorist attacks of] September 11 happened," he told David Ferrell for SecondAct. com (15 Apr. 2010). "At that point, everybody was talking about the Taliban and [Osama] bin Laden, and . . . I put the manuscript away." Roya once again provided encouragement. Hosseini recalled to Ferrell, "She said, 'All the stuff on the news has to do with terrorism and the drug trade . . . and your story is about regular people—it shows a different face of Afghanistan.'"

### THE KITE RUNNER

Cindy Spiegel, then a copublisher at Riverhead Books, a division of the Penguin Group USA, agreed with Roya's assessment. The company paid what industry insiders have characterized as a surprisingly generous advance for a fledgling writer, given that the manuscript of *The Kite Runner* required extensive editing and rewriting; some cynically suggest that Riverhead saw a marketing opportunity in Hosseini himself, a ruggedly handsome man with his own compelling life story.

*The Kite Runner* was published in 2003. It is the story of Amir, a wealthy young Pashtun boy from the Wazir Akbar Khan district of Kabul and his closest friend, Hassan, the son of his father's Hazara servant. During the waning days of Afghanistan's monarchy, they spend their time spinning tales and flying kites. One day Hassan is brutally attacked by a group of bullies, and Amir is too cowardly to come to his rescue. Even after he and his father settle in America, Amir is haunted by his disloyalty and inaction.

Years later Amir learns that the Taliban have murdered Hassan and his wife and that the fate of their son, Sohrab, is uncertain. Motivated by his longstanding guilt, he returns to Kabul, where he discovers that the boy has been enslaved by one of the former childhood bullies—now a prominent Taliban official. He also discovers a tangled web of family relationships and secrets that must be unraveled before he can win freedom for the boy and redemption for himself.

### CRITICAL AND POPULAR RECEPTION

Reviews were almost overwhelmingly positive. Calling *The Kite Runner* a "powerful first novel," Edward Hower wrote for the *New York Times* (3 Aug. 2003), "Khaled Hosseini gives us a vivid and engaging story that reminds us how long his people have been struggling to triumph over the forces of violence—forces that continue to threaten them even today."

The book's popularity spread, particularly through word of mouth. Independent bookstores touted it enthusiastically, and the large chains eventually followed. It was named book of the year 2003 by *Entertainment Weekly* and the *San Francisco Chronicle*, and while the hardcover edition had sold only about fifty thousand copies in its first print run, when the paperback

came out in May 2004, sales began to climb. It made its first appearance on the *New York Times* best-seller list in September 2004 and remained there for more than four years. The book has since been published in some seventy countries and, as of December 2008, had sold a reported eighteen million copies worldwide. In 2011 it was also successfully adapted for the graphic novel format.

Hosseini did not immediately give up his medical practice. "I was reluctant to let go of the security of a very stable life," he explained to Andrea Sachs for *Time* magazine (5 Dec. 2008). "[But] when I started seeing people at airports reading my book, and when my patients would come in to visit me, more out of a sense of getting a book signed than getting their diabetes treated, I started to see the writing on the wall."

*The Kite Runner* was made into a feature film in 2007. Hosseini has said he believes it to be the first major Hollywood film in which all of the main characters are Muslim and portrayed as ordinary people. As a precaution against anticipated Afghan anger over a depiction of male rape in the film, the producers agreed to relocate the young actors to the United Arab Emirates, procuring visas for their entry and arranging for the boys' ongoing education and shelter, as well as for their guardians' employment. The film's release date was even pushed back until the young teens were safely away from Afghanistan. Afghan response to the film ultimately proved minimal; in the United States the film received a Golden Globe nomination for best foreign language film.

### SUBSEQUENT BOOKS

In 2003 Hosseini returned to Afghanistan to visit. "When I went to Kabul, the things I heard were really astonishing. Women had seen their children starve to death. A woman's sister had been raped and killed herself. There were women living in abject poverty who were beggars," he told Dylan Foley for the *Denver (Colorado) Post* (15 July 2007). He had also seen "a rather famous video out of Afghanistan," which includes "a grainy shot of a woman wearing a burqa being led to a spot in a soccer stadium. The Taliban guy behind her shoots her in the head rather casually. She collapses. It disturbed me, but the writer in me thought, 'What was her crime? Who was she? What kind of dreams did she have? What was she like as a child?'"

Upon his return to the United States, Hosseini began work on his next book, this one focused on the plight of Afghan women. *A Thousand Splendid Suns*, as the sophomore effort was titled, was published in 2007. It tells the story of Mariam and Laila, two women from different generations brought together by their forced marriages to the same brutal husband. Calling it "a forceful but nuanced portrait of a patriarchal despotism where women are agonizingly dependent on fathers, husbands and especially sons," a reviewer for *Publishers Weekly* (26 Feb. 2007) wrote, "His [Hosseini's] tale is a powerful, harrowing depiction of Afghanistan, but also a lyrical evocation of the lives and enduring hopes of its resilient characters." *A Thousand Splendid Suns* was often included on lists of the best books of the year, and it remained on the *New York Times* best-seller list for some seventy weeks, a large portion of that time in the number-one spot.

In May 2013 Hosseini published the eagerly awaited *And the Mountains Echoed*, a multigenerational family saga that takes its characters from Kabul to Paris, San Francisco, and the Greek islands. Much like his first work, Hosseini's latest publication focuses on betrayal, loss, and redemption, as well as Afghan identity in diaspora. Early critical reviews by *Library Journal*, *Publishers Weekly*, *Kirkus Reviews*, and *Booklist* noted the complexity of the plot, some finding that its many intersecting subplots did not cohere sufficiently. Nevertheless most praised Hosseini for his characterizations and powers of description, the narrative strengths that have become his signature style.

### HUMANITARIAN ACTIVITIES AND PERSONAL LIFE

On June 20, 2006, Hosseini was given a humanitarian award and invited to speak at World Refugee Day, in Washington, DC. Shortly thereafter, he was named a goodwill envoy by the United Nations High Commissioner for Refugees (UNHCR), an agency that was established in 1950 to coordinate international action to protect and aid refugees. In that capacity, Hosseini has visited several countries to hear the stories of those forced from their homes and has capitalized upon his literary fame to spread awareness of their plight.

During a 2007 trip he made to Afghanistan with the UNHCR, Hosseini was horrified to see a refugee camp consisting of makeshift open huts, with no water or medical care for its inhabitants. An elder explained that each winter several children simply froze to death there. Inspired by that trip Hosseini and his wife established the Khaled Hosseini Foundation, which provides shelter, health care, schooling, and economic opportunities to the people of his native country. "It's not a nation of beggars," he told Catherine Lutz for the *Aspen Business Journal* (25 June 2011). "Give an Afghan a stick of gum and he'll make a business out of it."

Hosseini told Michael Mechanic for *Mother Jones* (19 May 2009), "For a novelist, it's kind of an onerous burden to represent an entire culture." Still, he said, he is grateful that his success has put him "in a unique position to speak on behalf of Afghanistan on certain issues that I feel are important."

Hosseini and his wife, who chairs his eponymous foundation, have a son, Haris, and a daughter, Farah. The family lives in Sunnyvale, California.

### SUGGESTED READING

Ferrell, David. "Doctor Savors Second Career as Novelist." *SecondAct*. Entrepreneur Media, 15 Apr. 2010. Web. 3 May 2013.

Guthmann, Edward. "Before *The Kite Runner*, Khaled Hosseini Had Never Written a Novel. But with Word of Mouth, Book Sales Have Taken Off." *San Francisco Chronicle*. Hearst Communications, 14 Mar. 2005. Web. 3 May 2013.

Hosseini, Khaled. "Khaled Hosseini, Kabul's Splendid Son." Interview by Michael Mechanic. *Mother Jones*. Mother Jones, 19 May 2009. Web. 3 May 2013.

Hosseini, Khaled. "Two Afghan Wives Salvage Joy amid Strife." Interview by Dylan Foley. *Denver Post*. Denver Post, 15 July 2007. Web. 3 May 2013.

Hower, Edward. "The Servant." Rev. of *The Kite Runner*, by Khaled Hosseini. *New York Times*. New York Times, 3 Aug. 2003. Web. 3 May 2013.

Sachs, Andrea. "Khaled Hosseini." *Time*. Time, 5 Dec. 2008. Web. 3 May 2013.

### SELECTED WORKS

*The Kite Runner*, 2003; *A Thousand Splendid Suns*, 2007; *And the Mountains Echoed*, 2013.

—Mari Rich

# Billy Hunter

**Born:** November 5, 1942
**Occupation:** Executive director of the National Basketball Players Association

On February 16, 2013, player representatives of the National Basketball Players Association (NBPA), the union for National Basketball Association (NBA) players, voted unanimously to fire the union's executive director, Billy Hunter. NBPA president Derek Fisher headed the effort to remove Hunter after allegations of mismanagement and questionable business practices surfaced during an independent audit. "Going forward, we will no longer be divided, misled, misinformed," Fisher said (qtd. in *New York Times* 16 Feb. 2013). "This is our union, and we have taken it back." Hunter refuted the allegations and said that he would challenge his ouster.

Hunter had once enjoyed a positive reputation as the NBPA's executive director and had

Justin Lane/EPA/Landov

distinguished himself as one of the most power-ful men in sports. A tough and relentless fighter known for his no-nonsense negotiating skills, Hunter worked to protect the rights of NBA players, and had been credited for building unity among players in the wake of owner-imposed lockouts that delayed the start of the 1998–99, and 2011–12 seasons. "What Billy's done, he's listened," the Boston Celtics guard and NBPA vice president Keyon Dooling told Jeff Zillgitt for *USA Today* (28 July 2011). "He's done a great job of listening and getting through the facts. What his genius has been is the way he's been able to relate to players, and get the message out, and let the players be engaged in this process."

Hunter had a long and diverse career prior to the scandal: he had a brief stint as a profes-sional football player in the National Football League (NFL) with the Washington Redskins and Miami Dolphins. After leaving professional football, he made his name in the legal field, first as a public prosecutor in the San Francisco Bay Area, and then as a US attorney for the Northern District of California. He spent over a decade in private practice, heading a firm that represented a number of high-profile athletes, entertainers, and sports-related businesses. In 1996, Hunter became the fourth executive director of the NBPA, and two years after that, he formed the NBPA's sister union, the Women's National Bas-ketball Players Association (WNBPA), for which he also served as executive director. Around the time of the latter organization's inception, David Stern, the commissioner of the NBA, described Hunter to Ellen Chase for the Newark, New Jersey, *Star-Ledger* (1 Feb. 1998) as a "fine man. He's a dedicated man, an accomplished attorney. He understands the issues extraordinarily well, and he is firmly devoted to his clients."

## EARLY LIFE AND EDUCATION
George William "Billy" Hunter was born on No-vember 5, 1943, in Delaware Township, New Jersey (now Cherry Hill Township). Hunter's family history is steeped in a tradition of fighting for justice and liberty. His great-great grandfa-ther, William Still, was a noted abolitionist who played a vital role in building the Underground Railroad, the network of secret routes and safe houses used by slaves from the South to escape to northern free states and Canada. Widely con-sidered to be the "Father of the Underground Railroad," Still helped up to sixty slaves a month escape to freedom and later published a book, titled *The Underground Railroad* (1872), which chronicled his experiences working with fugitive slaves. "As a young kid growing up in the 1940s and 1950s, you never really thought about it," Hunter said of his family heritage to Mike Wise for the *New York Times* (2 Aug. 1998). "Black history hadn't come into fruition or being. It wasn't taught, so there was no relevance. No one was promoting black contributions to America. But then the '60s came along and Alex Haley's 'Roots.' It made you think about your past."

Hunter came from humble beginnings. He was raised by his maternal grandparents, John and Loretta Holmes, in the "poorest part of town," as he noted to Zillgitt. Despite growing up in a segregated community, Hunter has said that many of his childhood friends were white. Naturally athletic, he would often leave his black neighborhood to play various sports with children in predominantly white neighborhoods. When Hunter was twelve years old, he was part of the first integrated team to play in the Little League World Series, held annually in South Wil-liamsport, Pennsylvania. He pitched and played infield for a Delaware Township team that made it all the way to the 1955 Little League World Series championship game; his team, however, would lose to the Little League of Morrisville, Pennsylvania, 4–3, in seven innings, in the first-ever extra-inning championship game. Dur-ing the tournament, Hunter and his two black teammates were segregated from the rest of their team and forced to stay with a local black fam-ily for a southern regional final in Front Royal, Virginia, where they heard death threats and ra-cial slurs from people in the stands. At that time, racial segregation was still very much a part of Southern society, but Hunter told Zillgitt that the experience ultimately "opened my eyes to the world and what you could be."

## HIGH SCHOOL AND COLLEGE YEARS
Hunter attended Delaware Township High School (now Cherry Hill High School West) in Cherry Hill, where he was a four-sport star, let-tering in football, basketball, baseball, and track. As one of about twenty African-Americans in the 3,000-member student body, he fell in not only

with his fellow black students but also with a small group of Jewish kids. "[T]hat coalition of minorities was sometimes forced to protect its honor the old-fashioned way—in fistfights with less-progressive white students," Howard Beck wrote for the *Daily News of Los Angeles* (20 Dec. 1998).

After graduating from Delaware Township High, Hunter earned a football scholarship to Syracuse University in New York. At Syracuse, he became a roommate, teammate, and friend of future Hall of Fame tight end John Mackey (1941–2011), who would later become the first president of the NFL Players Association (NFL-PA). Mackey remembered Hunter as "a hard worker on the field and in the classroom," as he told Peter May for the *Boston Globe* (30 Oct. 1998). "He kept saying that he came to Syracuse not just to score touchdowns but also to score in the classroom. He knew how important it was." Hunter played running back and defensive back for Syracuse and was a captain on the 1964 Orangeman team that played in the Sugar Bowl. He was widely expected to be a first-round NFL draft pick, until an injury during his senior season curtailed those chances. During his time at Syracuse, Hunter involved himself in social activism, and helped circulate a petition among black athletes to boycott Southern schools with segregated stadiums. He told Sam Smith for the *Chicago Tribune* (10 Oct. 1998), "I realized the role athletes can play in shaping public opinion and affecting issues." He received a bachelor's degree in political science from Syracuse in 1965.

## FOOTBALL CAREER AND LAW SCHOOL

Despite going undrafted in the 1965 NFL Draft, Hunter went on to a brief career in the NFL as a defensive back and kick returner after graduating from Syracuse. He played for the Washington Redskins in 1965, and the Miami Dolphins during their 1966 inaugural season, before a series of knee injuries ended his NFL career. Hunter has said that because the NFL did not have a players' association at that time, players were sometimes exposed to racial prejudice, and injustice, and not always financially protected when they suffered injuries. "What I learned in the NFL was just that it was very political," he told Jonathan Abrams for the sports and pop culture website *Grantland* (27 July 2011), "that you thought once you arrived at the pro level, it would be all about skill and ability, but the politics at the pro level, once you're involved with the teams back then, was just kind of endemic. . . . What they did back then was, there were limited positions that brothers could play."

Following his NFL career, Hunter played a brief stint in the Canadian Football League (CFL) with the Montreal Alouettes before returning to school to study law. He noted to Sam Smith, "I realized early on I had to get an education." After receiving his JD degree from Howard University Law School in 1969, Hunter attended the Boalt Hall School of Law at the University of California, Berkeley, where he received a master of laws degree in 1970. Afterwards he spent several years working as a prosecutor for the Alameda County District Attorney's office, before becoming the chief assistant in the San Francisco District Attorney's office. During that time, Hunter handled a wide range of misdemeanor and felony cases, including drug offenses, thefts, robberies, rapes, and homicides.

## US ATTORNEY IN CALIFORNIA

In 1977, Hunter was appointed to serve as the US Attorney for the Northern District of California by President Jimmy Carter, after being recommended to him by the California Democratic Senator Allan Cranston (1914–2000), who was then serving as Senate Majority Leader. At that time Hunter, who was barely in his mid-thirties, was one of the youngest lawyers to ever hold the position, noting to Stephen A. Smith for the *Philadelphia Inquirer* (28 June 1998), "I couldn't believe how quickly I'd risen, but it didn't come easy and without challenges." As a US attorney in San Francisco, Hunter oversaw a number of high-profile cases, including one involving the Hell's Angels Motorcycle Gang, and the Black Panther Party. Hunter was also involved in the case involving the People's Temple, a cult whose members died in a mass suicide-murder after drinking cyanide-laced Kool-Aid under the direction of their leader, Jim Jones (1914–78). The suicide occurred on November 18, 1978, at a settlement called Jonestown in the South American nation of Guyana. Hunter traveled to Guyana to investigate the so-called "the Jonestown massacre," with US representative Leo Ryan (1925–78), and four other members of a congressional team. He eventually prosecuted one of Jones's surviving associates, Larry Layton, for conspiracy to commit murder. (Layton served eighteen years in prison before being released in 2002.)

During his stint as a US attorney, Hunter also served as an emissary to President Jimmy Carter in the pardoning of newspaper heir Patty Hearst, who had been convicted and sent to prison on armed bank robbery charges with members of a left-wing terrorist organization called the Symbionese Liberation Army (SLA). Hearst, who opted to join the SLA shortly after being kidnapped by them in 1974, was sentenced to thirty-five years in jail for her actions. Her sentence was later reduced to seven years, and she was released after serving twenty-two months of that term. Hunter ultimately convinced President Carter to pardon Hearst after meeting with her several times at the federal prison she was staying at Pleasanton, California. "I remember talking to her and saying, 'Your grandfather is William Randolph Hearst, and I'm from a poor, black environment,'" he recalled to Sam Smith. "'And here we are at this point.'"

## PRIVATE LAW PRACTICE

Hunter left his job at the US attorney's office in 1984 to start a private practice in Oakland, California, which he ran until his appointment with the NBPA. His firm specialized in municipal finance, high-profile civil and entertainment litigation, and white-collar criminal defense. Hunter represented athletes and entertainers like MC Hammer, Bobby Brown, Pebbles, Rickey Henderson, and Deion Sanders, as well as big tobacco companies like R.J. Reynolds and Philip Morris, among other high-profile clients. As a private practice lawyer, Hunter developed a reputation as an extremely loyal, tireless, and relentless client advocate, often taking on pro bono cases to help friends, neighbors, and local church members. One of his former partners, Bill Webster, remembered him being almost "loyal to a fault," as he told Mike Wise. Hunter also became active in local and national politics, serving for a time as president of the Oakland Port Commission, and running unsuccessfully as a Republican for California's Ninth Congressional District in 1990.

## JOINING THE NBPA AS EXECUTIVE DIRECTOR

The idea of leading the National Basketball Players Association as its executive director first struck Hunter in the mid-1990s, after his friend and former Syracuse classmate, Hall of Fame basketball player Dave Bing, suggested he apply for the job based on his diverse work background and experience as a professional athlete. Bing, now the mayor of Detroit, Michigan, told Zillgitt about Hunter, "He understands the give and take that goes into negotiations between players and owners. I thought he could do a good job for the players." Hunter applied for the job and beat out two other finalists, sports agent Bill Strickland and former Continental Basketball Association (CBA) commissioner Terdema Ussery, to become the fourth executive director of the NBPA, which was founded in 1954. Despite being a basketball outsider with little experience in labor negotiating, Hunter was viewed by members of the NBPA as someone who could stand up to Stern, the powerful and sometimes autocratic NBA commissioner who had helped grow the NBA into one of the richest and most popular sports leagues in the world in the 1980s and 1990s. NBPA attorney Ron Klempner told Peter May, "Coming in from the outside, he had a fresh perspective. He just made it so easy for everyone. He's straight with you. He cuts right to it. People can warm up to him."

## DEVELOPING TRUST AND SOLIDARITY

Soon after stepping into the NBPA's top spot, in July 1996, Hunter began visiting with players from every team in the league in the effort to develop trust and solidarity. As head of the NBPA, which is based in Manhattan, he oversaw 450 players and worked with thirty owners around the league. In his role as executive director of the WNBPA, he oversaw every WNBA player from each of the twelve WNBA teams. These virtues that had been largely absent under the union's previous director Simon Gourdine (1940–2012), who "was widely held as a Stern puppet," as Ian O'Connor noted for the New York *Daily News* (16 Nov. 1997). Gourdine had become executive director of the NBPA in 1995, after his predecessor Charles Grantham resigned amidst contentious labor negotiations on a new collective bargaining agreement, as well as for alleged misuse of funds. In the summer of 1995, Gourdine negotiated an end to an eighty-day owners-imposed lockout that had resulted from those negotiations and helped create the NBA's first rookie wage scale. The deal he reached with NBA owners, however, dissatisfied many players, so much so that they circulated a petition for an election to decertify the union, which ultimately failed in a vote of 226–134. Gourdine was offered a contract to remain executive director, but player representatives rejected it, and he was eventually ousted by the union in early 1996. In February of that year, former Denver Nuggets star and NBA Hall of Famer Alex English was appointed the union's interim executive director, and by the time Hunter succeeded him, "the union was a certified mess," as O'Connor wrote. Hunter explained to Mark Heisler for the *Los Angeles Times* (30 Oct. 1998) that while he was working to unify players around the league "[they] wanted to know, did I have any other agenda . . . I just said, 'I've always prided myself on being fair, being a hard worker, objective and professional. And if I accept you as a client, it's always been my position to give you 110%.' And I also assured them that I could hang in there if I had to, that I could be tough." He added to Beck, "When I go into a locker room, I talk to every guy. I don't just go to the superstars. Everybody is important to me."

As the NBPA executive director, Hunter won the respect of his NBA constituency for his toughness and unwillingness to back down from league management and owners in the defense of players' rights. For example, in one of his first major actions as executive director, he helped Latrell Sprewell successfully take on the NBA after receiving an unprecedented one-year suspension from the league, and having his contract with the Golden State Warriors voided, after attacking and choking Warriors coach P. J. Carlesimo during a practice on December 1, 1997. Hunter led an appeal to the league that argued against the severity of the punishment. Sprewell's one-year ban reduced to seven months, and his lucrative multimillion dollar contract was returned.

## NEGOTIATING LOCKOUTS AND CBAS

Hunter also made waves when he persuaded all twelve members of the US men's national basketball team (known as the "Dream Team") to boycott the 1998 FIBA World Championships in Athens, Greece, in retaliation over tenuous labor negotiations that led to the 1998–99 NBA lockout. The lockout lasted 204 days, and resulted in a shortened fifty-game season, marking the first time the league lost regular season games due to a work stoppage. Proving early on to be Stern's "equal in the art of the deal," as Howard Beck wrote, Hunter played a chief role in negotiations during the lockout, and helped players and owners come to terms on a new collective bargaining agreement (CBA) in 1999. He later became actively involved in the ratification of another new CBA in 2005. Dave Bing told Zillgitt that Hunter has been "the type of person who doesn't run away from problems. He's been one of those guys who's solved problems."

Hunter guided NBA players through a second work stoppage in 2011, when owners imposed another lockout on players after the previous CBA expired. During the 162-day lockout, which lasted from July 1, 2011, to December 8, 2011, he briefly dissolved the NBPA, turning it into a trade association in order to pursue antitrust lawsuits against the NBA, before restoring it as a union when owners and players ratified a new CBA. Because of the 2011 NBA lockout, the 2011–12 regular season was reduced to an abbreviated sixty-six-game schedule, resulting in the second shortened season in league history. The season began on December 25, 2011. Under the new ten-year CBA, which includes a mutual opt-out in 2017, players received a revenue split of just over 51 percent of basketball related income (BRI) during the 2011–12 season, and will receive 49 to 51 percent of BRI in later seasons. Other terms in the deal include an amnesty provision, allowing teams to waive one player prior to the start of each season in order to clear cap space, a plan to triple the amount of revenue-shared money. The agreement also includes a new minimum team salary, a luxury tax, and new free agency rules.

After the negotiations concluded, Hunter felt that although no side was satisfied with the deal, it was equitable. "They say that when you're negotiating and neither side is really happy about the deal, then it's a fair deal," he said (qtd. in *New York Times* 25 Dec. 2011). Among the dissatisfied were players and agents who criticized Hunter for his handling of the lockout. Some thought that the players should have disbanded the union sooner and that it might have been possible to secure a deal without having to cancel any games.

## RIFT WITH DEREK FISHER

One of the casualties of the 2011 lockout was Hunter's relationship with WNBA president Derek Fisher. As William C. Rhoden, writing for the *New York Times* (25 Dec. 2011), said, "The rift with Derek Fisher . . . was so deep that Hunter refused to discuss the relationship, and his job seemed as if it might be in jeopardy." Hunter's relationship with Fisher further deteriorated the following year, as Fisher suspected that Hunter was engaged in nepotism—at the time, all three of Hunter's children held positions affiliated with the NBPA—and had used union funds without approval from the executive committee. In April 2012, Fisher requested an independent audit of the NBPA's financial practices. He did so without the NBPA executive committee's permission or an official vote, however. Furthermore, he refused to participate in a discussion about his concerns with the committee and Hunter. Hunter was able to convince the executive committee at the time that Fisher's concerns were unfounded and they voted unanimously to ask Fisher to resign; Fisher, however, refused, and retained the law firm Paul, Weiss, Rifkind, Wharton & Garrison to conduct the audit.

## SCANDAL AND OUSTER FROM THE NBPA

On January 17, 2013, Paul, Weiss released the results of their 469-page independent review of Hunter and the NBPA. The report did not find criminal offenses, but alleged that Hunter engaged in nepotism and other suspect hiring practices. Of particular concern was the NBPA's lack of a written contract governing its relationship business with Prim Capital, where Hunter's son Todd works. The Paul, Weiss report also charged that Hunter's contract extension was improperly approved and that he did nothing to remedy the situation once he was made aware of it.

In response to the audit, on January 30, 2013, Hunter announced reforms to union business practices, including an anti-nepotism policy and the termination of his family members from their NBPA posts. Despite this, the NBPA's executive and advisory committees put Hunter on indefinite leave on February 1, 2013, and a NBPA team representative vote to fire him was passed unanimously by the union's new executive committee—including Derek Fisher, who remained as union president—on February 16. Separate criminal investigations into his management of the union are ongoing.

Hunter decried his dismissal, questioned the validity of the new executive committee, and vowed to seek redress. "The current interim regime in control of the NBPA has set a terrible precedent for the union. It violates every tenet of fairness upon which the union was founded. Now that this has occurred, I will continue to examine all of my options, including whether the fairness that was absent from the NBPA process might be available in a different forum" (*Christian Science Monitor* 16 Feb. 2013). In

May 2013, Hunter filed a lawsuit in California against the NBPA, Fisher, and Jamie Wior, Fisher's publicist and business partner. The suit seeks compensation and punitive damages for breach of contract, intentional interference with contractual relations, intentional misrepresentation, and several other allegations.

## PERSONAL LIFE

Hunter and his wife, Janice, a former vice principal at Berkeley High School in California, divide their time between their homes in New York City and Oakland. They have three children: a son Todd, and daughters Robyn and Alexis. In his spare time, Hunter enjoys reading, studying history, and spending time with his family and grandchildren.

## SUGGESTED READING

Abrams, Jonathan. "From Patty Hearst to David Stern." *Grantland.com*. ESPN Internet Ventures, 27 July 2011. Web. 13 Aug. 2012.

Beck, Howard. "Hunter: He Has Kept His Troops in Line." *Daily News* [Los Angeles] 20 Dec. 1998: Sports. Print.

Heisler, Mark. "State of His Union; Billy Hunter Has Proved to Be More Than a Worthy Adversary for Stern." *Los Angeles Times* 30 Oct. 1998: Sports D1. Print.

Mahoney, Brian. "NBA Players Union Ousts Executive Director." *Christian Science Monitor*. Christian Science Monitor, 16 Feb. 2013. Web. 14 Mar. 2013.

Rhoden, William C. "In N.B.A., Games Begin, but Time Will Determine Who Won." *New York Times*. New York Times Co., 25 Dec. 2011. Web. 14 Mar. 2013.

Zillgitt, Jeff. "Billy Hunter Fired by NBA Players Union." *USA Today*. Gannett, 16 Feb. 2013. Web. 14 Mar. 2013.

—*Chris Cullen*

# Walter Isaacson

**Born:** May 20, 1952
**Occupation:** Biographer; president and CEO of the Aspen Institute; former CEO of CNN

When biographer and media executive Walter Isaacson was named one of the most influential people of 2012 by the editors of *Time* magazine (18 Apr. 2012), the citation, written by former Secretary of State Madeleine Albright, explained: "The age of landmark biographies had, we might assume, long since passed, replaced by one of short attention spans, interactive gadgets and fewer bookstores. Enter Walter Isaacson and his trio of brilliant works about men of genius—[Benjamin] Franklin, [Albert] Einstein

Devid Grunfeld/The Times-Picayune/Landov

and [Steve] Jobs. This is influence of the best species, educating us while demonstrating the continued fascination of the seriously examined life, rendered by Isaacson with the objectivity of a true historian and the flair of a born storyteller." She continued: "Both as an author and as president of the intellectually fertile Aspen Institute, Isaacson is a purveyor of knowledge, a supplier to addicts who seek a deeper understanding of all manner of things."

Isaacson is arguably best known for his book-length biographies—particularly the volume on Apple cofounder Steve Jobs, published in 2011, just weeks after the tech giant's death from cancer. He has also had a long career in journalism. Starting as a newspaper reporter, he climbed to the top of the masthead at *Time* before being named head of CNN—a post that made him "arguably the most powerful television news journalist in the world," in the words of Paul Farhi for the *Washington Post* (10 July 2001). Since 2003, Isaacson has been the president and chief executive officer (CEO) of the Aspen Institute, a think tank whose mission, as stated on its website, is "to foster leadership based on enduring values and to provide a nonpartisan venue for dealing with critical issues."

## EARLY YEARS

Walter Isaacson was born on May 20, 1952, at the Touro Infirmary, in New Orleans, Louisiana. His father, Irwin, ran an engineering firm; his mother, the former Betsy Seff, worked as a real estate broker. Isaacson has a younger brother, Lee, now a computer consultant. (Betsy died in 1985; Isaacson has a stepmother, Julanne, with whom he shares a warm relationship.) The family lived in a cottage on Napoleon Avenue in the New Orleans neighborhood of Broadmoor. Politically liberal, Isaacson's parents helped organize the Broadmoor Improvement Association; one of its goals was racial integration. Isaacson has said he became aware of racial issues at an early age, when he went to a local park with a black housekeeper and her son and saw a Whites Only sign on a carousel. When it dawned on him that his companions could not go on the ride, the injustice rankled him.

## EDUCATION

Family and friends have told journalists that Isaacson, who was known as Waldo or Wally, was always a bright and precocious child. He attended the Isidore Newman School, a private, non-denominational day school in New Orleans, graduating in 1970. While there, he served as class president and was voted "most likely to succeed." The year before he graduated, he was featured in the New Orleans *Times-Picayune* column Terrific Teens, which detailed his efforts to rally black and white students to work together to tutor poor children and to reopen a local pool.

After leaving the Newman School, Isaacson entered Harvard University, where he studied history and literature and developed an early love for computers and technology. "[Harvard] really opened up the world to me since I had barely been north of the Mason-Dixon Line as a kid," he told a writer for the *Harvard Crimson* (8 June 1999). There, he was the president of the Signet Society, an organization whose members are chosen based on character, intellectual achievement, and literary or artistic talent. He was also on the staff of the *Harvard Lampoon*, the undergraduate humor publication. During his summers, he worked as a reporter at the *States-Item*, a New Orleans newspaper that later merged with the *Times-Picayune*, and in England at the *Sunday Times* of London. He also worked for a time as a stevedore on the New Orleans docks, thinking that a stint in that rough-and-tumble environment would broaden his horizons as a writer.

The acclaimed author Walker Percy was the uncle of one of Isaacson's friends and served as something of a mentor. Isaacson told Holly A. Phillips for the Louisiana State University website (Mar. 2010) that Percy had once given him the best advice he had ever received: "There are two types of people that come out of Louisiana: preachers and storytellers. Be a storyteller; there are plenty of preachers."

Isaacson graduated from Harvard in 1974. He next attended Pembroke College, a constituent college of the University of Oxford, as a Rhodes Scholar studying politics, philosophy, and economics (PPE). When applying for the Rhodes program, one of his interviewers was future US president Bill Clinton, then a young politician.

## EARLY CAREER IN JOURNALISM

When he had completed his Rhodes studies, Isaacson returned to New Orleans to work at the *Times-Picayune/States-Item*. Isaacson covered city government and politics and has credited his stint as a newspaper journalist for teaching him to be a sensitive interviewer and good listener. As a young reporter, he lived on Decatur Street, in the French Quarter, renting an apartment in the area's historic and picturesque Pontalba Buildings.

In 1978, Isaacson joined the staff of *Time* as a political correspondent, and his byline appeared on hundreds of stories. He gradually moved up the ranks, becoming first the magazine's national editor and then, in 1993, editor of new media. In the latter capacity he oversaw Pathfinder, an ill-fated Internet portal. Isaacson explained to Evan I. Schwartz for *Wired* (March 1996), "When you're swamped with information and you have 1,000 different sources for each piece of data, you look to certain brand names [such as *Time*] and a certain type of journalism you trust to make sense of it, to be your intelligent agent, to sort it out." He continued, "Pathfinder began as an umbrella for a variety of Web services we wanted to create. In the end, what we have is just like what's in any of the popular online services: a great package of material put together in a coherent way, with old and new brand names." Pathfinder was famously referred to by Time Warner executive Don Logan as a "black hole" of unprofitability, and it now functions only as a landing page, with links to the conglomerate's major websites, including *People*, *EW*, and *Cooking Light*.

## HIGH-PROFILE PROMOTIONS

In 1996, in a widely publicized move, Isaacson accepted a post as *Time*'s managing editor, the top spot on the masthead. A popular choice, he was credited with improving staff morale during his tenure and with reviving the publication's somewhat stodgy reputation with the reading public.

In 2000 he received yet another high-profile promotion, when he was made editorial director of Time Inc. Isaacson's new job put him in charge of strategic planning for all of Time Inc.'s publications. He was also slated to serve as a liaison of sorts between Time Inc. and the cable network CNN, which was owned by a newly merged AOL Time Warner. Norm Pearlstine, the head of Time Inc., explained to Gabriel Snyder for the *New York Observer* (20 Nov.

2000), "If you look at Walter's background and temperament, he did spend three years running Time Inc. New Media and clearly has an understanding and an affinity for the digital world. . . . In that prior life, before becoming managing editor, he forged some pretty good relationships with AOL, and certainly as managing editor of *Time* magazine he forged some good relationships with CNN."

It caused considerable media buzz when in mid-2001, Isaacson was named chairman and CEO of the CNN News Group, moving from New York City to Atlanta to accept the post. In that capacity he oversaw not only CNN but more than a dozen other cable and satellite news networks around the world, forty-two global bureaus, several CNN-sponsored websites, and some four thousand employees. Although his appointment was considered refreshing by many of CNN's reporters, who saw the ascension of a serious print journalist as a validation of their profession, others within the company bemoaned his lack of television experience.

## FROM CNN TO THE ASPEN INSTITUTE

In the wake of the terrorist attacks of September 11, 2001, ratings were good, but within months the network had been overshadowed by the more conservative and bellicose Fox News. Isaacson tried to stem that tide by hiring star anchors like Connie Chung and Paula Zahn and tempting the enormously popular Larry King with a $30 million contract, and he vociferously insisted that CNN remain above the type of ideological diatribes for which Fox was known. "Fox does a different formula than what we are trying to do. When you hire a Connie Chung, the goal isn't to go after the same viewer who might be watching a Bill O'Reilly or a Chris Matthews. The goal is to bring in a different type of viewer," he explained to Allison Romano and John Higgins for the trade publication *Broadcasting & Cable* (17 Feb. 2002). "You can create networks based on ideological talk. You can base it on people parachuting into various places around the world, or you can base it on a long-term commitment to covering the world. We've done the latter. We offer credibility to viewers and advertisers, and that will build a great loyalty."

Despite that optimistic attitude, Fox continued to attract greater ratings; its audience grew by more than a third in 2002, while CNN's dropped by almost a tenth during the same period. Thus, when Isaacson announced in 2003 that he was leaving the network to assume leadership of the Aspen Institute, many observers posited that he was backing away from a losing battle. He denied that the heated ratings war had influenced his decision, asserting to Jennifer Harper for the *Washington Times* (14 Jan. 2003) that the post at the think tank was "exactly the type of job I have long wanted" and that he was

very much looking forward to "writing, exploring ideas, engaging in policy issues, and seeking solutions to social and international problems."

## BIOGRAPHIES

Most members of the public know Isaacson not from his long tenure as a journalist and media executive but from his work as a biographer. In 1986, while still at *Time*, he coauthored (with Evan Thomas) *The Wise Men: Six Friends and the World They Made*, a look at a group of presidential advisors whose doctrine of Communist containment became the foundation of American foreign policy: diplomat Averell Harriman, Secretary of State Dean Acheson, Secretary of Defense Robert Lovett, banker John McCloy, and Soviet ambassador Charles Bohlen. In the *Los Angeles Times* (30 Nov. 1986), reviewer Bryce Nelson called it "highly impressive" and wrote, "This book is full of fine stories, anecdotes, and quotations; it is almost compulsory reading for anyone wishing to understand modern American foreign policy."

Isaacson's next book-length effort was *Kissinger: A Biography* (1992), later published as *Kissinger: A Life*, a comprehensive examination of the controversial former secretary of state. He followed that with *Benjamin Franklin: An American Life* (2003), which reviewer Janet Maslin called "a well-organized, highly user-friendly book with an emphasis on the contemporary rather than the quaint" in her assessment for the *New York Times* (3 July 2003). Many reviewers pointed out that Isaacson shared something of a career trajectory and certain personal traits with his subject. "So here's a guy who starts as a writer, becomes a media baron, moves to a public-thinker career midlife, is known as a great networker, has a good sense of humor," Jesse Oxfeld wrote for *Book* magazine (Nov. 2003). "Who's this book about, anyway?" When confronted with the question, Isaacson replied, "Somebody once said that all biography is autobiography. You're certainly attracted to subjects who mirror the virtues you'd like to acquire, and perhaps you even play up those attributes in the person that most interest you."

Isaacson, who has expressed a strong interest in science, next chose to write about Albert Einstein. *Einstein: His Life and Universe* (2007) is now considered one of the most authoritative volumes on the legendary physicist ever written. Praising the book, Janet Maslin wrote for the *New York Times* (9 Apr. 2007), "The story of Albert Einstein's life calls for a protean biographer, not to mention a fearless one. Conveying the magnitude of Einstein's scientific achievements is tough enough, but that's just the start. His geopolitics, faith, cultural impact, philosophy of science, amorous affairs, powers of abstraction and superstar reputation are all part of this subject."

## STEVE JOBS

After *American Sketches: Great Leaders, Creative Thinkers, and Heroes of a Hurricane* (2009)—a collection of essays on such figures as Bill Gates, Ronald Reagan, Mikhail Gorbachev, Hillary and Bill Clinton, and Walker Percy—Isaacson tackled what was arguably his most daunting subject to date: Steve Jobs, the visionary and iconoclastic leader of Apple. Jobs had approached Isaacson in 2004 about cooperating on a biography. Isaacson, just beginning to write about Einstein and reasoning that Jobs was a relatively young man with only half his career behind him, encouraged the tech mogul to wait several years before embarking on the project. It was not until 2009 that Isaacson found out from Jobs's wife, Laurene, that the Apple founder had undergone a liver transplant and was dying of cancer. He immediately embarked upon an unprecedented series of interviews with the notoriously prickly genius, and the resulting biography, titled simply *Steve Jobs*, was published in 2011, just weeks after his subject's death.

The book made no attempt to whitewash Jobs, who initially denied paternity of one of his children, screamed mercilessly at his workers, cried when he did not get his way, and mistreated waitresses, among other notorious anecdotes. Still, Isaacson greatly admired his subject, writing: "The saga of Steve Jobs is the Silicon Valley creation myth writ large: launching a startup in his parents' garage and building it into the world's most valuable company. He didn't invent many things outright, but he was a master at putting together ideas, art, and technology in ways that invented the future. . . . Some leaders push innovations by being good at the big picture. Others do so by mastering details. Jobs did both, relentlessly." The book became the basis for a highly anticipated 2013 biopic starring Ashton Kutcher.

## OTHER WORK

Isaacson is the emeritus chair of the nonprofit organization Teach for America, which recruits young graduates to teach in poor communities. In 2009, President Barack Obama appointed him as the chairman of the Broadcasting Board of Governors, a US government agency that oversees Voice of America, Radio Free Europe, and other international broadcasts sponsored by the US government; he held that post until 2012. Isaacson is also a vice chair of Partners for a New Beginning, a group whose aim is to strengthen ties between the United States and the Muslim world. From 2005 to 2007, following Hurricane Katrina, he helped chair the Louisiana Recovery Authority, a job he accepted because of his deep love for his native state.

## PERSONAL LIFE

Isaacson and his wife, Cathy, a lawyer by training, live in the Georgetown section of Washington, DC. They have a daughter, Betsy, named after his late mother. A graduate of Harvard, the young Betsy Isaacson works as a technology writer.

There has been much speculation on what Isaacson will write next. He has told interviewers that he has toyed with the idea of exploring the life of jazz great Louis Armstrong and would one day like to write a book focused on New Orleans. Being raised there "allowed me to see the joy in everything," he told a writer for *New Orleans Magazine* (Mar. 2000), admitting that he asks his father to send him regular shipments of the local crawfish. "It made me love good music, food, interesting ideas. It showed me the diversity of people."

## SUGGESTED READING

Albright, Madeleine K. "The World's 100 Most Influential People 2012: Walter Isaacson." *Time*. Time, 18 Apr. 2012. Web. 13 Sept. 2013.

Ball, Millie. "Steve Jobs' Biographer Is Hometown Son Walter Isaacson." *NOLA.com*. NOLA Media Group, 11 Dec. 2011. Web. 13 Sept. 2013.

Elmer-DeWitt, Philip. "The Man Who Won Steve Jobs' Trust." *Fortune*. Cable News Network, 10 Apr. 2011. Web. 13 Sept. 2013.

Isaacson, Walter. "*Time*'s Pathfinder." Interview by Evan I. Schwartz. *Wired*. Condé Nast, Mar. 1996. Web. 13 Sept. 2013.

Snyder, Gabriel. "Walter Isaacson Moves On Up to the 34th Floor at Time Inc." *New York Observer*. New York Observer, 20 Nov. 2000. Web. 13 Sept. 2013.

## SELECTED WORKS

*The Wise Men: Six Friends and the World They Made*, 1986 (with Evan Thomas); *Kissinger: A Biography*, 1992; *Benjamin Franklin: An American Life*, 2003; *Einstein: His Life and Universe*, 2007; *American Sketches: Great Leaders, Creative Thinkers, and Heroes of a Hurricane*, 2009; *Steve Jobs*, 2011

—Mari Rich

# Jonathan Ive

**Born:** February 1967
**Occupation:** Industrial designer

Jonathan Ive has designed some of the most recognizable products in the world, although he is rarely recognized in public. As the senior vice president of industrial design at Apple Inc., Ive is the man behind every one of the company's innovations, from the curved edges of an iPod to the handy magnetic plug of a MacBook. A glance around the open laptops in any coffee

Wirelmage

shop in the world is a testament to the ubiquity of the Apple brand and the commercial success of Ive's designs, and his powerfully simple aesthetic has garnered him a number of prestigious artistic and cultural awards as well. As Shane Richmond wrote in part two of his interview with Ive for the London *Telegraph* (23 May 2012), "It's hard to over-estimate the influence of Jonathan Ive."

The genius of Ive, coupled with the astute eye of the late founder Steve Jobs, set Apple apart as being a design-driven company. "In most people's vocabularies, design means veneer," Jobs told *Fortune* magazine for their January 24, 2000, cover story. "But to me, nothing could be further from the meaning of design. Design is the fundamental soul of a man-made creation that ends up expressing itself in successive outer layers."

Jobs famously referred to Ive as his "spiritual partner": the two men were tuned in to the same creative wavelength, and during Jobs's tenure, they communicated daily. When asked about Ive, Jobs's widow, Laurene Powell, told Walter Isaacson for his biography, *Steve Jobs*, "Most people in Steve's life [were] replaceable. But not Jony." As Jobs explained to *Fortune*, "[Ive] has more operational power than anyone else at Apple except me. There's no one who can tell him what to do, or to butt out. That's the way I set it up."

The collaboration was obviously a successful one. The game-changing, candy-inspired iMac in 1998, the iPod in 2001, the iPhone in 2007, and the iPad in 2010 were all fruits of the Jobs/Ive partnership. But after Jobs's death in 2011, outsiders began to wonder what role Ive would

play in the company's future. There was some speculation that Ive would take over as Apple's CEO, but that distinction went to Apple's business expert Tim Cook. Famous for streamlining Apple's production processes, Cook could be the logistical yin to Ive's creative yang.

## EARLY LIFE AND EDUCATION

Jonathan Ive, known to friends and colleagues as Jony, was born in February 1967 in Chingford outside of London and raised in Staffordshire. His father was a teacher, silversmith, and furniture maker. When he was a child, Ive's father brought him to his workshop, and Ive was allowed to make whatever he wanted with his father's tools as long as he drew the desired object by hand first. "I always understood the beauty of things made by hand," Ive told Isaacson. "I came to realize that what was really important was the care that was put into it. What I really despise is when I sense some carelessness in a product."

Ive attended Walton High School in Stafford. He was a rugby player and played a stint as a drummer in a rock band, but teachers recall his superior skills as a draftsman. Ive initially wanted to design cars, and he enrolled in London's prestigious Central St. Martins Art School. He then transferred to Newcastle Polytechnic (now known as Northumbria University) in 1985 and majored in industrial design. He interned at the design consultancy firm, the Roberts Weaver Group, where he created a pen with a ball on the top. Staffers were intrigued by the object's playful simplicity. "We began to call it 'having a Jony-ness,'" Clive Grinyer, Ive's colleague and classmate told Peter Burrows for *Businessweek* (24 Sept. 2006), "an extra something that would tap into the product's underlying emotion."

## EARLY AWARDS AND DESIGNS

For his final project at the school, Ive designed a microphone and earpiece in white plastic to help hearing-impaired children communicate. His apartment was covered with foam board to construct the nearly one hundred models his final presentation required. According to Grinyer, most students built only six.

During his time at Newcastle, Ive twice won the student award for design from the Royal Society of the Arts. The first time he won, he designed an automated teller machine for Pitney Bowes, the award's sponsor. He served a brief internship at the company, located in Stamford, Connecticut, but also used his time in the United States to fly to California and interview with several Silicon Valley design firms. Robert Brunner, then of Lunar Design, recalled that Ive brought a beautifully constructed, question-mark-shaped phone to the interview. Beyond the phone's sleek appearance, Brunner was impressed by Ive's understanding of the phone's internal engineering.

Ive graduated with a bachelor of arts degree from Newcastle in 1989. The same year, he and Grinyer founded a design consultancy firm called Tangerine Design. Among their clients was Apple Computers, where Brunner had become chief of design. Ive stayed with Tangerine for several years, but eventually he realized he wanted to go somewhere where he could focus on making things for people who cared as much about design as he did.

## APPLE COMPUTER

Ive began work with Apple in 1992, but the company was far from the monolith it is today. Jobs had been forced to resign from his position as CEO in 1985, and the company's value was steadily declining. Still, Ive was personally attracted to the company. He recalls his first encounter with an Apple computer in design school. At the time, he considered himself "technically inept," he told Jessica Guynn for the *Los Angeles Times* (5 Sept. 2011). But he was surprised by how easily he operated the machine. "I could just use the product straightaway," he said. "It was really a profound moment. I don't think I ever had actually quite the same sense of 'wow' with a product before."

Ive worked as the creative studio manager and helped Brunner build a design team at Apple. Ive put in a lot of work, but he was frustrated. He was designing Newton PDAs and printer trays, but his own ideas weren't coming through. He didn't speak publicly about it at the time, but he later lamented that the company had lost its identity. Instead of the trendsetting company Jobs had envisioned, Apple was quickly fading into the background and was struggling just to keep up with the competition. "Apple does really badly when it plays to other people's criteria," Ive told John Markoff for the *New York Times* (5 Feb. 1998).

Brunner left Apple in 1996 and suggested that Ive take his job as chief of design. Despite his misgivings about the direction of the company and despite his age (he was only twenty-nine), Ive accepted the position. In 1997, Jobs returned as interim CEO, and he had big plans. He purged the company of a number of its employees and sought out new blood to revitalize the brand. Jobs also slashed the number of Apple's product offerings from over sixty to just four. He was particularly interested in shaking up the design department, but when he paid a visit to the Apple studio, he was surprised to find a kindred spirit there waiting for him. Before he became the official CEO in 1998, Jobs promoted Ive to vice president of industrial design.

## IMAC AND IPOD

Jobs tasked Ive with building a computer unlike any other on the market. Apple was in trouble, and the company needed a bold new idea to have a chance against their competition. Ive considered the array of PCs available to consumers at the time and decided that they all had one thing in common: They were all atrocious to look at, and Ive believed Apple could do better. He envisioned an all-in-one computer that looked more like a gumdrop than it did office equipment. The jewel-toned iMac came in five "flavors": strawberry, grape, blueberry, tangerine, and lime. Through its translucent shell, users could see the hardware inside. Much like the pen that had amused his coworkers a number of years before, Ive was hoping that the consumers would see the iMac as a product that would be fun to use. But nothing about the production of the new computers was easy. Ive and his team visited candy factories to perfect the color consistency of the iMac's shell. Its manufacture required an entirely new assembly process and cost almost three times the amount of a more generic model. Despite all of the potential drawbacks, Apple rolled the dice on the iMac and won big. The company sold 150,000 units the weekend the iMac was introduced, and 800,000 by the end of the year. The iMac changed the way people felt about their home computer and in turn, the way they felt about Apple. In 2001, Apple phased out the color palette of the original iMacs and unveiled an upgraded iMac made out of titanium that incorporated Ive's design for a sleek, monochromatic style.

Also in 2001, Apple released the new cigarette pack-sized iPod. From a business perspective, the iPod was another game changer. It was easy to use with Apple's iTunes online store, which forever changed the way people purchased music, and from a design perspective, the iPod made the MP3 player a fashion statement. From its clean white surface with discreet buttons arranged in a circle to its sleek white "ear buds," the iPod was instantly and enormously successful.

## IPHONE AND IPAD

The iPhone was launched in 2007, but according to Ive, it almost never saw the light of day. "There were multiple times where we nearly shelved the phone because we thought there were fundamental problems that we can't solve," he told Gideon Spanier of the London *Independent* (31 July 2012). But the iPhone was too important to Jobs to give up on. "We have been, on a number of occasions, preparing for mass production and in a room and realised we are talking a little too loud about the virtues of something," Ive continued. "You have that horrible, horrible feeling deep down in your tummy and you know that it's OK but it's not great. And I think some of the bravest things we've ever done are really at that point when you say, 'that's good and it's competent, but it's not great.'"

Apple anticipated that the iPhone would do well before they released it. Unlike most Apple products, consumers knew it was coming and they were excited. In 2008, after Apple had lowered the price tag, the company sold over ten million iPhones in five months. Again, from a business perspective, the iPhone was significant because it combined the abilities of Apple's two most successful products—the computer (with Internet capabilities) and the iPod—with all the capabilities of a handheld cellular phone. Subsequent generations of the iPhone are more powerful, lighter, thinner, and more refined.

Apple's latest technological innovation is the iPad. Introduced in 2010, the tablet computer has been garnering praise for its simplicity. Because Apple is able to control every aspect of a product, from its hardware to its software to its materials and the processes in which devices are built, they can seamlessly integrate the functions of multiple devices into one. "We try to develop products that seem somehow inevitable," Ive told Richmond.

## APPLE DESIGN STUDIO

Ive draws inspiration from unusual sources— gumdrops (the original iMac), water droplets (the mouse for the iMac), and sunflower stalks (the mountings for the iMac)—and he scours the globe for appropriate materials to recreate those sources. Often, Apple will have to invent the factory process to assemble the device, like the 2009 MacBook, which was built out of a single piece of aluminum.

But Ive's work doesn't stop with the completion of the product. He and Jobs were both concerned about packaging. The two men patented several aspects of the packaging for the iPod and iPhone. Ive says that the "ritual" of opening the product is just as important as the quality of the product itself. "I love the process of unpacking something," he told Isaacson. "You design a ritual of unpacking to make the product feel special. Packaging can be theatre, it can create a story."

The design studio at Apple is an almost sacred space. Separated from the rest of the Apple campus, Ive and his team work behind tinted windows and with a private kitchen to discourage them from discussing their ideas at the more public Apple cafeteria. Most of Apple's employees have never been inside. People speculate that designers are working on another stab at a television. If this is the case, consumers can expect it to be as multifunctional and as beautiful as the Apple products that came before. "There's no other product that changes function like the computer," Ive told John Arlidge for the *Observer* (21 Dec. 2003). "The iMac can be a jukebox, a tool for editing video, a way to organise photographs. You can design on it, write on it. Because what it does is so new, so changeable, it allows us to use new materials, to create new forms. The possibilities are endless. I love that."

## PERSONAL LIFE AND AWARDS

Ive met his wife, historian and writer Heather Pegg, at Walton High School. They married in 1987, have twin sons, and currently live in San Francisco, California.

In 2003, Ive was awarded the Design Museum's first Designer of the Year prize. Three years later he was appointed Commander of the Order of the British Empire (CBE) for his contributions to the design industry, and the following year Ive received a National Design Award in product design for his work on the iPhone. In 2008, he received the Mobile Data Association (MDA) award for personal achievement, and in 2012, Ive was made Knight Commander of the British Empire (KBE) for his "services to design and enterprise." Ive was named Apple's senior vice president of design in 2005.

At the height of his career, Ive seems poised to retain his powerful position within the company, possibly expanding his influence to software design as well. But the modest, soft-spoken Ive isn't power hungry and prefers the pronoun *we* when discussing his accomplishments with Apple. His words recalled an early speech from Jobs when he addressed a panel in London, as quoted by Spanier: "Our goal is not to make money—that may sound a little flippant but it happens to be true. Our goal, and what makes us exist, is to make great products."

## SUGGESTED READING

Burrows, Peter. "Who Is Jonathan Ive?" *Businessweek*. Bloomberg LP, 24 Sept. 2006. Web. 15 Mar. 2013.

Guynn, Jessica. "Apple Designer Jonathan Ive Enters a New Era." *Los Angeles Times*. Los Angeles Times, 5 Sept. 2011. Web. 15 Mar. 2013.

Isaacson, Walter. *Steve Jobs*. New York: Simon, 2011. Print.

Markoff, John. "At Home With: Jonathan Ive; Making Computers Cute Enough to Wear." *New York Times*. New York Times Co., 5 Feb. 1998. Web. 15 Mar. 2013.

Richmond, Shane. "Jonathan Ive Interview (Part One): Apple's Design Genius Is British to the Core." (London) *Telegraph*. Telegraph Media Group Ltd., 23 May 2012. Web. 13 Mar. 2013.

Spanier, Gideon. "Sir Jonathan Ive: We Nearly Axed the iPhone, It Wasn't Enough to be Good . . . We Knew It Had to be Great." *Independent* (London). The Independent, 31 July 2012. Web. 15 Mar. 2013.

—*Molly Hagan*

# David Ives

**Born:** July 11, 1950
**Occupation:** Playwright

The playwright David Ives made his mark on the New York City theater scene in 1993 with *All in the Timing*, a collection of six short plays. Ives was praised by critics for creating a unique brand of theater that blends laugh-out-loud comedy with philosophical insight. In the mid-1990s, *All in the Timing* went on to become the most produced play in America, second only to the works of William Shakespeare. Ives was again praised for *Mere Mortals and Others* (1997), another collection of short, clever and funny plays. Ives has also had success as a writer for the Broadway stage, particularly with his adaptation of the Mark Twain play *Is He Dead?* (2007) and his own seductive drama-comedy *Venus in Fur* (2010), which was nominated for a Tony Award for best play in 2012. In March of that year, the award-winning composer Stephen Sondheim announced that he and David Ives were working on a musical, though he did not announce a release date for the show.

Getty Images

## GROWING UP

David Ives was born David Roszkowski in 1950 in Chicago, Illinois. He grew up on the south side of Chicago, where he was raised by his father, Walter, a machinist, and his mother, Regina, a secretary. Ives began writing stories and plays around the age of nine and he has revealed in many interviews that his parents did not understand his passion, primarily because they did not know anyone who was making a living as a playwright. His was a working class family that did not fully comprehend Ives's ambition.

## EDUCATION AND EARLY WORK

Ives remained in his home state of Illinois to pursue his bachelor's degree. He studied English at Chicago's Northwestern University, where he made his first attempt at becoming a playwright. He read the plays of such theater greats as Harold Pinter, Samuel Becket, and Eugène Ionesco, who inspired him to create a new, ambitious kind of theater.

After graduation, Ives lived briefly in Germany, Boston, and Los Angeles, before settling in New York City in the mid-1970s. Through a friend, he was hired as a junior editor at the magazine *Foreign Affairs*. Despite the fact that he knew very little about diplomacy, international politics, and foreign relations, Ives stayed on at the magazine for three years. In the meantime, he was also writing stories and plays. An example of the latter is *St. Freud*, an ambitious play about the psychoanalyst Sigmund Freud, which has more than fifty scenes. Ives also wrote a play

about Harry Houdini, another ambitious work, and there were others. Those plays, however, were never staged.

Eventually, Ives decided to go back to school. In 1981, he began his studies at the Yale School of Drama in New Haven, Connecticut. He received his master of fine arts three years later. After unsuccessfully pursuing a career in television writing and movie writing, Ives began to focus more on short, one-act plays.

## MANHATTAN PUNCH LINE FESTIVAL

Starting in the late 1980s, Ives's plays began to be staged in New York City as part of the Manhattan Punch Line's Festival of One-Act Comedies. *Words, Words, Words*, about three chimpanzees—named Swift, Milton, and Kafka—in a room trying to write *Hamlet*, premiered in 1987. The idea for the play comes from the well-known humorous suggestion that if chimpanzees were put in a room with typewriters, they will be able to produce *Hamlet*, given enough time. The following year, also at the Punch Line festival, Ives's *Sure Thing*, a fifteen-minute play about the possibilities involved in talking to a member of the opposite sex, received positive reviews. Ives's short, one-act play *Philip Glass Buys a Loaf of Bread* premiered at the Punch Line festival in 1990. That year, in a piece for the *New York Times* (11 Feb. 1990), Mel Gussow included Ives as one of three American playwrights who have been revitalizing the country's theater scene: "Language is reaffirming itself in the American theater, and the harbingers are Mac Wellman,

Eric Overmyer, and David Ives. In a reaction against the recent emphasis on performance art, they value words . . . In common, their dialogue has an imaginative intellectual base."

### ALL IN THE TIMING

All in the Timing, which consists of six one-act plays, opened off-Broadway in 1993 at the Primary Stages Company. Five out of its six plays had already been performed elsewhere, but this marked the first time they were all performed together on the off-Broadway stage. Words, Words, Words, about three chimps locked together with three typewriters, is a platform for smart, literary humor. Philip Glass Buys a Loaf of Bread, about the avant-garde composer Philip Glass buying a loaf of bread, is both a parody and homage to the composer well known in the classical music world for his use of repetition. Variations on the Death of Trotsky examines, both with humor and with philosophical depth, the last day in the life of exiled Russian revolutionary Leon Trotsky, who was killed by an ax at his home in Mexico City. The Philadelphia, which takes place at a New York diner, is a funny philosophical discussion between two people about language and possibility.

Possibility is also a major theme in Sure Thing. In that short play, a man sees an attractive woman sitting alone in a coffee shop and strikes up a conversation. Yet every time something goes wrong in the conversation—and that happens many times—a bell rings offstage, and the two resume the conversation from before it took a wrong turn. Universal Language is about Dawn, a woman who stutters. She attends a class, which unbeknownst to her is a sham, on the universal language Unamunda, a made-up language in which popular names and brands represent words. For example, "Velcro" means "welcome," "John Cleese" means "English," and "Harvard U" means "how are you?" Not long after the lesson begins, Dawn starts to make up her own Unamunda words and the evening progresses toward the more comically absurd.

All in the Timing received great reviews and essentially launched Ives's theater career. Ben Brantley of the New York Times (3 Dec. 1993) called all six plays "utterly delightful," later adding, "There is indeed a real heart beneath Mr. Ives's intellectual tomfoolery, which may explain why one leaves the theater without the slight pangs of emptiness that sometimes follow determinedly clever revues. There is sustenance as well as pure entertainment here." In February 1994, the play transferred to the John Houseman Theater, a bigger venue, where it ran for more than a year. For the play, Ives won the 1994 Outer Critics Circle Award. Around this time, All in the Timing became the most produced play in the United States, coming in second only to Shakespearean plays.

### DON JUAN IN CHICAGO AND ANCIENT HISTORY

Ives's next off-Broadway offerings were the plays Don Juan in Chicago and Ancient History. The latter, a three-act play that combines the stories of Don Juan and Faust, premiered in 1995 and was over two hours long, which most critics found to be too long for its own good. Robert Stanton, who was one of the actors in All in the Timing, directed the play, the majority of which is written in rhyme. The play's character makes a deal with Mephistopheles in 1599 for an eternal life, on the condition that he sleeps with a different woman every night. This goes on for centuries. "Laughs or no laughs, the payoff is as unsatisfying as everything that has gone before it," wrote Jeremy Gerard for Daily Variety (27 Mar. 1995). Brantley offered a similar criticism in the New York Times (25. Mar. 1995), pointing out that Don Juan's lesson—that sex is better with someone you love—and the story are banal. Brantley's review concludes, "There are enough moments of original wit, as well as an underlying chord of a deeper wistfulness, to recall just how good Mr. Ives can be. Certainly no one should write him off after this. All writers have their lost moments in a creative purgatory."

The following year saw the revival of Ancient History, which had originally premiered in New York in 1989. The two-act play is the story of a clever, erudite couple that, at first glance, seems to get along well. However, as the play moves along, it becomes apparent that they are no perfect match. The man is not well off and is divorced, and the woman is successful and looking to get married. As other differences emerge, insults and bitter, personal attacks start flying. The short, one-act play English Made Simple opened for Ancient History. The play did receive better reviews than Don Juan, but not nearly the praise bestowed upon All in the Timing.

### DAVID COPPERFIELD, THE RED ADDRESS, AND MERE MORTALS

Ives made his Broadway debut as a writer in 1996 with David Copperfield: Dreams and Nightmares, a show of magic and entertainment by the illusionist David Copperfield. Ives wrote the book of the show, which in theater jargon means he wrote the spoken dialogue. (The person who writes the lyrics that people sing is known as a librettist.) The book, considered by most critics to be unessential to the show, was added so that Copperfield's performance would better fit the expectations of a Broadway audience.

In January of the following year, Ives returned to off-Broadway theater with The Red Address, a play from 1991 that he had rewritten. The Red Address is about a man who works a regular job during the day but likes to wear women's clothing—lingerie and high heels—at night. The play examines the seemingly unexplainable mystery of why a heterosexual man would want to wear women's lingerie. Peter Marks of the *New York Times* (15 Jan. 1997) observed, "It's always a pleasure to savor Mr. Ives's wordplay, but in this case, the words don't create a world." Marks found the play unfulfilling.

However, a few months later, in a review of Ives's next off-Broadway production, *Mere Mortals and Others*, Marks offered nothing but praise in his *New York Times* review (13 May 1997). The critic proclaimed the collection of six short plays to be "ferociously funny comedies" and stated that Ives was "back at the top of his game." Overall, *Mere Mortals* elicited similar praise as *All in the Timing*. In the title play, *Mere Mortals*, three construction workers sitting high above New York City imagine themselves to be—or somehow magically are, since ambiguity is a frequent theme in Ives's work—Marie Antoinette, a descendant of a Russian czar, and the adult version of the Lindbergh baby. *Speed the Play* spoofs the plays of David Mamet, including *American Buffalo* (1975), *Oleanna* (1992), and *Speed-the-Plow* (1988). *Time Flies* features two mayflies in conversation about their extremely short lifespan. In *Degas, C'Est Moi*, an average man imagines himself as the French artist Edgar Degas. *Foreplay or: The Art of The Fugue*, which is set at a miniature golf course, provides funny, clever observations on romantic rituals in both dating and sexual relations.

### POLISH JOKE AND THE OTHER WOMAN

Following the closing of *Dance of the Vampires* (2002), a Broadway musical comedy that turned out to be a flop, Ives returned to off-Broadway theater with the 2003 comedy *Polish Joke*. The play starred Malcolm Gets as Jasiu Sadlowski, a Polish American struggling with his identity. Jasiu tells the audience his life story, in which he changes his name and becomes a novelist. Although the play is not explicitly autobiographical, the *Polish Joke* program points out that Ives is of Polish origin. Despite Jasiu's efforts, his Polish identity stays with him, often manifesting itself in strange and humorous ways.

Also in 2003, a revival of the 1953 musical comedy *Wonderful Town* appeared on Broadway; Ives adapted the script, and the show ran for more than a year. In 2006, Ives's one-act play *The Other Woman* premiered in New York as part of the Ensemble Studio Theatre's annual festival of one-act plays. In the play, a man named Thomas stays up late, writing novels, while his wife Emma sleeps in another room. One night, Emma sleepwalks and appears to be not herself—as if she is another woman. She seems troubled, so Thomas consoles her, and they then proceed to have sex. Yet in the morning, Emma does not remember anything.

In a review for the *New York Times* (29 May 2006), Charles Isherwood called the play "a cleverly wrought yarn that also possesses real emotional depth." He added that "*The Other Woman* generates both edge-of-your-seat suspense and a measure of compassionate wonder about the mysterious frailty of the mind, and of the married state. It is seriously spooky, and good fun, but it's also a sensitive, sorrow-tinged parable about the secrets and lies that can create dangerous fissures in a seemingly firm relationship."

### IS HE DEAD? AND NEW JERUSALEM

In 2003 Shelley Fisher Fishkin, an English professor at Stanford University, found and published an archived manuscript of Mark Twain's 1898 play *Is He Dead?*, which had never been staged during the author's lifetime. Ives was brought in to adapt the play for a Broadway staging. He tightened the manuscript, making it crisper and funnier; he also cut out some parts and better developed the main character. Ives began working on the play in 2005 and it premiered on Broadway in December 2007. The play takes place in Paris in 1846 and features as its hero Jean-François Millet, a painter not recognized in his own time. Desperate for income and for recognition, Millet fakes his own death and then pretends to be his fictional twin sister, the widow Daisy Tillou. This takes place early in the play. For the rest of the show, Millet is in drag disguise, during which Millet's art dealer is not only after his paintings but is also after his "sister." The play was well-received. In a review for the *New Yorker* (17 Dec. 2007), John Lahr wrote, "Ives understands the seriousness of a light touch; he's swift and smart. He doesn't camp up Millet's camouflage; his laughs—there are a lot of them—are within character. The Widow's efforts to keep her life story straight are terrific fun."

The next play Ives wrote is a serious work. *New Jerusalem: The Interrogation of Baruch de Spinoza at Talmud Torah Congregation: Amsterdam, July 27, 1656* premiered at the Classic Stage Company in 2008. Baruch de Spinoza, a Jewish philosopher living in Amsterdam during the seventeenth century, expressed ideas that were considered blasphemous by most Jews and Christians of the time. Through his own method of mathematical and rational thinking, Spinoza proposed that God is Nature, which includes not only all space and everything within that space, but also all time—past, present, and future. As the name of the play indicates, Spinoza, threatened with expulsion from the city's Jewish community, was interrogated by the city's lead rabbi and several others, as if in a court of law. Because no transcripts of the interrogation exist, Ives had plenty of creative freedom. Isherwood observed that the play is "possibly his most challenging yet" and stated that "for the most part the debate makes for lively if dense listening" (14 Jan. 2008).

### VENUS IN FUR

Following the Broadway staging of *Irving Berlin's White Christmas* (2008, 2009), a musical comedy for which Ives wrote the book, and *Finian's Rainbow* (2009), a revival of a 1947 musical comedy that Ives adapted for Broadway, Ives saw an explosion of critical praise for his next play, *Venus in Fur*. The play opened off-Broadway in January 2010. *Venus in Fur* takes place in the present and is a comedy-drama that originally starred Wes Bentley and Nina Arianda. A playwright named Thomas, having written an adaptation of Leopold von Sacher-Masoch's erotic novel *Venus in Furs* (1870), is auditioning women for the lead role. A woman named Vanda enters, who insists that she be given an audition. She seems to know just what to say and how to act.

"And, as soon as she starts to read, she's no longer Vanda but Wanda, a measured woman with impeccable Continental diction," wrote Hilton Als for the *New Yorker* (8 Feb. 2010). "The transformation is subtle and not so subtle—acting is Vanda's bag, and it becomes ours, too, as we watch Thomas become more and more powerless in the presence of her unconquerable vitality, her seductive energy. Ultimately, it's that powerlessness which interests Thomas." The play goes beyond an exploration of male and female to focus on actor-writer and actor-director relationships. Called "intelligent and sometimes frightening" by Als, *Venus in Fur* ran for two months. The following year, the play moved to Broadway, where it continued to receive generally excellent reviews. On Broadway the role of Thomas was played by Hugh Dancy. *Venus in Fur* was nominated for the 2012 Tony Award for best play.

Off Broadway, Ives's period comedy *The School for Lies*, written in verse, ran during the month of May 2011 at the Classic Stage Company. The play is an adaptation of Moliere's *The Misanthrope* (1666), set in the 1660s. In a review for the *New York Times* (2 May 2011), Isherwood called *The School for Lies* "delightful." In addition to the plays cited above, Ives is also the author of three novels for young adults: *Monsieur Eek* (2001), *Scrib* (2005), and *Voss* (2008).

Ives has been married to Martha Stoberock, an illustrator, since 1997. Ives's first marriage ended in divorce.

### SUGGESTED READING

Als, Hilton. "The Whip Comes Down." *New Yorker*. Condé Nast, 8 Feb. 2010. Web. 11 Sept. 2012.

Brantley, Ben. "Merrily Sputtering Along." *New York Times* 3 Dec. 1993: C1. Print.

Collins, Scott. "Talk About Your Good Timing." *Los Angeles Times*. Los Angeles Times, 27 Oct. 1996. Web. 11 Sept. 2012.

Isherwood, Charles. "So, Young Mr. Spinoza, Just What Is Your Thinking About God?" *New York Times*. New York Times, 14 Jan. 2008. Web. 11 Sept. 2012.

Lahr, John. "Devil May Care." *New Yorker*. Condé Nast, 17 Dec. 2007. Web. 11 Sept. 2012.

Marks, Peter. "A Man of Few Words Is Sent Up by a Man of Few Acts." *New York Times* 13 May 1997: C11. Print.

—*Dmitry Kiper*

---

# E. L. James

**Born:** 1963
**Occupation:** Author

E. L. James is the author of the best-selling book *Fifty Shades of Grey* and its two equally successful sequels, *Fifty Shades Darker* and *Fifty Shades Freed*. She has been widely praised—and widely vilified—for popularizing sexually explicit fiction. "[James] has electrified women across the country, who have spread the word like gospel on Facebook pages, at school functions, and in spin classes," Julie Bosman wrote for the *New York Times* (9 Mar. 2012). "[She is] introducing women who usually read run-of-the-mill literary or commercial fiction to graphic, heavy-breathing erotica. In the cities and suburbs of New York, Denver, and Minneapolis, the women who have devoured the books say they are feeling the happy effects at home."

Many detractors object to James's work not on moral grounds, but because they believe she is a poor writer of prose. Even those who applauded the frankly sexual content in her books have conceded that her writing skills leave something to be desired. "The 'E L,' it is safe to assume, does not stand for 'English literature,'" Steve Johnson quipped in the *Chicago Tribune* (3 May 2012).

Despite the controversy and differences of opinion surrounding her work, James's sales figures are inarguably impressive. Her books have topped best-seller charts in Europe and the United States. Shortly after its release, the paperback edition of *Fifty Shades of Grey* became the fastest-selling paperback in history, topping a record set by J. K. Rowling's *Harry Potter* series. In 2012, James was named one of the Time 100, a list of the one hundred most influential people in the world compiled annually by the editors of *Time* magazine. She was also named Publishing Person of the Year for 2012 by the editors of *Publishers Weekly*.

dapd

## EARLY LIFE AND EDUCATION

E. L. James is the pen name of Erika Leonard (née Mitchell). She was born in 1963 in Buckinghamshire, a county in the southeast of England. It is widely known as the home of Anne Boleyn. Following James's publishing successes, several journalists tried to posit a connection between the ordinary middle-aged writer responsible for igniting the libidos of millions of readers and the ordinary-looking woman who captivated Henry VIII.

James's late father was of Scottish descent and made his living as a camera operator for the British Broadcasting Company (BBC). She has not publicly revealed her father's name. Her mother, Alexandra, a retired sales representative, is of Chilean descent. Alexandra has suggested to interviewers that her daughter's erotic writing is an expression of her "fiery" Chilean spirit.

By all accounts, James, who has one brother, enjoyed a happy, normal childhood. She has told interviewers that she and her family shared a rollicking sense of humor and a love of books. James is bilingual, having learned Spanish from her mother. As a child, she loved to write and was often asked by her teachers to read her tales aloud to the class. Her mother remembers with particular fondness one short story, written when James was she was about ten years old, which detailed the adventures of a flying snowman.

James attended the University of Kent, where she majored in history and took several courses in English literature. She was an organized student who earned good grades and showed a marked facility for mathematics. She has intimated during speaking engagements that at some point during her student years, she was

involved in an "inappropriate" romantic relationship, and many have speculated (without further evidence) that this period in her life inspired the sadomasochistic relationship that forms the basis of the *Fifty Shades* trilogy.

After graduating from the University of Kent, James joined the National Film and Television School in Beaconsfield, where she worked as a studio manager's assistant.

## MARRIAGE AND TELEVISION CAREER

At the National Film and Television School, James met Niall Leonard, an affable Irishman who shared her sense of humor. They married in 1987, moving to a home in a West London suburb. Leonard embarked on a successful career as a scriptwriter. He became known for penning such BBC programs as *Spender* (1993), a police drama; *Pie in the Sky* (1997), a popular detective comedy starring the British actor Richard Griffiths; and *Ballykissangel* (on which he worked from 1997 to 1998), a long-running series about an English priest who is transferred to a small Irish village.

In the meantime, James settled into the life of a middle-class homemaker. Their marriage is a happy one, although James has joked to interviewers about her husband's occasionally grumpy nature. Leonard has admitted to being an unromantic person. He told a reporter that he once gave his wife an electric can opener as a Christmas gift.

James gave birth to the couple's first son in 1992, and a second son followed in 1994. As the boys got older, she began to feel somewhat bored and decided to enter the workforce. Leonard did his writing from home most of the time and could be counted on to provide childcare, making James free to seek a full-time job. She worked for a time as a production manager for an independent television company called Shooting Stars, owned by the comedians Vic Reeves and Bob Mortimer.

As both her father and her husband had found fulfilling work with the BBC, James eventually applied there and was hired as a production manager on the comedy series *Funny Turns*, with responsibilities in such areas as budgeting and scheduling. She later worked on the television movie *Goodbye 2000* (2000), the documentary *There's Only One Madonna* (2001), and the television series *Bodies* (2004) and *Room 101* (2004). From 2003 to 2006, she served as head of production for *Have I Got News for You*, a televised political quiz show based on events in the news. In 2009, James became the head of production for a short-lived series called *Naked*.

Her workday was often stressful, so James took to reading novels to relax during her commute on the London tube. She frequented a bookshop on Charing Cross Road that specialized in genre fiction and she soon became hooked on the romance novels informally known as "bodice-rippers." Because many of the covers featured lurid scenes of bare-chested men, and women with exposed cleavage, James would bend back the covers so fellow commuters could not tell what she was reading.

She particularly loved the *Twilight* series, by Stephenie Meyer. The *Twilight* books, which center on a dashing vampire named Edward Cullen and Bella Swan, the mortal young woman who loves him, sold an estimated 100 million copies and spawned a global craze for supernatural romance. Originally intended for the teen market, the series became popular with female readers of all ages.

## THE *FIFTY SHADES* PHENOMENON

The *Twilight* books inspired a flood of fan fiction, or stories that employ the characters or settings of an established author, written by fans of the original work. James began writing sexually explicit fan fiction featuring Edward and Bella. In 2009, she began posting her work on FanFiction. net, an extensive website that allows fans to post stories where others can read them. The site also provides an active fan fiction discussion forum.

James initially wrote under the screen name Snowqueens Icedragon and she called her tale "Master of the Universe." She imagined Edward as a millionaire executive and sexual sadist and Bella as a virginal college student who is lured into a sadomasochistic lifestyle because of her love for him. So popular was the tale with readers of the site, who continually clamored for further installments, that in December 2010 James moved from FanFiction.net to her own website, 50Shades.com. Her fan fiction had attracted more than thirty-seven thousand readers who left reviews on the site, and presumably many thousands more who read her installments but did not leave a review.

In May 2011, the Writer's Coffee Shop, a tiny independent company, published the first *Fifty Shades* under the pen name E. L. James. The book was originally made available as an e-book and print-on-demand paperback. Thanks to word-of-mouth buzz and positive reviews on websites such as Goodreads, the popularity of *Fifty Shades of Grey* exploded.

James received an e-mail from a Hollywood studio asking if the film rights to *Fifty Shades of Grey* were available. She contacted Valerie Hoskins, her husband's London-based agent. Realizing that the Writer's Coffee Shop would never be able to meet the growing demand, Hoskins helped James land a lucrative publishing deal with Random House's Vintage Books imprint, which began publishing the *Fifty Shades* series in March 2012. Between March and December of that year, the trilogy sold more than 70 million copies (in combined e-book or trade paperback formats), reportedly accounting for one

out of every ten books sold by Random House in 2012. The publisher posted record profits, exceeding $420 million in revenue, which marked a 75 percent increase from 2011.

## CRITICAL RECEPTION

Following its publication by Random House, thousands of readers wrote positive reviews on GoodReads, Amazon, and other websites—with many touting the boost the books had given their own sex lives. In a piece for the London *Guardian* (6 July 2012), Zoe Williams explained, "James's sex scenes are not incidental, they are the meat of the plot, the crux of the conflict, the key to at least one of and possibly both the central characters." "It is a sex book," writes Williams of *Fifty Shades of Grey*, "not a book with sex in it. The French author Catherine Millet wrote: 'For me, a pornographic book is functional, written to help you to get excited. If you want to speak about sex in a novel or any 'ambitious' writing, today, in the 21st century, you must be explicit. You cannot be metaphorical any longer.' I'm not sure James's writing is that ambitious, but she has certainly understood the bit about not being metaphorical."

Professional critics were much less kind to James than the average reader. Many cited the line "My inner goddess is doing the merengue with some salsa moves," uttered by the female lead, as proof of James's poor writing style. Maureen Dowd opined in a piece for the *New York Times* (31 Mar. 2012), "James writes like a Brontë devoid of talent. . . . [She] cleaves to hoary conventions out of Harlequin: powerful and wealthy heroes with a sense of entitlement who need to be rescued; smart and strong-willed heroines who tame their men."

Jo Bryant echoed that frustration in a piece for the *Seattle Post-Intelligencer* (21 Sept. 2012), writing, "Where do I start? . . . Christian with the grey eyes. How many ways are there to describe grey eyes? A lot it seems. There's grey, intensely grey, dark and grey, serious and grey, super grey. Need I go on?" The review continued, "Then there is Ana's inner goddess, who glares, is thrilled, dances, nods, jumps, stops jumping, glows, is surprised, is pleased, is not pleased, smacks her lips, does back flips, bounces, wakes, pleads, stares open mouthed, prostrates herself, spins, has a do not disturb sign on her door, is beside herself, grins, pouts, scowls, basks, gazes, swoons, is hopeful, and she also drove me to drink."

James's selection as 2012 Publishing Person of the Year by *Publishers Weekly*, an honor once bestowed to Jeff Bezos, founder of Amazon, surprised many. Nevertheless, as the editors reiterated in a letter dated November 30, 2012, "[She was chosen] because the success of the series continues to reverberate throughout the industry in a number of ways—among other things, the money it's brought in helped boost print sales in bookstores and turned erotic fiction into a hot category."

## OTHER PROJECTS

In March 2012, James sold the film rights to her trilogy to Universal Studios for $5 million. The report caused fevered speculation among fans and the entertainment media about which actors will play the leads. Emilia Clarke and Emma Watson were named among the favorites to portray Ana, though Watson has adamantly denied having any interest in the role. Actors Ian Somerhalder and Robert Pattison have also been named in speculation about who will be cast as Christian. James has told interviewers that she has no control over casting and that she cannot comment publicly, but that she has her own favorites in mind.

EMI Classics released *Fifty Shades of Grey: The Classical Album* in late 2012. All of the music on the album is mentioned in the trilogy. Label executives have noted that the books' references to classical compositions have encouraged sales of those pieces, even propelling "Spem in Alium," a sixteenth century motet for forty voices by Thomas Tallis, to the top of the classical charts in the United Kingdom.

In April 2013, James published *Fifty Shades of Grey: Inner Goddess (A Journal)*, in which she discusses the inspiration behind her series and gives tips for aspiring writers.

## PERSONAL LIFE

James and Leonard live near Ealing with their teenage sons and a West Highland terrier named Max. During the late 2000s, Leonard wrote for the television series *Wire in the Blood* (2004–2008) and *Wild at Heart* (2007–2012).

James's appearance and demeanor often surprise those who are meeting her for the first time. "As the writer of the most successful erotic novel in history, one would imagine that E. L. James lounges around in a kittenish silk negligee, perhaps dangling a leather bondage whip from her perfectly manicured fingers. The reality is rather different, however," Zoe Brennan wrote for the London *Telegraph* (7 July 2012). "Instead of a leopard skin-clad dominatrix, she resembles a suburban school dinner lady."

James's life, Brennan wrote, "is a million miles away from her hero Christian's 'red room of pain' hidden in his luxury penthouse. In Twitter chats, [the author] has revealed that she drives a Mini, her favourite tipple is Oyster Bay sauvignon blanc—around £8 a bottle—and she loves eating Nutella with a spoon. Her husband snores, and she is not a morning person."

## SUGGESTED READING

Bosman, Jill. "Discreetly Digital, Erotic Novel Sets American Women Abuzz." *New York Times.* New York Times Co., 9 Mar. 2012. Web. 29 Mar. 2013.

Brennan, Zoe. "E. L. James: The Shy Housewife behind *Fifty Shades of Grey.*" *Telegraph.* Telegraph Media Group, 7 July 2012. Web. 29 Mar. 2013.

Bryant, Jo. "Book Review: *Fifty Shades of Grey* by E. L. James." *Seattle Post-Intelligencer.* Hearst Communications, 21 Sept. 2012. Web. 29 Mar. 2013.

Dowd, Maureen. "She's Fit to Be Tied." *New York Times.* New York Times Co., 31 Mar. 2012. Web. 29 Mar. 2013.

Johnson, Steve. "Who is E.L. James?" *Chicago Tribune.* Tribune, 3 May, 2012. Web. 29 Mar. 2013.

Williams, Zoe. "Why Women Love *Fifty Shades of Grey.*" *Guardian.* Guardian News and Media, 6 July 2012. Web. 29 Mar. 2013.

—Mari Rich

# Carly Rae Jepsen

**Born:** November 21, 1985
**Occupation:** Singer-songwriter

"Hit songs aren't difficult to generate, especially with help from a hot producer or hired-gun songwriter," Mike Devlin wrote for the *Times Colonist* (17 Oct. 2012). "But a worldwide smash—the type that happens once in a career—is often at the mercy of countless mitigating factors, some of which are impossible to discern, let alone predict." For Canadian singer-songwriter Carly Rae Jepsen, a third-place finish in the fifth season of the now-defunct *Canadian Idol* and the 2008 release of the album *Tug of War* brought modest success, but it was a series of unpredictable events—and an infectiously catchy single—that propelled Jepsen into the spotlight.

Released in Canada in late 2011, Jepsen's single "Call Me Maybe" quickly caught the attention of fellow Canadian singer Justin Bieber, who generated worldwide buzz for the song after mentioning it on the social networking site Twitter and lip-synching it in a video posted on YouTube. Selling more than 13 million copies worldwide, "Call Me Maybe" not only became a number one hit in both the United States and Jepsen's native Canada, but also achieved the same feat in more than fifteen other countries, including Australia, Finland, and South Korea. Despite the apparently meteoric nature of her rise to fame, Jepsen has acknowledged that it was the result of many years of work. "This is what I've been chasing since I was seven," she told Ky Henderson for *Cosmopolitan* (Jan. 2012). "I wake up and have to pinch myself."

Landov

## EARLY LIFE AND EDUCATION

Carly Rae Jepsen was born on November 21, 1985, in Mission, British Columbia. The second of three children born to Alexandra and Larry Jepsen, she has an older brother, Colin, and a younger sister, Katie. Jepsen's parents, both of whom were educators, divorced when she was three years old.

Growing up, Jepsen was exposed to a steady diet of folk and rock music by such artists as Bruce Springsteen, James Taylor, and Cat Stevens. She developed a love of performing at an early age; with her parents' support, she took part in her first talent show when she was seven years old. "That was my first taste of being on-stage," Jepsen told Henderson. "I sang 'Eternal Flame' and 'Beauty and the Beast.' I don't think I understood it, but I remember being onstage in the spotlight, feeling totally at home and comfortable, and knowing it was what I was meant to do."

Jepsen starred in productions of *The Wiz*, *Annie*, and *Grease* while attending Heritage Park Secondary School. However, her interest in musical theater was short lived. "I didn't want to go on stage and play somebody else," she explained to Alan Sculley for *The Morning Call* (1 Nov. 2012). "I just wanted to be me." Jepsen applied to a few music-related programs at Capilano College and the University of British Columbia with the idea of pursuing a career

as a music teacher, but she decided instead to focus on writing and singing her own music. "I knew I didn't really want that," she told Devlin. "I wanted to be performing."

At the suggestion of Beverly Holmes, Heritage Park Secondary School's drama teacher, Jepsen, who received her first guitar at age seventeen, enrolled in the Canadian College of Performing Arts (CCPA) in Victoria, British Columbia. She devoted herself to her studies, attending school six days each week. "I spent the year training nonstop," Jepsen recalled to Devlin. "You couldn't keep me away from it. I loved it." Upon completing her musical training at CCPA, Jepsen moved to Vancouver, where she played the pub circuit and also founded a swing band. She supported herself financially by working several odd jobs, including bartending at the live music lounge the Media Club.

### CANADIAN IDOL

In 2007, after several years of performing in Vancouver, Jepsen auditioned for the competitive singing show *Canadian Idol*, again with Holmes's encouragement. "She was like 'Carly, I know you're trying everything, but try this. Why not? It could be a bit of exposure. Worst-case scenario, you go to audition and it doesn't work and you just keep doing whatever you do,'" Jepsen recalled to Sculley. "It wasn't until season five that I finally caved in to her suggestion and went and tried it." Performing "Sweet Talker," an original acoustic composition, Jepsen made a positive impression on the show's four judges, Farley Flex, Jake Gold, Sass Jordan, and Zack Werner. She was among the 212 contestants invited to compete in Toronto, where she vied successfully for a spot as one of the show's top 22 finalists.

Like its American counterpart, *Canadian Idol*, the fifth season of which premiered in early June 2007, was modeled after the British series *Pop Idol*. Each week, the contestants performed songs and received frank critiques from the judges, who determined which contestant or contestants would be eliminated from the competition. Viewers also had the opportunity to vote by telephone for their favorite performers on a weekly basis.

Jepsen impressed audiences with her interpretations of songs by such artists as Corinne Bailey Rae, Ella Fitzgerald, and the Bee Gees, earning a place among the season's top ten contestants. In September 2007 Jepsen was eliminated after performing two songs, one selected by the judges (Janis Ian's "At Seventeen") and another chosen by the public (Dido's "White Flag"). She ultimately finished in third place, behind Jaydee Bixby and eventual winner Brian Melo. In November 2007 Jepsen embarked on a tour with Melo and Bixby.

## TUG OF WAR

Upon completion of the *Canadian Idol* concert tour, Jepsen returned to British Columbia to concentrate on writing and recording music for her demo record and assembling a backup band, with which she toured Canada for two years. Jepsen's demo eventually found its way into the hands of Jonathan Simkin, cofounder of Vancouver-based record label 604 Records. Although Simkin agreed to meet with Jepsen, he had no initial interest in signing her to his label. "I assumed she didn't write her own songs," he admitted to Jason Lipshutz for *Billboard* (25 June 2012). Intrigued by Jepsen's songwriting ability, Simkin decided instead to serve as her manager. Jepsen ultimately signed with MapleMusic Recordings, a Toronto-based independent label, and its distribution arm, Fontana North, as well as music publishing company Dexter Entertainment.

Jepsen entered the studio with songwriter and producer Ryan Stewart, who shared coproducer duties with Josh Ramsay on her folk-inspired debut album. She wrote eight of the ten songs on the disc, which also included a cover of the John Denver hit "Sunshine on My Shoulders." Released on September 30, 2008, *Tug of War* produced two gold singles: the title track, which reached number thirty-six on the Canadian Hot 100 list, and "Bucket," which peaked at number thirty-two. For the latter single, Jepsen incorporated elements of the children's song "There's a Hole in My Bucket." "It was a last minute idea. We were looking for a bridge," she told Kei Baritugo and Amalia Nickel for the *Vancouver Observer* (17 Apr. 2010). "I started singing it as a joke and we were, like, can we get away with that?" In 2009 Jepsen performed headlining shows across Canada in support of *Tug of War*, which went on to sell more than ten thousand copies in Canada and earned song of the year honors at the 2010 Canadian Radio Music Awards. Jepsen was later nominated for songwriter of the year and new artist of the year at the 2010 Juno Awards, the Canadian equivalent to the Grammy Awards.

## "CALL ME MAYBE"

Following the modest success of Jepsen's freshman album, Simkin signed her to his 604 Records label. In early 2011 Jepsen reunited with Stewart and Ramsay to begin work on her second album. The trio collaborated on all the album's tracks, including "Call Me Maybe," a song that Jepsen cowrote with Ramsay and Tavish Crowe, a member of her backup band. Jepsen initially presented the song to Ramsay, who kept the catchphrase ("Here's my number, so call me maybe") but rewrote almost everything else and also changed the folk-inspired arrangement to a more dance music–inspired one. "I showed Carly [Annie Lennox's] 'Walking on Broken Glass'

as an example of how a string riff could be cool in a dance tune," he told Sean Michaels for the *Globe and Mail* (21 May 2012).

On September 20, 2011, "Call Me Maybe" was released as the lead single of Jepsen's second album, after much persistence from Simkin. "That was me having to fight for that one—the Universal radio team, that wasn't their first choice, " he told Lipshutz. "It wasn't anybody's first choice, except me. I just knew there was something about that song." The single received extensive radio airplay across Canada and quickly reached the top of the Canadian Hot 100 chart. Three months later the Canadian pop singer Justin Bieber, who was home for Christmas, heard "Call Me Maybe" and fell so in love with the infectious pop hit that he endorsed it on the popular social media website Twitter. Bieber later appeared in a video in which he and various other singers and actors lip-synched to the song. Bieber's manager, Scooter Braun, shared Bieber's sentiment, and in February 2012 he signed Jepsen to an American deal with his Schoolboy Records/Interscope label. In March 2012 "Call Me Maybe" debuted at number thirty-eight on the Billboard Hot 100. That same month Jepsen made her first US television appearance, performing the song on *The Ellen DeGeneres Show*. "Call Me Maybe" entered the top ten on the Billboard chart in April; two months later, it reached the top spot, where it remained for nine straight weeks. The track also held the number one position on the Billboard Digital Songs chart.

## CURIOSITY

Although they initially planned to release Jepsen's follow-up as a full-length album, the executives at 604 Records made the last-minute decision to release it as an extended play (EP) disc. *Curiosity* debuted on February 14, 2012. The six song EP featured five original songs, including "Call Me Maybe," as well as a cover of Joni Mitchell's "Both Sides Now."

In June 2012 Jepsen released the single "Good Time," a collaboration with electronic pop musician Adam Young, better known as Owl City. Within a month the song had reached number eight on the Billboard 100, becoming Jepsen's second US top ten hit. The song went on to sell more than two million copies in the United States, achieving double platinum status, and was generally praised by critics for its catchy sound. Grady Smith wrote for *Entertainment Weekly* (20 June 2012), "With the production-friendly voices of Owl City and Jepsen, the instantly hooky chorus, and the 'Whoa-oh-oh-oh-oh' refrain, 'Good Time' goes down easier than a frozen margarita at a beachfront tiki bar."

## KISS

In September 2012 Jepsen released *Kiss*, her second full-length studio album and first international record. The album, which featured two songs from *Curiosity*, debuted at number six on the Billboard 200. Jepsen cowrote ten of the album's twelve tracks. "The songwriting aspect is the one thing that never changes and is always there for me," she told Gary Graff for the *Oakland Press* (13 June 2013). "It's something that kind of keeps me grounded through all of it." To promote the album, Jepsen served as the opening act for Bieber during his Believe Tour, performing in North America and Europe.

A modest success, *Kiss* went on to sell over 225,000 thousand copies by early 2013. That year Jepsen was nominated for the Grammy Awards for song of the year and best pop solo performance. She won the awards for top pop song of the year and top digital song at the 2013 Billboard Music Awards and also took home the Juno Awards for single of the year, album of the year, and pop album of the year.

Jepsen made headlines in March 2013 for refusing to perform at the Boy Scouts of America's national jamboree in protest of the group's controversial ban against gay scout leaders and members. A few months later she embarked on her first headlining tour, writing songs for her next album while on the road.

Jepsen is in a relationship with fellow musician Matthew Koma. In addition to performing and recording music, she has served as a spokesperson for the apparel brand Candie's and the skin and hair product company Burt's Bees.

## SUGGESTED READING

Baritugo, Kei, and Amalia Nickel. "Juno Exclusive: Carly Rae Jepsen Talks about Big Dreams and Small Pleasures." *Vancouver Observer.* Observer Media Group, 17 Apr. 2010. Web. 16 July 2013.

Devlin, Mike. "Carly Rae Jepsen: It Takes a Few Years to Be an Overnight Sensation." *Canada. com.* Postmedia Network, 17 Oct. 2012. Web. 16 July 2013.

Henderson, Ky. "Carly Rae Jepsen Is Our January Cover Girl!" *Cosmopolitan.* Hearst Communications, Jan. 2013. Web. 16 July 2013.

Lipshutz, Jason. "Carly Rae Jepsen: The Billboard Cover Story." *Billboard.* Billboard, 25 June 2012. Web. 16 July 2013.

Sculley, Alan. "Carly Rae Jepsen Riding High on Tails of 'Call Me Maybe.'" *Morning Call.* Tribune, 5 Oct. 2012. Web. 16 July 2013.

## SELECTED WORKS

*Tug of War*, 2008; *Curiosity*, 2012; *Kiss*, 2012

—Bertha Muteba

# Jon Jones

**Born:** July 19, 1987
**Occupation:** Mixed martial artist

When charismatic mixed marital artist Jon Jones appeared on the *Tonight Show with Jay Leno* on March 24, 2011—just after his March 19 victory over Mauricio Rua, for which he became the youngest Ultimate Fighting Championship (UFC) light-heavyweight champion—the mainstream media glimpsed what many in mixed martial arts (MMA) circles had known since Jones first began fighting for the UFC in 2008: an athletic prodigy with the personality to complement his varied skill set, Jones was a major star who would increase the exposure of his organization and further legitimize a popular but oft-maligned sport. On the *Tonight Show* he exuded confidence, charm, and a sense of humor as he both discussed his prevention of a robbery the day of his championship bout and flirted with guest Kirstie Alley. He also exhibited great spokesmanship, defining what the sport of MMA is and discussing his training regimen and biographical background with a humility that belied his physical power and prowess in the ring.

By the end of 2012, the six-foot-four, 205-pound Jones had defended his light heavyweight title on four occasions and was preparing to face Chael Sonnen on April 27, 2013. He and Sonnen had developed a rivalry over several months; both Jones and Sonnen are coaches on the television show *The Ultimate Fighter 17*, which debuted on FX on January 22. On the show the twenty-five-year-old Jones trains a group of aspiring fighters, dispensing knowledge and inspiring the individual members of his team. "I'm a guy who is not going to be stingy with my success. I'm going to try and motivate others with [t]his success and share [t]his success and ultimately bring up the whole sport of mixed martial arts," Jones told John Morgan for the *Ithaca Journal* (2 Jan. 2013). Assuming that he beats Sonnen in their April 27 match, Jones also plans to defend his title at least once more in 2013, while continuing to promote UFC to a global market.

## EARLY LIFE AND EDUCATION

Born on July 19, 1987, in Rochester, and raised in Endicott, New York, Jones grew up with his two brothers and one sister (who died of cancer as a teenager) in a strict religious household. His father was a pastor, and his early life revolved around the church. As Jones has discussed in several interviews, his parents limited their children's experiences and exposure to negative aspects of their community, often using corporal punishment to instill both a sense of right and wrong and an understanding of the

Getty Images

sometimes brutal nature of the world. "My parents kept us pretty sheltered," Jones explained to Jack Encarnacao for SherDog.com (2 Dec. 2009). "We were never allowed to spend the night at our friends' house, not once. We were always taught to take care of our family and do the right thing." Jones's rigid upbringing influenced his impression of both himself and the world and was a primary cause of his professional discipline and focus.

Jones started wrestling in junior high school, finding his niche as an athlete early and in a sport removed from the mainstream, though he did play football in high school. Discussing his early obsession with wrestling with Encarnacao, Jones said, "I never took time off from the time it started. When kids would get one season in a year, I'd get three . . . I would be doing freestyle and Greco." His early exposure to various types of wrestling styles is evident in his UFC fights; one of his greatest advantages over his opponents has been his ability to integrate various martial arts into a cohesive and, to his opponents, often befuddling blend.

In high school Jones earned the nickname Bones from his football teammates—it is a nickname that he continues to use in his professional fighting career as a tribute to his hometown and his friends there. Laden with shoulder pads and a helmet, Jones's noticeably long, thin, and seemingly skeletal legs were exposed, hence the nickname. Though once the inspiration for fraternal hazing from high school teammates, Jones's legs became a source of advantage over many of his wrestling opponents, as he learned how to flick and kick from a protected distance into the midsection, legs, and head of other fighters. As a high school wrestler Jones dreamed of becoming the New York state champion, a

goal he realized as a senior in 2005. Winning his state's championship enabled him to compete at the national level. Coming into the tournament, he "was ranked 11th in the country and I ended up taking 4th," he told Encarnacao. "I got looked at by a lot of Division 1 schools." He had not performed well enough academically to attend a Division I school, however. The University of Iowa and Iowa State University, both with elite wrestling programs, set him up at Iowa Central Community College, with the intention of recruiting him when he established himself as a more serious student.

There Jones was first introduced to the sport of MMA. His roommate Joe Soto, who later became a successful professional fighter, provided the impetus for Jones's burgeoning interest in the sport. As Jones explained to Encarnacao, Soto "would just sit there and watch YouTube videos and have fighting on all the time. . . . Honestly, I thought he was kind of crazy for being so brave to fight people." In 2006 Jones won the National Junior College wrestling championship and was named to the Greco-Roman All-American team. Jones planned to earn a degree in criminal justice with the intention of returning to Endicott to join the local police force. He received an associate's degree and planned to enter a university, while also training as an MMA fighter. However, given his innate physical capabilities and his ability to learn and assimilate new martial arts tactics, he decided to give professional fighting a chance.

## SWIFT RISE THROUGH THE UFC RANKS

Many MMA fighters work for years to earn an invitation to a major UFC event, but through a combination of skill and good fortune, Jones was given an early opportunity to fight at an advanced professional level. Jones debuted as a MMA fighter in 2008, winning with a technical knockout in the first round against Brad Bernard. In fact, in his first six fights, all of which predated his ascension to UFC, Jones finished opponents off in the first round of four of them, taking just fourteen seconds to defeat Ryan Verrett with a flurry of punches in May 2008. In July of that year, by defeating Moyses Gabin by technical knockout, Jones became the United States Kickboxing Association heavyweight champion.

Marveling at Jones's domination, UFC president Dana White offered Jones his first UFC fight, scheduled for August 9, 2008, on short notice after the injured Tomasz Drwal was unable to fight. At UFC 87, Jones was the unanimous victor, going three rounds with the favored André Gusmão. Jones fought three times in 2009, tallying his first victory by submission against Jake O'Brien in UFC 100. However, he suffered his first and, through 2012, only loss in a controversial match against American Matt Hamill.

Jones dominated the fight, bloodying Hamill with repeated elbows to the face. "I think after 14 or 15 unanswered punches, it should [have] been stopped," Jones later said, as quoted by Michael David Smith for *SB Nation* (5 Dec. 2009). "It was awkward to keep hitting him like that. I was like 'C'mon, let's stop this.'" However, Jones was disqualified after the first round because instant replay revealed that he had used several illegal downward-thrusting elbow blows. Hamill had a dislocated shoulder and was thus unable to defend himself. Despite Jones's evident disappointment about losing to a clearly inferior opponent, after the fight, Jones was in a philosophical and relatively positive mood. He told Smith, "I've heard so many times that when you lose, you come back a better, stronger person . . . I try to look at everything at life for the best, but now I'm not worried about being undefeated." The loss seemed to embolden Jones, and he went on to defeat three high-profile opponents en route to a shot at the light heavyweight championship.

**TITLE SHOT**
After Jones defeated Vladimir Matyushenko at UFC Live on August 1, 2010, in a surprising first-round technical knockout, Dana White had high praise for the young Jones: "This kid is one of the top eight in the world in that weight division. He's got to keep his head together, stay focused . . . He's smart, good looking and bad ass" (qtd. in *MMA Mania*, 2 Aug. 2010). It was clear that White was determined to make Jones part of his plan for the expansion of UFC's popularity, and he pitted Jones against highly regarded, undefeated Ryan Bader in his following match. In UFC 126 it took Jones under two rounds to defeat Bader, forcing him to tap out after locking him in the brutal guillotine choke hold, which, applied properly, cuts off the flow of air and can potentially kill the opponent.

Jones's history of hard work and good luck coalesced in early 2011, and his rapid UFC ascension culminated in an opportunity to face the light heavyweight champion, Mauricio Rua. Rashad Evans, Jones's friend and training partner, whom he vowed never to fight, had been scheduled to fight Rua but suffered a knee injury that precluded him from participating in the championship match. Evans gave Jones his blessing to proceed with the March 19 fight. In his first title defense, Rua was manhandled, suffocated by the relentless onslaught of Jones's swift, strong, and diverse attack. Known for his creativity and use of such devastating maneuvers as ax kicks and spinning elbows, Jones connected with a flying knee early in the first round.

Jones struck Rua seventy-five times, absorbing only nine of Rua's shots, and scored three takedowns before finally earning a technical knockout in the third round after he connected with a knee to Rua's head. Rua was bloodied, with welts covering his body. By defeating Rua, Jones, then not yet twenty-four years old, became the youngest light-heavyweight champion.

**RIVALRY WITH EVANS AND TITLE DEFENSES**
In his first defense of his light-heavyweight title, at UFC 135 on September 24, 2011, Jones faced veteran fighter and former champion Quentin "Rampage" Jackson. Jones exposed Jackson's one-dimensional fighting style, kicking him repeatedly in the legs, connecting with Jackson's face with a spinning elbow, and forcing him to submit in the fourth round after applying a rear naked choke hold; the loss was Jackson's first ever by submission. The contrast between Jackson's slugger style and Jones's high-flying and precise techniques was glaring and highlighted Jones's unique ability to incorporate power, finesse, and ingenuity to force an opponent into defensive positions. Jones followed up his fight with Jackson by defending his title in December 2011 against Lyoto Machida, whom Jones rendered unconscious through a standing guillotine hold.

A year later, reflecting on his accomplishments in 2011, Jones told Duane Finley for *Bleacher Report* (18 Dec. 2012), "It was a phenomenal year. . . . Because I was having so much fun I guess I didn't realize how much work I had put it. I wouldn't take it back for the world, and hopefully I can duplicate that year in the future." Though 2011 was the year that Jones came to mainstream prominence, 2012 proved challenging in other ways, as he was forced to face his friend-turned-rival, Rashad Evans, and incurred the wrath of the UFC president for his decision to decline a high-profile fight.

Evans, who was the UFC light-heavyweight champion for a brief period in 2008–9, welcomed Jones to Greg Jackson's MMA training facility when the latter was first beginning to show promise as a young fighter. The two wrestlers became friends, training together and vowing never to face each other in the ring; before Jones defeated Rua, Evans even hinted that he would consider switching to another weight class to avoid having to fight against his friend. The rivalry between Evans and Jones seemed to develop immediately after Jones became champion, but it had probably been brewing for some time, given that Jones replaced the injured Evans in the title match.

Jones and Evans, now archrivals, finally faced each other on April 21, 2012, at UFC 145, going the distance in a hard-fought five-round contest that Jones won by unanimous decision. Jones outstruck Evans 105 to 45 and essentially ended speculation that a rematch would be necessary to determine the better fighter.

In the summer of 2012, Jones was scheduled to fight Dan Henderson at UFC 151, but Henderson suffered a knee injury and had to drop out. UFC attempted to replace Henderson on short notice, but Jones refused to fight, citing that he was not given enough time to prepare. White was forced to cancel UFC 151, an embarrassing action for which he seemed to blame Jones. For his part, Jones, who felt he was being forced into a fight he was not ready for, claimed the UFC was treating him "like a piece of meat," as reported by Thomas Myers in *SB Nation* (7 Jan. 2013). Later, White responded by calling Jones a "diva." Though his rise through the UFC was rapid, Jones was learning that staying at the top sometimes necessitated making difficult decisions and enduring criticism from fans, fighters, and even his employer.

### PERSONAL LIFE AND FUTURE ENDEAVORS

Jones is not the only famous athlete in his family. His older brother, Arthur, is a defensive end for the Baltimore Ravens, and his younger brother, Chandler, is a defensive end for the New England Patriots. In fact Chandler was the team's first-round draft pick in 2012 and was named the NFL Defensive Rookie of the Month in September 2012. Jones has said that he and his brothers are close and that Chandler, especially, could be a successful MMA fighter.

If Jones successfully defends his championship title against Sonnen, with whom he stars opposite in *The Ultimate Fighter 17*, in April, he will tie Chuck Liddel for most defenses of the UFC Light Heavyweight title. Even at twenty-five, Jones has been compared to the great fighters who have preceded him, and he seems poised for additional success inside the ring as well as in other facets of his life. He has been sponsored internationally by Nike, another indication of the rapid rise in popularity of the UFC, a phenomenon for which Jones is partially responsible. Jones explained to Duane Finley for *Bleacher Report* (18 Dec. 2012), "Legacy is definitely something that is always on my mind, and it is a big reason why I fight. I'm already the champion, so I don't fight to be the champion. I fight to be remembered. I fight to conquer records." Speculation has surfaced that Jones will be involved in a superfight with either middleweight champion Anderson Silva or heavyweight champion Cain Velasquez. In fact, Jones has indicated that, as he ages and naturally puts on weight, he will begin fighting at the heavyweight level. Bright, articulate, handsome, and determined, Jones has become the mixed martial artist on which the future prosperity of the UFC depends.

Jones and his fiancée, Jessie Moses, reside in upstate New York with their three daughters.

### SUGGESTED READING

Cofield, Steve. "Hours before the Biggest Fight of His Life, Jones Subdues a Robber." *Cagefighter*. Yahoo! Sports, 19 Mar. 2011. Web. 7 Jan. 2013.
Encarnacao, Jack. "Twelve Questions for Jon Jones." *SherDog.com*. CraveOnline Media, 2 Dec. 2009. Web. 7 Jan. 2013.
Finley, Duane. "The Fighting Life: Jon Jones Balancing the Pressure and Promise of Expectation." *Bleacher Report*. Bleacher Report, 18 Dec. 2012. Web. 7 Jan. 2013.
Iole, Kevin. "Jones Steamrolls Rua, Becomes Youngest UFC Champ." *Yahoo! Sports*. Yahoo! Inc., 20 Mar. 2011. Web. 7 Jan. 2013.
"Jon Jones Next Fight against 'One of the Top Eight Guys in the World.'" *SB Nation*. MMAmania.com, 2 Aug. 2010. Web. 7 Jan. 2013.
Morgan, John. "Jon Jones Teaching Lessons on 'TUF.'" *Ithaca Journal*. TheIthacaJournal.com, 2 Jan. 2013. Web. 7 Jan. 2013.

—*Christopher Rager*

# Rashida Jones

**Born:** February 25, 1976
**Occupation:** Actor

When Rashida Jones launched her acting career in 1997, she initially struggled to find roles. "I definitely had casting directors say to me, 'You're too white for this part.' I remember going in for a black character and a [casting director] saying to me, 'What are you doing here?'" Jones told Jenelle Riley for *Backstage* (8 Aug. 2012). "Other times I would go in for the girl next door, and I was too exotic for that. I was too quirky to be the popular girl but not nerdy enough to be the sidekick. I was stuck somewhere in the middle, and part of that was because I was biracial."

Jones briefly considered returning to school before landing her breakthrough role in *The Office*, the NBC adaptation of the British series; she was a series regular in 2006 and 2007, and reprised her role for episodes in 2009 and 2011. She has worked steadily ever since, amassing film credits with roles in several high-profile comedies, including *Brief Interviews with Hideous Men* (2009); *I Love You, Man* (2009); *The Social Network* (2010); *Our Idiot Brother* (2011); *The Muppets* (2011); and, most recently, *Celeste and Jesse Forever* (2012). She has been a small-screen fixture since 2009 with her supporting role as nurse Ann Perkins opposite actress Amy Poehler in the acclaimed NBC series *Parks and Recreation*.

### EARLY LIFE

Rashida Leah Jones was born in Los Angeles, California, on February 25, 1976. (Her first name means "rightly guided" in Arabic.) The younger daughter of Peggy Lipton, an actress, and the legendary music producer Quincy Jones, she grew up in the affluent, gated community

AJM/PA Photos/Landov

I naturally gravitated towards that culturally and religiously, which was cool because I didn't have a bat mitzvah."

Jones made headlines in 1992 when she penned an angry letter to the hip-hop magazine *The Source*, responding to comments made by the rapper Tupac Shakur, who blamed interracial unions for destroying the black community and criticized her parents' marriage. "I basically confronted Tupac for making a really foul comment about my dad. I basically said he wouldn't be anywhere if my dad hadn't paved the way for artists like him," she told Mike Einziger for *Malibu* magazine (Apr./May 2011). Jones eventually met and became friends with Shakur, who went on to date her older sister, to whom he became engaged.

## EDUCATION

Jones was an outstanding and highly motivated student in high school. "I was social, I was overachieving. I was a cheerleader, I was in the math club, I was in the National Honor Society. I was in every club; I was like a teacher's pet," she told Bennett Marcus in an August 2, 2012 interview for *Vanity Fair*. After graduating from the Buckley School in 1994, Jones, whose classmates voted her "most likely to succeed," was admitted to Harvard University, in Massachusetts, where she majored in religion and philosophy. She eventually decided not to pursue the field further because of the school's failure to acknowledge Eastern philosophy.

Jones abandoned an initial interest in law following her disappointment with O. J. Simpson's acquittal in his high-profile 1995 murder trial. "I hated the fact that Simpson was in any way representing justice for black people in California. I had wanted to be a lawyer, but after that I decided to do something else," she told Amy Wallace for *Los Angeles Magazine* (16 Feb. 2011). Instead, Jones decided to pursue the performing arts, after spending a summer at the Royal Academy of Dramatic Arts in London. At the time, she served as musical director for Harvard's a cappella group, the Harvard-Radcliffe Opportunes, and also joined the Harvard Radcliffe Dramatic Club and the Hasty Pudding Theatricals. As a member of the latter club, she composed scores for some of their productions, including their "Man of the Year" award.

## EARLY ACTING CAREER

After graduating from Harvard in 1997, Jones moved to New York City, where she signed with an agent. She initially struggled while making the audition rounds, partly, as she told Jenelle Riley, because of her ambiguous racial identity. Jones's professional debut came in the television miniseries *The Last Don* (1997), which was based on Mario Puzo's novel of the same name. A year later, Jones first appeared on the big screen in the

of Bel Air, where there were very few interracial marriages at the time. While her older sister, Kidada, who had brown skin, brown eyes, and short, curly hair, looked more like their African American father, Jones more closely resembled their white mother, with her lighter skin, green eyes, and straight hair. She also inherited her father's musical talent, singing and playing the classical piano since the age of five.

Jones, whose mother is Ashkenazi Jewish, received a progressive upbringing. "My parents were kind of hippies and I went to a Montessori school [where] everyone had different religions and cultural backgrounds. I had Jewish friends, I had black friends, I had Asian friends. So it didn't really occur to me that it was odd in any way," she told Gerri Miller in an interview for *American Jewish Life* magazine (Jan./Feb. 2007).

Jones's parents divorced when she was ten years old, and she moved to Brentwood with her mother. During this period she had started going to a meditation ashram and a Buddhist temple after meeting a meditation teacher. By the time Jones began attending the Buckley School, a prestigious college preparatory school in Sherman Oaks, she began to increasingly explore the Jewish faith. "Junior year, I started dating a guy who was Conservative and had an Orthodox brother and practiced more than I did, was more devout than I was," she revealed to Miller. "We had a group of friends who were Jewish so independent drama *Myth America* (1998), Galt Niederhoffer's directorial debut. She followed that with a role in another independent feature: *East of A* (2000).

Jones next portrayed a feminist in *If These Walls Could Talk 2* (2000), the sequel to the HBO anthology drama, which takes place during three different eras and chronicles the lives of lesbians living in the same house. After a guest appearance as high-school bully Karen Scarfolli in the NBC cult comedy *Freaks and Geeks*, which also starred Jason Segel, Jones had a costarring role with Adam Brody in the comedic short film *Roadside Assistance* (2000).

That same year, Jones raised her profile considerably when she was cast as Louisa Fenn, the sarcastic assistant to the principal in David E. Kelley's acclaimed high-school drama *Boston Public*, which aired on the Fox network. During her two years on the weekly series (2000–2002), Jones, whose contract was not renewed, received an NAACP Image Award nod. In addition to showcasing her vocal talents on several of the show's episodes, she served as a backup vocalist on *Songs about Jane*, the debut album from the pop group Maroon 5, and as a guest vocalist on *The Rose That Grew from Concrete* (2000), a tribute album dedicated to Shakur, who was the victim of a fatal drive-by shooting in Las Vegas.

Following her stint on *Boston Public*, Jones began to mostly tackle comedic projects. She followed up a small, uncredited part in Steven Soderbergh's *Full Frontal* (2002), a satire on the fashion industry, with a supporting role in the romantic comedy *Now You Know* (2002), in which she played a woman who calls off her engagement, to the bewilderment of her fiancé. Jones also costarred, alongside her mother and her mother's brother Robert Lipton, in the play *Pitching to the Star*, which had a six-week run at the Lee Strasberg Institute in Los Angeles. In 2003 she appeared in the Damon Dash–directed mockumentary *Death of a Dynasty* (2003), a satirical look at the hip-hop industry, and *Chappelle's Show*, comedian Dave Chappelle's short-lived sketch comedy show on Comedy Central. From 2003 to 2004 she also served as a contributing editor for *Teen Vogue*.

### THE OFFICE AND MAINSTREAM SUCCESS

In 2004 Jones, whose scenes in the HBO drama *Strip Search* had ended up on the cutting-room floor, returned to the big screen as gynecologist Dr. Rachel Keyes in *Little Black Book*. The romantic comedy is about an insecure woman (played by Brittany Murphy) who investigates her boyfriend's past girlfriends after she finds his electronic organizer. Her next project was the seven-part British drama *NY-LON* (2004), in which she starred as Edie Miller, a New York–based record store clerk who pursues a long-distance romantic relationship with a London

stockbroker (played by Stephen Moyer). Shot in both cities, this series was broadcast on Channel Four in the United Kingdom and BBC America in the United States. The following year Jones played the part of Karen, the downstairs neighbor in the pilot for the 2005 improvisational Comedy Central series *Stella*, which lasted for only ten episodes before it was cancelled. She also appeared in another short-lived television series: the TNT police drama *Wanted*, in which she played Carla Merced, a government agent and hostage negotiator.

Jones gained more widespread attention in 2006, when she joined the cast of the NBC comedy *The Office*, an American adaptation of the British television series of the same name. At the time, she had considered returning to school. Jones was cast as Karen Filippelli, Pam Beesley's (Jenna Fischer) rival for the affections of Jim Halpert (John Krasinski), but she was almost passed over because of her looks. "When we were looking for Karen and I saw Rashida's name on the audition list, I [thought], 'This is a friend of people who work here, so let's be nice, but it's just not going to be her,'" executive producer Greg Daniels told Daniel Fierman in a February 9, 2007, interview for *Entertainment Weekly*. "But the thing that's great about her is that she's very beautiful but doesn't seem aware of her beauty. She leads with her intelligence. And she felt like a good contrast to Pam. When she read scenes with Jenna [Fischer], that's when we said, 'This is cool.'" Jones, who appeared regularly in season three, also garnered headlines for her brief, off-screen involvement with Krasinski. She made brief appearances as Karen in episodes in 2007, 2009, and 2011.

After two failed television pilots—an untitled project with Paul Reiser (2006) and *Our Thirties* (2006)—Jones appeared in two projects by David Wain: the ensemble comedy *The Ten* (2007), on which she also served as a coproducer, as well as a first-season episode of Wain's Internet video series *Wainy Days*. In February 2007, she reprised the role of Karen on *Saturday Night Live* (SNL), appearing in a parody of *The Office*, alongside SNL host and *Office* costar Rainn Wilson in the opening monologue. Jones continued to hone her comedic chops with her costarring role in the short-lived Fox sitcom *Unhitched* (2008), produced by the Farrelly brothers; and a recurring part in the Showtime comedy *Web Therapy* (2008), starring Lisa Kudrow. She was also among several celebrities who appeared in *Prop 8: The Musical* (2008), a satirical take on California's initiative against same-sex unions.

### PARKS AND RECREATION AND THE SOCIAL NETWORK

The following January, Jones lent her voice to several characters in an episode of the Adult Swim comedy *Robot Chicken*. Also in 2009, she reteamed with Krasinski, appearing in his directorial debut: the big-screen adaptation of David Foster Wallace's 1999 short-story collection *Brief Interviews with Hideous Men*. She then played the female lead, opposite former *Freaks and Geeks* star Segel and Paul Rudd, in the 2009 comedy *I Love You, Man*. "From the minute I got the script I loved it and wanted to be a part of it," she told Joel Amos in an interview for *Sheknows.com* (19 Mar. 2009). "You don't generally—especially if the focus is men—you don't get the girlfriend who is in any way dynamic. She is usually wallpaper to hear a voice that is not a guy. This is a really well carved out interesting specific integral character who has a point of view. She has her own mind and her own friends. It's really, really, really nice to play someone like that."

Also in 2009, Jones returned to weekly television with the role of nurse Ann Perkins on the critically acclaimed NBC comedy series *Parks and Recreation*. While creators Greg Daniels and Michael Schur (who also worked on *The Office*) were developing the series, Jones, who had been already been cast, could not appear in any other film or television projects. "I waited and waited, and it was kind of torturous. So I was just trying to write myself out of a painful, dark place," she told *SheKnows.com*. The result was a screenplay about divorcing high-school sweethearts who try to remain friends; in a case of life imitating art, Jones spent several months cowriting the script with Will McCormack, whom she briefly dated. *Parks and Recreation*—a mockumentary-style comedy about the local government of the fictional town of Pawnee, Indiana—eventually premiered on April 9, 2009. Though the show's short first season received mixed reviews from fans and critics, it eventually became known as one of the best comedies on television and was renewed for a sixth season in 2013. The Emmy-nominated series stars Amy Poehler, along with actors Aziz Ansari, Nick Offerman, Adam Scott, Aubrey Plaza, Chris Pratt, and Rob Lowe.

Jones returned to Harvard University, at least in the figurative sense, for her next film, *The Social Network*—an adaptation of Ben Mezrich's book *The Accidental Billionaires* (2009), which chronicles the founding of the social media site Facebook. Jones played Marylin Delpy, part of Facebook founder Mark Zuckerberg's legal defense team. The screenplay was written by Aaron Sorkin and the movie was directed by David Fincher. The cast also featured many up-and-coming actors of young Hollywood, including Jesse Eisenberg, Andrew Garfield, Rooney Mara, and Justin Timberlake. *The Social Network* was lauded by critics and received an Academy Award nomination for best picture and won for best adapted screenplay. It also won the Golden Globe for best motion picture–drama, as well as for best director and best screenplay.

Jones was very much in demand in 2011, appearing in several high-profile comedies, including *Our Idiot Brother*, her second film with Paul Rudd; *Friends with Benefits*; *The Big Year*; and *The Muppets*, her third project with Segel. During a hiatus from *Parks and Recreation*, she spent twenty-two days filming *Celeste and Jesse Forever*—the screenplay she cowrote with Will McCormack while waiting for *Parks and Recreation*. Jones starred in *Celeste and Jesse Forever* opposite actor Andy Samberg and the film was positively reviewed by critics. An upcoming project includes a screenplay adaptation (with McCormack) of her comic book series cowritten with Nunzio DeFilippis and Christina Weir, *Frenemy of the State*, about a socialite turned CIA agent; it is currently under development at Universal and Imagine Entertainment.

## PERSONAL LIFE

An ardent Democrat, Jones has campaigned for presidential candidates John Kerry and Barack Obama. In addition to Krasinski, she has dated actor Tobey Maguire; Jon Favreau, President Obama's former speechwriter; and Mark Ronson, to whom she was previously engaged.

## SUGGESTED READING

Amos, Joel. "Rashida Jones: Hollywood's New It Girl." *SheKnows.com*. SheKnows, 19 Mar. 2009. Web. 12 May 2012.

Einziger, Mike. "Rashida Jones." *Malibu Magazine*. Malibu Magazine, Apr./May 2011. Web. 13 May 2013.

Fierman, Daniel. " Paper Doll." *Entertainment Weekly*. Time, 9 Feb. 2007. Web. 12 May 2013.

Marcus, Bennett. "Rashida Jones: I Was 'That Girl' Who Did Math Club, Cheerleading, and National Honor Society in High School." *Vanity Fair*. Conde Nast, 2 Aug. 2012. Web. 12 May 2013.

Miller, Gerry. "The Daughter of Q." *American Jewish Life Magazine*. Genco Media, Jan./Feb. 2007. Web. 12 May 2013.

Riley, Jenelle. "'Parks and Recreation' Star Eyes Film Stardom." *Backstage*. Backstage, 8 Aug. 2012. Web. 12 May 2013.

Wallace, Amy. "Rashida Jones." *Los Angeles Magazine*. Los Angeles Magazine, 16 Feb. 2011, Web. 12 Mar. 2012.

## SELECTED WORKS

*Boston Public*, 2000–02; *NY-LON*, 2004; *The Office*, 2006–11; *I Love You, Man*, 2009; *Parks and Recreation*, 2009– ; *The Social Network*, 2010; *Our Idiot Brother*, 2011; *The Big Year*, 2011; *The Muppets*, 2011; *Celeste and Jesse Forever*, 2012

—*Bertha Muteba*

# Anish Kapoor

**Born:** March 12, 1954
**Occupation:** Sculptor

Since he began working in the 1970s, Anish Kapoor has developed a reputation as one of the world's foremost contemporary artists for his larger-than-life sculptures and installations and his innovative use of materials, which range from the traditional (stone, glass, wax) to the high tech (stainless steel, PVC, fiberglass). Among his most ambitious and identifiable public works are the bean-shaped *Cloud Gate* (2004), a stainless-steel sculpture located in Chicago's Millennium Park; the concave satellite-shaped *Sky Mirror* (2006), a temporary sculpture that was installed at Rockefeller Center in New York City; *Marsyas* (2002), a trumpet-shaped installation commissioned for the Tate Modern; *Leviathan* (2011), an enormous womb-like structure that he created for the Grand Palais in Paris; and *ArcelorMittal Orbit* (2012), a winding red tower commissioned for the 2012 Summer Olympics in London.

## EARLY LIFE

Anish Kapoor was born on March 12, 1954, in Mumbai, India, the son of an Iraqi Jewish mother and a Punjabi father. His maternal grandfather was cantor of the Pune synagogue. Kapoor and his two younger brothers had a peripatetic, middle-class upbringing due to his father's career as a hydrographer, or ocean mapmaker, in the Indian Navy. Kapoor attended the Doon School in Dehradun, a renowned all-boys boarding school that is comparable to the elite Eton College in the United Kingdom.

During his late teens, Kapoor moved to Israel to explore his Jewish roots. After a two-year stay on a kibbutz, from 1971 to 1973, he studied electrical engineering for six months before embarking in another direction. "I went back to the kibbutz and decided I had to be an artist," he told Jackie Wullschlager for the *Financial Times* (5 May 2012). He added, "My parents weren't over the moon. I was so young and so naive. I'd hardly looked at any art, hardly ever seen a painting."

Kapoor subsequently enrolled at Hornsey College of Art in London, where he studied under British Romanian sculptor Paul Neagu, from 1973 to 1977. He then spent a year at the Chelsea School of Art, now the Chelsea College of Art and Design.

## DRAWING INSPIRATION FROM HIS HOMELAND

In 1979, Kapoor landed a teaching position in the fine-art department at Wolverhampton Polytechnic's School of Art and Design. He also earned extra income by designing furniture for London-based interior designer and socialite Nicholas Haslam. That same year, Kapoor made

Stefan Wermuth/Reuters/Landov

a visit to his homeland, which was reflected in his early works. "I suddenly realized all these things I had been making . . . had a relationship to what I saw in India," he told Charlotte Higgins for the *Guardian* (7 Nov. 2008). "It was a certain attitude to the object. I was making objects that were about doing, about ritual."

Kapoor's fascination with primary colors, form, and scale was reflected in his first notable series, *1000 Names* (1979–80), a collection of striking abstract geometric objects supported by wood, fiberglass, or plaster and completely saturated with loose pigment powder. The brightly hued pigments he used are reminiscent of the spices commonly found in Indian markets. The organic shapes could be traced to the unusual architecture of Jantar Mantar, an eighteenth-century astronomical observatory in New Delhi.

The sculptures also appeared to be emerging outward, from the surface of the floor and the walls. "I began to evolve a reasoning, which had to do with things being partially revealed. While making the pigment pieces, it occurred to me that they all form themselves out of each other," Kapoor told Amina Meer for *BOMB* magazine (Winter 1990). He explained, "The powder on the floor defines the surface of the floor and the objects appear to be partially submerged, like icebergs. That seems to fit inside the idea of something being partially there."

By the mid-1980s, Kapoor's use of raw pigments and intensely bright hues remained a distinguishing feature of his sculptures, including *As If to Celebrate I Discovered a Mountain Blooming with Red Flowers* (1981); *Part of the Red* (1981); *White Sand, Red Millet, Many Flowers* (1982); *Red in the Centre* (1982); *The Chant of Blue* (1983); and *Mother as a Mountain* (1985).

## INTERNATIONAL ATTENTION

Kapoor's pigment series earned him international recognition. In 1980 he held his first ever solo exhibition in Paris, France, at a studio owned by Patrice Alexandre. Two years later he served as an artist-in-residence at the Walker Art Gallery in Liverpool, England, and was one of Britain's representatives at the 1982 Paris Biennale, along with Stephen Farthing and Bill Woodrow. The following year, his work was also exhibited at the seventeenth São Paulo Art Biennial in Brazil. In 1986 Kapoor was the subject of solo exhibitions at the Barbara Gladstone Gallery in New York City; Kunstnernes Hus in Oslo, Norway; and University Gallery at the Fine Arts Center of the University of Massachusetts Amherst.

During the late 1980s Kapoor started to focus less on the outward forms associated with his pigment pieces and more on the interior spaces, or cavities, of objects. He also began to incorporate stone, most notably sandstone, limestone, and marble, into his work. Much of his work from this time seems religiously inspired, such as *Adam* (1988–89), a giant freestanding sandstone sculpture with a pigment-filled rectangular center that suggests an endless opening or void. Other, similar installations include *Angel* (1990) and *A Wing at the Heart of Things* (1990), two pieces made of slate and pigment; *The Healing of St. Thomas* (1989), a deep, bloodstained opening in the wall filled with powdered pigment; *Madonna* (1989–90), an ode to the Virgin Mary made of fiberglass and pigment; and *It Is Man* (1989–90), a human-scaled totem composed of sandstone and pigment.

## EARNING RECOGNITION AND EXPLORING INTERACTION

Another of Kapoor's installations—*Void Field* (1989), a group of sixteen crude sandstone blocks, each weighing between four and six tons and containing a hollow black hole on top—was selected by the British Council to be part of the British Pavilion exhibition at the 1990 Venice Biennale. It was a turning point for Kapoor, who won the prestigious Premio Duemila prize. "There comes a moment when you don't have to tell the world what you're doing. They tell you what you're doing," he said to Anna Coren for CNN.com (7 Dec. 2012). "I experienced that in a very real way in Venice at the Bienniale. . . . That was a real revelation." Kapoor made history the following year when he became the first Indian-born artist to receive the Turner Prize, for the sandstone-and-pigment piece called *Untitled* (1991).

Kapoor continued to explore the notion of the void with *Descent into Limbo* (1992), which he exhibited at the Documenta IX in Kassel, Germany. This work consists of a walk-in cube leading into a dark room, with a black carpet in the middle of the room that closely resembled a bottomless pit. "There were people who went into that room and were . . . terrified of the idea that this kind of homme phalos at the center of this room would suck them in," he told John Tusa in a BBC Radio 3 interview (6 July 2003).

Kapoor drew inspiration from a visit to Australia's Uluru (Ayers Rock) for his first white-on-white piece: *When I Am Pregnant* (1992), an interactive form, or installation, subtly protruding from a wall. Another work that alludes to the human figure is the void piece titled *My Body Your Body* (1993), a large blue wall installation with a sunken center. Two years later, *When I Am Pregnant* was part of Kapoor's solo exhibition at De Pont Foundation for Contemporary Art in Tilburg, Netherlands.

## EXPERIMENTS WITH MIRRORED SURFACES

By the mid-1990s Kapoor had begun working with industrial materials such as polyvinyl chloride (PVC), fiberglass, and stainless steel, as well as concave and convex shapes. He had also developed a fascination with curved, reflective surfaces that provide viewers with distorted images. "I think disorientation—or reorientation one should say—causes one to pause and I think part of the purpose has to be to somehow slow time down, to make that moment of pause as long as possible," he said in an interview for BBC News (4 May 1998).

This was evident in *Turning the World Inside Out* (1995), a stainless-steel sphere with an indentation in the center, and its companion pieces: *Turning the World Inside Out II* (1995), a floor installation boasting a funnel-shaped center that disappears into the floor, similar to a whirlpool; and *Turning the World Upside Down III* (1996), a mirrored ball with a hollow center that is on display in the lobby of London's Deutsche Bank headquarters.

In the late 1990s, optical effects remained a feature of Kapoor's works, including *Double Mirror* (1998), two concave steel discs facing each other; *Her Blood* (1998), three triangularly positioned concave discs, one with a dark red finish; *Iris* (1998), a convex floor piece resembling an eye; and *Yellow* (1999), a concave wall piece that looks like the sun and gives its viewers the feeling of being sucked into a void.

## LARGE-SCALE INSTALLATIONS

By the late 1990s, Kapoor had cultivated a loyal following around the world and was widely sought after for commissions. Among his first large-scale installations was *Taratantara* (1999–2000), a collaborative effort with structural engineer Neil Thomas. The sculpture was commissioned by the Baltic Centre for Contemporary Art in Gateshead, England. It was on display for eight weeks and viewed by more than sixteen thousand people before being displayed in the Piazza del Plebiscito in Naples, Italy.

A year later Kapoor unveiled *Parabolic Waters* (2000), a structure containing rapidly rotating colored water that was installed outside London's Millennium Dome. His next outdoor public art project was *Sky Mirror* (2001), a concave, reflective stainless-steel disc that was commissioned by the Nottingham Playhouse. "By making a concave form mirrored, what I found was that this wasn't just a mirrored object, this was, in a way, a space full of mirror," he told Coren. "It then occurred to me that maybe one could turn it up to the sky and have it reflect the sky. . . . And it became . . . almost like a landscape painting. And I was fascinated by that." Other versions of *Sky Mirror*, including his 2006 piece, have been exhibited at New York City's Rockefeller Center, London's Kensington Gardens, and Saint Petersburg's State Hermitage Museum.

In 2002, Kapoor debuted *Marsyas*, a massive installation that he and structural engineer Cecil Balmond had created by extending a red, skin-like PVC membrane across three enormous steel rings, each forming a trumpet-like opening. The sculpture is named after a man who was skinned alive by the Greek god Apollo, who was jealous of his superior flute-playing skills. Commissioned for the Unilever Series, *Marsyas* spanned the entire length of Turbine Hall at London's Tate Modern. It was viewed by more than 1.8 million people over the course of a year, making it one of the world's most visited sculptures. Another of Kapoor's steel works that received worldwide attention was his 2004 piece *Cloud Gate*, a thirty-three-foot-high concave, reflective structure that became a centerpiece in Chicago's Millennium Park. Nicknamed "The Bean," *Cloud Gate* was Kapoor's first public art installation in the United States and has the distinction of being the world's most expensive public commission, costing $25 million to make.

## RED WAX
During the early part of the 2000s, Kapoor started incorporating red wax into his work, which he also began to increasingly integrate within his surroundings. One such installation was *My Red Homeland* (2003), a circular platform twelve inches in diameter that contained twenty-five tons of blood-colored wax, Vaseline, and pigment constantly being stirred and reshaped by a large motorized arm. It was among the works featured in solo exhibitions at Kunsthaus Bregenz in Austria and the National Archaeological Museum in Naples. During this time, Kapoor also collaborated with the architectural firm Future Systems to design the entrances to Naples's Monte Sant'Angelo and Triano subway stations.

Kapoor followed up *My Red Homeland* with other wax pieces, including *Negative Box Shadow* (2005), a block of crude red wax that appears to have been hollowed out by a large metal disc; and *Moon Shadow* (2005), a crescent-shaped

form suspended on the wall and bisected by a flat wood board. He also collaborated with his friend, the renowned author Salman Rushdie, on *Blood Relations* (2006), marking Kapoor's first time working with text. The installation comprised two gigantic bronze boxes connected by red wax and inscribed with the first two paragraphs of Rushdie's text.

Arguably one of Kapoor's most challenging works was *Past, Present, Future* (2006), a massive half-dome composed of deep red wax and oil-based paint whose spherical form is maintained by a slowly rotating semicircular arch. Equally ambitious was his 2007 installation *Svayambh* ("self-generated" in Sanskrit), a thirty-five-ton train-shaped block of red crude wax slowly gliding along a matching track system and through narrow archways that span the entire length of the gallery halls. Originally commissioned by the Musée des Beaux-Arts de Nantes, *Svayambh* was shown at the inaugural 2007 Estuaire exhibition in France before being exhibited at the Haus der Kunst in Munich, Germany, and the Royal Academy in London.

Kapoor used weathering steel for the first time to produce his next installation, *Memory* (2008), a twenty-four-ton, submarine-shaped, rust-colored sculpture wedged into one room with an open end built into one of the gallery walls. On the other side of the wall, the aperture looked like a two dimensional painting. The piece was commissioned for the Deutsche Guggenheim in Berlin, Germany.

## RETROSPECTIVES
The following year, Kapoor assumed the role of guest artistic director at the Brighton Festival. There, he debuted *Imagined Monochrome* (2009), an interactive massage performance, and *The Dismemberment of Jeanne d'Arc* (2009), a site-specific commission in which he used red wax to represent body parts, including an enormous pit to represent the womb and two piles to represent the breasts. They were shown along with four of his other works: the 2001 version of *Sky Mirror*, *Blood Relations*, *1000 Names*, and *C-Curve* (2007).

In September 2009 Kapoor was the first living artist to be the subject of a career retrospective at the Royal Academy of Arts, where he had an entire floor devoted to his artwork. He took the opportunity to display his latest sculptures, including *Greyman Cries, Shaman Dies, Billowing Smoke, Beauty Evoked* (2008–9), a three-dimensional printer that is computer operated and expels cement according to a design formulated by the artist; *Tall Tree and the Eye* (2008–9), a sculpture with seventy-five hanging stainless steel spheres; and *Shooting into the Corner* (2008–9), an installation made up of a steel cannon in the middle of a white room, loudly firing red wax pellets into the corner at twenty-minute intervals. "Artists have to claim the ridiculous as part of their process of discovery," he told Zehra Jumabhoy for *Time Out Mumbai* (26 Nov. 2010). The major solo exhibition attracted more than 275,000 visitors in less than three months.

In late 2009 Kapoor's *Memory* traveled to New York's Guggenheim Museum before moving on to the Guggenheim Museum Bilbao in March 2010. Kapoor returned to India in November 2010 to take part in the first ever exhibition of his work in his homeland. The dual retrospective was held over a three-month period at the Mehboob Studio, a famed Bollywood film and recording studio in Mumbai, and the National Gallery of Modern Art in New Delhi. Also in 2010, he landed a commission to create a permanent landmark for London's Olympic Park.

## RECENT PROJECTS
In the summer of 2010, Kapoor unveiled *Temenos* in the English town of Middlesbrough, the first of five public sculptures commissioned by Tees Valley Regeneration and intended to be created throughout the Tees Valley area of North East England. *Temenos*, which looks like elongated butterfly nets, is the largest public artwork in the world. The rest of the project was eventually shelved due to lack of funding.

In 2011 the French Ministry of Culture and Communication enlisted Kapoor to produce a six-week installation for the annual *Monumenta* exhibition at Paris's Grand Palais. It was the first time in thirty-one years that Kapoor had returned to Paris. The result was *Leviathan* (2011), an enormous globular and tunnel-like structure with spherical extensions that project out into the three parts of the hall. He dedicated the piece to Chinese dissident artist Ai Weiwei. Milan's Fabbrica del Vapore was the site for his next sculpture, *Dirty Corner* (2011), a narrow, unlit steel tunnel that is one hundred feet long. In 2012, Kapoor garnered worldwide acclaim for *ArcelorMittal Orbit*, a 377-foot-high tower that he built with Cecil Balmond for the London Olympics. The tower features a red steel lattice tube curling around the central vertical structure.

## PERSONAL LIFE
Kapoor has received numerous honors for his work, including Commander of the Order of the British Empire (CBE) in 2003, Commandeur dans l'Ordre des Arts et des Lettres in 2011, the Padma Bhushan in 2012, and a British knighthood in 2013. He lives in London and has two children, Alba and Ishan, with art historian Susanne Spicale, whom he married in 1995.

## SUGGESTED READING
Higgins, Charlotte. "A Life in Art: Anish Kapoor." *Guardian*. Guardian News and Media, 7 Nov. 2008. Web. 17 July 2013.

Jumabhoy, Zehra. "Show Business." *Time Out Mumbai*. Time Out Group, 26 Nov. 2010. Web. 17 July 2013.

Kapoor, Anish. Interview by Anna Coren. *CNN.com*. Cable News Network, 7 Dec. 2012. Web. 17 July 2013.

Kapoor, Anish. Interview by John Tusa. *BBC Radio 3*. BBC, 6 July 2003. Web. 17 July 2013.

Kennedy, Maev. "Anish Kapoor Takes His Art to India." *Guardian*. Guardian News and Media, 3 Nov. 2010. Web. 17 July 2013.

Wullschlager, Jackie. "Lunch with the FT: Anish Kapoor." *Financial Times*. Financial Times, 5 May 2012. Web. 17 July 2013.

—*Bertha Muteba*

# Tawakkol Karman
**Born:** February 7, 1979
**Occupation:** Journalist and human rights activist

In 2011, at the age of thirty-two, Tawakkol Karman became not only the youngest Nobel Peace Prize laureate, but also the first Arab woman to be awarded the honor. She won the prize for her work advocating for peace-building and women's rights, as well as for her commitment to nonviolence as a Yemeni journalist and a political activist during the Arab Spring through 2010 and 2012. Often called the Mother of the Revolution in Yemen, Karman is also a member of the Islamist opposition party Islah and holds a position on its Shura Council. An outspoken advocate for issues including freedom of speech, freedom of the press, the release of political prisoners, and women's rights, Karman is an international symbol of Yemen's revolution. As both a conservative Muslim and a mother of three, Karman is challenging representations of Middle Eastern women both in her home country and abroad.

A voice for women and youth that speaks in favor of peace and nonviolence, Karman used her Nobel lecture to reiterate her worldview and her "belief that peace will remain the hope of mankind forever, and that the best hope for a better future for mankind will always drive us to speak noble words and do noble deeds" (10 Dec. 2011).

## EARLY LIFE AND EDUCATION
Tawakkol Abdel-Salam Karman (whose first name is alternately spelled Tawakkul or Tawakel) was born on February 7, 1979, in Mekhlaf in Yemen's southern Ta'izz province. The family later moved to the city of Sana'a, where her parents raised her along with her sister, Safa, and brother, Tariq. Her father, Abdel-Salam Karman, is an attorney and a politician who at one time worked

WireImage

as the legal affairs minister under President Ali Abdullah Saleh before resigning.

Throughout her childhood Karman witnessed turmoil in Yemen. She was born one year after Saleh took control over the Yemen Arab Republic (North Yemen), and the conflict between the two Yemeni states permeated her early life. The unification of North and South Yemen—forming the Republic of Yemen under Saleh—occurred in 1990 and was followed by a civil war between those factions in 1994. The north defeated the south and assumed control over the country, repressing the southern area of the country and its calls for independence and secession.

During that period of increasing unrest and unpopularity for Saleh, Karman attended the University of Science and Technology in Sana'a, where she graduated with a bachelor's degree in commerce in 1999. She remained in the capital to complete her graduate degree in political science from the University of Sana'a. Karman decided to pursue life as an activist in response to the corruption of tribal sheikhs. She told Tom Finn for the *Guardian* (26 Mar. 2011), "I watched as families were thrown off their land by corrupt tribal leaders. They were a symbol to me of the injustice faced by so many in Yemen. It dawned on me that nothing could change this regime, only protest."

## WOMEN JOURNALISTS WITHOUT CHAINS

In March 2005 Karman cofounded the Women Journalists without Chains (WJWC), a nongovernmental human rights organization, with seven other woman journalists. WJWC works to protect freedom of expression (including the freedom to protest), to improve media efficiency, and to promote training for journalists in Yemen. In its mission to protect human rights, the group also tracks freedom of the press in Yemen, documenting attacks on newspapers and reporters under the authoritarian regime. The protection of citizens seeking involvement in journalism—such as through newspaper or radio—is another goal of WJWC, especially in cases relating to women and youth. A 2011 Reporters without Borders study ranked Yemen 171 out of 179 countries in its Press Freedom Index—its worst ranking ever. WJWC released its own report in 2007 that listed abuses against freedom of the press—information the organization had been collecting since its inception.

During the period in which she helped form WJWC, Karman was also affiliated with *Al-Thawra* state-run newspaper and was a member of the Yemeni Journalists' Syndicate. Later in 2005 Karman traveled to the United States to participate in an exchange program administered by World Learning (a decades-old organization supporting intercultural exchange and education) and funded by the State Department's International Visitor Leadership Program. During the three-week program Karman and twenty-four other international journalists studied investigative journalism and its crucial role in democracies.

## WEEKLY PROTESTS

In May 2007 Karman began organizing weekly protests in Sana'a, often outside a cabinet building. Every Tuesday she and other demonstrators—sometimes only a handful, sometimes dozens or even hundreds—called for broad reforms and protested government repression and corruption, demanding inquiries into social and legal injustices and political change. Such issues include human rights abuses and the detention of political prisoners. Though the number of protestors varied, theirs was a consistent presence for over three years.

In a February 1, 2010, letter to the organization Women without Borders, Karman explained her efforts to promote human rights and tolerance while avoiding extremism and terrorism: "A Yemeni woman cannot be part of terrorism because she herself is suffering from terrorism. She is banned from taking part in public life, fearing she will mingle with men (which is forbidden). The intellectual terrorism that is practiced against women by a large segment of men in the Yemeni society makes her ineffective in the public domain either politically or socially." She added that, instead of being excluded from helping develop Yemen, women are essential to challenging terrorism and evoking change.

Many regular demonstrations were sit-ins held in Sana'a's Tahrir Square, referred to by Karman as "Change Square" or "Freedom Square." A controversial figure in Yemen, Karman's fellow protestors saved her from an assassination in 2010 when a woman armed with a *jambiya* (a type of curved dagger) tried to stab her. In addition to attacks on her person, threats, and arrests, Karman has also drawn the ire from opponents because she fails to conform to many expectations of Muslim women. Instead of wearing a full *niqab* (a face-covering veil that only leaves the eyes visible), Karman often wears only a colorful *hijab* (head scarf) covering her hair, allowing her to be, quite literally, the international face of her movement. She told Tom Finn for the *Guardian* (26 Mar. 2011), "I discovered that wearing the veil is not suitable for a woman who wants to work in activism and the public domain." She added, "People need to see you, to associate and relate to you. It is not stated in my religion to wear the veil; it is a traditional practice so I took it off."

## ARAB SPRING

The Arab Spring refers to a wave of protests and demonstrations that occurred in Arab countries beginning in December 2010 and continuing into 2013. During the course of the uprisings, leaders were ousted from countries including Egypt, Libya, and Tunisia, while major unrest has occurred in countries such as Syria, Jordan, and Bahrain. Protests in Yemen began during January 2011, with citizens initially calling for political and economic reform and eventually the resignation of President Saleh. Karman was outspoken in calling on university students to march for peace.

On January 23 Karman was taken from her car and detained by three police officers without a warrant. She was charged with inciting disorder and undermining peace. Her arrest was protested the next day, and eighteen other activists were also taken into custody; Karman was released on January 24. While the arrests were meant to be a warning, the movement was instead invigorated; Karman called for February 3 to be a "Day of Rage" via a massive protest. Over twenty thousand demonstrators participated in the cities of Sana'a and Aden. Similar protests against Saleh were held on February 11 and 18, each with tens of thousands of Yemenis taking to the streets of major metropolitan areas. These February demonstrations coincided with the resignation of Egyptian leader Hosni Mubarak after violent large-scale protests of his rule. Speaking to *Time* magazine (6 Feb. 2011), Karman discussed the motivation for her activism: "The combination of a dictatorship, corruption, poverty and unemployment has created this revolution." She added, "It's like a volcano. Injustice and corruption are exploding while opportunities for a good life are coming to an end." As a result of the uprising that winter, Saleh announced that he would not seek reelection in 2013—after more than thirty years in power—but would finish his current term and bow out. Throughout February and March, protests continued and ministers

in Saleh's government resigned, and the president fired his cabinet on March 20.

In addition to arrests and death threats, Karman has been pilloried by the media in Yemen, giving further credence to her calls for balanced journalism and freedom of the press. Living in an encampment in Change Square, however, her movement continued to draw both more supporters and more pushback from the government. On March 18 forces opened fire on the demonstration and killed approximately fifty protestors, wounding hundreds more; Saleh denied that his security forces carried out the attack. Despite the attacks Karman remained staunchly dedicated to peaceful protest and nonviolence. Inspired by the likes of Mahatma Gandhi, Martin Luther King Jr., and Nelson Mandela, Karman refused to meet violence with violence.

## SALEH'S HOLD

In April 2011 Saleh agreed to step down and establish a transitional government in exchange for immunity. By mid-May, however, no agreement had been reached; Saleh backed out on the deal to transfer power and instead remained in office. He was eventually forced to leave the country for medical treatment in Saudi Arabia after a rocket attack on his compound in early June, but still did not step down from office, despite global calls for him to do so.

In a June 18, 2011, op-ed in the *New York Times*, Karman noted that, while Saleh had fled the country, the revolution was far from complete: "Following months of peaceful protests that reached every village, neighborhood and street, Yemen is now facing a complete vacuum of authority; we are without a president or parliament. Mr. Saleh may be gone, but authority has not yet been transferred to a transitional presidential council endorsed by the people." In the article she criticized the role of the United States in Yemen and its support of Saleh's administration. She called for the United States to cut its ties with Yemen's security forces, which, she states, were supported by American counterterrorism efforts. Karman instead asked the United States to use its influence and join with the Yemeni people in ending Saleh's corrupt regime. She added, "On behalf of many of the young people involved in Yemen's revolution, I assure the American people that we are ready to engage in a true partnership. Together, we can eliminate the causes of extremism and the culture of terrorism by bolstering civil society and encouraging development and stability."

## NOBEL PEACE PRIZE

In October 2011 it was announced that Karman had won the Nobel Peace Prize for her "non-violent struggle for the safety of women and for women's rights to full participation in peace-building work." She won the award along with two other women activists: Ellen Johnson Sirleaf, the president of Liberia and first woman to be elected as the head of state in Africa, and Leymah Gbowee, a Liberian peace activist. Karman, who was protesting in Change Square when she heard the news, was the first Yemeni person and the first Arab woman to win the prize; at the age of thirty-two, she also became the youngest Nobel Peace Prize laureate. "I didn't expect it. It came as a total surprise," she told Alan Cowell for the *New York Times* (7 Oct. 2011). She added, "It is a victory for Arabs around the world and a victory for Arab women." Speaking from her tent, Karman also told the Associated Press that the prize "is not for Tawakkul, it is for the whole Yemeni people, for the martyrs, for the cause of standing up to [Saleh] and his gangs. Every tyrant and dictator is upset by this prize because it confronts injustice" (7 Oct. 2011).

In an interview with Nadia Al-Sakkaf, editor of the *Yemen Times*, just days after winning the prize, Karman noted that the publicity would not only bring in more supporters, but also more international support. She praised the bravery of those who protest by her side and affirmed her commitment to their cause. "I want a future where my children feel safe and appreciated and proud to be who they are," she told Al-Sakkaf for the *Daily Beast* (9 Oct. 2011). "My heart is one with all the Arab Spring heroes no matter how small they think their role is. I know they believe like me that we are working for a world whereby an Arab can live with the other in a respectful and dignified way. We as Arabs, finally after many decades of weakness, have proved to the world that we have greatness in our hearts."

Karman's prize was praised for not only recognizing the importance of the Arab Spring uprisings, but also for highlighting the importance of youth and women in protests. Her fight for democracy and human rights as a Muslim woman challenged international views on Muslims. Being a *peace* prize, specifically, also highlighted the success of nonviolence in the face of attacks and repression. As Karman told Al-Sakkaf, "The Nobel Prize for Peace says that we are peaceful protesters, and hence the regime and its partners can't call us rebels and shoot us down in cold blood."

## AFTER SALEH

President Saleh formally stepped down from office on February 27, 2012, after thirty-three years in power; his deputy, Abd Rabbuh Mansur al-Hadi, was sworn in as head of state. In ceding power Saleh became the fourth head of state to be ousted in the Arab Spring, following Tunisia's Zine El Abidine Ben Ali, Egypt's Hosni Mubarak, and Libya's Muammar Qaddafi.

The end of Saleh's rule and the election of President Hadi did not, however, mean an end to Karman's activism and demonstrations in Sana'a.

Her tent has remained a fixture in Change Square. She remains in part because family members of Saleh, such as his son and nephew, are still in power. The Saleh family's nepotism is seen as a threat to Hadi's government. Speaking to Bobby Ghosh for *Time* magazine (17 July 2012), Karman said, "As long as even one of his family remains in government, they will threaten the political transition and destabilize the country."

Aside from her unfinished business with the Salehs to assure the legitimacy of Hadi's presidency, Karman has also remained in the square to challenge unmet calls for change. Lingering issues include unemployment, poverty, and political corruption, as well as the challenge of keeping the country in the international spotlight. She is an advocate for the alienated youth population and has also campaigned to set a minimum age at which a woman can marry to help prevent forced marriages and give young women more rights and opportunities. In a conversation with Samira Shackle for *New Statesman* (26 Mar. 2012), Karman said that "stepping down the dictator is just the first goal, it isn't the end." She added, "The revolution is something continuous. We win when we achieve all our goals—reaching democracy, creating a constitution that guarantees human rights."

## PERSONAL LIFE

Humble about her role in Yemen's revolution, Karman saw her Nobel Peace as a broader form of recognition, saying in her Nobel lecture that the prize "did not come only as a personal prize for Tawakkol Abdel-Salam Karman, but as a declaration and recognition of the whole world for the triumph of the peaceful revolution of Yemen and as an appreciation of the sacrifices of its great peaceful people" (10 Dec. 2011). In her speech she reiterated her commitment to the youth revolution and to lasting peace and change. Karman was awarded an honorary doctorate of international law from the University of Alberta on November 20, 2012. When she is not leading protests or speaking internationally, Karman spends time with her family. Her sister, Safa Karman, is a journalist and news editor for the Al Jazeera television network, and her brother, Tariq Karman, is a poet. Karman has been married to Mohammed al-Nahmi since 1996, and he often camps in Change Square with her, while their son and two daughters remain with Karman's mother.

In terms of her future, Karman demurred in March 2011 when asked by the *Guardian*'s Tom Finn if she planned to one day run for president, saying, "My aim for now is to lead a peaceful revolution to remove this regime. I think if I can be in the street with the people I can achieve more than if I am the president" (26 Mar. 2011). That was over six months before receiving her Nobel

Peace Prize, and with Saleh out of office and her international profile growing, Karman's responses to questions regarding a potential presidential run were much more confident in December 2011. She has expressed not only interest in running for president of Yemen, but has also stated that, if she is allowed to be a candidate, she will win.

## SUGGESTED READING

Finn, Tom. "Tawakul Karman, Yemeni Activist, and Thorn in the Side of Saleh." *Guardian.* Guardian News and Media, 26 Mar. 2011. Web. 9 Jan. 2013.

Ghosh, Bobby. "The Arab Spring's Nobel Laureate Says the Revolution Isn't Over." *Time.* Time, 17 July 2012. Web. 9 Jan. 2013.

Karman, Tawakkol. "Yemen's Unfinished Revolution." *New York Times* 19 May 2011: 10. Print.

Shackle, Samira. "The Two Revolutions of Yemen's Women." *New Statesmen* 26 Mar. 2012: 11–12. Print.

—*Kehley Coviello*

# Christine Karumba

**Occupation:** Country director of Women for Women International's DRC chapter

Christine Karumba, country director for Women for Women International's DRC (Democratic Republic of Congo) chapter, works tirelessly to ensure that the women of her West African nation are given the tools, support, and education necessary to break free of the emotional, physical, and financial oppression they have endured since the early 1990s when civil wars broke out across the country and region. Unlike the majority of women in the DRC, Karumba is college educated. She holds two degrees: one from the Institute of Rural Development in Bukavu, DRC, and another from Miracle Bible College, Robert Kayanja Ministries in Kampala, Uganda.

## EARLY LIFE AND CULTURAL BARRIERS

Karumba has many happy memories of her early years growing up in the West African nation of Zaire, now called the Democratic Republic of Congo (DRC). She recalls travelling from village to village with her mother and grandmother and watching them interact with other women. By observing the older women work and in listening to them talk, she began to learn the necessary skills for a growing girl in that culture: cooking, fetching fresh water, growing and harvesting food, and—most importantly—bearing children. For young girls in the DRC, there was never any question of the importance of learning these practical skills, nor was there

Associated Press

seemingly any possibility that a girl could hold any other role when she grew to be a woman. As Karumba explained in a speech to the World Affairs Council of Northern California in October of 2006, women growing up in the villages of the DRC experience huge cultural barriers: "When a woman is born, she is born a mother. . . . She doesn't have another choice than to be a mother." Karumba went on to explain that young girls are raised in a culture that "doesn't treasure education" for women because if a young girl does not marry (and many girls are married as young as ten or twelve years old), she cannot help the family financially. If a girl was educated, her family assumes she would move away and would no longer help to support them. Karumba explained her belief that illiterate and ignorant women can only be expected to raise ignorant children, which is a bitter and crippling cycle for the people of her country.

## CIVIL WAR

Following the ethnic civil war in neighboring Rwanda and the mass genocide of approximately 800,000 people in that country, displaced Rwandan militia escaped to eastern Zaire in the mid-1990s and joined forces with the local militia against opposing ethnic tribal members. The armed rebels also joined with Ugandan forces to overthrow Zaire's President Mobutu Sésé Seko. The DRC is rich in natural resources such as diamonds, copper, and gold, and the coalition hoped to gain control of these minerals, which was one cause of the country's First Congo War. The Second Congo War, which began in 1998 and lasted until 2003, has been called the deadliest war in modern African history. As reported by Palash Ghosh for the *International Business Times*, (2 Jan. 2012), at least five million people were killed, mostly from disease and starvation.

Karumba told Rahim Kanani for *Forbes* (15 Nov. 2011) that her memories of the years leading up to the war are of a "growing climate of uncertainty." And once war began, her life changed dramatically. As she explained to Jerry Fowler for the United States Holocaust Memorial Museum (1 Nov. 2007), her family (which consisted of her parents and nineteen brothers and sisters) was starving, and with bullets flying past and bombs exploding, "you don't know if . . . the last bomb will be your house, your family."

Health centers had been destroyed, and with the lack of running water and proper hygiene and sanitation, people were dying from untreated injuries and diseases. Karumba told Kanani that she and her family "lived not knowing if [each day] would be our last, and for women the threat of violence was an ever-present reality."

## GENDER-BASED VIOLENCE

The people of the DRC suffered greatly during the two civil wars, and the women of the DRC were especially affected when the rebel soldiers began using gender-based violence as a war tactic, replacing traditional armed combat as a means of force. Fowler reports that in one year alone, there were close to 27,000 reported cases of rape in eastern DRC. As conflicts between Kabila's government and various rebel groups persist, rebels have continued to use rape and other forms of gender-based violence as a weapon of war.

Karumba reported for the international women's advocate organization Women for Women that women of the DRC "are raped, mutilated and kept as sex slaves, then they are turned away from their families and left with no hope to rebuild their lives." No one is spared, as young girls and old women have been reported as being raped. Additionally, men and children are often forced to watch the rape and mutilation of their wives and mothers. Karumba explains that in using rape as a weapon and involving men and children in the violence, the entire community is demoralized and degraded. As she clarified to Fowler, "When you touch a woman you have touched the heart of the community. This is a weapon against the community, the weapon to destroy an entire community."

Karumba believes, however, that the soldiers who commit gender-based violence are also victims of war and are not carrying out these acts due to cultural norms. Others agree. Matthew Clark reports for the *Christian Science Monitor* that soldiers in Eastern Congo rape for several reasons: They have been in the bush and away from women for an extended period; they are seeking revenge against their enemy; and to punish and discourage suspected spies. Karumba added to Fowler that a gun also allows the soldier to feel in a position of power over a vulnerable woman, and he has not been taught that rape is wrong. She believes that it is imperative "to provide the knowledge to our community so

[men] may understand . . . because men have to change their . . . attitude."

## WOMEN FOR WOMEN INTERNATIONAL

In "Speaking Out about Rape," a page on Women for Women International's website, Karumba recalls that she witnessed two types of death among women in the DRC: physical death and emotional death. "The physical death is when you are no longer alive to walk the earth, and the emotional death is where you no longer see signs of hope and are dead inside" (n.d.). It was after seeing the daily suffering among Congolese women and the two types of death they endured that Karumba, as she recalled to Kanani, "was forced to be a leader."

In 2004, the international women's advocate organization Women for Women International (WFW) opened its first office in the DRC. Karumba had already been working for over six years on community development and gender issues for other relief organizations such as UNICEF and Christian ministries in Uganda when she joined WFW, and when she began her position as country director for the organization, it was with the often voiced belief that "One woman can change things. Many women can change everything."

Founded in 1993 to work with women survivors of war and conflicts around the world, WFW works to empower women so that they no longer feel as if they are victims but are instead an active part of their respective communities. The group pairs each woman in a country's program with a female sponsor in another country (primarily from the United States and Great Britain), and for the following year, the two "sisters" (as WFW refers to its members) correspond via letters. The sponsor-sister provides direct aid and emotional support. Program members also receive access to vocational skills training, rights awareness and leadership training, and literacy and math education. The belief among WFW administrators is that stronger women build stronger nations.

Women for Women International also believes that working with male leaders in the various communities is crucial in order to educate them in the negative and destructive impact of rape on the entire community, and under Karumba's leadership, the DRC office has incorporated male-based programs into its community office. As Karumba reported to Fowler, "We help [men] to become the advocate for the women's rights. . . . They have to be [taught] . . . to receive knowledge to change their attitude."

Through Karumba's leadership and dedication, Women for Women International–DRC has served tens of thousands of women in rural and urban areas across the country. She has implemented the foundational programs in the DRC offices for direct financial aid and rights education. In 2004, women voted in the first democratic elections held in the DRC in forty years. Karumba has witnessed the change in her country and in its women. As she explained to Kanani, "Every day we see changes in the lives we have touched and how the program is transforming who they are and who are they becoming, manifesting a hope that is slowly becoming a reality." For its work aiding women in areas ravaged by war, Women for Women International received the 2006 Conrad Hilton Humanitarian prize, receiving over one million dollars in aid for their organization.

## SUGGESTED READING

Clark, Matthew. "Congo: Confronting Rape as a Weapon of War." *CSMonitor*. Christian Science Monitor, 4 Aug. 2009. Web. 19 Dec. 2012.

De Capua. "Both Women and Men Victims of Rape in Eastern DRC." *VOA*. Voice of America, 1 Nov. 2009. Web. 18 Dec. 2012.

Fowler, Jerry. "Women for Women in the Congo." *United States Holocaust Memorial Museum*. USHMM, 1 Nov. 2007. Web. 19 Dec. 2012.

Ghosh, Palash R. "Congo: The 'World War' Nobody Knows About." *International Business Times*. International Business Times Inc., 2 Jan. 2012. Web. 18 Dec. 2012.

Kanani, Rahim. "Courageous Leader Profile: Christine Karumba of Women for Women International." *Forbes*. Forbes.com LLC, 15 Nov. 2011. Web. 19 Dec. 2012.

Karumba, Christine. "Republic of Congo: War, Education and Culture." The Other Side of War. World Affairs Council, Northern California. Speech. *Fora.tv*. FORA.tv, 24 Oct. 2006. Web. 19 Dec. 2012.

---. "Speaking Out about Rape." *Women for Women*. Women for Women International, n.d. Web. 19 Dec. 2012.

United States Institute of Peace. *Speaker Bios—Women and War*. 3 Nov. 2012. Web. 19 Dec. 2012.

—*Robin Hogan*

# Eugene Kaspersky

**Born:** October 4, 1965
**Occupation:** Information security specialist; CEO of Kaspersky Lab

In the not-too-distant past, most computers were massive mainframes that took up entire rooms, and they were located mainly in government offices and research institutions. Today, however, digital data is essential not only to the functioning of the government and academia but to almost every facet of our lives, from our personal finances and healthcare to our jobs.

STR/Reuters/Landov

Because of this increasing reliance on information technology (IT), cybersecurity is becoming ever more crucial. President Barack Obama even declared in his May 29, 2009, speech that the "cyber threat is one of the most serious economic and national security challenges we face as a nation" and that "America's economic prosperity in the twenty-first century will depend on cybersecurity," as quoted on the official White House website.

Eugene Kaspersky is at the forefront of this field. He is the cofounder and CEO of one of the largest cybersecurity firms in the world, Kaspersky Lab, whose products and technologies help some 300 million individuals and 250,000 corporate clients protect their computer systems from unauthorized access and attack.

## EARLY LIFE AND EDUCATION

Kaspersky was born on October 4, 1965, in Novorossiysk, Russia, a port city on the Black Sea. As a young child, he was deeply interested in mathematics, and later, one of his favorite pursuits became solving puzzles and quizzes published in technical magazines—a hobby at which he excelled and that provided him with a great sense of accomplishment. Once in high school, he signed up for an extracurricular program organized by the Moscow Institute of Physics and Technology, and during his junior and senior years, he attended math and physics classes that were organized for gifted students and were sponsored by Moscow State University.

In 1987 Kaspersky graduated from the Russian Institute of Cryptography, Telecommunications and Computer Science, where he had specialized in computer technology and mathematical engineering. Some journalists, attempting to assign nefarious purposes to the Institute, have asserted that it was backed by the KGB, the primary Soviet security service from 1954 until 1991. Kaspersky generally ignores such innuendo, and today the school is considered within Russia to be a prestigious center for the study of information security.

Kaspersky then joined the Russian Army as an intelligence specialist. Some observers, playing on Cold War–era fears, refer to his role during this period as "Russian spy." His official biography on the Kaspersky Labs website states simply that after graduating he "started work at a Ministry of Defense research institute."

## KASPERSKY'S FIRST VIRUS

In late 1989 a virus infected Kaspersky's computer at the research institute. Called Cascade, the virus made the characters on his screen tumble to the bottom—a seemingly harmless prank rather than an attempt to do serious damage. Kaspersky was intrigued and began trying to understand the computer code and reverse engineer the virus. *Reverse engineering* refers to the process of breaking something down in order to build a duplicate, improve it, or just understand it better. Any time a new virus appeared, he studied it intently and created a "disinfection" program to disable it. "I soon became rather well-known around the facility as the 'guy who kills viruses,' and soon people were regularly drifting into my room bringing other strangely behaving files," he wrote on his blog, *Nota Bene* (Italian for "note well"). He added that "despite it then only being the early dawn of the computer era, within a couple of months I had analyzed dozens of viruses, and continuously improved my disinfection utility, called '-V.' With each new virus my interest in this phenomenon grew and soon I realized this was more than just a hobby."

"For Eugene, it was an addiction," his friend and later business colleague Alexey De-Monderik told Noah Shachtman for *Wired* (23 July 2012). "[He would] sit in front of the computer for 20 hours straight." Today, Kaspersky's database of viruses contains more than a million records and is considered one of the most complete virus repositories in the world.

Kaspersky felt an urge to study viruses full time, but it was notoriously difficult to win a discharge from the Russian military. Shachtman has asserted that the only way to leave the army at that time was to get sent to prison, do something extremely incompetent, or fall seriously ill. Kaspersky, however, was able to negotiate an honorable discharge with the help of an old teacher at the Institute of Cryptography, Telecommunications and Computer Science— a turn of events that some observers, including Shachtman, see as proof of Kaspersky's opaque government ties.

Released from his military obligations, Kaspersky joined the KAMI Information Technologies Center, which sold computers and various other items. It was reportedly owned by the former professor who had helped him obtain his military discharge. De-Monderik (a graduate of the Moscow Aviation Institute) and Kaspersky's wife, Natalya (a 1989 graduate of the Moscow Institute of Electronic Engineering), eventually joined him there.

At the company, the three embarked on the AntiViral Toolkit Pro (AVP) project, and in November 1992, the team's first product, AVP 1.0, was released. That year Kaspersky took part in his first foreign information technology exhibition, CeBIT, which is held annually in Germany. In a 1994 test conducted by Hamburg University, Kaspersky's program had a higher virus-detection rate than several of the more established antivirus programs of the day, and within a few years, companies from around the globe were approaching him to license his technology.

## KASPERSKY LABS

In 1997 Kaspersky, his wife, and De-Monderik founded their own company, calling it Kaspersky Lab. Kaspersky initially headed the research department, while Natalya served as CEO and De-Monderik led product development. Although the Kasperskys divorced the following year, Natalya remained CEO until 2007, when she stepped down to run a similar company, InfoWatch. Kaspersky then took over Kaspersky Lab as CEO. Despite his new title, he has remained active in research.

In 1999 Kaspersky Lab expanded internationally, opening an office in the United Kingdom. Today, the firm, which employs some three thousand people, operates in almost two hundred countries and territories around the globe, with headquarters in Moscow and the holding company registered in Great Britain. Regional offices can be found in Germany, France, Spain, Italy, Japan, China, Poland, the Netherlands, Sweden, Romania, the United States, South Korea, Australia, and other places.

When Kaspersky software is installed by a purchaser, it completes a scan of every application and file on the computer for signs of malicious activity. Recognized malware is automatically deleted. If a scan detects a suspicious program it doesn't recognize, it sends an encrypted sample of the virus to the lab's servers. The cloud-based system then checks the code against a "white list" of 300 million items it knows are trustworthy and an equally lengthy "black list" of confirmed malicious items. If the code is not on either of the lists, the system analyzes the program's behavior for any suspicious activity. If it's designed to make unauthorized changes to the computer's configuration options or constantly contacts a remote server, the system will deem it untrustworthy and delete it. If the system becomes stumped—not a frequent occurrence—one of Kaspersky's virus researchers will quickly become involved, analyzing the malware code and figuring out a way to spot it and delete it in future scans. Within minutes, a software update with the information is sent to Kaspersky's millions of users.

## THE BIGGER THREAT

Although protecting businesses and individual computer users is an important part of his mission, Kaspersky keeps his eye on more universal threats as well because, as he points out repeatedly to interviewers, criminals and hackers are no longer content to merely steal your personal data for financial gain; they could easily precipitate a massive global crisis for political or philosophical reasons. Among the biggest threats facing the world, he says, is cyberwarfare. If cybercriminals decided to target power plants, "we would be taken 200 years back, to the pre-electricity era," he told Katia Moskvitch for BBC News Technology (25 Apr. 2012). "And there is nothing—nothing—anyone could do about it." He continued, "It is possible that a computer worm doesn't find its exact victim—and since many power plants are designed in a similar way [and often use the same systems], all of them could be attacked [at the same time], around the world."

Kaspersky does not like to see himself as a fear-monger but feels it's his duty to speak out publicly. His initial catalyst for doing so came from an unexpected quarter: *Live Free or Die Hard*, a 2007 blockbuster starring Bruce Willis as John McClane, who is in a battle against a terrorist planning a massive cyberattack that would disable the 911 emergency call system, cripple the financial markets, and hinder many other computer-controlled infrastructures nationwide. "I watched the movie for 20 minutes, then pressed pause, got a cigarette and a glass of Scotch. To me it was really scary: they were talking about real scenarios. It was like a user guide for cyber terrorists," Kaspersky recalled to David Braue for the *Sydney Morning Herald* (28 May 2012). "We came to the [potential] of cyber terrorist attacks years before *Die Hard 4.0*. But it was forbidden in my company to explain it to journalists, because I didn't want to open Pandora's Box. I didn't want to let people think that my business is the business of fear. And I didn't want the bad guys to learn from these ideas."

In addition to cyberwarfare, Kaspersky sees other threats, including the use of sites like Twitter and Facebook to nefariously manipulate the general public. He explained to Moskvitch, "During the Second World War, airplanes were used to drop propaganda leaflets over enemy territory—and the same is already happening with social networks." He pointed to an incident in which rumors of a possible coup in China were spread by bloggers, some of whom reported tanks and gunfire throughout Beijing. "There weren't any tanks, it was all a lie. But if such information is put out by someone of high authority and somewhere where millions can read it, it may create a panic," Kaspersky said.

## GOVERNMENT-CREATED WORMS

Kaspersky Lab has been responsible for discovering several major "worms." (Unlike a virus, a worm does not have to attach itself to an existing program in order to replicate and do harm.) Among the most notable of these was Stuxnet, a 500-kilobyte worm that infected the software of more than a dozen industrial sites in Iran, including a uranium enrichment plant. It was discovered in mid-2010 by Kaspersky Lab researchers who unraveled its mysteries. They found that Stuxnet first targeted Microsoft Windows networks, repeatedly replicating itself. Then it sought out the software used to program industrial control systems and compromised them. The worm's creators could then spy on the industrial systems and even cause machinery—like the centrifuges at the uranium-enrichment plant—to damage itself, totally unbeknownst to the workers at the plant. Two more high-profile worms, Flame and Gauss, infected thousands of computers in the Middle East not long after.

The size and complexity of Stuxnet led experts to assert that it could have been created only by a national government, and leaks to the press strongly suggested that the United States and Israel, acting in concert, were responsible. Some observers faulted Kaspersky for revealing the existence of Stuxnet and other such worms, arguing that he was working against the national interests of the United States. He responded in an article posted on *Nota Bene*, "No IT Security company would remain silent on the discovery of a cyber-weapon, no matter who the author might be. . . . The logic of the IT Security industry is to focus on keeping customers safe—regardless of their origin, or the origin of the malware."

Noah Shachtman is among the observers who fear that Kaspersky may have ill intentions. He wrote, "[Kaspersky Lab is run] not all that different from the way US security companies like Symantec or McAfee operate globally. Except for the fact that in Russia, high tech firms like Kaspersky Lab have to cooperate with the *siloviki*, the network of military, security, law enforcement, and KGB veterans at the core of the Putin regime." Kaspersky answered that charge on his blog, asserting, "All three of the world's leading security companies—Symantec, McAfee/Intel, and Kaspersky Lab—work with law enforcement bodies worldwide to help fight cyber-crime. The ITU, CET, FBI, FSB, US Secret Service . . . we all have a duty to help them solve criminal cases. . . . We provide EXPERTISE. Nothing more."

## PERSONAL LIFE

By all accounts, Kaspersky is an almost larger-than-life figure, known for throwing lavish annual parties for his employees and jet-setting around the world to visit his regional operations. An entire section of his blog is devoted to his travels, and journalists scheduled to interview him often find themselves squeezed into the scant available time between international flights.

Since 2010, Kaspersky Lab has been a sponsor of Ferrari's Formula 1 racing team, and Kaspersky is often in attendance at the track. "Despite our recent alliance with Ferrari, I have to settle for fulfilling my passion for fast driving with a BMW M3—public roads in Moscow still leave much to be desired and are not suited to the Italian supercars one bit," he wrote on his blog. He is an avid skier, and when he is not traveling for business, he can often be found in the Alps.

Kaspersky, who resides in Moscow, is the father of three. On April 19, 2012, his twenty-year-old son, Ivan, a college student, was kidnapped while walking the short distance from his Moscow apartment to his internship. He was forced to call his father with his captors' demands for three million euros in ransom money. Kaspersky turned to Russian law enforcement after receiving the call, and with their help Ivan was rescued five days later from a country house in a small town forty miles northeast of Moscow. Kaspersky's detractors have cynically pointed out that he must maintain very strong ties to the Russian Federal Security Service (FSB) to have gotten such quick and effective help from the agency.

Despite the controversy that sometimes surrounds Kaspersky, he has been the recipient of numerous accolades, including the National Friendship Award of China (2009), the State Prize of the Russian Federation (2009), the Strategic Brand Leadership Award from the World Brand Congress (2010), a Lifetime Achievement Award from *Virus Bulletin* (2010), CEO of the Year honors from *SC Magazine* (2010), the World's Most Powerful Security Executive title from SYS-CON Media (2011), a listing as one of the Top 10 Innovators of 2011 from CRN (2011), and an honorary doctoral degree from the United Kingdom's Plymouth University (2012).

## SUGGESTED READING

Braue, David. "Be Afraid: *Die Hard 4* Reveals a Real Threat." *Sydney Morning Herald.* Fairfax Media, 28 May 2012. Web. 2 Apr. 2013.
Moskvitch, Katia. "The World's Five Biggest Cyber Threats." *BBC News Technology.* BBC, 25 Apr. 2012. Web. 2 Apr. 2013.
Reed, John. "What Keeps Eugene Kaspersky Up at Night?" *Foreign Policy.* FP Group, 28 Sept. 2012. Web. 2 Apr. 2013.
Schofield, Jack. "The Russian Defence against Global Cybercrime." (London) *Guardian.* Guardian News and Media Limited, 30 Jan. 2008. Web. 2 Apr. 2013.
Shachtman, Noah. "Russia's Top Cyber Sleuth Foils US Spies, Helps Kremlin Pals." *Wired.* Condé Nast, 23 July 2012. Web. 2 Apr. 2013.

—*Mari Rich*

---

# Jay Keasling

**Born:** 1964
**Occupation:** Bioengineer

Over the course of a two-decade-plus career, synthetic biology researcher Jay Keasling has revolutionized malaria treatment by developing an inexpensive antimalarial drug from genetically engineered microorganisms. He has also come to be regarded as one of the leading experts in turning microbes into fuel factories. Synthetic biology is an extension of the genetic engineering methods that have been in practice since the late 1970s. Keasling, one of its foremost pioneers, views each cell as a potential chemical factory, capable of transforming the simplest materials into highly complex and valuable products if given the right set of DNA instructions.

Keasling oversees the Physical Biosciences, Genomics, and Life Sciences Divisions at the Lawrence Berkeley National Laboratory and heads the Joint BioEnergy Institute. He has also cofounded three biotechnology startups, Amyris, LS9, and Lygos, and has earned several awards and honors for his groundbreaking work in the fields of medicine and alternative energy.

## EARLY LIFE

Jay D. Keasling was born in 1964 to Max and Karen Keasling and grew up in Harvard, Nebraska, a rural town whose population is under one thousand people. He lived there with his parents and sister on a pig farm that has been in his father's family for five generations.

At the age of eleven, Keasling experienced a life-changing event, when his mother, a breast cancer survivor, was involved in a fatal car accident while returning home from her final doctor's appointment. Both she and the other driver, her own first cousin, died as a result of the crash. Keasling, whom his father describes as having been very close to his mother, credits her with instilling in him a sense of determination and focus, which later served him well professionally.

The tragic loss of Keasling's mother forced him to assume more adult responsibilities. "For me, it meant taking on work in the house—cooking,

© Mike Kepka/San Francisco Chronicle/Corbis

cleaning, etcetera—in addition to studying, practicing for sports and piano, and everything else," he told Tom Abate for the *San Francisco Chronicle* (12 Nov. 2010). "There was very little time for fun and games," he recalled to Neil deGrasse Tyson for the PBS program *Nova scienceNow* (23 Feb. 2011). "That's served me pretty well, I think, because right now, there's pretty much no amount of work that seems insurmountable."

## STUDIES IN CHEMICAL AND GENETIC ENGINEERING

Despite the circumstances Keasling thrived at Harvard High School, where he joined the wrestling team and was elected class president. After being named valedictorian of his graduating class in 1982, Keasling attended the University of Nebraska-Lincoln (UNL), on a Regents Scholarship.

Keasling, a chemical engineering major, experienced a memorable turning point as a first-year student working at the Cedar Point field station at Ogallala. "I spent the summer after my freshman year there, and it was great fun," he recalled in a UNL alumni profile. "I took classes in field biology, and that changed my interests; I went to the university thinking I would go on to medical school, but that summer experience really convinced me to go into research."

After receiving his bachelor's degree in chemistry and biology in 1986, Keasling studied chemical engineering at the University of Michigan in Ann Arbor. He also served as a research assistant in the school's chemical engineering department—a position he held while earning his master of science degree in 1988 and his PhD degree three years later. Under the guidance of microbiology professor Stephen Cooper, Keasling learned genetic engineering, which involves isolating and genetically manipulating an organism's genome by introducing foreign DNA into the host organism.

From 1991 to 1992 Keasling conducted postdoctoral research with Nobel Prize winner Arthur Kornberg at Stanford University's Department of Biochemistry.

## EARLY CAREER AT UC BERKELEY

In 1992, following his yearlong postdoctoral stint, the twenty-eight-year-old accepted an assistant professorship in the chemical engineering department of the University of California (UC), Berkeley. There he also served as a researcher at the Lawrence Berkeley National Laboratory (Berkeley Lab), a Department of Energy (DOE) facility managed by the university.

At that time, "biological components were relatively crude, making the engineering of microorganisms time-consuming and costly. But my colleagues and I had the idea that one could engineer microorganisms into chemical factories that produce nearly any important chemical from sugar. Unfortunately, there were few tools available to us," he remarked during a hearing on synthetic genomics before the House Committee on Commerce and Energy (27 May 2010).

Over the next decade, Keasling studied plasmids, the DNA rings used to introduce foreign genes into bacteria. He also discovered how to get microorganisms to generate copious amounts of a specific protein and created potent chemical "switches" that enable him to initiate the production of a protein. During this period Keasling was promoted to associate professor (1998–2001) and served as vice chair (1999–2000) of the university's chemical engineering department.

## EXPERIMENTS WITH ARTEMISININ

In 2000 Keasling began investigating isoprenoids, a group of chemicals that influence the odors, tastes, and appearances of many plants. At the time one of his graduate students brought to his attention a paper profiling the chemical amorphadiene synthase, which is used in the treatment of drug-resistant malaria, a mosquito-borne disease that affects over 200 million people and kills more than half a million every year, especially impoverished African children under five years old. "He told me that it was a precursor to artemisinin, an effective antimalarial. I had never worked on malaria," Keasling explained to Michael Specter for the *New Yorker* (28 Sept. 2009). "So I got to studying and quickly realized that this precursor was in the general class we were planning to investigate. And I thought, Amorphadiene is as good a target as any. Let's work on that."

Around 2002 Keasling partnered with postdoctoral fellows Neil Renninger, Jack Newman, and Kinkead Reiling to study ways of synthesizing amorphadiene—work that would soon lead them to establish the renewable-products startup Amyris Biotechnologies, with the goal of commercializing products that would cure millions of people. They came up with the idea of producing the drug artemisinin from a microbe, or single-celled organism, rather than extracting it from the sweet wormwood plant (*Artemisia annua*), which is a time-consuming process that can set the cost of the drug at as much as twenty times the price of other antimalarials. Although the wormwood plant produces higher levels of artemisinin, crop availability fluctuates and there is not enough of the drug to meet global demand; the low-yielding plant, native to East Asia, is sensitive to ultraviolet light and proper water levels. Keasling's strategy involved reprogramming or converting yeast cells to produce a synthetic, more affordable version of artemisinin. "I see no reason why we can't completely reimagine the chemical industry," he told Jeneen Interlandi for *Newsweek* magazine (19 Dec. 2008). "We don't have to just accept what nature gives us."

## MAKING STRIDES IN TREATING MALARIA

In 2003 Keasling and his team published their initial results in *Nature Biotechnology*, in which they explained how they introduced, or transplanted, genes from yeast and wormwood plants into the *Escherichia coli* (*E. coli*) bacteria and, through a constructed metabolic pathway, induced it to produce amorphadiene, a precursor chemical that can be converted into artemisinin. As a result of this work, the Bill and Melinda Gates Foundation presented the San Francisco–based nonprofit Institute for OneWorld Health, with a $42.6 million grant in December 2004, through which it and Keasling's lab, Amyris Biotechnologies, could collaborate with each other on developing a synthetic, inexpensive version of artemisinin. The Berkeley Lab would conduct research, OneWorld Health would oversee drug development, and Amyris would handle large-scale industrial production and commercialization.

In 2005 the World Health Organization (WHO) advocated artemisinin-based combination therapies (ACTs), or the use of artemisinin along with another malaria drug, as the first line of treatment against malaria. The following year researchers from the Berkeley Lab, Amyris Biotechnologies, and the California Institute of Quantitative Biomedical Research began collaborating on a microbe capable of producing significant amounts of artemisinic acid and enabling scientists to make low-cost artemisinin. They were successful in genetically engineering common brewer's yeast, *Saccharomyces cerevisiae*, to be able to yield high levels of arteminisic acid instead of ethyl alcohol.

In March 2008 Amyris entered into an agreement with OneWorld Health and Sanofi-Aventis, a French pharmaceutical firm, to develop artemisinin-based drugs. Under the deal, Amyris granted Sanofi royalty-free use of its artemisinic acid–producing yeast strains, while Sanofi provided expertise on industrial-scale fermentation; and OneWorld Health concentrated on public policy and global access goals. In May 2013 WHO approved Sanofi's new synthetic version of artemisinin. Sanofi plans to produce a sufficient amount of semisynthetic artemisinin for up to 150 million ACT treatments per year by 2014. In keeping with the stated mission of making it affordable for the poorest patients, the new drug will be sold at cost.

## SPEARHEADING THE BIOFUEL MOVEMENT

Encouraged by Keasling's success with artemisinin, Amyris has focused on using synthetic biology tools to produce biofuels and renewable chemicals as petroleum alternatives. In 2006 the Silicon Valley investment firms Khosla Ventures and Kleiner Perkins invested $20 million into Amyris to uncover renewable energy sources. A year later Keasling was part of a group of scholars who were awarded $500 million over ten years from oil giant British Petroleum (BP) to establish the Energy Biosciences Institute, a research firm specializing in biofuels and clean energy.

In 2007 Keasling was selected to run the Synthetic Biology Research Center, the country's first such research facility. The following year the DOE appointed Keasling as CEO of its newly created Joint BioEnergy Institute (JBEI), a bioenergy research center tasked with producing efficient, low-emission liquid biofuels, with energy outputs comparable to those of diesel and jet fuel, from basic ingredients like sugar cane and grass. Keasling, whose father grows corn to produce the less-efficient gasoline additive ethanol, is very aware of the land-use and food production constraints facing the emergent biofuels industry. He and his colleagues at JBEI are seeking to use the cellulose-rich plant "waste," such as corn stalks, grasses, shrubs, and the like, as their base material. In 2011 Keasling's JBEI team achieved a major milestone when they engineered the world's first strains of *E. coli* bacteria that eat the cover crop switchgrass and synthesize its sugars into either gasoline, diesel, or jet fuels—without adding enzymes. That year the startup Lygos spun off from JBEI to optimize and commercialize the process. These successes undoubtedly contributed to the April 2013 DOE announcement that it would renew JBEI's funding for another five years.

Over the course of his career, Keasling has earned several accolades. These honors have included the *Discover* magazine Scientist of the Year Award in 2006; the Biotechnology Industry Organization's Biotech Humanitarian Award in 2009 and its George Washington Carver Award in 2013; the International Metabolic Engineering Award in 2012; and a Heinz Award in 2012. He is also a fellow of the American Institute of Medical and Biological Engineering and of the American Academy of Microbiology.

## PERSONAL LIFE

In his *Nova scienceNow* interview, Keasling admitted that he struggled as a closeted gay youth and did not come out until after his move to Berkeley in the early nineties. Keasling is now the father of two boys, whom he adopted with his former partner, James. In March 2009 he participated in a UC Berkeley panel discussion about LGBT experience in the sciences aimed at encouraging openness about sexuality in order to foster a more welcoming work atmosphere.

In his spare time, Keasling maintains a fitness regimen, plays piano, and enjoys twice annual visits to family back in Nebraska.

## SUGGESTED READING

Abate, Tom. "Jay Keasling Hits Jackpot with Biofuel Startup." *San Francisco Chronicle*. Hearst Corporation, 21 Nov. 2010. Web. 15 Sept. 2013.

"Featured Husker: Jay Keasling." *UNL*. University of Nebraska-Lincoln, 2013. Web. 15 Sept. 2013.

Harris, Richard. "Put Down Oil Drill, Pick Up Test Tube: Making Fuel from Yeast." *NPR.org*. Natl. Public Radio, 28 June 2013. Web. 15 Sept. 2013.

Interlandi, Jeneen. "Jay Keasling: Saving the World, One Molecule at a Time." *Newsweek*. Newsweek/Daily Beast Co., 19 Dec. 2008. Web. 15 Sept. 2013.

Keasling, Jay. "Hearing on Developments in Synthetic Genomics and Implications for Health and Energy." Committee on Energy and Commerce, US House of Representatives, 27 May 2010. PDF file.

Leuty, Ron. "Jay Keasling: Making a Synthetic Biology Antimalarial Drug Is Only First Step." *San Francisco Business Times*. American City Business Journals, 5 Apr. 2013. Web. 15 Sept. 2013.

Specter, Michael. "A Life of Its Own: Where Will Synthetic Biology Lead Us?" *New Yorker*. Condé Nast, 28 Sept. 2009. Web. 15 Sept. 2013.

Zimmer, Carl. "Scientist of the Year: Jay Keasling." *Discover*. Kalmbach Publishing, Dec. 2006. Web. 15 Sept. 2013.

—*Bertha Muteba*

# Keb' Mo'

**Born:** October 3, 1951
**Occupation:** Contemporary blues musician

Throughout a career that has spanned three decades, musician Keb' Mo' has played the role of archivist and innovator. Having grown up listening to gospel, blues, and R&B, he exhibits a range of influences in his work as a songwriter and instrumentalist. Keb' Mo' combines his deep reverence for traditional Delta blues music with

© Andrew Goetz/Corbis

a willingness to adapt and innovate, creating a modern R&B sound that is all his own. A frequent collaborator, he has worked with a variety of well-known artists, including Bonnie Raitt, Buddy Guy, Amy Grant, Eric Clapton, Vince Gill, India.Arie, Willie Nelson, and the Dixie Chicks.

Over the course of his career, Keb' Mo' has earned numerous award nominations and received the Grammy Award for best contemporary blues album on three occasions. He has performed all over the world with his signature red guitar and has written music for a variety of television productions, including a collection of sixteen songs released in conjunction with the 2003 documentary film series *The Blues*, produced by Martin Scorsese. In addition to his work as a popular musician, he has written music for children, performed as a television and film actor, and worked with the group Musicians United for Safe Energy, an organization that seeks to limit the spread and use of nuclear power.

## EARLY LIFE AND CAREER

Keb' Mo' was born Kevin Moore on October 3, 1951, in Los Angeles, California. His parents had previously relocated to California from the South. During his childhood, they instilled in him a love of various blues music traditions, from the guitar- and harmonica-based Delta blues sounds of Mississippi to the horn- and piano-infused blues of New Orleans. Although his parents later divorced, Moore's early musical experiences would remain with him throughout his life.

Moore dedicated himself to his musical career from a young age, performing regularly as a guitarist, steel drum player, and horn player by his early twenties. When he was twenty-one, his first band—a calypso group named Zulu—was hired as the opening act for blues violinist Papa John Creach, widely known for his work with the rock band Jefferson Airplane. At the age of twenty-four, Moore was hired by Almo Music, a publishing arm of A&M Records, as an arranger and contract musician. Moore released his first record, *Rainmaker*, in 1980. Unlike his later recordings, *Rainmaker* was released under the name Kevin Moore.

Moore continued to perform and record as a session player throughout the 1980s and 1990s. He played guitar regularly in saxophonist Monk Higgins's Whodunit Band. In 1990, Moore received a role in *Rabbit Foot*, a theatrical production about the Delta blues, which further strengthened his interest in the genre. During this period, Moore occasionally sat in on performances of jazz drummer Quentin Denard's band. Denard shortened Moore's name to Keb' Mo'. The nickname stuck, and Moore began working and performing under that name.

## SUCCESS AS KEB' MO'

Keb' Mo' released a self-titled album of acoustic guitar–based Delta and country blues music in 1994. The album *Keb' Mo'* features eleven original compositions and two covers of songs written by blues legend Robert Johnson, "Come On in My Kitchen" and "Kind Hearted Woman Blues." Writing for the website AllMusic, Thom Owens praised the album as "an edgy, ambitious collection of gritty country blues." The album was named the best country/acoustic blues album of the year by the Blues Foundation of Memphis, Tennessee. Keb' Mo's success in music led to opportunities in film, and he went on to portray Johnson in the 1998 documentary film *Can't You Hear the Wind Howl? The Life and Music of Robert Johnson*, directed by Peter Meyer. The film, which is narrated by actor Danny Glover, features commentary from music legends such as Robert Cray, Keith Richards, and Eric Clapton.

In 1996, Keb' Mo' released the record *Just Like You*. Unlike his self-titled album, which features solo acoustic blues, *Just Like You* incorporates the sound of a full backing band. The album includes another cover of a Johnson song, "Last Fair Deal Gone Down," and the title single features singers Jackson Browne and Bonnie Raitt. In his review of the record for the Pennsylvania radio station WVIA-FM (19 June 1996), George Graham noted that the record is "by no means a strict blues record." Keb' Mo', Graham explained, "is an artist whose interests and experience range widely. . . . About a third [of] the album qualifies as pop music, with the rest a mixture of fine acoustic guitar pieces and more electrified blues and R&B." The following year, *Just Like You* was named best contemporary blues album at the Grammy Awards.

Keb' Mo' followed *Just Like You* with 1998's *Slow Down*, which, like the two records before it, features a rendition of a Johnson song ("Love in Vain"). The album also features a song written by Keb' Mo' and colleague Patrick Shepard titled "Rainmaker"—an homage to Keb' Mo's 1980 record of the same name. In his review of *Slow Down* for WVIA-FM (26 Aug. 1998), Graham described the record as "a first-rate recording that continues [Keb' Mo's] sophisticated but largely acoustic blend of blues, with pop and rock." Comparing Keb' Mo' to blues musician Taj Mahal, Graham praised the artist for having "no qualms about going off into a melodic love song or a funky groove" and "walking the line between a traditional sound and more sophisticated pop elements." In 1999, *Slow Down* earned Keb' Mo' a second Grammy Award for best contemporary blues album.

## FOLLOW-UP ALBUMS AND COLLABORATIONS

The following year Keb' Mo' released *The Door*, a collection of original Delta blues music that features a track cowritten with musician Bobby McFerrin. Also in 2000 he released a live collection titled *Sessions at West 54th: Recorded Live in New York*, which features performance material recorded in 1997. Keb' Mo' also made an appearance on country music legend Willie Nelson's album *Milk Cow Blues* (2000), lending his voice to the song "Outskirts of Town." *Big Wide Grin*, a collection of children's songs, was released in 2001. Following its release, Keb' Mo' appeared on the children's television program *Sesame Street* to perform a song from the record.

In 2005 Keb' Mo' earned his third Grammy Award for best contemporary blues album for the album *Keep It Simple* (2004). His effort to fuse popular music with blues stylings led reviewer Steve Leggett, writing for the website AllMusic, to call him "the James Taylor of blues." Keb' Mo's 2004 record *Peace . . . Back by Popular Demand* primarily features cover songs, including renditions of the songs "Imagine" by John Lennon and "The Times They Are A-Changin'" by Bob Dylan. In 2005, he was featured alongside Tracy Chapman and Buddy Guy on a recording of the Bill Withers song "Ain't No Sunshine." Keb' Mo' also wrote a song, "I Hope," for the Dixie Chicks record *Taking the Long Way* (2006). Proceeds from the digital sales of the single benefited relief efforts following Hurricane Katrina, and the song was ultimately nominated for the Grammy Awards for best country song and best country performance by a duo or group with vocals.

Keb' Mo' released his eighth studio album, *Suitcase*, in 2006. *Suitcase* was produced by John Porter, best known for his work with the English rock group the Smiths and blues musicians R. L. Burnside and John Lee Hooker. Three years later, he released the album *Live & Mo'*, the first album to be released on his own independent record label, Yolabelle International. *Live & Mo'* is untraditional in that it features both live recordings and studio work, and this unconventional mix proved disappointing to some critics. In his review of the record for the website Pop Matters (31 Jan. 2010), Justin Cober-Lake criticized the album for taking few risks musically and for being neither a live record nor a studio work. "Having been an important voice for the better part of a generation," he wrote, "[Keb' Mo'] had the opportunity to do something bold, and he chose to do something odd." All the same, Cober-Lake gently praised *Live & Mo'* as a "step into new indie territory."

### THE REFLECTION
In 2011, Keb' Mo' released *The Reflection*, a collection of R&B material that includes a cover of the Eagles song "One of These Nights." The album features guest performances by country musician Vince Gill, vocalist India.Arie, bassist Victor Wooten, and saxophonist Dave Koz. Writing for the website Blogcritics (29 July 2011), Richard Marcus praised the record as "some of the finest R&B you'll have heard in ages." He continued, "One of the distinguishing marks of the great soul and R&B singers was the apparent effortlessness of their delivery. Keb' Mo' is no exception. . . . When you listen to him sing you don't only hear his lyrics—you feel the emotion behind them." Marcus concluded, "There are still a few performers out there who understand what it means to sing R&B. . . . It's only when you hear someone like Keb' Mo' performing that you realize how much of the heart has been cut out of the music by most people."

After making a guest appearance on singer-songwriter David Bromberg's 2011 album, *Use Me*, Keb' Mo' performed at the concert Robert Johnson at 100, a tribute to Johnson's life and work held at the Apollo Theater in New York in March of 2012. The event featured numerous artists, including Elvis Costello, Chuck D, Todd Rundgren, Macy Gray, and the Roots.

### FILM AND TELEVISION WORK
Following his appearance in *Can't You Hear the Wind Howl?*, Keb' Mo' continued to act throughout the 1990s and 2000s. He appeared in several episodes of the television drama *Touched by an Angel* between 1997 and 2002 and also appeared regularly as a musical performer in television shows such as *The West Wing*. He has served as a musical guest for late-night talk shows such as *Conan* and *The Late Late Show with Craig Ferguson*. Keb' Mo' acted in several films throughout the 2000s, including *All the King's Men* (2006), *Honeydripper* (2007), and *Who Do You Love* (2008), and appeared in numerous documentary film and television projects, including *Lightning in a Bottle* (2004) and *Bonnie Raitt and Friends* (2006).

Keb' Mo' also found success as a composer, creating music for a variety of television productions, including the series *Freddie* and *Memphis Beat*. His song "I See Love" was used as the opening theme for the CBS sitcom *Mike & Molly*, for which he also served as composer in 2010.

### PERSONAL LIFE
When asked during an interview published in *Rolling Stone* magazine (June 2011) what the blues means to him, Keb' Mo' stated, "The blues is life. It comes out of life experience." Describing his guitar playing style to Joe Moran for *Guitar World* magazine (29 Sept. 2011), he explained, "I'm not a flashy player, so I don't have any flashy stuff to put out to play." For Keb' Mo', knowledge is secondary to execution. "It's not necessarily the vocabulary," he told Moran, "but how you use what you know."

Despite his numerous achievements, Keb' Mo' has managed to keep a relatively low profile. Robbie Brooks Moore for *Nashville Arts Magazine* (1 Nov. 2010) described him as "famously under the radar." Moore wrote, "If asked by a person on the street, 'What do you do?' he responds with a shy grin and says 'I'm a guitar picker.'" Nevertheless, Keb' Mo' remains a well-known and influential figure in the blues community, and the guitar makers C. F. Martin and Company and Gibson Guitar Corporation have both released limited-edition Keb' Mo' model instruments. Keb' Mo' has one son, Kevin, and resides in Nashville, Tennessee.

### SUGGESTED READING
Graham, George. "Keb' Mo': *Just Like You*." *GeorgeGraham.com*. Graham, 1996. Web. 16 Sept. 2013.

Huey, Steve. "Keb' Mo'." *AllMusic*. All Media Guide, n.d. Web. 16 Sept. 2013.

Marcus, Richard. "Music Review: Keb' Mo'— *The Reflection*." *Blogcritics*. Technorati, 29 July 2011. Web. 16 Sept. 2013.

Moran, Joe. "Interview: Keb' Mo' Discusses Gear, Influences, and 'The Reflection,' His New Album." *Guitar World*. Harris Publications, 29 Sept. 2011. Web. 16 Sept. 2013.

Moore, Robbie Brooks. "Keb' Mo' Room to Breathe." *Nashville Arts Magazine*. St. Claire Media Group, 10 Nov. 2010. Web. 16. Sept. 2013.

### SELECTED WORKS
*Keb' Mo'*, 1994; *Just Like You*, 1996; *Slow Down*, 1998; *The Door*, 2000; *Sessions at West 54th: Recorded Live in New York*, 2000; *Big Wide Grin*, 2001; *Martin Scorsese Presents the Blues: Keb' Mo'*, 2003; *Keep It Simple*, 2004; *Suitcase*, 2006; *The Reflection*, 2011

—*Josh Pritchard*

# Andrew Keen

**Born:** 1960
**Occupation:** Entrepreneur and author

Andrew Keen is a British-born Internet entrepreneur and controversial media critic. His first book, *The Cult of the Amateur: How Today's Internet Is Killing Our Culture* (2007), pitted him against enthusiastic supporters of what was then known as the Web 2.0 culture. Though the term has fallen out of popular jargon, it referred to the era of user-aggregated Internet content such as the website Wikipedia; social networking sites such as Facebook (though it was MySpace, an earlier social media site, that was Keen's target of choice at the time); video-sharing sites such as YouTube; and the citizen journalistic nature of blogs.

Keen argued that the rise of the amateur (anyone with an opinion and Internet access) would bring an end to the expert. The latter title he defined somewhat loosely, stretching it to fit professionals such as book editors and academics but also including cultural gatekeepers such as Hollywood producers and record executives. Part of Keen's problem with Web 2.0 culture was that the content was free. People were offering their talents without compensation, and in doing so, Keen argued, they were threatening the paying jobs of those who could possibly perform the same service better. "I'm sure there is some quite good writing on the Internet, written by people who don't care about making money out of it, and who have something interesting to say," he told Tim Dowling for the London *Guardian* (19 July 2007). He added that he was "very uncomfortable with the radical altruism—in some ways, it's a legacy of the hippy culture—that lies at the heart of Web 2.0, the idea that we're all happy to give it away. I don't think that's the case. I think the majority of us need to work for money."

## EARLY LIFE AND EDUCATION

Keen was born in 1960 in Hampstead, England. His great uncle was Reuben Falber, the assistant general secretary of the Communist Party of Great Britain (CPGB) from 1968 to 1979, who later became famous for having accepted funds on behalf of CPGB from the Communist Party of the Soviet Union. Falber was a large influence on Keen, and though their political beliefs would never align, Keen fondly recalls walking through a park in London with his great uncle and talking about Karl Marx, Friedrich Engels, and Vladimir Lenin as well as the American filmmaker Alfred Hitchcock. The two shared a passion for Hitchcock's 1958 thriller, *Vertigo*, starring James Stewart and Kim Novak. The film, widely considered one of the director's best, is a disturbing take on temptation and conspiracy set in San Francisco.

© Colin McPherson/Corbis

Keen attended London University, where he studied history under the late Hugh Seton-Watson, a historical and political scientist who specialized in eastern European and Russian history. After graduating with a first-class honors degree in modern history, Keen traveled to eastern Europe as a British Council Fellow and studied at the University of Sarajevo in what was then Yugoslavia. At the time, the city was growing, though ethnic tensions were high. "In Sarajevo, I found the most effective antidote to the xenophobia of the street in the work of dystopian East European writers," Keen wrote in "Keen on Keen: My Story," a January 15, 2006, post on his former blog, *The Great Seduction*. He read the works of Milan Kundera, Josef Škvorecký, Czesław Miłosz, Danilo Kiš, and Jaroslav Hašek, but he was particularly captivated by the work of Franz Kafka and often refers to Kafka in his own writing.

After Sarajevo, Keen moved to the Bay Area in California to earn his doctoral degree in political science at the University of California, Berkeley, where he was especially influenced by professor Ken Jowitt, a political scientist who studied the nature of communist regimes and provided for Keen a "glitteringly original reading of modern history." With Jowitt as his inspiration, Keen graduated from Berkeley and moved to the Boston area to teach political science and modern history at Tufts University, Northeastern University, and the University of Massachusetts.

## THE GREAT SEDUCTION

In the early 1990s, Keen caught wind of the financial possibilities of the World Wide Web. He explained on his blog that these possibilities were "the greatest seduction since the dream of world communism." Keen moved to Silicon Valley and founded a website called Audiocafe. com with the help of investments from Intel, a prominent manufacturer of computer chips, and the software corporation SAP. Keen acted as president and chief executive officer of the site, which combined the sale of audio-related products and technologies, such as MP3 players and stereos, with music news. Keen acknowledged how the Internet was beginning to change the music industry when he explained to the Music Industry News Network (29 Nov. 1999), "While the pace of this technological change is exciting, it is very confusing to the mainstream consumer. Audiocafe.com is the first and only company to fully integrate online retail with a content-rich web site dedicated to educating consumers about the convergence of audio, technology, and music."

In 2000, Audiocafe.com was one of the first companies to close when the dot-com bubble burst. Keen has since referred to the proverbial gold rush of the early Internet age as a childish fantasy. He went on to play a role—"grown-up business roles," as he calls them—in several other companies, including Pulse 3D, Santa Cruz Networks, Jazziz Media, and Pure Depth.

After the dot-com collapse, Keen began to reexamine his enthusiasm for building an Internet community. His musings culminated in a February 2006 article, "Web 2.0: The Second Generation of the Internet Has Arrived. It's Worse Than You Think," published in the *Weekly Standard*. The article, which would serve as the seed of Keen's first book, compared Marxism to the democratization of the creation of content, specifically the availability of tools to create web-based content for sites such as Blogger or YouTube. In the article, he identified several problems with Web 2.0 and argued that "militant" language such as *empower* and *redistribute* used by advocates of Web 2.0 was reminiscent of Marx's "promises of self-realization." In other words, Keen expressed particular dismay at the prospect of upending mainstream business models and hierarchies of power.

### THE CULT OF THE AMATEUR

Keen's book *The Cult of the Amateur: How Today's Internet Is Killing Our Culture* was published in 2007. Its rhetoric was even more abrasive than that of the *Weekly Standard* article, as was Keen when speaking about the book. Asked if he used harsh words, *amateur* being one of them, to sell more books, Keen told Dowling, "I don't know if it necessarily sells books because I don't think bloggers read." *The Cult of the Amateur* predictably divided readers and garnered criticism for being sloppily fact-checked, which was ironic in light of Keen's criticisms of misinformed bloggers. (One writer gleefully pointed out an anecdote in the book that Keen misrepresented but that Wikipedia got right.) Surprisingly, Keen responded to the criticism by explaining that his book was meant to be a conversation starter rather than a detailed argument.

After the book was published, Keen eased his position on gatekeepers, admitting to Dowling that he might have "idealized mainstream media," but declared his endeavors a success. He added, "Even my biggest enemies agree that there is a need to have this discussion."

Keen was invited to the Technology, Entertainment, and Design (TED) Conference in 2007, where he was awarded the 2007 TED Prize and his book was featured as the conference's "book to read." For many intellectuals and authors, being asked to participate in a TED conference is a milestone in their career. The ubiquity of TED ("TED talks" are recorded and broadcast across the Internet) pulls many from relative obscurity. *The Cult of the Amateur* became a bestseller and Keen, who has since given a number of TED talks, has parlayed his teaching skills and controversial opinions into a successful career as a lecturer and public speaker.

## CONTINUED CRITICISM

Several years after the publication of *The Cult of the Amateur* and the barrage of criticism that followed, Keen eased his position to one of cautious acceptance. "I don't have to admire or improve what's happening, but I can't be a Luddite, either," Keen told Patrick Tucker for the *Futurist* (Mar./Apr. 2010), referring to a nineteenth-century movement of artisans against new labor-reducing technologies. The term is often applied to those who stoke fear in the face of technological advancement and is commonly associated with Keen. His arguments have found some traction, however, particularly those in his most recent book, *Digital Vertigo: How Today's Social Revolution Is Dividing, Diminishing and Disorienting Us* (2010). Keen argues, as others have before him, that Internet culture—with all of its encouragements to share, tweet, and "check in"—is blurring the line between public and private.

Keen was inspired to write the book while touring University College in London, where the mummified body of philosopher Jeremy Bentham was on display since his death in 1832. As Keen recounted to Jeanne Destro for *USA Today* (2 Oct. 2012), he wondered to himself why Bentham would "prefer everlasting exposure to the eternal privacy of the grave." As the thought came to him, he began to tweet it, and immediately he saw the uneasy correlation between the corpse and his own desire, or perhaps instinct, to put himself on display. Indeed, much of the book, according to Keen, is about his own dependence on social networking technology. He has often been asked to justify his use of sites such as Twitter and has responded that his online presence is a necessary part of the marketing of his brand and, by extension, his job. "There is a balance to the way these tools are used and what we choose to share on them," Keen told Nick Bilton for the *New York Times* (22 May 2012). "As a writer, Twitter is imperative to my business. Any writer who is not on Twitter should have their writing hands chopped off."

### DIGITAL VERTIGO
Keen, who has dubbed himself the "Anti-Christ of Silicon Valley," published his second book, *Digital Vertigo*, in 2012. Though inspired by Jeremy Bentham's mummified corpse, the book draws its title from Keen's favorite film. Keen uses the plot of Hitchcock's *Vertigo* as a metaphor for the seduction of social media. He argues that sites such as Facebook are too good to be true. They encourage users to share copious amounts of personal information that executives then sell to advertisers. "Consumers need to grow up and understand that free is never really free," he told Destro. "Data is the new oil, and the consumer has become the product." The book is marketed as a critique of Web 3.0, with the third generation differing from the first two in its focus: individualization. Users can tailor content to suit their preferences and interests, and sites such as Google employ software to track those preferences, in turn tailoring each search to each user.

Keen often appears on the news network CNN and writes for the network's website. He is also the host of an interview and chat program called "Keen On" for Techcrunch.com. Keen lives in Berkeley, California, with his family.

### SUGGESTED READING
"Audiocafe.com Launches the Internet's First Audio E-Commerce Web Site and Music Portal." *Music Industry News Network*. Music Industry News Network, 29 Nov. 1999. Web. 8 May 2013.

Bilton, Nick. "One on One: Andrew Keen, Author of 'Digital Vertigo.'" *New York Times*. New York Times, 22 May 2012. Web. 6 May 2013.

Keen, Andrew. "Keen on Keen: My Story." *The Great Seduction*. Andrew Keen, 15 Jan. 2006. Web. 13 May 2013.

Keen, Andrew. "Web 2.0: The Second Generation of the Internet Has Arrived. It's Worse Than You Think." *Weekly Standard*. Weekly Standard, 14 Feb. 2006. Web. 7 May 2013.

Tucker, Patrick. "Reinventing the Luddite: An Interview with Andrew Keen." *Futurist*. World Future Society, 1 Apr. 2010. Web. 7 May 2013.

—*Molly Hagan*

# Paula Kerger
**Born:** December 20, 1957
**Occupation:** President and chief executive of the Public Broadcasting Service (PBS)

Paula Kerger is the current president and chief executive officer (CEO) of the Public Broadcasting Service (PBS), the nation's largest noncommercial television network with more than 350 member stations. A veteran television administrator with significant experience in nonprofit management, Kerger was seen as having the potential to reinvigorate the struggling television network by helping to modernize the network's programming approach. Prior to her work for PBS, Kerger was president of the PBS station WNET in New York, where she led the company, in 1997, to completing the most successful endowment campaign in the history of public television. Under Kerger's leadership, PBS has expanded its programming with new online viewing options and a host of new children's, drama, and documentary programs. After her appointment as CEO of PBS, Kerger said at a press conference to the National Press Club, "if ever there were a medium fundamentally equipped to empower individuals, it is the one to which I—and thousands of other Americans—are dedicated. Public television. Or, what would be better called at this juncture, public media."

As CEO of PBS, Kerger has overseen the debut of the network's best programming lineup in the past twenty years, and her financial team has initiated innovative partnership agreements with iTunes, Amazon, BitTorrent, and Netflix in an effort to modernize the network's approach to digital media. In addition, Kerger helped to spearhead the PBS Foundation, a separate nonprofit organization dedicated to increasing private funding by soliciting grants and gifts from donors. By 2013, PBS programming reached an estimated 99 percent of American households and the network was ranked among the top in documentary and children's programming. Kerger has received numerous honors for her work, including being named multiple times to the Hollywood Reporter's Women in Entertainment Power 100, a ranking of television's most influential women executives. In 2008, Kerger received the Woman of Achievement Award from the New York–based Women in Development organization and, in 2012, Kerger was honored with the Brand Builder Award from PromaxBDA. To the National Press Club, Kerger said, "For those of us in public media—who are now, like you, caught up in this whirlwind of change—I think the one thing we must do is keep our sights set on that which anchors us—our mission to use the media as a tool for education and growth, for the betterment of individuals and our society."

Roger L. Wollenberg/UPI /Landov

## EARLY INTEREST IN PUBLIC BROADCASTING

Kerger was born on December 20, 1957, near Baltimore, Maryland. She has repeatedly said in interviews that her grandfather, Ed Arnold, was an important influence on her life and her decision to become involved with public media. Arnold founded the public radio station WBJC in Baltimore and was a strong proponent of public television and radio. Kerger has said in interviews that some of her strongest memories of her childhood were of watching pivotal programs like *I Claudius*, *The Forsythe Saga*, and *Brideshead Revisited* on public television. In her remarks to the National Press Club on May 23, 2006, Kerger said of this formative relationship, "From an early age, I can remember sitting close to my grandfather at night, listening to radio programs transmitted from far away. To a little girl, it felt like magic. Indeed it was."

## EDUCATION AND NONPROFIT WORK

Kerger attended the University of Baltimore, where she earned her bachelor's degree in 1979. After graduating, Kerger moved to Washington, DC, and took a job working for the US Committee for the United Nations Children's Fund (UNICEF) as a program development officer. After three years, Kerger was asked to move to New York City for a position in UNICEF's head office, where she continued to work in the organization's fund-raising department.

In 1984, Kerger was hired as director of development and alumni affairs for the New York–based nonprofit International House, a program that provides housing for graduate students around the world in addition to educational and cross-cultural exchange programs. During her time with International House, Kerger raised more than $30 million for the organization. In 1989, Kerger left International House to take a position with the New York Metropolitan Opera Association as the director of principal gifts and the coordinator of the organization's Silver Anniversary Fund capital drive.

## WNET

In 1993, Kerger was recruited to WNET, a PBS flagship station headquartered in New York City, as director of development. WNET, also known as Thirteen, is one of the most important programming providers of PBS and a longtime flagship for the network and reportedly the most watched public television station in the country. Founded as a private, for-profit station, WNET had fallen into bankruptcy until a group of commercial broadcasters decided to pool their money along with public collection drives to purchase the station in an effort to create an arm of broadcast media that would provide educational programming for the benefit of the public. After the broadcasters' initial investment, the local community raised the money to get the station on the air. The model created for WNET—a blend of corporate sponsorship, federal funding, and individual philanthropy—became the working model for public television around the country.

In a 2012 interview for WNET's *Pioneers of Thirteen* series, Kerger spoke about her effort to establish an endowment for the station to ensure a resource base that could be used to seed new projects and to protect the future of the station in situations where federal funding was reduced. Kerger was the most successful fund-raiser in the history of WNET and her endowment project earned more than $79 million for the network, which, at the time, was the largest endowment achieved by any public television station. Kerger called individual philanthropy, including private membership contributions to the station, the most important source of funding for public television and described her efforts to create an endowment as a continuation of this idea, using the endowment model common to universities and many other public arts organizations.

During Kerger's tenure with WNET, she was closely involved in decisions regarding new programming on the network. In 2000, Kerger was promoted to vice president and station manager and, in 2004, she became chief operating officer. Under her leadership, WNET significantly expanded its list of original programs and explored a variety of new angles on the station's traditional history and science-based educational programming. In her *Pioneers of Thirteen* interview, Kerger said of WNET's mission, "It's about a place where extraordinarily creative people—that have wonderful vision and aspirations—create content that is not just entertaining, but is inspiring."

## CEO OF PBS TELEVISION

In 2006, PBS organized a search committee to hire a new president and CEO of the network. With federal funding reductions and flagging levels of individual contributions to the network, it was believed that the network needed a new direction and had to choose an individual with significant experience in fund-raising. Before hiring Kerger, the PBS board interviewed fourteen candidates and reviewed more than 125 résumés. The head of PBS's search committee, Rod Bates, said that Kerger's name was brought to the search committee's attention more than any other candidate as they asked for recommendations, and she was the first to be selected for an interview. The president of WNET, Bill Baker, who was Kerger's immediate supervisor, described her as a "highly regarded, fair and disciplined manager" in an interview with Karen Everhart for *Current* (6 Feb. 2006). "She is very mission-conscious, and she knows the unique nature of public television," Baker added, describing her as the best available candidate for the position.

In her remarks to the National Press Club in 2006, just after her appointment, Kerger said, "I could tell you so many stories of people's lives that have been changed by public television," referring to the many teachers, students, professionals, and artists who credit public television stations with playing an important role in their education and careers. Kerger added, "It is these people that I want to focus on in my new position."

## GOING LOCAL AND DIGITAL

In her first year as president and CEO, Kerger attempted to improve the relationship between the parent company, PBS, and member stations by returning to the original model of member-station ownership. To this end, Kerger made efforts to ensure that member-station representatives played a more significant role in determining the future direction of the network. "Localism is our calling card," Kerger said in 2006 to the National Press Club, referring to the need for PBS to remain rooted in community programming chosen for and aimed at members of local communities.

At the same time, Kerger's development team engaged in a number of simultaneous efforts to enhance the station's involvement in alternative and digital media distribution. Kerger understood that the challenges of adapting to new media would be difficult, and she recommended corporate partnerships as the best way to address the issue. In 2007, it was announced that PBS would partner with BitTorrent by making select PBS programs, including a number of the network's most popular children's programs, available online through the BitTorrent network. Once a site for the peer-to-peer sharing

of unlicensed media, BitTorrent has evolved through prominent corporate partnerships to become a leader in providing peer-assisted downloads of licensed content. PBS also signed deals to provide streamed video and digital downloads through Netflix, Amazon, and iTunes, thereby vastly increasing their representation in the digital marketplace.

## CHILDREN'S PROGRAMMING

Children's programming has always been one of the cornerstones of PBS programming and, during Kerger's tenure as CEO, PBS expanded digital and online programming for children. In 2006, PBS launched Viva, a twenty-four-hour Spanish-language channel for PBS viewers who speak or are learning Spanish, with a focus on children's programming and education. On March 6, 2013, Kerger wrote an article for the *Huffington Post* about the network's expansion of their PBS Kids programming in an effort to increase the network's focus on science and math education. Kerger cited statistics indicating that the United States ranks twenty-fifth among thirty-four countries in math education as part of the inspiration behind the network's "It All Adds Up" initiative, which provides free educational resources aimed at helping parents integrate science and math lessons into daily activities. Kerger cited her grandfather's technique of teaching mathematics as part of working in the family garden as an example of how the network's mathematics resources could be put into practice.

## PRIME-TIME OFFERINGS AND UK PARTNERSHIPS

Between 2006 and 2013, Kerger and the development team at PBS also placed an increased focus on reinvigorating the network's prime-time television offerings. One of the PBS network's most popular programs, *Downton Abbey*, a coproduction with the UK-based ITV and Carnival Films that debuted in 2010, was a surprise hit that brought PBS programming back into the mainstream media spotlight. At the 2012 Emmy Awards, the series won six awards in categories that have been dominated by HBO original programming for much of the preceding decade. Speaking to Melissa Guthrie for the *Hollywood Reporter* about the success of *Downton Abbey* Kerger said (17 Feb. 2012), "it's a combination of good content and hitting at the right time." In an interview with David Hinckley for the *Daily News* (4 Jan. 2012), Kerger remarked, "I've had people tell me PBS is cool again," adding, "Of course, I always thought it was."

In her interview for the *Hollywood Reporter*, Kerger said that cooperative ventures were the key to maintaining funding for PBS programs. To support this, Kerger described how executive producer Rebecca Eaton, who is responsible for the station's *Masterpiece* series, including

*Downton Abbey*, and *Sherlock*, has a strong working relationship with Julian Fellowes of the BBC and Channel 4. Partnerships between PBS and British television networks have been mutually beneficial and profitable. In 2011, thanks to donations from an anonymous philanthropist, PBS launched a new US news and history channel that will air through British satellite services. As the network will air only through paid television providers in the United Kingdom, it was intended as a source of continued profit for PBS, potentially providing additional revenues that can be used to fund domestic projects. Kerger said that the new network was meant to provide a realistic version of American television and news that will help to counter the misconceptions about American culture transmitted internationally through Fox News and other commercial news agencies.

## REALITY TELEVISION

In 2012, Kerger announced that PBS would begin competing in the reality television market with a new series *Market Warriors*, which is a spinoff of the popular *Antiques Roadshow* program. In her interview for the *Daily News*, Kerger said she believed there was room for more informative and accurate reality programming, especially as many of the cable and networks have altered much or all of their history and arts programming to focus on "lowbrow shows that sell better." By contrast, Kerger reemphasized her commitment that, even as the network begins competing in the reality-show market, PBS will remain "the only source for real arts programming on television."

## FEDERAL FUNDING ISSUES

The 2012 electoral season brought public television funding to the center of the national economic debate when the Republican presidential candidate, Mitt Romney, declared that he would cut funding to the Corporation for Public Broadcasting (CPB) if elected and that stations like PBS would be forced to seek advertising revenues in order to stay on the air. In response, PBS issued a press release stating that the network was "stunned" at the way in which Romney had singled out their network as an example of governmental mismanagement. In the press release, released on October 4, 2012, PBS defended its position by saying that PBS television stations are publicly and locally owned and that the individuals running the stations are experts in making the most of limited resources, adding that "for every $1.00 of federal funding invested, they raise an additional $6.00 on their own—a highly effective public-private partnership." The PBS press release also noted that a 2012 Harris Interactive poll confirmed that Americans considered the PBS network to be the most trusted public institution in the nation and the second

most valuable use of public funds after national defense spending.

In 2010, the CPB was the largest contributor to PBS, donating an estimated $75.3 million out of the network's budget of $355.2 million. Kerger responded to these figures in her interview for the *Hollywood Reporter*, saying that the contribution of federal funding through the CPB works out to about $1.35 per American household, which Kerger described as "not even the cost of a cup of coffee." In an interview with the *Guardian* (16 Oct. 2011), Kerger asserted that 85 percent of the network's budget is derived from charitable foundations and individuals and that federal funding provided to the network is small compared to the amount dedicated to public broadcasting in England, where the BBC has an annual budget of more than three billion British pounds.

Kerger has described defending federal funding for public television as the most difficult part of her job. In her *Hollywood Reporter* interview, Kerger said, "I don't mean to say that our funding from the federal government is insignificant, and I know people have to make tough decisions. On the other hand, it's such a good investment." Adding, "when Mitt Romney says, we're not going to kill Big Bird, we're just going to make him take commercials, it's frustrating because it shows a lack of truly understanding the impact we have." During her tenure in the position, Kerger has placed emphasis on updating the network's funding model. Part of this effort was the creation of the PBS Foundation, which seeks to increase funding by drawing on charitable corporations and donors at a higher level.

In Kerger's opinion, the federal funding received by PBS is insignificant compared to the positive benefit that the network and its more than 350 member stations provide to the public. Kerger cites the wide variety of people, from artists to educators, who have been inspired to follow their careers and interests through public television programming. "Those of us who work in this business do so because it is good. It is necessary," Kerger told the National Press Club. "And our country is better for it."

Kerger lives in Washington, DC, with her husband, Joseph Kerger.

## SUGGESTED READING

Guthrie, Melissa. "How *Downton Abbey*, Mitt Romney Are Suddenly Making PBS Topic A (Q&A)." *Hollywood Reporter*. Hollywood Reporter, 17 Feb. 2012. Web. 2 May 2013.

Hinckley, David. "PBS President Paula Kerger Says Network Will Remain a Key Source of Quality Programming." *Daily News*. NYDailyNews.com, 4 Jan. 2012. Web. 2 May 2013.

Kerger, Paula. "It All Adds Up: Using Media to Help Kids Love Math." *Huffington Post*.

TheHuffingtonPost.com Inc., 6 Mar. 2013. Web. 2 May 2013.

Kerger, Paula. "Remarks to National Press Club." *About PBS News*. Public Broadcasting Service, 23 May 2006. Web. 2 May 2013.

"Meet Paula Kerger." *PBS*. Public Broadcasting Service, n.d. Web. 2 May 2013.

Sabbagh, Dan. "Interview: PBS Boss Paula Kerger on Launching a UK Channel." *Guardian*. Guardian News and Media, 16 Oct. 2011. Web. 2 May 2013.

—*Micah Issitt*

Courtesy of Daisy Khan

# Daisy Khan

**Born:** 1958
**Occupation:** Executive Director of the American Society for Muslim Advancement

Daisy Khan gained national attention when she and her husband, Imam Feisal Abdul Rauf, proposed an Islamic cultural center and mosque in New York City near the site of the terrorist attacks of September 11, 2001. Rauf and Khan serve as moderate voices for Islam. They were married in 1996, and the following year they founded the American Society for Muslim Advancement (ASMA). The organization has tried to forge an American-Islamic identity while keeping an awareness of both Islamic history and the experience of other immigrant faith communities that have assimilated into American life and culture. The nonprofit's website states that the organization is "dedicated to strengthening an authentic expression of Islam based on cultural and religious harmony through interfaith collaboration, youth and women's empowerment, and arts and cultural exchange."

Citing the example of Jewish and Roman Catholic newcomers to a predominately Protestant country and gradually gaining acceptance into a pluralistic society, Khan explained to *Sojourners* magazine's Jim Wallis, "I firmly believe that the core values of Islam—faith in and obedience to the Divine, reverence for individual rights and communal well-being, compassion and justice, respect for pluralism and diversity—are entirely resonant with American values."

Her quest is to change the too-frequent caricature of Muslims as people who practice a backward religion rooted in ignorance and intolerance. Her work with WISE (Women's Islamic Initiative in Spirituality and Equity), begun in 2006, is a global effort to merge contemporary plurality with timeless tradition. Khan steadfastly advocated for an Islamic center near the site of the September 11 attacks in New York City, despite death threats against her and her husband. "What gives me strength," she told Sally

Quinn for the *Washington Post* (19 Aug. 2010) is that "we are in a history-making moment. Our ideals must prevail. We have to fight for a bigger society."

A frequent speaker and lecturer, Khan is also a regular *Washington Post* contributor for its On Faith column. She has also been a contributor to and an adviser on several documentaries, such as PBS's "Muhammad: Legacy of a Prophet," the Hallmark Channel's "Listening to Islam," and National Geographic's "Inside Mecca." In acknowledgment of her community work, Khan was chosen by the online site Women's eNews as one of their "21 Leaders for the 21st Century" and has also received the annual Faith Leaders Award, the Auburn Seminary's Lives of Commitment Award, and the Interfaith Center's Award for Promoting Peace and Interfaith Understanding.

## EARLY LIFE AND EDUCATION

Born Farhat Khan in Kashmir, India, into a devout Muslim family, Khan came to the United States at the age of sixteen to study. Her grandfather, a student of civil engineering at Harvard during the 1920s, had told her stories of America. Nazir Khan, her father and a former soccer player, encouraged his daughter to train for the Olympics. Khan regards her grandmother as a role model for the strength and kindness she drew from her faith as she faced stereotypes of women and inequality.

Wanting to study art and design, professions closed to women in Kashmir, Khan went to live with her aunt and uncle in New York in order to pursue her interests. She excelled in field hockey, which gave her the opportunity to make friends, and she learned the guitar. Feeling herself a "flower child" and wanting to blend in, she dropped her given name, choosing instead to be called Daisy. Khan explained to Michael Grynbaum for the *New York Times* that babysitting taught her about US pop culture; she absorbed what American children watched on television and what they wanted read to them at bedtime.

Khan attended the primarily Jewish Jericho High School on Long Island and explained to Grynbaum that she was inundated with questions from her classmates about India and her Muslim religion. In many ways, this was her first experience as an advocate for Islam.

Khan earned her bachelor of fine arts degree in interior architecture from the New York School of Design. After graduation, she moved permanently to Manhattan and began an intense period of work as an architectural designer.

## EARLY EMPLOYMENT AND MARRIAGE

Kahn was the interior designer for the Islamic Center of Long Island, which broke ground in 1990 and opened in 1993 in time for Ramadan, the Muslim month of fasting. An unusual feature of the prayer space in the center was that men and women prayed together, rather than the women being separated by a partition or praying in another room. In a February 25, 1993, article for the *New York Times*, Khan clarified that "there are some conservative Muslims from the region who have come and been offended. They had to realize that the women are not a threat but an asset here, and that their values will not get broken down the way they fear."

Although there was some initial resistance to the idea of a mosque in the neighborhood, community opinion has been favorable. Khan's uncle, Faroque Khan, was one of the founders of the mosque, and the mosque serves not only as a place a prayer, but also as a gathering place.

During her twenties, Khan struggled with her faith, in part because of the theocracy of Iran where women's rights were suppressed. She decided to abandon Islam rather than try to defend it, yet she was not content.

In 1987, she was working as a project manager at Shearson Lehman Brothers on the 106th floor of the World Trade Center. She passed a mosque daily on her lunch break. After meeting the Imam, Abdul Rauf, whose emphasis on inclusion and meditation intrigued her, she began regularly attending Friday afternoon prayers. The Imam later began courting Khan; they married in 1996.

## AMERICAN SOCIETY FOR MUSLIM ADVANCEMENT

Khan and her husband, seeing the struggles immigrant Muslims experienced in order to adapt to life in the United States, founded the American Society for Muslim Advancement (ASMA) in 1997. The organization aims to build bridges between Muslims and other religions.

In an article for *Newsweek* (30 July 2007), Khan and her husband commented that there should be no conflict between the ideals of classical Islam and those of the United States: "Both the country and the religion were founded on the principle that individual freedom is a God-given, inalienable right. . . . They share a central belief in the strength that comes from embracing diversity."

The ASMA offers cultural events such as a 2001 art exhibit that Khan herself organized in response to the recent September 11 attacks. Attended by more than six hundred people from the tri-state area, "Reflections at the Time of Transformation: Muslim Artists Reach Out to New Yorkers" highlighted works of art created by Muslim poets, musicians, filmmakers, and visual artists.

After more than two decades spent working for Fortune 500 companies as an interior architect, Khan decided in 2005 to devote herself full-time to activism. Her outreach activities have included the Cordoba Bread Fest, an annual interfaith event that brings together Muslims, Jews, and Christians for a meal.

## WOMEN'S ISLAMIC INITIATIVE IN SPIRITUALITY AND EQUITY

In November 2006, Khan convened a gathering of Islamic women from around the world. The Ford Foundation, the Booth Foundation, and Rockefeller Brothers provided initial funding for what would become the Women's Islamic Initiative in Spirituality and Equity (WISE), which seeks to encourage Muslim women in making decisions about families and career paths. As Khan told Maureen Fiedler in an interview for Fiedler's 2010 book, *Breaking the Stained Glass Ceiling*, "We began to see images of women who were repressed, leaving a very strong perception in America that Muslim women are repressed throughout the world." WISE seeks to uncover and dispel gender-based inequality using the principles of Islam; belief and tradition then become balanced with current social realities. Islam in many parts of the world is struggling to adapt to modernity, just as other major world religions have struggled.

Muslim women in the United States have had considerable success in the quest for equality. Speaking to Maureen Fiedler, Khan referred to the WISE Project as "a Muslim women's reclamation movement." She continued, "We are reclaiming our faith. We're asserting our rights within Islam." Although women do not serve in leadership roles as Imams, they have been presidents of mosques—the Islamic faith does not ordain a separate clergy class. A woman has also served as the leader of the Islamic Society of North America. Women are permitted to be jurists who have the authority to issue legal opinions based on Islamic law as well. These jurists, rather than the Imams, have the power to shape social change.

## GLOBAL MUSLIM WOMEN'S SHURA COUNCIL

Along with founding WISE in 2006, Khan used the group two years later to organize the first all-women Shura Council. A Shura Council is a gathering of advisers—often jurists, scholars, and judges—who work to effect social change. Meeting online, the council strives to improve the lives and opportunities of Muslim women, particularly those living in countries where women remain largely uneducated.

According to the council's website, their work "affirm[s] our conviction that the Muslim woman is worthy of respect and dignity, that as a legal individual, spiritual being, social person, responsible agent, free citizen, and servant of God, she holds fundamentally equal rights to exercise her abilities and talents in all areas of human activity." Khan's belief is that American Muslims can take advantage of the religious freedoms afforded in the United States in order to have an effect on Muslim women from other cultures.

One example of the issues that the forty-member Muslim Women's Shura Council is addressing is that of female genital cutting (FGC), believed by many Muslims to be ordained by the Qur'an. The WISE Shura Council issued an argument against the practice and is offering religious education and economic incentives to end FGC. Other issues that concern the Shura include rape laws and honor killings.

Khan has a list of "ten deadly sins," as she terms them. They are customs that directly affect women and are often carried out in the name of Islam. Speaking in February 2013 at a conference sponsored by the US Institute for Peace (USIP), Khan addressed the topic and challenged the audience to work toward eliminating these ten practices over the next ten years.

## IMAM TRAINING PROGRAM TO END VIOLENCE AGAINST WOMEN

The Imam Training Program to End Violence Against Women (ITP), another WISE initiative, began in 2009 with Afghani Imams. The program is designed to educate the highly respected Imams in the rights of women and in the inclusion of women's rights in the Qur'an and hadiths. Imams from thirty Afghani mosques were chosen to participate and were trained in the five rights the Qur'an guarantees to women: an education, the right to inherit, marriage only by choice, participation in the social sphere, and ownership of property. During an evaluation of the program's effectiveness in 2012, Khan reported in her blog for the *Huffington Post* (2 Feb. 2012) that an Imam commented, "We respect the Quran, yet we have a major lack of understand of [it]. . . . Through this program, we are slowly opening to

a new understanding of the rights of women in Islam."

## PARK51

Following the September 11 attacks at the World Trade Center in New York City and the Pentagon in Washington, DC, American public opinion seemed to excoriate all followers of Islam. Khan and her husband worked to reverse the hatred and scapegoating that followed the attacks: Imam Feisal, who served at the al-Farah Mosque in Lower Manhattan's Tribeca neighborhood, had already begun the Cordoba Initiative, which was named for the Spanish city where Christians, Jews, and Muslims lived together in peace during the medieval times. The organization focused on civil dialogue, education, cultural exchange, and policy initiatives to bring harmony between the United States and Islam.

One of the ideas that the couple suggested following the attacks was that an Islamic cultural center be built several blocks from the site of the attack on the World Trade Center. The erupting firestorm led to death threats for Khan and her husband, and after protests erupted regarding the proposed name of Cordoba House, the name was changed to Park51, a reference to the address on Park Place, which was privately held land. Both President Barack Obama and New York's mayor Michael Bloomberg supported the rights of Muslims to build the center, although some prominent politicians and surviving family members did not. When asked about the effects that the death threats and hate mail had on her, Khan told Grynbaum, "I believe this affliction, even though it has taken a personal toll on us, is going to result in something better for all of us."

In an interview with Tamer El-Ghobashy for the *Wall Street Journal* (2 Aug. 2010), Khan responded to the question of Park51's goal by saying it was "to create a deep tolerance in intrafaith affairs. It's a place for Muslims to come together in a place where divisions would gradually peel away and a new vision of Islam that is culturally American would emerge."

Park51 Community Center opened on September 21, 2011, the International Day of Peace, with a special exhibit by photographer Danny Goldfield. The NYChildren Project captures images of children from every nation then living in New York City. It highlights the diversity and common humanity of the city's population.

## SUGGESTED READING

El-Ghobashy, Tamer. "Ground Zero Mosque Founder: 'We Want to Repair the Breach.'" *Wall Street Journal*. Dow Jones & Co., 2 Aug. 2010. Web. 3 Apr. 2013.

Fiedler, Maureen E., ed. *Breaking Through the Stained Glass Ceiling: Women Religious Leaders in Their Own Words*. New York: Seabury, 2010, 105–7. Print.

Kirkwood, Peter. "Muslims' Ground Zero Home." *Eureka Street*. EurekaStreet, 8 Sept. 2011. Web. 21 Mar. 2013.

Quinn, Sally. "Daisy Khan: 'When Will Muslims Be Accepted?'" *Washington Post*. Washington Post, 19 Aug. 2010. Web. 10 Apr. 2013.

Rauf, Imam Feisal Abdul. *Moving the Mountain: Beyond Ground Zero to a New Vision of Islam in America*. New York: Free, 2012. Print.

—*Judy Johnson*

Bloomberg via Getty Images

# Salman Khan

**Born:** October 11, 1976
**Occupation:** Educator and founder of the Khan Academy

Salman Khan, a former hedge fund analyst, is the founder of the Khan Academy, a nonprofit organization whose mission, according to its website, is to "chang[e] education for the better by providing a free world-class education for anyone anywhere." To that end, Khan has made thousands of videos on topics ranging from simple mathematics to cosmology, and has posted them online. "All of the site's resources are available to anyone," states Khan Academy's website. "It doesn't matter if you are a student, teacher, home-schooler, principal, adult returning to the classroom after twenty years, or a friendly alien just trying to get a leg up in earthly biology."

Since he quit his job and began operating the site full-time in 2009, Khan's more than 2,200 videos have been viewed, collectively, approximately 250 million times by users all over the world, who are also given access to practice drills and a dashboard that tracks their progress. "With so little effort on my own part, I can empower an unlimited number of people for all time," Khan told James Temple for the *San Francisco Chronicle* (14 Dec. 2009). "I can't imagine a better use of my time."

Microsoft founder Bill Gates called Kahn, who was named one of "The World's 100 Most Influential People" by the editors of *TIME* magazine in 2012 (18 Apr. 2012), "my favorite teacher," an accolade that has since been repeated regularly by journalists. While Gates has been instrumental in providing funding for the site, which he enthusiastically uses with his own children, the praise Kahn earns from his less famous students is just as gratifying to him. "[I get] feedback like, 'You know, my child has dyslexia, and this is the only thing that's getting into him,'" he told Sanjay Gupta for a *60 Minutes* segment (11 Mar. 2012). "I get letters from people saying, 'You know, we're praying for you and your family.' That's pretty heady stuff. People don't say that type of stuff to a hedge fund analyst normally."

## EARLY LIFE AND EDUCATION

Salman Khan, whose first name is generally shortened to "Sal," was born on October 11, 1976, in Metairie, Louisiana, a suburb of New Orleans. (He is not to be confused with the Bollywood superstar who shares the same name—a coincidence, the educator has joked, that drives many people to his site by mistake.) His father, a doctor, hailed from Barisal, a port city in Bangladesh, and his mother was a native of Kolkata (Calcutta), India.

Khan's father split up with his wife when Kahn was two years old. His mother struggled to raise Khan and his older sister with the meager income she earned working in convenience stores and other such jobs. "My dad moved to Philadelphia and was more of a notion than a person: I met him once for an evening when I was twelve and he passed away when I was thirteen," Khan recalled to Helena de Bertodano for the London *Telegraph* (28 Sept. 2012). He has credited his mother with making sure that the family always had a place to live and adequate food and clothing, but admitted to de Bertodano, "We lived at the poverty line and I was on free school lunches. . . . My mother . . . is always very embarrassed when I say that but I love that about this country: people don't care where you come from."

Khan, who enjoyed math and art, attended his area's public schools, which he remembers as varying widely in quality. He found some teachers engaging but others decidedly less so. Once, he told de Bertodano, he took a class from a geography teacher "who would make us recite the countries in a continent in alphabetical order—without telling us where they were or their history."

## THE MASSACHUSETTS INSTITUTE OF TECHNOLOGY

Always a high-performing pupil, Khan dreamed sometimes of becoming a theoretical physicist like Richard Feynman. He was placed in his school's gifted-and-talented section when he was nine years old. "Most of my really formative memories come from that programme," he told de Bertodano. "That's where I learnt to play chess, where I learnt about the great artists." As a high school student, Khan took advanced-placement courses at the University of New Orleans, and upon graduating he earned a scholarship to the Massachusetts Institute of Technology (MIT). There he played the guitar in a heavy-metal band and served as president of his senior class. In 1998 he earned bachelor's degrees in mathematics, electrical engineering, and computer science. Khan remembers his years at the school fondly; during a commencement address he gave to MIT's graduating class on June 8, 2012 (*MIT News*), he said, "MIT is the closest thing to being Hogwarts—Harry Potter's wizarding school—in real life. The science and innovation that occurs here looks no different than pure magic to most of the world."

During his 2012 MIT commencement address, Khan pointed out that his mission—to make education available to everyone, free of cost—was inspired in large part by an initiative first undertaken at MIT in 2001: OpenCourseWare (OCW), the online publication of virtually all of the university's course content, available totally without charge to anyone in the world with access to the web. Khan greatly admired what he saw as the administration's moral clarity and willingness to place principle over profit.

Khan found work at a series of Silicon Valley dot-coms before entering Harvard Business School in 2001. As at MIT, he served as president of his class. Khan told Clive Thompson for *Wired* magazine (15 July 2011) that he entered Harvard mainly to find his future wife. "I'm dead serious," he said. "Silicon Valley in the late '90s was the absolute worst place to find a wife or girlfriend." In 2003 he graduated with a master's degree in business administration.

## A CAREER IN HEDGE FUNDS

Khan put his MBA degree from Harvard to use as a financial analyst, working at the Boston office of the small firm Wohl Capital Management. He found the job both intellectually challenging and lucrative, but his later career path came as little surprise to his coworkers, who saw firsthand that Khan had a real affinity for teaching. "I'd come back to the office and giant math equations were scrawled across the board," his boss, Dan Wohl, recalled to Thompson, noting that Khan was explaining to the junior staff members the finer points of hedge fund analysis. "It's not the usual cutthroat Wall Street thing to do. But he had this natural gift and a really selfless approach."

One day in 2004, in what has become an oft-told tale of Khan Academy's genesis, Khan's cousin Nadia, then thirteen years old, asked him for his help in math. She was entering seventh grade at her school in New Orleans and had not been placed on the advanced math track. One issue, in particular, was giving her trouble on the test: unit conversion—turning gallons into liters, for example, or ounces into grams. Her parents, used to their daughter being a stellar student, were understandably distressed.

Kahn had long been known within the family for his math abilities, and he agreed to tutor Nadia over the phone. During their tutoring sessions, the two would log onto Yahoo's instant messaging service, and he would draw problems on the screen using a program called Yahoo Doodle. He subsequently wrote some computer code that generated sets of problems she could complete on her own for practice.

## THE EARLY DAYS OF TUTORING ONLINE

Nadia's skills grew enormously, and soon her younger brothers, Arman and Ali, asked for tutoring of their own. As word spread, other family members began clamoring for help for their own children, and soon his relatives' friends had become interested. Khan kept up as well as he could, but soon the sheer numbers of youngsters requesting help—combined with his work demands and their busy extracurricular schedules—made that impossible. Rather than continuing to use instant messaging, Kahn recorded his presentations and posted them on the video-sharing site YouTube. Initially, he scoffed at the idea of posting math tutorials on YouTube. The website, he thought, was only for videos of "dogs riding skateboards" (*Wired* 3 May 2011) or "cats playing the piano" (*New York Times* 11 Dec. 2011), as he has told journalists.

Ultimately, however, he decided to give it a try. In late 2006—employing a PC, an electronic pen that cost about $80, and $20 worth of screen-capture software that he set up in a closet at his home—he uploaded his first video, which explains the basics of least common multiples. Nadia and the other students loved that video and the ones that followed. They could watch the videos at their convenience, pausing or replaying them repeatedly when they needed to. "The worst time to learn something," Khan told Thompson, "is when someone is standing over your shoulder going, 'Do you get it?'"

Each video is about ten to fifteen minutes long and features colored diagrams on a black background reminiscent of a classroom blackboard. Kahn's voice can be heard in the background, explaining the steps he is taking. He never appears in his videos, preferring instead to maintain the effect that he is right at the viewer's shoulder, speaking directly into his or her ear, rather than standing at the front of a room lecturing.

## KHAN ACADEMY TAKES OFF

Khan holed up in his closet and recorded several lessons an evening, after finishing work at Wohl Capital. By 2009, however, it was dawning on him that he was attracting tens of thousands of viewers, and he quit his analyst's job to devote all of his time to the educational venture. Though his following had grown incredibly since that first video in 2006, he financed Khan Academy, as he calls his site, with his own savings. When asked by Robert Siegel in a National Public Radio *All Things Considered* interview (28 Dec. 2009) about funding in those early years, he joked that his major supporter was "the Salman Khan Bank of America Checking Account."

Small donations eventually began to trickle in, however, and fans wrote to tell him that his videos had kept them from failing courses or dropping out of school. To his surprise, he also got letters from adult learners who were using the videos to brush up on material they should have mastered years before. Some were even being motivated to complete long-abandoned college coursework. One day Khan received a $10,000 check in the mail from Anne Doerr, the wife of Silicon Valley investor John Doerr. Flabbergasted by her generosity, he wrote to thank her. She was equally flabbergasted to learn that hers had been the largest donation he had gotten to date and that he was living on his savings. She promptly wrote him a second check, this one for $100,000.

## THE SUPPORT OF BILL GATES AND GOOGLE

Other backers followed. During the June/July 2010 Aspen Ideas Festival, Anne Doerr texted Khan to tell him that Bill Gates was talking about him onstage. Gates was telling the audience that his own children were hooked on Khan Academy videos and that he watched alongside them. Soon after, in September, the Bill and Melinda Gates Foundation gave Khan $1.5 million. Gates later joined Khan onstage at the March 2011 TED (Technology, Entertainment, and Design) conference, an annual gathering of the world's most creative and influential figures. He told the audience after Kahn's speech, "You just got a glimpse of the future of education." Kahn got one of the biggest rounds of applause of the day when he admitted during his presentation, "Here I was an analyst at a hedge fund. It was very strange for me to do something of social value."

Gates continues to be an outspoken booster of Kahn's mission, particularly as it pertains to math education. "Math is the killer," Gates told Clive Thompson. "If you ask people, 'Hey, there are these open nursing jobs, why don't you go and get one?' math is often the reason they give for not applying. . . . 'Why didn't you pass the police exam?' Math."

Gates was not the only large institutional donor; when the Internet behemoth Google asked its users in 2010 what types of projects deserved the company's support, many voted for making educational content available free online. (Other top picks included making government more transparent and encouraging innovation in public transport.) Google subsequently awarded $2 million to Khan that September to enable him to create more courses and to translate a core portion of the video library into other widely spoken languages.

## KHAN ACADEMY IN THE CLASSROOM

In late 2010 the Los Altos (California) School Board agreed to a pilot program in which two fifth-grade classrooms and two seventh-grade classrooms would begin using Khan's videos as part of the official curriculum. The project involves a concept called "flipping the classroom," wherein students watch the videos in the evening and then complete the drills—exercises that might traditionally be considered homework—during the day, when their teacher is available to guide them.

With the money received from the Gates Foundation and Google, Kahn hired programmers who developed a "dashboard" that allows teachers to monitor student performance and progress. The dashboard displays which subjects the student is studying, the number of videos he or she has seen, what problems have been completed, and the length of time the student has spent using Khan Academy at home. Students, in turn, can jump in to help struggling classmates and compare the virtual badges that they have earned for mastering certain skills. Khan told Gates during his TED talk that the badge system produces interesting results: "Just the wording of the badging or how many points you get for doing something, we see on a system-wide basis, like tens of thousands of fifth graders or sixth graders going one direction or another, depending on what badge you give them." Khan expects that other school districts will join in eventually. He has stressed that his aim, as he explained to de Bertodano, "is not about replacing teachers, it's about empowering teachers."

## CRITICS OF THE ACADEMY

Khan Academy has its share of detractors. As David A. Kaplan wrote for CNN's *Money* magazine (24 Aug. 2010), "Online critics question whether he amounts to a dilettante who's turning learning into pedagogical McNuggets." In disagreement, Kaplan wrote, "But while you obviously don't learn calculus in one session—the subject is divided into 191 parts, which doesn't include thirty-two more in precalc—Khan's components seem to hit the sweet spot of length and substance."

Some critics also do not believe that it is possible for one man to know enough about such a wide range of subjects to teach others: Khan has branched out from his original focus on math and science to include lessons on such topics as the Napoleonic War, the US Social Security system, and the ramifications of underfunded pension plans. Khan maintains that he is able to master many topics on his own. He explained to Jeffrey R. Young for the *Chronicle of Higher Education* (6 June 2010) how he prepared, for example, for a video on entropy: "I took two weeks off and I just pondered it, and I called every professor and everyone I could [think of to] talk to and I said, Let's go have a glass of wine [and talk] about entropy. After about two weeks it clicked in my brain, and I said, now I'm willing to make a video about entropy."

## "LIBERATING THE CLASSROOM"

"Part of [Khan's] appeal is the polymathic mastery issue," Larry Berger, the chief executive of digital education company Wireless Generation, told David Gelles for the *Financial Times* (28 Oct. 2011). "It's nice to learn chemistry from someone who also seems to know his math and history and physics. Part of the fun is being able to dip into videos on such different topics taught from the same mind." Still, Khan does hire experts to give tutorials. One series of videos on art history, for example, features Steven Zucker and Beth Harris, historians who lead a humanities-focused team for him.

Among Khan's most vociferous critics are those in the education world who feel that he is merely promoting rote drill. Students will lose interest in math, this group holds, because Khan is taking a mechanical, joyless approach to the topic. "It's the exact opposite!" Khan told Thompson, stressing that the more students watch his videos at home, the more class time is freed up for creative activities like arts and games. "You're actually liberating the classroom; you're making it more human." Khan's supporters have also pointed out that Khan's enthusiastic, encouraging delivery is a hallmark of the videos, making them far from boring. To help communicate the benefits of his approach, Kahn wrote a book that "fleshes out the story and the vision that began with [his] talk at TED" (*TED Blog* 3 Oct. 2012). *The One World Schoolhouse: Education Reimagined* was published in 2012.

## PERSONAL LIFE

Khan and his wife, Umamia, a physician, have one son and one daughter. Speaking of his decision to keep Khan Academy as a nonprofit venture, he often tells journalists that he has a nice home, two serviceable cars, and a wonderful family, so he doesn't feel the need to make billions of dollars. "The incremental cost [of what I'm doing] is so much lower than the incremental value," he told Ethan A. Solomon for the MIT news publication the *Tech* (6 Dec. 2011). "The incremental value is almost priceless." In an editorial written for *TIME* magazine on the occasion of Khan's listing as one of the world's one hundred most influential people (18 Apr. 2012), Bill Gates concurred: "[Khan] started by posting a math lesson, but his impact on education might truly be incalculable."

## SUGGESTED READING

Bertodano, Helena de. "Khan Academy: The Man Who Wants to Teach the World." *Telegraph* [London]. Telegraph Media Group, 28 Sept. 2012. Web. 12 Mar. 2013.

Gupta, Sanjay. "Khan Academy: The Future of Education?" *60 Minutes*. CBS Interactive, 11 Mar. 2012. Web. 12 Mar. 2013.

Kaplan, David A. "Bill Gates' Favorite Teacher." *CNN Money*. Cable News Network, 24 Aug. 2010. Web. 12 Mar. 2013.

Temple, James. "Salman Khan, Math Master of the Internet." *San Francisco Chronicle*. Hearst Communications, 14 Dec. 2009. Web. 12 Mar. 2013.

Thompson, Clive. "How Khan Academy Is Changing the Rules of Education." *Wired*. Condé Nast, 15 July 2011. Web. 12 Mar. 2013.

Young, Jeffrey R. "College 2.0: A Self-Appointed Teacher Runs a One-Man 'Academy' on YouTube." *Chronicle of Higher Education*. Chronicle of Higher Education, 6 June 2010. Web. 12 Mar. 2013.

—*Mari Rich*

# Angus S. King Jr.

**Born:** March 31, 1944
**Occupation:** Politician

As Maine's governor from 1995 to 2003, Angus King was a social progressive and fiscal conservative who gained widespread popularity during his first term and was reelected by one of the largest margins in state history. After taking a nearly ten-year leave from politics, King decided to run for the US Senate seat vacated by Senator Olympia Snowe, who announced her retirement in 2012, citing the "hyperpartisan" environment in Washington as the reason for her departure. King, an independent politician, saw an opportunity to work across the aisle for positive change in the Senate, believing that he could act as a "bridge senator" to bring together legislators from the two major opposing parties.

In his campaign for Senate, King pledged to tackle political obstructionism in Washington, DC, particularly through election and filibuster reforms. "We've got all these problems—fiscal

Roll Call/Getty Images

problems, health care, energy, immigration—but the system itself that's set up to solve these problems wasn't working," King said in an interview with Lloyd Grove for the *Daily Beast* (31 Jan. 2013), explaining his reasons for reentering politics. "That's what led me to say we're gonna do this. It's uncharted territory, but maybe somebody who's not affiliated with either of the parties, but who's also had political experience, can nudge the process toward a little bit better functionality. That's what we're trying to do. That's the motivation."

### EARLY LIFE
Angus Stanley King Jr. was born in Alexandria, Virginia, on March 31, 1944. King was the first son and youngest child of Angus Stanley King Sr., who goes by his middle name, and Ellen Ticer King. His father worked as a small-town lawyer and went on to become a US commissioner and federal magistrate. King's mother was a schoolteacher and an active member of St. Paul's Episcopal Church in Alexandria, who once served as president of the Episcopal Church Women of the Diocese of Virginia. King described his parents as traditional "Roosevelt Democrats" in an interview with Andrea L'Hommedieu for the George J. Mitchell Oral History Project at Bowdoin College (3 Nov. 2009). King comes from a family of politicians; his grandfather had been mayor of Alexandria during the 1930s and his uncle had served on the city council while King was a boy. His father also chaired Alexandria's school committee and Rotary Club.

King grew up in a neighborhood on the outskirts of Alexandria, on the slope of Seminary Hill. King attended Hammond High School, where he played football and was elected class president as a junior and senior. In 1961, at the age of seventeen, King attended Boys State, the American Legion's model government program, where he was elected "governor" of Virginia by his peers. The *Washington Post* ran a photograph of the young King shaking hands with Virginia's then-governor, James Lindsay Almond. In an interview with Colin Woodard for the *Portland Press Herald* (23 Sept. 2012), a former classmate of King, George M. Williams Jr., recalled, "Everybody knew who Gus was, and we assumed he wanted to be a politician. He was a natural-born leader of that sort and had the ability to get people to work with him on a cooperative basis without looking like he was getting them to work for him. He didn't have to expend effort or advertise himself to do this."

### POLITICAL AWAKENING
In 1959, during King's freshman year of high school, a federal court ordered Hammond High to integrate. While other schools in the state opted to temporarily close their doors rather than desegregate, King was inspired by the positive leadership he witnessed at Hammond. In his interview with Woodard, King recalled the scene when two black students arrived at Hammond for their first day of classes, "It was absolutely silent, and nobody knew what to do. After this long pause there was a voice saying, 'Excuse me, excuse me,' and it was Mike Vopatek, who was senior class president. . . . He didn't make a speech or anything, he just came up to the Raglands and said, 'Hello, I'm Mike Vopatek, can I help you find your class?' That moment could have turned ugly, but that set the tone and defused the moment." This strategy of cultivating friendships would later become a hallmark of King's political style. "I'm a great believer that we have better and worse angels of our nature," King told Woodard. "We can be led in either direction, and leadership is so important. People can be moved to be generous and tolerant and all those things, and can also be moved to be hateful." King has cited this moment as a major milestone in his leadership development, as it demonstrated to him the power and importance of positive leadership.

### COLLEGE EDUCATION
King graduated from high school in 1962 and enrolled at Dartmouth College in Hanover, New Hampshire. There, he met the woman who would later become his first wife, Edie C. Hazard. At Dartmouth, King was active in the school's student government organization and was involved in radio broadcasting there. He earned his bachelor's degree in 1966 and went on to the University of Virginia Law School. While at law school, King worked as a campus

coordinator for Senator Robert F. Kennedy's 1968 presidential campaign, until the senator's assassination in June of that year. While still at the University of Virginia, King joined a legal aid clinic that provided free legal assistance to low-income individuals across Virginia. King also took an internship at a corporate law firm in Washington, DC. When he did not pursue employment at the firm following his graduation in 1969, his mother was shocked and disappointed, but King was determined to continue his work with the legal aid clinic.

## EARLY CAREER

After receiving his law degree, King joined the National Legal Services Program and was given the choice of continuing his work at a legal aid clinic in Maine, Louisiana, or South Dakota. At the behest of his wife, Edie, who had been raised in Vermont, King chose Maine. He started his career at Pine Tree Legal Assistance in Skowhegan, in central Maine, where he worked as a staff attorney. King continued his work at Pine Tree for the next three years, but became frustrated when he could not address many of the problems faced by his clients. "I could deal with their legal problems, but I couldn't deal with their lack of dental care, their lack of care for an autistic child, their total lack of education, all these other things," he told Woodard. "It made me think: If you're going to help people, you're going to have to try to deal with a larger segment of who they are." This realization prompted King to leave Pine Tree Legal Assistance and join the campaign staff of William Hathaway in his race for a US Senate seat.

After Hathaway won the election, King joined the senator's staff in Washington, DC, as a legislative assistant in January 1973. In this role, King was responsible for reviewing various bills and advising the senator on education, labor, and transportation policies. It was at this point in his career that King began to question his Democratic Party affiliation. When tasked with reviewing a recently proposed bill regarding camp safety, King quickly became disillusioned with the bill's overreliance on government regulation. "It got down to how many latrines you had to have per camper and that the path to the waterfront had to be paved with a certain kind of paver, and I thought this is just stupid," he said to Woodard. "I can almost date it from that moment, where I thought: the federal government and regulation is not the answer to everything. There are countervailing values."

In 1974, at the age of twenty-nine, King was diagnosed with melanoma, one of the deadliest forms of skin cancer. The cancer was discovered in its early stages at a routine physical and promptly treated, but the ordeal gave King a newfound perspective on life. "There were two things that were important: family and friends.

Everything else you could deal with," he told the *Daily Beast*'s Grove. In 1975, King returned to Maine with his wife and two young children, settling in Topsham. King started a small law practice called Smith, Loyd and King in Brunswick. During this time, he became involved with the Maine Public Broadcasting Network and hosted a show called *Maine Watch*. He was also an active lobbyist at the state legislature in Augusta for energy and conservation-related issues. In 1982, King and his first wife divorced, yet remained on good terms.

## NORTHEAST ENERGY MANAGEMENT

In 1983, one of his law firm's former clients offered King a position as vice president of an alternative energy development company, Swift River/Hafslund. Swift River's focus was on rehabilitating or supplementing power plants at hydroelectric dams. In 1984, King married Mary Herman, the former head of the Maine Women's Lobby. In 1988, Swift River was forced to lay off forty of its forty-four employees, including King. However, King retained the rights to an idea he had been working on for Swift River: to offer energy-conservation consultations to utility companies rather than offer ways to supplement their energy supply. As King explained in his interview with L'Hommedieu, "I went to CMP [Central Maine Power] and said, 'You ought to consider this, because it costs half as much to save power than it does to generate power. So instead of paying eight cents a kilowatt-hour for new power, you can pay me three cents a kilowatt-hour for saved kilowatt-hours that you can then resell.'" The following year, in 1989, King took out a second mortgage on his home to found Northeast Energy Management Inc. Over the next five years, King and his company helped utility plants, companies, and colleges across Maine to save tens of thousands of dollars each year by upgrading and replacing energy-inefficient equipment. The sale of Northeast Energy Management in January 1994 made King a multimillionaire.

## GOVERNOR OF MAINE

The sale of Northeast Energy afforded King the freedom to pursue his longtime interest in politics. In 1986, he had seriously considered running for Congress, but tabled the idea in order to focus on his family and business. "I'd always been interested in politics and expected to be involved, but it just didn't happen because of children and a young family and I kind of gave up on the idea," King told Woodard. "Then all of a sudden all the stars were in alignment." King used the money he had earned from his energy-consultation business to fund about half of his $1.6 million campaign. King launched a number of television ads to bolster his name recognition. "Without the money that I contributed I couldn't have been elected. . . . I had 9 or 10 percent name recognition when I started and Joe Brennan, who was my [Democratic] opponent, had 94 percent," King said to L'Hommedieu. Running as an independent candidate, King won the election following a close three-way race against Brennan and Republican candidate Susan Collins. King was sworn in as Maine's seventy-first governor on January 5, 1995.

King's governorship oversaw a period of economic growth and prosperity, and Mainers appreciated King's nonpartisan approach. King had campaigned on the promise of curtailing partisanship in Maine's government; in 1991, the Republican governor and Democratic state legislature could not resolve their differences over the state's budget, resulting in a partial shutdown of the state's government. King lived up to his independent affiliation, embracing fiscally conservative and socially progressive policy initiatives. As Woodard noted, "While governor he at one time or another irritated liberals by vetoing minimum-wage increases and social conservatives by backing gay rights initiatives." An article printed on October 29, 1998, in the *Economist* commended King's first term as governor, "He has produced results: lower taxes, leaner government, and a budget surplus." In 1998, King was reelected by a forty-point margin, one of the largest margins in Maine's history. The two major-party candidates, Republican James Longley and Democratic Thomas Connolly, split only a third of the total vote.

During his two terms as governor, King accomplished meaningful reforms in education, environmental protection, and health care, and successfully fostered economic development and job growth in the state. He also actively fostered the sense of community among politicians in August, hosting weekly bipartisan breakfasts for state legislators. "It wasn't policy stuff," King said of the breakfast meetings in his interview with Grove. "It was, how are you doing? How are your kids doing? What's going on in the district? Because a system like ours has to be based on relationships."

## PRIVATE LIFE

In January 2003, King left politics in pursuit of a more "private life." He and his wife, Mary Herman, embarked on a six-month, cross-country tour of the United States in an RV with their two adopted children, Ben and Molly. Upon returning to Maine, King spent the following years practicing law, lecturing at colleges across the state, and pursuing several business opportunities, becoming part owner of the alternative-energy provider Independence Wind and serving on the board of W. P. Steward, a Bermuda-based investment fund from 2004 to 2010. In 2010 he joined the board of directors of the Bank of Maine. In 2011, King released a book about his

family's cross-country RV trip, *Governor's Travels: How I Left Politics, Learned to Back Up a Bus, and Found America*, and was planning a second RV trip when Senator Olympia Snowe of Maine unexpectedly announced she would not seek reelection in 2012.

Snowe, a moderate Republican, had been an extremely popular and effective senator. She cited the hyperpartisan environment and political gridlock in Washington as one of the primary reasons for her retirement. Prior to Snowe's departure, King had never considered running for the Senate. In his interview with Grove, King explained he had never considered challenging Maine senators Snowe and Susan Collins, stating "We have two really good senators, and the only reason for me to run against them would be ego." After Snowe announced her retirement, many Mainers were concerned about the impact of losing Snowe's moderate voice in Washington, DC. King announced his intention to run for Snowe's vacated Senate seat on March 5, 2012.

## US SENATE

King ran as an independent to win with 53 percent of the vote against the two major-party candidates, former Maine secretary of state Charlie Summers, a Republican, and former state senator Cynthia Dill, a Democrat. King was sworn in as Maine's first independent senator on January 3, 2013. King hoped that being politically independent would help him rise above the political fray and work with colleagues on both sides of the congressional aisle. While King has chosen to caucus with the Democratic Party, he has nevertheless maintained his nonpartisan, community-building approach that characterized his governorship. According to Grove, in King's first month as senator he had already "visited with more than thirty of his fellow senators from both parties, including a long chat with Republican leader Mitch McConnell. It's King's political MO" (*Daily Beast* 31 Jan. 2013).

King's moderation is refreshing to many US legislators at a time when many Americans are concerned that US politics are becoming increasingly divisive and dysfunctional. "Angus has got a tremendous reputation for working across the aisle and getting things done," West Virginia Senator Joe Manchin told Grove. "He's looking at the issues, not the politics. He's going to be a real problem solver."

## PERSONAL LIFE

King has five children, Angus III, Duncan, James, Ben, and Molly, as well as five grandchildren. He lives in Brunswick with his wife, Mary Herman. King loves riding motorcycles, and even completed a six-hundred-mile campaign tour from Fort Kent to Kittery on his Harley Davidson V-Rod in the months leading up to the 2012 election.

## SUGGESTED READING

Grove, Lloyd. "Angus King: New Senator Aims to Build Bridges amid Washington Dysfunction." *Daily Beast.* Newsweek/Daily Beast Co., 31 Jan. 2013. Web. 9 Feb. 2013.

King, Angus. Interview by Andrea L'Hommedieu. *George J. Mitchell Oral History Project.* Bowdoin College Digital Commons, 3 Nov. 2009. Web. 9 Feb. 2013.

"King Angus." *Economist.* Economist Newspaper, 29 Oct. 1998. Web. 9 Feb. 2013.

Seelye, Katharine Q. "Maine Race Complicates Struggle for the Senate." *New York Times.* New York Times Co., 30 June 2012. Web. 9 Feb. 2013.

Woodard, Colin. "The Making of a Man without a Party." *Portland Press Herald.* Maine Today Media Inc., 23 Sept. 2012. Web. 9 Feb. 2013.

—*Mary Woodbury*

Steve Broxterman, World Access for the Blind

# Daniel Kish

**Born:** March 19, 1966
**Occupation:** Echolocation expert and president of World Access for the Blind

Daniel Kish, the founder and president of the nonprofit group World Access for the Blind (WAB), is the first blind orientation and mobility specialist in the world. Commonly referred to as O&M, the field of orientation and mobility focuses on teaching people with blindness or visual impairment to safely navigate the environments they encounter. While other O&M specialists typically teach their students to rely on the use of a long cane, a trained guide dog, or help from a sighted person, Kish advocates adding the innovative technique of echolocation, or sensing objects by bouncing sound waves off them—in this case by subtly clicking the tongue. The process can result in unprecedented independence for those who master it, allowing practitioners to navigate city streets and mountain bike or hike on challenging wilderness trails. It is similar to the method of echolocation used by bats, and as a result, Kish has earned the nickname "Batman." The sobriquet is sometimes applied admiringly and sometimes disparagingly; many disapprove of Kish's work and doubt its effectiveness, and the National Federation of the Blind, one of the largest such groups in the world, refuses to endorse him. "The blindness field is firmly based in tradition and dogma and is very slow to evolve," Kish explained to Michael Finkel for *Men's Journal* (1 Mar. 2011). "It's been traditionally dominated by sighted people who feel the need to tell blind people what to do."

## EARLY LIFE

Kish was born on March 19, 1966, in Montebello, California. He was diagnosed as an infant with retinoblastoma, a rare and virulent form of ocular cancer that is readily treatable today but was less so several decades ago. In an effort to save Kish's life, doctors removed both of his eyes by the time he was thirteen months old; Kish now wears prosthetic eyes. The disease is genetic, and Kish's younger brother, Keith, was also affected; however, doctors were able to help him retain some of his vision. In addition to their health issues, the boys faced other difficulties: Their father, a mechanic, drank heavily and could be abusive; their mother separated from him when Kish was six years old.

At about the age of two, Kish has recalled, he discovered intuitively that he could get feedback on his surroundings by making noises—in his case by clicking his tongue. That discovery is not uncommon among blind children, who might clap their hands, stamp their feet, or snap their fingers if allowed. Such behaviors are often swiftly and methodically discouraged, however, because conventional wisdom deems them antisocial or off-putting. In Kish's case, his mother discerned that the clicking was of benefit to him, and so she never tried to prevent him from doing it. Friends and family got used to Kish clicking his tongue, and they began to refer to the resulting sounds as his "radar."

A rambunctious child, Kish did not allow his lack of vision to prevent him from engaging in typical boyhood activities. He loved to explore his neighborhood and once climbed out of his bedroom window in the middle of the night to do so. When he was discovered wandering around a backyard on the other end of the block, having climbed over several fences, the panicked homeowners called the police to retrieve him. He also loved to ride his bicycle. "I used to go to the top of a hill and scream 'Dive bomb!' and ride down as fast as I could," he told Finkel, recalling how the neighborhood children would scatter wildly to avoid being plowed down. "One day I lost control of the bicycle, crashed through these trash cans, and smashed into a metal light pole. It was a violent collision. I had blood all over my face. I picked myself up and went home." He explained, "Running into a pole is a drag, but never being allowed to run into a pole is a disaster. Pain is part of the price of freedom."

## EDUCATION

Despite such mishaps, his mother never became overprotective, and Kish, an accomplished singer and avid reader of Braille books, was sent to mainstream schools, where he was expected to be self-reliant. In middle school he was named smartest in his class, and in high school he was voted "most likely to succeed." In 1984 he graduated with an almost-perfect grade point average and entered the University of California at Riverside. Kish earned a bachelor's degree in 1988 and decided upon a career in psychology.

In 1990 Kish suffered a tragedy that had a great impact on him. He owned a black Labrador retriever named Whiska, and although he relied heavily on echolocation to navigate, the dog was meant to help him as well. One day, as they were walking together, she was hit by a car and killed. He blamed himself. "I spoiled her rotten and took over her job. She forgot to watch for traffic, because I'd always done that for her," he wrote in a journal that he allowed Finkel to read. Except for one other brief, abortive attempt, he has not owned a dog since.

In 1995 Kish earned a master's degree in developmental psychology from California State University (CSU) at San Bernardino. Although he had little interest in entering a field specifically relating to blindness, he wrote his master's thesis on the history and science of echolocation. He included an explanation of a training program he had devised, which he believed would enhance the ability of blind children to navigate when combined with more conventional methods. He was asked to present his thesis findings at a conference of the California Association of Orientation and Mobility Specialists. In the audience was Diane Fazzi, the chair of CSU's O&M program, based at the school's Los Angeles campus. She asked Kish if he was interested in becoming certified as an O&M specialist. While he had intended to follow a different path entirely, he was intrigued by her suggestion. He remembered how resistant he had been to using a cane as a teen and believed that he could identify with and help other young people who were similarly reluctant.

Before World War II, few agencies or schools provided anything but rudimentary instruction in independent travel for the visually impaired. During the war, however, as increasing numbers of blinded servicemen required rehabilitation, the US Veterans Administration began addressing the issue, with good results. Thanks to a surge of interest in O&M, the first university training program for specialists was started in the 1960s. Since then, it has been a growing field of study, usually at the graduate level and typically as a component of special-education or rehabilitation programs. In 1996 Kish graduated with a second master's degree, this one in special education, and a certificate in O&M from CSU Los Angeles, becoming the first blind O&M specialist in the world.

## WORLD ACCESS FOR THE BLIND

Kish began working on an itinerant basis, traveling to work with those willing to hire a blind O&M expert. At times he contracted with state-run or privately owned rehabilitation agencies, school districts, and even individuals. His clients ranged in age, but most were school-aged children. He later became the youth outreach coordinator at the Blind Children's Learning Center in Los Angeles.

In 2000 Kish founded a nonprofit organization called World Access for the Blind; its motto is "Our Vision Is Sound." As stated on its website, the organization's philosophy is that "blindness is not as disabling as is commonly believed." The site continues, "Barriers to functioning associated with blindness arise more from poor interaction between blind people and society than from intrinsic deficiency. We characterize blindness as a condition of lifestyle with specific challenges requiring a strong capacity to adapt. Blindness should not deny access to all the experiences and opportunities of the world." To that end, Kish and a small team of coworkers travel all over the world teaching students with visual impairments to use echolocation, which he has given the more stylized name of "FlashSonar."

Although WAB operates on a budget of less than $200,000 a year, Kish tries not to turn down anyone who requests his services. To date he has helped well over five hundred students, either meeting a few times a month for sessions or conducting intensive week-long training. He has taught in Mexico, Scotland, Armenia, South Africa, and Switzerland, among other countries.

## IN THE MEDIA SPOTLIGHT

Human echolocation is not a recent discovery. "For centuries, scientists have been working on the question of how blind people compensate for their loss of vision," Daniel Engber wrote for *Slate* (1 Dec. 2006). "[Philosopher Denis] Diderot's 'Letter on the Blind' from 1749 described an 'amazing ability' to navigate in the absence of sight, which later became known as 'facial vision.'" Psychologist Winthrop Kellogg published a study on human echolocation in 1962. Nevertheless, the phenomenon periodically captures the attention of the media. In 2006, print and television journalists began reporting on the abilities of a teenager named Ben Underwood, who could skateboard, ride horses, and navigate the hallways of his high school as well as any sighted student. He was the subject of an admiring profile in *People* magazine, headlined "The Boy Who Sees with Sound" (24 June 2006). Kish was quoted in the piece as a "blind psychologist and leading teacher of echo-mobility among the blind." Kish, an expert sportsman himself, cautioned Alex Tresniowski, the *People* reporter, that Underwood was out of the ordinary, asserting, "His skills are rare. Ben pushes the limits of human perception." Underwood and Kish were featured together on the ABC News program *Primetime* later that year, in an episode devoted to medical mysteries.

In 2011 Kish was again thrust into the media spotlight when he was featured on CNN. He used the opportunity to tout the benefits of echolocation. "It isn't that difficult to teach. It really isn't," he told a reporter, as quoted on the CNN wire service (9 Nov. 2011). "I believe that the brain is already at least partly wired to do this. All that needs to happen is the hardware needs to be awakened. It needs to be activated, and we believe we've found ways of doing this." News footage abounds of Kish performing some of his most amazing feats; journalists seem to particularly favor shots of him biking or navigating traffic-filled streets. Still, he told the CNN reporter, "This is not aiming at making our students daredevils or 'super-blind' or anything like that. It's really aimed at opening opportunities and helping students . . . to lead day-to-day lives."

## PERSISTENCE IN THE FACE OF OBJECTIONS

Many in the blind community have not embraced Kish; at one point he estimated that he had approached more than one thousand agencies and gotten only ten positive responses. "Many O&M specialists believe that even the most talented echolocaters would be better off—that is, safer—with a more conventional mode of navigation," Engber explained. Also, many with visual impairments, according to Engber, have "been working for years to dispel the long-standing 'myth' that people without sight can compensate for their deficit with superhuman hearing or touch." Others fear that the clicking itself will brand blind people as freakish or odd. Kish discounts such thinking, asserting that such objections arise because organizations for the blind are staid and resistant to innovation. "I think that has a lot to do with a dogmatic adherence to tradition," he told the CNN reporter.

Despite such objections, many of those who have trained with World Access for the Blind are true believers in the power of echolocation. As of September 2012, more than five hundred students worldwide had taken WAB's course in FlashSonar. Asked by *Current Biography* to name a few stellar students, Kish is loath to single anyone out, but he mentions one woman in Australia who was an accomplished vocal instructor and choral conductor despite her limited mobility and anxiety. Learning about World Access for the Blind from a documentary on Ben Underwood, she raised the funds to bring Kish to Queensland for a month. While the local schools and agencies she contacted were skeptical at first, she persevered and was able to book several presentations and demonstrations for him. The response was so overwhelmingly positive that a movement has sprung up in Queensland to spread the word about echolocation training. "In over five hundred students, I don't know that I can say that any of them have taken so much initiative on our behalf, as well as shared their benefits with so many others, so quickly, and so decisively," Kish said.

## VISIONARY

Kish, who was included in *Utne Reader*'s list of "Fifty Visionaries Who Are Changing the World" in 2009, admits that animals are better at echolocation than humans. "A bat can determine an object the size of a gnat from so many meters away," he explained to the CNN reporter. "For me, the object has to be at least the size of a softball. So bats definitely have the edge on humans in terms of their use of ultrasound." He believes that situation could be improved with further research, however. Working with Leslie Kay, a scientist who experimented with underwater sonar for the British navy during the Cold War, Kish helped develop a product called the K-Sonar, a small device that attaches to a blind person's cane and emits ultrasonic pulses that are then digitally transmitted to the user through earphones.

In 2011 Kish was invited to give a presentation on human echolocation at the PopTech conference, an annual event founded by former Apple CEO John Sculley at which new ideas in science and technology are explored. That year Kish also submitted himself to MRI testing, the results of which suggested that he processes the echoes of his clicking with parts of the brain usually devoted to sight, rather than hearing. "I am enthusiastically hopeful that [the test results] will point the way toward a better and more realistic and accurate understanding of sensory processing and imaging, with a more respectful perspective on nonvisual processing," he told Ed Yong for *Discover* magazine's *Not Exactly Rocket Science* blog (25 May 2011).

## PERSONAL LIFE

Kish is a deeply spiritual person who says he is happiest when surrounded by nature. He owned a small cabin tucked away in California's Angeles National Forest until 2007, when it burned down due to a faulty wood-burning stove. Despite the cabin's isolation, Kish was able to summon help quickly, preventing the blaze from spreading throughout the canyon.

A vegan, Kish made the decision to avoid all animal products several years ago, during a seven-day fast in the mountains. He told *Current Biography*, "I [realized] I would need to make a fundamental change to my body chemistry and to my relationship with the planet—to detach myself from all exploitive energy and take into my system only life energy, not the energy of death, decay, or despair." Despite his spiritual nature, he has been characterized by some of his friends as a "bridge-burner," and he has little patience for sighted people he feels are being patronizing. "I have felt beaten and pummeled by many things," he once wrote on his website, "misplaced kindness foremost among them." Kish told *Current Biography* that he hopes his work will help blind people achieve autonomy in a society that is not fully prepared to offer it. "Freedom must be claimed; it cannot be granted," he said.

## SUGGESTED READING

Bermudez, Caroline. "Bat Navigation Inspires Charity's Approach to Aiding the Blind." *Chronicle of Philanthropy* 6 Oct. 2011: 11. Print.

Engber, Daniel. "The Mystery of Sonar Boy." *Slate*. Slate Group, 1 Dec. 2006. Web. 14 Mar. 2012.

Finkel, Michael. "The Blind Man Who Taught Himself to See." *Men's Journal*. Men's Journal, 14 Mar. 2011. Web. 5 Feb. 2012.

Kremer, William. "Human Echolocation: Using Tongue-Clicks to Navigate the World." *BBC News Magazine*. BBC 12 Sept. 2012. Web. 13 Mar. 2013.

Lombrozo, Tania. "Be Like a Bat? Sound Can Show You the Way." *NPR: 13.7 Cosmos & Culture*. NPR 28 Jan. 2013. Web. 13 Mar. 2013.

Ramirez, Marc. "Eight-Year-Old Lewisville Boy Destined for Blindness Learns Some New Tricks." *Dallas Morning News*. Dallas Morning News, 19 June 2011. Web. 14 Mar. 2012.

Rosenblum, Lawrence. "Mountain Biking with the Blind." *Psychology Today*. Sussex Publishers, July 2009. Web. 14 Mar. 2012.

—*Mari Rich*

# Maria Klawe

**Born:** 1951
**Occupation:** Computer scientist and president of Harvey Mudd College

Maria Klawe is a mathematician and computer scientist, though she is best known for her administrative prowess as the president of Harvey Mudd College in Claremont, California. Since her hiring in 2006, Klawe has completely revamped the school's computer science department with the aim of attracting more students, particularly women, to the field.

Female graduates in computers and technology have become few and far between. Katie Hafner for the *New York Times* (3 Apr. 2012) reported that in 1985, 37 percent of the field's graduates were women. In 2005, that number had dwindled to 22 percent, while the percentage of women in related subjects rose. Even women who begin technology-related studies often drift to other subjects such as biology, according to Klawe, who has spent her career as an educator waging what Ari Levy for *Bloomberg Businessweek* (22 Sept. 2011) called a "quiet revolution" to correct these disparities. With Klawe's guidance, the computer science program at Harvey Mudd has tripled its number of female graduates. Her strategies for attracting students of both genders to computer- and technology-related fields have been borrowed by other prestigious colleges, including Duke University, Northwestern University, the University of California at Berkeley, and Bucknell University.

As a mathematician and theoretical computer scientist, Klawe has made significant contributions to a number of fields, such as functional analysis, discrete mathematics, and human-computer interaction. She described her work in a Public Broadcasting Service (PBS) *NOVA* video (12 Mar. 2013) as "simple problems that have hard answers." Klawe has held leadership positions in a number of organizations, including the American Mathematical Society, the Computing Research Association (where she was the first woman to serve on the board), the Society for Industrial and Applied Mathematics, the Anita Borg Institute for Women and Technology, and the Canadian Mathematical Society, and is on the boards of Microsoft, Broadcom, and the nonprofit Math for America. Klawe has won a number of awards and holds honorary doctorates from five different universities.

Courtesy of Harvey Mudd College

## EARLY LIFE AND EDUCATION

Klawe was born in Toronto, Canada, in 1951. (She became a naturalized US citizen in 2009.) She is the second oldest of four sisters. Her mother, Kathleen Klawe, was an Irish-born professor of economics who taught at the University of Edinburgh (Scotland) and at the University of Alberta (Edmonton, Alberta, Canada) while Klawe was growing up. Klawe's father, Janusz Klawe, was a Polish-born cartographer and geographer. He was also a professor at the University of Alberta. When Klawe was four years old her family moved to Scotland, where she attended George Watson's Ladies College (now George Watson's College), a day school in Edinburgh. She recalls being extremely lonely at school as a young girl. She read constantly, and her affinity for building forts and having adventures was out of step with the interests of other girls her age. In fact, Klawe has said that she consciously pursued activities deemed "for boys," and she hated activities such as playing with dolls. Her father thought of her as a son. "I spent the first thirty years of my life trying to be more male than any male," she told Levy.

Klawe returned to Edmonton, Canada, with her family when she was twelve and enrolled in a coeducational school. Her eccentricities were not as well tolerated in Canada as they had been in Scotland, and she felt even more isolated. Boys teased her incessantly, and she was friendless for over a year. She even contemplated suicide at the time. But then a music teacher—Klawe played the trumpet, among other instruments—took her under her wing and introduced her to a group of girls in the school. Klawe still remembers the kindness of that teacher and tries to emulate her in her own role as an educator.

Klawe was naturally gifted academically. She graduated from Strathcona High School as valedictorian of her class in 1968. In her graduation speech, Klawe surprised teachers and administrators by criticizing the school for "spoon-feeding" its students, and she called on students to think for themselves and make their own decisions about the world. The speech was inspired by the burgeoning student protest movement, which would become an important part of Klawe's college life.

## COLLEGE YEARS AND PROTESTS

Klawe applied to a few different colleges but decided to attend the University of Alberta, where her parents were both professors, for financial reasons. Several days before classes began, Klawe switched her major from engineering to honors mathematics, losing a large scholarship in the process. She fell in love with high-level mathematics, joined student council, and became heavily involved in the student protest movement. One summer, she visited the campus of the University of California, Berkeley, and was arrested while protesting the shooting of James Rector, a Berkeley student who was killed by police during a student protest in May 1969. After the arrest, her parents issued an ultimatum, she told Stephen Ibaraki in an interview for *IT Manager Connection* (24 Oct. 2011): "Either I gave up politics, sex, and drugs, or I'd have to move out and stay away from the family when I turned eighteen because they were afraid I was going to destroy my two younger sisters' lives by getting them involved with politics, drugs, and sex."

In response, Klawe left home to live with her older sister, Anna. Her parents offered to support her financially; she accepted the support for two months and then never accepted any money from them again. She made a living teaching mathematics and art courses and worked as an art consultant for a small film company in Edmonton for a few years. Academically, she began enrolling in graduate classes during her junior year. She loved pure mathematics, but its esoteric nature did not fit with her passion for politics and social change. She wanted to change the world, and she felt that she could not accomplish this goal as a mathematician.

## TRAVELING ABROAD

Klawe decided to drop out of school midway through her junior year, and she and her boyfriend planned to spend the next year traveling throughout Europe and Asia. While the travelers were visiting Klawe's parents, who were spending the year in India for her father's work, war broke out between India and Pakistan. The conflict later became known as the Indo-Pakistani War of 1971. Animosity toward North Americans was high, and there was talk of a widespread evacuation. Klawe's parents begged her to stay at the house during the episode, and Klawe, who was hoping to mend her relationship with them, agreed.

After three months, tensions between Klawe and her father were running high. He was particularly upset that she was living with a man to whom she was not married. To remedy the situation, Klawe and her boyfriend decided to marry; they would later divorce. The marriage seemed to satisfy her father, and after the war ended, Klawe and her husband left her parents, on good terms, to travel. They traveled around India, Iran, and Afghanistan; before that, they had hitchhiked from Scotland to Venice. Klawe has stated that the months she spent in transit—living on little more than twenty-five cents a day—were some of the most important of her life. After a while, however, Klawe realized that she missed mathematics; she knew this was the case because she was reading mathematics texts for recreation and playing chess, which, as she told Ibaraki, she ordinarily did not enjoy.

## RETURN TO MATHEMATICS

Klawe wrote to the University of Alberta and asked if she could return to the school as a doctoral student. The school told her that she would have to finish her undergraduate degree, of which she had only completed two full years, before applying for her PhD. As a compromise, she could complete her undergraduate degree by taking graduate courses. If she did well in those classes, the school agreed to give her a degree in honors mathematics after her first year. Klawe accepted the offer. To her surprise—mathematics had always come easily to Klawe—the graduate courses were extremely difficult, and she had no choice but to put in hours of work to keep up. "[The experience] changed me from someone who, you know, had basically just sort of coasted through everything to someone who loved working really, really hard," she told Ibaraki. "And that was just a phenomenal change . . . I became a fundamentally different person."

Klawe received her bachelor's degree in honors mathematics in 1973 and enrolled in the school's graduate program. She worked with mathematician Tony Lau, who later oversaw her thesis, and solved several long-standing proofs in functional analysis during her third year. She spent the fourth year of her PhD writing her thesis at the University of British Columbia in Vancouver.

## STUDYING COMPUTER SCIENCE

After earning her doctorate in 1977, Klawe accepted a tenure-track position as an assistant mathematics professor at rural Oakland University in Michigan. She had applied to eighty-three jobs teaching pure mathematics in the United States and Canada. Oakland was the only tenure-track position available, and on the advice of Lau, she took it. Klawe was unhappy at the university, which she told Ibaraki "was in the middle of a field," and missed the culture of her hometown. During her time there, she realized that positions for computer science professors abounded, and she decided to work toward a second PhD in theoretical computer science.

Klawe began her studies at the University of Toronto in the fall of 1978. She showed such promise in her first few months that by the next summer, the university had hired her as an assistant professor. It was there that she met computer scientist Nick Pippenger, a guest speaker at the school. They were engaged four months after their meeting and married in 1980. That year, the couple moved to San Jose, California, where they took positions in the Almaden Research Center at IBM. Klawe worked there for eight years, helping to build one of the top three theoretical research centers in the world.

## GAME DESIGN AND THE UNIVERSITY OF BRITISH COLUMBIA

In 1988, Klawe and her family moved to Vancouver, where she took a position with the University of British Columbia. She remained with the school until 2002, serving in a variety of positions, including dean of science, vice president of student and academic services, and head of the Department of Computer Science. From 1997 to 2002, she held the IBM-NSERC Chair for Women in Science and Engineering.

In 1993, Klawe founded the collaborative Electronic Games for Education in Math and Science (EGEMS) project to design computer games for children in grades four through nine. Klawe recruited designers and writers as well as scientists and computer engineers to create games that develop problem-solving and critical-thinking skills as well as hard math skills. Klawe, who believes that video games and other interactive computer games are wonderful tools for learning, was concerned by a disturbing trend: video games had been deemed "for boys." "Even before students get into high school, they already have a sense of whether computer-type related careers are a male thing or a female thing," Klawe told Eve Lazarus for the Canadian *Globe and Mail* (10 Dec. 1998). "And the first experience for most children is playing games."

At the time, there were several games available that were marketed to girls. A few of them revolved around shopping; Klawe referred to these offerings derisively as "pink software" in

*Newsweek* (28 Oct. 1996). While she admitted that any time girls spend with the computer is valuable, she thought she could create a better game—designed to encourage players to look for patterns and test hypotheses—that would appeal to both boys and girls. The result was a sophisticated game called *Phoenix Quest*. With a story arc created by children's fiction writer Julie Lawson, the game was a far-reaching quest in which players interacted with computer-simulated characters and solved logic problems to unlock clues for their journey. Though popular with children, the game was ultimately deemed too fun for school and too educational for home. "It doesn't fit the way we market to the schools—it doesn't have thirty-six lessons, each of which is graded . . . it's a game," a frustrated Klawe told Lazarus.

## PRINCETON UNIVERSITY

In 2002, Klawe was recruited to become the dean of engineering and applied sciences at Princeton University. On one of her first days on the job, an angry male professor told her that he did not have to listen to her because she was not a real dean and had only gotten the job because she was a woman. But Klawe was more heartened by the number of female faculty members in the school of engineering—almost 10 percent, which she considered high. She was surprised when she learned that most were terribly unhappy. They felt that their work was not being taken seriously, and many were considering leaving. Klawe worked hard to address their problems and change the atmosphere. "It was actually just listening carefully, understanding what the issues were, trying to figure out what the background was, and then acting with the people who were in power to actually change them to change them," Klawe told Ira Flatow for National Public Radio's *Talk of the Nation* (26 Aug. 2005).

## HARVEY MUDD COLLEGE

During her tenure at Princeton, Klawe was regularly contacted regarding administrative opportunities at other institutions. She was thankful, though largely dismissive. "A lot of times it's not that they care about you, but they need a credible female candidate," she told Hafner. In 2005, however, an e-mail arrived from the small liberal arts school Harvey Mudd College. Klawe felt compelled to leave her Ivy League job for Claremont, California, where she became president of the school. Harvey Mudd, named after a mining engineer and founded in 1955, focuses on science, mathematics, and engineering. Klawe's first order of business was to revamp the school's introductory computer science course—a task that had begun a year prior to her hiring. The college requires all students to take a computer science course, but the retention rate—the

number of students who pursued other courses in computer science or pursued the subject as a major after taking the course—was poor. The number of female students in the field was abysmally low.

Prior to the revamp, the class focused on high-level programming and favored students who were already familiar with computer programs, mostly young men, and alienated those who were not—mostly young women. Under Klawe's guidance, the faculty decided to divide the class into two sections, denoted by the school's colors, for students with and without prior programming experience. The course's goals were then broadened to demonstrate to students that computer science "has intellectual depth and connections to other disciplines," Ran Libeskind-Hadas, the chairman of the department, told Hafner. Klawe also instated a program wherein the school pays for every female freshman to attend the Grace Hopper Celebration of Women in Computing conference, named after the pioneering female programmer.

## "THE MOST AMAZING SCHOOL YOU'VE NEVER HEARD OF"

Klawe's strategic planning at Princeton and Harvey Mudd includes students at every stage. Her approach to educational administration and the way she interacts with students are hugely influenced by the student protest movement of her youth. Harvey Mudd admits an annual incoming class of about two hundred students. Using flashcards, Klawe works to memorize all of their names before the first day of classes.

Interest in the school has grown since Klawe's hiring. Still, she is known as a Harvey Mudd evangelist. When traveling, she wears a T-shirt that reads, "The Most Amazing School You've Never Heard Of," with the school's name on the back. She takes seriously her role as an administrator and role model for women in mathematics and computer science. She is particularly candid about her own life experiences, which she describes as "turbulent" yet rewarding, and tries to use her story as a teaching tool. "I feel that one of the ways you can help other people is by really acknowledging difficulties you've been through in your life," she told Ibaraki, "because I think people look at people who have been successful . . . and they sort of go, 'Well, that person never really had any problems.'"

## PERSONAL LIFE

Klawe and Pippenger have two adult children, Sasha and Janek. A lifelong artist and painter, Klawe completes thirty to forty paintings a year. Until she was forty years old, she never told anyone about her paintings, as she was worried that other mathematicians would not take her seriously if they found out that she was serious about art. Klawe often paints during meetings;

she explained in the PBS *NOVA* video that the activity makes her a better listener. She also loves video games and can often be seen skateboarding around the Harvey Mudd campus.

## SUGGESTED READING

Flatow, Ira. "Women in Science, Climbing the Career Ladder." *Talk of the Nation*. National Public Radio, 26 Aug. 2005. Web. 16 Apr. 2013.

Hafner, Katie. "Giving Women the Access Code." *New York Times* 3 Apr. 2012: D1. Print.

Ibaraki, Stephen. "Dr. Maria Klawe: Pioneering World-Renowned Computer Scientist and Executive Leader, Shares Her Early Years." *IT Manager Connection*. Microsoft, 24 Oct. 2011. Web. 16 Apr. 2013.

Lazarus, Eve. "Getting Girls into the Game: New UBC Science Dean Hopes Her Software Will Boost Women's Numbers in Technology." *Globe and Mail* [Canada]. Globe and Mail, 10 Dec. 1998. Web. 13 Apr. 2013.

Levy, Ari. "A Campus Champion for Women in Computer Science." *Bloomberg Businessweek*. Bloomberg, 22 Sept. 2011. Web. 16 Apr. 2013.

—*Molly Hagan*

# Brian Kobilka

**Born:** May 30, 1955
**Occupation:** Professor and scientist

Known to friends and colleagues as much for his modest, self-effacing manner as for his passion for the structure of protein molecules, Stanford scientist Brian Kobilka won the 2012 Nobel Prize in Chemistry for his discoveries, along with Duke University biochemist Robert Lefkowitz, pertaining to G-protein-coupled receptors (GP-CRs), which are key facilitators of cellular communication. "I work on a family of proteins that are very important in communication within the body," Kobilka explained to Elizabeth Dunbar for Minnesota Public Radio (10 Oct. 2012). "These proteins respond to hormones and neurotransmitters, things that you might have heard of like adrenaline, dopamine, serotonin, so they're very important in almost every aspect of normal human physiology. As a result they're also important targets for drug development for a number of diseases."

Kobilka's success was more than two decades in coming, though—two decades during which he often seemed to be laboring in vain to unlock the secrets of our cells' portals to the outside world. Then, a series of breakthroughs beginning in 2007 and culminating in his Nobel win thrust the normally shy Kobilka into the spotlight. Childhood friend Tom Stoy told Terry Lehrke for the *Morrison County Record* in

Getty Images

Minnesota (10 Oct. 2012), "I think he's right up there with Charles Lindbergh"—another native of Kobilka's hometown of Little Falls, Minnesota—"How many people from the state of Minnesota have gotten a Nobel Prize?"

## EARLY LIFE AND EDUCATION

Brian Kent Kobilka was born on May 30, 1955, in the small rural community of Little Falls in central Minnesota, to Franklyn A. and Betty L. (Faust) Kobilka. He has one sister, Pamela Elconin. Franklyn Kobilka, who died in 2004, was the longtime owner of the Sanitary Bakery in downtown Little Falls, a business he inherited from his father and ran until he sold it in 1985. The bakery was a family operation where young Brian and Pamela helped their parents. Brian Kobilka would later credit the bakery business with helping him succeed in the business of science. "Running a lab involves getting a lot of people to work together for a common goal," Kobilka told Paul Walsh and Alejandra Matos for the Minneapolis *Star Tribune* (11 Oct. 2012). "I learned a lot from my father in that sense, even if it was a different operation." His sister told Walsh and Matos that her brother "never got in trouble and always tried to do the right thing," and that he had always been interested in science; as a child, "his favorite gift was a microscope."

Kobilka, a Catholic, went to St. Mary's Grade School in Little Falls and graduated from Little Falls High School in 1973 before going on to the University of Minnesota Duluth (UMD), where he studied biology and chemistry. He said UMD biology professor Conrad Firling was "very important in teaching me how to think about science, how to work and do things properly." He also met his future wife, Tong Sun Thian, in a

UMD developmental biology lab, where they constructed a tissue-culture hood (intended to prevent the contamination of samples) using scrap plastic sheeting from the Kobilka family bakery. "He always topped the curve," Tong Sun told Lizzie Buchan for the journal *Nature* (24 Aug. 2011). "But he was also so modest and quiet, you'd never know."

Another professor who influenced Kobilka at UMD was chemist Robert Carlson, who together with Firling helped Kobilka bring together both disciplines—biology and chemistry—in his studies. Carlson told Walsh and Matos that he and Firling "set up a collaboration so Brian could do chemistry and molecular biology research. It was the first time we set up that kind of interdisciplinary cooperation."

In 1977 Kobilka graduated from UMD with a BS in biology and chemistry. Despite his interest in research, he went on to medical school at Yale University, where he finished his MD in 1981, followed by a residency in internal medicine at Barnes Hospital at the Washington University School of Medicine in St. Louis, Missouri, which he finished in 1984. In medical school, according to Buchan, he "developed an interest in intensive-care medicine and the drugs used in life-or-death situations that act on GPCRs."

Wanting to do more research on G-protein-coupled receptors, Kobilka sought and obtained a postdoctoral fellowship with Robert Lefkowitz—the man with whom he would one day share a Nobel Prize—at Duke University in Durham, North Carolina. He stayed there until 1989, and the following year joined Stanford University's Faculty of Medicine and Molecular and Cellular Physiology, where he remains.

## CAREER

Scientists have long known that all manner of stimuli, from light to hormones, communicate with the cells of the human body without actually entering the cells. This communication was eventually understood to happen through protein structures embedded in cell membranes, called receptors, which act as intermediaries between external stimuli and the internal mechanisms of the cell. Most drug treatments do their job by acting on these receptors to produce a desired result, but the details of how the receptors actually work have been poorly understood, which is why many drugs are only partially effective or produce undesirable side effects. Understanding how the largest class of these receptors, GPCRs, operate has been Brian Kobilka's life's work.

In an August 24, 2011, profile of Kobilka for *Nature*, Lizzie Buchan wrote: "Nearly every function of the human body, from sight and smell to heart rate and neuronal communication, depends on G-protein-coupled receptors (GPCRs). Lodged in the fatty membranes that surround cells, they detect hormones, odours, chemical neurotransmitters and other signals outside the cell, and then convey their messages to the interior by activating one of several types of G protein. . . . Working out [GPCRs'] atomic structure will help researchers to understand how this central cellular-communication system works, and could help drug-makers to design more effective treatments."

Kobilka joined Lefkowitz at Duke in the 1980s because Lefkowitz was doing intriguing research on receptors for adrenaline, specifically the beta-2 adrenergic receptor, involved in triggering the body's fight-or-flight response—it is one of the receptors targeted, for example, by the class of drugs known as beta blockers. In his first major contribution to working out the GPCR puzzle, Kobilka played a lead role in helping Lefkowitz's team determine the genetic sequence of the beta-2 adrenergic receptor. In the process, the researchers discovered that the receptor protein snaked in and out of the cell membrane seven times—just like another ostensibly very different receptor, rhodopsin, which responds to light in the retina. Lefkowitz has called this a "eureka moment," because the researchers realized that these receptors were all part of a large family of proteins, now known as "seven transmembrane receptors," or G-protein-coupled receptors.

Because of the apparently great number and variety of GPCRs (there are now known to be nearly a thousand) and thus their high importance for understanding cellular communication, Kobilka's object was to determine the three-dimensional structure of the beta-2 adrenergic receptor, which would reveal more about how they work, and hopefully provide a model for discerning the structure of other GPCRs. The method for identifying the atomic structure of a molecule such as protein is x-ray crystallography, in which proteins are compressed together into a crystalline structure and hit with x-rays that diffract in a way that shows the arrangement of the protein's atoms. Wrote Buchan: "It was an audacious goal. To produce an intelligible x-ray diffraction pattern, Kobilka first needed to crystallize the receptor—a formidable process of packing millions of identical copies of protein so tightly that they form a solid that looks like a microscopic shard of glass."

Kobilka took up this task at Stanford. The task was daunting because crystallizing the receptor would involve dislodging it (millions of copies of it, in fact) from the cell membrane that allowed it to hold its shape. Driven by Kobilka's single-minded focus, his team at Stanford spent years becoming intimately familiar with the beta-2 adrenergic receptor, but with little success in crystallizing it. The expensive research and limited results began to raise eyebrows. A longtime colleague of Kobilka's, Henry Bourne, now a professor emeritus at the University of California, San Francisco, told Buchan, "People viewed what he was doing as dotting i's and crossing t's. And for a while it was sort of that. He wasn't getting published in fancy journals."

Meanwhile, Kobilka and his wife were raising two young children, and he had started working weekends as an emergency room doctor to help pay their mortgage. By the 2000s, his lab was starting to suffer financially as his funding started to dry up. "I don't think I ever considered giving up," Kobilka told Buchan. "I admit that it was frustrating at times, but I enjoyed the challenge and I wanted to know the answer." He said one of his friends described his attitude as "irrational optimism."

## A BREAKTHROUGH

In 2004, after nearly fifteen years, his team finally succeeded in growing tiny GPCR crystals, but they were too small to properly diffract the x-ray beams. The task of building sufficiently large crystals was incredibly complicated, but eventually—with fresh funding from the US National Institutes of Health—Kobilka's team was able to hold floppy segments of the receptors in place with another kind of protein, T4 lysozyme, and secure the entire crystalline structure with a fatty scaffolding. In 2007, Kobilka and his colleagues finally published a trio of papers detailing the structure of the beta-2 adrenergic receptor in the journals *Nature* and *Science*.

In an August 2008 interview with the website ScienceWatch, Kobilka characterized the significance of his achievement: "The adrenaline receptor is structurally similar to receptors for serotonin, dopamine, histamine, and many other hormones and neurotransmitters. The technology developed and applied to obtain the adrenaline receptor structure may be applied to obtain structures for other receptors. These structures may be useful for the development of more effective drugs for a broad spectrum of diseases."

Almost immediately, Kobilka moved to capitalize on his success. He had captured x-ray images of the receptors in their inactive states, but now he wanted to see them when they were activated—at the moment of sending their messages to the G proteins inside the cell. This required even larger, more complex crystals. After thousands of attempts at protein engineering under varying crystallization conditions, in 2011 Kobilka's team finally reached this goal as well, and he was able to publish three-dimensional images of the atomic structure of an activated beta-2 adrenergic receptor. In 2012, the Nobel committee called the image a "molecular masterpiece." Since 2011, similar techniques have revealed the structures of a handful of other GPCRs, and

the process is expected to continue, with exciting implications for drug development.

On October 10, 2012, the Royal Swedish Academy of Sciences announced that Lefkowitz and Kobilka were being awarded the Nobel Prize in Chemistry, and its accompanying $1.2 million prize, for their work with G-protein-coupled receptors. "Today, we know what this receptor looks like down to the finest molecular detail," thanks to Lefkowitz and Kobilka, said Nobel chemistry prize committee chairman Sven Lidin, quoted by Robert Lee Hotz for the *Wall Street Journal* (10 Oct. 2012). "Think of a disease, and there is probably a medicine there that affects the G-protein-coupled receptor. This work can provide the tools to make better drugs with fewer side effects."

In her 2011 profile, Buchan wrote: "When asked why he is so captivated by GPCRs, Kobilka struggles for an answer. 'I'm just inherently fascinated by these proteins. I don't know. I just want to know how they work,' he says. The only time he becomes animated is when describing the conformation of the receptor gripping its G protein. 'It's a fantastic structure,' he says, a grin across his face. 'It's just amazing. I really enjoy talking about it.'"

Bourne told Buchan, "Brian is a fascinating character. He's so driven, and enormously intense. But you don't get any feeling of—nor is there any—self-aggrandizing, pushiness, show-offiness. There is absolutely none of that. It's quite refreshing and rare."

Tong Sun Kobilka, a physician and researcher like her husband, works with Kobilka in his Stanford lab—"She was absolutely a part of the process as well," he told Lehrke for the *Morrison County Record* after learning of his Nobel win. The Kobilkas also cofounded, nearly a decade ago, a biotechnology company called ConfometRx, which works with pharmaceutical companies to help them develop drugs targeting specific GPCRs. The Kobilkas have two grown children, Jason and Megan.

## SUGGESTED READING

Buchen, Lizzie. "Cell Signalling Caught in the Act." *Nature*. Nature, 19 July 2011. Web. 19 Feb. 2013.

Chang, Kenneth. "Two American Scientists Win Nobel Prize in Chemistry." *New York Times*. New York Times Co., 10 Oct. 2012. Web. 19 Feb. 2013.

Hotz, Robert Lee. "Unlocking Cells Yields Prize." *Wall Street Journal*. Dow Jones, 10 Oct. 2012. Web. 19 Feb. 2013.

Lehrke, Terry. "Little Falls Native Wins Nobel Prize for Chemistry." *Morrison County Record* [MN]. ECM, 12 Oct. 2012. Web. 19 Feb. 2013.

Stimson, Daniel. "The Structure of an Important Drug Target Made Crystal Clear." *National Institute of Neurological Disorders and Stroke.*

National Institutes of Health, 5 Dec. 2007. Web. 19 Feb. 2013.

Walsh, Paul, and Alejandra Matos. "Little Falls Bakery Helps Deliver a Sweet Reward: Nobel Prize." [Minneapolis] *Star Tribune*. StarTribune, 11 Oct. 2012. Web. 19 Feb. 2013.

—*Adam Groff*

# Daphne Koller

**Born:** 1968
**Occupation:** Professor at Stanford and AI researcher

Hector Garcia-Molina

Born in Jerusalem, Daphne Koller arrived in the United States to pursue her PhD at Stanford University on Independence Day, 1989. Her family set an example of academic achievement; Koller is a third-generation PhD. She completed her degree and did postdoctoral work at University of California, Berkeley, before returning to Stanford, where she is the Rajeev Motwani Professor in the computer science department and an Oswald Villard University Fellow in Undergraduate Education; she also has a courtesy appointment in the pathology department. At Stanford, Koller has helped to develop Stanford's biomedical computation major and the CURIS summer internship program for undergraduates.

In a February 2004 article in *Technology Review*, Koller explained the appeal of working with computer programs that study gene regulation: "People are limited in their ability to integrate many different pieces of evidence. . . . Computers have no such limitation," Koller's research and the technology she developed have resulted in many applications in medicine, as well as other fields. Later that year, Koller received a MacArthur Fellowship, commonly called a "genius grant," which carries a grant of $500,000.

In 2012, Koller made news again as the cofounder of Coursera, a provider of free online college courses. The first three computer-science courses that Coursera offered drew a quarter of a million students from more than 170 nations. More than forty-four thousand students from around the world signed up for her online course Probabilistic Graphical Models.

## EARLY LIFE AND EDUCATION

Born to an English-professor mother and a botanist father, Koller found school to be less than challenging. When she was twelve, the family spent a year at Stanford for her father's work; she began programming on a Radio Shack personal computer that she and another student shared. When she and her family returned to Jerusalem, Koller explained to her father that she needed something more challenging than high school. Six months later, she began taking classes at Hebrew University in Jerusalem. There she studied mathematics and computer science, completing her undergraduate degree in 1985, when she was just seventeen. By that time, she was teaching a database class for the university. The following year she earned a master's degree from the same institution. After serving in the Israeli army, she headed to Stanford for doctoral work.

Koller dislikes the stereotype of the computer nerd. As she told John Markoff for the *New York Times* (3 May 2008), "I find it distressing that the view of the field is that you sit in your office by yourself surrounded by old pizza boxes and cans of Coke, hacking away at the bowels of the Windows operating system. . . . I spend most of my time thinking about things like how does a cell work or how do we understand images in the world around us?"

## STANFORD UNIVERSITY

After completing her doctoral degree at Stanford, Koller briefly did postdoctoral work at University of California, Berkeley, before returning to her alma mater to teach. She has convened a research group she playfully calls DAGS, Daphne's Amazing (or Approximate) Group of Students. These graduate and postgraduate students have gone on to faculty appointments at prestigious universities, as well as to positions at companies such as Facebook and Google. The group regularly meets for lunch and discussion.

Koller was responsible for instituting the major in biomedical computation in 2001. She also founded the Stanford computer science department's undergraduate summer internship program, known as CURIS. She is a member of the faculty at the Stanford Artificial Intelligence Lab (SAIL), whose stated goal is to turn data into usable information about projects that concern laypeople. Her three major areas of research include bioinformatics, probabilistic inference, and machine learning. She applies the two latter areas to better understand the behavior of genes.

One of her projects involved studying gene regulation, attempting to discover why some cells behave differently when all the cells have the same DNA. Why are the genes activated in some cells, but not in others? This study has implications for understanding how cancer develops. In 2003 the journal *Nature Genetics* published an article that Koller coauthored with Eran Segal and Nir Friedman, a Stanford alumnus who went to Hebrew University. The team developed a computational method that examined large collections of genetic measurements to determine their regulatory circuits. The circuits tell the cells to turn off or on the capacity to make protein. Applying the method, the genetics department at Stanford conducted experiments to characterize three genes that had been previously uncharacterized.

### NEW USES FOR AN OLD THEORY

The eighteenth-century minister Thomas Bayes could not have imagined that the theory he put forth would become a keystone of computer science and medicine. The Royal Society of London received Bayes's memoir on probability and causal relationships in 1763, two years after his death. Other mathematicians built on his work; Bayesian statistics interpret probability based on the confidence placed on a proposition. If a hypothesis is deemed true, then greater confidence in the probability exists. All probabilities do not need to be considered; nodes of the interconnecting networks of information can be dropped if they are not applicable.

Computer programs that rely on Bayesian statistics can work with large bodies of data to deduce probable networks of relationships. Koller used Bayesian algorithms to analyze gene regulation, which may assist in getting drugs approved more rapidly. Also, predicting a patient's probable response to a drug depends on a multiplicity of factors, including the strain of the disease and other drugs being taken. Bayesian probability allows for all of these variables to be considered in decision making. One of the values of Bayes's theorem is that it allows for estimates of probability to be updated as new information becomes available. Many fields have found Bayes's theorem to be useful in quantifying information. Applications have been made not only in medical research but also in natural language processing and weather forecasting.

### CHANGING TEACHING METHODOLOGY

Koller argued in the *New York Times* (5 Dec. 2011) for a change in the way students are educated. Claiming that educational practice has remained largely unchanged since the Renaissance, she wrote, "Presenting content in short, bite-size chunks, rather than monolithic hour-long lectures, is better suited to students' attention spans, and provides the flexibility to tailor instruction to individual students."

Koller calls the idea of students moving at their own pace through the material, with a faculty member on video, the "flipped classroom." She cites evidence showing that students improve in proficiency when this method is implemented. In addition to improving regular classroom performance, she concludes that "for the millions here and abroad who lack access to good, in-person education, online learning can open doors that would otherwise remain closed."

### FOUNDING COURSERA

Koller joined forces with Andrew Ng, her colleague at Stanford, to develop an advanced free online classroom delivery system that went live in 2012. Prior to offering the classes at large, Ng opened three computer classes; he reached more than 100,000 students, a total that would have required 250 years of teaching in the traditional classroom.

Coursera refers to itself as a social entrepreneurship company, partnering with the world's major universities. Their goal is nothing short of improving the lives of individuals, families, and communities through education. Professors from Stanford and more than thirty other institutions teach most of the classes, which are offered in every subject area. More than a million people worldwide have taken Coursera's classes.

Coursera classes focus on mastery learning, a concept developed by Benjamin S. Bloom in 1984. Mastery learning allows students to retain information rather than simply memorizing—and soon forgetting—facts and ideas. By taking the time they need to understand concepts, students can achieve mastery. Frequent evaluation helps to reinforce the learning.

Rather than relying on the traditional fifty-minute lecture, which has been shown to be a less than effective method of presenting material, courses are designed to include active learning practices. Attendance increases and grades improve when active learning techniques are incorporated.

Developed by Stanford undergraduate and graduate students, Coursera software differs from that used in most online class formats. For example, it pauses during presentations to allow students to answer questions; when students resume the video, they receive instant feedback. This allows students to track comprehension of the material in real time, rather than waiting for days or weeks to receive the results of exams or papers. It also allows students to ask questions about the material, both of other students and of the professor. The median response time for receiving an answer was less than half an hour, which in many cases betters the time in a traditional setting.

Some class content does not lend itself well to being graded by computer, so Coursera teaches peer evaluation techniques for courses in the humanities and social sciences. Students learn to use a rubric to grade essays or poems. At least two students grade each homework assignment. This process improves the chances of fair assessment, which does not always occur when a single teaching assistant is responsible for grading and returning a mass of essays in a timely manner.

## EVALUATING THE ONLINE EXPERIMENT

Online courses are not new; they are sufficiently established to have earned their own acronym, MOOC, which stands for "massive open online courses." Although objections to the efficacy of online learning have sometimes been raised, in 2010 the US Department of Education examined forty-five studies and found that MOOC is at least as successful as face-to-face classroom time. Used in combination with traditional classrooms, as is happening at some universities where Coursera students are enrolled, MOOCs offer an even stronger mode of teaching.

As Koller commented for CNN (23 Sept. 2012), discussing her interest in online learning, "it had become clear that changes in higher education were desperately necessary. A high-quality education is now a critical need for most people who aspire to a better life, while it continues to be out of reach for many." Her comment highlighted two populations that online classes hope to affect: those of low income, for whom college courses are prohibitively expensive, and nontraditional older students needing retraining.

In November 2012, the American Council on Education (ACE) decided to look into the question of whether MOOCS could be taken in fulfillment of a college degree. Their College Credit Recommendation Service (CREDIT) evaluates courses for credit worthiness, although individual institutions have the final say on each course. More than two thousand colleges and universities rely on this service. When Coursera became a client of ACE, Koller stated, "We believe strongly in the value of a college degree and, by offering these high-quality courses to students in a way that opens the potential of college credit, we hope to ease the path for students toward graduation."

As Molly Corbett Broad, ACE's president, wrote on the organization's website (13 Nov. 2012), "MOOCs are an intriguing, innovative new approach that holds much promise for engaging students across the country and around the world, as well as for helping colleges and universities broaden their reach. But as with any new approach, there are many questions about long-term potential, and ACE is eager to help answer them—questions such as whether MOOCs can help raise degree completion, deepen college curricula and increase learning productivity."

## MOOC GOES MAINSTREAM

With funding from the Bill and Melinda Gates Foundation and the cooperation of several key people and organizations, including Coursera, ACE began a research and evaluation process. Part of that process included creating a Presidential Innovation Lab, so that presidents of colleges and universities could meet to discuss the implications of this new learning environment, particularly as it relates to degree completion and educational achievement for low-income young adults.

Because a second objective for the Coursera program has been the collection of data in real time to discover which methods of teaching work and which do not, an unprecedented amount of data is now available for analyzing ways of improving teaching. This data was also made available to ACE as it addressed three major questions about MOOCs: Are low-income young adults and older adult learners being served? How satisfied with their learning experience are those enrolled in MOOCs? Can MOOCs lead to attaining certification or degrees?

In February 2013, ACE recommended that five Coursera MOOCs receive credit. Four of them were for college-level work, while one was a developmental math vocational course. The approved courses were from Duke University; the University of California, Irvine; and the University of Pennsylvania. Duke University's provost, Peter Lange, commented on a Coursera blog (7 Feb. 2013) highlighting this news, "We are excited by this opportunity to experiment with new ways of using our MOOC courses to extend our educational reach and provide credit for students who would not otherwise have access to our faculty. MOOCs, often in combination with the creativity of individual universities, have much potential to open and enrich the educational offerings available to students across the United States and the globe."

## ONGOING PROJECTS, PUBLICATIONS, AND AWARDS

Koller's current projects at Stanford focus on artificial intelligence. She looks at machine learning and probabilistic models to develop practical applications in fields such as medicine and for problems with computer vision. Koller has served as program cochair and general chair of the Neural Information Processing Systems (NIPS) conference, an annual event that draws more than nine hundred scientists in various disciplines. She is also on the NIPS Foundation board, which plans the conferences.

Koller is a prolific writer, with more than 180 publications in journals to her credit. With Friedman, she is coauthor *Probabilistic Graphical Models: Principles and Techniques*, published in 2009. Alan Bierman served as coauthor on an article entitled "Computer Game Playing: Beating Humanity at Its Own Game," published in the 2004 compilation *Computer Science: Reflections on the Field, Reflections from the Field*. That same year, Koller also collaborated with a number of others, including Coursera cofounder Ng on the article "Simultaneous Mapping and Localization with Sparse Extended Information Filters: Theory and Initial Results." It appeared in the collection *International Workshop on Algorithmic Foundations of Robotics*. In addition to her writing, Koller has also worked as an associate editor for both the *Journal of Artificial Intelligence Research* and *Machine Learning*.

Koller's many awards, in addition to the 2004 MacArthur Foundation Fellowship, include the IJCAI Computers and Thought Award in 2001 and the 2008 ACM/Infosys Foundation Award in Computing Sciences. In 2011, she was inducted into the National Academy of Engineering. Her teaching has also been recognized; she received the 2003 Cox Medal for excellence in fostering undergraduate research at Stanford and was named a Bass University Fellow in Undergraduate Education in 2004.

## PERSONAL LIFE

Koller lives in California with her husband, Dan Avida, who is involved in Silicon Valley projects, and their two daughters. Her hobbies include hiking, reading, and listening to music. The family enjoys taking vacations in exotic locales, where they engage in activities such as sailing, hiking, and scuba diving.

## SUGGESTED READING

Koller, Daphne. "Death Knell for the Lecture: Technology as a Passport to Personalized Education." *New York Times*. New York Times Co., 5 Dec. 2011. Web. 15 Feb. 2013.

Koller, Daphne. "Top College Courses, for Free?" *CNN.com*. Turner Broadcasting System, Inc., 23 Sept. 2012. Web. 15 Feb. 2013.

Levy, Ari. "Daphne Koller Brings the World into Stanford Classes." *Bloomberg Business Week*. Bloomberg LP, 1 Mar. 2012. Web. 14 Feb. 2013.

Markoff, John. "Pursuing the Next Level of Artificial Intelligence." *New York Times*. New York Times Co., 3 May 2008. Web. 18 Mar. 2013.

—*Judy Johnson*

# Dave Koz

**Born:** March 27, 1963
**Occupation:** Jazz saxophonist

For Dave Koz, playing the saxophone is more than just a hobby or even a profession; it is an extension of his person. From the moment he first picked up the instrument at a young age, Koz immediately felt as though he had found a missing part of himself. Not only did the saxophone provide him with a valuable outlet for creative expression, it also offered him a way to cope with his sexuality, an issue he struggled with as a young man.

The product of a musical family, Koz displayed a natural talent for performance from an early age. He played a variety of instruments before settling on the saxophone. After his penchant for playing jazz led him to pursue a career in the music industry, Koz found himself playing with numerous top-tier musicians. His solo debut in 1990 marked the beginning of a long and successful career that has included numerous albums and several Grammy Award nominations.

In addition to his work as a musician, Koz is also a dedicated philanthropist, serving as an ambassador of the Starlight Children's Foundation, an organization that works to provide care and support to seriously ill children and their families. As part of his commitment to the charity, Koz created his own brand of fine wine. Koz donates all of the profits from his wine sales to the Starlight Children's Foundation.

Whether recording albums, performing on the jazz-themed cruises he frequently headlines, or working on behalf of his favorite charities, Koz has led a multifaceted career that has been as beneficial to his fans as it has been to him.

## EARLY LIFE AND EDUCATION

Koz was born in Los Angeles, California, on March 27, 1963. He grew up in the San Fernando Valley as part of a musically oriented family. The Koz household was filled with the sounds of various styles of music, ranging from Frank Sinatra and Nat King Cole, to rock-and-roll hits from bands such as Genesis and Earth, Wind, and Fire. Koz developed a keen interest in music from an early age and was eager to perform— a desire that was fueled significantly by his brother, who was in a band that Koz desperately wanted to join.

Koz's earliest experiences playing musical instruments came as a result of his mother's insistence that he take up playing the piano. He disliked the instrument and began playing drums as a small act of defiance. When it became clear that neither the piano nor the drums were a good fit, Koz gave them up and began looking for another instrument.

Associated Press

Koz's search to find an instrument he could play in his brother's band led him to the saxophone. Although he was new to the instrument, Koz felt an immediate familiarity with it. In a 2004 interview with the *Advocate*'s Adam B. Vary, Koz described the saxophone's instantaneously transformative effect on his musicianship. "I didn't really feel like I had a lot of musical aptitude until I picked up the sax," Koz said. "[It was] really like finding another part of my body. It was an extension of me immediately."

For Koz, the impact of discovering the saxophone went far beyond just improving his musical ability. The instrument entered his life when he was thirteen years old and coping with many of the emotional and social challenges that young teenagers face. In addition, Koz was struggling to come to terms with his own sexuality and the realization that he was gay. The saxophone provided Koz with a crucial outlet for feelings he did not understand and could not otherwise express. "The saxophone became my best friend, my most trusted ally, because it enabled me to communicate feelings that I didn't have the words for," Koz writes on his website, "In many ways, it saved my life."

After graduating from Taft High School in the Woodland Hills area of Los Angeles, Koz went on to the University of California, Los Angeles (UCLA), where he earned a degree in mass communications. Almost immediately after finishing college, he made the decision to pursue a career as a professional musician and set about making his first serious foray into the music industry.

## LAUNCHING HIS CAREER

Just weeks after leaving UCLA in 1986, Koz kicked off his professional career by joining singer-songwriter and multi-instrumentalist Bobby Caldwell's band for a series of live performances. Following the tour with Caldwell, Koz found work as a session musician. As he continued to make a name for himself, he embarked on tours with other musicians, including keyboardist and smooth jazz composer Jeff Lorber and pop singer Richard Marx. The time Koz spent working with Marx played an important role in his development as a musician and prepared him for heading up his own band, as he told Will Harris of the *Virginian-Pilot* (1 Dec. 2012). "Richard was one of the most important experiences that I've ever had musically," Koz said. "I learned good things, and I learned things that, if I was leading a band, I wouldn't want to do as well."

Koz rounded out his résumé by earning a spot in the house band of the short-lived CBS late night program *The Pat Sajak Show*. Though the show was cancelled, it provided another useful learning experience for Koz that further readied him for the next stage of his professional career. "The chance to get to play with that amazing band was a tremendous learning experience and so much fun," Koz said in his interview with Harris. "And being on TV every night didn't hurt!"

## GOING SOLO

In 1990, Koz began his own solo recording career. After signing with Capitol Records, he began work on his first album, a self-titled debut album that featured "Emily," one of his best-known compositions. The success of *Dave Koz* introduced him to the smooth jazz community and helped set the tone for his future work. His sophomore album, *Lucky Man*, was released in 1993. The record solidified Koz's standing as one of the leading smooth jazz artists of his time.

After *Lucky Man*, Koz released *Off the Beaten Path* in 1996 and *The Dance* in 1999, before going on to produce one of his most ambitious and lauded albums to date, *Saxophonic*, in 2003. On that album, Koz created an entirely original smooth jazz sound infused with the flavors of electronica, R & B, hip-hop, funk, African folk, and other genres. Thanks to Koz's creative ingenuity, *Saxophonic* was a critical success, earning him two Grammy nominations.

Koz followed *Saxophonic* with *At the Movies*, a 2007 album on which Koz offered personal renditions of well-known Hollywood movie theme songs. Some of the tracks he covers on the album include "Over the Rainbow" from

*The Wizard of Oz* and "As Time Goes By" from *Casablanca*.

In 2010, Koz left Capitol Records and joined Concord Records. His 2010 album, *Hello Tomorrow*, was inspired in part by his decision to switch recording labels. Koz made the concept of change one of the album's major themes. He explained to Solitaire Miles in a *Chicago Music Guide* interview (6 Dec. 2011) that change came to play a significant role in *Hello Tomorrow* because of ongoing changes in his own personal life and changes he saw in the world around him. "The more people I talk to, the more I realize that there are millions of people with a similar story—the loss of a job in an economic downturn, the end of a marriage, the beginning of a new career, any circumstances that force them to take a step in a different direction or reinvent themselves in some way," Koz said. "They're reaching a certain point where they see a life ahead of them that they never expected. Many of us are at the beginning of a new era, and we'd be wise to embrace it."

In 2009, Koz received a star on the Hollywood Walk of Fame. He was delighted to have his name placed among those of many of the entertainment industry's greatest luminaries. Appropriately, his star was placed directly in front of the Capitol Records building, the very place where his career was born almost twenty years earlier.

## RADIO, TELEVISION, CONCERTS, JAZZ CRUISES, AND MORE

Over the course of his career, Koz has spent a considerable amount of time focusing on projects outside the recording studio and the regular touring circuit. In addition to hosting annual Christmas concerts and sponsoring regular jazz-themed cruises, Koz also made numerous television appearances and established himself as a notable radio personality.

Just as much a fan of smooth jazz as he was one of its most renowned practitioners, Koz decided to take on a larger role in promoting the genre by starting his own radio show, *The Dave Koz Radio Show*, in 1994. The show was a syndicated program blending talk and smooth jazz music that aired on radio stations in markets around the nation. After leaving that show, Koz began hosting *The Dave Koz Morning Show* on Los Angeles's 94.7 FM until 2007. For a time, he also hosted a third radio program on the Smooth Jazz Network.

Although *The Pat Sajak Show* did not pan out well for Koz, he has never shied away from the medium of television. Over the course of his career, he has appeared on numerous talk shows and television dramas, including *Desperate Housewives*, *Family Matters*, and *Melrose Place*. His most notable return to television since his stint on *The Pat Sajak Show* came when he

signed on to be the bandleader for celebrity chef Emeril Lagasse's *The Emeril Lagasse Show* for a short time in 2010.

Although he is Jewish, Koz has always had an affinity for Christmas and Christmas music. Beginning with 1997's *December Makes Me Feel This Way*, Koz has recorded numerous Christmas albums, including *A Smooth Jazz Christmas* and *Memories of a Winter's Night*, in between his regular releases. In 1997, Koz put on his first Christmas concert, which has since become an annual event. He was inspired to undertake his first holiday tour that year thanks to some urging from David Benoit, a fellow musician and close friend of Koz's. In the midst of his 2012 holiday tour, Koz told Michelle Humphrey of Examiner.com (11 Dec. 2012) about how the holiday tour concept got started and what it came to mean to them. "[Benoit] had the idea that we could do some shows around Christmas time for something positive," Koz said. "We have built this into a tradition for us."

Always looking for innovative ways to share his love of music with his fans, Koz began performing on jazz-themed cruises. In 2005, he began the Dave Koz & Friends Jazz Cruise. Since that time, the jazz cruise has become an annual tradition for Koz, during which he shares the cruise ship stage with many of his contemporaries and provides fans with an entertaining, jazz-filled getaway. In October 2006, Koz explained to Janine Coveney for the website JazzTimes why his jazz cruises have been such a success. "If you're a smooth jazz fan, you are able to see ten or twelve different artists over the course of a week," Koz said. "You can see them in their big show and then also see them in more intimate venues doing things you could never see elsewhere. You can eat with these people, you can travel to exotic locations with these people, and everybody on board—here's the key part—everybody on board shares the same passion as you."

## PERSONAL LIFE AND PHILANTHROPY

Koz overcame a major hurdle in his personal life in 2004 when he publicly announced in an interview with the *Advocate* that he is gay. Though he first realized he was gay as a child, he had a difficult time dealing with his feelings during his adolescence. He dated women throughout high school and college despite being fully aware of his real sexual orientation. As he grew older, however, he eventually learned to accept who he was and gradually became more comfortable with expressing his true feelings, due in no small part to his love affair with the saxophone. In time, he came out to his family, including his father—something he told Adam B. Vary in his interview with the *Advocate* that he wished he had done much sooner. "[I]t was the biggest nonissue, especially with my dad," Koz said. "If I could bottle the energy I spent for those years worrying about telling my dad—seeing his response, I felt like such a fool that I had wasted all that energy."

Coming out publicly was a more daunting prospect, however, and something that Koz was considerably less sure about doing. Part of the reason he was reluctant to reveal himself publicly was the potential impact on his career. An early manager, who reacted negatively to rumors about Koz's sexuality, exacerbated this worry. "I couldn't actually be who I really was, and I went along with it for a long time, until it was just too much to take, and I couldn't deal with it anymore," Koz said in his interview with Vary. "I got new management, and there was this great weight that was lifted because of that." Coming out publicly was ultimately a very important personal step forward for Koz that was both empowering for him and inspirational to the gay members of his fan base.

Inspiring fans with his personal bravery is far from the only way Koz has reached out to others. He has also been a longtime ambassador of the Starlight Children's Foundation, a charitable organization committed to making life better for kids affected by chronic or terminal illness or serious injury. As part of his association with the foundation, Koz visits hospitalized children across the country, sharing his music and distributing gifts. He has also worked to support the Starlight Children's Foundation by introducing his own line of fine wines, known as KOZ Wines. Koz donates all of the proceeds from his wine business to Starlight to help fund the organization's efforts.

## SUGGESTED READING

Barton, Chris. "Hollywood Star Walk: Dave Koz." *Los Angeles Times*. Los Angeles Times Media Group, 27 June 2010. Web. 10 Apr. 2013.

Coveney, Janine. "Come Sail with Me: Artists Take the Helm of Jazz Cruises." *JazzTimes*. JazzTimes, Oct. 2006. Web. 12 Apr. 2013.

Harris, Will. "Saxophonist Dave Koz Has a Few 'Secrets.'" *Virginian-Pilot*. Landmark Media Enterprises, 1 Dec. 2012. Web. 10 Apr. 2013.

Humphrey, Michelle. "Exclusive Interview with Saxophonist Dave Koz." *Examiner.com*. Clarity Digital Group, 11 Dec. 2012. Web. 10 Apr. 2013.

Miles, Solitaire. "Interview with Dave Koz." *Chicago Music Guide*. Chicago Music Guide, 6 Dec. 2011. Web. 10 Apr. 2013.

## SELECTED WORKS

*Dave Koz*, 1990; *Lucky Man*, 1993; *Off the Beaten Path*, 1996; *The Dance*, 1999; *Saxophonic*, 2003; *At the Movies*, 2007; *Hello Tomorrow*, 2010; *Live at the Blue Note Tokyo*, 2013

—Jack Lasky

# Nadine Labaki

**Born:** February 18, 1974
**Occupation:** Actor and film director

"Lebanon may be known more for its civil strife than its fledgling movie industry, but Nadine Labaki hopes to change all that," Jenny Barchfield wrote for the Associated Press (14 Sept. 2011). "The director-actress is out to transform the way the world sees her native country." Labaki is best known for the two feature films she has directed, *Caramel* (2007), which tells the interwoven stories of a group of Lebanese women who congregate at a local beauty salon, and *Where Do We Go Now?* (2011), which follows a group of women who will do anything to distract their men from fighting.

"It's a battlefield to make a film in Lebanon," Labaki told Lynda Gorov for the *Boston Globe* (20 May 2012). She explained that although most people assume that it is particularly difficult for her as a woman, that is not the case; male and female Lebanese filmmakers find the process equally challenging. "There's no film industry, no structure, no funding, no nothing," she said. Still, she believes the struggle is worthwhile. "Cinema is a very powerful nonviolent weapon to make change," she asserted to Gorov. "You start believing this could have been me. This could have been somebody I know. This could be a situation I was in. It does have an impact on your life when you start thinking, 'It's not a fiction. It's reality.'"

## EARLY LIFE

Nadine Labaki was born on February 18, 1974, in Baabdat, Lebanon, a tiny town not far from the capital city of Beirut. (Lebanon is a small country, about the size of Connecticut, located at the eastern end of the Mediterranean Sea, with Israel to the south and Syria to the east.) Her father's uncle was the local *hakawati*, or storyteller, a figure of great importance in Arab culture who is responsible for passing down family histories, cultural myths, and other tales. Labaki credits her great-uncle's influence for her own love of narrative. She also cites her father, Antoine, a telecommunications engineer, as a role model. He had purchased a camera with his first paycheck and continued to enjoy photography throughout his life; he especially loved to make home movies and could often be found wielding a camera, recording the youthful exploits of Labaki and her sister, Caroline.

Although he and Labaki's mother, Antoinette, a homemaker, tried to normalize family life as much as possible, the girls' childhoods were marked indelibly by Lebanon's seemingly interminable civil war. The country had undergone intermittent periods of political turmoil throughout its history, but in 1975 a civil war broke out that would last more than fifteen years. Neighboring

Associated Press

entities, including Israel, Syria, and the Palestine Liberation Organization (PLO), got involved and began to stage their own conflicts in the already beleaguered nation. Despite periods of relative calm, the strife continued until 1991, when most of the major militias (except Hezbollah) were dissolved and the nonsectarian Lebanese Armed Forces began to rebuild. More than 100,000 people had been killed during the conflict, and some 900,000 had been displaced from their homes, either temporarily or permanently.

Against that backdrop, Labaki came of age. "Because of the war, we used to spend a lot of time at home as kids—no school, nothing to do, bored—so I started developing a special relationship with my TV," she told Barchfield. Despite frequent power outages, she enjoyed watching such popular Western programs as *Dynasty*, *Dallas*, *Magnum P.I.*, and *Moonlighting*. She became entranced by the glamorous settings of the prime-time dramas and the fast-paced action of the detective shows. "Very soon, I understood that to be able to create these worlds that were very different from my reality was to become a filmmaker. Very early, everybody in my family knew this was the thing I wanted to do," she recalled to Barchfield. Some reporters have noted that Labaki's early years were also somewhat peripatetic because of the war; although she was not permanently displaced, as many Lebanese citizens were, she lived at various times in Canada, France, and Cyprus.

**THE DRIVE FOR A FILM CAREER**

Labaki chose to attend Saint Joseph University in Beirut, a city often called the Paris of the Middle East. Despite periodic wars and conflicts,

Lebanon's geographical location has made it a hub of culture and commerce in the Middle East, and Beirut has served as its epicenter.

Although Lebanon had no film industry to speak of, the university housed the Institute for Scenic and Audio-Visual Studies. Labaki immersed herself in her studies, and in 1997, she directed a well-regarded senior project, the thirteen-minute-long *11 Rue Pasteur*, which examines a small slice of street life as seen through the sight of a gun. In Paris the following year, it was named best short film at the Biennale of Arab Cinema at the Institut du Monde Arabe (IMA or Arab World Institute). In 1998, Labaki attended the Cours Florent, a private French academy of drama, where she trained as an actress.

Labaki subsequently embarked on a successful career as a director of commercials for clients such as Coca-Cola and music videos for such recording artists as Pascale Machaalani and Katia Harb. "That was the only way for me to learn," she told Ann Hornaday for the *Washington Post* (11 May 2012). "You know, there's no film industry in Lebanon. So when you dream of making films, the only way to learn when you come out of university is to work on music videos and commercials."

She became particularly well known for the music videos she made with Lebanese pop star Nancy Ajram, a multiplatinum-selling singer who is sometimes compared in stature to Western megastars such as Beyoncé. In their first video together, for the 2003 track "Akhasmak Ah," which translates to "I Will Upset You," Ajram portrays a seductive waitress working in a coffee shop. The video, tame by Western standards, so offended censors in the Egyptian government that an official decree banned its airing for a time.

Labaki and Ajram went on to make several other music videos together, including ones for the title track to Ajram's breakthrough album *Ya Salam* (2003), in which she plays a Marilyn Monroe–type figure with a troubled love life; the infectiously bubbly "Sehr Oyouno," in which she portrays a young girl falling in love at first sight with a handsome stranger; "Ah w Noss," the title track from Ajram's 2004 album; "Lawn Ouyounak," which features Ajram as a joyful bride; "Inta Eih," which tells the tale of a tragically wronged wife; and "Ya Tabtab," in which she comically plays a carnival entertainer.

**CARAMEL**

In 2004, thanks to the involvement of French producer Anne-Marie Toussaint, whom Labaki had met at a Beirut film festival the previous year, Labaki attended the Résidence du Festival de Cannes, an annual program in which a dozen young directors, out of a pool of more than one thousand candidates, are invited to work on their first or second feature films. There, Labaki penned the script for *Caramel* (*Sukkar Banat*). The film debuted in Cannes in May 2007 and went on to be shown at festivals in Canada, Denmark, Brazil, and the United Kingdom, among other countries. It enjoyed a limited release in the United States in early 2008.

In Labaki's native Lebanon, the film became a blockbuster hit. "I don't know one [Lebanese] person who doesn't travel with four or five DVDs of *Caramel* and they give it to all the people they know abroad," Labaki told Barchfield. "It has become a sort of ambassador for Lebanon."

The film, which was made for a modest $1.6 million and earned more than $14 million worldwide, takes its name from the Middle Eastern practice of removing unwanted hair on the face or body with a hot sugar mixture, which is applied to the skin and then ripped off. As many reviewers pointed out, the mixture is sweet to the taste but painful to the touch—a fitting representation of the bittersweet nature of life for the film's characters.

*Caramel* is the story of a group of women who work in or frequent a small Lebanese beauty parlor. Labaki, one of the only trained actors in the film, plays Layale, a young beautician engaged in an affair with a married man. A fellow beautician, Rima, is secretly gay, while their coworker Nisrine is worried that her fiancé will discover that she is not a virgin before their wedding. Their customers include Jamale, who is desperate to appear youthful, and Rose, a dressmaker who must care for her eccentric older sister.

"Together these characters embody various ages and phases and female troubles, all illustrating the position of women in a culture that is caught—in complicated, sometimes contradictory ways—between tradition and modernism," Alison Gillmor wrote for the *Winnipeg Free Press* (20 Mar. 2008). "This approach could easily become formulaic, but somehow never does, thanks to Labaki's deft, low-key filmmaking style and her palpable affection for her characters and for the city of Beirut. . . . *Caramel* is grounded in the casual rhythms of conversations in kitchens and bedrooms and in the natural, emotionally accessible work of a solid non-professional cast. These women talk—in French and Arabic, and sometimes a fluid mix of the two—expressing feelings of vanity, insecurity, sisterly solidarity and subversive humour." Gillmor's sentiments were widely echoed by other reviewers. Philip French, writing for the London *Observer* (17 May 2008), added, "It's good to see a movie from Lebanon in which people aren't dodging shells every couple of minutes."

*Caramel* was Lebanon's official submission for best foreign-language film at the Academy Awards, and it won several honors at the San Sebastian Film Festival, including the Youth Award, the Audience Award, and the Sebastiane Award. Labaki and her female cast mates also won the Black Pearl Award for best actress at the Abu Dhabi Film Festival. Also in 2007, Labaki was named the Variety Middle East Filmmaker of the Year.

## WHERE DO WE GO NOW?

After the success of *Caramel*, Labaki turned down several offers to make English-language films with larger budgets, choosing instead to film in Lebanon with a cast of predominately nonprofessional actors. Her second feature, *Where Do We Go Now?* (*Halla La Wayn?*), was written while she was pregnant with her first child. Referring to an incident in which Shiite militiamen from Hezbollah and other pro-Syrian groups entered Beirut and engaged in a series of violent clashes with Sunni Muslims, she explained in an interview for *Regal Cinema Art Film Guide* (13 Apr. 2012), "I found out that I was expecting a baby on May 7, 2008. On that day, Beirut once again slipped into war mode, with road blocks, the airport closed, fires and so on. Violence broke out all around." She continued, "People who had lived for years in the same building, who'd grown up together and attended the same schools, were suddenly fighting each other because they didn't belong to the same religious community. I said to myself, if I had a son, what would I do to prevent him from picking up a gun and going out into the street? How far would I go to stop my child from going to see what's happening outside and thinking he had to defend his building, his family or his beliefs? The idea for the film grew out of that."

Starring Labaki as the owner of a small café, *Where Do We Go Now?* takes place in an unspecified Middle Eastern village where Muslim and Christian women band together to keep the men of the village from fighting. They employ every tactic they can think of, including hiring a band of Ukrainian strippers to serve as a distraction and lacing the men's food with hashish. Many critics compared the plot to that of ancient Greek playwright Aristophanes's play *Lysistrata*, in which the women of Greece withhold sexual favors from their husbands and lovers in order to convince them to end their warfare.

Like *Caramel*, *Where Do We Go Now?* was a massive hit in Lebanon, and it garnered several international prizes, including the Audience Award at the San Sebastian Film Festival, the Audience Award at the Toronto International Film Festival, and best screenplay honors at the Stockholm Film Festival. American critics were warmly appreciative of the movie's message, although, like most foreign films, it played in the United States mainly at small art houses in limited runs. In a review for the *New York Times* (10 May 2012), Stephen Holden called it a "jolly, galumphing crowd-pleaser," and Barchfield wrote in a review for the Associated Press (19 May 2011) that it was "touching and laugh-out-loud funny in equal measures."

## OTHER WORK
In addition to acting in her own films, in 2005 Labaki starred in Philippe Aractingi's *Bosta*, a musical about a composer-choreographer who returns to his native Lebanon to organize a troupe of performers. In 2010, she played a reluctant bride in *Stray Bullet* and had a part in Italian director Ricky Tognazzi's *The Father and the Foreigner*. Labaki played Miriam in Laïla Marrakchi's comedic drama *Rock the Casbah* (2012).

Labaki has also acted on the stage. In 2012, when it debuted in Beirut, she starred in American playwright Neil LaBute's dark comedy *Reasons to Be Pretty*, which touches on the themes of aging, beauty, and romantic relationships.

## PERSONAL LIFE
While relatively unknown in the United States, Labaki is a major star in her native country. She is frequently featured in Middle Eastern entertainment and gossip magazines, and she is often included in lists of the most powerful Middle Eastern figures in the media. Journalists regularly comment on Labaki's sultry beauty, and she has been widely praised for her style and sense of fashion. Her sister, Caroline, is also deeply interested in fashion and has worked as a costume designer on Labaki's films.

Labaki is married to the composer Khaled Mouzannar, who wrote the music for both *Caramel* and *Where Do We Go Now?* They have one young son. The family divides its time between Beirut and Baabdat.

While she is devoted to her family and is an exceptionally hands-on parent, Labaki has no intention of giving up filmmaking or abandoning her mission of introducing the complexities and beauty of Lebanon to international audiences, who might otherwise see Lebanon only on the evening news. "I think for Lebanese women everywhere we still have a long way to go," she told Beverly Andrews for *Middle East* (1 Dec. 2007). "We are struggling between the images we see of women in the West, while still dealing with the weight of thousands of years of tradition and religion on our shoulders. It is a very difficult balance and I suppose I am very much like the characters you see in my film, caught between these two very different worlds and, of course, struggling to find a way to navigate between them."

## SUGGESTED READING
Gillmor, Alison. "Salon Setting Gets Lovely Makeover in Warm Film about Women." *Winnipeg Free Press*. Winnipeg Free Press, 20 Mar. 2008. Web. 8 May 2013.
Gorov, Lynda. "Shrewdly Naive Filmmaker Takes On War." *Boston Globe*. New York Times, 20 May 2012. Web. 8 May 2013.
Hornaday, Ann. "Labaki's Latest Film Hits Close to Home." *Washington Post*. Washington Post, 13 May 2012. Web. 8 May 2013.
Turan, Kenneth. "Cannes 2011: A Personal Project for Nadine Labaki." *Los Angeles Times*. Los Angeles Times, 19 May 2011. Web. 8 May 2013.
"Where Do We Go Now? Directed by Nadine Labaki." *Regal Cinema Art Film Guide* (Summer 2012): 4–5. Print.

## SELECTED WORKS
*Caramel*, 2007; *Stray Bullet*, 2010; *The Father and the Foreigner*, 2010; *Where Do We Go Now?*, 2011; *Rock the Casbah*, 2012

—*Mari Rich*

# Ray LaMontagne
**Born:** June 18, 1973
**Occupation:** Singer-songwriter

Ray LaMontagne burst onto the music scene following the release of his 2004 debut album, *Trouble*, which achieved instant cult status based largely on the strength of the hit title track. The singer-songwriter, whose soulful, raspy voice and raw delivery have evoked comparisons to Otis Redding and Van Morrison, followed his critically acclaimed gold disc with two additional albums, *Till the Sun Turns Black* (2006) and the Grammy-nominated *Gossip in the Grain* (2008). In 2010, LaMontagne released his most successful record to date, *God Willin' and the Creek Don't Rise*, which reached the number-one spot on the Billboard digital, rock, and folk charts. It also won LaMontagne his first Grammy Award, for best contemporary folk album.

Despite his success, LaMontagne prefers to remain private and does his best to shun the limelight. "Simply put, I have no interest in fame," he told Ashley B. Howard for *Los Angeles Confidential* (18 Aug. 2010). "My self worth is not tied to other people's opinions of me—I have a strong sense of self. Music for me is not a vehicle for fame; I just love music."

## EARLY LIFE AND EDUCATION
Raymond LaMontagne was born on June 18, 1973, in New Hampshire. He grew up in a turbulent household where his father, a musician, was abusive. "My father came home drunk and angry and frequently shared his misery with me," LaMontagne revealed in an interview for *The Sun* (3 Aug. 2007). When LaMontagne was

© Tim Mosenfelder/Corbis

five, his father abandoned the family. His mother raised him and his five half siblings, frequently relocating them to different states, including Tennessee, Minnesota, Utah, Nebraska, and New York. In addition to sleeping in cars and tents, they lived in a converted chicken coop and a concrete-block shell on a horse ranch.

Although LaMontagne was bitten by the music bug at an early age, he did not immediately pursue his passion. "Growing up, whenever I would show an interest in music I would be told my father was a musician. But then when I was not such a good kid, I would be told I was just like my father," he recalled to Jonathan Perry for the *Boston Globe* (14 Jan. 2005). "So I pushed music away completely because I didn't want to be like my father at all. I had to discover it on my own."

By his early teens, LaMontagne had settled in Utah. The self-described misfit found it difficult to fit in during high school, often getting into fights with fellow students and skipping classes. Despite these difficulties, LaMontagne committed himself to attending classes regularly during his senior year in order to graduate.

### FINDING MUSICAL INSPIRATION

After receiving his diploma, LaMontagne moved away from his family. He drifted around for several years before settling in Lewiston, Maine. LaMontagne initially worked as a carpenter before accepting a job in a shoe factory. His work routine consisted of getting up at four o'clock in the morning and working until nightfall. On his days off, LaMontagne, who struggled with periods of deep depression, indulged in self-destructive behavior. "Acid, mushrooms, drinking fairly heavily, lots and lots of pot and whatever else I

could get my hands on that was available," he told Eric R. Danton for the *Hartford Courant* (13 Jan. 2005).

LaMontagne's life took a fateful turn one morning, when he awoke to his alarm clock playing the song "Tree Top Flyer" by Stephen Stills. "It's like a light went off and everything became very clear to me," he explained to Andy Tennille in an interview for *American Songwriter* (1 Sept. 2006). "That period of my life was a dark, dark time, but I knew at that moment exactly what I wanted to do; I wanted to play music." Instead of going to work that day, LaMontagne drove to local record stores in search of the Stills album *Stills Alone* (1991), which contained the single. He eventually tracked it down at Enterprise Records, a vinyl-only record shop in Portland, Maine. However, it was his discovery of another Stills album, *Manassas* (1972), that inspired LaMontagne to quit his shoe-factory job to pursue a career as a singer-songwriter.

### PURSUING A CAREER IN MUSIC

While working part time as a carpenter's apprentice, LaMontagne immersed himself in music, listening to a wide range of artists, including the Band, the Grateful Dead, Bob Dylan, Neil Young, Joni Mitchell, Otis Redding, Ray Charles, Nina Simone, and Crosby, Stills, and Nash. He also bought an acoustic guitar, which he taught himself to play, and decided to put pen to paper. "I knew it was the next step," he told Richard Harrington for the *Washington Post* (8 Dec. 2006). "Writing songs became a passion and I just kept doing it, and then it got to the point where I thought, 'I've got fifteen, twenty, twenty-five songs, maybe I should try to play them for people and see what happens.'"

In 1999, LaMontagne entered a local recording studio and recorded a ten-song demo tape, titled *Raycharles Lamontagne*, which he sent to local music venues. His demo caught the attention of Mike Miclon, the owner of the Oddfellow Theater in Buckfield, Maine, who offered the painfully shy LaMontagne the opportunity to serve as the opening act for touring folk musicians John Gorka and Jonathan Edwards. LaMontagne, who also played gigs at small coffee shops as well as clubs in Vermont and New Hampshire, often performed in his work clothes and never made eye contact with the audience. Over the next four years, he released four more demos: *Acre of Land* (2001), *Green* (2002), *One Lonesome Saddle* (2002), and *Introducing Ray Lamontagne* (2003).

While performing at a local fan's company cookout in Portland, Maine, LaMontagne caught the attention of the state's governor, who forwarded *Introducing Ray Lamontagne* to Jamie Ceretta of Chrysalis Music Publishing. After their first face-to-face meeting, during which LaMontagne performed four songs on his acoustic guitar, Ceretta immediately signed him to a publishing deal. "Ray wasn't at all part of the current formula," Ceretta told Celeste Fremon for *LA Weekly* (31 Mar. 2005). "He was outside the grid. His voice was amazing. And the stuff he was writing was timeless."

## MAJOR-LABEL DEBUT

Ceretta decided that Chrysalis would produce LaMontagne's full-length debut album and recruited Ethan Johns, a Grammy Award–winning producer who had previously worked with Ryan Adams and the Kings of Leon, to produce a more refined demo that Chrysalis could subsequently shop to major record labels. On a shoestring budget, LaMontagne and Johns spent two weeks recording LaMontagne's debut album at the Sunset Sound and Sound Factory Recording Studios in Los Angeles, California. The majority of the songs from *Introducing Ray Lamontagne* were rerecorded live; LaMontagne handled both vocal and guitar duties, while Johns played drums, bass, and piano. They also drafted Jennifer Stills, Stephen Stills's daughter, to provide backing vocals on one of the album's tracks.

Once completed, LaMontagne's album sparked a bidding war between several labels that was eventually won by RCA Records. After signing LaMontagne to a recording deal, RCA released *Trouble* in September 2004. In a review for *Esquire* (1 Oct. 2004), Andy Langer wrote that the album "is populated by the same demons that made so many people evangelical over Jeff Buckley and Elliott Smith, only LaMontagne seems poised to touch so many more of us. . . . His voice will stop you dead in your tracks."

In 2005, LaMontagne hit the road to promote his debut album. While on tour, he made television appearances on NBC's *Late Night with Conan O'Brien* as well as CBS's *The Early Show* and *The Late Show with David Letterman*. LaMontagne also performed several tracks from his album on an episode of the PBS music series *Austin City Limits*. *Trouble* was a modest commercial success, achieving gold status in the United States. The title track was featured on the soundtrack of the big-screen comedy *A Lot Like Love* (2005). Later that year LaMontagne released an EP of his performance at the Bonnaroo Music Festival. He was also among the musicians who performed at a New York City charity fundraiser for Hurricane Katrina victims, held at Radio City Music Hall.

## TILL THE SUN TURNS BLACK

LaMontagne again collaborated with Johns for his sophomore effort, which the duo recorded at Allaire Studios in upstate New York and Three Crows Studios in North Hollywood, California. *Till the Sun Turns Black* was a clear departure from his acoustic debut album. "LaMontagne is one of those artists for whom gloominess is an avocation," Allison L. Stewart wrote for NPR (15 Sept. 2006). "*Till the Sun Turns Black* is in many ways darker and more mournful than its predecessor."

In addition to incorporating strings and horns in several of the album's eleven self-penned tracks, LaMontagne adopted a different approach to songwriting. "I began to realize that I didn't want to just have a collection of songs that didn't really connect with each other or relate to one another," he told Tennille. "I wanted to try to have a more complete piece, a record that was greater than each individual song on its own."

Released in August 2006, *Till the Sun Turns Black* sold twenty-eight thousand copies during its first week and climbed up the Billboard 200 chart, peaking at number twenty-eight. It went on to sell nearly three hundred thousand copies, according to Nielsen SoundScan.

## GOSSIP IN THE GRAIN

In 2008, LaMontagne followed his sophomore disc with *Gossip in the Grain*, which he recorded with Johns at Peter Gabriel's Real World Studios in England. The album became his highest-charting record in the United States to date, reaching the top spot on the Billboard top rock albums and independent albums charts while also peaking at number three on the Billboard 200 chart.

The first album to feature LaMontagne's live band, the Pariah Dogs, *Gossip in the Grain* was praised by critics for its more dynamic sound. "His latest release . . . suggests that LaMontagne . . . has either worked through some of his demons, or merely chosen to reveal a different side of himself," Colleen A. Ericson wrote for *Mlive* (16 Apr. 2009). "It's true that he still shows a proclivity for navel-gazing and ruminative atmospherics on tracks like 'Winter Birds' and the title song. But several tracks move to livelier tempos, and some songs reveal a playfulness not heard in his previous work."

Greg Kot was equally complimentary in a review for *Entertainment Weekly* (14 Oct. 2008): "On *Gossip in the Grain*, he slides effortlessly between horn-inflected R&B and hushed Nick Drake-like folk, with stops in between for string-band country, flute-flavored chamber pop, and harmonica-stoked blues." The album earned Grammy nominations for best engineered album and producer of the year.

## GOD WILLIN' AND THE CREEK DON'T RISE

For his fourth studio album, *God Willin' and the Creek Don't Rise*, LaMontagne made the surprising decision to serve as producer rather than collaborate with Johns. "There was . . . a real sense of freedom that I hadn't felt before because there wasn't another producer. It was just me," he told Ellen Sterling for the *Huffington Post* (2 Sept.

2010). LaMontagne spent two months writing songs for the album. *God Willin' and the Creek Don't Rise* was recorded over a five-day period at his home studio, located in an early nineteenth-century barn on his remote western Massachusetts property, which was formerly owned by writer Norman Mailer.

Critics hailed LaMontagne's producing debut. "It's one of the stand out releases of the year," Jim Farber wrote for the *New York Daily News* (17 Aug. 2010). "Normally, his strategy involves inverting the common soul mode. Instead of the genre's usual yelps, LaMontagne creates intensity through a dark, slow brood. While most of the new CD holds to that strategy, the disc stands out by stressing country lilts over ones built on blues and soul."

Reviewer Steve Morse echoed that sentiment. "New Hampshire native Ray LaMontagne returns with his fourth studio album—and it's an absolute gem," he wrote for the *Boston Globe* (16 Aug. 2010). "It exudes a homespun, rootsy intimacy as he shares his profound talent for rustic storytelling and a haunting voice that crosses the rasp of Gregg Allman and the spiritual intensity of Richard Manuel of The Band."

*God Willin' and the Creek Don't Rise* was released in August 2010 and debuted at number three on the Billboard 200. It claimed the top spot on the Billboard digital, rock, and folk charts, selling more than 345,000 copies. Later that year, LaMontagne embarked on a coheadlining tour with fellow singer-songwriter David Gray. In 2011, LaMontagne was awarded his first Grammy Award, in the category of best contemporary folk album.

LaMontagne lives on his farm in rural western Massachusetts with his wife and two children.

**SUGGESTED READING**

Danton, Eric R. "A Wake-Up Call from Stephen Stills." *Hartford Courant*. Tribune Company, 13 Jan. 2005. Web. 11 Aug. 2013.

Fremon, Celeste. "It's No Shame about Ray." *LA Weekly*. Voice Media Group, 31 Mar. 2005. Web. 11 Aug. 2013.

Harrington, Richard. "Ray LaMontagne, Finding His Place." *Washington Post*. Washington Post, 8 Dec. 2006. Web. 11 Aug. 2013.

Howard, Ashley B. "Ray LaMontagne Finds Beauty in Music." *Los Angeles Confidential*. Niche Media, 18 Aug. 2010. Web. 11 Aug. 2013.

Langer, Andy. "One Sweet-Sounding Season." *Esquire*. Hearst Magazines, 1 Oct. 2004. Web. 11 Aug. 2013.

Perry, Jonathan. "Saved by Music: Ray LaMontagne Digs Deep into His Rough Past for Inspiration." *Boston Globe*. New York Times, 14 Jan. 2005. Web. 11 Aug. 2013.

"Ray's Life Less Ordinary." *The Sun*. News UK, 3 Aug. 2007. Web. 11 Aug. 2013.

Tennille, Andy. "Ray LaMontagne: Centered By Solitude." *American Songwriter*. American Songwriter, 1 Sept. 2006. Web. 11 Aug. 2013.

**SELECTED WORKS**

*Trouble*, 2004; *Till the Sun Turns Black*, 2006; *Gossip in the Grain*, 2008; *God Willin' and the Creek Don't Rise*, 2010

—Bertha Muteba

# Denis Lavant

**Born:** June 17, 1961
**Occupation:** Actor

Denis Lavant is a French actor known for the physicality of his acting and his work with director Leos Carax. Their most recent collaboration is the 2012 film *Holy Motors*, in which Lavant plays eleven different characters, including a sewer-dwelling troll, an old woman in rags, and an ordinary, middle-aged man trying to communicate with his teenage daughter. The film garnered both boos and wild cheers at the Cannes Film Festival and was included in many critics' lists of the best films of the year. In her review for the *New York Times* (17 Oct. 2012), film critic Manohla Dargis called it "a dream of the movies that looks like a movie of dreams." Her statement refers to the film's metaphorical subject, the history of cinema, but the film's real subject is Lavant. Elbert Ventura for *Slate* (18 Oct. 2012) called *Holy Motors* "a gushing tribute to the incomparable Lavant," who appears in nearly every frame.

The loose plot centers on a man named Monsieur Oscar (Lavant), who spends his day traveling the Paris streets in a white stretch limousine, chauffeured by a woman named Céline, played by César Award–winning actress Édith Scob. Oscar travels to various "appointments," for which he undergoes one mesmerizing transformation after another. These in-between moments, in which the limousine grows to surreal proportions to allow him to get into "character" for each scene of the film, are where Lavant's talents as a mime, clown, and all-around physical artist really shine. He began his performance career in the circus, but his ability to convey such a depth of emotion through movement is reminiscent of the great silent film actors. "If Denis had said no [to the role]," Carax told Michael Phillips for the *Baltimore Sun* (7 Dec. 2012), "I would have offered the part to Lon Chaney or to [Charlie] Chaplin."

Associated Press

## EARLY LIFE AND CIRCUS TRAINING

Lavant was born to theater-loving parents, a pediatrician and a psychologist, in Neuilly-sur-Seine, a western suburb of Paris, on June 17, 1961. Growing up, he was fascinated with mimes and clowns, particularly renowned French mime Marcel Marceau. As a teenager, he studied juggling, miming, and clowning with a student of the legendary mime. At one time, Lavant considered becoming a dancer, but then he joined his high school's theater troupe. After graduation, he enrolled in the École Nationale Supérieure des Arts et Techniques du Théâtre (ENSATT), a prestigious conservatory of the dramatic arts. The conservatory was also known as the White Street School at the time, as it was located on rue Blanche (White Street) in Paris; the school relocated to Lyon in 1997. Only a year into his training, however, Lavant dropped out of school and joined a Belgian circus called les Baladins du Miroir. He traveled with the group for six months, performing as an acrobat.

Lavant returned to the conservatory to finish his studies in the early 1980s. In 1982, Robert Hossein, a French film actor and director, approached Lavant, asking him to appear in his film adaptation of the Victor Hugo novel Les Misérables. This was Lavant's introduction to film; he played the small role of Montparnasse. He also appeared in the television movie L'ombre sur la plage that year. Although he began appearing

in films early in his career, Lavant still considers himself first and foremost an actor of the stage. He has appeared in a number of plays, including well-received French productions of Anton Chekhov's The Seagull and William Shakespeare's Romeo and Juliet and Richard II.

## THREE CHARACTERS NAMED ALEX

Though Lavant met Carax around the time he returned to the conservatory, the two did not collaborate until Carax's first feature film, Boy Meets Girl, in 1984. At the time, both actor and director were only in their mid-twenties. Carax saw Lavant as an alter ego, a representation of himself in front of the camera while he stood behind it, and even named Lavant's character Alex after himself. Carax's real name is Alex Christophe Dupont; his stage name is an anagram of Alex and Oscar, the latter of which is a nod to the Academy Awards. Lavant would play a character named Alex in Carax's next two films as well, and in Holy Motors, he plays Oscar.

In Boy Meets Girl, Alex is a lonely filmmaker who wanders the streets of Paris at night. He encounters a depressed waitress named Mireille, played by Mireille Perrier. Characteristic of Carax's films, there is little more plot than that, but the film's artistry and the quiet power of its stars drew significant critical praise. Ventura quoted the influential film critic Serge Daney as writing that Boy Meets Girl is evidence "that the cinema will go on, will produce its Rimbauds in spite of everything." However, not everyone was equally impressed; Vincent Canby for the New York Times (11 Oct. 1985) wrote that the film lacks identity and draws too heavily from the new wave auteurs of the past. But, he added, "at its best, the film looks at life through Alex's cinema-blurred eyes."

## BAD BLOOD AND LOVERS ON THE BRIDGE

Lavant and Carax's next film together was Bad Blood, titled Mauvais sang in France, which premiered at the Berlin Film Festival in 1986. The film, which stars Lavant opposite a young Juliet Binoche, is a stark departure from the more impressionistic Boy Meets Girl—it is a thriller. Lavant plays Alex, a card player drawn into a plot to steal a special disease-curing serum, only to fall in love with the crime boss's mistress (Binoche). In what became the most famous scene of the film, Lavant runs down an empty city street to the sounds of David Bowie's 1983 song "Modern Love." The film garnered three Cèsar Awards, the French equivalent of the Academy Awards.

The third "Alex" film was the ill-fated Les amants du Pont-Neuf, or The Lovers on the Bridge (1991), once again starring Lavant and Binoche. The film takes place in Paris, though it was filmed in Montpelier, in the south of France. Carax demanded the construction of a replica of the Parisian bridge Pont Neuf, putting the project outrageously over budget; one report at the time called it the most expensive film in French cinema history. Rumors of the spending and delays in filming tainted the film's reception, and it was dismissed by critics and promptly buried by the mortified Carax, who went into self-imposed exile for nearly a decade.

Interestingly, in 1999, the year of Carax's first (though unsuccessful) comeback, American audiences discovered the film and were delighted by it. Ventura called *The Lovers on the Bridge*, which is set during the 1989 French bicentennial, a monumental celebration of Paris in the mold of American filmmaker Woody Allen's ode to New York, *Manhattan* (1979), and "one of the great city symphonies of our time." In the film, Lavant plays a vagrant named Alex who falls in love with an artist (Binoche) who is going blind. In a reference to his circus days, Lavant's character is also a fire-breather.

## BEAU TRAVAIL

During Carax's hiatus, Lavant worked on a number of projects with other directors. In 1999, he teamed up with French filmmaker Claire Denis to make the film *Beau Travail*. (The title translates to "Nice Work.") The film is an adaptation of American writer Herman Melville's unfinished nineteenth-century novella *Billy Budd*. The book describes sailors in the late 1700s, but Denis's version takes place among French Foreign Legion officers in Djibouti, a small country in northeastern Africa. "Denis Lavant is mesmerizing as Galoup, a forty-ish career soldier with a hard body, a hard face, and an attitude that he is 'unfit for life . . . unfit for civil life,'" Marke Andrews wrote for the *Vancouver Sun* (29 Jan. 2001). Lavant's character subtly spars with Grégoire Colin's character, Sentain, a new recruit who could be compared to Melville's Budd. However, the film is more of a compilation of snapshots—the isolation of the desert, the choreography of group calisthenics, the monotony of military life—than a plotted tale. *Beau Travail* won praise from critics around the world; it won a Cèsar Award and was named the best film of the year 2000 by New York's *Village Voice*. It also won top awards at several international film festivals.

The same year, Lavant starred in the experimental German film *Tuvalu*. In the film, Lavant and Russian actress Chulpan Khamatova play on a dreamscape reminiscent of turn-of-the-century German expressionist art. In 2004, Lavant worked with *Amélie* and *Delicatessen* director Jean-Pierre Jeunet on the film *Un long dimanche de fiançailles*, or *A Very Long Engagement*, starring Audrey Tautou. The film, which was generally well received, takes place during World War I.

## MISTER LONELY

In 2007, American indie director Harmony Korine enlisted Lavant to play a Charlie Chaplin impersonator in the film *Mister Lonely*. The film is about, among other things, a Michael Jackson impersonator who moves to a commune of fellow impersonators in the Scottish Highlands. Along with the Pope, Abraham Lincoln, and Madonna, he falls in with Marilyn Monroe (whose daughter is Shirley Temple) and her husband, Charlie Chaplin. After having seen Lavant in Carax's films, Korine wrote the part with him in mind. He later called Lavant his favorite actor, comparing him to Buster Keaton, Humphrey Bogart, and James Dean.

Lavant accepted the role happily, though the language barrier—Lavant does not speak any English—made filming difficult. Through an interpreter, he told Louise Catier for *France in London* (19 Mar. 2008) that he never wanted to learn the language because he believes it is "kind of commercial." He only had to speak in one scene of the film, and he opted to attend an intensive English class before filming it. Still, he enjoyed playing Chaplin because Chaplin's process was so similar to his own. "I love all my body to play," he told Catier. "For me, a role isn't just a face and a voice, and the great actors that I admire are those who use their body to give a shape to their character."

## HOLY MOTORS

*Holy Motors*, which premiered at the Cannes Film Festival in 2012, was a comeback on a grand scale for Carax and a major career milestone for Lavant. "I was rather apprehensive about taking on so many roles," Lavant told Kate Muir for the London *Times* (26 Sept. 2012). "The masks, the identities, the makeup, and staying sympathetic to each character, but the key is to stay relaxed and unruffled." Lavant's attitude seems humorous in light of his task—to embody eleven characters who represent the evolution of cinema. In one scene, he dons a full bodysuit for motion-capture dance. In another scene, he is serenaded by Australian pop singer Kylie Minogue in a tribute to the musical. As the flower-eating sewer troll Monsieur Merde—a character whom Lavant portrays in a short Carax film included in the anthology film *Tokyo!* (2008)—he kidnaps a model (Eva Mendes) in the middle of a fashion shoot.

The array of images and characters communicated through Lavant's full-body portrayal has baffled and delighted audiences. "Like cinema itself, Denis comes from the stage, the fairground, and the circus," Carax told Muir. "When I film his body on the move, I feel the same pleasure I imagine [English motion photographer Eadweard] Muybridge felt watching his galloping horse."

The film won a staggering number of awards and was named the number-one film of 2012 by the influential French film journal *Cahiers du cinéma*. It was included in over forty end-of-the-year top-ten lists across the globe. A number of film critics, journalists, and bloggers campaigned for a best actor nomination for Lavant at the Academy Awards, though to no avail. However, he was nominated for a Cèsar Award for his role in 2013.

### SUGGESTED READING

Andrews, Marke. "Foreign Legion Film Is Beefcake-o-Rama." Rev. of *Beau Travail*, dir. Claire Denis. *Vancouver Sun* 19 Jan. 2001: D7. Print.

Catier, Louise. "*Mister Lonely*: Interview with Denis Lavant." *France in London*. FranceinLondon.com, 19 Mar. 2008. Web. 17 Apr. 2013.

Dargis, Manohla. "It's Not about the Destination, But about the Dizzying Ride." Rev. of *Holy Motors*, dir. Leos Carax. *New York Times* 17 Oct. 2012: C1. Print.

Muir, Katie. "Denis Lavant, Star of the Arthouse Hit *Holy Motors*." Rev. of *Holy Motors*, dir. Leos Carax. *Times* [London]. Times Newspapers, 26 Sept. 2012. Web. 17 Apr. 2013.

Phillips, Michael. "A Man of Many Faces: Denis Lavant Is a Shape-Shifting Wonder in '*Holy Motors*.'" Rev. of *Holy Motors*, dir. Leos Carax. *Baltimore Sun* 7 Dec. 2012: 18T. Print.

—*Molly Hagan*

WireImage

# Jennifer Lawrence

**Born:** August 15, 1990
**Occupation:** Actor

Jennifer Lawrence is an Academy Award–winning actress, best known for her divergent roles in *Winter's Bone* (2010), *X-Men: First Class* (2011), *The Hunger Games* (2012), and *Silver Linings Playbook* (2012), for which she won an Oscar for best actress in 2013. Offscreen, the outspoken twenty-two-year-old has garnered an Internet following for her riotous non sequiturs, deadpan humor, and refreshing candidness about her own fame. Jim Windolf, who interviewed Lawrence for *Vanity Fair* (Feb. 2013) wrote that her charm is rare in Hollywood; she is a "a celebrity who sound[s] more like a human being than a well-coached witness."

Lawrence never saw herself as a professional actress until the first time she held a script in her hands at a cold read-through for a Reese's Peanut Butter Cup commercial when she was fourteen. She had been spotted on the street by a modeling scout but made the hasty (and wise) decision that she would only take acting gigs if she got an agent. According to Lawrence, her rise was a bit of a whirlwind. Joking about her lack of formal training, she told Melena Ryzik for the *New York Times* (9 Nov. 2012), "That's how I can go about life free as an idiot: because I have no idea what I'm doing." But Gary Ross, the director of *The Hunger Games*, characterized her talent differently: "She doesn't make it too complicated for herself," he said. "She doesn't have anything approaching a self-indulgent process. She's very relaxed, she's chatty, she's almost part of the crew in some ways because she's so confident in what she's doing. She doesn't have a lot to be nervous about."

Her attitude about acting might seem casual, but her work—and her choice of projects—is anything but. Of her breakout performance as gritty, squirrel-butchering teenager Ree Dolly, trying to hold her family together in *Winter's Bone*, *New York Times* (10 June 2010) reviewer A. O. Scott wrote, "In Ms. Lawrence's watchful, precise and quietly heroic performance, Ree is like a modern-day Antigone, making ethical demands that are at once entirely coherent and potentially fatal." For her role in the poignant comedy *Silver Linings Playbook*, Manohla Dargis, also for the *New York Times* (15 Nov. 2012), wrote that Lawrence's performance was "aching, tender [and] lovely."

Lawrence's ascension to global celebrity, particularly for her starring role in the *Hunger*

*Games* trilogy, has been quick, and she admits that the changes in her life are, at times, daunting. But her talent is formidable. As Windolf pointed out, the actress has excelled in drama (*Winter's Bone*) and comedy (*Silver Linings Playbook*) and has anchored two action franchises. As far as movies go, "[s]he's a triple threat," he wrote.

## EARLY LIFE

Jennifer Shrader Lawrence was born on August 15, 1990, in the Indian Hills neighborhood near Louisville, Kentucky, where her family owned a horse farm. Her mother, Karen, runs a summer camp called Camp Hi-Ho, and her father, Gary, used to own a concrete-contracting business. Her family says that Lawrence was the first girl born to her father's side of the family in fifty years. She has two older brothers, named Ben and Blaine, and her parents admit they raised her in a similar vein. "I didn't mind if she was girlie," Karen Lawrence told Josh Eells for *Rolling Stone* (12 Apr. 2012), "as long as she was tough." As a child, Lawrence was indeed tough—in preschool she was not allowed to play with the other girls because she was too rough—and incredibly energetic. Her family nickname was Nitro.

Lawrence attended Kammerer Middle School, where she was voted "Most Talkative." She played the oboe in the school band and played softball, basketball, and field hockey. She was also a cheerleader.

Lawrence made her stage debut at the age of nine in a church play based on the book of Jonah. Her performance as a prostitute from Nineveh stole the show. She continued to act in plays and musicals at her church and school, but her earliest ambition was to become a doctor. Indeed, Lawrence has been known to have moments of misgiving about her ultimate career choice. She told Windolf, "Not to sound rude, but it *is* stupid. Everybody's like, 'How can you remain with a level head?' And I'm like, 'Why would I ever get cocky? I'm not saving anybody's life. There are doctors who save lives and firemen who run into burning buildings. I'm making movies. It's stupid.'"

## DISCOVERY

When she was fourteen, Lawrence traveled with her mother to New York City for spring break. It was a trip that would change both of their lives. While watching break-dancers in Union Square Park, Lawrence was approached by a man with a camera who said that he was a modeling scout for H&M. He asked to take Lawrence's picture. "I didn't know that kind of thing was creepy," Lawrence told Stephen Heyman for the *New York Times T Magazine* (2 Feb. 2010). Lawrence gave the man her mother's phone number. The two were there to meet with a couple of modeling agents, only one of which also focused

on acting. Before she and her mother left Louisville, Lawrence had appeared at the city's Walden Theatre as Desdemona in *Othello*. The trip, as her mother put it to Josh Moss for *Louisville Magazine* (Dec. 2010), was for Lawrence to get the acting bug "out of her system." That endeavor was an unsuccessful one. Lawrence began getting calls from agents, and she begged her parents to let her move to New York to pursue her dream. The family finally agreed—at the urging of a number of agents who stressed Lawrence's unusually high talent—to let her go to the city for two months during the summer. They rented a Manhattan apartment, and the family members took turns staying with her. Her brother Blaine, who was nineteen at the time, was the first, but when Lawrence started booking gigs, her mother moved in.

Though her career was progressing, it was a difficult period for Lawrence and her family. She was taking classes online, and would eventually earn her GED, but she was lonely. "Our friends thought we were nuts. We thought we were nuts," Karen told Eells. The acting world seemed so foreign and impenetrable to the sports-obsessed Lawrences. "But her brothers told us, 'This is her baseball diamond. You've gotta let her play.'"

## EARLY CAREER

Lawrence landed bit parts in commercials and on a number of television shows including *Cold Case*, in which she played a victim's daughter, and *Monk*, where she played a school mascot. She appeared in the pilot for a show called *Not Another High School Show* in 2007. According to the Internet Movie Database (IMDB), she played "Frantic Girl," though she joked that her character might as well have been "Girl with the Boobs," for the push-up bra they made her wear. She also did a photo shoot for the retailer Abercrombie & Fitch. She was disappointed that the company did not use any of her shots in the final ad, and her father called to find out why. The photographer sent Lawrence the negatives as if they were an explanation in themselves. For the shoot, she had been asked to toss around a football on the beach with a number of other girls. The other models were posing; a red-faced Lawrence was snapped midair going for a tackle. The tomboyish Lawrence has a handful of similar anecdotes, but her plight is revealing of the roles that were available to her at the time. "It's very hard to find a role that's not stupid, especially for a young blond girl," Lawrence later told Vince Talotta for the *Toronto Star* (18 June 2010). "They're all supposed to be stupid and they're all following a man. It's all the same. The movies I've been in, I found them very interesting and I was drawn to them."

In 2007, Lawrence landed the part of the smart-alecky daughter on the TBS sitcom *The*

*Bill Engvall Show.* The fifteen-year-old Lawrence signed a seven-year contract, but the show lasted only three seasons. The job loss turned out to be a boon for the actress, though. She was already finding her way to meatier roles in independent films. In 2008, two films were released in which Lawrence was cast as a principal character. Neither film reached a wide audience, but Lawrence had the chance to cut her chops alongside some household names. The first was called *The Burning Plain*, which was written and directed by Guillermo Arriaga of *21 Grams* (2003) and *Babel* (2006) fame. Lawrence played a hardscrabble youth (her signature role) with Oscar-winning costars Kim Basinger and Charlize Theron. She also starred in Lori Petty's semiautobiographical film *The Poker House* (2008), about a girl coming of age in a brothel with a drug-addicted mother, played by Selma Blair.

Lawrence also appeared in the Jodie Foster film *The Beaver* (2011), starring Mel Gibson. As another woman who came of age on the screen, Foster told Eells: "One of the great things about Jen is she's been very picky. Usually 21-year-olds get a job and suddenly they're doing every bad movie—a romantic comedy, a musical, a cameo in a break-dancing movie. They don't know who they are yet, so they think they can be everything. But she's been very specific about what she's wanted to do."

## BREAKTHROUGH ROLE

Lawrence was almost passed over for star turn in *Winter's Bone*, a dark mystery based on a novel by Daniel Woodrell set in the Ozark Mountains. The casting directors thought she was too pretty. But Lawrence, who had read the book years before on the recommendation of her mother, was determined to win the part. After a red-eye flight from Los Angeles, she braved the New York City sleet to make it to the audition with a runny nose and unwashed hair. (They gave her the part, though they still painted her teeth yellow during shooting.) Written and directed by Debra Granik, the film is about a teenager named Ree Dolly who must hunt down her deadbeat father, who is accused of cooking methamphetamine, so that she and her family do not lose their house to the bail bondsman. To play Ree, Lawrence learned to chop wood, handle a gun, and, infamously, gut a squirrel. It was not her physical actions in the film that earned her so much praise, however, though they did garner a lot of attention. The steely yet maternal Ree complimented Lawrence's own nature. She was drawn to Ree, she told Moss, because Ree did not "take no for an answer."

*Winter's Bone* premiered at the Sundance Film Festival in 2010, where it won the prestigious Grand Jury Prize. Lawrence was nominated for a slew of awards for her role—including best actress at the Academy Awards, Golden Globes, Screen Actors Guild Awards, and the Independent Spirit Awards. At the age of twenty, she was one of the youngest Oscar nominees for best actress ever. It was an exciting, but also terrifying, moment for Lawrence. "It was so much, so fast," she told Ryzik.

Lawrence did not win that year, but she got her first taste of fame on a grand scale. She was doing more interviews, being considered for more roles, and being chased by more cameras.

## THE GIRL ON FIRE

After filming *Winter's Bone*, Lawrence began work on a film that could not have been more different from the dark indie. She was cast as the blue mutant superhero, Mystique, in *X-Men: First Class*. To prepare for the role, Lawrence spent nearly eight hours every day getting into makeup. On set, Lawrence befriended costars Zoë Kravitz, the daughter of singer and actor Lenny Kravitz, and Nicholas Hoult, whom she dated for nearly two years.

During the 2011 Oscar season, Lawrence was intensely focused on another book recommendation from her mother, a trilogy by Suzanne Collins called *The Hunger Games* (2008–10). In the books, protagonist Katniss Everdeen inhabits a dystopian society in which children are chosen to fight to the death in a nationally televised gladiatorial game. The popularity of the books rivaled that of the *Harry Potter* (1997–2007) and the *Twilight* series (2005–08). According to Eells, Lawrence told one reporter that she could not wait to get back to her hotel room to read. "They're adapting it," she said of the books. "They're gonna start auditioning and stuff."

Lawrence later said that she sympathized with Katniss who, after offering herself as "tribute" to fight in place of her younger sister, is submitted to a hasty makeover before she is presented to the world on primetime television. In *The Hunger Games*, the tributes are treated like contestants on a reality show, pressured to embody their carefully crafted personas for the viewers at home. During Oscar season, Lawrence had her own bevy of stylists and pressures of her own. Her instant fame could even be said to have spawned the same nickname Katniss was given when she was introduced to the world in a flaming gown: "the Girl on Fire."

Director Ross has said that after he saw Lawrence audition, he could not think of any other actress more suited to the part. When it was offered to her, Lawrence knew it was another watershed moment in her career. "It was a very bizarre time to be presented (with a part) that could make me arguably the most famous person my age, a year from now," she told Jay Stone for the Montreal *Gazette* (3 June 2011) of her immediate reaction to the news. "I remember sitting in a coffee shop in London, thinking, if I say yes to this job, next year, at this time, people will be here, taking pictures of me with their phones. And I couldn't find a bright side in it. But I didn't want to say no to a script that I loved because I was scared."

Lawrence spent months training for the role. In the books, Katniss is a skilled archer, and Lawrence learned how to handle a bow and arrow from a four-time Olympian. The film was shot in Asheville, North Carolina, where Lawrence celebrated her twenty-first birthday at a local bar.

*The Hunger Games* was released in March 2012 and grossed $155 million its opening weekend. Lawrence began filming the second film in the four-part series in 2012. It will be called *Catching Fire*, and it will be released in 2014. The third installation, *Mockingjay*, will be shot as two films.

## SILVER LININGS PLAYBOOK

Before her stint as Katniss Everdeen, Lawrence shot a film called *Silver Linings Playbook*, a dark romantic comedy directed by David O. Russell. Her costars included Bradley Cooper and Robert De Niro. Lawrence plays a sex addict and widow named Tiffany who falls for Cooper's Pat Solitano, a mentally unstable former teacher. Director Russell was drawn to Lawrence in her audition, which was partly conducted over Skype, but producer Harvey Weinstein was worried that she was too young for the part. Cooper, her love interest in the film, is thirty-seven. But Russell pushed for her. "There's an expressiveness in her eyes and in her face, that many stars have to work for, that's ageless," he told Ryzik.

The film opened to positive reviews, but most of the praise was reserved for Lawrence and Cooper, who were both nominated for Golden Globes and Academy Awards. Lawrence won both; Cooper won neither. Throughout the 2013 Oscar season, Lawrence was the favorite to win against actresses Naomi Watts and Jessica Chastain. Still, Lawrence looked surprised when they called her name. On her way to the stage, she famously tripped over her gown. When she reached the podium, the audience gave her a standing ovation. "You guys are just standing up because you feel bad that I fell," she joked. "That's really embarrassing."

Lawrence's next project, a Depression-era film called *Serena*, in which she stars with Cooper again, will be released in 2013. She lives alone, and divides her time between New York City and Los Angeles.

## SELECTED WORKS

*The Bill Engvall* Show, 2007–9; *The Burning Plain*, 2008; *The Poker House*, 2008; *Winter's Bone*, 2010; *Like Crazy*, 2011; *The Beaver*, 2011; *X-Men: First Class*, 2011; *Devil You Know*, 2012; *The Hunger Games*, 2012; *Silver Linings Playbook*, 2012; *House at the End of the Street*, 2012

## SUGGESTED READING

Dargis, Manohla. "The Calm before the Kablooey." *New York Times*. New York Times, 15 Nov. 2012. Web. 16 Mar. 2013.

Eells, Josh. "Jennifer Lawrence: America's Kick-Ass Sweetheart." *Rolling Stone*. Rolling Stone, 12 Apr. 2013. Web. 17 Mar. 2013.

Heyman, Stephen. "The Nifty Fifty: Jennifer Lawrence, Actress." *New York Times T Magazine*. New York Times, 2 Feb. 2010. Web. 16 Mar. 2013.

Moss, Josh. "Too Young for Methods: Louisville's Academy Award-Nominated Actress Jennifer Lawrence." *Louisville Magazine*. Louisville.com, 1 Dec. 2010. Web. 17 Mar. 2013.

Ryzik, Melena. "Shooting the Sass Easily as an Arrow." *New York Times*. New York Times, 9 Nov. 2012. Web. 17 Mar. 2013.

Scott, A. O. "Where Life Is Cold, and Kin Are Cruel." *New York Times*. New York Times, 10 June 2010. Web. 17 Mar. 2013.

Talotta, Vince. "Tough Roles an Easy Choice." *Toronto Star*. Toronto Star Newspapers, 18 June 2010. Web. 16 Mar. 2013.

Windolf, Jim. "Girl, Uninterruptible." *Vanity Fair*. Condé Nast, 1 Feb. 2013. Web. 15 Mar. 2013.

—*Molly Hagan*

# Tan Le

**Born:** May 20, 1977
**Occupation:** Technology entrepreneur

As a lawyer and community activist without any formal science or technology background, Tan Le seems an unlikely technology entrepreneur. But Le, who has cofounded three successful companies, has never allowed her circumstances to limit her potential. When Le was a small child, her family fled communist-controlled Vietnam, risking their lives for a chance to start over. This calculated risk paid off; the family settled in Australia, where Le's mother overcame poverty and the language barrier to become a successful businesswoman and eventually mayor of a suburb of Melbourne. Le herself excelled in school and was named Young Australian of the Year in 1998 in recognition of her volunteer work with the Vietnamese immigrant community.

Although she was admitted to the bar in 2000 and was hired by one of Australia's most established law firms, Le found her legal career to be unfulfilling. "There was a technology revolution going on, and I didn't want to just be a facilitator," she told David H. Freedman for

Getty Images

the magazine *Inc.* (1 Dec. 2008). "I wanted to be part of the creating." Entering the risky but rewarding world of technology start-ups, Le co-founded the communications company SASme before partnering with a number of scientists to found Emotiv, a neuroengineering company dedicated to facilitating brain-computer interaction. In 2009 the company introduced its EPOC neuroheadset, which allows users to interact with computer programs using only their thoughts and facial movements. Although the technology is currently limited to select gaming and research applications, Le believes that the EPOC headset will have a great impact on both technology and society as a whole. "We see it becoming a totally ubiquitous device, allowing you to interact in a seamless way with everything else in the world," she told Freedman.

## EARLY LIFE

Tan Le was born in southern Vietnam on May 20, 1977, the first of two daughters born to Hoan Le, a pharmacist, and Mai Ho. Her mother, the daughter of a staunch anticommunist, worked for years to convince her family to attempt to leave the country, the southern portion of which had fallen to communist North Vietnamese forces only two years before Le's birth. When Le was four, she left Vietnam with her mother, younger sister, grandmother, aunt, and uncle. Her father stayed behind in order to arrange transport for his siblings and was ultimately imprisoned for a time when he attempted to leave himself.

Leaving Vietnam was illegal at the time, so in order to avoid detection, Le's family and more than one hundred other refugees hid in the hold of a vessel disguised as a fishing boat. The voyage was a dangerous one, as the family risked capture by both Vietnamese officials and the pirates that targeted boats in the South China Sea. Determined to save her daughters in the event

that the ship was captured by pirates, Le's mother carried a bottle of poison, from which they would all drink if the boat was taken. "She didn't tell us about any of the horrible stuff, but she didn't have to," Le told Freedman. "You see the fear on people's faces, and you know." Despite the family's fears, the bottle of poison remained unopened. After five days of sailing, the boat ran out of fuel off the coast of Malaysia. A nearby oil tanker rescued the passengers and transported them to a refugee camp, where Le and her family remained for several months.

Given the opportunity to choose which country to immigrate to, Le's mother decided to move her family to Australia. They eventually settled in Footscray, Victoria, a suburb outside of Melbourne, where Le's mother worked a variety of jobs while she learned English. She went on to start a series of small businesses and eventually run for public office. Le has identified her mother as her greatest source of inspiration. "She worked on a farm picking vegetables just to make ends meet, then worked at a factory, and then got two university degrees and went on to become mayor of our city, which is pretty incredible," she explained in a video released in conjunction with Monash University's 2011 Distinguished Alumni Awards.

## LIFE IN AUSTRALIA

Le's early years in Australia were difficult at times, as her mother struggled to provide for her family and educate herself. "We were poor," Le explained in a December 2011 talk about her immigration experience at the TEDxWomen conference. "All the dollars were allocated and extra tuition in English and mathematics was budgeted for regardless of what missed out, which was usually new clothes; they were always secondhand." Footscray had a significant Vietnamese population, and the working-class town was made up of immigrants from all over. Still, Le has noted that she experienced some racism and occasionally encountered the small minority of Australians who believed that immigrants had no place in the country. Although the prejudice she faced was painful, Le resolved to overcome it. "Something stiffened inside me," she explained at TEDxWomen. "There was a gathering of resolve and a quiet voice saying, 'I will bypass you.'"

After completing primary school on an accelerated schedule, Le enrolled in Mac.Robertson Girls' High School, a selective school in Melbourne from which she graduated at sixteen. She went on to enroll in Monash University, where she studied commerce and law, and graduated with honors in 1998. Le credits her time at Monash with preparing her for her multifaceted career. "Those five years at Monash were those years in which I really had the opportunity to explore who I wanted to be and what I wanted to become," she said in the Distinguished Alumni Awards video. After graduating from Monash, Le pursued a career in law and in 2000 was admitted as a barrister and solicitor.

## YOUNG AUSTRALIAN OF THE YEAR
Throughout her teen years, Le was heavily involved in efforts to support and educate the Vietnamese immigrant community. She worked alongside her mother to provide Vietnamese immigrants with community services and, at eighteen, she was named president of the Vietnamese Community of Footscray Association (later known as the Australian Vietnamese Services Resource Centre), which provided job training and other resources. In 1998, Le's community work led her to be named Young Australian of the Year, an honor sponsored by the National Australia Day Council and intended to recognize Australians between the ages of sixteen and thirty who have made significant contributions to the country.

As Young Australian of the Year, Le was abruptly thrust into the spotlight. "Tan Le, anonymous Footscray resident, was now Tan Le, refugee and social activist," she explained in her TEDxWomen talk. Now in demand as a public speaker, she was invited to prestigious events and asked to speak before large groups. Le was overwhelmed by this sudden change, but her mother convinced her that she could handle it. "She reminded me that I was now the same age she had been when we boarded the boat. No had never been an option. 'Just do it,' she said, 'and don't be what you're not.' So I spoke out on youth unemployment and education and the neglect of the marginalized and the disenfranchised. And the more candidly I spoke, the more I was asked to speak."

In addition to speaking about the immigrant and refugee experience within Australia, Le was offered the opportunity to represent Australia abroad. She traveled to the United Kingdom on the invitation of the British High Commission and the Foreign and Commonwealth Office, and she also worked with the Australian Youth Ambassadors for Development program, a volunteer foreign aid initiative managed by the Australian Agency for International Development. While serving as goodwill ambassador to Asia, Le returned to Vietnam for the first time. There, she briefly reunited with her father, who had learned of his daughter's achievements from the newspaper.

## CAREER
Shortly after graduating from Monash, Le took a position with Freehills (now Herbert Smith Freehills), one of Australia's largest law firms. Although she had previously thought that she wanted to be a lawyer, she found that practicing law did not satisfy her creatively. "One of the things that motivates me in my life is to live a life that's meaningful," she told Jenny Brockie for the Australian television program *Insight* (8 Mar. 2011). "I wanted to be really involved in innovating, in creating new technologies."

Le soon left Freehills and, like her mother before her, turned her attention toward entrepreneurship. For her first venture, she partnered with Vietnamese-born technologists Nam Do, Duc Ngo, and Duc Tran to found SASme. While they originally intended to focus on integrating bar-code scanners with Short Message Service (SMS) text messaging in a project known as Scan and Send Me, the source of the company's name, the team abandoned that project in favor of developing technology that could handle large volumes of text messages.

The first major test of this technology came when SASme partnered with the soccer-oriented television program *The Footy Show* to carry out a phone poll in which votes were submitted via text message, becoming the first company in Australia to use SMS technology for this purpose. In subsequent years, SMS-based voting became a key part of television programs such as *American Idol*. SASme proved successful, and the company licensed its platform to a number of other companies and opened international offices in Vietnam and Poland. In addition to its SMS-related work, SASme also carried out research regarding chips used in communications systems as well as other technologies. Le and her partners sold SASme in 2003.

## EMOTIV
After leaving SASme, Le partnered with Do, Marconi Prize–winning scientist Allan Snyder, and chip designer Neil Weste to found the neuroengineering company Emotiv, which seeks to develop technology that allows the human brain to interface with computers. "Our vision is to introduce this whole new realm of human interaction into human-computer interaction so that computers can understand not only what you direct it to do, but it can also respond to your facial expressions and emotional experiences," she explained in a talk delivered at the TEDGlobal conference in July 2010. "And what better way to do this than by interpreting the signals naturally produced by our brain, our center for control and experience."

Although Le and her collaborators founded Emotiv in Australia, they ultimately decided to establish Emotiv's headquarters in the United States in order to benefit from the vast body of knowledge and the technological infrastructure available in California's Silicon Valley. "It's been very important for us to have moved to Silicon Valley, where there is a hub of activity and there's a system in place for launching new technologies and new companies," she told Brockie. "We have really had to go to the Valley for the expertise and the experience." Emotiv also operates facilities in Hong Kong, Mauritius, and Vietnam and remains connected to its Australian roots, maintaining a research and development office in Australia.

## NEUROHEADSETS

As president of Emotiv, Le supervised the development of the Emotiv EPOC neuroheadset, a headset with fourteen built-in sensors that detect both electrical signals within the brain and facial movements. When using specific computer programs designed by Emotiv and various developers, the headset allows users to play games and manipulate digital objects without physically touching any controls. Emotiv initially marketed this product toward video-game enthusiasts, emphasizing the EPOC's ability to facilitate a new kind of gaming experience.

Le and her partners faced a number of challenges when developing the EPOC, including negative publicity following a disastrous demo in 2008 in which the headset malfunctioned. In addition, some users experienced difficulties using the device even under controlled conditions, a fact that concerned Le. "We have an opportunity to revolutionize the way people interact with technology," she told Freedman. "But we won't get a chance to do that unless we provide the right experience in the beginning." Despite these setbacks, Emotiv continued to improve the technology and made the headset available for purchase in late 2009.

Emotiv followed the EPOC with an electroencephalogram (EEG) headset, which has many of the same applications as the EPOC. Unlike the EPOC, however, the EEG headset allows users to collect and access data from the brain that is not accessible to users of the earlier model. The EEG headset is intended for use by researchers and, as a portable and relatively inexpensive alternative to large and costly EEG equipment, has been a key tool in a number of medical studies.

While Emotiv has facilitated significant research by giving scientists easy access to data from the brain, Le wants to perform even more in-depth investigations into the brain's functions and capabilities. "We are really only scratching the surface of what is possible today," she noted at TEDGlobal. In 2011, she founded an affiliated bioinformatics company, Emotiv Lifesciences, which focuses on brain research. The company, for which Le serves as chief executive officer (CEO), provides researchers with crowdsourced data related to the brain's functions.

## RECOGNITION AND PERSONAL LIFE

Le has been recognized by a number of organizations for both her work in technology and her service to Australia's immigrant community. The magazine *Fast Company* named her one of the most influential women in technology in 2010, and *Forbes* included her in its 2011 list of names its readers should know. Her immigration story has been featured in exhibits on immigration in several Australian museums, and she has been awarded Monash University's distinguished alumni award and honored as a young global leader by the World Economic Forum. In 2012, she received the Advance Global Australian Award, an award that recognizes the work of Australians living abroad, for her contributions to information and communication technologies.

Le lives in San Francisco, California. Although her work with Emotiv and speaking engagements keep her busy, she has noted that balancing her work and her personal life is easier than some might think. "I do something that I'm totally passionate about," she explained to Brockie, "so it's not really about balancing or juggling. It's more about doing the things that I enjoy." In her free time, she enjoys playing piano. "It's very relaxing," she told Brockie. "That's my me time."

## SUGGESTED READING

Freedman, David H. "Reality Bites." *Inc.* Mansueto Ventures, 1 Dec. 2008. Web. 15 Feb. 2013.

Le, Tan. "Tan Le: A Headset That Reads Your Brainwaves." *TED.* TED Conferences, July 2010. Web. 15 Feb. 2013.

Le, Tan. "Tan Le: My Immigration Story." *TED.* TED Conferences, Dec. 2011. Web. 15 Feb. 2013.

Pollack, Neal. "Mind Control: How a £200 Headset Is Redefining Brain-Computing Interaction." *Wired.co.uk.* Condé Nast, 23 Nov. 2010. Web. 15 Feb. 2013.

"Three Women." *Insight.* Narr. Jenny Brockie. SBS, 8 Mar. 2011. Web. 15 Feb. 2013. Transcript.

—Joy Crelin

# Adam Levine

**Born:** March 18, 1979
**Occupation:** American singer-songwriter, front man of Maroon 5

Adam Levine had always wanted to be a musician since he was a young child, and he always had the confidence and star power to make his dream a reality. The singer-songwriter, with his devastatingly good looks and smooth, soulful vocals, was signed to his first record label while he was still in high school. "Ever since he was twelve, I'd say, pretty firmly, that he hasn't basically changed," Levine's bandmate Mickey Madden told Angus Batey for the *Guardian* (15 Nov.

FilmMagic

2007). "I would maybe say that fame has justified his personality."

After his first band dissolved, Levine continued to evolve as a musician, eventually regrouping with his original bandmates to form Maroon 5. Levine has a great ear for melody, and he and his bandmates penned all the songs for their debut album, *Songs about Jane*, which went on to top the charts and propel Maroon 5 to fame. Levine quickly rose to sex-symbol status, with one interviewer even calling him "a Lothario who's rarely out of the tabloids" (*Telegraph* 26 Aug. 2007). Although he once developed a reputation for his perceived arrogance, Levine's image has softened over the years. "Cocksure as he comes across onstage, Levine is, in fact, exceedingly polite and self-deprecating in person." Finn-Olaf Jones wrote in an article for *Architectural Digest* (Mar. 2012). "This is not a Top 40 flavor of the month who arrived in LA with a session tape and a prayer, but a homegrown talent who has had to hone his craft and earn every bit of his success."

## EARLY LIFE

Adam Noah Levine was born in Los Angeles on March 18, 1979, to Patsy Noah and Fred Levine. His father owned a men's fashion boutique clothing chain in Los Angeles, called M. Fredric, and the Levine family was very well off. When Levine was five years old, his parents divorced. Levine inherited his love of rock music from his mother. "My mom was insane about the Beatles. . . .We'd sit in her car—it was a little red BMW 320i—and we'd listen to *Abbey Road*, and she'd quiz me about which Beatle was singing a certain song," Levine recalled to Austin Scaggs in an interview for *Rolling Stone* (15 Apr. 2004). He attended his first concert with his father while he was in fifth grade, seeing the hair-metal band Warrant during their Dirty Rotten Filthy

Stinking Rich tour at the Santa Monica Civic Auditorium. Even as a child, Levine had a passion for music and dreamed of becoming a musician. "I used to have a karaoke machine when I was nine. I sat in front of a mirror with a microphone singing 'I Wanna Sex You Up,' making up my sexy moves," he told Scaggs (15 Apr. 2004).

Suffering from bad acne, Levine was a self-conscious and somewhat shy teenager, even as he pursued his musical ambitions. "He has a tremendous rapport with the audience, but it took him eight years to develop," his mom, Patsy Noah, explained in an interview with Christian Hoard for *Rolling Stone* (10 June 2004). "At his first performances, he performed with his back to the audience." Levine has cited Stevie Wonder, the Rolling Stones, U2, Prince, Talking Heads, Michael Jackson, Quincy Jones, and Herbie Hancock as early and major influences on his musical development.

## KARA'S FLOWERS

Levine attended the prestigious, private Brentwood School in Los Angeles for middle and high school, where he befriended classmates Mickey Madden, Jesse Carmichael, and Ryan Dusick. The four friends formed a band called Kara's Flowers in September 1995, with Levine as lead vocalist and guitarist, Madden as bass guitarist, Carmichael as keyboardist and guitarist, and Dusick as percussionist. Levine had his stage debut at age fifteen, playing a school dance. With Dusick, Levine increasingly began writing music for the group, and their collaboration produced the bulk of Kara's Flowers material. The alt-rock quartet steadily developed a hometown following, and eventually came to the attention of Reprise Records. Reprise signed the band while Levine was still only a senior in high school. Levine and his bandmates worked with producer Rob Cavallo to record Kara's Flowers first and only album, *The Fourth World*, which was released in the summer of 1997. The band filmed a music video for the album's lead single, "Soap Disco," which featured Levine and his bandmates decked out in matching suits—a 1990s garage-rock band channeling the early Beatles. The group even made a cameo performance on *Beverly Hills 90210*. Nevertheless, while Kara's Flowers received some critical praise, their album was a commercial failure. Reprise dropped Kara's Flowers from its label in late 1998, and the band split up in 1999.

Despite this setback, it was around this time that Levine heard the 1998 hit single "Are You That Somebody?" by Aaliyah and Timbaland, and he was blown away by the song's sophisticated blend of genres. "That is one of the most revolutionary-sounding songs ever recorded," Levine told Steve Appleford for the *Los Angeles Times* (20 Oct. 2010). "We heard that song, and we thought to ourselves, 'Whoa, there has never been anything like this before.'" In several interviews, Levine has acknowledged the profound impact that song has had on his evolution as a musician.

## FORMING MAROON 5

Following the breakup of Kara's Flowers, Levine attended Five Towns College, a liberal-arts college in Dix Hill, on Long Island, New York, with former bandmate Jesse Carmichael. The college is known for its business, communications, and music programs, and Levine's music was influenced by his exposure there to hip-hop, soul, and R & B. "That's when I started waking up to the whole hip hop, R&B thing. We had friends named Chaos and s——. It was *not* Brentwood High," Levine said in an interview with *MTV News* in 2002.

Taking inspiration from his time in New York and his new passion for R & B and soul, Levine returned to Los Angeles, where he regrouped with Madden, Carmichael, and Dusick. It was around this time that the songs that would form the group's next album, *Songs about Jane*, were beginning to be written, with most of the inspiration for the album coming from Levine's breakup with his ex-girlfriend Jane. In 2001, with a handful of demo songs recorded, the group signed with A&M Octone Records, and guitarist James Valentine joined the band to free Levine up as lead singer and front man—the band's producers at Octone had already recognized Levine's potential star power—and to allow Carmichael to transition to keyboards. With a new composition and fresh sound, the group renamed itself Maroon 5. "Maroon 5 are the rare rock band to appeal across modern rock, Top Forty, and adult-contemporary radio," James Diener, the executive who signed them to Octone, said in an interview with Christian Hoard for *Rolling Stone* (10 June 2004).

Levine explained the shared vision between his band and label to Craig Rosen for *Billboard* (4 June 2005), "We had the same vision, the same ideas about where we wanted to take everything, and we seemed to all be on par with each other. . . . They wanted to put us on the road, and we wanted to work our asses off for a long time. We were ready to go." Levine further explained to Rosen the importance Maroon 5 placed on establishing itself as a touring band before seeking radio and video success, "That was the goal behind the band in the first place. We had to establish ourselves as a band first and foremost, and all the other stuff would come into play later, like MTV and radio. The record was out a year before they even paid attention to us at all."

Maroon 5 completed recording *Songs about Jane* at Rumbo Recorders in Los Angeles. In 2002, Maroon 5 left Los Angeles to begin a grueling tour schedule that would stretch over the next few years. Levine recalled leaving Los Angeles in an interview with Finn-Olaf Jones for *Architectural Digest* (Mar. 2012): "I was sharing a house, renting a bedroom for $800 a month. I left to go on tour and had no money and had to give up my room." After a few years of touring for *Songs about Jane*, the album went multiplatinum and Levine returned to Los Angeles a chart-topping star. "I suddenly had a career," Levine told Jones, "but nowhere to live."

### SONGS ABOUT JANE

Maroon 5's debut album, initially released in June 2002, would not crack into the Billboard Top Ten until more than two years after its release. In an article for the *Guardian* (15 Nov. 2007), Angus Batey explains that *Songs about Jane* "was the ultimate 'sleeper' hit, turned into a huge success by relentless, unforgiving touring." For three and a half years, Levine and his bandmates embarked on a nearly nonstop tour. Their performance schedule was so demanding that Dusick, the band's drummer, developed tendinitis and was forced to ice his elbows, wrists, and shoulders after each show to keep up with touring demands.

Beginning in 2003, Maroon 5 began opening for John Mayer, the chart-topping singer-songwriter, whom Valentine had met while the two musicians were both students at Berklee College of Music in Boston, Massachusetts. Mayer recalled Maroon 5's rapidly growing fan base in an interview with Christian Hoard for *Rolling Stone* (10 June 2004), "I remember looking out and thinking, 'This band has the crowd in their seats.' It got to the point the house was almost full before they came on." Some seventeen months after *Songs about Jane* was released, the album's lead single "Harder to Breathe" began getting regular airplay on major radio stations in the United States, peaking at number 18 on the Billboard Hot 100 in late 2003. "Harder to Breathe" was followed shortly by the success of the single "This Love." *Songs about Jane* entered into the Billboard Top Ten in August 2004, about twenty-five months after its initial release. In 2005, Maroon 5 won the Grammy Award for best new artist.

The popularity of the music video for "This Love," featuring steamy scenes of Levine and his then-girlfriend Kelly McKee, and the follow-up success of the singles "She Will Be Loved" and "Sunday Morning" propelled the album to quadruple-platinum status. In an interview with Sylvia Patterson for the *Telegraph* (26 Aug. 2007), Levine explained that he had channeled his hero Prince for inspiration for the highly sexualized "This Love" music video. "An overt sexuality confuses people," he told Patterson. "The video was a very 'pop star' thing to do." Levine took well to his newfound fame, as he had the rock-star attitude and confidence to match. "Levine is a weird combination of mature reflection and fast-talking, youthful energy," Christian Hoard wrote of the up-and-coming star for *Rolling Stone* (10 June 2004). As the band's fame mounted, Levine increasingly became the center of attention in interviews and photo shoots—sometimes to the annoyance of his bandmates.

## ON FAME

"Adam is particularly suited for this type of life," Valentine explained to Sylvia Patterson for the *Telegraph* (26 Aug. 2007). "He acted like Adam living in 2007 back in 2000 when I met him. He always had the strut, the confidence, and the ego. He always felt entitled to this sort of success. The sex-symbol thing, that's gone from hilarious to . . . kind of annoying. There's a weird concern where, I think, 'What do our contributions matter if it's about this other thing?'" As Levine's bandmates grappled with their fame and the changing dynamics among the group, Levine took to celebrity life like a duck to water. "I'm not one of those reluctant really successful people," Levine told Patterson. "My life-long dream fulfilled, how awful," he added sarcastically.

As Maroon 5's fame grew, Levine appeared with increasing frequency in tabloid magazines for his many Hollywood hookups, including singer Jessica Simpson, actress Lindsay Lohan, and lingerie model Anna Vyalitsyna. "I never struggled with the opposite sex, it always came naturally, but now it's been magnified tens of thousands of times," he gushed to Patterson for the *Telegraph* (26 Aug. 2007). Through the mid-2000s, interviewers increasingly described Levine "cocksure" or "arrogant." As Levine's rise to fame began to outpace that of his band, a number of magazines asked for interviews with only Levine—at the exclusion of his bandmates. In 2007, Levine turned down an offer from *Rolling Stone* to appear on the magazine's cover alone. After Levine had established a reputation for his arrogance, he began to soften his image. "The biggest thing I've realized is that image plays into everything. And that's true whether you're Ke$ha or Bob Dylan," he told Melissa Maerz in an interview for *Entertainment Weekly* (17 Feb. 2012).

### *IT WON'T BE SOON BEFORE LONG* AND *HANDS ALL OVER*

As Maroon 5 neared the end of touring for *Songs about Jane*, Dusick was often unable to play shows due to his wrist and shoulder injuries. In 2006, Dusick officially left the band. He was replaced by Matt Flynn, the former drummer for Gavin DeGraw. Soon after, Maroon 5 returned to the recording studio to complete their second album, *It Won't Be Soon Before Long*, which was released in May 2007. Within the first week of its release, the album sold more than 100,000 copies on iTunes alone, breaking an iTunes sales record. The album went double-platinum, propelled by the popularity of the top-charting single "Makes Me Wonder," which reached number 1 on Billboard's Hot 100. Nevertheless, the album proved to be less critically acclaimed and commercially successful than *Songs about Jane*.

Maroon 5's follow-up album, *Hands All Over*, was released in September 2010. The group's third album proved even less popular than *It Won't Be Soon Before Long*. Though the album would go on to sell more than one million copies in the years following its release, *Hands All Over* sold only 142,000 copies in its first week, compared to the first-week sales for *It Won't Be Soon*, which were nearly triple that amount. Mikael Wood for the *Los Angeles Times* (24 June 2012) described *Hands All Over* as the "album that temporarily stalled the ascent of this LA–based pop-rock group." Levine explained to Wood, "I don't think we knew what kind of record we were making. It was such a hodgepodge—all these disparate ideas and songs that didn't make any sense together." The group had travelled to Switzerland to work on the album with producer Robert Lange, who owns a lakeside studio near the Swiss Alps. "We were in this idyllic paradise, which is a horrible place to make a record," Levine told Wood. In 2010, during this lull in Levine's career and in Maroon 5's success, Levine was approached by NBC about joining a new talent-search reality show as a judge.

### JUDGING *THE VOICE*

In March 2011, Levine announced he would be joining NBC's reality singing show *The Voice*, which debuted the following month. Levine stated he had no previous interest in signing on to a reality singing competition, but that NBC approached him at the right time. "To be quite frank, I wasn't interested in being part of one," Levine told Ramin Setoodeh for the *Daily Beast* (7 Sept. 2012). "Timing is such an interesting thing. What seemed like a cool idea at one point in my life might have seemed like a joke at another." Despite his initial disinterest, Levine's participation on *The Voice* has helped to relaunch the singer's career and to rehabilitate his reputation. "Of the four artists on NBC's *The Voice*, he's probably benefited the most," Setoodeh wrote. "Once America got to know Maroon 5's frontman as a laidback jokester with a competitive streak, his singing career has been on fire."

Levine has said that being on *The Voice* has helped to give him a voice of his own, unfiltered by the impressions of his interviewers. "Singers don't get the chance to talk very often," he told Melissa Maerz for *Entertainment Weekly* (17 Feb. 2012). "I like that I'm not perceived as just a bimbo." Maerz seems to agree with Levine's assessment, writing, "On paper, Adam Levine is kind of hard to like: He's a cocky rock star who dates a lingerie model and lives in a bachelor pad with suede floors. But on TV"—as a coach on NBC's hit *The Voice*—the Maroon 5 singer is "funny, charming, and (dare we say it?) sweet." As Levine mentors the show's contestants, his fans have been able to see another, softer side of the singer. "I think it absolutely has helped our career." Levine said to Setoodeh (*Daily Beast* 7 Sept. 2012). "I think there's no doubt about that. Things were fine with the band. . . . But people discovered and rediscovered who we were and what we did and got to know me. I always felt like I was slightly misrepresented."

In June 2011, all the members of Maroon 5 appeared on *The Voice* to debut the band's latest single, "Moves like Jagger," which features vocals by Levine's *Voice* costar Christina Aguilera. The song would go on to top the charts in eighteen different countries and sell more than five million copies in the United States alone. "'Jagger' saved us," Levine acknowledged in his interview with Wood (*Los Angeles Times* 24 June 2012). "It totally revived the band." The group later re-released *Hands All Over* with the new single.

### OVEREXPOSED

In June 2012, Maroon 5 released the group's fourth album, *Overexposed*. The album demonstrates Maroon 5's evolving sound, as the group moves away from its earlier rock and soul influences to allow for more pop and hip hop influences. The band also opened itself up more to collaboration, working on the album with a number of giants in pop music, including producers Max Martin, Ryan Tedder, and Benny Blanco. "It's kind of like a reinvention," John Ivey, a program director at Los Angeles–based radio station KIIS-FM, said of the band's evolving sound in an interview with Wood for *the Los Angeles Times* (24 June 2012). "I think they reached a fork in the road, and they took the right path. But it doesn't feel like a sellout. They just contemporized their sound." The album's lead single, "Payphone," featuring rapper Wiz Khalifa, debuted on *The Voice*. The follow-up single, "One More Night" reached number 1 on the Billboard Hot 100 in late September. As Rob Sheffield wrote in his review of the album for *Rolling Stone* magazine (26 June 2012), "Maroon 5 go all the way pop with heavyweights like Max Martin and Benny Blanco. It's top-shelf radio sucrose." Sheffield adds, "It's their best yet."

An ardent yoga enthusiast, Levine lives in Hollywood Hills with his golden retriever, Frankie. His home, an "immaculately refurbished 1940s ranch-style dwelling" decorated with art by Jean-Michel Basquiat, Shepard Fairey, Andy Warhol, and others, was featured in the March 2012 issue of *Architectural Digest*.

### SUGGESTED READING

Batey, Angus. "The Band They Hate to Love." *Guardian*. Guardian News and Media, 15 Nov. 2007. Web. 10 Jan. 2013.

Hoard, Christian. "A Whiter Shade of Funk." *Rolling Stone* 10 June 2004: 43–44. Print.

Maerz, Melissa. "All the Right Moves." *Entertainment Weekly* 10 Feb. 2012: 40–43. Print.

Patterson, Sylvia. "Maroon 5: They Will Be Loved." *Telegraph*. Telegraph Media Group, 26 Aug. 2007. Web. 10 Jan. 2013.

Setoodeh, Ramin. "Adam Levine Dishes on *The Voice, American Horror Story*, and Getting Naked." *Daily Beast*. Newsweek/Daily Beast Company, 7 Sept. 2012. Web. 10 Jan. 2013.

—*Mary Woodbury*

# Jeremy Lin

**Born:** August 23, 1988
**Occupation:** Basketball player

On January 17, 2012, point guard Jeremy Lin scored twenty-eight points for the Erie Bay-Hawks of the National Basketball Association (NBA) Development League. Four weeks later he had become an international sensation as a member of the New York Knicks and was playing in the Rising Stars Challenge during the NBA's All-Star Weekend. During his first five games in the NBA, Lin scored more points than any rookie player had in over thirty-five years. At the peak of his remarkable run, Lin was at the center of a global craze known as "Linsanity," which reinvigorated the Knicks fan base and drew the attention of sports fans from all over the world. Lin's ethnic background served to augment the story of his astonishing debut; he is the first Taiwanese American player in league history. "It's a sport for white and black people," Lin stated to *San Francisco Chronicle* reporter Byran Chu, during his years as a college player for Harvard, "You don't get respect for being an Asian American basketball player in the US" (16 Dec. 2008). Speaking about his college recruitment experience, Lin added, "I think if I were a different race, I would've been treated differently."

Lin's debut in the NBA might not have materialized had Knicks rookie guard Iman Shumpert not suffered a sprained knee in late December 2011. The team claimed Lin off waivers following Shumpert's injury. Knicks head coach Mike D'Antoni had lined up Shumpert as a replacement for veteran point guard Baron Davis, who was experiencing complications in his recovery from an injured back. Despite the fact both Davis and his back up were injured, the Knicks had two other options at guard: Toney Douglas and Mike Bibby. The team nearly released Lin

ChinaFotoPress via Getty Images

among the best in the conference in scoring, rebounding, steals, blocked shots, and free throws. On December 6, 2009, the Harvard Crimson were defeated by the nationally ranked Connecticut Huskies, 79–73. Fans and basketball analysts nationwide took note of Lin's thirty-point performance. Lin graduated from Harvard in 2010, taking a bachelor's degree in economics. After graduation he played in the NBA Summer League, based in Las Vegas, Nevada. His play in the summer league was good enough to draw the attention of several NBA franchises.

## JOINING THE NBA

After finishing college Lin was not selected in the NBA draft. Nevertheless, in July 2010 Lin signed a two-year contract with the Golden State Warriors. Although he reportedly received higher offers to play for other NBA teams, Lin elected to sign a deal with the Warriors because they were his favorite team as a kid. Upon joining the Warriors, Lin became the first Taiwanese American in history to join an NBA roster and the first Asian American in the NBA in over sixty years. Even before playing in his first NBA game, Lin was a fan favorite among California's Asian American communities. As Lin's teammate David Lee told Anna Katherine Clemmons for ESPN, "I've never seen that kind of reception for a rookie. Jeremy has a cult following" (9. Mar. 2011). As a rookie Lin made occasional appearances for the Warriors, usually during the last minutes of regular season games. He also played games for the Warriors' development league affiliate, the Reno Bighorns. Lin appeared in twenty-nine NBA games during his first year in the league. At the end of the season, the Warriors placed him on waivers, making him available as a selection to any NBA team willing to acquire his contract.

Lin was selected off waivers by the Houston Rockets on December 12, 2011, but played in just two preseason games before being released on waivers again. He was claimed off waivers by the New York Knicks on December 24.

## LINSANITY

Ironically, Lin made his debut as a member of the New York Knicks in a game against the Golden State Warriors on December 29, 2012. By mid-January he was playing for the Bay-Hawks, the Knicks affiliate in the development league. On January 20, 2012, he scored twenty-eight points with the BayHawks against the Maine Red Claws, earning eleven rebounds and twelve assists. His performance in that game and a rash of injuries on the Knicks roster resulted in his return to the NBA in February. The Knicks' poor play in February 2012 made head coach D'Antoni more willing to take a shot on an upstart like Lin. "He got lucky," D'Antoni told Berman for the New York Post, "because we

to make room for another free agent shooting guard, J. R. Smith. D'Antoni later told New York Post reporter Marc Berman that without the rash of injuries, Lin would have likely never seen the floor in an NBA game. "He wouldn't have gotten the chance probably," he said. "I like to think if someone is true to his profession and works hard, he'll get his chance, but I don't think that it always works out that way" (12 Feb. 2012). Lin made his Knicks debut against the New Jersey Nets on February 14, 2012.

## EARLY LIFE AND EDUCATION

Jeremy Shu-How Lin was born on August 23, 1988, in Los Angeles, California, to Lin Gie-Ming and Shirley Lin, both dual citizens of Taiwan and the United States. Raised in a devout Catholic family in the San Francisco Bay area, Lin learned the sport of basketball at young age, when his father would play with him at the YMCA. "Religion is and has been a big part of my life," he told Rick Chandler for NBC Sports (9 Feb. 2012). He attended Palo Alto High School, where as a senior he helped his team win the California Interscholastic Federation Division II state championship. Lin's parents made sure that he focused as much on his education as his basketball. Following his senior year Lin had hopes of attending Stanford University or the University of California, Los Angeles. However, neither school expressed interest in Lin's basketball skills. Lin enrolled at Harvard in 2005.

During his sophomore year at Harvard, Lin played well enough to earn a spot on the All-Ivy League Second Team. He made the All-Ivy League First Team his junior year, after ranking were playing so bad. You have to have luck in this league and he got a bunch of luck" (12 Feb. 2012). Lin scored twenty-five points, earning five rebounds and seven assists in a Knicks victory over the New Jersey Nets on February 4. The following game he scored twenty-eight points in a win against the Utah Jazz. "I don't think anyone," Lin told reporters after the game, according to Howard Beck for the *New York Times*, "including myself, saw this coming" (8 Feb. 2012). On February 8, Lin scored twenty-eight points and earned ten assists in 107–93 win over the Washington Wizards.

While Lin's run of excellent play had begun to earn attention from basketball fans in New York, it was his performance in a February 10 Knicks victory over the Los Angeles Lakers that started what would become a phenomenon. Lin outscored Lakers superstar Kobe Bryant in the game, scoring a career-high thirty-eight points. Four days later, after being named Eastern Conference Player of the Week, Lin sank a buzzer-beating, game-winning three-point shot to secure a 90–97 Knicks win over the Toronto Raptors. Thus, "Linsanity" was born.

After the game Lin's teammate Jared Jeffries told the Associated Press, "He continues to impress every night. Every game he plays better, he does more and more to help us win. You can't ask any more of a kid coming into this situation" (14 Feb. 2012). Lin's play against the Raptors made him the first rookie in NBA history to score twenty points or more in his first five NBA starts. Lin earned thirteen assists in the following game against the Sacramento Kings, helping to earn the Knicks their seventh consecutive victory. Lin's rise to stardom was made complete by February 23, when Lebron James and the Miami Heat made Lin the focal point of their defensive scheme and, in doing so, caused him to make just one of eight shots from the floor. Lin later told Will Leitch for *GQ* that the experience was "flattering . . . and terrifying" (Nov. 2012). At the height of his notoriety during the 2011–12 season, basketball analysts throughout the nation began lobbying for Lin to make the Eastern Conference team in the NBA All-Star team. Instead he appeared in the league's Rising Star Challenge.

In November 2012 President Barack Obama used a basketball analogy to describe his campaign's preparation in the face of Republican Party challenger Mitt Romney. "We're the Miami Heat," Obama told Jodi Kantor for the *New York Times*, "and he's Jeremy Lin" (2 Sept. 2012). Although Obama put Lin on the losing side of his analogy, Lin was struck by the mention. He told Leitch, "It's weird that the president knows who I am."

In March 2012 Lin was forced to have surgery on a tear in his left knee, which put him out for the remainder of the regular season.

Nonetheless, his amazing play over twenty-six games with the Knicks helped to revitalize the franchise and earned worldwide media attention. During Lin's run of success, television audiences for NBA games in China increased nearly 40 percent. Lin also appeared on the cover of two consecutive issues of *Sports Illustrated*.

## ETHNICITY AND SUPERSTARDOM

Lin's rise to superstardom resulted in a debate about ethnic stereotypes and racial profiling among both the sports media and traditional news outlets. Boxer Floyd Mayweather caused controversy by remarking on Twitter, "Lin is a good player but all the hype is because he's Asian. Black players don't get the same praise" (13 Feb. 2012). The MSG Network, the television network that covers Knicks games, was criticized for showing a fan with a sign depicting Lin's image with a fortune cookie reading "The Knicks Good Fortune." ESPN fired a reporter who, in reporting a Knicks loss to the Charlotte Hornets on February 17, used a blatantly racist term in a headline that read "Chink in the Armor." ESPN removed the headline from its website within forty minutes of its publication. Lin reported that he regularly heard racist taunts and jeers from fans of opposing teams. Lin handled the debate surrounding his ethnicity with grace. During All-Star Weekend in late February 2012, when asked about whether his ethnicity played a role in how he was perceived by basketball fans and analysts Lin stated, "I think it has something to do with it," as quoted by Steve Aschburner for *NBA.com* (24 Feb. 2012). "But I think that's fine. It's something that I embrace, and it gives me a chip on my shoulder. I'm very proud to be Asian American." *Time* magazine named Lin one of the Top 100 Most Influential People in the World in April 2012. In June 2012 the NBA awarded him with the first annual Social Breakout Player of the Year Award, in recognition of his popularity on social media websites such as Twitter and Facebook.

## LATER CAREER

Lin became an unrestricted free agent at the end of the 2011–12 season. In the off-season he signed a contract with the Houston Rockets. Although he struggled as a starter, he scored thirty-eight points in a Rockets victory over the San Antonio Spurs on December 10, 2012. Lin returned to Madison Square, home of the Knicks, on December 17, 2012. Before Lin's return Knicks forward Steve Novak described the impact his 2011–12 season had on basketball fans. "He's one of those guys people will remember for his time here," he told Bertrand for the *New York Post* (17 Dec. 2012). "It wasn't a very long time, but it was special. He touched a lot of people who will be in the stands." Jeff Zillgitt for *USA Today* reported that twelve New

York–area Chinese and Taiwanese organizations bought tickets to see Lin's return performance, to which Lin responded, "The Asian community has exceeded all my expectations with their support. The craziness they have, the enthusiasm. I've seen it in full force here, other cities, and Asia. It's a lot of fun" (17 Dec. 2012).

## SUGGESTED READING

Beck, Howard. "From Ivy Halls to the Garden, Surprise Star Jolts the N.B.A." *New York Times* 8 Feb. 2012: A1. Print.

"Lin Dazzles with 30 Points But No. 13 UConn Hangs On, 79–73." *Harvard Men's Basketball.* Harvard U, 6 Dec. 2009. Web. 17 Dec. 2012.

Zillgitt, Jeff. "Jeremy Lin Seeks Closure in Return to New York." *USA Today Sports.* USA Today, 17 Dec. 2012. Web. 17 Dec. 2012.

—*Josh Pritchard*

Martin Roe/Barcroft Media/Landov

# Liu Bolin

**Born:** 1973
**Occupation:** Artist

Liu Bolin is a performance and visual artist who is known to the art world as the "Invisible Man." Using his own body as his medium, his work combines photography, painting, and performance; with the aid of several assistants, Liu, who lives in Beijing, paints his clothed body in such a way that it allows him to seem to disappear into different environments, ranging from the Great Wall of China to a supermarket shelf display. The paintings are uncanny in their level of detail, and it is difficult to spot Liu in the resulting photographs, but Liu's art encompasses the entire process of painting and disappearing. The whole event, during which Liu must remain completely still, can take as long as ten hours. "What Liu does may be a gimmick," Fred Bernstein wrote for the *New York Times Style Magazine* (17 May 2011), "but it's a gimmick taken to fascinating lengths, and one in which viewers can read all kinds of ideas about dislocation and anonymity."

Liu graduated with a master's degree in sculpture from a prestigious art academy in Beijing in 2001, but the impetus for his disappearing act came in November 2005, when the Chinese government demolished his art studio along with approximately one hundred others in Suojiacun, an artists' community in Beijing, ostensibly to make way for redevelopment related to the 2008 Summer Olympics. Artists from the community suspected that the city government was punishing them on ideological grounds. The demolition made Liu realize to what extent his environment—where he was born, where he lived, where he was educated—controlled his life. Liu's work is his way of illustrating the intangible and often disquieting relationship between society and the individual and of making the invisible visible. "My intention was not to disappear in the environment," he said in a 2011 press release for Galerie Paris Beijing, "but instead to let the environment take possession of me."

## EDUCATION AND INTRODUCTION TO CHINESE CONTEMPORARY ART

Liu Bolin was born in 1973 in China's coastal Shandong province. He attended the Shandong University of Arts in Jinan, where he studied realist painting and earned his BFA in 1995. Liu received his MFA in sculpture from the prestigious Central Academy of Fine Arts (CAFA) in Beijing in 2001. At CAFA he studied under Sui Jianguo, the former chair of the academy's department of sculpture and a famous contemporary artist. Sui, who is considered among the first generation of Chinese contemporary artists, was influenced by the waning years of the cult of Mao; his Mao-jacket sculptures explore his own complicated relationship to China's former leader. Sui trained in Socialist Realism—a didactic genre of art that originated in the Soviet Union—during China's bloody Cultural Revolution. As a child, Sui regarded Mao as a god, and he told Jesse Hamlin for the *San Francisco Chronicle* (16 Feb. 2005) of his work *Sleeping Mao*, which recalls iconic images of a sleeping Buddha, "I'm putting him to rest. This way, I can grow up."

The specter of China's Communist past in Sui's work—and also the work of Liu, who later became his assistant—is significant because it is indicative of the social and cultural upheaval in which Chinese artists continue to create. The government still exercises great control over contemporary artists, who look for ways to reconcile Chinese artistic traditions and Western influences. To what degree they succeed is a source of heated debate within the community. The Chinese artist and dissident Ai Weiwei argues that Chinese contemporary art must address contemporary Chinese issues such as unemployment, poverty, and homelessness. In an article for the *Guardian* published on September 10, 2012, Ai called many purportedly contemporary works from China (and specifically those in a show featuring the work of Chinese artists in London in 2012) "propaganda" that "casts no critical eye. It is like a restaurant in Chinatown that sells all the standard dishes, such as kung pao chicken and sweet and sour pork. People will eat it and say it is Chinese, but it is simply a consumerist offering, providing little in the way of a genuine experience of life in China today." Ai is not alone in drawing a distinction between Chinese art that is merely new and contemporary art. One former Suojiacun resident, a sculptor named Zhang Jianhua, told Mark Magnier for the *Los Angeles Times* (9 Dec. 2005), "Since Mao's day, art was supposed to serve the government. But contemporary art is critical of contemporary society and often seen as subversive."

Liu credits Sui with introducing him to contemporary art, and much of Liu's work does address contemporary Chinese issues. For example, in his 2006 piece *Laid Off*, Liu posed six unemployed workers—just a few of the 21 million workers who were laid off between 1998 and 2000 as China transitioned to a market economy—against the wall of the factory where they had worked for their entire lives. In the photograph, the viewer can see a Communist slogan written above their heads, a vestige of their once-guaranteed employment.

## DEMOLITION OF SUOJIACUN

After graduate school, Liu returned to Shandong to teach, and in 2005, he became Sui Jianguo's assistant in Beijing. He began his *Hiding in the City* series after the destruction of his art studio at the hands of the Chinese government that year. Liu was living in an artist's village called Suojiacun in northeastern Beijing. According to Liu, the government did not like the idea of artists congregating or living together and in June 2005 threatened to destroy the village of painters, sculptors, and photographers, claiming that it did not have proper permits. There was a public backlash, and government officials backed down, only to return several months later. (Engineered ownership disputes abound in China though there is officially no private property in the country.) In November 2005, with only twenty-four hours notice, Liu's studio loft and about one hundred others were destroyed.

The demolition of Suojiacun also occurred under the auspices of the city's rapid modernization before hosting the Summer Olympics in 2008. After its selection in 2001, Beijing spent over $40 billion renovating the entire city, often steamrolling over private homes to make way for luxury hotels and high-end retailers in anticipation of the crowds of Olympic athletes and spectators. But the ruins of Suojiacun were never put to any use. Peter Fimrite, a reporter for the *San Francisco Chronicle* (8 Aug. 2008) who visited the site during the games, reported that an official-looking woman was escorting American journalists out of the village. He suggested that it was a source of embarrassment to city officials and a reminder of Beijing's outmoded past. "Dozens of sculptures sit inside one locked gate amid overgrown weeds," he observed of the remains of the artists' workshops. "Flying goddesses, dragons and nymph-like characters peek out of the brush."

## HIDING IN THE CITY

Liu's first piece in what would later become his *Hiding in the City* series features (or more accurately, obscures) Liu amid the rubble of his former home and studio in Suojiacun. He told Vourazeri that his inspiration for the series actually came after his graduation from CAFA. He felt alone on a personal level—"For a long time I had no family, no job and no love in my life," he said—and on a professional level, as he struggled to make ends meet as an artist. These existential feelings of displacement were physically realized several years later, when the destruction of his studio rendered him homeless. His situation was not unusual in China, where the state has been scrambling to modernize, sometimes without paying heed to the well-being of its citizens, but his mode of expression was strikingly unusual. *Hiding in the City*, which grew to include famous Chinese landmarks as well as nameless yet meaning-laden construction sites, tapped into a festering sense of displacement among the Chinese people and, as Charles Schultz wrote for *Whitehot* magazine (Apr. 2008), "crystallized a decisive moment of destruction in China's path towards cultural development."

The series was an immediate and international success for Liu, even in China, though he told Sam Gaskin for the online art magazine *Blouin Artinfo* (14 May 2013), "In China people take it as a game—where is the person in the piece? Overseas, people think I am an artist who dares to speak out about social phenomena." Liu has continued to add pieces to the series, including a series of pieces featuring the structures and signs erected for the 2008 Olympic Games in

Beijing. Around the same time, Liu began to seek environments outside of China for his series, including locations in Paris, Venice, and New York City. He even collaborated with a number of prominent fashion designers—including Jean Paul Gaultier, Angela Missoni, Alber Elbaz for Lanvin, and Maria Grazia Chiuri and Pier Paolo Piccioli for Valentino—each of whom he painted into their own famous designs for a 2011 series for *Harper's Bazaar*, *Lost in Fashion*, which was exhibited in the spring of 2012.

Though the *Hiding in the City* series is most successful for its succinct description of life in present-day China, Liu insists that the basic concept of his work remains the same wherever he chooses to create it. "I question the relation between man and its environment," he told Marine Cabos for *Photography of China* (2 Feb. 2012), citing pieces in which he poses in front of a rack of magazines or a dizzying section of a shelf packed with plush panda toys. "My body is a tool that enables me to inform the audience that in the end all the things created by our own hands make us disappear."

**OTHER WORKS**

Following the initial success of *Hiding in the City*, Liu presented a series of realist paintings called *China Report: 2007*, in which he meticulously recreates, in paint on canvas, images from popular Chinese media. In China, the government controls the media, but Liu carefully chose ten images that fall into three categories: stories about natural disasters, stories about population, and stories about politics and military drills. "If you look at media pictures from thirty years ago it's all the same stuff, nothing has really changed," he told Schultz. "Even the drills of the military, they're the same as they were thirty years ago." From this perspective, his work touches on the saying "the more things change, the more they stay the same." He even cited the country's move to a socialist-oriented market economy and lamented that foreign investors have overrun the country, polluting the environment and negatively affecting the lives of Chinese citizens. It is a theme that a number of contemporary Chinese artists have examined through their work—the idea that Chinese citizens were oppressed under a Communist regime but are now oppressed in another sense by the byproducts of capitalism.

Liu has found success with a number of sculptural works as well. *Red Hand* (2006–8) is a group of shining red and white figures of young boys cast in patriotic or playful poses. Upon a closer look, the boys are missing eyes or have large red hands covering their faces. Several figures have other physical deformities, suggesting unease for the viewer, and for the figures, a blithe unawareness of their surroundings. *Olympic Warrior* is a series of bronze sculptures meant to recall the thousands of clay soldiers—known as the terra cotta army—buried alongside the first emperor of China. In Liu's work, the soldiers are posed as if they were at the starting blocks of a race; they are cast in bronze and painted in the five colors of the Olympic rings. *Mask* (2013) is a series of sculptures that reinterpret traditional Peking Opera masks. Historically, the masks were used in performance and represented Chinese heroes and gods as symbols of Chinese values. In Liu's work, the masks are emblazoned with food and drink advertising logos, suggesting China's increasing commercialization.

Liu has lived in Beijing since 1999. He is represented by the New York gallery Eli Klein Fine Art and Galerie Paris-Beijing in Beijing, Brussels, and Paris.

**SUGGESTED READING**

Ai Weiwei. "Ai Weiwei: 'China's Art World Does Not Exist.'" *Guardian*. Guardian News and Media, 10 Sept. 2012. Web. 9 Sept. 2013.
Batet, Janet. "Liu Bolin: Vigilance, Survival Instinct and Simulation." *Artpulse*. Artpulse, 2013. Web. 9 Sept. 2013.
Bernstein, Fred A. "Liu Bolin's Disappearing Act." *New York Times Style Magazine*. New York Times, 17 May 2011. Web. 9 Sept. 2013.
Fimrite, Peter. "Dirt and Poverty, Minutes from Olympic Glitz." *San Francisco Chronicle*. Hearst Corporation, 8 Aug. 2008. Web. 9 Sept. 2013.
Gaskin, Sam. "Interview: Liu Bolin on the Inferno and Paradiso of Cell Phones." *Blouin Artinfo*. Blouin Artinfo, 14 May 2013. Web. 9 Sept. 2013.
"Invisibility Cloaked—Liu Bolin." *Emaho Magazine*. Emaho Magazine, 11 Apr. 2013. Web. 9 Sept. 2013.
Magnier, Mark. "Wrecking Ball Casts Shadow on Arts Colony in Beijing." *Los Angeles Times*. Los Angeles Times, 9 Dec. 2005. Web. 9 Sept. 2013.

**SELECTED WORKS**

*Hidden in the City*, 2005–; *Urban Camouflage*, 2006; *Red Hand*, 2006–8; *China Report 2007*, 2007; *Burning Man*, 2007; *Dragon Series*, 2010; *Lost in Fashion*, 2011; *Mask*, 2013

—Molly Hagan

# Abraham (Avi) Loeb

**Born:** 1962
**Occupation:** Theoretical physicist and educator

Abraham Loeb, who goes by the name Avi, is a well-known astrophysicist, cosmologist, and author. A native of Israel, he is the Frank B. Baird Jr. Professor of Science at Harvard University in

Jon Chase/Harvard Staff Photographer

Cambridge, Massachusetts. In addition to working as a professor of astronomy, Loeb also serves as the chair of the Department of Astronomy and the director of the Institute for Theory and Computation (ITC), a part of the Harvard-Smithsonian Center for Astrophysics. The focus of Loeb's work is the beginnings of the universe and he is considered an authority on what happened after the big bang. His first book, a textbook entitled *First Light in the Universe*, was written with Andrea Ferrara and Richard S. Ellis and published in 2008. In 2010, Loeb published his second book, entitled *How Did the First Stars and Galaxies Form?* His third book, *The First Galaxies in the Universe*, written with Steven R. Furlanetto, was published in 2013. "If we want to trace our origins—the scientific version of the story of Genesis—then we need to understand how the first stars formed and how they produced heavy elements," Loeb told Linda Shiner for the Smithsonian's *Air & Space Magazine* (Sept. 2010). "The first galaxies were the building blocks of the Milky Way, and the desire to understand them is a search for our roots."

Loeb's strengths lie in his creativity and his thirst for hard data in a theoretical field. His fascination with space and the universe grew out of his love of philosophy and the questions he fostered as a child growing up on a farm in Israel. "Avi is the only person I know who has more good ideas for research than he has fingers and toes," the late astrophysicist John Bahcall told William J. Cromie for the *Harvard Gazette* (9 Jan. 1997)

when Loeb earned tenure at Harvard. "In addition, he can calculate just about anything that is calculable."

## CHILDHOOD AND EDUCATION

Loeb was born in Israel in 1962 and raised on a farm in the village of Beit-Hanan, about twelve miles from Tel Aviv. His father, David, was the head of Israel's pecan industry and his mother, Sarah, worked on the family farm raising chickens and growing oranges and grapefruits. She returned to school in the 1990s and earned her doctorate in comparative literature. Loeb has two older sisters, Shoshana and Ariela. As a child, Loeb would load the family tractor with books about philosophy and drive out into the fields to read after completing his chores. He was a bright student and excelled at sports.

In 1979, at the age of eighteen, he was selected as one of only twenty-five other boys for the elite Talpiot training program in the Israel Defense Forces (IDF). The program, then in its first year, aimed to foster the creativity of the country's most talented young mathematicians and scientists. Loeb earned his undergraduate degree in physics and mathematics from the Hebrew University in Jerusalem while participating in basic training. "I parachuted, I drove tanks," Loeb told Abigail Klein Leichman for the online magazine *ISRAEL21c* (11 Jan. 2011). "The purpose [of the Talpiot program] is for participants to get to know what goes on in the army before starting to develop devices for army use." Young Israeli men are required to serve three years in the country's military and members of the Talpiot program are required to serve a total of six years, though they spend that time developing new technologies rather than serving in combat. In total, Loeb was a participant in the Talpiot project from 1980 until 1988.

Early in his service, while working at the Soreq Nuclear Research Center, Loeb developed a way to propel projectile missiles using electric rather than chemical energy, increasing their speed by a factor of ten. From 1985 to 1988 he headed the research group on electromagnetic propulsion. He was asked to present his findings to US Air Force General James Abrahamson, the first director of President Ronald Reagan's Strategic Defense Initiative. Abrahamson agreed, on behalf of the United States, to provide financial backing for a project that was to be headed by Loeb, who was still earning his doctorate.

Loeb earned his MSc in physics in 1986 and received the faculty's "Best MSc Student" award. Loeb went on to earn his PhD in plasma physics from the Hebrew University of Jerusalem in 1986 at the age of twenty-four.

## EARLY TEACHING CAREER

Loeb's association with the Strategic Defense Initiative brought him to the United States in 1986, where Abrahamson introduced him to plasma physicist Marshall Rosenbluth. Through Rosenbluth Loeb met astrophysicist John Bahcall at Princeton University's Institute for Advanced Study (IAS). After a lunch meeting, Bahcall invited Loeb to stay at IAS for four weeks. Bahcall eventually convinced Loeb to switch his area of study to astronomy and in 1987 offered him a five-year position at the IAS. "I owe him my career," Loeb told Robert Irion for *Science Magazine* (12 Apr. 2013) of Bahcall.

In the early 1990s, Loeb and other theorists attempted to simulate the early universe using computers in an effort to understand how the first stars formed. It was the beginning of Loeb's career-long fascination with the dawn of the universe. In 1993, he accepted a job as an assistant professor at Harvard University. Loeb became an associate professor in 1995, and he soon began to get tenure offers from other departments at schools like Cornell University, the University of California, San Diego, and the Weizmann Institute in Israel. Harvard had not awarded tenure to an associate professor in the astronomy department in decades, but to Loeb's surprise, the school offered him tenure in 1996, a mere three years after hiring him.

As a professor of physics, Loeb encourages his students to ask questions and be innovative. He has urged his students to devote twenty percent of their research to riskier work, or what he calls "venture capital" projects. Although this is not always a popular point of view among his colleagues, Loeb believes that creative questions yield the best research.

## THE DARK AGES OF THE UNIVERSE

Loeb is a cosmologist. Simply described, cosmologists study the universe, but Loeb provides a more detailed description in an article he wrote for *Scientific American* (Nov. 2006). "Cosmologists are addressing some of the fundamental questions that people attempted to resolve over the centuries through philosophical thinking," writes Loeb, "but we are doing so based on systematic observation and a quantitative methodology." He poses questions such as: How did life begin? Why is there "something" instead of "nothing?" Loeb himself is interested in what he calls the "dark ages" of the universe—the transitional period between the big bang and the formation of the cosmos. Loeb refers to this period as the dark ages because the universe was suffused with hydrogen gas that swallowed any form of light.

Because the universe is expanding, scientists can look to deep space (literally back in time) to begin to understand its origins. In the 1960s, scientists discovered something called the cosmic microwave background (CMB)—radiation that began to permeate the entire universe about

four hundred thousand years after the big bang. The discovery of CMB confirmed the theory of the big bang. Writing in *Scientific American* Loeb compares CMB to an ultrasound photograph that portrays what the universe looked like after the big bang—the moment the hot gases from the big bang cooled enough to emit radiation. However, the release of the microwave background did not bring with it the galaxies and stars seen today. The first light from a star was detected nearly two hundred million years later. As a cosmologist Loeb questions what happened in between.

The short answer is everything, though that view has not always had the widespread support in the scientific community that it has now. Throughout his career, Loeb has spearheaded the effort to understand this moment in the universe's history. "The cosmic dark age is one of the great mysteries of astronomy," Nobel Prize laureate John Mather told Marcus Chown for *New Scientist* magazine (7 Feb. 1998). "We have no direct evidence of how galaxies were formed, how the first stars formed without the help of the prior generations of stars, how galaxies evolved, [or] whether they were formed from aggregations of smaller units or from subdivisions of large ones. Everything happened in the cosmic dark age. It goes right to the heart of the question of how we got here."

Scientific advancements in the twentieth and twenty-first centuries have allowed cosmologists the once unthinkable opportunity to begin to figure out how the dark ages set the stage for what is observable in space today. The universe moved out of its formless state and emerged from the darkness with a slew of new elements and young galaxies. It underwent a process of reionization during which the hydrogen atoms were broken apart into protons and electrons. This period of reionization has been fodder for a number of theories and Loeb admits that computer simulations regarding this period are imperfect. According to Loeb in his *Scientific American* article, "observers may well see reionization before theorists are able to forecast what they should see."

## MILKOMEDA GALAXY

In the 2000s Loeb and his Harvard colleague T. J. Cox worked to build models of the earth and its galaxy to see what they might look like billions of years into the future. Using computer simulations, they found that the earth's galaxy, the Milky Way, was on a collision course with the Andromeda galaxy, which is currently situated a comfortable 2.5 billion light years away. They discovered that in about five billion years, the two galaxies will merge creating one large galaxy that Loeb has dubbed "Milkomeda." The arrangement might, they hypothesize, push Earth's solar system nearly one hundred thousand light years from the new galaxy's center. The position and the rate of the expansion of the universe would render the night sky nearly empty for future astronomers. The prospect is difficult to fathom. Indeed, the distant future is a concept that many people have trouble imagining, but studies like these appeal to Loeb. "There is much more to the universe than meets the eye on earth. As an astrophysicist, I have the privilege of being paid to think about it and it puts things in perspective for me," he wrote for *Scientific American*. "There are things that I would otherwise be bothered by—my own death, for example. Everyone will die sometime, but when I see the universe as a whole, it gives me a sense of longevity." The January 2008 issue of *Astronomy* magazine named Loeb's paper on Milkomeda one of the top ten space stories in 2007. Cox and Loeb's paper, "The Collision Between the Milky-Way and Andromeda Galaxies," was published in 2008 in the *Monthly Notices of the Royal Astronomical Society*.

## OTHER PROJECTS

For several years, Loeb has been working with astronomy professor Dan Maoz of Tel Aviv University on a means for finding life on other planets. Since the early 1990s, scientists have been searching for Earth-like planets near stars similar to Earth's own sun. Nevertheless, a star the size and brightness of the sun would make it incredibly difficult to observe the characteristics of a planet the size of Earth when the two bodies are aligned. Instead of stars similar to the sun, Loeb suggested that scientists seek out dying stars known as white dwarfs. White dwarfs can still have the same surface temperature of the sun—and thus retain the ability to sustain life on a nearby planet—but are much smaller in size (about the size of the earth, actually) and thus fainter in observation. Observing a planet next to a white dwarf, Loeb told Lemonick for *Time* magazine (6 Mar. 2012), "you could detect biomarker molecules like oxygen in just a few hours of observation time."

The most exciting aspect of Loeb and Maoz's proposal is that it can be executed before the end of the decade. The highly sophisticated James Webb Space Telescope, successor to the Hubble Space Telescope, will launch in 2018. Equipped with a special infrared telescope, the Webb will not only be able to provide information about life on other planets, but will also inform Loeb's theories about the formation of the universe's first galaxies. The Webb and other telescopes like it, he told Shiner, "promise to supply a flood of data about the infant universe during its first billion years after the Big Bang." "This emerging interface between theory and observation," he added, "will constitute an ideal opportunity for students considering a research career in astrophysics or cosmology."

## ACCOLADES AND PERSONAL LIFE

In addition to his tenure at Harvard and role as the director of the ITC there, Loeb's many other academic roles include being named the Salpeter Lecturer at Cornell University in 2006, the Merle Kingsley Distinguished Visitor at Caltech in 2007, and the Australian Institute of Physics Lecturer at University of Melbourne in 2007. In 2011 he was awarded the Las Cumbres Prize Lectureship at the University of California, Santa Barbara, as well. Loeb also holds a visiting professorship at the Weizmann Institute of Science and a Sackler senior professorship at the School of Physics at Tel Aviv University.

Loeb is the recipient of many prestigious awards. He was awarded the Kennedy Prize for his doctoral research in 1987 and received a fellowship from the Guggenheim Foundation in 2002. In 2012 he was elected as a member of the American Academy of Arts and Sciences. In addition to being the author of more than four hundred research articles, Loeb has been featured in cover stories in *Time* magazine and *Smithsonian Magazine*.

In the 1990s Loeb traveled between Cambridge and New York City to be with his wife, Israela, who was a PhD student at Columbia University. The two divorced around the same time that Loeb received his promotion at Harvard. Several months later, he met a lawyer named Ofrit Liviatan in Israel. The two married in 1999 and live in Lexington, Massachusetts, a suburb of Boston. Liviatan lectures in Harvard's Department of Government. They have two young daughters, who are bilingual, named Klil and Lotem.

## SUGGESTED READING

Chown, Marcus. "Let There Be Light." *New Scientist*. Reed Business Information, 7 Feb. 1998. Web. 9 May 2013.

Cromie, William J. "Dark Age of the Universe: Abraham Loeb Lights It up with His Research." *Harvard Gazette*. President and Fellows of Harvard College, 9 Jan. 1997. Web. 9 May 2013.

Irion, Robert. "From Cosmic Dawn to Milkomeda, and Beyond." *Science Magazine* 12 Apr. 2013: 136–37. Print.

Leichman, Abigail Klein. "Getting paid to think about the sky." *ISRAEL21c*. Israel21c, 11 Jan. 2011. Web. 9 May 2013.

Lemonick, Michael D. "Could Tiny Stars Be Home to Mirror Earths?" *Time*. Time, 6 Mar. 2013. Web. 9 May 2013.

Loeb, Abraham. "The Dark Ages of the Universe." *Scientific American* Nov. 2006: 46–53. Print.

Shiner, Linda. "A&S Interview: Avi Loeb." *Air & Space Magazine*. Smithsonian Institution, Sept. 2010. Web. 9 May 2013.

## SELECTED WORKS
*First Light in the Universe* (with Andrea Ferrara and Richard S. Ellis), 2008; *How Did the First Stars and Galaxies Form?*, 2010; *The First Galaxies in the Universe* (with Steven R. Furlanetto), 2013.

—*Molly Hagan*

# Kevin Love

**Born:** September 7, 1988
**Occupation:** Basketball player with the Minnesota Timberwolves

Minnesota Timberwolves' six-feet-ten forward Kevin Love is study in contrasts: he hails from a famous family and played at UCLA, a university with perhaps the most fabled college basketball program in history, but he is often credited for his grasp of basketball fundamentals and not for the flashy play of many of his contemporaries in the National Basketball Association (NBA). Love is what might be termed an "old school" player for his focus on passing and rebounding and his ability to score from multiple spots on the court, and he has modeled his game on such NBA legends as Bill Walton, Elgin Baylor, and Wes Unseld, a teammate of Love's father, Stan, with the Baltimore (later Washington) Bullets during the early 1970s. However, Love has embraced the technological trappings of modern society, and is an active contributor on Twitter.

Though Love credits his father for instilling in him the work ethic, knowledge, and tenacity necessary to be a successful professional athlete, his most famous immediate relative is his uncle Mike Love, the leader singer and an original member of the Beach Boys, a band that also included the Love brothers' cousins, Brian, Dennis, and Carl Wilson. Though of different generations and different fields, Love and his uncle Mike share the similar abilities of excelling in the spotlight and managing fame. "I've always liked the Beach Boys," Love admitted to John Branch for the *New York Times* (18 Mar. 2008). "I just never liked to say it in front of my friends back home." However, it seemed only natural, given his family's connection to Southern California, that Love would return to Los Angeles, doing so for his brief, but highly regarded stint at UCLA.

Love started his NBA career during the 2008–09 season, but began to establish himself as a premier player in the league in his third season, leading all players in rebounds per game, posting career highs in five statistics categories, and earning the NBA's award for Most Improved Player. He began the 2012–13 season on the sidelines, suffering a broken hand during training camp, but, having signed a lucrative contract

Getty Images

extension in January 2012, Love has become the focus of the Timberwolves' franchise.

## EARLY LIFE AND EDUCATION
Love was born on September 7, 1988, in Santa Monica, California, and moved with his family to Lake Oswego, Oregon, the following year. He is the middle child; his brother Collin, is two years older, and his sister, Emily, is five years younger. Love grew up in a household immersed in basketball. His father had been a star player at the University of Oregon and played several years of professional basketball, first in the NBA for the Bullets and the Los Angeles Lakers and briefly in the American Basketball Association (ABA) for the San Antonio Spurs (before the NBA and ABA merged in 1976).

Stan Love encouraged his son's basketball abilities from a young age, teaching him not only the basics of the sport but also schooling him the history of the NBA. "When most kids were watching Big Bird, my Dad had me watching Larry Bird. He taught me not only what he knew, but what he learned from Wes Unseld and Earl Monroe and Jerry West, Gail Goodrich, George Gervin, and other Hall of Famers," Love told Ollie Burruss for *1859 Oregon Magazine* (17 July 2012). When he was a senior in high school, Love told Arash Markazi for *Sports Illustrated* (2 Mar. 2007) that he began watching video of classic NBA footage when he was "about four or five" but that he "started grasping it when I was in the third or fourth grade."

In addition to his natural athletic ability as a child and his father's tutelage, Love had a strong desire to excel in the sport, needing little prodding to practice on his own before school and even in the inclement rainy weather for which Oregon is notorious. "You would always hear that ball dribbling out there, shots going up, rain, sleet or snow it didn't matter," Love told Marc J. Spears for *Yahoo! Sports* in a March 15, 2011 interview. The synthesis of physical and intellectual abilities and hard work made Love the best (at least statistically) high school basketball player in Oregon state history.

## HIGH SCHOOL CAREER

At Lake Oswego High School, Love established himself as one of the most dominant high school basketball players of all time, winning numerous awards and establishing the Oregon state scoring record by compiling 2,628 points over his four-year career. He led his team, the Lakers, to the state championship game in three consecutive years, from 2005 to 2007; the team won the 2006 championship against South Medford High School. His statistical output improved each of his four seasons, culminating in per-game averages for his senior season of almost 34 points, 17 rebounds, and 4 assists. He averaged 26.8 points and 14.5 rebounds per game during his high school career.

Love's father videotaped his Lake Oswego games, allowing Love to review games and improve upon his performances by correcting mistakes that he found in his game. However, the videos also served as promotional tools for Love as colleges began to recruit him. What became most apparent from the videos was Love's passing ability, including his full-court, two-handed passes, which require strength and precision. Love told Markazi "passing comes the most natural. It is something I've worked on, but it's something I've been blessed with; being able to see things that other players might not be able to see. It's really an instinctive thing." Love's passing skill seemed to separate him from other players, adding to his reputation as a unique and fundamentally sound player.

Despite scoring 37 points and grabbing 15 rebounds in the final game, Love could not lead the Lakers to another state championship, as the team lost to South Medford in 2007. However, Love earned numerous accolades his senior season as many anticipated his arrival in Westwood as he planned to join the UCLA Bruins team. In 2007, Love was named player of the year by several businesses and institutions including Gatorade, *USA Today*, *Parade* magazine, and Naismith Prep.

## COLLEGE CAREER

Ben Howland, the head basketball coach of the UCLA Bruins, began recruiting Love before he even entered high school. Stan Love, who played basketball at Morningside High School in Inglewood, a South Los Angeles suburb, had wanted to play at UCLA, but was not recruited by the Bruins, who, at the time, were in the midst of a historic run of ten national championships during a twelve-year period. With the Love's ties to Los Angeles, Stan's adolescent dream of playing for the Bruins, and Howland's aggressive recruitment, UCLA seemed like the right fit for Love. As Karen, Love's mom, told Branch, "We had our hearts set on UCLA all along."

Love choose UCLA for these reasons and several others, including the facts that the school was the alma mater of Bill Walton, a center to whom Love has often been compared, and the former domain of legendary basketball coach John Wooden, who, despite being in his late nineties, was still a presence at UCLA basketball games and an icon whom coaches and players revered. Love told Markazi that he "got to sit down and talk to Coach Wooden when I made my decision." When asked what he has taken away from Wooden, who died in 2010, he told Spears that he had learned "how to act on the court and off the court. . . . When you're on the court there [are] certain things that you would do that you wouldn't do off the court. When you get off, you obviously have to be gracious and a humble person. When you are on the floor be a team player."

Love joined a team that had advanced to the Final Four the previous two seasons, only to lose to the University of Florida Gators on both occasions (in the final game in 2006 and in the semifinal game in 2007). With the addition of Love at the center position, the Bruins were expected to return to the Final Four, at least, if not win the championship outright.

Love's college career was short and did not end the way he and UCLA fans would have hoped, but he nonetheless established himself as one of the finest players in UCLA's illustrious history. During his freshman, and only, season at UCLA, Love averaged 17.6 points and 10.7 rebounds per game. He also shot .565 from the field and had 53 blocks. The Bruins lost only four games overall and two in the conference during the season and won both the Pacific 10 conference and tournament. The team earned one of four top seeds in the NCAA basketball tournament, advancing for the third consecutive season to the Final Four. However, the Bruins were beaten in the semifinal round by the University of Memphis Tigers, who, incidentally, in 2009, had to forfeit their entire 2007–08 season because of rules infractions. This fact was little consolation to Love and the Bruins at the time, as the team had again failed to win a championship.

For the season, Love earned Pac 10 Player of the Year and Pac 10 Freshman of the Year honors. Many hoped that Love would return for a sophomore season at UCLA, but he decided to forgo the remainder of his college career and enter the NBA Draft. As his mother stated to Branch, "I'm pro-school . . . but there are those factors, you know. If you're going to be a lottery pick . . . how can you not go? That's more money than people make in their lifetime. You have a chance to stay and get injured. There's so much to weigh."

## FIRST TWO SEASONS WITH THE NBA

In June 2008, the Memphis Grizzlies picked Love fifth in the NBA Draft, trading him and others to the Timberwolves for O. J. Mayo, who had been picked third, and three other players. The Timberwolves had traded Kevin Garnett to the Boston Celtics in 2007 and had struggled through a 22–60 record in 2007–08. The team continued to struggle at the start of the 2008–09 season, prompting General Manager Kevin McHale, a former Celtics player, to take over head coaching duties.

Love and McHale bonded immediately. "He's so far advanced for a 20-year-old it's ridiculous," McHale commented to the *Los Angeles Times* (20 Jan. 2009). Jerry Sloan, the longtime coach of the Utah Jazz, also praised Love during his rookie season, stating, as Steve Aschburner for *NBA* reported on December 11, 2009, "He knows how to play basketball. He passes the ball, he sets screens, he does whatever it takes to try to play the game. It's not that difficult, but we make it difficult because we think we have to do something sensational. . . . Those guys play for years and years in this league." Players and coaches were beginning to take notice of Love's burgeoning stardom.

During his first season, Love averaged 11.1 points and 9.1 rebounds per game, had twenty-nine "double-doubles" (ten or more in two statistical categories), and was the Rookie of the Month in March. Though his second season would turn out to be even better than his first, he missed eighteen games at the start of the 2009–10 season after breaking his left hand in a preseason contest.

Though Love's game minutes did not increase dramatically (he averaged about twenty-five in his first season and about twenty-nine in his second), his three-point-field-goal percentage went from 11 to 33 and he averaged a double-double for the season, with 14 points and 11 rebounds, for the first time in his career. Perhaps most surprising, he led the league in rebounds per forty-eight minutes (the length of an NBA game), besting the Orlando Magic's superstar Dwight Howard.

## THE 2010–11 SEASON

Many followers of the NBA knew that Love was a rising star in the league, but few could have predicted the streak he established in 2010–11. From November 19, 2010, to March 13, 2011, Love had a double-double in each game, fifty-three in all, falling two short of the record set by Elvin Hayes in 1973–74 but surpassing Moses Malone's post-merger record of fifty-one, set during the 1979–80 season. Though the double-double is not an official statistic of the NBA, the accomplishment underscored Love's value to his team and the city of Minneapolis. However, after the streak came to an end in a game against the Golden State Warriors, Love seemed relieved. "I thought I was doing it for myself but a lot of it was for the fans and everybody watching. I feel a big weight off my shoulders" (*USA Today*, 14 Mar. 2011).

Earlier in the 2010–11 season, Love joined elite company by scoring more than 30 points and collecting more than 30 rebounds in a game. Only eighteen other players had accomplished the feat previously, and the last player to do so was Malone in 1982. By grabbing 31 rebounds, Love also became the first player in the association with more than 30 rebounds in a game since Denver Nuggets center Dikembe Mutombo had 31 in March of 1996. In February 2011, Love became an all-star for the first time, replacing injured Houston Rockets center Yao Ming on the active roster.

The 2010–11 season represented Love's ascension from a young player with potential to a legitimate star. During the season, he averaged more than 20 points and 15 rebounds, becoming the first player to do so since Malone in 1982–83. At the end of the season, he was voted the NBA's Most Improved Player, after leading the league in rebounding with a 15.2 per-game average.

Though Love had risen to become one of a handful of stars under the age of twenty-five, the Timberwolves continued to struggle as a team. In Love's first three seasons, the team had a combined record of 56–190, winning only fifteen games in 2009–10 and seventeen in 2010–11. In 2009, the Timberwolves had drafted Spanish guard Ricky Rubio, one of the premier young European players; however, they were not able to persuade him to join the team until after the 2010–11 season. With Rubio and other talented young players, such as forward Derrick Williams, who was the second pick in the 2011 NBA draft, the Timberwolves appeared to be on the road back to competitiveness.

## THE 2011–12 SEASON

After a league-wide lockout abbreviated the 2011–12 NBA season, the Timberwolves and Love began play with a sense of optimism. Love picked up where he left off, dominating the backboards and starting the season with fifteen consecutive games in which he had a double-double. His rebounding average for the season fell to 13.3, but his scoring average jumped by almost six points a game, to 26.0, placing him fourth in the league in points per game, after Kevin Durant, Kobe Bryant, and LeBron James. He also averaged thirty-nine minutes of playing time per game, the most of his career.

Soon after the season began, in January 2012, Love signed a contract extension with the Timberwolves, worth $62 million over four years. He was eligible to become the team's "designated" player, which would have given him a five-year guaranteed contract. However, the two sides eventually settled on the four-year deal; the fourth year of the contract is a player option, giving Love the choice to return to Minnesota or leave the team as a free agent. "Did I want the five years? Of course," Love told Marc Stein and Chris Broussard for *ESPN* on January 27, 2012. "It was something I felt strongly about, but at the end of the day, a four-year deal is still great. I like the direction the team is headed . . . I like the youth. I like the pieces, like we're knocking at the door and we're close in a lot of games." Love's statement echoed the optimism in Minneapolis surrounding the home team, a feeling that had been missing since Kevin Garnett was traded after the 2007 season.

The momentum that the Timberwolves were creating during the 2011–12 season came to halt, however, when, on March 9, Rubio tore two knee ligaments during a game against the Los Angeles Lakers. Rubio missed the remainder of the season, and the Timberwolves failed to make the playoffs for the eighth consecutive season.

### THE OLYMPICS, DISCONTENT, AND INJURY

In 2010, Love helped Team USA win a gold medal in the FIBA World Championships, his first taste of international basketball. In the summer of 2012, Love joined Team USA in the London Olympics, as the team hoped to defend its gold medal from the 2008 Beijing Olympics. On a roster that included Bryant, James, Durant, and Carmelo Anthony, it was uncertain how much playing time Love would have during the Olympics. However, he became an integral member of the group, collecting 61 rebounds during the tournament (the most on the team) and scoring 9 points and grabbing 9 rebounds in the gold-medal game against Spain, which Team USA won 107–100.

Being a member of Team USA prompted Love to voice his concerns about the Timberwolves franchise, given that the team had not been competitive since he joined. Speaking during the preparation for the Olympics, Love discussed with Spears the fact that he was the only player on the roster without playoff experience (8 July, 2012). "My patience is not high. . . . Would yours be, especially when I'm a big proponent of greatness surrounding itself with greatness? All these [Team USA] guys seem to have great players around them. . . . It's tough seeing all these guys that are young and older who have all played in the playoffs. When they start talking about that, I have nothing to talk about. If I don't make the playoffs next year I don't know what

will happen." Love was certainly voicing his frustration over the state of the team as well as the injury to Rubio, which cost the Timberwolves a chance at the playoffs, but he also seemed to indicate that the clock was ticking for the Timberwolves to become a successful franchise with Love as the centerpiece. Unfortunately, during training camp, while preparing for the 2012–13 season, Love broke his right hand while doing knuckle pushups, an exercise he has done since childhood on his father's advice. Regarding his injury, Love, as the Associated Press reported on October 31, 2012, stated, "I do feel like I'm a big part of this team, and for me not to be out there the first few or several games, it kills me."

Despite the Timberwolves' struggles and Love's injury, which was to keep him from playing for about six weeks, Love is quickly becoming one of the most talked about players in the league, not only for his basketball abilities but also for his charitable endeavors and sense of humor. Chris Palmer, a contributing writer for ESPN tweeted on March 24, 2012, "Kevin Love is the 3rd best player in the NBA behind Kobe and LeBron. No question."

### PERSONAL LIFE

Love has two siblings, brother Collin, with whom he lived during his season at UCLA, and his sister Emily. When Love and Collin lived together, Collin usually kept house so Love could focus on his studies and basketball. Love has credited his family for helping to mold him into the person he has become. As he told Beth Harris for the Associated Press on February 9, 2008, "I am a good kid and I'm not going to make any bad choices because I was raised right by my parents."

The lessons that Love learned from his family as well as mentors such as Wooden and Howland have prompted him to be involved with charitable causes in both Minnesota and other parts of the United States. Joining the Salvation Army and Comcast, each winter, Love participates in an event called Kevin Love's Coat Drive, during which coats are distributed to needy families in the Minneapolis area. Furthermore, Love became involved with St. Jude's Research Hospital in Memphis, Tennessee, an institution focused on curing and treating pediatric cancer.

Through his work with St. Jude's, Love befriended Dylan Witschen, a teenager suffering from cancer. "Being able to put my hands on the whole thing and develop a relationship with a kid who's been through it all, it's pretty special to me. It makes me kind of hold everything closer," Love told Ken Berger for *CBS Sports* (4 Mar. 2010). Love invited Dylan to visit the Timberwolves locker room, and the two have corresponded by email.

Though Love has rapidly become one of the most respected athletes in the NBA, his style belies the contemporary fascination with style over substance. Though he has become a prolific scorer, he is best known among NBA circles for performing the often underappreciated aspects of basketball. He strengths are passing, rebounding, foot work, court vision, and the comprehension of strategy. Coupled with his jovial nature, these are the attributes that are causing basketball fans to take an interest in the future of the Minnesota Timberwolves and to speculate about where Love will rank among the greats as his career continues to unfold.

## SUGGESTED READING

Aschburner, Steve. "From Minnesota with Love: Wolves Finally Looking Better." *NBA*. NBA Media Ventures LLC, 11 Dec. 2009. Web. 5 Nov. 2012.

Berger, Ken. "St. Jude Utilizes Power of Love, NBA in Fight against Cancer." *CBS Sports.* CBS Interactive, 4 Mar. 2010. Web. 5 Nov. 2012.

Bolch, Ben. "Kevin McHale Really Likes Kevin Love." *Los Angeles Times.* Los Angeles Times, 20 Jan. 2009. Web. 5 Nov. 2012.

Branch, John. "Having Fun, Fun, Fun as a Freshman at U.C.L.A." *New York Times.* New York Times Co., 18 Mar. 2008. Web. 5 Nov. 2012.

Markazi, Arash. "Feelin' the Love: Old School Hoops Phenom Turning Heads All Over." *Sports Illustrated.* Time Inc., 2 Mar. 2007. Web. 5 Nov. 2012.

—*Christopher Rager*

# Lex Luger

**Born:** March 6, 1991
**Occupation:** Record producer

Lex Luger was just nineteen years old when the first song featuring his beats hit the radio in May 2010. That song was "Hard in da Paint," a thumping, crunk-inspired track from Atlanta-based rapper Waka Flocka Flame's debut album, *Flockaveli.* Luger's production on that song—and on the majority of the tracks on that album—helped to popularize Waka Flocka Flame and his brand of loud, unpolished, in-your-face rap. The song's success also contributed to a renewed interest in the Southern rap subgenre known as "trap music," which features beats characterized by layers of heavy bass, synthesizers, and accelerated hi-hat percussion and lyrics. Luger, a self-taught producer, was praised for his distinctive version of trap beats on *Flockaveli.* "Mr. Luger's tracks are cluttered and loud—always loud—but unfold with grace, nobombastic drum out of place," music critic Jon Caramanica wrote in a review of the *Flockaveli* for the *New York Times* (9 Oct.

2010). "Several songs on *Flockaveli* feature the signature Luger effect, a quickly accelerating series of tinny synth darts—like an airplane on a runway—right up until Waka Flocka Flame jumps in with the opening line of his first verse like a heavy-booted kick to the sternum."

After *Flockaveli*, Luger garnered attention for supplying the beats for Rick Ross's popular 2010 single "B.M.F." and for "H.A.M.," the lead single off *Watch the Throne*, a 2011 collaboration album by rappers Kanye West and Jay-Z. Today, Luger is one of the most in-demand producers in hip hop, collaborating with both emerging and established artists and inspiring numerous producers to imitate his style. His contributions have been recognized by the hip-hop industry with numerous awards and nominations, including the title of producer of the year at the 2011 BMI Urban Awards and BET Hip Hop Awards. Luger has said that when making his beats, he draws from events in his life—including painful ones. He told Jayson Rodriguez, Christopher Schafer, and Samuel Rogers for MTV's *Mixtape Daily* (21 Jan. 2011), "Day-to-day stuff, stress, family, everything—I put that all in my beats. Life—I put life in my beats."

## EARLY LIFE

Luger was born Lexus Arnel Lewis and raised in Suffolk, Virginia, in the state's southeastern region. Several other notable hip hop artists and producers originated in southeastern Virginia, including Timbaland, Missy Elliott, and Pharrell Williams. In an interview with Alex Pappademas for the *New York Times Magazine* (6 Nov. 2011), Luger pointed out that unlike those artists, he came from an area that was more rural and poor. "Suffolk is *country*," Luger told Pappademas. "The countryest, out of all of 'em."

Several members of Luger's family were musical. His mother and grandmother played the piano, and his father played the drums. Luger was introduced to percussion by his father when he was a toddler and went on to play drums in his local church band growing up; with this early experience, Luger learned the basics of rhythm and meter. He later began to create more complex beats using *MTV Music Generator 3: This Is the Remix*, a 2004 PlayStation video game that allows users to create and sample original music and provides tutorials on how to create remixes. After mastering that game, Luger moved on to a Music Production Center (MPC) 2000 sampler. That device allowed Luger to assign sound snippets to different drum pads. Initially, Luger did not let anyone listen to his beats. "I wasn't sure if they'd be as good to anyone besides me, so I kept whatever I was working on to myself," Luger said, as quoted on PRLog.org (27 Dec. 2010). "But once I did let people hear, they gave me some good feedback and told me to keep working, so that's what I did. I worked, worked, worked and worked some more."

## FIRST BEATS
Creating beats became a popular activity among Luger's social circle after a friend of Luger's, Black (short for "Ur Boy Black"), returned from a visit to North Carolina with a pirated copy of the sound mixing program known as Fruity Loops. (The software has since been renamed FL Studio, due to a conflict with the Kellogg Company.) That copy of Fruity Loops was copied multiple times over and, for a period of time, it seemed that everyone in Suffolk had become an aspiring hip-hop producer, according to Luger. Luger told Pappademas that his peers even began adopting producer nicknames. Luger dubbed himself "Lex Luger," after the professional wrestler of the same name.

While most of his friends lost interest in mixing music after a while, Luger's interest persisted. He could spend hours on end creating beat after beat on Fruity Loops. He was quick, too; he could make an original beat in a matter of minutes and then spend hours perfecting it.

Luger ultimately dropped out of high school after his sophomore year to pursue a career in music. Having read about hip-hop producers who got their start through social media, Luger began posting beats on his MySpace page and sending samples to rappers through e-mail. He did not have immediate success. "I was sending my music out, but nobody wanted to hear it," he told *Mixtape Daily*. "There was a time I was sending my music out to Waka [Flocka Flame] and [rapper OJ da] Juiceman and nobody cared because I didn't have no name." Nevertheless, Luger persisted. "I was just real hungry and was reaching out to any and everybody," he told PRLog.org (27 Dec. 2010).

## BREAKOUT TRACK
The first artist to express interest in Luger's beats was the Atlanta-based rapper Waka Flocka Flame, whose debut single, "O Let's Do It," had reached number 7 on the Billboard Rap charts after its December 2009 release. Waka, whose given name is Juaquin Malphurs, quickly became known for his blunt lyrics, aggressive delivery, and his overall unpolished, raw sound. His music contrasted with the smoother sounds, poetic lyrics, and sophisticated rhyme schemes of many other popular rappers at the time. Waka flew Luger to Atlanta to collaborate with him on his debut album. Luger told Pappademas that at the time he was working with Waka, he was "broke as a joke" and considering quitting music. Luger created hundreds of beats in Waka's basement, where the two spent their downtime playing video games or watching movies. After Luger returned to Virginia, Waka contacted him and asked him to create just one more beat, which ultimately became the basis of the album's first single, "Hard in da Paint."

Luger first heard the completed version of "Hard in da Paint" while driving home from the airport in the spring of 2010. "I don't listen to the radio or go out that much; I just work," Luger explained to *Mixtape Daily*. "When I got to Atlanta . . . my boy turned on the radio. My boy was like, 'Yeah, this is it.' I said, 'Turn it up,' and it felt crazy." Driven by Luger's hard, dramatic beat, "Hard in da Paint" features Waka rapping about the impact of his younger brother's death on his life. That song outperformed Waka's first single, reaching number 2 on the Billboard Rap and Hip Hop/R & B charts.

Critics generally received *Flockaveli* positively; embracing Waka's unconventional—even vulgar—rap style. Some declared the record the strongest crunk album in years—a genre characterized by heavy bass lines and lyrics delivered in loud, shouting, call-and-response style. Luger's beats, which were featured on the majority of the album's tracks, were considered by critics to be the highlight of the album. Critic Jon Caramanica, in his review for the *New York Times* (9 Oct. 2010), described Waka and Luger as "a dream pair." He continued, "Often it sounds as if they're engaged in a cage match, or a street brawl: the rapper holding forth on weapons, jewelry and gang signs, while the producer toys with all the cinematically inclined presets on his keyboard and drum machine. Just two hyped-up maximalists out for some mayhem."

## HIGH-PROFILE COLLABORATIONS
Luger next supplied the beat for Miami-based rapper Rick Ross's single "B.M.F. (Blowin' Money Fast)" from Ross's fourth studio album, *Teflon Don* (2010). In the song, Ross compares himself to real-life gangsters Demetrius "Big Meech" Flenory, the leader of notorious Detroit-based

gang Black Mafia Family, and Larry Hoover, the leader of the Chicago street gang called the Gangster Disciples. Critic Chris Richards reviewed the track for the *Washington Post* (5 Apr. 2011), noting that "the song sounds anything but dreamy—it's propelled by apocalyptic drum machine thunder, crafted by the imaginative young producer Lex Luger." Released on June 29, 2010, the song reached number 4 on the US Billboard Rap chart and was ranked number 4 on MTV's list of the best songs of 2010. The song also won Luger two BET Hip Hop Awards, including track of the year.

At just nineteen, Luger had suddenly become a highly in-demand producer. Through the rest of 2010, he created beats for dozens of artists, ranging from well-known street artists Fat Trel and OJ da Juiceman to better-known stars such as Soulja Boy. His growing popularity notwithstanding, Luger was surprised when he was invited to collaborate with Kanye West, one of the best-known and most-respected rappers and producers in the industry. Luger was in Atlanta on his way to pick up Chinese food when he received a call from West asking him to collaborate with him. Luger told *Mixtape Daily* that he talked to West about beats for about thirty minutes before he realized who he was speaking to. After a two-hour conversation, Luger agreed to fly to New York City to work with him on some beats. "I played him a lot of beats," Luger told *Mixtape Daily*, "but he liked the ones that I didn't expect him to like." One of Luger's beats was included on West's 2010 track "See Me Now," a collaboration with R & B singers Beyoncé and Charlie Wilson. Released as a single in August 2010, it debuted at number 2 on Billboard's Bubbling Under R & B/Hip-Hop Singles chart. The track also became a bonus iTunes track on West's fifth album, *My Beautiful Dark Twisted Fantasy* (2010).

Luger worked with West again on "H.A.M.," the first single to be released off West's 2011 collaboration album with Jay-Z, *Watch the Throne*. Luger never heard the completed song until after it was released in January 2011. "Working with Kanye was crazy," Luger told *Mixtape Daily*. "I can't really explain it. He's a perfectionist. He has to have everything perfect and out the ordinary, 10 times greater than everything. He's a crazy guy, but he's fire." Both "H.A.M." and the album were widely praised. Describing Luger's dramatic production on the song, critic Jody Rosen wrote for *Rolling Stone* (11 Jan. 2011) that the song "starts out big—twitchy synths giving way to spooky opera ululating—and then gets humungous, with a choir booming over what sounds like a dozen symphony orchestras. You expect God, or Gandalf, to come striding out of the mist."

### FURTHER SUCCESS

Luger went on to create beats for numerous notable artists in 2011, among them Snoop Dogg, Wiz Khalifa, Rick Ross, Fat Trel, Ace Hood, Young Jeezy, DJ Khaled, and Soulja Boy. One artist Luger was particularly excited to work with was the West Coast–based rapper known as the Game, who was protégé of Dr. Dre, Luger's favorite producer. Luger created a beat for the song "Bottles & Rockin' J's" for Game's fourth studio release, *The R.E.D. Album* (2011). The track also featured Lil Wayne, DJ Khaled, Busta Rhymes, Rick Ross, and Fabolous.

Also in 2011, Luger joined with Atlanta-based producer Southside—another frequent Waka Flocka Flame collaborator—to form the hip-hop production supergroup 808 Mafia with Waka's label, Brick Squad Monopoly. (The group has created a number of mix tapes featuring a revolving cast of up-and-coming producers.) Since its formation, 808 Mafia has produced tracks for artists such as 2 Chainz, Meek Mill, and Soulja Boy. In 2011 the group produced the song "She Be Puttin' On" for *Ferrari Boyz*, Waka Flocka Flame's collaboration album with Gucci Mane. 808 Mafia released its debut, self-titled mixtape in 2012, featuring the work of several of the group's newest producers. In 2013, Luger and several other group members produced a number of tracks for Gucci Mane's album *Trap God*.

Luger's talents were recognized with several nominations and awards in 2011. Two songs produced by Luger were nominated for BET Hip Hop Awards; "Hustle Hard" by Ace Hood and "No Hands" by Waka Flocka Flame were nominated for best club banger, with "No Hands" winning in that category. Luger himself was honored as producer of the year at the BET Hip Hop Awards that year. Also in 2011, Luger became the youngest person ever to be named producer of the year at the BMI Urban Awards.

By 2012, Luger had begun creating beats with higher quality software and production systems, namely Pro Tools and Maschine. He continued to produce influential beats throughout 2012 for artists such as Rich Ross, Fat Trel, Gucci Mane, Tay Don, Juicy J, Schoolboy Q, Wiz Khalifa, Game, and many others. He created the beat for one song on Waka Flocka Flame's 2012 album, *Triple F Life: Fans, Friends & Family*, which was dedicated to Waka's friend Slim Dunkin, who had recently been murdered. The song, "Round of Applause," featuring Drake, was the album's lead single. It was widely considered a highlight of the album. The single was released in October 2011 and reached number 15 on Billboard's US Hip Hop/R&B Songs list.

### ONGOING WORK

Since 2010, Luger has been signed with the management and production company Mizay Entertainment, which is headed by Waka's mother, Debra Antney. (Mizay also represents artists OJ da Juiceman and Gucci Mane, and formerly Nicki Minaj.) He is also a member of

VABP—short for Virginia Boyz Productionz—a rap group he started with his childhood friends in Virginia. VABP released the mixtape *On Da Moon Remix* in 2009.

Luger is known for his ability to create beats quickly. Pappademas, who observed Luger's routine while spending time with him for his *New York Times* article, noted that the producer can create a new beat in a matter of minutes. When Pappademas observed that Luger had created a track in just twenty-two minutes, Luger responded with disappointment, "Twenty-two minutes? Psssh. I'm gettin' old." Pappademas also noted that Luger works while smoking copious amounts of marijuana. "Because he turns out music at an assembly-line clip (while really, really stoned), sometimes he'll forget about a beat entirely until it turns up on the radio as somebody's new single." Luger's rapid production pace and simple equipment—combined with the popularity of the trap style he has championed—have made him a target for imitators. There are many videos on YouTube demonstrating how to make a Lex Luger–style beat.

Luger is sensitive to the criticism that the beats he creates sound too similar to one another. Rather than avoid reading criticism, Luger seeks it out and attempts to defy the expectations of his critics. "I go on websites, and I look at what people got to say about the previous record that I dropped, and . . . I try to cater to the haters' needs and their minds," Luger told Nadine Graham for HipHopDX (23 Aug. 2011). "That's what I like doing. I like seeing [someone] say, 'Oh, Lex Luger wack. All his beats sound the same.' [I like to] prove him wrong, you know what I'm saying? That's what really keeps me going, trying to go to the next level really." Luger is eager to expand his range outside of rap and hip hop to pop, R & B, and other genres. "My sound is hard. My sound is trap, very hard," he told *Mixtape Daily*. "But I want people to hear another side to that. I got R & B, pop, everything—I got everything—and I want people to see that, hear that."

**PERSONAL LIFE**

As of late 2011, Luger owns a waterfront home in Norfolk, Virginia, near his hometown of Suffolk, where he lives with his girlfriend and two young daughters. He has said that providing for his daughters was the main reason that he was so persistent in pursuing music as a career. Luger has an impressive work ethic. "I wake up four or five in the morning sometimes, and just go into the studio—boom—and make beats till about ten, twelve," Luger told *Mixtape Daily*. "Go back, go to sleep. Chill with my kids and my family. Go back to the studio, make some more beats, come back home, do the same thing."

Pappademas observed that Luger is naturally a shy person. "He has the tunnel vision of a hardcore gamer or a programmer, someone who can wire into an interface and shut off his perception of time's passage—someone who feels more comfortable doing that than he does living in the world," Pappademas noted. "And having his picture taken and answering questions about his craft ultimately takes him out of the zone where he's most comfortable, the one where everything else falls away and it's him and the screen and the beat."

**SUGGESTED READING**

Caramanica, Jon. "The Newest Rap: Intense, Authentic and Accidental." *New York Times* 10 June 2012, New York ed.: AR22. Print.

Caramanica, Jon. "Bam! Pow! A Loud Young Rapper Rekindles Rap's Old Fighting Spirit." *New York Times* 9 Oct. 2012, New York ed.: C5. Print.

Graham, Nadine. "Lex Luger Recalls Working with Game on 'R.E.D.,' Says His Sound Comes from Pain." *HipHopDX*. Cheri Media Group, 23 Aug. 2011. Web. 10 Mar. 2013.

Pappademas, Alex. "Lex Luger Can Write a Hit Rap Song in the Time It Takes to Read This Article." *New York Times Magazine* 6 Nov. 2011: MM26+. Print.

Rodriguez, Jayson, Christopher Schafer, and Samuel Rogers. "Jay-Z, Kanye West's 'H.A.M.' Beatsmith Lex Luger Looks Ahead." *Mixtape Daily*. Viacom Intl., 21 Jan. 2011. Web. 10 Mar. 2013.

—*Margaret Roush Mead*

# Marisa Acocella Marchetto

**Born:** ca. 1962
**Occupation:** Cartoonist

In 2004, Marisa Acocella Marchetto interpreted her cancer diagnosis as a challenge to overcome, which then led to opportunities to help other women battling the same illness. Rather than wallow in despair and self-pity when she learned she had breast cancer, Marchetto fought the disease and used her skills as a comic artist to share her story. In the graphic novel *Cancer Vixen: A True Story* (2006), Marchetto utilized humor to chronicle her battle and to literally illustrate how other women could fight theirs as well.

Marchetto's road to *Cancer Vixen* and her other works began with a childhood interest in drawing that eventually led to a career as a comic strip cartoonist. Throughout her years as a cartoonist, which took her from *Mirabella* magazine to *Glamour*, the *New Yorker*, and the *New York Times*, Marchetto focused her attention on capturing a woman's point of view on everything from fashion to romance. By the early 2000s, she had built a reputation as a respected

Fitzroy Barrett/Landov

and accomplished cartoonist whose work regularly appeared in national and international publications.

In 2004, however, Marchetto's career was nearly derailed when she was diagnosed with breast cancer. When her editors at *Glamour* learned of her diagnosis, they suggested she document her fight and that it be published in the magazine. Marchetto enthusiastically obliged, and when she emerged from her treatments cancer-free, her journey appeared in the magazine's pages as *Cancer Vixen*. Hoping to share her story with an even wider audience, Marchetto released an expanded version of *Cancer Vixen* in the form of a full-length graphic novel. "I really wrote this book from my heart for the women out there. I was plugging into the healing energy of the unstoppable creative life force," Marchetto explained to Wayne Beamer for Comics Alliance.com in 2007.

Though her own battle is seemingly behind her, Marchetto continues the fight against breast cancer for women everywhere and continues to create wickedly funny cartoons that leave the world around her a little brighter.

## EARLY LIFE AND EDUCATION

Born in the early 1960s, Marchetto grew up in Roselle Park, New Jersey, where her father was a pharmacist. Her mother, Violetta, was employed as a women's shoe designer, and at age

three, Marchetto began imitating her mother's drawings, which was a hobby she continued for the next several years. By the time she was beginning to grow bored with sketching women wearing shoes, however, Marchetto's family took a trip to Bermuda and stayed in the vacation cottage frequented by renowned *New Yorker* cartoonist and short story author James Thurber. Many of Thurber's captioned drawings decorated the walls of the cottage, and Marchetto was captivated by them, explaining to Jane Gordon of London's *Mail on Sunday*, "I just thought it was so cool because I had never seen a cartoon before," and she soon realized that the fashionable yet boring ladies she'd been sketching could be more interesting if she gave them something to say. Additionally, as she told Wayne Beamer of ComicsAlliance in 2007, Marchetto found old *New Yorker* issues and many of Thurber's books in the cottage, and she "stayed up all night that night reading . . . and woke up with the sensation of things crawling all over me. I jumped out of bed and saw four hundred red ants in it. It was then that I was bitten by the cartoonist bug."

Although she remained passionate about cartooning well into adulthood, Marchetto did not immediately pursue it as a profession. After graduating from college, she entered the advertising industry, represented a number of major clients, and helped found the Kirshenbaum Bond ad agency (now Kirshenbaum Bond Senecal + Partners) with Richard Kirshenbaum. Fate again intervened to remind her of her love for cartooning. Kirshenbaum introduced Marchetto to former *Vogue* editor in chief Grace Mirabella, who was then the editor of the women's fashion magazine *Mirabella*. Mirabella offered to publish Marchetto's comic strip, and with that, Marchetto, who by then was a vice president at Young & Rubicam, embarked on what was soon to become her new career.

## CARTOONING CAREER

When Marchetto made her debut with *Mirabella* in 1993, she introduced SHE, an original character who became one of the artist's most well-known creations. An upper-middle-class product of postfeminism suburbia, SHE playfully rejected and defied the gender expectations that society expected her to fulfill. Rather than simply accept the implied limitations of her womanhood, the ever-trendy SHE challenged the world head-on and made it very clear that she could do anything she wanted.

SHE was a hit with readers almost immediately and quickly elevated Marchetto's reputation in the cartooning industry, especially after one of her cartoons, which lamented Vice President Al Gore's marital status, actually produced a response from Gore himself. "[He] wanted a copy, and I got some attention," Marchetto said in a 2006 interview with Toni Schlesinger for the *New York Observer*. Within a year of making her first appearance in *Mirabella*, SHE became so popular that Marchetto was able to publish a full-length graphic novel based on the character, *Just Who the Hell Is SHE, Anyway?* From 1996 to 1997, SHE also appeared in the international fashion magazine *Elle*.

Marchetto's success with SHE eventually caught the attention of Robert Mankoff, the cartoon editor of the *New Yorker* magazine. In 1998 Mankoff offered Marchetto the opportunity to become one of the magazine's regular cartoon contributors, which led to a long-time association with the *New Yorker* that not only provided her with a high-profile showcase for her cartoons but also afforded her the chance to try her hand at reporting. One of her stories took readers inside the New York Knicks locker room on opening night and helped Marchetto land a job with the *New York Times*. During her brief time there, Marchetto produced the paper's first regular cartoon feature, *The Strip*. Shortly after her departure from the *New York Times* in 2001, Marchetto began producing a single-panel cartoon in *Glamour* magazine's Dos & Don'ts feature called *Glamour Girls*.

In addition to *Mirabella*, *Glamour*, the *New Yorker*, and the *New York Times*, Marchetto's work has also appeared in a variety of other magazine genres including *Modern Bride* and *ESPN Magazine*.

## CANCER DIAGNOSIS

By May 2004, Marchetto's cartooning career was moving ahead at full speed with no sign of slowing down. Her personal life was also busy: she was engaged to Silvano Marchetto, the long-time owner of New York's Tuscan-cuisine Italian restaurant, Da Silvano, and their wedding was fast approaching. About a month before the wedding, however, Marchetto discovered a lump in her breast. In an interview with Roy Edroso in 2009 for the *Village Voice*, Marchetto described the moment of discovery and her subsequent decision to ignore the lump because she didn't have health insurance. "I found something, a lump, when I was swimming in April of 2004, but I ignored it because I was just hoping it was a pimple or something." The following month, Marchetto went to the doctor complaining of a cold, and during a routine chest exam, the doctor's stethoscope "bumped into the lump. . . . I walked into his office thinking I had a cold, and walked out wondering if I had cancer."

The diagnosis was indeed breast cancer, and though it was understandably devastating, Marchetto was determined from the start not to let the disease get the better of her. She was equally determined not to let her condition put a damper on her flair for fashion, frequently wearing designer heels to her chemotherapy treatments

hoping that keeping up her stylish appearance would lift her spirits. "I figured if I looked good, I'd feel good," Marchetto commented to *New York Times* reporter Lola Ogunnaike in 2005.

## CANCER VIXEN

Not long after Marchetto learned she had breast cancer, an editor at *Glamour* approached her with an idea. She suggested that Marchetto document her experience in cartoon form. Marchetto agreed and began doing just that. For the entire eleven months that Marchetto spent in treatment, from her cancer diagnosis and her confession to Silvano about not having health insurance to being deemed cancer free and her victory over the disease, she recorded the experience.

Marchetto often sketched the scenes and people around her, even while receiving chemotherapy treatments, and documented many of the most unnerving and occasionally bizarre moments of her journey such as a conversation with two fellow breast-cancer patients who accused her of not taking a heavy enough dose of chemotherapy after noticing that she still had long hair in the midst of her treatment. Marchetto also re-created an incident with another woman who, apparently believing that Marchetto would soon be much sicker and perhaps dead, made romantic overtures toward the cartoonist's husband right in front of her.

Though many of these moments were painful for Marchetto, she eventually found the humor in them with some coaxing. As she revealed to Ogunnaike, "Some of the moments were not funny when they were actually happening to me . . . but my mom would be, like, 'Material, material!'"

When she was finally declared cancer-free in May 2005, Marchetto's story appeared in *Glamour* as a six-page comic spread called *Cancer Vixen*. Touching the hearts of readers and critics alike, *Cancer Vixen* quickly generated an overwhelmingly positive response. Marchetto was so encouraged by the reaction to her work that she decided to turn six pages into a full-length graphic novel. Released in 2006, the expanded version of *Cancer Vixen* was widely popular and critically acclaimed. That same year, it earned Marchetto a nomination for Best Graphic Novel of the Year by the National Cartoonists Society. In addition, it was announced in 2013 that actress Cate Blanchett would produce and star in the film version of *Cancer Vixen*, which would be developed by HBO.

## ADVOCACY AND PHILANTHROPY

The real reward for Marchetto in *Cancer Vixen*'s success has been in helping others. While the book allowed her to empower women battling breast cancer, she was also grateful, as she explained to Edroso, to have been covered under her husband's insurance and she "felt a sense of obligation and enormous gratitude" to the doctors who had helped her recover. Marchetto decided the best way to give back was to help the women who would be fighting future battles and she donated a portion of the profits from *Cancer Vixen* to the Breast Cancer Research Foundation, an organization operated through St. Vincent's Hospital in Manhattan, where she underwent treatment.

Marchetto didn't stop there, however. One of her most terrifying experiences of the previous year had been the thought of fighting the disease without the benefit of health insurance, and Marchetto was struck by the reality that many women were not as fortunate as she had been. Even with regular breast exams and early detection, a higher percentage of women die from the disease if they do not have health insurance. As Marchetto pointed out in her 2009 *Village Voice* interview, "[Ninety-eight] percent of the time, if you find breast cancer early, you can beat it. Early detection is the closest thing we have to a cure. But women diagnosed with breast cancer who have no insurance have a 49 percent greater risk of dying from [it]. If they're diagnosed with cancer, they are unable to fund the treatment." To help alleviate the problem, Marchetto set up the Cancer Vixen Fund at St. Vincent's Comprehensive Cancer Center. The program allows the hospital to hold free semiannual breast cancer screenings and also offers a variety of support services for uninsured or underinsured breast cancer patients.

While Marchetto has advocated for regular breast cancer screenings and early detection of the disease, she also strongly believes that once diagnosed, the most critical part of the fight it is to stay positive and not become overwhelmed with the negative emotions cancer can bring. As she explained to Edroso, "Any way you're able to, transform the energy from a negative to a positive. It's important to do that—instead of seeing yourself as a victim, become a vixen."

In the fall of 2006, Marchetto was presented with the Humanitarian Award at the Breast Cancer Research Foundation Symposium and Awards Luncheon. She is currently working on her third graphic novel, which is fiction.

## SUGGESTED READING

Beamer, Wayne. "Talking to Marisa Acocella Marchetto, the 'Cancer Vixen'." *ComicsAlliance*. ComicsAlliance, 4 Oct. 2007. Web. 13 June 2013.

Edroso, Roy. "Q&A: Marisa Acocella Marchetto on *Cancer Vixen*, Her Fund, and FREE Mammograms This Friday." *Village Voice*. Village Voice LLC, 14 Oct. 2009. Web. 13 June 2013.

Marchetto, Marisa Acocella. *Cancer Vixen Fund*. CancerVixen, 2009. Web. 13 June 2013.

Ogunnaike, Lola. "A Vixen Cartooning in the Face of Cancer." *New York Times*. New York Times Co., 14 Apr. 2005. Web. 13 June 2013.

Publishers Weekly. Review of *Just Who the Hell Is SHE, Anyway? Publishers Weekly*. PWxyz LLC, 29 Aug. 1994. Web. 13 June 2013.

Schlesinger, Toni. "Cancer Vixen Tells All." *New York Observer*. New York Observer LLC, 2 Oct. 2006. Web. 13 June 2013.

## SELECTED WORKS

*Just Who the Hell Is SHE, Anyway?*, 1994; *The Strip*, 2000; *Glamour Girls*, 2002; *Cancer Vixen: A True Story*, 2006

—Jack Lasky

# Susana Martinez

**Born:** July 14, 1959
**Occupation:** Governor of New Mexico

Susana Martinez was elected governor of New Mexico in 2010. She is the first Latina governor in US history and the first female governor of New Mexico. In 2013, *TIME* magazine named her one of their 100 Most Influential People in the World.

Multiple publications have used the phrase "tough as nails" to describe Martinez, a Republican, who spent nearly four terms as the district attorney of Doña Ana County, the second-largest county in New Mexico. She won her first term in 1996, beating her former boss after switching her party affiliation from Democrat to Republican. Although criticized for the switch, she has nevertheless remained a loyal Republican, even if she does not always agree with her party on all issues. In 2012 she supported Mitt Romney for president despite being offended by his proposition to create strict measures that would encourage illegal immigrants to "self-deport." Still, Martinez largely toes the party line; for example, in 2011 she supported a measure to reverse New Mexico's policy of issuing drivers licenses to illegal immigrants and, via executive order, instructed New Mexico police officers to check the immigration status of each person they arrest.

As the Republican Party has been criticized for supporting a number of policies that negatively impact Hispanics and women, Martinez has been held up as the new face of the GOP. She spoke at the Republican National Convention in 2012 amid speculation that she might be chosen as Romney's running mate. Martinez has embraced the spotlight and her more prominent role within the party—she was named a member of the Republican Governors Association's

© Lynn Goldsmith/Corbis

leadership committee in 2011—and indeed, she has dreamed of participating in national politics since she was a child. Even so, she has been wary of being touted as the country's first female Hispanic governor, or even as a role model for young Hispanic women. "I embrace the fact that I am a woman who is Hispanic, has a law degree, and is accomplished in a field where it's 95 percent men. I embrace that," she told Deborah Baker for the *Albuquerque Journal* women's magazine, *Sage* (1 Jan. 2011). "But I didn't do it because I'm a woman, or Hispanic. I did those things because I worked hard, because I found education to be very important, because I tackled the issues or the problems in a logical way."

## EARLY LIFE AND INTEREST IN LAW

Susana Martinez was born on July 14, 1959, in El Paso, Texas. She grew up in a working-class neighborhood called Thomas Manor in El Paso's Lower Valley, though when Martinez was first born the family lived in public housing. Her father, Jacobo "Jake" Martinez, was a local boxing legend who served in the Korean War. After starting a family, he coached boxing and spent thirteen years as a deputy with the El Paso County Sheriff's Office. Her mother, Paula, worked as a secretary for an insurance company. According to Baker, Martinez is the great-granddaughter of Toribio Ortega, a Mexican general who served under Pancho Villa, and who is "credited with firing the first shot of the Mexican Revolution."

Martinez is the youngest of three siblings. Her brother, Jake Martinez Jr., is the owner of an El Paso uniform store. Her older sister, Leticia,

is developmentally disabled and lives with Martinez and her husband. Both of her parents worked full-time when she was a child. "[W]e were what is termed latchkey kids," Martinez Jr. told Ramón Rentería for the *El Paso Times* (24 Oct. 2010). But the independence suited Martinez, a girl who earned the nickname *la abogadita* or "little lawyer" from her family at the age of five. Her father was active in the local Democratic Party, and Martinez accompanied him to hand out campaign literature or to stuff envelopes for candidates. She dreamed of being a politician and decided early on that the best route to working in government was to study law. "I didn't have anybody to ask, to say how do you get there, how did that happen?" she told Colleen Heild for the *Albuquerque Journal* (12 Sept. 2010). "But I realized a lot of [politicians] were lawyers. So that's when my goal became to become an attorney so that I could then maybe get involved in national politics."

## EDUCATION AND WORK ETHIC

Martinez attended a Catholic elementary school and later, the public Riverside High School. She was a cheerleader and a member of the school's drill team. During her senior year, a group of students approached her to run for secretary of the student council on their ticket, but she turned them down. She decided that she would rather be student body president and ran against the group that tried to recruit her. She won, and according to Heild, took her post so seriously that she once "chastised the school janitors about keeping the grounds clean."

The future governor also excelled academically; she graduated as one of the top ten students of her class in 1977. It was an impressive feat considering the slew of responsibilities that awaited her outside of the classroom. Martinez spent evenings and summers caring for her older sister, and when she was seventeen years old, her parents started their own security business with only $400 in the bank. The family's new entrepreneurial role was a frightening one for Martinez, who told Heild that it made her realize for the first time that they were living paycheck to paycheck. Martinez took an active role in the family business. She was certified to carry a firearm before she turned eighteen and patrolled parking lots at church bingo games as an armed security guard.

While attending the University of El Paso, Martinez continued to work for her family's business. She graduated with a degree in criminal justice in 1981. Later, she attended law school at the University of Oklahoma at Norman, where she was one of only a handful of Hispanic students. "People would ask me what I was, and I had never been asked that question, having been raised in El Paso," she told Heild. She earned her juris doctorate in 1986 and moved to Las

Cruces, New Mexico, a town about forty minutes north of her family home in El Paso, Texas.

## DOÑA ANA COUNTY DISTRICT ATTORNEY'S OFFICE

New Mexico's Third Judicial District Attorney's Office, based in Las Cruces for Doña Ana County, hired Martinez as an assistant district attorney in 1986. There, she specialized in cases involving victims of child abuse, domestic violence, and rape. She told Baker that two weeks into her new job, the district attorney (DA) brought her three young children and asked her to figure out if they were "telling the truth." It was implied that she was selected for the task because she was the only woman in the office. "I realized very quickly I did not know what I was doing," she said, and she convinced her boss to let her train in interviewing techniques. Those skilled paid off during her first trial, when she was able to convict a child molester on the testimony of a three-year-old girl.

Being a tenacious prosecutor helped Martinez's career progress quickly. She became deputy district attorney to two-term district attorney Doug Driggers, a Democrat, and worked on his reelection campaign in 1992. Driggers lost in the Democratic primary to a Las Cruces defense attorney named Gregory Valdez. Martinez's time in the new Valdez administration was short; she was fired after she received a subpoena to testify against him in a private hearing regarding the termination of a district attorney investigator. "My first question to him when he handed me my [termination] papers was, 'Does this have anything to do with the [subpoena]?'" she recalled to Heild. "[A]nd his response was, and I'll never forget it, 'I'm not going to tell you either way.' I grabbed my letter and I left." She filed a civil rights lawsuit against Valdez and settled out of court for $120,000.

## PARTY SWITCH FROM DEMOCRAT TO REPUBLICAN

Martinez next served as an attorney for the state's Children, Youth, and Families Department from 1993 until 1996, when she ran against Valdez for the Doña Ana County district attorney seat. Before her campaign began in earnest, she switched her party affiliation—from Democrat to Republican—and at election time "won handily," according to Heild, with nearly 60 percent of the vote. Martinez was accused of changing her party affiliation for political gain, but she denied the charge, noting that Democrats significantly outnumbered Republicans in Doña Ana County.

In an interview with Michael Haederle for the *Los Angeles Times* (1 Jan. 2011), Martinez attributed the switch to a genuine shift in values. She originally planned to run against Valdez as a registered Democrat, but when the local Republican Party got wind of her plans, they invited her to a lunch to discuss touchstone party issues like the death penalty, taxes, and government spending. Martinez knew they were trying to recruit her and remembered telling her husband, "We're going to be very polite. We're going to say thank you very much and we're going to leave," as she recalled to Haederle. Afterward, she said, "We got in the car, we looked at each other and said, 'Oh my God, we are Republicans! Now what do we do?'" Martinez added that she expected to lose the election after officially registering as a Republican, but she drew enough crossover votes—most likely because she was well-known within the community—to win the election.

## TENURE AS DISTRICT ATTORNEY AND KATIE'S LAW

As DA, Martinez developed a reputation for her aggressive tactics. She continued her work for victims of abuse and during her tenure personally prosecuted a man named Gabriel Avila for the brutal rape and killing of a graduate student named Kate Sepich in 2003. The case had been unsolved for several years, but in 2006, a DNA sample tied Avila, who had been convicted of robbery in 2003, to Sepich's murder. He pled guilty to Sepich's murder after being confronted with this DNA evidence.

Avila had been required to provide a DNA sample because he was convicted of a felony, but victim advocates like Sepich's parents reasoned that if DNA samples are taken after suspects are arrested for felonies, cases like Katie's could be solved more quickly and more often. After the trial, Martinez joined Sepich's family in a campaign to require New Mexico to employ such DNA sampling, and the state passed Katie's Law in 2006. The law initially required people arrested for violent felonies, like kidnapping, rape, and murder, to provide DNA samples to the state. After her term as the governor of New Mexico began in 2011, Martinez signed into law an expansion of Katie's Law requiring people arrested for any felony in New Mexico to provide DNA samples to the state.

A federal version of Katie's Law, the Katie Sepich Enhanced DNA Collection Act of 2012, was first proposed in 2010 by New Mexico Representative Harry Teague and revived in 2012 by California Representative Adam Schiff. The bill was signed into law by President Barack Obama in January 2013. The act allows for the federal government to provide grants to state law enforcement for the creation or expansion of DNA collection programs; the intent is for these programs to take samples upon the arrest of those suspected of serious crimes.

During her tenure as district attorney, Martinez was twice named "Prosecutor of the Year" in New Mexico. She was reelected three consecutive times: in 2000, 2004, and 2008. Martinez beat Democratic challenger Kent E. Yalkut in

2000, with 52 percent of the vote; beat Valdez again in 2004, with 60 percent of the vote; and ran unopposed in 2008.

## GOVERNOR OF NEW MEXICO

Martinez had considered a run for governor for several years before throwing her hat into the race in 2010. Governor Bill Richardson, a Democrat, was leaving office after serving two consecutive terms. He had once enjoyed tremendous popularity in the state, but by 2010, after allegations of corruption, he was somewhat of a political pariah. Martinez faced Democrat Diane Denish in the general election. Denish had served two terms as Richardson's lieutenant governor, and it was easy for Martinez to frame the election as a referendum on an unpopular outgoing governor and his administration. The campaign garnered national attention because each candidate stood to become the state's first female governor. Republicans poured money in Martinez's campaign, including a whopping $450,000 contribution from a Houston developer. She also brought in popular conservative personality and former Alaska governor Sarah Palin to speak at one of her rallies. With the heft of the national party behind her, Martinez bested Denish by a margin of nearly 54 percent to 46 percent of the vote.

Sworn into office in January 2011, Martinez has since developed a dual reputation. She is strongly pro-business yet maintains the appeal of being a populist governor. She has pushed forward a bold agenda while working hard to undo much of her predecessor's legacy. She has touted her bipartisan history and yet is generally averse to compromise. Perhaps most conspicuously, she has won the support of the Hispanic community while championing harsh anti-immigration legislation.

Weeks after her inauguration, Martinez issued an executive order requiring state police officers to check the immigration status of each person they arrest. Rachel LaZar, the executive director of an immigration rights group called El Centro de Igualdad y Derechos, told Marc Lacey for the New York Times (30 Aug. 2011), "People ask, 'Why would someone who came from where we came from do this?'" It was a common sentiment across the state, and Martinez had a ready response. "I understand as a Latina not all Hispanic people are criminals," Martinez told Lacey. "Of course, I understand that. This isn't an immigrant issue. It's a public-safety issue." The order has continued to face criticism.

Martinez began raising funds for her 2014 reelection campaign in early 2012. She has denied rumors about running for president in 2016.

## PERSONAL LIFE

Martinez met her first husband in law school at the University of Oklahoma. They divorced after three years. She then married retired Doña Ana County Undersheriff Chuck Franco in 1991, whom she met while working for the DA's office and Franco was an undercover officer for the sheriff's department. Martinez has a stepson named Carlo from Franco's previous marriage. The couple lives in Las Cruces with Martinez's disabled sister Leticia, or Lettie. Martinez has said that her decision not to have children was partly due to knowing that she would be her sister's caretaker later in life. "I knew that after my mother died, Lettie would come back to me, and she would still be five," she told Champ Clark for People magazine (5 Aug. 2013).

## SUGGESTED READING

Baker, Deborah. "From Bordertown Neighborhood to State's Highest Elected Office." Sage. Albuquerque Journal, 1 Jan. 2011. Web. 16 Sept. 2013.

Clark, Champ. "Gov. Susana Martinez: Caring for Her Sister." People 5 Aug. 2013: 130–34. Print.

Haederle, Michael. "A Rising GOP Star in Santa Fe." Los Angeles Times. Los Angeles Times, 1 Jan. 2011. Web. 16 Sept. 2013.

Heild, Colleen. "Tough as Nails." Albuquerque Journal. Albuquerque Journal, 12 Sept. 2010. Web. 16 Sept. 2013.

Lacey, Marc. "New Mexico Governor Rushes to Undo the Agenda of Her Predecessor." New York Times 30 Aug. 2011: A11. Print.

Rentería, Ramón. "'Bossy' El Paso Girl Susana Martinez a Born Leader." El Paso Times. Texas/New Mexico News Group, 24 Oct. 2010. Web. 16 Sept. 2013.

—Molly Hagan

# Misty May-Treanor and Kerri Walsh Jennings

**Occupation:** Professional beach volleyball players

## MISTY MAY-TREANOR
**Born:** July 30, 1977

## KERRI WALSH JENNINGS
**Born:** August 15, 1978

Misty May-Treanor and Kerri Walsh Jennings, former women's professional beach volleyball partners, are widely considered to be the greatest beach volleyball duo of all time. Over the course of their eleven-year partnership—from 2001 to 2012—May-Treanor and Walsh Jennings, both of whom were decorated indoor volleyball players before they made the switch

Diego Azubel/EPA/Landov

to sand, racked up more accolades, accomplishments, and awards than any other women's beach volleyball team in history. They were known as "volleyball's version of Montana-to-Rice—two supreme athletes who have an uncanny awareness of what the other is going to do," Mark Emmons wrote for the *San Jose Mercury News* (14 Sept. 2007), referring to the San Francisco 49ers' legendary quarterback-receiver tandem of Joe Montana and Jerry Rice.

May-Treanor and Walsh Jennings were the first and, to date, the only duo of either gender in their sport to capture gold medals at three consecutive Olympic Games and three consecutive Fédération Internationale de Volleyball (FIVB) Beach Volleyball World Championships. They have been credited with transforming women's beach volleyball with their rare combination of size, speed, and skill, as well as for putting the sport on the map, growing it from a niche event to "the hippest sport in the Summer Games," as Jason Diamos noted for the *New York Times* (10 July 2004). May-Treanor retired from beach volleyball following the 2012 Olympic Games, but Walsh Jennings continues to compete on the sport's professional circuit.

## MAY-TREANOR'S EARLY LIFE

May-Treanor was born Misty Elizabeth May on July 30, 1977, in Los Angeles, California. She is the only child of Bob and Barbara May, but she has two stepbrothers, Brack and Scott, from her father's first marriage. Both of May-Treanor's parents were distinguished athletes. Her father played on the men's US indoor volleyball team that placed seventh at the 1968 Summer Olympics and was a highly regarded professional beach volleyball player. Her mother, who died of cancer in 2002, was a nationally ranked tennis player at the University of California, Los Angeles, before becoming a standout beach volleyball player in her own right.

May-Treanor was raised in Santa Monica, California, on Muscle Beach, a world-famous site known for its outdoor exercise areas and many high-level basketball and beach volleyball courts. By the time she was born, her parents were totally immersed in beach volleyball and the wild and effervescent culture that went with it, meaning she was being practically raised in the sport. "From the moment I took my first breath, my life has been about the beach," May-Treanor said in her memoir, *Misty: Digging Deep in Volleyball and Life* (2010), which she cowrote with the sportswriter Jill Lieber Steeg. "The sand was, and always has been, my playground. Or more accurately, when I was a baby, my play-pen." May-Treanor fondly recalls being "lulled to sleep by the sounds of the Pacific Ocean crashing against the sand and the batting of volleyballs back and forth across the nets."

Growing up around some of the best beach volleyball players in history, legends such as Kathy Gregory and Karch Kiraly, May-Treanor was fated to play beach volleyball. When she was four years old, her father, using a balloon, started running her through volleyball drills in the family living room. At eight, she competed in her first beach volleyball tournament, playing with her father in a mixed-doubles event in which they finished fifth. At ten, she started playing indoor volleyball.

May-Treanor's development as an elite volleyball player came quickly, thanks to her playing almost exclusively with and against older competition. Throughout her early indoor volleyball career, she was nearly always forced to compete against children in older age divisions because of her advanced skills. May-Treanor's athletic talents, however, were not just limited to volleyball. As a youth she also excelled in such sports and activities as dance, soccer, swimming, track, and tennis. Despite growing up in a household that lived paycheck to paycheck, May-Treanor has said that her parents, who for a time ran a pizza stand on Muscle Beach and coached women's indoor volleyball at Santa Monica College, never prevented her from participating in a sporting activity because of lack of money.

## WALSH JENNINGS'S EARLY LIFE

Walsh Jennings, born Kerri Lee Walsh on August 15, 1978, was raised in California and grew up in an athletic family. Her father, Tim, was a six-foot-eight minor-league baseball pitcher in the Oakland Athletics organization and a former semiprofessional basketball player; her mother, Marge, was a volleyball star at Santa Clara University, where she was twice named most valuable player (MVP). Walsh Jennings has an older brother, Marte, and two younger sisters, Kelli and KC, all of whom were collegiate athletes.

Extremely shy and introverted as a child, Walsh Jennings found her niche in sports. She grew up a fan of the San Francisco Giants and, taking after her father, initially fostered dreams of becoming a professional baseball player. Those dreams changed, however, after she discovered indoor volleyball, which she started playing at the age of ten. Despite her reserved nature, Walsh Jennings quickly became a standout in the sport, largely because of her height, which gave her an immediate advantage over other competitors. As an adult Walsh Jennings is six-foot-three, making her one of the tallest female players in the sport. Unlike May-Treanor, who continued to play on beach volleyball club teams throughout her indoor career, Walsh Jennings did not take up the outdoor discipline until much later in her career. "Growing up, I'd avoid it," she recalled to David Leon Moore for *USA Today* (12 Aug. 2004). "I was really awkward, and I couldn't move. I felt like I was pretty good at indoor, and I didn't want people to see me weak. So I made a conscious effort to avoid it."

## RIVALS BEFORE PARTNERS

When May-Treanor was in the eighth grade, she moved with her parents to Orange County, California. She attended Newport Harbor High School, in Newport Beach, where she was a standout in volleyball, soccer, and track. While playing for Newport Harbor's varsity women's volleyball team May-Treanor first crossed paths with Walsh Jennings. Walsh Jennings attended Archbishop Mitty High School in San Jose, where she played for the school's girls' varsity volleyball team. During her sophomore season she played against May-Treanor for the first time, while competing in a volleyball tournament held in Stockton, California. By that time, May-Treanor had already developed a reputation around California as a volleyball prodigy, so much so that Walsh Jennings idolized her, even though the two were only one year apart in age. "It was magical watching her," Walsh Jennings said to Donald Deane in an interview for the TSM Interactive website (22 July 2012). "She could do anything." At the Stockton tournament, Walsh Jennings went so far as to ask May-Treanor for an autograph, to which the surprised May-Treanor complied.

May-Treanor and Walsh Jennings met again during the former's senior year, when their high school volleyball teams squared off at the Santa Barbara Tournament of Champions, one of the longest-running and most prestigious girls varsity volleyball tournaments in California. At the tournament, Newport Harbor High lost to Archbishop Mitty High in the quarterfinals. The defeat marked Newport Harbor's only loss of that season, in which May-Treanor led the team to a 33–1 record and a California Interscholastic Federation Division I state championship. As a senior May-Treanor was named Mizuno High School National Player of the Year and earned

Division I state MVP honors for a second consecutive year, after setting a national record with 548 kills and recording 302 digs and ninety-two assists. (In volleyball parlance, a "kill" is a successful point-scoring spike, and a "dig" is a defensive save or pass of a hard-driven ball from the other team.) In her four years on Newport Harbor's varsity squad, May-Treanor helped the team post an overall record of 106–12. During her junior and senior seasons, she further honed her volleyball skills as a member of the elite Ichiban Volleyball Club team, which is based in Long Beach, California.

Walsh Jennings, whom May-Treanor described in *Misty* as being "the Northern California version of me" in high school, also had a decorated high school career. From her sophomore through senior seasons, she led Archbishop Mitty High to three consecutive indoor state titles; during her senior year, she was named Gatorade National Player of the Year. Like May-Treanor, she also participated in club volleyball and played on the San Jose-based Team Mizuno club volleyball team. In 1995, she helped Team Mizuno capture a gold medal at the Junior Olympics in Orlando, Florida.

## COLLEGE ALL-AMERICANS

By the time they finished high school, May-Treanor and Walsh Jennings were two of the most highly touted women's volleyball players in the country. May-Treanor received more than three hundred recruiting letters and was courted heavily by the nation's volleyball powerhouses, including Stanford University, the University of the Pacific, and Long Beach State University. Despite verbally committing to Pacific as a sophomore, she ultimately chose to remain close to home, enrolling at Long Beach State. One of the main reasons May-Treanor chose to attend the school was to train under assistant coach Debbie Green—a two-time All-American volleyball star at the University of Southern California and former US national volleyball team member who is also widely regarded as the greatest women's volleyball setter of all time. Coming out of high school, the five-foot-nine May-Treanor had been considered one of the nation's top outside hitters, but she decided to become a setter in college, since the position would better complement her height at the professional level. (Despite her above-average height, May-Treanor is considered short by professional volleyball standards. Outside hitters are generally players who are set up for spikes over the net, while setters are responsible for running the offense of the team.)

Under the tutelage of Green and head coach Brian Gimmillaro, May-Treanor developed into one of the best setters in collegiate volleyball history. During her four-year career at Long Beach State, she was twice named the American

Volleyball Coaches Association (AVCA) Division I player of the year (1997 and 1998) and earned first-team all-American honors on three occasions (1996–1998). As a senior, May-Treanor captained a Long Beach team that posted a perfect 36–0 record, en route to defeating Penn State University in the 1998 National Collegiate Athletic Association (NCAA) Division I Women's Volleyball Tournament; she was named the tournament's co-MVP, as Long Beach became the first NCAA women's volleyball team in history to finish a season undefeated. That season, May-Treanor was named AVCA Division I player of the year for the second consecutive year, becoming the first back-to-back winner since Long Beach State's Tara Cross in 1989 and 1990, and she received the Honda Broderick NCAA athlete of the year award.

While May-Treanor was racking up accolades at Long Beach, Walsh Jennings was putting together a record-breaking career of her own at Stanford. As a four-year starter at outside hitter for Stanford, she led the school to consecutive NCAA titles in 1996 and 1997 and was a four-time, first-team all-American (1996–1999), becoming only the second player in NCAA history to receive such an honor all four seasons. She was named MVP of the NCAA championship tournament as a freshman in 1996 and was named co-national player of the year as a senior in 1999. During her junior season, Walsh Jennings played against May-Treanor for the third time, when she led Stanford to victory over Long Beach in the semifinals of the 1997 NCAA championship tournament; Stanford later defeated Penn State to win that year's NCAA championship. Like May-Treanor, Walsh Jennings was credited with helping to transform her position with her rare mix of skills and was heralded as one of the greatest collegiate players of all time.

## TURNING PRO AND 2000 SUMMER OLYMPICS

May-Treanor and Walsh Jennings both joined the American professional volleyball circuit after finishing their college careers. May-Treanor, who majored in kinesiology and physical education at Long Beach, became a full-time member of the US women's national indoor volleyball team in June 1999, but she left the team only two months later to join the professional beach volleyball tour. By that time she had become exhausted from the constant grind of indoor volleyball; as a member of the US national team, she was required to participate in twice-daily practices and an intensive weight training and cardio program. "You get burned out after a while playing indoors," May-Treanor told Moore. "I was starting to lose that fire." That "fire" was further lost after head coach Mick Haley told her that she would have to wait at least a year and a half before she could become the team's starting setter.

May-Treanor's departure from the national indoor team came shortly before Walsh Jennings was added to the team. Walsh Jennings, who majored in American studies at Stanford, played under Haley on the women's national indoor team for two seasons (1999–2000), during which she competed at the 2000 Olympic Games in Sydney, Australia. As a right-side hitter on the Olympic women's indoor squad, she led her team to a respectable, but ultimately disappointing, fourth-place finish. Afterward, Walsh Jennings, feeling burned out, began contemplating her own indoor future. She told Diamos, "My parents knew I was kind of drained. . . . I kind of hit the point at the Olympics where the game had become very stressful to me. I loved the sport so much. But I needed a change. And I didn't want to play professionally in Europe."

May-Treanor also qualified for and competed in the 2000 Olympic Games, but she did so as a beach volleyball player. Leading up to the Games, she formed a partnership with Holly McPeak, then the best female beach volleyball player in the world; the two enjoyed a meteoric rise to the top of the sport, after having dominated much of their competition in numerous events on different professional beach volleyball circuits, including FIVB, the Association of Volleyball Professionals (AVP), USA Volleyball, and Beach Volleyball America (BVA). May-Treanor and McPeak earned a number-four seed at the 2000 Olympics, where they were expected to contend for a medal. However, they failed to advance to the medal round and finished in a disappointing fifth place, which happened largely because May-Treanor was hampered by a nagging abdominal injury that prevented her from playing at the peak of her abilities.

## RECORD-BREAKING PARTNERSHIP

Following the 2000 Olympic Games, May-Treanor, as suggested by her parents, parted ways with McPeak to become partners with Walsh Jennings. Both women had reached crossroads in their careers after unsatisfying performances in Sydney and had been looking for an exciting change of pace—May-Treanor from the motherly restraint of her workaholic, more seasoned partner, and Walsh Jennings from the rigorous demands of indoor volleyball. "We both kind of left there [Sydney] wanting more," Walsh Jennings told Diamos. Despite her early career reservations about playing on sand, Walsh Jennings quickly picked up the discipline under May-Treanor's tutelage, and the duo began competing in tournaments in 2001. In April of that year, they competed in their first tournament together, a BVA event in Clearwater, Florida, in which they placed seventh. They then competed in and won a BVA event in Oceanside, California, before embarking on the elite FIVB tour. The duo won four medals in eight FIVB events. At the 2001 Beach Volleyball World Championships in Klagenfurt, Austria, the pair finished ninth.

Though May-Treanor and Walsh Jennings experienced typical struggles in their first year of competition together, the duo soon emerged as the best women's beach volleyball team in the world. In 2002, they won the FIVB tour, becoming the first US team to do so. In 2003, their first year playing on the AVP tour, they won all eight AVP events in which they competed, winning all thirty-nine matches and losing only five sets, to complete the first undefeated season in the tour's history. May-Treanor and Walsh Jennings were subsequently named AVP team of the year, an honor they would earn in each of the next five years. Meanwhile, in addition to that year's AVP tour, the duo won five of the eleven tournaments in which they competed on the FIVB tour. At the 2003 FIVB Beach Volleyball World Championships in Rio de Janeiro, Brazil, May-Treanor and Walsh Jennings won the gold medal.

During the 2004 season, May-Treanor and Walsh Jennings amassed one of the most remarkable winning streaks in beach volleyball history. They entered that season having won their previous nine tournaments (on both the AVP and FIVB tours), and then they won six more tournaments (four AVP, two FIVB) before finally losing in the semifinals of a tournament in Manhattan Beach, California, in June 2004; during the course of their winning streak, which lasted eleven months, they won a then-record eighty-nine straight matches. May-Treanor and Walsh Jennings finished the 2004 season winning seven of ten AVP tournaments and four of five FIVB tournaments. Their dominating season culminated at the 2004 Olympics in Athens, Greece, where they took home the gold medal in convincing fashion by sweeping all seven of their opponents. May-Treanor and Walsh Jennings became the first US women's duo to capture gold, let alone any medal, in beach volleyball.

## SECOND OLYMPIC GOLD MEDAL

After the 2004 Olympics, May-Treanor and Walsh Jennings became minor celebrities, thanks to primetime coverage of their matches on television, which in true beach volleyball fashion, featured bikini-clad competitors, blaring music, and raucous fans. "That exposure made us who we are more than anything," Walsh Jennings noted to Emmons. The duo only continued to raise their profile in 2005, when they won their second consecutive FIVB Beach Volleyball World Championships gold medal. That year they also won eleven of the fourteen AVP tournaments they entered and six of seven FIVB tournaments.

In 2006, May-Treanor and Walsh Jennings set the AVP tour single-season record for wins

(thirteen) and captured three FIVB titles. In 2007, they won their third consecutive world title, at the FIVB Beach Volleyball World Championships in Gstaad, Switzerland, becoming the first team to accomplish such a feat. That year they matched their AVP tour single-season record for wins and added seven more FIVB titles to their collection. May-Treanor and Walsh Jennings each finished the year ahead of McPeak on the beach volleyball all-time wins list, moving into first and second place, respectively.

During the 2008 season, May-Treanor and Walsh Jennings recorded "one of the most astonishing winning streaks in any sport," as Kelli Anderson noted for *Sports Illustrated* (29 Dec. 2008). The duo eclipsed their own record by winning 19 consecutive tournaments and 112 consecutive matches. The streak lasted more than a year and carried into the 2008 Olympic Games, in Beijing, China, where the pair again dominated the competition, sweeping all seven of their opponents en route to winning a second consecutive gold medal. With their Beijing triumph, May-Treanor and Walsh Jennings were the first women's beach volleyball team to win consecutive Olympic gold medals.

## SEMIRETIREMENT AND THIRD OLYMPIC GOLD MEDALS

Following the 2008 Olympics, May-Treanor and Walsh Jennings both took brief sabbaticals from beach volleyball to focus on other endeavors. May-Treanor, who by that time had had reservations about competing again in another Olympics, became a contestant on the seventh season of ABC's television series *Dancing with the Stars*. She was forced to drop out of the show after only three weeks, when she ruptured her left Achilles tendon in rehearsals. The injury required her to undergo surgery, which kept her sidelined for most of the 2009 season. In *Misty*, May-Treanor called her ruptured Achilles tendon rehabilitation "the most difficult" of her athletic career.

While May-Treanor recovered from her injury, Walsh Jennings settled down to start a family with her husband, professional beach volleyball player Casey Jennings, who she married in December 2005. She gave birth to two sons, Joseph and Sundance, over a twelve-month span, in 2009 and 2010, respectively. Upon returning to the women's professional beach circuit in late summer 2010, Walsh Jennings partnered with Nicole Branagh, who had been a member of the other US women's beach volleyball team at the 2008 Olympics (with her partner Elaine Youngs). The two competed in the final two FIVB events of the 2010 season, placing fifth at a tournament in China and winning a tournament in Thailand.

May-Treanor had also partnered with Branagh during the first part of the 2010 season, while

Walsh Jennings recovered from the birth of her second child. The pair won two events on the AVP tour, but after going winless in nine FIVB tournaments, May-Treanor contemplated sitting out the 2011 season as a way to evaluate her future. She only changed her mind after having an inspirational conversation with her husband, the major-league baseball catcher Matt Treanor, who ultimately convinced her that her career was not yet over. (The two had married in November 2004.)

In 2011 May-Treanor and Walsh Jennings reunited as partners and competed in eleven events on the FIVB World Tour, finishing with three titles and four second-place finishes. They won two more events on the FIVB tour in 2012 to secure the number-three seed in the Olympic qualification rankings.

At the 2012 Olympic Games, in London, May-Treanor and Walsh Jennings—who sought help from a sports psychologist before the Games to help rekindle their magic as partners—won their third consecutive Olympic beach volleyball gold medal, when they defeated fellow Americans and 2009 FIVB world champions April Ross and Jennifer Kessy in the gold-medal match. May-Treanor and Walsh Jennings lost only one set in the entire competition and finished their Olympic career with a perfect 21–0 record. Commenting on the duo's third Olympic gold medal victory, May-Treanor said, as quoted by Rick Maese for the *Washington Post* (8 Aug. 2012), "The first two medals, I think was more volleyball . . . The friendship we had was there, but it was all volleyball, volleyball. This was so much more about the friendship, the togetherness, the journey. . . . I don't know if you can write this script the way that it turned out. . . . But we believed."

### PERSONAL LIVES

May-Treanor retired from professional women's beach volleyball immediately after the 2012 Olympic Games, as part of plans to raise a family with her husband. At the time of her retirement, she was the most successful female beach volleyball player in history, with 112 career victories (winning 69 in the United States and 43 internationally), and more than $2 million in career prize winnings. She and her husband reside in Long Beach, California.

Walsh Jennings, who revealed that she had been five weeks pregnant while competing at the 2012 Olympics, gave birth to her third child, daughter Scout, in April 2013. She has announced plans to compete at the 2016 Olympics in Rio de Janeiro, Brazil, in hopes of taking home a record fourth gold medal. By the end of the 2012 season, she was ranked second to May-Treanor on the all-time women's beach volleyball wins list, with 109 (winning 65 in the United States and 44 internationally). She lives in Manhattan Beach with her husband and their three children.

### SUGGESTED READING

Anderson, Kelli. "A Sand Slam." *Sports Illustrated* 29 Dec. 2008: 45. Print.

Emmons, Mark. "Six Feet of Sunshine: Walsh Enjoying the Beach Volleyball Life." *San Jose Mercury News*. MediaNews Group, 14 Sept. 2007. Web. 25 Mar. 2013.

May-Treanor, Misty, and Jill Lieber Steeg. *Misty: Digging Deep in Volleyball and Life*. New York: Scribner, 2010. Print.

Moore, David Leon. "Beach Volleyball's Dynamic Duo." *USA Today*. USA Today, 12 Aug. 2004. Web. 25 Mar. 2013.

Ostler, Scott. "Partnership Endures through Sands of Time." *San Francisco Chronicle* 1 Aug. 2012: B1. Print.

*— Chris Cullen*

# Andrew McCutchen

**Born:** October 10, 1986
**Occupation:** Baseball player

Pittsburgh Pirates center fielder Andrew Mc-Cutchen is, as J. Brady McCollough wrote for the *Pittsburgh Post-Gazette* (31 Mar. 2013), "the face—and the hair—of the [Pirates'] franchise, his long locks having become a symbol of hope for a fan base that has had to take loyalty to new levels over two decades." A quintessential "five-tool" player known for his world-class speed, ability to hit for both average and power, and superb defensive skills, McCutchen has lived up to extremely high expectations since joining the Pirates' organization in 2005, straight out of high school. After spending three and a half years in the minor leagues, McCutchen made his major-league debut with the Pirates in 2009 and has since established himself among the premier all-around players in the game. He has been named to two all-star teams and has been singlehandedly responsible for leading the Pirates, a long-struggling but once-glorious franchise, back to respectability. McCutchen had a breakout year in 2012, when he finished among the National League (NL) leaders in a number of statistical categories and contended for that league's Most Valuable Player (MVP) Award. When asked about his teammate, Pirates infielder Neil Walker told Tyler Kepner for the *New York Times* (26 July 2012), "In my opinion he's the best player in the league, and the fact that he plays here in Pittsburgh, he's probably lost some of that exposure, because we don't play on national television that much. . . . You stick him in a place like New York or Boston, he may be the face of this entire league."

© Jeanine Leech/Icon SMI/Corbis

## EARLY LIFE

Andrew Stefan McCutchen was born on October 10, 1986, in Fort Meade, Florida. He has a younger sister, Lauren. When McCutchen was born, his parents, Lorenzo and Petrina, were still in high school. As a result he spent his early years living in a close-quartered Fort Meade home with his mother, grandmother, aunt, and several cousins. McCutchen later moved with his parents to a mobile home in the nearby city of Bartow before eventually returning to Fort Meade, where he was raised in a deeply religious, tight-knit household. His father worked at a phosphate mine before becoming a youth pastor; his mother is a juvenile case-records manager for the Polk County Sheriff's Office.

Both of McCutchen's parents were athletes. His father was a standout football, basketball, and baseball player at Fort Meade High School and earned a football scholarship to Carson-Newman College in Tennessee. Lorenzo had dreams of playing professionally in the National Football League, but he gave up those plans to be closer to his family and left college without playing a single down of football. McCutchen's mother played volleyball at Polk County Community College but eventually left college for the same reasons. The couple married on August 1, 1992, when McCutchen was five years old.

At an early age McCutchen learned the value of hard work and perseverance from his parents, who sometimes struggled to make ends meet. "I had everything I needed or wanted," he told Lisa Olson for *Sporting News* (27 Sept. 2012). "I didn't know anything different. I learned to be a hard worker. I learned that things aren't going to be given to you on a silver platter." That mindset carried over to baseball, for which McCutchen developed an early passion. He grew up about an hour away from the Pirates' spring-training facility in Bradenton, but he rooted for the Atlanta Braves and idolized the Seattle Mariners' Ken Griffey Jr. McCutchen started playing T-ball at the age of five and quickly progressed through other youth leagues as he got older. He

was taught the fundamentals of the game by his father, who pitched to him on a daily basis to develop his batting skills. "He was always there," McCutchen said of his father to McCollough. "His father was in and out of his life, and I think he pretty much made a promise to himself that if he had kids he was going to be supportive, and that's what he did."

## HIGH SCHOOL CAREER

McCutchen's baseball talent was evident from the start, and by age eleven, he was routinely outshining teenagers on Amateur Athletic Union summer travel teams. Around this time McCutchen caught the attention of Jeff Toffanelli, the head baseball coach at Fort Meade Middle-Senior High School. Toffanelli was so convinced about McCutchen's ability that he named him Fort Meade High's starting varsity shortstop when McCutchen was still in the eighth grade. The youngest member of the team, McCutchen went on to lead all Polk County high schools in hitting with a .507 batting average and earned first-team all-county honors.

At Fort Meade High, McCutchen became a star not only on the baseball team but also on the football and track teams. As a freshman he earned first-team all-county honors in baseball once again and helped the school's track team win the state title. McCutchen played wide receiver on the junior-varsity football squad and won particular attention for his performance in the team's season finale, during which he scored five touchdowns. He was promoted to Fort Meade's varsity football team as a sophomore and earned first-team all-county honors, even though his season ended early because of a knee injury. The injury required him to have surgery and forced him to miss his entire sophomore baseball season.

When McCutchen returned for his junior season, Toffanelli moved him to the outfield at the suggestion of major-league scout Don Jacoby. The move to the outfield was meant to take advantage of his speed; by that time McCutchen was being clocked at a blazing 6.2 seconds in the sixty-yard dash. McCutchen proved to be a natural fit for the outfield, and as a center fielder during his junior season, he batted .474 with eight home runs, forty runs batted in (RBIs), and forty-five stolen bases.

During his senior season McCutchen put up numbers that read "more like fantasy than reality," as Bruce Keidan for the *Pittsburgh Quarterly* (2010) noted. He led Polk County in every offensive category, batting .709 with sixteen home runs, forty-two RBIs, eight doubles, and three triples, while drawing twenty-three walks to just six strikeouts. He was named the Gatorade Florida High School Player of the Year and was ranked by *Baseball America* as the top high school baseball prospect from the state of Florida. Despite being heavily recruited by colleges to play both baseball and football, McCutchen decided to enter the 2005 MLB amateur draft.

## PITTSBURGH PIRATES

Throughout his high school career McCutchen was scouted heavily by a number of major-league organizations, but none more so than the Pirates, representatives of which reportedly attended every one of his senior-season games. The Pirates scout credited with discovering McCutchen, Rob Sidwell, told Kepner, "He had lightning-fast hands, and he could really generate bat speed. . . . He had the quickest hands I've ever scouted, and he could hit it a long way. He was a five-tool guy, even as a young, skinny, small-town kid." Despite McCutchen's "five-tool" ability, Pirates top executives still expressed reservations about his height (roughly five feet ten) and the fact that he competed in Florida's class 2A division, the second lowest of the six high school baseball levels in the state. As a result he was forced to prove himself further to Pirates brass in a workout held at the team's spring-training facility in March 2005, early in his senior season. McCutchen's performance in that workout, in which he outperformed Rajai Davis, then a highly touted minor-league outfield prospect, ultimately helped persuade the team to draft him. In June 2005, the Pirates selected McCutchen eleventh overall in the draft's first round and awarded him a contract that included a signing bonus of $1.9 million.

McCutchen's arrival in Pittsburgh came with extremely high expectations. Despite being one of the storied franchises in baseball history, the Pirates were in midst of their thirteenth consecutive losing season. Since their last winning season in 1992, the Pirates had consistently failed to find a player who could lift them from the depths of the National League. To many in the Pirates organization, McCutchen was the player to break the long stretch of futility. His signing with the Pirates "was just the perfect storm," McCutchen told Kepner. "Their spring training field was an hour from where I was from. My high school had the same colors as the Pirates' colors. . . . I felt like it was just the perfect place for me."

## RISE TO THE MAJOR LEAGUES

McCutchen moved through the Pirates' farm system rather quickly. In the summer of 2005 he reported to the Pirates' rookie-level Gulf Coast League team in Bradenton, batting .297 in forty-five games; he subsequently moved up to the organization's Pennsylvania-based short-season A affiliate, the Williamsport Crosscutters. McCutchen opened the 2006 season with the A-level Hickory Crawdads of the South Atlantic League and was selected to participate in the league's midseason all-star game. He played the last twenty games of the season with the AA Altoona Curve. At nineteen years and ten months, McCutchen became the youngest player in Curve history, and he was named the Pirates' Minor League Player of the Year.

In 2007, *Baseball America* rated McCutchen the thirteenth-best prospect in the game and the best position player in the Pirates' farm system. As a result, he was invited to the Pirates' annual spring-training camp to compete for a spot on the team's twenty-five-man roster. However, after failing to make the team, McCutchen returned to Altoona, where he struggled for the first time in his career. He began the 2007 season by going hitless in his first fifteen at bats, en route to posting a dismal .189 average for the month of April. Determined to regain both his swing and his confidence, McCutchen began working with Gregg Ritchie, the Pirates' roving minor-league hitting coordinator, and Brandon Moore, Altoona's hitting coach, on his hitting mechanics. "I believed in them," he told Joe Lemire for *Sports Illustrated* (18 June 2012). "Anyone can be coachable if you just accept the fact that you need to change." Under Ritchie and Moore's instruction, McCutchen, who is known to possess remarkable bat speed for a player his size, started holding his hands closer to his body rather than high up, which helped him level out and give more power to his swing.

McCutchen quickly saw the effects of his adjustments, hitting .307 over his final forty-one games with Altoona before moving up to the AAA Indianapolis Indians of the International League. He spent the entire 2008 season with the Indians and hit .283 with nine home runs, fifty RBIs, and 134 stolen bases in 135 games.

## ROOKIE STANDOUT

McCutchen returned to the Indians to start the 2009 season, but after batting .303 in forty-nine games with the club, he was deemed ready for the major leagues. The Pirates traded starting center fielder Nate McLouth to the Atlanta Braves two months into the season, and McCutchen was called up to replace him, making his major-league debut in a game against the New York Mets on June 4, 2009. In his debut, he hit leadoff and collected two hits in four at bats, a walk, three runs scored, one RBI, and one stolen base. Five days later McCutchen became the Pirates' everyday starting center fielder and leadoff hitter, collecting four hits, including two triples; he went on to hit a major-league best five triples for the month of June.

McCutchen continued to impress throughout his rookie year. The highlight of his season came on August 1. With his parents in attendance on their seventeenth wedding anniversary, McCutchen hit three home runs and knocked in six runs, to go along with a single and four runs scored in a Pirates victory. He became the first Pirates rookie ever to hit three home runs in one game and the tenth Pirates player overall to accomplish the feat. Though the Pirates finished last in the NL Central Division for the fifth time in six seasons, McCutchen was recognized for his performance following the regular season. He finished fourth in the voting for the NL Rookie of the Year Award and was named *Baseball America*'s Major League Rookie of the Year.

McCutchen followed his auspicious rookie debut with an even better year in 2010, his first full season in the majors. He produced an identical .286 batting average, hit sixteen home runs with fifty-six RBIs, and led the Pirates in hits, doubles, triples, runs, walks, and stolen bases. McCutchen's hit total was second among NL center fielders, and his double and stolen base totals both marked career highs. However, the Pirates posted their eighteenth consecutive losing season, with the worst record in the majors. Consequently, manager John Russell was fired and replaced by former Colorado Rockies manager Clint Hurdle.

Under Hurdle the Pirates enjoyed a mild resurgence in 2011, when they unexpectedly emerged as playoff contenders for the first time in nearly two decades. The Pirates entered the season's midpoint with a 47–43 record and were first in the NL Central Division in late July, but they collapsed during the final two months. Nonetheless, the team enjoyed a fifteen-game improvement from the previous year. Leading the turnaround was McCutchen, who earned his first career all-star selection. He set career highs and led the Pirates in home runs and RBIs, with twenty-three and eighty-nine, respectively. He also led the club with twenty-three stolen bases, becoming the eighth player in franchise history to record at least twenty home runs and twenty stolen bases in the same season. In addition, he continued his superb defensive play and finished second in the NL in outfield assists with nine.

## MLB ALL-STAR

During the off-season McCutchen made a long-term commitment to the Pirates, agreeing to a six-year contract extension worth $51.5 million. The deal was the second largest in club history and runs through the 2018 season. That same off-season McCutchen worked to open up his batting stance, which allowed him to see the ball better and hit more effectively to all fields. "His biggest adjustment is the mind-set of staying within his swing and not trying to destroy every pitch," Pirates general manager Neal Huntington explained to Kepner. "His mentality is to make the pitcher come to him and essentially hit the ball where it's pitched."

Armed with his new contract and approach to the plate, McCutchen emerged as one of the best players in the game in 2012, putting together "one of the finest seasons in recent memory," Will Graves declared for the Associated Press (19 Mar. 2013). He established career highs in nearly every offensive category, hitting thirty-one home runs with ninety-six RBIs and finishing first among all NL players in hits (194). He also tied for second in the league in runs (107) and finished in second place in batting average (.327), on-base percentage (.400), slugging percentage (.553), total bases (328), and wins-above-replacement (7.2). He was named to his second consecutive all-star team, finished third in the NL MVP voting, and won consecutive NL Player of the Month awards, in June and July. He also received his first career NL Silver Slugger Award as well as his first Rawlings Gold Glove Award, after leading all NL center fielders with a .997 fielding percentage.

With McCutchen anchoring the team's offense and defense, the Pirates again contended for an NL Central title and flirted with making the playoffs for the second consecutive year. However, the team had another inglorious second half of the season, losing eighteen times in their final twenty-three games. Despite tying their best record since the 1997 season, the Pirates clinched their twentieth consecutive losing season, the longest such streak in MLB history.

By the 2013 season McCutchen had become one of the major leagues' highest-profile players. He was voted by fans to appear on the cover of the popular video game *MLB 13: The Show*, for which he appeared in a commercial, and his jersey ranked among the best sellers in baseball. Such exposure has helped the Pirates become relevant again after spending much of the last two decades in baseball obscurity. "The way I look at it, people are going to notice you for one of two reasons, if you do something good or you do something bad," McCutchen said to Graves. "At least, they're noticing me for doing something good."

## PERSONAL LIFE

In addition to his dreadlocks, McCutchen is known for his calm and humble demeanor and many charitable activities. He serves as the official spokesman for the Habitat for Humanity of Greater Pittsburgh and established the Cutch's Crew community outreach program to assist inner-city youths and families. In 2013, McCutchen received the Dapper Dan Sportsman of the Year Award, awarded annually to a Pittsburgh sports figure with nationally recognized achievements.

## SUGGESTED READING
Graves, Will. "Pirates OF McCutchen Deals with Stardom in Stride." *Big Story*. Associated Press, 19 Mar. 2013. Web. 20 May 2013.

Keidan, Bruce. "Eye on the Ball: Centerfielder McCutchen." *Pittsburgh Quarterly*. Pittsburgh Quarterly, 2010. Web. 20 May 2013.

Kepner, Tyler. "The Man Powering the Pirates." *New York Times*. New York Times, 26 July 2012. Web. 20 May 2013.

Lemire, Joe. "Being the Natural Isn't Enough." *Sports Illustrated*. Time, 18 June 2012. Web. 20 May 2013.

McCollough, J. Brady. "Center Fielder Andrew McCutchen Is Now the Face of the Pirates Franchise." *Pittsburgh Post-Gazette*. PG, 31 Mar. 2013. Web. 20 May 2013.

Olsen, Lisa. "Andrew McCutchen Is Living the American Dream." *Sporting News*. Sporting News, 27 Sept. 2012. Web. 20 May 2013.

Sheehan, Joe. "It Was a Very Good Year." *Sports Illustrated*. Time, 18 June 2012. Web. 20 May 2013.

—*Chris Cullen*

# Jane McGonigal

**Born:** October 21, 1977
**Occupation:** Game designer and researcher

Alternate reality game designer and "future forecaster" Jane McGonigal wants to make the world a better place—through gaming. The top of her website's home page states, "My #1 goal in life is to see a game designer nominated for a Nobel Peace Prize. I've forecast that this will happen by the year 2023." As she explains in her doctoral thesis, in her best-selling book *Reality Is Broken* (2011), and during numerous conferences and other public speaking engagements, McGonigal believes that collaborative gaming encourages problem solving, which can help people change the way they live their lives. McGonigal designs alternate reality games, or ARGs, for Fortune 500 companies, nonprofits, and individuals, all of which require socialization among players to solve simulated—or real—problems. One of McGonigal's game simulations, called World Without Oil, ran for a total of thirty-two days in 2007, during which players had to figure out how to survive during an energy crisis. Another game, SuperBetter, has helped individuals achieve health goals such as smoking cessation and weight loss.

In addition to designing games, McGonigal works as a research affiliate for the Institute for the Future. The nonprofit formulates future forecasts with the goal to help organizations bring about positive change in the world.

## EARLY LIFE AND GAMING INTEREST

Born on October 21, 1977, to two public school teachers, Jane Evelyn McGonigal and her iden-tical twin sister Kelly grew up in Moorestown, New Jersey. McGonigal was highly competitive growing up, partly because of her parents' way of fostering learning at home; allowance money was given based on the number of books the children had read, for example. The environment "was both good and stressful," Kelly McGonigal, a professor of psychology at Stanford University, told Whitney Joiner for *Elle* (22 June 2011). The twins' mother, Judith McGonigal, "never treated us like we were gifted. It was like, 'You have to work hard all the time.'"

McGonigal's childhood activities included debate, novel writing—she wrote a young-adult novel the summer before starting high school—and gaming or programming (coding in Basic+) on the family's Commodore 64 computer. "I was super-geeky," she told Bruce Feiler for the *New York Times* (27 Apr. 2012). McGonigal would spend hours playing on the Commodore 64, rather than the more popular Nintendo or Sega gaming systems at the time, because she liked the problem-solving aspect of the computer's text adventure games.

Games were important for McGonigal from an early age: she created a board game called Prom Night in fourth grade, would win nearly every time she played the card game Spit— "People would sit in a circle and watch Jane play," her sister told Joiner—and even designed a dice game based on her relationship with her high school boyfriend. Kelly McGonigal told Feiler that her sister "decides what's interesting, then convinces everyone else it's interesting, too." McGonigal explained to Joiner that, as a child, she "liked that you could take a bunch of people and they'd have this experience together and get excited. Maybe it's because I was geeky," she added, "but I liked that people who wouldn't ordinarily talk or be nice to each other would be on the same team."

## FURTHER EDUCATION
As an undergraduate at Fordham University, McGonigal majored in English literature and media studies. Active both on and off campus, she edited the news section of Fordham's student newspaper, the *Observer*, and during her senior year interned with New York City's Department of Parks and Recreation, running games at outdoor festivals in Central Park. McGonigal graduated in 1999 at the top of her class.

After earning her bachelor's degree, McGonigal spent one year working for Student Advantage as a discussion forum moderator and a features writer for the company's website. In her spare time, she volunteered as an off-Broadway stage manager. McGonigal then decided to return to school, this time to study theater; she began a PhD program in performance studies at the University of California at Berkeley in 2001. McGonigal's interests soon returned to gaming, however, and she changed the focus of her doctoral research to match. She also delved into game design.

McGonigal's first project, from 2001 to 2002, was as a writer and game designer for Wink Back's The Go Game, an urban scavenger hunt that provides players with clues through the web browser on their mobile phones. The game has been used as a team-building exercise for such companies as Cisco. "It seemed to change the players afterwards," McGonigal told Joiner. "You'd play this game in North Beach, and then any time you came back to North Beach, you were full of optimism and curiosity, going into strange shops and talking to strangers. I thought, Wow, games really stay with you."

## THE "PINOCCHIO EFFECT"
In 2003, McGonigal wrote a paper on the use of physical spaces in digital gaming. The paper discusses what she terms the "Pinocchio effect," or the desire for games to become reality, or for reality to become a game. McGonigal draws on The Go Game as an example of this effect, as well as The Beast, an ARG created by 42 Entertainment to promote Steven Spielberg's film *A.I. Artificial Intelligence* (2001). The paper so impressed 42 Entertainment that the company hired McGonigal to design I Love Bees (also called ilovebees), an ARG promotion for and companion to Microsoft's Halo 2. Approximately six hundred thousand people played the game after its release in 2004, ranking it as one of the most popular ARGs at that time; the game also won the International Academy of Digital Arts and Sciences Webby Award for gaming and the

Game Developers Choice Award for innovation. "These were collaborative games that were tremendously positive," Sean Stewart, lead writer for The Beast at the time, told Joiner. "People came from all kinds of places and found themselves in a common cause, united together. That's what always appealed to Jane."

McGonigal founded Avant Game, her personal business for commercial ARG design, in 2003. One notable commercial ARG was Tombstone Hold 'Em, a promotional event for Activision's game Gun. During this event, held in October 2005, players traveled to historic cemeteries and used tombstones (instead of cards) to play poker. Another notable commercial ARG, The Lost Ring, ran during the 2008 Summer Olympics in Beijing as a marketing campaign for McDonald's. The Lost Ring was played by an estimated two million participants worldwide. McGonigal has designed games and game workshops for other major companies as well, such as Nike, Disney, and Nintendo.

## "HACKING HAPPINESS"
McGonigal's doctoral thesis, completed in 2006, focuses on how the combination of experimental game design with ubiquitous computing—ubiquitous gaming, which involves interaction in both a virtual world and in the real world—has led to a number of games that change the way people think and how they relate to everyday life. "How can we intervene against the widespread public alienation and lack of engagement in the complex world of everyday life, and bring these two worlds together?" McGonigal asked during her presentation at the O'Reilly eTech Emerging Technology Conference on March 27, 2007. Her answer lies in creating alternate realities, or as she often calls it, "hacking happiness"; this can promote community and result in improvements in people's lives. In 2006, at age twenty-eight, McGonigal was named by the *MIT Technology Review* as one of the year's "35 Innovators Under 35." The honor had a huge impact on McGonigal. "Most of the other people who won were inventing solar ovens for women in Africa or doing molecular biology to cure cancer, and I felt fairly unworthy," she told Joiner.

## INSTITUTE FOR THE FUTURE
To foster her growing belief that gaming can change people's lives, McGonigal left 42 Entertainment in 2007 to become a research affiliate for the Institute for the Future (IFTF). This nonprofit think tank uses various analysis, scenario, and diagnostic tools to formulate "future forecasts," or insights that can help organizations bring about change. McGonigal became IFTF's director of Games Research and Development in 2008. In this role, she has worked on how games can be used to positively affect the way people live.

One of the first games that McGonigal designed with this purpose in mind was World Without Oil. The game, conceptualized by writer Ken Eklund, simulated a worldwide energy crisis. Sponsored by the Center for Public Broadcasting, World Without Oil ran from April 30 to June 1, 2007. Nearly two thousand participants had to figure out how to survive as if the world had almost no petroleum left, energy was at an extreme shortage, and millions of jobs were lost. Players explained how they would deal with these changes through social media websites such as YouTube and Blogger; some players even changed their lifestyles to match the scenario. "A dramatic decrease in oil availability is not at all far-fetched," McGonigal told Eliza Strickland for *Salon* (10 July 2007). "We thought we could play our way to a set of ideas about how to manage that crisis, if it were to happen."

"Gamification" is the term used to describe games that seek to solve real-world problems. These games are also used by businesses as a tool to measure user behavior. But McGonigal does not like that term. "I don't do 'gamification,' and I'm not prepared to stand up and say I think it works," she told Feiler. "I don't think anybody should make games to try to motivate somebody to do something they don't want to do. If the game is not about a goal you're intrinsically motivated by, it won't work."

## LEARNING HOW TO SAVE THE WORLD

The following year saw McGonigal's next major simulation, Superstruct, played by employees of major corporations such as Procter & Gamble and National Semiconductor. In the game, set in 2019, players were asked to imagine various crises that might occur, such as a global food shortage or a pandemic, and worked collaboratively on ways to solve these crises. "We're using games to help people focus," McGonigal told Reena Jana for *Bloomberg Businessweek* (10 Nov. 2008). "The quality of engagement in games is more intense than in real life. . . . Plus, games offer metrics and feedback, and they push people to action."

Another notable project, EVOKE, was sponsored by the World Bank Institute. The game consisted of a graphic novel set in the year 2020 and the players' choice of social media. From March 3 to May 12, 2010, players collaborated to solve the issues of poverty and disease in sub-Saharan Africa. Those who completed all of the game's challenges were named the World Bank's social innovators. EVOKE also resulted in fifty entrepreneurial ventures funded by the organization, some of which have remained in business.

## "JANE THE CONCUSSION KILLER"

In early 2009, McGonigal took a sabbatical from her job at the Institute for the Future to spend time writing what would become the *New York Times* best seller *Reality Is Broken: Why Games Make Us Better and How They Can Change the World* (2011). That summer, she accidentally banged her head against an open cabinet door and ended up with a serious concussion. Post-concussion syndrome left McGonigal feeling mentally fogged; her doctor informed her that the symptoms—an aching head, dizziness, blurred vision, and memory loss—would last for a month. McGonigal was told not to read, write, run, or work at all until those symptoms cleared. When symptoms persisted after that first month, she was depressed to hear that the next target for recovery was three months to a year. "My mind was telling me I wanted to die," she told Feiler.

Depression can exacerbate the problem, however, and McGonigal wanted to break out of what could become a vicious cycle. "I am either going to kill myself or turn this into a game," she decided, as she recalled to Feiler. Thus the game SuperBetter was born. In it, she was "Jane the Concussion Killer," who recruited allies—her family and friends—to help her tackle one issue at a time. They would call her with "missions" to complete, such as walking a few steps more than she had the day before. "The main thing that worked was I stopped feeling helpless," she told Feiler. "It made me feel optimistic and like I had agency."

## SUPERBETTER LABS

People read about SuperBetter on McGonigal's blog and later in her book, and many wanted to try it for themselves. With funding provided by the Ardmore Institute of Health, McGonigal was able to expand the game so that it would help people with more than just concussions. In January 2011, McGonigal cofounded and became creative director for Social Chocolate, which designs social adventure games that are based on the science of positive emotion and human connection. SuperBetter became its first game, for which McGonigal serves as chief creative officer. The online social game helps people face major health challenges like depression, quitting smoking, losing weight, and other challenges.

"I still believe really strongly that gamers can solve some of the world's toughest challenges, but some of the world's toughest challenges are very personal," she told Peter Hartlaub for the *San Francisco Chronicle* (4 Mar. 2012). "Things like depression and obesity are global challenges." Whether people are tackling a personal challenge or a global one, McGonigal told Feiler that "What I really want to do is help people suffer less." She added, "What games do successfully is help you tap into certain gamer traits like optimism, resilience and learning from failure that are really useful to have when you're tackling a tough challenge. It's because gamers develop these giant calluses that help you work harder in the face of failure."

## BEING "GAMEFUL"

In February 2010, McGonigal gave a TED (Technology, Entertainment, and Design) Talk that led many people, inspired by her words, to ask if they could be involved in her development of ARGs, whether as designers or as participants. McGonigal responded that October with Gameful, "A Secret HQ for World-Changing Game Developers." According to its website, Gameful is a central hub for game developers, or for anyone else, to collaboratively design games that change the world.

"'Gameful' is a word I coined to describe what it feels like to have the heart of a gamer, as opposed to just 'playful,' which sounds like you're not taking something seriously," McGonigal told Amanda Bensen for *Smithsonian* magazine (Feb. 2011). "When you're gameful, your creativity is sparked, your curiosity is sparked and you're more likely to collaborate with others. You're more likely to stick with a tough problem, even if you fail at first." Gameful would later partner with Games for Change, a similar nonprofit company founded in 2004. McGonigal serves on the advisory board for Games for Change, as well as the advisory board for the annual Serious Games Summit at the Game Developers Conference in San Francisco.

## HONORS FOR INNOVATION

McGonigal has received many honors for her innovative ARG designs. In addition to the Game Developers Choice Award and the Webby Award her team won for I Love Bees in 2005, she also won the 2008 SXSW Interactive Award for activism. Her promotion of ARGs as a way to improve the world landed her not only in the *MIT Technology Review*'s "35 Innovators Under 35" list in 2006, but also in the number one slot for *BrandWeek*'s 2008 "Bright Idea of the Year," in the *Harvard Business Review*'s top twenty "Breakthrough Ideas for 2008," in *Fast Company*'s "100 Creative People in Business" (2009), and in *Entrepreneur* magazine's "2013's Entrepreneurial Women to Watch," among other lists.

A popular public speaker, McGonigal has given the keynote address at a number of major conferences and other events. Notable addresses include one for the World Economic Forum in 2012 as a Young Global Leader and Davos Speaker, as well as her 2010 TED Talk, which ranked at number sixteen out of 835 that year for the "All-Time Most Engaging TED Talk."

McGonigal lives in San Francisco with her husband, Kiyash Monsef, an Emmy-nominated producer, director, and writer.

## SUGGESTED READING

Feiler, Bruce. "She's Playing Games with Your Lives." *New York Times*. New York Times, 27 Apr. 2012. Web. 15 Feb. 2013.

Hartlaub, Peter. "Jane McGonigal: Game on with 'SuperBetter.'" *San Francisco Chronicle*. Hearst Communications, 4 Mar. 2012. Web. 15 Feb. 2013.

Joiner, Whitney. "Super Girl." *ELLE*. Hearst Communications, 22 June 2011. Web. 15 Feb. 2013.

Saletan, William. "The Computer Made Me Do It." *New York Times*. New York Times, 11 Feb. 2011. Web. 15 Feb. 2013.

Strickland, Eliza. "Play Peak Oil Before You Live It." *Salon*. Salon Media, 10 July 2007. Web. 15 Feb. 2013.

—Julia Gilstein

# Dalton McGuinty

**Born:** July 19, 1955
**Occupation:** Premier of Ontario, Canada

Dalton McGuinty, the twenty-fourth premier of the Canadian province of Ontario, has spent the better part of his professional life in the political sphere, first assuming the provincial legislative seat left vacant by his father, after his sudden death in 1990. After twenty-two years, however, McGuinty is transitioning away from politics, abruptly announcing his resignation in October 2012, shocking his party and his constituency. Though the reasons for his departure from public office are debated, McGuinty has cited personal reasons, wishing to spend more time with his wife, his four adult children, and his extended family. However, critics and colleagues alike point to clear political reasons for the abandonment of his post, including scandals surrounding the cancellation of two power plants, a gridlocked legislature, and the increasing fiscal insolvency of his province.

Considered by most to be a fiscally moderate but socially liberal representative of Canada's Liberal Party, McGuinty initially ran for premier on the platform of health and education reform, fiscal responsibility, and infrastructural investment. Speaking in December 2012, after he had announced his resignation, he reflected on his administration's years in power. Charles Lammam for the *Huffington Post* quoted McGuinty as saying, "Our government hasn't been perfect. . . . But when it comes to the big things that families count on us to get right—schools, health care, the environment, and the economy—we've gotten it right every time" (13 Dec. 2012). McGuinty's focus over his two-plus terms in office has been these issues, but, as Lammam highlights in his editorial, McGuinty's claim about making the right decision each time, especially as it relates to Ontario's provincial economy, is disputable, and may be an example, of the "gap

Bloomberg via Getty Images

between rhetoric and reality." Nonetheless, after McGuinty's announcement that he was leaving office, politicians along the political spectrum, including John Tory, the former leader of the Progressive Conservative Party in Ontario, praised him for his leadership and his commitment to the people of his province.

## EARLY LIFE AND EDUCATION
McGuinty was born on July 19, 1955, in Ottawa, Ontario, Canada, and grew up in the Alta Vista neighborhood of the provincial capital. One of ten children (six boys and four girls) in an Irish Catholic family, McGuinty was raised with the values of education and community service, both of which helped structure his political outlook. His father, Dalton McGuinty Sr., was an English professor at the University of Ottawa who eventually entered politics, representing the Ottawa South district in the Ontario provincial parliament until suffering a fatal heart attack in 1990. McGuinty replaced his father as the Ottawa South Member of Provincial Parliament (MPP). McGuinty's mother, Elizabeth worked full time as a nurse.

McGuinty attended St. Patrick's High School, where he met his future wife, Terri, marrying her in 1980. He studied biology at McMaster University, earning a bachelor of science degree, and went on to study law at the University of Ottawa. After passing the bar exam in 1983, he entered private practice and, later, taught business law classes at Carleton University.

## CAREER IN POLITICS BEGINS
McGuinty's road to politics might have seemed a natural one, given his legal experience and his father's political career. However, because of his father's untimely death, McGuinty felt a sense of urgent obligation toward his father's constituency and desired to carry on his father's legacy. At the time of his election, McGuinty found himself in the legislative minority and was the only first-time Liberal Party representative. Though young, he quickly became a leader of the opposition. Reelected as MPP in 1995, McGuinty emerged as one of four candidates to be the official leader of the Liberal Party. McGuinty's prospects of election did not initially look favorable, as he finished last in the first and second ballots among the four candidates, holding firm to his moderate to right-wing economic stances. It took five ballots, but McGuinty eventually won enough votes to secure leadership of the party, besting the left-wing progressive Gerard Kennedy, who later became Ontario's minister of education during McGuinty's first term as premier.

In 1999, McGuinty was up for reelection again, and early polling indicated that the Liberal Party might have a chance to gain the legislative majority from the Progressive Conservatives, a party led by Premier Mike Harris and one that had been successful by campaigning for a "common sense revolution," in which government programs were cut and taxes were lowered in an attempt to diminish the fiscal deficit. During the campaign, the Progressive Conservatives cast McGuinty as an inexperienced leader, and though McGuinty won reelection, his party was again outnumbered in the provincial parliament, forcing McGuinty to act as the leader of the minority opposition to the Progressive Conservatives.

A series of events helped to tilt the balance of power over the following election cycle, including McGuinty's ability to articulate to the voting public the Liberal Party's agenda, which began to resonate with the majority of the Ottawa population. Furthermore, the Progressive Conservative Party was having difficulty proving that its fiscal strategies were beneficial for the populace at large. Harris was forced to resign in 2002, partly because of what became known as the Walkerton scandal, in which lack of government oversight was faulted for the *E. coli* contamination of the city of Walkerton's water, resulting in several deaths and widespread illness. Ernie Eves replaced Harris, but the door was open for the Liberal Party to take political control of the province, and McGuinty was poised to fill the role of premier.

## 2003 ELECTION AND PREMIER MCGUINTY'S FIRST TERM
In the previous four years, McGuinty had helped develop a platform that he hoped would allow

the Liberal Party to take over leadership of Ontario. The party was helped in its quest by Harris's resignation and poor campaigning on the part of Eves and other Progressive Conservatives. In October 2003, McGuinty's Liberals became the first to unseat an incumbent Conservative government in Ontario since Mitchell Hepburn's 1934 election. The Liberals gained 72 of the 103 representative positions.

While running for election, McGuinty promised to "hold the line" on taxes, a promise that seemed ill-conceived by the following year. McGuinty had made the restructuring and the resurgence of Ottawa's health care system one of the four primary points of his party's platform (the other issues were education, infrastructure, and the economy). McGuinty's promises, on one hand, to equalize the health care system for all of Ottawa's residents and, on the other, not to introduce any new taxes were not congruous. Contrary to his campaign guarantee, McGuinty imposed on citizens a health premium—essentially a new tax—that varied according to income. McGuinty's decision to implement this program, though ostensibly done to effectuate policy, was viewed by many as an example of the dishonesty of a duplicitous politician, a perception that may have subsequently hampered McGuinty's administration.

In addition to health care reform, McGuinty sought changes to the economic relationship between Ottawa and the Canadian federal government, noting that there was a significant difference between the amount of money Ottawa pays into the federal system and the goods and services it receives in return. This economic discrepancy was one of the issues that McGuinty discussed with Prime Minister Paul Martin in 2004. "[Ottawans] are proud to be a full partner in Confederation. . . . We ask only that the federal government be a full partner in health care," McGuinty stated (qtd. in CBC News 14 Sept. 2004). After much political wrangling, Martin committed $5.75 billion to Ottawa, to fund a variety of programs such as college education and job training, in addition to health care.

During his second year in office, McGuinty focused on education policy. The 2005 budget promised to cut class size and to provide more educational opportunities for low-income students, among other initiatives. Ontario's minister of finance Greg Sorbara, in the official budget released by the province, stated "I'm proud to announce today that this budget includes the largest multi-year investment in postsecondary education and training in 40 years—a historic investment in better universities, colleges and training that will result in new jobs and economic growth" (11 May 2005).

In the last two years of McGuinty's first term, the party concentrated on the environment,

energy policy, and transportation. The government spent significant sums of money to repair roads and bridges and to update the energy grid, stating that it would both invest in new nuclear reactors, to be built at Darlington, outside Toronto, and delay the closure of coal stations. The administration's energy plan proved controversial, especially in light of the revelation that the plan was exempt from a thorough assessment. In an attempt to qualm fears from environmental groups, Energy Minister Dwight Duncan responded, "Each of these projects will get a very thorough environmental review," as quoted by Martin Mittelstaedt for the *Globe and Mail* (16 June 2006). To complicate matters, the McGuinty administration was criticized for its lack of fiscal responsibility, as an increasing amount of money was being poured into social services and other programs without any indication of a balanced budget.

## SEEKING AND FINDING REELECTION

Perhaps the most important hurdle that McGuinty had to overcome in order to win reelection 2007 was acknowledgment of his 2003 campaign promise to not raise taxes, which he broke the following year. His major-party opponents, Progressive Conservative John Tory (who replaced Eves as his party's leader) and New Democratic Howard Hampton, were quick to use McGuinty's broken promise as a political wedge to open up the possibility of McGuinty's defeat. In a September 2007 debate, the CanWest News service reported that McGuinty broached the subject, sensing that the issue was on many voters' minds, "At the time of the last election I told Ontarians I wouldn't raise their taxes, and I broke that promise. I did raise their taxes, I hated making that decision. . . . I knew that people would be angry about that. I understand that and I accept that. I still think it was the right call to make. And because I did raise taxes I had the resources I needed to get more doctors, and more nurses and to build new hospitals" (21 Sept. 2007). McGuinty's candid confession perhaps gained him the political capital he needed to stay in power.

More important, the support for public funding of faith-based organizations, a seemingly fringe issue but one at the center of the Progressive Conservatives' platform, undid McGuinty's Conservative opponent and helped McGuinty secure another four years. "We do not want to see our children divided," McGuinty explained to supporters on election night, after his victory was secure, "We want publicly funded schools, not public funds for private schools" (CanWest). The general populace seemed to agree.

The Liberal Party's platform in 2007 highlighted many of the same issues that the 2003 platform had. Focusing on health care and the environment, the Liberal Party hoped to add doctors and nurses and reduce hospital wait times. Additionally, the plan provided incentives for energy efficiency and looked to update and expand the provinces public transportation, especially in Toronto, its largest city. As the second term unfolded, however, McGuinty looked less like a socially minded Liberal than one concerned with the widening economic deficit. He implemented the Harmonized Sales Tax, combining the goods and services tax with the provincial sales tax, a decision that proved unpopular. He also opposed an increase in the minimum wage, infuriating workers and workers-rights groups. Because of the backlash, he amended his decision: "When we talk about the minimum wage, we have to ask ourselves what it is that we owe both our workers and employers. I think clearly we owe them fairness. . . . Our commitment was to get the $10.25 an hour [in 2010] and we will honor that commitment" (qtd. in *The Star* 31 Mar. 2009).

The accomplishments of McGuinty's second term, including the implementation of an all-day kindergarten, were soon overshadowed by a scandal involving eHealth Ontario, an organization tasked with digitizing the medical records of Ontario's citizens. McGuinty had circumvented vetting protocols in order to hire Sarah Kramer as CEO of the company, upon the recommendation of Dr. Alan Hudson. Kramer resigned from her position in 2009 when it was revealed that she had approved contracts without entertaining competitive bids. Many accused her of being unqualified for the job and criticized McGuinty for his seemingly unethical role in her hiring.

## THE ROAD TO RESIGNATION

Despite the scandal and a second term in which he spent more time troubleshooting than attempting to implement meaningful policy, McGuinty was reelected to a third term, though the Liberal Party lost its parliamentary majority, leaving McGuinty to govern from a minority position. McGuinty tendered his resignation in October 2012, fueling speculation for his motivations. Despite several simmering scandals and a budget deficit that had tripled since he first entered office in 2003, he remained a respected politician, especially within the ranks of his own party.

In an attempt to trim the provincial budget, McGuinty introduced Bill 115, which sought to cut wages of public employees as well as their bargaining power. The legislation garnered immediate backlash. "Bill 115 appears to be the beginning of a greater agenda to erode the rights of hardworking Ontarians," claimed Ken Coran, president of the Ontario Secondary School Teachers' Federation (qtd. in CBC News 11 Oct. 2012). McGuinty's bill was condemned as "draconian" by Sam Hammond, president of the Elementary Teachers' Federation of Ontario, and seemed to signal McGuinty's retreat from the center into the right-wing reaches of his party (CBC News).

As McGuinty's popularity decreased, another scandal began to consume his administration. McGuinty had planned to develop seventeen new gas plants, part of the renovation of Ontario's electricity system. In 2011, Jane Taber for the *Globe and Mail* reported that he cancelled plans for two of the plants—to be located in Mississauga and Oakville—because of their unpopularity, a decision that cost the province millions of dollars. "We were in the midst of a massive renewal plan for our electricity system . . . we got two of those wrong" (22 Nov. 2012). However, the Progressive Conservatives claimed that the administration was not forthright about the details of the closures and that it had lied when it stated that all documents concerning the closures had been released. As it turned out, thousands of pages of documents had been withheld, and the Progressive Conservatives threatened Energy minister Chris Bentley with censure for refusing to release pertinent documentation associated with the issue. In response to the political pressure from the Progressive Conservatives, McGuinty said, "They decided to make some political hay out of it . . . they are entitled to do that . . . but it was the right decision. . . . We listened to the communities and got it right the second time" (22 Nov. 2012).

As the power-plant scandal developed further, on October 15, 2012, McGuinty announced that he was adjourning the legislature indefinitely and that he was resigning from office as soon as his party chose a suitable replacement. Opposition considered his proroguing of the parliament as a way of delaying the investigation of Bentley, but McGuinty said his decision was based on the contentious state of the parliament, where open-minded political debate has ceased to exist and where he has been unable to earn enough support for his proposed wage freezes. Furthermore, he wanted to engage labor groups "in a way that is free of the heightened rancour that has sadly too frequently characterized our legislature of late" (qtd. in CTV News 15 Oct. 2012).

His disaffection for the parliament seemed to be his primary motivation for resigning, given the fact that since the elections of 2011, his party has been in the minority, making it nearly impossible for him to gain the approval for any of his propositions, especially those concerning the economy. McGuinty offered another reason for his resignation: his desire to spend more time with his family. During the wedding of his daughter several months before his announcement, McGuinty made the decision to resign, feeling like the timing was right on both personal and political fronts. "The party is behind me . . . and my responsibility is to ensure we renew our party" (CTV News). His proroguing of the parliament and his resignation allowed the Liberal Party some time to reassess its direction.

## PERSONAL LIFE AND FUTURE ENDEAVORS
Family has always been a priority for McGuinty, and his political career seems to be bookended by the influence of two family members: His entry into politics was largely the result of his father's political career, and his exit was partially based on the realization that his children were growing older and that he needed to spend more time with them and his growing family. After resigning from the premiership, McGuinty spent a week contemplating his place in the Liberal Party, as many in his party hoped he would announce his candidacy for leadership of the federal Liberal Party, considering him a worthy competitor for Justin Trudeau.

After deliberating, however, McGuinty decided not to seek the federal position, again citing his desire to be with family. "My family has supported me throughout. So, it's time for me to take on challenges outside of politics and I am confident that I'm going to find other ways to serve my province." After thanking those who wanted him to run for federal leadership of the party, he added, jokingly, that his wife "thanks all those who were opposed" (qtd. in CBC News 23 Oct. 2012).

Though McGuinty has been criticized for excessive spending and for a contentious relationship with his state's workers, and though he was ranked in an Angus Reid Public Opinion poll as the least popular provincial premier in December 2012, McGuinty is credited with increasing environmental awareness through initiatives to combat climate change, innovations in education and health care, and a strong adherence to the democratic process.

## SUGGESTED READING
Benzie, Robert. "McGuinty: I Was Wrong." *The Star*. The Star, 31 Mar. 2009. Web. 17 Dec. 2012.
"Dalton McGuinty Rules Out Federal Liberal Leadership." *CBC News*. CBC News, 23 Oct. 2012. Web. 17 Dec. 2012.
Howlett, Karen, Adrian Morrow, and Paul Waldie. "Ontario Premier Dalton McGuinty Resigns." *Globe and Mail*. Globe and Mail, 15 Oct. 2012. Web. 17 Dec. 2012.
Lammam, Charles. "How Dalton McGuinty Botched Fiscal Policy." *Huffington Post*. Huffington Post Canada, 13 Dec. 2012. Web. 17 Dec. 2012.
"McGuinty Exit Triggers Liberal Leadership Renewal Process." *CBC News*. CBS News, 16 Oct. 2012. Web. 17 Dec. 2012.
Simpson, Jeffrey. "Dalton McGuinty, the Man Who Knew When to Go." *Globe and Mail*. Globe and Mail, 17 Oct. 2012. Web. 17 Dec. 2012.

—*Christopher Rager*

# Mark McNairy
**Born:** March 8, 1961
**Occupation:** Fashion designer

Mark McNairy is the irreverent designer behind the street wear label Mark McNairy New Amsterdam. A creative veteran of J. Press, a purveyor of East Coast "gentleman's" fashion, McNairy mixes American classics and Ivy League prep—with a flippant flourish. His latest collection included a men's camouflage jacket embellished with daisies and handkerchiefs with doodle-drawn phalli. "Most people in this business take themselves too seriously," McNairy told Jian Deleon and Nick Schonberger for *Complex* magazine (17 Jan. 2013). "I'm just having fun doing what I like to do. My clothes are fun but not funny." Perhaps Adam Tschorn for the *Los Angeles Times* (17 Feb. 2013) described McNairy's aesthetic best, writing that Mark McNairy New Amsterdam is an "American-made line with an Ivy League look and a National Lampoon sense of humor."

McNairy, who is sometimes referred to by the nickname "McNasty," launched his brand as a footwear label in 2008. His passion for a well-made shoe (he detests flip-flops) made him a cult favorite among fashion-forward men. McNairy's shoes—which include brogues, chukkas, loafers, and bucks—are handmade in Northampton, England. The styles are classic but not dated; his shoes often boast rubber soles or leopard-print cowhide. McNairy approached the dress shoe as another designer might approach a sneaker and, in doing so, has introduced a whole new crop of men to a grown-up but fashionable look. "A lot of the kids who buy my stuff have never owned a proper pair of shoes," he told Aaron Richter for *ACCLAIM* magazine (10 Oct. 2012). "They've worn sneakers all their lives and my shoes are an introduction to proper menswear."

The Mark McNairy New Amsterdam label has expanded to include full men's and women's clothing collections. The latter was inspired by McNairy's college-aged daughter, Daisy, and debuted in 2012. The younger McNairy serves as both a muse and a partner in her father's business. Though it might seem incongruous with his rough-edged persona, McNairy has fostered a number of successful collaborations over his long career. He is credited for resuscitating the

© Lee Clower

dying J. Press, and he serves at the helm of Woolrich Woolen Mills, another American fashion institution. In 2012, McNairy teamed up with the rapper and singer Pharrell Williams and his fashion line, the Billionaire Boys Club. Together they created Bee Line, a successful mash-up of traditional street wear and McNairy's signature Ivy League aesthetic. McNairy's other collaborators have included the Gap, Southwick, Spiewak, Bass, Keds, Engineered Garments, and Urban Outfitters.

### EARLY LIFE AND CAREER

McNairy was born in Greensboro, North Carolina, on March 8, 1961. His father, who repaired cash registers, wore a suit to work every day. McNairy began experimenting with clothing in junior high school. He screen printed T-shirts for art class, and at his after-school job at a sporting-goods store, he made jerseys. In high school, he began to shop at vintage stores, searching for military chinos and Brooks Brothers button-down shirts—a uniform he continues to wear today. Even though McNairy once told Peter Davis for *Papermag* (20 Aug. 2012) that Greensboro was "probably the most boring place on earth," his work is largely influenced by his hometown and what he calls Southern prep. McNairy has pointed out that the term *preppy* conjures a different image in different regions. Northeastern,

Ivy League prep, the kind on which McNairy is known to riff, is more conservative, he told the magazine *Slamxhype* (20 May 2010). The bright floral patterns of the late designer Lilly Pulitzer, favored by Jacqueline Kennedy Onassis, "is southern preppy," McNairy said, as are ribbon belts, chinos, and saddle oxfords. "Southern preppy is flashy, go-to-hell pants, that sort of thing," he explained.

McNairy graduated from Page High School in Greensboro in 1979 and attended college in Wilmington, North Carolina. His first job was as a traveling salesman, selling women's clothing in North Carolina and Virginia. He was miserable, so he traveled to New York City for a couple of days, where he went to the garment district and handed out his resume on the street. (In a similar fashion, he learned to make clothes by visiting clothing factories.) McNairy found a job in fashion sales and moved to the city in 1986. There, he met a fellow aspiring designer named Antoinette Linn, who was also working in sales. In 1987, the two quit their jobs and pooled two thousand dollars of their own money to launch a women's sportswear label called Finis (Latin for "the end"). Finis drew upon influences familiar to McNairy's work: flea markets, vintage, and prep. In spirit, the label called for a "finis" to high-concept, unwearable clothes. "We're not out to create new shapes, to come up with a jacket that has a pocket where there's never been one before," Linn told a reporter for *People* magazine (28 Mar. 1990). McNairy added that it was more important to him and Linn that their pieces could "be worn a million different ways."

The couple, who married in 1988, did introduce a few unusual flourishes outside of the McNairy oeuvre. One collection mixed tartan plaids and Senegalese printed fabrics. Another collection was inspired by the state of Tennessee; McNairy and Linn handed out bottles of Jack Daniels in the gift bags, and the show featured, among other pieces, a pair of gingham hip-huggers. By the early 1990s, the label appeared to be going strong. "It looked very successful from the outside," McNairy told Davis, "but we were a small, underfinanced mom-and-pop business." Finis lasted nearly nine years before problems fostering the label's growth caused McNairy to quit. He and Linn later divorced. After Finis, McNairy owned an Americana-inspired clothing business called 68 & Brothers. He then designed clothes for his own line, McNairy Brothers, a label he owned with his brother.

### J. PRESS AND AMERICAN IVY LEAGUE

In 2005, McNairy was hired as the creative director of J. Press. J. Press is considered the original clothier of New England "prepsters." Its first store was built in New Haven,

Connecticut, the home of Yale University; there is another store—one of four in the United States—in Cambridge, Massachusetts, near Harvard. Still, when McNairy was brought aboard, J. Press was facing a unique problem. Its most faithful customers, men in their sixties and seventies, were beginning to die off. Clearly, the company's offerings seemed stale. J. Press turned to McNairy because it needed someone who could make conservative dress appealing to a new generation.

McNairy's task—attract new customers with different tastes while retaining existing customers—was a difficult one by all accounts, but he pulled it off. "My idea was to step back to move forward," he told Lauren Murrow for *New York Magazine* (9 Feb. 2010). McNairy resurrected the iconic J. Press look while slyly throwing a few of his own pieces into the mix. He brought back J. Press basics such as the Shaggy Dog Shetland sweater and the three-button sack suit but also introduced subtly rebellious pieces such as a tie printed with a skull and crossbones, "not a nod to Yale's secret [Skull and Bones] society," Rosencranz Baldwin wrote for the *New York Times* (17 Sept. 2006), "but a wink to the new customer who has a closet full of ironic T-shirts." McNairy's influence was never so overt as to offend the old guard, but it was strong enough to attract aspiring preppies.

During McNairy's tenure with J. Press, which was bought by a large Japanese company in 1986, the American Ivy League aesthetic exploded in Japan. According to a 2009 *New York Times* article, J. Press sold roughly six times more merchandise in the country than it did in the United States. J. Press's popularity there made McNairy a cult figure in Japan long before he would be described as such in the United States.

## MARK MCNAIRY NEW AMSTERDAM

Despite his success after four years with J. Press, McNairy was unsure if the company would renew his contract and began mentally mapping out a collection of his own. Around the same time, the owner of the English shoe factory that had worked with J. Press for McNairy's single shoe collection in 2006 came to New York. The two men met for coffee and began discussing a possible collaboration. McNairy was interested in making white and dirty bucks and saddle shoes—particular types of men's dress shoes that he wanted yet could not seem to find anywhere. After the initial meeting between McNairy and the factory owner in December 2008, McNairy's line was immediately set in motion. McNairy flew to London the following week and worked for two days designing the collection. By January 2009, just a month later, McNairy was showing samples of his shoes to stores in New York. The collection of bucks and saddle shoes

boasted a number of models with red brick bottoms. McNairy, who left J. Press in 2009, called the collection Red Brick Soul.

McNairy expanded his footwear collection to include brogues, boots, and loafers. He also launched capsule (limited-edition) collections with Engineered Garments, stoking demand for his designs. The shoes are still made by the same small factory in England and are known for their exceptional craftsmanship. "We can do small runs of my shoes for stores because they're basically handmade," he told *Slamxhype*, adding of his second collaboration with Engineered Garments in 2010, "[It's] a legitimate collaboration—no one else will have those shoes."

McNairy's earliest collection was certainly more in step with the aesthetic he had revitalized at J. Press, but he soon began to experiment with bolder colors, prints, and materials. McNairy did not see his designs as audacious, however. "Camo is like a floral print for guys," he told David Hellqvist for the MTV District website (21 Feb. 2012). "Sometimes you feel like a nut, sometimes you don't."

## FAMILY BUSINESS

McNairy expanded his label to include buttondown shirts, ties, and cargo pants in 2010. Though he had designed menswear countless times before, the small offering served as a proverbial toe in the water for his successful brand. "I debated whether I wanted to do clothes again or not," he told Murrow. "But it's in my blood, I couldn't control myself." He soon branched out to a full menswear collection. His style could be described as J. Press with a blue-collar edge; McNairy draws inspiration from not only threepiece suits but also American work wear and military garb. His aesthetic is most influenced by the iconic American designer Ralph Lauren, whom he described to Murrow as "God," and the avant-garde Japanese fashion label Comme des Garçons.

Mark McNairy New Amsterdam was a thriving menswear and footwear label, but in his spring 2013 collection, McNairy decided to introduce clothing for women as well. The move was partly inspired by his daughter, Daisy, who grew up in New Orleans, Louisiana, splitting her time between her quiet life with her mother, Finis partner Linn, and visiting her father amid the swirl of the New York fashion world. Daisy began attending Rutgers University in New Jersey, with dreams of entering medical school. But as she spent more time with her father—working as an assistant during fashion week, a stylist, and, later, a runway model—she realized her true passion for the family business.

Father and daughter share similar tastes, and Daisy served as a consultant while McNairy designed his first women's collection.

"When I first started working on the women's collection, every piece she saw, she wanted," McNairy told Andrew Bevan for *Teen Vogue* (21 May 2012). "So I thought I must be doing something right." The well-received collection included the infamous daisy-studded camouflage jacket as well as other pieces embellished with the flower. Daisy is not the only family member to inspire McNairy. After the birth of his son, Ryder, McNairy began offering his shoes in children's sizes.

## WOOLRICH WOOLEN MILLS

In 2011, McNairy succeeded Daiki Suzuki as the creative director of Woolrich Woolen Mills. The American outerwear company, which was founded in 1830, has done a brisk business selling thick wool plaids to outdoorsy New Englanders and supplying Civil War reenactors with material for costumes. But the company's solid reputation also put them in a unique position to cash in on the growing popularity of Americana in men's fashion. Suzuki began the fashionable offshoot of the company in 2006. McNairy's first line with Woolrich drew heavily from what the company does best—hardy outerwear with a military bent—and added a light collegiate touch. The collection offered mishmashed plaid button-downs, tailored wool jackets (often with a bow tie or wool scarf peeking out), trench coats, fitted khakis, and even a wool hoodie.

McNairy lives in Weehawken, New Jersey, with his wife, Analia, their son, Ryder, and his mother-in-law.

## SUGGESTED READING

Baldwin, Rosecrans. "American Brandstand." *New York Times*. New York Times, 17 Sept. 2006. Web. 11 May 2013.

Bevan, Andrew. "Daisy McNairy Creates a New Collection with Her Father, Mark McNairy." *Teen Vogue*. Condé Nast Digital, 21 May 2012. Web. 12 May 2013.

Davis, Peter. "Nasty Boy: The Cult of Mark McNairy." *Papermag*. Paper, 20 Aug. 2012. Web. 12 May 2013.

Murrow, Lauren. "Mark McNairy Champions Preppy Style, English Footwear." *New York Magazine*. New York Media, 9 Feb. 2010. Web. 12 May 2013.

"They Put Bravado in Your Bracket." *People*. Time, 28 Mar. 1990. Web. 12 May 2013.

Tschorn, Adam. "Spotlight on Mark McNairy: The 'Eagle' Flies High." *Los Angeles Times*. Los Angeles Times, 17 Feb. 2013. Web. 12 May 2013.

—*Molly Hagan*

# Jim Messina

**Born:** 1969
**Occupation:** Campaign manager, political adviser

According to White House communications director Dan Pfeiffer, Jim Messina is "the most powerful person in Washington that you haven't heard of" (qtd. by Ari Berman in *Nation* Apr. 2011). Messina began working with the Obama administration in 2008, and earned the nickname "The Fixer" for his ability to resolve internal campaign disputes and manage politically sensitive negotiations. In 2009, President Obama named him White House Deputy Chief of Staff. Messina played an important role in the success of the Obama administration's first term legislative agenda, including the passage of the health care reform bill known as Obamacare. According to Berman, the appointment of Messina to a role within the administration caused some controversy, because many viewed him as an expert in business-as-usual law-making tactics, and methods of political deal making that ran contrary to the political philosophy of Obama's 2008 presidential campaign. In addition, many progressives worried that Messina would steer the Obama administration away from issues related to gay rights, thinking he would likely view them to be politically and culturally controversial.

## EARLY LIFE AND EDUCATION

Jim Messina was born in 1969 in Denver, Colorado. He was raised in Boise, Idaho, where he attended Boise High School. After graduating from high school in 1988, he enrolled at the University of Montana and earned a bachelor's degree in political science in 1993. When he was still a senior in college, Messina managed the reelection campaign of Mayor Dan Kemmis in Missoula, Montana. Democratic Senator Max Baucus of Montana hired Messina in 1995. In 1999, Congressman Carolyn McCarthy of New York hired him as chief of staff.

In 2002, Senator Baucus hired Messina to run his re-election campaign. Gay rights advocates have criticized Messina for his role in producing a political advertisement against Baucus's challenger, Republican Mike Taylor. Writing for *Salon* (15 June 2012), columnist David Sirota called the advertisement "one of the most homophobic ads in American history." Taylor ended his campaign shortly after the advertisement aired. Following Baucus's re-election, Messina became chief of staff for Senator Byron Dorgan of North Dakota. Senator Baucus named Messina as his chief of staff in 2005.

In 2008, Illinois Senator Barack Obama named Messina as chief of staff of his presidential campaign. Obama's campaign manager, David Plouffe, was impressed by Messina's work in

opposing President George W. Bush's efforts to privatize social security. Messina later described his work with the 2008 Obama campaign to Ryan Lizza for the *New Yorker* (17 Nov. 2008), saying, "I spend the money, so everything's gotta go through me to get spent, which is the best job ever. It's like getting the keys to a Ferrari." "I spend a lot of time making sure the trains run on time," he said, "making sure that Barack and the staff get to where they need to go and the message is right, and making the [campaign] departments talk to each other." Messina added, "We've grown from a small business to a Fortune 500 company and that's probably the biggest piece of what I do." Nevertheless, many people within the Democratic Party and inside Obama's circle of advisers were leery of Messina joining the campaign. He was widely viewed as a Washington insider, adept at the very practices of politicking and lobbyist negotiation that many members of the campaign staff openly renounced. Following Obama's successful 2008 presidential campaign, Messina became Deputy Chief of Staff under White House Chief of Staff Rahm Emanuel. When Emanuel left the White House in the fall of 2010, in order to run for mayor of Chicago, Messina ended his tenure at the White House as well.

## CAMPAIGN MANAGER

President Obama asked Messina to manage his 2012 re-election campaign in late 2010. After accepting the position, Messina left Washington DC, and established an office at Obama's campaign headquarters in Chicago, Illinois. "Jim is a great campaign technician," Obama's chief political consultant David Axelrod told the *Washington Post* (n.d.), "He's a great manager, he's a great organizer, he understands every element of the campaign and how they fit together." Speaking with Jeff Zeleny for the *New York Times* (2 Apr. 2011), Messina shed light on his philosophy for the 2012 campaign. "I really believe that the president is the art and I am the science," he said. "You have to start out with the assumption that this will not be 2008 again."

The Obama administration's 2012 re-election campaign began December 2008, one month following Obama's victory over Arizona Senator John McCain in the 2008 general election. Jeremy Bird, who had operated Obama's 2008 campaign in Ohio, led a group of mid-level campaign officials in a thorough analysis of the 2008 campaign. In addition to a review of logistics and field strategy, the review included a detailed review of voting data, and phone interviews with thousands of campaign organizers and volunteers. The work conducted by Bird and colleagues beginning in late 2008—and, in particular, its focus on data—would directly influence the strategy of Obama's 2012 campaign. Data analysis became central to Obama's 2012 campaign strategy. "Politics always has room for feel and instinct," Plouffe told Joshua Green for *Bloomberg BusinessWeek* (14 June 2012), "but there is so much more that's measurable now." Plouffe praised Messina's focus on data analysis as Obama's 2012 campaign manager. "We think from a technology and data perspective that what Jim has built will be the best that politics has ever seen," said Plouffe.

In addition to focusing on metrics, Messina met with numerous business leaders and technology innovators in the years leading up to the 2012 presidential election. These included Steve Jobs of Apple, Eric Schmidt of Google, *Vogue* magazine editor Anna Wintour, and filmmaker Steven Spielberg. "I went around the country for literally a month interviewing these companies and just talking about organizational growth, emerging technologies, [and] marketing," Messina told Green. According to Green, Jobs counseled Messina in the development of the campaign's mobile communication strategies, while Spielberg advised him on how best to capture an audience's attention.

## NEW STRATEGIES

In an article for *Buzzfeed* (9 Nov. 2012) Ruby Cramer discusses how the social media landscape during Obama's 2012 reelection campaign was vastly different from what the campaign experienced in 2008. In 2008, the iPhone was still a relative newcomer, and Facebook had just one-tenth of its 2012 user population. Messina spoke frankly to Cramer about the 2008 campaign's view of Twitter. "We thought it was some stupid technology that would never go anywhere," he said. Although the campaign sent just one tweet on election day of 2008, Twitter would become an integral part of its communication and fundraising in 2012. In September 2012, Reuters reported that Obama's acceptance speech at the Democratic National Convention generated 52,756 tweets per minute after it ended, setting a record. Messina chose to invest $100 million dollars in the campaign's technology apparatus. This allowed Obama's organization to increase the breadth and scope of its social network, and develop a proprietary software system that allowed campaign workers to work remotely, away from central campaign offices.

The campaign also invested in systems that allowed them to operate their own polling mechanisms. Cramer reports that the Obama analytics team would run the campaign through a computer simulation 66,000 times each evening in order to measure its efficacy. "Every morning," Messina told Cramer, "we would come in and spend our money based on those simulations." Breaking with tradition, the Obama campaign did not rely on traditional polling metrics from Gallup and the Associated Press. According to Messina, the campaign "spent a whole bunch of time figuring out that American polling is broken." Many tradition polls predicted that minority populations and young voters would not turn out again in support of Obama in the way they did in 2008. However, following the election, voting data showed that each group supported the president's re-election in larger numbers than in four years previous.

## CAMPAIGN CHALLENGES

In light of the Great Recession of 2007–8, and high unemployment numbers in the United States, the US economy became the central issue of the 2012 presidential election. The campaign of Republican Party challenger, former Massachusetts Senator Mitt Romney, was highly critical of Obama's economic record. Romney repeatedly challenged Obama for increasing government spending and overseeing an economy in which growth was faltering and unemployment was increasing. As Steven T. Dennis reported in *Roll Call* (4 Sept. 2012), Messina and other Obama campaign officials negotiated these criticisms by maintaining that Obama's grade on the economy was "incomplete." Deputy campaign manager Stephanie Cutter expounded upon this concept in Dennis's article, saying, "We're on a path forward. We're on our way up. There's a lot more that [President Obama] wants to get done. He's not done yet." Messina and other campaign officials continually maintained that the Romney campaign supported an economic plan that would provide tax cuts for the wealthiest Americans while increasing taxes on the middle class.

During the first presidential debate of the 2012 campaign, President Obama was widely criticized for appearing unenthused and detached. Meanwhile, Romney was praised for offering simple but energized explanations of his economic platform. While the first debate was viewed as a blow to the Obama campaign, Messina worked to put the incident in a positive light for his candidate. In speaking with Allison Sherry for the *Denver Post* (16 Oct. 2012), Messina alluded to the idea that the formal setting of the first debate better suited Romney. Obama's missteps, according to Messina, served as evidence of "why he likes to get out of Washington to talk to regular voters." "He always been a candidate of the middle class," said Messina, "he's just like these voters, he has the same struggles."

The Obama administration was criticized by its GOP opponents following the September 11, 2012, attack on the US consulate in Benghazi, Libya, in which US Ambassador J. Christopher Stevens was killed. The Romney campaign pointed to the attack as an example of Obama's weakness on security issues, and a representative of his inability to manage his foreign policy staff. In defense of Obama's foreign policy record, Messina told Sherry that the attack was "another example of why you need a strong commander in chief, a steady hand at the wheel." "We're going to contrast that with Governor Romney's record and how he went to Europe and managed to offend [America's] biggest ally," added Messina, in reference to statements Romney made while touring the London Olympics that questioned the United Kingdom's preparedness for a security threat.

In late October 2012, one week before the general election, both the Obama and Romney campaigns endured the challenge of a natural disaster in the form of Hurricane Sandy. While the press reveled in various predictions about how the storm might impact voting, Messina ensured that the president and his re-election campaign maintained an air of control and determination. Under the leadership of Messina and other campaign officials, President Obama successfully negotiated his roles as candidate and commander in chief. As the storm approached the northeast coast of the United States, Obama advised the public to listen to the advice of their local officials. During a White House press conference (29 Oct. 2012), when Obama was asked for his thoughts on how the storm might impact the election, he stated, "I'm worried about the impact on families and our first responders. The election will take care of itself next week. Right now our number one priority is to make sure that we are saving lives."

## NOVEMBER SUCCESS

In the days leading up to the general election on November 2, 2012, the media and traditional polling outlets continued to report that the race between Obama and Romney was too close too call. Reporting in *USA Today* (4 Nov. 2012) two days before election, David Jackson wrote, "No one knows what's going to happen in what could turn out to be a historically close presidential election." However, such predictions proved false. In the final analysis, Obama was reelected to a second term by a fairly significant margin of votes. He earned 51 percent of the total vote to Romney's 47.2 percent, nearly 5 million more votes nationwide. The margin in the Electoral College was even wider, with Obama earning 332 electoral votes to Romney's 206.

The Associated Press (8 Nov. 2012) reported that Obama earned 70 percent of Hispanic votes and more than 90 percent of votes from black Americans. Obama earned an 11 percent margin over Romney among female voters.

Writing for *Politico* (20 Nov. 2012), Ginger Gibson called Obama's 2012 campaign "the most technology-heavy campaign in history." However, Messina was quick to underplay the campaign's technological infrastructure and political know-how, stating that Obama was re-elected because his message resonated with voters. "It's about the candidate," Messina told Gibson. "It's about the message. That's why millions of Americans went online and signed up for Obama for America. It wasn't because they got a t-shirt [or] bumper sticker. It was because they deeply believed in Barack Obama."

## POLITICAL FUTURE

Following Obama's successful re-election bid in November 2012, Messina told *Politico*'s Mike Allen (20 Nov. 2012) that he planned to "go to Italy and hang out." "I've taken one vacation in five years, and it is time to restore my energy. The president and I were joking recently about how bad I look, and it's time to take a vacation." Messina claimed that he wanted to help Obama accomplish his second term goals, but that he would likely do so outside of the White House. "I think my future is probably outside the White House," he told Allen, "helping [the president] and becoming a part of whatever happens to our social movement to help advocate for his agenda."

## PERSONAL LIFE

Despite the public nature of his work in politics, Messina has managed to maintain privacy about his personal life. He is not married and does not have any children, but it has been reported that he has a girlfriend who lives in Los Angeles.

## SUGGESTED READING

Corn, David. *Showdown: The Inside Story of How Obama Battled the GOP to Set Up the 2012 Election.* New York: Morrow, 2012. Print.

Lizza, Ryan. "Battle Plans: How Obama Won." *New Yorker* 17 Nov. 2008. Rpt. in *Best American Political Writing 2009*. Ed. Royce Flippin. Boulder: Public Affairs. 2009. Print.

---. "The Final Push: The Obama Team's High-Risk Strategy." *New Yorker*. Condé Nast, 29 Oct. 2012. Web. 14 Jan. 2013.

Zeleny, Jeff. "An Obama Insider, Running the Race from Afar." *New York Times*. New York Times, 2 Apr. 2011. Web. 16 Jan. 2013.

—*Joshua Pritchard*

# Anne Akiko Meyers

**Born:** May 15, 1970
**Occupation:** Violinist

Anne Akiko Meyers has been called one of the most innovative and skillful violinists of the modern age. Over the course of her career, Meyers has toured and been a featured soloist with many preeminent symphony orchestras including London's Philharmonia Orchestra, Los Angeles Philharmonic, Boston Symphony Orchestra, New York Philharmonic, Vienna Symphony, Orchestre de Paris, and Tokyo's NHK Symphony. Her prominence in the world of concert violin is such that she was recently awarded lifetime use of the Vieuxtemps Guarneri del Gesú violin, one of the world's most sought after instruments, even though she performs on two world-renowned Stradivarius violins.

Having played on the professional stage since childhood, Meyers has garnered high praise from critics and fans over the years. In a review of her performance of Mendelssohn's Violin Concerto in E Minor, Anthony Bannon for the *Chautauquan Daily* wrote, "It was played not for drama, but for delectation; not for flash, but for all that is fine. Her artistry has no need for razzmatazz." In a February 2011 article for the *Austin Statesman*, critic Luke Quinton wrote, "Meyers possesses a tone so pure that it emerges just a few times in a generation." Her solo and ensemble recordings have also garnered significant critical praise, the *American Record Guide* quoted as saying, "there seems to be no limit to the colors she can draw from her instrument." Conductors praise Meyers's skill and her interaction with the orchestra to create successful performances. Peter Bay, music director for the Austin Symphony Orchestra, said of Meyers, "There's a certain fire she brings to the stage, which creates a great energy with the orchestra, conductor and audience."

While Meyers has become a seasoned veteran of the classical music community, she has also become an important ambassador for the violin. For many, Meyers represents the best of

© Lisa Marie Mazzucco

the modern generation of instrumentalists: she is able to navigate between musical genres and is able to blend her personality and skill to become a leading voice in modern music while keeping past traditions alive.

## CHILD PRODIGY AND EDUCATION

Anne Akiko Meyers was born in San Diego, California, in 1970, and is the daughter of Richard Meyers, who served as president of several universities, and Japanese-born painter Yakko Meyers. Meyers first started taking formal violin lessons when she was four, though according to Meyers, her introduction to classical music began before she was born. As she explained in a 2012 interview for National Public Radio (NPR), "My mother played a lot of music for me when she was pregnant with me . . . [and when] I was born and especially when she fed me, I would associate the pleasure of food and eating with music." In a 2008 interview with St. Louis, Missouri, television station KETC, Yakko Meyers said that while she was not necessarily hoping her children would become musicians, she introduced them to music at an early age so they would grow to have an understanding and appreciation of music as an art form.

Meyers displayed innate skill with the instrument early on, and by age eleven, performed with the Los Angeles Philharmonic. She performed with Zubin Mehta and the New York Philharmonic a year later at age twelve. She was put in charge of the Angels Ensemble of California Quartet, a popular group of child prodigies in the Los Angeles area. After appearing on the *Tonight Show* with Johnny Carson in 1981, the members of the Angels Ensemble became minor television celebrities. They were asked to return to the *Tonight Show* twice, and performed at the Emmy Awards in 1982, among other appearances.

Meyers's formal education included lessons at the Colburn School of Performing Arts in Los Angeles, California, under the tutelage of violin instructor Alice Schoenfeld, a famed international recording artist and violin virtuoso, and chamber music coach Eleonore Schoenfeld. As a tribute to Eleonore Schoenfeld, Meyers wrote on her website that her "standard for excellence was unparalleled," and that "this combination of tireless dedication to her art and her students will forever motivate me." In the early 1980s, Meyers studied with Russian virtuoso Josef Gingold at Indiana University.

Meyers's family made significant sacrifices in order to allow her to continue developing her skills. Her mother reportedly drove more than 150 miles each way to bring her daughter to lessons, and when Meyers was invited to attend the Juilliard School to study with Dorothy DeLay at the age of fourteen, Anne relocated to New York City with her mother and sister. Her father, then president of Western Oregon University, stayed behind. At Juilliard, Meyers studied with Viennese virtuoso Felix Galimir, Japanese American soloist Masao Kawasaki, and Dorothy DeLay, who is regarded as one of the most influential violin instructors of the twentieth century. Meyers has spoken highly of all of her instructors, saying that each one imparted essential lessons that she repeatedly uses as a professional.

## CAREER AND RISE TO PROMINENCE

When Meyers was sixteen, she was signed by International Creative Management (ICM) and began touring professionally. Meyers made her first solo recording when she was eighteen, an album of the Barber Violin Concerto and Bruch Violin Concerto No. 1, with Christopher Seaman and the Royal Philharmonic Orchestra. At age twenty, Meyers signed a multiple-record contract with RCA Red Seal.

In 1993, at age twenty-two, Meyers was the sole recipient of the prestigious Avery Fisher Career Grant, providing her with $10,000 to further her career. By this time, Meyers had been featured with many of the world's leading orchestras and was recognized as one of the top violin virtuosos of her era. Among dozens of performances she gave before the age of thirty, Meyers was a featured soloist with the Boston Symphony Orchestra, Philadelphia Orchestra, London's Philharmonia Orchestra, Royal Philharmonic Orchestra, New York Philharmonic, and the Royal Concertgebow Orchestra. Meyers was also asked to perform in many high-profile settings, including a performance for the emperor and empress of Japan and an Australian bicentennial celebration in front of 750,000 people at Sydney Harbour.

## SOLO RECORDING AND PERFORMANCE CAREER

From her recording debut through the first decade of the twenty-first century, Meyers has been featured in more than twenty recordings. Over the years, Meyers became passionate about recording music from new composers and experimenting with alternative musical genres like jazz and fusion. She premiered new works by composers including Mason Bates, Karl Amadeus Hartmann, John Corigliano, Wynton Marsalis, Akira Miyoshi, Somei Satoh, and Joseph Schwantner, and has also frequently commissioned emerging composers to write new works for her to record and perform. Meyers has performed with jazz trumpeter Chris Botti, the pop vocal group Il Divo, and pianist Ryuchi Sakamoto, among others.

Meyers's versatility has won her praise from fans and fellow musicians around the world. Acclaimed pianist Anton Nel explained to Jeanne Claire van Ryzin for the online magazine *Austin 360* (17 Feb. 2011) that Meyers "is someone who can easily and fearlessly perform standard repertoire, as well as contemporary music, and even cross over into popular styles." Meyers told KETC television that it was important for a musician to play new work in addition to the classical pieces expected of a violinist. "You need the new work in order to enrich the old work," she said, adding, "It gives me fuel."

Many of Meyers's most celebrated recordings are interpretations of classical recordings. But Meyers also plays and records modern and alternative selections. Her 2008 album *Smile* contained songs that Meyers described in an interview with Minnesota Public Radio as being "music that I have absolutely loved for a very long time." The album's title track was made famous in the 1936 Charlie Chaplin movie *Modern Times* and was composed by Chaplin for the film. Speaking about the album, Meyers said on Minnesota Public Radio, "This music definitely comes from within a very deep place within myself. . . . It's music that has always moved me, and I think it has the ability to move just about everybody." *Smile* also contains Meyers's arrangement of a traditional Japanese song called "Moonlight over the Ruined Castle," one of her grandmother's favorites.

In 2010, Meyers released the album *Seasons . . . Dreams . . .* in which she chose a selection of classical and contemporary pieces related to the various seasons of the year. The album contains works by composers such as Wagner,

Beethoven, Gershwin, Debussy, and Faure, and includes the songs "Autumn in New York" by Vernon Duke, and a critically lauded recording of "Silent Night," composed by Alfred Schnittke, which Meyers described to Chris McGovern of the arts-centered website *The Glass* as an "eerie spin on one of the most traditional songs ever composed." Meyers went on to explain that, "music shouldn't be all pretty and on the surface. Music should make one dream but also feel, and the [rendition of "Silent Night"] has both elements—even if it makes one squirm."

Meyers's 2012 recording *AIR: The Bach Album* garnered substantial praise from critics worldwide and was a top selling recording of 2012. Her performance of Bach's Violin Concerto for Two Violins, was unique because Meyers recorded both parts of the concerto herself, using her two famed Stradivarius violins. "It was like having a tennis match with myself," Meyers told McGovern. Meyers recorded the first part of the concerto with her famed 1697 Molitor Stradivarius accompanied by the English Chamber Orchestra in London. In New York several months later, Meyers, wearing headphones, accompanied herself and recorded the second part using her 1730 Royal Spanish Stradivarius.

## FAMOUS VIOLINS

Because world-class instruments are very costly, professionals often play instruments owned by foundations or private sponsors. In 2005, Meyers was able to purchase her own world-class violin, a 1730 Stradivarius known as the Royal Spanish, which was once owned by the King of Spain. "There's nothing like ownership. There's nothing like being able to own your voice," Meyers said in a 2010 interview with WQXR Radio, adding, "I've been saving up for it my whole life."

In October 2010, Meyers made international news when she acquired a second famous instrument, the 1697 Molitor Stradivarius, paying $3.6 million, which at the time was the highest price paid at auction for a concert instrument. (The Molitor got its name from Count Gabriel-Jean-Joseph Molitor, a general in Napoleon's army, whose family owned the instrument for more than a century.) "It has an extraordinary sound," Meyers told the Van Ryzin. "It's so clear, so piercing in its purity."

Meyers likes alternating between the two instruments for their unique and individual characteristics. She described the sound of the Royal Spanish as having "a little more masculine tone to it." By contrast, the Molitor, or "Molly," as Meyers has nicknamed the violin, "has a very pure, beautiful, crystalline voice."

In January of 2013, an anonymous sponsor gave Meyers lifetime use of the 1741 Vieuxtemps Guarneri del Gesù, which has a reported value of $18 million. "I have never heard another violin with such a beautiful spectrum of color," Meyers said in a 2013 press release, adding, "I am honored and humbled to receive lifetime use of the instrument, and I look forward to taking the violin to audiences all over the world." Named for its most famous owner, nineteenth-century Belgian violinist and composer Henri Vieuxtemps, the instrument is widely considered to be one of the finest violins ever made.

Meyers has repeatedly said in interviews that the pedigree of an instrument is less important than the qualitative measure of the instrument's sound. "There are a lot of great contemporary makers today," Meyers told WQXR, adding that when looking for an instrument, musicians will have an emotional reaction to it and will know that it suits them. "It's pretty instantaneous when it does happen."

### PERSONAL LIFE

Meyers lives with her family in Austin, Texas. She often travels with them in tow and she reported to Van Rysin that her oldest daughter has specific musical tastes of her own. "My Beethoven Spring Sonata immediately stops any melt down. I can't even stand hearing my own recording of it anymore, but if it works for her, I'll go with it." In a 2012 concert at New York's Rubin Museum of Art, Meyers debuted a new composition by John Corigliano entitled, "Lullaby for Natalie," which she commissioned to honor her daughter's birth. Meyers intends to record the composition with the London Symphony Orchestra with Leonard Slatkin conducting in September, 2013.

### SUGGESTED READING

Amacher, Julie. "New Classical Tracks: Love Letter to Composers." *MPR News*. Minnesota Public Radio, 17 Mar. 2009. Web. 8 Apr. 2013.

Bannon, Anthony. "CSO, Meyers Leave Audience Amazed at the Wonder." *Chautauquan Daily*. Chautauqua Inst., 4 Aug. 2012. Web. 8 Apr. 2013.

Van Ryzin, Jeanne Claire. "Famed Violin Makes Local Debut This Weekend." *Austin360*. Cox Media Group, 17 Feb. 2011. Web. 7 May 2013.

"Violinist Anne Akiko Meyers: From Playing in Knee Socks to Owning Two Strads." *Deceptive Cadence*. Natl. Public Radio, 6 Feb. 2012. Web. 7 May 2013.

Vittes, Laurence. "AIR: The Bach Album." *Strings*, July 2012. Web. 8 Apr. 2013.

### SELECTED WORKS

*Smile*, 2008; *Seasons . . . Dreams . . .* , 2010; *AIR: The Bach Album*, 2012

—Micah Issitt

# Yuri Milner

**Born:** November 11, 1961
**Occupation:** Russian entrepreneur and venture capitalist

When a relatively unknown Russian investor named Yuri Milner swooped into Silicon Valley to claim a 2 percent stake in Facebook for $200 million in May 2009—giving the social network a then-unbelievable overall valuation of $10 billion—most technology investors thought he was mad. "Many people thought Facebook at a $10 billion valuation at the bottom of the market was expensive," Milner told Rupert Neate for the London *Telegraph* (22 May 2010). "But our thesis is to find the best companies in their categories and invest in them. The better companies that we look at tend to be expensive." Milner's pragmatic assessment of Facebook's potential value paid off in spades, nearly quintupling in value over the next three years. Milner, through his international investment firm, DST Global, has also invested in other Internet giants, including Twitter, Groupon, Spotify, and Zynga, among others. "Today his various investment funds are worth an estimated $12 billion, and his private worth is set at $1 billion," Geoff Brumfiel wrote for *Nature* magazine (31 July 2012). Milner's uncommon investment strategy, in which he often refuses a seat on the board or other perquisites, has baffled and impressed investors in Silicon Valley. "How is it that an outsider has spotted opportunities that the Valley's best investors missed?" Michael Wolff asked in an article for *Wired* magazine (21 Oct. 2011).

"The way Milner plays the venture game has rocked the tidy Sand Hill Road cabal because it's a style unlike any they've seen. Milner's three secretaries rotate on eight-hour shifts. DST Global's two dozen employees, many ex-Goldman Sachs bankers, scout deals and raise money from Singapore, Dubai, and London," Parmy Olson wrote for *Forbes* magazine (28 Mar. 2011). As the most successful investor in social media, Milner grew his fund by $12 billion in US assets in less than two years, beginning with his prescient and well-timed investment in Facebook. "We chose a strategy of total and unconditional focus on the consumer Internet, and I would say, even the social Internet," Milner explained to Andrew E. Kramer for the *New York Times* (3 Jan. 2011). "Global investors with this level of focus, it turns out, are few. People usually think more broadly, and then have to follow a large number of sectors and process lots of information." Despite his level of focus, Milner is still dealing with an information overload, regardless of how adeptly he manages it. According to Olson, the walls of Milner's home and office are loaded with flat-screen televisions tuned

Bloomberg via Getty Images

to various news channels, such as CNBC and CNN, as well as various Twitter feeds that mention Milner or his investment firm. While Milner is focused on analyzing the market, technology investors around the world are focused on Milner, waiting to see what his next move will be.

## EARLY LIFE

Yuri Milner was born into a Jewish family of Moscow intellectuals on November 11, 1961. Milner's father, Boris, was a business professor, who, during the course of his career, wrote or edited more than fifty books on American management practices. Milner's mother, Betty, worked as a physician at the Moscow Department for Disease Prevention. Milner has one older sister, an architect.

Milner was interested in computer technology even as a teenager, and he took programming classes three nights a week during high school to learn to code. He later enrolled at Moscow State University, graduating with a degree in theoretical physics in 1985. He went on to study particle physics at the Lebedev Institute at the Russian Academy of Sciences, where he studied under Nobel laureates and other highly esteemed scientists. Describing himself as a "failed physicist" to Dennis Overbye for the *New York Times* (10 Dec. 2012), Milner decided to drop out of his PhD program in 1989.

At this time, the Soviet Union was beginning to collapse and inflation was running rampant. Through a friend of his, Milner landed a job selling personal computers, where he was able to earn a decent wage. But his father disapproved

and encouraged him to enroll in an MBA program at the University of Pennsylvania's Wharton School of Business, where a colleague and friend worked. In 1990, Milner took a scholarship to attend Wharton. Milner would later admit to Michael Wolff in 2011 that he never completed his degree at Wharton, falling just a few credits short. Nevertheless, after leaving Wharton, Milner was able to secure a job at the World Bank's financial branch in Washington, DC, where he spent three years in the early 1990s. In an interview with Parmy Olson for *Forbes* (28 Mar. 2011), Milner described them as his "lost years," as he watched, with jealousy and anger, the rapid privatization of the Soviet government's holdings in Russia's natural resources, including oil, minerals, agriculture, and lumber, which greatly enriched a small class of well-connected Russian oligarchs.

## EARLY INVESTMENT CAREER

Milner eventually left the World Bank and returned to Moscow. In 1995 he met Mikhail Khodorkovsky, one of the richest men in Russia and founder of the oil company Yukos. Greatly impressed by Milner, Khodorkovsky offered him a position at his brokerage firm, Alliance-Menatep, where Milner would successfully manage Menatep's brokerage and investment banking divisions. In 1995 Milner organized an attempted takeover of the Russian candy maker Red October, which had recently been released from government control. "We are in the process of creating a first legal precedent for public bids in Russia, and hope that this operation will serve as a basis for future regulation in this area," Milner told John Shepherd for the *Independent* at the time (12 July 1995).

In 1998 Milner organized a group of investors to purchase a macaroni factory. The Russian government had just defaulted on its debt, and Milner understood that the price of imported foods would skyrocket. Also around this time, Milner met Gregory Finger, who managed the Moscow office of New Century Holdings, a US hedge fund. The two investors clicked, as both had interests in various technology opportunities in Russia and the United States. Milner approached Finger about starting a venture fund together. New Century Holdings agreed to put up $2.25 million for a venture fund, as long as Milner and Finger were willing to each invest $750,000 of their own money. Milner, through the stock market and the income from his macaroni factory, had made enough money to fund his share. In 1999 Finger and Milner established the venture fund NetBridge and began investing in a number of Russian Internet firms, including an online auction site called Molotok and another online retailer known as 24x7. When the dot-com bubble burst, Milner was forced to shut down 24x7 in 2001. Nevertheless he capitalized

on the downturn by organizing a merger between NetBridge and the online portal Port.ru,
formerly the largest Internet company in Russia.
Following the merger, Port.ru became known as
Mail.ru and, beginning in 2001, was headed by
Milner as chief executive officer. Over the next
few years, Mail.ru steadily gained market share,
eventually becoming one of the three major Internet companies in Russia. Milner also oversaw
Mail.ru's early experimentations with online
gaming services, instant messaging, and virtual
credits.

### MAJOR INVESTMENTS

In 2005 Milner created an investment holding
company called Digital Sky Technologies with
Gregory Finger and Mikhail Vinchel. Digital
Sky took a controlling stake in Mail.ru. Between
2005 and 2011 Mail.ru invested nearly a billion
dollars in thirty businesses, including several European social networks and an instant-messag-
ing service. At the end of 2008, as the markets
were recovering from the global financial crisis
that began in 2007, Milner sought investors to
establish a new investment fund, which would
be called DST Global. He secured early backing
from Alisher Usmanov, a controversial figure in
finance and one of the richest men in the world.
Milner had his sights set on taking a stake in
Facebook and approached the social network's
chief financial officer, Gideon Yu, in January
2009. As Parmy Olson notes in *Forbes* (28 Mar.
2011), "Yu politely rebuffed Milner, suggesting
it wouldn't be worth his time to fly all the way
out to Palo Alto." Undeterred Milner boarded a
plan from Moscow and showed up at the Facebook offices the next morning anyway. When Yu
met with Milner, he was so impressed by the
investor's knowledge of social media and Internet start-ups that he brought Milner in to see
Facebook CEO Mark Zuckerberg. A few months
later, in May 2009, Silicon Valley investors were
bowled over when DST Global announced it had
taken a 2 percent stake in Facebook for $200
million, valuing the social network at $10 billion.
"A number of firms approached us, but DST
stood out because of the global perspective they
bring, backed up by the impressive growth and
financial achievements of their Internet investments," Zuckerberg stated in a May 26, 2009,
press release. Milner was able to secure the deal
by ceding the voting rights on those shares to
Zuckerberg. "Ultimately, it was my comfort with
DST that led to the deal," Zuckerberg said in an
interview for *USA Today* (27 May 2009).

Milner's decision to refuse a seat on the
boards of the companies he invests in is part of
his overall strategy. According to Olsen, "Milner
makes huge bets at high valuations. Once in, he
refuses to take a board seat. The entrepreneurs
behind Facebook, Groupon, or Zynga may not
hear from him for weeks or months." While such

terms may seem foolish to traditional investors,
Milner seems to be more interested in creating
his own network among the giants of social media. "There is always something vaguely opposi-
tional about the relationship VCs have with the
companies they invest in," Michael Wolff wrote
for *Wired* magazine (21 Oct. 2011). "They are
trying to maximize their positions, to pay as little
as possible and cash out for as much as possible.
Milner . . . is not thinking about individual deals
but is aligning himself financially and strategically with the founders and reaping the benefits." Over the next two years, Milner made a
series of investments in Facebook, at one point
growing his stake to approximately 9 percent of
the company. Prior to Facebook's initial public
offering, though, Milner reduced his stake to
some 4.5 percent. The estimated worth of his
holdings, based on the midpoint of Facebook's
stock price, is roughly $2.5 billion. "Although
Milner seems to have made a chump's deal without all the protections that early-stage money is
usually entitled to, for a period of time he has
gotten one thing: a right of first refusal on any
other Facebook stock that changes hands. The
dumb money has just bought itself potentially
unlimited access to arguably the most important
company to hit the Internet in a decade," Wolff
wrote.

Six months after Milner's initial investment
in Facebook, in December 2009 Milner and
DST invested $180 million in Zynga, the online-
gaming service that produced Mafia Wars and
Farmville. Milner also developed a reputation for
just showing up and securing monumental deals.
"When Groupon was considering raising a Series
E venture round in March 2010, its cofounder,
[Eric] Lefkofsky, mentioned it to Milner during
a brief phone call. Milner told him to wait and
showed up in Chicago the next day. A few hours
after he landed the Groupon deal was done," Olson reported. Just a few months earlier, Groupon
had rejected a $6 billion acquisition deal from
Google. Milner and DST Global managed to negotiate a deal to take a 5 percent stake in the
company. In January 2011 Milner invested an
additional $125 million into Facebook, and six
months later he invested $100 million in Spotify,
an online music streaming service. One month
after that, Milner and DST Global invested
$112 million in Airbnb, an online rentals-listing
service. Also in July 2011 DST Global invested
$400 million into the popular microblogging site
Twitter.

### "INDUSTRIALIZING" INTERNET VENTURE CAPITAL

Danny Rimer, a partner at the London-based Index Ventures, told *Forbes* magazine's Parmy Olson (28 Mar. 2011), "Yuri is industrializing venture capital. For the first time in a long time, he
is approaching venture capital as an asset class

rather than as a profession." In 2010 Milner divided DST into two parts, taking Mail.ru public and renaming it Mail.ru Group. The stakes that Milner secured in Zynga, Facebook, and Groupon are shared between Mail.ru Group and DST Global, with Milner owning a minority interest in the combined assets of both companies. Milner has also invested hundreds of millions of dollars into the Chinese online retailer 360buy. com, the point-of-care and medical-scheduling website ZocDoc, and the Internet giant Alibaba Group. In March 2011 *Forbes* listed Milner among its list of the world's billionaires for the first time.

Speaking of his investments in social media, Milner explained his strategy to Rupert Neate for the *Telegraph* (22 May 2010), "Every single industry will get disrupted by the Internet. This is permanent, not cyclical. Music will never be the same again, the newspaper business will never be the same again. No matter what happens macro-economically, the Internet will continue to change the world. I am investing in disruptive companies, that just happen to be Internet companies." In January 2011 Milner announced that he would partner with the "angel-investing" fund SV Angel to create a fund called Smart Fund, which would invest $150,000 into every start-up company that emerged from Y Combinator, a seed investment company. In early 2012 Milner left the board of Mail.ru to focus more exclusively on his social-media investments. While Milner's social-media investments were first criticized as bad strategy and "dumb money," the investors of Silicon Valley have since adopted his deal structure—investing huge sums into late-stage and well-established start-ups with extremely lax deal terms. While some may wonder how a Silicon Valley outsider managed to change Internet venture capitalism so dramatically, Michael Wolff offered the following explanation in *Wired* (21 Oct. 2011): "Who would be more gobsmacked by the implications of social media—the prospect of everyone constantly talking to one another without an arbiter, mediator, or censor—than a citizen of the former Soviet Union? Likewise, who would see it as more revolutionary and valuable?" In September 2012 *Bloomberg* magazine named Milner to its list of the Most Influential 50 people in the world of finance. Milner is likely to continue to set the strategy—and the prices—in online investments for years to come.

## FUNDAMENTAL PHYSICS PRIZE

In July 2012 Milner announced the establishment of the Fundamental Physics Prize, beginning by awarding $27 million to be distributed among nine physicists for their work in fundamental theory. Milner selected the initial nine recipients of the prize himself after conferring with a number of celebrated physicists. In the future, third parties will be able to nominate physicists for the prize and the winner will be selected by a committee of the prize's previous winners. Previous prize winners will also be responsible for nominating a junior researcher for the $100,000 New Horizons Prize. The $3 million award represents nearly triple the amount of prize money given to winners of the Nobel Prize, the Kavli Prize, and other major awards in the field. "The intention was to say that science is as important as shares trading on Wall Street," Milner told Geoff Brumfiel for *Nature* magazine (31 July 2012).

Lyn Evans, director of the Large Hadron Collider and one of the initial recipients of the Fundamental Physics Prize, expressed her shock and delight in an interview with Ian Sample for the *Guardian* (10 Dec. 2012): "I was gobsmacked. The first thing you do is sit down. This is great for us, and it addresses some of the deficiencies of the Nobel Prize, which cannot go to more than three people." Another criterion that distinguishes Milner's award from the Nobel is that the contributions of physicists need not be experimentally verified in order to be eligible for the award. Milner hopes that this will provide researchers with the financial backing to pursue new ideas more easily and thoroughly. The only condition that comes with prize money is that the winners are required to offer at least one annual public lecture on their research, which will be posted to the Fundamental Prize's website. Stephen Hawking, one of the recipients of the inaugural prize, praised Milner's efforts to Sample, saying, "No one undertakes research in physics with the intention of winning a prize. It is the joy of discovering something no one knew before." He continued, "Nevertheless prizes like these play an important role in giving public recognition for achievement in physics. They increase the stature of physics and interest in it."

## PERSONAL LIFE

Milner, when he is not traveling, splits his time between his penthouse apartment in Moscow and his home in Los Altos Hills, California. His wife, Julia, is a former model who currently works as a photographer and artist. Together they have two daughters.

## SUGGESTED READING

Brumfiel, Geoff. "Theoretical Physicists Win Massive Awards." *Nature*. Nature Publishing Group, 31 July 2012. Web. 4. Jan. 2013.

Neate, Rupert. "Facebook Is Just the First Step, Say Russians." *Telegraph*. Telegraph Media Group, 22 May 2010. Web. 4 Jan. 2013.

Olson, Parmy. "The Billionaire Who Friended the Web." *Forbes*. Forbes.com, 9 Mar. 2011. Web. 4 Jan. 2013.

Sample, Ian. "Biggest Science Prize Takes Web Tycoon from Social Networks to String Theory."

*Guardian.* Guardian News and Media, 31 July 2012. Web. 4 Jan. 2012.

Wolff, Michael. "How Russian Tycoon Yuri Milner Bought His Way into Silicon Valley." *Wired.* Condé Nast, 21 Oct. 2011. Web. 4 Jan. 2013.

—*Mary Woodbury*

# Nicki Minaj

**Born:** December 8, 1982
**Occupation:** Rapper and television personality

Since collaborating with rapper Lil Wayne on a series of mix tapes from 2007 to 2009 and releasing her debut solo album, *Pink Friday,* in 2010, Nicki Minaj has become one of the world's most influential female hip-hop artists. "[She] turned a lot of heads by coming out of the gate as a supremely confident, powerful MC in any one of the many guises she has chosen to inhabit," Scott Plagenhoef wrote for the music magazine *Pitchfork* (24 Nov. 2010). "Avoiding easy categorization on her mix tapes and guest verses, Minaj has played the coquette, the powerhouse, the lady, the diva, the rapper's rapper, the fembot, and the comedian. . . . And while she plays fast and loose with her past, her inclination to slip into a number of characters is the work of a creative former theater kid rather than a myth-making rapper."

Indeed, Minaj receives as much attention for her fashion choices, madcap persona, and chameleon-like ability to reinvent herself as she does for her music. "[Minaj] has been difficult to miss, raking in music awards and posing on magazine covers in the Day-Glo wigs and makeup that summon up Japanese anime," Brent Staples wrote for the *New York Times* (7 July 2012). "She raps in hyper speed in British, Caribbean, and New York accents, and channels her engaging zaniness through alter egos, one known as Harajuku Barbie. . . . She is as much actor as musician, hopscotching among genres and personas more easily than most of her rivals. Look back at her earliest music video appearances, and you get the sense that she is driven to shed one role for another, maybe just to fend off boredom."

In 2010, even before her debut solo album was released, Minaj made history by having the most singles on *Billboard*'s Hot 100 chart at the same time. The record-setting seven tracks on which she was featured included Ludacris's "My Chick Bad," Lil Wayne's "Knockout," and Usher's "Lil Freak." She has since garnered numerous industry prizes, including BET Awards as best female hip-hop artist in 2010, 2011, 2012, and 2013; an MTV Video Music Award for best hip-hop video of 2011 (for her hit single "Super

Landov

Bass"); and a People's Choice Award as favorite hip-hop artist of 2013.

Minaj was introduced to a larger mainstream audience as a judge on the televised singing competition *American Idol* during its 2012–13 season. She made headlines for an alleged feud with a fellow judge, singer Mariah Carey. Many critics praised Minaj for adding a much-needed boost of excitement to the long-running show.

## CHILDHOOD

Onika Tanya Maraj was born on December 8, 1982, in Saint James, a district in Trinidad and Tobago's capital city, Port-of-Spain. Her parents are Trinidadians of African heritage—her father has some South Asian ancestry as well. The family surname, Maraj, is a Hindu term derived from the word *Maharaj,* or "great king." (Indians first arrived in Trinidad as contract laborers in the middle of the nineteenth century.)

Minaj is the product of a family with a tempestuous history. Minaj's mother was the tenth of eleven children, growing up in a crowded home in St. James, Trinidad and Tobago. She married at age twenty and later discovered that her husband often became abusive. Still, she tried to make the best of her situation, working as a bank teller and payroll clerk, and giving birth to two children: Minaj and a son. When she was twenty-four, she immigrated to the United States, leaving her children to be raised by their grandmother.

Six months after her arrival, wanting to keep the family together and knowing that she would need his help before sending for the children, she petitioned her husband to immigrate as well. He got a job at American Express, and the couple later purchased a home in the New York City borough of Queens. Minaj joined her parents in Queens when she was five. While living in Queens, Minaj's father began drinking heavily and using drugs.

One night in December 1987, he attempted to burn their house down. "When he set fire to the house, he was attempting to kill my mother," Minaj recalled to Jonah Weiner for *Details* (May 2010). "She got out before it burned all the way down. I've always had this female-empowerment thing in the back of my mind—because I wanted my mother to be stronger, and she couldn't be. I thought, 'If I'm successful, I can change her life.'"

## YOUNG ARTIST

Minaj's parents ultimately divorced. Her father has disputed accounts that depict him as an abusive drug addict, claiming that although he had some issues with anger, the performer and her mother have grossly exaggerated his behavior to the media.

During the years of their turbulent marriage, Minaj's mother moved frequently. "I would have to go to a new school, which meant I'd have to face the task of making new friends," Minaj told Eva Chen for *Teen Vogue* (June 2012). "I dreaded it. I had butterflies in my stomach each time: Are people going to like or hate me? Will they talk about me?" At times, she was bullied and had to call her older brother to defend her. She eventually learned to cope by ignoring her tormentors. "I always felt like I had other things going in my life outside of school, like church and extracurriculars—I was even on the softball team," she recalled to Chen.

Things changed markedly for Minaj once she entered LaGuardia High School, the storied New York City performing-arts institution that inspired the movie *Fame* (1980). "It was the first time I felt like I really fit in. Everyone there was creative," she told Chen. "For once, I didn't feel like there was something weird about me." She graduated from LaGuardia in 2002.

Minaj had little luck in the conventional workforce. "The last job I had was as an office manager in a little, tiny room where I literally wanted to strangle this guy because he was so loud and obnoxious," Minaj recalled to Mariel Concepcion for *Billboard* (12 Nov. 2010). "I would go home with stress pains in my neck and my back. That's when I went to my mother and said, 'Look, I'm not going back to work.' I'd been fired like fifteen times because I had a horrible attitude. I worked at Red Lobster before that and I chased a customer out of the restaurant once

so I could stick my middle finger up at her and demand that she give me my pen back. I swear to God I was bad."

## EARLY MUSIC CAREER

Minaj had written her first rap song at the age of twelve. She later began taking on gigs singing backup for local rappers and posting photos and videos on her MySpace page, which was discovered one day by the hip-hop impresario known as Big Fendi. Fendi oversaw a DVD "magazine," *The Come Up*, and Minaj, who had by then adopted her stage name, appeared in several editions, including one that spotlighted the rapper Lil Wayne.

Lil Wayne had joined Cash Money Records in 1991, at the age of nine, becoming the youngest member of the influential label. By the time he was introduced to Minaj, he had recorded several platinum albums. Impressed by the young female rapper, he featured her on a series of mix tapes, including *Playtime Is Over* (2007) and *Beam Me Up, Scotty* (2009), which featured the popular single "I Get Crazy." She also appeared on various remixes by other artists, including T.I.'s "No Matter What" and Jeffree Star's club track "Lollipop Luxury."

In 2009, Minaj made a memorable appearance in the music video for rapper Gucci Mane's "Five Star Chick," dancing provocatively and sporting vibrantly colored makeup and a Cleopatra-type hairstyle. "My hands just went on my hips and I became like a doll. I had never done that before or planned to do it," she explained to Concepcion. "After that I would go to shows and girls in the audience would do the whole 'Five Star Chick' dance. Afterward I thought, 'Maybe I'm on to something.'" Referring to an area in Japan known for its youth culture and trendy fashions, Minaj began calling herself the Harajuku Barbie and later dubbed her fans "Barbies."

In 2010, she contributed to the track "Monster," on Kanye West's album *My Beautiful Dark Twisted Fantasy*, an assignment that also allowed her to work with her longtime idol Jay Z. "I just feel blessed to be on a song with two living legends. Jay and Kanye are both icons, and I never in a billion years would've [dreamed of this]," she told Sean Ryon for *Hip Hop DX* (8 Sept. 2010). Of reviews that stated she had almost outperformed the two male stars, she said, "I'm happy that people think [that], [but] it just feels exciting to have been a part of [the record]."

## SOLO EFFORTS

In April 2010, Minaj released her first digital single, "Massive Attack," which peaked at number sixty-five on the Hot R&B/Hip-Hop Songs chart. Although she had originally intended it to be the lead single of her upcoming debut album, Minaj changed her mind after seeing its poor chart performance. Instead, "Your Love," was released as the album's first official single on June 1, 2010, and helped garner her the BET Award for best female hip-hop artist. The track topped the Hot Rap Songs chart for several weeks. Minaj became the first female artist in nearly ten years to occupy the number-one spot on Hot Rap Songs chart.

The album, *Pink Friday* (2010), was released in November in second place on the *Billboard* 200. It ultimately went platinum and spawned several hit singles, including "Super Bass," which quickly landed in the top-ten on the *Billboard* Hot 100 chart, marking Minaj's first top-ten placement there as a lead artist. In its first week alone, *Pink Friday* sold 375,000 copies—the second-highest initial sales week for a female hip-hop artist, behind Lauryn Hill's *The Miseducation of Lauryn Hill*, which had sold some 420,000 copies when it debuted in 1998.

The album received generally positive reviews. "Feed off the production, the great musical ideas, and Minaj's keen sense of her surroundings, and *Pink Friday* is an outstanding success," David Jeffries wrote for the website *All Music Guide* (19 Nov. 2010). "It's chock-full of new wave textures and diva attitude. . . . This is the Nicki the mixtape crowd fell in love with." wrote Jeffries. "Longtime fans familiar with her underground work won't even consider this her debut," he continued, "just an extravagant coming out party."

In 2012, Minaj released her sophomore effort, *Pink Friday: Roman Reloaded*, an album built around her alter ego "Roman Zolanski." "He's the boy that lives inside of me. He's a lunatic and he's gay," she explained to reporters backstage at the 2011 MTV Video Music Awards. The album included the hit single "Starships," a catchy Europop-inspired track. *Roman Reloaded* climbed to the top of the pop, R & B and rap charts, and later that same year, Minaj released a new version entitled *Pink Friday: Roman Reloaded—The Re-Up* (2012), with eight new tracks added.

## INFLUENCE

Even before her debut album was released, Minaj realized the impact she could have on the hip-hop world. She explained to journalists that if *Pink Friday* failed, record labels would use it as an excuse to avoid signing other female rappers. If she succeeded, however, it might provide the impetus for them to seek out other talented women.

Most observers believed she was correct about her importance. "A few years ago, before her rise began, there were hardly any female rappers of note; now, a new generation, including Azealia Banks, Brianna Perry, and Angel Haze, is rising quickly, working territory that she carved out," Jon Caramanica wrote for the *New York Times* (30 Mar. 2012). "This is a story about influence, to be sure, but also about the weakening of old walls, and the reshaping of the gates that the gatekeepers keep. Thanks to Nicki Minaj and the possibilities she has laid bare, and to hip-hop's stasis of masculinity it is, outrageously and unprecedentedly, a more exciting time to be a female rapper than a male one."

Some critics, however, believed that her music had become too mainstream and could not even fairly be considered hip-hop. The issue came to the forefront when morning show DJ Peter Rosenberg took the stage at New York's 2012 Hot 97 Summer Jam concert and criticized Minaj's song "Starships" and her fans. When Lil Wayne heard the comment, he pulled all Young Money artists from the concert lineup at the last moment. The feud percolated for a year but, in mid-2013, Minaj agreed to bury the hatchet and appeared as a guest on Rosenberg's show.

### AMERICAN IDOL

Another very public feud erupted in 2012, when Minaj was hired as one of the judges on the television show *American Idol*, where she sat on the panel with singer Mariah Carey. The pair appeared to feel an instant antipathy toward one another and engaged in a bitter argument during contestant auditions in North Carolina, which culminated in Minaj storming off stage. Carey later claimed that Minaj had threatened her with bodily harm, to which she responded by hiring extra security personnel. In one widely disseminated entry on her Twitter feed, Minaj called the other singer "insecure" and "bitter." Still, after both had decided to leave the show following a single season, the rapper said that the experience had been positive. "I had a wonderful time and I learned a lot about myself; I learned a lot about the world's perception of me," she told Jenna Mullins for *E! Online* (5 July 2013). "And I think it was a great thing for hip-hop to see me transcend, and then I can come back and still do the BET Awards and still be authentic in what I do." She added, "It was really inspiring . . . to see [young contestants] fulfill their dreams and be part of that."

### STYLE

Minaj is widely known for her candy-colored wigs and outlandish outfits. "Perhaps it was the brightly colored surgical mask that covered Nicki Minaj's pout at the MTV Video Music Awards last August. Or maybe it was the neon puffball tunic, which made her look as if she'd fallen into a bowl of Dippin' Dots, that she wore to Carolina Herrera's spring 2012 show in September," Laura M. Holson wrote for the *New York Times* (7 Jan. 2012). "But few in 2011 could take their eyes off Ms. Minaj, the Technicolor Barbie with the big voice and an elastic smile."

In late 2010, MAC, an edgy cosmetics brand, introduced Pink Friday, a lipstick color inspired by Minaj that sold three thousand tubes in just fifteen minutes thanks to the star's posts on Twitter and Facebook. She has also inspired a line of OPI brand nail polishes and a fragrance, which comes packaged in a bottle modeled on her head and torso. In 2012, Mattel created a one-of-a-kind Barbie based on Minaj—complete with bubblegum-pink hair and jewelry—which was auctioned off for charity.

In 2013, Minaj launched a highly anticipated clothing line in partnership with the retailer K-Mart. It includes form-fitting mini dresses, wildly printed leggings, metallic bustiers, and jeweled hats. "I'm doing this for women in general to feel beautiful and sexy. Any woman can wear it and feel confident," states Minaj in a promotional video.

## PERSONAL LIFE

Early in her career, Minaj claimed to be bisexual. She recently retracted that declaration, stating that she had merely been trying to get attention. "I think girls are sexy," she said, as quoted by Diane Anderson-Minshall in the *Advocate* (5 Sept. 2012). "But I'm not going to lie and say that I date girls." Minaj has been linked romantically with two men—aspiring rapper Safaree Samuels and fellow star Drake—but has asserted that journalists are mistaken about those relationships.

## SUGGESTED READING

Caramanica, Jon. "A Singular Influence." *New York Times*. New York Times, 30 Mar. 2012. Web. 5 July 2013.

Chen, Eva. "Nicki Minaj Speaks Her Mind about Everything from High School to Hollywood." *Teen Vogue*. Condé Nast, June 2012. Web. 5 July 2013.

Concepcion, Mariel. "Nicki Minaj: The *Billboard* Cover Story." *Billboard*. Prometheus Global Media, 12 Nov. 2010. Web. 5 July 2013.

Holson, Laura M. "It's Nicki's World." *New York Times*. New York Times, 7 Jan. 2012. Web. 5 July 2013.

Plagenhoef, Scott. *"Pink Friday* Review." *Pitchfork*. Pitchfork Media, 24 Nov. 2010. Web. 5 July 2013.

Staples, Brent. "Nicki Minaj Crashes Hip-Hop's Boys Club." *New York Times*. New York Times, 7 July 2012. Web. 5 July 2013.

Weiner, Jonah. "Nicki Minaj: Hip-Hop's Hottest Sidekick Goes Solo." *Details*. Condé Nast, May 2010. Web. 5 July 2013.

## SELECTED ALBUMS

*Pink Friday*, 2010; *Pink Friday: Roman Reloaded*, 2012; *Pink Friday: Roman Reloaded—The Re-Up*, 2012

—*Mari Rich*

# Lin-Manuel Miranda

**Born:** January 16, 1980
**Occupation:** Composer, rapper, lyricist, and actor

In 2007, Lin-Manuel Miranda went from a relative unknown to a household name with the premiere of *In the Heights*, his love letter to his New York City neighborhood of Washington Heights. The musical was written in response to the disappointment that Miranda experienced after seeing *The Capeman*, a musical based on the life of a Puerto Rican gang leader. "No one was going to write the Great Latino Musical. I thought I'd take a crack at it," he said in an interview with Robert Hofler for *Daily Variety* (28 Oct. 2008). That effort paid off in 2008, when *In the Heights* was the recipient of four Tony Awards, including best musical. A year later, the musical was named a finalist for the 2009 Pulitzer Prize in the drama category.

## EARLY LIFE AND EDUCATION

Lin-Manuel Miranda was born on January 16, 1980, in New York City to Luz Towns-Miranda, a psychologist, and Luis A. Miranda Jr., a political consultant and community activist. He grew up with his Puerto Rican–born parents and his older sister, also named Luz, in the northern Manhattan neighborhood of Inwood, which is adjacent to Washington Heights, a diverse, working-class community consisting of immigrants from predominantly Latin American countries, including Puerto Rico, the Dominican Republic, and Cuba.

Miranda's early introduction to music came from his family. "My parents had crates and crates of records, and I remember going through them and putting them on from a very young age," he recalled to Bobby Garcia for the *Philippine Star* (19 Mar. 2012). "Everything from El Gran Combo to [Michael Jackson's] *Thriller* to cast albums: *Man of La Mancha, Camelot.* I remember my mother blasting *Camelot* in the car, and how much the music moved her." Miranda, who also cites Rubén Blades and Juan Luis Guerra as musical influences, was equally fascinated by his sister's record collection, most notably the albums by the hip-hop groups De La Soul and A Tribe Called Quest.

Miranda's initial exposure to the theater occurred during the second grade, when he took in his first Broadway show, *Les Miserables*. Despite sleeping through much of the three-hour performance, he found himself instantly drawn to that musical. "I remember [my parents] bought the cast album, and I promptly memorized every song on it," Miranda told Beth Stevens for Broadway.com (17 Mar. 2008). He managed to stay awake during *Phantom of the Opera*, his second Broadway musical, which "really grabbed me," as he told Stevens.

© Corey Hayes/Corbis

While attending the exclusive Hunter College elementary and high schools, located on New York City's affluent Upper East Side, he displayed a natural talent for performing. Miranda, who studied piano while growing up, also sang in the school choir. When he was in the sixth grade, the twelve-year-old made his stage debut in a production that consisted of a medley of six popular musicals. He played multiple characters, including Captain Hook from *Peter Pan* and Bernardo from *West Side Story*.

## DEVELOPING A PASSION FOR PERFORMING AND WRITING

Miranda was encouraged to begin writing after his eighth-grade English teacher, Dr. Rembert Herbert, remarked favorably on an essay he penned, as well as a group assignment that involved teaching several chapters of Chaim Potok's 1967 novel *The Chosen*. For the latter project, Miranda wrote and recorded a number of musical compositions that were inspired by each chapter and lip-synched by the group members. With Dr. Herbert's support, Miranda successfully tried out for Brick Prison, Hunter College High School's student-run theater group.

Miranda experienced a turning point at age seventeen, when he attended a performance of the critically acclaimed, Tony Award–winning musical *Rent*. "I'd never before seen a musical that takes place today and that felt autobiographical, like the author was writing from his gut," Miranda confided to Mary Carole McCauley for the *Baltimore Sun* (21 Feb. 2010). "It was really a watershed moment for me, and it gave me permission to write musicals." By the time he reached his senior year, he had already written two twenty-minute musicals for the Brick Prison theater club and one play, while also directing a production of *West Side Story*.

In early 1998 Miranda was left disappointed after attending a trio of screenings for *The Capeman*, the critically panned Paul Simon musical that centered on Salvador Agrón, a Puerto Rican gang leader. "The themes in *The Capeman* broke my heart because there we were again; Puerto Ricans as knife wielding murderers," Miranda revealed to *Latina* (22 Feb. 2008). "The music stirred my soul but the subject matter didn't. I wanted to capture the Latino experience without the violence, because I felt like that had already been seen."

## NEW HEIGHTS AT WESLEYAN

After graduating from Hunter College High School in mid-1998, Miranda was accepted at Wesleyan University in Middletown, Connecticut, where he majored in theater studies. While there, he lived at La Casa de Albizu Campos, an on-campus residence. It proved to be a fulfilling experience for Miranda. In his conversation with McCauley, Miranda said, "Wesleyan was the first time I'd ever lived with other Latino kids my age. I didn't really have a lot of Latino friends in high school. I had friends from the neighborhood, but my close friends were my school friends, and none of them were Latino."

In his sophomore year, Miranda started writing a contemporary musical, which was inspired by *Fiddler on the Roof*. "It was about a community [that is] groping with change and has change thrust upon it," he told Hofler. He was also influenced by the experience of living among fellow Latino students—first-generation immigrants who similarly encountered difficulty navigating between their two cultures and who continually struggled to fit in, at home and at school. "I think *In the Heights* was in many ways my first attempt to reconcile those two different sides to my upbringing," Miranda said in an interview for the *Boston Globe* (10 Jan. 2010).

Miranda's nostalgic ode to his multicultural neighborhood also drew heavily upon the type of music he heard while growing up. "I wanted it to sound like 10 blocks in Washington Heights," he told Everett Evans in an interview for the *Houston Chronicle* (8 Aug. 2008). "If you walk from 183rd to 173rd Street, you'll hear hip-hop music blasting out of cars, you'll hear different kinds of Latin music, salsa and merengue and bachata."

During the winter of 1999, Miranda submitted an application to showcase *In the Heights* at Wesleyan's Patricelli '92 Theater, home to Second Stage, one of the country's oldest student-run theater organizations. He was scheduled to debut his musical production for a weekend in late April. Miranda, who had only written one song at the time, spent his winter break finishing up the first draft, which revolved around a love triangle between Nina, a Washington Heights native who is branded an outsider for her decision to attend a renowned college; Benny, Nina's African American love interest who is also considered an outcast because he is not Latino; and Lincoln, Nina's closeted gay brother who is infatuated with Benny.

When *In the Heights* premiered at Wesleyan in April 2000, the eighty-minute, one-act musical shattered the '92 Theater's box-office records. John Buffalo Mailer, a Wesleyan senior and son of the renowned author Norman Mailer, was among the audience members. Impressed by what he saw, John Mailer contacted Miranda; he casually informed him that after graduating from college, he planned to launch a production company and was interested in bringing *In the Heights* to New York City.

## REVISING AND REFINING HIS MUSICAL

Mailer returned to Wesleyan in 2002 to attend a production of Miranda's senior thesis and to express continued interest in his musical. Mailer then presented Miranda's script to his three partners at Back House Productions (and fellow alumna of Wesleyan), including the show's future director, Thomas Kail. After graduating with honors, Miranda met with Kail in the basement of the Manhattan-based Drama Book Shop. Kail suggested script changes to Miranda, who spent the next year rewriting his play while teaching seventh-grade English at his former high school and composing music for advertisements for local political candidates, including Eliot Spitzer, H. Carl McCall, and Fernando Ferrer.

*In the Heights* slowly evolved from a musical that centered on a love triangle to one that revolved around an entire multicultural neighborhood on the verge of change. Although most of the characters remained unchanged through these revisions, Miranda's newly revised script focused more on Usnavi, the Dominican owner of a corner bodega frequented by local residents, including Kevin and Camila Rosario, the owners of a struggling taxi dispatch service, and their daughter, Nina, a Stanford University dropout who further disappoints her family by becoming romantically involved with Benny, an African American who works for her parents. Among the other featured characters in the play are Sonny, Usnavi's lothario cousin; Vanessa, the motivated but money-challenged woman with whom Usnavi is infatuated; and Abuela Claudia, Usnavi's surrogate grandmother who dreams of winning the lottery so she can return to the Caribbean. (Miranda based the Abuela character on Edmunda Claudio, the Puerto Rican live-in nanny who raised Miranda and his older sister and who often played the illegal slot machines at the bodega.)

The first five readings of *In the Heights* were held at Back House Productions in 2003. Under the direction of Kail, Miranda also took on the role of Usnavi. "Tommy suggested I play the main character Usnavi because it would have been too hard for anyone else to remember all the lines on such short notice," he said in his interview for *Latina*. The readings elicited interest from veteran theatrical producer Jill Furman, as well as Kevin McCollum and Jeffrey Seller, the Tony Award–winning producing duo responsible for *Rent* and *Avenue Q*. In 2004, the Latina playwright Quiara Alegría Hudes was enlisted to write the novel version of the script. In 2005 *In the Heights* premiered in workshops at the Manhattan Theater Club and the Eugene O'Neill Theater Center in Waterford, Connecticut. After two years spent refining the musical's script, compositions, and choreography, the producers were ready for *In the Heights* to make its Off Broadway debut. In addition to investing $2.5 million into the production, they reserved the nearly five-hundred-seat theater at 37 Arts, a performing arts complex formerly owned by McCollum and Seller (now known as the Baryshnikov Arts Center).

## OFF BROADWAY SUCCESS

*In the Heights* premiered at 37 Arts in February 2007 to mostly positive critical acclaim. "Light and sweet are actually just the words to describe this amiable show, which boasts an infectious, bouncy Latin-pop score by a gifted young composer, Lin-Manuel Miranda," Charles Isherwood wrote in a review for the *New York Times* (9 Feb. 2007). "As you watch Mr. Miranda bound jubilantly across the stage, tossing out the rhymed verse currently known as rap like fistfuls of flowers, you might find yourself imagining that this young man is music personified." Equally complimentary was Jeremy McCarter, who wrote in a review for *New York Magazine* (28 May 2007): "The most obvious of the show's many virtues is that it doesn't sound like the half-assed pseudo-pop that clutters up Broadway. Miranda's score is rich and kaleidoscopic, as it needs to be."

However, the musical garnered some criticism for its inaccurate portrayal of life in Washington Heights. "People always ask, 'Why aren't there more drugs and crime in the show?'" Miranda told Christopher Wallenberg for the *New York Times* (10 Jan. 2010). "That's because the only time they hear Washington Heights is on the news. But that's not specific to our neighborhood. And it wasn't my experience. The only things I know about drug dealing are from rap music. I'd be writing a fiction if I tried to make my show about that."

Buoyed by the overwhelming reception, the producers unveiled plans in May to bring the show to Broadway. During its five-month Off Broadway run, *In the Heights* received numerous accolades, including two Drama Desk Awards; the Lucille Lortel Award for outstanding musical;

the Outer Critics Circle Award for outstanding Off Broadway musical; the Theatre World Award for outstanding debut; and the Obie Award for music and lyrics.

## BROADWAY AND BEYOND

On March 9, 2008, *In the Heights* made its Broadway debut, at the Richard Rodgers Theatre on Forty-Sixth Street. It became the first musical initially staged by a college theater program to appear on Broadway since *Godspell* debuted at Carnegie Mellon University in 1970. In early May, the musical amassed thirteen Tony Award nominations—the most of any production that season; a month later, it won four, including best musical, best direction, best orchestrations, and best original score. During his acceptance speech for best original score, Miranda launched into an impromptu rap that started with the lines: "I used to dream about this moment, now I'm in it / Tell the conductor to hold the baton a minute." In June 2008 the soundtrack album for *In the Heights* was released; Universal Pictures obtained the film rights to the musical in November but scrapped the plans for a film version nearly three years later. By January 2009, after ten months on Broadway, the show's producers announced that *In the Heights* had already recovered its initial $10 million investment.

Miranda gave his final Broadway performance as Usnavi in February—the same month that the *Heights* soundtrack won a Grammy Award in the best musical show album category. In late March he returned to Broadway—behind the scenes—to work on Arthur Laurents's revival of *West Side Story*, which had a nearly two-year run; Miranda penned the Spanish-language dialogue and collaborated with renowned composer and lyricist Stephen Sondheim to translate song lyrics from English to Spanish. In May, he was one of several performers invited to appear at the White House Evening of Poetry, Music, and the Spoken Word, where he performed a portion of *The Hamilton Mixtape*, a rap album based on the life of founding father and the first US treasury secretary, Alexander Hamilton.

In late June 2010 Miranda resumed his role as Usnavi when the national touring production of *In the Heights* performed in Los Angeles, California, and again in San Juan, Puerto Rico. He returned to the Broadway stage on Christmas Day 2010 and remained there until January 2011, when *In the Heights* ended its run on Broadway after 1,185 performances. That September, the musical had a limited run in Manila, Philippines. Miranda subsequently earned music and lyrics cowriting credits for *Bring It On: The Musical*, a stage adaptation of the 2000 teen comedy movie about rival cheerleading squads. After launching a national tour in October 2011, the production premiered on Broadway in August 2012 before closing four months later.

## OTHER ARTISTIC ENDEAVORS

In addition to his role as Usnavi, Miranda has also amassed other credits on the stage, as well as on the big and small screens. In February 2012 he appeared in a limited-run revival of the George Furth and Stephen Sondheim musical *Merrily We Roll Along*, held at the New York City Center. His television appearances include roles in several popular series, including the HBO drama *The Sopranos* and the long-running PBS children's educational series *Sesame Street* and *The Electric Company*.

In addition to guest-starring stints in the Fox medical drama *House M.D.* and the ABC comedy *Modern Family*, Miranda also played a doctor in the short-lived NBC drama *Do No Harm*. On the big screen, he had a supporting role, alongside Jennifer Garner, in the 2012 Disney film *The Odd Life of Timothy Green*. He starred in the romantic comedy movie *200 Cartas*, scheduled for release in 2013. Miranda is also a cofounder of Freestyle Love Supreme, a New York–based improvisational touring rap group whose song lyrics are derived from impromptu audience suggestions.

On September 5, 2010, Miranda married his high-school sweetheart, Vanessa Nadal, at the Belvedere Mansion in Staatsburg, New York. Miranda also has the distinction of being the youngest-ever recipient of an honorary doctoral degree in the history of Yeshiva University.

## SUGGESTED READING

Garcia, Bobby. "The Genius behind 'In the Heights' Comes to Manila." *Philippine Star*. PhilStar Daily, 19 Mar. 2012. Web. 21 Mar. 2013.

Hofler, Robert. "The Groundbreakers: Legit." *Variety*. Variety Media, 28 Oct. 2008. Web. 21 Mar. 2013.

Isherwood, Charles. "'In The Heights' Review." *New York Times*. New York Times, 9 Feb. 2007. Web. 21 Mar. 2013.

McCauley, Mary Carole. "A Community, In Its Own Words." *Baltimore Sun*. Tribune, 21 Feb. 2010. Web. 21 Mar. 2013.

Stevens, Beth. "Lin-Manuel Miranda." *Broadway.com*. Key Brand Entertainment, 17 Mar. 2008. Web. 21 Mar. 2013.

Wallenberg, Christopher. "Hometown Heart behind *The Heights*." *Boston Globe*. New York Times, 10 Jan. 2010. Web. 21 Mar. 2013.

## SELECTED WORKS

*In the Heights*, 2007–11; *Bring It On: The Musical*, 2012; *The Odd Life of Timothy Green*, 2012

—Bertha Muteba

# Janelle Monáe

**Born:** December 1, 1985
**Occupation:** American R & B/soul musician

The futuristic, multigenre stylings of performer Janelle Monáe defy all available description. The twenty-seven-year-old singer, musician, composer, and record producer baffled then charmed then completely blew audiences and critics away with her 2010 debut album *The ArchAndroid (Suites II and III)*. Her fans include Prince, Stevie Wonder (her own idol), Erykah Badu, and First Lady Michelle Obama—who included Monáe's hit single "Tightrope" on her workout playlist.

Monáe is noted for her clothing and overall look—she frequently wears what she calls a "uniform" of a black and white tuxedo and her signature hairstyle is a pompadour. This plays into her futuristic and science-fiction-influenced work in her music—*ArchAndroid* and her 2007 EP *Metropolis: Suite I (The Chase)*—as well as her performances and persona. Monáe's alter ego is a time-traveling android named Cindi Mayweather. In the year 2719, Mayweather has come to set people free from discrimination, but she is persecuted in the dystopian city of Metropolis for having human emotions. Unlike the alter egos of other artists, which usually herald a change in dress or musical genre, the more sophisticated Cindi Mayweather story functions as an allegory for racial, sexual, and class discrimination. But Monáe also insists that the story is a preemptive call for the equality of androids—she is a fan of futurist and Google executive, Ray Kurzweil, who predicts androids will not be the stuff of fiction for much longer.

Monáe has been nominated for a handful of Grammy Awards and, in 2013, she won song of the year, for "We Are Young," a collaboration with the indie pop band Fun., with whom she had once toured. Her tour mates and collaborators are an eclectic bunch that includes musician and poet Saul Williams and indie rock band Of Montreal. She has also toured with Prince and No Doubt. Monáe herself has been compared to Lauryn Hill, David Bowie, James Brown, and Grace Jones—though she does not like to be defined by comparisons, however flattering. Her genre- and gender-bending choices are all specifically cultivated to be forward-looking. "I [want] a new energy to be out there," she told Greg Kot for the *Chicago Tribune* (26 May 2010), "to focus on new ideas, and the future."

## EARLY LIFE AND EDUCATION

Janelle Monáe Robinson was born in Kansas City, Kansas, on December 1, 1985. She grew up in a tough neighborhood where her mother worked as a janitor and her father, Michael Robinson Summers, collected trash and drove

Getty Images for BET

a truck. He also struggled with a crack cocaine addiction during Monáe's childhood. He is clean now, but the remembrance continues to affect her outlook and Monáe does not do drugs. "I consider myself the drug," she told Kot. "It could've easily been the other way around, I could've easily been a product of my environment and played the victim. But I consider myself a thriver."

Monáe's extended family also played a significant role in her upbringing. She grew up watching old episodes of *The Twilight Zone* and Alfred Hitchcock movies with her grandmother; she also sang in the church choir with her father's aunt. Monáe comes from a musical family, but those around her realized that she was extraordinarily gifted at an early age. (Money she earned from singing competitions made her a breadwinner early on.) Summers told Danny Alexander for the *Kansas City Pitch* (21 Oct. 2010), that if the choir was having a hard time hitting a certain note, his aunt would say, "'Janelle, hit that note for me,' because she knew she could always do it."

Growing up, Monáe performed in musicals like *Cinderella* and *The Wiz*, but she also began writing her own musicals with the Coterie Theatre's Young Playwrights' Roundtable. One play that she wrote at the age of eleven or twelve was about a boy and girl falling in love with a plant, inspired by Stevie Wonder's soundtrack for the

1979 documentary *Journey through the Secret Life of Plants*. "She always had her own way of doing things," her aunt Loretta told Alexander.

Monáe attended F. L. Schlagle High School, where she continued to act. She and her friend Kinshasa Smith formed a singing duo; they won talent shows and played open mic nights at Kansas City haunts like the Blue Room and the Gem Theater. By the time she graduated, Monáe wanted to be on Broadway. She auditioned for the American Musical and Dramatic Academy (AMDA) in New York City and won a scholarship. There, she studied with vocal coaches and took classes in tap, jazz, and ballet, but soon became disillusioned with the future she saw before her. "I would go and watch the Broadway shows, and I'm African-American, and it's sad, but you get typecast," she told Nadia Pflaum for the *Kansas City Pitch* (4 May 2006). "So you go to an audition, and they go, 'Oh, it's an African-American girl.' You have *The Lion King*. You have *The Wiz*, if it came back out. *Aida*. Those roles are cool, but so many people have done them. So what's new?"

## WONDALAND ARTS SOCIETY

So, Monáe made a risky decision. She dropped her scholarship, packed her bags, and headed to Atlanta, Georgia. She was partly inspired by the band OutKast, who got their start in the city. She moved in with her cousins and then into a boardinghouse, and worked at Office Depot. Monáe began performing at Clark, Morehouse, and Spelman universities. "I literally did dorm room lounge tours," she told a reporter for the *Soul Train* website (18 Sept. 2012). After many months she recorded the songs she had written and, with a little money from her mother, pressed nearly two hundred CDs. To her surprise and delight, she sold them all at her next show.

During her college tours, Monáe met a number of like-minded artists including writer/producers Chuck Lightning and Nate Wonder. "It was a Matrix moment where we all locked eyes and it was almost like we were meant to be on the same team," she told Dorian Lynskey for the London *Guardian* (26 Aug. 2010). "We wanted to create a different blueprint." Together, the group—which includes visual artists and graphic novelists—formed a collective called the Wondaland Arts Society. The group also formed a record label of the same name.

One night, Monáe performed at an open mic at a now-closed club called Justin's owned by Sean "Diddy" Combs. She sang Roberta Flack's "Killing Me Softly" and received a standing ovation. Monáe did not realize it while she was performing, but rapper and producer Big Boi was watching her in the front row. When she left the stage, he grabbed her arm and told her that he wanted to sign her to Purple Ribbon Records, his new label. It was an offer any nineteen-year-old

aspiring star would kill for, but Monáe was cautious; she did not want to jeopardize the control she had over her creative future. She eventually signed onto the label after she had explained her larger vision and asserting that she and Wondaland would remain firmly in control.

Monáe's first introduction to a larger audience was in 2005 on the Big Boi produced compilation *Got Purp? Volume 2*. He included her song, "Lettin' Go," which she wrote when she got fired from Office Depot after responding to an e-mail from a fan. In 2006, OutKast featured her on two songs on the *Idlewild* movie soundtrack. Through it all, Monáe was honing her image and enjoying a growing fan base on Facebook and MySpace. Diddy himself contacted her through the latter, eventually signing her to a distribution deal with his own Bad Boy Records. He later said that it was one of the most important signings of his career.

## METROPOLIS

In 2007, Monáe cut her first EP: *Metropolis: Suite I (The Chase)*. Several record executives suggested changes to the seven-track album, so Monáe and Wondaland decided to release the album themselves online. "The record execs were not connected to the people," she explained to Lynskey. "They didn't know, they still don't know, what the people want." Monáe was rewarded for her diligence and was nominated for a Grammy Award for best urban/alternative performance for the song "Many Moons" in 2008. For the album as a unit, she was inspired by the silent German film *Metropolis* (1927), directed by Fritz Lang, which takes place in a future society sharply divided by class. "I started noticing similarities between the characters in the movie and myself, as well as the environment that I grew up in," she told Brian Davis for *Concrete Loop* (5 June 2006). "In the movie you have the 'have's,' who live this good and care-free life and then on the opposite side, you have the 'have-not's,' who are kept underground and struggle to rise to the top." Monáe is not the first artist to illustrate present-day problems, particularly the oppression of African Americans, with science fiction scenarios. She is inspired by the work of Afrofuturists like jazz impresario Sun Ra.

Monáe was also inspired by the 1932 Aldous Huxley novel *Brave New World*, as well as the work of science fiction writers like Octavia Butler and Isaac Asimov. But after *Metropolis* was released, her narratives broadened and deepened to include the paintings of Salvador Dali and visions from her own dreams. Often times, Monáe would wake in the middle of the night to record bits on her iPhone. Her process can sound a bit mystical at times—she says she "sees" songs in colors—but was certainly methodical about the music that would be included in Suites II and III. Even after the buzz she received from her

Grammy nomination, Monáe wanted to take her time creating. "My goal was not to become an overnight success," she told Bernadette Mc-Nulty for the London *Daily Telegraph* (26 June 2010). "You have to be ready and prepared and I took the time to complete my album and grow, to fully understand my purpose as an artist and to hone my craft."

## "THE ANDROID HAS LANDED"

The time she took completing *The ArchAndroid (Suites II and III)* with Wondaland certainly paid off. In his review, Seth Colter Walls of *Newsweek* (7 June 2010) called Monáe "a singer so exciting that writers are flipping deep into their adulation thesauruses looking for new ways to express the opinion." The eighteen-track album is a wild journey through a landscape of funk, pop, hip-hop, psychedelic rock, soul, jazz, R & B, and folk, with a touch of Broadway as well. But the record flows together almost as one seventy-minute track though it includes cameos by Big Boi, Of Montreal, and Saul Williams. She even samples composer Claude Debussy's "Clair de Lune." She calls the concept album as an "emotion picture," and the album has lived up to that description. *Pitchfork*'s reviewer Matthew Peretua wrote (20 May 2010): "The first listen is mostly about being wowed by the very existence of the fabulously talented young singer and her over-the-top record; every subsequent spin reveals the depths of her achievement."

*ArchAndroid* was released on May 18, 2010. That night Monáe appeared on the *Late Show with David Letterman* performing her hit single "Tightrope." A rarity for late night musical performances, *Pitchfork* wrote a separate article about it, labeling it a must-see. Decked out in her uniform, Monáe wailed and moved like a petite James Brown. Backed by a full band, she showed off her signature one-legged mashed potato in her saddle shoes, proving that she was a performer to be reckoned with. At the end of her performance, Diddy came out from backstage and bowed at her feet.

*ArchAndroid* was nominated for a Grammy for best contemporary R & B album in 2011; "Tightrope" was nominated for best urban/alternative performance.

## ARTISTIC AND BUSINESS PURSUITS

Monáe is currently working on the fourth suite of *Metropolis*, as well as a Wondaland Broadway musical and a graphic novel. In addition to her musical projects and performances, Monáe's appearances as a spokesperson have kept her busy. In 2012 she partnered with the digital company Sonos to appear in its commercials; she became a spokesperson for Cover Girl cosmetics that year as well. She has also appeared in commercials for the Gap clothing retail store and for Coca-Cola.

## PERSONAL LIFE

Monáe frequently wears a variation on a fitted black and white tuxedo—an outfit she calls her uniform. The look is inspired by film star Marlene Dietrich, but the consistency with which she wears it is a tribute, she told Rebecca Milzoff for *New York Magazine* (16 May 2010), "[to] my mother, who was a janitor, and my father, who drove trash trucks. It pays homage to how they put on a uniform every day and turned something into nothing." Her job might be more glamorous, she adds, but she does the same. Her signature up-do hairstyle is similarly consistent. "Some people call it a pompadour or a wompadour," she told Milzoff, "but it's a Monáe." Her androgynous uniform is more than a fashion choice. She has said that she wants to show young girls that they do not have to dress a certain way to be cool. "I want to redefine how a woman can dress, how she can wear her hair," she told Kot. "It's sad when you feel you have to change who you are to get your voice out there. We can have a better, happier society when people are accepted for who they are."

The uniform also fits neatly into her larger concept, the science fiction scenario that drives *ArchAndroid* and *Metropolis: Suite I (The Chase)*, as well as the persona of time-traveling android Cindi Mayweather. Monáe also, for better or worse, is known to keep up the Mayweather story in interviews. She told McNulty of her timeless tux: "I am a time traveler so I don't want my clothes to date me."

Monáe is also unapologetic about her political beliefs. She recorded a public service announcement about healthcare and education during the 2008 presidential election, and has performed at several campaign and White House functions for President Barack Obama in the past. She also hopes to open a performing arts school for disadvantaged youth in Kansas City in the future. As far as her romantic life, when asked about dating—several reporters have asked if she was gay—she told one reporter that she dates only androids.

## SUGGESTED READING

Alexander, Danny. "Janelle Monáe's Roots in One of Kansas City's Most Historic—and Troubled—Neighborhoods." *Kansas City Pitch*. Kansas City Pitch, 21 Oct. 2010. Web. 19 Mar. 2013.

Davis, Brian. "CL Exclusive Interview with Janelle Monáe." *Concrete Loop*. ConcreteLoop Media, 5 June 2006. Web. 18 Mar. 2013.

Kot, Greg. "Janelle Monáe, the Interview: 'I Identify with Androids.'" *Chicago Tribune*. Tribune Interactive, 26 May 2010. Web. 19 Mar. 2013.

Lynskey, Dorian. "Janelle Monáe: Sister from Another Planet." *Guardian* (London). Guardian News and Media, 26 Aug. 2010. Web. 19 Mar. 2013.

McNulty, Bernadette. "The Android Has Landed." *Telegraph* (London). Telegraph Media, 26 June 2010 Web. 18 Mar. 2013.

Pflaum, Nadia. "She's On It." *Kansas City Pitch*. Kansas City Pitch, 4 May 2006. Web. 19 Mar. 2013.

Walls, Seth Colter. "Pop Goes the Art House." *Newsweek* 7 June 2010: 52–53. Print.

—*Molly Hagan*

# Elisabeth Moss

**Born:** July 24, 1982
**Occupation:** Actor

Although Elisabeth Moss has been acting since she was a child and had a recurring role in the prime-time political drama *The West Wing* as a teen, she did not come to widespread fame until costarring in the blockbuster AMC series *Mad Men*, which premiered in 2007. Set in 1960s New York City, the critically acclaimed drama follows the lives and careers of the employees of a Madison Avenue advertising agency, and it has been widely lauded for its period detail and rich character studies.

Moss plays Peggy Olson, a naive young secretary who climbs her way to a post as a senior copywriter as the series progresses, thanks solely to her talent and hard work. "One of the things I like about Peggy's story line is she is the ultimate feminist and she is unaware of it," Moss explained to Tenley Woodman for the *Boston Herald* (16 Aug. 2009). "It's true of a lot of women at the time. [Her approach is] not 'There's the glass ceiling; let me break through it,' it is 'Let my voice be heard.'"

The show's female characters—including office siren Joan Holloway, played by Christina Hendricks, and suburban wife Betty Draper, played by January Jones—have been the subject of both near-constant cultural analysis, and many female observers find Moss's Peggy to be the most relatable and unambiguously admirable of the bunch. "Peggy has to figure things out for herself, renegotiate again and again the balance of power and the expectations which shift swiftly, noiselessly, every day between her, the ad men, the secretaries and her poor, bewildered mother," Lucy Mangan wrote for the British magazine *Stylist* (20 Mar. 2012). "Yet on she goes, because that's what pioneers do. She's a living, breathing, working feminist before the word started circulating anywhere near Madison Avenue's gleaming towers." Mangan concluded, "*Mad Men* is a brilliant, clever, subtle show and the creation of Peggy is the most brilliant, clever, subtle thing in it."

© Russ Elliot/AdMedia/AdMedia/Corbis

## EARLY LIFE

Elisabeth Singleton Moss was born on July 24, 1982, in Los Angeles, California. She has a younger brother, Derek, who now works as a video editor and writer. Their parents were both in the music industry. Ron Moss, their British-born father, is a jazz musician and artist manager. Among his most high-profile clients were bass player Kyle Eastwood, the son of screen legend Clint Eastwood, and soul singer Isaac Hayes. He was also the longtime manager of Chick Corea, a Grammy Award–winning keyboardist who joined jazz musician Miles Davis's band in the late 1960s. Corea, a Scientologist, introduced Ron to the controversial religion. Ron subsequently became a devout practitioner and was even ordained as a minister. Moss's mother, Linda, is a professional player of the blues harmonica who learned to play as a young girl and had been performing professionally since age fifteen, backing famed blues bands and singers such as Muddy Waters, Junior Wells, and Melissa Etheridge. She and her daughter have remained exceptionally close, and they try to see each other regularly, no matter how busy they are professionally.

Of her childhood in the Laurel Canyon area of the Hollywood Hills, Moss told Heather Hodson for the *Telegraph* (2 July 2013), "There were instruments everywhere and everyone stayed up late and slept in—it was total musician time. At Christmas we'd have people come over and there'd be jam sessions with someone on the piano and someone on the drums. . . . So it was an eclectic upbringing but to us it was normal and it definitely brought me up with this incredible appreciation of the arts."

A serious ballet student from ages five to fifteen, Moss attended the prestigious School of American Ballet in New York City and also studied with famed prima ballerina Suzanne Farrell at the Kennedy Center. Moss credits her mother with preventing her from developing the body-image problems and eating disorders that are sometimes found among young ballerinas.

## EARLY CAREER

At the age of six, Moss was seen dancing in a production of *The Sound of Music* by an agent, who suggested she try her hand at auditioning for commercials. She was serious about her career right from the start. "I felt the same about acting when I was [a child] as I do now. It wasn't, 'Oh, this is fun.' I felt I had a role, a character, I had a scene and emotions to play. I took it very seriously," she recalled to Hodson.

In 1990 Moss appeared in the television miniseries *Lucky Chances*, based on a pair of novels by Jackie Collins about the Las Vegas casino industry. In the miniseries, she portrays the main character, the daughter of a former mobster, at age six; the adult version of the character is played by Nicollette Sheridan. She next began to win small but regular roles in various television series and films. Among these projects were *Bar Girls* (1990), an unsold CBS pilot about two female lawyers, and *Picket Fences*, a small-town crime drama in which Moss appeared as the precocious Cynthia Parks from 1992 to 1995.

Moss went on to appear in the 1993 adaptation of the musical *Gypsy*. The television film stars veteran actor Bette Midler as notorious stage mother Mama Rose, and Moss plays the title character, vaudeville and burlesque performer Gypsy Rose Lee, as a young girl. She later told interviewers that she was thrilled to work with Midler, whom she admired even at that young age. Moss had the opportunity to work with another consummate professional when she appeared opposite Harvey Keitel in the 1994 film *Imaginary Crimes*. Set in 1950s Indiana, the film focuses on a small-time con man trying to raise his daughters (one played by Moss) on his own.

## CAREER ACCELERATES

Moss next took a role in the 1995 television film *Escape to Witch Mountain*, based on the 1968 science-fiction novel by Alexander Key about two siblings with otherworldly abilities; the novel had previously been adapted into a 1975 film by Walt Disney Productions. That same year she appeared in the made-for-television biopic about

the mother-daughter singing group the Judds, who were popular at the time. In *Naomi & Wynonna: Love Can Build a Bridge*, Moss plays the nonsinging member of the family, actor Ashley Judd, as a teen. Moss also found herself much in demand as a voice-over artist during her youth, lending her vocal talents to several cartoons and animated films, including *Frosty Returns* (1992), *Recycle Rex* (1993), *Batman* (1993), *Once Upon a Forest* (1993), *Animaniacs* (1993), and *Freakazoid!* (1995).

Although she was finding steady acting work, Moss continued to dance and did not discount the possibility of pursuing a career in ballet. This changed after she appeared opposite veteran actor Martin Landau in the 1999 film *The Joyriders*, about a trio of troubled teens who kidnap an elderly man. "I was just old enough to have friends on the set and the whole six-week experience was so fun," she recalled to Hodson. "When I looked at ballet I thought, yikes, that is such a scary life, and [acting] looked like such fun."

That year Moss also appeared in her best-known film role to date, playing a supporting role in the drama *Girl, Interrupted*. Based on a memoir by Susanna Kaysen, *Girl, Interrupted* stars Winona Ryder as a young woman admitted to a private mental hospital. Moss plays Polly, a fellow patient who has earned the cruel nickname Torch because she was badly burned. She later explained in interviews that she was attracted to the challenge of the substantial role.

## THE WEST WING

In October of 1999 Moss made her first appearance in the role of Zoey Bartlet, one of the president's daughters, in the hit political drama *The West Wing*, starring Martin Sheen as the commander in chief. She was particularly surprised and gratified to have won the role because in one of her auditions she competed against fellow actor Danica McKellar, who had costarred in *The Wonder Years*, one of Moss's favorite shows as a child.

Created by veteran screenwriter Aaron Sorkin, *The West Wing* enjoyed good ratings throughout its run and was said to be a favorite among Washington insiders. "[It] appeals so strongly, I suspect, because it offers up a vision of a government that works, or at least actually has the country's best interests in mind even when it fails, and a president who really is as smart and as caring as we want the Leader of The Free World to be," Graeme McMillan wrote for *Time* (19 Apr. 2003). "Both of those thoughts are very reassuring, especially considering the alternative offered by the reality. When it comes down to it, who wouldn't want to watch that on a weekly basis?"

Moss appeared in episodes of the show until 2006, when it ended its seven-season run. During the course of that time, her character dated an African American presidential aide who subsequently became the target of a white supremacist group, graduated summa cum laude from Georgetown University, and was kidnapped. When not filming the series, Moss occasionally accepted other roles, and she received particularly profuse praise for her portrayal of an innocent teen who finds herself pregnant in the independent film *Virgin* (2003).

### MAD MEN

In 2007 Moss began costarring in the career-making hit *Mad Men*. The show's notoriously exacting creator, Matthew Weiner, told Glenn Whipp for the *Los Angeles Times* (16 June 2011), "It was the very first day of auditions, and she was the second person to read. Not just for Peggy, but for the show, period. . . . She was so young, wearing this ingénue dress, with her hair long and straight. And all of a sudden, I just saw Peggy. She was just complete in every way." He continued, "After Elisabeth walked out, I said, 'So, we need to get two or three people like that and I'll pick the best one,' not realizing there wasn't going to be anyone else like her."

The program made history in 2012 when it became the first basic cable series ever to win the Emmy Award for outstanding drama series four years in a row. Among the other laurels it has received are Golden Globes for best television drama in 2008, 2009, and 2010. The ensemble cast has also won several Screen Actors Guild Awards. For her role as Peggy Olson, Moss was nominated for an Emmy for outstanding lead actress in a drama in 2009, 2011, 2012, and 2013; in 2010 she submitted herself in the supporting category and was nominated as well.

In 2013 Weiner announced that the show will end after its seventh season, scheduled to air in early 2014, spurring rampant speculation about what is in store for the employees of the Sterling Cooper & Partners advertising agency. Fans of Moss's character were especially abuzz after the sixth-season finale where she is shown wearing a pantsuit and working in her former boss's office—a sign that she may be in line to take the place of Don Draper, her mentor and the firm's creative director, in the company.

### OTHER WORK

While costarring in *Mad Men*, Moss has also taken on various film roles, including parts in the comedies *Did You Hear about the Morgans?* (2009) and *Get Him to the Greek* (2010). In 2008 she made her Broadway debut in the David Mamet play *Speed-the-Plow*, impressing theatergoers and critics with her stage presence. "When the curtain falls on this short and unsparing study of sharks in the shallows of the movie industry, it's as if you had stepped off a world-class

roller coaster," theater critic Ben Brantley wrote for the *New York Times* (24 Oct. 2008). "[Moss brings] a naked clarity to her unvarnished, tinny-voiced [character] that makes the play hang together in ways it didn't before."

In 2011 Moss made her West End debut in Lillian Hellman's *The Children's Hour*, in which she and British actor Keira Knightley played two teachers suspected of being lesbians. She went on to star in the highly acclaimed television miniseries *Top of the Lake*, directed by Jane Campion and Garth Davis. Moss plays Robin Griffin, a detective who specializes in sexual assault cases; in the series she is investigating a pregnant twelve-year-old girl in New Zealand who has gone missing. The miniseries was nominated for eight Emmy Awards, and Moss earned a nomination for the Emmy for outstanding lead actress in a miniseries, in addition to her nomination that year for *Mad Men*.

### PERSONAL LIFE

In late 2008, while making a cameo appearance in an episode of the sketch-comedy show *Saturday Night Live*, Moss met cast member Fred Armisen. The two began a relationship and married on October 25, 2009, but separated in June of the following year. Their divorce was finalized on May 13, 2011.

### SUGGESTED READING

Goodman, Lizzy. "Elisabeth Moss: How I Found My Inner Tough Guy." *Guardian*. Guardian News and Media, 2 July 2013. Web. 9 Sept. 2013.

Hodson, Heather. "Elisabeth Moss: Mad Men and Strong Women." *Telegraph*. Telegraph Media Group, 2 July 2013. Web. 9 Sept. 2013.

Mangan, Lucy. "Peggy Olson: Feminist Icon." *Stylist*. Stylist, 20 Mar. 2012. Web. 9 Sept. 2013.

Whipp, Glenn. "Elisabeth Moss Puts *Mad Men*'s Peggy Olson on the Career Track." *Los Angeles Times*. Los Angeles Times, 16 June 2011. Web. 9 Sept. 2013.

Woodman, Tenley. "No 'Mad' Woman." *Boston Herald*. Boston Herald, 16 Aug. 2009. Web. 9 Sept. 2013.

### SELECTED WORKS

*Gypsy*, 1993; *Imaginary Crimes*, 1994; *Naomi & Wynonna: Love Can Build a Bridge*, 1995; *Girl, Interrupted*, 1999; *The West Wing*, 1999–2006; *Virgin*, 2003; *Mad Men*, 2007–; *Did You Hear about the Morgans?*, 2009; *Get Him to the Greek*, 2010; *Top of the Lake*, 2013

*—Mari Rich*

# Siddhartha Mukherjee

**Born:** 1970
**Occupation:** Indian-born American oncologist and author

In the summer of 2003, while Siddhartha Mukherjee was beginning an advanced medical program at Massachusetts General Hospital and the Dana-Farber Cancer Institute in Boston, he began a personal journal to document an experience that consistently left him after his rounds "in stunned incoherence" as he put it. The project's scope soon became vast as Mukherjee struggled to answer questions from patients about whether the "war" on cancer could be won, about what exactly it was they were battling. As he stitched together his personal experience with cancer, and the experiences of his patients, with the history of cancer research from the first recorded mastectomy in 2500 BCE through the present day, Mukherjee transformed a highly technical subject into an extremely moving and human story, one that simultaneously examines the medical, literary, social, political, and scientific meanings and interpretations of cancer throughout history. The resulting book, published in 2010 as *The Emperor of All Maladies: A Biography of Cancer*, earned Mukherjee the 2011 Pulitzer Prize for general nonfiction. As Decca Aitkenhead wrote for the *Guardian* introducing her interview with Mukherjee, "How did a literary novice, with a full-time job and a young family teach himself to write so beautifully?" (4 Dec. 2011).

Mukherjee's first book is a remarkable accomplishment; prior to its publication, there were simply no other books on the market that encompassed the scope of *The Emperor of All Maladies*, and certainly none that offered such an accessible and compelling history of the disease and the efforts to treat it. As Aitkenhead remarks, it seems "scarcely possible that the author of *The Emperor of All Maladies* could really be an actual doctor and not a writer, so exquisitely is his book crafted and paced" (4 Dec. 2011). Mukherjee traces the progress and failures of cancer treatments, which were often as devastating to a patient's body as the disease itself, particularly the radical mastectomies of the late nineteenth century and early chemotherapy treatments advanced in the 1940s. Mukherjee explains that cancer cells are so difficult to target and treat because they are so similar to healthy cells. "If there's a seminal discovery in oncology in the last twenty years, it's that idea that cancer genes are often mutated versions of normal genes," Mukherjee explained to Terry Gross in an interview for NPR. "And the arrival of that moment really sent a chill down the spine of cancer biologists" (17 Nov. 2010). Cancer takes

Getty Images

full advantage of all of the human body's own survival tactics—its adaptability and persistence.

Mukherjee is currently an assistant professor of medicine at Columbia University, where he runs a lab studying acute myeloid leukemia and myelodysplasia, a preleukemic disease. He also sees patients as part of the oncology rotation at New York Presbyterian Hospital and regularly publishes articles to increase public awareness of cancer and cancer research.

## EARLY LIFE

Siddhartha Mukherjee was born in 1970 in New Delhi, where he grew up in the Safdarjung Enclave with his parents and older sister, Ranu. His father, Sibeswar Mukherjee, worked as an executive for Mitsubishi and his mother, Chandana, was a schoolteacher. Mukherjee attended a Roman Catholic school in New Delhi called St. Columba's School, where he recalls having to memorize a lot of poetry. He loved books and reading as a child. His aunt, who worked as an editor, would bring him to visit the bookstalls on College Street in Calcutta.

According to one of his former schoolteachers, as a schoolboy Mukherjee participated "in the very prestigious Govardhan Das Declamation competition and when he spoke, we were all floored" (*Hindustan Times* 21 Apr. 2011). In a June 2011 interview with *India Abroad*, Mukherjee's mother remembered her son as an extremely inquisitive and talented child with interests in everything, including art, music, literature, and science. When he was in the eleventh grade, Mukherjee traveled to visit relatives in California, where he was able to visit the campus of Stanford University. "He saw the parking spots for the Nobel laureates at the Lawrence Berkeley lab and made up his mind," his father recalled to *India Abroad* (June 2011). Mukherjee earned a remarkable score of 1580 out of 1600 on his Scholastic Aptitude Tests (SATs) and subsequently earned full scholarships to a number of Ivy League schools in the United States. As his father told Reshmi Dasgupta for the *Economic Times*, Mukherjee ultimately chose Stanford because he particularly wanted to work with Nobel-winning biochemist Paul Berg, who would later became Mukherjee's mentor.

## UNDERGRADUATE EDUCATION

In 1989 Mukherjee began as an undergraduate at Stanford, majoring in biology as a Daniel Starr Jordan scholar, a scholarship awarded to students with "exceptional academic abilities" according to a Stanford press release (5 Jan. 1992). As a sophomore, Mukherjee joined the research group of the biochemist Paul Berg, spending more than twenty hours a week in the laboratory studying the genetic causes of cancers in the immune system. In addition to his lab work and full course load, Mukherjee also served as a teaching assistant and tutor in math and science and as a staff writer and artist for the student-run newspaper *Stanford Daily*. He also volunteered as a resident assistant in his dormitory. He was active with the Stanford Indian Music Group, performing classical Indian music at several on-campus concerts, and he completed a psychedelic mural of musical instruments in a building on campus.

He wrote his thesis at Stanford on the 1974 book *The Lives of a Cell*, a collection of essays by the American biologist Lewis Thomas that imagines the entire planet as a single cell. In January 1992, Mukherjee was named a 1993 Rhodes scholar representing one of four students from India. Two other students from Stanford also earned Rhodes scholarships that year, both representing the United States. Mukherjee was attracted to the Rhodes scholarship and Oxford University because he was inspired by the work of British immunologist Alain Townsend. As Mukherjee explained to John Garth for the Michaelmas 2011 issue of *Oxford Today*, "Alain Townsend, who was to become my mentor at Oxford, had made one of the most seminal discoveries in immunology by solving the so-called 'inside-out problem,' which is that if the immune system exists outside our cells, how can we eliminate those viruses that hide inside our cells? He figured out our immune system scans the cell surface for foreign pieces of viruses."

## RHODES SCHOLAR AT OXFORD

Mukherjee initially had some trouble adjusting to Oxford University in England, describing the differences between Stanford and Oxford as "stark." His first-year residence was at Magdalen College in a first-floor room he described to John Garth as "quite dismal" and "a blackhole." In his first month at Oxford, he and a group of fellow students were beaten up by a group of thugs. "Part of it was to do with color, I think.

But Anthony Smith, the president of Magdalen, was unbelievably kind to me, and we've kept up an informal correspondence since then," he told Garth.

In his second year at Oxford, Mukherjee moved into a new apartment that overlooked Rose Lane, "the most beautiful place on campus," as he termed it. Mukherjee found made good friends with several other Rhodes scholars but was largely absorbed by his studies, which were focused on immunology. He spent most of his time at the laboratory at the Weatherall Institute of Molecular Medicine, where he worked with Townsend, Vincenzo Cerundolo, Sebastian Springer, and Judy Bastin.

Mukherjee's doctoral topic was on the "flip-side of Alain [Townsend]'s 'inside-out' question." As he explained to Garth, "There are some infections you never clear, such as the Epstein-Barr virus. . . . So the 'outside-in' problem is: why can your immune system not eliminate such viruses? Working with Alain, I found that whereas the influenza virus can be chopped up and displayed on the cell surface so the immune system can sniff it out, the EBV proteins are specifically designed not to be displayed." However, he was delayed in completing his doctorate because a professor would not approve his dissertation because it did not follow the Oxford format.

## MEDICAL TRAINING

In 1995 Mukherjee earned a full scholarship to Harvard Medical School and left Oxford without completing his degree. At Harvard, he solidified his interest in oncology and decided to specialize in cancer and stem cell research. In 1998, he resubmitted his dissertation at Oxford and earned his doctorate degree. He completed his MD program in five years, graduating in 2000. He completed an internship at Massachusetts General Hospital (MGH) in 2001 and residency there in 2003. Around this time, Mukherjee began the private journal that would become *The Emperor of All Maladies*. That fall, he began a fellowship in oncology at MGH and the Dana-Farber Cancer Institute in Boston. The two-year "full-time immersion" program marked an extremely difficult time in Mukherjee's life. As he wrote in *The Emperor of All Maladies*, "Medical school, internship, and residency had been physically and emotionally grueling, but the first months of the fellowship flicked away those memories as if all of that had been child's play." In May 2004, ten months into his fellowship, Mukherjee explained, "I felt as if I had gravitated to my lowest point. In those ten indescribably poignant and difficult months, dozens of patients in my care had died."

In the summer of 2005 Mukherjee and his wife, Sarah Sze, a Boston-based sculptor and former MacArthur fellow, had their first child. Their daughter Leela was born at MGH, across the hall from the oncology ward where Mukherjee had worked for the past several years. "I would like to see myself at my wife's side awaiting the miraculous moment of my daughter's birth as most fathers do. But in truth I was gowned and gloved like a surgeon, with a blue, sterile sheet spread out in front of me, and a long syringe in my hands, poised to harvest the maroon gush of blood cells from the umbilical cord," he recalled in *Emperor*. Mukherjee goes on to describe how umbilical blood is a rich source of blood-forming stem cells, which can be used for bone marrow transplants. It is "an intensely precious resource often flushed down a sink in hospitals," Mukherjee writes in *Emperor*. Even as a new father, Mukherjee remained committed to his patients and his work as an oncologist.

After completing his fellowship, Mukherjee began to develop a broadened perspective on the questions he has struggled to answer for his patients. He noted, "The questions about the larger story of cancer emerged with urgency: How old is cancer? What are the roots of our battle against this disease? Or, as patients often asked me: where are we in the 'war' on cancer? How did we get here? Is there an end? Can this war be won?" It was at this point that *The Emperor of All Maladies* began to take its shape.

### THE EMPEROR OF ALL MALADIES

What was initially intended to be a personal journal covering his medical training would earn the Pulitzer Prize for general nonfiction. Mukherjee claims he was inspired by a patient whose abdominal cancer had relapsed and said, "I'm willing to go on, but before I go on I need to know what it is that I'm battling," as Mukherjee recalled to Terry Gross for NPR. He continued, "It was a very humbling moment for me, because not only could I not answer her question, I couldn't point her to a book or a resource that would answer her question in the most fundamental sense" (17 Nov. 2010). At a time when one in three American women and one in two American men will develop cancer in their lifetime, Mukherjee recognized the need for a book that could offer a comprehensive narrative and history of cancer.

Because he had never written a book before, Mukherjee told Decca Aitkenhead for the *Guardian* how he "invented rules, such as you won't go through two chapters without meeting a real human character" in order to give himself some structure (4 Dec. 2011). That decision paid off in adding a human element to the book, which includes the stories of patients, surgeons, researchers, fundraisers, politicians, and the author himself in the five-thousand-year battle against cancer. "I couldn't write a book proposal because it was impossible to explain. How do you explain that there'll be a thread of memoir in it, which is small, and then the backdrop, which

is much, much larger? One of the things about the book is that the scale shifts very dramatically," Mukherjee explained to Aitkenhead. "The book lives in its seams, it lives in the connections in the shifts between scale, so it was really like writing a jigsaw puzzle. How do you fit all these moving parts together? You can't explain that in a book proposal. I thought: you know what, I'm just going to write the book" (4 Dec. 2011). After completing a few hundred pages, he began showing an early draft of the book to publishers. The book was released by Scriber, an imprint of Simon and Schuster, in November 2010.

The title is drawn from a quote by a nineteenth-century physician, who had written "cancer is the emperor of all maladies." The subtitle, "a biography of cancer" came from Mukherjee's desire to understand and explain the "personality" of cancer and to trace its various manifestations throughout history. The primary purpose of the book was to sketch "an intellectual history of cancer and in that process a social and cultural history of cancer as well," as Mukherjee told Amit Roy in an exclusive interview for the Calcutta *Telegraph*. "One of the important features of this book is not just writing a scientific history of cancer—some of which has been done before—but to synthesize the very complex and sometimes very charged and unpleasant history between science and medicine, which has been very much a feature of the history of cancer." Much of the book explores the delicate ethical implications of cancer treatment and research, particularly the sometimes competing interests of offering the best care for patients and offering the most cutting-edge treatments. In addition to the Pulitzer, *The Emperor of All Maladies* was named the 2011 Guardian First Book Award, beating out four novels on the shortlist. The book also earned the 2011 PEN/E. O. Wilson Literary Science Writing Award, and was listed among *Time* magazines All-Time 100 Best Nonfiction Books list, a listing of the "best and most influential books written in English since 1923, the beginning of *Time*."

### CAREER AT COLUMBIA UNIVERSITY

Mukherjee briefly served on the faculty at Harvard, but in the fall of 2009, he moved to Columbia University as an assistant professor of medicine at the Herbert Irving Cancer Center, where he organized a lab to study acute myeloid leukemia and myelodysplasia, a preleukemic disease. He also treats patients as part of the oncology rotation at New York Presbyterian Hospital. The focus of Mukherjee's research later shifted to the effect of the cellular environment on cancer development. "Cancer cells don't live in isolation," he told Ann Levin for the *Columbia University Record*. "They create homes for themselves, often by co-opting signals from other parts of the body. . . . What are these home-building cells? Can we attack them and thereby affect the biology of cancer?" In addition to his research, Mukherjee also maintains a blog to promote public awareness of cancer research and biotechnology news. He has also written articles for *Newsweek*, the *New York Times*, *Nature*, the *New England Journal of Medicine*, and the *New Republic*.

Mukherjee lives in New York with his wife, Sarah Sze, a professor of art at the Columbia University School of the Arts, and their two daughters, Leela and Aria.

## SUGGESTED READING

Aitkenhead, Decca. "Siddhartha Mukherjee: 'A Positive Attitude Does Not Cure Cancer, Any More than a Negative One Causes It.'" *Guardian*. Guardian News and Media, 4 Dec. 2011. Web. 14 Nov. 2012.

"An Oncologist Writes 'A Biography of Cancer.'" *NPR Books*. NPR, 17 Nov. 2010. Web. 15 Nov. 2012.

Garth, John. "Siddhartha Mukherjee—Magdalen College 1993." *Oxford Today* Michaelmas 2011: N. pag. Web. 12 Nov. 2012.

McGrath, Charles. "How Cancer Acquired Its Own Biographer." *New York Times* 9 Nov. 2010, New York ed.: C1. Print.

Mukherjee, Siddhartha. *The Emperor of All Maladies: A Biography of Cancer*. New York: Scribner, 2010. Print.

—*Mary Woodbury*

# Thomas Mulcair

**Born:** October 24, 1954
**Occupation:** Canadian politician and lawyer, leader of the official opposition in Canada

The Liberal and Conservative Parties (and, prior to 2003, the Progressive Conservative Party) have dominated Canadian politics for decades, frequently trading majorities in the Canadian House of Commons, one of the two houses of the Parliament of Canada. Although a number of minority parties have sought to break the stranglehold these parties have maintained on Canadian politics, none has come closer than the New Democratic Party (NDP), a center-left party that has been the official opposition since the 2011 election.

The NDP is headed by Thomas Mulcair, who succeeded beloved NDP leader Jack Layton following Layton's death in 2011. Having fought his way through the ruthless world of Quebec politics as a Liberal, Mulcair left the party of his youth and joined Layton's NDP because he believed its leadership represented the

Chris Wattie/Reuters /Landov

same progressive ideals for which he had long struggled. Since becoming a member of Parliament as a New Democrat in 2007, Mulcair has gained a reputation as a smart and tough political operative. When he won the leadership race to succeed Layton in 2012, many NDP insiders agreed it was the smart choice for a party looking to win a majority of seats in the next federal general election and form a government. "It's a very mature choice," Raoul Gebert, former president of the party's Quebec wing, told John Geddes for *Maclean's* (19 Sept. 2012). "The party knows where it wants to go and knows that Tom is the person who can bring us there."

## EARLY LIFE

Thomas Joseph Mulcair was born in Ottawa, the capital city of Canada, on October 24, 1954, the second of Henry Donnelly Mulcair and Jeanne Hurtubise's ten children. His father, who worked in insurance, hailed from an Irish family; his mother, a teacher, was a French Canadian. Both mother and father loved their large family and in fact wished they had more children. "When my mother would have a child," Mulcair said, as quoted by Geddes, "my father would always bring her fourteen roses, because they decided when they were married that they would have fourteen children." When Mulcair was just a toddler, his family lived in Hull (now part of Gatineau), Quebec. They moved to Montreal during his preschool years and remained there through much of his childhood. In the early 1970s, Mulcair's father, who had been vice president of an insurance company, lost his job and decided to give up city life and become a small-town insurance salesman. The Mulcairs then moved to Sainte-Anne-des-Lacs, a town about an hour's drive north of Montreal and not far from where the family had a summer cottage on Lac Marois.

Along with his parents and his older sister, Colleen, Mulcair cared for his younger siblings, putting them to bed, reading them stories, helping them with problems with school, and offering advice. "He essentially raised his younger siblings," his sister Deborah told Geddes. "He was quite attentive." In addition to his responsibilities at home, Mulcair worked hard at school, proving to be both a bright student and a gifted athlete. His family's Catholicism played a prominent role in his upbringing. In addition to attending morning Mass nearly every day before school, he was involved with the church's traditional social outreach.

Mulcair's interest in politics came through his parents. Both avid readers and supporters of Canada's Liberal Party, they encouraged him to study the political issues of the day and form his own opinions. By age fourteen, he knew he wanted to work in politics. As a student in the two-year preuniversity program at Vanier College in Montreal, he studied social sciences and participated in student politics. After completing his studies at Vanier in 1973, Mulcair was accepted into McGill University's law school.

Although younger than many of his law school classmates, Mulcair was able to keep up with them due to his intelligence and his willingness to work long hours. During his time there, he was elected president of the undergraduate students' association. He earned his bachelor of civil law degree in 1976 and his common law degree in 1977. Two years later, he was admitted to the Quebec bar.

## EARLY CAREER

Mulcair had moved to Quebec City, Quebec, immediately after earning his law degree, but he found no easy entry into the Canadian province's political system, in large part because he did not speak French as fluently as did many native Quebecers. (Growing up with an anglophone father and a francophone mother in officially bilingual Canada, he had spoken more English at home than French.) A career in the Quebec civil service would require him to be proficient in French. Mulcair asked his new wife, Catherine Pinhas, who had been raised in Paris, France, to help him master the language. Before long he was sufficiently fluent in French to move up through Quebec's political system, even though he did not support many ideas that were popular at the time, such as a 1980 referendum on whether Quebec should leave the Canadian federation.

Prior to his entry into elective politics in 1994, Mulcair held various positions as a lawyer and legal professor. He was a professor at St. Lawrence College from 1979 to 1982, a lawyer in the legislative affairs department of the Department of Justice and the legal affairs department of the Conseil supérieur de la langue française (Superior Council of the French Language) from 1980 to 1982, a director of legal affairs at Alliance Quebec from 1983 to 1985, and a professor of civil law at Concordia University in 1984 and 1985. He also served as a reviser of the statutes of Manitoba (1985–87), a commissioner on the Commission d'appel sur la langue d'enseignement (Appeals Committee on the Language of Instruction, 1986–87), and president of the Office des professions du Québec (Office of the Professions of Quebec, 1987–93).

However, Mulcair's most important lessons about the political world came through his relationship with Claude Ryan, then the provincial leader of the Liberal Party. When Ryan became education minister in 1985, he tapped Mulcair to help him solve a thorny issue related to English Catholic schools operating in Quebec in violation of the province's language laws. Mulcair worked out a compromise measure: allow the schools in existence to continue to operate but impose financial penalties to prevent additional ones from being established. With regard to this experience and other political issues, Mulcair has credited Ryan with helping him understand the importance of public oversight and administration.

## ENTERING POLITICS

In the 1994 Quebec election, Mulcair ran as a Liberal and won the Chomedey riding (electoral district), despite the fact that the provincial Parti Québécois trounced the Liberals in the election. Before long he was making a reputation for himself as a potent opposition fighter in the National Assembly of Quebec, allowing him to be reelected to his seat in 1998 and 2003. He worked under provincial Liberal leader Jean Charest, first as deputy of the opposition from December 1998 to March 2003. When the Liberals won a majority in Quebec and were able to form a provincial government following the 2003 elections, making Charest the premier of Quebec, Mulcair served in the Charest cabinet as environmental minister and deputy government House leader until February 2006.

Although Mulcair worked well under Charest for a time, their relationship soured while he was serving as environment minister. According to Mulcair, he quit the Charest government when he refused to agree to sign over public land in the Mont Orford provincial park to a condominium developer. According to some former colleagues, he quit because he had refused to accept a demotion to minister of government services. Regardless of whether the refusal to sign or the demotion came first, Mulcair has stated that he had his family's full agreement that he should quit the cabinet rather than give in to Charest's demands.

Following his departure from the cabinet, Mulcair did not find himself in the political wilderness. On the record as an independent-minded and principled statesman, he found himself being wooed by politicians of all stripes at the federal level, including members of the Liberal, Conservative, and New Democrat Parties. His greatest bond was forged with Jack Layton, leader of the New Democratic Party, a major progressive party with a socialistic history that had yet to lead the Canadian government or even become the official opposition, which is the party with the second-most seats in the House of Commons, behind the party in power. Layton wanted to broaden the NDP's outreach, particularly in Quebec, where he believed the party's progressive policies would appeal to Quebecers who wanted to remain a part of Canada.

In an interview with Kady O'Malley for *Maclean's* (27 June 2007), Mulcair recalled, "When I decided to leave cabinet in February 2006 . . . the first question that I had to find an answer to was whether I wanted to stay in politics. I'm an attorney and I could have returned to private practice. But I really felt strongly that I still had something to contribute." Mulcair had known Layton since Layton's tenure as the head of the Federation of Canadian Municipalities, from 2001 to 2002, and when Mulcair was asked to attend the NDP convention in Quebec City in September 2006, he told O'Malley, the two "hit it off." Mulcair had been invited to give a presentation on an environmental bill he had introduced in Quebec City. "I was really astonished by the reception I got," he said, "and it was quite clear to me that, no matter how detailed things were, people in the NDP knew the environment." This experience marked the beginning of Mulcair's move from the Liberal Party to the NDP.

## WITH THE NEW DEMOCRATS

Layton believed that Mulcair could help the NDP become a political party that could ultimately lead the Canadian national government. Since its formation in 1961, the NDP had long been considered Canada's "nudge" party—the principled center-left party that attempted to coax whichever party had formed a majority in the House of Commons to provide greater social justice to all Canadians, regardless of race, creed, economic status, or sexual orientation. The NDP also supports sustainable economic and environmental development and a foreign policy based on diplomacy and humanitarian aid.

To become a more credible presence in Quebec's political scene, the NDP needed at least one representative from the province in the House of Commons; as of 2006, it had none. In 2007, Mulcair ran under the orange NDP banner in a by-election for Montreal's Outremont riding and won it with an impressive 48 percent of the vote. (In the previous election, the NDP candidate had won just 17 percent of the vote.) Mulcair's victory was only the second time since

1935, when Outremont was first represented in the House of Commons, that a member of a party other than the Liberal Party had won the seat.

As a representative and the sole NDP member of Parliament (MP) from Quebec at the time, Mulcair sought to improve his new party's outreach in the province by eliminating badly translated and dated socialist-tinged pamphlets and replacing them with well-written French ones whose messages specifically targeted Quebecers. For example, he felt the national NDP emphasis on prescription-drug programs and government-funded daycare made little sense in Quebec, where such programs already existed on the provincial level. "That's why we pay pretty high taxes," he told Layton, as quoted by Geddes. "If you start promising a whole series of new social programs to Quebecers who are already paying for the ones they've got, they're not going to get it."

## TAKING QUEBEC BY STORM

Although no new NDP members were elected from Quebec during the 2008 election, Mulcair was reelected as an MP, in large part because he had earned a reputation as a formidable questioner of the Conservative government's policies on Parliament Hill in Ottawa. Back in Quebec, he helped give the NDP a face and a set of policies that many voters found quite appealing. During the 2011 election, the NDP's popularity increased exponentially, due both to Mulcair's high profile in Quebec and to Layton's national popularity, which was aided by his battle with cancer and his willingness to barnstorm across the country despite having recently broken his hip.

On May 2, 2011, the New Democratic Party became, for the first time in its history, the official opposition of the government, winning a record 103 seats, including 59 in Quebec. Since the 2008 election Layton had been telling Canadians that he was campaigning to become Canada's prime minister; following the 2011 election results, it looked as if he would do just that, if the NDP could demonstrate its leadership abilities as the official opposition by 2015. However, Layton died on August 22, 2011, following a second bout with cancer.

Prior to taking a leave of absence in July 2011, Layton had recommended Nycole Turmel, another MP from Quebec, for the position of interim leader; after his death, she remained in the role until party members could elect Layton's successor in March 2012. A number of party leaders, including Mulcair, vied to become the NDP's new leader and therefore the leader of the official opposition. Mulcair officially became a candidate for the post on October 13, 2011, and ran a hard campaign across much of Canada, hoping to broaden his appeal outside of Quebec, the province that knew him best.

## LEADER OF THE OPPOSITION

Some of Mulcair's rivals for the NDP leadership attempted to portray him as too temperamentally unsuited for the leadership, in part because of his reputation as a combative enforcer of party doctrine, while others suggested that he was too new a NDP member and was attempting to move the party too far to the center so it could be in a position to govern. In response, Mulcair's campaign focused on his qualities as a skilled debater and a media-savvy figure to sell him to the party faithful. He was elected party chief on March 24, having handily beaten his eight rivals for the top spot. Mulcair credited his background with helping him secure his victory. "Quebec City is a tough neighborhood to learn your politics in," he told Megan Fitzpatrick for CBC News (24 Mar. 2012). "It's very rough and tumble politics, so that's prepared me well for the work that I've done after."

In victory, Mulcair promised his fellow NDP members that he would present a plan to help Canada reduce greenhouse-gas emissions via a cap-and-trade system and advocate for reestablishing the long-gun registry. The registry, which was intended to be a record of all nonrestricted firearms, such as rifles and shotguns, in the country, was started in 1993 and struck down by the federal government in 2012. With an eye toward winning a majority in the House of Commons in the 2015 elections, Mulcair was reintroduced to the Canadian public during the party's policy convention in March 2013, at which NDP leaders sought to expand the party's brand by stripping out some dated socialist language from the preamble to their constitution.

Mulcair has also been a vocal critic of the proposed Keystone XL pipeline, which would send Canadian oil from Alberta's oil sands to the United States, Canada's largest trading partner. In 2011, the United States imported more than a full third of its oil from its northern neighbor. Mulcair believes that the oil-sands production is driving up the value of the Canadian dollar and making Canadian goods too expensive to compete on the international market. "Right now we think it's measurable and confirmed by studies that we are losing the balanced economy Canada had built up since the Second World War," Mulcair told Steven Mufson for the *Washington Post* (6 July 2012). "We're seeing the disappearance of manufacturing jobs that came with a good pension."

## PERSONAL LIFE

Mulcair met Catherine Pinhas in 1974, when Pinhas was visiting Quebec for a cousin's wedding. The two married in 1976, when they were both just twenty-one. Pinhas later became a psychologist. They have two sons: Matthew, a police officer with Quebec's provincial police, and Gregory, an aerospace engineer and college professor.

## SUGGESTED READING

Fitzpatrick, Meagan. "Thomas Mulcair Builds on His Quebec Base." *CBC News*. CBC, 24 Mar. 2012. Web. 16 Sept. 2013.

Geddes, John. "Smart, Tough and Nasty: The Definitive Portrait of Thomas Mulcair." *Maclean's*. Rogers Media, 19 Sept. 2012. Web. 16 Sept. 2013.

Matthews, Dylan. "Think Our Senate Is Horrible? Wait Til You See Canada's." *Washington Post*. Washington Post, 9 July 2013. Web. 16 Sept. 2013.

Mulcair, Thomas. "The Macleans.ca Interview: Thomas Mulcair." Interview by Kady O'Malley. *Maclean's*. Rogers Media, 27 June 2007. Web. 16 Sept. 2013.

Raj, Althia. "Thomas Mulcair's Family, Personal Side to Be Shown in New Light at NDP Policy Convention." *Huffington Post*. TheHuffingtonPost.com, 10 Apr. 2013. Web. 16 Sept. 2013.

—*Christopher Mari*

# Matt Mullenweg

**Born:** January 11, 1984
**Occupation:** Internet entrepreneur and web developer

Based on his background and childhood, it seems as if Matt Mullenweg was born to be an Internet mogul. The son of a computer programmer, Mullenweg developed a fascination with computers from a very early age and wasted no time in pursuing his newfound interest. From the time he was in middle school, Mullenweg was already knowledgeable enough to volunteer his services as an amateur computer repairman and had begun to tinker with programming. Just before finishing high school, Mullenweg got into the new field of blogging as a way to share his photography hobby with friends and family. This decision put him on the career path that led to him becoming one of the world's leading Internet entrepreneurs and a multimillionaire businessman.

When Mullenweg first started his blog in the early 2000s, he did so using free open-source blogging software. When the original developer of that software stepped away from the project, Mullenweg took the reins and eventually turned it into WordPress—a user-friendly online blogging tool. Before long, WordPress became one of the most popular and most widely used open-source blogging software programs available on the Internet.

AFP/Getty Images

Following a brief collegiate career and an equally brief run with online media giant CNET Networks, Mullenweg devoted himself full time to both WordPress and Automattic, the start-up company that powers WordPress. Since its founding, WordPress has become the go-to blogging software for private users and large corporate users alike. Some of its most prestigious clients include the *New York Times*, CNN, and the Coca-Cola Company. As Mullenweg continues his efforts to improve WordPress and explore new online ventures, he remains steadfastly committed to the concept of open-source software and the notion of a free and democratic Internet.

### EARLY LIFE

Matt Mullenweg was born in Houston, Texas, on January 11, 1984—the son of Chuck and Kathleen Mullenweg. His father, a Halliburton software engineer, was clearly the inspiration behind Mullenweg's early interest in computers. Dedicated to his craft, Mullenweg's father often brought his work home with him, and as a result, computers and other electronic equipment became a common sight in the family's home. Mullenweg's curiosity about computers was initially piqued simply because he was forbidden to touch his father's things. "The reason I got into computers is that I wasn't allowed to be on them when I was very young," Mullenweg explained in an October 28, 2004, interview with Cathy Matusow for the *Houston Press*. "So that's what I wanted more than anything."

By the time he was enrolled in classes at Johnston Middle School, Mullenweg's computer skills had progressed far beyond those of other students his age. One of his earliest computer ventures involved programming music on an early-model Macintosh system in use at the

school. Around the same time, his father, impressed with his son's obvious technological talent, began taking him to meetings held by the Houston Area League of PC Users (HAL-PC), an organization in which Mullenweg quickly became a full-fledged member. As part of his service to the club and his community, Mullenweg volunteered to fix ailing machines brought in by nonmembers.

### SECONDARY EDUCATION

Computers were not Mullenweg's only interest as a young man. He also became an avid jazz fan and musician. After learning to play the saxophone as a youngster and developing a strong passion for the jazz genre, Mullenweg decided to pursue music as a career path and chose to attend Houston's High School for the Performing and Visual Arts. Though he ultimately chose computers over music, Mullenweg believes jazz played an important part in the development of his computer coding skills. In his interview with Matusow, Mullenweg noted similarities between jazz musicians and computer code writers, describing how both must break down the work of others to learn how it was done. "It's like learning how [coders] do certain graphic effects, or why they use a certain code," Mullenweg said. "That's how you learn; that's how you get good."

As Mullenweg's skills progressed, however, a health setback not only almost sidelined his lofty career ambitions, but also nearly left him blind. From as early as fifth grade, Mullenweg suffered from increasingly debilitating migraines. It was not until his high school years that he was finally diagnosed with a sinus infection so severe that some of the bone and tissue around his sinus cavity was already dead. Scans showed that if the infection had spread even just a few millimeters further, it would have cost him his sight.

Once he recovered, Mullenweg was again able to resume his pursuit of a jazz career. In his final year at his arts-centric high school, Mullenweg took part in an economics competition hosted by the Federal Reserve in Washington, DC. During his stay in the city, he found himself taking picture after picture of the many sights to be seen in the nation's capital. Upon his return to Texas, he turned to blogging as a way to share his pictures with family and friends. This decision proved to be a turning point for Mullenweg. Drawn by the possibilities of the Internet, he set his sights on a career in the technology industry as his high school days came to an end.

### COLLEGE AND THE BIRTH OF WORDPRESS

After graduation in 2002, Mullenweg decided to move on to the University of Houston to study political science, economics, and philosophy. As he began his studies, he continued updating his blog, which he named *ma.tt*. By the end of that year, a change involving the software provider that powered the blog pushed Mullenweg to make what turned out to be the most important decision of his life.

Mullenweg first started publishing *ma.tt* using a piece of blog-building software known as b2. By late 2002, however, b2 creator Michel Valdrighi stopped his development of the software to move onto other work. Mullenweg, who had made some contributions to b2's code prior to Valdrighi's departure, decided to pick up where Valdrighi left off and to take over the development of b2. He planned to take the source code and begin updating it for his own use.

Mullenweg announced the takeover of b2 on his blog on January 24, 2003. In the post, he reflected on the best qualities of the various online publishing software packages of the day and which of those qualities would make for an ideal blogging experience. He wrote: "It would be nice to have the flexibility of Movable Type, the parsing of TextPattern, the hackability of b2 and the-ease-of-setup of Blogger," adding, "Someday, right?" Unbeknownst to those who followed his blog at the time, Mullenweg planned for "someday" to come very soon.

Following that announcement, Mullenweg joined forces with British programmer Mike Little to turn the b2 blogging software into WordPress—software that would allow users to easily create their own personal websites at no cost and with a wide range of customization features. WordPress was officially launched in May of 2003.

While Mullenweg continued his studies at the University of Houston, the popularity of WordPress began to grow. This growth was significantly accelerated in 2004 by the decision of Movable Type—a competitor program—to begin charging users for its service. Outraged by the move and unwilling to pay for a previously free service, hordes of bloggers jumped ship and switched to the still free WordPress. Thanks to both its own user-friendly approach and Movable Type's new fees, WordPress expanded to include approximately fifteen thousand users. This remarkable surge in interest brought both WordPress and Mullenweg himself to the attention of some of the major players in the online communications industry.

## SHIFTING FOCUS
One of the leading tech companies that took notice of Mullenweg's quickly rising star was CNET Networks. The CNET gurus were so impressed with Mullenweg's accomplishments that they offered him a job that would allow him to work for them  while still letting him work on WordPress—a special request Mullenweg asked of all the potential employers who expressed interest in hiring him. For Mullenweg, the CNET job offer was ideal, even though he would have to drop out of college to do it. Years later, he reflected on his choice in an interview with Michelle Klump for the University of Houston website: "It still wasn't an easy decision though, because my parents had always emphasized education so much, and also because my dad had worked so hard to go to school. It felt careless in a way to be throwing that away to focus on the Web and WordPress, which no one really knew was going to go anywhere." Despite his reservations about abandoning his academic pursuits, Mullenweg ultimately took the job and left Houston for CNET's San Francisco headquarters.

One of the main reasons that Mullenweg took the job at CNET, aside from the time his employer was willing to allot him for working on WordPress, was that he would be able to focus his attention and energy there on open-source software. Since his earliest blogging days, Mullenweg was a big supporter of open-source software, that is, software to which any user is welcome to contribute modifications. He strongly believed that open-source software was the most user-friendly and socially progressive technological tool available and one well worth supporting.

In spite of how pleased he was with his job at CNET and his work in support of open-source software, the continuing growth of WordPress forced Mullenweg to consider other career opportunities. Specifically, he wondered whether focusing on WordPress full-time was a viable option. He had been spending more and more time working on WordPress and the project had become an important part of his life. In the "About Matt Mullenweg" section of *ma.tt*, Mullenweg explains the sentiment that eventually drove him to leave CNET and compared it to his love of music. Mullenweg says: "Like eating, breathing, music, I can't not work on WordPress. The project touches a lot of people, something I've recently begun to appreciate. I consider myself very lucky to be able to work on something I love so much." Mullenweg resigned from CNET in October of 2005 and returned to Houston to begin the next phase of his career and life.

## RETURN TO WORDPRESS
To make WordPress a viable full-time career, Mullenweg had to reinvent its business model to make it more profitable. Though he remained strongly committed to maintaining WordPress's status as an open source web-building tool, Mullenweg recognized the need to somehow monetize the project. From the time that WordPress first became one of the leading blogging tools of its time, Mullenweg had received offers from an array of potential investors and large corporations looking to profit from WordPress or buy it out entirely. He regularly declined these offers in hopes that he might find a business partner who

shared his personal vision for the blogging tool. Mullenweg talked with *Forbes* contributor J. J. Colao about his reluctance to capitalize financially on WordPress in a September 24, 2012, interview, saying "part of my resistance to making it a business was that I hadn't met someone who could meld the business side of things with my philosophy." That all changed when he met Toni Schneider, an investor who had just made nearly $30 million selling his Oddpost web mail service to Yahoo!

Together, Mullenweg and Schneider devised a plan to turn WordPress into a profitable web-building tool that would still appeal to users. In 2005, the pair founded the web development corporation Automattic. Automattic was established to power the new WordPress.com, a website where anyone on the Internet could go to start a professional website without the hassle of dealing with hosting or servers. While this service remained free for the majority of users, advanced clients could pay a premium fee for access to top-of-the-line customization and other features.

## CONTINUING SUCCESS

In the first two years following the debut of its new business model, WordPress users launched an estimated two million new websites. By autumn of 2006, a number of major media outlets had expressed interest in creating their own WordPress blogs, including CNN, TechCrunch, and GigaOM. That September, Mullenweg finally invited them to join WordPress as VIP premium members.

Though initial profits were not exactly overwhelming, the company managed to make enough to turn down a substantial buyout offer in 2008, aided in part by the fund-raising efforts of some of its investors. Despite being able to claim responsibility for 18 percent of all web content, WordPress remains a relatively tightly run financial ship. The majority of its revenue comes from premium feature charges and special VIP client fees. Some revenue is also derived from embedded advertising provided through WordAds, a service Mullenweg created by way of a joint partnership between Automattic and Federated Media.

Though a concerted effort has clearly been made to make WordPress a financial success, Mullenweg insists that the company's profitability is only a secondary concern. In an interview with Jefferson Graham for *USA Today* (30 Jan. 2009) he said: "Our goal was never to make the most money possible, just enough to sustain our growth and contribute as much back to open source as possible."

## PERSONAL LIFE AND PHILANTHROPY

While he continues to work on WordPress and Automattic, Mullenweg still considers himself a jazz enthusiast and an avid amateur photographer, regularly posting pictures from his world travels on *ma.tt*. He has also remained close with many of the friends he grew up with, spending time with them whenever he is at home in Houston. Speaking to the *Houston Chronicle*'s David Kaplan for an August 4, 2012, article, Mullenweg's high school friend Elissa Rinehart marveled at how little fame and fortune have changed the young man who graduated just a year before she did. "It's incredible—he's still so humble," Rinehart said. "He's still the same dude, just better dressed."

In addition to his professional commitments, Mullenweg has also participated in a number of philanthropic endeavors. Most notably, he has been a strong supporter of Charity: Water, a non-profit organization that works to provide people in developing third world countries with clean drinking water.

More than anything else, however, Mullenweg remains singularly dedicated to supporting the continued use of open-source software—the very type of software that makes WordPress and many other web-building tools possible. He summed up the importance of open source in an interview with Erin Griffith of the website PandoDaily (24 May 2012). "I believe that open source is the most powerful invention of our generation," Mullenweg said. "You see it applied to software, you see it applied to hardware; it blows it up. In every way you can imagine, it destroys everything that came before. It's the most ultimate form of creative destruction."

## SUGGESTED READING

Colao, J. J. "With 60 Million Websites, WordPress Rules the Web. So Where's the Money?" *Forbes*. Forbes, 24 Sept. 2012. Web. 11 Mar. 2013.

Graham, Jefferson. "WordPress Creator Mullenweg Is Many Bloggers' Best Friend." *USA Today*. Gannett, 30 Jan. 2009. Web. 11 Mar. 2013.

Griffith, Erin. "Matt Mullenweg and the Cult of WordPress." *PandoDaily*. PandoDaily, 24 May 2012. Web. 11 Mar. 2013.

Kaplan, David. "Houston-Born Blog Guru Stays True to His Roots." *Houston Chronicle*. Hearst Communications, 4 Aug. 2012. Web. 11 Mar. 2013.

Klump, Michelle. "Former UH Student Helps People Find Their Voice on the Web." *University of Houston*. U of Houston, n.d. Web. 11 Mar. 2013.

Matusow, Cathy. "The Blog Age." *Houston Press*. Houston Press, 28 Oct. 2004. Web. 11 Mar. 2013.

—*Jack Lasky*

# Carey Mulligan

**Born:** May 28, 1985
**Occupation:** Actor

When Carey Mulligan was cast in her first leading role in Danish director Lone Scherfig's 1960s coming-of-age-drama *An Education* (2009), adapted by Nick Hornby from a memoir by British journalist Lynn Barber, little did she know that the film would change her life. Mulligan's performance in the film as Jenny Mellor, a precocious sixteen-year-old schoolgirl who gets swept off her feet by a charming older man (played by Peter Sarsgaard), won rave reviews from critics and earned her a slew of awards, including a British Academy of Film and Television Arts (BAFTA) Award for best actress; she also won Golden Globe and Academy Award nominations for the role. Mulligan, who made her screen debut in Joe Wright's *Pride & Prejudice* (2005), was instantly catapulted from relative obscurity to Hollywood "it girl" status and became one of the most in-demand and acclaimed actors of her generation. Joan Juliet Buck, writing for *Vogue* (Oct. 2010), called Mulligan "one of [Hollywood's] great talents, with an exceptional ability to convey profound emotional depth," while Nina Lakhani wrote for the London *Independent* (14 Feb. 2010), "Not since Helen Mirren has a British actress been received so well on the fickle world stage."

Mulligan reached wider audiences with roles in such mainstream films as *Public Enemies* (2009) and *Wall Street: Money Never Sleeps* (2010), directed by Michael Mann and Oliver Stone, respectively, as well as in provocative indies like Nicolas Winding Refn's *Drive* (2011) and Steve McQueen's *Shame* (2011). In 2013 she starred in Baz Luhrmann's 3-D film adaptation of the F. Scott Fitzgerald novel *The Great Gatsby*, as well as in Joel and Ethan Coen's folk music drama *Inside Llewyn Davis*. In addition to her film roles, she has occasionally performed in stage productions, most notably in a highly acclaimed revival of the Anton Chekhov play *The Seagull*, which ran in London in 2007 and on Broadway in 2008. Unlike many of her contemporaries, Mulligan has forged a career without formal acting training. She admitted to Nick Hornby, who interviewed her for *Elle* (15 Oct. 2009), "I've only really learned [how to act] by watching other people. That's been my drama school."

## EARLY LIFE AND EDUCATION

Carey Hannah Mulligan was born on May 28, 1985, in Westminster, a district in the central part of London, England. Her father, Stephen Mulligan, a British hotel manager, had met her mother, Nano Booth, a Welsh college lecturer, while they were both working at a hotel in

© Stephane Cardinale/People Avenue/Corbis

Amman, the capital and largest city of Jordan. Along with her older brother, Owain, Mulligan had a peripatetic childhood, growing up in a series of hotels that her father managed.

At the time of her birth, Mulligan's family lived in London's posh Mayfair Hotel; when she was three years old, they moved to Düsseldorf, Germany, after her father was hired to run the European arm of the InterContinental hotel chain. They lived in Germany for about five years before Mulligan's family moved back to England. In an interview with Elizabeth Sanderson for the London *Mail on Sunday* (2 May 2010), Mulligan, who grew up speaking German, said of her unusual yet privileged upbringing: "My mother would cook but we would get looked after by maids. It felt like we lived in these enormous houses with lots of guests. But it all felt normal. It was weirder when we lived in a house and got real keys to let ourselves in with."

Mulligan fostered dreams of becoming an actor from the time she was a child. When she was six years old, she made her acting debut alongside her brother in a production of Rodgers and Hammerstein's musical *The King and I* at the International School in Düsseldorf. Mulligan had initially been prevented from joining the musical because of her age, but the school eventually placated the heartbroken actor by putting her in the cast as a male chorus member. For Mulligan, who had to dye her blonde hair black for the role, it "was the beginning of my playing male characters," as she noted to Lynn Hirschberg for the *New York Times* (20 Aug. 2009).

When Mulligan was eleven years old, her parents sent her to the Woldingham School, an exclusive all-girls Catholic boarding school in Surrey. At Woldingham Mulligan became determined to follow her acting ambitions, a plan her parents did not encourage. There, she became a standout member of the drama department, while appearing almost exclusively in male parts in both musicals and plays. "Right from the word go, you could see there was a special quality about Carey," Mulligan's former drama teacher Judith Brown told Anita Singh for the London *Telegraph* (20 Feb. 2010). "She was talented and very natural" and "had an inner confidence and knew she could succeed, but was incredibly modest about her ability."

## MAKINGS OF AN INGENUE

While attending Woldingham, Mulligan saw Kenneth Branagh's live production of the William Shakespeare play *Henry V*. Moved by Branagh's performance as Henry V, she wrote a letter to him asking for advice and expressing her desire to become an actor. On the actor's behalf, his sister wrote back to Mulligan encouraging her to follow her dreams. By that time, Mulligan, despite being a straight A student, had grown "less and less interested" in school, as she told Graham Fuller for the *Arts Desk* (13 Oct. 2009). "All I wanted to do was go off and do acting."

Upon completion of her A-level exams (the equivalent of a high school diploma in the United States) in 2003, Mulligan went against her parents' wishes by applying to drama schools instead of universities. Rejected by all three of her choices—the Royal Academy of Dramatic Art (RADA), the Central School of Speech and Drama, and Drama Centre London—Mulligan, who made the rash decision of using a monologue about suicide from Sarah Kane's play *4.48 Psychosis* as her audition speech, was forced to reapply to university after her parents found out. She was subsequently accepted to the University of Reading, in Berkshire, England, but nonetheless remained dogged in her pursuit of an acting career.

A turning point for Mulligan came after she arranged a meeting with Julian Fellowes, the Oscar-winning screenwriter of *Gosford Park* (2001), whom she had first met when he gave a talk at Woldingham. "I wrote to [Woldingham's] headmistress explaining that I didn't want to go to university and wanted to get in touch with him," she recalled to Chloe Fox for the *Telegraph* (10 Nov. 2007). "I knew it was a bit of a long shot, but I was desperate." Soon afterward, Mulligan was invited to a dinner at London's upscale Le Caprice restaurant with Fellowes, his wife, and several other acting hopefuls. Struck by Mulligan's passion and recognizing her potential, Fellowes and his wife put her in contact with several agents and casting directors, and within days, she landed an audition for the supporting role of Kitty Bennet in Joe Wright's *Pride & Prejudice*, an adaptation of the Jane Austen novel.

## FILM AND TELEVISION DEBUTS

Mulligan had to audition three times before being cast as Kitty in *Pride & Prejudice*, which was released in 2005 and marked her feature film acting debut. At that time her only acting

training consisted of several weekend improvisation workshops. That lack of training notwithstanding, Mulligan, who was then working as a barmaid, proved she could hold her own opposite Keira Knightly, who starred as her older sister Elizabeth Bennet, and the film's other big-name stars, including her childhood idol Judi Dench. *Pride & Prejudice*, which follows five sisters from a privileged family in England at the turn of the nineteenth century, was both a critical and commercial success. The film received four Academy Award nominations, including one for Knightly for best actress. Mulligan, meanwhile, won notice for making the rebellious Kitty "a flurry of hormonal excitability," as Fuller wrote.

Mulligan also made her television debut in 2005 as the orphan Ada Claire in BBC's *Bleak House*, a critically acclaimed, BAFTA Award–winning miniseries based on Charles Dickens's satirical novel about the failure of the British legal system. The following year she appeared in a guest spot on the ITV murder mystery series *Agatha Christie's Marple*, and played the daughter of the title character in the BBC six-part drama *The Amazing Mrs. Pritchard*, about a supermarket manager who becomes the prime minister of England.

Mulligan amassed more British television credits in 2007, when she landed roles in the BBC series *Waking the Dead* and *Doctor Who*, as well as in the made-for-television dramas *Northanger Abbey* and *My Boy Jack*. The latter is based on the real-life disappearance and death of author Rudyard Kipling's only son, Jack, during the First World War. In that film, Daniel Radcliffe, the titular star of the Harry Potter film franchise, starred as Jack, while Mulligan played his sister Elsie.

## RISE TO ACTING PROMINENCE: *THE SEAGULL*

Concurrently with her film and television work, Mulligan has performed on stage. She earned the most attention for her turn as the naïve ingenue Nina in Ian Rickson's revival of the Anton Chekhov play *The Seagull*, which examines the creative and romantic struggles of four artists. The play, which also starred Kristin Scott Thomas as the fading actor Arkadina, Chiwetel Ejiofor as the tortured novelist Trigorin, and Mackenzie Crook as the lovelorn playwright Konstantin, opened at London's Royal Court Theatre in January 2007. It received rapturous reviews and enjoyed a highly successful two-month run, during which Mulligan suffered and recovered from a bout of appendicitis. Mulligan was originally given a recovery period of three to six weeks, but she returned to the stage after only one week.

Many reviewers singled out Mulligan for her tour de force portrayal of Nina, considered among the most difficult stage roles to play. Rickson said to Buck, in another article for

*Vogue* (Oct. 2009), that Mulligan made "an almost unplayable part completely coherent and deeply moving." Charles McGrath observed for the *New York Times* (10 May 2011) that the actor "brought such power and vitality to the part, suggesting both the youthfulness and the depth of Nina's ambition, that she was a big reason many critics called [the Royal Court production] the best *Seagull* in generations."

In the fall of 2008, *The Seagull* moved to the Walter Kerr Theater on Broadway in New York, where it enjoyed another successful three-month run. While Rickson and most of the original cast returned, Ejiofor was replaced by Mulligan's future *Education* costar Peter Sarsgaard in the role of Trigorin. For her Broadway debut, Mulligan received a Drama Desk Award nomination for best featured actress in a play. "The time I spent doing *The Seagull* was everything to me," she told Fox. "It was like falling in love with life."

## BREAKOUT ROLE IN *AN EDUCATION*

In between London and Broadway productions of *The Seagull*, Mulligan, who by this time had caught the attention of Hollywood, landed roles in a handful of feature films, including Lone Scherfig's *An Education*. Mulligan beat out hundreds of other hopefuls for the role of Jenny after impressing Scherfig with her audition DVD. "Carey stood out immediately," Scherfig said, as quoted by Stephanie Bunbury for the Melbourne, Australia, *Age* (12 Mar. 2011). "Not because she reminded me of anyone—more perhaps because she didn't."

Set in 1961 London on the cusp of the mod era, *An Education* follows Jenny, a model student at an elite private girls' school, as she develops a romantic relationship with Peter Sarsgaard's David Goldman, a charismatic thirty-something entrepreneur. David, a self-described graduate of the "University of Life," woos Jenny into a dazzling adult world outside of her sheltered adolescence and away from her overbearing parents (Alfred Molina and Cara Seymour) and unyielding headmistress (Emma Thompson), who have hopes of her attending Oxford University. Jenny briefly drops out of school and travels to Paris with David to celebrate her seventeenth birthday. Shortly after returning home, however, her love spell is broken when she discovers that David is not only a con man but is also married. When David disappears from her life, Jenny, with the aid of a compassionate teacher (Olivia Williams), continues down the academic path where she began.

## CRITICAL ACCLAIM FOR *AN EDUCATION*

*An Education* premiered at the Sundance Film Festival in January 2009, where it became a sensation, winning the audience choice and cinematography awards. Mulligan—who also had a small part in another film that debuted

at the festival called *The Greatest* (2009), a heartfelt indie drama starring Susan Sarandon and Pierce Brosnan—received widespread recognition for her performance, which drew comparisons to Audrey Hepburn's star-making turn in the 1953 William Wyler classic *Roman Holiday*. In a review for *Variety* (26 Jan. 2009) about Mulligan's "captivating" performance in the film, Todd McCarthy wrote that the actor "is completely convincing as sixteen going on seventeen . . . she tangibly communicates Jenny's thirst for knowledge, her attraction to culture and impatience at conservative ways of thinking and behaving. The way she tosses off little French phrases may be pretentious, but it adorably indicates where her head is. And when she finally gets to Paris and puts up her hair, you could almost swear you're watching Audrey Hepburn skipping through the same streets fifty years ago." Logan Hill, reviewing the film for *New York* (31 Aug. 2009), wrote, "Whip-smart yet naïve, charming without being cutesy, Mulligan captures a teenager's overheated emotions with endearing naturalism."

After making the rounds on the festival circuit, *An Education* received a wide release in the United States and England in October 2009. The film was a modest box office success and received critical acclaim, most of which was reserved for Mulligan, who earned a total of fourteen awards and twelve nominations for her performance. She won the BAFTA Award for best actress and also earned Golden Globe, Screen Actors Guild, and Academy Award nominations.

## HOLLYWOOD "IT GIRL"

For Mulligan, *An Education* was "a movie so perfectly attuned to her talents that it swept her up into that mysterious zeitgeist where new stars are spawned," Matt Mueller wrote for *Total Film* (Oct. 2010). On the heels of that movie's success, she was widely referred to in the media as an "it girl" and became one of the most in-demand young actors in Hollywood. Mulligan had already filmed small roles in Michael Mann's gangster epic *Public Enemies* (2009), as a bleached-blonde prostitute, and in Jim Sheridan's military thriller *Brothers* (2009), as a distraught war widow, when she was cast opposite *Prejudice* costar Keira Knightly and Andrew Garfield in Mark Romanek's well-received science fiction drama *Never Let Me Go* (2010). In the film, based on the novel by Kazuo Ishiguro and set in a dystopian England, Mulligan is a human clone named Kathy, who narrates the film and becomes entangled in a dangerous love triangle with two childhood friends and fellow clones, Knightly's Ruth and Garfield's Tommy.

Mulligan was subsequently cast as Winnie Gekko, the left-wing blogger and philanthropic-minded daughter of Michael Douglas's iconic corporate raider Gordon Gekko, in Oliver Stone's *Wall Street: Money Never Sleeps* (2010), the highly anticipated sequel to his 1987 classic *Wall Street*. The film is set to the backdrop of the 2008 financial crisis and follows Gekko as he takes Winnie's fiancé, a young New York City trader named Jacob Moore (Shia LaBeouf), under his wing. Gekko helps Moore plot revenge against a rival in return for Moore reuniting him with Winnie, long estranged from him after the suicide of her older brother. While the film received a polarizing response from critics, most of its cast—including Josh Brolin, Frank Langella, Eli Wallach, and Susan Sarandon—were recognized for giving strong performances. In her October 2010 article for *Vogue*, Buck wrote that Mulligan's Winnie is "the emotional heart of the movie."

## A PROLIFIC CAREER

In 2011, Mulligan played a conflicted single mother opposite Ryan Gosling in Danish director Nicolas Winding Refn's *Drive*, a highly stylized neo-noir crime drama about a Hollywood stuntman who moonlights as a getaway driver. She also costarred in British director Steve McQueen's challenging drama *Shame* (2011), as the troubled sister of a hopeless sex addict, played by Michael Fassbender. Both *Drive* and *Shame* garnered wide critical acclaim, and Mulligan received multiple award nominations for her performances in those films.

Mulligan also returned to the stage in 2011, in David Leveaux's off-Broadway play *Through a Glass Darkly*, based on Ingmar Bergman's 1961 Academy Award–winning film, which ran at the New York Theater Workshop. For her performance as Karin, a woman on the brink of insanity, Mulligan received her second career Drama Desk Award nomination for best actress. In a review for the *New York Times* (6 June 2011), theater critic Ben Brantley wrote that Mulligan is "one of the finest actresses of her generation" and that her performance in the play was "acting of the highest order."

In 2013 Mulligan played the coveted role of Daisy Buchanan, opposite Leonardo DiCaprio, in Baz Luhrmann's extravagant reimagining of F. Scott Fitzgerald's *The Great Gatsby*. She also portrayed Justin Timberlake's love interest in the Coen brothers' *Inside Llewyn Davis*, about struggling folk musicians in 1960s New York. Both films premiered at that year's Cannes Film Festival, the latter of which won the prestigious Grand Prix award.

Mulligan married the British musician Marcus Mumford, the lead singer of the folk band Mumford & Sons, in April 2012.

## SUGGESTED READING

Buck, Joan Juliet. "The Talented Miss Mulligan." *Vogue* Oct. 2010: 266–301. Print.
Fox, Chloe. "Carey Mulligan: All or Nothing." *Telegraph* [London]. Telegraph Media, 10 Nov. 2007. Web. 12 Aug. 2013.
Fuller, Graham. "Actress Carey Mulligan, Emotionally Speaking." *Arts Desk*. Arts Desk, 13 Oct. 2009. Web. 12 Aug. 2013.
Hornby, Nick. "She's the One." *Elle*. Hearst Communications, 15 Oct. 2009. Web. 12 Aug. 2013.
Lakhani, Nina. "Carey Mulligan: Hollywood's New Star Pupil." *Independent* [London]. Independent.co.uk, 14 Feb. 2010. Web. 12 Aug. 2013.
McCarthy, Todd. "*Education* Aces Test." Rev. of *An Education*, dir. Lone Scherfig. *Variety* 26 Jan. 2009: 35–42. Print.
Mueller, Matt. "There's Something about Carey." *Total Film* Oct. 2010: 116–20. Print.
Sanderson, Elizabeth. "The Miseducation of Carey Mulligan." *Mail on Sunday* [London] 2 May 2010: News 44. Print.

## SELECTED WORKS

*The Seagull*, 2007–8; *An Education*, 2009; *Public Enemies*, 2009; *Wall Street: Money Never Sleeps*, 2010; *Never Let Me Go*, 2010; *Drive*, 2011; *Shame*, 2011; *Through a Glass Darkly*, 2011; *The Great Gatsby*, 2013; *Inside Llewyn Davis*, 2013

—Chris Cullen

# Geoffrey Mutai

**Born:** October 7, 1981
**Occupation:** Long-distance runner

With his victories in the Boston and New York City Marathons in 2011, Geoffrey Mutai—who came to international attention after an exciting second-place finish in the 2010 Marathon Rotterdam—earned the distinction of being the first person to capture both major marathons in the same calendar year. However, Mutai did not fare as well in the early part of the 2012 season. After failing to complete the Boston Marathon, he was not selected to represent Kenya at the Summer Olympics in London. He rebounded later in 2012, however, with wins at two shorter-distance events, the Ottawa Race Weekend ten-kilometer (10K) race and the Boston Athletic Association (BAA) 10K race, as well as wins at the Berlin Marathon in September and the Pfixx Solar Montferland 15K in the Netherlands in December. In February 2013, he received the 2012 Association of International Marathons and Distance Races (AIMS)/ASICS World Athlete of the Year award for the second year in a row. He won the New York City Marathon again in November 2013.

© Craig Ruttle/ /AP/Corbis

## EARLY LIFE AND EDUCATION

Geoffrey Kiprono Mutai was born on October 7, 1981, in Mumberes, an administrative division in the Koibatek District, located in Kenya's Rift Valley Province. His father worked at Rivatex East Africa Limited, a textile-manufacturing company in the western Kenyan city of Eldoret. The oldest of nine children, Mutai took up running at age twelve. He competed in the 10,000-meter race while attending Tuiyotich Primary School in Nakuru and instantly fell in love with the sport. "I can say it came to me naturally . . . I used to train daily and with time, I could not do without running," Mutai said, as quoted by Mutwiri Mutuota and James Wokabi in a profile of the athlete for the International Association of Athletics Federations (IAAF) website (28 Feb. 2011).

However, after passing the 1998 Kenya Certificate of Primary Education (KCPE) exam, a standardized national test that is administered to primary-school graduates, Mutai was unable to pursue his secondary education due to financial constraints. "When I finished primary school, my father had lost his job at Rivatex when it closed down and I had no choice but to discontinue with my learning," Mutai revealed, also in his IAAF profile. As a result, running became his primary focus. "I remained with the running option only, and my specialty was the long distance," he told Jonathan Komen for Kenya's *Daily Nation*, the largest publication in East Africa (24 Apr. 2011).

## A CAREER NEARLY SIDELINED

In 1999 Mutai began supporting himself and his family by working as a farm laborer. His daily workout routine consisted of early morning runs. A year later, Mutai began training for the steeplechase, a middle-distance event in which competitors race for three thousand meters—just over seven laps—around a circuit that consists of four hurdles and one water jump during each lap, for a total of twenty-eight hurdles and seven water jumps.

In 2002 Mutai qualified to represent Kenya in the 3,000-meter steeplechase at the IAAF/Coca Cola World Junior Championships, held that July in Kingston, Jamaica. However, the Kenyan federation removed him from the team after he could not produce a birth certificate in order to secure a passport. Mutai's bad luck continued later that year when he sustained a severe injury to his Achilles tendon during a long run.

As a result of his injury, Mutai made the decision to put his running career on hold. He subsequently returned to Eldoret and began working for the country's public utility company, the Kenya Power and Lighting Company (KPLC), as a tree cutter. But Mutai did not completely abandon his favorite sport. After his tendon injury had healed properly, he continued to run recreationally. "I discovered I could not work without running," Mutai revealed in his profile article on the IAAF website. "I resumed training by going on long runs in the morning before reporting to work. Running was in my blood."

## RUNNING AGAIN

Mutai's tenure at the KPLC was short lived; in 2005, he was let go from his position. Following the loss of his job, Mutai made the decision to resume his running career. He became a member of the Kiptenden Athletics Club, a sports facility in Kericho, and unsuccessfully tried out for the club's training camp, which was then being led by renowned running coach David Kosgei.

After Mutai's failed training-camp bid, he returned home and joined the Kapng'entuny Athletics Club, which is based in Eldoret. In June 2006 Mutai entered the Kilimanjaro Half Marathon, a twenty-one-kilometer race that is held annually at the base of Africa's tallest mountain. He made a respectable showing, finishing in sixth place.

## MARATHON DEBUT

In December 2007 Mutai made his first full marathon appearance at Kenya's inaugural Kass Marathon, a forty-two-kilometer event that takes place in the Rift Valley Province between the towns of Kapsabet and Eldoret. "Although the course was quite tough to many runners, I found it easy since I had trained at the hilly areas of Kapng'etuny," he told Komen. Mutai's second-place finish, with a time of 2:12:22, caught the attention of Gerard van de Veen, an agent with the Netherlands-based athlete-management firm Volare Sports. Mutai subsequently signed with van de Veen, under whose guidance he began competing in high-profile global marathon competitions.

The following March, Mutai's international marathon debut came at the Monaco Marathon, also known as the Monaco and the Riviera Marathon, the world's only marathon in which participants travel through three different countries—France, Italy, and Monaco—during the course of the race. Mutai experienced his biggest win to date, finishing first with a time of 2:12:40. He followed up that result with a second-place finish at the Kenyan National Championships in June 2008. A month later Mutai fell short in his bid to represent his country at the Beijing Summer Olympics, following a disappointing ninth-place finish in the 10,000-meter event at the Kenyan trials, which were held at Nairobi's Nyayo National Stadium. He rebounded in October 2008 at the Eindhoven Marathon, where Mutai came first with a time of 2:07:50—a personal best and, at the time, a course record.

Mutai had one of his worst marathon career performances in March 2009 at the Seoul International Marathon in Korea, where he failed to cross the finish line. A month later he came in eighth at the Daegu Marathon, also in Korea. After these disappointing results, Mutai bounced back in mid-July with a strong effort at the Fortis Loopfestijn Voorthuizen, an annual 10K race held in the Netherlands. He came in first with a time of 27:39, topping the previous course record of 28:05. Mutai bested the second- and third-place finishers, fellow Kenyans Wilson Kipsang and Gilbert Kirwa, by nine seconds and forty-nine seconds, respectively.

In October 2009 Mutai successfully defended his title at the Eindhoven Marathon with a time of 2:07:01, again smashing both his own record and the previous course record. Mutai's 2009 season ended on a strong note with a first-place victory at the Valencia Half Marathon in Spain.

## INTERNATIONAL ATTENTION
The following year Mutai captured the attention of the worldwide running community. In February 2010 he overcame a field of 1,340 runners to win the Ras Al Khaimah (RAK) Half Marathon, a yearly competition held in the United Arab Emirates. With his winning time of 59:43, Mutai edged out Tadese Tola of Ethiopia by six seconds and earned $20,000 in prize money.

Mutai made headlines again in April, when he came in second—by a seven-second margin—to fellow Kenyan Patrick Makau at the 2010 Marathon Rotterdam. Mutai, who achieved a personal best of 2:04:55, was one of four men

who recorded an impressive time of less than 2:05:30; the other three were Kenya's Vincent Kipruto, Ethiopia's Feyisa Lelisa, and Makau. Mutai also became only the seventh man in history to complete a marathon in under two hours and five minutes.

A month later Mutai claimed the $15,000 first-place prize at Kenya's Sotokoto Safari Half Marathon. In late July he took home the bronze medal in the 10,000-meter race at the African Championships in Athletics. He also set a new personal best with a time of 27:33, finishing behind gold medalist Wilson Kiprop of Kenya and silver medalist Moses Kipsiro of Uganda.

## MAKING A NAME FOR HIMSELF
In September 2010, Mutai made his debut at Germany's prestigious Berlin Marathon, one of the five World Marathon Majors. (The others are the London Marathon, the Boston Marathon, the Chicago Marathon, and the New York City Marathon.) He was part of a deep field that included Kenyan rivals Makau and Eliud Kiptanui, the latter of whom had garnered attention with a record-setting breakthrough victory at the Prague Marathon, his second career marathon.

Despite adverse weather conditions in Berlin, including heavy rain and thick, dense fog, Mutai managed to keep pace with Makau in the home stretch of the race. In an exciting photo finish, Mutai was narrowly edged out by a margin of two seconds. For his second-place effort, he was awarded €20,000. Mutai, along with Makau and third-place finisher Bazu Worku of Ethiopia, received a bonus of €30,000 for achieving a time of less than two hours and six seconds.

At the end of November, Mutai appeared at the Delhi Half Marathon in India, where he posted a time of 59:38. Mutai fought off challenges from Ethiopians Yacob Jarso and Lelisa Desisa, the latter of whom he narrowly beat by one second to secure the $100,000 purse.

## THE MARATHON MAJORS
Mutai launched his 2011 season with January appearances at two local twelve-kilometer races, the KCB/Athletics Kenya National Cross Country Championships and the Kenya Police Inter-Divisional Cross Country Championships. His closest challenger at both events was Philemon Rono. In late March, Mutai competed in one of the world's most important cross-country races: the IAAF World Cross Country Championships, which were held that year in Punta Umbria, Spain. With a time of 34:03, he placed fifth in the men's twelve-kilometer race, which was won by Imane Merga of Ethiopia.

The following month Mutai competed at the Boston Marathon, the world's oldest annual marathon and one of the most prestigious road-racing events. He stunned observers by posting an impressive time of 2:03:02—almost a minute faster than the world-record time of 2:03:59, previously set by Ethiopia's Haile Gebrselassie at the 2008 Berlin Marathon. Mutai's winning time also shattered the marathon's previous course record of 2:05:52, formerly held by fellow countryman Robert Kiprono Cheruiyot.

Although Mutai had the fastest marathon time ever recorded, it was not counted as a world record since the Boston Marathon's largely downhill course, which spans 26 miles and 385 yards, does not conform to the standards of the IAFF, the international governing body of track and field. It was also determined that on the day of the race, Mutai's time was aided by a tailwind that was blowing fifteen to twenty miles per hour.

Mutai's next victory took place in June 2011 at the first annual BAA 10K event, which he won in 27:19. He followed that with a July appearance at Italy's prestigious Giro di Castelbuono, which is recognized as one of oldest road-running competitions in Europe. Mutai fared well in the inaugural 10,000-meter race, finishing first with a time of 29:05. A month later he won the Bogotá International Half Marathon, where he also set a course record of 1:02:20—more than two minutes faster than the second-place finisher, Deriba Merga of Ethiopia.

In November Mutai entered the New York City Marathon with his eyes trained toward the 2012 Olympic Games in London. He dominated the men's race, capturing first place with a time of 2:05:06. Mutai's performance eclipsed the event's decade-old course record, set by Ethiopia's Tesfaye Jifar. The victory made Mutai the first person to win both the New York City Marathon and the Boston Marathon in record time in the same year. His accomplishments in 2011 earned him the Association of International Marathons and Distance Races (AIMS) World Athlete of the Year Award.

## 2012 SEASON

Mutai had a strong start to the 2012 season, coming in second to Wilson Kiprop at the Discovery Kenya Cross Country championship, held in January in Eldoret, Kenya. In April, Mutai returned to the Boston Marathon in an attempt to defend his title. However, the uncharacteristically hot weather proved too much for Mutai, whose severe stomach cramps forced him to leave the race after reaching the eighteen-mile mark.

Mutai's failure to complete the marathon ultimately cost him the opportunity to represent his country at the 2012 Summer Olympics in London. "I really wanted so much to go to the Olympics, but . . . it was something beyond my control and there was really nothing I could do about my being left out," he told Justin Lagat for the *Competitor* (3 Aug. 2012). "It was painful when I heard the news, which came as a surprise to me because even after failing to finish at this year's Boston Marathon, the officials at Athletics Kenya (AK) had nevertheless assured me that they were going to include me on the team and had even given me the go-ahead to go and survey the course in London, and I did fly there directly from Boston."

Mutai quickly rebounded from his Olympic disappointment. After winning Puerto Rico's San Blas Half Marathon in February, he dominated the men's field at the Ottawa Race Weekend 10K, his first competition on Canadian soil. He posted a winning time of 27:41 at the Ottawa event, which is held annually in May. A month later Mutai mounted a successful defense of his title at the BAA 10K event, followed by a third-place finish at the Sotokoto Safari Marathon half-marathon race in July. In September 2012, he competed in the Berlin Marathon and edged out his training partner Dennis Kimetto for the win with a time of 2:04:15. Mutai's time was the fastest marathon time of the year and helped him take the World Marathon Majors overall men's prize for 2011–12. Mutai ended the year by setting the course record, 42:25, at the December 2012 Pfixx Solar Montferland 15K in 'S Heerenberg, the Netherlands.

## EARLY 2013

On February 14, 2013, Mutai received the men's 2012 AIMS/ASICS World Athlete of the Year award for a second consecutive year. "I am delighted to win this prestigious award for a second time . . . I would like to thank AIMS, their members, and award sponsors" (qtd. by IAAF 15 Feb. 2013). The award ceremony took place in Ras al-Khaimah, United Arab Emirates, where the following afternoon Mutai ran in the RAK Half Marathon, which he had won before in 2010. Although he led the pack during the middle of the race, he finished third with a time of 58:58, beating his 2010 winning time and coming in just four hundredths of a second behind the 2013 winner, Geoffrey Kipsang.

The self-coached Mutai spends the majority of his time training in the high-altitude town of Kapng'entuny, where he lives with his wife, Beatrice, and their two daughters.

## SUGGESTED READING

Douglas, Scott. "Leading Edge: Geoffrey Mutai's Mission." *Running Times*. Rodale, Apr. 2012. Web. 11 Sept. 2012.

Komen, Jonathan. "Rags to Riches." *Daily Nation*. Nation Media Group, 24 Apr. 2011. Web. 25 Aug. 2012.

Lagat, Justin. "Sneak Peek: Olympic Insights from Geoffrey Mutai." *Competitor*. Competitor Group, 3 Aug. 2012. Web. 11 Sept. 2012.

Springer, Shira. "How Geoffrey Mutai Trains for the Boston Marathon." *Boston.com*. New York Times Co., 13 Apr. 2012. Web. 11 Sept. 2012.

Vecsey, George. "Togetherness Helps Set Winner Apart." *New York Times*. New York Times Co., 6 Nov. 2011. Web. 11 Sept. 2012.

—*Bertha Muteba*

# Sue Naegle

**Born:** July 2, 1969
**Occupation:** Head of HBO Entertainment

Sue Naegle was hired as the president of HBO Entertainment, Home Box Office's entertainment division, in 2008, succeeding Carolyn Strauss. At that time, her main goal, as she told Michael Schneider and Josef Adalian for *Variety* (14 Apr. 2008), was "to bring in people who are passionate about their point of view and have a smart story to tell." Naegle's role at HBO is to oversee both the specials and the regular programming for each television season; in that role, she handles a budget of more than $100 million. *Newsweek* named Naegle among its top ten "Most Important People in 2010." In August 2012, Forbes magazine named Naegle as number forty-six in its list of "The World's 100 Most Powerful Women" (22 Aug. 2012).

Owned by Time Warner, HBO earns profits of more than a billion dollars annually. Under Naegle's leadership, HBO has had successes with *Boardwalk Empire*, *Game of Thrones*, and Aaron Sorkin's *The Newsroom*, which premiered in June 2012. In 2011, the network received 104 Primetime Emmy Award nominations, winning nineteen awards. In 2012, HBO Entertainment earned eighty-one nominations, which included a record half of the possible nominations in comedy for *Girls*, *Curb Your Enthusiasm*, and *Veep*. The network won twenty-three awards that year, marking the eleventh straight year that HBO won the most Primetime Emmy Awards of any network.

## CHILDHOOD AND EDUCATION

Born on July 2, 1969, in Rockaway, New Jersey, Naegle was a voracious reader as a child. She also watched a lot of television. Her father, a high school coach, and her mother, a medical market researcher, did not closely monitor their two daughters' television viewing. "They weren't restrictive about what we watched at all—*Dallas*, *Falcon Crest*, *Saturday Night Live*, and a lot of comedies," Naegle told Stacey Wilson for the *Hollywood Reporter* (5 Dec. 2012). She claims to do the opposite with her own daughters, who are not allowed to watch television during the week.

FilmMagic

In 1991, Naegle earned her bachelor of arts in comparative literature and telecommunications from Indiana University at Bloomington, a degree that she asserts put her in a good position for her life's work. Her first job after college, however, was as a waitress at the chain restaurant Bennigan's, back in New Jersey. Shortly thereafter, she interned at Orion Classics (now Sony Classics) in New York, but felt financially insecure and chose to move to Los Angeles, regardless of her lack of connections.

## UNITED TALENT AGENCY

Taking the advice of a family friend, Naegle applied and was hired to work in the mailroom at United Talent Agency in Los Angeles. In addition to corporations and top brand names, the agency—one of the largest of its kind—represents writers, actors, musicians, directors, and producers. Founded in 1991 through a merger of Bauer-Benedek and Leading Artists, UTA originally placed an emphasis on television, with special consideration to comedy writers.

UTA has a training program for new agents, all of whom begin in the mailroom. After only two months there, Naegle became a talent assistant in 1992, working with the agent Nancy Jones; two years later she became a full agent. In that role she was known as someone who was good at spotting new talent and who cared for and about her writers. In 1999, she was promoted to cohead of the television department and became a partner in the agency. She was twenty-nine years old, the youngest person ever to become a partner there.

Naegle was working at United Talent Agency when she was tapped for the HBO position. She had served at the agency for sixteen years. Part of Naegle's draw for HBO was her reputation as an agent who worked with some of the top television writers. For example, she worked with Alan Ball on *Six Feet Under* and the vampire drama *True Blood*, both shows for HBO, when she was an agent. UTA cofounder and board member Peter Benedek told Wilson, "I was totally bereft when she left us. She was a wonderful agent and took it very personally when buyers didn't get how amazing her clients were." When Naegle was hired at HBO, she defused the comments of those who were critical of the choice, claiming that both of her jobs were similar. For her, the move to HBO felt very comfortable, she told Josef Adalian for *Television Week* (17 Nov. 2008). "From the outside, it might look like a big leap," she stated. "But I knew everyone at HBO really well. It didn't feel like I was going to work with a company of strangers."

## HOME BOX OFFICE HISTORY

Home Box Office, best known as HBO, was founded in 1972 by parent company Time Incorporated and is the largest of the pay-TV channels. HBO originally offered commercial-free, uncut movies, requiring cable subscribers to pay an additional fee for access. It was the first network in the United States to deliver programs by satellite, beginning in 1975.

Cable television initially grew slowly, bogged down by lack of infrastructure and federal regulation, much of which had been developed by major networks that feared competition in terms of both audience and advertising revenue. In 1978, Time Inc. bought American Television and Communications Corporation (ATC), which was at the time the second-largest cable system operator in the United States. It was expected that many of Time Warner's subscribers would also buy into HBO. This acquisition fed a cycle of growth; with more subscribers, HBO could pay a better price for exclusive rights to movies, thus attracting even more subscribers. In the late 1970s, HBO paid for $35 million exclusive rights to a block of forty MGM/United Artists films, despite the risk that some of those films would not be successful. Movie studios feared that cable might lead to the death of the film industry.

This fear was unfounded, however; in 1982, HBO approached Columbia and CBS to create the first new studio in four decades, Tri-Star. HBO would have exclusive rights to the films that Tri-Star made. The following year, HBO began producing made-for-television movies and an original comedy program.

The media giant Viacom owned HBO's major competitor, Showtime. Viacom filed an antitrust suit against HBO in 1989. Ironically, the suit was brought by former HBO executives, who had moved on but charged that HBO was trying to force Showtime out of the cable market. The suit, which generated a great deal of negative publicity, came up as Congress was considering new cable regulations. It was not settled out of court until 1992.

## EXPANSION OF THE NETWORK

In light of the popularity of stand-up comedy, HBO developed the Comedy Channel, which debuted in 1989—the same year that Time Inc. merged with Warner Cable, a division of Warner Communications, creating the largest media corporation in the world. ATC was merged with Warner Cable in 1992, forming Time Warner Cable. Initially, the Comedy Channel broadcast excerpts from movies, situation comedies, and stand-up routines. Viacom's comedy channel, HA!, chose instead to broadcast entire segments of sitcoms. The two merged in 1990 to form Comedy Central.

Despite predictions that cable channels and pay-per-view television could not last, HBO expanded into licensing rights to broadcast sporting events, such as rights to the logo for the World Cup. By 1993, licensing comprised 28 percent of HBO revenues. That same year, HBO provided its parent company with eight percent of pretax profit. The company also moved into foreign markets, which helped to maintain profits.

In 1997, HBO made television history by becoming the first cable channel to garner more Emmy nominations—ninety—than any of the major broadcast networks. NBC narrowly took home the most awards that year. True success in the awards game, however, occurred only after the 1999 premier of *The Sopranos*.

In 2008 HBO experienced a major shakeup, with twenty-two-year veteran Carolyn Strauss stepping down as president of the entertainment division, though she continued to have a role in the company. That same year Chris Albrecht lost his position as chairman. Jobs were shuffled within the company, and Naegle, the first outsider to be hired at HBO in years, came on board.

## CHANGING THE SCOPE OF HBO

Naegle accepted the presidency of HBO Entertainment just as the phenomenally successful *The Sopranos*—which David Chase, a United Talent Agency client, had packaged, and Strauss had shepherded—was ending its run. A bit of a risk for the company, Naegle had no experience in developing or programming shows. She later claimed that her learning curve was vertical.

Hopes were high that Naegle could create another HBO original series hit at the success level of shows such as *Sex and the City* and *The Sopranos*. However, when Naegle began, she minimized the importance of doing so in an interview with Jacques Steinberg for the *New York Times* (10 Apr. 2008). "Not every show needs to reach the same size of audience, or same width, of a 'Sopranos,'" she said.

Naegle changed the process that HBO used to develop shows. Rather than making a pilot and waiting for audience reaction before developing the next show, she rolled out several new series at once, making sure always to have something in the pipeline. "We needed some choices," told Melissa Grego for *Broadcasting & Cable* (27 Apr. 2009). "In the past they would make a pilot, then pick it up and wait to try something new. It resulted in some amazing shows, but also left the pipeline empty and too much pressure on certain shows to work. To have so much pressure on something to go to series was not what I thought was an ideal way to work."

Naegle also broadened HBO's focus, adding comedy to the lineup. She told Andrea Morabito for *Broadcasting & Cable* (4 Apr. 2011), "Comedy's really difficult. It's difficult to develop, it's difficult to execute. A lot of people think that these higher-end, bigger-in-scope dramas are more difficult, but I would argue that comedy is as difficult to get right." Naegle's appreciation for comedy may be based at least in part on her admiration for comedian Flip Wilson, to whom she refers as an inspiration. Other sources of ideas include shopping malls and amusement parks. She has also added shows that feature strong male leads. As competition between the networks—namely HBO, Showtime, Starz, and AMC—has increased, this diversity has been necessary to retain market share.

### THE IMPORTANCE OF WRITERS

In addition, Naegle has encouraged more group processes. As she explained to Grego in another article for *Broadcasting and Cable* (27 Apr. 2009), "I ask for a lot more togetherness. We spend time talking about the scripts, and I am interested in anyone's view as long as they can make their case." At the same time, she has not been averse to retooling ideas, suggesting to Grego that another show similar to *Sex and the City* would be welcomed. She recalled gathering with women friends to watch the show and wanted to be able to offer that experience to others. With shows such as *Enlightened*, *Girls*, and *Veep*, she has succeeded.

In an interview with Gary Levin for *USA Today* (9 Apr. 2008) Naegle stated, "Everything starts with a great script, and I've been able to work with great writers and encourage them to do good work." Some of the writers in her stable, along with Alan Ball and Aaron Sorkin, have included big names such as Noah Baumbach, Jim Carrey, Martin Scorsese, and Tom Wolfe.

Naegle was optimistic about the future of HBO at the time she joined the network. "The strength of the place is it's been a haven for smart writers," she told Levin, "and I think that will continue." An insomniac, she continues to read—for pleasure as well as for work, always on the lookout for the next edgy show to bring to the network. She was the one who championed the fantasy *Game of Thrones* for HBO, which premiered in 2011. "[T]he hunger for knowing is what excites me. I get to geek out about editing, be on set, give notes to writers—I love it all," Naegle told Stacey Wilson. Combined with Cinemax, another Time-Warner cable company, HBO had reached approximately 114 million subscribers worldwide by early 2013—thanks in part to Naegle's approach.

### PERSONAL LIFE

Naegle is known for understated wardrobe choices from Rag and Bone or J. Crew. She lives with her husband, writer and actor/comedian Dana Gould—who has written for such shows as *The Simpsons*—in Los Angeles. They met in 1996 at Kathy Griffin's annual Christmas party. The couple has three daughters whom they adopted from China.

### SUGGESTED READING

Grego, Melissa. "Sue Naegle's New Recipe for HBO." *Broadcasting & Cable*. NewBay Media, 27 Apr. 2009. Web. 12 Mar. 2013.

Lafayette, Jon. "New Chief Unpacks HBO Pilots." *Television Week*. Crain Communications, 14 Apr. 2008. Web. 12 Mar. 2013.

Morabito, Andrea. "Programming Outside the Box." *Broadcasting & Cable*. NewBay Media, 4 Apr. 2011. Web. 12 Mar. 2013.

Schneider, Michael, and Josef Adalian. "Naegle Looks to Rev up HBO Skeins." *Variety* 14 Apr. 2008: 16. Print.

Wilson, Stacey. "Why HBO's Sue Naegle Didn't Lose Sleep Over 'Homeland's' Big Wins." *Hollywood Reporter*. Hollywood Reporter, 5 Dec. 2012. Web. 12 Mar. 2013.

—*Judy Johnson*

---

# Adela Navarro Bello

**Born:** 1968
**Occupation:** Journalist, general director of *Zeta* magazine

Adela Navarro Bello is an award-winning Mexican journalist and the general director of the Baja California weekly magazine *Zeta*. According to the nonprofit Reporters Without Borders, Mexico is one of the deadliest countries to work as a journalist. Navarro and her staff operate out of Tijuana, where she was born and raised. The city, located just across the US–Mexican border from San Diego on the Baja California peninsula, is historically known for its Prohibition-era cantinas, gambling, and prostitution. In the late

© César René Blanco Villalón

1980s, however, the city's illicit activities became much more sinister. Competing drug cartels—a part of northern Mexico's ongoing drug wars that have killed nearly 100,000 people—ravaged the city. The carnage, at its height, was difficult to fathom. William Finnegan for the *New Yorker* (18 Oct. 2010) reported: "During the last three months of 2008, nearly five hundred people were murdered here [in Tijuana], many in gruesome public displays: decapitations, dismemberments, corpses left hanging from bridges, piles of bodies with their tongues cut out. There were daylight shoot-outs between gangs using automatic weapons and rocket-propelled grenade launchers in downtown streets and shopping malls." In early 2007, the newly elected (now former) President Felipe Calderón sent in the Mexican army.

Civilian life has marginally improved in the city—though some worry that the relative calm indicates a larger organized crime operation, made up of several cartels that used to be at war—but violence and corruption still abound. Nowhere is this more apparent than in the city's news organizations. Only a handful of news outlets report on the daily violence in Tijuana; others will only report official government statements, and a disturbing number ignore events altogether for fear of retaliation. That fear is not unwarranted; according to the Press Freedom Index 2012, conditions for journalists have gotten worse in the past five years. Members of the media are commonly threatened, wounded, or killed in Tijuana almost without impunity; *Zeta* alone has lost two editors and a bodyguard to cartel assassins, most of whom are still at large. Many publications believe that self-censorship is the only way to survive. According to Arian Campo-Flores for *Newsweek* (1 Oct. 2010), the Mexican daily *El Diario de Juarez* "[felt]

compelled to publish front-page pleas to the cartels to 'explain what you want from us.'"

*Zeta* has taken on enormous risk for choosing not to bend to the will of the cartels. Staffers have gone so far as to publish the names and personal information of drug lords and corrupt officials, as well as (often lurid) details of their crimes. Though the magazine has been criticized for unduly praising the military (a charge that Navarro denies), the weekly tabloid's investigative journalism is unparalleled in Tijuana. Navarro is careful about her work—she does not discuss how many children she has, and the magazine's office, located on a quiet residential street, is protected by an armed guard—but she is also passionate. "I don't want to sound irresponsible, to say we are not afraid," she told Peter Rowe for the *San Diego Union-Tribune* (2 Dec. 2011). "But we know what we have to do. We know there is a risk in doing what we do. But the only way we can make a difference is through investigative journalism. That's our role."

## EARLY LIFE AND EDUCATION

Navarro was born in Tijuana in 1968. Her father, who worked as a rug merchant, was an avid newspaper reader and would read Navarro stories out loud before she could read. The practice instilled in her a passion for both writing and the news. Because she loved to write, as a child she often communicated with her father through letters even though they lived in the same house. Still, her first aspiration was the law; however, she told Julie Mandoyan for the *Global Journal* (18 May 2012) that lawyers had a poor reputation in Mexico during the 1980s. She eventually settled on journalism, "the best of both worlds," she told Mandoyan. "Through journalism, I could work towards social justice, open a window for those who are victims of injustice and publicly denounce what was happening to them."

Navarro studied communications in college. During her first semester, she researched news organizations in Baja California and decided that *Zeta* was the outlet that offered its journalists the most freedom to pursue the news that she was most passionate about: the government and crime. While Navarro was still a student, J. Jésus Blancornelas, *Zeta*'s cofounder and general director, visited her campus as a lecturer. She approached him and asked him for a job. He asked if she wanted to cover arts and entertainment. "No, no, no" she replied, according to Rowe. "I want politics."

## *ZETA* WEEKLY

Blancornelas and Héctor Félix Miranda founded *Zeta* in 1980. In 1977, Blancornelas had cofounded another muckraking weekly called *ABC*. The short-lived magazine printed articles about corrupt border officials but it was stormed by state police, who claimed they were intervening in a labor dispute, in 1979. At the time, journalists were censored and oppressed by Mexican government officials; the threat of censorship still exists although it pales in comparison to the visceral threats of cartel hit men. As a precaution against the forcible shutdown of *Zeta*, the weekly is printed in the United States in nearby San Diego. *Zeta* covered its very first drug-trafficking story in 1985. In 1988, Héctor Félix Miranda was shot and killed while driving to work. A man named Antonio Vera Palestina, the bodyguard of Jorge Hank Rhon, a prominent Tijuana businessman about whom Félix often wrote, was jailed for the crime. Rhon, who later became the mayor of Tijuana, has denied his involvement in the shooting. Still, since Félix's death, each issue of *Zeta* has included a full-page ad, featuring a photograph of Félix pointing at the viewer, asking Rhon, "Why did your bodyguard Antonio Vera Palestina kill me?"

Navarro began working for *Zeta* in 1990 and was named a member of the editorial staff in 1993. In 1994, she began writing her column, called *Sortilegioz* or "Charms" (the added "z" is a playful flourish). In 1999, the United States Information Agency invited Navarro to the United States to report on migration issues and American foreign policy. As part of her tour, she met with Immigration and Naturalization Service officials, observed Border Patrol training, and visited nongovernmental organizations. The experience, Navarro told Bill Manson for the *San Diego Reader* (23 Sept. 1999), allowed her to largely and objectively "understand the political apparatus regarding migration." Her newly enlightened opinion of that apparatus however, was quite low. Despite the kindness of the officials she encountered during her trip, particularly during Border Patrol training, she found a vast chasm between what officials were trained to do versus what they did in the field. "When they graduate and get to the border," she told Manson, "it's like two separate worlds."

## AN ASSASSINATION ATTEMPT AND TWO MURDERS

In 1997, Blancornelas was riding in his car, driven by his bodyguard Luis Valero Elizalde, when six gunmen of the Arellano-Félix cartel surrounded them on three sides and opened fire. Blancornelas, who was sixty-one, was shot in the hand and through his torso, where the bullet passed through his stomach, liver, and lung. Valero threw the car in reverse to escape the deluge, but was shot many times in the process. After the gunmen had fled, Blancornelas found his walkie-talkie and called for help. Valero died minutes later. Blancornelas spent three months in the hospital, and after arduous physical therapy, was able to walk with a cane. Navarro was in the office the day the Blancornelas's call

came through on the radio and rushed to the hospital. During his recovery, she kept the paper running.

In 2004, editor Francisco Javier Ortiz Franco was murdered as he was leaving a health clinic with his two young children. Ortiz had recently reported that drug traffickers were able to obtain fake IDs from the state attorney general. After the killing, Blancornelas decided that each drug-trafficking story would have his name in the byline regardless its actual author. Blancornelas was surrounded by bodyguards twenty-four hours a day and reasoned that he could handle the added risk. After Blancornelas died of cancer in 2006, stories about the cartels have featured the generic byline *Investigaciones Zeta* or "Zeta Investigations."

Before his death, Blancornelas appointed Navarro and his son César René Blanco Villalón as *Zeta*'s copublishers and senior editors. (Navarro has since taken over as the paper's public face.) The two debated whether to continue covering the cartels. Henchmen were killing reporters almost with impunity—despite overwhelming evidence no arrests were made in the murders of Valero or Ortiz. But Navarro knew they had little choice but to report what was happening all around them, particularly as other news outlets refused to do so. "Every time a journalist self-censors," she told Anne-Marie O'Connor for the *Washington Post* (26 Oct. 2011), "the whole society loses."

## NAVARRO'S *ZETA* AND NEW PRECAUTIONS

"Adela really has nerves of steel," Andrew Selee, the former director of the Mexico Institute at the Woodrow Wilson Center in Washington, DC, told Rowe of Navarro. "She is driven by the mission of the newspaper that she inherited, to publish the truth at all costs." In January 2010, a US law-enforcement official informed Navarro that the Arellano cartel was plotting to kill the top editors of *Zeta*. The threat, which was uncovered through an intercepted phone call, was confirmed and the Mexican army sent seven soldiers to guard the editors, including Navarro, around the clock for more than two months until the suspects were arrested. Navarro, who prides herself on keeping her work and home life completely separate, did not appreciate the invasion but realized its necessity. It was difficult to leave her house with a security detail, but it was even more difficult, she found, to do her job. Traveling with several armed guards hindered her ability to observe, interact with sources, and report.

Though Navarro no longer has a personal bodyguard, she has instituted a number of new safety precautions. *Zeta* staffers run background checks on new sources and an editorial board vets stories before reporters begin working on them. The *Zeta* building has its own private guard. Visitors must be on a list and then speak with a receptionist behind a bulletproof window to enter the office. Navarro routinely risks her life for a story, but she is quick to add to Rowe: "I am not a martyr."

Navarro appears in a documentary about *Zeta* called *Reportero*. Directed by Bernardo Ruiz, the film premiered on January 7, 2013, on PBS. Ruiz and his crew began filming in 2007. Despite the inherent dangers of documenting the goings-on behind closed doors at *Zeta*, Navarro believes that the film has proved helpful to the paper's cause on an international level. "The documentary, as well as the recognition of other international groups, is a form of protection for us," she said, as translated in a January 15, 2013, video on the *Reportero* website.

For all of *Zeta*'s good work, it does face criticism. Some say that the tabloid paints too rosy a picture of the army by omitting or downplaying allegations of corruption and torture within its ranks. Navarro denies these charges. Others have accused *Zeta* of sensationalizing cartel violence and playing into the hands of drug lords by making readers fearful of them. Ruiz does not agree with this assessment. He believes that Navarro and other *Zeta* reporters are attempting to humanize the violence in Tijuana, though he told an interviewer for the Latino Broadcasting Community website (13 Dec. 2012) that they were indeed "stuck between a rock and a hard place." He asked, "Are you fueling the violence by covering it? Do you pretend the drug war isn't happening and avoid covering the story?"

**PERSONAL LIFE**

Navarro is married to Carlos Mora, an executive at Mayan Resorts, a resort hotel chain. The two met in 1998 when Mora was running for Tijuana City Council. Navarro criticized him in *Zeta*, but Mora was drawn to her. When they met in person, Mora approached her and said, as quoted by Rowe, that he was her "fan Number One." Navarro replied that her number-one fan was her father and walked away. The two were married seven years later. (Navarro was previously married to a journalist who worked for the Tijuana newspaper, *Frontera*.) She has said that she has a daughter and has alluded to other children, though she refuses to be more specific for fear of endangering them. The family lives in Playas de Tijuana, a seaside suburb.

In 2012, Navarro was named one of Newsweek's 150 Women Who Shake the World. She also received the International Press Freedom award from the Committee to Protect Journalists in 2007 and the Courage in Journalism award from the International Women's Media Foundation in 2011. Internationally, she has been awarded the 2008 Ortega y Gasset Prize in Spain, the 2009 International Prize of Freedom of the Press in Argentina, and the Anna Politkovskaya Prize in Italy in 2009.

**SUGGESTED READING**

Finnegan, William. "Letter from Tijuana: In the Name of the Law." *New Yorker* 18 Oct. 2010. Web. 6 July 2013.

Manson, Bill. "Adela Does America." *San Diego Reader* 23 Sept. 1999. Web. 6 July 2013.

Navarro Bello, Adela. Interview by Julie Mandoyan. *Global Journal* 18 May 2012. Web. 7 July 2013.

O'Connor, Anne-Marie. "A Tijuana Editor's Peril-Filled Passion." *Washington Post* 27 Oct. 2011. Web. 5 July 2013.

Rowe, Peter. "A Mexican Journalist in the Crosshairs: Zeta's Adela Navarro Bello Persists in Risky Mission." *San Diego Union-Tribune* 2 Dec. 2011. Web. 5 July 2013.

—*Molly Hagan*

# Soraya Sarhaddi Nelson

**Occupation:** Foreign correspondent for National Public Radio

Soraya Sarhaddi Nelson has spent decades covering some of the world's most perilous regions, first as a foreign correspondent for various newspapers and then for National Public Radio (NPR). Her in-depth stories about the Middle East have earned her numerous awards and a legion of listeners drawn to her ability to make the most complicated stories comprehensible and humane. Since joining NPR in 2006, Nelson has covered the complexities of the war zones in Afghanistan and Iraq, stood with protesters fighting for more freedom and opportunity in Egypt, and watched as young women sought the right to vote in Saudi Arabia. Her work has been dangerous, not only because she is an American reporter working in nations that are often unfriendly to the United States but also because she is a woman reporting in strongly male-dominated cultures. Yet despite the dangers, which have included nearly being executed in Iraq as an American spy, she believes the risks she faces every day are both necessary and far less than those that her subjects face—be they US soldiers fighting to clear a Taliban stronghold in Afghanistan, protesters being clubbed or tear-gassed by riot police, or young girls seeking an education in a culture that forbids it. During her address as the 2011 Lovejoy Award recipient at Colby College (16 Oct. 2011), she recalled, "I became a foreign correspondent because I wanted to connect Americans to the rest of the world through compelling storytelling. And yes, to me it's worth it, even if it means a few premature gray hairs for my husband."

© Steve Barrett

## EARLY LIFE AND CAREER

Soraya Sarhaddi Nelson was born in Wisconsin, the daughter of an Iranian-born father. In 1985 she completed her education at the Philip Merrill College of Journalism at the University of Maryland in College Park, one of the top schools for undergraduates looking to pursue careers as reporters. Following her graduation, she became a newspaper reporter, starting out at the *Star Democrat*, a local daily newspaper in Easton, Maryland.

One of her first notable achievements as a reporter came during her three-year tenure as a reporter and editor for *Newsday*, a widely read daily newspaper that serves Nassau and Suffolk counties on Long Island, New York, and parts of New York City. With *Newsday* she reported on TWA Flight 800, a commercial jetliner that exploded and crashed in the Atlantic Ocean off Long Island on July 17, 1996, following its takeoff from New York's John F. Kennedy International Airport. All 230 people aboard were killed. Nelson and several of her *Newsday* colleagues earned the prestigious Pulitzer Prize for spot news reporting in 1997 for their coverage of the disaster.

Nelson then worked for a period at the *Los Angeles Times*, one of the largest metropolitan newspapers in the United States. She would later work for Santa Ana's daily *Orange County Register*, for which she reported on the prison system, state house, and administration of California governor Arnold Schwarzenegger, whose tenure as the state's chief executive lasted from 2003 to 2011.

## FOREIGN CORRESPONDENT

During her tenure at the *Los Angeles Times*, Nelson served as a foreign correspondent in Afghanistan and Iran. Her work as the newspaper publisher Knight Ridder's Middle East bureau chief from 2002 to 2005 also often had her reporting on Iran. Both of these assignments came in the wake of the al-Qaeda–sponsored terrorist attacks of September 11, 2001, which killed nearly three thousand at the World Trade Center in New York, the Pentagon in Washington, DC, and a hijacked jetliner in Shanksville, Pennsylvania. Following these attacks, the US government under President George W. Bush (2001–9) sought to deter additional terrorist attacks on the United States by waging war in Afghanistan and Iraq, where Nelson often worked as a foreign correspondent.

During these overseas assignments, Nelson often found herself in great danger. She recalled one particularly unnerving incident in her 2011 Lovejoy Award address: "I was arrested in 2004 in Iraq by the Mahdi Army run by radical Shiite cleric Muqtada al Sadr. I was the lone Western reporter in Najaf, which was under Sadr's control at the time. . . . Unbeknownst to me, Sadr's religious court in Najaf held a trial with me in absentia. The judges issued an execution warrant for me claiming I was an American spy. For more than six frantic hours, I pleaded with the black-clad gunmen to not take me to nearby Kufa Mosque where such executions were being carried out." She ultimately was released when Iranians working with Sadr became aware of her Iranian heritage. The danger did not abate when she returned to Baghdad, however; as she told Joseph Contreras and Rod Nordland for *Newsweek* (18 Oct. 2004), "There is no sense of safety anywhere in Baghdad. Journalists have become targets."

## MOVING TO RADIO

In 2006 Nelson became a foreign correspondent for the nonprofit media corporation National Public Radio (NPR). Aiding her in her transition from print to broadcast journalism was Loren Jenkins, Nelson's foreign editor at NPR, who spent a month helping to train her in editing audio recordings, writing transcripts, and voicing stories. By the end of the month, Nelson found herself in Afghanistan in the deepest part of winter, trying to record her stories with the electric generator switched off so its noise would not bleed into the background.

Because her work as a foreign correspondent has required her to spend a great deal of time in conservative Islamic countries such as Afghanistan, Iran, and Iraq, Nelson has frequently worn a full-body cloak called a burka (or burqa) or an abaya (a cloaklike dress) and a niqab (a face veil covering all but the eyes) while out in public. With the burka, a piece of transparent cloth is worn over the eyes, covering them but allowing the woman wearing the burka to see, although with limited peripheral vision. In strict Islamic countries, as Afghanistan was under the Taliban, women are required by law to be fully covered whenever they are outside their homes or in the presence of nonrelated men.

Although many women questioned her decision to wear a burka, Nelson felt that doing so was a necessary part of her job. "My rule is to defer to local customs and not become part of the story by drawing attention to myself, which would have happened if I had not worn a burka in most of Afghanistan's provinces," Nelson explained in her address. "Plus, the opaque polyester garment does offer anonymity when you are traveling in places where Taliban sympathizers would rather kidnap or behead you as opposed to being agreed to be interviewed with a big, furry microphone." In a June 10, 2009, interview with Renee Montagne for the NPR program *Morning Edition*, Nelson also noted, "When you explain to them [local Afghans], well, it's out of a sign of respect; it's out of, you know, protection for the people that I'm working with, then they calm down about it and it actually, you know, increases the rapport. You're able to have a dialogue with them and create some kind of connection."

### AWARD-WINNING STORIES

Nelson's stories have aired on a variety of NPR's programs—most notably *Morning Edition* and *All Things Considered*, the station's award-winning news programs that air during the morning and afternoon rush hours, respectively. After coming to NPR in 2006, Nelson established the station's permanent bureau in Kabul, the capital of Afghanistan. In addition to covering US and North Atlantic Treaty Organization (NATO) forces fighting in Afghanistan, she used her time there to gain a better understanding of Afghan society. She explained to Ricchiardi, "To help people understand why the war is going the way it is and why issues are the way they are, you need to talk to Afghans." Some of her stories have described the ways in which women have sought to develop their own identities and receive education in the years since coalition forces pushed the Taliban from power following the 2001 invasion. Others depict the ways in which many Afghans struggle with drug addiction, despite Islam's prohibitions against alcohol and drug use.

Nelson's work in Afghanistan earned her numerous awards, including the 2009 Lowell Thomas Award from the Overseas Press Club of America, a 2009 George Foster Peabody Award, and a 2010 Gracie Award, all of which were shared with her editors, Loren Jenkins and Doug Roberts. She was also granted an honorary doctorate of laws from Colby College in 2011. The Overseas Press Club, in its 2009 citation, noted that her "original and poignant stories about the lives of the Afghan people demonstrate her enterprise and ability to penetrate a complicated

society." The 2009 Peabody Award citation proclaims that Nelson's news stories "allow listeners to realize how narrow the parameters of American television coverage can be. . . . One day she may enlighten listeners about the 'creative' ways Kabul residents keep precious electricity flowing to their homes, another day she could be in a remote village trying to sort out whether civilian deaths in a battle were caused by the Taliban or US troops." Her 2010 Gracie Award was presented for her two-part story on opium and heroin addiction in Afghanistan. The story powerfully illustrated the wide reach of drug addiction by portraying a mother of six whose addiction prevented her from caring for her children and a nine-year-old boy who sought to rid himself of his heroin addiction for two years.

### A SOLDIER'S STORY

In early 2010 Nelson experienced the cold realities of warfare while she was traveling with US marines from India Company of the Third Battalion, Sixth Marine Regiment in Marjah in southern Afghanistan. The region was a hotbed of Taliban activity, and US and coalition troops often found themselves under sniper fire or removing hidden improvised explosive devises, or IEDs. During the time she was embedded with the regiment, she became friendly with Lance Corporal Alejandro Yazzie. Yazzie, who was twenty-three years old and from the Navajo Nation, was recently married and expecting a baby with his wife. Nelson described Yazzie to Montagne on *Morning Edition* (4 Mar. 2010): "What struck me about him, unlike the others, he was a little quieter, he was a little shyer, but very sincere, very nice . . . I could tell when he would just mention that he wanted to talk to his wife, his eyes would just light up in a way that I knew he was very much in love with her."

As the members of the regiment were out on patrol, they were ambushed. Nelson turned on her tape recorder so she could capture as much of the firefight as possible and watched as Lance Corporal Yazzie was struck and killed by a sniper's bullet. She discussed the attack, which was captured on tape and broadcast on NPR, with Montagne: "There were people crying and—I mean, I really wanted to portray this. I felt it was very important to chronicle what sacrifices these guys make. I mean, I felt it was part of this story of this patrol that had such a hard time just taking less than a half mile of land."

### COVERING THE ARAB SPRING

In July 2010 Nelson transferred from Afghanistan to Egypt, serving as bureau chief for NPR's Cairo office. Because she was based out of Cairo, the capital of Egypt, Nelson was an eyewitness to much of the Arab Spring, a wave of protests and demonstrations, both violent and nonviolent, that have spread across the Islamic world since January 2011, removing many long-time political leaders from power and sparking numerous civil uprisings and civil wars. As of mid-2013, leaders in Yemen, Egypt, Libya, and Tunisia have been removed from power, while protests of varying degrees have occurred in Syria, Algeria, Iraq, Jordan, Kuwait, Morocco, Sudan, Mauritania, Oman, Saudi Arabia, Djibouti, and Western Sahara. Most of the demonstrators are protesting the centralization of authority and the lack of political and economic opportunities in their countries. The protesters, who are mostly young, have used social media to help organize their movements. Many have been violently assaulted by forces loyal to their governments.

Nelson has been at the center of it all, capturing not only the large patterns of these national movements but also the more human stories. In Saudi Arabia she accompanied a group of women attempting to register at a voter registration center, even though women are not allowed to vote in the kingdom's largely symbolic elections. In Tunisia and Egypt she witnessed young people struggling against soldiers armed with batons, guns, and tear gas in order to procure more freedom and economic opportunity for themselves. One of her more surreal moments occurred in Libya, while she and other reporters were staying at the Rixos Hotel in Tripoli, the Libyan capital, as NATO forces bombed the city. In her Lovejoy Award address she recalled the challenges of objective reporting amid the conflict: "We were often forced to rely on government-organized excursions aimed at casting [now-ousted dictator Muammar] Gadhafi in the best light. Our minders would load us onto buses and take us to see staged rallies. On occasion they would show us rusty old bombs with Russian markings they would claim were dropped by NATO. They even used the same people to pose as ordinary Libyans for us to interview at different events in different places, as if we wouldn't notice." In the summer of 2012 Nelson moved on to assignments first in Kabul and then Berlin, Germany, ceding her place in Egypt to NPR newcomer Leila Fadel. However, she returned to Egypt to cover the unrest surrounding the ouster of President Mohammed Morsi by the Egyptian military in July 2013.

Nelson is married to fellow reporter Erik Nelson, with whom she has one son. She is a multilingual conversant in German, Farsi (Persian), and Dari, a Farsi dialect spoken in parts of Afghanistan.

## SUGGESTED READING

Brown, Emerson. "NPR News Wins Three 2010 Gracie Awards for Outstanding Series, Documentary and Podcast." *NPR*. National Public Radio, 24 Feb. 2010. Web. 25 July 2013.

Nelson, Soraya Sarhaddi. "2011 Lovejoy Award Recipient Soraya Sarhaddi Nelson." *Goldfarb Center for Public Affairs and Civic Engagement*. Colby College, 16 Oct. 2011. Web. 25 July 2013.

Nelson, Soraya Sarhaddi, and Renee Montagne. "Experiencing Life, Death with Marines in Marjah." *NPR*. National Public Radio, 4 Mar. 2010. Web. 25 July 2013.

Nelson, Soraya Sarhaddi, and Renee Montagne. "Reporting on, Living in Afghanistan." *NPR*. National Public Radio, 10 June 2009. Web. 25 July 2013.

Ricchiardi, Sherry. "Offscreen." *American Journalism Review* 30.5 (2008): 16–23. Print.

"Soraya Sarhaddi Nelson, International Correspondent, Cairo." *NPR*. National Public Radio, 2013. Web. 25 July 2013.

—*Christopher Mari*

# Cam Newton

**Born:** May 11, 1989
**Occupation:** Football player

Cam Newton of the Carolina Panthers is "android-perfect, a video-game avatar of a quarterback," Brett Martin wrote for *GQ* (Sept. 2012). Standing at six feet five inches and weighing 245 pounds, Newton possesses a combination of size, speed, power, and skills that clearly distinguishes him from other quarterbacks in the National Football League (NFL). Newton "is that thing known as the Whole Package," Martin continued. "On the field, a tantalizing glimpse of the One—a player who unifies the speed of the great modern running QBs like Michael Vick with the pocket skills of more traditional passers like Tom Brady. Off it, a star in the making."

Newton had a nomadic, scandal-plagued, and equally decorated college career that saw him spend two seasons at the University of Florida, one season at Blinn College in Texas, and a final season at Auburn University, where he won a Heisman Trophy and national championship. He was then selected by the Panthers as the number-one overall pick in the 2011 NFL Draft, but entered the league as an "enigma, a player with unquestioned physical tools but a questionable past," as Viv Bernstein noted for the *New York Times* (26 Aug. 2012). Newton became the first rookie quarterback in NFL history to pass for more than four thousand yards (4,051), the first player in league history with at least four thousand passing yards and five hundred rushing yards (706) in the same season, and set the league record for most rushing touchdowns by a quarterback (fourteen) in the same season, while breaking numerous other rookie and league records. He was named the 2011 Associated Press (AP) NFL Offensive Rookie of the Year and

© Chris Keane/Reuters/Corbis

earned a Pro Bowl selection as a reserve for the National Football Conference (NFC) squad.

Newton's statistics regressed slightly in 2012, when he threw for 3,869 yards and nineteen touchdowns, but led the Panthers with a career-high 741 rushing yards. While some have questioned Newton's maturity and leadership abilities, others believe he has the potential to redefine the quarterback position and make a lasting impact on the league. "Cam, his style of quarterbacking, I think it can go to another level," the Panthers coach Ron Rivera told Bernstein. "He's got some special attributes, combined with his size and his arm strength and his athleticism. He's just a different type of quarterback that we haven't seen in this league."

## EARLY LIFE AND EDUCATION

The middle of the three sons of Cecil Newton Sr. and Jackie (Wilder) Newton, Cameron Jerrell Newton was born on May 11, 1989 in Atlanta, Georgia. He grew up in College Park, an Atlanta suburb, in a religious, tight-knit family. His father, a Pentecostal minister, had met his mother, a former longtime AT&T employee, while attending Savannah State University, where he was an All-American safety and linebacker for the school's football team. After going undrafted out of college, Cecil Newton Sr. participated in the preseason camps of the NFL's Dallas Cowboys and Buffalo Bills in 1983 and 1984, respectively, but ultimately failed to make those teams' regular-season rosters.

Newton developed a passion for football early in life, and as a boy, spent countless hours playing catch with his father, who quickly recognized his special athletic ability. "He was throwing with such velocity," his father recalled to Phillip Marshall, in an undated article for the Auburn University sports fan site *Auburn Undercover*. "It would sting your hands, and he never seemed to get tired." Newton, like most NFL players, began his career playing Pop Warner football. At age seven he joined the North Clayton Eagles, a team comprised mostly of nine- and ten-year-olds and which included the future NFL player Morgan Burnett. Because of his large size, Newton initially started out playing tight end and linebacker before switching to the quarterback position. His competitive drive was such that he would try to score even while the "mercy rule"—which limits the scoring in lopsided games—was in effect.

Newton attended Seaborn Lee Elementary School and Camp Creek Middle School, both in College Park. According to accounts given by several of his former teachers, the hyperactive and popular Newton struggled academically, mainly because he was more focused on entertaining his classmates than completing homework assignments. As a student at Camp Creek, Newton boldly declared to his teachers that he would one day become a professional football player.

## HIGH SCHOOL FOOTBALL

In 2003, Newton enrolled at Westlake High School in Atlanta, which had a nationally known football program. As a freshman, he initially played quarterback for the junior varsity squad, but was later moved up to varsity as a backup quarterback during that season's playoffs. At that time, his older brother, Cecil Jr., who is three years older, was Westlake's senior starting center. (Cecil Jr. would earn a scholarship as a walk-on center at Tennessee State University before having off-season and practice-squad stints with several NFL teams from 2009 to 2012.)

Newton, who also played basketball in high school, earned several starts at quarterback for Westlake's varsity squad during his sophomore season, when the squad's starting and backup quarterbacks suffered injuries. It was not until his junior season that he blossomed into his full athletic potential. Around that time, Newton, who had already impressed coaches with his arm strength, pocket presence, instincts, and unflappable demeanor, underwent a growth spurt that added three inches and fifteen pounds to a once-lanky frame, putting him at six feet three inches tall and 205 pounds. "He just exploded," his high-school coach Dallas Allen noted to Thayer Evans for *Fox Sports* (10 Jan. 2011). As a junior, in his first season as a full-time starting quarterback, Newton threw for 2,500 yards and twenty-three touchdowns and rushed for 638 yards and nine touchdowns.

After establishing himself as one of the top dual-threat quarterbacks in the nation, Newton was recruited heavily by a number of NCAA Division I-A schools. Some of those schools, however, wanted to convert him from quarterback to tight end or defensive lineman, positions they felt would better suit his size and physical abilities. Therefore, Newton chose to accept a scholarship to the University of Florida (UF) in Gainesville, after then coach Urban Meyer guaranteed him an opportunity to compete for the starting quarterback position.

## UNIVERSITY OF FLORIDA

When Newton began his freshman season at Florida in the fall of 2007, the Gators were coming off an NCAA Bowl Championship Series (BCS) national title victory and looking to defend their title under the guidance of another immensely talented dual-threat quarterback, sophomore phenomenon Tim Tebow. Relegated to serving as Tebow's backup, Newton only appeared in five games, in which he passed for 40 yards on ten attempts and rushed for 103 yards on sixteen carries. Meanwhile, Tebow enjoyed one of the greatest regular seasons by a college quarterback in history and became the first sophomore to win the Heisman Trophy, awarded annually to the nation's best player.

Newton served as Tebow's backup again as a sophomore in 2008, but only appeared in the season opener before suffering an ankle injury. He was subsequently granted redshirted status (in order to maintain his remaining three years of college eligibility) for the rest of the 2008 season, which culminated with the Gators winning their second BSC national championship in three years.

Newton's already disappointing Gators' tenure was further complicated by two incidents: in November 2008 he was arrested for being in the possession of a stolen laptop, and later, was implicated in an academic cheating investigation. For the laptop incident, Newton was suspended indefinitely from the football team, but criminal charges (for grand larceny and obstruction of justice) against him were dropped after he completed a pretrial diversion program for first-time offenders.

## TRANSFER TO BLINN COLLEGE

Meanwhile, as he faced possible expulsion for his alleged academic cheating, and yet another season backing up Tebow (who returned for his senior season), Newton decided to leave Florida and transfer to Blinn College, a two-year junior college in Brenham, Texas. There, he revived his career under head coach Brad Franchione, who immediately designated him as the team's starting quarterback.

In his one season playing for Blinn, Newton passed for 2,833 yards and twenty-two touchdowns and rushed for 655 yards and sixteen touchdowns, leading the team to an 11–1 record and the 2009 National Junior College Athletic Association (NJCAA) national football title. He earned NJCAA honorable mention All-America honors and became the most recruited junior college quarterback in the nation. Newton has said that his time at Blinn allowed him to grow and mature as a man. "There were times at Florida that I just did immature things," he told Andy Staples for *Sports Illustrated* (28 May 2010). "I took a lot of stuff for granted. Being at Blinn, it humbled me . . . I was hard-headed, young and dumb."

## TRIUMPH AND TURMOIL AT AUBURN UNIVERSITY

After courting scholarship offers from such football powerhouses as the University of Arizona, the University of Oklahoma, and Mississippi State University, Newton chose to enroll at Auburn University, in Alabama, which he felt put him "in the best situation to play for the national championship," as he told Staples. Newton quickly picked up head coach Gene Chizik's hurry-up style offense, which catered to his explosive dual-threat abilities as a runner and passer, and he was named Auburn's starting quarterback in the spring of 2010.

That fall, during his junior season, Newton not only emerged as the best quarterback in the highly competitive Southeastern Conference (SEC) but also as the best college player in the country. In fourteen starts for Auburn, he passed for 2,854 yards and an SEC-record thirty touchdowns and led the team with 1,473 rushing yards and a school-record twenty touchdowns. He earned first-team All-America honors and was named SEC offensive player of the year. Newton also became only the third Auburn player to win the coveted Heisman Trophy Award (after Pat Sullivan in 1971 and Bo Jackson in 1985), and swept most of the other major college football awards, including the Maxwell Award and Davey O'Brien Award. Meanwhile, he helped Auburn rise from the bottom of the BCS top-25 rankings to the number-one team in the country, leading them to a perfect 12–0 regular-season record, an SEC title, and the 2010 BCS national championship.

In the midst of his glorious Heisman Trophy and BCS national title run, Newton found himself "embroiled in one of the most controversial issues in NCAA history," as Thayer Evans noted. In November 2010 Newton's father was implicated in a pay-for-play scheme with Mississippi State that alleged he had asked the school for $180,000 in exchange for his son enrolling there. Newton was briefly declared ineligible by Auburn, on the grounds that his amateur status had been breached, but was reinstated by the school and the NCAA after it was concluded that he had been unaware of his father's actions. Newton has said that, despite what his father did, the two grew closer as a result of the scandal.

## PANTHERS' NUMBER-ONE PICK

Three days after leading Auburn to its first national championship in fifty-three years, Newton announced that he would forgo his senior year to enter the 2011 NFL Draft. While many analysts and scouts projected him as a potential number-one overall pick, others advised NFL teams against taking him due to questions and concerns about his arm mechanics, limited experience, maturity, and character.

Leading up to the draft, Newton worked with the renowned San Diego–based quarterbacks coach George Whitfield Jr., who helped him polish his mechanics and fundamentals. However, character concerns about Newton increased when, on the eve of the 2011 NFL Scouting Combine, he declared to *Sports Illustrated*, as quoted by Peter King for that publication (7 Mar. 2011), that he viewed himself "not only as a football player but an entertainer and icon." The comment led many to see Newton as being arrogant, but it ultimately did little to dissuade the Carolina Panthers, which selected him with the number-one overall pick in the draft. Newton became the third player in history to be taken first in the draft in the same year that he won a Heisman Trophy and national championship. In July 2011 he signed a fully guaranteed four-year contract with the Panthers worth over $22 million.

## RECORD-SETTING ROOKIE SEASON (2011)

Despite having his development slowed by the 2011 NFL lockout, which lasted 136 days, Newton, who spent much of that off-season training at the IMG Academy in Bradenton, Florida, responded to his detractors and critics by having a rookie season for the ages. After beating out Jimmy Clausen and Derek Anderson for the Panthers' starting quarterback job during the team's summer training camp, Newton made his debut on September 11, 2011, in the season opener on the road against the Arizona Cardinals. In the game, which the Panthers lost 28–21, he threw for 422 yards and two touchdowns, becoming the first rookie in NFL history to throw for more than four hundred yards in his first career start and shattering Peyton Manning's 1998 first-game passing record of 302 yards. He fared even better in his next game, against the then reigning Super Bowl champion Green Bay Packers, when he threw for 432 yards and a touchdown and rushed for fifty-three yards and a touchdown. The Panthers lost that game as well, 30–23, but Newton set an NFL record and team record for

most passing yards in a game by a rookie, and also established a league record for most combined passing yards in his first two career starts (854).

While the Panthers went on to lose eight more games during the 2011 season, finishing third in the NFC South Division with a record of 6–10, Newton established himself as an NFL star and bona fide franchise quarterback. He started all sixteen games and set a litany of records. Among them was the NFL rookie record for most passing yards in a season, with 4,051 (broken by Andrew Luck in 2012); establishing a league record for most rushing touchdowns by a quarterback in a season, with fourteen; and breaking every Panthers single-game and season rushing record by a quarterback, including most rushing yards in a season, with 706. He also became the first player in league history to throw for more than four thousand yards and rush for more than five hundred yards in a single season.

At the end of the season, Newton was named the Associated Press offensive rookie of the year, earning forty-seven votes from a nationwide panel of fifty sportswriters. He also received the rare rookie honor of earning a selection to the Pro Bowl, as a backup quarterback for the NFL Pro Bowl squad.

## 2012 AND 2013 SEASONS

Newton again started all sixteen games for the Panthers during the 2012 season, in which his numbers dropped only slightly. That year he passed for 3,869 yards and nineteen touchdowns and led the Panthers with a career-high and team-record 741 rushing yards, to go along with eight rushing touchdowns. Equipped with a better understanding of NFL defenses and Rivera's complicated offense, Newton threw only twelve interceptions, as opposed to seventeen as a rookie, and amassed a career-best passer rating of 86.2. Meanwhile, he became the only person in league history to throw for more than five thousand yards and rush for more than a thousand yards, with at least twenty-five touchdown passes and fifteen rushing touchdowns, in his first two seasons. The Panthers, despite getting off to a rough 8–2 start, enjoyed an improvement from the previous year, going 7–9 and finishing second in NFC South.

Newton entered the 2013 season in hopes of taking on a more active leadership role with the Panthers. He also planned on improving his conduct—which was questioned at times during his first two seasons—both on the sidelines and in postgame press conferences. "Whether I'm watching film or just watching things that I can become a better person at," he explained to Jonathan Jones for the *Charlotte Observer* (28 June 2013), "I'm trying to polish things up to make me a better person and better player."

## PERSONAL LIFE

Newton, who owns a $1.6 million condominium in Charlotte, North Carolina, is known for his photogenic smile and large-than-life personality. Those attributes have helped him land endorsement deals with such high-profile brands as Under Armour and Gatorade. During the 2012 season he appeared in commercials for the NFL's "Play 60" campaign, which aims to prevent childhood obesity. He has been active in giving back to the local community and has established an eponymous charitable foundation that conducts football camps and sponsors tournaments for high school players.

## SUGGESTED READING

Barrows, Frank. "Barrows on Sports: The Making of Cam Newton." *Charlotte Magazine*. Charlotte Magazine, Sept. 2012. Web. 25 June 2013.

Bernstein, Viv. "Newton and Carolina Ready to Take Next Step." *New York Times*. New York Times Co., 26 Aug. 2012. Web. 25 June 2013.

Marshall, Phillip. "How It All Began for Cam Newton." *Auburn Undercover*. 247Sports, 2013. Web. 25 June 2013.

Martin, Brett. "QB1." *GQ*. Condé Nast, Sept. 2012. Web. 25 June 2013.

Person, Joseph. "Cam Newton's Drive to Compete Began Early." *Charlotte Observer*. Charlotte Observer, 29 Sept. 2012. Web. 25 June 2013.

—*Chris Cullen*

# Jonathan Nolan

**Born:** June 6, 1976
**Occupation:** Writer and producer

Though often overlooked in his partnership with his more famous older brother, screenwriter Jonathan "Jonah" Nolan has nevertheless developed a distinct voice as half of one of the most successful storytelling duos in entertainment. Before he even graduated from college, Nolan began writing the short story that would be the basis for *Memento*, one of the most enigmatic movies of the 2000s. Polishing his style and process, Nolan continued to collaborate with his brother and eventually cowrote two of the most successful films of all time, *The Dark Knight* and *The Dark Knight Rises*. Still only in his thirties, Nolan has a strong voice and a stellar reputation for combining gritty realism and thrilling moods with themes such as identity, justice, obsession, and the sometimes-gray area between good and evil.

In 2013, with a string of critical and commercial successes behind him, an ongoing television series, and several highly anticipated

Wirelmage

upcoming projects, Nolan is poised to continue this streak and further strengthen his distinctive creative voice. "A lot of writers find freedom in different places, and for me, it's the diversity of experiences, different ways to write that I'm tremendously interested in," he told Shira Gotshalk for the Writers Guild of America (WGA) website (14 Oct. 2011).

## EARLY LIFE AND EDUCATION

Jonathan Nolan was born on June 6, 1976, in London, England. His British father, Brendan, worked in advertising, and his American mother, Christina, worked as a flight attendant. Nolan was the youngest of three sons after older brothers Matthew and Christopher. In their Highgate neighborhood of North London, Nolan was exposed to filmmaking at a young age by Christopher and watched many of his brother's VHS tapes. In 1987 Nolan moved to a suburb of Chicago, Illinois, and he spent the rest of his childhood moving between the United States and the United Kingdom.

As a teenager in Chicago, Nolan struggled with his accent and spent hours watching television to Americanize his speech. In an interview for *Movies Online* he told Sheila Roberts, "I moved to Chicago with an English accent and that was very unpopular so I learned very quickly how to sound like a good Chicago kid." Nolan graduated from the Loyola Academy preparatory high school in 1994 and enrolled as a freshman at Georgetown University in Washington, DC. In the convocation address he gave at his alma mater in 2002, he noted that attending the university was an "arbitrary decision."

At Georgetown Nolan began his education at the Walsh School of Foreign Service (SFS) and worked as a writer for the *Hoya* student newspaper. He wrote a column for the paper and had a reputation as a prankster and a good friend among his fellow students. After two years Nolan left Georgetown to take some time off. He traveled to Spain and New Zealand, where he worked various jobs and read a great deal, notably the works of Herman Melville. In 1997 he returned to college and transferred from the SFS to Georgetown College, where he majored in English and took screenwriting courses under Professor John Glavin. Along with several friends, he wrote "Conflict in Satin and Silk," one-act play for the university's Donn B. Murphy One-Acts Festival. Nolan graduated from Georgetown in 1999.

## "MEMENTO MORI" AND *MEMENTO*

In a psychology class at Georgetown Nolan learned about anterograde memory loss, a condition that causes selective memory loss in which the patient cannot make new memories or recall new information. "I was drawn to it as a metaphor," Nolan told Daniel Fierman for *Entertainment Weekly* (30 Mar. 2001). He also called the disorder "a demonstration of how fleeting identity really is." Nolan played around with the idea of writing about anterograde memory loss until 1997, when he embarked on a cross-country drive from Chicago to Los Angeles with his brother Christopher. "Jonah told me the story," Christopher told Fierman. "It wasn't developed, just about a guy who can't make new memories who is looking for revenge. But I got excited and asked to write the screenplay." Christopher—who had just finished writing and directing his first film, *Following* (1998)—was eager for a new project. The brothers decided that Nolan would finish his short story and give Christopher a draft to turn into a screenplay.

After returning to college, Nolan wrote and rewrote what would eventually become the short story "Memento Mori." The story's protagonist, Earl, has anterograde amnesia and is forced to use notes and even tattoos to remember things—the most important of which is that he must escape the mental institution where he is confined to find the man who murdered his wife and take his revenge. The story shifts time frames and narrative voices, examining the roles of time and memory in identity; Nolan also meditates on the complexities of grief and vengeance, raising questions about the value of revenge if it will not be remembered. Christopher sent a copy of the story to *Esquire* magazine, and it was published in the March 2001 issue.

After leaving Georgetown, Nolan joined his brother in Hollywood and worked for him as a production assistant. "I was too dumb to realize how much of a chance I was taking," he told

Gotshalk. "My superpower is to be too stupid to understand the risk that I'm taking at any given moment. That kind of stupidity is very useful."

Christopher had also been working on the screenplay, in which the protagonist is named Leonard and the plot and execution are somewhat different, though the themes of memory, grief, and revenge are the same. The resulting film, *Memento* (2000), stars Guy Pearce, Joe Pantoliano, and Carrie-Anne Moss and was released by Newmarket Films and Summit Entertainment. *Memento* is an innovative psychological thriller that depicts the events of the story in reverse order, interspersed with a different sequence of scenes shown chronologically, to illustrate the main character's memory disorder. The movie premiered at the Venice International Film Festival and went on to perform successfully at the American box office. The film also won the praise of critics; it received an Academy Award nomination for best film editing, and the brothers were nominated for best original screenplay.

### THE PRESTIGE

For his next project Nolan worked with Christopher on another screenplay, this time adapting Christopher Priest's 1995 novel *The Prestige*. Christopher approached his younger brother with the novel in England in 2000, and the two felt that it was a good fit for their sensibilities. The book is set in England in the late 1800s and features an ongoing rivalry between rival magicians; it contains elements of both ghost stories and science fiction as well as themes of identity that were also present in *Memento*. Adapting the sprawling work, to be directed by Christopher, took the Nolans years to complete. "It's just a grind figuring it out," Nolan told John Horn for the *Los Angeles Times* (15 Oct. 2006). To Roberts, he added that the size and scope of the source novel "was a really big benefit" and gave them a significant amount of material to work with. The final screenplay is the result of passing drafts and revisions back and forth and arguing over storytelling devices and dialogue. "We are always talking," Nolan told Horn. "So there's a collaboration there in terms of setting both of our minds on the task. But we write separate drafts. This has been the way that it has worked." When the screenwriters cannot agree on a direction, however, they concede that the decision usually lies with Christopher as the director.

*The Prestige* was released in October 2006. The film stars Christian Bale and Hugh Jackman as the dueling illusionists and also features Michael Caine, Rebecca Hall, and Scarlett Johansson. The film earned positive reviews; critics applauded the storytelling, performances, and atmosphere as well as the way the screenwriters made the complex story accessible for audiences. Priest himself also approved of the adaptation.

## BATMAN

During the years in which the brothers were developing their screenplay for *The Prestige*, Nolan also collaborated with Christopher on another project. In 2003, Christopher and screenwriter David S. Goyer began working on a reboot of the Batman film franchise that Christopher would also direct. The film—*Batman Begins* (2005), starring Christian Bale, Michael Caine, Gary Oldman, Cillian Murphy, Morgan Freeman, Liam Neeson, and Katie Holmes—is an origin story for the character Bruce Wayne and his Batman alter ego and is darker and more realistic than the Batman films of the 1990s. Nolan served as a creative consultant for the script and was involved in his brother's rewrites. Though Nolan is not credited in the film, Christopher has been outspoken about his contributions.

*Batman Begins* was followed by a sequel, *The Dark Knight*, in 2008. Cowritten by the Nolan brothers and directed by Christopher, *The Dark Knight* continues themes from the first film, such as justice, vigilantism, revenge, and corruption, as well as conflicts such as good versus evil and order versus chaos. Most of the film's cast returned for the sequel, with the additions of Maggie Gyllenhaal, Aaron Eckhart, and, most notably, Heath Ledger. The popular film was praised by critics and audiences and named one of the best films of the year. Ledger—who died of an accidental drug overdose six months before the film's release—received raves for his portrayal of the Joker. His villainous performance earned a posthumous Academy Award for best supporting actor.

In an essay for *Empire* magazine (July 2010) about working with his brother on the movie, Nolan wrote, "Writing with Chris is writing at speed—on taxis, jumbo jets, boats, trams. London, LA, Chicago, Hong Kong. Chris has tech scouts, meetings with actors. I tag along. We figure out the script on the way—one long transcontinental argument, batting ideas back and forth. Bruce Wayne would be proud." He called the experience "an exhausting ride, exhilarating and heartbreaking in equal measure." Though overlooked for an Academy Award nomination for best screenplay, the Nolans shared writing awards including a Saturn Award, a Scream Award, and an Austin Film Critics Association award; they were also nominated for a Writers Guild of America award, a Chicago Film Critics Association award, and an Online Film Critics Society award.

To round out the trilogy, the Nolan brothers followed *Batman Begins* and *The Dark Knight* with 2012's *The Dark Knight Rises*. This final installment, again directed by Christopher, features the return of most of the previous films' casts with the additions of Anne Hathaway, Tom Hardy, Joseph Gordon-Levitt, and Marion Cotillard. The screenwriters knew that this would be their final Batman film and that they would finish the story with this last venture. *The Dark Knight Rises* grossed over $1 billion globally and became one of the most successful films of all time. On the whole experience, Nolan told Gotshalk that "working on Batman is a really, really fun thing to do." He added, "It's actually creatively an incredibly fulfilling place to be. You have all sorts of wonderful stories about this character, standing on the shoulders of literally hundreds or thousands of writers who have been thinking about this character for seventy plus years. It's a unique and incredibly satisfying experience."

## PERSON OF INTEREST

Following the tremendous success of the Batman films, Nolan made the switch from the big screen to the television screen. In 2010 he pitched the idea for the television series that would eventually become *Person of Interest*, a crime drama and thriller. The show is shot in New York City and features a former CIA agent (played by Jim Caviezel) and a tech billionaire (played by Michael Emerson), the latter of whom has developed a machine that can predict crimes before they occur. The protagonists use the machine to prevent these crimes from occurring. Like much of Nolan's work, *Person of Interest* features themes of identity, vigilante justice, obsession, and moral ambiguity in addition to contemporary issues of surveillance and paranoia in the post-9/11 United States.

As creator and executive producer and a writer for the show, Nolan has had to adapt his writing style to a procedural show that airs twenty-three episodes in a season. "I've long been jealous of the ability to tell stories about characters, build characters that you can continue deepening and changing year after year rather than just writing 120 pages," he told Gotshalk. He added, "It's staggering the amount of material that TV showrunners and TV staffs assemble in the course of shooting a season. And what's great about it is you really get a chance to try different ideas and try different approaches, which is incredibly exciting. A movie is a one-shot deal."

The show premiered on CBS on September 22, 2011, to generally positive reviews. *Person of Interest* was also successful in terms of viewership, winning its timeslot with its pilot and going on to be the fastest-growing drama of the 2011 and 2012 television season as it picked up more viewers. The show's success ensured that it would be picked up for a second season, which premiered on September 27, 2012. Nolan is happy with the show's success and the chance to keep using television as a form of storytelling. In an interview with Noelene Clark for the

*Los Angeles Times* (27 Oct. 2011) he explained, "I'm always interested in stories where you take a paradigm and turn it inside out or question it, and I think that's part of what we're doing here. There's a vigilante aspect to our show, but there are these characters who are very thoughtful and complicated, and they question these things. We get a chance to sort of see them breaking the genre apart and putting it back together."

## 2013 AND ONWARD

With *Person of Interest* renewed and his brother's Batman trilogy complete, Nolan is working on new projects and waiting for several scripts to finish their transition from the page to the screen. Both the Warner Bros. film *Hell and Gone* and the Paramount film *Interstellar* are in development with scripts written by Nolan. *Hell and Gone*, set to be directed by J. Blakeson, is about the Great Chicago Fire of 1871; Nolan has called it a story of revenge, and the script is reportedly a historical tragedy. *Interstellar* is a science-fiction film about time travel based on the work of theoretical physicist and astrophysicist Kip Thorne; the project will be directed by Christopher, and the film is set for release in November 2014. Nolan himself is not slated to direct a movie, or even an episode of *Person of Interest*, any time soon. In a 2006 interview with *Creative Screenwriting Magazine*, however, he told Jeff Goldsmith, "If you have enough success as a screenwriter, sooner or later someone will allow you to make a fool of yourself by directing a film. I fully expect to take advantage of that opportunity."

## PERSONAL LIFE

Nolan is married to writer Lisa Joy. Joy, who previously wrote for the acclaimed television series *Pushing Daisies*, is a writer and coproducer on the show *Burn Notice* and is developing a series of her own—*Athena*, set to debut in 2013. *Athena* is based on Joy's graphic novel *Headache*. Nolan, Joy, and their dogs live in Los Angeles.

While Jonathan and Christopher Nolan have been collaborating on films, their older brother, Matthew, has been in the headlines for criminal activity. In 2009 he faced extradition to Costa Rica on kidnapping and murder charges; he was also reportedly under investigation for check fraud, but charges were never filed. Though it was deemed that Costa Rican authorities did not have enough evidence for a conviction, he was eventually sentenced to two years of probation for his attempt to escape Chicago's Metropolitan Correctional Center.

Despite these family troubles, Nolan has remained positive about his life and work. In one of Yale University's famous Master's Teas in 2009, Nolan spoke to a group of young students about having a career path. "I think that you should feel free to pursue artistic endeavors, really whatever excites you and gives you a passion," he said. "It's better to fail at something that you enjoy than something you don't."

## SUGGESTED READING

Fierman, Daniel. "Memory Swerves." *Entertainment Weekly* 30 Mar. 2001: 20. Print.
Gotshalk, Shira. "The Power of Stupidity." *Writers Guild of America, West*. Writers Guild of America, 14 Oct. 2011. Web. 18 Feb. 2013.
Horn, John. "Chalk It All Up to Sibling Scribery." *Los Angeles Times*. Los Angeles Times, 15 Oct. 2006. Web. 18 Feb. 2013.
Nolan, Jonathan. "Memento Mori." *Esquire* Mar. 2001: 186–92. Print.
Nolan, Jonathan. "Part 6: Jonathan Nolan and *The Dark Knight*." *Empire*. Bauer Consumer Media, July 2010. Web. 18 Feb. 2013.

## SELECTED WORKS

### Screenplays
*Memento* (with Christopher Nolan), 2000; *The Prestige* (with Christopher Nolan), 2006; *The Dark Knight* (with Christopher Nolan), 2008; *Person of Interest*, 2011– ; *The Dark Knight Rises* (with Christopher Nolan), 2012

*—Kehley Coviello*

# Jacqueline Novogratz

**Born:** 1961
**Occupation:** Founder and CEO of Acumen Fund

Acumen Fund leader Jacqueline Novogratz has spent her career helping people lift themselves out of poverty. Novogratz's first job out of college in the 1980s was as an international credit analyst for Chase Manhattan Bank. She left that job after three years, disillusioned with the huge divide she had witnessed between rich and poor, and with the company's lack of interest in microfinance.

From the late 1980s onward, Novogratz has dedicated her life and her banking expertise to changing the world, not through charity, but through investments. Her work started in West Africa, where she reviewed and built microfinance institutions in partnership with the African Development Bank and UNICEF. As a fellow of the Rockefeller Foundation in the 1990s, she trained philanthropists to be problem solvers. In 2001, Novogratz founded Acumen Fund, an organization that invests thousands or millions of dollars from donors into entrepreneurial ideas in both Africa and South Asia. Acumen-funded businesses are designed to provide jobs, build capital, and, most importantly, provide

Bloomberg via Getty Images

people with basic necessities such as clean water and health care.

## EARLY LIFE AND EDUCATION

Jacqueline Novogratz was born in 1961 to a US Army officer and an antiques businesswoman. Her father's military career, which included serving in Korea and Vietnam, meant that the Novogratz family moved around a lot while she and her six younger siblings were growing up. When Novogratz was five years old, for instance, her family lived in Detroit; following that, the family lived just outside of West Point, New York. Novogratz attended high school in Alexandria, Virginia.

Even as a child, Novogratz had a strong work ethic. She was "the girl who sold the most scout cookies, got the best grades and worked all night on projects," her brother Bob told Helen Coster for *Forbes* (30 Nov. 2011). Novogratz sold Christmas ornaments at age ten, shoveled snow and mowed grass at age twelve, worked the ice cream counter at a Howard Johnson's at age fourteen, and bartended as a young adult. These odd jobs, as well as student loans, enabled Novogratz to matriculate at the University of Virginia in Charlottesville, where she earned a bachelor's degree in economics and international relations in 1983. Novogratz was not only hardworking, but "she was always hell-bent on changing people's minds about the world at a young age," Bob Novogratz told Coster.

After graduation, Novogratz had wanted to take time off to figure out her life before diving into a career. Her parents convinced her to apply for jobs related to her fields of study anyway.

At her first job interview, with Chase Manhattan Bank, Novogratz answered the interviewer's question about why she wanted to become a banker honestly, explaining that her parents had made her apply for the job. In her best-selling memoir, *The Blue Sweater* (2009), she wrote, "I don't want to be a banker. . . . I want to change the world" (5). The interviewer convinced Novogratz that working for Chase Manhattan would allow her to travel throughout the world. She finished the interview, got the job, and moved to New York City.

## CHASE MANHATTAN BANK

The next three years of Novogratz's life were dedicated to her job as an international credit analyst for Chase Manhattan Bank. She and a team of other recent college graduates would travel around the world, particularly in places with unstable economies, to review bank loans. Though Novogratz would travel to places like Singapore and Hong Kong, she spent much of her time focusing on the Latin American debt crisis, working in Chile, Peru, and Brazil.

While Novogratz was working in Rio de Janeiro, Brazil, she became disillusioned about her job, which essentially "was to write off millions of dollars in debt that would never be collected" (*Blue Sweater* 6). She spent what free time she had exploring the city, and in doing so saw firsthand the huge gap between the rich and the poor there. "I'd never experienced such poverty alongside such wealth before," she states in *The Blue Sweater*. "I'd also never felt such a strong desire to make a difference or felt so fully alive" (6). Novogratz asked her boss if the bank could provide small loans to Brazil's working class; she believed they would be more likely to pay off these loans, but her boss did not approve of her idea to experiment in microfinance. The practice of lending small amounts of money to low-income individuals, so that these individuals can work to get themselves out of poverty, was relatively uncommon at the time. Novogratz left Chase Manhattan in 1986.

## A CONSULTANT IN WEST AFRICA

Deciding to use her skills as a banking analyst to help those in poverty, Novogratz next set off for Africa as a representative of a New York–based nonprofit microfinance organization for women. She worked at the African Development Bank (ADB) located in Ivory Coast, where her goal was to help start local West African businesses. She quickly learned, however, that people did not like the presence of a foreigner trying to "save" them.

Novogratz's colleagues in the ADB treated her poorly, from blaming her for others' mistakes to even poisoning her food. After spending three days ill, Novogratz decided to leave the ADB. When she informed her colleagues that she was leaving, the ADB director told Novogratz that they did not like what her presence represented. "The North comes to the South and sends a young white woman without asking us what we want, without seeing if we already have the skills we need" (*Blue Sweater* 25).

Nevertheless, Novogratz returned to West Africa in early 1987. In Nairobi, Kenya, she spent time with a startup microfinance organization for women. After analyzing the organization's loan portfolio, she discovered that they were more than 60 percent in arrears. She offered to fix this problem, but then her report went missing. Discouraged with this lack of accountability, Novogratz accepted an offer to help build a credit program for Rwandan women. She would partner with UNICEF to first analyze whether a women's microfinance institution would be feasible there, and then, if so, to help create one.

## THE BLUE SWEATER STORY
An often-told story of Novogratz's is about the journey of her blue sweater. The sweater, which sported an image of two zebras in front of a mountain, was given to her by her uncle. It became her favorite piece of clothing, which she wore often through middle school and into high school. When she outgrew the sweater, both in size and in maturity, she donated it to Goodwill.

By complete chance, Novogratz would see that sweater again in early 1987 in Kigali, the capital of Rwanda, while out jogging. She spotted the sweater on a young boy, whom she guessed was about ten years old. "I grabbed him by the shoulders and turned down the collar," she recalls in *The Blue Sweater* (2). "Sure enough, my name was written on the tag of my sweater that had traveled thousands of miles for more than a decade." Novogratz took this as a sign of her purpose to help people help themselves. "At that point in my own journey, my worldview was shifting. I'd begun my career as an international banker, discovering the power of capital, of markets, and of politics, as well as how the poor are so often excluded from all three. I wanted to understand better what stands between poverty and wealth" (3).

## DUTERIMBERE
Inspired by her chance encounter with the boy wearing her blue sweater, Novogratz persisted in her work to establish a microfinance organization for Rwandan women. Given her experience thus far as a consultant, Novogratz understood that handouts were not the best way to help people. Instead, she hoped that by giving women loans with high expectations attached—and a fair interest rate—these women could responsibly support their families.

After meeting with aid workers, government officials, and various women of Kigali,

Novogratz and her team of twenty-nine women founded Rwanda's first microfinance institution. Duterimbere, which in Kinyarwanda means "to go forward with enthusiasm," was created in less than a year with political and financial support from Rwandan women, even though Novogratz had been warned that these poor women would not be able to give.

Duterimbere faced difficulties during its first year. One of its major backers was accused of stealing approximately US$3,000 from the organization. In addition, women were not paying back their loans—they viewed the nonprofit Duterimbere as a charity. Novogratz emphasized to customers that they were borrowing from fellow Rwandan women, insisting on "hold[ing] them accountable even if the rest of the world didn't" (*Blue Sweater* 55). This accountability paid off, and Duterimbere would become a success.

## AN ALL-WOMEN'S BAKERY
In 1988, Novogratz joined a women's project run by the Ministry for Family and Social Affairs in Kigali. The project, which enabled women to sell baked goods to government institutions and to sew dresses or make other crafts on order, was run similarly to a charity. Novogratz decided to turn it into a sustainable business. Instead of letting the women keep all of the money they earned, she instituted a regular wage plus commission. In a few months, the business became profitable, and the women were able to open up a real bakery. Eight months after opening their bakery, the twenty women who had participated in the ministry's project were earning a base pay of US$2 per day—four times what they had earned when their business first started. "Money is freedom and confidence and choice," Novogratz wrote of the women's success in her memoir (78). "Choice is dignity. The solidarity of the bakery also gave them a sense of belonging that made them even stronger."

Novogratz would stay in Rwanda for two years. She spent some of that time in Kenya as well, on behalf of UNICEF, reviewing and recommending changes for donor-funded women's enterprises. Novogratz discovered numerous problems with these enterprises; many projects were costing the locals more than they were helping them. For example, schools were empty because the cost of long-term teacher employment had been unaccounted for. Novogratz encountered similar problems with traditional aid in 1989 while on contract with the World Bank in Gambia for approximately nine months, where she worked with the Department of Agriculture to finalize a proposal for a soft loan package. There were, for instance, US$1 million–worth of broken down maize mills, because no one had been trained to repair them.

## THE ROCKEFELLER FOUNDATION

Although her work in Africa had often left her disheartened, Novogratz was determined to figure out a better way to help people create their own businesses. She applied for business school in the United States in order to learn more, and in 1989 was accepted at the Stanford University Graduate School of Business in California. It was before she began classes in the fall of 1989 that she partnered with the World Bank in Gambia. She remained in the United States to study for her degree, earning her MBA in 1991. After graduating, Novogratz became a fellow at the Rockefeller Foundation in New York, where she worked on strategies for enterprise development in low-income American communities.

In April 1994, while reading a newspaper during her subway ride to work, Novogratz learned about the massacres occurring in Rwanda at the time; the genocide of Tutsis and Hutu sympathizers lasted approximately one hundred days, from April into July 1994, and resulted in the deaths of an estimated 800,000 people. News about Rwanda upset Novogratz deeply. "The devastating impact of the Rwandan genocide on a people I'd come to love shrank my dreams even further," she states in her memoir (x). "I concluded that if I could only *nudge* the world a little bit, maybe that would be enough."

Novogratz continued to work on gearing philanthropy toward social change through the Rockefeller Foundation. In 1995, she founded the Philanthropy Workshop, which trains philanthropists from diverse backgrounds in "strategic" philanthropy, or problem solving. Originally part of Rockefeller, the Philanthropy Workshop would later become part of the Institute for Philanthropy in New York and London. While working at the Rockefeller Foundation, Novogratz also founded the Next Generation Leadership program in 1997. The fellows of this program collaborate on ways to make US democracy better, by focusing on issues such as immigration and globalization.

## RETURNING TO RWANDA

Between 1997 and 2000, Novogratz traveled to Rwanda four times to learn what had happened there in 1994—and specifically what had happened to the people she had worked with. She discovered that the bakery was no longer a bakery, but the home of an illegal Ugandan refugee. Most of the women who had worked there were dead. Two of the women she had worked closely with in 1987, Honorata and Liliane, had survived the massacres and had lived in refugee camps before being able to return home. Two other women Novogratz had been close with, Prudence and Agnes, were in prison for their roles in the genocide. Agnes, the major backer of Duterimbere who had stolen money from the organization, received a life sentence for having

allegedly incited murder. Prudence, whose only crime was remaining silent, would eventually be declared innocent and be released. Duterimbere itself survived the genocide, in spite of the fates of its founding members; with support from Women's World Banking, the organization has continued to operate.

## ACUMEN FUND

Returning to Rwanda after the genocide helped Novogratz understand "the extraordinary resilience of people for whom poverty is a reality not because they don't work hard, but because there are too many obstacles in their way" (*Blue Sweater* x). Novogratz wanted to create an organization that would help remove those obstacles, specifically one that would put philanthropic funding toward investments in new enterprises. These businesses would be run by low-income individuals and for low-income individuals—not as a charity, but a long-term way to solve the problems of poverty through the market. Novogratz began planning her venture capital fund in 1999. With backing from the Rockefeller Foundation, Cisco Foundation, and three private donors, Novogratz raised more than $8 million by 2001. Once she had a team and a business plan in place, Acumen Fund was founded that April.

Although Acumen Fund is officially a nonprofit, its donors are referred to as investors, because their money funds entrepreneurial ideas. Acumen invests in businesses that provide health care, clean water, alternative energy, and housing services to communities in need. The fund is not a microfinance institution but a major investor, providing equity and loans in thousands or millions of dollars. Novogratz told David Serchuk for *Forbes* (13 May 2009) that Acumen Fund "makes investments from $300,000 to $2 million, which is not your typical $30 to $100." This investment approach is built off of Novogratz's previous experience with charities: "Poor people seek dignity, not dependence," states Acumen's website. "Traditional charity often meets immediate needs but too often fails to enable people to solve their own problems over the long term. Market-based approaches have the potential to grow when charitable dollars run out."

However, Novogratz has recognized that the market alone cannot solve the issue of poverty. Instead, Acumen Fund provides what Novogratz terms "patient capital," which as she told Serchuk is to "take money, invest it in enterprises that are delivering water, helping with health care to low-income individuals, and then remeasure the change both financially and from the social perspective." Investments are long term, with projections up to ten years. Acumen understands risk and the likelihood of short returns. The organization is willing to partner with government and private organizations, provides management assistance to its businesses, and, overall, focuses on the social aspect of results rather than the financial. "It's a new twist on the old adage about teaching a man to fish, except that Novogratz wants to build an entire fish market," Helen Coster wrote for *Forbes* (30 Nov. 2011).

## PATIENT CAPITAL

Acumen's first investment was in Dr. Govindappa Venkataswamy's Aravind Eye Hospital in India, for the establishment of a telemedicine unit that enables rural farmers to receive eye examinations without needing to travel to the hospital. By 2008, one telemedicine unit had grown to sixteen units, providing eye care to thousands of people across India. In 2002, in Pakistan, Acumen invested in Tasneem Siddiqqui's company Saiban. This housing company offers low-income homeowners the option to buy small and then incrementally expand their homes over time, depending on what they can afford. By 2012, more than thirty thousand people were living in one of Saiban's earliest developments. Acumen has also invested in about twelve other companies in Pakistan, including Kashf Foundation, a women's microlender, and agricultural irrigation company Micro Drip.

In 2003, Acumen invested in A to Z Textiles in Tanzania. Through a partnership with UNICEF, the World Health Organization (WHO), ExxonMobil, and Sumitomo Chemical—the latter of which had developed bed nets treated with insecticide that can last for five years—A to Z began manufacturing long-lasting insecticide bed nets. By the end of 2012, A to Z had become Tanzania's largest employer. More than seven thousand workers, mainly women, produce 29 million bed nets annually—protecting millions of people from malaria. In 2004, Acumen invested in Amitabha Sadangi's idea for a drip irrigation system in India. The resulting company, Global Easy Water Products (GEWP), would in four years sell more than 275,000 systems, doubling the crop yield and income of the farmers who purchased them. Acumen also invested in WaterHealth International (WHI) that year, which works to bring safe drinking water to rural India. By the end of 2012, WHI had developed five hundred water systems for more than 500,000 people. In addition to these investments, Acumen Fund has seen numerous other successes across Africa and South Asia.

## THE RISKS AND REWARDS OF DONOR INVESTING

One of the reasons for the success of Acumen-funded companies is Novogratz's meticulous note taking during field visits. Her notes "give me insights and quantifiable data I can bring to conversations that have, frankly, been devoid of them for so long" she told Coster. "There's a real moral imperative in being an organization that takes the time to sit and listen to the customers and the people they're serving," she added. Granted, Acumen has experienced nearly $3 million in losses for enterprises that failed due to poor marketing, distribution, and other factors. One example is Mitry, which sold filters for the removal of excess fluoride from drinking water; the company had limited its sales to only Indian government institutions. "We know we're going to have losses," C. Hunter Boll, a volunteer director and donor-investor for Acumen, told Coster. Boll is a former managing director for private equity firm Thomas H. Lee. "We're investing in high-risk ventures in tough parts of the world." Boll added that while "it's difficult to find great entrepreneurs with a social mission and a business plan that makes sense," Acumen has still achieved success in "developing talent, leadership, influencing the world."

Acumen Fund has offices in New York City; Mumbai, India; Nairobi, Kenya; Karachi, Pakistan; and East Legon, Ghana. In just over a decade, the fund has invested more than $75 million in entrepreneurial ideas; a total of about seventy companies funded by Acumen have created nearly 60,000 jobs, leveraged $360 million, and have brought health care, clean water, and other services to millions of people. "I'd like Acumen to be remembered for helping people imagine a world beyond poverty," Novogratz told Elizabeth Dickinson for *Foreign Policy* (May/June 2010). "We need to move away from thinking, 'Oh, those poor people, we have to help them get out of poverty,' to thinking about, 'Can you imagine the world if we could release the energy of all of us to contribute to making it better?'"

## SPREADING THE WORD

Novogratz is a popular public speaker. She has given numerous lectures at conferences worldwide—including the Clinton Global Initiative, the World Economic Forum, and TED (Technology, Entertainment, and Design) Conferences—on the subjects of patient capital and social responsibility. Her honors include the 2008 Ernst & Young Entrepreneur of the Year Award, the 2009 CASE Leadership Award for social entrepreneurship, the 2009 AWNY Changing the Game Award, and the 2012 Women of Concern Humanitarian Award. Novogratz has been named one of *Foreign Policy*'s "Top 100 Global Thinkers" of 2009, one of the *Daily Beast*'s "25 Smartest People of the Decade" (30 Nov. 2009), and has appeared in *Forbes*'s lists of "The Five Most Powerful Women Changing the World with Philanthropy" (22 Aug. 2012) and "The Year's Seven Most Powerful Ideas" (2 Nov. 2011). She was also featured as the *Forbes* cover story for its December 19, 2011, issue.

Novogratz married the curator and leader of TED Conferences, Chris Anderson, in 2008. Their family lives in New York.

## SUGGESTED READING

Bryant, Adam. "When Humility and Audacity Go Hand in Hand." *New York Times*. New York Times Co, 29 Sept. 2012. Web. 13 Feb. 2013.

Coster, Helen. "Can Venture Capital Save the World?" *Forbes*. Forbes.com, 30 Nov. 2011. Web. 13 Feb. 2013.

Novogratz, Jacqueline. "A Banker for the World." *New York Times*. New York Times Co, 22 Aug. 2009. Web. 13 Feb. 2013.

"The Patient Capitalist." *Economist*. Economist Newspaper, 21 May 2009. Web. 13 Feb. 2013.

Serchuk, David. "Briefing Book: Jacqueline Novogratz." *Forbes*. Forbes.com, 13 May 2009. Web. 13 Feb. 2013.

—*Julia Gilstein*

Stephanie Berger

# Francisco J. Núñez

**Born:** April 23, 1965
**Occupation:** Artistic director and founder of Young People's Chorus of New York City

Musician, conductor, composer, and 2011 MacArthur fellow Francisco J. Núñez has decided to use his "genius grant" money toward doing what he has already been doing—leading the Young People's Chorus (YPC) of New York City. The internationally acclaimed choral group, which boasts over 1,200 singers ranging in age from seven to eighteen, is composed of children from different economic and cultural backgrounds who are there not only to excel at music, but also to foster diverse connections and to achieve personal growth.

Founded by Núñez in 1988, the YPC sings a variety of musical styles, from choral classics to contemporary compositions written specifically for them by award-winning composers. The latter, over seventy of which have been performed since Núñez first came up with the idea in 2001, are introduced to the public through the YPC's Transient Glory series. Transient Glory, a collection of concerts, recordings, publications, and symposia, showcases a repertoire of choral music for children. The success of the series has helped change the notion that music composed for children is not "serious" work.

The more important mission for Núñez, however, is to empower children through music. "When I take children to places from Rio to Tokyo, they come back so much bigger," he told Anthony Tommasini for the *New York Times* (3 Oct. 2011). "I want more of that." He added, "I want to fight poverty through music. I know that sounds romantic, but I've seen it happen."

## EARLY LIFE AND THE PIANO

Born on April 23, 1965, Francisco J. Núñez grew up in what he has described as a "close-knit" Dominican American household split between Washington Heights, a neighborhood of Manhattan in New York City, and the Dominican Republic. His mother, who had wanted to be both a ballerina and a pianist, had to leave school in seventh grade to work in the garment factory industry and support her family. She and her husband often traveled between the Dominican Republic and New York, so Núñez spent his childhood in both places. Núñez's father died when he was fourteen years old, after which he and his mother returned from the Dominican Republic to New York.

Núñez's home in the Dominican Republic had a piano, where his mother was his first piano teacher. Although poor, she bought her son a piano to practice on in New York as well. As Núñez explained to Jeffrey Brown for *PBS NewsHour* (23 Sept. 2011), he became interested in piano because "my mother wanted to keep me inside, because the kids downstairs were up to no good." He added later during the interview, "The best thing she could do was buy a piano. She bought a really rinky-dink piano at the Salvation Army, but that piano saved my life." Music, he told Tommasini, "brought me out of the barrio." Outside of school, Núñez dedicated his free time to practicing the piano. A musical prodigy, he spent six or seven hours practicing every day. In addition to his piano-playing talent, Núñez discovered a talent for musical composition. His first choral work, titled *Misa Pequeña*, was written at the age of fifteen.

## A SHARED MUSICAL EXPERIENCE

While playing the piano may generally be seen as a solo activity, Núñez's talent enabled him to perform at recitals and concerts, which put him in touch with other musically gifted children from different cultural and economic backgrounds. As he told Brown, there were "All types of children. And we all had so much in common because of the music, and we learned from each other." This connection with such a diverse group of children would influence Núñez's later career. "The instrument allowed me to speak to a different class of person," Núñez told Stuart Isacoff for the *Wall Street Journal* (15 Dec. 2011). "Classical music has always represented an educated sphere, whether you are poor or rich. And it taught me that you have to work hard to achieve something." Through his creation of the Young People's Chorus, Núñez would share that experience—and that lesson—with hundreds of children.

Núñez attended New York University (NYU) as a piano performance major. After graduating with a BS degree in 1988, he wanted to create a program that would allow the children of New York to have the same experience that he had growing up. "I wanted to create a program where I can take a kid from Harlem, from the Bronx and put them together with a kid from the Upper East Side or from Queens," he told Brown, "and let them learn about themselves by learning about others." That same year, he joined the Children's Aid Society of New York, where he would serve as the society's director of music for the next nine years. Through the Children's Aid Society, Núñez in 1988 founded the Young People's Chorus of New York City. He has served as the chorus's artistic director, as well as one of its composers and conductors, ever since.

## FORMATION AND EXPANSION OF THE YPC

Núñez's desire to bring together children of different cultural and economic backgrounds was achieved through his foundation of the Young People's Chorus. According to the YPC's website, "With music as the great equalizer, the diversity in the group resulted in new vocal colors and a confident urban style, creating not only a vibrant new choral sound, but also an avenue for children to succeed."

In order to attract members to the new program, Núñez traveled to different neighborhoods and their schools and after-school programs. In his interview with Brown, he recounted that he had told potential members, "If you join me, you'll get a T-shirt, and you'll get a jacket and one day you'll sing in Carnegie Hall." Years later,

children are the ones seeking out the YPC, which as of the end of 2012 boasted more than 1,200 members. And they do sing at Carnegie Hall. "At first, we sang terribly," Núñez told Isacoff, "the music wasn't the point yet." The point was—and still is—to bring children together so that they can learn about themselves and about others, and to give them an understanding of discipline. "Once they are with us, they make better decisions," Núñez told Isacoff. "It impacts their schoolwork, and it encourages them to seek out a diverse community."

The YPC has expanded over the years from its core after-school program, adding satellite programs in various New York City schools, a community chorus in Núñez's childhood neighborhood of Washington Heights, and affiliate programs in other cities in the United States. The chorus, which is broken into different age groups, accepts children ranging in age from seven to eighteen, who must audition for the program by singing a song of their choice. Auditions are made by appointment, and children need no prior music education in order to try out. Members are accepted based not only on their talent and their potential, but also on their level of experience and their cultural and economic background, in order to keep the YPC as diverse a group as possible.

## TRANSIENT GLORY

While Núñez has composed a number of pieces for the YPC to sing, he has also invited highly acclaimed composers—including winners of the Oscar, the Pulitzer Prize, and the MacArthur Fellowship—to write for the group. Many of these composers had not written for children before, as they did not want to be written off as unserious composers for doing so. Therefore, at first, many of these composers said no. However, in 2001, Núñez and the YPC changed that stigma, thanks to composer Ned Rorem's inclusion of the YPC at one of his concerts. Núñez told Rorem they wanted to call the YPC performance "Transient Glory." Núñez explained the name to Brown as "transient because it's during a time of a child's voice when it's just before he becomes an adult, and glory because it's glorious music." With Rorem's influence, Núñez was able to convince composers Michael Torke, John Tavener, Nora Kroll Rosenbaum, and Elena Kats Chernin to write pieces for the YPC's first Transient Glory series. The series' success helped the YPC grow in popularity, and soon other award-winning composers were writing for the group. By the close of 2012, the YPC had performed more than seventy music premieres through their Transient Glory series. The works composed for Transient Glory are not limited to the YPC, either. Each song and compilation is published by Boosey and Hawkes, where Núñez works in the role of editor, making this music available to anyone.

The YPC grew from singing "terribly" in its early days to becoming so impressive that it began receiving regular reviews from music critics. For example, a *New York Concert Review*, posted on the YPC website, states that "they sounded better than most professional choruses, singing . . . with impeccable intonation, exquisite blend of voicing and use of vibrato, excellent diction and precise rhythmic phrasing" (5 May 2008). In his interview with Núñez, Isacoff recounts that at one YPC concert, he "nearly fell out of his seat in astonishment." The YPC has performed at such renowned venues as Carnegie Hall, Orchestra Hall in Chicago, Jordan Hall in Boston, and the White House. They have also traveled around the world. The YPC was the first American youth choir to perform at the Adolf Fredrik Festival in Stockholm, Sweden, as well as the first American youth choir to sing at Polyfollia, an international choral showcase of fourteen choirs from around the world, held in Normandy, France. They went on tour in Japan in 2009 and 2010, represented the United States in 2005 at Kyoto's Seventh World Symposium, and represented North America at the 2012 World Choral Summit in Beijing.

## RADIO CHORUS AND RADIO RADIANCE

The success of Transient Glory inspired the creation of another performance series by the YPC, this time as the resident WNYC 93.9 Radio Chorus. At the YPC's radio debut, in October 2003, the group became the first resident chorus to perform at any New York radio station. The YPC is one of a handful of children's radio choirs across the United States, and it is the only one that performs new compositions exclusively for the radio. John Schaefer of WNYC has hosted the radio chorus since its first performance. In addition to being showcased in live radio performances, the YPC's songs have been recorded and aired again on WNYC's *Soundcheck*.

In 2009, WNYC and American Public Media (APM) partnered with the YPC and, with funding from the National Endowment for the Arts (NEA), created *Radio Radiance*, a radio and Internet program. The program is a combination of live-streamed music, recordings, and digital media. *Radio Radiance* runs on two-year cycles, during which the YPC promotes children's choruses across the United States—among them Ithaca, New York; Boston, Massachusetts; Miami, Florida; Seattle, Washington; Halstead, Kansas; and Atlanta, Georgia—who sing newly composed music on their local radio stations.

The music that the YPC performs ranges in style, from new and complex compositions to pop music arrangements, Broadway songs, spirituals, and choral classics. The group also performs a mix of music from different cultures. As Núñez told Isacoff: "I always wanted a hybrid . . . like bringing Indian raga and Inuit chant together with a backbeat of American pop. But we treated each style with respect: We didn't sing Brahms the way we did something that was Native American. And whenever we tackled a particular type of music—gospel, or Chinese, or Dominican—there would be kids from that particular background to help us get it right."

## THE REWARDS OF HARD WORK

The YPC choral program is intense, as Núñez and his team set high standards for their singers, including singing everything from memory. However, Núñez acknowledged to Brown that "the most important thing is when you are rehearsing together, after those rehearsals, you start asking each other questions: What do you want to do in life? What's next? And it opens up so many roads and paths. So the idea of that diversity coming together is life changing." The children also learn that hard work pays off, or as Núñez said in an interview for the National Arts and Humanities Youth Program Awards—of which the YPC was one of the winners in 2011—"doing something positive earns positive rewards." Núñez saw this lesson learned, for example, at the end of a concert that the YPC had performed with the New York Pops, which received a standing ovation. He overheard one of the shy performers say, "Listen, they're clapping for me. That's for me!"

Núñez has earned a number of his own "positive rewards" for his leadership. In 2005, he won the *New York Post*'s Liberty Ambassador Medal and was named one of the one hundred most influential Hispanics of 2005 by *Hispanic Business* magazine. Núñez and the YPC were given Chorus America's Education Outreach Award in 2006. In 2009, in addition to being named the 2009 man of the year" by La Sociedad Coral Latinoamericana, Núñez received a 2009 ASCAP Concert Music Award and the 2009 Choral Excellence Award from the New York Choral Society. In 2011, the YPC was honored with a National Arts and Humanities Youth Program Award, which was presented to Núñez by First Lady Michelle Obama. Núñez has won praise from fellow musicians as well. "He's like a pied piper for kids from all walks of life—he brings them together," Meredith Monk, the 2011 winner of Musical America's Composer of the Year award—and one of the composers who has written for the YPC—told Isacoff. "I think he is one of the greatest musicians we have, and these kids will never forget the experience."

## MACARTHUR FELLOW

In 2011, Núñez was named a MacArthur fellow and received a grant of $500,000. He has yet to decide what specifically to put all of the money toward, but he has acknowledged that, money aside, the MacArthur title is making more people aware of the YPC and its mission. This, in turn, will help him expand on that mission. "If you go to the richest schools, you will get more money and be able to hire great people," he told Isacoff, "but I want to bring the rich and poor together, as we did here." Núñez began expanding the YPC program into the Dominican Republic in 2011. A choir established in Capotillo became the first in the eventual creation of a national children's chorus in the Dominican Republic, to be comprised of youth choirs from neighborhoods across the country. "We already created one choir in a gang-run neighborhood, deep in the drug trade," Núñez told Isacoff. "I needed an armed escort. But I believe that music has the power to change society." Even if the MacArthur grant will only go so far in expanding the YPC, the important thing for Núñez is to continue empowering children, giving them the confidence to excel in every aspect of their lives. As he told Brown: "It was another MacArthur winner who did, I believe, the 52nd Street project. He had a beautiful quote. He said when children bow, when they come up, they come up taller. And it's true. It's an incredible feeling."

## OUTSIDE THE YPC

In addition to his leadership of the YPC, Núñez also conducts the University Glee Club of New York City (UGC). Established in 1894, the UGC is an all-men's choir made up of college graduates, both recent and from over fifty years ago, who live in the New York metropolitan area. The choir has approximately 150 active members who perform a range of musical styles at concert venues such as Carnegie Hall. Núñez, the group's fifth conductor, began leading the group in 2000. He also served as the director of choral activities at NYU from 2003 to 2010, and he has been a guest conductor, teacher, and music advisor nationwide. In 2012, he and the YPC collaborated with Carnegie Hall through the Weill Music Institute to establish a conducting fellowship program, a symposium to train choral conductors. The first two fellows selected became members of the YPC conducting team.

Núñez lives in Manhattan with his wife Elizabeth, a conductor for the YPC, and their two children.

## SUGGESTED READING

Brown, Jeffrey. "Conversation: Francisco Nunez, Choral Conductor for Kids." *PBS NewsHour.* MacNeil/Lehrer Productions, 23 Sept. 2011. Web. 10 Dec. 2012.
*Francisco J. Núñez.* Francisco J. Núñez, n.d. Web. 10 Dec. 2012.
Isacoff, Stuart. "The Power to Foster Social Renewal through Song." *Wall Street Journal.* Dow Jones & Co., 15 Dec. 2011. Web. 10 Dec. 2012.
Tommasini, Anthony. "Two Chosen 'Geniuses' Reflect on Label." *New York Times.* New York Times Co., 3 Oct. 2011. Web. 10 Dec. 2012.
*Young People's Chorus.* Young People's Chorus of New York City, n.d. Web. 10 Dec. 2012.

## SELECTED WORKS

*Transient Glory* (with Michael Torke, et al.), 2003; *Sing for Peace* (with Jim Papoulis), 2004; *Transient Glory II* (with Dominick Argento, et al.), 2007; *Coolside of Yuletide* (with Jim Papoulis), 2008; *Misa Pequeña para Niños*, 2009; *Francisco J. Núñez Schirmer Choral Series: Four Yeats Songs* (with Alice Parker), 2009; *Francisco J. Núñez Schirmer Choral Series: The Open Door* (with Theodore Wiprud), 2010; *How I Discovered America*, 2010; *What Is Christmas Made Of* (with Jim Papoulis), 2011.

—*Julia Gilstein*

# Bill O'Brien

**Born:** October 23, 1969
**Occupation:** Football coach

When Bill O'Brien was hired to replace football coaching legend Joe Paterno as the fifteenth head coach in Penn State University history, many observers within and outside the university scratched their heads. O'Brien, who spent fourteen years working with college football teams before spending five years as an assistant coach with the New England Patriots, had never served as a head coach at any level, had no previous ties to Penn State, and was a relative unknown outside of football circles. His selection, however, largely came by design. Penn State, in the midst of a child sex abuse scandal involving former assistant coach and now convict Jerry Sandusky, was looking for a new face to help rebuild their football program. The university was also hoping to guide the program into the future and away from the outdated methods of Paterno, who served as the school's head coach for forty-six years before being fired due to his involvement in covering up Sandusky's crimes.

In his first season with Penn State, O'Brien overcame numerous challenges, including severe sanctions imposed on the school by the National Collegiate Athletic Association (NCAA), to lead the team to an overachieving 8–4 record and a second-place finish in the Leaders Division. The team's performance earned O'Brien several national honors as well as the respect and support of alumni and fans.

O'Brien's coaching style has been described as intense and characterized by a hard-nosed,

Pat Little/Reuters/Landov

blue-collar approach. He is also "an X's-and-O's genius who is never unprepared, comprehends football's complexities, and teaches them passionately," Frank Fitzpatrick wrote for the *Philadelphia Inquirer* (8 Jan. 2012). A graduate of Brown University, O'Brien has placed just as much emphasis on academics as on football. He told Jon Birger for *Brown Alumni Magazine* (September/October 2012), "This [Penn State] will be a place where they play really competitive football, but they also learn values and appreciate the importance of a great education to their lives. Those values will never be sacrificed just to win."

## EARLY LIFE

William "Bill" O'Brien was born on October 23, 1969, in Dorchester, Massachusetts. The youngest of three brothers, he grew up in an Irish Catholic, upper-middle-class home in Andover, Massachusetts, where "the three common topics discussed at the dinner table were Brown University, Boston sports and politics," Stefanie Loh noted for the Harrisburg, Pennsylvania, *Patriot-News* (5 Feb. 2012). O'Brien's parents met while attending Brown in the early 1950s where his father was a standout defensive tackle. He later worked in the semiconductor industry and was active in local politics. O'Brien's mother was a librarian.

O'Brien developed an early love of sports through his older brothers, John Jr. and Tom. Both brothers were distinguished athletes and played football at Brown. Hypercompetitive and intense as a child, O'Brien frequently challenged

his much-older brothers to pickup basketball and hockey games in the family driveway. He went on to play in youth-leagues for football, basketball, and baseball, and he further channeled his passion for sports by voraciously reading the sports section of the *Boston Globe*. Rather than following in the footsteps of his childhood sports heroes, however, O'Brien fostered dreams of becoming a coach and has spoken of being indelibly influenced by his Andover youth-league coaches, who "were patient and competitive and taught you how to play the game," as he told Loh.

## EDUCATION

O'Brien attended St. John's Preparatory School, an exclusive Catholic school in Danvers, Massachusetts, where he was "a good athlete and a better student." He was a perennial honors student and a defensive tackle, linebacker, offensive center, and long snapper on the school's varsity football team. His coach, Jim O'Leary, described him to Loh as being "hard and hardnosed. He was a football coach's dream kid playing in high school. His tenacity and toughness, love of the game." During his high-school football seasons, O'Brien would normally have to do three hours of homework after practice each night and has credited St. John's with helping him to develop invaluable time management and organizational skills.

After graduating in 1988, O'Brien attended Brown University in Providence, Rhode Island, and worked that fall as a volunteer assistant coach under O'Leary at his high-school alma mater. In the winter of 1989, O'Brien became a matriculating student at Brown, where he continued to play football under head coach Mickey Kwiatkowski. From 1990 to 1992, O'Brien played at linebacker and defensive end under Kwaitkowski, who described him to Fitzpatrick as "the heart and soul" of the team and "a leader in every sense of the word—physically and emotionally." Though admittedly possessing only marginal talent on the field, O'Brien said to Birger that he "was always a team guy" and "was tough and didn't miss a lot of practices— your typical grinder." He graduated from Brown in 1992 with a double major in political science and organizational behavior management.

## PROFESSIONAL CAREER

Upon graduation, O'Brien stayed at Brown to take a job as a restricted-earnings coach, first working with the team's tight ends under Kwaitkowski in 1993 and then with the team's linebackers under Kwiatkowski's replacement, Mark Whipple, in 1994. Because of his "restricted-earnings" status, he earned only $150 a month "to live in a beer-soaked house," as Pete Thamel noted for the *New York Times* (25 Aug. 2012). During that meager time, O'Brien reportedly wrote letters to every NCAA Division I head coach in the country inquiring about prospective coaching positions. Among the coaches he heard from was Penn State's Joe Paterno, who promised him that he would keep his letter on file.

After spending two years as an assistant at Brown, O'Brien was hired by the Georgia Institute of Technology (Georgia Tech) to work as an offensive graduate assistant under head coach George O'Leary. O'Brien spent three seasons as a graduate assistant before being promoted to serve as the school's running backs coach in 1998. He held that role for three more seasons, during which the team ranked no worse than third in the Atlantic Coast Conference (ACC) in rushing. Meanwhile, he also spent two seasons as Georgia Tech's recruiting coordinator, from 1999 to 2000.

In 2001, O'Brien was promoted to the offensive coordinator and quarterbacks coach and finagled a meeting with New England Patriots' head coach Bill Belichick, who offered him football coaching tips and advice. Describing the meeting to Thamel as "one of the best football experiences I've had," O'Brien immediately became determined to work for Belichick. Afterwards, the two continued to remain in contact, with Belichick providing insight on football strategy in return for scouting reports on players in the ACC. "It was unbelievable," O'Brien told Thamel. "I just remember how good he was getting back to me. There's no one better, and as the relationship went forward, I knew I wanted to work for that guy no matter what the capacity would be eventually."

O'Brien was promoted to Georgia Tech's assistant head coach in 2002, and in 2003 he joined the coaching staff at the University of Maryland as a running backs coach. In his two years there, he helped guide the team to the second-best rushing attack in the ACC in 2003 and an overall record of 15–9.

## MOVE TO THE NEW ENGLAND PATRIOTS

Following a difficult two-year stint as offensive coordinator and quarterbacks coach at Duke University from 2005 to 2006, O'Brien left college coaching to work under Bill Belichick who offered him a spot as an offensive assistant. While the job paid less than half of his previous salary and entailed basic entry-level responsibilities like analyzing game films, O'Brien immediately seized the opportunity, which also allowed him to work in his native Massachusetts for the first time in his professional coaching career.

O'Brien rose rapidly up the Patriots' coaching ladder during the team's unprecedented run of success, and following their record-breaking 2007 season, Belichick promoted O'Brien to wide receivers coach, a role he held for one season. When the highly coveted Patriots offensive coordinator and quarterbacks coach Josh

McDaniels became head coach of the Denver Broncos in January 2009, O'Brien took over as quarterbacks coach (a position he held exclusively from 2009 to 2010), and in 2011, O'Brien was named offensive coordinator while continuing to serve as the team's quarterbacks coach.

O'Brien was the Patriots' primary play-caller in 2011 and helped sustain their reputation as an offensive powerhouse with the team finishing second in the NFL both in total offense (428.0 yards per game) and passing yards (317.8 yards per game) and finishing third in the league in total points scored (513). Meanwhile, quarterback Tom Brady threw for a career-best 5,235 yards and 39 touchdowns and became only the fourth quarterback in NFL history to throw for more than 5,000 yards in a single season, with his total marking the second-highest in history.

During his five-year tenure with the Patriots, O'Brien won over players and fellow coaches with his fiery intensity, gritty toughness, and unrelenting dedication. "It was clear pretty early on that he was going to do well, and he did," Bill Belichick recalled to Pete Thamel. "He worked really hard and didn't try to overstep his bounds." For his part, O'Brien has said that working for Belichick, whom he considers his biggest coaching influence, was similar to "getting a PhD in football," as he told Jon Birger. "As an assistant he gives you the parameters," he added, "but he lets you be creative and coach."

## REPLACING PATERNO

As the Patriots were steamrolling toward their second Super Bowl appearance in five seasons and their fifth under Belichick, Joe Paterno and his Penn State football program were experiencing one of the most shocking falls from grace in sports history. In November 2011, Jerry Sandusky, a former Penn State defensive coordinator and assistant coach who spent over three decades on Paterno's coaching staff before retiring in 1999, was arrested on numerous child sex abuse charges following a two-year grand jury investigation. Sandusky's arrest set in motion a stunning turn of events over the next nine months that included Paterno's firing, Penn State president Graham Spanier's resignation, a damning internal investigation report released by former FBI director Louis Freeh, and some of the most severe NCAA sanctions in history.

Less than two months after Paterno's dismissal, O'Brien, still in midst of the Patriots' Super Bowl run, was named as his successor on January 7, 2012, thus becoming the fifteenth head coach in Penn State's history. O'Brien was chosen over a number of other internal candidates, including Paterno's interim successor Tom Bradley, who had also interviewed for the job. The combination of O'Brien's lack of head coaching experience with his status as being a complete Penn State outsider drew the ire of many former Penn State players and alumni who had been expecting a candidate with more direct ties to the university. Nonetheless, university officials and members of the search committee were ultimately sold on O'Brien's character and confidence and his dedication to upholding the school's long tradition of excellence on the field and in the classroom. O'Brien, who had been prepped for the interview by Belichick, was signed to a five-year deal that gave him an annual base salary of $950,000.

### REBUILDING PENN STATE FOOTBALL

O'Brien faced many challenges in his first year as head coach. In July 2012, the NCAA hit the university and its football program with a litany of crippling sanctions, among them a four-year ban on postseason bowl games, a $60 million fine, and the loss of forty scholarships (ten a year over four years). All of Penn State's victories and bowl appearances from the 1998 to 2011 seasons were also vacated. As a result, Paterno, who died of complications from lung cancer just two weeks after O'Brien's hiring, went from being the winningest coach in Division I college football history to fifth in all-time Division I coaching victories. Furthermore, because of the severity of the sanctions, every member of the Penn State team was given an opportunity to transfer to another school where they would immediately be eligible to play. This action resulted in the departure of nine scholarship players.

Undaunted, O'Brien, whose contract was automatically extended four years through the year 2020 as a result of the sanctions, went ahead with his plans for rebuilding Penn State's football program and moving it into the twenty-first century, which included installing the complex offense he brought with him from New England and modernizing the university's training facility. Breaking with a long tradition, O'Brien also issued a uniform overhaul that added nameplates to players' jerseys to recognize and honor those who stayed at the school during the scandal.

O'Brien's impact on Penn State was immediate. Despite narrowly losing their first two games of the 2012 season, Penn State finished with a successful 8–4 record to finish second in the Leaders Division. They also posted a 6–2 record in the highly competitive Big Ten Conference. O'Brien's eight wins were the most by a rookie head coach in the school's 126-year history and resulted in him receiving a number of honors, including being named Bear Bryant Coach of the Year, Big Ten–Dave McClain Coach of the Year, ESPN.com's National Coach of the Year, Hayes-Schembechler Coach of the Year, and the Maxwell Football Club's Collegiate Coach of the Year. O'Brien was also a finalist for the prestigious Dapper Dan Sportsman of the Year award.

In January 2013, O'Brien interviewed for head-coaching vacancies with the Cleveland Browns and the Philadelphia Eagles, but he opted to remain at Penn State. Despite rumblings that O'Brien will leave for greener pastures, he has reinforced his commitment to the school and its players.

### PERSONAL LIFE

O'Brien met his wife, Colleen, while working as an assistant at Georgia Tech. They married in 1998 and have two sons, Jack and Michael. Their eldest son, Jack, was born with a rare brain disorder called lissencephaly, which severely limits his motor skills and causes him to have multiple daily seizures. "In a way, it was one of the best things that ever happened to us," O'Brien said to Pete Thamel about his son's disorder, which requires around-the-clock care. "It added so much perspective to our lives. We figured out what was important, and it brought us closer together and put in perspective the importance of football."

### SUGGESTED READING

Birger, Jon. "A Coach's Challenge." *Brown Alumni Magazine*. Brown University, Sept.–Oct. 2012. Web. 13 June 2013.

Fitzpatrick, Frank. "New Penn State Coach Bill O'Brien Known for Intensity." *Philly.com*. Interstate General Media, LLC, 8 Jan. 2012. Web. 13 June 2013.

Svrluga, Barry. "Bill O'Brien Keeps Penn State Job in Perspective." *Washington Post*. Washington Post, 31 Aug. 2012. Web. 13 June 2013.

Thamel, Pete. "As Tough as His Task." *New York Times*. New York Times Co., 25 Aug. 2012. Web. 13 June 2013.

—*Chris Cullen*

# Mark O'Connor

**Born:** August 5, 1961
**Occupation:** Violinist and composer

In a career spanning more than forty years, Mark O'Connor has demonstrated time and again that versatility and virtuosity can peacefully coexist in the same musician. Equally adept at a number of string instruments but best known for his work as a violinist, the award-winning musician and composer is known for his ability to play country, bluegrass, jazz, classical, and folk music with both dexterity and improvisation. He has also branched out from his roles as a performer and composer to begin work on a massive project: teaching others how to play their instruments through a method that he developed, which employs the improvisational skills honed by playing American music, rather than through more traditional, rote-memorization methods. "The biggest part of the last decade as far as my career

Associated Press

was about my performances, my playing, my music," he told Randy Lewis for the *Los Angeles Times* (15 Mar. 2009). "Now in my life it's more about what this music means to other musicians. It's becoming less about my performances as an artist and maybe more about being in a leadership position to steer in new ideas and bring new material for people to try out. It's a really, really gratifying development."

### EARLY LIFE

Mark O'Connor was born in Seattle, Washington, on August 5, 1961. His paternal ancestors had settled in Seattle in the late nineteenth century. His maternal ancestors had come to the Americas far earlier, in 1608, and traveled across the country until World War I, when his Memphis-born grandmother moved to Seattle. "So the journey west, both branches of my family took it, just like so many people," O'Connor told Martin Steinberg for the Associated Press (15 Mar. 2009). "And it was this journey out of our cities, towns, into whatever it was to get more land, just to get more breathing room or to get away from something. A lot of this movement was our cultural backdrop to make the music that we [Americans] have."

O'Connor came to music early, when his mother—a classical music lover who died when he was just twenty—bought him a guitar at age three. Two years later she found him a classical guitar instructor who taught him how to read music. By the age of nine or ten he was competing in classical guitar competitions, including a contest held at the University of Washington,

at which he competed against college-aged students and won second prize. During this period he became interested in the violin after seeing violinists and fiddlers performing on his local PBS television affiliate. He recalled to Peter Anick for *Fiddler Magazine* (21 Aug. 2010), "For three years, I begged them for a fiddle. They thought I was a little bit fickle and wasn't completely serious about my request. And it wasn't until I was trying to construct one out of cardboard around age ten, attempting to put my old set of guitar strings on it, that convinced my mother. It folded up on me and I ended up crying about it. So I finally got one at eleven."

It was clear from the start that O'Connor had an innate connection with the instrument. His mother began to take him on trips where he could hone his fiddling skills. His father, an alcoholic laborer whom O'Connor has described as somewhat domineering, approved of these trips because O'Connor usually won or earned money on them. "If it weren't for my musical talent, I would have been his slave, no doubt," he told Steinberg.

### EARLY MUSICAL EDUCATION

O'Connor's first lessons as a student of the fiddle were with Barbara Lamb, who had a musical background that included classical, bluegrass, and old-time fiddling. He then worked under John Burke, who sparked the improvisation and ingenuity he would later more fully develop under Stéphane Grappelli, the noted French jazz violinist considered by many music fans to be one of the instrument's greatest improvisers. Perhaps most significantly, he began taking lessons with the legendary Benny Thomasson, a champion fiddler who had won competitions for two decades in Texas. Thomasson lived two hours away from O'Connor's boyhood home in Seattle, so Thomasson and the O'Connors developed a unique arrangement. O'Connor explained to Anick, "My mother would drive me down to his house and my lesson would literally last an entire weekend. These excursions took place every other weekend. So I would learn from him hours and hours a day on a Saturday and half of Sunday, then come back home in order to go to school the next day. And we kept up that schedule more or less for a good three years."

O'Connor studied under Thomasson until he was fourteen years old. During that time he worked on about four or five songs per weekend. At the end of those three years, O'Connor had learned some 250 songs from the Texas fiddle master, as well as perfecting the style of Texas fiddling itself. He also competed in contests all over the country, at which he played about fifty of the tunes he had learned from Thomasson. Although he now claims to have lost about 75 percent of the contests he entered, O'Connor is remembered by many music fans as being the young winner of the Grand Master Fiddler Championship, which he won in 1975 at age thirteen. O'Connor beat numerous fiddling legends in that contest, including James "Texas Shorty" Chancellor, Lewis Franklin, and J. T. Perkins. According to his official website, he remains the only musician ever to win national championships on bluegrass guitar, fiddle, and mandolin.

O'Connor began a career as a session musician on country music records in Nashville, Tennessee, shortly after graduating from high school. Unfortunately, when he arrived in the early 1980s, Nashville music executives were trending against what were considered "old time" country instruments, such as steel guitars and fiddles. "Buddy Spicher, one of the great session players of the '60s and '70s, told me, 'Kid, you came to town at the wrong time—all the work has dried up,'" O'Connor recalled to Lewis. "But I had an idea that I could prove that a fiddle could play alongside a DX7 [synthesizer], a rock guitar, or a Fender Rhodes [electric piano]. I've been cross-pollinating for my entire career."

### SIDEMAN, BAND MEMBER, SOLO ARTIST

O'Connor's idea paid off. Over the next two decades, he had tremendous success as an in-demand session musician, or sideman. He has played on more than five hundred albums and has worked with such diverse musicians as Dolly Parton, Paul Simon, James Taylor, and Randy Travis, among others. From 1991 to 1996 the Country Music Association named him its musician of the year. He was also a member of several bands during this period. O'Connor joined the David Grisman Quintet, an acoustic string band, as a guitarist at the age of seventeen. Two years later, at nineteen, he served as a violinist and guitarist for the Dregs, a rock-fusion instrumental band of the 1980s. Also in the 1980s, he joined Strength in Numbers, an acoustic band with Sam Bush on fiddle and mandolin, Jerry Douglas on dobro, Béla Fleck on guitar and banjo, Edgar Meyer on bass, and O'Connor himself on fiddle, guitar, and mandolin. He then joined a pair of celebrated country bands, the American Music Shop house band and New Nashville Cats, in 1989 and 1990.

O'Connor's solo albums met with critical and commercial success as well. *The Fiddle Concerto* (1995) hit number six on the classical Billboard charts, *Liberty!* (1997) reached number eight on the same charts, and *Midnight on the Water* bested both of its predecessors, topping out at number five. O'Connor won Grammy Awards for his work with New Nashville Cats in 1992 and in 1996 released the chart-topping classical album *Appalachia Waltz*, a collaboration with cellist Yo-Yo Ma. In interviews O'Connor has expressed his belief that his success in so many styles of music is directly linked to his student days working

under Thomasson. He told Anick, "The theme and variations concept of Texas fiddling really is a very nice interesting musical bridge to other styles of music—jazz and classical, for instance."

### COMPOSER

Although he made excellent money as a session musician and enjoyed working with his various bands and as a solo artist, O'Connor spent much of his spare time writing and recording themes that were unconnected to the work he was doing with others. These themes, which he had begun working on in the early 1990s, would eventually evolve into his first forays into composing classical music infused with a wholly American style, combing bluegrass, classical, country, folk, and jazz. "When I started this I really thought . . . I was just going to write it for posterity. So I came from a lucrative session career where I made enough money to buy a very nice home and I quit my career cold turkey," O'Connor explained to Steinberg. "I just canceled everything. I said, 'That's it,' and I walked away—to a lot of people's dismay."

His first orchestral composition would eventually become his *Fiddle Concerto*, which he recorded in 1995 and has performed in concert more than two hundred times. By mid-2013, O'Connor had written more than forty classical works, including pieces for small musical ensembles and violin concertos. Most notably, he composed his *Americana Symphony*, which he completed in 2006 and released as an album in 2009. This masterwork drew heavily from both his varied musical influences and his personal family history in the United States, which he believes reflects the larger themes of average Americans living through the country's history. "I want to use jazz and blues and other vernacular music as the language on which classical compositions are built," O'Connor told Lewis. "It's the same thing [Astor] Piazzolla did in his native Argentina, what [Béla] Bartok did in Hungary, and what Tan Dun is doing in China. It's not a new concept. It's just new in American classical circles. It's so funny—it reveals some people's idea that our cultural musical heritage is somehow not important enough."

### TEACHING THE METHOD

In order to develop this national style of American music further, O'Connor aids emerging musicians by teaching at music programs at such prestigious institutions as the Aspen Summer Festival, Berklee College of Music, the Cleveland Institute of Music, the Juilliard School, Harvard University, Rice University, the University of Maryland, the University of Texas, and Tanglewood, among others. He also established the Mark O'Connor String Camp, which is held each summer; in 2013, it was held in Charleston, South Carolina. Most musical historians agree that O'Connor is not inventing a new approach to music but rather returning to an approach that had been employed by many musicians throughout the years. O'Connor, who concurs with that opinion, noted in the *Chicago Tribune* (2 Mar. 2010), "The music that we enjoy today is there simply because there were people who created musical styles that also ignored boundaries. People from Chuck Berry and Little Richard to Elvis Presley and Louis Armstrong to Jimmie Rodgers to Bob Wills to Bill Monroe. These guys were boundary-defiers."

In the fall of 2009 O'Connor introduced the O'Connor Violin Method, which breaks with the traditional, rote-memorization European and Japanese approaches to learning the instrument and instead promotes a more improvisational method that employs American music. The method is considered by many music teachers to be a revolutionary approach that helps to fill a gap in musical instruction. O'Connor explained in an interview with the *Huffington Post* (7 July 2013), "I think a complete and holistic music education is best for young students in today's challenging environments. That means that a music method book must join the technical with the creative. . . . Learning by rote, acquiring great technique, and using one's memory are all important, [but] I feel that it is an incomplete methodology if we continue to learn technically without learning to be musically creative."

## PERSONAL LIFE

Although O'Connor spends much of his time on the road, teaching or performing either solo or as part of an ensemble, he maintains a home in New York City as well as a country home in Pennsylvania. He lives with his partner, fellow string player Sadie Rose deWall, and their daughter, Autumn Rose O'Connor, who was born in 2010. He also has a son, Forrest, who in 2010 graduated from Harvard University, where he studied musicology and music composition. O'Connor was married to Forrest's mother, a former concert flutist named Suzanne, from 1987 to 1991.

While at home in New York, O'Connor tends to stay up very late working. He often works on his YouTube channel playlist and then goes out and has lunch and tea before returning to his apartment to work on new compositions or his method. He enjoys walking in Central Park, visiting famed jazz clubs such as Dizzy's and the Blue Note, and holding jam sessions with friends. Although he does not keep a traditional work schedule, O'Connor finds his routine tremendously helpful in his creative processes, particularly in perfecting his method. "The work it takes is incalculable," he noted in an interview with Sarah Harrison Smith for the *New York Times* (5 Jan. 2013). "I want to give stature to American string music and its history, culture,

creativity, the social aspects and the power of its being a vehicle for political change. That really hasn't been researched before."

## SUGGESTED READING

Anick, Peter. "Mark O'Connor: On Learning, Playing, and Teaching Strings, American-Style." *Fiddler Magazine*. Fiddler Magazine, 21 Aug. 2010. Web. 7 July 2013.

Harrison Smith, Sarah. "The Fiddler in the Cave." *New York Times*. New York Times, 5 Jan. 2013. Web. 7 July 2013.

Lewis, Randy. "Mark O'Connor, Genre Fiddler." *Los Angeles Times*. Los Angeles Times, 15 Mar. 2009. Web. 7 July 2013.

"Mark O'Connor: Violinist and Former Child Prodigy Celebrates Forty Years of Music." *Huffington Post*. Huffington Post, 9 June 2013. Web. 7 July 2013.

Steinberg, Martin. "First Symphony by Mark O'Connor Manifests the Fiddler's Destiny." *Seattle Times*. Seattle Times, 15 Mar. 2009. Web. 7 July 2013.

## SELECTED WORKS

*National Junior Fiddling Champion*, 1974; *Pickin' in the Wind*, 1975; *The Fiddle Concerto*, 1994; *Appalachia Waltz*, 1996; *Liberty!*, 1997; *Midnight on the Water*, 1998; *The American Seasons*, 2001; *Crossing Bridges*, 2004; *Americana Symphony*, 2009

—Christopher Mari

# Mikael Ohlsson

**Born:** December 27, 1957
**Occupation:** President and CEO of IKEA

In April 2009, Mikael Ohlsson was tapped to become president and chief executive officer (CEO) of IKEA, a company known for its modern and moderately priced furniture and its unique shopping experience, which guides customers through a long, labyrinthine showroom and asks them to load the flat-box-packed furniture from the warehouse. Ohlsson has spent his entire professional career at IKEA, beginning by selling carpets there when he was just twenty-two. Upon taking the company's top post in the midst of a global financial crisis, Ohlsson promised to focus on cutting costs and expanding into new markets in places such as India and China.

Keeping expenses low has always been a priority for IKEA, which was founded in Småland in 1943—during World War II—by Ingvar Kamprad when he was just seventeen years old. The culture of Småland, an impoverished rural area in southern Sweden, Ohlsson has said, is

Associated Press

reflected in the guiding principles of IKEA. "Smäland made people very thrifty, cost-consciousness, stubborn and humble. It fostered togetherness," he told James Lamont for the London *Financial Times* (4 Apr. 2011). "Part of that has grown into Ikea values. One is not to be satisfied, always to challenge and find new ways of doing things and never to feel that we are at the goal but rather on a journey." In his three years at the helm of IKEA, Ohlsson has helped the company weather a series of economic and public-image crises and enabled the notoriously private company to become more transparent, while remaining the number-one furniture retailer in the world.

Martin Hansson, who was IKEA's UK boss at the time, told Andrew Davidson for the London *Sunday Times* (23 Jan. 2011), "It's about understanding the space people live in, where size and affordability are key. . . . And Mikael is a good ambassador for Ikea values—down to earth, non-hierarchical, humble." In September 2012, Ohlsson announced that he would retire in September 2013 and would be succeeded by Peter Agnefjall, country manager of IKEA Sweden.

## EARLY LIFE AND EDUCATION
Ohlsson was born in Helsingborg, a coastal city on the southern tip of Sweden, near Denmark. His grandparents were farmers, and his parents were teachers. Ohlsson told Lamont that he likely would have become a farmer if his family still owned the land they once did. Ohlsson

studied industrial engineering, marketing, and management at the Institute of Technology at Linköping University in Sweden, earning a master of science degree.

Ohlsson was twenty-two and still in school when he took his first job at IKEA, selling carpet out of its Linköping store, a city in the middle of Sweden, in 1979. He remained in that position for two years before being promoted to store manager in Sundsvall, Sweden, in 1981. In 1984, Ohlsson became a training and development manager at IKEA Sweden, and by 1986, he had become a marketing manager. Ohlsson went on to serve as a country manager for IKEA Belgium (1988–91), a country manager for IKEA Canada (1991–95), and a managing director of IKEA Sweden (1995–2000).

Ohlsson's rise through IKEA coincided with a period of enormous growth for the company. When Ohlsson started working there, IKEA had established stores in Norway (1963), Denmark (1969), Switzerland (1973), Australia (1975), Canada (1976), Austria (1977), and the Netherlands (1979).

In 1982, IKEA created the unique ownership structure aimed at minimizing costs. It formed the IKEA Group, a collection of holding companies that each run different operations, such as merchandising and distribution. The IKEA Group was owned by the parent company, a foundation called the Stichting INGKA Foundation. The ownership structure allowed IKEA to reinvest its profit without paying any dividends to banks or investors. "That's one of the reasons I like it," Ohlsson told Davidson, "the aim is to satisfy customers, not stock markets." The structure also allowed the company to keep the level of its success private because it did not have to release earning statements and balance sheets to its investors.

## GROWTH AND CHANGES IN LEADERSHIP
The first IKEA in the United States opened in 1985. In 1986, Kamprad, IKEA's founder, retired to become an adviser to IKEA's parent company. He was replaced by Anders Moberg, who had held several positions within IKEA since 1979; Moberg went on to play a key role in the company's global expansion. Over the next several years, IKEA opened stores in the United Kingdom (1987), Italy (1989), Hungary (1990), the Czech Republic and Poland (1991), Spain (1996), and China (1998).

During that time, IKEA enjoyed great success, especially among the baby-boom generation, establishing a reputation for providing affordable quality furniture. IKEA was already the largest furniture retailer in the world by the 1990s, with more than ninety-five stores. The company was so popular that there were times that its stores struggled to keep up the supply with the high demand.

In 1999, Moberg was replaced by Anders Dahlvig, who had worked for IKEA since 1984. During Dahlvig's almost ten year as CEO, the pace of growth slowed for IKEA in part because it faced a global economic slowdown and in part because competitors such as Walmart were strategically lowering prices to target IKEA's dominance over the furniture market. It expanded into just three new markets—Russia (2000), Portugal (2004), and Japan (2006)—and at times had to come up with creative ways to entice buyers to spend, offering free breakfasts at its restaurant or implementing strategic promotions of top-selling products. During Moberg's time as CEO, Ohlsson served as regional manager of IKEA for southern Europe and North America, from 2000 to 2009.

## REACHING THE TOP

In April 2009, Ohlsson was named president and CEO of IKEA. According to Davidson, many former colleagues thought Ohlsson should have been selected to helm the company in 1999 but was passed over because he too often disagreed with Kamprad's leadership. Ohlsson has said that he did not expect the appointment; rather he was planning on working for a few more years in senior management before retiring.

At the time Ohlsson became CEO, the global economy was in crisis. IKEA annual sales growth was down to 3 percent from 10 percent. The company was also facing increased competition from large retailers that had cut their prices to adjust to the economic conditions. Still, Ohlsson remained confident that IKEA's success would continue. "Ikea is at its best when times are bad," he said, as quoted by the Canada *Globe and Mail* (25 Apr. 2009). "When wallets get thinner, for many, Ikea becomes an even better alternative." Ohlsson also promised that the company would be more open about its business practices than it had been in the past.

Ohlsson surprised many when he led IKEA to record profits even as other businesses struggled in the thick of the recession. In January 2011, IKEA profits were up 6 percent to $2.7 billion, and revenues, up 7.7 percent to $23.1 billion. Of its 280 warehouse stores, IKEA was most successful in Europe, selling about half of the new kitchens purchased in Norway and about one-third of every new kitchen sold in Sweden and France.

## FOCUS ON EXPANSION

IKEA earned an impressive net profit of $2.5 billion in 2010, but the vast majority of sales were concentrated in Europe. In an effort to reduce its reliance on its revenues from Europe, which was stuck in a recession, and to take advantage of its higher-growth emerging markets, Ohlsson focused on expanding to Russia, China, and especially India.

By 2012, IKEA had yet to open a single store in India because the country's many layers of regulation, including the requirement that any foreign-owned business be a joint venture, restricted foreign investment. "There is a real need of good home furnishings at [a] low price in India with what is happening in the coming 20 years in Indian cities," Ohlsson told Lamont. "There is a lot of need and people have relatively thin wallets in these cities." Ohlsson spent a significant amount of time consulting with both the Indian government and business community in an effort to persuade them that allowing foreign investors like IKEA would benefit their economy.

In late 2011, India's cabinet announced that, with some restrictions, it would begin allowing single-brand retailers—such as IKEA—to own 100 percent of their subsidiaries in India and multibrand retailers—such as Walmart—to own up to 51 percent of their India-based businesses. As Ohlsson expected, the ruling sparked outrage among small business and labor communities, as shares of local retailers plummeted in the wake of the announcement and isolationist sentiment swept the country. Ohlsson retreated from India before unveiling IKEA's investment strategy. After more than a year of deliberations over the matter, in January 2013, India's foreign investment ministry approved IKEA's plan to enter the country's market; IKEA was also expected to receive approval from the Indian federal cabinet. IKEA reportedly plans to invest $2 billion in India and open twenty-five stores.

Ohlsson also faced regulatory obstacles when attempting to expand in Europe. After announcing plans to spend 20 billion euros by the end of the decade in Europe by opening between twenty and twenty-five stores a year and creating 100,000 jobs, IKEA managed to open just eleven stores employing eight thousand workers in 2012. Ohlsson told Richard Milne for the London *Financial Times* (23 Jan. 2013), "We would like to move faster but the process of getting licences and going through the hidden and not hidden barriers is getting longer and longer. This red tape is holding back many investments and therefore job creation in Europe."

Meanwhile, IKEA has been successful in its efforts to expand in China. In April 2013, Ohlsson lowered its prices there and announced plans to add five new stores to its eleven already in the country—and to have forty in the country by 2020. "China will be Ikea's number two market relatively soon," Ohlsson told the Canada *National Post's Financial Post & FP Investing* (3 Apr. 2013), "and number one maybe in the long run."

## OPENING UP

In 2010, Johan Stenebo, a former IKEA executive, published *The Truth about Ikea*, in which he accused the company of valuing profits over ethics and establishing a group of managers that lacked diversity. In his January 2011 interview with Davidson, Ohlsson challenged the notion that IKEA was not diverse, pointing out that many of IKEA's country managers were local and 40 percent of his top two hundred managers were women. He also dismissed criticisms of the company's management structure. "We are run like any other company, with an executive management reporting to a board of directors," Ohlsson said. He added that the only difference from publicly listed companies was that IKEA's private ownership allowed it to adopt a long-term view when it came to serving customers.

While deflecting the recurrent criticism, Ohlsson also consciously moved toward making IKEA a more transparent company, providing information to the press about the company's unusual tax structure. In the fall of 2012, IKEA also published its financial results for the first time ever. When he was asked whether he thought IKEA had been overly secretive in the past, Ohlsson told the *Financial Times* (24 Sept. 2012), "I know it has been perceived like that. A lot of that is disappearing. We have focused always on our customers, on our range, on our suppliers. We have spent very little time to make interviews with the *Financial Times*."

### PLANS FOR THE FUTURE
In September 2012, Ohlsson announced he would retire in exactly one year but that IKEA's ten-year business plan would remain in place under the new CEO. Ohlsson has said that with his remaining time he will continue to focus on pursuing markets in Asia. He also told Milne that IKEA would squeeze out more waste from IKEA's already streamlined production system. "We want to drive unnecessary costs out of the system and price the products lower and lower," he said. "I see very big opportunities when it comes to industrialisation to help the cost picture and it will help the quality even further. We will keep the direction, but amplify it."

Additionally, Ohlsson is focused on continuing to invest in environmentally sustainable practices, including using photovoltaic systems and wind farms to provide power for stores—with the goal of eventually using 100 percent renewable energy. He has also stated his commitment to continuing IKEA's extensive charitable work, much of which is centered on mothers and children in India. After weathering a series of economic crises over the years, IKEA remains the number-one furniture retailer in the world, operating about 290 stores in twenty-six countries and increasing sales every year since 2001.

### PERSONAL LIFE
In his article, Davidson describes Ohlsson as "affable, bright and deceptively tough." He lives in Leiden, in the Netherlands, with his three children—two sons and one daughter—and his wife, a former banker. He also owns homes Helsingborg, Sweden, and Sitges, Spain. He drives a silver Audi A6. In his spare time, he enjoys playing guitar and the saxophone and taking photographs. Ohlsson's favorite music is by John Lennon, his favorite book is Keith Richards's 2010 autobiography *Life*, and his favorite film is *Australia* (2008), starring Nicole Kidman.

### SUGGESTED READING
Davidson, Andrew. "Ikea Chief Turns Up the Heat." *Sunday Times* [London] 23 Jan. 2011: 7. Print.

Lamont, James. "A Missionary of Soft Furnishing." *Financial Times* [London] 4 Apr. 2011: 16. Print.

Milne, Richard. "Red Tape Frustrates Ikea's Plans for Growth." *Financial Times* [London] 23 Jan. 2013, US ed.: 16. Print.

Ward, Andrew. "Retailer Still Strong on the Home Front." *Financial Times* [London] 14 Jan. 2011, Asia ed.: 15. Print.

—*Margaret Roush Mead*

---

# Jim O'Neill

**Born:** March 17, 1957
**Occupation:** Economist and former chair of Goldman Sachs Asset Management

In 2001 Jim O'Neill, a British economist working for the investment bank Goldman Sachs, made his mark on his field when he successfully argued that four very diverse countries—Brazil, Russia, India, and China—would, in the coming decades, use their fast-growing economies to alter the geopolitical landscape radically. O'Neill's thesis was a bold jab at the conventional economic thinking of the era, which held that these developing nations would be unlikely to rival the robust economies of nations such as the United States and the United Kingdom at any point in the near future. During the first decade of the twenty-first century, the BRIC nations, as O'Neill called them, played a vital role in the global economy and demonstrated that they would likely continue to do so. In 2009, these four nations joined together in a formal association, and a year later, South Africa joined the group, changing the acronym to BRICS.

Although the BRICS represented almost three billion of the world's seven billion people by early 2013 and had economies with a combined nominal gross domestic product (GDP) of 14.8 trillion in US dollars, O'Neill never imagined that the internal paper he wrote for Goldman Sachs concerning these nations would have a concrete impact on politics and economic

In 1982 O'Neill took his economic credentials into the financial world when he joined Bank of America, at the time a major holder of OPEC (Organization of Petroleum Exporting Countries) funds. He then took a position with Marine Midland Bank in 1983 and remained there until 1988. He began to be noticed in the financial world after joining Swiss Bank Corporation (SBC) in 1988, initially overseeing the corporation's fixed income research group. In 1991 he was tapped to serve as SBC's head of global research, a position he held for four years.

## GOLDMAN SACHS

In 1995 O'Neill joined Goldman Sachs, one of the wealthiest and most powerful investment banks in the world. The American multinational firm works primarily for international institutional clients in the fields of investment management and financial services; throughout its long history, many of its executives have gone on to work in a variety of government posts in nations around the world. During his tenure at Goldman Sachs, O'Neill worked in a number of positions, including chief currency economist, cohead of global economic research, and head of global economics, commodities, and strategy research. His first position involved deciding the bank's view on the US dollar. "Within a week, about two hundred other people at Goldman offered me their view on the dollar," he recalled to Ellen Kelleher for the *Financial Times* (31 Mar. 2013). "I'm like, 'Oh my God. They are all so bright.' But that's how the place is. It's amazing in that sense."

In 2001, O'Neill's fellow cohead of economic research left Goldman Sachs to become the chair of the British Broadcasting Corporation (BBC), the largest broadcaster in the world. In his cohead's absence, O'Neill felt that he needed to put his own stamp on the Goldman Sachs division and sought a way to do that. His inspiration came after the terrorist attacks of September 11, 2001.

O'Neill quickly realized that despite the terrorist attacks, globalization—the process by which nations' natural and cultural resources are exchanged worldwide at an ever-increasing rate due to technological advancement—would remain a major factor in the years ahead, and a number of emerging economies would make a considerable impact on the process. He recalled to Kowitt, "Around the horror of that event, the underlying message was that globalization was going to continue and thrive." He added, "It was going to have to be on a more complex basis, and it wouldn't effectively be about the Americanization of the world—because that was how it seemed to be in the eyes of many. Even though 9/11 wasn't a direct sign of this, it crystallized the thought in my head."

Sysoyev Grigory/Itar-Tass/Landov

policies at the highest levels. He told Beth Kowitt for *CNN Money* (17 June 2009), "It's transformed my own life. The impact really started to grow two years later, when we did our first piece looking at what the world could look like by 2050, which picked up on the theme of my earlier paper. We showed that some time between then and 2050, specifically 2037, the combined GDP of those four countries could become bigger than the G7. After that, interest from the international corporate community absolutely exploded, and it's been crazy ever since."

## EARLY EDUCATION AND CAREER

The son of a mail carrier and his wife, Terence James O'Neill was born in Gatley, in the Greater Manchester region of England, on March 17, 1957. A lifelong fan of the football (soccer) club Manchester United, O'Neill passed on an opportunity to matriculate at a local private secondary school because it did not have its own soccer team. He instead attended one that did, Burnage Comprehensive (later renamed Burnage Media Arts College), a less prestigious state school.

O'Neill next attended Sheffield University, a research university in Sheffield, England, where he chose to study geography and economics. He eventually decided to drop his geography courses and focus on economics, completing his bachelor's degree in that field in 1978. After graduating, he attended the University of Surrey at Guildford, in the southeastern part of England, where he earned his doctorate in economics in 1982. His thesis, titled "An Empirical Investigation into the OPEC Surplus and Its Disposal," was completed under the supervision of economist David Hawdon.

## COINING A NEW ACRONYM: BRIC

In November 2001, O'Neill wrote a paper for Goldman Sachs titled "Building Better Global Economic BRICs." An acronym coined by O'Neill, BRIC stands for Brazil, Russia, India, and China. In his 2001 paper, O'Neill argues that these four nations, though unalike politically, will grow at such a brisk economic clip in the coming decades that they will shift geopolitical power away from the G7. The G7, also known as the Group of Seven, is composed of seven of the wealthiest nations on earth—the United States, the United Kingdom, France, Germany, Italy, Canada, and Japan.

O'Neill's paper predicts that during the middle of the twenty-first century, the BRIC nations will have annual gross domestic products (GDPs)—the market value of goods and services produced by a given country—that will overtake those of the G7 and radically alter the global economic and political landscape. In short, O'Neill contends that the BRIC nations will help spur a trend toward a world in which no nation or group of nations can exert outsized influence on world events, as the United States and the Soviet Union did through the latter half of the twentieth century. One of O'Neill's predictions about the BRIC nations has already come true: in the decade ending in December 2012, the stocks in emerging markets outperformed those in developed markets, according to Vanguard, with annual returns of 16.2 percent for emerging markets and just 8.4 percent for developed markets other than the United States.

In September 2006, foreign ministers from each BRIC nation met for the first time in New York City, marking the beginning of what would soon become an official annual summit. The coalition's first major diplomatic meeting was held in Yekaterinburg, Russia, in May 2008; the first formal summit took place there in June 2009. Representatives from these nations meet each year to discuss their mutual interests and their group's emerging role in the world's economy. O'Neill, who has noted that his BRIC grouping gained considerable traction in the mainstream lexicon after 2003, has marveled at the idea that a concept he originally wrote about in an economic paper has become a political reality. "Who would have ever dreamt that there would be a BRIC political club? It certainly isn't something that I ever imagined," he told Nima Elbagir for CNN (5 Apr. 2011).

## FORMATION AND EXPANSION OF THE BRIC COALITION

Although the BRIC confederation is based on O'Neill's economic concept, the group has since expanded beyond that. In December 2010, after much lobbying by its government, South Africa was formally asked to join the group, now known officially as the BRICS, with the S standing for South Africa. O'Neill himself was initially puzzled by the addition. According to the World Bank, at the end of 2012 South Africa had a population of approximately fifty-one million people and a GDP of about $384 billion, both tiny figures when compared with the four original BRIC nations, which account for about 40 percent of the world's population.

"Being part of the BRIC political club doesn't guarantee that you are going to be regarded as a BRIC economically," O'Neill said to Elbagir. "At this particular point in time, just because South Africa has been accepted into that club doesn't change the way that I'll think about it in terms of how we focus on what constitutes a BRIC or not and whether it affects others in terms of investment flows." However, O'Neill has since softened his stance on South Africa's inclusion, having noted that the African nation's influence on the rest of the continent and its strong financial sector provide solid reasons for its inclusion in the BRICS. In 2011 the economist published *The Growth Map: Economic Opportunity in the BRICs and Beyond*, a book outlining his thoughts on these nations' futures.

In 2013, at the group's fifth annual meeting, the BRICS announced that they would establish a development bank, an international financial institution governed by international laws and designed to improve their member nations' economic outlook. O'Neill cheered the announcement of a BRICS development bank and published an article in the London *Independent* (8 Aug. 2013) giving suggestions about what such a development bank could do. After naming the three areas he believes emerging economies need in order to be successful—better government, better education, and access to modern technology—O'Neill advised the new bank to "set country-by-country targets for improving performance on each of these three measures over agreed periods. Make these scores the organizing principle, and use them to guide capital allocation." He concluded, "If a BRICS development bank adopted a rationale such as this, used it to focus minds and then followed through with its decisions, it could do its members, and others as well, a power of good."

## ASSET MANAGEMENT

In September 2010 Goldman Sachs announced that its executive board had tapped O'Neill to run the bank's asset management division, a unit that the bank had built up very quickly over the previous ten years. In 2007, just prior to the worldwide economic collapse known as the Great Recession, the asset management division had assets totaling $868 billion. When O'Neill took on the post, however, the asset management division managed some $802 billion in investors' money. O'Neill decided he would spend no more than two years in his position because he knew little about asset management, which was not his primary field of interest.

In February 2013, after about two and a half years on the job, O'Neill announced that he would be retiring from the bank later that year. O'Neill officially retired in late April. Despite his relatively short tenure, O'Neill helped raise the division's assets by more than $50 billion, though assets remained below prerecession levels. When asked by Kelleher if his decision to quit was related to the fact that the division had not returned to its all-time peak, he responded, "That hasn't influenced me at all. In the context of me making the decision to quit, last year was one of Goldman Sachs Asset Management's best-ever years in terms of performance, so I thought I could disappear and the consequences wouldn't be so bad."

## MANCHESTER UNITED AND BRITISH EDUCATION

In March 2010, O'Neill was part of a group of wealthy investors, dubbed the Red Knights Group, who sought to take over the Manchester United soccer club from the Glazer family, who had bought the team in June 2005. From 2004 to 2005 O'Neill had served as a nonexecutive director of the club. He raised concerns about the club's finances early in 2010, when the Glazer family sought to bring in new revenues through a bond issue that they hoped would decrease the team's debt repayments. For several months, the Red Knights and the Glazers sought to find the right price to allow a buyout; however, the price set by the Glazer family was too high for the Red Knights Group, and negotiations were put on hold indefinitely.

Since retiring from Goldman Sachs, O'Neill has served as an economics commentator, writing articles for various newspapers and appearing in a number of television programs. He has also taken up the chairmanship of Support and Help in Education (SHINE), a London-based educational charity he helped found in 1999. In addition to SHINE, O'Neill is a board member of Teach for All and other educational nonprofits. In July 2013, he was appointed to the UK Department for Education as a nonexecutive director and advisor to Michael Gove, the secretary of state for education. The ministry announced that O'Neill would begin work that September.

O'Neill lives with his wife in Barnes, a district of southwest London. They have two children.

## SUGGESTED READING

Blackhurst, Chris. "Goldman Star Who Is Shining for Charity Too." *London Evening Standard*. Evening Standard, 7 Oct. 2009. Web. 13 Aug. 2013.

Elbagir, Nima, and Teo Kermeliotis. "South Africa an Economic Powerhouse? 'Nowhere Near,' Says Goldman Exec." *CNN*. Cable News Network, 5 Apr. 2011. Web. 13 Aug. 2013.

Fletcher, Richard. "Jim O'Neill: Profile of Manchester United's Red Knight." *Telegraph*. Telegraph Media, 2 Mar. 2010. Web. 13 Aug. 2013.

Kelleher, Ellen. "I've Been Able to Be Me at Goldman." *Financial Times*. Financial Times, 31 Mar. 2013. Web. 13 Aug. 2013.

Kowitt, Beth. "For Mr. BRIC, Nations Meeting a Milestone." *CNN Money*. Cable News Network, 17 June 2009. Web. 13 Aug. 2013.

Smith, Randall. "Jim O'Neill, Prominent Goldman Economist, to Retire." *New York Times*. New York Times, 5 Feb. 2013. Web. 13 Aug. 2013.

Tett, Gillian. "The Story of the Brics." *FT Magazine*. Financial Times, 15 Jan. 2010. Web. 13 Aug. 2013.

—*Christopher Mari*

# Ronnie O'Sullivan

**Born:** December 5, 1975
**Occupation:** Professional snooker player

Ronnie "the Rocket" O'Sullivan has often been credited with bringing excitement back to snooker, a cue sport similar to English billiards. His fast and aggressive style of play is both thrilling to watch and extremely effective; the snooker star has won four World Championships and more than twenty other major titles. One of the most popular and controversial snooker players in the United Kingdom, O'Sullivan is known by some as much for his run-ins with snooker authorities and fellow players, stemming from his struggles with drug use and depression, as for the skills he brings to the table.

Despite these setbacks, O'Sullivan remains one of the most successful players in professional snooker. As of the beginning of the 2012–13 snooker season, he holds the world records for the youngest player to score a competitive maximum break (the maximum number of points that can be scored in one frame under normal conditions) and the fastest maximum break and is one of two players to hold the record for the most maximum breaks scored in competitive snooker. In recognition of his talent, O'Sullivan has been named player of the year by World Snooker and has also been inducted into the sport's hall of fame.

## EARLY LIFE AND EDUCATION

Ronald Antonio O'Sullivan was born December 5, 1975, in Wordsley, England, the first of two children born to Ronnie and Maria O'Sullivan.

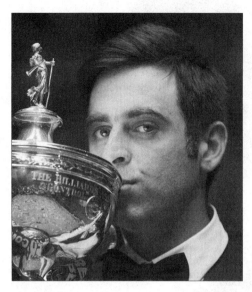

Getty Images

Ronnie Sr. owned a number of adult bookstores, while Maria worked as a waitress and later took over her husband's business. When O'Sullivan was young, his family moved to Chigwell, where he and younger sister Danielle grew up.

O'Sullivan began playing snooker as a child and soon fell in love with the game. He started going to snooker clubs at the age of eight or nine, and by his early teens, he frequently left Wanstead High School during lunch to play. His parents encouraged him to pursue his goal of playing professionally, going so far as to establish a dedicated snooker room in their home. O'Sullivan has named his father as his greatest influence during this period. "I believe that champions are made, not born. I have to give my dad the credit because he made me what I am," he told Matthew Syed for the *Times* (19 Apr. 2008). "Dad instilled in me how to be a winner."

### EARLY CAREER

O'Sullivan was signed by manager Barry Hearn in July of 1991, at the age of fifteen. Asked why he signed such a young, relatively inexperienced player, Hearn told Gordon Burn for the *Independent* (17 Oct. 1993), "Because he is going to be the best there's ever been." He added, "O'Sullivan is the front runner of a whole new breed. They're fearless."

Prior to signing with Hearn, O'Sullivan had competed in the English Amateur Championship and scored a maximum break, becoming the youngest player ever to do so. O'Sullivan began his professional career at the age of sixteen, winning 95 out of the 112 matches he played during the 1992–93 season. When not competing, he practiced every day at the Ilford Snooker Centre in Greater London. In addition to playing throughout the United Kingdom, O'Sullivan

traveled to Thailand to compete in the Asian Open and to the United Arab Emirates to play in the Dubai Classic. He won his first UK Championship in 1993, a month before his eighteenth birthday, and proceeded on to the World Championship, where he won ten matches but was eliminated relatively early.

Over the next several years, O'Sullivan took a number of prestigious titles, winning the British Open in 1994, the Asian Classic in 1996, the Scottish Open in 1998, and the China Open in 1999, among others. He won his second UK Championship in 1997 and proceeded to the World Championship every year between 1994 and 1999. He made it to the semifinal round in the World Championship in 1996, 1998, and 1999 but was bested by Peter Ebdon, John Higgins, and Stephen Hendry, respectively. O'Sullivan was also a key member of the English team that won the Nations Cup in January of 2000.

### STRUGGLE AND RECOVERY

O'Sullivan's early career was marked by controversy, as he was involved in conflicts with players and nonplayers, as well as with the law. Many observers, and at times even O'Sullivan himself, have suggested that his troubles during this period stemmed from the incarceration of his father. In 1992, his father was imprisoned for killing a man during an altercation in a London nightclub. O'Sullivan's mother was later convicted of tax evasion and sentenced to a year in prison, leaving her teenage son to care for his sister as well as the family business. Although his mother was soon released, the incarceration of his father had a lasting effect on O'Sullivan.

In the years following his father's conviction, O'Sullivan struggled with depression. "I lie there some mornings and think what's the point of even getting out of bed?" he told Donald McRae for the *Guardian* (13 Apr. 2009). "I end up lying there until one in the afternoon. I'll struggle up, have a cup of tea and that's pretty much it. Those are the days you just lose." Though O'Sullivan told reporters early in his career that he neither drank nor smoked because of his father's emphasis on physical fitness, he eventually began to abuse drugs and alcohol.

Although O'Sullivan's struggles with depression and drug abuse affected every aspect of his life, his troubles often seemed inextricably connected with his career, and he became known for several greatly publicized incidents during snooker matches. At the 1996 World Championship, O'Sullivan assaulted a tournament official, which led him to be fined and given a two-year suspended sentence. The same year, he generated controversy when he played left handed against Canadian player Alain Robidoux, who accused him of being disrespectful; the charge of bringing the game of snooker into disrepute was dropped, however, after O'Sullivan proved in a disciplinary hearing that he was fully capable of playing left handed. His troubles continued in 1998, when he was forced to give up his Irish Masters title after testing positive for marijuana.

Determined to regain control over his life, in mid-2000 O'Sullivan put his snooker career on hold and checked into the Priory, an exclusive mental health and rehabilitation facility known for treating many celebrities. Although he would go on to relapse on a few occasions in the years after leaving the Priory and would continue to struggle with depression, O'Sullivan has noted that since 2000, he has been in a much better place. "I'm a little better," he told McRae, "because, in the past, I used to drown my sorrows. Now I don't. I face them front on. I'm ready for them."

## WORLD CHAMPION

After leaving the Priory, O'Sullivan returned to the world of snooker with a vengeance. In late 2000, he placed second in the UK Championship, which allowed him to move on the 2001 World Championship. At the Crucible Theatre in Sheffield, England (known to snooker fans simply as the Crucible), O'Sullivan defeated Higgins 18–14 to become world champion. O'Sullivan dedicated his victory to his father. "He won't show it but I know exactly how he will be feeling—I can't describe just how good the feeling is but it makes all the tough days seem a million miles away," he told BBC Sport (8 May 2001). "We have been through some hard times but this makes it all worth it."

O'Sullivan returned to the World Championship every year through 2012 and achieved three more victories, defeating Graeme Dott in 2004 and Ali Carter in 2008 and 2012. In addition, he won a number of other tournaments, including the 2003 European Open, the 2005 Irish Masters, the 2008 Northern Ireland Trophy, and the 2012 German Masters. At the 2006 UK Championship, O'Sullivan walked out of his quarterfinal match against Hendry, later ascribing his behavior to his perfectionism. "I got so annoyed with myself that I lost my patience and walked away from a game that, with hindsight, I should have continued," he told BBC Sport (14 Dec. 2006). Despite this incident, O'Sullivan returned to the UK Championship the following year and ultimately won.

In addition to amassing numerous wins, O'Sullivan has published the autobiographies Inside the Frame (2001) and Ronnie (2003; written with Simon Hattenstone). His book More Ronnie O'Sullivan is scheduled for publication late in 2013. Clips of his games have been collected in a number of DVD compilations, and his likeness is featured in the iPhone game Ronnie O'Sullivan's Snooker.

## STYLE OF PLAY

O'Sullivan is known for a fast and aggressive style of play that led snooker fans and commentators to nickname him the Rocket. A record-breaking player, he received particular attention for one game in the 1997 World Championship in which he scored a maximum break in only five minutes and twenty seconds, setting a Guinness World Record that as of the beginning of the 2012–13 snooker season had yet to be broken. O'Sullivan is also known for his versatility. As he memorably demonstrated in his controversial match with Robidoux, he is comfortable playing with his left hand as well as his right, which allows him to take shots from a wide range of angles.

Snooker officials and other players have referred to O'Sullivan as a "character," and he has often been likened to notable players of the 1980s such as Alex Higgins, who was known for both his fast and exciting style of play and his run-ins with authority both at and away from the snooker table. O'Sullivan has lamented that this more engaging style of play and sense of personality are rare in modern snooker. "There's definitely a lack of characters now," he told Matt Majendie for the London Evening Standard (26 Oct. 2010). "With a lot of players years ago, you could really see what they went through and I think people could relate to that." He continued, "The problem is that today players just desperately don't want to lose and it can come across that they're not actually enjoying snooker. If you see someone enjoying it, you can relate to that and think I want to watch that."

Although O'Sullivan thrives when actively playing, the periods of waiting inherent to the game frustrate him. "Snooker gets in your head and there's nothing you can do when your opponent is at the table," he explained to McRae. "That's the frustration. You have to sit in that chair and pretend you're interested. But I just want to jump up and play." He has expressed his support for proposals to increase the number of snooker tournaments but decrease their length, noting that spending long periods of time waiting to play at such events can be demoralizing for players.

## WITHDRAWAL FROM THE WORLD SNOOKER TOUR

In late 2012, O'Sullivan announced that he was withdrawing from the remainder of the 2012–13 World Snooker Tour. "There are personal things I need to sort out before I can even think of a return," he told Andrew Dillon for the Sun (9 Jan. 2013). However, O'Sullivan has not been letting himself get rusty. "I am still playing every couple of weeks at my mum's house," he said. O'Sullivan has agreed to participate in a special Snooker Legends tournament in Belfast, Northern Ireland, in June of 2013, and a number of snooker players and officials have told the press that they expect O'Sullivan to return to the sport sooner rather than later.

After announcing his withdrawal from the season, O'Sullivan occupied himself with volunteer work, serving as a laborer on a farm near his home. "I didn't want stress, as that was what was made me pull out of snooker, so I decided to go and do something unpaid," he told Dillon. "It has been kind of the opposite to what I was going through in snooker and I am really enjoying it."

O'Sullivan has also occupied himself with spending time with his family, particularly his father. The elder Ronnie was released from prison on a temporary basis on several occasions in 2009 and returned to the family home in Chigwell permanently in 2010. O'Sullivan was delighted to reunite with his father and has noted that the family's reunion has brought back happy memories from his childhood and made him optimistic about the future. "When my dad came back and we had our first meal together it reminded me of when I was seven and we always had huge bowls of pasta and salad and bread," he told McRae. "It's good them days are coming back."

**PERSONAL LIFE**

O'Sullivan lives in Chigwell, not far from his parents' home. He is engaged to actress Laila Rouass, to whom he proposed in early 2013, and has three children from two previous relationships, daughters Taylor-Ann and Lily and son Ronnie. It seems no surprise that O'Sullivan, whose life and career have been so defined by his relationship with his father, treasures the experience of fatherhood himself. "My favourite time is with my kids," O'Sullivan told Majendie. "It really is the best feeling in the world."

When not playing snooker, O'Sullivan enjoys long-distance running, which he credits with helping him manage his depression. "I have tried many, many things to combat my demons and running is the one thing that does it for me," he told the BBC (11 Feb. 2009). He has noted that he tries to run about fifty miles each week and that if forced to choose between running and snooker, he would leave his snooker career behind. O'Sullivan also enjoys racing cars and has appeared on the BBC car program *Top Gear.*

**SUGGESTED READING**

Burn, Gordon. "Out of the Shadows Comes a Bright Star." *Independent.* Independent, 17 Oct. 1993. Web. 18 Feb. 2013.

Majendie, Matt. "How Being a Father Has Given Tough-Guy Ronnie O'Sullivan a Soft Side." *London Evening Standard.* Evening Standard, 26 Oct. 2010. Web.

McRae, Donald. "How Ronnie O'Sullivan Is Trying to Run Off 'Them Demons.'" *Guardian.* Guardian News and Media, 13 Apr. 2009. Web. 20 Feb. 2013.

Rendall, Jonathan. "Pocket Calculator." *Observer.* Guardian News and Media, 30 Oct. 2004. Web. 18 Feb. 2013.

Syed, Matthew. "Star Sentenced to Spend Life in His Father's Debt." *Times* 19 Apr. 2008: Sport 90. Print.

—Joy Crelin

# Jim Parsons

**Born:** March 24, 1973
**Occupation:** Actor

In 2010, when Jim Parsons won his first Emmy Award in the category of outstanding lead actor in a comedy series for his work on the hit sitcom *The Big Bang Theory,* announcer John Hodgman quipped, "As Jim Parsons walks to the stage, nerds across America are taking to the streets in joy, setting cars on fire, and then backing away, using their inhalers." The show, in which Parsons depicts a highly intelligent but socially maladroit physicist, does indeed have many fans among scientists, but its popularity extends far beyond that narrow group. Since the show's premiere in 2007, it has won both a large following among the general public and critical acclaim.

In an article headlined "I Love *The Big Bang Theory.* And You Should, Too," published in the *New York Times* (24 May 2013), Rob Hoerburger admits that he had avoided the show at first. To his great surprise, Hoerburger discovered that the show is exceptionally smart and well crafted. "It took roughly a week of nightly viewing before I realized how impoverished my life had been for the four years that I was oblivious to *The Big Bang Theory,*" he wrote. "The touchstone, the lodestar, the flypaper for me at first was, predictably, Parsons," he added. "Watching Parsons's every twitch, wiggle, full-body smirk, or social paroxysm . . . is alone worth any half-hour spent on the show."

**EARLY YEARS AND EDUCATION**

James Joseph Parsons was born on March 24, 1973, in Houston, Texas. His father, who died in 2001 in an automobile accident, owned a plumbing company. His mother, Judy, is a first-grade teacher for the Mittelstadt Elementary School, part of the Klein Independent School District in Harris County, Texas. Parsons has one younger sister, Julie, who teaches at the same school as their mother.

As a child, Parsons loved television, and he was particularly fond of such sitcoms as *Three's Company* and *Family Ties.* Parsons frequently forced Julie and her friends to act out scenes he had scripted. When he was six, he played a kola-kola bird in the Mittelstadt Elementary

© Armando Gallo/Retna Ltd./Corbis

production of Rudyard Kipling's "The Elephant's Child," wearing a pair of bright yellow tights and a feathered costume. Although he remembers himself as a shy, somewhat awkward child, he was a great success in the role. He attributes his early comfort with reciting lines to the fact that Judy regularly read aloud to him. Parsons later became passionate about *Star Wars*, and his mother recalled in a February 16, 2011, interview with *Entertainment Tonight* that their home was filled with Luke Skywalker and Darth Vader action figures, for which Parsons made buildings and vehicles out of discarded cardboard boxes.

Parsons, who took several years of piano lessons as a boy, attended Klein Oak High School in the town of Spring, Texas. He was an active participant in the drama department and has pointed to a junior-year production of Michael Frayn's *Noises Off*, in which he played the insecure but likeable character Freddy Fellowes, as a time in which he fully connected to a role and learned the value of working in an ensemble. In the February 2011 *Entertainment Tonight* interview, his high-school drama teacher, Margaret Locher, called him the funniest person she had ever known. Parsons graduated from Klein Oak in 1991. The school's website features a quote from Parsons about his time there: "I consider myself extremely fortunate to have been in an environment that exposed me to both theater and arts in general and also allowed me to explore my path in those areas—a path that continues to this day."

## UNIVERSITY AND INFERNAL BRIDEGROOM PRODUCTIONS

Before pursuing a career in acting, Parsons considered becoming a meteorologist; he was fascinated by extreme weather events such as hurricanes. After matriculating at the University of

Houston, he initially majored in television and radio and roomed with his best friend from high school, Greg Stanley, a theater major. Parsons has said that watching Stanley audition and rehearse was the final push he needed to switch his own major to theater. That decision was also influenced by the failing grade Parsons received in his one meteorology course because he was so busy with theater. Parsons appeared in more than a dozen plays during his time at the University of Houston and in 1996 earned a bachelor's degree in theater.

Parsons was a founding member of a Houston-based acting company called Infernal Bridegroom Productions, which later changed its name to Catastrophic Theatre. With that troupe he appeared in *The Threepenny Opera*, *Endgame*, and many other productions. "It was the first time I got to do [Samuel] Beckett and [Bertolt] Brecht on stage, working in different venues, warehouses and outdoors and parking lots and theaters," he explained to Andrew Dansby for the *Houston Chronicle* (22 Apr. 2010). "[These were] not necessarily the best conditions. So in a way it was a labor of love."

In 1999 Parsons enrolled in the University of San Diego, where he had been accepted into a highly selective two-year program in classical theater, taught in partnership with the Old Globe Theatre. He earned a master of fine arts degree in 2001. The school would later invite him to give a commencement address in 2009.

## A FLEDGLING CAREER

After earning his master's degree in San Diego, Parsons moved to New York City to pursue his career. He has described his life during this period as that of a typical struggling actor. He won occasional stage roles in off-Broadway productions and subsisted on unemployment benefits some of the time. When those benefits ran out, he worked briefly in a fabric store in the neighborhood of SoHo.

Parsons has also appeared in more than a dozen failed pilots—shows that no television network was willing to purchase. "My first pilot was *Blitt Happens* with Fox," he recalled to Luaine Lee for the McClatchy-Tribune News Service (4 Dec. 2007). "The Farrelly brothers directed. It didn't go. The next one was for CBS. It was *Taste*, Jane Krakowski's show. And that didn't go. But that's where I met up with CBS and did a holding deal with them for the next year."

Thanks to that deal, in 2004 Parsons obtained a recurring guest spot on the family drama *Judging Amy*, playing a young law clerk until the end of the show's run in 2005, and he also appeared in several CBS pilots for the following year. As with his previous efforts, those pilots failed to win over the network. Parsons also accepted work in commercials from time to time, including one for the sandwich chain Quiznos, in which he plays a man raised by wolves, and one for FedEx, in which he portrays an inefficient office worker. The spot for Quiznos required him to pretend to suckle from a "wolf," which was actually a trained Siberian husky. "That showed a willingness on my part to do anything," he told Nancy Mills for the New York Times Syndicate (9 Oct. 2011). "Maybe it had some effect on my career. It was certainly the beginning of a small wave of work."

Parsons got what many observers characterize as his big break in 2004, when he appeared in the independent film *Garden State*, written and directed by Zach Braff, who stars as a troubled man who returns home for his mother's funeral after being estranged from his family for years. Parsons appears in only one scene, and he is clad for much of his time onscreen in a full suit of armor. He plays a worker who has been "knighted" while at his low-level job at a medieval theme restaurant. Parsons also landed a small part in the film comedy *School for Scoundrels* (2006).

### THE BIG BANG THEORY

When Parsons received the script for the pilot of *The Big Bang Theory*, he sensed that there was something special about it. He spent the entire evening sitting on the floor of his tiny sublet apartment and going over the lines repeatedly. "I knew if I didn't get the part and felt I could've done more, I really couldn't live with myself because I just knew it was a wonderful fit—whether or not [the producers] thought so," he told Lee. The producers, however, agreed with him. In fact, his audition was so exceptional that Chuck Lorre, the show's creator, insisted upon a second audition immediately, to make sure the first had not been merely a fluke.

The show—which is filmed in a multicamera style in front of a live audience—debuted on CBS in 2007, with Parsons playing Caltech physicist Sheldon Cooper. The original cast also included Johnny Galecki as Sheldon's roommate, fellow scientist Leonard Hofstadter; Kaley Cuoco as Penny, their attractive blonde neighbor; Simon Helberg as aerospace engineer Howard Wolowitz; and Kunal Nayyar as astrophysicist Raj Koothrappali. Melissa Rauch joined the show in 2009 as microbiologist Bernadette Rostenkowski, who later marries Howard. Mayim Bialik became a lead member of the cast in 2010; she plays Amy Farrah Fowler, a neurobiologist whose relationship with Sheldon remains platonic thanks to his reluctance.

*The Big Bang Theory* is rife with science-related jokes and dialogue—for instance, at a poker game, a character is likely to announce, "I fold . . . like a protein"—and a physicist from the University of California, Los Angeles, is on staff to make sure that those parts are accurate. "He sends over this diagram on this white board and he'll throw in little inside jokes that I don't find funny because I don't know what the heck he's talking about," Parsons told Terry Gross for the National Public Radio show *Fresh Air* (28 Sept. 2010).

### THE CHARACTER OF SHELDON COOPER

In his *New York Times* review, Rob Hoerburger describes Sheldon as "a Nobel-craving, coitus-avoiding, Purell-packing, sarcasm-challenged, boy-man genius." The character has a markedly different self-conception. Told by Leonard to make himself scarce in episode two of the second season, he replies, "I am a published theoretical physicist with two doctorates and an IQ which can't be accurately measured by normal tests. How much scarcer could I be?" For his part, Parsons views Sheldon and his cohorts with a great deal of tenderness and sympathy. "[These are] truly special characters that we are bringing to life," he told Mills. "To say 'smart' or 'nerd' is not enough. They've got this ability and we don't. It's something to celebrate." Referring to the title of a popular book and film about the life of John Nash, a Nobel laureate in economics, Parsons often tells reporters that Sheldon and Leonard are "beautiful minds."

Many observers have noted that Sheldon appears to exhibit the signs of Asperger syndrome, a condition on the autism spectrum characterized by a failure to decipher social cues, a seeming lack of empathy, and an inability to recognize subtle differences in tone, pitch, and accent in the speech of others. The show's writers have repeatedly disavowed the notion that Sheldon has the condition—as well as obsessive-compulsive personality disorder (OCPD) and an asexual orientation—although he undeniably shares traits with those who do. Parsons explained to Allie Townsend for *Time* (23 Sept. 2010), "I think it was very smart of the writers to borrow a lot of those behaviors without nailing us down with some extra social responsibility to get this story right. It's more of a celebration of these kinds of characteristics and the fun, colorful side they offer."

Among the laurels Parsons has garnered for his work on *The Big Bang Theory* are Emmy Awards won in 2010, 2011, and 2013—he was nominated in 2009 and 2012 as well—and a Golden Globe in 2011. Parsons was nominated for another Golden Globe in 2013.

### OTHER ROLES

In addition to *Garden State* and *School for Scoundrels*, Parsons has appeared in such films as the comedy *The Big Year* (2011), which costars Owen Wilson and Jack Black, and *The Muppets* (2011). In a highly anticipated cameo in the latter, Parsons plays the human version of the Muppet Walter when Walter sings the musical number "Man or Muppet?" On the small screen, Parsons has had guest spots in *iCarly* and

*Family Guy*, among other shows, and appeared in *Sesame Street* in a science segment dealing with arachnids.

Parsons has also continued to pursue his stage career when time allows. In 2011 he appeared in the Broadway revival of *The Normal Heart*, a 1985 drama by Larry Kramer that takes place during the early years of the AIDS epidemic. While most critics were rapturous, some audience members who had purchased tickets just to see Parsons, unaware of the themes of the play, were reportedly disappointed to see him depicting an anguished gay man instead of some version of Sheldon. Parsons has been cast in a film version of the play scheduled for release in 2014.

Theatergoers hoping to see Parsons in a comic role had better luck the following year, when he starred in a Broadway revival of *Harvey*, taking on a role made famous in the 1950 film version by the legendary actor Jimmy Stewart. His character, the kind-hearted Elwood Dowd, is forced to contend with the title character, a rabbit who stands over six feet tall that no one else can see. "Mr. Parsons carries the weight of a role immortalized on film by the inimitable Jimmy Stewart as lightly as Elwood does the hat and coat he keeps on hand for his furry companion," Charles Isherwood wrote for the *New York Times* (14 June 2012), "Mr. Parsons possesses in abundance the crucial ability to project an ageless innocence without any visible effort: no small achievement for an actor in these knowing times."

## PERSONAL LIFE

Parsons received a flurry of press attention after a May 23, 2012, *New York Times* interview casually mentioned his partner of more than ten years, thereby revealing that he is gay. Few careful observers were surprised. The gay press had long covered Parsons, with the website of *Out* magazine asserting, "[Like many other stars] Parsons has lived as a gay man in his private life, but in his professional public life he skirted the issue." Parsons's partner, Todd Alan Spiewak, is an art director. The couple owns two condominium units in the upscale Gramercy Park neighborhood of New York City, which features a gated private park. The landmarked building in which they live was designed in 1908 and features Gothic arches and picturesque gargoyles.

Parsons remains close to his extended family and has told interviewers that when he is unable to make it home for the holidays, his mother seats a life-sized cardboard cutout of him at the table. He has two nephews, one of whom he says looks amazingly like him as a child.

By all accounts, Parsons is a kind and down-to-earth person who is loved by his coworkers for his humility, compassion, honesty, professionalism, and sense of humor. His only regret in playing Sheldon, he has said, is that the role has not improved his own grasp of science. "I've learned very little," he told Adam Tanswell for *Digital Spy* (5 Oct. 2011). "It's a shame but every time I get something scientific in the script, I read up to find out what I'm talking about—but then I'm on to the next script and it's forgotten. There's no absorption of information. I'm no smarter since appearing on the show. In fact, I might be a little dumber because I haven't had time to learn anything else."

## SUGGESTED READING

Healy, Patrick. "Stalked by Shadows (and a Rabbit)." *New York Times*. New York Times, 23 May 2012. Web. 15 July 2013.

Hoerburger, Rob. "I Love *The Big Bang Theory*. And You Should, Too." *New York Times*. New York Times, 24 May 2013. Web. 15 July 2013.

Lee, Luaine. "Jim Parsons Says If at First You Don't Succeed, Try Another Pilot." *PopMatters*. PopMatters Media, 4 Dec. 2007. Web. 15 July 2013.

Mills, Nancy. "Jim Parsons & *Big Bang Theory*." *Qatar Tribune*. Qatar Tribune, 9 Oct. 2011. Web. 15 July 2013.

Tanswell, Adam. "Jim Parsons Interview: Big Bang Theory Changed My Life." *Digital Spy*. Hearst Magazines, 5 Oct. 2011. Web. 15 July 2013.

## SELECTED WORKS

*Garden State*, 2004; *Judging Amy*, 2004–2005; *School for Scoundrels*, 2006; *The Big Bang Theory*, 2007–; *The Big Year*, 2011; *The Muppets*, 2011; *The Normal Heart*, 2011; *Harvey*, 2012

—*Mari Rich*

---

# Lyn-z Adams Hawkins Pastrana

**Born:** September 21, 1989
**Occupation:** Professional skateboarder

Lyn-z Adams Hawkins Pastrana is considered among the best female skateboarders in the world, but she has spent her career shooting for a different goal: to simply be the best. She began that quest early in her career when, as a teenager, she competed in the men's vert skateboarding event at the 2005 Tampa Am, a highly regarded amateur contest, and came in third. Since that time, she has racked up victories in professional competitions around the globe, including eight medals in the X Games, the extreme-sports equivalent of the Olympics. She has also become the first woman to execute several difficult skateboarding moves in competition, including a kickflip indy and a McTwist 540. Moreover,

© Paul Hebert/Icon SMI/Corbis

unlike many skaters who become skilled at one particular style of skateboarding, Pastrana has excelled in everything from street and vert to bowl and mega ramp.

Although best known as a professional skateboarder, she is also an avid surfer (her first love) and enjoys snowboarding and riding dirt bikes. Now the wife of daredevil stunt performer, motorsports competitor, and X Games medalist Travis Pastrana, she even took to the racetrack in October 2012 to win the Better Half Dash, a twenty-five-lap charity race against eleven other wives and girlfriends of Pastrana's fellow NASCAR drivers that benefited Speedway Children's Charities and Motor Racing Outreach. After the race, she told Steve Reed for the Associated Press (11 Oct. 2012), "I skateboard for a living, but this is very different. I was so nervous I don't think I could do more than one a year. I was white-knuckled the whole time, sweat dripping down my visor."

## EARLY LIFE

Pastrana was born Lyndsey Adams Hawkins in San Diego, California, on September 21, 1989; she began using the moniker Lyn-z in the fourth grade, when she became tired of writing out her full name. She grew up partly in Cardiff-by-the-Sea, a beach community in Encinitas, California, and partly in Sayulita, Mexico, where her family owned a bed-and-breakfast. An avid athlete from a very young age, she spent her childhood playing everything from baseball to basketball to soccer, as well as participating in gymnastics and surfboarding. In fact, Pastrana began surfing at a

surprisingly young age. "I got my first surfboard when I was five years old," she told Jade Kennedy for the *Townsville Bulletin* (24 Mar. 2011). "It was like the big, soft boards you use when you're learning to surf but in miniature. I grew up at the beach, so my parents used to take my brother and I to the surf with our boogie boards from about the age of two. Once we started learning how to stand up on our boogie boards our parents decided it was time to buy us surfboards."

Growing up near the skate park at the YMCA in Encinitas, she was able to quickly transfer the skills she had honed on a surfboard to skateboarding. For her sixth birthday, her older brother, Tyler, bought her a membership to the Encinitas Y, where she found herself watching legendary skateboarders like Tony Hawk and his son, Riley, skate. Her life would be skateboarding from there on out, despite the fact that so few girls were then involved with the sport. "I've been pretty lucky, though where I grew up, all of the top skaters live there and have basically watched me growing up and have been around to help me out and stick up for me and that sort of thing," she told Kennedy. "I've never had a problem, though, being a girl in a typically guy's sport, I know a lot of girls have had a much tougher time of it than me."

## EARLY CAREER

At age ten, Pastrana was dropped for the first time into a vert ramp—a form of half-pipe used in skateboarding, so named because it transitions from a horizontal plane at the bottom to a vertical one on each side. As much as she enjoyed, and continues to enjoy, street skateboarding (which focuses on doing tricks on objects found on city streets, such as benches, trash bins, railings, picnic tables, and stairs), she loves vert skateboarding even more—in part, she once claimed in an interview, because it does not hurt as much when she falls. "I love all skating, but everything just goes away when I am skating vert," Pastrana told Shanti Sosienski for *Sports Illustrated for Kids* (Sept. 2005). "It's like flying."

As it became clear that Pastrana had the skills needed to make it as a professional skateboarder, her parents allowed her to be homeschooled and, later, to study at the Carlsbad Seaside Academy, which was founded in 1998 as an alternative school that gives credits to students involved with sports. Many professional skateboarders, like Pastrana, have attended the academy, which maintains a flexible schedule that allows students to check in just once every three weeks while they are competing across the country (and, in some cases, around the world). For most young athletes involved in competitive sports, their only choices for continuing their education while competing are either homeschooling or alternative schools like Carlsbad Seaside Academy. Some simply drop out of school. The choices are indeed stark, but the opportunities are great for the few athletes capable of competing at the professional level. "Only six of forty amateurs are major competitors," Jimmy Button, a motocross-racer-turned-agent, said in an interview with Matt Higgins for the *New York Times* (20 Sept. 2006). "Only two will make it to the pro ranks, and maybe one will make a substantial living." Button added, "With no education and making 80–90 grand a year, after your career is over, after seven or eight years, you have nothing. It's sad."

Pastrana, however, would beat the odds and become one of the few amateurs to make it into the pros. At age eleven, she took first place in the amateur division of the 2001 All Girl Skate Jam in New York, a feat she repeated the following year. When she turned pro in 2002 and competed at the Slam City Jam in Vancouver, British Columbia, she came in fourth in the vert contest and fifth in the street—an impressive debut for someone so young.

## OFF TO A WINNING START

Despite being female in an overwhelmingly male-dominated sport, Pastrana worked hard and quickly found herself rising up the ranks in professional competitions. In 2003 she participated in numerous competitions, including the Slam City Jam in Vancouver and the Next Cup in Aguanga, California, but her most striking performances might have been at the X Games— the yearly sporting event run by the sports cable channel ESPN that focuses on "extreme sports" that involve a great risk of personal injury, such as motocross, skateboarding, surfing, and snowboarding. That year, for the first time, the X Games offered medals in women's street skating; Pastrana, who was just thirteen years old at the time, placed second. She also placed third in the vert competition. It was the first time that the press had begun to seriously take notice of young women in skateboarding competitions, and Pastrana was glad to have been part of the group that was making that happen. "It has taken a lot of time," she told Sal Ruibal for *USA Today* (16 Sept. 2004). "It should have happened a little earlier, but now we're progressing faster than the guys. We're stepping up and skating a lot better now."

In 2004 Pastrana stepped up her game at X Games Ten, where she placed fourth in the street competition but first in the vert—the first time she had done so. "Probably my proudest moment so far was winning my first X Games gold," she told Kennedy. "I was fourteen years old, I had never beaten the girls who won silver and bronze before and actually the girl who got silver had never been beaten by a girl before and was, like, twice my age. It was even more special because my dad had passed away earlier that same year, so that gold was for him." The same

year, in December, she became the first female skateboarder to successfully ride a mega ramp, a huge vert-style skateboarding ramp with a sixty-four-foot roll-in and a fifty-five-foot gap. Mega ramps have also been used at the X Games, where they are called "Big Air."

Pastrana competed against men at the 2005 Tampa Am in the vert competition and placed third. That season she also participated in the Globe World Cup in Melbourne, Australia, placing fourth in the street competition; at the Pro Tec Pool Party in Orange, California, placing fifth in the bowl competition; and at X Games Eleven, where she placed ninth in the street competition but second in the vert. At fifteen, she became the first female skateboarder to land the tricky kickflip indy move on vert. She was out of competition in 2006 due to injuries, but she stayed involved with the skateboarding world by serving as a commentator and lending her likeness to the video game *Tony Hawk's Project 8*.

## AMONG THE BEST

Since returning to competition in 2007, Pastrana has stunned the skateboarding world by chalking up impressive victories in competitions around the world. In 2007 alone, she placed second in the bowl competitions at both the Pro Tec Pool Party and at the Soul Bowl in Huntington Beach, California, and won the gold medal in the vert competition at X Games Thirteen. In 2008 she took silver in the vert at X Games Fourteen. In 2009, she came in first in the vert competitions at both the ISF Skateboarding World Championships, held in Boston, Massachusetts, and X Games Fifteen. She then placed second in the vert competition at X Games Sixteen in 2010. Overall, she has won eight X Games medals, including three gold. Also in 2009, Pastrana became the first female skateboarder to successfully land a McTwist 540, an extremely difficult aerial move in which the skater and board make one and one-half rotations in midair with one hand grabbing the toe side of the skateboard. Although she was unable to land the McTwist during the X Games, she was able to do it at the Tony Hawk Show in Paris, France, that November before thousands of thrilled fans.

Pastrana has also been a regular at the Nitro Circus, a so-called action sports collective developed by her husband, stunt performer and motorsports competitor Travis Pastrana, who has won ten X Games gold medals and has four Rally America titles under his belt. Nitro Circus began as a DVD collection in the early 2000s and has since spun off to be a television series and a 3-D film, featuring various athletes performing on the circus's world tour. The shows feature Travis Pastrana and his friends performing stunts, riding dirt bikes, BASE jumping, and skateboarding. The couple began dating in 2010 but had known each other for a number of years beforehand, having met at various events. Pastrana explained to Alex Prewitt for the *Boston Globe* (14 July 2012) what had attracted her to her husband: "[He was] such a happy, goofy, I-don't-care-what-people-think kind of guy, and I really admire that. People in action sports are so caught up in image and what people think of them. It was so refreshing to hang out with someone who just didn't care."

## PERSONAL LIFE

The Pastranas' engagement took place on June 4, 2011, before a crowd of thousands at the Nitro Circus Live World Tour in Las Vegas, Nevada. After Pastrana fell on her first run, one of the Nitro Circus crew carried her off to the base of the takeoff ramp, where Travis was waiting on bended knee. The couple was married on October 29, 2011, at a small ceremony before close family members and friends.

On February 26, 2013, the couple announced via their Facebook and Twitter accounts that they were going to be parents for the first time. "Travis Pastrana and I are stoked to announce Baby Pastrana expected to be 'Dropping In' to this world 9/2013," Pastrana wrote in her Facebook post. When asked how they will pass down their love of sports, Travis Pastrana told Alyssa Roenigk for ESPN.com (28 Feb. 2013), "Lyn-z will be the go-getter, getting them on bikes and boards early. I think that sounds scary. Lyn-z is good at conventional sports, but I never learned how to throw. She'll be the coach of all the teams. I can pass down driving and motorcycles. Go to your mom to learn how to throw."

Although Pastrana has been out of competition due to her pregnancy, she remains ranked among the best skateboarders in the world. And even if she should never return to competitive skateboarding, she is one of the pioneering women of the sport; among other records, she was one of the first women to skate the DC Mega Ramp and the Nitro Giganta Ramp. She has also been featured as a playable skater in several of Tony Hawk's video games.

## SUGGESTED READING

Higgins, Matt. "For New-Sport Athletes, High School Finishes 2nd." *New York Times*. New York Times Co., 20 Sept. 2006. Web. 15 July 2013.

Kennedy, Jade. "Fearless Female." *Townsville Bulletin*. North Queensland Newspaper Co., 24 Mar. 2011. Web. 15 July 2013.

Langer, Anna. "Vertical Horizons." *Cooler*. Mpora, 30 Aug. 2012. Web. 15 July 2013.

Prewitt, Alex. "Travis Pastrana Driven to Succeed." *Boston Globe*. New York Times Co., 14 July 2012. Web. 15 July 2013.

Roenigk, Alyssa. "Diapers and Other Changes Due for Pastranas." *EPSN.com*. ESPN, 28 Feb. 2013. Web. 15 July 2013.

Ruibal, Sal. "Teen Takes Quick Ride to Top of Skateboarding World." *USA Today*. Gannett, 16 Sept. 2004. Web. 15 July 2013.

Sosienski, Shanti. "Skater Grrrl." *Sports Illustrated for Kids* Sept. 2005: 54. Print.

—*Christopher Mari*

# Oren Peli

**Born:** 1970
**Occupation:** Film director and producer

With his debut film, the haunted-house thriller *Paranormal Activity* (2007), Oren Peli became known as the master of the slow-burn horror film, the kind of movie with an eeriness that builds gradually through subtlety and psychological suggestion rather than gory scenes or "gotcha" scares. "Doors crash closed, the bed sheets billow, prints are found in the white powder scattered on the polished floor," Amy Raphael wrote in a review of the film for the London *Guardian* (20 Nov. 2009). "There is no monster, virtually no blood. There are tantalizingly long moments of silence, and static shots are preferred to the usual jerky, handheld frenzy of DIY horror movies. The film looks, sounds, and feels very homemade. Yet it's scary as hell."

*Paranormal Activity* became the most successful horror movie of the decade and has since been followed by three other installments, *Paranormal Activity 2* (2010), *Paranormal Activity 3* (2011), and *Paranormal Activity 4* (2012). A former computer programmer who had never made a film before his remarkable debut, Peli has become a notable talent among horror filmmakers and has gone on to contribute to other films in the horror genre, including the 2010 film *Insidious*, which he produced, the 2012 thriller *Chernobyl Diaries*, which he wrote and produced, and the short-lived sci-fi ABC series *The River* (2012), which he also wrote and produced. Peli's films typically have low budgets and few special effects, and many make use of the found-footage format, in which the film itself is composed of seemingly amateur footage supposedly made by the characters.

## EARLY LIFE AND EDUCATION

Peli was born in Israel to parents who were both teachers. He was eleven when he first watched *The Exorcist*, William Friedkin's classic 1973 horror film about a girl who becomes possessed by a demon and undergoes an exorcism. Peli was deeply affected by the film, which is widely considered among the scariest of all time. "It totally freaked me out," he told Raphael. "After that I couldn't watch any movie that had anything to do with haunting or a ghost. I was in my

Paul Buck/EPA/Landov

mid-teens when *Ghostbusters* [1984] came out and although I knew it was a comedy, I couldn't handle the idea of it. I didn't see another horror film until I was well into my twenties."

Peli dropped out of high school at the age of sixteen, and with his friend Amir Zbeda, he designed a computer program and sold it for $120,000. The two friends used that money to travel to the United States in 1990 to achieve "the American dream," as he told a writer for the *Irish Times* (20 Nov. 2009). Peli initially lived in Salt Lake City, Utah, for about four years before moving to California, first living in Los Angeles and then San Diego. He studied animation and graphic design and then embarked on a two-decade career as a video game designer and computer programmer.

### INSPIRATION FOR *PARANORMAL ACTIVITY*

In 1999, Peli met and began dating twenty-five-year-old Toni Taylor, who at the time worked setting up phone systems for businesses. In January 2003, they moved into a four-bedroom house in suburban San Diego. Not long after they started living there, however, Peli and Taylor began to notice unusual sounds in the house when no one else was there. "The house, or the ground around it, was settling; things were falling off shelves in the middle of the night," Peli told the New South Wales *Coffs Coast Advocate* (3 Dec. 2009). "I'm not saying there was a ghost or anything, because the incidents, or whatever you would call them, were happening months apart." Taylor, who was bothered by the incidents more than Peli, even claimed to sense a strange presence and to feel someone whispering in her ear when no one was there. With his tech background, Peli thought it would be interesting to investigate the strange sounds by setting up video cameras in the house and recording what was going on when no one was there. "If those cameras caught something good," Peli told the *Advocate*, "I thought that could make a pretty interesting movie."

Though he never actually set up the cameras, Peli did decide to try to make a movie about a couple who went through with such a plan. Peli had had ideas for movies in the past, but he had never attempted to make a film before. He was inspired by the success of a number of low-budget films, especially *The Blair Witch Project* (1999), the wildly popular horror movie about three teenagers who disappear while attempting to film a documentary about a legend in the Black Hills of Maryland. Peli bought a camera for about $3,000 and spent a year researching ghosts, demonic possession, and filmmaking; he also scrutinized the styles of several classic horror films. After crafting a storyline, he held open auditions in Hollywood for the story's two main characters, attracting 150 aspiring actors. Peli selected Katie Featherston and Micah Sloat because of their natural chemistry together. "They were among the very few actors we saw who slid right into character when we threw them our standard question, which was 'So tell me why you think your house is haunted?'" Peli told the *Advocate*. He continued, "They were absolutely convincing as a couple that had been together for years. They were telling stories about their vacations, talking about how Katie's mom didn't approve of them living together. They came up with elaborate back stories for their characters on the spot."

### INITIAL REACTIONS

To save money and for the sake of overall convenience, Peli decided to shoot the film at his and Taylor's house. Before he began filming, Peli embarked on a series of home improvements. He also hung pictures on the walls and rearranged some of the rooms to accommodate the shots he wanted. Peli shot the movie in just one week for a cost of about $15,000, not counting what he paid for the home improvements. Each of the main actors was paid just $500. Though he had a storyline, Peli had no formal script. "When filming, I would give them the scene, we'd discuss it, then they would use their own lines," he told the *Irish Times*. "It was a very collaborative process. They became storytellers as well as actors." Peli spent about a year editing seventy hours of footage, adding in computer-generated imagery and mixing the audio on his computer. Every so often during the editing process, he showed a version of the film to friends for feedback; once, he lent a copy to a neighbor and the neighbor's seventeen-year-old son. To Peli's delight, the adolescent reported that he had trouble sleeping after watching the film. "So right from the start we knew we had something," Peli told Craig Mathieson for the Melbourne *Age* (4 Dec. 2009). "For this film, nightmares means real potential."

Peli began submitting the completed film to festivals in 2007; though it was rejected by the San Diego Film Festival, it was accepted by many others, including Screamfest, a small horror film event in Los Angeles. The viewers who saw *Paranormal Activity* at festivals posted rave reviews on blogs and on Twitter, creating early word-of-mouth anticipation for the film's wide release. Peli sent his film to a number of production companies and received many rejections before attracting the interest of DreamWorks, the company founded by acclaimed filmmakers Steven Spielberg, David Geffen, and Jeffrey Katzenberg and which was owned at the time by Paramount Pictures. DreamWorks producers had intended to reshoot the movie entirely, but upon witnessing the near-hysterical reactions of test audiences, they decided to release the film essentially as it was. When Spielberg himself took *Paranormal Activity* home to watch, not only did he find the film scary, he reported that after having watched it one of the doors in his house was inexplicably locked from the inside, forcing him to call a locksmith. Spielberg approved of releasing the film, but suggesting filming a new, simpler ending. Peli told Mathieson that Spielberg "said it's one of the scariest films he'd ever seen." He added, "His ending works extremely well. If you get advice from Steven Spielberg it's worth following it."

### PARANORMAL'S SUCCESS
Although DreamWorks left its partnership with Paramount Pictures in 2008, Paramount Pictures retained rights to *Paranormal Activity*. Prior to the film's release, Paramount launched an interactive marketing campaign that allowed fans to bring the film to their local movie theater by clicking a "Demand It" button on Facebook or the film's website. Paramount also launched a "Tweet your scream" campaign, asking fans to post footage of their reactions to the movie on the Internet. Footage of movie theater audiences was also featured in the film's trailers. "The marketing automatically relied on the fact that people would see the movie, enjoy it, and tell their friends," Peli told Raphael. "Without word-of-mouth, the film would have done nothing." *Paranormal Activity* was shown in twelve theaters in September 2009, and thanks to fan demand, it was released nationwide the following month.

Based on Peli's and Taylor's experiences after they moved into their San Diego home, *Paranormal Activity* follows Katie and Micah, a young couple who set out to investigate the strange noises they begin to hear after moving into their San Diego home. The film is entirely composed of footage the couple supposedly collects using cameras they set up around their home. To add another layer of realism, the movie begins with text that thanks "the families of Micah Sloat and Katie Featherston." *Paranormal Activity* became the decade's most successful R-rated horror film in the United States, grossing about $190 million worldwide. Many critics praised the movie for the effectiveness of its slowly building suspense, as well as the performances of the two relatively new actors. In a review for the *Chicago Sun-Times* (7 Oct. 2009), Roger Ebert called *Paranormal Activity*, "an ingenious little horror film, so well made it's truly scary." He went on to note, "It illustrates one of my favorite points, that silence and waiting can be more entertaining than frantic fast-cutting and berserk f/x. For extended periods here, nothing at all is happening, and believe me, you won't be bored."

### INSIDIOUS
The success of *Paranormal Activity* made Peli a big name in horror filmmaking. Though he could have garnered any number of big-budget projects, he opted instead to produce a small-budget horror movie that gave filmmakers full creative control without any large studio influence. He contacted James Wan and Leigh Whannell, the creators of the horror movie *Saw* (2004), the first in a series of movies that revolves around a serial killer who puts his victims in gruesome, sadistic scenarios. Enthusiastic about Peli's idea, Wan and Whannell submitted a script to Peli and began filming about four months later, with Peli as executive producer.

Made for just over $10 million, the resulting film, *Insidious* (2010), starring Rose Byrne and Patrick Wilson, follows a family whose son inexplicably falls into a coma after a series of strange incidents that take place in their new house. The completed film drew comparisons to the classic horror film *Poltergeist* (1982) and received mixed reviews. Writing for the *San Francisco Chronicle* (1 Apr. 2011), Mick LaSalle called *Insidious*, "a respectable attempt at a type of horror movie they don't make anymore—that is, horror that is scary and not merely disgusting." He went on to note, however, that it was "hampered throughout by little inconsistencies. . . . Director James Wan falls too in love with his own effects, to the point that sequences get stretched and drained of tension." Despite this and other mixed reviews, the film earned more than $97 million worldwide, making it the most profitable film of the year.

### PARANORMAL ACTIVITY FRANCHISE AND THE RIVER
After the completion of *Insidious*, Peli went on to serve as executive producer and cowriter of the next two films in the *Paranormal Activity* franchise, both of which are, like the original, made up of supposedly found footage. Directed by Tod Williams, *Paranormal Activity 2* (2010), a prequel to the first film, focuses on Kristi, the sister of Katie, and her husband Daniel. They set up video cameras in their house after being burgled, leading them to discover that their house is possessed by a demonic entity. The third film in the series, *Paranormal Activity 3*

(2011), was directed by Henry Joost and Ariel Schulman, makers of the hit 2010 documentary thriller *Catfish*. Set in 1988, the third film follows the haunting of Kristi and Katie as children. Though neither prequel was as warmly received by critics as the original, both performed well at the box office, each earning more than $100 million.

Peli next entered the realm of television with *The River*, a sci-fi horror television series set on an uncharted region of the Amazon River. Peli, who had initially conceived of the project as a film rather than a television show, had set the project aside for a couple of years before successfully pitching the series to Dream-Works. Spielberg had also earlier suggested that he and Peli work together on a television show. In September 2010, ABC won a bidding war with NBC for the project. Starring Bruce Greenwood, Leslie Hope, and Joe Anderson, *The River* follows Emmet Cole, an adventurer and the host of a wildlife nature series called *Undiscovered Country*, who goes missing while exploring the Amazon River. When, after six months, Cole's emergency beacon goes off, his wife and part-time cohost, Tess; his son, Lincoln; and a team of explorers travel to the Amazon River to investigate what happened to Cole. They also bring a production crew to record the journey on film.

In the style of Peli's found-footage films, *The River* consists mostly of unsteady camera footage that is supposedly captured by the documentary team. The series premiered on ABC to American and Canadian audiences on February 7, 2012, and in the days that followed, it debuted in numerous countries around the world—a global release designed to prevent piracy in foreign countries. The first two episodes of *The River* received a lukewarm review from Mike Hale for the *New York Times* (6 Feb. 2012), who noted, "*The River*, ABC's deadly serious and profoundly silly new spook show, is a horror hybrid, an escapee from Dr. Moreau's island of television beasts." Despite high anticipation, the show suffered from low ratings from the start and was cancelled in May 2012 after its eight-episode first season.

### CHERNOBYL DIARIES

Peli came upon the idea for his next film project, *Chernobyl Diaries* (2012), after stumbling upon videos on YouTube made by people who had embarked on "extreme tourism" day trips to the abandoned town of Pripyat, Russia. The city was the setting of the notorious 1986 Chernobyl nuclear reactor disaster, in which an explosion set off the worst nuclear accident in history. As a result, an enormous amount of radioactive contamination was released into the atmosphere over western Soviet Union and Europe—more than four hundred times the radioactive material released by the atomic bomb dropped on Hiroshima. The population of Pripyat was forced to evacuate quickly, leaving the city essentially as it was. "People basically didn't have a chance to pick up their belongings," Peli told Robert Bianco for *USA Today* (24 May 2012). "They all just vanished overnight, and there's not a place like that on Earth." Intrigued by the history of the abandoned town, Peli thought it would be an excellent setting for a horror film. He initially wanted to film on location in Pripyat before learning that in 2011, the Ukrainian government had banned people from going there. The film was instead shot in Serbia and Hungary and made use of computer graphics imagery to insert images of the actual city.

*Chernobyl Diaries* follows six adventurist Americans who embark on an excursion to Pripyat with a local guide. When their van breaks down and their guide proves useless, the tourists become stranded in the supposedly deserted town. As the sun goes down, mysterious mutated things begin to emerge in the darkness. Directed by Bradley Parker, with a script cowritten by Peli, and starring Jonathan Sadowski, Jesse McCartney, Olivia Taylor Dudley, and Devin Kelly, the film was released in May 2012 to mediocre reviews. Claudia Puig wrote for *USA Today* (25 May 2012), "Despite an unlikely setting and a moderately intriguing premise, *Chernobyl Diaries* proves to be a generic horror flick where young tourists are systematically victimized in unoriginal and not terribly scary ways." Neither was the film a box office success; it grossed about $18 million worldwide.

### OTHER PROJECTS

Following *Chernobyl Diaries*, Peli produced *Lords of Salem*, a horror film about a coven of witches that visits the Massachusetts town. Written and directed by Rob Zombie, the film was shown at the Toronto International Film Festival in September 2012. Peli also produced and cowrote *Paranormal Activity 4*, which was released in October 2012. The fourth *Paranormal* installment, like the third, was directed by Joost and Schulman. Peli is also the producer, writer, and director of *Area 51*, a film about the mysterious military base thought to house evidence of extraterrestrials, which is set for a November 2013 release.

Peli does not comment on projects he's working on while they are still in development, a practice he began while making his first film. "Even when I was making the first *Paranormal Activity*, I didn't tell anyone I was making it, not my friends or neighbors or coworkers," he told Mekado Murphy for the *New York Times* (25 May 2012). "I just kind of found that there was nothing to be gained by announcing to the world that you're doing something. I believe you just go ahead and do it and when it's ready to present to the world, then you can talk about it."

## PERSONAL LIFE

A writer for the *Irish Times* described Peli as "a sober man who rarely laughs [and] comes across like an efficient, only mildly enthusiastic junior sales manager." Though Peli has said he was quite happy with his computer programming career before he began making films, he reportedly quit after the success of his first film. Peli and Taylor, the girlfriend whose experiences helped inspire the *Paranormal Activity* franchise, broke up in 2007, soon after the film's release. She is credited as a producer in the film.

## SUGGESTED READING

Ebert, Roger. "Paranormal Activity." *Chicago Sun-Times*. Sun-Times Media, 7 Oct. 2009. Web. 18 Sept. 2012.

Murphy, Mekado. "What Scares Oren Peli?" *New York Times*. New York Times, 25 May 2012. Web. 18 Sept. 2012.

Puig, Claudia. "'Chernobyl Diaries': Skip the Trip to Toxic Wasteland." *USA Today*. Gannett, 25 May 2012. Web. 18 Sept. 2012.

Raphael, Amy. "How *Paranomral Activity* Became a Frightening Success." *Guardian* [London]. Guardian News and Media, 20 Nov. 2009. Web. 18 Sept. 2012.

Yadav, Hans. "Oren Peli Explains Why 'Paranormal Activity' Will Keep You Up at Night." *Michigan Daily*. Michigan Daily, 27 Sept. 2009. Web. 18 Sept. 2012.

## SELECTED WORKS

*Paranormal Activity*, 2007; *Insidious*, 2010; *Paranormal Activity 2*, 2010; *Paranormal Activity 3*, 2011; *Chernobyl Diaries*, 2012; *Paranormal Activity 4*, 2012; *The Lords of Salem*, 2012; *The River*, 2012; *Area 51*, 2013.

—*Margaret Roush Mead*

# Roger Penrose

**Born:** August 8, 1931
**Occupation:** Mathematical physicist

Sir Roger Penrose is a British mathematical physicist, mathematician, and philosopher as well as an emeritus Rouse Ball Professor of Mathematics at Oxford University and a best-selling author. He is widely considered one of the leading scientific thinkers of the age as he has made fundamental contributions to geometry and to the science of consciousness and has proposed his own theory for the unification of Einstein's theory of general relativity and quantum field theory. Penrose and his collaborator and friend Stephen Hawking received the Wolf Prize in 1988 for their work on black holes. Penrose has also received the Dannie Heineman

Associated Press

Prize in 1971, the Dirac Medal in 1989, and the Albert Einstein Medal in 1990. In 1994, Penrose was knighted for his services to science.

Many of Penrose's ideas—his rejection of inflationary cosmology, for example, which was a tenet of the big bang theory, or his proposal that the human mind obeys laws similar to those that govern subatomic particles—are considered highly controversial, but he enjoys a large and diverse following. As an author, he is praised for his ability to relate to the common reader. His books, which bear daunting titles like *The Road to Reality: A Complete Guide to the Laws of the Universe* (2004), are international best sellers. As an academic, he is respected among his peers for his profoundly complex yet elegant mathematics. Even the Dutch graphic artist M. C. Escher (1898–1972) was a fan. Several aspects of Escher's most recognizable pieces, including the "impossible staircase" featured in *Ascending and Descending*, were based on the work of Penrose and his father.

Much of Penrose's work stems from his own intricate drawings. He eschews PowerPoint presentations in the classroom in favor of carefully rendered slides, sometimes layering them in complex schemes to illustrate a concept. Even his own theories about consciousness and his argument for why computers could never fully replace the human brain could be said to find their root in an artist's understanding of inspiration. Citing Kurt Gödel's incompleteness theorem, he wrote in his book *Shadows of the Mind: A Search for the Missing Science of Consciousness* (1994), as quoted by Christopher Lehmann-Haupt for the *New York Times* (31 Oct. 1994), "Human intuition and insight cannot be reduced to any set of rules." In his next book *Shadows of the Mind: A Search for the Missing Science of Consciousness* (1994), Penrose argued that even current physical laws could not adequately describe human consciousness, though he is certain that scientists will one day solve the mystery. "I'm trying to say that in consciousness we are actually using some physics that physicists don't know yet," he told John Schwartz for the *Washington Post* (1 Dec. 1994).

## EARLY LIFE

Penrose was born on August 8, 1931, in Colchester, Essex, England. His parents, Lionel Sharples Penrose and Margaret Leathes, both studied mathematics and medicine. Penrose's grandfather was a talented artist, and his uncle, Sir Roland, was the cofounder of the Institute of Contemporary Arts in London. His father was a medical geneticist who studied mental illness and was an elected Fellow of the Royal Society. His mother loved geometry and according to Penrose, she was very talented, but she devoted her life to her husband and children. "[My father] wanted her at home," Penrose told Judy Siegel-Itzkovich for the *Jerusalem Post* (1 May 2005). "There were embarrassing arguments over this, and it was so hard for her. She loved to play chess, and applied for the British Ladies Championship, but my father forbade it." All of Penrose's siblings, including his brothers Oliver and Jonathan, and a sister Shirley, were scientifically inclined and went on to study math, psychology, and medicine. Jonathan is a ten-time British chess champion and Oliver is a highly respected theoretical physicist.

When Penrose was eight years old, his family moved to Philadelphia. His father was a pacifist and decided to keep the family in North America for the duration of World War II. Lionel Penrose became the director of psychiatric research at Ontario Hospital in London, Ontario, Canada. After the war, the family moved back to England where he became a professor of human genetics at University College, London, and Penrose attended a private school associated with University College.

Penrose's upbringing was strict. He didn't read novels, but he picked up the habits of his father, he told Susan Kruglinski for *Discover* magazine (6 Oct. 2009), who didn't distinguish "any boundary between his work and what he did for fun." Penrose's father made puzzles and games for his children and taught them calculus. As a young man, Penrose made puzzles for fun, too, and his recreation culminated in some exciting geometric principles for which he later became famous.

## UNDERGRADUATE WORK AT UNIVERSITY COLLEGE

Penrose studied mathematics at University College, London, but his father, who was a professor at the school, was not supportive of the decision. He believed that "mathematics was something you did only if you were fanatical and weren't interested in other things," Penrose explained in a January 24, 1989, interview with Alan Lightman for the Niels Bohr Library and Archives. Hoping to deter Penrose from the field, his father arranged to have him take a difficult entry exam with a University College lecturer before enrolling. To his father's disappointment, Penrose did very well.

Penrose met Dennis Sciama, a renowned Cambridge cosmologist, while still an undergraduate at University College. Penrose asked Sciama about a problem that had been bothering him concerning the belief at the time that galaxies disappeared from view when they reached the speed of light. Penrose drew Sciama a picture from a geometrical perspective demonstrating why he thought that this could not be the case. Sciama was intrigued and showed Penrose's work to his partner, astronomer Fred Hoyle (who coined the term *big bang*). They found that Penrose was correct. "When I did go to Cambridge as a research student, in quite a different area (in pure mathematics), I think Dennis [Sciama] felt it was his duty to look after me," Penrose told Lightman. Sciama fostered Penrose's enthusiasm for physics and cosmology.

## GRADUATE WORK AND TEACHING CAREER

Penrose received a bachelor's degree with first-class honors in mathematics from University College and decided to pursue a graduate degree in pure mathematics at St. John's College, Cambridge, and studied algebraic geometry with Sir William Hodge. After a difference of opinion and a divergence of interest, he parted ways with the great mathematician and studied under John Arthur Todd. In 1955, Penrose published the first of several papers on what would become known as the Moore–Penrose pseudoinverse, all the while maintaining his interest in physics and cosmology.

In 1956, he taught as an assistant lecturer in pure mathematics at Bedford College at the University of London. After earning his PhD, he was appointed as a research fellow at St. John's College. He remained there for three years. During his fellowship at Cambridge, Penrose received a NATO Research Fellowship that allowed him to travel to the United States and teach from 1959–61 first at Princeton University and later at Syracuse University. He returned to England as a research associate at King's College, London, and in 1963, he spent an academic year as a visiting associate professor at the University of Texas at Austin. In 1964, Penrose was appointed reader of mathematics at Birkbeck College, London, and in 1966 he became a professor of applied mathematics.

In 1973, Penrose was named Rouse Ball Professor of Mathematics at the University of Oxford; in 1998 he was named Emeritus Rouse Ball Professor of Mathematics at Oxford and was appointed Gresham professor of geometry at Gresham College, London. Penrose is officially retired though he still teaches and remains active in academia.

## M. C. ESCHER AND PENROSE TILING

During his second year at Cambridge, Penrose attended the International Congress of Mathematicians in Amsterdam where he was shown a print of M. C. Escher's woodcut *Night and Day*. In *Night and Day*, birds fly in opposite directions and their color and pattern give the impression that the setting is both night and day. Penrose was inspired by a subsequent visit to one of Escher's exhibitions. "I decided to try and draw some impossible scenes myself and came up with this thing that's referred to as a tri-bar," he told Kruglinski. "It's a triangle that looks like a three-dimensional object, but actually it's impossible for it to be three-dimensional." Penrose showed his work to his father and the two men designed what Penrose called "impossible buildings." They published an article about their work, acknowledging Escher's influence, in the *British Journal of Psychology*.

Escher saw the article and used some of the Penroses' principles in his subsequent works. The tri-bar appears in his 1961 lithograph *Waterfall*, and an "impossible staircase" of Lionel Penrose's design appears in *Ascending and Descending* (1960). Penrose later met the artist and gave him some tiles and a challenge: the tiles would make a repeating pattern only after correctly fitting twelve of them together. Eventually, Escher solved the puzzle and contacted Penrose to understand the geometry behind it. The concept is illustrated in Escher's last tessellation *Ghosts* (1971).

Throughout his career, Penrose continued to devise pattern puzzles in his spare time. Until the 1960s, it was thought to be impossible to create a pattern that, when laid down on a plane, could go on forever in all directions without repeating itself. This is known as an aperiodic tiling. Penrose tiles, and indeed all totally aperiodic tilings, are significant because they represent "an area of mathematics that is beyond the reckoning powers of computers," Alison Boyle wrote for *Plus* magazine (1 Dec. 2000). In 1973 Penrose developed a set of six tiles that could be arranged to be totally aperiodic. He then developed a tiling that consists of only two rhombuses. The tiling exhibits an important concept known as quasiperiodicity, in which "some parts of the pattern could be periodic on local scales, but the whole pattern . . . is not periodic. Such order within disorder is known as quasiperiodicity," Boyle explained.

"My interest in the tiles has to do with the idea of a universe controlled by very simple forces, even though we see complications all over the place," Penrose told Kruglinski. "The tilings follow conventional rules to make complicated patterns. It was an attempt to see how the complicated could be satisfied by very simple rules that reflect what we see in the world."

## SINGULARITY THEOREMS AND TWISTOR THEORY

Penrose began seriously studying physics as a research fellow and began publishing papers on cosmology in 1959. In 1965, he produced the mathematics that illustrates how dying stars collapse to form black holes. His findings proved that Einstein's theory of general relativity breaks down when confronted with the nature of black holes, and, along with the work of physicist Stephen Hawking, resulted in the Penrose–Hawking singularity theorems. The work led Penrose on a quest to construct a "theory of everything" that would reconcile general relativity and quantum field theory. In an article for *New Scientist* (31 July 2004), Penrose described the two theories as "the two greatest 20th-century revolutions in physical understanding." Though he adds, "there are serious inconsistencies in each of the great theories separately, and there are reasons for believing that each could benefit from its union with the other. The main reason is that in certain situations, the theories just don't make any physical sense." To combine them in any satisfying and coherent way might provide a glimpse of the fundamental structure of the universe. In 1967, Penrose put forth his own theory of everything known as "twistor theory," which interprets space-time through the lens of geometry and the mathematics of complex numbers.

## *THE EMPEROR'S NEW MIND* AND *SHADOWS OF THE MIND*

In 1989, Penrose published *The Emperor's New Mind: Concerning Computers, Minds and the Laws of Physics*, which contained what he believes was the most controversial idea of his career. Penrose argues in the book that true artificial intelligence, a computer that can function like a human brain, is impossible. Consciousness, he asserts, is not merely computational; the human brain employs a level of insight that a computer cannot match. The book, which was awarded the 1990 Rhône-Poulenc Prizes for Science Books, became a surprise best seller and drew criticism from biologists and computer scientists. The late biologist John Maynard Smith, as quoted by Schwartz, suggested that the book only told readers what they wanted to hear: "Most people do not want to see themselves as lumbering robots programmed to ensure the survival of their genes. . . . To be told by someone with impeccable scientific credentials that they are nothing of the kind can only be pleasing."

In *Shadows of the Mind: A Search for the Missing Science of Consciousness* (1994), Penrose's follow-up to *The Emperor's New Mind*, he expanded his argument and responded to his critics. He introduced the possibility that the human mind could obey the strange laws of quantum mechanics (as opposed to classical physical laws), but he also outlined his own criticisms of quantum theory: "Our brains," he writes in the book, "have somehow contrived to harness the details of a physics that is yet unknown to human physicists" (373).

## THE ROAD TO REALITY

*The Road to Reality: A Complete Guide to the Laws of the Universe* (2005) is widely considered Penrose's "grand opus," as Siegel-Itzkovich describes it, and is as daunting and as complete as the subtitle suggests. Although Penrose is a patient teacher for lay readers, one of those readers, a critic named Therese Littleton, quipped in a very positive review of the book as quoted by Siegel-Itzkovich, "The number of people in the world who can understand everything in it could probably take a taxi together to Penrose's next lecture." Still, the book went on to be an international best seller.

Penrose's next book, *Cycles of Time: An Extraordinary New View of the Universe* (2011), expounds on a tenet of twistor theory—the idea that a chain of universes like our own have come and gone through never-ending cycles of birth, through an event like the big bang, and death by black hole. His next project is purportedly a collection of a series of lectures with the working title of *Fashion, Faith, and Fantasy*, with each descriptor matching a current school of scientific thought. "Fashion" represents the ubiquitous string theory, much of which Penrose dismisses as passing fad. "Faith" represents problems with the paradoxical yet highly valued quantum theory, which, as Penrose complained to Michael Brooks for *New Scientist* (13 Mar. 2010), "is so successful and so non-intuitive that people think they can have any old theory they like and it could be perfectly true." Finally, "fantasy" represents Penrose's ideas regarding inflationary cosmology, or the widely accepted idea that the universe expanded after the big bang from, as Brooks put it, "the size of a pea to the size of the Milky Way."

## PERSONAL LIFE

Penrose married American Joan Isabel Wedge in 1959. They have three grown sons. He is currently married to his second wife, Vanessa, who teaches mathematics at a boy's school. They have one young son.

## SUGGESTED READING

Boyle, Alison. "From Quasicrystals to Kleenex." *Plus Magazine.* Millenium Mathematics Project, 1 Dec. 2000. Web. 12 July 2013.

Brooks, Michael. "Happy-Go-Lucky, No Strings Attached." *New Scientist* 205.2751 (2010). 28. Print.

Kruglinski, Susan. "Discover Interview: Roger Penrose Says Physics Is Wrong, from String Theory to Quantum Mechanics." *Discover.* Kalmbach Publishing Co., 6 Oct. 2009. Web. 9 Jul. 2013.

Lightman, Alan. "Oral History Transcript—Dr. Roger Penrose." *Niels Bohr Library & Archives.* American Institute of Physics, 24 Jan. 1989. Web. 10 July 2013.

Penrose, Roger. "Strings with a Twist: Do We Really Need Half-a-Dozen Hidden Dimensions? Not Any More, Says Physicist Roger Penrose." *New Scientist.* New Scientist, 31 July 2004. Web. 8 July 2013.

## SELECTED WORK

*The Emperor's New Mind: Concerning Computers, Minds and the Laws of Physics,* 1989; *Shadows of the Mind: A Search for the Missing Science of Consciousness,* 1994; *The Nature of Space and Time* (with Stephen Hawking), 1996; *The Large, the Small and the Human Mind* (with Abner Shimony, Nancy Cartwright, and Stephen Hawking), 1997; *The Road to Reality: A Complete Guide to the Laws of the Universe,* 2004; *Cycles of Time: An Extraordinary New View of the Universe,* 2010

—*Molly Hagan*

---

# Kamla Persad-Bissessar

**Born:** April 22, 1952
**Occupation:** Prime minister of the Republic of Trinidad and Tobago

Kamla Persad-Bissessar took office on May 26, 2010, as the first female prime minister of the Republic of Trinidad and Tobago. This momentous occasion came after a long series of political firsts for the seasoned Hindu politician, who had already broken the glass ceiling on a number of cabinet-level government posts in the late 1990s and early 2000s. Upon becoming prime minister, she also became the first woman to assume the mantle of chairperson-in-office for the Commonwealth of Nations.

The Republic of Trinidad and Tobago is a small Caribbean nation roughly the size of Delaware. The two main islands, Trinidad and Tobago, are geographically close but were colonized separately by various European powers starting in the sixteenth century. In the early nineteenth century, both islands became holdings in the British Empire, and the British government combined them into one colonial administration. Soon after the empire abolished slavery, indentured servitude grew on the islands' sugar plantations, bringing migrants from faraway locations such as India, Sierra Leone, China, and Portugal and adding to the existing mix of Spanish, French, Dutch, and British inhabitants.

Independent since August 1962, Trinidad and Tobago was ruled nearly continuously by the

India Today Group/Getty Images

People's National Movement (PNM) for over four decades. The country's balance of power radically shifted in the spring of 2010, however. Amid accusations of government corruption and public outrage at high government spending, PNM prime minister Patrick Manning suddenly called a snap election in April 2010, only halfway through his five-year term. On May 24, the United National Congress (UNC) candidate Kamla Persad-Bissessar and her multiparty coalition enjoyed a landslide victory.

Committed to protecting and empowering all Trinidadians and Tobagonians, Prime Minister Persad-Bissessar is well known for women's- and children's-rights activism and for championing women as agents of change. In a Commonwealth Day message delivered in her capacity as chairperson-in-office, Persad-Bissessar credited "change in the social, economic and political status of women throughout our world" to the small actions of "many dedicated sisters, daughters, mothers and grandmothers of every little community in every country in our world" (12 Mar. 2011).

### EARLY LIFE AND EDUCATION

One of eight children, Kamla Persad-Bissessar was born in Siparia, Trinidad, in 1952. Her parents were descendants of indentured servants who had migrated from India to Trinidad in the late nineteenth and early twentieth centuries. In a January 2012 speech given during a visit to India, Persad-Bissessar recognized the challenges her ancestors had faced and the enduring gifts they had bestowed on their progeny. "When they went, they had no gold, no diamond, no traveller cheque, and they had no facility of cell phone, Internet, Blackberry, and Facebook.

What they took with them was Ramayan, Gita, and Koran and the lifestyle, tradition, values from this land," she said, as quoted by Faizan Ahmad in the *Times of India* (11 Jan. 2012). She later implored the listening crowd to "get [their] daughters educated," saying, "For future generations, do what my ancestors did: give education to children."

Persad-Bissessar grew up in the district of Penal in a rural, underdeveloped area of southwestern Trinidad. At Indian Arrival Day festivities in late May 2010, she publicly recalled the communal spirit shared among her hometown's diverse members, saying, "I remember sharing meals from the same pot with neighbours of different racial, ethnic, social and economic backgrounds. . . . We all managed. If one had, then all had. Because then we were intuitively and instinctively our brother's keepers," as quoted by BBC correspondent Nazma Muller (24 June 2010).

After graduating from Iere High School, Persad-Bissessar went on to pursue postsecondary studies, thanks in large part to the efforts of her mother, who advocated for her continued education. Persad-Bissessar's father, a firm adherent to traditional Indian gender roles, opposed this. Nonetheless, Persad-Bissessar attended college at the University of the West Indies and then enrolled at the Norwood Technical College in London.

Persad-Bissessar's experiences in the United Kingdom would have lasting effects on her life. As a student, she took a job in social work with the Church of England Children's Society of London, no doubt inspiring her long-standing interest in children's issues. As a person of color, she endured racial prejudice, which influenced her decision to pursue social justice throughout her career. It was also in Britain that she met the man who became her husband, Dr. Gregory Bissessar.

### AN ADVOCATE FOR THE PEOPLE

Gregory Bissessar's medical studies took the couple to Jamaica, where they settled for fourteen years, a period corresponding to the rise of the black-power movement in that country. During the 1970s and 1980s, Persad-Bissessar taught students at St. Andrew High School in Kingston and at the University of the West Indies in Mona. At this time, she also witnessed gun battles between rival gangs and fell in love with the music of reggae artist Bob Marley, whose song "No Woman No Cry" later served as a political anthem of sorts for her.

Returning to Trinidad after an absence of nearly twenty years, Persad-Bissessar decided to return to the classroom, first as a teacher and then once more as a student. She obtained a diploma in education and a bachelor's degree in law from the Hugh Wooding Law School in

Trinidad and Tobago. After six years of teaching law, she moved to practicing law full time.

In the late 1980s, she made her entrée into politics, serving as the National Alliance for Reconstruction alderman for St. Patrick County Council from 1987 to 1991. Three years later, she was elected to Parliament as the UNC representative for the town of Siparia, not far from where she grew up in Penal. The late 1990s and early 2000s saw her rise to a variety of prominent government positions. In 1995, Persad-Bissessar was appointed minister of legal affairs, a post she held through 1999 and again in the fall of 2001. Her background in teaching became important when Prime Minister Basdeo Panday made her the minister of education in 1999. Persad-Bissessar also had the distinction of being the first woman attorney general of Trinidad and Tobago, serving from 1995 to 1996 and in fall 2001. On April 26, 2007, she was made leader of the opposition, another first for women in Trinidadian politics.

The gender discrimination Persad-Bissessar faced as a young woman in the 1960s unequivocally informed her views on the role of women in politics. In a 2007 speech, Persad-Bissessar summed up what she felt was her duty as a woman in a male-dominated political area, saying, "In that sea of men who argued and cussed each other . . . I knew I had to be the rare voice of fairness, nurturing, caring, and love. I knew that my vote was always influenced by the thought of how those policies or stances would affect the heart, mind and bodies of the country," as quoted by Aliyyah Eniath and Sasha Mohammed in *Caribbean Belle* magazine. Named among the top female world leaders in 2010 by *Glamour* magazine, Persad-Bissessar told reporter Lynn Harris, "As a woman, my style defines my leadership. It's a gentler, more compassionate approach . . . I consult, I listen, and I compromise where it's in the best interest of the citizens" (1 Nov. 2010).

## A DRAMATIC VICTORY

On February 25, 2010, following a fierce, often-vitriolic campaign against her former political mentor, Basdeo Panday, Persad-Bissessar was once again named leader of the opposition for the UNC. Calling Panday's strategies a "smear campaign of lies, half-truths, and innuendoes," Persad-Bissessar defiantly asserted, "Smear campaigns do not win elections. Sticks and stones may break my bones but words cannot hurt me," as quoted by BBC News correspondent Nazma Muller (24 June 2010). Evidently the battle for UNC leadership served her well, as a mere three months later, on May 26, she was sworn into office as prime minister of Trinidad and Tobago, becoming the first woman to hold the position.

The May 2010 election marked a significant change in power dynamics not only between political parties but also between racial and ethnic groups in the country. During the campaign, Persad-Bissessar and her minoritarian party, which has a predominantly South Asian–descended base, successfully mobilized a multi-ethnic five-party coalition known as the People's Partnership to defeat the PNM, historically largely supported by African-descended Trinidadians and Tobagonians, and unseat PNM prime minister Patrick Manning. On May 24, the Trinidadian and Tobagonian voting population decided overwhelmingly in favor of the coalition: of the forty-one seats in Parliament, the People's Partnership took twenty-nine, or 70 percent control, in a dramatic reversal of the PNM's former majority of twenty-six to fifteen. Reflecting the cooperative spirit of the coalition victory, just before taking office, Persad-Bissessar said, "We will build on our collective strength and character and everyone of us will rise; no one will be left behind," as quoted by Tony Fraser for the Associated Press (25 May 2010).

## MOTHER OF THE NATION

In her 2007 Bob Marley–inspired "No Woman No Cry" speech, Persad-Bissessar stated that throughout her political career she has considered it her "duty to assume the natural role of mother when it came to national issues." "My maternal instincts made me choose sometimes not by my head, but my heart. But as any true mother, those instincts were never wrong," she said, as quoted by Eniath and Mohammed. Since taking office, Prime Minister Persad-Bissessar has used those "maternal instincts" to implement social programs aimed at addressing destitution, children's issues, and gender-related problems. Her achievements in office include the establishment of the Helping Hand Initiative, a collaborative effort among Caribbean governments, nongovernmental organizations, and companies to offer intraregional disaster relief, and the creation of the Children's Life Fund, through which poor, critically ill children can receive special medical treatments in the United States. In May 2012, Persad-Bissessar's newly created Ministry of Gender, Youth and Child Development announced its National Gender Policy on child care, domestic and sexual violence, teen parenthood, reproductive health, and the growing gap between women and men in secondary education and employment, among other gender- and sexuality-related issues.

Perhaps more visible than any other issue she has tackled is Persad-Bissessar's aggressive stance on crime, one of voters' two major concerns during the 2010 election. As a result of Trinidad and Tobago's geographical proximity to South America, crime related to international drug trafficking has plagued the country in recent years. According to a BBC News report on August 23, 2011, the country's murder rate in 2011 was thirty-six per hundred thousand.

Madison Gray, writing for *Time* magazine, went so far as to call it the "murder capital of the Caribbean" (25 May 2010).

In August 2011, nearly a dozen murders occurred within a few days' time, prompting Persad-Bissessar to declare a state of emergency in certain "hot spots" throughout the country. BBC News correspondents quoted her as stating, "The nation will not be held to ransom by marauding gangs of thugs bent on creating havoc on our society" (23 Aug. 2011). An overnight curfew lasting from 9 p.m. until 5 a.m. was instituted in the affected areas, and police powers to search and arrest were enhanced. By late November, Persad-Bissessar estimated in a media release that 7,269 arrests had been made under the state of emergency and announced that a vast amount of contraband, including over $1.5 billion in drugs, had been confiscated. In the statement, she reaffirmed her resolve, claiming, "These nefarious elements, with support from others whose names will also come to light in time, are finally confronted by a government which possesses the political will, courage and strength of conviction to stoutly defend and protect the citizens of our country. We will not cow to them, nor negotiate with them nor give any quarter to them. . . . For far too long these criminals have been allowed to flourish as the untouchables, some with their sinister connections of legitimacy. The intense pressure brought to bear by our initiatives will be intensified and I will stop at nothing to return Trinidad and Tobago to the peaceful state we once enjoyed." The apparent success of the administration's anticrime initiatives may account for an unsuccessful plot on the lives of the prime minister and her cabinet in November 2011. The limited state of emergency expired in December of that year, proving wrong the fear that the assassination plot would give the government an excuse to extend it.

Like many other Caribbean countries, Trinidad and Tobago has the death penalty, though no one has been executed there since 1999. Although capital punishment enjoys widespread popular support at home, the possibility that executions might resume in Trinidad and Tobago has garnered criticism from international human-rights groups. Persad-Bissessar has openly supported the country's mandatory death sentence for murder convictions as a means to fight the rising crime rate, but what her ultimate legacy will be in this area remains to be seen.

### PERSONAL LIFE

Vidwatie Newton, Persad-Bissessar's sister, has frequently received a per diem from the state to accompany the prime minister as her travel assistant on international state visits, for which Persad-Bissessar has been severely criticized. Persad-Bissessar has vociferously defended the practice and claims that her sister's compensation comes from private funds, not those of the government. "I do give her some of my own money because she has to live," she reportedly told interviewers for the *Sunday Express* on September 25, 2011. Persad-Bissessar added, "She [Newton] was gainfully employed for many years and I am very grateful to her for helping me. I can trust her with my personal things: my food, my clothing."

One key reason given for Newton's assistance is the prime minister's poor health. After she was unexpectedly hospitalized in October 2011, it was revealed that Persad-Bissessar suffers from diabetes and high blood pressure. While visiting Barbados the following May, she was again hospitalized and underwent a series of tests. An elevator was installed in early 2012 at the Diplomatic Centre in St. Ann's, Trinidad, where Persad-Bissessar and her husband, Gregory, reside, to assist the ailing prime minister.

The Bissessars have one son, Kris, and Persad-Bissessar enjoys spending time with their two grandchildren.

### SUGGESTED READING

Eniath, Aliyyah, and Sasha Mohammed. "She Has Risen: Getting to Know the Honourable Prime Minister, Kamla Persad-Bissessar." *Caribbean Belle Magazine*. Safari, n.d. Web. 17 Nov. 2012.

Fraser, Tony. "Kamla Persad-Bissessar: Trinidad and Tobago Elects First Female Prime Minister." *Huffington Post*. TheHuffingtonPost.com, 25 May 2010. Web. 17 Nov. 2012.

Gray, Madison. "Trinidad Elects Its First Female Prime Minister." *Time*. Time, 25 May 2010. Web. 17 Nov. 2012.

Muller, Nazma. "Trinidad's PM Breaks the Cultural Mould." *BBC News*. BBC, 24 June 2010. Web. 17 Nov. 2012.

Persad-Bissessar, Kamla. "Commonwealth Day Message from the Chair-in-Office." *Commonwealth Secretariat*. Commonwealth Secretariat, 12 Mar. 2011. Web. 19 Nov. 2012.

"Trinidad PM Persad-Bissessar: Assassination Plot Foiled." *BBC News*. BBC, 24 Nov. 2011. Web. 17 Nov. 2012.

—*Céleste Codington-Lacerte*

# Markus Persson (Notch)

**Born:** June 1, 1979
**Occupation:** Video game designer and philanthropist

Although only in his early thirties, Markus Persson—also known online as Notch—is already one of the most successful video game programmers and designers in history, thanks to his

Yui Mok/PA Photos/Landov

idiosyncratic and addictive game *Minecraft*. Described by JP Mangalindan for *CNNMoney* (5 Apr. 2012) as a "digital sandbox" in which players are able to build entire worlds out of their imaginations, *Minecraft* has sold tens of millions of copies since its 2009 release and has created an army of loyal fans who regularly post their creations on the Internet. Persson—a self-effacing man with an antiestablishment streak who expected to earn no more from his game than enough money to make another—has become an industry celebrity, in large part because of the way he single-handedly developed, programmed, and sold his pioneering game online. When the demand for *Minecraft* became too much for him to handle alone, he established his own company, Mojang, which now produces follow-up game titles in addition to managing *Minecraft*'s sales and future development. Persson has used his wealth and influence not only to aid his employees and favorite charities but also to promote other independent video game studios and challenge the major video game publishers, whom he believes stifle designers' creativity in their pursuit of profits.

Persson is admittedly conflicted about his newfound wealth and influence. In a comment on the social news website Reddit, as quoted by Dave Thier in *Forbes* (4 Feb. 2013), Persson explained, "Well, on one hand I don't mind having loads of money at all. On the other, it's a bit strange that I can create something once and keep getting paid over and over and over for it. If you build a car, you can only sell it once. If you paint a fence, you only get paid for it once. If you create a piece of software that's essentially free

to reproduce, you can keep getting paid over and over perpetually."

## EARLY LIFE AND EDUCATION

Markus Persson was born on June 1, 1979, and grew up in Edsbyn, Sweden, a small town near his home country's east coast. In interviews he has described his family as being relatively poor and recalled that they had to save up for things such as a new computer or video game console. But his first recollections center on his father, a railroad worker. "My strongest early memory is of my dad dragging me through very deep snow on a sled," Persson recalled to Simon Parkin for the *New Yorker* (5 Apr. 2013). "I looked up at him and he seemed annoyed at me. Perhaps it was tough work, dragging me, or perhaps I had been crying. And I realized that . . . he's actually a real person, with his own perception of things."

When Persson was very young, his father taught him how to use a Commodore 128, which was the family's home computer. Transfixed by computers and, in particular, early video games, Persson began reading computer magazines, which often printed strings of computer code, thereby allowing their readers to create playable video games on their home computers. "My sister would read the lines out to me and I would tap them into the computer," Persson told Parkin. "After a while, I figured out that if you didn't type out exactly what they told you then something different would happen, where you finally ran the game. That sense of power was intoxicating."

Persson's interest in computer programming increased exponentially after the family moved to Stockholm when he was seven years old. At age thirteen, he began competing against classmates to see which of them could produce the best effects on their Atari ST computers. During his teen years, his parents separated, largely because of his father's alcoholism, which had been hidden from both Persson and his sister. Persson's father moved from Stockholm to the Swedish countryside, where he believed he could get sober as well as isolate himself from temptations. He remained estranged from his children for a few years before reconnecting when they were a bit older.

## EARLY CAREER

By 1994, Persson had decided to become a video game designer. He was encouraged in this pursuit by his father. His teachers, however, suggested that he study graphic design, so he subsequently took his first job as a web designer. He did not remain in the position for long. "I didn't stay there, because I was a bit arrogant and thought I could just go and make games," he explained to Parkin. "But then the dot-com crash happened [in 2000] and I couldn't get a job." After living with his mother for two years, he found a new job as a programmer with King.com, where he created some thirty Flash games, including *Funny Farm*, *Luxor*, and *Carnival Shootout*, before moving over to the Internet photo album website jAlbum.

During his four-and-a-half years at King.com, he began to develop the ideas that would lead to the creation of *Minecraft* in early 2009. At some point in the game's early development, Persson showed it to Carl Manneh, who was then CEO of jAlbum, but Manneh was less than impressed at the time. "I didn't see any potential in it, and that's the honest truth," Manneh recalled to Mangalindan.

## DEVELOPING *MINECRAFT*

Confident that he was on to something, Persson reduced his hours at jAlbum to part time in order to spend more time perfecting *Minecraft*. On June 1, 2010, his thirty-first birthday, he resigned from his day job in order to concentrate on developing his game full time and selling it via digital download. Before long he realized he was unable to keep up with demand working on his own, so he asked Manneh and Jakob Porsér to partner with him to found Mojang, meaning "gadget" in Swedish, an independent studio that would both refine *Minecraft* and develop subsequent video games. Seeing *Minecraft*'s brisk sales, Manneh became convinced of the game's potential and readily agreed.

To its legion of fans, *Minecraft* is unlike any of the video games currently on the market. Its graphics and sound effects, which are primitive looking, recall the video games of the 1980s. Because it is not as hyperrealistic as most modern video games, it can be played on almost any device, from home computers to smartphones, without slowing down. This low-tech approach has allowed the game to become enormously popular with players of all ages. According to data collected by Mojang, the majority of *Minecraft* players are under fifteen, but its serious devotees range in age from nine to seventy.

Also unlike most video games on the market, *Minecraft* has no single objective or story line. Instead, players are allowed to build whatever they wish out of polygonal cubes. The playable, unnamed builder has the ability to transform raw materials such as rocks, dirt, and trees into building materials with which to construct whatever he or she likes—during the daytime. When night falls, however, players must hide in caves or else fend off attacks by various creatures, including creepers, green monsters with the ability to blow up whatever structure or object the player has been working on.

## A SMASH SUCCESS

Since the game's initial release in 2009, *Minecraft* has sold in excess of twenty million copies across various formats. By early 2013, Mojang was selling ten thousand copies of the computer version each day, at $27 per unit. Because the game is sold via digital download, Mojang has little overhead or upfront costs for shipping, storage, or distribution. The game's success, combined with low overhead, contributed to the company's reported $80 million in revenues and $13.5 million in profits for 2011. In 2012, the company had revenues in excess of $235 million and netted $90 million in earnings. Persson is said to have earned $100 million in 2012 from a game he had once hoped to earn him enough money to allow him the time and space to develop another.

"There is no analogy for *Minecraft*'s success, there are multiple story-lines that you can get attached to and think why it's successful," Nabeel Hyatt, a partner with the investment firm Spark Capital, told Matthew Lynley for the *Wall Street Journal* (1 Feb. 2013). "On the one hand it's the story of a single developer building a game in a community with the community watching him start from the first line of code. It's also the story of a huge community which uses that game and starts to build . . . their own multiplayer servers."

## A DEVOTED FAN BASE

Persson and his partners readily agree that *Minecraft*'s success stems from its devoted fan base. The game has approximately 25 million registered users, but millions more play the game regularly. These dedicated fans have organized everything from an annual convention (MineCon, which drew about 4,500 people, including Persson and Manneh, to Disneyland Paris in November 2012) to detailed postings online on websites such as YouTube, which have highlighted players' more remarkable creations. Players are able to create whatever structures they like—inspired by their imaginations, real life, or popular culture—while at the same time exploring the bounds of their creativity and honing their survival skills by hunkering down each night, hoping that whatever they have created will keep the monsters at bay. "Infinite power just isn't very interesting, no matter what game you're playing," Persson told Parkin. "It's much more fun when you have a limited tool set to use against the odds. Usually, a new player to *Minecraft* doesn't make it through the first night. They're just not prepared for the danger. It's a hard lesson but it establishes the rules."

The game's popularity—and Mojang's profit margins—have made the company a key target for both investors and larger video game companies interested in acquisition. To date, Mojang's owners have expressed no interest in either being bought out or invested in. They have, however, partnered with several companies to promote *Minecraft*, including Lego, which offers *Minecraft*-themed building-block toys. Although Persson has left operational control of the company to his partners, his antiestablishment philosophy pervades the Mojang office and inspires its twenty-nine employees. The company itself maintains both flexible working hours and a flat management structure.

## OTHER PROJECTS

In late 2011, Persson designed a *Minecraft* sequel of sorts, *Minicraft*, as part of the Ludum Dare contest, a competition that requires contestants to develop a game from scratch in just two days. Compared to *Minecraft*, *Minicraft* is a more action-oriented game with a specific goal: the player is tasked with killing a character known as the Air Wizard.

Mojang also helped develop an adventure roll-playing game called *Scrolls*, which uses aspects of traditional board games and collectible card games. Persson and the game's primary designer, Jakob Porsér, were inspired to create the game because they felt that a video game having such elements would fill a gap in the gaming market. *Scrolls* went on sale in June 2013 and works on multiple gaming platforms.

Persson is at work on a new game titled *0x10c*, pronounced "Ten to the C," which has been described as a science-fiction sandbox game set in a far-future spacefaring society. The game was inspired in part by the short-lived, cult favorite science-fiction television show *Firefly* (2002). Like its predecessors, *0x10c* will be available on multiple platforms. A release date has yet to be set, in part because Persson is suffering under the pressure of producing a follow-up to such a massive hit as *Minecraft*. "I definitely think *Minecraft* is a freak thing," he told Parkin. "There's no way you could replicate it intentionally. And yes, I'm starting to feel writer's block as a result. . . . With *Minecraft* it was just easier, because nobody knew who I was. Now I post a new idea and millions of people scrutinize it."

## PERSONAL LIFE

In recent years Persson has faced personal challenges as well as professional ones. His father committed suicide in 2011. Then, in 2012, he and his wife—a former moderator on the *Minecraft* forums—divorced after about a year of marriage. Persson has also had to adjust to the fact that he is now a person of means and influence. His success has enabled him to do many things he has long wanted to do—specifically, provide for his family and aid causes he is passionate about, including children's charities and charities devoted to protecting freedoms. He has also been generous to Mojang's employees. In 2011, he divided up and gave them the equivalent of $3 million, which he had earned as dividends. His reasoning is simple. "I still like playing games and programming, and once I had the latest computer and consoles, there really isn't

much more to spend the money on [other] than traveling," he explained in a comment on Reddit, as quoted in *BBC News Technology* (4 Feb. 2013).

Persson has also used his influence to promote video games he has enjoyed playing, particularly ones made by independent designers like himself. Being "notched" by Persson via a positive online review all but guarantees that an independent game will receive an additional boost in sales, usually in the tens of thousands. He has also served as a public and outspoken critic of video game publishers, whom he believes are more interested in securing profits than in producing the most creative games. In December 2012, he donated $250,000 to the Electronic Frontier Foundation (EFF), a nonprofit group dedicated to protecting Internet-based freedom of speech as well as digital rights.

## SUGGESTED READING

"Being Rich Is Weird, Says *Minecraft* Creator." *BBC News Technology*. BBC News, 4 Feb. 2013. Web. 26 May 2013.

Lynley, Matthew. "The Big Money behind Hit Game *Minecraft*." *Wall Street Journal*. Wall Street Journal, 1 Feb. 2013. Web. 25 May 2013.

"Notch!" *Mojang*. Mojang AB, n.d. Web. 25 May 2013.

Parkin, Simon. "The *Minecraft* Creator Markus Persson Faces Life after Fame." *New Yorker*. New Yorker, 5 Apr. 2013. Web. 25 May 2013.

Thier, Dave. "*Minecraft* Creator Markus 'Notch' Persson Made $100 Million Last Year, Is a Little Confused How." *Forbes*. Forbes, 4 Feb. 2013. Web. 26 May 2013.

—*Christopher Mari*

# Kyra Phillips

**Born:** August 18, 1968
**Occupation:** CNN news anchor and journalist

Broadcast journalist Kyra Phillips served for thirteen years (from 1999 to 2012) as an anchor for the afternoon portion of *CNN Newsroom*, the cable news station's seven-hour weekday broadcast of major stories that includes live and taped reports, interviews, and expert analyses. In addition to her reports from behind the anchor desk, Phillips has become known for her in-depth reporting in national and international conflict zones and other adventurous locales. Notably, she served as an embedded journalist on the USS *Abraham Lincoln* aircraft carrier in the Persian Gulf in 2002 and 2003, giving viewers an exclusive look at the United States Navy's preparations for the Iraq War. She later

Wirelmage

filed numerous CNN reports during four tours in the war-ravaged country. Among her most praised stories was her work on the 2007 CNN Special Investigations Unit documentary called *Judgment in Jena*, in which she investigated race relations in the small town of Jena, Louisiana, whose high school became the site of intense racial controversy beginning in August 2006. Phillips, who has won numerous awards over the years—including five Emmy Awards—moved to CNN sister network HLN in August 2012.

### EARLY LIFE AND EDUCATION

Phillips was born in rural Illinois. When she was in the fourth grade, she moved with her family to San Diego, where her parents both worked as professors at San Diego State University. Phillips attended what had formerly been an all-black elementary school as part of a federally mandated racial integration program. "So as a kid I was already involved in diversity and integration issues," she told Tom Blair for *San Diego Magazine* (Apr. 2008). "And it was tough. This was the first time in San Diego that black students had whites coming to their schools, and it was a fascinating dynamic." Phillips was sometimes a target of violence at school, and she had to learn quickly how to protect herself.

Phillips enjoyed talking to people even as a little girl. As a child she would request to sit next to strangers on airplanes while traveling with her family so that she could meet new people. "I had two pen pals by the time I got off the plane," she said in an interview with Jeremy Rosenberg for the University of Southern California (USC) Annenberg Alumni website. Phillips knew from a young age that she wanted to be a journalist and started a newspaper at her elementary school.

Her very first interview was with the famed children's author and illustrator Dr. Seuss. The author, whose given name is Ted Geisel, had had his piano tuned by the father of one of Phillips's friends. Phillips scoured the Rolodex of her friend's father to find Geisel's phone number. "I called him up; said I was doing a story for my elementary school newspaper," Phillips told Blair. "He was not happy. Not friendly to me. But I told him, 'I love your books; this is going to be my first interview.' And I talked him into it. He gave me about six minutes—and my career was off and running."

Phillips attended the University of Southern California's Annenberg School of Communications and Journalism, where she was a member of the Delta Gamma sorority. During her time in college, Phillips interviewed the political cartoonist and humorist Art Buchwald for the school newspaper, the *Daily Trojan*, striking up a friendship that continued until Buchwald's death in 2007. She graduated with a bachelor's degree in broadcast journalism in 1990.

### STARTING OUT AS A JOURNALIST

After graduating, Phillips was an intern at KGTV Channel 10, the local San Diego television station, where she got the opportunity to interview Mother Teresa while accompanying reporter Leonard Villarreal to Tijuana, Mexico. Phillips, a Christian, was in awe of the beloved Roman Catholic nun. "That is the most memorable moment of my life," Phillips told Blair. "Mother Teresa put her hand on my head and blessed me. She gave me a rosary, and to this day it hangs in my office."

Phillips's first full-time reporting job was in Lubbock, Texas, a city located in the northwestern region of the state. During this time, she observed a fraught relationship between the local news stations and law enforcement when journalists accompanied them on missions. To remedy that relationship, she sought out SWAT and special weapons training. "It was a huge challenge," Phillips told Blair. "And so I said to myself, 'I'm going to learn to understand the mentality—what they do, how they train—so when [I'm called to report on a SWAT call] like this again I'm going to know the right language, the right procedures, when to roll the camera and when not to.'" The training paid off, and Phillips was given greater access by law enforcement and developed a greater sense of trust. "It was tremendous for my career," she said.

Over the next few years, Phillips served as a reporter in several different stations across the country, including WLUK-TV in Green Bay, Wisconsin; WDSU-TV in New Orleans, where she was also a weekend anchor; and KCBS-TV in Los Angeles, where she worked on the special assignment team from 1995 to 1999. In 1996, Phillips investigated whether it would be possible for a predator to obtain personal information about children. She contacted Metromail, a large data firm based in Chicago and a subsidiary of R. R. Donnelley & Sons Company, and was able to obtain names, phone numbers, addresses, and ages of 5,500 Pasadena-area children with a $277 money order and no proof of identification. Phillips even gave the name of "Richard Allen Davis," a moniker shared by a convicted child molester and confessed murderer, who was at the time on trial for kidnapping and murdering a twelve-year-old girl. Phillips's acclaimed story won the Bill Stout Memorial Award for enterprise reporting. As a direct result of her reporting, United States Senator Dianne Feinstein of California introduced the Children's Protection and Parental Empowerment Act of 1996, to prohibit the sale of personal information about children without parental consent. (The bill ultimately died in the Senate and was not passed.)

## JOINING CNN

In October 1999, Phillips joined the cable news station CNN, headquartered in Atlanta, as coanchor of its afternoon desk. Serving in that role for more than a decade, Phillips covered a variety of major news stories, becoming particularly known for her adventurous on-the-scene reporting and her ability to secure exclusive access to sources. In the aftermath of the terrorist attacks on September 11, 2001, Phillips traveled to a naval base in Fallon, Nevada, where she reported on the navy's preparation for war in Afghanistan. Phillips became the first network correspondent to be granted access to the elite navy air wing Combat Applications Group (CAG), also known as the Delta Force. In a series of reports in September 2001, she gave viewers exclusive access to the group's preparations for war, including glimpses into the cockpits of strike fighter jets and discussions of the team's training methods.

Phillips spent the month of January 2002 filming a *CNN Presents* documentary in Antarctica. The documentary, "Harsh Continent: Life in Antarctica," debuted in February 2003. Phillips lived at McMurdo Station, the American research center on Ross Island and the largest home for scientists and other workers on the continent. Cameras followed Phillips as she became acquainted with the history and culture of those who live in Antarctica. With her team, Phillips also embarked on a number of dangerous adventures, including trekking to the South Pole and traversing into an ice crevasse.

## EMBEDDED REPORTING FROM IRAQ

During the military's preparations for the Iraq War in late 2002 and early 2003, Phillips reported while embedded aboard the USS *Abraham Lincoln*. The aircraft carrier had been monitoring Saddam Hussein's compliance with United Nations resolutions as part of Operation Southern Watch when its deployment was extended from January to May to take part in Operation Iraqi Freedom. Phillips interviewed naval officers about the difficulties of lengthy deployments and reported on the latest weaponry on F-14 strike fighters, which included satellite-guided bombs and other precision weapons designed to minimize civilian casualties. In October 2002, Phillips's inclusion in an F-14 air-to-air combat training mission over the Persian Gulf was the first such flight by a female journalist. She also gave audiences exclusive glimpses into Special Operations Command and the training of Naval Special Warfare Combatant Crewmen and Navy SEALs. She continued to file reports from the USS *Abraham Lincoln* as the war began in late March as strike fighters launched from the carrier for missions in Baghdad.

Phillips served four tours in Iraq during the seven-year war, reporting on the experiences of the Iraqi people during the conflict. Her subjects ranged from the population's use of drugs as an escape from stresses of the war to the challenges faced by children attending Baghdad's only school for the blind. Phillips would later identify those stories about the Iraqi people as the ones she was most proud of. "People back home in the U.S. and at work are starting to say to me, 'Wow. We're finally getting a glimpse of what it's really like in Iraq—what it takes for a typical Iraqi to get through the day,'" she told Blair. In March 2008, Phillips took a tour of the vacated prison cell that had been occupied by deposed Iraqi dictator Saddam Hussein between his 2003 capture and his 2006 execution. Marine Major General Doug Stone, the overseer of American military detention operations in Iraq, showed Phillips excerpts from Saddam's private diary and the small garden he was permitted to keep. Phillips also learned, among other things, that prison guards referred to Saddam as "Vic," which stood for "very important criminal."

## REPORTING LIVE

From March 11 to March 12, 2005, Phillips contributed to live reporting of the two-day manhunt for Brian Nichols, who was facing trial for rape at the Fulton County Courthouse in Atlanta, Georgia, when he stole the gun of woman deputy officer and entered the courtroom; Nichols shot and killed the judge on his case, a court reporter, and a sheriff's deputy before fleeing the courthouse. (Nichols, who later shot and killed a federal agent, was ultimately apprehended after a woman whose apartment he had entered called the police.) From June 24 to June 26, 2005, Phillips reported from the last New York City revival held by Billy Graham, the highly influential Christian evangelist. Graham, who rose to national prominence in 1957 when he hosted a sixteen-week revival at Madison Square Garden, hosted his last New York City revival at Flushing Meadow–Corona Park in Queens. During Phillips's one-on-one interview with the eighty-six-year-old Graham, who was suffering from a number of health problems at the time, the preacher stated that he had no unfinished business left on Earth—noting, as quoted on CNN Live From . . . (24 June 2005): "The only unfinished business would be to hug my children and kiss my wife again."

Phillips committed a memorable gaffe on August 29, 2006, during CNN's live coverage of a somber speech by President George W. Bush, who was marking the first anniversary of Hurricane Katrina. Footage of Bush's speech was interrupted by audio of Phillips, who had accidentally left her microphone on while chatting with a colleague in the restroom. During the ninety-second conversation, Phillips could be heard telling her colleague: "My husband is handsome and he is genuinely a loving, you know, no ego, you know what I'm saying . . . just a really passionate, compassionate, great, great human being. And they exist. They do exist. They're hard to find . . . but they are out there." Phillips went on to discuss her brother and her sister-in-law—noting "I've got to be protective of him. He's married, three kids, and his wife is just a control freak." She turned her microphone off quickly afterward, and CNN later issued an apology to viewers and to the White House for the mistake. Though the blunder was widely mocked by the media, Phillips took the criticism in stride, laughing it off in several interviews. She even appeared in a skit on the television program Late Night with David Letterman that poked fun at the incident.

### "JUDGMENT IN JENA"

Phillips hosted a widely praised CNN Special Investigations Unit documentary called "Judgment in Jena" that aired on September 20, 2007. The small town of Jena, Louisiana, became the site of intense racial controversy in August 2006, when three nooses were hung from a tree in front of local high school by three white students, apparently in response to a gathering of black students under the tree, which was understood by the black students to be a hangout spot unofficially reserved for white students. The students who had hung the nooses were initially expelled, but the school board overturned their expulsions after their parents complained. Instead, the three students received less than a week of suspension and counseling sessions—a punishment thought by many to be far too lenient given the racial overtones of the act. Over the next few weeks, a series of fights that seemed to be racially motivated broke out in Jena, the most serious of which took place in December 2006, when Justin Barker, a white Jena High School student, was severely beaten

by a group of black students. The six students arrested for the beating—dubbed the "Jena Six"—were initially charged with attempted second-degree murder and conspiracy to commit second-degree murder. In June 2007, one of the accused teens, Mychal Bell, was convicted of aggravated second-degree battery and conspiracy to commit second-degree battery, which carried a possible prison sentence of twenty years.

The conviction sparked widespread protests across the country; protesters accused Jena's law enforcement of using double standards for blacks and whites. Civil rights activists descended on the town of Jena in the summer of 2007 prior to Bell's scheduled sentencing in September 2007. Phillips's report—which included numerous interviews with Jena residents, one school board member, and the parents of some of the young men involved in the disputes—revealed differing interpretations of the events in Jena and highlighted the complicated history of race relations in the town. It concluded with scenes from the largest civil rights protest in decades, held in Jena in September 2007. "Judgment in Jena" won a top documentary award from the Society of Professional Journalists in 2007. The same year, Phillips was named Atlanta Press Club's National Reporter of the Year.

### RECENT CAREER HIGHLIGHTS AND TRANSITIONS

In early September 2008, Phillips spent several days in Anchorage, Alaska, reporting on the background of Sarah Palin, the little-known Alaskan governor who had been named the running mate for Republican presidential candidate Senator John McCain on August 29. On July 6, 2010, Phillips gained a worldwide exclusive interview with United States Coast Guard Admiral Thad Allen, the national incident commander for the BP Deepwater Horizon oil spill in the Gulf of Mexico. Phillips discussed with Allen developments in the government's efforts to stop the oil, which was ultimately successfully capped on July 15 after spewing a total of 4.9 million barrels of oil into the gulf, making it the largest accidental oil spill in the history of the petroleum industry.

More recently, Phillips reported on a story for CNN Presents that aired on April 26, 2012, about allegations of rape and sexual harassment in military academies. The story, "Betrayal of Trust? Allegations of Rape at West Point, Annapolis," focused on two young women who alleged they were raped while attending the Military Academy in West Point, New York, and the Naval Academy in Annapolis, Maryland, respectively. In each case, the women had reported the incidents to authorities and requested investigations, but the perpetrators were never punished. According to the story, the women's lawsuits claimed that "former Secretary of Defense Robert Gates, former superintendents of the two academies, and the current secretaries of the Army and Navy [were] 'personally responsible' for failing to 'prevent rapes and sexual assaults at the Naval academy and West Point.'" Phillips noted in her story that, according to the Department of Defense, although sexual assault reports were increasing, very few investigations ever resulted in a court-martial. Secretary of Defense Leon Panetta told Phillips in an exclusive interview, "We've got to train commanders to understand that when these complaints are brought, they've got to do their damnedest to see that these people are brought to justice." A week after the interview with Phillips, Panetta announced the creation of a special victims unit to investigate allegations of sexual assault.

In August 2012, Phillips left CNN and joined HLN, a spinoff cable news network (formerly known as CNN2 and CNN Headline News) devoted only to the day's top stories. As HLN anchor, Phillips has been leading the network's coverage of the 2012 presidential election.

In addition to those previously mentioned awards, Phillips has been the recipient of five Emmy Awards, two Edward R. Murrow Awards for investigative reporting, and several Golden Microphones.

### PERSONAL LIFE
Phillips's first marriage to investment banker A. John Assad ended in divorce at some point after 2006. In June 2010, Phillips became engaged to John Roberts, a fellow broadcast journalist at CNN, who joined FOX News—a rival network—in February 2011. "There's always a little bit of competition in every relationship, I think that's what keeps it fresh," he told the *Huffington Post* (25 Feb. 2011). "The fact that we may be television competitors is an interesting dynamic, but we don't get angry at each other." Regarding their plans to marry, he said, "There's no plan for a wedding. I call her my wife; she refers to me as her husband. . . . At our age, fiancée just doesn't sound right." On March 15, 2011, Phillips gave birth to fraternal twins, daughter Sage Ann and son Kellan Clay. At forty-two years old, she underwent in vitro fertilization therapy in order to get pregnant, a topic she discussed in depth on a March 3, 2012, CNN special report called "Baby Quest."

Phillips is an avid golfer. She has participated in the Big Brothers/Big Sisters of America mentoring program since 1992. Phillips also serves on the board of The Brain Tumor Foundation for Children.

### SUGGESTED READING
Blair, Tom. "Kyra Phillips: Dialogue with Tom Blair." *San Diego Magazine*. San Diego Magazine, Apr. 2008. Web. 18 Sept. 2012.

"Largest Database Marketing Firm Sends Phone Numbers, Addresses of 5,000 Families with Kids to TV Reporter Using name of Child Killer." *Electronic Privacy Information Center.* Business Wire, Inc., 13 May 1996. Web. 18 Sept. 2012.

Phillips, Kyra, and Aaron Brown. "Harsh Continent." *CNN Presents. CNN: Transcripts.* Cable News Network/Turner Broadcasting System, 9 Feb. 2003. Web. 18 Sept. 2012.

--- and Carol Costello. "Judgment in Jena." *CNN Special Investigations Unit. CNN: Transcripts.* Cable News Network/Turner Broadcasting System, 20 Sept. 2007. Web. 18 Sept. 2012.

Rosenberg, Jeremy. "Kyra Phillips, Storyteller." *USC Annenberg School for Communication and Journalism: Annenberg Alumni.* U of Southern California, 2010. Web. 18 Sept. 2012.

*—Margaret Roush Mead*

## Mark Pincus

**Born:** February 13, 1966
**Occupation:** Internet entrepreneur and cofounder of Zynga

Internet entrepreneur Mark Pincus has started several companies: FreeLoader, SupportSoft, Tribe Networks, and Zynga. The latter, founded in July 2007 with a team of other entrepreneurs, has released such popular social games as FarmVille, Words with Friends, and Draw Something. Millions of players access Zynga's games through Facebook. The company's games are also accessible on other social media networks, such as Google Plus, and can be played as standalone games on tablets and smartphones. As Zynga's CEO, Pincus led the company in less than five years to billions of dollars in success—making him a billionaire in the process.

Pincus has helped popularize something that did not exist, at least not in the mainstream, prior to Zynga: social gaming. "We invented social gaming," Pincus told Matt Hendrickson for *Details* magazine (May 2010). "We were the first ones to figure out virtual goods and social pay, and we've helped the whole industry."

### EARLY LIFE AND FINANCIAL SERVICES
Mark Pincus was born on February 13, 1966, in Chicago, Illinois. His father, Theodore Pincus, worked as a business columnist and public relations advisor, and his mother was an architect. He graduated summa cum laude from the University of Pennsylvania's Wharton School of Business in 1988.

After earning his bachelor's degree, Pincus spent the next six years in financial services and venture capital. He worked as an analyst

Getty Images

for Lazard Freres & Co. for two years, and then moved to Hong Kong to serve as a vice president for Asian Capital Partners. That position also lasted two years. Pincus then moved to Boston, Massachusetts, to attend Harvard Business School. While studying at Harvard, he worked during the summer of 1992 as an associate for Bain & Co. He was asked to leave the company in the middle of the summer, because he did not get along with his managers. "I went out of my way to tell people they were stupid if I thought they were. People loved me or hated me," Pincus told Hendrickson. "In hindsight, I was forcing myself to be an entrepreneur—I was shutting all the doors."

Thus, Pincus's pattern of short-term positions continued. He earned his MBA in 1993, after which he managed corporate development at Tele-Communications Inc. (which later became AT&T Cable). He switched jobs after one year as manager, becoming senior vice president of Columbia Capital in Washington, DC. At this venture capital firm, Pincus worked on investments in software start-ups and new media. The position also lasted only one year.

## FREELOADER AND SUPPORTSOFT
Pincus left finance in 1995 to become his own boss. In October, he cofounded FreeLoader Inc. with investor and entrepreneur Sunil Paul. FreeLoader is an offline web delivery service that downloads content from the Internet to users' computer hard drives. The first web-based push service of its kind, the company offers such services as the categorization of websites, usage

pattern tracking, and the generation of detailed reports about a company's clients. The company was sold in June 1996, seven months after its creation and initial success, to Individual Inc. for a reported $38 million. FreeLoader has remained in operation as a branch of Individual Inc.

After the sale of FreeLoader, Pincus partnered with entrepreneurs Scott Dale and Cadir Lee to launch his second start-up, Support.com, in August 1997. The original idea behind the company was to fix problems with Windows desktop systems. Under Pincus's leadership as chairman and CEO—and after his partnership with enterprise software company builders Robert Amaral and Tony Rodoni—the company grew to become a leading global provider of online tech support and of software that automates the resolution of computer problems. Support.com developed what are called "DNA Probes," software algorithms that remotely diagnose and fix PC software problems. Pincus brought the company public in July 2000, and in 2002, its name was changed to SupportSoft Inc.

In January 2000, Pincus and Martin Roscheisen founded the incubator Tank Hill. However, they decided to close the firm after nine months and returned most of their investors' funds. "Pretty sure we were the only incubator to ever give the money back," Pincus wrote in the company background information listed on his Typepad blog.

## TRIBE NETWORKS
In early 2003, Pincus cofounded, with Valerie Syme and Paul Martino, his third company. Tribe.net, or Tribe Networks, is one of the first social networks. The network connects people with similar interests—such as music, travel, business, and sports—who live in the same metropolitan area. By the time Pincus bought a social networking patent in 2004, Tribe was primarily concentrated in the San Francisco Bay Area. Since then, it has expanded to numerous cities in the United States and abroad.

Tribe, funded at first through venture capital and backed by major local newspapers, grew to over half a million members by the fall of 2006. However, the company was struggling financially, and in April 2006, the majority of Tribe's employees were laid off. Pincus, who had been chairman and CEO of the company but had stepped back from his CEO role for a time, returned in August 2006 in response to Tribe's problems. He formed Utah Street Networks, a new corporation specifically created to buy the assets of Tribe Networks. He also had the website redesigned with a customizable user interface. Pincus's intervention only helped for a short while, as the site had a number of technical problems during the course of 2008 and

2009, and many of its users migrated to different social networks. Cisco Systems acquired Tribe's technology assets in March 2007, enabling Pincus to pay back Tribe's debt to his investors. The site has continued to run since then.

In an article Pincus wrote for *Bloomberg Businessweek* (12 Apr. 2012), he states the reasons for Tribe's failure: "We came up with ideas purely based on intuition, and it could take us three to six months to build it and launch. Those bullets were expensive, and many of them were not on target. Tribe reached the point where the investors literally gave up, resigned from the board, and walked away." Despite this failure, Pincus's experience with Tribe helped him understand how social networks function—which led to his creation of Zynga.

## THE RISE OF SOCIAL GAMING: ZYNGA AND *FARMVILLE*

After selling Tribe.net, Pincus founded his fourth start-up: the Zynga Game Network. As Pincus explained to new employees during a talk held in July 2010, and reported on by Miguel Helft for the *New York Times* (24 July 2010), Pincus wanted to build an Internet company that was "synonymous with fun." He told employees, "I thought, it's 2007, and this can't be all the Internet is meant to be . . . a garage sale, a bookstore, a search engine and a portal." With the help of nine supporting founders, Pincus launched Zynga under the name Presidio Media in April 2007. Since then, he has served as the company's CEO and chief product officer. In July, Pincus renamed the company after his American bulldog, Zinga. That spelling was already taken by another company, so he went with Zynga instead.

Zynga released its first game, Zynga Poker, in July 2007 on Facebook. With $39 million invested by several venture capital firms in 2008, Zynga was able to expand and acquire other games and companies, such as YoVille in July 2008 and Bonfire Studios in October 2010. By April 2009, the company was the top Facebook application developer, with about forty million users playing its games monthly. Zynga launched FarmVille in June 2009. In just two months, the game was being played by ten million Facebook users on a daily basis; by October it had twenty million active players. FarmVille was the first Facebook game to reach these numbers. The following month, the game was modified so that it could be used on platforms other than Facebook. In two and a half years, Zynga reached 100 million users—it had taken Facebook more than twice the time to reach that number. "Social networks are like cocktail parties: You bring all these people together and there's nothing to do," Pincus told Hendrickson. "We've given them something to do."

## HOW TO MAKE MONEY, FAST: ZYNGA'S ADVERTISING SCANDAL

In March 2009, while discussing Zynga's rapid financial success with aspiring web entrepreneurs at a bar in Berkeley, California, Pincus let slip that he did "every horrible thing in the book to just get revenues right away." The comment was recorded on video, leaked online, and quoted by a number of tech blogs and news websites. "Web 3.0 had its first villain," wrote Hendrickson, "and his name was Mark Pincus." The "horrible things" Pincus referred to were advertisements, in which users would earn game points by signing up for advertised services, such as credit cards or a recurring subscription, or by downloading software. Users sometimes signed up unwittingly or downloaded software that they did not really want and that proved difficult to uninstall. Michael Arrington of *TechCrunch* called Zynga's advertising scheme "Scamville" (31 Oct. 2009), claiming that it was earning Zynga millions in revenue. According to one Zynga executive, third-party advertising had accounted for a third of the company's revenue, including legitimate advertisers such as Netflix.

Pincus had allowed the advertisements because he "wanted to control my own destiny," as he told his Berkeley audience. Pincus has had a general dislike of venture capitalists, due to previous history with them. He blamed investors of Support.com, for example, of plotting to oust him as CEO. Still, Zynga responded to the public outcry over Zynga's advertising scams, as well as a class action suit from users, by pulling the questionable ads and downloads. As for Pincus, he told Helft that he "never meant to imply you should do anything unethical." Normally blunt in his statements, Pincus realized that, because of his company's popularity, he needed to be more careful with what he said. "As the company has had more exposure and visibility, I have had to realize that more people take what I say seriously," he told Helft. "I've had to grow up."

## FROM PRIVATE TO PUBLIC, AND PARTNERING WITH HASBRO

With the acquisition of mobile game developer Newtoy Inc. in December 2010, Zynga became the owner of such popular games as Words with Friends. That same month, CityVille became Zynga's most popular game, with over sixteen million players daily. By July 2011, the company had grown to two thousand employees. "We're at the dawn of the new Web business plan," Pincus told Hendrickson. "We've created a whole new industry." Pincus decided to make his private company public, and Zynga began trading on NASDAQ in December 2011. At the time, Zynga was valued at $9 billion. Business analysts expected that the company's transition from private to public would earn it $1 billion, making its IPO the largest since Google. "I admire

Google," Pincus had told Hendrickson back in May 2010. "I want Zynga to be one of the five or six brands that matter in people's lives. We are the skyscrapers of the 21st century."

In February 2012, an announcement was made that Hasbro and Zynga would be partnering to create games and toys from Zynga's more popular online games, for the mutual benefit of both companies. That month, Hasbro's Scrabble had an estimated one million players, whereas Zynga's Words with Friends had thirteen million. The partnership, which became official in October, received criticism from some who saw it as another example of Zynga's lack of originality—Zynga's history has often consisted of game acquisition and the copying of previously existing ideas. Jon Fox for *IGN* (2 Oct. 2012) was one critic of the Zynga-Hasbro plan to create the "board game version of board game apps." Zynga decided to sell, for example, a copycat version of Scrabble—Words with Friends—and with the partnership, FarmVille would become the board game Hungry Hungry Herd, reminiscent of Hungry Hungry Hippos.

Pincus does not view Zynga's "lack of originality" as a problem, however. As he told Bob Safian in an interview at the Innovation Uncensored Conference in San Francisco in November 2012, reported on by Owen Thomas for *Business Insider* (8 Nov. 2012), "For us, innovation is about making games more accessible, more social, more fun, and more free—giving you more value for your time and money." He added, "We don't define innovation by whether or not our Words with Friends game looks different enough from Scrabble. We think it's an innovative game because it's connected tens of millions of people together." Pincus's "copycat" strategy has proven successful for much of Zynga's existence.

## THE ROCKY ROAD OF NASDAQ

In March 2012, Zynga acquired OMGPOP, creators of the popular social game Draw Something, six weeks after the game was released. Zynga's share price, initially offered at $10, peaked at $14.69 that month. Pincus, now worth $1.8 billion, made *Forbes'* 2012 list of the world's billionaires. Pincus cashed out sixteen million of his Zynga shares during this time. However, taking the company public did not prove as successful as Pincus had hoped. After March, Draw Something began to lose players, Zynga's stock plummeted, and Pincus's fortune plummeted along with it, as he had owned a reported 87.4 million Zynga shares. By October 2012—seven months later—Pincus's wealth had fallen more than 80 percent. Zynga, over the course of 2012, lost more than 75 percent of its shares.

Due to its losses, Zynga had to close some of its offices, beginning in October 2012, and laid off 5 percent of its three thousand employees. Some of the senior employees confronted Pincus, and others walked out. Product director Jonathan Liu, for example, confronted Pincus about dipping company morale. "People couldn't articulate what the main strategy was, or why they were coming to Zynga on a day-to-day basis," Liu told Evelyn M. Rusli for the *Wall Street Journal* (15 Nov. 2012).

The popularity of Zynga's online games lessened in part because of changes by Facebook that have made Zynga less visible on the social networking site. In addition, Pincus and Mark Zuckerberg of Facebook came to an agreement in November 2012 that allows Facebook to develop its own games. Pincus assured the public that this did not mean he and Zuckerberg were no longer on good terms. As he explained to *CBS This Morning* cohosts Charlie Rose and Gayle King (5 Dec. 2012), "Facebook has been an amazing accelerator of growth for social gaming. . . . But as I said, the future is really on mobile, phones and tablets. For us, this is really about making the social available, the social opportunities for our players—anything they want."

## CHANGES AT ZYNGA

Pincus has outwardly remained optimistic about his company's future, even stating in July 2012 at a *PandoDaily* event in San Francisco that he intends to keep Zynga, no matter what happens. "I was upfront with everybody," he said, according to Olga Kharif for *Bloomberg* (22 Aug. 2012). "I said, 'We're never going to sell the company. There is no exit. . . . My only exit is by natural causes.'" However, Rusli reported that Pincus was struggling with employee confrontations, executive defections, and other internal strife. Pincus, who as CEO has owned 50.2 percent of Zynga's voting control, hired Bill Campbell of Apple Inc. in November 2012 to coach him in his management and communication skills. Campbell told Rusli that Pincus was trying to save his company and "felt terrible about what was happening; he felt the turmoil," even to the point that he "was near tears."

With help from Campbell and other outside advisers, Pincus reworked Zynga's internal structure and his executive team. He planned to have the company focus on making new games, with a particular focus on mobile apps. "One thing I learned is that while your vision should never change, you should keep trying different strategies until one works," he wrote for *Bloomberg Businessweek*. "If you can fine-tune your instinct and have confidence in it, then you can keep taking different bites of the apple and keep approaching the problem in different ways until you get it right." He added, "I think failing is the best way to keep you grounded, curious, and humble. Success is dangerous because often you don't understand why you succeeded. You almost always know why you've failed."

## GAMBLING FOR SUCCESS

In December 2012, Pincus and his team at Zynga announced another course of action to save the company: online gambling. That news, along with Zynga's application to obtain a Nevada gambling license, helped the company's stock rise. The previous month, Zynga had signed an agreement with Bwin.party, allowing Zynga to introduce 180 online gambling games to the United Kingdom in 2013.

Despite various criticisms of Pincus and of Zynga, the company has ranked among Facebook's top ten applications, and its games are popular downloads on iTunes. "I have a very high-stress life," financial analyst Alena Meeker told Helft. "I love relaxing with the games." In October 2012, FarmVille 2, which had been released in September, reached 50 million players and became the most popular app on Facebook. While the first version of FarmVille had peaked at 83 million players, the numbers for FarmVille 2 proved significant in an increasingly competitive social gaming industry.

## ZYNGA FOR CHARITY

Pincus founded a charitable organization through Zynga, called Zynga.org, in October 2009. Purchases of certain virtual goods on Zynga games translate to money for Zynga.org's partner organizations, such as Habitat for Humanity, Save the Children, and DirectRelief International. Zynga.org provided disaster relief funding to Haiti in October 2009 and January 2010, and to Japan in March 2011. By the end of 2012, Zynga.org had raised more than $13 million for its partner organizations.

A controversy occurred in March 2010, when Brazilian news service Folha Online reported that 50 percent of Zynga.org's Haiti relief funding went straight to Zynga rather than to Haiti. The story went viral online. However, the news service had confused Zynga.org's two separate Haiti fundraisers. The earlier one, according to Pincus, had explicitly stated that 50 percent of the proceeds would go to FATEM.org and Fonkoze.org; the second one donated 100 percent of proceeds to the UN's World Food Programme. "It's really reprehensible," Pincus told Hendrickson. "I feel morally offended that we get attacked by the media for doing something good and no one else is outraged when these people are wrong."

Pincus has been an angel investor in a number of companies, such as Napster, Twitter, and Facebook. Pincus invested $40,000 in the latter in 2004. During the 2009 TechCrunch Crunchies awards, he was named CEO of the Year, and for the 2010 Crunchies he was named Founder of the Year.

Pincus lives in San Francisco with his wife, Ali, the founder of One Kings Lane—a furniture and home accessories retailer—and twin daughters.

## SUGGESTED READING

Helft, Miguel. "Will Zynga Become the Google of Games?" New York Times. New York Times Co., 24 July 2010. Web. 13 Dec. 2012.
Hendrickson, Matt. "Why You Should Love the Most Hated Man on Facebook." Details. Condé Nast, May 2010. Web. 13 Dec. 2012.
Peterson, Steve. "Zynga Interview: Mark Pincus Part 2." GamesIndustry International. Eurogamer Network, 17 July 2012. Web. 13 Dec. 2012.
Rivlin, Gary. "Zynga's IPO Will Make Mark Pincus Silicon Valley's Next Billionaire." Daily Beast. Newsweek/Daily Beast Co., 14 Dec. 2011. Web. 13 Dec. 2012.
Rusli, Evelyn M. "Behind Mark Pincus's Bid to Save Zynga." Wall Street Journal. Dow Jones & Co., 15 Nov. 2012. Web. 13 Dec. 2012.

—Julia Gilstein

# Alvin Plantinga

**Born:** November 15, 1932
**Occupation:** Analytic philosopher; author

For more than a half century, the American author, educator, and philosopher Alvin Plantinga has argued that religious belief in general, and Christianity in particular, has a rational basis despite popular assumptions to the contrary. In the decades leading up to the mid-twentieth century, when many expressed disdain toward any expression of religious fervor, Plantinga was carefully establishing a vigorous defense of not just his Christian faith but of theism as a whole. Today, his free-will defense is considered by philosophers as a model way to explain the existence of evil, and his work as an author and educator is regarded as having influenced and inspired a new generation of Christian philosophers. Plantinga has had his fair share of detractors, however, including notable atheists such as philosopher Daniel C. Dennett and zoologist Richard Dawkins, who believe his theories to be wholly irrational. "To call a philosopher irrational, those are fighting words," Plantinga said to Jennifer Schuessler for the New York Times (13 Dec. 2011). "Being rational is a philosopher's aim. It's taken pretty seriously."

Plantinga has written passionately that his religious faith is compatible with his belief in Darwinian evolution but that many atheists combine evolutionary theory with their own naturalistic views and then offer that as proof

Associated Press

that science has concretely established there is no God or supreme deity. Plantinga told Rachel Martin for NPR (12 Jan. 2012), "I think science is . . . the most impressive intellectual episode of the past half a millennium. . . . I also am a Christian. If there is an alleged incompatibility between them, well, that disturbs me."

## EARLY LIFE

Plantinga was born in Ann Arbor, Michigan, on November 15, 1932, the son of Cornelius A. Plantinga, an immigrant from the province of Friesland in the Netherlands, and the former Lettie Bossenbroek, a native of Alto, Wisconsin, whose family emigrated from the Netherlands during and in the decades after the American Civil War. At the time of his son's birth, Cornelius Plantinga was a graduate student of philosophy at the University of Michigan.

Christianity was the central component of Plantinga's early life. Both sets of grandparents were members of Calvinist churches, and to them, faith was the main focus of life and was not something attended to only on Sundays and forgotten during the week. In addition to participating in two services on Sunday (a morning service in English and an afternoon one in Dutch), the Plantinga's family discussed scripture vigorously, lived lives based on the concept of Christian charity, and received all formal education through the filter of their faith. None of them believed in secular education.

Plantinga's family moved to Jamestown, North Dakota, when he was in junior high school and remained there during high school while his father was a professor of philosophy, psychology, Latin, and Greek at Jamestown College. The family worshiped at Jamestown's Presbyterian church, and Plantinga often accompanied his father to nearby towns while he preached or taught at weekly catechism classes. Plantinga also attended Sunday school, weekly young people's meetings, and church-sponsored summer bible camps. In a 1993 essay, "A Christian Life

Partly Lived," Plantinga recalled of these camps, "I found the girls more interesting than the sermons, and for me (and others) the stimulation was by no means exclusively spiritual. As I remember those camps, there was a sort of fervid, febrile atmosphere, shimmering and throbbing with energy and excitement that was as much sexual as spiritual" (49).

## EDUCATION

At his father's suggestion, Plantinga enrolled at Jamestown College before his seventeenth birthday and began his undergraduate education there in the fall of 1949. In January of 1950, he transferred to Calvin College in Grand Rapids, Michigan, where his father was professor of psychology. Plantinga then won a two-year scholarship to Harvard University in Cambridge, Massachusetts, and began there in the fall of 1950.

At Harvard, Plantinga encountered a wide variety of opinions on religious faith, including those of many nonbelievers. "I liked it a great deal," Plantinga explained to Myrna Anderson for the Calvin College website (6 Dec. 2012), "and I met a great many people of a different sort than I met at Calvin." He was, however, conflicted and taken aback by fellow classmates and professors who were often contemptuous of his Christian beliefs. For a time, his respect for them clashed with his own beliefs, and he began to have doubts and question whether his classmates and professors were right. Then, one windy and rainy night while returning to his dormitory from dinner, he had a singular experience that helped to end his confusion. "I heard, so it seemed, music of overwhelming power and grandeur and sweetness; there was light of unimaginable splendor and beauty. . . . I suddenly saw or perhaps felt with great clarity and persuasion and conviction that the Lord was really there and was all I had thought," he writes in "A Christian Life Partly Lived." "I was still caught up in arguments [with students and professors] about the existence of God, but they often seemed to me merely academic, of little existential concern" (51–52).

On a spring break from Harvard, he returned home and sat in on several of Professor Harry Jellema's philosophy classes at Calvin College. Jellema had been Cornelius Plantinga's philosophy professor when he had been a student, and the experience was a revelation to the younger Plantinga. Here was a man—an intelligent and thoughtful Christian—who sought to connect his religious beliefs with modernity and demonstrate, unlike the prevailing view at Harvard, that Christianity was not an outmoded concept in a more scientific age but was something relevant to the challenges humanity faced in the modern world. After sitting in on three of Jellema's classes, Plantinga decided to transfer from Harvard back to Calvin, where he graduated in 1954 with a double major in philosophy and psychology.

Plantinga attended graduate school at the University of Michigan in January 1954, earning a master's degree in philosophy in 1955. He earned his doctorate from Yale University in 1958.

## TEACHING CAREER

After graduating from Yale, Plantinga joined the philosophy department at Wayne State University in Detroit, Michigan. Despite working amongst people openly hostile to his beliefs, Plantinga feels that their honesty and intellectual rigor helped to deepen and sharpen his own religious theories: It was during his time at Wayne State that he developed his free will defense, which he expanded on in 1974 with the publication of *God, Freedom, and Evil*, that counters the atheistic argument that God cannot exist because of the presence of evil in the world. Plantinga explained in "A Christian Life Partly Lived" that "even if God is omnipotent, there are nonetheless possible worlds he could not have actualized" (64).

In 1963, Plantinga's former mentor Harry Jellema was planning his retirement from the philosophy department at Calvin College, and Plantinga was approached by the college to replace him. After much thought and to his Wayne State colleagues' disbelief, he decided to accept the offer for several reasons. "I endorsed the Calvinist contention that neither scholarship nor education is religiously neutral; I was therefore convinced of the importance of Christian colleges and universities. I wanted to contribute to that enterprise, and Calvin seemed an excellent place to do so" (65).

Plantinga remained at Calvin until 1982, when he was offered a position at Notre Dame in Indiana as the John A. O'Brien Professor of Philosophy and director of the Center for Philosophy of Religion. He remained at Notre Dame until his retirement in 2010. He also served as a visiting professor at several universities, including the University of Illinois, Harvard University, the University of Chicago, the University of Michigan, Boston University, Indiana University, and Syracuse University.

## BOOKS AND AWARDS

During his long career, Plantinga has authored more than a dozen books that have discussed the nature of God, evil, religious faith in general, and Christian faith in particular. Plantinga explained to Schuessler that while he has no proof that God exists, "Belief in God . . . is what philosophers call a basic belief: It is no more in need of proof than the belief that the past exists, or that other people have minds, or that one plus one equals two."

Plantinga has been presented with honorary degrees from numerous universities such as Glasgow University, Calvin College, North Park College, and Free University of Amsterdam, and he has received multiple fellowships from such places as the Center for Advanced Study in the Behavioral Sciences, the Guggenheim Foundation, the American Academy of Arts and Sciences, and the National Endowment for the Humanities. In 2012, Plantinga was awarded the Rescher Prize, a prestigious award that honors the systematic study of philosophy.

As an educator and author, Plantinga is widely credited with helping to foster a new generation of Christian philosophers who have established their careers on the rigorous approach to philosophy that Plantinga established. Before him, there were few philosophers who were public Christians and fewer still who made their faith part of their philosophical careers. "It would be very difficult to exaggerate the impact Al has had both on the profession of philosophy and the lives of younger Christian philosophers," explained philosophy professor Kevin Corcoran to Anderson. He added, "Christian philosophers of my generation and younger would likely not be doing what we're doing and the way we're doing it, were it not for the pioneering work of Al Plantinga."

## RECENT WORK

Plantinga in recent years has turned his attention to refuting the atheistic evolutionary/Darwinian contention that all life evolved from lower forms through a process of natural selection, which in turn disproves God's existence. Plantinga, who like most Christians accepts the scientific theory of evolution, argues that atheists have misused Darwin's theories to support naturalism—the philosophical belief that nothing exists beyond the natural world, including a supreme being or deity. Plantinga clarified to John Wilson for *Christianity Today* (15 Dec. 2011), "Some people seem to think that if . . . science doesn't say that God is guiding the process of evolution, then science is really saying that God is *not* guiding the process. But that's ridiculous. Science doesn't say anything about it one way or the other."

In his book, *Where The Conflict Really Lies: Science, Religion, and Naturalism* (2011), Plantinga suggests that there is no real argument between theistic belief and the scientific theory of evolution—that God could have created the world through whatever means he chose, including natural selection. Moreover, Plantinga contends, there never has been a true debate between Christianity and Darwinism; he notes that nineteenth-century theologian Charles Hodge made this point not long after Darwin first published *On the Origin of Species* in 1859. Plantinga notes in his interview with Martin that "science started off in the bosom of Christian belief in the West. The early scientists—Newton, Boyle, and so on—were all believers in God and they saw science as a way of exploring the world that God has created. I think that the present emphasis on conflict arises . . . because a number of thinkers tried to co-opt science into the service of atheism. And they want to use science as a kind of weapon in the battle between atheism and theistic religion."

## PERSONAL LIFE

Plantinga met Kathleen DeBoer when she was a senior at Calvin College in 1953. Although DeBoer had grown up on a farm near Lynden, Washington, her family, like Plantinga's, hailed from Dutch Christian Reformed immigrants. They married in June 1955 and had four children: Carl, Jane, Harry, and Ann. Driving through North Dakota to his wife's family in Washington, Plantinga discovered what would become an enduring passion, rock climbing and mountaineering.

## SUGGESTED READING

Anderson, Myrna. "Plantinga Wins Prestigious Rescher Prize." *Calvin*. Calvin College, 6 Dec. 2012. Web. 18 Sept. 2013.

Martin, Rachel. "Exploring the Real 'Conflict': Science vs. Naturalism." *NPR*. NPR, 12 Jan. 2012. Web. 18 Sept. 2013.

"Modernizing the Case for God: Philosophers Refurbish the Tools of Reason to Sharpen Arguments for Theism." *Time* 7 Apr. 1980: 65. Print.

Plantinga, Alvin. "A Christian Life Partly Lived." *Philosophers Who Believe: The Spiritual Journeys of 11 Leading Thinkers*. Ed. Kelly James Clark. Downers Grove: InterVarsity, 1993. 45–82. Print.

Schuessler, Jennifer. "Philosopher Sticks Up for God." *New York Times*. New York Times Co., 13 Dec. 2011. Web. 18 Sept. 2013.

Wilson, John. "Q & A: Alvin Plantinga on Conflict Resolution with Science." *Christianity Today*. Christianity Today, 15 Dec. 2011. Web. 18 Sept. 2013.

## SELECTED WORKS

*God and Other Minds: A Study of the Rational Justification of Belief in God*, 1967; *The Nature of Necessity*, 1974; *God, Freedom, and Evil*, 1974; *Does God Have a Nature?*, 1980; *Warrant: The Current Debate*, 1993; *The Analytic Theist: An Alvin Plantinga Reader* (with James F. Sennett), 1998; *Warranted Christian Belief*, 2000; *Essays in the Metaphysics of Modality* (with Matthew Davidson), 2003; *Where the Conflict Really Lies: Science, Religion and Naturalism*, 2011

—Christopher Mari

# Tala Raassi

**Born:** December 17, 1982
**Occupation:** Fashion designer

When *Newsweek* made a list of the 150 most fearless women in the world in 2012, it included such figures as Hawa Abdi, one of the first female gynecologists in Somalia, and Sue Akers, a high-ranking official at Scotland Yard. Some readers might have considered it unusual to find on that list Tala Raassi, a designer of bikinis. But to the courageous and resilient Raassi, swimwear represents more than mere style.

As a teenager living in Iran, Raassi had been discovered wearing a miniskirt and listening to Western-style music at the home of a friend. For that transgression, she was sentenced to forty lashes by Iran's religious authorities. Reasoning that leaving the country would provide her with a chance to heal emotionally, her parents later sent her to live with a relative in Washington, DC. "Surrounded by American women who were free to wear what they want and think what they want, I knew exactly what I wanted to do," she explained to Michele Shapiro for *Marie Claire* (May 2010). "I would become a fashion designer. Because to me, fashion equaled freedom."

## EARLY YEARS AND EDUCATION

Tala Raassi was born on December 17, 1982, in Silver Spring, Maryland. Her family had moved there from Iran shortly before she was born because her brother, then three years old, required open-heart surgery that was best performed in the United States. They moved back to Iran when Raassi was about two years old and her brother, by then recuperated, was five. "Because I was so young, my memory of the United States was limited," she told *Current Biography*. "But I always cherished the pictures and memories my parents shared with me."

Raassi's childhood was a happy one. She delighted in watching her mother, an interior designer by trade, sew curtains and decorative pillows and tried to emulate her by making outfits for her Barbie dolls. Simply owning the curvaceous fashion doll was considered a dangerous indiscretion, because such toys were banned by authorities, and it was impossible to find extra doll clothing in Iranian stores. Raassi has recalled wanting to use only the finest fabrics, and she was sometimes chastised by her parents for snipping bits of leather from the bottom of the family sofa or pieces of mink from the hem of her mother's coat to use in her creations.

The educational system in Iran was stringent, and some of Raassi's high school courses were akin to American college offerings. Students were required to study both English and Arabic and to choose a major in order to prepare for their future careers. Raassi has joked that

Prince Raassi Photography

Iranian parents consider only medicine, law, and engineering to be acceptable choices, and she ultimately settled on law, because she liked to talk and possessed a quick wit. However, despite her close family ties and good education, Iran was far from a perfect place to come of age.

## A REPRESSIVE REGIME

In 1984, when Raassi's family returned to Iran from the United States, the country was being ruled by Ayatollah Ruhollah Khomeini, a proponent of the Shi'a version of radical Islamism. Khomeini had been exiled in 1964 because of his opposition to the totalitarian rule of Mohammad Reza Shah Pahlavi, but after the shah left Iran because of civil unrest and his own ill health, Khomeini returned and seized power in 1979.

Although Khomeini had originally promised to mold Iran into a representative democracy, he instead formed an Islamic republic and declared himself ruler for life. Implementing a fearsomely harsh version of Sharia (Islamic law), he set about banning foreign books and movies, persecuting gay people, severely limiting elections, and torturing or executing anyone who spoke out against him.

Under Sharia, Iranian women were forced to dress very modestly, often in the full-body cloak known as the chador. In high school Raassi and her female classmates were each required to wear a *roo-sari* (head-scarf) and *roo-poosh* (knee-length coat), with matching pants underneath the coat. They were prohibited from painting their nails, waxing their eyebrows, or donning the Converse All-Star sneakers or Dr. Martens

boots then so popular in the West. "As a fashion-conscious young girl, this was incredibly difficult for me as I had (and still have) a deep desire to express my individuality through my clothing style," she told *Current Biography*. "I was frequently in trouble for breaking dress code and was even kicked out of one high school because of it!" Deeper trouble was soon to come.

## A FAR-FROM-SWEET SIXTEEN

On Raassi's sixteenth birthday, she attended a party at a friend's home. As was usual among her friends, the girls arrived at the party in the modest clothing dictated by Sharia law. Once inside the private residence, they took off the garments to reveal fashionable Western-style clothing—in Raassi's case, a miniskirt and black T-shirt not unlike clothing worn by teens in the United States. Party activities consisted of chatting and listening to pop songs; there were no illicit drugs or alcohol present. Unbeknownst to the thirty or so guests, however, one boy, possibly disgruntled because he had not received an invitation, notified Iran's notoriously brutal religious police of the gathering. Without warning, the police raided the party, bursting violently through the front door. Panicked, Raassi and a friend escaped out the back door. They ran from neighbor to neighbor, begging to be allowed in to hide, to no avail. (The religious police, who wielded great power under Khomeini, were almost universally feared.)

When one policeman yelled that he would shoot if the teens did not stop running, Raassi, certain that he would not hesitate to carry out the threat, obeyed. According to her account, he then struck her with the butt of his gun, knocking her to the ground before dragging her back to the scene of the party, where she joined her frightened group of friends. The police then searched the guests' bags and purses, looking for drugs or alcohol. Upon finding Raassi's copy of the Qur'an, one officer taunted her with the assertion that she had defied Islamic law. (There is some dispute among religious scholars as to what the Qur'an dictates regarding women's clothing.) While not strictly devout, Raassi told Shapiro that she always carries the book with her, enjoying the sense of comfort and safety it provides.

Despite the absence of illicit substances, the situation was grave. The young people had undeniably been wearing prohibited clothing, listening to forbidden music, and fraternizing with members of the opposite sex. All were handcuffed and thrown roughly into the back of a van to be transported to a local jail.

## IMPRISONED AND FOUND GUILTY

Upon their arrival, the boys and girls were separated. Raassi and the other girls were ushered into a dank cell several feet underground, which was already occupied by a pregnant woman, a woman holding an infant, and even one prisoner who had apparently been arrested at her own wedding, as she was still wearing her white gown. There they spent the night, with no food or water—and little idea what might be in store for them. They spent their time trying not to think about the rats they could hear scratching across the floor and listening to the screams of fellow prisoners housed in other cells. They were forced to use rudimentary squat toilets in the corridors of the jail, visible to anyone who happened to look, and because there were no sinks in the facility, they were unable to wash their hands afterward. Making the situation even harder to bear, the older women spread tales of the rapes that had taken place there, further frightening the already petrified girls.

The next day, Raassi and her friends were allowed to have visitors, and some of the mothers arrived, bearing meals of meat kebabs and rice. Although she loved the dish, Raassi was barely able to enjoy that one small comfort, because as she ate, the prisoners who had not received visitors eyed her food hungrily.

Raassi and her friends were imprisoned for five days. Each day, during *adhan*, the call to prayer, they were made to line up and told that they would soon be lashed for their supposed crimes. After standing for almost an hour, they were dismissed, with the threat still hanging over them. Raassi recalled to Shapiro, "I'd always loved the adhan and found it beautiful, but that week, I came to dread it."

On the fifth day, the young inmates were taken to a Tehran courthouse. They were neither allowed to retain lawyers nor permitted to speak in their own defense. A judge summarily deemed them guilty and sentenced them to be lashed—fifty strokes for each boy and forty for each girl.

## FORTY LASHES

Although many of the parents tried to negotiate on behalf of their children, the judge did not change the sentences. Some parents did manage, however, to slip some money to the guards, who promised to wield their whips more lightly in exchange. "I don't think the guards upheld their end of the deal, though," Raassi told Shapiro. "I don't see how the beating could've been any worse."

The wait itself was excruciating. Handcuffed to one friend, Raassi could hear others being whipped and loudly screaming. In turn, her friends emerged, weeping and bloody. Barely able to breathe because of the anxiety, she was finally summoned by a chador-clad guard. Raassi wore a T-shirt and underwear during the whipping. Every time one of her two female torturers drew back their leather whips to strike again, the fabric was ripped away from her raw and bloodied flesh, intensifying the pain. Equally as unbearable as the physical pain was the emotional anguish of knowing that her parents were right outside the door, forced to listen to her agonized cries. "I [kept] thinking, 'I can't believe this is happening to me. I'm a good student; I come from a great family. I'm not a criminal,'" she recalled to Shapiro.

After the forty lashes were administered—a process that took less than ten minutes but that Raassi has said seemed interminable—she and her parents drove home, all of them deeply shaken and unable to speak. The moment they arrived at the house, Raassi dove into the shower, huddling on the tile floor for hours as the warm water washed over her wounds.

## LEAVING IRAN

Although her high school threatened to expel her in the wake of the incident, she was allowed to complete her senior year and graduate with her class. After graduation, Raassi, still traumatized, traveled to Dubai to stay with family friends. She began to consider abandoning her plans for a law career. Within a few months she left the Middle East to live with a relative in Washington, DC, where she became determined to enjoy her hard-won autonomy and pursue a career in fashion.

Raassi took a job in a boutique to help make ends meet and set about learning all she could about the fashion industry. The task was made difficult by her poor English-language skills and lack of business training, but she eagerly took English classes and bought books about developing a business plan. She also visited factories, showrooms, and fabric distributors, admitting her inexperience and asking for help. She eventually earned a degree in business management.

## DAR BE DAR TAKES OFF

Raassi, who is also a licensed makeup artist, was at a party in 2005 when a fellow guest admired the black cotton T-shirt she was wearing, which featured a silver pocket and studded hem. When she explained that she had made it herself and that she was trying to launch a clothing line, he asked her why she was only "trying" and not actually "doing." He soon became her first major investor when she started her own company, Tala Raassi, LLC, that same year.

Raassi called her fashion line Dar Be Dar, which means "door to door" in Farsi, choosing the name because in her effort to learn about the industry, she had, quite literally, gone door to door. In a colloquial sense, the phrase also means "all over the place," and Raassi has pointed out that it applies to her because in the beginning, she handled every aspect of the business herself, from designing to sourcing materials to cutting patterns to merchandising.

In 2006 she opened a trendy boutique called Profile Fashion in a converted row house just off U Street in Washington, DC. Although the shop caused a buzz among the city's fashionistas, Raassi later sold her interest in it to focus on Dar Be Dar. During a buying trip to Brazil, she became enamored of the sense of style and joy exhibited by the people she saw. "I felt like I was finally seeing what it meant to be a confident, independent woman," she told Leila Antakly for the blog *Ninu Nina* (June 2009). "Exploring the exotic beaches of South America, I was inspired by the bright colors and various styles of bikinis." Upon her return, she decided to focus on swimwear.

In 2010 Dar Be Dar was chosen as the official swimwear sponsor of the Miss Universe pageant, an honor that required Raassi to make four hundred bikinis in just two months. She was subjected to some criticism for accepting the assignment but vehemently refutes her detractors. "The pageant is about celebrating beauty, not the subjectivity of women," she said in an interview with Susan McClelland for *Elle Canada* (April 2011). "For me, Miss Universe is a sign of peace and freedom. In Iran, women aren't allowed to take part in such competitions. Millions of Iranian girls would trade places with them in an instant. Western women who criticize beauty pageants are entitled to their freedom of expression, but they also need to remember that many women in the world are dying to be able to express themselves through fashion and through their beauty."

## PERSONAL LIFE AND FUTURE PLANS

Raassi, who remains confident and optimistic despite her travails, is currently single and lives in the Washington, DC, area. She looks forward to falling in love, settling down, and having children one day. She cites clothing designer and former pop singer Victoria Beckham as a particular inspiration because of the way in which she combines a successful career in fashion with family life.

Raassi plans to publish a memoir one day that will include tales from her frequent travels. Also in the works is a T-shirt line she envisions calling Lipstick Revolution, after the protests that were sparked during the 2009 Iranian election. (Journalists conceived the name after noting the number of women taking part in the demonstrations.) Proceeds from the shirts would be used to support other female entrepreneurs. "Although the fashion industry appears glamorous and luxurious, the behind-the-scenes aspects are grueling and gut-wrenching. However, if I can accomplish this dream, then I truly believe anyone can," she told *Current Biography*. Asked what advice she would give aspiring businesswomen, she replied, "Embrace failure! I have done everything wrong at some point in this journey, but that has helped make me the success I am today."

## SUGGESTED READING

Frank, Madeline. "Fashionable Life: Q&A with Designer Tala Raassi." *Washington Life Magazine*. Washington Life Magazine, 10 June 2010. Web. 20 May 2013.

McClelland, Susan. "*Elle* World: Designing Women." *Elle Canada* Apr. 2011: 154. PDF file.

"150 Fearless Women." *Newsweek* 12 Mar. 2012: 50. Print.

Raassi, Tala. "Jailed for Wearing a Miniskirt—Now I'm a Top Fashion Designer." *Look* 24 May 2010: 54. Print.

Raassi, Tala, and Michele Shapiro. "How I Survived Forty Lashes." *Marie Claire*. Hearst Communication, 7 Apr. 2010. Web. 20 May 2013.

—*Mari Rich*

# Victoria Ransom

**Born:** 1976
**Occupation:** Internet entrepreneur

New Zealander Victoria Ransom is the cofounder and CEO of Wildfire Interactive, a social media marketing suite that runs campaigns such as sweepstakes across any social media website. First developed in 2008, the application went live in August 2009. Since then, the company's customer base has grown to about 21,000. Wildfire's clientele, which ranges from small mom and pop stores to about thirty of the world's fifty top brands, includes such companies as Pepsi, Sony, AT&T, Microsoft, Virgin Atlantic, and Facebook.

Wildfire began as an application to run a giveaway for Ransom's previous start-up, Access Trips, on the company's Facebook fan page. In July 2012, Google approached Ransom and Alain Chuard, her cofounder and then fiancé; they sold Wildfire to Google for a reported $350 million. The couple announced that they would continue to run Wildfire for at least a few years, although Ransom has stated that she "already feels that entrepreneurial itch," according to her profile on *Fortune*'s annual forty-under-forty list (17 Oct. 2012).

Before Wildfire, Ransom worked as a media analyst for Morgan Stanley. After less than two years with the company, she decided to quit in September 2001, and with Chuard founded Access Trips, a sports adventure travel company for young professionals like themselves. In 2006, the cofounders stepped away from the company in order to attend business school. It was during this time that Wildfire was born.

## EARLY LIFE AND EDUCATION

Born in 1976, Victoria Ransom grew up in the small rural village of Scotts Ferry in the Manawatu

Bloomberg via Getty Images

region of New Zealand's North Island. As a child, she picked asparagus at her family's farm and then sold it to fishermen on the Rangitikei River. Her primary school had only twenty-five students. "It was a wonderful upbringing," Ransom stated in an interview with business strategy consultant Sramana Mitra (29 Mar. 2012), posted on Mitra's website. "It was a very supportive and a small environment. I felt I could do anything. Neither of my parents went to college, but they instilled in me a 'reach for the stars' attitude."

At the age of seventeen, Ransom received a scholarship to attend the United World College (UWC) in Montezuma, New Mexico. The UWC is a network of twelve colleges located across the globe, which fosters international relations through pre-university education and community service. Ransom was one of two hundred students representing ninety different countries at the UWC in New Mexico. After two years at UWC, Ransom attended Macalester College in St. Paul, Minnesota. There, she met her future business partner and fiancé, Alain Chuard, a professional snowboarder from Switzerland.

Although Ransom graduated from Macalester with a degree in psychology, by that time she had realized that she did not want to pursue a career in the field. During her last year of college, she gained business experience through an internship with a consulting firm. After graduation, Ransom moved to London to work for that firm. Six months later, she applied to various investment banks. By January 2000, she was living in New York City, working on Wall Street as a media analyst for Morgan Stanley.

## FROM MORGAN STANLEY TO ACCESS TRIPS

Ransom left Morgan Stanley in September 2001. "Going through round after round of layoffs, I decided that there had to be something better in life," she told Helen Coster for *CNN Money* (19 Oct. 2012). Chuard, who had been working as an analyst for Salomon Smith Barney, quit at the same time. Before they left their respective companies, the couple had been planning a vacation during which they intended to learn to surf. Unfortunately, they could not find what they were looking for on the Internet. "[A]ll I found were package vacations with no instruction or high-volume surf camps that appeared to be more focused on partying than learning," Ransom told Christian L. Wright for the *New York Times* (1 May 2006). "I did find some quality surf camps, but they didn't provide any real opportunity to explore and experience the country where I would travel."

Chuard and Ransom decided that, since no sports adventure travel company seemed to exist for young professionals, they would create one themselves. After some initial planning, they decided to risk the recession, quit their jobs, and moved to New Zealand. There, they built what would become Access Trips, an "instructional adventure tour" company for young professionals aged twenty to forty-five, according to the company's website. Ransom and Chuard spent two months driving around New Zealand to plan their first trip. "Our office was a combination of youth hostels, Internet cafes and the back seat of our car," Chuard told Wright. That first trip, a fourteen-day ski and snowboard vacation in New Zealand's South Island, attracted thirty people. At the end of a successful two weeks, their customers expressed interest in more. The next trip was established in Switzerland, and a year later, the couple had planned five more vacations.

In just a few years, Ransom and Chuard had grown their business into a global network of trips. This growth enabled the couple to step back from leading every trip and focus instead on marking and client services for the company. They would sell the company in July 2010, staying on in only an advisory role. By 2012, Access Trips was offering instructional vacations to small groups in thirteen countries across the globe. They also expanded beyond sports instruction—snowboarding, skiing, mountain biking, and surfing—to offer instructional culinary cooking tours as well.

## ENTERING THE WORLD OF SOCIAL MEDIA

In August 2006, Ransom and Chuard distanced themselves from Access Trips in order to attend business school—Chuard at Stanford University's Graduate School of Business and Ransom at Harvard Business School. The couple continued to promote Access Trips online while working toward their MBAs. They also looked for a safe technological solution to send out travel and insurance information and to collect payments from customers. Once again, they could not find what they were looking for, so they decided to build it themselves. Ransom told Mitra, "It was eye-opening to realize that in order to build a good software product, you don't need to be a good coder. You need to understand a business process very well and have a good intuition for a clear user experience." She and Chuard decided to expand their customer management software product and make it available for other businesses.

The launch of Facebook fan pages for businesses in November 2007 provided Ransom and Chuard with another opportunity to promote Access Trips and to connect with the company's demographic. The couple decided it would be a great idea to give away a free trip. However, in order to do so, they would need to build an application that could run a sweepstakes on Facebook and let people share that sweepstakes with their friends. To solve this issue—for both Access Trips and for other small and medium-sized businesses—they hired software developers from Estonia.

"We were told when we first started Wildfire that a great coder can be worth tens times the value of a mediocre coder," Ransom told Laura Forrest for *Women 2.0* (8 Aug. 2011). "[I]t is without question more cost effective in the long run to pay for smart, reliable, productive developers, even if they cost a lot more." She added: "In a start-up it is critical that you hire top notch performers for every key role and an exception shouldn't be made for the founders. So if the founder is not a rock-star coder, or designer, or marketer she should find people who are and focus on the areas that she can add the most value to the business."

## WILDFIRE INTERACTIVE

What had started as a side project to benefit small businesses quickly spread to larger companies that had heard about Ransom and Chuard's Wildfire Promotion Builder application and were interested in using it. After completing their MBAs in June 2008, the couple launched Wildfire Interactive and moved to Silicon Valley in California. The business, a downloadable application, allows users to design promotions such as contests and sweepstakes, which are run across social media networks like Facebook and Twitter. The name Wildfire comes from the marketing viral power that the company promises. According to the company overview on their Facebook fan page, Wildfire's technology helps companies "integrate proven promotion techniques like sweepstakes, contests and coupon giveaways with the viral features of the social web to create engaging promotions that

spread like wildfire." Zappos and Kayak were among the first of the larger companies to use Wildfire. To connect with Zappos, Ransom and Chuard contacted an employee who had traveled with Access Trips. Kayak heard about Wildfire separately, and the couple made use of their business school networks for further outreach.

Ransom and Chuard knew that Wildfire needed to form a close relationship with Facebook in order to be successful. They contacted business school acquaintances who worked for the company, convincing them that Wildfire would make marketing more effective on Facebook. They next ran marketing campaigns for Facebook's legal and international growth departments. They also applied for the Facebook fund (fbFund), a grant from Accel Partners and the Founders Fund that enables entrepreneurs to build applications for Facebook. After four months of competition—during which they submitted written and video applications, were interviewed, produced a working version of their application, and waited for the public to vote—they won a $250,000 grant at the end of 2008. The money and publicity helped the business gain credibility and grow.

Despite the rapid growth of social media at the time, few investors were willing to risk dealing with these Internet businesses. Ransom and Chuard had to bootstrap Wildfire and worked from their living room until they were able to rent office space above a Mexican deli. Their sales force at the time was a combination of recent college graduates and senior salespeople who received cheap salaries but generous commissions. In less than a year, the business achieved profitability.

## FROM FACEBOOK ONWARD

In April 2009, Wildfire was a winner of the first Facebook Site Governance Vote, a Facebook user vote on the company's terms of use. Wildfire had designed the application for voting, which can be run across multiple social media platforms. This win earned them a second grant from the fbFund. After Facebook's investment in Wildfire, Summit Partners and 500 Startups followed suit, providing the company with $14 million in funds. The money enabled Wildfire to redesign and expand its software.

In addition to the campaign-enabling capabilities of Wildfire—sweepstakes, votes, contests, and games—companies can use Wildfire to run advertisements and messages across social media networks. Companies can also perform social media analyses, such as monitoring what their customers are saying about them. Tracking followers helps companies make sure, for example, that the same person does not vote twice.

In August 2009, the Wildfire web application software transitioned from beta, wherein customers had to be invited to try the technology prototype, and went live. Once that happened, a few hundred customers grew to several thousand. At the beginning of 2010, the company had seven employees. By October 2012, Wildfire was employing nearly four hundred employees and serving 21,000 customers. The company, based in Redwood City, California, expanded to locations in Los Angeles, New York, and Chicago. Offices were also opened internationally, in London, Paris, Munich, and Singapore.

Wildfire offers businesses different services and pricing, from $5 for each promotion at $0.99 a day, to $250 a promotion at $4.99 a day. Campaigns designed and run fully by Wildfire are charged at $2,500 per month upward, depending on the client. Wildfire is designed to run on any social media platform simultaneously with other social media platforms, such as Facebook, Twitter, Google Plus (Google+), LinkedIn, Pinterest, and YouTube. In addition to its application, Wildfire Interactive offers support and services such as custom CSS design and help with driving traffic to a company's campaign. Wildfire's biggest feature is the Wildfire Social Marketing Suite, a platform that allows brands to manage all of their social media marketing in one place. This includes fan pages, applications, tweets, advertisements, promotions, and videos.

## WILDFIRE BY GOOGLE

Google noticed Wildfire's rapidly growing success and decided to make Ransom and Chuard an offer. On July 31, 2012, an announcement was made on both companies' websites that Wildfire was being sold to Google. Ransom and Chuard had not actually been looking to sell, but part of the deal with Google was that Wildfire would remain running as it was, with Ransom and Chuard still leading the company as a new branch of Google's advertising sector. The acquisition—a sale of reportedly $350 million and $100 million in retention bonuses—was complete two weeks later. "That's when I thought, 'I'm going to remember this for a very long time,'" Ransom told Coster. In an interview discussing the acquisition with Hamish Fletcher for the *New Zealand Herald*, her father, John Ransom, stated, "She's come from a very modest background . . . it's a fairytale if you knew what Scotts Ferry was, a tiny settlement of about 40 households" (3 Aug. 2012). Ransom has told reporters that she and Chuard intend to stay with Wildfire for a few years. After that, they may start another company.

Google was the third in a series of companies that bought social software companies like Wildfire in 2012. Vitrue was sold to Oracle in May, and Buddy Media was sold to Salesforce.com in June. Google approached Wildfire because of the company's connection to Facebook, since Google has not had the success it hoped for with its social media products: Google Plus, Google Wave, and Google Buzz. Nate Elliott, vice president and principal analyst at Forrester Research, explained to Coster: "What would be interesting to Google is seeing what kind of data Facebook has access to, having a peek at how the technology works, and understanding how Facebook is communicating information about social users to third parties."

## WORKING AS A TEAM

When talking about the success of Wildfire, Ransom never takes full credit for the venture. In her role as CEO, she focuses on marketing, business development, and the general running of the company. Her cofounder, Chuard, leads product management and design. Ransom has noted that their success stems partly from entering the social media marketing business early. She told Tom Pullar-Strecker for *Business Day* (New Zealand) that Wildfire's success also stems from "the quality of people we hired, the company culture we built, which enabled us to attract and retain top-notch people, our focus on being a software company and not an agency, and our investment in building out a large sales team" (8 July 2012). Wildfire was named one of the top ten best places to work by the *San Francisco Business Times* in 2011. The newspaper, along with the *Silicon Valley/San Jose Business Journal*, named Wildfire in their list of the 125 best places to work" in 2011 as well. The company was also a runner-up for the TechCrunch Crunchies Award for the best bootstrapped start-up of 2010.

Ransom has been asked a number of times what it is like to work with her significant other. "I don't know why people make such a big deal about it," she told Mitra. "Our skill sets are very different and it is very clear who does what in our company. Alain is a product visionary and he has a real eye for design. We both collaborated on the product, but he really ran the engineering and oversaw the development. I did the selling and everything else. What is critical for cofounders is to have different skill sets and a very clear delineation of roles. I think it works very well for us."

## RECOGNITION FOR ENTREPRENEURIAL LEADERSHIP

Ransom has won a number of honors for her entrepreneurial success. In 2010 and 2011, she was named in Accenture's list of twenty-five women to watch in the technology sector. In 2011, she also won the Techfellow Award for general management, was a finalist for the Women in Technology Leadership Awards, and was named the 2011 Ernst & Young Entrepreneur of the Year (New Zealand). In 2012, Ransom was nominated for the 2012 Small Business Influencer Awards in the leaders category, was named one of *Fortune*'s 10 most powerful women entrepreneurs, and shared a spot with Buddy Media cofounder Michael Lazerow in *Fortune*'s forty under forty list.

## PERSONAL LIFE

Ransom and Chuard live in San Francisco. The couple enjoy traveling and sports such as snowboarding, rock climbing, hiking, surfing, and mountain biking. They made plans to marry in Ransom's native New Zealand during the autumn of 2012. Ransom once spent six weeks living with a tribe in the Amazon region of South America and five months living in a Brazilian favela (shack). She has also spent many of her summers working with teenagers. In addition to starting another entrepreneurial venture, Ransom and Chuard have expressed an interest in philanthropy.

## SUGGESTED READING

Coster, Helen. "Victoria Ransom's Wild Ride." *CNN Money*. Cable News Network, 19 Oct. 2012. Web. 15 Nov. 2012.

Douglas, Jeanne-Vida. "Beginnings: Victoria Ransom." *BRW* [Australia]. Fairfax Media, 24 Aug. 2011. Web. 15 Nov. 2012.

Forrest, Laura. "How to Be a Tech Entrepreneur Without Knowing How to Program." *Women 2.0*. Women 2.0, 8 Aug. 2011. Web. 15 Nov. 2012.

Mitra, Sramana. "From New Zealand to Silicon Valley: Victoria Ransom's Wildfire Journey." *Sramana Mitra*. Sramana Mitra, 29 Mar. 2012. Web. 15 Nov. 2012.

Wright, Christian L. "Have Fun, Learn a Skill." *New York Times*. New York Times Co., 1 May 2006. Web. 15 Nov. 2012.

—*Julia Gilstein*

# Eric Ripert

**Born:** March 2, 1965
**Occupation:** Chef and restaurateur

World-renowned French chef, seafood expert, and television personality Eric Ripert is the co-owner of the famed seafood restaurant Le Bernardin in New York City. Consistently ranked among the city's, and indeed the world's, best restaurants, Le Bernardin has won more James Beard Awards than any other New York restaurant, has earned and kept three Michelin stars since the guide first ranked the restaurant in 2005, and has retained four stars from the *New York Times* since it opened in 1986—the longest-held record of any New York restaurant.

In addition to his career as a chef and restaurateur, Ripert partnered with the Ritz-Carlton

Wirelmage

Hotel Company to open three restaurants in 2005, 2007, and 2008: Blue by Eric Ripert in the Cayman Islands, 10 Arts Bistro and Lounge in Philadelphia, Pennsylvania, and Westend Bistro in Washington, DC. He is the chair of the City Harvest food council, an organization that provides food to homeless shelters across New York. He is also the author of several cookbooks and has become a well-known television personality. Ripert has been a frequent guest judge on Bravo's *Top Chef*, made numerous guest appearances on talk shows such as the *Late Show with David Letterman* and on food shows such as *Anthony Bourdain: No Reservations*, and hosted his own award-winning cooking show on PBS, *Avec Eric*.

## EARLY LIFE AND EDUCATION

Eric Ripert was born on March 2, 1965, in Antibes, a coastal town of southeastern France, to a banker father and a clothing-importer mother. When he was a young boy, his family moved to Andorra, a small country located on the border between France and Spain. Ripert has cited the cuisines of both regions as major influences on his later career as a chef.

While Ripert learned how to cook at home—his first lessons were in his grandmother's kitchen—he would also request that his family eat at well-known restaurants on special occasions, such as his birthday, so that he could sample their menus. On one such occasion the family traveled to Hotel Le Café de Paris in Biarritz, France, where he went through the restaurant's entire tasting menu, sampled six à la carte items, and sampled all thirty desserts. Given Ripert's childhood passion for food, he seemed destined to become a chef: when he was ten years old, a psychic visited Ripert's family in Andorra and told him that "he would become a chef in a grand restaurant," he recalled to Samantha Miller and Julia Campbell for *People* magazine (3 Aug. 1998).

## CULINARY TRAINING

At the age of fifteen, Ripert left home to attend culinary school in Perpignan, France. A good palate, Ripert told Sarah Ball for *Newsweek* (5 Oct. 2009), is "born," though he qualified, "It's like a nice voice. If you don't train it, you have a nice voice—but you'll never be Pavarotti." In 1982, after two years of training, Ripert moved to Paris, where he became a cook at La Tour d'Argent, a renowned Parisian restaurant with a history that allegedly dates back to 1582.

Ripert spent two years at La Tour d'Argent before Joël Robuchon—who would be touted as the "chef of the century" by the French Gault & Millau guides in 1989—hired him to work at Jamin. The restaurant had a remarkable three Michelin stars at the time, the highest ranking that the Michelin guides give (even one Michelin star is a mark of prestige). Ripert was quickly promoted to assistant *chef de partie* (station chef or line cook), in charge of a particular area. He had to leave Jamin in 1985 to fulfill his military service; once he completed his service, he returned to the restaurant at the request of Robuchon, who appointed Ripert as *chef poissonier* (fish chef).

## JOINING LE BERNARDIN

In 1989 Ripert was given the opportunity to work as a *sous-chef*—the second-in-command of a kitchen—under Jean-Louis Palladin at the Watergate Hotel in Washington, DC. Two years later he moved to New York City, where he worked as sous-chef for David Bouley for just under a year, before siblings Maguy and Gilbert Le Coze recruited him as *chef de cuisine* (head chef) for Le Bernardin. Begun as a fish-only restaurant in Paris by the Le Cozes in 1972, the restaurant achieved two Michelin stars in 1980, the highest rating a seafood restaurant can achieve. (For three stars, a restaurant must serve more than one type of meat.) The siblings opened Le Bernardin in New York in 1986, with Gilbert as executive chef and Maguy overseeing the restaurant's finances.

After Gilbert Le Coze died in 1994, Ripert, who had become a close friend of theirs, took over the kitchen as head chef. "Right away you could see he was going to be a leader," Maguy Le Coze told Samantha Miller and Julia Campbell for *People* magazine (3 Aug. 1998). Le Coze had Ripert step in as co-owner of the restaurant

as well. Ripert, at twenty-nine, garnered his first four-star rating for Le Bernardin from the *New York Times* in 1995. "He stepped up to the plate and kept standards absolutely where they had been," *New York Times* critic Ruth Reichl said in her April 1995 review, as quoted by Miller and Campbell. Subsequent reviews would follow in 2005 and 2012, awarding four stars each time. "Now, as before, it is a high church of reverently prepared fish," Frank Bruni wrote of Le Bernardin in his March 16, 2005, *New York Times* review.

## LE BERNARDIN: THE BEST OF THE BEST

Three months after its opening in January 1986, Le Bernardin was awarded four stars by the *New York Times*, the highest ranking the newspaper gives. The restaurant has retained that ranking ever since. As one of only six four-star restaurants in New York City, Le Bernardin is also the only New York restaurant to have maintained four stars for more than twenty years. Ripert's insistence on excellence is what has kept the restaurant at the top for so long. "I'm a tough cookie," Ripert told Miller and Campbell. "I don't like mediocrity."

Le Bernardin has received numerous other awards and honors, including more James Beard Awards—the Oscars of Food—than any other New York restaurant. The James Beard Award for outstanding restaurant was given to Maguy Le Coze in 1998; in 2009 the restaurant was awarded for its outstanding wine service; and in 2012 the restaurant earned a James Beard Award for the best restaurant design—Ripert and Le Coze had hired New York architecture and design firm Bentel & Bentel to redesign Le Bernardin in 2011. Ripert has personally received accolades as well: in 2003 the James Beard Foundation named Ripert outstanding chef of the year.

When in 2005 Michelin gave its first-ever reviews of New York restaurants, Le Bernardin received three Michelin stars, a ranking it has retained ever since. The restaurant has also been top rated in the best food category of the New York Zagat guides for eight consecutive years, and in Zagat's 2012 and 2013 editions is named New York's most popular restaurant. In an interview with James Mulcahy for Zagat's website (3 Oct. 2012), Ripert explained what has kept Le Bernardin on top for so long: "We're in New York City, and it's always reinventing itself, it's a very competitive city. I see competition as a blessing, not as a threat. . . . We have to look at ourselves and what we have done here and say, 'This is not enough.'" He added, "We always update ourselves, rejuvenate ourselves, reinvent ourselves." Le Bernardin's worldwide standing is also impressive: in a 2012 listing of the world's fifty best restaurants, San Pellegrino ranked Le Bernardin at number nineteen.

## RIPERT CONSULTING

In 1999 Le Coze and Ripert founded Ripert Consulting, which has helped restaurants across the United States. Ripert and his consulting team advise restaurant owners on every aspect of operating a restaurant, from menu design to back-of-house training. Ripert Consulting also partnered with the Ritz-Carlton Hotel Company, opening Blue by Eric Ripert at the Ritz-Carlton in Grand Cayman, Cayman Islands, in 2005, the Westend Bistro in Washington, DC, in 2007, and 10 Arts Bistro and Lounge in Philadelphia, Pennsylvania, in 2008. While Ripert has not run those Ritz-Carlton restaurants in person, he has acted as their consulting chef. He left Westend and 10 Arts at the end of 2012, however, because "a project in New York affiliated with his famed Le Bernardin required too much of his time," as reported by Michael Klein of *Philly.com* (30 Nov. 2012). Ripert did not reveal any details of the project.

While Ripert's influence extends far through his consulting business, he owns only Le Bernardin in New York. "I've had many offers to open Le Bernardin somewhere else," he told Lisa Fickenscher for *Crain's New York Business* (19 June 2011). "At the end of the day, what matters is to be satisfied, and I am very satisfied with what I am and what I have." As he told Hara Estroff Marano for *Psychology Today* (1 Nov. 2010), "We excel, and you can't duplicate excellence without being on-site often. . . . How much money do you need? I'm not willing to compromise standards. I have found balance."

## *TOP CHEF, AVEC ERIC,* AND OTHER TV APPEARANCES

Owning one of the most highly acclaimed restaurants worldwide—and keeping it that way—is not the only thing satisfying Ripert. He has also become a popular television personality, though, unlike many of his peers, he did not actively seek out celebrity. "You don't become a chef to become famous," he told Jenny Comita for *W* magazine (Sept. 2009). "You become a chef because you like cooking." Ripert's guest appearances include the *Late Show with David Letterman* (2008–11), the *Today* show (2007, 2012), and *Anthony Bourdain: No Reservations* (2008, 2010), among others. He has also played himself on HBO's *Treme* (2010–12), a show about the people of New Orleans after the 2005 Hurricane Katrina disaster. Ripert's best-known role, however, is as a regular guest judge on Bravo's *Top Chef* (2007–12). The *Top Chef* fan favorite turned down an opportunity to become a permanent judge for the show's eighth season (2010–11), after one of his employees, 10 Art's chef de cuisine Jennifer Carroll, became a contestant for the second time.

In addition to those guest appearances, Ripert has also hosted his own television shows. His first show, *Avec Eric*, ran on PBS for two seasons, from 2009 to 2010. *Avec Eric* is part travel show, part cooking show. The episodes follow Ripert from his restaurant to the source of inspiration for a particular dish; he then provides a lesson on how to cook that dish. When asked by *Newsweek*'s Sarah Ball why he wanted to do his own show when he was already popular on *Top Chef*, he replied, "I wanted to do something a bit different. I wanted to try television myself, even though I don't speak English [well]" (5 Oct. 2009). He added that *Avec Eric* is "more myself. It's basically taking people with me on an adventure. It creates more intimacy, and it's a different vision than what you would expect. A wild-boar hunt? I haven't seen that on TV yet." *Avec Eric* earned two Daytime Emmy awards, one in 2010 for outstanding achievement in main title and graphic design, and one in 2011 for outstanding culinary program. The show also earned a 2011 James Beard Award for best television program on location.

Ripert became the host of Reserve Channel's YouTube show *On the Table* in July 2012. On each episode of the show, Ripert hosts a celebrity friend, such as Anthony Bourdain, in his home kitchen, and together they cook the guest's signature dish.

## COOKBOOK PUBLICATIONS

Ripert has published several cookbooks. *Le Bernardin Cookbook: Four-Star Simplicity*, the first Le Bernardin cookbook, was written with Maguy Le Coze and published in 1998. Ripert published a *Return to Cooking* in 2002; a collaboration between Ripert, author Michael Ruhlman, photographers Shimon and Tammar Rhothstein, and artist Valentino Cortazar, the book was named one of the best books of the season by *Newsweek*. In 2008, Ripert published *On the Line* with Christine Muhlke, who in 2011 became executive editor of *Bon Appétit*. As part of the *Avec Eric* television series, Ripert published *Avec Eric: A Culinary Journey with Eric Ripert*, a compilation of recipes inspired by his travels, in 2010.

## CITY HARVEST

While working as chef and co-owner of Le Bernardin, Ripert learned about City Harvest, a food rescue organization—the first of its kind—founded in 1982; he would later become chair of the organization's food council. City Harvest delivers food to shelters and other agencies that feed New Yorkers who cannot afford to buy their own food. The food comes from restaurant donations across New York City as well as from individual monetary donations. Le Bernardin, for example, donates unused food every day to City Harvest.

City Harvest's food council works to bring together members of New York City's food industry in order to increase the amount of high-quality food gathered and to raise funds for and aware-ness of the organization. In October 2011 City Harvest released a smartphone application called Great Food, Good Hearts, which allows users to look up restaurants that donate to City Harvest and then make reservations through OpenTable, an online restaurant-booking service.

## CONVERSION TO BUDDHISM

A practicing Buddhist, Ripert first began explor-ing the religion after picking up a book on Bud-dhism at the Charles de Gaulle airport in Paris, when he was about to embark on his first trip to the United States. The Buddhist karmic ideal for eating is vegetarianism. However, as the chef of a seafood restaurant, Ripert has worked to find a middle road. "I never pressure myself to do something I don't want to do," he told Jenny Co-mita for *W* magazine (Sept. 2009). At Le Bernar-din, Ripert promotes sustainability and respect for food. For example, he tries to make sure his restaurant only buys fish caught in a way that does not disturb fragile sea beds. "The nature of human beings is to eat meat and fruits and veg-etables, and therefore we have to kill animals," he told Sarah Ball for *Newsweek* (5 Oct. 2009). "I don't have a problem with that. But it's a sa-cred moment. It's a gift of life. When we kill a lobster here, I always say, do it humanely. I don't want the lobster to have pain." He added, "If you burn the lobster or you totally oversalt it or don't do a good job, you don't pay homage to that life. It's an insult."

## BUDDHISM IN THE KITCHEN

Converting to Buddhism also changed the way that Ripert runs his kitchen. Having been trained in Paris, where "the goal is to break down a cook, then rebuild him," as Ripert told Hara Estroff Marano for *Psychology Today* (1 Nov. 2010), he learned that "engaging in verbal abuse, scaring the cooks, and being a dictator was the right way." He even once threw a plate at pastry chef François Payard. However, after joining Le Bernardin, Ripert began to lose staff, and those who remained were all unhappy—including him. "I contemplated what was wrong," Ripert told Marano. "And I concluded I was wrong."

A restaurant kitchen is a fast-paced, high-stress environment. Ripert eventually managed to incorporate a Zen-like attitude into that en-vironment, enabling him to maintain high stan-dards while not driving his staff away. "I use Buddhist principles in the way I run the restau-rant without bringing in the Buddhist religion," he explained to Marano. Incorporating those principles has led to two-thirds of Le Bernardin's staff staying on for more than three years—some have been with Ripert for more than twenty.

In May 2010 Ripert had the honor to cook for the Dalai Lama when he visited New York. Le Bernardin hosted a lunch benefit for the Dalai Lama, and the proceeds of the fundraiser went toward the creation of a cultural center for Tibetan immigrants in the city. Ripert has cooked for a number of distinguished persons, including as a guest chef at the French embas-sies in Mexico and Venezuela and for the New York City Ballet.

Ripert became a recipient of France's high-est civilian honor, the Legion d'Honneur, in March 2009. He lives in New York with his wife, Sondra, and his son.

## SUGGESTED READING

Comita, Jenny. "Eric Ripert: Out of the Kitch-en." *Wmagazine*. Condé Nast, Sept. 2009. Web. 11 Jan. 2013.
Marano, Hara Estroff. "Kitchen Karma." *Psy-chology Today* 43.6 (2010): 44–45. Print.
Miller, Samantha, and Julia Campbell. "A Fin Romance." *People* 50.3 (1998): 95. Print.
Mulcahy, James. "NYC Survey Results: Eric Ripert Talks Le Bernardin—Secrets of a No. 1 Restaurant." *Zagat*. Zagat Survey, 3 Oct. 2012. Web. 11 Jan. 2013.
Rothstein, Mervyn. "Four-Star Chef." *Cigar Afi-cionado*. Cigar Aficionado Online, Sept./Oct. 2006. Web. 11 Jan. 2013.

## SELECTED WORKS

### Books
*Le Bernardin Cookbook: Four-Star Simplicity* (with Maguy Le Coze), 1998; *A Return to Cook-ing* (with Michael Ruhlman), 2002; *On the Line* (with Christine Muhlke), 2008; *Avec Eric: A Cu-linary Journey with Eric Ripert*, 2010

### Television and Internet Series
*Top Chef* (guest judge), 2007–12; *Avec Eric*, 2009–10; *Treme*, 2010–12; *On the Table*, 2012

—Julia Gilstein

# Yves Rossy

**Born:** August 27, 1959
**Occupation:** Aviator and inventor

He has been known as Airman, Rocketman, Fusionman, and most commonly, Jetman. Ever since childhood, Swiss pilot Yves Rossy has want-ed to fly. As an adult, his first step toward achiev-ing that dream was his career as a military pilot. He then became a commercial flight captain for Swiss International Air Lines. But piloting air-planes proved not to be enough: Rossy wanted to fly through the air without the confines of a vehicle. He began working on a wing for himself in the early 1990s. After more than ten years of

Getty Images

development and fifteen prototypes, Rossy in 2006 became—and remains—the first man to fly with only the aid of a jet-powered wing.

Since then, Rossy has continued to improve his invention and push the limits of human flight. In May 2008, with the world watching, he took a five-minute flight across the Swiss Alps. That September, Rossy made another highly-publicized flight, this time across the English Channel. In November 2009, he attempted to cross continents, from Morocco to Spain via the Strait of Gibraltar, but poor weather conditions prevented him from achieving his goal. This failed attempt did not stop the aviator from continuing to fly, however. In May 2011, Rossy flew over the Grand Canyon, and a year later he flew for eleven minutes over Rio de Janeiro. He has also flown in formation with military aircraft.

While some have viewed the aviator as an attention-seeking daredevil, Rossy does not see himself that way. "I am just a normal man," he told Eric Hagerman for *Popular Science* (Feb. 2009), "who has realized his dream to fly a little bit like a bird." Rossy has continuously worked to improve and test his designs for better safety and maneuvering. He hopes that in the near future his technology will be available to anyone.

## EARLY LIFE AND PILOT CAREER
Yves Rossy was born in Neuchâtel, Switzerland, on August 27, 1959, to Paule Rossy and Swiss Railway employee Henry Rossy. He cites the age of thirteen as when he was first inspired to fly. Rossy's parents took him and his brother Phillipe, two years his senior, to an air show near their hometown, Penthalaz. After admiring the

military jet planes at the show, he decided he wanted to fly them. As he told Jeff Pearlman for *Sports Illustrated*: "Then the thing begins, and I am taken away. . . . I'm fascinated. Just so fascinated. At the end they had this amazing finale, with . . . Switzerland's version of the Blue Angels. They did this formation, where the planes swooped down so low and so fast. At that moment I knew—I absolutely knew—that I wanted to be the man in the machine like that" (15 May 2012).

In 1977, at the age of eighteen, Rossy joined the Swiss Air Force. His first airplane as a fighter pilot was the Hawker Hunter, followed by the Mirage III supersonic and other airplanes. After about seventeen years in the military, Rossy switched to commercial flying, becoming a pilot for Swiss Air and flying Airbus and Boeing airliners. When the company went bankrupt in 2002, he became a pilot for Swiss International Air Lines, which took over as the flag carrier for Switzerland. Rossy has remained a flight captain for the company ever since.

Despite Rossy's skill as a pilot, he wanted to find a way to fly "in the most natural way possible," according to his *Jetman* website. He began to experiment with free fall, what "winged stuntrepreneur" (*Popular Science* Feb. 2009) Felix Baumgartner of Austria is known for. Free fall does not allow for complete control over one's trajectory and how long one spends in the air, however. For that reason Rossy began to develop his own mode of flight in the early 1990s.

## FIRST ATTEMPTS AT FLYING
Rossy's first flying experiments, from 1992 to 1998, included skysurfing, in which skydivers attach a board to their feet to perform aerial aerobatics, and wingsuit flying, the use of a special suit designed to act like the webbing of a bat's wings or between a flying squirrel's limbs. Rossy placed second in the first Skysurfing World Championships, held in September 1993 in Empuriabrava, Spain. There, he met Patrick de Gayardon, a Frenchman who was working on a design for a winged skydiving suit, made of nylon. Inspired by Gayardon's attempts at stalling freefall, Rossy created board five feet in width on which to "surf" the air. The plank proved too dangerous, and Rossy had to cut himself free and unfurl his parachute to land safely.

The next flight experiments, from about 1999 to 2003, were with an unpowered inflatable wing. Rossy had first tried an inflatable wing in 1992, but then had switched his focus to skysurfing and wingsuit flying. He then returned to the inflatable wing, which was able to lift his body and keep him in the air, allowing him to glide. The wing could take him long distances. For example, during one flight in 2002, Rossy leaped off an airplane and glided over Lake Geneva for approximately 7.5 miles. Still, gliding does not enable the flier to maneuver, climb, and dive to the extent that Rossy desired. To do so, the pilot would need to employ the jet engine, which has enough force to propel a human body forward in the air—too much force for an inflatable wing. Rossy switched to a wing made of carbon fiber, but the material proved unstable. After twice redesigning the wing, he still had work to do. In addition to lift (upward force) and thrust (propulsion), for a successful flight the pilot needed to work with drag (backward force), caused by air's resistance to a moving object. To fight air drag, he attached first two and then four jet engines to his wing.

## DEVELOPING THE WING

After designing, testing, and discarding various prototypes between the early 1990s and the mid-2000s, Rossy eventually ended up with a carbon fiber skeleton covered by a fiberglass shell. In addition, the wing has an electronic control unit and two fiberglass fuel tanks—which for his 2008 flight across the English Channel contained 3.5 gallons of jet fuel each. Four jet engines (turbines) are attached to the underside of the wing. The only other piece to the "jet pack" is a lever that Rossy uses to increase or decrease the engines' thrust.

The wing was custom-made for Rossy, by himself and by Alain Ray of ACT Composites, a company based in Geneva, Switzerland. Rossy designed the mechanical parts, while Ray took care of the wing's structure. The turbines of the wing were designed by German manufacturer JetCat, as modifications of the type produced for military drones and model airplanes. JetCat covered the turbines in Kevlar, a type of para-aramid synthetic fiber often used in body armor, to protect the wing's wearer from shrapnel if a turbine ever explodes.

According to *Jetman*, the wing, including fuel, weighs 55 kilograms, or just over 121 pounds. Its tanks hold about four gallons of fuel each. The wing originally spanned about eight feet across after unfolding, but by November 2010, Rossy and RUAG, a Swiss technology company, had redesigned it to about 6.5 feet across, without the need to unfold. It can fly an average of 125 miles per hour—though it can reach up to 190 miles per hour—for approximately ten minutes, given the limited amount of fuel carried. Other than that, Rossy's body is the rest of the "airplane." He wears a skydiving suit and a fully enclosed helmet for protection, and he maneuvers his body to deflect the airstream.

In November 2006, Rossy flew for nearly six minutes near the town of Bex, Switzerland. "It was fantastic," he told Stephen Battersby for *Current Science* (25 Feb. 2011). "After years of testing and building prototypes, I finally did it; I was flying." Since the success of the four–jet engine version, Rossy has continuously worked to improve the wing design for greater and greater success.

## ACROSS THE ALPS AND THE CHANNEL

On May 14, 2008, Rossy strapped on what became called his "wingsuit," boarded an airplane that lifted him up over the Swiss Alps, and jumped off when the plane reached 7,500 feet. He unfolded his wing and accelerated to 186 miles per hour, flying over the mountains for about five minutes before landing with the help of a parachute. This was his first pre-publicized flight. His mother was in the audience, fully confident in her son's ability to fly safely. "He knows what he's doing," Paule Rossy told reporters, according to Frank Jordans of the Associated Press (*NBCNews.com*, 14 May 2008). Rossy described the wingsuit as being "like a second skin," he told reporters after the flight. "If I turn to the left, I fly left. If I nudge to the right, I go right."

The next challenge for Rossy was crossing the English Channel. He successfully achieved this feat on September 26, 2008, when the first man to fly with a jet-propelled wing became the first man to do so over the English Channel. The stunt was broadcast on live television by the National Geographic Channel. Rossy was flown up to a height of 8,202 feet before jumping out of the airplane and flying at about 125 miles per hour. He traveled from Calais, France, to the White Cliffs of Dover in England, a twenty-two mile distance that took approximately thirteen minutes. Rossy had enough fuel at the end of his flight to perform aerobatic celebratory loops before landing.

## "WHOOPS" MOMENTS AND OTHER SETBACKS

Crossing continents was Rossy's next big goal. The then fifty-year-old set out to do so on November 25, 2009. He started from the air above Tangiers, Morocco, at 6,500 feet, and flew toward Atlanterra, Spain, across the Strait of Gibraltar, a distance of twenty-three miles. Unfortunately, engine trouble and poor weather conditions, namely the strength of the wind, prevented him from achieving his goal. Rossy had to abandon his flight and land in the Mediterranean Sea. The aerobat was rescued by a helicopter; his wing was picked up by the Spanish coast guard later on.

Rossy has had various setbacks during the creation of the wingsuit and during his flying attempts, including at least twenty instances of ending up in an uncontrollable spin. Even so, he has remained confident. "I've had many 'whoops' moments," he told Jordans, adding, "My safety is altitude" (14 May 2008). Altitude is not his only safety, however. His confidence comes from being prepared. "The truly crazy part?" wrote Eric Hagerman for *Popular Science* (Feb. 2009), "Through all the testing, he's never been injured.

Like any good pilot, Rossy is meticulous about safety. His first order of business was to build a cutaway harness [made of seatbelts] that would make it easy to eject the wing."

## THE GRAND CANYON

By the time Rossy crossed the Grand Canyon in Arizona, on May 7, 2011, he was already a popular stuntman. He jumped from a helicopter at eight thousand feet above the canyon floor, and then flew from a height of about two hundred feet above the canyon's rim. His US flight was announced well in advance so that the media and other spectators could claim viewing spots on the Skywalk at Grand Canyon West, a glass-bottomed deck four thousand feet above the canyon's floor. The Hualapai Nation, the owners of the Grand Canyon West tourist spot, gave Rossy permission to fly there. The event was sponsored by Swiss watchmaker Breitling, Rossy's sponsor.

Rossy was scheduled to fly on May 6; he instead flew one day later. The surprise May 6 cancellation meant that reporters were not present for his achievement. However, there is video footage that proves Rossy's flight over the canyon did indeed occur. Breitling claimed that Rossy delayed his flight because he had to wait for optimal wind conditions. Tim Neville for the Swiss news website Swissinfo reported that the pilot had been nervous about the location and all the attention. "This is a very challenging place," he said, according to Neville (10 May 2011). "Big air currents, steep walls. Without training, I don't want to take the risk of presenting something unprofessional." He added, "I have a knot in my body. Sorry for that. I'm human."

Popular Science reporter Clay Dillow wrote that one reason for the delay was because the Federal Aviation Administration (FAA) was uncertain how to certify Rossy for flight in the United States, and they gave approval at the last minute. The FAA decided to forgo the usual test flight time required because of Rossy's experience, classifying Rossy and his jet wing as a registered aircraft instead.

## OTHER AERIAL STUNTS

In early November 2010, Rossy jumped from a hot-air balloon at 7,200 feet over Denezy, Switzerland. With an audience watching, he performed his first aerobatics show with his then new 6.5 foot wing. The balloon, named Esprit Breitling Orbiter, was flown by British balloonist Brian Jones. In March 1999, Jones had won a nonstop round-the-world balloon race; he and Swiss balloonist Bertran Piccard became the first to achieve this feat. Jones maneuvered the balloon in coordination with Rossy's aeronautics, enabling Rossy to loop around the balloon.

After Rossy's flight across the Grand Canyon in May 2011, his next foreign flight occurred on May 3, 2012, over Rio de Janeiro, Brazil. He jumped out of an airplane toward the cityscape and flew across the city, performing a barrel roll along the way. Eleven minutes later, he landed by parachute on Copacabana Beach.

In addition to flying solo—albeit with a helicopter nearby in case of emergency—Rossy has also flown in formation with various aircraft. He flew with two Aero L-39c Albatros jets, piloted by the Breitling Jet Team, in November 2011 in Switzerland. He also flew alongside a vintage 1940s passenger Breitling Douglas DC-3 over Switzerland's Lake Lucerne in June 2012. That September, during the Bex aerodrome's annual "fly-in" near Geneva, Switzerland, Rossy flew in formation with a Spitfire MH434, an iconic type of British fighter plane made for World War II, piloted by Nigel Lamb.

## DAREDEVIL OR INNOVATOR?

Critics of Rossy's public flying displays have generally dismissed him, describing him as an attention-seeking daredevil. Richard Laermer, CEO of American public relations firm RLM, said of Rossy: "He's a stunt guy like Donald Trump . . . do what you can to get attention, and then after the check is cashed run back to the cave and start all over again," he told Daniel B. Wood for the Christian Science Monitor (11 May 2011). "None of this is real or adds value."

While Rossy does like to perform aeronautics during his flights to show off his and his wingsuit's ability, he has stated that publicity is not his sole purpose for flying: "I built this wing to realize my own dream: to fly like a bird," he said in a press release from his marketing firm, Centigrade Inc, quoted by Wood. "Flying is a passion. I always wanted to fly since I am a child. My inspiration has always been to realize my dream." Following his passion is not all that Rossy wants to achieve. He also hopes to make his technology available to the public. "Speed is not the great motivator," he told Jeff Pearlman for Sports Illustrated (15 May 2012). "Living is. Feeling is. Experiencing is—and then sharing that experience with others. That's why I do this. That's the only reason why."

Rossy's fans look forward to the future they believe he is helping to bring. "This is the future promised to us since the end of World War II, and I, for one, am still waiting for jet packs and flying cars," Robert Thompson, founder of the Bleier Center at Syracuse University in New York, told Wood. Christian Landry, a skydiving tandem instructor at aerodrome Yverdon, located near Lake Neuchâtel and where Rossy performed some of his first tests with his wing, told Hagerman: "With that type of guy, things become possible. I don't know exactly in the future if he can bring something important for everybody with the technology, but only with people who live more than 100 percent can society go forward. In French we say, metro, boulot, dodo:

subway, work, sleep. If all people are like this, we are like sheep and nothing comes better. And we need some people like Yves."

## PERSONAL LIFE
Rossy lives in Nyon, north of Geneva. He is divorced and has no children. Instead, he devotes his time to his passion: flying. As he told Pearlman: "It can catch people by surprise, because what I'm doing is unique. But once people understand, I think they are moved. This is a man living his dream. I am the richest person in the world."

## SUGGESTED READING
Battersby, Stephen. "Rocket Man." *Current Science* 25 Feb. 2011: 4–5. *Academic Search Complete*. Web. 1 Nov. 2012.
Hagerman, Eric. "Wingman." *Popular Science* Feb. 2009: 36–43; 76; 79. *Academic Search Complete*. Web. 1 Nov. 2012.
*Jetman Yves Rossy*. Jetman, 2012. Web. 1. Nov. 2012.
Pearlman, Jeff. "It's a Bird, It's a Plane, It's Jetman." *Sports Illustrated*. Time Inc., 15 May 2012. Web. 1 Nov. 2012.
Wood, Daniel B. "'Jetman' Zooms along Rim of Grand Canyon in First US Flight." *Christian Science Monitor*. Christian Science Monitor, 11 May 2011. Web. 1 Nov. 2012.

—*Julia Gilstein*

Associated Press

# Stephanie Ruhle

**Born:** December 24, 1975
**Occupation:** Television anchor and journalist

Bloomberg Television anchor Stephanie Ruhle cohosts the midday programs *Market Makers* and *Lunch Money*, both of which feature high-profile guests commenting on the news of the day and its implications for financial markets. Ruhle arrived at Bloomberg in October 2011 after almost fifteen years on Wall Street, where she was elbow-deep in the trading of the complex financial instruments known as credit derivatives. As a brand new business journalist with a lively manner and this level of firsthand experience in a crucial sector of the securities industry—unusual for anyone, but especially so for a woman—Ruhle's arrival attracted attention. "She's been at the network for just over a month, and in that short time it's become clear that she's the most important new name in financial television," wrote Joe Weisenthal for *Business Insider* in November 2011. "While there have been plenty of folks on TV who are ex–Wall Street, there aren't many who bring the metabolism and perspective of the trading floor to the screen like Ruhle."

## EARLY LIFE AND EDUCATION
Stephanie Ruhle was born the younger of two girls in Park Ridge, New Jersey, to a stay-at-home mother and a father who owned a mechanical engineering company. Raised in a loving and supportive environment, she told the website I Want Her Job (21 Aug. 2012), "I grew up with a mom who said every day, 'You can do anything you set your mind to. I believe in the American Dream.'"

Armed with this strong family foundation and an intensely competitive nature—"When I was five, I knew I wanted to win," she told *Working Mother* magazine (Sept. 2009)—she set off for college at Lehigh University in Bethlehem, Pennsylvania, where she studied international business. Wanting to travel, she spent two of her college years abroad, in Guatemala, Kenya, and Italy.

Her first experience with Wall Street was a summer internship with Merrill Lynch. She told Joe Weisenthal, for the website *Business Insider* (10 Nov. 2011), that she worked "in the bowels of derivative documentation, some truly horrible file-room internship, and one day I had to make a delivery onto a trading floor, just a manila envelope. And on that day, at that moment—and this happens to a lot of people—I was bit by the trading floor bug. I said, 'I don't know what anyone here does for a living but this is what I'm going to do when I grow up.'"

## CREDIT SUISSE
Acting on that urge, Ruhle joined the sales and trading program at the financial services firm

Credit Suisse upon graduating in 1997. She was hoping to go abroad again, but instead was given a position in corporate bond sales in New York, a job she described to Weisenthal as "totally vanilla," but "they had a seat, it was open and I took it."

Around this time, securities markets were beginning to trade more heavily in credit derivatives—innovative financial instruments designed to spread around the risk from various kinds of debt by securitizing it and selling it to investors. Ruhle met some of the people at Credit Suisse who dealt in credit derivatives, and she was intrigued. "They basically said we'll teach you credit derivatives if you get us access to the clients," she told Weisenthal, and so Ruhle began handling sales of credit derivatives to corporate clients. About a year or so later, always drawn to where the action is, Ruhle moved to working with hedge funds, ultimately becoming Credit Suisse's highest-producing credit derivatives salesperson in the United States.

Speaking to Julia La Roche for *Business Insider* (21 May 2012), Ruhle later reflected that it was "amazing to have been at the forefront of the credit derivatives markets and boom in hedge funds during this historic time in the markets." She told Weisenthal that the novelty of the credit derivatives market was part of the key to her rapid rise in the business: "I think for young people and I think for women it's great to work in new products and derivatives products, because if you work in a plain vanilla product it's going to take you decades to get to a level where other people are. If you work in a brand new business, no one is more experienced than you are." In other words, as she summarized to *Working Mother*, "There can't be an old boys' network at a new game."

## DEUTSCHE BANK
Continuing her upward trajectory, after six years at Credit Suisse, Ruhle took a job at Deutsche Bank in April 2003, calling the company "just a much bigger derivatives platform than [Credit Suisse] was" (to Weisenthal). Ruhle stayed at Deutsche Bank for eight and a half years, seemingly propelled by her own momentum. "When I first started I said, I want to be a managing director when I'm thirty, and then that's it. And then I'm gonna go home, I'm gonna pack it in," she told Weisenthal. "And I made [managing director] when I was thirty but by no means did I think I was going to leave at that point. I felt like, hey, I'm, just getting warmed up."

Ruhle remained Deutsche Bank's managing director in structured credit sales through the financial crisis of 2008, an event for which the credit derivatives on which she had built her career received a significant portion of blame. Ruhle seemed unfazed, however, conceding to

*Working Mother* in 2009 only that "in the good times, both individuals and institutions took on more debt than we could handle." Regarding the ensuing wave of public scrutiny and moves to bolster government regulation of the securities markets, she continued, "I make a concerted effort to be positive. . . . The clients I work with are very sophisticated, and now they're under intense scrutiny, so they need to feel they can trust me. . . . I introduce them to resources that can solve their problems."

Nonetheless, by 2011, Ruhle found she was ready to strike out in a bold new direction. She loved her job in Wall Street securities trading, but wanted to work with the bigger picture. She told Wiesenthal that she was drawn to "having a seat at the table. Sitting at roundtable discussions, roundtable dinners, understanding what seven different people with seven different perspectives have to say." A good place to do that seemed to be broadcast journalism, to which Ruhle said a part of her had always been attracted. At a forum for women leaders, she voiced this interest, and Melinda Wolfe, head of human resources for Bloomberg LP, was at the table. "I sat down with her and she said, is this something you could really want to do," Ruhle told Wiesenthal. "I said I don't know, maybe, if I got the right seat, sure. And then she introduced me to [Bloomberg Media Group CEO] Andy Lack and we talked about it for awhile and the rest is history."

## BLOOMBERG TELEVISION
Ruhle joined Bloomberg Television in October 2011, initially coanchoring the morning show *Inside Track* with Erik Schatzker before moving to *Market Makers* and *Lunch Money*. She told the website I Want Her Job why she loves the position so much: "Bloomberg is the media outlet that every professional in the industry uses. The weight of this job is massive to the markets. You can provide information and insights that change the way people look at companies and the economy. And that's really heavy."

Ruhle's Wall Street experience was an immediate asset to the network, and when she began commenting on credit derivatives with the knowledge of an insider, people noticed. Her presence meant that "there's someone on financial TV that sees the news through the lens of people who it's intended for, something that can't be said for many on TV," wrote Weisenthal. She told him, "In many instances I'm still working with so many of the people I've always worked with. Almost every day I have a guest on who's either a colleague or a [former] client of mine. So it's not like I'm having different conversations—I'm having more of them. This is an exciting place to sit. People now more than ever, in large part because they're so mad at Wall Street, they want to understand it. Again, I'm not saying

I have the answer, but I think I have an insider's perspective."

Thus far, Ruhle said her proudest day at Bloomberg has been helping to break the April 2012 story of the "London Whale," the nickname given to a securities trader named Bruno Iskil who worked for JPMorgan Chase in the banking company's London office, and who was responsible for over $2 billion in credit derivatives trading losses. Ruhle told Wiesenthal (11 May 2012) that she began hearing from sources about enormous trades in credit default swaps—a type of credit derivative—being made at JPMorgan at a time when most banks were moving away from such complicated, risky instruments. "These trades just weren't JPMorgan's modus operandi. And they raised pretty basic questions," she said. "I couldn't testify to exactly what was wrong, but I knew it didn't pass the smell test." The April 6 story she published with Bradley Keoun and Mary Childs alleged that Iskil's trades were so large they were distorting prices in the $10 trillion derivatives market. Eventually, JPMorgan CEO Jamie Dimon was forced to go public with the size of the losses the company suffered, and Iskil's trading privileges were revoked.

## ADVOCATE FOR WOMEN IN BUSINESS

As a highly successful woman in a male-dominated profession, Ruhle is passionate about encouraging the professional advancement of other women in her industry. As she bluntly stated to *Working Mother*, "I agree with our first female U.S. secretary of state, Madeleine Albright, who said that there's a place in hell reserved for women who don't help other women. I really live by that."

Accordingly, while at Deutsche Bank, Ruhle founded the company's Global Markets Women's Network and served on the steering committee for the annual Women on Wall Street conference hosted by the firm. She is also active in the White House Project, a nonprofit organization aimed at encouraging the rise of women in business and politics, as well as 100 Women in Hedge Funds and the Women's Bond Club. She also serves on the board of Girls Inc. of New York and the corporate council of the mentorship program iMentor. "I am the *most* proud of driving women's initiatives and helping move the needle for women in the industry," she told La Roche for *Business Insider*.

Ruhle brims with advice for up-and-coming professional women. "You need to be open-minded, driven, ignore stereotypes, be fearless," she told I Want Her Job. "Most importantly, be respectful. Never do you have to treat someone badly or disrespectfully. You never have to step on anyone in order to climb the ladder. What you need are people around you to help build that ladder."

She told *The Glass Hammer* that mentorship is incredibly important. "Make the time and plan for networking—it will open doors for you in the future. You will experience different trajectories and plateaus along your career path. Those are times when you will need to tap into the experience and assistance of your mentors. Achieving success is a collaborative effort and having the support of those above and around you is key." She added: "No one wants to see a woman get a job because of a diversity initiative. We want her to get the job because she is the best candidate. I want to help increase the number of women we bring into the business and those who are eligible for prized senior jobs."

## PERSONAL LIFE

Ruhle met her husband, Andy Hubbard, in the global training program at Credit Suisse in the 1990s. He stayed at Credit Suisse and is charge of the company's US structured credit derivatives trading—making them something of a credit derivatives household. Ruhle told Wiesenthal, "I'm a credit derivatives person who's married to a credit derivatives person. So every angle [at Bloomberg] I have is, 'Oh my God, what did you think about sovereign [credit default swaps] today,' and people are like, 'Unlike you Stephanie, I didn't talk about it at dinner with my spouse.' And I'm like, 'Oh, I forgot, I did.'"

Ruhle and Hubbard have two sons, Harrison (b. 2006) and Reese (b. 2009), and they live in the Tribeca section of Lower Manhattan, not far from Wall Street. She discussed with *Working Mother* the issues professional women still face in raising a family. "I see that my husband's [work/life] balance is easier to achieve because his place in the world as a man is widely accepted," she said. "He's allowed to work fifteen-hour days, entertain clients at night and have few responsibilities at home. The traditional family dynamic saw no issue with fathers and husbands putting work first. But this is completely unacceptable for women, hence our dilemma." She does not accept that she needs to sacrifice either her career or her role as a mother, however. "I hate it when I hear some great working moms say they know they'll never be the best mom," she said. "The best mom is a happy mom. It's not about martyring yourself. You don't need to change ten diapers a day to be an excellent parent."

## SUGGESTED READING

Anderson, Melissa J. "Voice of Experience: Stephanie Ruhle, Managing Director, Relationship Management, Deutsche Bank." *The Glass Hammer*. Evolved People Media, 1 Aug. 2011. Web. 19 Nov. 2012.

Ruhle, Stephanie. Interview. *I Want Her Job*. Burrowes Media, 21 Aug. 2012. Web. 19 Nov. 2012.

---. Interview by Joe Weisenthal. "Meet Bloomberg's Stephanie Ruhle, the Most Important New Face on Financial TV." *Business Insider*. Business Insider, 10 Nov. 2011. Web. 19 Nov. 2012.

"Stephanie Ruhle Hubbard." *Working Mother*. Working Mother Media, Sept. 2009. Web. 19 Nov. 2012.

—*Adam Groff*

# Douglas Rushkoff

**Born:** February 18, 1961
**Occupation:** Media theorist

Writer Douglas Rushkoff has made a career out of analyzing how technology affects culture and society. In the 1990s, his work focused on the pioneers of cyberspace—the subculture of computer scientists, mathematicians, and engineers using new technologies to simultaneously create and explore the new frontier of the Internet. During the early years of the World Wide Web, when computer networking was still regarded by many as an unfamiliar novelty, predictions regarding how web-based technologies and virtual reality would change politics, economics, and entertainment reverberated widely. In the preface of his book *Cyberia: Life in the Trenches of Cyberspace* (1994), Rushkoff describes this phenomenon as "the cyberian renaissance." "Thanks to technologies like the computer, the modem, interactive media, and the Internet," he writes, "we no longer depend on printed matter or word of mouth to explore the latest innovations or discoveries."

In the mid-to-late 1990s, speculation regarding how the web would affect the world began to have a significant impact on the world economy. Entrepreneurs and business leaders across the globe raised trillions of dollars in the hopes of establishing lucrative web-based enterprises. The move to invest massive amounts of money in web-based companies came to be known as the dot-com bubble. Following the bursting of the dot-com bubble, Rushkoff's work focused on the ways in which corporate interests shaped the development of digital media and the larger economy. While he became known as a critic of the influence of business interests on the evolution of the Internet, Rushkoff also established himself as a proponent of the opportunities for cooperation and collaboration afforded by technology in a networked world. "Interactive technologies offer us a ray of hope," Rushkoff writes in *Open Source Democracy* (2003), "for a renewed spirit of genuine civic engagement." In addition to his work as a media theorist, Rushkoff has also written on religion, produced graphic novels and

© Seth Kushner/Retna Ltd./Corbis

works of fiction, and collaborated with various radio and documentary television productions. In 2013, he published *Present Shock*, an analysis of how attitudes, behaviors, and popular culture are influenced by the hyperconnectivity of mobile devices and social media.

## EARLY LIFE AND EDUCATION

Douglas Rushkoff was born on February 18, 1961, in New York City. His father, Marvin, worked as a hospital administrator. His mother, Sheila, was a social worker. Rushkoff, who would later write abundantly on teenagers and the psychology of branding, attended Scarsdale High School in Westchester County, where he was criticized by some classmates for failing to dress in accordance with current trends. "I wore Keds. Everybody else wore Pumas and Adidas," he told the *Bat Segundo Show* (31 July 2009) podcast. "We couldn't spend the money on [them] and I was teased actively and relentlessly." After graduating from high school in 1979, Rushkoff enrolled at Princeton University, where he studied English and theater. He graduated from Princeton in 1983 with a bachelor's degree. Pursuing an interest in film studies, Rushkoff next enrolled at the California Institute of the Arts (CalArts) in Valencia, California. After earning a master of fine arts in directing from CalArts in 1986, he took a postgraduate fellowship with the American Film Institute (AFI). As an AFI fellow, Rushkoff worked as an intern on the set of director Brian De Palma's film *The Bonfire of the Vanities* (1990). He later travelled to New Zealand on a Fulbright scholarship, where he worked as a lecturer on narrative. Rushkoff completed his PhD at Utrecht University in the Netherlands in 2012.

## CYBERIA

HarperCollins published Rushkoff's first book, *Cyberia: Life in the Trenches of Hyperspace*, in March 1994. The book is a series of interviews with people—many of whom were Rushkoff's friends and colleagues—who were helping to design and build the Internet during the early days of its existence. These include writer and metaphysical theorist Terrence McKenna and R. U. Sirius, cofounder and editor of *Mondo 2000* magazine. *Cyberia* tells the story of how early Internet culture was shaped by computer scientists, musicians, artists, and hackers who existed on the fringes of mainstream culture but began collaborating by way of computer networks. Rushkoff infers similarities between the counterculture of 1960s America and the early culture of the web. The book review magazine *Kirkus Reviews* (1 Apr. 1994) praised *Cyberia* as a "wide-ranging survey of the current state of interface between the longings of youth and the wild potentials of computer technology." Rushkoff published a second collection of interviews later in 1994 entitled *The GenX Reader*.

## PLAYING THE FUTURE, COERCION, AND CRITICISM

In 1996, Rushkoff published *Playing the Future: What We Can Learn from Digital Kids*, an in-depth analysis of seemingly innocuous or offensive cultural trends and the ways in which they reveal changing norms about communication and cooperation—particularly among young people. As Vanessa E. Domine of Montclair State University writes in a review of the book (*RCCS* Feb. 2000), while "adults may complain about the short attention span of the screenager,"—a term Rushkoff coined—"Rushkoff reframes it as an evolutionary survival mechanism that in reality helps kids process the massive amounts of information available to them." "Kids are leading us in our evolution," adds Domine, "past linear thinking and toward a dynamic culture."

Where *Cyberia* and *Playing the Future* celebrated the potential of the new media landscape to encourage cooperation and the democratization of ideas, Rushkoff's *Coercion: Why We Listen to What "They" Say* (1999) inhabits a more critical, foreboding viewpoint. In a review for *Booklist* (Aug. 1999), David Pitt summarizes Rushkoff's thesis. Through relentless exposure to media in the contemporary world, "we're bombarded," Pitt writes, "by appeals to our vanity, our desire to belong to a group, [and] our need for approval." "Rushkoff reveals all the tricks we use on one another," he continues, "and reminds us that, no matter how clever we think we are, we're always, inevitably, being manipulated." *Coercion* was awarded the 2002 Marshall McLuhan Award for Outstanding Book in the Field of Media Ecology. The book's focus on consumerism and corporatization, and the influence of these

forces in the larger culture, would inform much of Rushkoff's work during the next decade.

In 2003, Rushkoff published a work of religious criticism entitled *Nothing Sacred: The Truth about Judaism*, in which he argues that Judaism is losing its cultural vibrancy through a strict adherence to conservative ideals. That same year Rushkoff published *Open Source Democracy: How Online Communication Is Changing Offline Politics*, a political treatise in which he argues that the collaborative problem-solving methodology used to create open-source software on the web can be utilized to enact political change. The concept of cooperation is also central to his 2005 book *Get Back in the Box: Innovation from the Inside Out*. Contrary to trends in management philosophy stressing the importance of unconventional thinking in the pursuit of relentless growth, Rushkoff advises that organizations should focus on their established strengths and promote internal collaboration.

## FRONTLINE EPISODES

In 2001, Rushkoff served as a producer for an episode of the PBS television series *Frontline* entitled "Merchants of Cool." The program investigates the relationship between teenagers, the media, and the marketing efforts of corporations. "Merchants of Cool" suggests that despite its reputation for being subversive and cutting edge, much of youth culture is the by-product of precision market analysis and brand manipulation of major corporations. "Today," Rushkoff narrates, "five enormous companies are responsible for selling nearly all youth culture. These are the true merchants of cool." "Merchants of Cool" utilizes interviews with writers, marketers, and business leaders to demonstrate the complex relationship between marketing experts, content providers, and audiences. Those featured include social science theorist Malcolm Gladwell, MTV executive Brian Graden, and music critic Ann Powers. Writing for the *Boston Globe*, television critic John Koch comments that "Merchants of Cool" "is to be commended for raising important, scary questions about the corporatization of teen culture and whether it has displaced virtually everything honest and original." The production, which helped to raise the profile of Rushkoff's work, was generally praised by critics for its efforts to increase media literacy among young people.

In 2004, Rushkoff served as a correspondent for a second episode of *Frontline* entitled "The Persuaders." The program investigates the field of neuromarketing—the effort by marketing and public relations firms to utilize data from psychological studies, behavioral analysis, and brain-imaging technology in advertisements. "Advertisers now imagine a target audience not as pests but as spirits in need of uplift," writes

Ned Martel in a review of the program for the *New York Times* (9 Nov. 2004). "This so-called mission marketing," Martel continues, "has produced cultish brand loyalists [and] the sort of customer devotion and sense of purpose that companies want."

## MEDIA VIRUS

In 2005, Rushkoff published his first significant work of media criticism and social theory, entitled *Media Virus!: Hidden Agendas in Popular Culture*. Building on the ideas of celebrated media critic Marshall McLuhan, Rushkoff speculates that during the early to mid-twentieth century, government and industry used print and television media to co-opt public opinion in the name of politics and marketing. Later media theorists, including Rushkoff, suggest that by the century's last decade, the general public's tolerance for such messaging had been exhausted.

In *Media Virus*, Rushkoff explores the viral nature of memes in the Information Age—the new age of web- and television-based connectivity. He uses the term "datasphere" to refer to the vast territory of ideas and information created by the Internet and twenty-four-hour broadcast news that is "as open as the globe was five hundred years ago." A key element in the new media landscape, according to Rushkoff, is audience participation and audience self-analysis. In the preface of the book, he describes the 1994 televised pursuit of murder suspect and former football star O. J. Simpson in Los Angeles as a pivotal moment in media history. "Thousands of residents, watching a chase on television, realized that O. J. was going to pass their homes," writes Rushkoff. "They ran out into the street," he continues, "and onto their television screens. The viewing public participated in the event as observers and subject matter all at the same time."

While many criticized cable news, controversial talk shows, and reality television in the early 1990s as exploitative, Rushkoff theorizes that each represented new avenues for mass audiences to subvert traditionalism and begin spreading their own ideas and messages. The new media landscape, Rushkoff states, represents a paradigm shift in the realm of media activism—allowing once-suppressed ideas to be spread in a way that is similar to the biological evolution of viruses. In a review for *Mediamatic.net*, Jules Marshall summarizes Rushkoff's thesis. "The explosion in DIY [Do-It-Yourself] media," writes Marshall, "from zines to camcorders to bulletin boards, coupled with ever greater degrees of interactivity, means that media-wise Gen Xers are no longer content to let the media simply wash over them." Marshall praises *Media Virus* for avoiding both naïve positivity and pessimism in its survey of the emerging modern

media landscape. He commends Rushkoff for suggesting "media can serve to foster new cultural growth and accelerate our evolution."

## LIFE INC.

In 2009, Rushkoff published *Life Inc.: How Corporatism Conquered the World, and How We Can Take It Back*. The book follows the history of the corporation from its beginnings in the fifteenth century through the global economic crisis of 2008. As Sarah Jaffe of *Global Comment* (24 May 2009) notes, "Rushkoff lays bare the history of corporations and how our society became shaped in their image. He theorizes that corporatism has such a hold on us that we tend to live our entire lives like miniature corporations, thinking only of the short-term value of things and seeing other people solely as assets to be managed." Modern society and consumerism, Rushkoff argues in *Life Inc.*, has degraded the public's sense of self-worth. In an interview with Jaffe, Rushkoff discusses his view that the reach and power of multinational corporations has resulted in the corporate model being mirrored by labor groups and other activists, which overshadows the importance of small-scale activity. "Those of us in activism, trying to do good things, are now stuck believing that unless the thing we're doing is big, then it's not real or not worth anything," says Rushkoff. "That's an awful trap," he adds, "because often it's real, up until it gets to be big." In his review of *Life Inc.* for the *Guardian* (31 July 2009), Pat Kane criticizes Rushkoff for over-generalizing life in contemporary society, claiming he "bundles together complex trends into a monolith called 'corporatism.'" "For [Rushkoff]," Kane writes, "corporatism isn't just a form of commercial enterprise. It's also a kind of permanent civilization war" that pits "local, face-to-face virtue" against "universal, faceless vice." Kane argues that the reality is less black-and-white than *Life Inc.* portrays it. He cites as an example the use of Internet platforms by political dissidents in Iran. Other viewers praised *Life Inc.* for posing difficult questions about the relationship between business and culture. Author Jonathan Lethem called it "Rushkoff's best and most important book."

## PRESENT SHOCK

In 2013, Rushkoff published *Present Shock: When Everything Happens Now*. The book examines how popular culture and community psychology have been impacted by the hyperconnectivity and endless streams of information in today's digital society. Combining his interest in media criticism and sociology, Rushkoff theorizes that where public consciousness in the late twentieth-century was relentlessly forward-looking and anticipating the next miraculous technological breakthrough, the beginning of the twenty-first century represented a great arrival and a new obsession with the present, or "nowness." There has been "a diminishment of everything that isn't happening right now," writes Rushkoff. In her March 12, 2013, review for the *New York Times*, Janet Maslin writes that *Present Shock* is "one of those invaluable books that makes sense of what we already half-know. The future arrived a little while ago. Now it's here." Among the concepts that Rushkoff explores in the book are the collapse of the use of traditional, linear narratives in movies and television, and the effects of the digitally connected life on natural biological relationships with time, or "chronobiology."

## OTHER WORKS AND ACHIEVEMENTS
Rushkoff published his first novel, *Ecstasy Club*, in 1997. The novel tells the story of a group of twenty-somethings organizing a rave in an abandoned piano factory. His second work of fiction, *Exit Strategy* (2002), is a science fiction story influenced by the dot-com boom. Rushkoff is also the author of three graphic novels, including *Club Zero-G* (2004), *Testament* (2005–8), and *A.D.D.* (2011).

In addition to his best-selling books, Rushkoff has written for the *Guardian, Daily Beast*, and *New York Times*, and has hosted a podcast called *The Media Squat* (2008–9) for WFMU in New York. He teaches at the New School University in Manhattan. In 2004, he received the Neil Postman Award for Career Achievement in Public Intellectual Activity from the Media Ecology Association. He and his wife, Barbara, have one daughter.

## SUGGESTED READING
Domine, Vanessa E. Rev. of *Playing the Future* by D. Rushkoff. *Resource Center for Cyberculture Studies*, Feb. 2000. Web. 16 Sept. 2013.
Jaffe, Sarah. "*Life Inc.*: An Interview with Douglas Rushkoff." *Global Comment*. Global Comment, 24 May 2009. Web. 16 Sept. 2013.
Kane, Pat. Rev. of *Life Inc.* by D. Rushkoff. *Independent*. Independent.co.uk, 31 July 2009. Web. 16 Sept. 2013.
Koch, John. "Preying on Teen Culture for Profit: *Frontline* Explores How MTV Keeps Cool and Makes Millions." *Boston Globe*. New York Times Co., 26 Feb. 2001. Web. 16 Sept. 2013.
Marshall, Jules. "Media Virus—Hidden Agendas in Popular Culture." *Mediamatic*. Mediamatic, 1 Oct. 1996. Web. 12 Sept. 2013.
Maslin, Janet. "Out of Time: The Sins of Immediacy." *New York Times*. New York Times Co., 12 Mar. 2013. Web. 12 Sept. 2013.
Pitt, David. Rev. of *Coercion: Why We Listen to What "They" Say* by D. Rushkoff. *Booklist Online*. Booklist Publications, Aug. 1999. Web. 16 Sept. 2013.

## SELECTED WORKS
*Cyberia*, 1994; *The GenX Reader*, 1994; *Playing the Future*, 1996; *Coercion*, 1999; "The Merchants of Cool," 2001; *Open Source Democracy*, 2003; "The Persuaders," 2004; *Media Virus*, 2005; *Life Inc.*, 2009; *Present Shock*, 2013

—Josh Pritchard

# Paul Ryan
**Born:** January 29, 1970
**Occupation:** Politician

A Wisconsin congressman by age twenty-eight and the 2012 Republican vice-presidential nominee by forty-two, Paul Ryan's rise in national politics has been both spectacular and unanticipated. More a self-described "policy wonk" than a politician, Ryan has exerted enormous influence on his party by sticking to fundamental conservative principles—lower taxes, smaller government—with scant regard for the political consequences. His visionary, policy-over-politics approach led him to present a version of the federal budget in 2008—radically curtailing popular entitlement programs like Social Security and Medicare—that was initially regarded by all but a few of his colleagues as too hot to touch. However, it won the hearts of conservative ideologues and opinion makers, and by 2011, the "Ryan budget" had become party orthodoxy, embraced by the overwhelming majority Republicans in Congress as well as Republican presidential nominee Mitt Romney, who ultimately selected Ryan as his running mate in a strong though ultimately unsuccessful bid to unseat President Barack Obama in 2012. Despite his first-ever electoral defeat, Ryan was positioned at the start of 2013 to wield extraordinary influence in the Republican Party in Congress.

## BACKGROUND AND EDUCATION
Paul Davis Ryan was born and raised in Janesville, Wisconsin, the youngest of four children in an Irish Catholic family with deep local roots. His great-grandfather established an earthmoving company in Janesville in 1884, and today Ryan Incorporated Central is a national concern. Paul Ryan's branch of the family, however, left the family business, his grandfather and father becoming lawyers instead.

A formative experience early in Ryan's life was the death of his father from a heart attack when Ryan was sixteen. "It was just a big punch in the gut. I concluded I've got to either sink or swim in life," Ryan told Ryan Lizza for the *New Yorker* (6 Aug. 2012) of the event. "I grew up really fast." He dove into his schoolwork and extracurricular activities and was elected class

Getty Images

president his junior year. He also began cultivating his lifelong habit of consuming thick volumes of literature that appealed to him, discovering the works of twentieth-century Russian American novelist and philosopher Ayn Rand, a radical exponent of laissez-faire capitalism. "What I liked about her novels was their devastating indictment of the fatal conceit of socialism, of too much government," he told Lizza. In 2005, speaking before a group of Rand devotees called the Atlas Society, he said, "The reason I got involved in public service, by and large, if I had to credit one thinker, one person, it would be Ayn Rand." (Ryan has, however, been careful to distance himself from Rand's atheist beliefs.)

In 1988, Ryan enrolled at Miami University in Ohio, where he double majored in economics and political science, delving deeper into the works of libertarian and free-market philosophers such as Rand, Friedrich Hayek, and Milton Friedman. The summer before his junior year, he got his first taste of national politics when he secured an internship in the office of Wisconsin senator Bob Kasten. Ryan reported to Republican staff director Cesar Conda, who told Stephen Hayes for the *Weekly Standard* (23 July 2012), "Paul at age nineteen was the exact same person he is today. Earnest, personable, and hard-working, with an insatiable appetite for discussing policy ideas." The following summer, he returned to intern with the House Small Business Committee, on which Kasten sat.

## EARLY CAREER

After graduating in 1992, at the invitation of Conda, Ryan briefly joined Kasten's staff as an

economist with the Small Business Committee. The following year, he took a job as a policy analyst and speechwriter with Empower America, a think tank run by conservative activists Jack Kemp and William Bennett, who both became important mentors for Ryan. During this time, Ryan supplemented his income by waiting tables at Tortilla Coast, a Tex-Mex restaurant on Capitol Hill.

In 1995, following the Republican takeover of Congress under House Speaker Newt Gingrich, Ryan, at the young age of twenty-five, was hired as legislative director for freshman congressman Sam Brownback of Kansas, and he immediately began making his mark as a policy expert. Brownback recalled to Hayes that the young Ryan "was very puritanical on economic policy," consistently advocating for a small-government approach with little appreciation for the give-and-take of practical politics. "It's all policy to him," said Brownback. "People don't appreciate just how much of a policy guy Ryan is and how little of a politician he is."

Ryan was not a politician at all until 1997, when Republican congressman Mark Neumann of Wisconsin's First District decided to run for Senate and suggested that Ryan run to fill his seat. With five years of policy and staff work behind him, Ryan took up the challenge, running in the 1998 election and winning the House seat he has held ever since. At twenty-eight, he was at the time the second-youngest member of Congress.

## FIRST YEARS IN CONGRESS

Of Ryan's new job, Jennifer Steinhauer and Jonathan Weisman wrote for the *New York Times*, "He did not arrive in Congress as a superstar, but he did possess a skill that would make him one: a genuine interest in the federal budget." Assigned to the House Budget Committee, Ryan set to work in his junior position. Former Democratic representative John M. Spratt Jr. of South Carolina told Steinhauer and Weisman, "When he first got there, he did his yeoman's work as a backbencher. He mastered a lot of budget."

Hayes wrote in the *Weekly Standard*, "Ryan was regarded as a quiet policy wonk in the early stages of his congressional career—a respected conservative reformer but not necessarily someone his colleagues envisioned as a party leader. He brought to office the same interest in economics and spending that had driven him as a staffer and quickly acquired a greater appreciation of the trade-offs involved in pushing for free-market policy outcomes while also seeking to serve constituents."

Ryan made many such trade-offs during the administration of President George W. Bush, including voting for Bush's Medicare prescription-drug benefit in 2003—a vote he justified by saying the president was intent on signing some version of the plan into law, so Ryan backed a bill containing amendments with free-market reforms he supported. In 2008, he also supported the Troubled Asset Relief Program (TARP), the multi-billion-dollar bank bailout launched in response to the subprime mortgage crisis. Ryan later told Lizza that votes such as these made him "miserable" and that he had vowed "to do everything I can to make sure I don't feel that misery again."

But as he made these compromises, Ryan also set about putting his core principles into action. During Bush's 2004 reelection campaign, Ryan worked on a plan to privatize Social Security—one of the most enduringly popular entitlement programs and therefore, despite its tremendous cost, long considered a third rail of domestic politics. Since 1935, the program, financed by payroll taxes, has guaranteed government payments to the elderly and disabled, keeping millions out of poverty and making proposals to alter it extremely politically risky. Ryan's plan, the premise of which had been bandied about in conservative think tanks but had not entered mainstream political discourse, involved allowing workers to keep a portion of their payroll taxes and invest them in private retirement accounts. Conservative activists from Kemp to Gingrich loved the idea and put pressure on the president and reluctant congressional Republicans to back it. In 2005, Bush released a watered-down version of the plan that was savagely attacked by Democrats and failed to win widespread public support. In the 2006 midterm elections, Republicans lost their majority in Congress. "What some might interpret as the failure of an unpopular idea Ryan insisted was mostly a communications problem," wrote Lizza, quoting Ryan as saying the proposal was poorly received because the Bush administration "did a bad job of selling it."

## ROADMAP FOR AMERICA'S FUTURE
Undeterred, Ryan returned for his fifth term and persuaded then–house majority leader John Boehner and other party leaders to make him the ranking Republican on the House Budget Committee, leapfrogging over twelve other Republicans with more seniority. This position gave him a larger staff and access to the Congressional Budget Office, which could crunch the numbers of any budget proposal Ryan came up with.

In 2007 and early 2008, Ryan and his team worked on crafting an alternative to the Democratic budget. He named it the Roadmap for America's Future and introduced it as legislation in May 2008. "When I wrote this, I didn't ask the leadership for permission," Ryan told Hayes. "I figured, ask for forgiveness later and not permission first." The introduction to Ryan's Roadmap read like a conservative manifesto:

America faces a choice between two fiscal and economic futures. In one, the Federal Government attempts to satisfy the multiple needs of a changing population, in a rapidly changing world, with outdated policies that demand ever-rising levels of public spending. The effort overwhelms the government's capacities, and smothers the economy under crushing burdens of debt and high taxes. It is a future in which America's best century is the past century.

The second future calls for a transformation—or more accurately, a restoration of the principles that created America's freedom and prosperity. It is the path set out in a plan I have developed called A Roadmap for America's Future.

In particular, summarized Lizza, "Ryan recommended ending Medicare, the government health-insurance program for retirees, and replacing it with a system of direct payments to seniors, who could then buy private insurance. . . . He proposed ending Medicaid, the health-care program for the poor, and replacing it with a lump sum for states to use as they saw fit. Ryan also called for an end to the special tax break given to employers who provide insurance; instead, that money would pay for twenty-five-hundred-dollar credits for uninsured taxpayers to buy their own plans. As for Social Security, Ryan modestly scaled back his original proposal by reducing the amount invested in private accounts, from one-half to one-third of payroll taxes."

## A RISING PROFILE
Conservative think tanks and commentators lauded the Ryan plan, but Republicans in Congress backed away from it. Later that year, Barack Obama won the presidency. As the country battled an economic crisis and Obama pushed through an economic stimulus package, Ryan shelved his budget plan until early 2010. In January, he produced an updated version of the Roadmap, and his profile began to rise as he engaged the president directly on budget issues, first at a retreat for House Republicans in Baltimore at which Obama was a guest and again at a health-care summit hosted by the administration in February. Here was a relatively young congressman, not even in his party's leadership, matching wits with the president of the United States over major budgetary issues.

While most congressional Republicans remained skeptical about the political viability of the Roadmap, Ryan's ability and willingness to engage the Obama administration with facts and figures garnered increasing support from conservative opinion makers, and pressure began to grow on elected leaders to back the plan. In the November 2010 elections, the Republicans recaptured the majority in the House of Representatives, with many seats going to upstart "Tea Party" candidates who swept into office on a tide of red-state alarm about federal deficits and government spending. Ryan seemed to have just the plan these incoming freshmen were looking for, and he worked hard to sell it to them, as well as to party leaders facing new pressure for dramatic change. "I think the validation of the 2010 elections gave [Republican] leadership the courage to proceed—2010 woke people up," Ryan told Hayes. "The eighty-seven new freshman were a welcome burst of energy, and I think leadership understood that they had two choices: They could lead the parade, or they could get out of the way."

Steinhauer and Weisman wrote, "Whether Mr. Ryan helped galvanize the Tea Party with his tough-medicine budget ideas or simply rode its wave is a matter of debate. But there is no question that the rising concern over the deficit and the arrival in 2010 of eighty-seven Republican freshmen who were loyal to Mr. Ryan's ideas made him the intellectual leader of the House's majority party."

## THE PATH TO PROSPERITY

As if to confirm his new stature, in January 2011, Ryan, now chairman of the House Budget Committee, was selected to deliver the Republican response to Obama's State of the Union Address; in his speech, Ryan said the national debt is "out of control" and that "what was a fiscal challenge is now a fiscal crisis" that must be met with serious spending cuts. In April, he rolled out an updated version of his budget plan, titled the Path to Prosperity. The Ryan budget, many of whose central proposals his colleagues had deemed unworthy of consideration only three years earlier, was now the official Republican budget proposal for fiscal year 2012. This version dropped the modifications to Social Security but retained plans to scale back Medicaid and Medicare and added provisions for the repeal of the Patient Protection and Affordable Care Act, Obama's national health-care law, widely denounced by Republicans as akin to European-style socialism. Ninety-seven percent of the Republicans in both houses of Congress voted in favor of the budget (which failed in the Democrat-controlled Senate). An updated version was submitted again in March 2012 as the Republican proposal for fiscal year 2013.

With congressional Republicans in full support of the Ryan budget as of spring 2011, the slate of 2012 Republican presidential candidates could not avoid taking a position on it; the prestige it had attained was demonstrated by the implosion of the campaign of Newt Gingrich, attributed in part to his characterization of the Ryan budget in May 2011 as "right-wing social engineering." The eventual Republican nominee, Mitt Romney, went further than endorsing the budget; in a bold move, he selected Ryan as his running mate in early August 2012.

## VICE-PRESIDENTIAL CANDIDATE

"Vice Presidential nominees rarely shape the course of a campaign," Michael Crowley wrote for *Time* magazine (22 Oct. 2012). "But Romney's selection of a Congressman famous for budget blueprints so austere that President Obama called them 'social Darwinism' stirred unusual passions from the start. The Obama campaign called Ryan 'radical' and 'extreme,' while conservatives saw something closer to deliverance and geared up for an epic clash of policy visions."

The Romney and Obama campaigns did clash over unemployment, social issues, and Medicare, among other issues—although the Medicare debate seemed to hover around which side's plan would damage it more, the Ryan budget or the Obama health-care law—but both sides avoided dwelling in detail on the specifics of their own plan to rein in spending on the popular entitlement program. Some conservatives wanted to hear a full-throated defense of Ryan's approach, but Republican strategists considered that too risky.

"Liberals say there's an obvious reason for muffling the Ryan message," Crowley wrote. "The public doesn't support balancing the budget through huge spending cuts. Columnists may extol Ryan's budgets as visionary and hardheaded, but their particulars have never been popular. For instance, only 18 percent of Americans would support major cuts to Medicare to reduce the deficit, according to a June 2011 Kaiser Family Foundation poll."

Policy details aside, Ryan's youth, good looks, and folksy Midwestern demeanor were also considered an asset to the Romney campaign. In October, less than a month before the November election, Ryan met Vice President Joe Biden for the campaign's only vice-presidential debate. The candidates locked horns over US policy in the Middle East as well as taxes, health care, and entitlement programs. Public opinion following the debate gave a slight edge to Biden, but Ryan's respectable showing against a man who had been in national politics since Ryan was a toddler earned widespread admiration as well.

On November 6, however, Barack Obama was reelected convincingly, leaving Republicans to sort out what went wrong. For Ryan, who was also elected to an eighth term in the House, it was his first-ever electoral defeat; he told Bill Glauber for the *Milwaukee Journal Sentinel* (12 Nov. 2012) that it was "a foreign experience; it's tough to describe." Questions immediately arose about whether Ryan himself might consider a run for the presidency in 2016, but he brushed aside such speculation. "Right now, I look at what I've just been reelected to do, to represent Wisconsin, to be the chairman of the Budget Committee, to deal with these budget and fiscal and economic issues," he told Juana Summers for *Politico* (12 Nov. 2012). "I'm going to throw myself back to that work because it's work that needs to get done."

## PERSONAL LIFE AND FAMILY

In 2000, Ryan married Janna Little, a Washington lobbyist from a prominent Democratic family in Oklahoma. A lawyer and tax specialist who has represented major firms such as PricewaterhouseCoopers and Blue Cross Blue Shield, Janna Ryan gave up her Washington career to join her husband in Janesville and raise a family. Though their families are on different sides of the political divide—Janna's first cousin is former Oklahoma Democratic congressman Dan Boren—Paul and Janna Ryan share midwestern conservative values and a love of hunting and fishing. They have three young children, Liza, Charlie, and Sam.

Paul Ryan is a well-known fitness buff, a lifestyle choice he attributes to his father's and grandfather's deaths from heart attacks at relatively young ages. Ryan's devotion to the P90X intensive cross-training fitness program was well documented during the presidential campaign.

## SUGGESTED READING

Chait, Jonathan. "The Legendary Paul Ryan." *New York Magazine*. New York Media, 29 Apr. 2012. Web. 14 Nov. 2012.

Crowley, Michael. "The Phenom." *Time Magazine*. Time, 22 Oct. 2012. Web. 14 Nov. 2012.

Gilbert, Craig. "Ryan Shines as GOP Seeks Vision." *Milwaukee Journal Sentinel*. Journal Sentinel, 25 Apr. 2009. Web. 14 Nov. 2012.

Hayes, Stephen F. "Man with a Plan: How Paul Ryan Became the Intellectual Leader of the Republican Party." *Weekly Standard*. Weekly Standard, 23 July 2012. Web. 14 Nov. 2012.

Lizza, Ryan. "Fussbudget: How Paul Ryan Captured the GOP." *New Yorker*. Condé Nast, 6 Aug. 2012. Web. 14 Nov. 2012.

—*Adam Groff*

# Joe Sacco

**Born:** October 2, 1960
**Occupation:** Cartoonist, journalist

"What hits me in the gut is an interesting story," Joe Sacco told Duncan Campbell for the London *Guardian* (22 Oct. 2003), and he has traveled to some of the most dangerous places in the world in pursuit of an interesting story. The work of

AP Photo

the award-winning comic journalist represents a unique cross of the graphic novel (a term he eschews) with wartime reporting. The genre, while small, is not new. The first and best-known example of comic journalism—with a postmodern twist that is absent in Sacco's realistically rendered work—is the graphic novel *Maus* (1980) by Art Spiegelman. Spiegelman wrote the book about his father's experiences in a Nazi concentration camp during World War II.

Sacco immerses himself in the lives of his subjects and presents their narratives, unembellished, in the structure of long-form comics. The taste of Palestinian tea as well as the taunts of American soldiers (as remembered by Iraqi prisoners) are details that find a home in his stories. But perhaps the most unusual detail is Sacco himself, whom he draws as a cartoonish, self-effacing figure with eyes hidden behind the glare of his glasses, conducting interviews and exploring peoples' homes. In his books, Sacco seeks to uncover what Rebecca Tuhus-Dubrow for *January Magazine* (June 2003) called "the overlooked minutiae of oppression," but he also seeks to understand the root of ongoing violence among humans. In *Footnotes in Gaza* (2009), Sacco comes close to that understanding. The book details two largely forgotten (and in some circles, disputed) mid-twentieth-century massacres of Palestinians by Israeli soldiers in the Gaza Strip towns of Rafah and Khan Younis. Events such as these, Sacco writes (as quoted by Patrick Cockburn for the *New York Times*) "often contain the seeds of the grief and anger that shape present-day events."

Fans of Sacco's work praise his effective blend of art and journalistic prose; like a documentary filmmaker, he is able to capture the perspective of each "character" through composition and careful editing. Sacco often spends years rendering a single book (*Footnotes in Gaza* took him nearly seven years), but he views the time spent as a responsibility to the people he has interviewed who are often telling their personal histories for the first and only time. "When you draw, you can always capture that moment," he told Hillary Chute for the *Believer* magazine (June 2011). "You can always have that exact, precise moment when someone's got the club raised, when someone's going down. I realize now there's a lot of power in that."

Sacco won the prestigious American Book Award in 1996 for *Palestine*, and his book, *Safe Area Goražde: The War in Eastern Bosnia 1992–1995* won the Eisner Award in 2001 for best graphic album. Sacco is also the recipient of a Guggenheim Fellowship.

**EARLY LIFE AND TRAVELS**

Sacco was born in Kirkop, a village on the Mediterranean island of Malta, on October 2, 1960. (He holds dual citizenship in Malta and the United States.) As a child, he listened to his mother's stories about Malta during World War II. She was six years old when the war began, and Sacco was struck by the violence she was exposed to. He asked his mother to recount her experiences to him in a series of letters, and based on the letters, he wrote "More Women, More Children, More Quickly," first published in 1990 in *Yahoo* for Fantagraphics Books. (*Yahoo* was incorporated into the anthology *Notes from a Defeatist* in 2003.) The title of the story—about the civilian bombings in Malta—comes from a quote by British prime minister Stanley Baldwin. Addressing the House of Commons in 1932, Baldwin warned of the dangers of airpower and the defenselessness of civilians against it. "The bomber will always get through," he said. "The only defense is offense, which means that you have to kill more women and children, more quickly than the enemy if you want to save yourselves" (Marshall 9–10).

Sacco began reading and drawing at the age of seven; his other childhood interests included military history and following the war in Vietnam. (Sacco was a preteen at the height of the war.) He even wrote his own comic about the Vietnam War while he was still in high school. He submitted it to Spiegelman's alternative-comic magazine, *RAW*, for publication. It was rejected.

When Sacco was an infant, his family—which included his mother, his father, and older sister Maryanne—moved to a suburb outside of Melbourne, Australia. When Sacco was twelve, they moved to Los Angeles, California, and then settled in Beaverton, Oregon, where Sacco graduated from Sunset High School. Influenced by writers like George Orwell and Michael Herr, the author of the Vietnam War book *Dispatches*, Sacco chose to study journalism at the University of Oregon. He completed his BA degree in three years and graduated in 1981.

**SACCO'S FIRST COMICS**

After graduation, Sacco worked for the National Notary Association in Los Angeles but found the work boring. He decided to return to Malta in 1983, and for a year he worked for a local publisher writing guidebooks. He convinced the publisher to produce several of his romance comics under the title *Imhabba Vera* ("True Love"). It was Malta's first comic book series.

When he returned to the United States several years later, Sacco coedited a free humor magazine called the *Portland Permanent Press* with Tom Richards, who is now the curator of Portland's Faux Museum. The publication folded after fifteen issues due to a lack of funds. (Sacco, by his own account, spent most of his twenties and thirties borrowing money from friends and family because he made so little money.) In 1986, Sacco began working for Los Angeles comics publisher Fantagraphics Books. He edited the humor magazine *Honk!* and he re-created it as the more comic-oriented *Centrifugal Bumble-Puppy*, named for the children's game featured in Aldous Huxley's 1932 novel *Brave New World*. He also edited the news section of the *Comics Journal*. He left the country again in 1988.

Throughout the late 1980s, Sacco traveled and worked on his own comic series titled *Yahoo*—a name that he associated with eighteenth-century satirist Jonathan Swift. The series is largely autobiographical. His European travels as a roadie with the punk band the Miracle Workers, his mother's World War II experiences, and the breakup with his girlfriend are all documented. (Stories about the Miracle Workers as well as other stories about music have also been compiled in the 2006 anthology *But I Like It.*) One story in particular, which Sacco still considers his best, is called "How I Loved the War." Sacco was living in Berlin at the time, and the story offers a detailed account of the first Gulf War and reflects on Sacco's feelings toward it. Still in Europe, Sacco became fascinated with the Israeli-Palestinian conflict during the first intifada in the early 1990s. In the same manner of his previous work, he told Sam Adams for the *A.V. Club* (10 June 2011), "I just thought I would do comics about my experiences, then go to the Middle East."

**PALESTINE**

Sacco's travels to the Middle East eventually engendered a very different kind of story. "When I was there, something clicked in my head," he told Dave Gilson for the magazine *Mother Jones* (July/Aug. 2005). "I found myself interviewing people, searching out facts and figures." He spent two months during late 1991 and early

1992 traveling with Palestinians through Jerusalem and the occupied territories. Sacco then traveled to Palestine to talk to the people there because, as he recounts in *Palestine*, "I've heard nothing but the Israeli side most of my life."

Still, Sacco recalls nervously telling people he was working on a comic, fearing that they would laugh at him. On several occasions, he described his early demeanor as "bumbling" and, as told to Rachel Cooke for the *Guardian* (21 Nov. 2009), as if he was committing "commercial suicide." His fears were not without merit. *Palestine* was originally published as a series of nine comics beginning in 1993, and each installment sold worse than the one before. The last, according to Sacco, sold less than two thousand copies in the United States. The slow and painful disappointment of *Palestine* was a key factor in Sacco's decision to publish his next project, *Safe Area Goražde: The War in Eastern Bosnia 1992–95* (2000), as a single volume.

## SAFE AREA GORAŽDE

*Safe Area Goražde* was the first of three books that Sacco would write about the Balkan conflicts. He made four trips to Goražde, a Muslim area and the United Nations (UN) designated "safe" zone under siege in Bosnia, in the winter of 1995 and early 1996. By his own concession, *Safe Area Goražde* represented not only a shift toward a more journalistic methodology—Sacco takes pictures of his surroundings as well as willing interviewees so he can accurately render them later—but it was also a shift to a more realistic style of drawing. The book, which won the 2001 Eisner Award for best graphic album, gained national attention. Ironically, the book's success came at a time when Sacco was reassessing his career. "I'd say the turning point came when the book was reviewed by the *New York Times Book Review*," he told Adams. (The *New York Times* named *Safe Area Goražde* a notable book of the year.) Soon, other publications were reviewing the book. The attention elevated Sacco from the relative obscurity of the comic world to a mainstream audience. He received a fellowship from the Guggenheim Foundation and, he added, "I stopped having to worry about next month's rent." The popularity of *Safe Area Goražde* also brought renewed interest to *Palestine*. According to Sacco, sales figures show that the latter has long outsold the former. "I think [*Palestine* will] be the book I'm remembered for," he told Cooke.

*Palestine* won the prestigious American Book Award in 1996; in 2001, Fantagraphics Books released *Palestine* as a single volume. In the forward to that edition, the late Palestinian intellectual Edward Said wrote, "With the exception of one or two novelists and poets, no one has ever rendered this terrible state of affairs better than Joe Sacco."

Sacco's follow-up to *Safe Area Goražde* was called *The Fixer: A Story from Sarajevo* (2003). The book is named for an army veteran named Neven, known as "the fixer," with whom Sacco discusses the horrors of the war in 2001. Sacco's third book about the Balkans was *War's End: Profiles from Bosnia 1995–96* (2005). The book is comprised of two stories, previously published separately, from Sacco's experiences in Bosnia. The first was called "Christmas with Karadzic," and the title refers to the Bosnian Serb leader Radovan Karadzic. Sacco met Karadzic, who is sometimes called the "Butcher of Bosnia," on Christmas in 1996. The episode was chilling in its ordinariness, Sacco reports. "That story is really about the fight between being a journalist and being someone who actually cares about what they write about," Sacco told Gilson regarding the man who had committed so many atrocities. (Karadzic was later indicted by The Hague on charges of genocide.) The second story, "Šoba," is about the life of a Sarajevo man of the same name.

## OTHER WORKS

In 1998, *Details* magazine and its comics editor Art Spiegelman commissioned Sacco to cover the Bosnian war crimes trials in The Hague, Netherlands. The resulting story, which won widespread praise, was called "Portrait of The Hague as a Young Court." In 2000, Sacco went on tour with the late American blues singer and guitarist, R. L. Burnside. The result was a piece called "The Rude Blues," which was later collected in *But I Like It* (2006). Perhaps Sacco's most ambitious creation, *Footnotes in Gaza*, was published by the mainstream publisher Metropolitan Books in 2009. Split into two parts, the work examines the massacres that took place during the Suez crisis in 1956 in the Gaza towns of Rafah and Khan Younis. Sacco was inspired to write the book after he and journalist Chris Hedges collaborated on a story for *Harper's Magazine* about Khan Younis during the second intifada. They wrote about the 1956 massacres, but magazine editors, believing the story to be irrelevant, cut any mention of it from the published article. The events are largely forgotten to history and are adamantly disputed by several Israeli scholars. However, as Sacco's painstakingly rendered work shows, the events left as profound an impact on the survivors and their families as the current violence between Israelis and Palestinians does in 2012. For those survivors and even their children, Sacco believes, the events are not "history" at all. "It gives you this idea, especially in the particular case of the Palestinians, that history hasn't really stopped. They've never had the luxury of looking back and isolating things, and thinking about it and coming to terms with it," he told Chute. "Every generation is somehow brutalized, and their parents are transmitting bitterness and frustration." The book received the Ridenhour Book Prize in 2010.

*Journalism* (2012) is a collection of Sacco's short pieces that have appeared in other publications. "The Unwanted," is about African migrants in Malta and was originally published in the *Virginia Quarterly Review*; "Chechen War, Chechen Women" examines female refugees during the war in Chechnya and was originally published in Mia Kirshner's book *I Live Here* (2008); and "Kushinagar" explores India's Untouchables and was originally published in the French magazine *XXI*.

### DAYS OF DESTRUCTION, DAYS OF REVOLT

Sacco has partnered with the Pulitzer Prize-winning journalist Chris Hedges on numerous articles in the past; in 2012, they collaborated on the book *Days of Destruction, Days of Revolt*. It was Sacco's first major project that focused on life in the United States. The two journalists traveled to the Pine Ridge Lakota reservation in South Dakota; the tomato fields of Florida; the post-industrial town of Camden, New Jersey; and the area surrounding Blair Mountain in West Virginia, hoping to capture the faces of American poverty in the twenty-first century. By all accounts, the depictions are bleak, and Hedges concludes the book, somewhat controversially, with a call to arms. Referring to the conditions and depth of American poverty, Hedges wrote, as quoted by Philipp Meyer in a review for the *New York Times* (17 Aug. 2012), "There are no excuses left. Either you join the revolt or you stand on the wrong side of history."

Sacco lives in Portland, Oregon. He loves music, and he cites the Rolling Stones and the American New Wave punk group Devo as major influences.

### SUGGESTED READING

Adams, Sam. "Interview: Joe Sacco." *A.V. Club.* Onion Inc., 10 June 2011. Web. 15 Sept. 2012.

Campbell, Duncan. "I Do Comics, Not Graphic Novels." *Guardian.* Guardian News and Media Ltd., 22 Oct. 2003. Web. 15 Sept. 2012.

Chute, Hillary. "Joe Sacco: Comics Journalist." *Believer.* The Believer, June 2011. Web. 15 Sept. 2012.

Cockburn, Patrick. "They Planted Hatred in Our Hearts." *New York Times* 27 Dec. 2009: BR13. Print.

Cooke, Rachel. "Eyeless in Gaza." *Guardian.* Guardian News and Media Ltd., 21 Nov. 2009. Web. 15 Sept. 2012.

Gilson, Dave. "The Art of War: An Interview with Joe Sacco." *Mother Jones.* Mother Jones and the Foundation for National Progress, July/Aug. 2005. Web. 14 Sept. 2012.

Marshall, Monica. *Joe Sacco.* New York: Rosen, 2005. Print.

Tuhus-Dubrow, Rebecca. "January Interview: Joe Sacco." *January Magazine.* January Magazine, 1 June 2003. Web. 16 Sept. 2012.

### SELECTED WORKS

*Palestine*, 1993; *Safe Area Goražde: The War in Eastern Bosnia 1992–95*, 2000; *The Fixer: A Story from Sarajevo*, 2003; *Notes from a Defeatist*, 2003; *War's End: Profiles from Bosnia 1995–96*, 2005; *But I Like It*, 2006; *Footnotes in Gaza*, 2009; *Days of Destruction, Days of Revolt* (with Chris Hedges), 2012; *Journalism*, 2012

—Molly Hagan

# Maritza Sáenz Ryan

**Born:** ca. 1960
**Occupation:** Professor and head of the department of law at the US Military Academy

Of the many institutions that have been traditionally phallocentric, perhaps the military holds the distinction as being most guilty of male-centered exclusivity. According to the Women in Military Service for America Memorial Foundation (based on statistical information from the Department of Defense and Coast Guard), in 2011, women comprised 14.6 percent of active-duty military personnel, a relatively large number considering women were allowed to make up only 2 percent of the US military until 1967. It was within this social time frame that Maritza Sáenz Ryan entered the United States Military Academy at West Point as part of the class of 1982, only the third class to admit female cadets. As Sáenz Ryan writes in her 2009 essay "In Blood and Spirit," her inclusion at an institution known as a male sphere of influence was groundbreaking and was recognized as such by her family and fellow cadets. "The West Point name is inseparable from the tradition of Duty, Honor, Country, and every male who came here was seen as fulfilling that tradition. For a woman at that pivotal time in our nation's history, however, it seemed a revolutionary act."

Sáenz Ryan, who went on to complete a law degree, has made a lifetime commitment to both the US military and that revolutionary ideal that women soldiers should rank on par with their male counterparts. She has risen to the rank of colonel and is the head of the department of law at West Point, becoming the first woman (and Hispanic) to be appointed the head of any department in West Point's long history, along the way advocating for the increased presence of women in the workforce, specifically in the military and legal realms. A wife and mother of

Visual Information/DPTMS U.S. Army Garrison, West Point

two boys, Sáenz Ryan has come to epitomize the modern woman, whose strengths and commitments can be evenly distributed among domestic and professional lives, and she has become an inspiration to a generation of students and military personnel, both female and male, who grasp the importance of a balanced military that allows for equal opportunities for women.

## EARLY LIFE AND EDUCATION

Sáenz Ryan was born in New York City, in approximately 1960, to immigrant parents. Her father emigrated from Puerto Rico and her mother from Spain. She grew up in Manhattan and, because of her obvious academic gifts, received a scholarship to a girls' preparatory high school. During high school, she and her classmates took a field trip to West Point, at a time when the academy was still exclusively for men. Though she dreamed of attending the military academy, exclusionary policies made such a notion seem impossible. However, by the time Sáenz Ryan graduated from high school, West Point had abolished its guidelines that forbade female attendees, based on Public Law 94-106, a congressional provision that called for the secretary of the military to institute practices that allowed for female admission to military academies; Sáenz Ryan was accepted to the academy as part of the third class to allow women.

"Frankly, the thought that I could make it through West Point, become colonel, and then be selected the first woman department head, was not a thought that would have entered my mind" at the time of her enrollment at the school (qtd. by R. A. Burks in *ABNow*, 25 July 2011).

However, her admittance to West Point sparked one fortuitous opportunity after another. After graduating, Sáenz Ryan was commissioned as a second lieutenant and given her first assignment, joining the First Armored Division at Pinder Barracks in what was then West Germany. While at West Point, she had discovered her passion for law; while in West Germany, because of her academic achievements and unblemished military record, she was granted the opportunity to pursue her interest in the legal profession, as she was chosen to be part of the Army's Funded Legal Education Program.

Sáenz Ryan attended Vanderbilt University Law School in Nashville, Tennessee, where she graduated with a law degree and became part of the Order of the Coif, an honor society for graduates in the ninetieth percentile of their class. Admitted to the New York bar, she decided to join the Judge Advocate General's Corps, the military division tasked with matters of military law, and moved to Fort Sill, Oklahoma, to become a prosecutor.

## MIDDLE EAST DEPLOYMENT, PROFESSIONAL ADVANCEMENT, AND CANCER

In 1991, as part of the US military operations Desert Shield and, then, Desert Storm, the US Army deployed Sáenz Ryan, then a captain, to be legal counsel for a field artillery brigade serving in the Middle East from 1991 to 1992. She was one of only a few women out of the brigade's one thousand soldiers. After her deployment she returned to her alma mater, West Point, as an assistant professor in the law department, filling the position from 1992 to 1994. Though she left West Point for a string of positions as a judge advocate, she would return less than a decade later in historic fashion.

In 1995, she took a position in Hawaii, serving as the officer in charge of the Twenty-Fifth Infantry Division at Fort Shafter, becoming the chief of military justice at the Schofield Barracks in Hawaii in 1997. Her rapid rise through the ranks was hastened when cancer was discovered in her leg in 1999. While she was at staff school in Fort Leavenworth, Kansas, doctors discovered soft-tissue sarcoma cancer and started her on an aggressive, and ultimately successful, schedule of chemotherapy and radiation. Sáenz Ryan's cancer could have taken away her military career, not to mention her life. The Army "easily could have said I was medically retired. I would have understood and gone on," Sáenz Ryan explained to Burks (25 July 2011). However, Brigadier General Malinda Dunn compiled a list of military personnel to look after Sáenz Ryan, who in 2000 had become the judge advocate at the Army Medical Department Center and School in Fort Sam Houston, Texas, a trying time that could have been made more difficult if not for the compassion and loyalty of colleagues. "I had to go to Texas, my family was up in Kansas and so I was basically alone," she said to Burks. "My sister came as much as she could but basically I had a bunch of attorneys taking care of me."

In 2001, Sáenz Ryan applied for a professorship at West Point, still recovering from the cancer and treatment. She got the job, and was appointed the deputy head of the law department, a newly created position, reporting to department head Brigadier General Pat Finnegan, who was one of her staunchest supporters. However, during the transition period from Texas to New York, Sáenz Ryan experienced a setback from the cancer that could have again ended her military career. As part of her treatment, doctors inserted a metal rod in her affected leg, which became infected because of her weakened immunity resulting from rounds of radiation and chemotherapy. "I was basically looking at being in a wheelchair for the rest if my life if they couldn't do a hip replacement," she explained to Burks.

Her ongoing health problems meant that she could not assume her West Point post at the scheduled time. However, Finnegan allowed her the proper time to recover, illustrating the value he placed on her healthy presence at the academy and his understanding that, most times, health concerns outweigh professional duty. Cancer-free, she was able to assume her post, helping to usher in an unprecedented era at the law department at West Point.

## DEPARTMENT HEAD AND ACTIVISM

After serving as a professor and deputy head of the law school, in 2006, at the recommendation of Finnegan, who stepped down to become the academic dean of West Point, Sáenz Ryan became the first woman to hold the post of department head of the US Military Academy law department, a position that requires a nomination by the president of the United States and congressional confirmation. By assuming the position, she not only was the first female department head but also the first Hispanic to fill such a role, becoming the highest-ranking Hispanic judge advocate in the United States.

Sáenz Ryan has used her power to become what some might call an "activist" department head. In 2008, she helped start the West Point Center for the Rule of Law (CRL), which examines issues of military law that affect the entire global community. She has lobbied extensively for the advancement of women to high-ranking civilian and military posts and has been an outspoken critic of the US military's Combat Exclusion Policy that forbids female soldiers from engaging in frontline military operations.

The CRL has hosted distinguished speakers such as journalist Dan Rather, who discussed the Afghani practice of disguising girls as boys, called *bacha posh*. Sáenz Ryan has headed the initiative to send cadets on educational field trips to heighten their awareness of the social situations that affect the military decision making of the US Army. One such field trip was taken to Liberia in the wake of that country's civil war in order to study the legal issues facing the postwar regime. Under Sáenz Ryan, West Point also hosted the Brigadier General Telford Taylor Memorial Conference in September 2010, which gathered international legal experts to examine issues of international criminal law. One participant, professor Kevin Govern from the Ava Maria School of Law in Florida, said the conference "was the best run and most meaningful" he had ever been part of, and Sáenz Ryan discussed the importance of the event, stating that it "epitomize[s] the continuing role of the West Point Center for the Rule of Law as the world leader in the analysis and development of legal issues affecting the military and society" (qtd. by R. Meyer in *Army*, 29 Sept. 2010).

As homage to the female pioneers, such as Justice Ruth Bader Ginsburg, who paved the way for her successful career, Sáenz Ryan has used much of her clout to raise awareness of gender and women's issues. In April 2011, the CRL hosted a conference dubbed Gender Justice: Toward Achieving Equality. In "In Blood and Spirit," Sáenz Ryan notes the entrenched belief in the inferiority of women, writing that an "'accepted doctrine' prevalent in the military as in society had long held that women can't fight and certainly couldn't lead in combat—this despite many women across various cultures, including our own, having done so successfully, if mostly anonymously, throughout history." It is from this perspective that she has attempted to spotlight the inherent inequality of the Combat Exclusion Policy.

## QUEST FOR GENDER EQUALITY

In 2011, the American Bar Association Commission on Women in the Profession gave Sáenz Ryan the Margaret Brent Women Lawyers Achievement Award, an award named after the first female lawyer in America and given for "remarkable achievements and accomplishments of distinguished women lawyers," as commission chair Roberta D. Liebenberg stated, according to Burks. The award was recognition for Sáenz Ryan's aggressive gender-equality policies at West Point, where she has pushed for an increased number of female cadets at West Point and soldiers in the US Army.

In a 2009 *Women Lawyers Journal* essay entitled "'Some Leaders Are Born Women': Gender Diversity and Leadership," Sáenz Ryan writes that "until not too long ago in America, gender stereotypes were routinely used to justify legally excluding women entirely from the public sphere, and certainly from the professions and career paths to positions of leadership in society." From this position, she has attacked the intrinsically gender-biased Combat Exclusion Policy. Established by the Pentagon in 1994, the policy limits the roles that women can perform in the military, specifically denying them access to participation in direct ground combat. While this might seem to be to the advantage of female soldiers because it removes them from direct harm, it is both based on a gendered assumption that women, because of either their physical or mental makeup, are unable to engage in frontline combat with male counterparts and precludes them from advancing to higher-ranking positions because they lack combat experience.

In "In Blood and Spirit," Sáenz Ryan calls the Combat Exclusion Policy "anachronistic" and writes, "So long as military service, and the intangible attributes it implies—courage, tenacity, patriotism, and, . . . leadership—continues to be a hallmark of full membership in society as American citizens, and as long as our country needs leaders . . . we will need women to lead alongside our male colleagues." She has stressed that in all facets of professional life, not just in the legal and military professions, society will increasingly rely on the leadership of women, noting in "'Some Leaders Are Born Women'" that "a consensus is building that women . . . bring a more inclusive and communicative style" to leadership, highlighting her relentless advocation of opportunities for women.

In January 2013, to implement policy that coincided with the reality of combat in Afghanistan and other locations where the US military is engaged, Secretary of Defense Leon E. Panetta announced plans to lift the ban on women's participation in combat, a step that was widely applauded by advocates for equal opportunity for female soldiers.

## PERSONAL LIFE AND COMMENDATIONS

Sáenz Ryan met her husband, fellow cadet Robert Ryan, while a student at West Point. The couple has two boys, both adults; Alexander and his younger brother Andrew have both pursued military careers. In 2006, *Hispanic* magazine labeled Sáenz Ryan one of its top one hundred influential Hispanics, and in 2012, the Women in the World Foundation, as part of the International Women's Day, named her as one of the "150 Fearless Women" in the world.

Sáenz Ryan has garnered numerous military awards, including the Meritorious Service Medal, the Joint Services Commendation Medal, the Army Commendation Medal, and the Army Service Ribbon. She also possesses an Air Assault Badge and a Parachutist Badge. Highly admired for both her military and legal careers, she continues to set an example for those who fight

against long odds to accomplish their life's goals, and she is certain to continue to be a voice for pragmatic military policy making and cadet and officer advocacy.

## SUGGESTED READING

Burks, Rabiah Alicia. "Veteran Female Lawyer Fought Cancer, Discrimination to Lead." *ABA Now*. American Bar Association, 25 July 2011. Web. 14 Jan. 2013.

Bumiller, Elisabeth. "Pentagon Allows Women Closer to Combat, but Not Close Enough for Some." *New York Times*. New York Times, 9 Feb. 2012. Web. 14 Jan. 2013.

"Maritza S. Ryan." *American Bar Association*. American Bar Association, n.d. Web. 14 Jan. 2013. PDF file.

Meyer, Rich. "Legal World Converges at West Point." *Army*. US Army, 29 Sept. 2010. Web. 14 Jan. 2013.

Sáenz Ryan, Maritza. "In Blood and Spirit." *The Shriver Report: A Woman's Nation Changes Everything*. By Maria Shriver. Ed. Heather Boushey and Ann O'Leary. Washington, DC: Center for Amer. Progress, 2009. PDF file.

---. "'Some Leaders Are Born Women': Gender Diversity and Leadership." *Women Lawyers Journal* 94.3 (2009): 17–20. Print.

—*Christopher Rager*

# Nate Silver

**Born:** January 13, 1978
**Occupation:** Statistician, psephologist, and writer

A day or so after the 2012 elections, Nate Silver, political analyst and writer for the *New York Times*'s *FiveThirtyEight* blog, was out with friends on Manhattan's Lower East Side when he was recognized by people sitting near him at the bar, much to his surprise. "Is this going to happen every day, as opposed to once a month? I still have to get accustomed to this," he said in an interview with Jocelyn Noveck for the Associated Press (9 Nov. 2012).

For those who follow *FiveThirtyEight*, however, Silver's celebrity is no surprise. In the week before the election, 71 percent of the viewers of the *New York Times* News and Politics section visited Silver's blog. On Election Night, he had predicted the presidential election results in each state and almost all of the US Senate results with stunning accuracy. In fact, throughout the 2012 election season, he had projected that the odds were in Obama's favor, though not by a huge margin, even when many other political analysts were saying that the race was too close to call and closer to fifty-fifty than seventy-thirty

FilmMagic

Nate Silver is named for one of his mother's forebears, a Nathaniel Read who was born in Sudbury, Massachusetts, in the early eighteenth century. According to Nate Bloom, a writer for the *InterfaithFamily* website (and Silver's father, who commented on Bloom's article), Nate Silver comes from a long line of "intellectually and professionally distinguished men and women," including his maternal great-grandfather Harmon Lewis, who headed the Alcoa Steamship Company; his paternal grandfather, an aerospace engineer; his paternal uncle, a Caltech professor emeritus of geology who trained Moon-bound Apollo astronauts to collect samples from the lunar surface; and his maternal grandmother, who graduated from Columbia University with a bachelor of architecture degree (13 Nov. 2012).

## AN EARLY PASSION FOR NUMBERS AND BASEBALL

Silver's parents encouraged their son's precocious gift with numbers, which was already evident to them by the time he was a toddler. Brian Silver remembers that when Nate was two years old, he counted to twenty when his mother asked him to count to three. By the time he was four, he knew what negative numbers were. He learned his numbers before his letters, and was able to solve double-digit multiplication problems in his head. "His mind had a little calculator in it," said his mother, Sally Silver (qtd. in *Detroit Free Press*, 11 Nov. 2012).

Another of Silver's passions, baseball, developed early as well. William Hageman reported for the *Chicago Tribune* that "Silver caught the baseball bug when he was 6, growing up in East Lansing, Michigan. It was 1984, the year the Detroit Tigers won the World Series. The Tigers became his team and baseball his sport" (4 Jan. 2006). It didn't take long for Silver's two interests to merge into a greater whole. "If there's anything that goes hand in glove with baseball, it's numbers," Hageman writes. Or as Silver put it, "It's always more interesting to apply [numbers] to batting averages than to algebra class." Silver's father took him to Tigers games during their championship season, and Silver tracked the team's season all the way to the World Series. As he grew older, his analysis became more sophisticated. According to the *New York Times*'s Stephanie Clifford: "By 11, he was conducting multivariate analysis to figure out if the size of a baseball stadium affects attendance (it doesn't). By age 13, he was using statistics to manage a fantasy baseball team" (10 Nov. 2008). Silver's interest in fantasy baseball would continue into high school, college, and his early career.

## HIGH SCHOOL DEBATE TEAM STANDOUT

Silver did well as a student at East Lansing High School, where he was a writer and editor for the student newspaper. He was also a member of the

or, by election night, 90.9 to 9.1. Republicans such as Joe Scarborough of MSNBC's *Morning Joe* were outraged by Silver's projections before the election, while left-leaning celebrities such as John Legend, Salman Rushdie, and Michelle Pfeiffer read his blog for "stability and sanity," as Legend put it according to a writer for *Hollywood Reporter* (9 Nov. 2012). After the election, he was hailed by *Daily Show* host Jon Stewart as "the lord and god of the algorithm" (qtd. in *Guardian* 17 Nov. 2012). Pundits on the political left and right deemed Silver the "other winner" of the 2012 presidential election, one who, as Noveck put it, "silenced doubters and proved the value of a cool-headed, math-based approach."

## A DISTINGUISHED FAMILY TREE

Silver's wry, often self-deprecating humor was evident in his tweet on the subject of his birthday: "I was born on a Friday the 13th (1.13.78). Which explains a lot" (13 Aug. 2010). Nathaniel Read Silver was indeed born on January 13, 1978, in East Lansing, Michigan, where he was raised with his younger sister, Rebecca Gard Silver (also known as Becca), in an interfaith/agnostic household. His father, Brian D. Silver, who is Jewish, works at Michigan State University as a professor of political science and grew up in Connecticut. Silver's mother, Sally Thrun Silver, a community activist, traces her family in America back to the 1630s as well as to nineteenth-century non-Jewish German immigrants.

debate team for all four years of high school. As his father told Jocelyn Noveck for the AP (9 Nov. 2012), "On the debate team it was OK to be a geek." In 1996, he took the first prize of $1,500 in a statewide annual debate contest sponsored by the *Detroit Free Press*—although, according to his high school debating partner Kathryn Hoffman, he put much more effort into what his debate coach called "grinding amounts of research" than he did into his physical appearance. Silver himself estimates that he devoted sixty hours a week to debate prep during the season. "Clothes didn't matter to him," Hoffman said. "He was opposed to worrying about them. He viewed them as shallow" (qtd. in *Detroit Free Press* 11 Nov. 2012)—which is perhaps why she and others who knew Silver and how smart he was back in the day were still surprised to see his rise to news media stardom. "That's not the area where you expected him to excel," Hoffman said.

Despite a busy schedule, Silver also found time to play Scoresheet Baseball, a form of fantasy baseball, with one of his friends. The two used their analysis of player statistics—similar to that featured in the book (also a film) *Moneyball*—to create one of the best teams in the fantasy league.

## COLLEGE YEARS

After graduating from high school, Silver went to the University of Chicago, from which he would graduate in 2000 with honors and an AB in economics. In addition to his studies, he wrote for two campus publications, the *Chicago Maroon*, for which he wrote about sports, and the *Chicago Weekly News*. He also was a contributor to BaseballHQ, a website for fantasy baseball enthusiasts trying to figure out which players they should add to their fantasy team rosters.

Silver spent his junior year (1998–99) at the London School of Economics. When he returned to the United States from London, he came out to his parents as being gay. Silver, who was named *Out* magazine's person of the year for 2012 and was one of the magazine's Out 100 in 2010, says that while he was growing up, being a geek made him feel like more of a misfit than being gay did. Yet, perhaps one key to Silver's aplomb as a celebrity is his acceptance of what he calls his own "dorkiness." As he mentioned to the UK *Guardian*'s Carole Cadwalladr, "I've always felt like something of an outsider. I've always had friends, but I've always come from an outside point of view" (17 Nov. 2012). "For me, I think the most important distinguishing characteristic is that I'm independent-minded," he said in an interview with Aaron Hicklin for *Out* (18 Dec. 2012). Silver continues, "I'm sure that being gay encouraged the independent-mindedness, but that same independent-mindedness makes me a little bit skeptical of parts of gay culture, I suppose." In his conversation with

Hicklin, Silver also recalled a memorial plaque for Keith Haring in Chicago's Boystown, one of several such plaques. "There was one little plaque for Keith Haring, gay American artist . . . and I was like, Why isn't he just an American artist? I don't want to be Nate Silver, gay statistician, any more than I want to be known as a white, half-Jewish statistician who lives in New York."

## KPMG, PECOTA, AND BASEBALL PROSPECTUS

In 2000, Silver took a position with KPMG, a global network of audit and tax advisory firms, as an economic consultant, or as he said in an interview with Rich Lederer for *Baseball Analysts*, "one of those consulting jobs that an economics grad from the U of C might be expected to take" (12 Feb. 2007). Silver found himself bored with the work, however.

In 2002, he started developing his own method for forecasting the performance of individual baseball players. Silver's method became known as PECOTA, which stands for Player Empirical Comparison and Optimization Algorithm, an acronym that pays tribute to Bill Pecota, "a .303 lifetime hitter against Detroit" (*Baseball Analysts* 12 Feb. 2007). Although Silver says that the original version of the algorithm focused on pitchers, he expanded it based on feedback from one of his supporters, Gary Huckabay, who was then head of Baseball Prospectus (BP), a firm that publishes baseball player stats, analysis, and prospect rankings for use by baseball professionals as well as fantasy league enthusiasts. As Silver explains it, PECOTA "uses comparable player data to provide an objective estimate of the probability of a marked improvement in the player's performance" (BP 29 Jan. 2003) and is used by analysts to identify players who have a high probability of performing better than they have in prior seasons. In January 2003, Silver sold PECOTA to BP, which was looking for a new projection system for the premium subscription services it was planning to launch. He also started writing and providing baseball analysis for the company.

In April 2004, Silver left his consulting job at KPMG to devote more of his time to online poker. According to Hicklin, Silver made $400,000 in a little over two years when he realized that the easy money wouldn't necessarily last forever. On one memorable night near the end of 2006, he lost about $75,000 in a single game. Silver described the scene to Dan Amira for *New York* magazine online: "Well, I was playing games where you're betting $200 per betting round, so you start to make some bad decisions and kind of go on tilt a little bit, and those losses add up. But poker, I played limit hold 'em, which is actually a really swingy game, you have a really small edge. So if you're off your game even a little bit—and frankly, that night, I was probably off by more than a little bit—then you're probably a favorite to lose money."

During his poker playing days, Silver also became BP's executive vice president upon Huckabay's departure in 2004. Silver told Lederer what it was like to run the company: "Probably the most challenging part of running an independent business like BP is that you necessarily need to be a jack of all trades. It seems to me the only way to get anything done is to be willing to trust your intuition." In addition to managing the company, Silver wrote a weekly column, "Lies, Damned Lies"—a reference to the phrase, "There are three kinds of lies: lies, damned lies, and statistics," often attributed to either Mark Twain or Benjamin Disraeli.

### FIVETHIRTYEIGHT AND THE 2008 ELECTION

Silver was still working at Baseball Prospectus in October 2007 when he started blogging as "Poblano" on the *DailyKos*, a left-leaning political website. He started the blog because he wanted to use quantitative analysis to dissect politics in a way that non-math wonks could comprehend. The idea for *FiveThirtyEight* occurred to him while he was stranded between flights in New Orleans, when he saw an opportunity to improve on what he saw as simplistic analysis of political polls and demographics. His forecasts of the 2008 presidential primary contests attracted notice and were cited by other political commentators, including William Kristol, op-ed columnist for the *New York Times*.

Having gained a substantial following while blogging for the DailyKos, Silver started his own blog, *FiveThirtyEight*, on March 7, 2008. He wrote under the pen name Poblano until May 30, 2008, when he posted, "My real name is Nate Silver and my principal occupation has been as a writer, analyst and partner at a sports media company called Baseball Prospectus. What we do over there and what I'm doing over here are really quite similar. Both baseball and politics are data-driven industries. But a lot of the time, that data might be used *badly*. In baseball, that may mean looking at a statistic like batting average when things like on-base percentage and slugging percentage are far more correlated with winning ballgames. In politics, that might mean cherry-picking a certain polling result or weaving together a narrative that isn't supported by the demographic evidence." In addition to publishing on *FiveThirtyEight*, he also analyzed the 2008 presidential campaign for newspapers, magazines, and on television.

In an effort to allow his readers to decide for themselves whether his election analysis was biased, Silver disclosed his own political leanings on *FiveThirtyEight*'s FAQ page. "I vote for Democratic candidates the majority of the time (though by no means always). This year [2008] I have been a supporter of Barack Obama."

Indeed, according to Sasha Issenberg's *The Victory Lab* (2012), Silver had come to the attention of the Obama campaign, which decided to share its polling information with him in exchange for signing a confidentiality agreement. On election night 2008, Silver correctly predicted Obama's popular vote win within 1.1 percent, as well as the presidential election returns in forty-nine states. He also called all 2008 US Senate races. The accuracy of his predictions increased Silver's prominence as a political forecaster and set a high bar not only for other political analysts and pundits, but for himself.

### MOVING TO NEW YORK AND THE *NEW YORK TIMES*

In 2009, Silver moved to New York City after living in Chicago for about twelve years. The following summer, he announced *FiveThirtyEight*'s three-year partnership agreement with the *New York Times*, under which *FiveThirtyEight* would keep its identity but would no longer have its own web domain once it became part of the *New York Times* website under its News: Politics section. Silver would also write for the paper's print editions. Silver's blog, named *FiveThirtyEight: Nate Silver's Political Calculus*, moved to the *New York Times* on August 25, 2010. Silver admitted that the transition required some adjustment on his part, but felt that it was a positive change overall. Challenges for Silver have included getting used to the paper's journalism standards—some of which he disagrees with—and taking on more of the blog's day-to-day writing workload, now that he has fewer co-contributors, some of whom have not passed the paper's vetting process for various reasons. On the positive side, writing for the *Times* has allowed him to cover topics beyond politics. And, instead of pixilated cuttings and pastings from Microsoft Excel, he is able to work with the paper's graphic design staff to elevate the blog's look and feel.

### 2010 MIDTERM ELECTIONS

The 2010 midterm campaigns for congressional seats and state governorships were in full swing when *FiveThirtyEight* migrated to the *New York Times*. Silver's models for the midterm races were based on demographics, electoral history, and polling results. However, compared to his forecasts for the 2008 elections, Silver's 2010 midterm predictions were not as accurate. On September 10, he posted that his model showed that the GOP had a two-in-three chance of taking control of the House of Representatives, and predicted a net gain of forty-five to fifty seats for the Republicans. As he live-blogged election night, Silver's model gave real-time updates based on exit polling and early returns. Over the course of the evening, the model's forecast of the number of House seats gained by Republicans steadily increased from an initial prediction of fifty-four to fifty-five seats to sixty-five seats. The actual Republican gain was 63 seats, once all of the results were in, including those in contested states. His projections were also wrong about Senate races in Alaska, Colorado, and Nevada.

## 2012 ELECTIONS
After the 2010 midterm election misses, Silver had the sense that his forecasts for the 2010 presidential and congressional races could make or break his reputation as a political analyst. Thus, the pressure was on when political pundits, both progressive and conservative, began questioning Silver's methodology. As Election Day approached, Silver's model showed that based on the strength of President Obama's advantage in swing states like Ohio, his chances of winning the election rose well above 70 percent. On election night, this percentage increased to a 90.9-percent likelihood that Obama would win. Despite the fact that Silver's prediction was mostly in line with what other political betting markets were giving as odds, backlash came from conservatives who claimed that Silver's poll aggregation model was somehow biased against Romney. Many political pundits thought the race was too tight to call and were outraged. MSNBC's Joe Scarborough said "Anybody [who] thinks that this race is anything but a toss-up right now is such an ideologue. . . . They're jokes" (qtd in *Newsweek* 19 Nov. 2012). Silver responded to Scarborough's critique by saying, "All you have to do is take an average, and count to 270. It's a pretty simple set of facts. I'm sorry that Joe is math-challenged." Silver bet Scarborough $2,000 that Obama would win—a bet which Scarborough declined to accept. Others also questioned whether a statistical model could make better election forecasts than a human analyst. One such critic, *Politico*'s Dylan Byers (29 Oct. 2012), wrote that Silver "could be a one-term celebrity" if his predictions were off. "Should Mitt Romney win on November 6, it's difficult to see how people can continue to put faith in the predictions of someone who has never given that candidate anything higher than a 41 percent chance of winning."

As it turned out, Silver's projections for the 2012 election were even more accurate than his 2008 projections. His forecast of the presidential election returns in all fifty states and almost all of the US Senate races was extremely accurate. "You know who won the election tonight?" asked the progressive-leaning MSNBC TV news anchor Rachel Maddow. "Nate Silver" (qtd. in *Guardian* 17 Nov. 2012).

Vindicated by his success, Silver suddenly became a popular television guest. His new book, *The Signal and the Noise: Why Most Predictions Fail—but Some Don't* (released Sept. 2012) began its rapid ascent to the top of several best seller lists, including that of the *New York Times*; Amazon lists it as its most popular business and advertising book. The book is the first of two for which Silver's publisher Penguin reportedly paid him an advance of $700,000.

## 2012 AND BEYOND
According to Ezra Klein, a writer for the *Washington Post*'s *Wonkblog*, Silver's success with the 2012 elections not only vindicated Silver himself, but was a win for political forecasters in general. "My guess is Silver and his successors will win this one, if only because, for all the very real shortcomings of models, election forecasters have better incentives than homepage editors. For instance, note that all these attacks on Silver take, as their starting point, Silver's continuously updated prediction for the presidential election, which includes point estimates for the popular vote and electoral college, and his predictions for the Senate races. Those predictions let readers check Silver's track record and they force Silver, if he wants to keep his readers' trust, to make his model as accurate as he can. That's a good incentive structure—certainly a better one than much of the rest of the media has—and my guess is his results, over time, will prove it" (30 Oct. 2012).

Before Election Day 2012, Silver was somewhat vague about what his postelection plans might include, besides getting more rest. He told Jason Zengerle for *New York* magazine that he would probably have a better idea after the election, but hinted that someone else might be in charge of *FiveThirtyEight* in 2016. "I'm 97 percent sure that the *FiveThirtyEight* model will exist in 2016 . . . but it could be someone else who's running it or licensing it" (30 Sept. 2012). After his partnership with the *New York Times* expired in August 2013, Silver left to join ESPN, bringing along his *FiveThirtyEight* blog to the sports network.

## HONORS AND PERSONAL LIFE
Silver has many honors and awards to his credit. In addition to being named *Out* magazine's Person of the Year for 2012, he has most recently won a Webby Award for best political blog (2012) from the International Academy of Digital Arts and Scientists, was featured as one of *Crain's New York Business*'s "Forty under Forty" young entrepreneurs, and was named a Game Changer in 2012 by *Rolling Stone* magazine.

Silver lives in Brooklyn with his sister, Becca Silver, who characterized his work style as "trance-like" (*Detroit Free Press* 11 Nov. 2012).

## SUGGESTED READING
Bloom, Nate. "Interfaith Celebrities: Nate Silver, Another Bond, and Happy Endings." *InterfaithFamily*. InterfaithFamily.com, 13 Nov. 2012. Web. 17 Dec. 2012.

Cadwalladr, Carole. "Nate Silver: It's the Numbers, Stupid." *Guardian* [UK]. Guardian News and Media, 17 Nov. 2012. Web. 3 Dec. 2012.

Clifford, Stephanie. "Finding Fame with a Prescient Call for Obama." *New York Times*. New York Times, 10 Nov. 2008. Web. 18 Dec. 2012.

Hicklin, Aaron. "Nate Silver: Person of the Year." *Out*. Here Media: 18 Dec. 2012. Web. 18 Dec. 2012.

James, Bill. "Scientists and Thinkers: Nate Silver." *Time Lists: The 2009 TIME 100*. Time, 30 Apr. 2009. Web. 3 Dec. 2012.

—*Lisa Phillips*

Courtesy of Julie Smolyansky

# Julie Smolyansky

**Born:** 1975
**Occupation:** CEO of Lifeway Foods

When Julie Smolyansky was appointed president, chief executive officer (CEO), and director of Lifeway Foods in June 2002, she became—at twenty-seven years old—the youngest woman to head a publicly traded company in American corporate history. The Ukrainian-born Smolyansky was thrust into the positions after her father, Michael Smolyansky, who founded the Illinois-based company in 1986, died unexpectedly of a heart attack at the age of fifty-five. "Suddenly, it all fell on my shoulders," she told Jonathan Black for *UIC Alumni Magazine*, the alumni magazine of the University of Illinois at Chicago (UIC), from which she graduated in 1996. "I had no one to go to for advice and support. My dad used to tell me what to do. But failure wasn't an option."

Since taking over as president and CEO of Lifeway Foods, which specializes in the production of the yogurt-like drink kefir, Smolyansky has not only managed to hold her own in her father's former role but also helped fulfill his dream of turning the company into a household name. Under her direction, Lifeway has expanded its product line, entered into new markets, and formed lucrative partnerships and has grown from a small but successful seventy-employee business with $12 million in annual sales to a nearly 350-employee enterprise projected to hit over $90 million in sales by the end of 2013. Smolyansky's mission at Lifeway, as she explained to Christina Dreher for *Crain's Chicago Business* (6 June 2011), is "to innovate and create fully healthy, good-for-you food."

## EARLY LIFE

Smolyansky was born in 1975 in Kiev, Ukraine, then part of the Soviet Union. She immigrated to the United States with her parents, Michael and Ludmila, when she was one year old. Julie and her younger brother, Edward, grew up in Rogers Park, a diverse neighborhood in Chicago. Smolyansky's parents did not speak English when they arrived in the United States, but they nonetheless quickly found work, her father as a mechanical engineer and her mother as a hairdresser and manicurist. Her parents eventually learned to speak English fluently, and Smolyansky grew up speaking both Russian and English.

In the late 1970s Smolyansky's parents opened a Russian delicatessen, one of the first of its kind in Chicago, to cater to the growing Russian population in the area. Smolyansky's mother oversaw the deli's day-to-day operations, handling everything from accounting to the unloading of goods and sundries. Her father, meanwhile, relieved her mother at the deli each day after completing his regular nine-to-five shift as an engineer. Smolyansky and her brother also occasionally helped out and were assigned small tasks such as labeling canned goods. Smolyansky's parents eventually came to own and operate a chain of five Russian delis throughout Chicago, as well as an import and distribution business specializing in Eastern European foods. She told Jennifer Okelmann for the blog *All Things Mothering* (28 June 2012), "I learned at a young age that I could have any life I wanted—a career I loved, a beautiful family—anything was possible."

## LIFEWAY FOODS

The idea of producing and selling kefir first struck Smolyansky's parents in the mid-1980s, when they were reintroduced to the cultured, enzyme-rich drink at a trade show in Germany. Kefir originated in the North Caucasus region of Eastern Europe thousands of years ago and is made by combining kefir grains—a combination of live bacteria and yeasts—with milk. It has a taste and texture somewhat similar to that of yogurt. Because kefir was not commercially available in the United States at the time, Smolyansky's parents saw an opportunity to market it to the growing Russian population in Chicago. Not long after returning home from the trade show, Smolyansky's father began experimenting with kefir recipes in the family basement, using cultures directly imported from Russia. "My younger brother and I were his guinea pigs," she recalled to Amy Zipkin for the *New York Times* (23 Aug. 2008). "He was always asking us whether the consistency was too thick or the taste too sweet. We also went to trade shows and poured the product into cups."

Smolyansky's father soon opened a factory and started selling batches of kefir to local retailers. In 1986 he quit his job as an engineer and founded Lifeway Foods to produce and sell kefir. The company grew quickly and went public on the NASDAQ stock exchange in 1988. Smolyansky recalled to Lindsey Gerdes for *CNNMoney* (1 July 2004) that her father "didn't even know what it meant to go public." She continued, "But he needed financing and somebody said he should. He researched it in the library."

Adopting her parents' strong work ethic, Smolyansky started working in her early teens. While attending Niles North High School in the Chicago suburb of Skokie, she babysat, managed the concession stand at a local pool, and worked at a Russian restaurant her father had opened. She was also involved in tennis and figure skating and in charitable activities, such as working at a battered women's shelter in the nearby city of Evanston. "I was always leading people, and I was always overbooked in my calendar," she told Marc Hogan for *Bloomberg BusinessWeek* (18 Dec. 2006). "It was almost a kind of training for me to do what I'm doing now."

## EDUCATION AND EARLY CAREER

After graduating from high school in 1993, Smolyansky enrolled in UIC to study psychology, with a minor in women's studies. While in college she taught aerobics classes and continued to babysit and work at her father's restaurant to help pay her tuition. Smolyansky graduated from UIC in three years, earning her bachelor's degree in 1996. She explained to Black, "I was determined to graduate quickly and get out in the real world."

Intending to study clinical psychology, Smolyansky enrolled in graduate school in Chicago. Around that time she started working part-time at Lifeway, helping with data entry and marketing. Although she had previously assisted her father on weekends and during breaks from school, Smolyansky had not planned on making a career at Lifeway. Nonetheless, she quickly became drawn to the business and left graduate school after a year to become Lifeway's director of sales and marketing. "I didn't really know my father growing up," she told Gerdes. "He was starting a company. But when I fell in love with it myself, I got to see what he was doing when he wasn't around. It healed our relationship."

As director of sales and marketing, Smolyansky was trained in all facets of the business. She helped lead the company through a period of rapid growth, expanding the reach of its flagship kefir product into the mainstream natural health-food market. "I was my dad's right-hand person," she noted to Black. "If it weren't for that, the company might be in a very different place today."

## CEO

When her father died unexpectedly of a heart attack on June 9, 2002, Smolyansky was elected his successor by Lifeway's board of directors, becoming Lifeway's president, CEO, chief financial officer (CFO), and treasurer, as well as a member of the board. Then twenty-seven years old, Smolyansky became the youngest female CEO of a publicly traded company in history. At that time Lifeway was a thriving business, with seventy employees and $12 million in annual sales. However, when Smolyansky's appointment was announced, Lifeway's stock fell considerably, trading as low as two dollars per share as investors, company insiders, and even family members questioned her ability to run the company. Recalling the painful and trying experience, Smolyansky, who was also forced to hide company records the day of her father's death out of fear that they would be stolen by competitors, told Hogan, "Overnight my life changed just unbelievably. Not only was I mourning the loss of my father, but I was also trying to keep the company together and leading our staff and suppliers to make sure they knew that everything was OK. Even at my father's funeral, I'd heard people behind my back saying, 'There's no way a little girl's going to run a company like this.'"

Saddened but undaunted by the sudden loss of her father, Smolyansky channeled all of her grief and energy into making sure Lifeway would succeed, and in her first year as CEO, the company's gross annual sales rose from $12 million to $14.8 million. Working up to twenty-two hours per day, she focused on marketing kefir to younger, health-conscious consumers and introduced different versions of the drink to help expand the company's product line. She also increased Lifeway's distribution channels by striking up partnerships with such health-food stores as Whole Foods and Wild Oats. Smolyansky has said that she adopted a "tough-girl" persona—one that exudes assertiveness and confidence—and drew on her wide range of skills to lead Lifeway through a difficult but fruitful time.

"Because of some of my training in psychology and crisis management, I had a pretty decent grasp on crisis management," she explained to Hilary Farrell for the website *Benzinga* (9 July 2012). "I think that what I learned was to really use my skill set—the things that I'm really good at—to my advantage. The things that I'm not good at or don't enjoy, [I] find really great people to support me on those sides." In 2004 Smolyansky relinquished the positions of CFO and treasurer to her brother, who also serves as the company's controller. Her mother serves as chair of Lifeway's board of directors.

## EXPANSION AND GROWTH

In the decade since Smolyansky took the helm, Lifeway has enjoyed significant and steady growth. Much of that growth has been attributed to Smolyansky's strong emphasis on product development and innovation. Under her guidance, Lifeway has vastly expanded its line of kefir drinks and launched other products. The company offers kefir in a number of varieties, including original, low fat, nonfat, whole milk, and organic, and in such flavors as pomegranate, blueberry, strawberries and cream, raspberry, and chocolate truffle. It also sells ProBugs, a line of organic whole milk kefir for children; Green Kefir, a line of organic kefir made with a blend of probiotic nutrients and vegetables; BioKefir, a line of 3.5-ounce shots containing enhanced kefir; Low Carb Kefir, a line of kefir smoothie blends sweetened with Splenda; and gluten-free dessert varieties such as Frozen Kefir and Greek Style Fro-Yo.

Lifeway's products, which also include a line of farmer cheeses, are sold at health-food stores, supermarket chains, membership-only clubs, and other retailers throughout the United States. In 2008 Lifeway launched Starfruit Café, an Illinois chain of kefir boutiques that offers a range of kefir parfaits, smoothies, and other frozen treats. In 2012 Smolyansky announced plans to expand the chain outside of Illinois, testing a new Starfruit kiosk concept at a Whole Foods store in the Boston suburb of Wellesley, Massachusetts.

Smolyansky has been lauded for helping Lifeway achieve most of its growth during a global economic recession. Instead of cutting back on costs, she spent more money on the business, investing more in advertising and marketing and using social media to recruit skilled and experienced people who had been laid off. "I hired at discount prices and took advantage of the availability of highly qualified people from incredible backgrounds," she explained to Elizabeth Burke for the blog *Levo League* (8 Aug. 2012). "I pushed through." In 2009 Smolyansky led Lifeway's acquisition of its biggest competitor, the Pennsylvania-based kefir maker Fresh Made Dairy, which it

purchased for $14 million. The following year, she led the company through its acquisition of the New Jersey–based First Juice, a maker of organic beverages for children. The former move has allowed Lifeway to bolster its East Coast market presence; the latter has helped the company build upon its entry into the children's market. Thanks to such key business moves, Lifeway achieved nearly $80 million in gross sales in 2011. That year Smolyansky rang the closing bell on the NASDAQ stock exchange in honor of Lifeway's twenty-fifth anniversary.

In June 2012 Smolyansky announced in a press release commemorating the tenth anniversary of her father's death that Lifeway had surpassed $2 million in weekly sales. The company, which is headquartered in Morton Grove, Illinois, with additional offices and warehouse facilities in the nearby town of Niles, has been regularly listed among the fastest-growing small businesses in the United States by *Forbes*, *Fortune*, and *Crain's Chicago Business*. Smolyansky explained to David Wolinsky for NBC Chicago's startup blog *Inc.Well* (5 Jan. 2012) that being a CEO entails not only helping a company succeed but also helping people. "I think that when you're in this role, it's all about the people around you making sure that they're safe, that they have the support that they need," she said. "To me, this is like a family. And so I would do anything for my family."

## PERSONAL LIFE

Smolyansky lives in Chicago with her longtime partner, jewelry designer Jason Burdeen, and their two daughters, Leah and Misha. She is an avid fan of the rock band Pearl Jam and has seen them in concert more than twenty times. She is also a devoted runner and has completed several marathons. A self-proclaimed insomniac, Smolyansky typically gets fewer than four hours of sleep per night and has been known to do most of her e-mail correspondence after midnight.

Smolyansky is involved with several humanitarian organizations and has been dedicated to raising awareness about health and human rights issues. She holds board memberships with the Anti-Defamation League (ADL), the Illinois Holocaust Museum and Education Center, and the International Probiotics Association, among other organizations. She was recognized as one of *Crain's Chicago Business's* forty leaders under forty years old in 2005 and was named a finalist for the Ernst and Young Entrepreneur of the Year Award in 2010. In February 2013, she joined the United Nations Foundation's Global Entrepreneurs Council. Smolyansky and Lifeway partnered with supermodel-turned-activist Christy Turlington Burns and her Every Mother Counts organization in 2011 to raise awareness for maternal and child health. "I live with purpose," she told Lauren Shapiro for the women's online magazine *Cheeky Chicago* (28 Feb. 2011). "I want to continue to positively shape our health and the way we eat and live."

## SUGGESTED READING

Farrell, Hilary. "Four Keys to Successful Business Strategy with Julie Smolyansky." *Benzinga*. Benzinga, 9 July 2012. Web. 30 July 2012.

Shapiro, Lauren. "Meet the Cheekiest and Youngest CEO in the Country." *Cheeky Chicago*. Cheeky Chicago, 28 Feb. 2011. Web. 30 July 2012.

Wolinsky, David. "Lifeway's Julie Smolyansky on Inheriting the Family Business." *Inc.Well*. NBCUniversal, 5 Jan. 2012. Web. 30 July 2012.

Zipkin, Amy, and Julie Smolyansky. "A Taste of Kefir." *New York Times*. New York Times Co., 23 Aug. 2008. Web. 30 July 2012.

—*Chris Cullen*

---

# Rebecca Soni

**Born:** March 18, 1987
**Occupation:** Swimmer

Rebecca Soni is known in competitive swimming circles as "the breaststroke queen" for her sustained dominance in individual breaststroke events at the national and international level. Soni has had a virtual stranglehold on the 200-meter breaststroke event since the 2008 Olympic Games, held in Beijing, China, where she won the gold medal and set a world record in that event. At those Games, she also won a surprising silver medal in the 100-meter breaststroke and another silver medal as a member of the US women's 400-meter-medley relay team. Following her breakthrough performance in Beijing, Soni became one of the faces of US swimming and one of the top female breaststrokers in the world. Soni went on to reach a competitive pinnacle at the 2012 Olympic Games in London, where she captured her second consecutive gold medal in the 200-meter breaststroke, becoming the first American swimmer of either gender to successfully defend an Olympic title in the breaststroke discipline. More significantly, in the gold-medal 200-meter breaststroke final, she eclipsed her own world record in the event and became the first woman to break the two-minute, twenty-second barrier, which had long been considered "one of the hallowed barriers in swimming," as Lisa Dillman noted for the *Los Angeles Times* (19 Mar. 2013). In London, Soni also picked up a second consecutive silver medal in the

Brian Kersey/UPI/Landov

100-meter breaststroke and another gold medal in the 400-meter-medley relay.

A six-time National Collegiate Athletic Association (NCAA) champion at the University of Southern California (USC) from 2006 to 2009, Soni has differed from the vast majority of her peers in one major respect: her swimming technique is considered highly unusual. Pedro Moura wrote for ESPN.com (27 July 2012): "Her breaststroke, with an abbreviated kick but an accentuated, fine-tuned shoulder jerk, is unprecedented in world-class swimming and impossible to copy." Soni, who in 2006 underwent a heart procedure called cardiac ablation to correct debilitating bouts of rapid heartbeat, has been equally known for her unrivaled dedication to training and for possessing a fiery competitiveness that belies an otherwise calm, unassuming personality. Her head swim coach at USC, Dave Salo, told Kelli Anderson for *Sports Illustrated* (30 Apr. 2012), "Someone asked me what animal I would characterize her as, and I said a lioness. . . . There's that quietness, but you know if she wants to strike, you're going to get full bore."

## EARLY LIFE

Rebecca Soni was born on March 18, 1987, in Freehold Borough, New Jersey, the younger of the two daughters of Peter Soni, a realtor, and Kinga Soni, a nurse. Of Hungarian descent, her parents immigrated to the United States from Romania in the 1980s. Soni and her older sister, Rita, were raised in the central New Jersey town of Plainsboro. They both participated in gymnastics from an early age. Soni switched from gymnastics to swimming at age ten, in part because her parents wanted her to become involved in a sport that she would not outgrow as a teenager. She eventually, reluctantly, followed

2

her sister onto a local swim team after deciding that it would be a better option to swim than to wait around for her sister's practices to end. "At first I didn't want to switch over," Soni recalled to Mike Greger for *Metro.us* (15 July 2012), "but I grew to love it."

When Soni first started swimming, she admittedly knew little about the sport. She was unaware of basic swimming strokes and events and was unprepared for the strenuous training and practices required by the sport. Nonetheless, Soni soon became dedicated to the sport. At thirteen, she joined the elite Scarlet Aquatic Club (now Scarlet Aquatics: Rutgers Division). By that time Soni had given up one of her other passions, the piano, in order to focus solely on swimming. Her early development as a swimmer was fostered by Tom Speedling, the head coach at Scarlet Aquatics, who quickly saw her potential for greatness.

## AN UNUSUAL STYLE

The breaststroke is the slowest of the four main strokes in competitive swimming, but it is widely considered to be the most difficult to master and teach. The stroke requires swimmers to lie face-down in the water, leaning on their chests at a slight angle, then use a strong circular arm pull motion with a whip or "snap" kick that resembles that of a frog. Because the stroke naturally increases a swimmer's drag and resistance in the water, the timing and rhythm of the arms and legs are critical for effectiveness and fluidity.

While many of the world's top breaststrokers are known for either their distinctive pulls or kicks, Soni relies more on her core strength to propel herself in the water. "Where others surge through the water with long glides," Anderson writes, "Soni skims along the surface like a water skeeter, her abbreviated pull and narrow snap kick giving her a quick tempo few swimmers can maintain." Speedling explained to Anderson, "When she first got here [at Scarlet Aquatics], she had a very different stroke, she was throwing her hands out of the water. . . . I like to tell the kids about how Michelangelo would look at a piece of marble and see the David in it—he just cut away the excess stuff that wasn't necessary. That's what we did with her stroke; we tried to base it on her core strength." When Soni was an age-group swimmer with Scarlet Aquatics, her unorthodox but highly effective breaststroke so perplexed deck officials in swim meets that they would sometimes disqualify her from races because her stroke seemed simply too fast to be legal.

Under Speedling, Soni refined her stroke to complement her core strength and altered her approach in races to make better use of her below-average size for a swimmer. Speedling had her switch from a full to a more abbreviated pull and shortened the motion of her kick by having her keep her knees closer together. Also, instead of using a long underwater pullout after jumping off the starting block, Speedling got her to start doing a quick pullout at the outset in order to launch immediately into her stroke.

## HIGH SCHOOL AND COLLEGE SWIMMING

Speedling's changes paid off, and Soni developed into one of the top female breaststrokers in the country. She participated in her first US nationals meet when she was thirteen, and at sixteen, she was a finalist in the 100- and 200-meter breaststroke events at the 2003 US Summer Nationals. At seventeen, Soni qualified for the 2004 US Olympic Trials, finishing in fifteenth and eleventh place, respectively, in the 100- and 200-meter breaststroke. She then won her first national title at the 2005 US Summer Nationals, placing first in the 200-meter breaststroke. As a member of Scarlet Aquatics, Soni also set New Jersey state records in the 100- and 200-yard breaststroke.

Though Soni was making waves in the swimming world, she seldom spoke of her achievements while attending West Windsor–Plainsboro High School North. In fact, many of her high school classmates, were unaware that she even swam. Unlike some elite competitive swimmers, Soni did not swim for her high school, instead dedicating all of her free time to training, both independently and with Scarlet Aquatics. Throughout high school she would normally wake up each day at three o'clock in the morning and drive from Plainsboro to Princeton to swim; she would swim again after school with Scarlet Aquatics. Her dedication was such that she would routinely swim even while she was sick. "I didn't have much of a social life," Soni recalled to Greger. "Going to the pool was my social time."

Recruited by the renowned swim coach Mark Schubert, Soni chose to attend USC after graduating from high school in 2005. As a freshman, Soni went undefeated in the 200-yard breaststroke, winning both NCAA and Pacific 10 Conference (Pac 10) titles in the event. She also won a Pac 10 title in the 100-yard breaststroke while notching second-place finishes in that event and the 400-yard medley relay at the 2006 NCAA Swimming and Diving Championships.

Shortly after the 2006 NCAA Championships, Schubert left USC to become USA Swimming's national team director. He was replaced by another renowned swim coach, Dave Salo, who had developed an impressive number of Olympic swimmers as the longtime head coach of the prestigious Irvine Novaquatics swim club. Despite his resume and reputation for developing world-class breaststrokers, Soni was unaccustomed to Salo's radical coaching style and philosophy. His style revolved around high-intensity, low-yardage training and espoused accountability and self-sufficiency. Soni, who relished the high-yardage, endurance-based workouts implemented by Schubert, Speedling, and most swim coaches in general, considered transferring to another school, out of fear that Salo would try to change her stroke and training regimen.

## BEATING ADVERSITY

As Soni tried to adjust to Salo's new coaching style and workout sessions, she decided to correct an energy-depleting heart condition that had affected her since her midteens. The condition, called supraventricular tachycardia, frequently caused her to suffer heartbeat irregularities during intense training sessions, in which her heart rate sometimes increased to more than two hundred beats per minute; as a result she would often have to sit out practice because of exhaustion. Soni's heartbeat irregularities became more frequent as she entered college, and they eventually came to a head at a meet in Mission Viejo, California, in May 2006, when her condition suddenly crept up before a race. That July she underwent a relatively minor and otherwise routine procedure known as cardiac ablation to correct the condition; Soni has since had a normal heartbeat.

Less than a month after having her ablation, Soni competed at the 2006 US Summer Nationals, placing tenth in both the 100- and 200-meter breaststroke. Though she failed to defend her national 200-meter breaststroke title, she successfully defended her NCAA title in the 200-yard breaststroke during her 2006–7 sophomore season at USC. She also reached the finals in the 100-yard breaststroke for the second consecutive year. However, Soni performed disappointingly in her events at the 2007 Pac 10 Championships, coming in second in the 200-yard breaststroke (the only time in her collegiate career that she lost her signature event) and fourth in the 100-yard breaststroke. Undaunted, Soni bounced back at the April 2007 Duel in the Pool, an international exhibition meet that pitted the US team against the Australian team; she won a silver medal in the 200-meter breaststroke with a personal-best time and a bronze medal in the 100-meter breaststroke. Later that summer, she notched a gold-medal sweep of those events at the 2007 US Summer Nationals.

By the fall of 2007 Soni had bought into Salo's vision for her, after trepidation. "It took me a long time to understand what he was doing," she explained to Karen Crouse for the *New York Times* (20 Mar. 2008). "Before Dave, I never really thought of anything for myself. I just followed what the coach said. With Dave, it's like you have to learn what you have to do for yourself." Keeping Salo's principles in mind, Soni enjoyed a breakout year in 2008, sweeping the 100- and 200-yard breaststroke events at the NCAA and Pac 10 championships and winning the 200-meter breaststroke title at the US Olympic

Trials. Her victory in the 200-meter breaststroke guaranteed her a spot on her first Olympic team. Meanwhile, despite finishing fourth in the finals of the 100-meter breaststroke at the trials, Soni was granted a spot on the Olympic team in that event when first-place finisher Jessica Hardy tested positive for a banned substance.

## UNLIKELY OLYMPIC HEROINE

Heading into the 2008 Olympic Games in Beijing, Soni was relatively unknown outside of national swimming circles. Her profile, however, rose considerably after she left the Games with three medals. First, Soni earned a surprising silver medal in the 100-meter breaststroke. Then, three days later, she shocked both the swimming world and herself when she won the gold medal in the 200-meter breaststroke, finishing with a world-record time of 2:20.22. Soni later described her 200-meter breaststroke performance in Beijing to Anderson as "the best race of my life." She added another silver medal as a member of the 400-meter-medley relay team.

While the 2008 Games were largely dominated by discussion of American swimming phenomenon Michael Phelps winning a record eight gold medals, Soni left Beijing as one of the new faces of US swimming and the undisputed "breaststroke queen." In the spring of 2009, she culminated her college career by sweeping the 100- and 200-yard breaststroke events at the NCAA and Pac 10 championships, to win her fifth and sixth NCAA and Pac 10 titles. She finished her career at USC as the school record holder in the 100-yard breaststroke, 200-yard breaststroke, 200-yard-medley relay, and 400-yard-medley relay; the American, NCAA, and Pac 10 record holder in the 200-yard breaststroke; and the NCAA and Pac 10 record holder in the 100-yard breaststroke. In May 2009, Soni graduated from USC with a degree in communications.

That summer Soni continued her breakthrough run at the US National Swimming Championships, where she swept the 100- and 200-meter breaststroke events, setting an American record in the former. Then, at the 2009 World Championships in Rome, Italy, Soni set a world record in the 100-meter breaststroke, winning the gold medal. She also claimed a silver medal in the 50-meter breaststroke but finished in a disappointing fourth place in her signature event, the 200-meter breaststroke, despite getting off to a record-breaking start and leading most of the race. Soni's poor performance in the 200-meter breaststroke was largely attributed to her wearing a polyurethane bodysuit, which "made the race feel easier than it probably was," as she told Anderson. She started out the race uncharacteristically fast before slowing down considerably and ultimately tiring out during the last 50 meters, the portion of the race where she normally pulls away from the field.

## DEFENDING HER TITLE

Following the 2009 World Championships, Soni was recognized as the American Female Swimmer of the Year by *Swimming World Magazine* and landed an endorsement contract with the European-based swimsuit maker Arena. In 2010, she went undefeated in the 100-meter breaststroke, winning gold medals in the event at the US Nationals and Pan Pacific Championships. She also won gold medals in the 200-meter breaststroke at those meets. In December of that year, Soni won three gold medals and one silver medal at the FINA Short Course World Championships, sweeping the 50-, 100-, and 200-meter breaststroke events and placing second in the 400-meter-medley relay. She was named the American Female Swimmer of the Year for the second consecutive year, as well as World Swimmer of the Year.

At the 2011 World Championships in Shanghai, China, Soni defended her gold medal in the 100-meter breaststroke, earned her first world title in the 200-meter breaststroke, and added a third gold in the 400-meter medley relay. The relay team set a new American record in the event. Soni also garnered a bronze medal in the 50-meter breaststroke. For her achievements, she earned her third consecutive American Swimmer of the Year honor and second straight World Swimmer of the Year honor.

In contrast to 2008, Soni was widely expected to win gold in both the 100- and 200-meter breaststroke at the 2012 Olympic Games in London. She secured a trip to the Games after qualifying for both events and for the 400-yard-medley relay at the 2012 Olympic Trials. In London, Soni was upset in the 100-meter breaststroke, losing by 0.08 seconds to Lithuanian Ruta Meilutyte. However, she easily defended her 200-meter breaststroke title several days later, first breaking Canadian Annamay Pierse's world record in the semifinals; she then broke her own world record in the finals. Soni finished more than a second ahead of second-place finisher Satomi Suzuki of Japan. Soni culminated her second Olympics by winning her third career gold medal as a member of the 400-meter-medley team, which established a new world record in the event.

Following the 2012 Olympics, it was revealed that Soni had swum with a painful cyst on her tailbone for two months before the Games. The condition caused slight nerve pain in her right leg and limited her flexibility. As a result, Soni took an extended period off from competitive swimming after returning home from London in order to recover physically and to focus on other endeavors, including working toward a graduate degree in nutrition at USC. Though

Soni has yet to commit to the 2016 Olympics in Rio de Janeiro, Brazil, she has not ruled out the possibility of competing and continues to train under Salo.

## PERSONAL LIFE

Soni lives in Manhattan Beach, California, with her longtime boyfriend, Ricky Berens, a fellow US Olympic swimmer who won gold medals at the 2008 and 2012 Olympics. Since 2010, Soni has served as a global ambassador for the United Nations Foundation's Girl Up program, which aims to improve the lives of young women around the world. She is fluent in Hungarian and enjoys hiking, reading, going to the beach, and hanging out with friends and family in her spare time.

## SUGGESTED READING

Anderson, Kelli. "Stroke of Genius." *Sports Illustrated*. Time Inc., 30 Apr. 2012. Web. 15 May 2013.

Crouse, Karen. "A Breaststroke That Is Hard to Imitate and All but Impossible to Beat." *New York Times*. New York Times Co., 21 Aug. 2010. Web. 15 May 2013.

Dillman, Lisa. "Swimmer Rebecca Soni's Olympic Heroics Have a (Painful) Back Story." *Los Angeles Times*. Tribune Co., 19 Mar. 2013. Web. 15 May 2013.

Greger, Mike. "Rebecca Soni: Swimming into Pool of Expectations." *Metro.us*. Metro, 15 July 2012. Web. 15 May 2013.

Moura, Pedro. "Rebecca Soni Cools Down." *ESPNW Summer Olympics*. ESPN Internet Ventures, 27 July 2012. Web. 15 May 2013.

—*Chris Cullen*

# Morgan Spurlock

**Born:** November 7, 1970
**Occupation:** Filmmaker

Morgan Spurlock first came to widespread attention as a filmmaker with *Super Size Me* (2004), in which he documented a thirty-day period—from February 1 to March 2, 2003—during which he ate only fast food from McDonald's for breakfast, lunch, and dinner. The film explored the negative effects the diet had on his weight, health, and psyche, and it also took a hard look at the fast food industry's relentless drive for profit in the face of a growing obesity crisis in the United States and elsewhere.

The picture earned Spurlock a reputation as a unique and even outrageous filmmaker; "There is almost nothing Morgan Spurlock will not do for public attention," Genevieve Roberts wrote for the London *Independent* (1 Apr. 2012). He

Associated Press

cemented that reputation with his subsequent work, which includes *Where in the World Is Osama Bin Laden* (2008), in which he went on a personal search for the terrorist mastermind; *The Greatest Movie Ever Sold* (2011), which explores in comic detail the world of paid product placement; and *Mansome* (2012), a look at male grooming—and an exceptionally fitting project for Spurlock, as one of his trademarks is his distinctive horseshoe-shaped mustache. "I have spent the past few years putting myself into situations that are usually very difficult and at the same time somewhat dangerous," he explained in 2011, during his talk at the TED (Technology, Entertainment and Design) conference, an annual event that attracts thought leaders from around the world. "In fact, most of my career, I've been immersing myself into seemingly horrible situations for the whole goal of trying to examine societal issues in a way that makes them engaging, that makes them interesting, that hopefully breaks them down in a way that makes them entertaining and accessible to an audience."

## EARLY LIFE

Morgan Valentine Spurlock was born on November 7, 1970, in Parkersburg, West Virginia. He has described his Methodist household as very traditional, with "a dead animal on the table at every meal," as he told Ariel Leve for the London *Guardian* (18 Feb. 2012). Among his early memories is the time he hunted and killed a squirrel, which was then served for dinner. He remains quite close to all of his family members, but, acknowledging that they are more conservative

than he is now in most respects, he continued, "We just don't talk about religion or politics."

He has cited his mother as a particularly influential figure; during his childhood she introduced him to her favorite British comedies, including *Fawlty Towers*, *Blackadder*, and *Monty Python's Flying Circus*. "I was doing funny walks round the house at six or seven," he recalled to Roberts. He knew at a very young age that he wanted to be a professional entertainer. "I never wanted to do anything else," he recalled to Leve. He realized that he would probably did not have the makings of a superstar. "I was awkward as a kid," he continued. "I wasn't the best looking or the most athletic or the funniest." Still, he was a persistent and tenacious youth, and he is grateful to his parents for instilling those attributes in him. "The one thing I never saw my father do in the midst of failure was quit. I don't ever remember seeing him depressed," he told Leve. "I was never allowed to quit anything—once you started, you carried it through to the end. Period."

## EDUCATION

When he graduated from Woodrow Wilson High School, in Beckley, West Virginia, in 1989, he began investigating film schools. He had narrowed his career choice to filmmaker when he was a young teen, and the director John Sayles was shooting his 1987 release, *Matewan*, a film about an embattled mining community, about a half an hour away from the Spurlock home. Spurlock and his mother drove to the set and watched the filming for hours. "To me it was the most magical thing I'd ever seen because at that moment movies suddenly became real," he recalled to Peter Biesterfeld for *Videomaker Magazine* (Dec. 2012). "Suddenly they weren't these things that were so far away and were only made in Hollywood. . . . Once I learned that I could go to college and actually study film, I said, 'Hold on, that's exactly what I want to do.'"

His persistence and tenacity served him well as a college student. He initially attended the University of Southern California, and each semester he applied for admission to the school's film program. He was rejected each time. Finally, after two years he made the decision to transfer to New York University's Tisch School of the Arts, whose other notable alumni include the filmmakers Charles Kaufman, Chris Columbus, and Martin Scorsese.

Spurlock found the entrepreneurial spirit of New York City invigorating. Every film student at Tisch was expected to raise the money to make his or her own movie, a requirement that Spurlock felt helped prepare him for the real world. "When you graduate, the chances of you coming out of college with a film degree and an idea and somebody walking up to you and giving you a check for a million dollars to go make a movie, are few and far between," he told Biesterfeld.

"Mostly what's going to happen to you when you come out is that you're going to have to hustle to find somebody who likes your idea, you have to find a place to sell it and you have to find a crew."

## A FLEDGLING CAREER
After graduating from Tisch in 1993, Spurlock began seeking work as a production assistant and found jobs on such films as Luc Besson's *Léon: The Professional* (1994) and Woody Allen's *Bullets Over Broadway* (1994). He found working with the iconic filmmakers revelatory but eventually began to "burn out," as he has put it, as a production assistant. His student thesis film had been accepted at several film festivals, and he was working in a field he loved, in close proximity to some of the most talented cinematic artists of the day, but life was not as fulfilling as he had imagined it would be. One day, while he was laboring on the set of Barbet Schroeder's *Kiss of Death* (1995), a casting agent suggested that he audition for a spokesperson job with Sony Electronics, which was mounting a large promotional tour. He got the gig, and when executives speculated that it would be good to make a video about the tour, he revealed that he had been to film school and would like to take on the task.

That led to directing commercials for Sony's Digital Mavica, a camera that used floppy disks, and he also made a multimillion dollar presentation video that was used during the annual Consumer Electronics Show in Las Vegas. (He has recalled that it was the most expensive thing he had made up until that time.) He served at one point as an announcer for the Bud Light Pro Beach Volleyball League, which was sponsored by Sony, and went on to a similar role at ESPN, announcing various extreme sports.

Spurlock later found work directing commercials and music videos, and in his spare time he wrote plays. One 1999 piece, *The Phoenix*, was mounted at several theater festivals that year and took home an audience award.

At about that time, Spurlock became interested in the possibilities of the burgeoning Internet, so he raised the money to start his own production company, sleeping in a hammock in his office when his budget was too tight to pay the rent on an apartment. His first Internet venture was the web series *I Bet You Will*, on which people were paid to perform disgusting or outrageous acts, like eating a hairball made of butter and their own hair or slurping an entire bottle of cod-liver oil. In 2002, he sold the series to MTV, where it aired for one season.

### SUPER SIZE ME
In 2002 Spurlock visited his family in West Virginia for Thanksgiving. While there he watched a television news story about two girls suing McDonald's, on the grounds that the fast food chain's products had contributed to their obesity. Ambushed by reporters for a comment, a McDonald's representative responded, "Our food is nutritious." The exchange gave Spurlock the idea to eat only items from McDonald's for an entire month to see how he fared and to document the process on film; he required himself to accept whenever a clerk gave him the option of "super-sizing" his meal, meaning that he got the largest available portions of French fries and soft drinks. In good physical condition at the start of the experiment, he found himself gaining more than twenty pounds and suffering from dangerously high cholesterol. He interspersed footage of himself with a segment about young children who could identify a picture of Ronald McDonald but not one of Jesus and a graphic look at an actual stomach-reduction surgery. The documentary, *Super Size Me*, which Spurlock both produced and directed, was shown at the 2004 Sundance Film Festival, where it won Spurlock the award for best director in the documentary competition; he also received an Oscar nomination in the category of best documentary film.

Critics, while repulsed, were generally impressed. "*Super Size Me* is a deliciously amusing socio-culinary prank," Owen Gleiberman wrote in a representative review for *Entertainment Weekly*. "[It] is witty, gross, smart, outrageous, and so clever it just about pops. The movie lays bare the insidiousness of American fast-food culture by feasting on it in big, hungry bites."

The movie elicited such an outcry that in response, McDonald's discontinued the practice of super sizing. It is still shown in high school health classes and remains the film with which Spurlock is most closely identified. "I'll be that guy till I die," he told Roberts.

### DOCUMENTARIES AND OTHER PROJECTS
Spurlock followed that with a well-received television series called *30 Days*, which aired from 2005 to 2008 and which he executive produced. Each episode of the documentary series chronicled the experiences of a person who has agreed to live for thirty days in a situation completely different from his or her norm. In one installment, for example, a Christian man from West Virginia moves in with a Muslim family in Michigan; in another, a border guard moves in with a family of illegal immigrants. Spurlock himself appears in an episode, which showcases his attempt to live on a minimum-wage salary.

Spurlock next directed and produced *Where in the World Is Osama Bin Laden*, in which he documented his ostensible search for the September 11 mastermind who had eluded capture by American forces for almost a decade. Traveling throughout the Middle East, he interviewed several Arabs who did not subscribe to the doctrines of radical Islam and concluded that people were much the same all over the world. The documentary was considered didactic and self-indulgent by most reviewers and made little of the splash that *Super Size Me* had.

After directing and producing the animated *Simpsons Twentieth Anniversary Special: In 3-D! On Ice!* in 2010, Spurlock, whose production company is called Warrior Poets, returned to the documentary format to direct *Freakonomics* (2010), based on a popular book of the same name.

The following year he executive produced and directed *The Greatest Movie Ever Sold*, a film that garnered him almost as much media attention as *Super Size Me*. In a stunt that journalists seemed to find irresistible, Spurlock had financed a documentary about branding, advertising, and product placement by selling branding opportunities, advertising, and product placement to major companies, including the beverage firm Pom Wonderful, which paid $1 million to have its name at the top of the marquee. In one of his more audacious moves, Spurlock paid the city of Altoona, Pennsylvania, to change its name to Pom Wonderful Presents: The Greatest Movie Ever Sold, Pennsylvania for ninety days. (The funds were earmarked for the city's financially strapped police department.)

Mark Holcomb wrote for the *Village Voice* (20 Apr. 2011), "As agreeable as it is insidious, Morgan Spurlock's latest exposé of corporate control via immersive humiliation is his best, most formally inventive project yet." Stephen Holden also gave a positive assessment in his review for the *New York Times* (21 Apr. 2011), writing, "Cocky with an undertone of ironic self-deprecation that forestalls accusations of insincerity, [Spurlock] is a superb promoter of himself as a brand. In *The Greatest Movie Ever Sold* he may look ridiculous wearing clothes plastered with corporate logos, but he lets us in on the joke."

## RECENT AND ONGOING WORK

Spurlock's most recent projects include producing and directing *Comic-Con Episode IV: A Fan's Hope* (2011), a documentary focused on the thousands of fans who descend on San Diego, California, each year to attend one of the world's largest comic book conventions; producing and directing *The Dotted Line* (2011), an inside look at the world of sports agents; and producing and directing *Mansome*, whose tagline asks, "In the age of manscaping, metrosexuals, and grooming products galore—what does it mean to be a man?" The last film was widely reviewed, but those reviews tended to be decidedly mixed. For example, Marc Savlov wrote for the *Austin Chronicle* (18 May 2012), "*Mansome* is frequently laugh-out-loud funny, thanks in large part to canny interviews with the likes of Judd Apatow, Adam Carolla, and pro wrestler Shawn Daivari. But as a documentary dissertation on all

that it means to be male in the modern world, you'd be better off investing in the complete works of Ernest Hemingway."

British television is now airing another Spurlock project, *New Britannia*, which is described on the website of Sky Atlantic TV as "a lively new show in which the acclaimed American humourist will dissect the eccentricities of British culture." Spurlock's latest web project is the *Failure Club*, an Internet reality series that brings together seven people every week for a year and follows their efforts to help each other overcome fear of failure. The participants include a homemaker who wants to start her own business, a businessperson who wants to become a stand-up comic, and a middle-aged mother who wants to train as an equestrian.

Some observers have expressed surprise that Spurlock is currently producing and directing *One Direction: This Is Us*, a 3-D documentary about the popular boy band. Scheduled for release in mid-2013, the film follows the members of One Direction as they rehearse, perform, and go about their daily lives.

## PERSONAL LIFE

From May 2006 to 2011 he was married to Alexandra Jamieson, a vegan chef who appeared with him in *Super Size Me*. She devised the diet that helped him shed his excess weight and restored him to good health when the experiment was over; she later wrote the book *The Great American Detox Diet: Feel Better, Look Better, and Lose Weight by Cleaning Up Your Diet* (2005). They share custody of a son, Laken, who was born in December 2006.

When Spurlock is not traveling, he makes his home in Fort Greene, a neighborhood in the New York City borough of Brooklyn. He is an avid art collector and has curated occasional gallery shows. He is also the author of *Don't Eat This Book: Fast Food and the Supersizing of America*, which was published in 2006.

## SUGGESTED READING

Biesterfeld, Peter. "Morgan Spurlock: Inspired by the Need to Find Answers." *Videomaker*. Videomaker, Dec. 2012. Web. 26 Mar. 2013.

Gleiberman, Owen. "Movie Review: *Super Size Me*." *Entertainment Weekly*. Entertainent Weekly, 1 Feb. 2005. Web. 26 Mar. 2013.

Leve, Ariel. "Morgan Spurlock: 'I wasn't the best looking kid—I was just tenacious'" *Guardian*. Guardian News and Media, 18 Feb. 2012. Web. 26 Mar. 2013.

Roberts, Genevieve. "Morgan Spurlock: 'I was doing funny walks around the house aged six.'" *Independent*. Independent, 1 Apr. 2012. Web. 26 Mar. 2013.

Rothman, Lily. "Morgan Spurlock on Mustaches, Mantyhose and *Mansome*." *Time*. Time, 26 Apr. 2012. Web. 26 Mar. 2013.

## SELECTED WORKS
*Super Size Me*, 2004; *Where in the World Is Osama Bin Laden?*, 2008; *The Simpsons Twentieth Anniversary Special: In 3-D! On Ice!*, 2010; *Freakonomics*, 2010; *The Greatest Movie Ever Sold*, 2011; *Comic-Con Episode IV: A Fan's Hope*, 2011; *Mansome*, 2012

—*Mari Rich*

---

# Steven Stamkos

**Born:** February 7, 1990
**Occupation:** Hockey player with the Tampa Bay Lightning

Getty Images

After being drafted first overall by the Tampa Bay Lightning in the 2008 National Hockey League (NHL) draft, Steven Stamkos developed a reputation as one of the game's most lethal scorers. "Stamkos is the complete player," wrote Adam Bass, senior writer for the sports website *Bleacher Report* (20 May 2008), "He has unbelievable speed and great movement. He has a huge wrist shot with a quick release. . . . He shows no weakness, and he has the great ability to make everyone around him better." He earned his first Maurice "Rocket" Richard Trophy, awarded annually to the league's top goal scorer, following his second season in the NHL. Stamkos became widely known for his use of the shot known as the "one-timer," which involves meeting a teammate's pass with an immediate shot on goal. Making regular use of the one-timer, he scored sixty goals in 2011–12. As of 2013, Stamkos is one of twenty players in league history to score sixty or more goals in a single season. Among the other players to achieve this milestone are NHL legends Wayne Gretzky and Mario Lemieux. "There's people who work hard and there are people who are relentless. He is relentless," Lightning coach Guy Boucher told Sarah Kwak for *Sports Illustrated* (13 Feb. 2013). "He might have a bad game, but it will never be because of his work ethic." In addition to his presence on the ice, Stamkos has established himself as a big presence among Tampa Bay's charitable and nonprofit organizations. He was described in the *South Tampa-Hyde Park Patch* (18 May 2012) as "one of Tampa Bay's most visible and benevolent athletes."

## EARLY LIFE AND EDUCATION
Steven Christopher Stamkos was born on February 7, 1990, in Markham, Ontario, to Chris and Lesley Stamkos. His father, a Canadian of Macedonian descent, worked for the financial services corporation American Express. His mother, who is of Scottish descent, worked as a telemarketer. Stamkos has a younger sister named Sarah. Stamkos was raised in a section of Markham known as Unionville, and attended Central Park Public School and Brother Andre Catholic High School. His father introduced him to the game of hockey at age two. In addition to hockey, Stamkos enjoyed playing sports of all kinds, including baseball, soccer, lacrosse, and golf. As a young hockey player, Stamkos modeled his game after renowned scorer Joe Sakic of the Colorado Avalanche. In addition to work on his hockey skills with his father (who earned a scholarship as a college player), Stamkos also attended training programs.

Even as a player in the local Pee Wee league, Stamkos's talents on the ice were evident. Stamkos began playing hockey for the Markham Waxers of the Ontario Minor Hockey Association at the age of fifteen. In just sixty-six games with the Waxers during his first season, Stamkos scored 197 points. In 2005, Stamkos joined the Sarnia Sting of the Ontario Hockey League (OHL). During the 2006–07 season, he scored forty-two goals and finished second in the voting for OHL Rookie of the Year. He scored fifty-eight goals during his second season in the OHL. Stamkos's success in the OHL made him one of the hockey world's most widely known prospects. He ranked first on the International Scouting Ranking from December 2006 until the 2008 NHL draft.

## JOINING THE NHL

The 2008 NHL Draft took place on June 20–21 at Scotiabank Place in Ottawa, Ontario. In total, the NHL's thirty teams selected ninety-one elite prospects. With the first pick of the first round of the draft, the Tampa Bay Lightning selected Stamkos. Following the draft, he signed a three-year, $8.5 million contract with the team, in addition to an endorsement deal with Nike. He made his NHL debut on October 4, 2008, in a game played in Prague, Czech Republic. On February 17, 2009, Stamkos earned his first career hat trick, scoring three goals against the Chicago Blackhawks. In his inaugural season, he scored twenty-three goals, setting a new record for Lightning rookies. He also earned twenty-three assists en route to collecting a total of forty-six overall points.

The 2009–10 season was Stamkos's breakout year as a professional hockey player. Prior to the start of the season, he trained with recently retired NHL veteran Gary Roberts. In addition to working on the ice, Stamkos hit the gym to build up his strength and endurance. The hard work paid off. "I knew he was going to be good," former Lightning coach and NHL veteran Rick Tocchet told the *Examiner* (27 Jan. 2011), "I didn't know he would develop this quickly." During the 2009–10 season, the strength and accuracy of Stamkos' shots became a phenomenon among hockey fans and analysts. Former NHL executive and NHL Network analyst Craig Button described Stamkos' shot to *NHL Insider* (27 Oct. 2010). "It's so fast off his stick and so heavy, that even though the goalie knows where he has to get to, the shot literally beats the goalie," said Button. The goalies know it's coming, but Stamkos gets the better of them. . . . He moves around, too. . . . Steven can be watching the puck and everybody around it." Following his fifty-one goal 2009–10 performance, Stamkos finished fifth in the league-wide scoring rankings. He earned forty-four assists and scored a total of ninety-five points. He was jointly awarded the Rocket Richard Trophy with Sidney Crosby of the Pittsburg Penguins, who also scored fifty-one goals.

## NHL ALL-STAR

Stamkos scored nineteen goals in the first nineteen games of the 2010–11 season. He generated much excitement among hockey fans during the opening months of the season, many of whom thought he might reach the elusive "50-in-50" mark, or fifty goals in fifty games. Although Stamkos fell short of 50-in-50, he again proved himself to be one of the league's best players. In January 2011, he was named to the NHL All-Star team. Stamkos finished the season with forty-five goals, again finishing fifth in the league in scoring, with forty-six assists and ninety-one points overall. He also made his Stanley Cup Playoffs debut in the 2011. The Lightning defeated the Pittsburg Penguins in seven games in the conference quarterfinals. The Lightning won four consecutive games to sweep the Washington Capitals in the conference semifinals. During game 7 of the Eastern Conference Finals against the Boston Bruins, Stamkos was hit in the face with a slapshot, resulting in a broken nose. Although Stamkos remained in the game, the Lightning were defeated and eliminated from the playoffs.

In June 2011, Stamkos was selected to appear on the cover of the EA Sports video game *NHL 12*. In July 2011, Stamkos re-signed with the Lightning, earning a five-year contract worth $37.5 million. His sixty-goal performance in the 2011–12 season solidified him as one of the NHL's elite players. He scored an NHL record five overtime goals during the year, although the Lightning failed to make the playoffs. In addition to his work in the NHL, Stamkos has represented Canada numerous times in international play throughout his career, including appearances in 2009 and 2010 at the International Ice Hockey Federation's (IIHF) World Championships. He was named to the IIHF's World Championships All-Star team in 2009.

## JOINING THE NHL'S ELITE

Over the course of his first few seasons in the NHL, Stamkos has come to be known as the on-ice leader of the Lightning. He has appeared in every game (eighty-two each year) in the three seasons following his debut as a member of the Lightning. His name is regularly mentioned along with the Penguins' Crosby in conversations among fans and analysts about who is the best offensive player in the league. "He goes about his seasons in a workman-like way," writes Eric Stietz for *Bleacher Report* (12 Oct. 2012), "He plays. He produces. He leads and he wins. Stamkos . . . has earned the trust and respect of his teammates through his consistency." Speaking with the Damian Cristodero for the *Tampa Bay Times* (23 Sept. 2011), Stamkos revealed how his team's tough loss in the 2011 playoffs changed him as a player. "I learned it doesn't always take scoring a couple of goals or getting a couple of assists to have a good game," he says, adding "I've been in this league awhile. . . . I'm comfortable that I've earned the respect of the veteran [players]." According to Cristodero, Lightning head coach Boucher said that during Stamkos's 2010–11 campaign, "he went from being a star, to a winner."

In April 2012, Andrew Khatchaturian of *Bleacher Report* listed Stamkos third on his list of the NHL's Top 100 Players. "The gap between the top three players in the league and the rest is pretty wide," writes Khatchaturian, "Steven Stamkos is going to make Tampa Bay Lightning fans smile for years to come."

In 2012, Stamkos was awarded the Award of Excellence from Ronald McDonald House Charities of Tampa Bay. Previous recipients of the award include General Norman Schwarzkopf, basketball analyst Dick Vitale, and New York Yankees owner George Steinbrenner. In addition to working with the Lightning Foundation, his team's charitable organization, Stamkos has served as a leader of the Kids Are Heroes program at Tampa's St. Joseph's Children's Hospital.

## THE 2012–13 LOCKOUT
The beginning of the 2012–13 NHL season was delayed by a lockout, during which league officials and player representatives worked out the details of a new collective bargaining agreement. Stamkos remained active during the delay by playing hockey in his father's beer league, and staying active with his charity work. In December 2012, Stamkos led a team of NHL players in an appearance at a charity game to raise money for the NHL Players' Association's Goals & Dreams fund and the Royal Bank of Canada's Play Hockey fund. Speaking about the game with ESPN.com (12 Dec. 2012), Stamkos described the event as "a great opportunity to share the joy and excitement of hockey with our fans . . . while helping to raise funds to benefit local hockey programs across the country."

Following the end of the 2012–13 lockout, Stamkos got off to a slow start. Some were critical of his lack of offensive production. However, Stamkos was undeterred. "You have to adjust your game," he tells *Sports Illustrated*'s Kwak. "That's something I learned from [teammate] Marty [St. Louis]. You have to reinvent your tendencies on the ice." As part of this reinvention, Stamkos has come to rely less on the one-timer, which many NHL defenses now expect from him. "A lot of people still to this day think I score a lot of goals on the one-timer," Stamkos said to Kwak. "In reality, in the last couple years, I could probably count on both hands the number of times I've scored that way."

## PERSONAL LIFE
Stamkos, who is unmarried, turned twenty-three in February 2013. Outside of hockey, he enjoys watching baseball, in particular, the Toronto Blue Jays. He is also a fan of the National Football League's Buffalo Bills. Stamkos, who is still known among teammates and hockey fans by his childhood nickname, "Stammer," is also a music fan.

## SUGGESTED READING
Kwak, Sarah. "Steven Stamkos Remains a Work in Progress." *SI.com*. Time, 15 Feb. 2013. Web. 19 Feb. 2013.

Pashman, Althea. "Lightning's Steven Stamkos Gears Up for First All-Star Appearance." *Examiner*. Clarity Digital Group, 27 Jan. 2011. Web. 21 Feb. 2013.

Rosen, Dan. "How Does Stamkos Do It? Practice, Practice, Practice." *NHL Insider*. NHL, 27 Oct. 2010. Web. 21 Feb. 2013.

Steitz, Eric. "Will Steven Stamkos Pass Sidney Crosby as Best in NHL This Season?" *Bleacher Report*. Bleacher Report, 20 Jan. 2013. Web 19 Feb. 2013.

"Steven Stamkos #91." *Tampa Bay Lightning*. Lightning Hockey, 2011. Web 19 Feb. 2013.

—*Josh Pritchard*

# George Steinmetz
**Born:** 1957
**Occupation:** Photographer

Professional photographers are ever on the lookout for a new angle—some way of capturing their subjects that makes us reevaluate not only what they have shot but also the world at large. George Steinmetz found his new angle by sailing hundreds of feet into the air in a propeller-driven kite-like device called a motorized paraglider and snapping away with a single digital camera equipped with a wide-angle zoom lens. Since the late 1990s, he has captured breathtaking images from all over the world with a profound and fresh intimacy. His photographs depict everything from South America's Altiplano to wide stretches of the open Arabian Desert, the slums sprawling out of Cape Town, South Africa, and the Korowai and Kombai tree-dwellers of Papua, Indonesia.

Steinmetz's work, which demonstrates the skills of both an artist and a documentarian, has garnered him numerous awards and honors, as well as multiple write-ups in major newspapers and magazines. Steinmetz, however, is quick to assert that his aerial photography is not just a gimmick or something he does simply for recognition. As he explains in an article published in *National Geographic Adventure* (Dec. 2008/Jan. 2009): "I'm a photographer who flies, not a pilot who takes pictures. I do this kind of flying because it gives me the opportunity to photograph remote areas in a way they have never been seen before. And from my vantage point in the sky, there is always more to explore, to question, and, ultimately, to understand."

## EARLY LIFE AND EDUCATION
George Steinmetz was born into a well-to-do family in Beverly Hills, California, in 1957, the youngest of his parents' four children. Because he lived in the show business capital of the world, he often came into contact with celebrities through his friendship with Todd Fisher,

© George Steinmetz

the son of actress and singer Debbie Reynolds and entertainer Eddie Fisher. Once, while playing ball, he was nearly run over by comedian Groucho Marx.

Steinmetz's mother was the former Verna Pace, who graduated from Stanford University in 1945; his father, David Henry Steinmetz III, the heir to a lumber fortune, worked as a stockbroker and collected art. Although David Steinmetz worked in business, he had earned his degree in mechanical engineering from the California Institute of Technology (Caltech) in Pasadena, California. His passion for both the outdoors and for machinery would help inspire his son George's career.

Steinmetz's parents divorced when he was just five years old. Although he lived with his mother, Steinmetz remained close to his father, who would take him, along with older siblings Don, Julie, and Diane, up in his Cessna airplane for weekend visits to the family home in the Sierra Mountains. This early exposure to travel helped foster Steinmetz's own interest in traveling. During his junior year at Harvard-Westlake School, a private school for grades seven to twelve in Los Angeles, he spent some months in Tokyo as an exchange student.

## COLLEGE YEARS AND TRAVELING ABROAD

Following his graduation from Harvard-Westlake, Steinmetz began his undergraduate studies at his mother's alma mater, Stanford, but the university life did not appeal to him. During the summer following his sophomore year, he and a friend bought Eurail passes and traveled across the European continent together. "We rented mopeds and drove around with these big bottles of cheap wine and slept on the beach," Steinmetz recalled to Lauren Collins for the *New Yorker* (19 Apr. 2010).

Because the pass was also good for Morocco, he was able to visit North Africa as well. During

this first trip to Africa, Steinmetz dreamed of flying above it, snapping pictures. "I wanted to get into that landscape," he told Abigail Tucker for *Smithsonian* (Jan. 2009). "I wanted to see Africa in 3-D."

After his trip around Europe, Steinmetz returned to Stanford—but not for long. Three years into his undergraduate studies in geophysics, he dropped out at age twenty-one in order to explore Africa. What began as a brief interlude in his education ultimately became a twenty-eight-month sojourn around the continent, during which he developed his love of photography with a 35-mm. Olympus OM-1 camera borrowed from his brother. As Steinmetz traveled, he would mail film canisters back to his mother in California, who would then have them developed. While she was less than pleased about his career choice, she eventually began giving him her critical opinions of his developed photographs.

## PROFESSIONAL PHOTOGRAPHER

Although Steinmetz returned to Stanford to complete his degree in geophysics, he was convinced that he could forge a career as a professional photographer. After a brief internship at an oil company, he returned to Africa, hoping to sell his pictures to magazines. When that did not pan out, he moved to San Francisco, working first for a studio photographer and then for photojournalist Ed Kashi. Though Steinmetz was fired from both positions, Kashi remained friends with his young former employee and started feeding him jobs. Through Kashi, Steinmetz earned his first professional paycheck as a photographer doing a portrait photo shoot of a psychic stockbroker for *California* magazine.

Before long, Steinmetz's photos were featured in *Forbes*, *Fortune*, and *Rolling Stone*. His big breakthrough came in 1986 when he was assigned by *GEO*, a monthly magazine with editions in Germany and France, to document the grand opening of Caesars Palace in Las Vegas. It would become the first of many assignments; by mid-2013 Steinmetz had done some twenty-five stories for *GEO*, including photo essays of the Salt Desert of Iran and the Empty Quarter of Saudi Arabia.

In the mid-1980s, Steinmetz began a long relationship with *National Geographic*, a magazine he had long dreamed of working for. One of his first assignments looked at oil exploration around the world through the eyes of those working the oil fields and rigs. Another, done in 1995, enabled him to photograph the tree-dwelling Kombai and Korowai tribes of Irian Jaya, Indonesia (now Papua, Indonesia). In 1998 and then again in 2002, Steinmetz's expeditions to the Gobi and Sahara deserts were aired on the *National Geographic Explorer* television show.

All told, by mid-2013, Steinmetz had completed thirty-one photo essays for *National Geographic*, including three magazine covers.

In addition to doing photo shoots for magazines, Steinmetz has also had great success in advertising and corporate photography for clients that have included General Motors (GM), Sigma Camera, Toshiba, and Union Bank of Switzerland. Yet his passion—particularly since taking up paragliding—has been photographing the natural world from the air. In interviews, Steinmetz has described this, his life's work, as "exploration photography." He told James Estrin for the *New York Times* (13 Dec. 2012): "You're seeing things that in many cases nobody's ever seen before. You're flying in areas that it's never been possible to fly into. In this world we think everything's been seen and done. There's a lot of fantastic things just waiting to be seen—and photographed."

## MOTORIZED PARAGLIDING

Steinmetz took up motorized paragliding after an aborted attempt in 1996 to photograph the Sahara Desert for *National Geographic* by flying over it in a small plane. He grew frustrated trying to explain to his pilot what he wanted to shoot, and the plane itself could not slow down long enough for him to get the kind of photos he wanted. Moving at more than sixty miles an hour and shielded from his subject by Plexiglas, he realized he could not shoot the desert the way he had envisioned. When the pilot quit the project, Steinmetz searched for an answer to his problem. Then he learned about motorized paragliding.

At first, Steinmetz dismissed the notion as being far too risky. But the few people he knew who had done motorized paragliding told him it would be a fairly easy thing for him to learn— and he did not need a pilot's license to do it. The device resembles a large kite; the pilot hangs beneath it in a harness with a gas-powered motor strapped to his back and steers with cables attached to his arms. At around sixty-five pounds, the paraglider can be broken up into its three main components (the kite wing, the motor, and the harness) and packed into three large duffle bags, which allows it to travel with traditional baggage on most commercial flights. While the paraglider can only fly in the mornings or at dusk when the air is calm and has a fairly limited range—between fifty to one hundred miles, depending on the fuel tank—it does allow Steinmetz to dip into places an airplane or helicopter never could, without disrupting things on the ground the way those aircrafts' motors would. After learning how to pilot his paraglider in Arizona in 1997, Steinmetz had his first solo flight above the hedgerows outside Paris on his fortieth birthday. Before long, Steinmetz was using it to capture amazing photographs of some of the world's most difficult terrains, including deserts, with his digital camera and a wide-angle zoom lens.

## CAPTURING THE WORLD FROM ABOVE

Steinmetz recognizes that taking photos while flying at thirty miles an hour is tricky. Because he needs both hands to hold his camera as well as steer, he must take his hands off his controls in order to snap photos. In calm breezes and at an adequate height off the ground, it poses little problem, but in high winds or when he is too low to the ground, it can be fairly intense. He outlines the benefits of using his motorized paraglider in his article for *National Geographic Adventure*, explaining that "it provides me with an unrestricted 180-degree view in both horizontal and vertical directions, like a flying lawn chair. It's also relatively quiet in flight (it sounds like a moped), and it lets me fly low and slow over the land with a minimum of disturbance to the people and animals below." There are additional benefits as well: "For takeoff, I don't need an airfield, only a small patch of open terrain slightly larger than a basketball court, with enough running room and no trees or power lines in front of me," he wrote. "While I can gain as much as 6,000 feet on a flight, I prefer to shoot at 100 to 500 feet above ground."

Motorized paragliding both literally and figuratively opened up the world to Steinmetz's camera. Able to traverse even forbidding places like deserts and oceans in his "flying lawn chair," he has since captured everything from remote villages in Mali, to elephants grazing in Namibia, to vast swatches of sand dunes in the Empty Quarter of the Arabian Desert. Moreover, because the paraglider is not an aircraft, he has been able to work even in restrictive countries like China, Saudi Arabia, Iran, and Libya, where he would never have gotten permission from the local authorities to take aerial photos in a traditional aircraft. "Most aerial photographers work from helicopters or little planes, but he goes up on this crazy little thing," said Ruth Eichhorn, director of photography for the German edition of *GEO*, as quoted by Tucker. "He can go very low, so he can photograph people in the landscape, and he will go to places that nobody else will go. It's very, very dangerous work, but I think it's worth it."

## PHOTOGRAPHY BOOKS

The photographs that Steinmetz took over Africa in his paraglider were first published in magazines like *Smithsonian*, *GEO*, and *National Geographic*, but after adopting a digital workflow to organize his work, Steinmetz began to see them in a new light, as a book. As he recalled in an interview with Steve Casimiro for *Adventure Journal* (15 Jan. 2009): "I was organizing a big shoot I had done for *National Geographic Magazine* to submit to my picture agents, and thought why not throw in some older aerial work in Africa . . . some odds and ends from different projects over the years. As I saw it all come together on the computer screen I realized that I had a pretty representative mosaic of the whole continent." Steinmetz then got to work on his book proposal. "I took the proposal to Abrams in New York, and then Hervé de La Martinière in Paris, who owns Abrams," he told Casimiro. "When Hervé heard of my unusual method of flying and saw pictures of me with pygmies thirty years ago, he said it should be a personal book, which gave rise to the long introduction in the front of the book."

That first book, *Africa Air*, was published in 2008 to great success and gave rise to two additional volumes: *Empty Quarter: A Photographic Journey to the Heart of the Arabian Desert* (2009) and *Desert Air* (2012). The photographs in the latter volume result from fifteen years planning, organizing, and ultimately making trips to twenty-seven countries in order to capture each of the world's deserts. In the *New York Times*, Estrin calls the book "a result of passion, obsession, and ample amounts of time and stubbornness."

### PERSONAL LIFE

Steinmetz remains passionately committed to his exploratory photography, in the hopes of finding new ways to see our planet. Yet, no matter how often he flies into remote areas or how badly he wants to get the right shot, he is all too aware that mishaps occur or that a sandstorm could force him to make an emergency landing. To that end, he makes sure to fly only under optimum conditions because, as he explains in *National Geographic* (Nov. 2012), "it's always better to be on the ground wishing you were in the sky than in the sky wishing you were on the ground."

George Steinmetz has received many awards for his photography throughout his career, including two first prizes in science and technology from World Press Photo in 1995 and 1998, as well as honors from the Overseas Press Club, Pictures of the Year, and the Alfred Eisenstaedt Awards for Magazine Photography. He was also the 2006 recipient of a grant from the National Science Foundation, with which he documented scientific work being conducting in the McMurdo Dry Valleys and volcanoes of Antarctica. When not traveling on assignment, Steinmetz resides in Glen Ridge, New Jersey, with his wife, Lisa Bannon, an editor for the *Wall Street Journal*; his daughter, Nell; and twin sons, John and Nicholas.

### SUGGESTED READING

Casimiro, Steve. "Photography: The Aerial Art of George Steinmetz." *Adventure Journal*. Adventure Journal, 15 Jan. 2009. Web. 2 May 2013.

Collins, Lauren. "Angle of Vision." *New Yorker* 19 Apr. 2010: 70–83. Print.

Estrin, James. "Floating in the Desert Air." *New York Times*. New York Times, 13 Dec. 2012. Web. 2 May 2013.

Steinmetz, George. "Africa's Eye in the Sky." *National Geographic Adventure*. National Geographic Society, Dec. 2008/Jan. 2009. Web. 2 May 2013.

Steinmetz, George. "Sailing the Dunes." *National Geographic*. National Geographic Society, Nov. 2012. Web. 2 May 2013.

Tucker, Abigail, "Africa on the Fly." *Smithsonian*. Smithsonian, Jan. 2009. Web. 2 May 2013.

### SELECTED WORKS

*Africa Air*, 2008; *Empty Quarter: A Photographic Journey to the Heart of the Arabian Desert*, 2009; *Desert Air*, 2012

—*Christopher Mari*

---

# Emma Stone

**Born:** November 6, 1988; Scottsdale, Arizona
**Occupation:** American actor

When Emma Stone was only fifteen years old, she created a PowerPoint presentation in an attempt to convince her parents to allow her to relocate to Los Angeles and pursue film acting. Stone was so determined and persuasive in her proposal that her mother agreed to come with her to California, where the two rented a small apartment and pursued countless auditions over the next three years. Little did Stone or her parents know that within a few years of the move, Stone would become one of the most sought-after actors in Hollywood. After a few false starts with short-lived television roles, Stone earned her first film credit in the 2007 comedy *Superbad*, starring Jonah Hill and Michael Cera. Since her film debut, Stone has become renowned for her crossover appeal in both dramatic and comedic roles and with both male and female audiences.

"Emma Stone has no reservations about balancing that fine line between dorky and cool, sharp-tongued and sexy," according to her online profile for *People* magazine. Known for her excellent comedic timing, down-to-earth personality, smoky voice, and widespread relatability with audiences, in the six years since her film debut Stone has garnered major film roles and critical accolades. Her quick wit, spontaneity, and authenticity have endeared her to countless interviewers, costars, and fans. As Nathan Heller describes the young star in *Vogue* (18 June 2012), "Stone has become a kind of celebrity ambassador, a high-wattage movie star who nonetheless seems as if she might show up at

Wirelmage

to make people laugh. Comedy was my sport. It taught me how to roll with the punches. Failure is the exact same as success when it comes to comedy because it just keeps coming. It never stops."

Stone started performing in plays with the Valley Youth Theatre in Phoenix. In her first on-stage performance, Stone played the role of Otter in a production of *The Wind in the Willows* in 2000. Her former director and drama mentor Bobb Cooper recalled Stone's first audition in an interview with the *Daily Mail* (4 Nov. 2011). "It was in 1999 and she auditioned for *The Wind in the Willows*. She came into the theater and she had a very deep raspy voice, which was intriguing for a little girl. She really knew how to project. She was very loud." After casting Stone in his play, Cooper was impressed by Stone's acting abilities and willingness to take on various roles. "Pretty much everything I threw at her she was able to take on. She had a great comedic timing and great sense for comedy," recalls Cooper. "She had an innate ability and we just had to kind of refine her."

Between the ages of eleven and fifteen, Stone performed in sixteen shows at the theater. At age twelve, she convinced her parents to begin homeschooling her so she could pursue additional auditions. Stone's last show at the Valley Youth Theatre was in 2003, during her freshman year at Xavier College Preparatory High School, when she and her mother relocated to Hollywood. Since finding success, Stone has donated thousands of dollars to the Valley Youth Theatre.

## MOVE TO HOLLYWOOD

After Stone created a PowerPoint presentation to persuade her parents to allow her to relocate to Los Angeles, Stone's mother packed up her entire life in Scottsdale and moved to Hollywood with her teenaged daughter. Stone remembers her early years living in California, where she was homeschooled and continually attended auditions. "I went up for every single show on the Disney Channel and auditioned to play the daughter on every single sitcom" recalled Stone, as quoted in her online profile for *People* magazine. "I ended up getting none." Though Stone was determined to pursue acting, she was not initially interested in film acting. In an interview with Ben Barna for *BlackBook* magazine (2 Oct. 2009), Stone recounts, "The dream was not actually movies since I was young—it was sketch-comedy. I wanted to do comedy, and then I thought I wanted to do theater, so I wanted to do musical theater, and then I took voice lessons for like eight years, and I sucked at singing, so I was like, 'Alright, never mind.'" Stone worked part time at a bakery making specialized dog treats and she enrolled in several online classes. She studied American Sign Language as part of her foreign-language requirement, and she has said

your next dinner party, someone who sees what you see even as she scales the distant peaks of Hollywood fame."

## EARLY LIFE AND EDUCATION

Emma Stone was born Emily Jean Stone on November 6, 1988, in Scottsdale, Arizona. Her only sibling, a brother named Spencer, was born two years later. Her father, Jeff, worked as a contractor, and her mother, Krista, was a homemaker. Stone was born with a hiatal hernia, a condition in which part of the stomach protrudes into the chest cavity through an opening in the diaphragm. The hernia caused Stone to experience severe stomach pain as an infant, which she credits with causing her signature raspy, deep voice to develop. "I had terrible stomach aches the first six months of my life, so I screamed myself hoarse every day when I was awake," she explained in an interview with Marlow Stern for *Newsweek* (2 July 2012). "I gave myself nodules before I could talk, so my voice was at this pitch as a toddler."

Stone describes herself as an anxious child; she recalls having her first panic attack at the age of eight. "I was just kind of immobilized by it," she told Nathan Heller for *Vogue* (18 June 2012). "I didn't want to go to my friends' houses or hang out with anybody, and nobody really understood." She attended therapy sessions for several years before getting into improvisation comedy with a local theater troupe at the age of eleven. Stone recalled in her interview with Heller how comedy helped her to overcome her childhood anxiety: "It gave me a sense of purpose. I wanted that sign language was great in honing her acting skills. "I had a deaf tutor," Stone told *People*. "It's an incredible language, especially as an actor, drawing on body language and facial expressions to convey things without speaking."

In an interview with Alexandra Wolfe for the *Vanity Fair* website (28 June 2011), Stone recalled her worst moment during her time in Hollywood as a teenager. Stone had attended an audition for the NBC television series *Heroes*. She recalled, "I could hear that, in the other room, a girl had just gone in and they were saying, 'You are our pick. . . . On a scale of 1 to 10 you're an 11.'" Stone remembered actor Hayden Panettiere leaving the room having just landed the role of Claire Bennet. "I went home and just had this meltdown," Stone said, adding that the experience was her "rock bottom" moment in Hollywood. It was also around this time that Stone changed her first name from Emily to Emma. She had gone to register at the Screen Actors Guild and found that there was already an Emily Stone registered there. To avoid confusion, Stone registered under the name Emma Stone and has been credited as such ever since. However, Stone told Andrea Mandell for *USA Today* (27 July 2011), "Everyone at home calls me Emily, people who know me really well."

In 2004, Stone's luck in Hollywood began to turn. Her mother encouraged her to try out for a VH1 talent-search competition called *In Search of the New Partridge Family*. As Stone told Marlow Stern for *Newsweek* (25 June 2012), "It was totally, 100 percent a reality show. My mom had never pushed me to audition for anything, but she saw a commercial on TV for it and said, 'You look like Susan Dey a little, and just dyed your hair brown. . . . Why don't you give this a shot? I have a weird feeling.'" Stone ended up winning the competition and landing the role of Laurie Partridge for the 2005 VH1 show *The New Partridge Family*, which never made it past the pilot episode. Despite being short-lived, Stone is thankful for the experience. "Thank God I did it. You're not so worried about making a silly choice in a movie when you were already Laurie Partridge, playing the air keyboards. It gives you a lot of humility," she told *Entertainment Weekly* (9 July 2010). A number of minor television roles followed, and from 2005 through 2006 she made appearances on *Malcolm in the Middle, Medium*, and several other shows. In 2007, Stone portrayed the character of Violet Trimble on the Fox miniseries *Drive*.

## FILM DEBUT

Stone came to prominence following her role in the 2007 comedy *Superbad* as Jules. Speaking of her rise to fame with Mandell for *USA Today*, Stone credits *Superbad* producer Judd Apatow. "I think Judd Apatow is who I owe most everything

to. I think without that, most of this probably wouldn't have occurred." Executive producer Matt Tolmach recalled to Nathan Heller his initial reaction to Stone's audition: "She came in to see me, and what I got is exactly what you get in that movie when Jonah meets her: She's as funny as or funnier than you are; she's so quick; she's stunning, so she's disarming; and she's just cool. You'll say anything to her because you just want her to be your best friend." Although she was only eighteen years old at the time, Stone was sure that she was moving in the right direction in Hollywood. "I did *Superbad* in what would've been my senior year," she told Wolfe for *Vanity Fair* (28 June 2011). "I was playing a senior, and had I graduated I would've missed that opportunity, and had I missed that opportunity I wouldn't be here right now."

"It's no surprise that her career is taking off," *Superbad* director Greg Mottola told Alexandra Wolfe in the August 2011 issue of *Vanity Fair*, after the film's release. "Emma is very, very smart. It's clear in the choices she made. She knows what she's done well but has really pushed herself and challenged herself." A number of other film roles followed. In 2008, Stone appeared in the comedy films *The Rocker* and *The House Bunny*. In 2009, she appeared in *Ghosts of Girlfriends Past* and *Paper Man*. Also in 2009, Stone landed the role of Wichita in the horror-comedy film *Zombieland*, in which she performed alongside Woody Harrelson, Jesse Eisenberg, and Bill Murray. Stone garnered praise for the role, particularly for her versatility and crossover appeal. "She's managed to avoid standard rom-coms, finding her niche in rowdy movies with crossover boy appeal," wrote Kyle Buchanan and Claude Brodesser-Akner for *New York* magazine (22 Aug. 2011). Her costars Murray and Harrelson also sang her praises. Harrelson wrote in *Entertainment Weekly* (16 Dec. 2011), explaining how Billy Murray had said, "'That Emma is pure gold.'" Harrelson added, "It's a much bigger statement than it sounds like because Bill doesn't ever say that . . . He was knocked out by her. He really thought the sky was the limit for her—and it absolutely is. We're just *beginning* to see what she's capable of." Around this time, Stone relocated from Los Angeles to New York City.

## STAR STATUS

In 2010, Stone landed her first starring role as Olive in the comedy *Easy A*, in which Stone's character pretends to have had sex with her gay friend in order to spare him from bullying. Stone said that she was drawn to the role because of the positive message the script sends about acceptance. As she told *Advocate* magazine (Aug. 2011), "I grew up with a ton of gay friends and witnessed their struggles. One of the most wonderful things about doing *Easy A* was that we got to tackle issues that many gay teenagers face."

The role earned Stone a 2011 MTV Movie Award for best comedic performance and a Golden Globes nomination. In his review of *Easy A*, Roger Ebert wrote that the film "takes the familiar but underrated Emma Stone, and makes her, I believe, a star" (15 Sept. 2010).

By the following year, Stone had reached top-billing status and appeared in three major movies released in the summer of 2011. She had a minor role in *Friends with Benefits*, starring Justin Timberlake and Mila Kunis. She also landed the lead role in the 2011 romance *Crazy, Stupid, Love*. After Stone auditioned for the part of Hannah, Ryan Gosling, the film's male lead, said that the script suddenly began to make sense to him. Gosling told Mandell for *USA Today*, "The whole movie depends on who plays that role. My character is supposed to give it all up for her. So when Emma walked in, I thought, 'Show me someone who wouldn't give it all up for Emma Stone, and I'll show you a liar.'"

Stone's role in the 2011 blockbuster *The Help*, an adaptation of Kathryn Stockett's novel about racial discrimination in the 1960s, was her first major break from comedy. Stone's costar in the *Help*, Allison Janney, explained Stone's versatility and appeal to Aili Nahas for *People* magazine (15 Aug. 2011): "She can be completely goofy and gawky and geeky, and she can be drop-dead gorgeous." As with Olive in *Easy A*, Stone was drawn to the role of Skeeter Phelan in *The Help* because of the character's tenacity and drive to address injustice. Stone explained to *Advocate* magazine, "I'm the least eloquent person on the planet. . . . But that's what's so wonderful about good movies and writers: I can be a part of a project that says what I wish I could say. My ultimate goal is to continue doing movies with some sort of message that can make a change."

### THE AMAZING SPIDER-MAN

While still on the set of *The Help*, Stone received a call informing her that she had been offered the part of Gwen Stacy in the 2012 film *The Amazing Spider-Man*. Recalling the brief phone call to Mandell for *USA Today*, Stone said, "It was like someone goes, 'Your life changed, bye!'" The film would go on to gross a staggering $750 million worldwide. As her first action movie, *The Amazing Spider-Man* is the first time audiences saw Stone in a truly vulnerable role. "The damsel-in-distress aspect appealed to me for the first time," Stone told Brian Hiatt for *Rolling Stone* (31 May 2012). "I love that [Gwen's] not 100 percent confident."

Despite her interest in portraying a more sensitive and vulnerable character, Stone was nevertheless challenged by the role. *The Amazing Spider-Man* truly marks Stone's development and maturation as an actor as she delves into more serious and painful topics. "Comedy is really vulnerable, but the second something falls flat, you pick up and continue. You're flashing skin for little seconds. Whereas you're totally naked in something that isn't funny," she explained to Heller for *Vogue*. "There was a day like that on *Spider-Man*, where Andrew [Garfield] and I were sitting on the floor, and there was a scene in my bedroom, and it was just the two of us, and it was an incredible feeling. . . . How to live in that place without making a joke."

Although Stone was drawn to her character's vulnerability, director Marc Webb says Stone's comedic ability is why he ultimately cast her. Her costar, Andrew Garfield, who plays Peter Parker, is a very serious actor, and Webb hoped that Stone would help him to relax. "She could make him laugh," Webb explained to Nathan Heller for *Vogue*. "A lot of young actresses are either very serious and morose or they're very doe-eyed and bat their eyelashes and are trained to seduce the camera. Emma sidesteps that." Garfield agreed with his director's assessment of Stone: "Working with Emma was like diving into a thrilling, twisting river and never holding on to the sides. From the start. To the end. Spontaneous. In the moment. Present. Terrifying. Vital. The only way acting with someone should be." After the movie was released, Stone and Garfield reportedly began dating seriously. In November 2012, the couple purchased a home in Beverly Hills together.

### OTHER EFFORTS

In 2011 *People* magazine named Stone one of the twenty-five "most intriguing" people of the year. In 2012, Stone took home the inaugural MTV Trailblazer Award. In announcing her win, Josh Wigler asked, "How many other 23-year-old stars have zombie apocalypse, stoner comedy, racially charged Oscar-attracting drama and superhero credits to their name?" Drawing on her background in improv comedy, Stone hosted and performed on *Saturday Night Live* in October 2010 and November 2011, an experience she has called a "dream come true." Stone has also become a spokesmodel for Revlon, and in 2012 she appeared in a public-service advertisement with her mother, a breast cancer survivor, in an effort to raise awareness regarding cancer screenings and the importance of early detection.

Stone has a number of upcoming film projects, including *The Amazing Spider-Man 2*, due to be released in 2014; the animated film *The Croods*; and the period crime drama *Gangster Squad*, which will open in January 2013. Despite her widespread success, Stone told Jessica Pressler for *New York* magazine (25 June 2012) that she is still adjusting to her fame: "It's weird. I don't actually recognize the person that's out there. It's like there's this outside person, and there's me."

## SUGGESTED READING

Barna, Ben. "*Zombieland*'s Emma Stone Dreams of SNL and Mexican Food." *BlackBook*. BlackBook, 2 Oct. 2009. Web. 13 Dec. 2012.

Heller, Nathan. "Emma Stone Makes Her *Vogue* Cover Debut in the July Issue." *Vogue*. Condé Nast, 18 June 2012. Web. 13 Dec. 2012.

Pressler, Jessica. "Emma Stone's Spidey Sense." *New York* 45.22 (2012): 50–54. Print.

Stern, Marlow. "Emma Stone, Revealed." *Daily Beast*. Newsweek, 25 June 2012. Web. 13 Dec. 2012.

Wolfe, Alexandra. "Hollywood Is Her Oyster." *Vanity Fair*. Condé Nast, Aug. 2011. Web. 12 Dec. 2012.

—*Mary Woodbury*

Rebecca Cook/Reuters /Landov

# Ndamukong Suh

**Born:** January 6, 1987
**Occupation:** Football player

The Detroit Lions' Ndamukong Suh is one of the most dominant defensive tackles that the National Football League (NFL) has ever seen. "On the football field, Suh is fire, heat, a constant explosion of violent desire," Jeanne Marie Laskas wrote for *GQ* (Sept. 2012). "He is science fiction; six feet four, 307 pounds, a speeding machine of humanity intent on devouring mankind." In his first three seasons with the Lions, Suh, who enjoyed a record-breaking career at the University of Nebraska, established himself as one of the NFL's best defensive linemen. During the 2010 season, he led the Lions, as well as all rookies and defensive tackles, with ten sacks, en route to being named the Associated Press (AP) Defensive Rookie of the Year. He also earned selections to the AP First-Team All-Pro and National Football Conference (NFC) Pro Bowl teams. Suh returned in 2011 to help the Lions earn their first playoff berth in twelve years and went on to earn his second career All-Pro and Pro Bowl selections during the 2012 season.

Despite these accolades, Suh has often been criticized for an overly aggressive style of play, which has led many observers to perceive him as a "dirty" player. During the 2011 season, Suh received multiple fines and a two-game suspension from the NFL for a series of illegal hits. In the process he became "an unintended lightning rod, a helmet-ripping, personal-foul-accumulating referendum on what constitutes dirty play in a game that venerates raw brutality," Judy Battista noted for the *New York Times* (23 Nov. 2011). To some, however, Suh, who is known for being cerebral, soft-spoken, and thoughtful off the field, is simply misunderstood. The Lions' defensive coordinator, Gunther Cunningham, who has coached in the NFL for more than three decades, told Damon Hack for *Sports Illustrated* (10 Oct. 2011), "The problem with the league is, they've never seen a defensive tackle like this. He's the best football player at that position I've ever seen."

## EARLY LIFE

Ndamukong Suh was born on January 6, 1987, in Portland, Oregon, to a Cameroonian father and a Jamaican mother. He has a sister, Ngum (known as "Gum"), who is four years his senior. Suh, whose first name means "House of Spears," is named after his paternal great-grandfather, who was a police chief in the Ngema tribe of Cameroon. Suh's father, Michael, is a mechanical contractor, and his mother, Bernadette, is an elementary school teacher. His parents divorced when he was about two years old. Nonetheless, Suh was raised in "a loving and learning environment with each parent," as Jason Quick noted for the Portland *Oregonian* (23 Nov. 2011). Both of Suh's parents instilled in him the importance of discipline and education.

Quiet yet highly inquisitive as a boy, Suh developed an early fascination with taking things apart and putting them back together. Suh's curiosity also lent itself to sports. His first love growing up was soccer, a popular sport in his family; his father was a former semiprofessional soccer player, and his sister was a standout forward at Mississippi State University and a member of Cameroon's national team.

Suh's athletic gifts were evident early on, as was his size. By age eight he already stood five feet eight inches tall—the same height as his father. As a youth-league soccer player, Suh was reportedly so much larger than the children he played against that his mother had to have his birth certificate on hand at games when questions came up about his age. It has also been noted that officials, unsure of what to make of his size and physicality, would frequently, and unnecessarily, penalize him for making even just slight contact with other children on the field. "He could breathe on someone and knock them over," his sister told Battista. Suh ultimately gave up soccer for good in the eighth grade, after coming to the realization that the sport was incompatible with his aggressive style of play.

## HIGH SCHOOL FOOTBALL

Suh started playing football during his sophomore year at Grant High School in Portland. (He was allowed to join the team after convincing his initially apprehensive parents that he could maintain a 3.0 grade point average or higher as a freshman.) Football proved to be a natural fit and welcome change for Suh, whose size, strength, quickness, and nimble feet left coaches and fellow teammates in awe. "When I first started playing," he recalled to Laskas, "I was surprised at the fact that I was allowed to hit people as hard as I could and not get in trouble."

During his senior season, Suh, who played both offense and defense at Grant High, emerged as one of the top defensive tackles in the nation. (A defensive tackle, also known as a nose tackle or defensive guard, lines up either directly across from or slightly to the side of the ball on the interior defensive line and holds the primary responsibilities of stopping the run and pressuring the quarterback.) He made sixty-five tackles, ten sacks, and four fumble recoveries and was named the Oregon Class 4A Defensive Player of the Year. After being heavily recruited by major football powerhouses all over the country, Suh enrolled at the University of Nebraska, in Lincoln, which he chose for its exceptionally strong engineering program.

During his time at Grant High, Suh was also a standout on the varsity basketball and track teams. He was selected as an all-league honorable mention in basketball during his junior and senior seasons and won the state Class 4A shot put title as a senior after establishing a school record with a throw of sixty-one feet and four inches.

## UNIVERSITY OF NEBRASKA

Suh's first three years at the University of Nebraska were relatively undistinguished. As a freshman during the 2005 season, he played in the Cornhuskers' first two games before suffering a knee injury that required season-ending surgery. This resulted in him being granted a medical redshirt for the remainder of that season, which allowed him to maintain his four years of athletic eligibility.

When Suh returned in 2006, he served as the Cornhuskers' backup nose tackle and came off the bench in all fourteen of their games. Nonetheless, he recorded nineteen tackles, eight tackles for loss, three and a half sacks, one forced fumble, and one interception and was named to *Sporting News*'s Big Twelve Conference All-Freshman squad. Suh then started in eleven of twelve games during the 2007 season, in which he recorded thirty-four combined tackles. The Cornhuskers, hampered by one of the worst defenses in school history, went 5–7 in those games to finish with just their second losing record since 1961 and second in four seasons. Offensive-minded head coach Bill Callahan, who had guided Nebraska to a disappointing 27–22 record during his four-year tenure at the helm (2004–7), was fired at the end of the season and replaced by Mark "Bo" Pelini.

Following the 2007 season, Suh, frustrated with his lack of progress at Nebraska, considered transferring. He ultimately decided to stay after the hiring of Pelini, a defensive guru who had spent the previous three seasons as the defensive coordinator for Louisiana State University. Pelini hired his brother, Carl, to serve as defensive coordinator, and the two began working closely with Suh to improve various aspects of his game. Under the Pelini brothers, Suh adopted a more aggressive style of play and became a devoted student of the game. At that time, Carl Pelini explained to Hack, "[Suh] was used to more of a penetration system. . . . He became more about defeating blocks to make plays. It became a craft. He was always looking for an edge, studying opponents, almost to where it would drive you crazy."

## RECORD-BREAKING SEASONS

Suh's newfound approach paid immediate dividends. As a redshirt junior during the 2008 season, he led the Cornhuskers with seventy-six tackles and seven and a half sacks and tied for the team lead with two interceptions, starting all thirteen games at nose tackle. He also showcased his athleticism in other roles, blocking two kicks as a member of the special-teams unit and scoring one offensive touchdown as a short-yardage fullback in a game against the University of Kansas. He was selected to the All-Big Twelve First Team and was named the Cornhuskers' Defensive Most Valuable Player (MVP). Meanwhile, Nebraska won nine of thirteen games and defeated Clemson University in the 2009 Gator Bowl.

Suh returned for his senior season in 2009. He started in all fourteen games and again led the Cornhuskers with eighty-five tackles and twelve sacks, also leading the team with twenty-four tackles for loss, twenty-six quarterback pressures, and three blocked kicks. He set a single-season school record for most passes defended by a defensive lineman with ten, leading the nation for a player at his position.

While anchoring a defense that finished ninth in the nation, Suh led Nebraska to a Big Twelve runner-up finish, with a record of 10–4, and a blowout victory over the University of Arizona in the 2009 Holiday Bowl. Suh was a unanimous All-American and All-Big Twelve First-Team selection and was named the Big Twelve Defensive Player of the Year. He also became the first defensive player ever to win the AP College Player of the Year Award, finished fourth in the voting for the Heisman Trophy, and swept most of the other major college football defensive awards, including the Outland Trophy and the Rotary Lombardi Award. According to Carl Pelini, Suh's success was due to his eagerness to master not only the intricacies of his position but also those of every other defensive role. "He thought about the overall picture and scheme," Pelini told Hack. "The scouts started coming around and asking me, 'Will he be a good pro?' I'd say, 'He already is.'"

## NFL DRAFT

Many scouts and analysts considered Suh to be a potential number-one pick in the 2010 NFL Draft, and at the very worst, a top-five pick. Those projections proved to be accurate when the Detroit Lions selected Suh as the second overall pick in the draft. In August 2010 Suh, who graduated from Nebraska with a degree in construction management, signed a five-year deal with the Lions worth $68 million and including $40 million in guaranteed money.

Suh was one of the most highly anticipated players to arrive in Detroit since the electrifying Hall of Fame running back Barry Sanders, who served as the face of the Lions franchise from 1989 to 1998. When the Lions drafted Suh, the team envisioned him serving as the centerpiece and savior of their 4–3 defense (a defensive scheme featuring four down linemen and three linebackers), which had finished ranked last in the NFL during the 2009 season. Though the Lions had long been the symbol of NFL futility, as they were coming off their ninth consecutive losing season and were only two years removed from compiling the first 0–16 season in league history, the team was considered to be on the rise. Led by second-year head coach Jim Schwartz, the Lions featured a young foundation of potential superstar players that included not only Suh but also second-year franchise quarterback Matthew Stafford (the number-one overall pick in the 2009 draft) and fourth-year receiver Calvin Johnson. Together, they were widely expected to bring the Lions back to respectability as well as spearhead the team's return to the playoffs.

## DETROIT LIONS

Suh announced his arrival to the league in ferocious fashion during the Lions' third game of the 2010 NFL preseason against the Cleveland Browns. In that game he made a vicious hit on Browns quarterback Jake Delhomme by grabbing his facemask, twisting his neck, and then slamming him down to the ground. The hit drew a personal foul penalty and subsequently earned him a $7,500 fine from the league. For Suh, it would be the first in a series of violent and illegal hits that would contribute to his reputation as a "dirty" player. Nonetheless, Suh enjoyed arguably the greatest season by a rookie defensive tackle in history. During his rookie year in 2010, he started all sixteen games and finished with sixty-five tackles and a team-best ten sacks, which led all rookies and defensive tackles. He also recorded forty-one quarterback pressures, three passes defensed, one interception, one forced fumble, and one fumble recovery, which he returned for his first career touchdown.

Despite putting up spectacular numbers, Suh repeatedly drew negative attention for his aggressive style of play. He was fined $5,000 by the league for committing an unsportsmanlike conduct penalty during a game against the New York Jets and was later fined $15,000 for delivering a forearm hit to the back of Chicago Bears quarterback Jay Cutler's head. Those incidents notwithstanding, Suh was named the AP Defensive Rookie of the Year and was the only rookie named to the AP All-Pro Team. He was also selected as a starter for the NFC Pro Bowl squad. Though Suh missed the annual Pro Bowl game after undergoing off-season shoulder surgery, he became the first Lions rookie since Barry Sanders to be named a Pro Bowl starter. Thanks to a vastly improved defense, the Lions enjoyed a four-game improvement from the previous year, finishing third in the NFC North division with a record of 6–10.

## VILLAIN OF THE LEAGUE

By the start of his second NFL season in 2011, Suh had established himself as one of the best defensive tackles in the league. Suh's numbers dropped considerably, but he continued to be a disruptive force on the Lions' interior defensive line and was named a Pro Bowl alternate for the NFC squad. Meanwhile, the Lions, powered by an explosive offense that set a franchise record with 474 points scored, went 10–6 to finish with their first winning record since 2000 and advanced to the postseason for the first time since the 1999 season. The Lions were defeated by the New Orleans Saints in the NFC wild-card playoff round, 45–28.

While the Lions' 2011 season was considered a success, Suh's otherwise solid sophomore campaign was marred by several widely publicized incidents involving violent hits, which further bolstered his reputation as a dirty player. One incident occurred during the first game of the Lions' 2011 preseason, when Suh was penalized and fined $20,000 by the league for slamming Cincinnati Bengals rookie quarterback Andy Dalton down to the ground by his helmet. Two months after that incident, Suh told Battista that he had been designated "the villain of the league" but noted, "When my parents, close friends, family, teammates tell me I'm crossing the line, then will I care about it."

Suh's play did, in fact, egregiously cross the line during the Lions' Thanksgiving Day game against the Green Bay Packers. During the third quarter, after following an incomplete pass thrown by Matthew Stafford, Suh pounded Packers offensive lineman Evan Dietrich-Smith's helmet into the ground three times and then stomped on his right arm after the whistle had blown. Suh was immediately ejected from the game and was then suspended for two games without pay, which cost him $164,000. After the game, Suh said that his actions against Dietrich-Smith were inadvertent, but he later issued an apology on his Facebook page.

## 2012 SEASON

Suh entered the 2012 season with the hope of repairing his image, which was further tarnished by several traffic-related incidents. His on-field aggressiveness, however, once again seemed to get the best of him. In yet another Thanksgiving Day outburst, Suh kicked Houston Texans quarterback Matt Schaub in the groin area during a first-quarter play. The league fined Suh $30,000 for the kick, which he again insisted was done inadvertently and without malicious intent, despite video evidence to the contrary. Around that time he was voted the dirtiest player in the league in a poll of NFL players conducted by *Sporting News*, marking the second consecutive year that he finished first in the poll. Despite that dubious distinction, Suh's dominant play continued to speak for itself. He was named to the AP All-Pro Second Team and earned his second career Pro Bowl selection after finishing the season with thirty-five tackles, eight sacks, and more than fifty quarterback hurries. The Lions, however, failed to build on their success from the previous year, losing their last eight games to finish with a disappointing 4–12 record.

While Suh has endured harsh criticism for his aggressive style of play, he has maintained that he is not a dirty player. "A dirty player is somebody who ultimately is trying to hurt somebody," he told Laskas. "There's a huge difference. There's no gray in that. Like, you have no conscience, no nothing, no guilt. I don't have that mean streak in me. I don't play angry." Suh has also said that the NFL needs to adapt to how he plays because of his unprecedented combination of size, speed, and skills. He told Hack,

"Nobody's seen a specimen like myself. . . . When you combine speed and power, things are going to look bad when I hit somebody."

## PERSONAL LIFE

During the off-season, Suh lives in Portland in a home he shares with his sister, Ngum, who serves as his business manager. He has endorsement deals with Nike, Chrysler, Dick's Sporting Goods, Omaha Steaks, and Subway and has appeared in national television commercials for each of those companies. Suh has also been involved in numerous charitable activities. In 2011 he was named the most charitable athlete in the United States by the Giving Back Fund for his many generous donations, including a $2.6 million gift to the University of Nebraska. He has established the Ndamukong Suh Family Foundation, which implements programs to assist local communities.

## SUGGESTED READING

Battista, Judy. "Suh Pushes the Line and Anchors the Lions." *New York Times*. New York Times, 23 Nov. 2011. Web. 6 Aug. 2013.

Crossman, Matt. "The Legend of Ndamukong Suh." *Sporting News* 1 Mar. 2010: 28–34. Print.

Hack, Damon. "Remade in Detroit." *Sports Illustrated*. Time, 10 Oct. 2011. Web. 6 Aug. 2013.

Laskas, Jeanne Marie. "He Didn't Mean to Hurt You." GQ. Condé Nast, Sept. 2012. Web. 6 Aug. 2013.

Quick, Jason. "Ndamukong Suh Has Learned to Navigate the Storm." *Oregonian*. Oregon Live, 23 Nov. 2011. Web. 6 Aug. 2013.

—*Chris Cullen*

# Ron Suskind

**Born:** November 30, 1959
**Occupation:** Journalist and political writer

Ron Suskind has had a prolific career as an investigative journalist in the tradition of Bob Woodward, burrowing deep inside the lives of his subjects and crafting highly readable, award-winning narratives, first for national publications such as the *Wall Street Journal* and *Esquire* magazine, and then in a series of bestselling, nationally acclaimed books. The level of detail he gathers allows him to present nonfiction narratives that read like novels, placing the reader inside the heads of his subjects. He described his technique to John Wihbey for the website *Journalist's Resource* (29 May 2012) as follows: "I'll first offer the reader the most stunning example of something, and then once I have them with that hook, I drag them into the

Courtesy of Ron Suskind

lake. And then they end up swimming after a while. The reader ends up walking in the shoes of characters with whom he or she may have nothing in common. While doing that, the goal is to define the choice and consequences we make as individuals, as Americans, or as important public actors whose decisions affect the lives, in many cases, of millions of people. It's all about those choices—what flows into those choices. The goal is to learn what we can learn in this short life."

## EARLY LIFE AND EDUCATION

Ronald Steven Suskind was born on November 30, 1959, into a Jewish family in Kingston, New York, to Walter and Shirley Suskind. The family subsequently moved to Wilmington, Delaware, where Suskind graduated from Concord High School in 1977. He then graduated from the University of Virginia with a degree in government and foreign affairs, putting his political education to work in 1981 as a field coordinator with Chuck Robb's successful Democratic gubernatorial campaign in Virginia, and again the next year as campaign manager for Democrat John Downey's failed bid for a US Senate seat in Connecticut.

Suskind then attended the Columbia School of Journalism in New York City, graduating with a master's degree and beginning his journalism career in 1983 as an interim business writer for the *New York Times*. In 1985 he went to work as a staff writer for the *St. Petersburg Times* in Florida, and in 1988 he became the editor of the now-defunct *Boston Business* magazine. Another Boston journalist, Peter Kadzis, later told Mark Jukowitz for the *Boston Globe* (27 Jan. 2004)

that "[Suskind's] ambition always had an effervescent quality. It was like champagne. He was always a big game hunter." In 1990, Suskind became a staff reporter in Boston for the *Wall Street Journal* before becoming the paper's senior national affairs writer from 1993 to 2000.

In 1986, Suskind married fellow writer Cornelia Anne Kennedy. The couple has two sons, Walter and Harold.

### A HOPE IN THE UNSEEN

Suskind first came to national attention when he won the 1995 Pulitzer Prize in Feature Writing for a series of articles published the previous year in the *Wall Street Journal* about Cedric Jennings, an African American honors student trying to survive a violent inner-city high school in Washington, DC, and make it into a good college. Suskind expanded on this work by following Jennings through his first year at Brown University and publishing the book *A Hope in the Unseen: An American Odyssey from the Inner City to the Ivy League* (1998). In it, Suskind painted detailed pictures of the beleaguered but determined youth, his hardworking mother, his incarcerated, drug-dealing father, and many of his classmates—including gang members with undisguised hostility toward Jennings for "selling out" to mainstream white culture. Widely acclaimed, the book, written in a genre described by some as "biographical novel," became required reading at many colleges and was credited with influencing the national debate on affirmative action, which was a major issue at the time.

### THE PRICE OF LOYALTY

In the 2000s, Suskin returned to politics for his subject matter, specifically the administration of President George W. Bush. Having left the *Wall Street Journal* in 2000, over the next few years he published a number of high-profile articles in publications like *Esquire* magazine and the *New York Times*. A pair of articles that ran in Esquire garnered notice in particular: In July 2002, Suskind wrote about the departure of Bush advisor Karen Hughes, which he characterized as a blow for moderates in the Republican White House, and part of the rise of archconservative Republican strategist Karl Rove, whom Suskind further profiled for the magazine in January 2003. With these articles, Suskind further established his knack for getting people in high places to talk to him; in particular, he found dissatisfied members of the Bush team willing to go on record with the basic elements of the narrative that came to be widely espoused by opponents of the administration: that it operated according to a hardnosed political calculus based on a black-and-white view of the world that was not open to adjustment based on new information.

A key administration official whose confidence Suskind gained was Treasury Secretary Paul O'Neill, who was in office for the first two years of Bush's first term before being forced out over policy disagreements. Based on extensive interviews with O'Neill and other administration officials, as well as a large volume of government documents, in 2004 Suskind published *The Price of Loyalty: George W. Bush, the White House, and the Education of Paul O'Neill*, which reached number one on the New York Times Best Seller list. Among the book's revelations was that the administration had been formulating plans to invade Iraq months before the terrorist attacks of September 11, 2001.

When the book was published, the administration launched a campaign to discredit Suskind, which he saw as part of a larger effort by factions within the Republican Party to discredit mainstream American journalism in general. He told Eric Boehlert for *Salon.com* (20 Oct. 2004), "The news strategies of those in power are really born of a dark corner of the American ideal, which is kill or be killed, which is to rely on assertion rather than authenticity and to use power as best you can to get to the agreed-upon ends. That's what this is about."

Suskind followed *The Price of Loyalty* up in October 2004 with an article in the *New York Times* magazine called "Faith, Certainty and the Presidency of George W. Bush," which furthered the theme of narrow-mindedness within the administration, and also ignited controversy with the disclosure that Bush was planning to release a proposal to privatize Social Security in his second term. A particularly famous quotation from the article, which Suskind wrote "gets to the very heart of the Bush presidency," came from a Bush aide other commentators later identified as Rove. The aide described people like Suskind as being part of "the reality-based community," people who "believe that solutions emerge from your judicious study of discernible reality." The aide asserted, however, that "that's not the way the world really works anymore," because "we're an empire now, and when we act, we create our own reality. And while you're studying that reality—judiciously, as you will—we'll act again, creating other new realities, which you can study too, and that's how things will sort out. We're history's actors . . . and you, all of you, will be left to just study what we do." For critics of the Bush administration, this became a defining sentiment.

### THE ONE PERCENT DOCTRINE AND THE WAY OF THE WORLD

In 2006, Suskind published *The One Percent Doctrine: Deep inside America's Pursuit of Its Enemies since 9/11*, about the war on terror the Bush administration launched following the September 11 attacks. The "one-percent doctrine," attributed to Vice President Dick Cheney, asserted that the threats to the United States were so great that a highly proactive defense policy was necessary to counter it. Suskind quoted Cheney as saying, as an example, "If there's a 1-percent chance that Pakistani scientists are helping al-Qaeda build or develop a nuclear weapon, we have to treat it as a certainty in terms of our response."

Suskind's third and last book on the Bush administration, published in 2008, was *The Way of the World: A Story of Truth and Hope in an Age of Extremism*. In it, he described the state of global politics and, again, the US war on terror by telling the stories of a variety of actors both high and low, from an Afghan youth studying in the United States to former Pakistani prime minister Benazir Bhutto. The most explosive revelation in the book concerned the "Habbush letter," a document Suskind said was forged at the behest of the CIA and attributed to Iraqi intelligence chief Tahir Jalil Habbush al-Tikriti, asserting that Mohammad Atta, one of the September 11 bombers, received training in Iraq. Roundly denied by the CIA and the Bush administration, the letter was presented as further evidence of the administration's vain struggle to establish a connection between Iraqi leader Saddam Hussein and the terrorist attack on the United States, to retroactively justify the US–led invasion of Iraq that began in 2003. Both books, *The One Percent Doctrine* and *The Way of the World*, reached number three on the New York Times Best Sellers list.

### CONFIDENCE MEN

For his next book, Suskind turned his attention to Bush's successor, Barack Obama, who took office in 2009 as the nation was reeling from its greatest economic crisis since the Great Depression. Suskind again conducted hundreds of interviews with key players on the president's team, specifically the ones responsible for crafting a response to the crisis. The result was 2011's *Confidence Men: Wall Street, Washington and the Education of a President*. If Suskind's readers suspected that his previous books critical of the Bush administration were born out of partisan bias, *Confidence Men* adjusted this perception, as it too described a flawed national leadership. Among its charges were that the Obama administration was a boys' club that was hostile to its female members, and, more particularly, that Obama was an inexperienced leader who was manipulated by an economic team—chief economic advisor Larry Summers, Treasury Secretary Timothy Geithner, and Chief of Staff Rahm Emanuel, among others—that was by turns fractious and beholden to Wall Street financial interests. Among the book's assertions that garnered national attention was the allegation that Obama ordered the nationalization of the troubled financial giant Citigroup, and Geithner "slow walked"—carried out so slowly that it did not happen—the directive.

In contrast to his books critical of the Bush administration, *Confidence Men,* which reached number two on the New York Times Best Sellers list, was heavily criticized not just by the administration, but by a number of commentators in the press. Writing in the *New Yorker* (3 Oct. 2011), Hendrik Hertzberg wrote, "[*Confidence Men*] has the virtues and the limitations of its Woodwardian genre: contemporary, still unfolding history, filtered through the aesthetic conventions of the mass-market novel. That means an omniscient, seemingly eyewitness, mind-reading narrator; an irresistible penchant for conflict and drama; and a linear, character-driven story. . . . It's a type of nonfiction that might be labeled, with only a little exaggeration, 'Based on a True Story.'"

## REPORTING TECHNIQUE

Suskind has spoken to numerous writers about how he gets his sources to go on the record with groundbreaking quotes. "I make them believers in truth, and it takes a while," he told Howard Kurtz for the *Washington Post* (9 Dec. 2002). "I make them feel comfortable that it is a privilege for them to tell me what they believe in their hearts." He elaborated on this approach in his interview with Boehlert for *Salon,* describing how sources move from talking on background to allowing Suskind to print some of their most revelatory comments: "There is a moment of both fear for them, but also liberation. People think, 'Goddamn it. I'm finally going to say it. I've been walking around with a lump in my throat and a tightness in my chest. I'm a grown-up, and I worked hard. When things have worked out in my life, I've trusted truth.' In almost every case, the source will take ownership of the quote, or if they don't, they will throw out what are transparently non-denial denials. Most readers get that: the 'Washington walk-back,' they call it."

As with all successful journalists, Suskind has built his career on establishing a relationship of trust with his sources. He told Wihbey for *Journalist's Resource,* "I respect the fact that people need to stay in the shadows, and I would do anything, including go to jail, to protect them. I will do everything to protect my sources, and that gives them comfort." Of his craft, he told Boehlert, "It is part of our professional creed to be open to searching for the modest truths we're able to know in life and to render them effectively in what we write and what we say. That is a long and venerable tradition in this country."

## SUGGESTED READING

Boehlert, Eric. "Reality-Based Reporting." *Salon. com.* Salon Media Group, 20 Oct. 2004. Web. 19 Dec. 2012.

Hertzberg, Hendrik. "The Book on Barack." *New Yorker.* Condé Nast, 3 Oct. 2011. Web. 19 Dec. 2012.

Jurkowitz, Mark. "Ire Starter: Ron Suskind's In-Depth Writing often Sparks Controversy." *Boston Globe.* New York Times Co., 27 Jan. 2004. Web. 19 Dec. 2012.

Kurtz, Howard. "Ron Suskind, the Confident Confidant." *Washington Post.* Washington Post, 9 Dec. 2002. Web. 19 Dec. 2012.

Wihbey, John. "Research Chat: Ron Suskind on Investigative Reporting, Interviewing and Documents." *Journalist's Resource.* Shorenstein Center, 29 May 2012. Web. 19 Dec. 2012.

## SELECTED WORKS

*A Hope in the Unseen: An American Odyssey from the Inner City to the Ivy League,* 1998; *The One Percent Doctrine: Deep inside America's Pursuit of Its Enemies since 9/11,* 2004; *The Price of Loyalty: George W. Bush, the White House, and the Education of Paul O'Neill,* 2004; *The Way of the World: A Story of Truth and Hope in an Age of Extremism,* 2008; *Confidence Men: Wall Street, Washington and the Education of a President,* 2011

—Adam Groff

# Katie Taylor

**Born:** June 2, 1986
**Occupation:** Boxer and footballer

Katie Taylor is one of Ireland's most accomplished and beloved athletes and perhaps the greatest female boxer of all time. Described by Kieran Shannon for the *Irish Examiner* (11 Aug. 2012) as "the Goliath of women's boxing," Taylor, who competes in the women's 60-kilogram (132-pound) lightweight division, emerged from a working-class upbringing in Ireland to become a preeminent figure in her sport. In 2001, at age fifteen, she made history by participating in Ireland's first ever officially sanctioned women's boxing match, defeating Alanna Audley of Belfast at the National Stadium in Dublin. Afterward, Taylor boxed in a number of international competitions before achieving her breakthrough at the 2005 Women's European Amateur Boxing Championships in Tønsberg, Norway, when she won the gold medal in the lightweight division, becoming the first Irish woman to capture top honors at the competition. She went on to win gold at the next four European Amateur Boxing Championships, in 2006, 2007, 2009, and 2011. In 2006, she won the first of four consecutive world amateur lightweight titles at the International Boxing Association (AIBA) World

Niall Carson/PA Photos /Landov

Amateur Boxing Championships in New Delhi, India. She has also won four consecutive gold medals at the European Union Amateur Boxing Championships (2008–11).

A three-time winner of AIBA's World Female Boxer of the Year Award, Taylor is considered a trailblazer for women's boxing worldwide and credited with being a driving force behind the International Olympic Committee's decision to introduce women's boxing as an official sport at the 2012 Summer Olympic Games in London, England. At those games, she realized a life-long dream by winning an Olympic gold medal, becoming the first female boxer to take home gold in the lightweight division and only the ninth gold medalist in Ireland's history. Over the course of a career that has included nearly 150 amateur fights, Taylor, also a talented footballer (soccer player) who has played as a midfielder for the Republic of Ireland women's national team, has amassed well over a hundred victories in the ring, with only a handful of defeats.

### EARLY LIFE

The youngest of four children of Peter and Bridget Taylor, Katie Taylor was born on June 2, 1986, in Bray, a town in county Wicklow, Ireland, and grew up on a council estate in the working-class Bray suburb of Ballywaltrim. She comes from a family with a deep passion for boxing: her father was a decorated amateur boxer who won the 1986 Irish senior light heavyweight championship; her mother was one of the first women to serve as a boxing judge in Ireland; and her brothers, Lee and Peter, were also accomplished boxers. After retiring from amateur

competition, Taylor's father, who worked as an electrician, opened the St. Fergal's Boxing Club in Bray, where he was a youth boxing coach and trainer.

A self-confessed tomboy growing up, the extremely competitive Taylor naturally gravitated toward sports. Early on she played soccer and became involved with the Gaelic Athletic Association (GAA), where she joined clubs for such sports as camogie and Gaelic football. She developed an early interest in boxing through her father and two brothers and started boxing at around the age of ten. Taylor actually first entered the ring by accident, when her father was forced to bring her to his boxing club one evening after failing to find a babysitter to watch her. While her father trained other local boys, she started doing skipping exercises and hitting punching bags before sparring with boys herself.

Taylor became instantly mesmerized by the sport. "There was something great about getting into the ring and one-on-one combat," she said in a 2010 interview with Adrienne Murphy for *Hot Press*, republished on the magazine's website on August 9, 2012. Physically and mentally tough as well as agile and technically adept, Taylor quickly proved to be a natural in the ring. "When she donned the first pair of gloves, you knew she could box," her father told Peter McDermott for the *Irish Echo*, a weekly Irish American newspaper based in New York, in a 2009 interview republished on August 10, 2012. Taylor got her first pair of boxing gloves as a Christmas present and soon started sparring with boys on a regular basis. One of her biggest inspirations growing up was the Irish track-and-field legend Sonia O'Sullivan, arguably the country's greatest sportswoman, who won a silver medal in the 5,000-meter event at the 2000 Olympic Games in Sydney, Australia. Taylor dreamed of one day following in O'Sullivan's footsteps and representing Ireland in the Olympics, but she wanted to do so as a boxer, despite the fact that women's boxing at that time was not even sanctioned in Ireland, let alone as an Olympic sport.

### FEMALE BOXING TRAILBLAZER

With no girls to fight during the first few years of her career, Taylor sparred exclusively with and against boys, which she has said proved invaluable in her development as a boxer. Despite being weaker and slower than most of her male counterparts, it has been noted that she was normally the one inflicting pain in the ring. Ian Earls, one of Taylor's early sparring partners, remembered her as always having "great speed and technical ability as a boxer," as he told Jason O'Toole for his book *Katie Taylor: Journey to Olympic Gold* (2012). During her early teens, Taylor went undefeated in a series of unofficial exhibition matches against boys at St. Fergal's Boxing Club.

On October 31, 2001, at age fifteen, Taylor made her mark as a trailblazer for female boxing in Ireland when she participated in the country's first officially sanctioned female bout at the National Stadium in Dublin. In the fight, which was one of three female matches on a sixteen-bout amateur card, she defeated Alanna Audley of Belfast in three ninety-second rounds with a 23–12 decision. Taylor's historic victory was described by Irish Amateur Boxing Association (IABA) president Dominic O'Rourke as "a momentous day for Irish boxing," according to McDermott. Following the victory, Taylor began boxing on the international circuit, at which point her father quit his job to become her full-time coach and trainer. Her father was part of a group of local boxing coaches and enthusiasts who were credited with helping to lobby the IABA to recognize women's boxing as a sport in Ireland.

From 2002 to 2005, Taylor competed in amateur boxing tournaments all over Europe. During this time, she dominated many of her opponents, most of whom competed in the sixty-kilogram lightweight division. One of Taylor's more noteworthy bouts occurred in February 2004, when she scored a knockout victory over then-undefeated Lorna Cooper of Wales in an event sponsored by the Fermoy Boys and Girls Boxing Club in county Cork, Ireland; the fight lasted just thirty seconds and has since gone down as the shortest of her career. In June of that year, she defeated Canadian Jennifer Ogg, the 2002 world amateur lightweight champion, in the final of the Torneo Italia in Cascia, Italy, in which she also took home the award for best boxer of the tournament. The bout was "a big stepping stone for me," Taylor told McDermott. Then, at the 2004 European Amateur Boxing Championships in Riccione, Italy, she put up a strong showing against the Russian fighter and future sixty-three-kilogram super lightweight world champion Yuliya Nemtsova but ultimately lost a questionable 27–12 decision.

Taylor's profile rose considerably when she won the gold medal in the lightweight division at the 2005 European Amateur Boxing Championships in Tønsberg, Norway, in which she scored a third-round technical knockout (TKO) over Eva Wahlström of Finland. (A TKO occurs when a boxer is judged to be unable to safely continue fighting.) With her victory, the then-eighteen-year-old Taylor became the first Irish woman to win gold at the prestigious competition. She went on to reach the quarterfinals in the lightweight division at the 2005 AIBA World Amateur Championships, which were held in Podolsk, Russia.

Taylor attended St. Kilian's Community School in Bray, which her older siblings also attended. There, she played soccer, Gaelic football, basketball, and netball, a variation of basketball. After completing her leaving certificate,

or final secondary school exam, in 2005, she enrolled in the arts program at University College Dublin. She would later leave the university to focus on her boxing career.

## SOCCER CAREER

During her swift rise to the top of women's boxing, Taylor enjoyed just as much success on the soccer pitch. In her teens, after playing for the Lourdes Celtic and St. James's Gate clubs in the Dublin Women's Soccer League (DWSL), she earned a spot in the elite Peamount United soccer club, which is based in Newcastle. Taylor played for Peamount United in the 2005 Football Association of Ireland (FAI) Women's Cup, where they finished as the runners-up behind Dundalk City WFC. She also played as a midfielder for Ireland's under-seventeen and under-nineteen squads before being promoted to the country's senior squad in 2007 for the Fédération Internationale de Football Association (FIFA) World Cup qualifying tournament.

Taylor would play for the Irish women's national team until early 2010, when she took an indefinite hiatus from soccer to concentrate on boxing training for the 2012 Olympic Games. In all, she appeared in more than forty international matches with the team, including qualifying tournaments not only for the World Cup but also for the Union of European Football Associations (UEFA) Cup. Olivia O'Toole, the former captain of the Irish women's national team, compared Taylor to one of Ireland's most celebrated male soccer players, telling Mark Hilliard for the *Irish Independent* (10 Aug. 2012), "Boxing always came first, but when she did play for us it was like putting Roy Keane on the pitch—it was like having two extra players. . . . She could have been a superstar."

## FIRST WORLD AMATEUR BOXING TITLES

Back in the boxing ring, Taylor retained her gold medal in the lightweight division at the 2006 European Amateur Boxing Championships in Warsaw, Poland, with a fifteen-point mercy ruling in the second round against Russian fighter and then-defending world amateur lightweight champion Tatiana Chalaya. (In women's amateur boxing, the fifteen-point mercy rule is enforced by the referee when a boxer gains a fifteen-point advantage over her opponent.) She then defeated Chalaya again in the semifinals of that year's AIBA World Amateur Boxing Championships in New Delhi, India, before overcoming Anabella Farias of Argentina with a 31–14 decision in the final to win her first world amateur lightweight title. In the process, Taylor became the first Irish woman to win a world amateur title. Soon afterward she became one of the most recognizable and dominant female boxers in the world. "If you had a medal," Chris Mannix wrote for *Sports Illustrated* (8 Aug. 2012), "she was coming to get it."

In 2007 Taylor won her third consecutive European amateur lightweight title at the European Amateur Boxing Championships in Vejle, Denmark, after stopping Swiss opponent Sandra Brugger on the fifteen-point mercy rule in round two. In her four fights in the tournament, she collected a remarkable forty-nine points and conceded only four.

By this time Taylor had become the top-ranked female boxer in the world in her weight class, with dubious judging the only impediment standing in the way of her success. For instance, in May 2007, Taylor lost a highly controversial 16–13 decision to the Turkish fighter Gülsüm Tatar in the final of the Ahmet Comert Tournament in Istanbul, Turkey, despite dominating much of the fight. Nonetheless, after the loss, Taylor would rack up an amazing forty-two consecutive victories before losing, in March 2010, to the Russian fighter Sofya Ochigava in the semifinal of a tournament in the Czech Republic, in yet another controversial decision. It was later revealed that two of the five ringside judges for the fight were Russian nationals. Of Taylor's six defeats on record, all have been marred in some way by controversy regarding the judging. Despite this, she refuses to exercise her right to object to the presence of certain judges prior to a fight. "We never even look at the judges' names," her father explained to Vincent Hogan for the *Irish Independent* (16 Apr. 2012). "We don't care. Just go in and box to the best of your ability, that's our attitude."

## ROAD TO RECOGNITION

Taylor has displayed a similar attitude toward money, turning down lucrative endorsement deals to maintain her amateur status in the hopes of being able to compete for a gold medal at the Olympics. Those hopes were delayed when the International Olympic Committee (IOC) decided against introducing women's boxing as an official sport at the 2008 Olympics in Beijing, China. Despite being upset about the decision, Taylor nonetheless agreed to participate in media events promoting the games that year, and she served as a panelist for local television coverage of the games. She went on to win a second consecutive world amateur lightweight title at the 2008 AIBA World Amateur Boxing Championships in Ningbo, China, defeating Chinese fighter Cheng Dong with a convincing 13–2 decision. Several weeks after the tournament, Taylor, who also won the first of four consecutive European Union amateur lightweight titles in 2008, was named AIBA World Female Boxer of the Year at a ceremony held in Moscow, Russia. She was also recognized as the Irish Times/Irish Sports Council Sportswoman of the Year for the second year in a row.

Taylor was finally given a chance to realize her childhood dream in August 2009, when the IOC announced its decision to include women's boxing in the 2012 Olympics in London. While the announcement was met with some derision, many embraced it, including Ireland's former world featherweight champion Barry McGuigan. Once opposed to the idea of women's boxing, McGuigan was admittedly swayed after witnessing Taylor's boxing prowess firsthand. "My personal considerations were blown away the first time I saw Katie train," McGuigan wrote for the *Daily Mirror* (15 Aug. 2009). He added, "Her skill, power, speed, technique and attitude are all top class. . . . Double left hooks, right hands over the top, just extraordinary." Taylor expressed her elation with the IOC's decision at the 2009 European Amateur Boxing Championships in Mykolaiv, Ukraine, where she thoroughly handled all three of her opponents without conceding a single point, en route to winning a fourth consecutive European amateur lightweight title.

Despite female boxing's new Olympic status, Taylor, as the face and ambassador of the sport, still had to contend with outright sexism leading up to the 2012 Olympics, as officials tried to implement ploys that they believed would better market the sport and help distinguish it from the men's discipline. The most egregious of these ploys occurred at the 2010 AIBA World Amateur Boxing Championships in Bridgetown, Barbados, where, prior to Taylor's semifinal match with the American fighter Quanitta "Queen" Underwood, each fighter was presented with a skirt and tight-fitting vest to wear during their bout. Taylor vehemently refused to wear the new uniform and threatened to forfeit her title defense before officials acquiesced to her terms; as a result of her protests, the new uniforms are now optional and not mandatory for female boxers. She went on to narrowly defeat Underwood in a close 18–16 decision, then defeated Cheng Dong again in the final to claim her third consecutive world amateur lightweight title and hundredth career win. She was subsequently named the 2010 AIBA World Female Boxer of the Year, the second time in as many years. (The award was not given in 2009.)

## 2012 OLYMPIC GAMES

After capturing her fifth straight lightweight title at the 2011 European Amateur Boxing Championships in Rotterdam, Netherlands, Taylor entered the 2012 Olympic Games as the clear gold-medal favorite in her weight class. She officially qualified for the games at the 2012 AIBA World Amateur Boxing Championships in Qinhuangdao, China, on May 16, 2012, after her intended opponent in the quarterfinals, Mihaela Lăcătuş of Romania, withdrew due to a neck injury. Three days later, she won her fourth consecutive world title after beating Sofya Ochigava in the lightweight final by an 11–7 margin.

Taylor was chosen to serve as Ireland's flag bearer at the London 2012 Olympics opening ceremony, becoming the first female boxer and only the third boxer in the country's history to be given the honor. The ceremony welcomed more than four thousand of the world's top athletes from over two hundred countries and was viewed by an estimated nine hundred million people around the world. Extremely high expectations surrounded Taylor's long-awaited Olympic debut, with many viewing anything less than a gold medal as a failure. Undaunted, Taylor wasted little time living up to the hype. After receiving a first-round bye, she squared off against Great Britain's Natasha Jonas in the quarterfinal round. She went on to defeat Jonas in convincing fashion, scoring a 26–15 decision.

Receiving overly enthusiastic support from a predominantly Irish crowd at the ExCeL London arena, where all of the 2012 Olympic boxing matches were held, Taylor quickly dispatched her semifinal opponent, Tajikistan's Mavzuna Chorieva, to advance to the gold-medal round. In the Olympic women's lightweight final, she faced the Russian fighter Sofya Ochigava, her longtime adversary, who had stirred up controversy heading into the match by accusing her Irish opponent of receiving favoritism from judges. The two fought a tight, back-and-forth bout, but Taylor ultimately emerged victorious, scoring a 10–8 decision to capture the gold and realize her lifelong dream. Taylor became the first female boxer in history to win a gold medal in the lightweight division and Ireland's first gold medalist since 1996; her gold was also only the ninth in Ireland's history.

After the Olympics, Taylor was welcomed as a national hero in her hometown of Bray, where she was greeted by an estimated twenty thousand fans. She received the 2012 AIBA World Female Boxer of the Year Award for a record third time and was also named 2012 Sports Person of the Year at Ireland's annual People of the Year Awards.

Following the 2012 Olympics, some speculated that Taylor would retire from amateur competition to join either the professional boxing or soccer ranks, but she has continued to retain her amateur status in hopes of defending her title at the 2016 Olympic Games in Rio de Janeiro, Brazil. Taylor's boxing legacy is nonetheless already firmly in place. "She is going to go down as one of the best boxers in history," USA Boxing coach Basheer Abdullah told Mannix. "Not just female boxers, the best boxers. She can do it all. She can box, she can fight, she is a true world champion."

## PERSONAL LIFE

Taylor, who has been described as "shy," "softly spoken," "genuine," and "humble," lives in Bray with her family. She is a devout, born-again Christian, teetotaler, and nonsmoker and is a member of St. Mark's Pentecostal Church in Dublin. Taylor has spoken frequently about how her faith has kept her grounded in life and how it has helped her serve as a better role model for children. She explained to Hogan, "Obviously I'd love to go down in history as one of the greatest female boxers. But I'd like to be remembered for being a good person too and for my faith in God. I don't want people to define me by my medals, but by how I live my life."

## SUGGESTED READING

Bearak, Barry. "Striking a Blow for Ireland." *New York Times*. New York Times, 9 Aug. 2012. Web. 13 May 2013.

Hillard, Mark. "She Could Have Been a Star in Any Sport She Chose." *Irish Independent*. Independent.ie, 10 Aug. 2012. Web. 13 May 2013.

Mannix, Chris. "Ireland's Taylor May Be Most Popular Athlete at London Olympics." *SI.com*. Time, 8 Aug. 2012. Web. 13 May 2013.

McDermott, Peter. "Katie Taylor: Born to Win." *Irish Echo*. Irish Echo, 10 Aug. 2012. Web. 13 May 2013.

O'Toole, Jason. *Katie Taylor: Journey to Olympic Gold*. Dublin: Gill, 2012. Print.

Taylor, Katie. Interview by Adrienne Murphy. *Hot Press*. Hot Press, 9 Aug. 2012. Web. 13 May 2013.

"Women's Boxing: Katie Taylor Biography." *WBAN*. WBAN, 16 Dec. 2012. Web. 13 May 2013.

—*Chris Cullen*

# Mike Trout

**Born:** August 7, 1991
**Occupation:** Baseball player

In the history of Major League Baseball (MLB), few players have had a more dominant and impactful rookie season than the Los Angeles Angels of Anaheim's outfielder Mike Trout. Known for his rare combination of size, speed, and power, the six-feet-two, 230-pound Trout, who made his major-league debut with the Angels in July 2011 at the age of nineteen, emerged in 2012 as "the best player in baseball," Tom Verducci declared for *Sports Illustrated* (27 Aug. 2012). Despite spending the first month of the 2012 season in the minor leagues, Trout led not only all rookies in virtually every major statistical category but also the majors in several statistical categories.

During the 2012 season, Trout achieved a number of distinctions. He became the first player in MLB history to achieve at least thirty home runs, forty-five stolen bases, and 125 runs

John Green/CSM /Landov

and shoulder problems. Jeff, who had a career minor-league batting average of .303, later became a history teacher at his alma mater, Millville Senior High School, where he also coached baseball and football.

Trout developed a passion for baseball at an early age. He began playing the sport competitively at the age of five, and by eight, he was intently watching full-length nine-inning games on television. Growing up, Trout was reportedly so fond of baseball that he would sleep in his uniform after T-ball games. When Trout was young, his father, who for a time served as Millville High's varsity head baseball coach, brought him along to Millville team practices, where he would help shag fly balls during batting practice. "He basically grew up in the locker room," his father told Ramona Shelburne for ESPN Los Angeles (11 July 2010). Trout also played football and basketball, and he grew up a fan of Philadelphia's four major sports teams: the Phillies, the Eagles, the Flyers, and the 76ers.

As Trout got older, his baseball talent became clearly evident, and he routinely stood out in games against older children, often hitting towering home runs. One of the major influences in his baseball development was his mother, also a teacher at Millville High, who encouraged him to play on seasonal travel teams that competed in tournaments throughout New Jersey. "We never had to force him to play, and he always loved it," his mother told Marc Narducci for the *Philadelphia Inquirer* (13 June 2012). While Trout honed his baseball skills in both local and travel leagues, he learned greater truths about the game from his father, who used the example of his own career as a way to teach his son about hard work, dedication, perseverance, and acceptance of failure.

## HIGH SCHOOL CAREER

Like his father, Trout attended Millville Senior High School, where he was a four-year starter on the varsity baseball team. He also played football during his freshman year and basketball all four years. Armed with a ninety-mile-per-hour fastball, Trout initially made his mark in baseball as a pitcher and, when he was not on the mound, as a shortstop, but he was moved to the outfield after his junior year because his coaches thought it would better complement his speed, size, and athleticism. In an interview with Bob Behre for the Newark, New Jersey, *Star-Ledger* (19 June 2009), Roy Hallenbeck, the head baseball coach at Millville, described Trout as having "top-of-the-lineup speed in a linebacker's body." J. J. Cooper, writing for *Baseball America* (7 Sept. 2011), pointed out Trout's imposing "physicality" and noted that watching him run "was like watching a massive Mercedes with a big engine under the hood." In high school, Trout reportedly ran the sixty-yard dash in 6.38 seconds,

in a single season. He was selected to play in the 2012 MLB All-Star Game and was credited with almost singlehandedly turning around an underperforming team. After winning four out of the six American League (AL) Rookie of the Month honors during the season, Trout was a unanimous selection for the 2012 AL Rookie of the Year Award. Oakland Athletics general manager Billy Beane told Verducci about Trout, "He's the best player in the game. . . . He's the most exciting talent I've seen come into the game since A-Rod [Alex Rodriguez] and [Ken] Griffey Jr. There's a 0.1 percent chance of finding a player like this. It happens once every fifteen, twenty years—if that." Despite such rarefied comparisons, Trout, who is known as much for his electrifying defensive plays as for the infectious enthusiasm that he brings to the baseball diamond, has remained grounded. "My mindset is, don't worry about numbers," he told Scott Miller for CBS Sports (27 Mar. 2013). "Do everything you can to help your team win."

## EARLY LIFE

Michael Nelson Trout was born on August 7, 1991, in Vineland, New Jersey, to Jeff and Debbie Trout. He has an older sister, Teal, and an older brother, Tyler. Trout grew up in the southern New Jersey town of Millville, and he has baseball in his roots. His father was a standout switch-hitting infielder at the University of Delaware and was selected in the fifth round of the 1983 MLB Draft by the Minnesota Twins. Jeff Trout spent four years in the Twins' organization, advancing to the AA level before being forced to retire from baseball because of recurring knee which is considered remarkably fast for a player at any age.

Trout first appeared on the radar of major-league scouts during his junior year at Millville High, when he earned all-state honors as a pitcher, posting an 8–2 record and a 1.77 earned run average (ERA) with 124 strikeouts and only forty walks in seventy innings. He also put up remarkable numbers as a hitter, batting .530 with nine home runs and thirty-five runs batted in (RBI). During the summer after his junior year, Trout began competing in tournaments all over the country that showcased some of the top high school baseball prospects in the nation. Among those who saw him play was Greg Morhardt, then the Angels' Northeast scout. Morhardt, who had been a minor-league teammate of Jeff Trout while the two played for the AA Orlando Twins, told Tyler Kepner for the *New York Times* (22 June 2012), "Of all the players I've seen at seventeen, eighteen, nineteen years old, I've never seen a better athlete for strength and speed than Michael—ever. I remember playing against Jose Canseco in the Southern League, but he was on juice. Michael was a freak of nature."

### RECRUITMENT AND MLB DRAFT

By the time Trout entered his senior year, he had already been recruited by more than one hundred schools, including such baseball powerhouses as the University of San Diego and Arizona State University. Nonetheless, he signed a letter of intent to attend the lower-profile East Carolina University, in Greenville, North Carolina. The school's head baseball coach, Billy Godwin, envisioned Trout serving as the cornerstone of East Carolina's baseball program, but those visions were short lived.

Trout made a seamless transition to the outfield, and as a center fielder during his senior season, he hit .531, with a state-record eighteen home runs, forty-five RBI, and nineteen stolen bases; he also posted a 5–1 record with a 1.71 ERA as a pitcher. He earned all-state honors for the second consecutive year and was named New Jersey High School Player of the Year. Trout's staggering senior-year numbers solidified his status as an elite prospect, and he ultimately chose to forgo college to enter the 2009 MLB Draft.

Leading up to the draft, Trout drew serious interest from a number of major-league teams. However, some teams' scouts expressed reservations about Trout's unusual, coiled batting style and remained unconvinced that a baseball player of his caliber could hail from New Jersey, a cold-weather state not known for breeding top-level prospects. Despite these concerns, the Angels drafted Trout as the twenty-fifth overall pick in the 2009 draft. Morhardt, whose strong conviction about Trout ultimately persuaded the Angels' top executives to draft him, explained to

Kepner, "In my mind, Mike was it. . . . My chips were in: he was an everyday big league player who had the chance to be a Hall of Fame player." One month after the draft, Trout agreed to terms with the Angels on a signing bonus of $1.215 million, which was a standard figure for his draft spot but significantly lower than what his agents had tried to negotiate for him.

### LOS ANGELES ANGEL

Trout enjoyed a rapid ascension through the Angels' farm system. In the summer of 2009, he reported to the Angels' rookie-level Arizona League team in Tempe, where he immediately made an impression, hitting .360 in thirty-nine games. After being named the Arizona League's top prospect, Trout was moved up to the Angels' A affiliate, the Cedar Rapids Kernels of the Midwest League, where he finished the 2009 season. He returned to the Kernels to open the 2010 season and batted .362 with six home runs, thirty-nine RBI, and forty-five stolen bases in eighty-one games. In the summer of 2010, Trout was selected to participate in the Sirius XM All-Star Futures Game, which was part of that year's MLB All-Star Game festivities in Anaheim, California. In the game, a showcase of the best young baseball prospects from the United States and abroad, he collected two hits in four at bats and scored two runs. Following the game, the Angels decided to keep Trout in California, sending him to play with the organization's advanced A affiliate, the Rancho Cucamonga Quakes of the California League, with whom he batted .306 in fifty games. At the end of the 2010 season, Trout was named the top prospect of both the Midwest and California Leagues. He also received the J. G. Taylor Spink Award as the Topps Minor League Player of the Year, becoming, at nineteen years old, the youngest-ever recipient of the award.

Trout entered the 2011 season ranked by MLB.com as the game's best prospect and by the magazine *Baseball America* as the second-best prospect. That spring he attended the Angels' annual training camp, and afterward he was sent to play with the Arkansas Travelers in the AA Texas League. In seventy-five games with the Travelers, Trout batted .324 and compiled a near-perfect fielding percentage of .994. By that time the Angels were confident that he was ready to play in the major leagues. Trout earned his first call-up to the majors on July 8, 2011, when the team's starting center fielder, Peter Bourjos, went on the disabled list. At nineteen years and eleven months old, Trout became the youngest player in the majors and the youngest player to debut for the Angels since Andy Hassler in 1971. In his major-league debut, Trout went hitless in three at bats. He went on to appear in thirteen more games for the Angels before returning to Arkansas. However, Trout's return to Arkansas lasted less than three weeks, and on August 19, he was recalled by the Angels to play for the remainder of the season. In forty games with the Angels that year, he hit just .220 in 123 at bats.

Despite underperforming by his standards at the big-league level in 2011, Trout established himself as a force with which to be reckoned in the minors. After batting .326 with eleven home runs, thirty-eight RBI, thirty-three stolen bases, and eighty-two runs scored in ninety-one total games with the Travelers, he was named the minor-league player of the year by both *Baseball America* and *Sporting News*. In 2012, Trout was invited back to the Angels' spring-training camp, where he was offered a chance to compete for a spot on the team's twenty-five-man roster. Those chances were dashed after a viral infection and a shoulder problem limited him to just six spring-training at bats. As a result, Trout opened the 2012 season with the Salt Lake Bees, in the AAA Pacific Coast League. He batted .403 in twenty games before being called up to the Angels for good on April 28, 2012.

## THE ROOKIE PHENOM

When Trout joined the Angels in late April 2012, the team was in disarray. Despite entering the 2012 season with lofty expectations and the fourth-highest payroll in baseball, the Angels posted a dismal 6–14 record through the first twenty games, one of the worst starts in franchise history, which put them in last place in the AL West Division. At the center of the Angels' struggles was nine-time all-star and three-time most valuable player (MVP) Albert Pujols, who had joined the team during the 2012 MLB off-season after signing a record contract. At the time of Trout's arrival, Pujols was batting just .225 with no home runs and two RBI. Meanwhile, the Angels' second-highest-paid player, the three-time all-star outfielder Vernon Wells, was also underperforming, batting only .230 with five home runs and eight RBI through the team's first twenty games.

Trout quickly galvanized the Angels by "authoring the greatest rookie season in baseball history," Miller wrote. Immediately designated as the team's starting center fielder and leadoff hitter, he batted a rookie-best .324 with five home runs and sixteen RBI in twenty-seven games for the month of May and was named the AL Rookie of the Month. He was named Rookie of the Month for June also, after batting .372 with three home runs, seven doubles, fourteen stolen bases, sixteen RBI, and twenty-seven runs scored, making him the first Angels rookie to win consecutive Rookie of the Month awards. By that time, Trout had become one of the biggest stories in baseball, not only for the unprecedented numbers he was compiling but

also for the highlight-reel plays that he seemed to make on a nightly basis. Many of his dazzling plays went viral on the Internet, and he became a mainstay on ESPN's *SportsCenter* and on the MLB Network. The most noteworthy of Trout's plays occurred on June 26, in a game against the Baltimore Orioles, when he jumped halfway up a seven-foot wall and fully extended his body to rob shortstop J. J. Hardy of a home run. "Were there a Louvre for great catches," Verducci wrote, "this one would hang prominently." The home run–robbing catch was recognized as the MLB Play of the Year at various sports-related awards shows.

## SECOND HALF OF A RECORD-BREAKING SEASON

Trout entered the midpoint of the 2012 season hitting .341 with twelve home runs, fifteen doubles, forty RBI, and twenty-six steals in sixty-four games. In those games, the Angels enjoyed a dramatic turnaround, posting a record of 40–24, which helped them climb back into the AL West Division race. Trout was one of three rookies selected to represent the American League in the 2012 MLB All-Star Game; he was also only the sixth Angels rookie to be selected for an all-star team. Following the game, Trout continued his record-breaking tear, hitting .392 with ten home runs, twenty-three RBI, and thirty-two runs scored in twenty-five July games, garnering his third consecutive Rookie of the Month honor and his first AL Player of the Month Award; he became the first AL player in history to win both awards in the same month. He went on to earn a fourth straight AL Rookie of the Month honor for the month of August, after batting .284 with seven home runs, nineteen RBI, and eleven stolen bases.

Though the Angels ultimately missed the playoffs, finishing five games behind the Oakland Athletics, Trout finished the year ranked at or near the top of most AL batting categories. He finished second in the American League in batting average (.326) and third in both slugging percentage (.564) and on-base percentage (.399), and he led the majors in runs scored (129), stolen bases (forty-nine), and wins above replacement (10.7), an advanced baseball statistic that measures a player's true value to his team. He also had thirty home runs, eighty-three RBI, twenty-seven doubles, eight triples, and sixty-seven walks. Trout became the first player in baseball history to hit thirty home runs, steal forty-five bases, and score 125 runs in a single season; he also was the first to post a batting average of .320 or better with at least thirty home runs and forty-five steals in a single season.

In November 2012, Trout was unanimously selected as the AL Rookie of the Year. He received all twenty-eight first-place votes from the Baseball Writers' Association of America, making him only the eighth unanimous AL rookie of the year pick in history. He also finished second in the AL MVP voting, behind Detroit Tigers third baseman Miguel Cabrera. Many believed that Trout was more deserving than Cabrera of the MVP award; nonetheless, his second-place finish marked the best by a rookie in MVP balloting since the Seattle Mariners' Ichiro Suzuki won the award in 2001. Reflecting on his meteoric rise to MLB superstardom, as well as on his sudden celebrity, Trout told Daniel Riley for *GQ* magazine (Mar. 2013), "At the airport at the end of the [2012] season, I'm coming home, buying a pack of gum or something. And there were all these magazines. And I see this little kid looking at the cover of *ESPN The Magazine*. Looks at it and looks at me; looks at it, looks at me. And he finally goes, 'Is that you?'"

Prior to the 2013 season, Trout had his contract renewed by the Angels for $510,000. Though his contract is just $20,000 over the MLB minimum salary, many ultimately expect him to be properly compensated by the club in the not-too-distant future. Trout was moved from center field to left field during the 2013 season.

**PERSONAL LIFE**

Trout owns a condominium in Anaheim, near Angel Stadium, but he plans to buy a house in Newport Beach, California. He spends much of his time during the off-season with his family in Millville, where he enjoys hunting and fishing. Trout has signed endorsement deals with the beverage brand BodyArmor, the sportswear giant Nike, the food and beverage manufacturer J & J Snack Foods, and the Subway sandwich chain, for which he appeared in a commercial that aired during Super Bowl XLVII and the 2013 NCAA Men's Division I Basketball Tournament.

**SUGGESTED READING**

Behre, Bob. "Mike Trout Is New Jersey's Finest Baseball Player." *Nj.com*. New Jersey On-Line, 19 June 2009. Web. 17 Apr. 2013.

Kepner, Tyler. "Mike Trout, the Angels' Prodigy, Is Enjoying the Ride." *New York Times*. New York Times, 22 June 2012. Web. 17 Apr. 2013.

Narducci, Marc. "Mike Trout, 20, Is Diving Into the Future with Talent and Confidence." *Philly.com*. Philadelphia Media Network, 13 June 2012. Web. 17 Apr. 2013.

Riley, Daniel. "The MVP in Mom's Basement." *GQ*. Condé Nast, Mar. 2013. Web. 17 Apr. 2013.

Verducci, Tom. "Kid Dynamite." *Sports Illustrated*. Time Inc., 27 Aug. 2012. Web. 17 Apr. 2013.

—*Chris Cullen*

# Cenk Uygur

**Born:** March 21, 1970
**Occupation:** Talk show host and political commentator

Cenk Uygur, a Turk whose family immigrated to the United States when he was a child, hosts a web-based talk-radio show known as *The Young Turks*. A former lawyer, Uygur quit his day job to pursue a full-time career in talk radio in the late 1990s. He made his dream a reality in 2002 when he and a friend created the progressive talk-radio show *The Young Turks*, the first original talk show to air on Sirius Satellite Radio. The show later moved to Air America Radio and was broadcast on XM Satellite Radio.

Uygur began posting clips of *The Young Turks* online to the video-sharing website YouTube. The clips were very popular, and the show eventually became an Internet-based show in the mid-2000s. On the Internet, the show became massively popular, receiving more than half a billion views. Uygur then formed the TYT Network, which hosted the flagship *The Young Turks* along with other web-based talk shows featuring political, pop culture, comedic, and lifestyle content.

In 2011 Uygur brought his talents to *MSNBC Live* as a political talk show host. The stint was short-lived, however, and he left the network after about six months. By the end of 2011, he had a new job, hosting a television version of his talk-radio show on Current TV. The show, *The Young Turks with Cenk Uygur*, was similar to the format of his online show. After the sale of Current TV in early 2013, Uygur then focused solely on *The Young Turks* Internet show as well as his other shows on the TYT Network. He also served as a blogger for the *Huffington Post* and contributed to other publications.

**EARLY LIFE AND EDUCATION**

Cenk Uygur (pronounced Jenk Yoo-ger) was born on March 21, 1970, in Istanbul, Turkey. His family moved to the United States when Uygur was just eight years old. They settled in East Brunswick Township, New Jersey, where he attended East Brunswick High School. After high school, Uygur studied political science and entrepreneurial management at the University of Pennsylvania's Wharton School, from which he graduated in 1992. He then received a law degree from Columbia University Law School and worked for various law firms and radio stations.

**EARLY RADIO CAREER**

After graduating from law school, Uygur worked as a weekend and fill-in talk show host at WRKO radio in Boston, Massachusetts. He then landed a job as an associate at the law firm of Drinker,

Getty Images

Biddle & Reath LLP in Washington, DC. In his spare time, Uygur worked as a weekend talk-show host at WWRC radio. His show—which he called *The Young Turk*—dabbled in politics, news, and pop culture. He then moved to New York City, where he worked as an entertainment lawyer for Parcher, Hayes & Liebman. During this time, he also worked on political campaigns. He eventually left his law career to pursue work as a full-time radio talk-show host. Uygur told Andrea K. Hammer in an August 25, 2010, interview for the *Pennsylvania Gazette* that "life took twists and turns that were unimaginable—the first one being that I became a talk-show host. But when I worked on political campaigns briefly, I was intensely uninterested. So I wanted an outlet to express my opinions but without the drudgery of going through the political campaigns."

### THE YOUNG TURKS

In 1999 Uygur worked as a commentator and writer for the news show *The Times* at WAMI-TV in Miami, Florida. There he worked with Ben Mankiewicz, with whom he quickly became friends. The two decided to develop their own talk-radio show. After the September 11, 2001, terrorist attacks and the resulting war with Iraq, Uygur—who had been a Republican—began questioning the administration of President George W. Bush. Uygur disassociated himself from the Republican and Democratic parties, calling himself an anti-Republican and siding with liberal and progressive views.

In 2002 Uygur and Mankiewicz made their dream a reality and moved to Los Angeles, where they debuted their show *The Young Turks* on Sirius Satellite Radio. Uygur said they chose the name of their show because they considered themselves young rebels who disagreed with the views

of the country's administration. Uygur told Hammer, "The minute that I did my own show, I knew that was what I wanted to do for my life. The rest of it was incredibly hard work. . . . As long as you know what your goal is—I don't want to say that it gets easier, but at least you know where you're going. So the road gets more bearable."

Uygur said his strategies with the show were honesty and originality. Instead of reading news from a teleprompter, he said that he wanted to do something different and give his real views and opinions. He felt that this was the main reason that the younger generation was generally disinterested in news, and he wanted to do something to lure these younger viewers. In the early days of the show, Uygur read a great deal of newspaper and online articles, choosing ones that he thought were interesting enough to discuss. As the show progressed, his staff added audio clips of politicians saying interesting or absurd things. Uygur would play the clips and then comment on them. This helped boost the show's popularity.

In 2005 Uygur decided to stream his radio show online. With help and financial assistance from family and friends, he and show staff members at the time—Ben Mankiewicz, Dave Koller, Jill Pike, Jesus Godoy, and Jayar Jackson—began filming interviews and posting them on their website TheYoungTurks.com and other sites such as YouTube. Some of the individuals on the show during this time included former Speaker of the House Nancy Pelosi and actor Mel Brooks. Uygur knew that many people did not want to spend hours watching or reading news, so he began to expand his web presence by uploading short clips from his three-hour shows to YouTube. The clips were an instant hit and were shared through social media sites Facebook and Twitter, further spurring the show's popularity.

The radio show moved to the all-talk Air America Radio, which was broadcast on XM Satellite Radio, in 2006. Around this time, Mankiewicz left the show to pursue other interests and was replaced by Ana Kasparian, who cohosted *The Young Turks* with Uygur. Koller and Pike later left the show, and Steven Oh was hired. Other hosts and staff members included Malcolm Fleschner, Tom Hanc, Kim Horcher, John Iadarola, Irina Nichita, Mark Register, and Rick Strom. *The Young Turks* last aired on the radio in 2010, when it became a solely web-based show.

### TYT NETWORK

The online talk show later evolved into the TYT Network, which formed partnerships with online media groups including AOL News, TidalTV, and YouTube. In addition to politics, the network covered economics, lifestyle and social trends, and popular culture, as well as added new video talk shows, podcasts, and web series to cover these issues. The TYT Network included the YouTube channels Pop Cultured and Town Square. Pop Cultured featured the pop culture and gossip show *Pop Trigger* while Town Square included the weekly panel discussion *The Point*. Some of the network's other shows included *TYT Comedy*, which streamed funny videos and news stories; *TYT Interviews*, which featured interviews from everyday people to celebrities and politicians; *TYT Sports*, which covered sports news; *TYT Undergound*, which showed humorous videos and news about various TYT staff members; *TYT University*, which covered topics important to college students such as dating, fashion, and studying; *Nerd Alert*, which was about gaming news and other geek culture; and *What the Flick?!*, which featured movie reviews. The network later added *Absurdity Today*, *TYT Regulators*, *The Lip TV*, *The David Pakman Show*, *Take Action News with David Shuster*, and *Sam Seder's Majority Report*.

As of 2013, the TYT Network had more than thirty million views a month and more than a billion total video views since its inception; The Young Turks YouTube channel alone had more than half a billion total video views. In a December 2, 2011, interview, Uygur explained to Kevin Lincoln for *Business Insider* why he thinks the network is so popular. "We've been really lucky—all this time, we've gotten great feedback from the audience saying that they've learned something from [our show]," Uygur said. "Basically what you're doing is, you're providing a service for them, because they don't have time to read 30, 40, 50 articles on the news every day. We distill that down to what's really important, and hopefully give them some analysis that they're not going to find anywhere else because we can give them the right context."

In addition, Uygur, the TYT Network, and *The Young Turks* show have been recognized with several award nominations and awards throughout the years. At the Mashable Awards in 2009, TYT Network was named the best political news site. *The Young Turks* show was named the best political podcast at the 2009 Podcast Awards. In 2011 the show received the News/Politics Shorty Award and the People's Voice Webby Award for best news and politics series. The following year, *The Young Turks* show won best video podcast at the Podcast Awards. Also in 2012, the American Humanist Association awarded Uygur the Humanist Media Award.

## MSNBC

When MSNBC had a slot opening for a new show in 2010, Uygur called on his fans for their support. They sprang into action, sending e-mails and writing letters to MSNBC on Uygur's behalf. It worked, and in 2010 Phil Griffin, the head of the network, called Uygur for a meeting. In late 2010, Uygur served as a fill-in host and commentator for MSNBC. By January of 2011,

he received a trial position hosting an evening political talk show as part of *MSNBC Live*.

Although Uygur generally had favorable reviews and high ratings, after about six months he was told he would no longer host on *MSNBC Live* and was offered a job hosting a weekend show instead. His show's ratings had beaten CNN's *The Situation Room* in the eighteen to thirty-four demographic. Uygur told Ed Rampell in the August 2012 issue of the *Progressive*, "I had a conversation with Phil Griffin, and he said I'd done everything he'd asked me to do and my ratings were clearly good. My last quarter at MSNBC beat Ed Schultz's numbers from the year before, and Ed Schultz is terrific. But I didn't get the slot, and they told me they were going to move me to the weekends."

Uygur did not accept the new position—although it was rumored to come with a hefty pay increase—and left MSNBC in July of 2011. Afterward Uygur claimed that Griffin and other company executives were not happy with the way he criticized US president Barack Obama's administration and that he did not book enough Republican guests on the show. Griffin and MSNBC disputed the claims, saying that the company was unhappy with Uygur's hosting abilities.

## CURRENT TV

Shortly after Uygur left MSNBC, Current TV's new head of programming, David Bohrman, approached Uygur about hosting a new political talk show. The network was looking for shows with similar liberal views to compete with the likes of CNN and MSNBC. Current TV was interested in Uygur because of his enormous web presence and was hoping to lure some of those numbers to its programming.

*The Young Turks with Cenk Uygur* debuted in late 2011 in the 7:00 p.m. time slot, directly before *Countdown with Keith Olbermann*. The show was similar to the format of his Internet-based *The Young Turks*, and it sometimes featured his cohosts. To help keep the television show separate from the online entity, both production staffs met to decide which stories would go online and which would be seen on television. The television show enabled Uygur to use detailed graphics and elaborate introductions; it also gave him more access to guests and experts—luxuries his Internet show lacked because of resources. Because of this, he was able to give his television viewers a broader range of perspectives on certain topics. Uygur told Lincoln of the major differences in working on television and online. "If it's a story on Newt Gingrich today, the old way of doing it would've been just to tell the story, the new way of doing it is to create value-added stuff visually, now that we can," he said. He went on to explain that television "gives a whole different way of telling the story that I think will help the process."

In January of 2013, Current TV's owner, former US vice president Al Gore, sold the channel to Al Jazeera, which will transition the network into Al Jazeera America. Uygur and other hosts were told to continue broadcasting their shows until the takeover is complete. Uygur told *Politico*'s Mackenzie Weinger in a January 15, 2013, interview, "Right now, we plan to keep doing the show, as we are, for about a three-month period, roughly. And then we'll see if there's something we can do with Al Jazeera or another cable network, and we'll take it from there."

## WOLF PAC

A supporter of the Occupy Wall Street protests, Uygur created the political action committee (PAC) Wolf PAC in 2011. The goal of Wolf PAC is to amend the constitution to remove private funding from politics. Uygur claimed that private campaign donations cause corruption and insisted that private money should be separated from politics. He said that this would end corporate involvement in politics and put the decisions back into the hands of the voters. Uygur explained his reasoning for the creation of the PAC in an October 20, 2011, *Huffington Post* article, saying, "Every single issue gets decided by who gives the most donations. We have, in a sense, lost our democracy. The only determining factor is money. We must pass a constitutional amendment to get money out of politics. It's not even a democracy anymore, it's an oligarchy."

## PERSONAL LIFE

Uygur married Wendy Lang, a marriage and family therapist who was born in Hong Kong, on December 6, 2008. The couple's first child, Prometheus Maximus Uygur, was born on July 12, 2010. They had a daughter, Joy Uygur, on October 15, 2012. The family resides in Los Angeles, California.

## SUGGESTED READING

Huffington Post. "Cenk Uygur Launches New Effort to Separate Money and Politics." *Huffington Post*. TheHuffingtonPost.com, 20 Oct. 2011. Web. 12 Mar. 2013.

Lincoln, Kevin. "Meet the Host of 'The Largest Online News Show in the World.'" *Business Insider*. Business Insider, 2 Dec. 2011. Web. 12 Mar. 2013.

Rampell, Ed. "An Interview with Cenk Uygur." *Progressive*. Progressive Mag., Aug. 2012. Web. 12 Mar. 2013.

Taintor, David. "The TPM Interview: Current TV Host Cenk Uygur." *Talking Points Memo*. TPM Media, 8 June 2012. Web. 12 Mar. 2013.

Weinger, Mackenzie. "Bill Press on Future of Current TV Hosts." *Politico*. Politico, 15 Jan. 2013. Web. 12 Mar. 2013.

—*Angela Harmon*

# Sofía Vergara

**Born:** July 10, 1972
**Occupation:** Actor and entrepreneur

When Sofía Vergara was growing up in Colombia, her ambitions did not include a career in front of the camera. "I didn't want to be an actress. I wanted to be a dentist, but you never know what life will bring you," she told Francis Rodríguez in an interview for the *New York Daily News* (20 Mar. 2008). "But I can't complain," she added. "I'm happy with what I've achieved." After starting out as a host on Spanish-language television, Vergara was introduced to US audiences in the comedy film *Chasing Papi* (2003). After landing a development deal with ABC, she costarred in several short-lived series for the network: *Hot Properties, Knights of Prosperity,* and *Dirty Sexy Money*. She finally found success in 2009, when she was cast in the hit television series *Modern Family*.

## EARLY LIFE AND EDUCATION

Sofía Margarita Vergara was born on July 10, 1972, in Barranquilla, an industrial port city located on the northern coast of Colombia. Vergara's mother, Margarita Dávila de Vergara, was a homemaker, while her father, Julio Enrique Vergara Robayo, raised cattle for the local meat industry. She grew up with her five siblings in a devoutly Catholic but tumultuous middle-class home. "My parents were together on and off until they divorced in 1993," Vergara told Dotson Rader for *Parade* (24 July 2011). "Fighting, leaving, coming back. Such craziness is worse than divorce."

As a teenager, Vergara attended Marymount School in Barranquilla, a private Catholic and coeducational bilingual school, where she learned to speak English. Much to her dismay, she was also a late bloomer, earning the childhood nickname "Palillo," the Spanish word for toothpick. "In my culture, a skinny girl has nothing going on," she told Steven Baker and Lauren Effron in an interview for *ABC News* (2 Nov. 2011). "So I was very scared, always concerned that I was never gonna fill up. . . . I would never even wear skirts or anything because I thought I was too skinny."

## FIRST ON-SCREEN APPEARANCE

Vergara's figure started to fill out by the time she reached the age of seventeen, and in 1989, she attracted the attention of modeling scouts, who spotted Vergara on a beach while she was vacationing with her family in the town of Santa Marta. "They said, 'Oh, let's take a picture of you. We're looking for somebody for a Pepsi commercial,'" Vergara said to Rader. "I was like, 'No, the nuns would kill me.' I was in my senior year. And my mother said, 'Yeah! Take the picture!'"

Associated Press

Vergara was ultimately cast in the Pepsi television advertisement, which became quite popular, garnering her more offers to act and model.

In 1991, after graduating from Marymount, Vergara married her high-school sweetheart, José González, and enrolled in dental school. In 1992 she gave birth to their son, Manolo, whom she named after a character in the 1983 Al Pacino movie *Scarface*. Soon after, Vergara and González amicably split; the couple divorced in 1993.

### LAUNCHING HER TELEVISION CAREER
In 1994, with only two years of dental school remaining, Vergara dropped out and moved with her son from Colombia to Miami, Florida, in pursuit of an entertainment career. Within a year she had landed a gig hosting *Fuera de serie* (Out of the ordinary), a half-hour, Spanish-language travel series that was broadcast worldwide on Univision, the largest Spanish-language television network in the United States. "We traveled around the world on prime time. It was a family show to show interesting things and facts in a way that everybody could watch," she told Luaine Lee for the Fredericksburg, Virginia, *Free Lance-Star* (31 Dec. 2006).

Vergara's acting debut came in 1995, with an appearance in the Mexican telenovela *Acapulco, cuerpo y alma* (Acapulco, body and soul). She continued to cohost *Fuera de serie* until its cancellation in 1998—the same year that her family was struck by personal tragedy. Her older brother, Rafael, was killed in Bogotá, Colombia, following a kidnapping attempt. "He was kidnapped two years before and he paid the ransom and they tried to kidnap him again two years later," she explained to Lee. "And by that time

he was already carrying guns and had left his bodyguards in the house. They shot him when he went to reach for his gun."

Fearing for her family's safety, Vergara brought her mother, her sister Victoria, and her brother Julio to live with her in Miami. "I got a big house and we all lived together. I am so grateful to be in this country," she told Rader for *Parade*. In 1999 she assumed hosting duties for another Univision television series, *A que no te atreves* (I dare you), a game show in which contestants are dared to perform wild and crazy public stunts in exchange for money.

### HOLLYWOOD BREAKTHROUGH
Vergara experienced her own personal tragedy a year later, in 2000, when she was unexpectedly diagnosed with thyroid cancer—a battle that she kept secret at the time. "Because I have a family history of type 1 diabetes—my five siblings have it—I know what it's like to have injections every day and to have craziness happen to your body. So I took my son to an endocrinologist to be checked out early. While we were there, the doctor wanted to check me, too, and he found a lump in my neck," she told Jennifer Graham Kizer in an interview for *Health* magazine (21 Apr. 2008). After undergoing successful surgery to remove her thyroid gland, Vergara, who was left with a visible scar on her neck, received radioactive iodine treatment while still keeping her illness a secret. "I didn't want publicity because of that. Having cancer is not fun. You don't want to deal with anything else while you're going through it," she revealed to Kizer.

However, Vergara's health setback did little to stall the momentum in her budding career. In 2002, she made her feature film debut, alongside actors Tim Allen and Stanley Tucci, in the ensemble comedy *Big Trouble*, an adaptation of the 1999 Dave Barry novel of the same name. That same year she guest-starred in an episode of the now-defunct ABC comedy *My Wife and Kids*. Vergara also served as a spokesmodel for a Miller Lite print campaign, and starred in a Spanish-language television advertisement for the beer and in another for McDonald's.

Vergara landed her first notable role in *Chasing Papi* (2003), a big-screen romantic comedy with a predominantly Latino cast. The blonde-haired Vergara was asked to dye her hair darker to play Cici, a Miami cocktail waitress and the girlfriend of a womanizer, who is also seeing two other women in different cities. "I'm a natural blonde, like my siblings," she told Rader. "In L.A. they're used to Latin women looking more Mexican. But if you go to Uruguay, Argentina, and Colombia, everybody is blond." Vergara followed up her breakthrough role with a small part as a flight attendant in *Soul Plane* (2004), another ensemble comedy.

## CREDITS ON THE BIG AND SMALL SCREENS

The following year Vergara, who had signed a development deal with ABC, made her television series debut in the network's short-lived comedy *Hot Properties* (2005). Her supporting role as Lola Hernandez earned notice from Alessandra Stanley of the *New York Times* (7 Oct. 2005), who wrote: "Ms. Vergara is sultry but silly—a throwback to Charo of cuchi-cuchi fame." Next came big-screen appearances in the gritty drama film *Lords of Dogtown* and the John Singleton–directed urban thriller *Four Brothers*, both released in 2005. Her personal life also became a subject of interest when she briefly dated actor Tom Cruise that year.

After a supporting role as a seductress, in which she acted opposite Ray Romano and Kevin James in the direct-to-video release *Grilled* (2006), Vergara returned to Univision—and weekly television—in *Amas de casa desesperadas*, the Colombian version of the hit ABC dark comedy *Desperate Housewives*. Vergara, who also served as executive producer, played Alicia Oviedo, the show's narrator and a suburban housewife whose sudden and mysterious suicide leaves her four closest friends determined to solve her mysterious death. She narrated all twenty-three episodes of the first season, which aired in 2007.

Also in 2007, Vergara landed the female lead in another short-lived ABC comedy, *The Knights of Prosperity*, in which she played a disgruntled waitress at a diner in the New York City borough of Queens who teams up with a band of celebrity-worshipping misfits to steal items from various celebrities, including Rolling Stones front man Mick Jagger. A guest appearance on the premiere episode of the fourth season of the HBO ensemble dramedy series *Entourage* gave her another opportunity to show off her comedic chops. She then landed a recurring part on the ABC prime-time soap *Dirty Sexy Money*. Vergara remained a fixture on the small screen, with her recurring appearances on the Mexican telenovela *Fuego en la sangre* (Burning for revenge) in 2008 and her guest-starring role in two episodes of the comedy *Men in Trees*, which also aired on ABC.

## MAINSTREAM SUCCESS ON *MODERN FAMILY*

For her next film role, Vergara costarred opposite Angela Bassett in the Tyler Perry film *Meet the Browns* (2008). She played against type for her next film role, teaming with Perry again for *Madea Goes to Jail* (2009), the big-screen adaptation of his 2006 play. In the comedy, Vergara took on the role of T.T., a serial killer and the cellmate of the title character (played by Perry himself).

Vergara finally found mainstream success that year, following a meeting with writers and producers Christopher Lloyd and Steven Levitan, who were looking for an actress to play Gloria Pritchett-Delgado, the sexy, much younger trophy wife of an older man (played by *Married with Children*'s Ed O'Neill) in a comedy series entitled *Modern Family*. Lloyd and Levitan immediately cast Vergara in the role, and they also incorporated elements of the actress's real life into the plot line; like Vergara, Gloria is a single mother from Colombia with a son.

On September 23, 2009, *Modern Family* debuted on ABC to rave reviews. "Mr. O'Neill exquisitely portrays the straight man to the fire engine of Ms. Vergara, whose performance is a tonally perfect sendup of the Hispanic hot-mama stereotype," Ginia Bellafante wrote in a review for the *New York Times* (22 Sept. 2009). The following year Vergara received a Primetime Emmy Award nomination in the category of outstanding supporting actress in a comedy series. Consecutive Emmy nominations followed in 2011 and 2012, along with three Golden Globe nods between 2011 and 2013 in the category of best performance by an actress in a supporting role in a series, miniseries, or motion picture made for television. Vergara shared three Screen Actors Guild Awards with the cast of *Modern Family* in 2011, 2012, and 2013 for outstanding performances by an ensemble in a comedy series.

In addition to her role on *Modern Family*, Vergara costarred in the ensemble comedy *New Year's Eve* (2011) and the 2012 comedy film *The Three Stooges*. She has also lent her voice to several animated television series and films, including the Fox comedies *The Cleveland Show* and *Family Guy*; *The Smurfs*; and *Happy Feet Two*. She has three films in postproduction that are due to be released in 2013: *The Smurfs 2*; *Fading Gigolo*; and *Machete Kills*.

In 2012, *Forbes* magazine listed Vergara as the highest-earning woman on television, having earned an estimated $19 million that year, in part due to her endorsement deals with Pepsi and CoverGirl cosmetics, as well as her clothing line with Kmart.

## PERSONAL LIFE

A philanthropist, Vergara is the founder of the nonprofit organization Peace and Hope for the Children of Colombia, which she established in 2001. She also cofounded her own talent-management and marketing firm, Latin World Entertainment, in 1998 with producer Luis Balaguer. Vergara became engaged to businessman Nick Loeb in July 2012.

## SUGGESTED READING

Bellafante, Ginia. "I'm the Cool Dad and Other Debatable Dispatches from the Home Front." *New York Times* 23 Sept. 2009, New York ed.: C3. Print.

Kizer, Jennifer Graham. "Sofia Vergara Beats Thyroid Cancer." *Health*. Health Media Ventures, 21 Apr. 2008. Web. 14 Apr. 2013.

Rader, Dotson. "Sofia Vergara: Not Just Another Pretty Face." *Parade*. Parade Publications, 24 July 2011. Web. 18 Apr. 2013.

Rodríguez, Francis. "Sofia Vergara Stars in 'Meet the Browns,' Strives for a Lead Role." *New York Daily News*. NYDailyNews.com, 20 Mar. 2008. Web. 18 Apr. 2013.

Woods, Vicki. "Sofía Vergara: Dangerous Curves." *Vogue*. Condé Nast, 13 Mar. 2013. Web. 18 Apr. 2013.

—*Bertha Muteba*

Getty Images

# Melanne Verveer

**Born:** June 24, 1944
**Occupation:** US ambassador at large for global women's issues

Describing her latest role to Moira Forbes for *Forbes* magazine (28 Sept. 2012), Melanne Verveer explained, "As the first ever US ambassador for global women's issues, my most important obligation is really to integrate issues affecting women and girls across the US State Department in our far-flung missions around the world and in all of the work that we do in Washington, from economics to regional issues to human rights." The ambassadorship was created by President Barack Obama shortly after his inauguration in 2009, reflecting an unprecedented commitment in US foreign policy efforts to integrate and engage women and girls in the political, economic, and social advancement of their respective countries and the world at large. As Verveer wrote in a May/June 2012 article for *Foreign Policy* magazine, "Promoting the status of women is not just a moral imperative but a strategic one; it's essential to economic prosperity and to global peace and security."

According to a study published by the World Economic Forum, there is a clear correlation between gender equality—as measured by women's economic and political participation and their access to education and health care—and gross domestic product (GDP) per capita. "When women have equal access to agricultural resources, 100 million to 150 million fewer people will go hungry," Verveer wrote in an article with Penny Abeywardena for CNN (24 Sept. 2012). "When women participate equally in the workforce, the GDP in the United States, the Eurozone, and Japan will experience a double-digit spike." Verveer points to US foreign policy efforts of recent decades that failed because policymakers did not heed the concerns and contributions of women, such as de-mining efforts that targeted landmine removal along roadways but ignored the fields where most women work.

As director of the State Department's Office of Global Women's Issues, Verveer works tirelessly to provide women around the world with the access to capital, credit, and training that will allow them to participate more fully in the economic and political advancement of their countries. Ambassador Verveer and the Office of Global Women's Issues are also focused on ending human trafficking, obtaining equal legal protections for women, promoting political participation and economic opportunities, and securing human rights. "She seeks power to empower others," Alyse Nelson, a former colleague of Verveer, told Sandra McElwaine for the *Daily Beast* (11 June 2009). "She really gets it and knows how to work with people across the divide." At her confirmation hearing on April 6, 2009, Verveer emphasized the importance of her efforts, saying, "It remains a simple fact that no country can get ahead if half of its citizens are left behind."

## EARLY LIFE AND EDUCATION

Melanne Starinshak Verveer was born on June 24, 1944, in Pottsville, Pennsylvania, and was raised in the nearby town of Shamokin. Her four grandparents were Ukrainian immigrants who had settled in Pennsylvania at the turn of the twentieth century. Her mother, Mary, was a homemaker, and her father, Walter Starinshak, ran a post office and insurance company and was actively involved in the local community. He would often help his neighbors, many of whom were recent immigrants to the United States, to coordinate with local, state, and federal government agencies. "He gave me a sense of government as responsive to people, as enabling them to improve their lives," Verveer recalled to the Associated Press (7 Dec. 1999). Verveer attended the Transfiguration Ukrainian Catholic School and later received her high school diploma from St. Mary's Villa Academy in Sloatsburg, New York. Verveer was interested in politics even as a child. She started a civics club at St. Mary's and spent a lot of her spare time reading the *New York Times*, *Time*, and the *Congressional Record*.

In an interview with Moira Forbes for *Forbes* magazine (28 Sept. 2012), Verveer recalled how her parents helped her to develop a strong sense of self: "As I was growing up, my parents and particularly my father always said to me, 'You can do whatever you set yourself to doing.'" Her active participation at school, from giving speeches at assemblies to greeting visiting school officials, helped her to develop confidence and to feel comfortable in a leadership role. She told Forbes, "I think that nurtured in me a sense that you can do these things, and it wasn't alien, and it wasn't something that was out of the norm. And I think, going back to that, how important it is for us to be able to nurture, particularly in girls . . . that sense that they can prevail, they can. They have enormous talents. They can make a difference." In her junior year of high school, Verveer attended a school field trip to Washington, DC, where she was impressed with Georgetown University. A couple years later she enrolled in the Georgetown School of Languages to study Russian.

It was at Georgetown, in a sophomore-year theology class, that she met Philip Verveer. "We hit it off immediately. She was smart, energetic, and positive—a real extrovert," Philip Verveer told Sandra McElwaine for the *Daily Beast* (11 June 2009). He added that he admired his wife's "preternatural level of efficiency. She tries to help everyone." Philip Verveer proposed marriage in their junior year of college, around the same time the young couple was getting to know a classmate named Bill Clinton, then a freshman at Georgetown. Verveer earned her bachelor's degree from Georgetown in 1966 and completed a master's degree in Russian there in 1969.

## ENTERING POLITICS

After graduation Verveer began work at several nongovernmental organizations (NGOs). She worked as a field manager for Common Cause, a nonpartisan, nonprofit advocacy organization dedicated to improving the political process. In 1972 Verveer joined the presidential campaign of Democratic senator George McGovern, where she began working with Hillary Rodham Clinton. In 1981 Verveer became a founding member of the Coalition on Human Needs, an organization that advocates policies to support the needs of low-income and other vulnerable populations. She also served on the boards of the Leadership Conference on Human Rights and the Advocacy Institute and Public Allies. In 1982 Verveer began work as a legislative director to Democratic representative Marcy Kaptur. She also worked as a coordinator for civil rights and urban affairs at the US Catholic Conference's national office, where she played a key role in organizing a grassroots coalition to support the passage of the Voting Rights Extension Act of 1982.

In 1987 she was named executive vice president of People for the American Way, a constitutional-liberties nonprofit organization. In that capacity she helped support the passage of several important civil rights bills and was instrumental in organizing the rejection of President Ronald Reagan's Supreme Court nominee Robert Bork in 1987. In 1989 she was listed among *Beacham's Guide to Key Lobbyists* in recognition of her enormous influence and ability to work with lawmakers and other organizations to effect change. Verveer took leave from People for the American Way in 1992 to help with the presidential campaign of Bill Clinton, who defeated the incumbent, President George H. W. Bush.

## CHIEF OF STAFF TO FIRST LADY HILLARY CLINTON

Verveer joined the Clinton White House in early 1993, where she worked as deputy assistant to the president and deputy chief of staff to First Lady Hillary Rodham Clinton. Many political commentators have noted that Hillary Clinton was one of the most politically active and influential First Ladies since Eleanor Roosevelt. Verveer, well known for her coalition-building skills, was instrumental in organizing the First Lady's vast network of individuals and interest groups. The *National Catholic Reporter* called Verveer "the First Lady's official problem-solver and team-builder" (9 Sept. 1994). Of First Lady Hillary Clinton's many policy initiatives, from health care to women's issues to foreign policy, it was "Verveer's responsibility to do much of the detail work and policy formation to try to implement these objectives," reported the Associated Press (7 Dec. 1999). "No First Lady's staff has ever had a political operative of the caliber and experience of Melanne Verveer," the *National Catholic Reporter* wrote (9 Sept. 1994).

In September 1995 Verveer helped to plan Hillary Clinton's speech at the United Nations' World Conference on Women in Beijing, China, in which the First Lady famously stated, "It is no longer acceptable to discuss women's rights as separate from human rights." Many members of the Clinton administration thought that the speech would be too risky and politically sensitive, and Verveer and Hillary Clinton were discouraged from their plans. "They gave us lots of flak," Verveer told Michelle Cottle for *New York* magazine (6 Aug. 2007). When the speech inspired a standing ovation and drew accolades from around the world, many formerly hesitant members of the Clinton administration embraced the speech. "Sometimes we would initiate something and the boys would take credit for it," she told Cottle archly. At that time Verveer helped to establish the Interagency Council on Women in order to coordinate the policy initiatives related to women's progress that had been announced at the UN World Conference on Women. Speaking of Verveer's success at coordinating Hillary Clinton's policy efforts, Neel Lattimore, former press secretary to Clinton, described Verveer to the Associated Press as "the stealth weapon of the First Lady's office."

## VITAL VOICES

In 1997 Verveer was involved in the creation of the Vital Voices Democracy Initiative with Hillary Clinton and former secretary of state Madeleine Albright. The initiative partnered with the United Nations, the World Bank, and other agencies to promote emerging female leaders from around the world and to provide them with the training and resources they needed. Due to the success of the initiative, Verveer decided to continue the effort after the Clinton administration left the White House. In June 2000, as President Clinton neared the end of his second term, Verveer launched the Vital Voices Global Partnership to continue to train and empower women leaders around the globe. "I think private organizations have an important role to play in women's issues," Verveer said in an interview with WhoRunsGov of the *Washington Post* (21 Dec. 2011). "The government can't do everything, we need allies." The Vital Voices Global Partnership continues to provide training and networking opportunities to women entrepreneurs, as well as advocacy efforts aimed at promoting the political, legal, and economic involvement of women around the world. Verveer's dedication to furthering that initiative after the Clintons left the White House demonstrates her deep commitment to women's advancement. "She's a real treasure, a deeply passionate, effective and compassionate person," Bobbie Greene McCarthy, who worked with Verveer at the White House, told Sandra McElwaine for the *Daily Beast* (11 June 2009).

After she left her post as chief of staff to the First Lady, Verveer dedicated herself to the global partnership, serving as the organization's chair and chief executive officer for the next nine years. As Verveer told Anne Orleans for the *Washington Report on Middle East Affairs* (Sept. 2004), "This initiative will equip women leaders from Morocco to Afghanistan, from Turkey to Yemen, with the skills, confidence, and resources they need to participate effectively in the economic, social, and political progress of their

countries and the region." Madeleine Albright, who watched Verveer transform their State Department initiative into an NGO with an annual budget of ten million dollars, described Verveer to McElwaine as a "voice for the voiceless, a true champion for women." Albright added, "The impact of her work can be seen in the thousands of women who have benefited from the tools, information, and leadership provided by Vital Voices, a remarkable organization whose success can be largely attributed to Melanne."

## 2008 PRESIDENTIAL CAMPAIGN

In 2006 Verveer joined Hillary Clinton's 2008 presidential campaign as a faith outreach coordinator. She was able to speak to Clinton's experience as a First Lady, asserting to Matt Stearns for *McClatchy Newspapers* (27 July 2007) that the former First Lady's time in the White House and her diplomacy efforts abroad were not all "photo ops and fancy dinners." She elaborated, "It was going to villages, to cities, looking at the tough challenges facing people. . . . That gave her a very broad perspective and a sophisticated vision of America's place in the world." When Hillary Clinton conceded the Democratic presidential nomination in the summer of 2008, Verveer pledged her support for the Democratic presidential candidate, then senator Barack Obama, who would go on to win the presidency that November.

## AMBASSADOR AT LARGE FOR GLOBAL WOMEN'S ISSUES

Shortly after President Obama's inauguration, in March 2009, the White House announced Verveer's nomination as the first ambassador at large for global women's issues. Verveer was confirmed to that appointment on April 6, 2009. The ambassadorship was created to ensure that issues related to the advancement of women are fully implemented into US foreign policy efforts through the State Department. Speaking of her new appointment, Verveer told Lois Romano for the *Washington Post* (19 Nov. 2009), "It's an effort to truly integrate these concerns into the overall operations of the State Department." Verveer added that the efforts "really are about the kind of world we want to create." Through the State Department Ambassador Verveer continues to work closely with Hillary Clinton, who was confirmed as the sixty-seventh secretary of state shortly before Verveer's confirmation.

As ambassador Verveer has traveled to dozens of countries around the world to promote women's rights and to coordinate US foreign policy in that area with individual leaders and government agencies worldwide. "As a growing body of research shows," Verveer wrote for *Foreign Policy* magazine (May/June 2012), "the world's most pressing economic and political problems simply cannot be solved without the participation of women. That's why Secretary of State Hillary Clinton is working to ensure that advancing the status of women and girls around the world is fully integrated into every aspect of US foreign policy." In the spring of 2012, Verveer worked with Clinton to implement the first secretarial policy directive on gender for all US diplomats, which outlines specific steps to promote gender equality and the advancement of women through US embassies and bureaus worldwide.

"Girls and women do indeed perform 66 percent of the work and produce 50 percent of the world's food. But they earn only 10 percent of the world's income and own a dismal 1 percent of its property. And women everywhere experience less access to credit, training, technology, markets, role models, and protection under the law," Verveer wrote in an article for CNN with Penny Abeywardena (24 Sept. 2012). Through the State Department Verveer mobilizes support for initiatives that aim to secure equal access to education and health care for women, to prevent rape and domestic violence, to end human trafficking, and to provide the credit, training, mentorship, and legal protections that women around the world need to advance themselves, their communities, and their countries. Emphasizing the importance of engaging more women in global economic and political issues, Verveer stated at her April 6, 2009, confirmation hearing, "Democratic institutions cannot thrive and survive without their participation. Economies cannot grow and prosper without their inclusion. And it remains a simple fact that no country can get ahead if half of its citizens are left behind."

## PERSONAL LIFE
Verveer's husband, Philip, works at the State Department as deputy assistant secretary for International Communication and Information Policy. Together they have three grown children, Elaina, Alexandra, and Michael Verveer. The Verveers' commitment to public service continues with their children as well: Alexandra, a lawyer, at one time served in the Justice Department, while Michael has been a city alderman for Madison, Wisconsin, since 2005.

## SUGGESTED READING
Cottle, Michelle. "Hillary Control." *New York*. New York Media, 6 Aug. 2007. Web. 3 Jan. 2013.
Farmer, Ann. "Speaking for the Women Who Can't." *Perspectives* 19.3 (2011): 8–14. Print.
McElwaine, Sandra. "Hillary's Secret Weapon." *Daily Beast*. Newsweek/Daily Beast, 11 June 2009. Web. 4 Jan. 2012.
Orleans, Anne. "Mideast Women Leaders Speak Out." *Washington Report on Middle East Affairs* 23.7 (2004): 77. Print.
Verveer, Melanne. "The World's Ambassador for Women." Interview by Moira Forbes. *Forbes*. Forbes.com, 28 Sept. 2012. Web. 4 Jan. 2013.

## SELECTED WORKS
Verveer, Melanne. "Why Women Are a Foreign Policy Issue." *Foreign Policy* 193 (2012): 1–4. Print.
Verveer, Melanne, and Penny Abeywardena. "Lift up Women to Lift the World." *CNN*. Cable News Network, 24 Sept. 2012. Web. 4 Jan. 2013.

—*Mary Woodbury*

# Alexa von Tobel
**Born:** 1984
**Occupation:** Founder and chief executive officer of LearnVest

Young women seeking advice on how to manage their personal finances need to look no further than Alexa von Tobel. The entrepreneurial financial guru von Tobel is the founder of LearnVest, a personal finance website designed specifically for women. Named "the next Suze Orman" by *Bloomberg Businessweek*, von Tobel was inspired to establish her rapidly growing start-up after she came to the stunning realization that her Harvard education had left her woefully unprepared to handle even the simplest of financial tasks. Believing the same was true for most other young women, she set out to create an online resource where women could go to find helpful financial advice without having to invest a small fortune beforehand. In relatively short order, von Tobel made LearnVest one of the Internet's top financial advice websites and one of the only sites to cater specifically to the financial needs of women.

Using her savvy and sharp business acumen, von Tobel managed to grow LearnVest into a multimillion-dollar venture, and has established herself as one of the most trusted voices among young investors and entrepreneurs alike. Her efforts have been lauded by many of the financial sector's leading publications, including *Forbes* and *Bloomberg Businessweek*, and have led her to become a highly sought-after expert for television appearances and speaking engagements. More important, however, thanks to her sound advice and dedication to LearnVest, von Tobel has helped more than one million women take charge of their financial futures.

## EARLY LIFE AND EDUCATION
Born in 1984, Alexa Leigh Marie von Tobel was raised in Jacksonville, Florida, and was

© Ramin Talaie/Corbis

determined to succeed from the time she was just a young girl. Her mother, Darlene Marie von Tobel, worked as a nurse practitioner at the Southside Family Medical Center in Jacksonville, and her father, Harry von Tobel, was a developmental pediatrician. Von Tobel developed strong leadership skills early on in life, thanks in part to her two older brothers, Travis and Brandon, who both became the targets of her organizational prowess and who pushed her to take risks and think outside the box. As von Tobel explained in a 2011 interview with Bianca Bosker for the *Huffington Post* (23 July 2011), "My parents used to joke I was the one who was always trying to organize them because they were always getting in trouble," she said of her siblings. "I always wanted to hang out with them so [I] always made sure I was comfortable doing things like playing sports that I had no interest in playing, and putting myself out of my comfort zone."

After graduating from high school, von Tobel's soaring ambitions quickly set her on the path to real success. She earned an AB degree in psychology and graduated with honors from Harvard College and entered the business world, taking a position as a trader with Morgan Stanley. While she was finishing school and preparing to head to Wall Street, von Tobel had a stunning realization: Though she was about to begin working in the stock market, she barely knew anything about handling her own finances. That unlikely fact only became more evident after she began her job with financial giant Morgan Stanley, as she remarked to Jacob Brody in an interview for *VentureBeat* (27 July 2010). "Here I was responsible for millions and millions of dollars and I didn't know the first thing about getting a credit card or insurance," von Tobel said. "I needed tools like these." She set out to educate herself about personal finance, but nearly all the available financial guides were targeted at

older adults who had already amassed significant amounts of assets. "I was reading every book I could find," she told April Joyner for *Inc.* magazine (19 July 2010). "But none of them spoke to me."

The idea that she and other young women should have a better grasp on their personal finances stayed with von Tobel throughout the two valuable years she spent learning the ins and outs of the financial world at Morgan Stanley, before she left to become the head of business development at a New York City start-up called Drop.io.

Despite her apparent success, von Tobel was strongly motivated by her sudden realization, which prompted her to pursue the idea of starting a business centered on providing financial advice, particularly to women. In hopes of making her newfound dream a reality, she enrolled at Harvard Business School in 2008.

## THE INITIAL SUCCESS OF LEARNVEST

While studying at Harvard Business School, von Tobel entered a business plan competition sponsored by Astia, a nonprofit organization dedicated to providing support to up-and-coming female entrepreneurs. Upon winning the contest, von Tobel realized the time was right to get her idea off the ground. Taking a leave of absence from Harvard, she used $75,000 of her own money to found LearnVest, an upstart through which she intended to provide women with financial advice, so that they might be able to enjoy a greater degree of financial freedom and security. In her interview with Bosker for the *Huffington Post*, von Tobel explained why taking control of one's finances is so crucial and, in turn, why founding LearnVest was so important to her. "Having command over your finances is a huge aspect of taking command over your life, from changing jobs to who you end up with, to having the courage to ask for raises," von Tobel said.

After officially beginning her venture in November 2008, von Tobel enlisted the help of a circle of trusted advisors as she worked toward bringing LearnVest online. She also sought out additional funding from investors, including Goldman Sachs, from whom she received $1.1 million in seed funding in January 2009. In September 2009, LearnVest was officially launched, quickly earning the distinction of being named a TechCrunch50 company. LearnVest was off and running.

Since its debut, the company has been an overwhelming success. With several hundred thousand users and an estimated 360,000 unique visitors every month, LearnVest has become a highly visible and increasingly popular financial advice resource for women everywhere. Growth came quickly to LearnVest, with von Tobel's meager staff expanding to include ninety employees by 2013. Financial growth was equally as quick—as of 2013, the company had raised about $25 million from various investors, most notably Accel Partners.

To von Tobel, however, the most important sign of LearnVest's success has been in what her company has done for the women the company serves. According to the LearnVest website, von Tobel and her team have helped more than one million women take charge of their financial portfolios. Von Tobel expressed this sentiment herself in an open letter she posted on Learn-Vest on July 26, 2011. "When I started Learn-Vest almost two years ago, I dreamed of creating a smart and accessible one-stop resource for women who want to take control of their finances," von Tobel wrote. "We've grown faster than I could have imagined—LearnVest is now the leading financial website for women, and I'm proud of all the ways we've helped women gain confidence with their money."

### EXPANDING LEARNVEST
Von Tobel has striven to make LearnVest as powerful a tool for women as possible. In addition to the budget tracker, retirement progress reports, and other basic tools that can be found on many other financial advice websites, LearnVest also provides users with the opportunity to directly communicate with financial advisors through video chats, e-mail, or by phone. This type of person-to-person interaction allows LearnVest to provide each of its individual users with customized advice tailored to their specific needs. Furthermore, this support is also designed to meet clients' unique financial needs as women in modern society—an important and often-ignored area of need, as von Tobel pointed out in an interview with Samantha Lear for *More* magazine (16 Sept. 2011). "Women are getting married much later, running their own finances into their thirties and forties and divorce is at an all-time high," von Tobel said. "Financial planning shouldn't be a luxury. Everyone should have a financial plan."

LearnVest's offerings do not stop there, however. Von Tobel and the LearnVest staff also provide interactive "boot camps" for users on a number of key finance-related topics, including cost cutting, wealth building, and debt relief. As part of these boot camps, users receive daily e-mails that offer helpful information related to the specific topic they are focusing on and simple tasks designed to easily guide them toward their monetary goals. In her interview for *VentureBeat*, von Tobel explained that the boot camps were designed to make learning about finances easier and more affordable for those who need help making the right financial choices. "It's cheaper than *Personal Finance for Dummies* and easier to understand and accomplish," von Tobel said of the boot camps. "We don't want users to be overwhelmed."

In 2011, LearnVest also began offering online courses on various money-related topics for users who wish to gain an even firmer grasp of their personal finances. Through an interactive multimedia curriculum, LearnVest allows users to learn about financial topics on their own time and at their own pace. As with all of LearnVest's services, these courses reflect von Tobel's personal belief that knowledge is the key to financial stability and, ultimately, a better quality of life.

### VON TOBEL MEETS THE PRESS
Thanks to LearnVest's success and her own effervescent attitude, von Tobel quickly became something of a media darling. Admired for her accomplishments and respected for her vast financial knowledge, von Tobel became a frequent guest and expert commentator on such television programs as *Today*, *Good Day New York*, *ABC News*, and *Fox Business News*, among others.

As von Tobel's public persona grew, she was recognized by a wide variety of print publications and received many significant accolades. She was named an Inc. 30 Under 30 Honoree in 2010, and was similarly recognized by *Marie Claire* in 2010 and *Forbes* in 2011. She was even named a Young Global Leader by the World Economic Forum in 2011.

With her emergence as a leading financial advice maven, many media personalities began to compare her to Suze Orman—one of the most respected voices in the world of finance, especially for women—and often referred to von Tobel as "the next Suze Orman" or "Suze Orman 2.0." Von Tobel appreciated the comparison and even drew inspiration and a sense of direction from it, as she stated in her interview with Joyner for *Inc.*, "Suze Orman helps 45-year-old women get out of debt," von Tobel said. "Why not reach 20-year-olds to keep them from getting into debt?"

Despite her sudden fame, von Tobel has been sure to make two things very clear: her enthusiasm for her work is absolutely real and that her work remains her most important focus. She emphasized these points while talking with Nick Summers in an interview for *Bloomberg Businessweek* (14 Feb. 2013). "This is a genuine, genuine passion, and so this isn't an upbeat persona that I have to really put on," von Tobel explained. "The world could fall apart around me, our money could go away, and I would still be sitting here doing the exact same thing."

Now that LearnVest is a proven success, von Tobel is keen to see her company become the go-to source for women who are ready to control their own finances, as she told Brienne Walsh for GoGirlFinance.com (13 Apr. 2012). "I'd like the website to become like Weight Watchers for personal finance," von Tobel said. "I want financial help to be readily available to those who are looking for it, and I want our advice to be easy to follow. That's our goal as a company, and I think we can achieve it."

## PERSONAL LIFE

Von Tobel married Michael Clifford Ryan Jr. on March 23, 2013, at the Ritz-Carlton Hotel in Amelia Island, Florida. Von Tobel met Ryan, who currently serves as vice president at the investment firm Riverstone Holdings in New York, while they were both still students at Harvard, in 2003. Her brother Brandon officiated at the ceremony. Von Tobel's first book, *Financially Fearless: The LearnVest Guide to Worry-Free Finances*, will be published in December 2013 by Random House.

## SUGGESTED READING

Brody, Jacob. "LearnVest's Founder: Is Alexa von Tobel Suze Orman 2.0?" *VentureBeat*. VentureBeat, 27 July 2010. Web. 19 Apr. 2013.

Joyner, April. "Alexa von Tobel, Founder of LearnVest." *Inc*. Mansueto Ventures LLC, 19 July 2010. Web. 19 Apr. 2013.

Summers, Nick. "In Financial Advice, Alexa von Tobel May Be the Next Suze Orman." *Bloomberg Businessweek*. Bloomberg LLP, 14 Feb. 2013. Web. 19 Apr. 2013.

Von Tobel, Alexa. "Letter from Alexa von Tobel, LearnVest CEO." *LearnVest.com*. LearnVest, 26 July 2011. Web. 19 Apr. 2013.

Walsh, Brienne. "LearnVest's Alexa von Tobel Talks to GGF about Women and Finance." *GoGirlFinance.com*. Go Girl LLC, 13 Apr. 2012. Web. 19 Apr. 2013.

—*Jack Lasky*

# Kah Walla

**Born:** February 28, 1965
**Occupation:** Cameroon's first major female presidential candidate

Like many women in countries where gender equality is not the norm, the young Kah Walla probably did not anticipate becoming one of her nation's most influential political voices. However, she did exactly that. Since establishing herself as an accomplished entrepreneur, Walla has risen to become one of her native Cameroon's most outspoken political activists and a well-known proponent of reforms aimed at increasing government accountability and reducing corruption. Though she has faced considerable opposition, Walla has never backed down.

Long before she ever dreamed of stepping into the political arena, Walla focused her attention on becoming a success in the business world. Realizing that her educational options

© Jan Haas/dpa/Corbis

in Cameroon were limited, she headed to the United States to attend college. She returned home with an MBA and she began working for a consulting agency. Though she rose through the company's ranks in short order, the agency went out of business. Some might have seen this as a setback, but Walla perceived it as an opportunity to use what she had learned to start her own business. She founded STRATEGIES!, a consulting firm that served a wide variety of both domestic and foreign clients. Although Walla made the firm a success, the difficulties she experienced dealing with government officials while trying to run her business convinced her to take a more serious interest in politics.

After beginning her political career as a community organizer, Walla took her first significant step as a government leader when she was elected to the municipal council of the First District of Douala. In that position, she fought aggressively for improved governmental transparency and electoral reform. As her public profile grew, Walla faced increasing resistance to her policies, particularly from her own government, and repeatedly found herself the target of harassment, beatings, and even kidnappings. Unwilling to cave to the intense pressure from her adversaries, she announced her candidacy for the Cameroonian presidential election in 2011. Though she ultimately lost the presidential race, Walla remains an outspoken critic of government corruption and one of Cameroon's leading advocates of reform.

## EARLY LIFE

Born Edith Kabbang Walla on February 28, 1965, Walla spent time growing up in both her native Cameroon and in the Ivory Coast (Côte d'Ivoire). At an early age, Walla developed a keen interest in business and a desire to have a successful professional career. As she grew older, however, it became clear that gender inequality in Cameroon would make it difficult for her to get the education she would need to establish a career in the business world. Determined to see her dreams come to fruition, Walla left Cameroon for the United States, where she studied business and earned an MBA at Howard University in Washington, DC. With degree in hand, she returned to Cameroon in 1989, eager to put what she had learned to good use.

Walla's return to Cameroon coincided with a radical shift in gender equality in the country. Women gained new rights and freedoms that made it much easier for them to run their own businesses. Suddenly, Walla and countless other women like her felt empowered and optimistic about their future. Walla commented in an interview that appeared in the 2008 World Bank report *Doing Business: Women in Africa*, "You got a sense that women felt liberated in a very literal way." Walla's initial entry into the business world came when she landed a position with a local consulting firm. At first, her work with the company went quite well, and she quickly climbed the ranks to the office of managing director. When she finally assumed control, however, Walla learned that business was not doing as well as she thought and, as a result of prior mismanagement, the firm closed.

**STRATEGIES!**
When the firm where she had been working went out of business, Walla decided to start her own company. To that end, she founded STRATEGIES!, a business management consulting firm much like her former employer. STRATEGIES! started small—so small, in fact, that Walla initially had to operate out of her father's dining room. With an equally small staff of dedicated supporters, Walla took her first steps into the local marketplace and began to establish her brand. Her strategy was to bring the high-quality consulting services available on the international market to Cameroon; she wanted to focus on the specific needs of businesses in that market, such as team building and recruiting. Before long, STRATEGIES! had become a success in Cameroon.

Having established a firm foothold in the local market, Walla's next move was to begin looking for business opportunities elsewhere. "One of our biggest successes came when one of our consultants, Sophie, asked why we were just working in Cameroun," Walla told Soetan. "She proposed going to Chad to seek out clients, a trip that would cost $3000, money we couldn't afford to waste. We eventually agreed and it turned out to be the best decision we ever made." By 2013,

more than 80 percent of the firm's business was being generated from foreign markets.

Achieving and maintaining success proved to be a continual uphill battle for Walla, principally because of the restrictive business environment in Cameroon. Of particular concern was the country's tax system, which was poorly regulated and rife with corruption. Complex and frequently changing regulations, as well as a lack of clear communication, made dealing with taxes nearly a full-time job for Walla. "There is no transparency," she said in her *Doing Business: Women in Africa* interview. "Well-qualified tax consultants have a very hard time telling you whether what is being asked of you by the taxation officer is right or wrong. There is an enormous amount of interpretation in the system and it really is extremely arbitrary." To make matters worse, some tax officials expected Walla to offer them bribes because she was a woman. She refused to do so and took legal action against a number of officials. While these and other troubles with corruption in Cameroon made operating STRATEGIES! more difficult for Walla, they also inspired her to start thinking about taking a more active role in local politics.

**GETTING INTO POLITICS**
Frustrated with Cameroon's dysfunctional taxation system and male-dominated political culture, Walla increasingly felt the need to start doing something to help bring about change. Her earliest foray into politics came as an activist and community organizer. Walla became an ardent leader and supporter of several grassroots campaigns aimed at stemming corruption, making it easier to operate businesses, and improving quality of life in Cameroon. One of her most significant grassroots accomplishments was founding Cameroon Ô'Bosso, a citizenship movement that implemented a number of key electoral reforms, such as instituting a voter registration program. Another of Walla's noteworthy campaigns saw her work with the nongovernmental organization Vital Voices to provide training in business registration, tax procedures, and space management to more than five hundred female traders at Sandaga, which is one of the largest produce markets in Douala—Cameroon's largest city and its leading economic center.

Despite how much she seemed to be accomplishing, however, Walla came to believe she could do more to effect change by becoming directly involved in politics as an elected official. In her interview with Soetan, Walla said that while she had never previously considered taking this step, she knew it was the right choice: "I used to say to myself back when I started my business, 'anything but politics!'" Walla added: "But it became clear to me as time went on and as I ran my business that at the end of the day, I always came up against the government. The government was always somehow a stumbling block or obstacle to running my business effectively whether in form of its policies, operations or officials. It became clear that I couldn't make change from the outside."

Walla began her journey into politics in 2007 as a candidate for the Social Democratic Front (SDF). She had been an active supporter of the SDF for many years. Walla successfully campaigned for a seat on the municipal council of the First District of Douala. After winning the election, she quickly became one of the council's most outspoken and progressive members. Walla pursued an agenda that emphasized increased governmental transparency and improved budgetary management while continuing to be a strong proponent of electoral reform. She also became a vocal critic of a constitutional amendment proposed in 2009 that was designed to do away with presidential term limits. In time, Walla became one of Cameroon's most recognized political figures and began to consider taking her political career to the next level.

## PRESIDENTIAL CAMPAIGN

After establishing herself as a politician, Walla began considering the possibility of running for her nation's highest office in 2011. As she told the *Huffington Post*'s Stephenie Foster (13 Feb. 2012), she believed she had what it took to do the job. "After working for 20 years in the private sector and as a civil society activist, I realized that my country's main problem is one of political leadership and governance," Walla said. "I [had] the right combination of grassroots experience, knowledge and expertise in a broad range of development issues and the courage and capacity to lead. It was time to demonstrate that Cameroon has innovative, efficient leaders capable of putting the country's best interest at the forefront of their agenda."

After leaving the SDF in October 2010 and aligning herself with the Cameroon People's Party (CPP), Walla announced her candidacy for the office of president. Her biggest opponent was incumbent President Paul Biya, who has served as president of Cameroon since 1982. Though she was well aware that her bid for the presidency was a long shot, Walla and her supporters remained hopeful. Moreover, Walla was steadfast about running a campaign that did not rely on bribery or electoral fraud to succeed. Instead, she focused on generating support among women and young Cameroonians through her platform of change.

When the election returns came in, Biya was ushered into another term as president. Suspecting that there may have been some foul play involved, Walla and several other candidates contested the results but they were eventually forced to concede. Though she garnered relatively few votes in comparison with Biya, Walla

was proud of her performance and of her supporters' enthusiasm.

Although she failed to win her the presidency, Walla told Foster that her campaign succeeded in planting the seeds of change in Cameroon. "Our 'Time Is Now' campaign definitely ignited a new spark all across Cameroon and within the Diaspora," Walla said.

## CONTINUED ACTIVISM

Even after losing the presidential election, Walla continues her work as a leading political activist in Cameroon. Indeed, the exposure the election afforded her allowed Walla to position herself as a major figure in the fight for political and economic reform. Unfortunately, it also made her a highly visible target for those who oppose such reform. Walla has repeatedly been the victim of harassment and violence intended to discourage her from continuing her activism. She has been blasted with chemical-laced water cannons, beaten by police officers, and was even kidnapped by government agents. Despite this, Walla has refused to give in to her tormentors' demand for silence. She views everything that has happened to her as a sign that she is making an impression on the current government. As Alyse Nelson, president and CEO of Vital Voices, pointed out in an interview with Anna Louie Sussman of the Women in the World Foundation (21 Sept. 2011): "[Walla] joked to me that that meant she had a chance at winning." Adding, "to her, getting kidnapped was a sign that the party in power is taking her candidacy seriously."

Regardless of whatever adversity she might have to overcome, Walla has made it clear that she is still determined to bring real, substantive change to Cameroon. Though she is unceasingly optimistic, Walla is acutely aware that achieving real progress will be a daunting challenge, as she made clear to Foster. She said, "Change is such a simple word . . . and so difficult to actually effect."

## SUGGESTED READING

Doyle, Anne. "Kah Walla's Voice from Cameroon Calls Women Everywhere to Embrace Power." *Forbes*. Forbes.com, 27 Feb. 2012. Web. 5 June 2013.

Foster, Stephenie. "Cameroon's Kah Walla on Her Candidacy, the Arab Spring, and More." *Huffington Post*. HPMG News, 13 Feb. 2012. Web. 5 June 2013.

Nkem-Eneanya, Jennifer. "Kah Walla: Entrepreneur Going on President." *Konnect Africa*. Konnect Africa, 22 May 2013. Web. 5 June 2013.

Soetan, Folake. "Unleashing Africa's Potential with Cameroon's Kah Walla." *Ventures*. Ventures Publ. Intl., 2 Mar. 2013. Web. 5 June 2013.

—*Jack Lasky*

# Bubba Watson

**Born:** November 5, 1978
**Occupation:** Professional golfer

Born Gerry Lester Watson Jr., Bubba Watson is known throughout professional golf for his epic drives, unbelievable shots, laid-back (and some say childlike) personality, and his commitment to raising awareness and funds for charities nationwide.

Watson was named after his father, who nicknamed his son Bubba after professional football player Bubba Smith. Although Watson was an accomplished athlete and loved to play baseball and basketball, he devoted himself to golf, a sport in which he excelled despite a lack of formal training and instruction.

Watson decided to become a professional golfer during his last year in college, and after several rocky years spent struggling to earn a professional tour card and then several more years without a tournament win, Watson's game began to blossom and flourish. At the 2012 Masters he made what many called an impossible golf shot to win one of the game's most prestigious major tournaments, which was even more remarkable given his lack of training. As Bob Harig for the ESPN website reports, Watson has never wanted a coach: "I want to do it on my own. . . . I've never [sought] out advice of a coach or anything on my swing. I just swing funny and somehow it works." (10 Mar. 2012).

## EARLY LIFE AND EDUCATION

Bubba Watson was born on November 5, 1978, in the small working-class town of Bagdad just north of Pensacola in Florida's Panhandle. His father, Gerry Lester Watson Sr., was a Vietnam War veteran and a lieutenant in the Green Berets' Special Forces who later worked as a plant supervisor. Watson's mother, Molly, held down several jobs during Watson's high school years in order to help support her son's love of and talent for golf.

Watson's father introduced Bubba to the game when he was six years old, and the few lessons the largely self-taught Watson has had came from his father. As Chris White for *OnlineAthens* explained, "His father taught him . . . to swing hard [and] the rest . . . would work itself out later" (11 Apr. 2012).

Watson played his early game with a cut-down 9-iron, and, as he is quoted as saying on the PGA Tour website, he practiced golf shots by hitting Wiffle balls around the house and the yard playing "non-stop every day from six to twelve years old . . . instead of playing with trucks out in the yard, I'd play with a ball and a club." By the time he was twelve years old, Watson could hit a drive fifty yards further than other kids his age. He was also developing his flair for

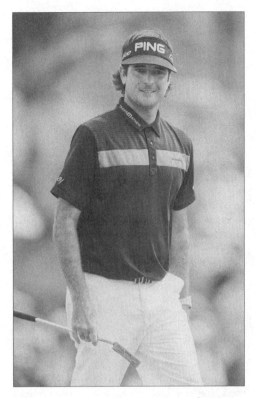

Getty Images

brightly colored clothing and often wore fluorescent pink shirts, brightly colored golf knickers, and pink socks when he played. Chris Haack, then American Junior Golf Association (AJGA) director, told White that he first met Watson when he was in the AJGA's thirteen-to-fourteen-year-old grouping, and "even then . . . he really stood out . . . [and] you could tell he was a nice kid with a lot of talent and a lot of personality to go with it." It was during this time that Watson also discovered his love for trick shots, and he practiced hitting shots that would first bounce off roofs or curve around buildings before landing in a desired spot. And as Erik Matuszewski and Dex McLuskey for Bloomberg explained, what many viewed as "goofing off" would later be labeled "Bubba golf" and would help prepare Watson for a life-changing playoff victory many years later.

Although Watson had the physique and talent in high school to pursue a career as a professional baseball pitcher, his first love was golf. He played as a freshman for Pace High School's golf team and then moved to Milton High School, playing on that school's team for the next three years.

After graduation in 1997, Watson attended Faulkner State Community College in Alabama and was named first-team junior college All-American. He then transferred to the University of Georgia on a golf scholarship and helped the team win its 2000 Southeastern Conference title. Watson left school a year early to turn professional in 2001.

## QUALIFYING FOR A TOUR CARD

Watson struggled during his first two years as a professional golfer to make enough money to qualify for his tour card. In 2003 he joined the Nationwide Insurance Tour (now called the Web.com Tour), which was developed in 1990 by the Professional Golf Association (PGA) for golfers who were either unable to score well in the tour's qualifying school (the "Q-School") or who were unable to win enough money the previous season to retain their PGA tour card. Golfers who finished in the top twenty-five of the money list on the Nationwide Tour received PGA tour cards for the following season. After not qualifying in 2003 and 2004, Watson finished in twenty-first place in 2005, earning $202,437 and his card.

In 2006, and on the PGA tour, Watson's game began to thrive. Although he missed the cut in over half of the tournaments that year, he was the tour leader in driving distance. He also finished as one of the top ten players in three tournaments, and he finished in third place in the Chrysler Classic in February. His winnings for the season were just over $1 million, which allowed him to retain his card and assured him a place on the 2007 PGA Tour.

The following year brought Watson fewer missed cuts, more top-ten finishes, and more earnings (over $1.5 million) than in 2006. He tied for second place in the Shell Houston Open in March, and in June, Watson tied for fifth in the prestigious US Open Championship. He was also the lead player in driving distance for the second consecutive year.

## WINNING HIS FIRST TOURNAMENT

The next two years on the tour brought similar earnings and tournament placements, but Watson had yet to win a tournament. In June of 2010, however, he won the Travelers Championship at TPC River Highlands in Cromwell, Connecticut, after the second hole of a sudden-death playoff against veteran golfers Corey Pavin and Scott Verplank. Watson dedicated his victory to his father, who was ill with throat cancer at the time.

In August during the PCA Championship tournament, Watson again faced a playoff, this time against Germany's Martin Kaymer, who beat Watson by one stroke after the third hole. In October Watson played in the prominent Ryder Cup as a member of the US team. Shortly after the tournament, however, his father passed away. "My dad got to see me win and play for [the] USA in the Ryder Cup," Watson tweeted on October 14, 2010. Added the devout

Christian, "God gave my family my best year and worst year!"

Watson won two more tournaments in 2011—the Farmer's Insurance Open in January and the Zurich Classic of New Orleans in April, which he won after another playoff, this time against Webb Simpson. Watson was also chosen as a member of the US team for the elite President's Cup, a biannual PGA Tour event similar to the Ryder Cup. He had his highest earnings of his professional career thus far with a total of just under $3.5 million.

The 2012 PGA tour began well for Watson. He made the cut for the first seven tournaments he participated in, finishing in the top ten in three of them. It would be Watson's eighth tournament of the season, the prestigious Masters Tournament, which would change his life and would bring him international attention.

## THE 2012 MASTERS TOURNAMENT

Established in 1934 and played the first full week in April at Augusta National Golf Club in Georgia, the Masters is one of four major PGA championships. In addition to the prize money and prestige involved in winning, the top player receives automatic invitations to the other three major tournaments (the US Open, the British Open, and the PGA Championship) for the next five years, a five-year membership on the PGA Tour, an invitation to the Players Championship for five years, a lifetime invitation to the Masters tournament, and an honorary membership to Augusta National.

The 2012 Masters Tournament began with odds on former three-time Masters winner Phil Mickelson and four-time winner Tiger Woods. By the end of regular play on the final day of the tournament, however, it was Bubba Watson, not the traditional favorites, who had the chance to win the tournament.

After the final hole of regulation play on Sunday, Watson was tied for the lead with South Africa's Louis Oosthuizen, which automatically initiated a sudden-death play-off round. The sudden-death component of the tournament, first used in 1979, occurs when players are tied for the lead at the end of the tournament. They then continue to play, and the first player to post the lowest score on a completed hole wins the tournament.

Watson and Oosthuizen both missed birdie shots (one stroke under par) to par the first play-off hole. From the next tee, they each hit their drives to the right and into the trees. Oosthuizen's ball bounced back into the rough, leaving him a 230-yard shot to the flag. He was just short of the green with his next shot and recorded a bogey (one stroke over par) for the hole.

Watson's first shot into the trees landed deep in the woods, or as the *Washington Post* sports editors put it, "Jail" (9 Apr. 2012) but Watson had "Bubba golf" on his side and the personal mantra that if he could swing the club, he had a shot. What followed is what Karen Crouse for the *New York Times* has called both "majestic" (8 Apr. 2012) and "preposterous" (10 June 2012) and what Oosthuizen described later as "an unbelievable shot" (*Bloomberg* 9 Apr. 2012). Watson hit the ball so it not only cleared the trees, but then began to rise before it "hooked" (curved) dramatically and landed on the green within ten feet of the hole. He then two-putted to par the hole for an emotional tournament win after which he stood sobbing and embracing his mother. The *Washington Post* quotes Watson as saying afterward, "I've never had a dream go this far" (9 Apr. 2012).

## CHARITY WORK

In addition to his love for golf, Bubba Watson loves to help others, and he does so by raising thousands of dollars through fundraisers and corporate endorsements and sponsorships. As Tracey McManus reported for the *Augusta Chronicle* Masters Tournament website, Watson intends to "raise money for three types of charities: cancer research, military causes, and anything to do with children. . . . His goal is to raise $1 million" in 2012 (8 Apr. 2012), and he named the cause Bubba & Friends Drive to a Million.

One way Watson devised to meet his million-dollar goal was by developing the Grand Slam Drive for Charity with US clothing manufacturer Travis Mathew Apparel. During 2012, Travis Mathew produced a limited number of polo shirts that matched the shirts Watson wore during each of the major tournaments that year. All of the proceeds were donated to various charities, and for every limited edition shirt that sold out, Travis Mathew donated to charity an additional $50,000 per major tournament.

Also in 2012, Ping, an American golf equipment manufacturer, worked with Watson to create an all-pink driver. Watson has used a pink-shafted driver for years, and he approached Ping in 2011 to create an all-pink driver in an effort to raise funds for his Drive to a Million cause. Ping initially donated $10,000 and also agreed to donate an additional $300 for every shot over 300 yards that Watson made with the club. In April of 2012, Ping announced it would sell five thousand limited-edition all-pink drivers, with five percent of the proceeds going to Watson's Drive to a Million fund.

In addition to his endeavors to reach one million charitable dollars that year, Watson also supported military charities such as Birdies for the Brave. He donated $50,000 to aid in the relief for victims of the 2011 earthquake in Japan, and he raised over $25,000 for a summer camp for seriously ill children. As Watson says on his website, "I've always felt the need to give back . . . [and] helping these charities . . . can be more rewarding than winning a golf tournament."

## PERSONAL LIFE

Watson met his future wife, Angie Ball, when they both attended the University of Georgia (UGA). Angie Watson is a six-feet-four former UGA basketball player who also played professionally for the WNBA and in Europe. They were married in 2004, and since an injury forced her to quit basketball, Angie has served as Watson's agent. They adopted their son Caleb in March of 2012.

During the summer of 2008 and without telling any friends or family, Watson completed his undergraduate degree from UGA. As he explains on his website, he "wanted to be able to encourage kids to get an education and pursue their dreams and . . . felt it was important to set an example."

## SUGGESTED READING

Harig, Bob. "Bubba Watson Driving Toward 4th Win." *ESPN Golf.* ESPN Internet Ventures, 10 Mar. 2012. Web. 26 Nov. 2012.

Matuszewski, Erik, and Dex McLuskey. "Bubba Watson Wins Masters in Playoff for First Major Golf Title." *Bloomberg.* Bloomberg LP, 9 Apr. 2012. Web. 21 Nov. 2012.

McManus, Tracey. "Bubba Watson's Clothing to Be Sold for Charity." *Masters. Augusta.* Augusta Chronicle, 8 Apr. 2012. Web. 21 Nov. 2012.

White, Chris. "Watson First Had to Master Himself." *OnlineAthens.* Athens Banner-Herald, 11 Apr. 2012. Web. 21 Nov. 2012.

*Robin Hogan*

# Alisa Weilerstein

**Born:** April 14, 1982
**Occupation:** American cellist

American cellist Alisa Weilerstein has been making a name for herself in the classical-music world since her professional debut with the Cleveland Orchestra at age thirteen. Born into an accomplished musical family, Weilerstein picked up her first "cello"—really a toy made from an empty cereal box—when she was two years old and started playing the real thing less than two years later. Though her parents were careful never to push her and to let her learn at her own pace, Weilerstein says she always knew what she wanted to do with her life. "I don't remember a single moment of my life where I ever questioned that I was going to be a cellist," she told Scott Simon in an interview for National Public Radio (27 May 2011).

Boston Globe via Getty Images

Weilerstein has performed as a soloist, a recitalist, and a chamber musician. She also performs with her parents as the Weilerstein Trio; the three first played in concert together when Weilerstein was six years old. Weilerstein, who studied at the Juilliard School and graduated from Columbia University in 2004, won the 2006 Leonard Bernstein Award and a 2008 Martin E. Segal Award in recognition of her exceptional talent and promising future. In 2009, she was invited by First Lady Michelle Obama to perform and lead musical seminars at the White House.

In April 2010, Weilerstein performed Edward Elgar's Cello Concerto in E Minor with the Berliner Philharmoniker under the direction of conductor Daniel Barenboim. The performance was a historic one, as it was Barenboim's wife (and Weilerstein's idol), Jacqueline du Pré, who had performed the definitive version of the concerto, and Barenboim had not conducted another female cellist in the role since du Pré's death in 1987.

In October 2010, Weilerstein became the first cellist in over thirty years to sign with renowned music label Decca Classics. The following year, she was one of twenty-two recipients of a MacArthur Fellowship, a $500,000 prize recognizing exceptionally outstanding work in one's field.

## EARLY LIFE

Alisa Weilerstein was born on April 14, 1982, in Rochester, New York, the oldest child of violinist Donald Weilerstein and pianist Vivian Hornik Weilerstein. At the time, Donald was the first violinist of the Cleveland Quartet, which he had helped found in 1969, while Vivian frequently performed as both a soloist and a chamber musician. "I listened to my parents practicing in the house from the time I was just a few days old," Weilerstein told Colin Eatock for the *Houston Chronicle* (18 May 2011). "My mom is very disciplined: she was practicing again almost immediately after I was born. And I heard my father's quartet in the house until I was seven years old."

Growing up surrounded by music, Weilerstein fell in love with it at an early age. Speaking about her parents to David Abrams for the Internet Cello Society (Apr. 2005), she said, "I loved listening to them practice so much that apparently I'd have terrible tantrums if my mother practiced less than three hours a day. I also was a very precocious concert-goer; apparently I was six weeks old when I first went into a concert hall." Her love affair with the cello began when she was two years old and sick with chicken pox; both her parents were out of town performing, and her grandmother, to cheer her up, made her a toy string quartet (two violins, a viola, and a cello) out of cereal boxes. "The cello, made out of a Rice Krispies box with an old toothbrush for an end pin, was the instrument I immediately fell in love with," Weilerstein told Abrams. "I ignored the others completely. So I was happy when my parents returned to their normal routines of practicing and rehearsing, because now I could participate."

Weilerstein was four years old when she convinced her parents to replace her cereal-box cello with a real one. "Both my parents were reluctant at first because they were sure I was too young, but they soon relented," she told Abrams. "I began lessons a couple of months after that, and I instinctively knew that this was what I wanted to do." At age six, Weilerstein began performing with her parents as the Weilerstein Trio. When she was seven, her family moved to Cleveland, where she began playing in the Cleveland Institute of Music's preparatory recitals. She had had several cello teachers by that time, but her lessons had not been very structured. "My first teachers instilled good habits, but also gave me a wonderful sense of freedom," she said to Abrams, adding, "I really ran wild in my first years." At age nine, Weilerstein began studying with celebrated cello teacher Richard Aaron. "He was the first teacher who told me and my parents that I needed to be much more disciplined in the way that I practiced," she told Abrams. "He told my parents (and eventually he told me) that I was too talented to just run wild—I had to have a structured practice routine. He basically told my parents to listen to me with the same standard that they would use for a talented conservatory student." She began practicing with her father for two hours a day; soon, her practice time increased to four hours.

## A YOUNG PROFESSIONAL

In 1995, Weilerstein made her professional debut when, at age thirteen, she won a competition to perform with the Cleveland Orchestra. Despite her young age, her performance attracted the attention of management firm ICM Artists. "It built gradually, with not too many concerts at first, so I could still go to high school and have a normal life," she said to Jessica Duchen for the *Jewish Chronicle* (7 Oct. 2010). Also at age thirteen, she entered the Young Artist Program at the Cleveland Institute of Music. "That meant I went to regular public school in the mornings and took conservatory-level classes and practiced in the afternoon," Weilerstein explained to Abrams. She graduated from Cleveland Heights High School in 1999, two years after making her Carnegie Hall debut with the New York Youth Symphony and one year after releasing her debut CD with EMI Records.

After high school, Weilerstein attended Columbia University, where she studied Russian history. "I had dreams of pursuing an academic degree early on—I think as early as middle school," she told Abrams. "I was surrounded by musicians and was taking classes in theory and music history . . . and I realized I wanted something entirely different for my college experience. I had a terrible fear of becoming a very isolated musician who knew nothing of the rest of the world." In 2000, she received an Avery Fisher Career Grant, the majority of which she put toward her tuition. She did not neglect her musical studies, however, taking advantage of Columbia's New York location to work with Joel Krosnick at the Juilliard School. She also continued to perform during this time. "My college life felt like I had about three full-time jobs," she said to Abrams. "When I wasn't playing concerts I was either going to class or writing papers, and vice versa. . . . I literally wrote papers on planes, trains, buses, and automobiles and e-mailed them to my professors, who were (with a couple of exceptions) very understanding of my situation." During her first year at Columbia, Weilerstein lived across the hall from actor and fellow student Julia Stiles. "She said she liked hearing me practice while she was studying, but I don't know whether she was just saying that to be nice," she told Beth Satkin for *Columbia College Today* (May 2002).

## RECOGNITION, COLLABORATION, AND ADVOCACY

Following her graduation in 2004, Weilerstein continued to perform as a soloist, recitalist, and chamber musician, as well as with her parents as the Weilerstein Trio; the three of them released their first recording in 2006. Also in 2006,

Weilerstein was presented with the Leonard Bernstein Award at the Schleswig-Holstein Musik Festival in Germany, the first cellist to receive the honor. The award is given annually to a promising young artist and comes with a prize of ten thousand euros. In 2008, the Lincoln Center named Weilerstein one of two winners of that year's Martin E. Segal Awards, another prize that recognizes outstanding achievements by young artists.

In summer 2007, Weilerstein made her debut at Lincoln Center's annual Mostly Mozart Festival playing Osvaldo Golijov's cello concerto *Azul*, originally performed by world-famous cellist Yo-Yo Ma the year before. Prior to the Mostly Mozart performance, Golijov collaborated with Weilerstein to completely rework the piece. "I was unhappy with some of the music in the concerto," he told Steve Smith for the *New York Times* (31 July 2007). He explained, "Originally the piece was very, very still all the time"—a stillness that did not mesh with Weilerstein's energetic performance style. Describing the experience to Louise Lee for *Strings* magazine (Feb. 2010), Weilerstein said, "I got the final score just two days before the performance. . . . It was an exhilarating, and kind of scary, process, but it was very natural. It had evolved in a very unselfconscious way." Since then, she has worked directly with several composers, including Lera Auerbach and childhood friend Gabriel Kahane. Weilerstein enjoys the collaborative process, telling Lee, "Each composer has become a friend."

Weilerstein became a celebrity advocate for the Juvenile Diabetes Research Foundation in November 2008. She was diagnosed with juvenile (type 1) diabetes at age nine, and though she did not hide her diagnosis from friends, for a long time she kept it a secret from her professional colleagues—including her manager. "I never even told my manager until three years ago, because the perception of diabetes is that you're on dialysis or going blind or facing amputation," she said to Donna Perlmutter for the *Los Angeles Times* (20 Mar. 2011). "I wanted to prove I could have my music, my career, and encourage other young people who were as scared as I was in the beginning."

In November 2009, Weilerstein was one of four musicians invited by First Lady Michelle Obama to perform at the White House and provide instruction for young musicians. "It was Michelle Obama's initiative, first to have music in the White House, but also to have some seminars," she told Duchen. She continued, "We talked a lot about the state of music education in the US, where there's not much government support for the arts; the National Endowment for the Arts is miniscule. This was a great day for classical music—it attracted the most press attention I've ever seen for classical music in the US."

## FOLLOWING IN HER IDOL'S FOOTSTEPS

Weilerstein achieved a major turning point in her career when she performed Edward Elgar's Cello Concerto in E Minor under the conductorship of Daniel Barenboim—the husband of famed late cellist Jacqueline du Pré, whose performance of the concerto had made it a world-famous best seller and whom Weilerstein had idolized from a young age. "I was kind of obsessed with her. I had a poster of her on my wall. I could quote her interviews. I saw every single bit of film footage on her by the time I was ten," Weilerstein told David Patrick Stearns for the *Philadelphia Inquirer* (13 Dec. 2012). "But when I started to learn the concerto on my own, I had to put the recordings away. They were so seductive."

Since du Pré's death in 1987 from multiple sclerosis, Barenboim had conducted the Elgar concerto only once, for Yo-Yo Ma. When Weilerstein first met Barenboim in December 2008, she was initially determined not to play the concerto for him; the following May, conductor Asher Fisch, who had introduced the two, convinced her otherwise. "He said, 'Well, I hear that you're playing for Maestro [Barenboim] a lot, you really ought to play the Elgar concerto for him. And I said, 'No way. I can't play the Elgar for him possibly.' And he said, 'No, no one knows the piece the way he does. You'll learn so much from him," Weilerstein recalled to Julie Subrin for the *Tablet Magazine* podcast *Vox Tablet* (20 Nov. 2012). She added, "Probably the hardest thing that I ever did was to play the Elgar for him for the first time."

Nevertheless, her playing impressed Barenboim, and he immediately asked her to play the concerto with him and the Berliner Philharmoniker the following year. "I was just in complete shock," Weilerstein told Rick Schultz for the *Jewish Journal* (21 Nov. 2012). "Of course, I gave a very enthusiastic yes, but afterward I walked out of Carnegie Hall with my cello and wound up somewhere in Central Park. I was so completely stunned." She made her debut with Barenboim and the Philharmoniker on April 27, 2010.

## LIFE AFTER ELGAR

In October 2010, Weilerstein signed a contract with the prestigious record label Decca Classics, becoming the first cellist to be signed by the label in over three decades. Her first recording with Decca, released in fall 2012, features the Elgar concerto as conducted by Barenboim as well as a concerto by Elliott Carter, written in 2000. Shortly after the album's release, on November 5, Carter died at age 103. Weilerstein had met with him in summer 2012 to discuss her performance for the album, due to be recorded in September; the meeting, which Weilerstein recorded on video, proved to be the last videotaped interview of the composer and is available online.

In 2011, Weilerstein received her most significant award to date: a MacArthur Fellowship, a no-strings-attached award of $500,000 paid out over five years. Yet she almost did not hear the news, dismissing the MacArthur Foundation's first attempt to contact her, an e-mail from an unfamiliar address promising good news and asking her to call, as spam. "I thought it was one of those, you know, 'I'm your long-lost Nigerian grandparent who wants to give you a million dollars,' that sort of thing," she told Timothy Mangan for the *Orange County Register* (30 Nov. 2012).

Weilerstein is particularly noted for her physical, passionate performances onstage; Zachary Woolfe, a critic for the *New York Times*, described her as performing "with soulful expression and physical abandon" (2 Oct. 2011). "When I was first starting out, many people used to say, 'Oh, you move around so much on stage, you make so many faces, you're so expressive.' And I really had no idea," Weilerstein told Simon. She explained, "I try to use the analogy, you know, if you go to, like, a rock concert . . . you see the rock musicians on stage are going crazy. I mean, they're bouncing all over the walls and dancing. It always struck me as sort of surprising that people would find that strange in classical music."

Weilerstein is dating Venezuelan conductor Rafael Payare. She and her parents, the Weilerstein Trio, have been a trio in residence at the New England Conservatory of Music in Boston, Massachusetts, since 2002. Her brother, Joshua Weilerstein, born in 1987, studied violin at the New England Conservatory before becoming an assistant conductor with the New York Philharmonic in 2011.

## SUGGESTED READING

Abrams, David. "Conversation with Alisa Weilerstein." *Internet Cello Society*. Internet Cello Society, Apr. 2005. Web. 17 Dec. 2012.

Duchen, Jessica. "The New Jacqueline du Pré? Barenboim Might Just Agree." *Jewish Chronicle Online*. Jewish Chronicle, 7 Oct. 2010. Web. 17 Dec. 2012.

Eatock, Colin. "Cellist Alisa Weilerstein on Center Stage with Symphony." *Houston Chronicle*. Hearst Communications, 18 May 2011. Web. 17 Dec. 2012.

Perlmutter, Donna. "Cello Virtuoso Alisa Weilerstein Is Always at the Head of Her Class." *Los Angeles Times*. Los Angeles Times, 20 Mar. 2011. Web. 17 Dec. 2012.

Schultz, Rick. "Cellist Weilerstein Brings Worldly Depth to SoCal Stages." *Jewish Journal*. Tribe Media, 21 Nov. 2012. Web. 17 Dec. 2012.

—*Randa Tantawi*

# Bradley Wiggins

**Born:** April 28, 1980
**Occupation:** Professional cyclist

Bradley Wiggins is widely considered to be one of Great Britain's greatest all-around cyclists. He enjoyed a highly distinguished career on the track, capturing gold medals in the individual pursuit event at the 2004 and 2008 Olympic Games, before making a transition to road cycling, where he has established himself as a legitimate stage racer. He gained worldwide recognition in 2012 when he became the first British cyclist to win the Tour de France, the most prestigious stage race in the world. That year Wiggins had also become the most decorated British Olympian of all time after he picked up a record seventh Olympic medal at the 2012 Olympic Games in London.

Professional cycling has been marred by numerous scandals related to the use of performance-enhancing drugs but Wiggins, an outspoken anti-doping advocate, is seen as an example of what is right in his sport. Many refer to him as the "people's champion." Addressing the subject of doping in an article for the London *Guardian* (13 July 2012), he wrote, "What I love is doing my best and working hard. If I felt I had to take drugs, I would rather stop tomorrow, go and ride club ten-mile time trials, ride to the café on Sundays, and work in [British supermarket chain] Tesco stacking shelves."

## EARLY LIFE

Bradley Marc Wiggins was born on April 28, 1980, in Ghent, Belgium, to an Australian father and a British mother. His father, Garry, was a distinguished professional track cyclist who competed on the six-day circuit, which holds six-day races on an inclined indoor oval track called a velodrome. Garry Wiggins, infamous in cycling circles for his violent temper, proclivity for fighting other riders, and voracious appetite for alcohol and amphetamines, abandoned Wiggins and his mother, Linda, when Wiggins was two years old. "As far as Garry was concerned we didn't exist," Wiggins wrote in his 2008 memoir *In Pursuit of Glory* (20). The cyclist died under suspicious circumstances in Australia in 2008.

Wiggins was raised by his mother, a school secretary, and his maternal grandparents in the Kilburn and Maida Vale neighborhoods of northwest London. Growing up, he developed a close relationship with his grandfather George, who took him to greyhound races several times per week and stepped in as a father figure. "He became my male role model in a family that was predominantly women," Wiggins told Simon Hattenstone for the *Guardian* (2 Nov. 2012), referring to his mother's two sisters. When Wiggins

Phil Noble/Reuters /Landov

was seven, his mother had a second son, Ryan, with her then partner, Brendan. In addition to his half-brother, Wiggins has two half-sisters on his father's side, Shannon and Madison.

## EDUCATION AND CYCLING BEGINNINGS

Wiggins's first passion growing up was soccer, and like most of his peers, he started playing the sport early on. After attending St. Augustine's Primary School, in Kilburn, Wiggins enrolled at its affiliated school, St. Augustine's Church of England High School. There, he played goalie on the soccer team and competed in cross-country running.

During the summer of 1992, Wiggins, then twelve, attended a six-week soccer camp in the East Ham district of London. While there he watched the British track cyclist Chris Boardman win a gold medal in the individual pursuit event at the 1992 Summer Olympic Games, held in Barcelona, Spain. Captivated by Boardman's performance and the sheer spectacle of the Games, Wiggins immediately shifted his sporting interests to cycling and began pursuing the sport in earnest. "I wanted to do something with my life," he said to Simon O'Hagan for the London *Independent* (23 Feb. 2003).

Wiggins first started honing his cycling skills around the Serpentine, a lake in London's Hyde Park. Then, with the help of his mother, he joined a local cycling club that held racing competitions on an unused part of the Hayes bypass, a dual carriageway in West London. Through the club Wiggins came into contact with Stuart Benstead, an organizer and coach for the Archer Road Club, based at the famed Herne Hill Velodrome in south London. Benstead had helped Wiggins's father launch his track cycling career at Herne Hill in the mid-1970s, and he suggested that the twelve-year-old Wiggins start training and racing there himself. Wiggins soon became a regular at Herne Hill and other local racing venues, including the Crystal Palace National Sports Centre.

By the time Wiggins was fifteen, he was dominating the local track cycling circuit. He was the national schoolboy champion in the points race event at the British Cycling National Track Championships in 1995, and the following year he was the national junior champion in the one-kilometer time trial at those championships. By 1997, Wiggins was training regularly with the national junior track cycling squad in Manchester. Around this time he left school to focus on his cycling career.

In 1997 Wiggins achieved a so-called grand slam at the Championships upon winning junior titles in the one-kilometer time trial, individual pursuit, points race, and scratch race events. Later that year he was the only British cyclist selected to compete at the UCI Juniors Track World Championships in Cape Town, South Africa, where he placed sixteenth in the individual pursuit and fourth in the points race.

Wiggins solidified his status as one of track cycling's brightest young talents in 1998 when he won the individual pursuit title at the UCI Juniors in Havana, Cuba. That same year, after defending his titles at the British Championships, he was promoted to the national senior squad for the Commonwealth Games in Kuala Lumpur, Malaysia. At those Games, Wiggins finished fourth in the four-kilometer individual pursuit and won a silver medal in the team pursuit. Shortly thereafter, he received a National Lottery grant from British Cycling's World Class Performance Programme (WCPP) that paid him £20,000 per year until he began his professional career in 2000.

## FIRST OLYMPIC MEDAL
Wiggins spent all of 1999 training with Great Britain's pursuit squad in preparation for the 2000 Olympic Games in Sydney, Australia. As part of his conditioning, he participated in that year's Tour of Britain (then known as the PruTour), a weeklong, multistage road race spanning Great Britain. Wiggins then competed at the 1999 UCI Track World Championships, held in Berlin, Germany, placing fifth in the team pursuit and partnering with Rob Hayles to finish tenth in the madison, a team event normally consisting of two riders. Those performances helped him qualify for the Olympic Games in both events.

In Sydney, Wiggins won his first Olympic medal by capturing a bronze in the four-kilometer team pursuit, with teammates Bryan Steel, Paul Manning, and Chris Newton. The quartet finished the race in four minutes and 1.979 seconds, thus establishing a new British record.

"The excitement of that bronze medal still remains one of the highlights of my career," Wiggins states in his memoir (44). Meanwhile, he narrowly missed out on another Olympic medal, placing fourth in the madison with Hayles.

Following the 2000 Olympic Games Wiggins had planned on turning his full attention to road racing, with the goal of competing in and ultimately winning the Tour de France, the crown jewel of cycling and widely considered to be the most difficult of the three Grand Tours; the other two are the Giro d'Italia (Tour of Italy) and the Vuelta a España (Tour of Spain). However, the thrill of winning a medal for his country led Wiggins to reevaluate his sporting ambitions. Yearning for more Olympic medals, particularly gold, he immediately made the 2004 Games in Athens, Greece, the next major focus of his career. He closed out the first year of the new millennium by winning a silver medal in the team pursuit at the 2000 UCI World Championships in Manchester, England.

## PROFESSIONAL ROAD CYCLIST
In the years leading up to the 2004 Olympic Games, Wiggins launched his professional road cycling career. In November 2000 he signed a contract with the British-based Linda McCartney Racing Team. Despite high expectations brought on by its distinguished group of cyclists, the team folded in early 2001 due to insurmountable financial problems. Consequently, Wiggins had his lottery funding reinstated and returned to the British Cycling national team, with whom he began competing in road races all over Europe. Former British professional cyclist John Herety, then the national team manager, remembered Wiggins as "a gifted athlete who managed to find the right people to help him at the right time," as he told Sam Wallace for the *Independent* (21 July 2012). "He was astute."

After the 2001 road race season, which was highlighted by first-place finishes in the Cinturón a Mallorca, in Mallorca, Spain, and the Flèche du Sud, in Luxembourg, Wiggins signed a contract with the French cycling team Française de Jeux (FDJ), based in Nantes, a city in western France. Not long after moving to Nantes, however, Wiggins grew homesick and frustrated. In contrast to the system put in place for the British national team, FDJ's training facilities and accommodations were second-rate, and Wiggins was largely unhappy with his role as a domestique for Australian team leader Brad McGee. A domestique, which translates as "servant," is a rider who holds the responsibility of aiding the team leader during races.

Following a poor road racing season in 2002, Wiggins was not selected by FDJ for that year's Tour de France, leading him to return to the British national team for the Commonwealth Games in Manchester. There, he claimed silver medals in the individual pursuit and team pursuit. Wiggins then competed in the 2002 UCI World Championships in Copenhagen, Denmark, where he placed a disappointing fifth in the individual pursuit and won a bronze medal in the team pursuit.

After making his Grand Tour debut with FDJ at the 2003 Giro d'Italia, where he was eliminated after the eighteenth stage, Wiggins captured his first world title in the individual pursuit at the 2003 UCI World Championships in Stuttgart, Germany. He also won a silver medal in the team pursuit. Later that fall Wiggins won the prologue stage of the Tour de l'Avenir (Tour of the Future), held in France.

Prior to the 2004 season, Wiggins left FDJ to sign with the French-based team Crédit Agricole. During the first half of the 2004 season, he performed poorly due to lackluster training and conditioning. As a result he did not compete at the 2004 UCI World Championships in Melbourne, Australia. Nevertheless, Wiggins returned to form in time to earn a spot on the British cycling squad for the 2004 Olympic Games in Athens, Greece.

Heading into the 2004 Games, Wiggins was considered one of the heavy favorites to win gold in the four-kilometer individual pursuit. In the qualifying round for that event, he achieved a personal best and set an Olympic record with a time of four minutes and 15.165 seconds. He then handily defeated rival Brad McGee in the final by more than four seconds to win his first career Olympic gold medal. After collecting two more medals, a silver in the team pursuit and a bronze in the madison with Hayles, Wiggins became the first British athlete in forty years to win three medals in a single Games. With that achievement, he was named an officer of the Order of the British Empire (OBE).

## RETURN TO THE ROAD

Following the 2005 road racing season, Wiggins ended his relationship with Crédit Agricole, which had soured, by agreeing to a deal with another French team, Cofidis. Under the terms of the deal, Wiggins was automatically preselected for the 2006 Tour de France, at which point he took a hiatus from track competition to concentrate on road racing. He ended up placing 124th in his first Tour, which was won by the American cyclist Floyd Landis—later stripped of his title for doping.

Wiggins next competed in the 2007 UCI World Championships in Palma de Mallorca, Spain. He collected two gold medals, winning his second career world title in the individual pursuit and a first career world title in the team pursuit. Afterward, Wiggins recommenced his training for the 2007 Tour de France. He placed fourth in the Tour's opening prologue time trial, held in London, but was then forced to withdraw

from the race after the fifteenth stage, along with the rest of his Cofidis team, when it was revealed that Italian team member Cristian Moreni had failed a drug test. In the aftermath, Wiggins and his fellow team members were arrested and interrogated by the French police. "I remember traveling back from Pau [Pyrénées Airport in France], and throwing all my team kit in the [waste] bin," Wiggins recalled to Chris Harvey for the London *Telegraph* (18 June 2010). Shortly after returning home, he excoriated dopers and the Union Cycliste Internationale (UCI), cycling's world governing body, in a widely publicized press conference.

## 2008 OLYMPIC GAMES

Wiggins permanently severed ties with Cofidis and decided to forgo riding in the 2008 Tour de France. He turned his attention back to the track and the British national team to prepare for the 2008 Olympic Games in Beijing. Five months before those Games, he competed at the 2008 UCI World Championships in Manchester, where he defended his individual pursuit world title, claiming gold in the event for the third time. He was also a member of Britain's gold medal–winning team pursuit squad and added a third gold in the madison with partner Mark Cavendish.

In Beijing, Wiggins successfully defended his individual pursuit title, first breaking his own Olympic record in qualifying, with a time of four minutes and 15.031 seconds, before defeating Hayden Roulston of New Zealand in the gold-medal match. He became the first British cyclist in history to win consecutive gold medals in the same event. Wiggins then won a second gold medal as a member of Britain's world record–breaking team pursuit squad. His attempt to win a third gold, however, came up short, when he and Cavendish placed a disappointing ninth in the madison. That result notwithstanding, with the addition of two more Olympic medals Wiggins brought his career total to six, thus matching rower Steve Redgrave for the most medals in British Olympic history. He was subsequently promoted to commander of the Order of the British Empire (CBE).

## EMERGENCE AS TOP ROAD BICYCLE RACER IN THE WORLD

After the 2008 Olympics, Wiggins rededicated himself to road racing. For the 2009 season he signed with the Girona, Spain–based American team Garmin-Slipstream (now Garmin-Sharp). He then placed fourth in the 2009 Tour de France, finishing less than a minute behind third-place finisher Lance Armstrong, who had returned to the Tour after a three-year absence. In the process Wiggins tied for the best-ever finish by a British rider in the Tour, matching Robert Millar's fourth-place finish in 1984. He was later promoted to third place overall after Armstrong's result was voided by the UCI for his role in leading a systematic doping program.

Following his stellar 2009 Tour performance, Wiggins was recruited to the newly formed Team Sky, a British-based team managed by British Cycling's performance director Dave Brailsford. He was immediately designated team leader and was signed to a contract that paid him over £1 million per year. With Wiggins's signing, Team Sky announced that they hoped to win a Tour de France within five years. Wiggins, however, underperformed in his first year with the team. Despite taking the opening time trial stage at the 2010 Giro d'Italia, he placed a disappointing twenty-fourth in that year's Tour de France, finishing almost forty minutes behind winner Alberto Contador of Spain. Wiggins was later promoted to twenty-third place after Contador was disqualified for failing a doping test.

Wiggins was expected to fare better in the 2011 Tour de France following his first-place finish in that year's Critérium du Dauphiné, an annual eight-stage road race held in the Dauphiné region of France. However, he was forced to withdraw during the Tour's seventh stage after breaking his collarbone in a crash. Wiggins recovered in time to participate in the 2011 Vuelta a España, and in his first time racing in the event, he placed third, then his best-ever finish in a Grand Tour. With this achievement he and Sky teammate Chris Froome, who finished second, became the first British competitors to stand on a Grand Tour podium.

### FIRST BRITON TO WIN TOUR DE FRANCE AND MORE OLYMPIC GLORY

In 2012 Wiggins enjoyed a historic, record-breaking season. In March of that year he became the first British rider since 1967 to win the prestigious Paris-Nice, a one-week stage race held in France. Then, in April, he became the first Briton in history to win the Tour de Romandy, which runs in the Romandy region of Switzerland. After successfully defending his Critérium du Dauphiné title, Wiggins came into the 2012 Tour de France as one of the pre-race favorites. He opened the Tour with an impressive second-place finish in the prologue and then won the stage nine and stage nineteen time trials en route to becoming the first Briton to win the Tour de France. Combining "methodical mountain rides with explosive time trial performances," Jon Brand noted for the *New York Times* (23 July 2012), Wiggins finished the grueling three-week, 2,173-mile race three minutes and twenty-one seconds ahead of Froome, the runner-up.

One week after his Tour win, Wiggins competed in the 2012 Olympic Games, held in his home city of London. Despite not being given an opportunity to defend his title in the individual pursuit, which had been removed from the

Olympic program, he won his fourth Olympic gold medal after winning the road cycling individual time trial event. With that win, Wiggins increased his Olympic medal tally to seven, surpassing Redgrave and matching fellow track cyclist Chris Hoy, who also collected his seventh medal at the 2012 Games, as Britain's most decorated Olympian. He also became the first cyclist in history to win the Tour de France and an Olympic gold medal in the same year.

In 2013 Wiggins did not defend his Tour de France title because of a lingering knee injury and other various ailments, which forced him to miss the race. With the emergence of Team Sky's Chris Froome, who won that year's Tour, he has said that he may not return to the race, but has not ruled out other cycling endeavors.

### PERSONAL LIFE

Wiggins lives with his wife, Catherine, whom he married in 2004, and their two children, Ben and Isabella, in the village of Eccleston, in Lancashire, England. He is known for his affinity for 1960s mod culture and his penchant for collecting, including guitars, vintage scooters, and boxing memorabilia. He has received many awards and honors, including being named the 2012 BBC Sports Personality of the Year and receiving a knighthood in Queen Elizabeth II's 2013 New Year's honors list.

### SUGGESTED READING

Brand, Jon. "Taking Control Early, Wiggins Is First Briton to Win Race." *New York Times* 23 July 2012: D2. Print.

Hattenstone, Simon. "Bradley Wiggins: 'Kids from Kilburn Aren't Supposed to Win the Tour.'" *Guardian*. Guardian News, 2 Nov. 2012. Web. 18 Sept. 2013.

Lewis, Tim. "Bradley Wiggins: The Undisputed King of the Road." *Observer*. Guardian News and Media, 21 July 2012. Web. 19 Sept. 2013.

Wallace, Sam. "Tour de France: The Making of Bradley Wiggins." *Independent*. Independent.co.uk, 21 July 2012. Web. 26 Aug. 2013.

Wiggins, Bradley. *In Pursuit of Glory*. London: Orion, 2008. Print.

—*Chris Cullen*

---

# Kristen Wiig

**Born:** August 22, 1973
**Occupation:** Actor, comedian

Actor and comedian Kristen Wiig "doesn't exactly fit the mold of a traditional leading lady—she is more like America's eccentric aunt than its sweetheart," Susan Dominus wrote for the *New York Times* (28 Apr. 2011). Similar sentiments

Francis Specker/Landov

were expressed by Kate Meyers, who interviewed Wiig for *Women's Health* magazine (7 Dec. 2009); Meyers wrote, "You could say that Kristen Wiig is a one-woman homage to wacko. This is someone who takes the little things—tics, accents, weird gestures—and creates a full-on personality out of them."

Wiig has been widely celebrated for her seven seasons on the long-running sketch-comedy show *Saturday Night Live*, generally known by the acronym *SNL*. Appearing from 2005 to 2012, she garnered four Primetime Emmy Award nominations in the category of outstanding supporting actress in a comedy series. The show's producer, Lorne Michaels, has famously counted her among the top cast members ever to be affiliated with the program—particularly high praise considering that over the course of *SNL's* decades-long history, he has nurtured such iconic performers as Bill Murray, Gilda Radner, and John Belushi.

Wiig has also made a splash on the big screen. *Bridesmaids* (2011), which she cowrote and starred in, has been credited with introducing audiences to the idea that an all-female cast can carry an uproarious gross-out comedy in the vein of *National Lampoon's Animal House* (1978) or *The Hangover* (2009). Film critic Roger Ebert elaborated in his review for the *Chicago Sun-Times* (11 May 2011), "*Bridesmaids* seems to be a more or less deliberate attempt to cross the Chick Flick with the Raunch Comedy. It definitively proves that women are the equal of men in vulgarity, sexual frankness, lust, vulnerability,

overdrinking and insecurity." Of a scene in which Wiig is forced to climb over a high fence to reach her car after a night of meaningless sex, David T. Friendly wrote for the *Hollywood Reporter* (19 June 2011), "As far as metaphors go, it might represent the watershed moment when female-centric comedy broke down the Hollywood gates."

### EARLY YEARS

Kristen Carroll Wiig was born on August 22, 1973, in Canandaigua, a town in the Finger Lakes region of New York State. Her father, Jon, ran a marina, and her mother, Laurie, was an artist. She has an older brother, Erik, who is generally described in the press as "mentally handicapped." She is, by all reports, exceptionally devoted to him. "He's not aware of a lot of things," Wiig told Kate Meyers. "He has his own world, and there's this innocence about him. He's always happy and a joy to be around. He's also hilarious. He calls me his favorite sister in New York."

Wiig's family moved to Lancaster, Pennsylvania, when she was about three years old. When asked about a "giggle-worthy" childhood memory, Wiig recalled to Meyers, "I used to carry my dad's empty guitar case around the neighborhood because I wanted people to think I played the guitar. I would put Flintstones vitamins in it in case I got tired, so I could pop some and keep walking." Jon and Laurie divorced when Wiig was nine years old, and she and Erik moved to Rochester, New York, with their mother a few years later.

While she sometimes dreamed of being like the actresses in such popular 1980s sitcoms as *Family Ties* and *The Cosby Show*, Wiig never seriously considered a performing career, in large part because of her shy nature. "If I had to give a speech in class, I would try anything to get out of it," she told Alec Baldwin for his WYNC radio show *Here's the Thing* (9 Apr. 2012). "I hated talking in front of people. I still, actually, don't really like doing that." Despite her shyness, she was relatively popular, and she generally enjoyed her time at Rochester's Brighton High School.

Though not far from a serious student academically, Wiig completed a semester in Mexico at the National Outdoor Leadership School, which organizes remote wilderness expeditions and teaches its participants outdoor skills and teamwork. She refers to the program as one of the most challenging but important things she has ever done.

### LEARNING TO PERFORM

Like her mother, Wiig had always been artistic, and she subsequently entered an arts program at the University of Arizona, partly due to her desire to travel and partly because of what she described to Alec Baldwin as "a boyfriend thing." She majored in studio arts, and one of the requirements of the course was to take offerings in other areas. "I just tried this class called Performance Art, which was like writing poems and doing very weird light changes and things like that, which was like my first experience of being on a stage, even though it was like this tiny, little box in front of a class," she recalled to Baldwin. "It was literally Acting 101." Wiig greatly impressed her teacher, who encouraged her to hone her talent and keep performing.

With that seed planted, Wiig decided against a career in the visual arts. In an often-repeated tale, she had accepted a job at a plastic surgery clinic, preparing before-and-after sketches of prospective patients, but decided against showing up for her first day of work. Instead, she packed up her car on the spur of the moment and moved to Los Angeles, where she took a string of odd jobs while trying to break into acting. These included stints at a farmer's market, a flower-design studio, and a mall. She also waited tables in the executive dining room at Universal Studios, prepared the window displays at the upscale retailer Anthropologie, worked for a catering company, and babysat. Her shortest-lived job consisted of a single day spent manning the complicated phone system at a law firm. At one point, she took three months off work to travel in India.

## THE GROUNDLINGS

Wiig also tried acting classes but found that their traditional methods and exercises did not really engage her. One day, a friend took her to see a show put on by the Groundlings, a legendary Los Angeles–based improvisation and sketch-comedy troupe founded by Gary Austin in 1974. Renowned for launching the careers of dozens of performers, the Groundlings count several *SNL* members, including Will Ferrell, Phil Hartman, Maya Rudolph, and Julia Sweeney, as alumni.

Excited by the improvisational nature of the work, Wiig auditioned for a spot training with the troupe and was accepted. She took progressively more advanced classes, some of them focused on penning comedic material. There she met Annie Mumolo, who would later become her writing partner. Some aspiring performers who attend classes with the Groundlings are invited to join a junior group, called the Sunday Company, before being asked to be a part of the main company. Working her way up, Wiig was eventually asked to join the main group, and there she began developing some of the characters that would become popular on *SNL*.

## JOINING *SNL*

While working with the Groundlings, Wiig acquired a manager, Naomi Odenkirk, for whom she had babysat during her early days in Los Angeles. Odenkirk sent a tape of Wiig performing to the producers of *SNL*, who invited her in to audition. Their requirements were extremely specific: Wiig was to rehearse five characters and three impressions and be prepared to display them in only five minutes. "I [had only been] to New York once, when I was in eighth grade. To Hard Rock Café or something like that," she told Baldwin. Of her audition, she said, "I bought a stopwatch because I really thought they were going to just turn the lights off at five minutes, because they said, 'It's five minutes. Please don't go over.' So I practiced in the mirror with a stopwatch." When her five minutes were over, she "felt pretty good," she recalled. "They laughed a little bit. I was warned, 'It's going to be quiet. Just do it.' It's a tough crowd. . . . If anything, I just felt happy that I did it, because I was so terrified and shaking, I couldn't sleep. I couldn't eat."

Wiig heard nothing for about six weeks, and then she was invited back for a second audition to meet Lorne Michaels. He was warm and encouraging—he later told reporters that hers had been among the best auditions he had ever seen—but said he had no immediate openings, so Wiig was surprised to get a call to join the cast after the fourth show of the 2005 season. She moved from Los Angeles to New York City with a week's notice and made her debut on the show on November 12, 2005. She quickly gained a reputation as one of the hardest-working, most versatile members of the cast.

## POPULAR CHARACTERS

Among Wiig's most popular characters have been an overly enthusiastic Target clerk with a bad haircut and a cloying voice; Aunt Linda, an acerbic amateur film critic whose tastes run to insipid movies other critics are panning; Gilly, a diabolical young girl in an Orphan Annie wig who winsomely apologizes after each dangerous prank she pulls on a classmate; and Penelope, who feels the need to one-up everyone with increasingly outlandish claims. (Told by a friend that she just got a speeding ticket, Penelope claims to have gotten ninety-nine such tickets and to have once driven so fast she broke the sound barrier.) According to Susan Dominus, "Many of Wiig's characters are embarrassingly enthusiastic about something: a surprise party or the physical appeal of a love interest. . . . Their unchecked excitement—the raw wanting— makes the characters painfully nervous; and the combination of emotions bumping up against one another makes for comedy."

Wiig has taken inspiration for her characters from a variety of sources. She says, that she has an acquaintance very much like Penelope, and that she once actually met a Target clerk with a voice like that of her character. Wiig also performed several popular impersonations, including one of financial expert Suze Orman—in one sketch, Wiig's Orman advises viewers to soak in beef bouillon for a cheap self-tan—and perky talk-show host Kathie Lee Gifford, whom Wiig portrays as perennially tipsy.

## CRITICAL ACCLAIM AND DEPARTURE

Wiig remained with *SNL* for seven seasons, until 2012. During that time she was nominated for four Primetime Emmy Award nominations in the category of outstanding supporting actress in a comedy series, in 2009, 2010, 2011, and 2012. In 2009 the editors of *Entertainment Weekly* named her one of the twenty-five funniest actresses in Hollywood.

Wiig's final appearance on the program came on May 19, 2012. That show closed with Rolling Stones front man Mick Jagger presiding over a mock graduation. As the band Arcade Fire performed a cover of the Rolling Stones' "She's a Rainbow" in the background, Wiig removed her graduation cap and gown and danced, first with Jagger and then the rest of her cast mates in succession. The show concluded with everyone joining in to sing the Stones' song "Ruby Tuesday," which features the repeated line "Still I'm gonna miss you," and Wiig, who wiped away tears several times during the segment, dancing with Lorne Michaels. "The show was seven years of my life and a six-day work week, and you're constantly with your friends all day, all night," she said weeks later, as quoted by Erin O'Sullivan for *Access Hollywood* (19 Apr. 2013). "You sort of live and breathe the show. Then, when it's over, you kind of feel a little lost. . . . It was definitely an adjustment."

## FILM CAREER

Wiig's departure from *SNL* came as little shock to observers; she had been appearing with some regularity in big-screen projects, and particularly after the blockbuster success of *Bridesmaids*, speculation had been rampant that she would leave the show to focus on films.

After a handful of small parts in independent, little-seen films, Wiig made her major movie debut in 2007 with *Knocked Up*, a Judd Apatow picture starring Seth Rogen and Katherine Heigl. In it she appears as a catty television executive who tells Katherine Heigel's already-slim character, "We don't want you to lose weight, we just want you to be healthy. Y'know, by eating less." "*Knocked Up* is a movie filled with slapstick, screaming and shtick, and yet Wiig, with nothing more than her small, tight smile and death-by-platitude lines, practically stole the show with that two-minute scene," Dominus opined.

That year Wiig also appeared in *The Brothers Solomon*, *Meet Bill*, and the Apatow-penned *Walk Hard: The Dewey Cox Story*. The following year, she played a ditzy yoga instructor in the hit romantic comedy *Forgetting Sarah Marshall*, though her character only appears in the unrated version, and a crackpot surgeon in the Ricky Gervais picture *Ghost Town*. She remained busy in 2009, appearing as an eccentric theme-park owner in *Adventureland*, playing opposite Jason Bateman in *Extract*, and portraying roller-derby queen Maggie Mayhem in the Drew Barrymore-helmed *Whip It!* In 2010 she had a role in the action comedy *MacGruber*, starring *SNL* alum Will Forte. As in *Knocked Up*, Wiig's parts in most of these pictures may have been small, but critics were generally impressed and often referred to her scene-stealing abilities.

## BRIDESMAIDS

While filming *Knocked Up*, Apatow asked Wiig if she had ever considered writing her own screenplay. In response, she began collaborating with fellow Groundling Annie Mumolo on a story about two friends, one planning a wedding and the other trying to be supportive while her own life deteriorates. Apatow produced the film, and in 2011, *Bridesmaids* debuted, starring Wiig and an ensemble cast that included Melissa McCarthy, Rose Byrne, Maya Rudolph, Ellie Kemper, and Wendi McLendon-Covey. Wiig and Mumolo's original screenplay was nominated for several awards, including an Oscar.

Some critics objected to seeing women engaged in such crude physical comedy—one oft-mentioned scene takes place in a tastefully decorated bridal emporium, where the group is hit with severe gastrointestinal distress thanks to a restaurant meal Wiig's character has insisted upon. (The entire cast won Best Gut-Wrenching Performance honors at the MTV Movie Awards.) Still, others felt the picture heralded a new age. "It's a strange day when our social movements coalesce around a movie comedy that appears, from its trailer, to hinge largely on an explosive farting scene, but Hollywood's warped gender politics seem to make each day stranger than the last," Rebecca Traister wrote for *Salon* (12 May 2011). "This week, with a viral enthusiasm usually applied to marches on Washington, grassroots presidential campaigns or saving Planned Parenthood from House Republicans, women (and men) who believe in a future that includes movies for and about women have turned the comedy *Bridesmaids* . . . into a cause."

In 2011 Wiig also appeared in the films *Paul*, an oddball comedy in which two sci-fi geeks meet an alien, and *Friends with Kids*, which explores relationships and parenting issues among three couples. She has a slew of other films in various stages of production, including *Girl Most Likely*, an independent comedy that debuted at the Toronto International Film Festival in 2012 and is expected to have a limited US release in mid-2013; *The Secret Life of Walter Mitty*, based

on the famed story by James Thurber and sched-
uled to appear in theaters in late 2013; and the
Will Ferrell comedy *Anchorman: The Legend
Continues*, also expected in late 2013.

Wiig frequently works as a voice-over artist
for animated films, and her credits include *Ice
Age: Dawn of the Dinosaurs* (2009), *How to Train
Your Dragon* (2010), and *Despicable Me* (2010).
Since 2011 she has also voiced the character of
Lola Bunny on the *Looney Tunes Show*, which
updates the adventures of the classic Warner
Bros. characters.

## PERSONAL LIFE
Wiig was married to the actor Hayes Hargrove
from 2005 to 2009. Since her divorce, she has
been linked romantically to actor and filmmaker Brian Petsos and Strokes drummer Fabrizio
Moretti.

Despite her professional success and sometimes zany public persona, Wiig retains a degree
of shyness. "People are surprised when they
meet me that I'm not telling jokes and talking
in different voices," she told James Mottram for
the *Irish Independent* (17 June 2011). "For me,
it's what I love to do when I'm at work. But as a
person, I may be in the room for a while at the
party before you notice that I'm there."

## SUGGESTED READING
Dominus, Susan. "Can Kristen Wiig Turn on the
    Charm?" *New York Times*. New York Times,
    28 Apr. 2011. Web. 20 Apr. 2013.
Traister, Rebecca. "Seeing *Bridesmaids* Is a So-
    cial Responsibility." *Salon*. Salon Media, 12
    May 2011. Web. 20 Apr. 2013.
Wiig, Kristen. "Getting Funny with *SNL*'s Kris-
    ten Wiig." Interview by Kate Meyers. *Women's
    Health*. Rodale, 7 Dec. 2009. Web. 20 Apr.
    2013.
Wiig, Kristen. Interview by Nathan Rabin. *The
    A.V. Club*. Onion, 30 March 2009. Web. 20
    Apr. 2013.
Wiig, Kristen. "My Brilliant Career: Kristen
    Wiig." Interview by Rachel Rosenblit. *Elle*.
    Hearst Communications, 19 Mar. 2010. Web.
    20 Apr. 2013.

## SELECTED WORKS
*Saturday Night Live*, 2005–2012; *Knocked Up*,
2007; *Walk Hard: The Dewey Cox Story*, 2007;
*Ghost Town*, 2008; *Adventureland*, 2009; *Whip
It*, 2009; *Bridesmaids*, 2011; *Friends with Kids*,
2011; *Paul*, 2011; *The Looney Tunes Show*,
2011–

—*Mari Rich*

# Sunita Williams
**Born:** September 19, 1965
**Occupation:** NASA astronaut

On July 21, 1969, a nearly four-year-old Sunita
Williams watched Neil Armstrong and Edwin
"Buzz" Aldrin become the first men to walk on
the moon. At the time, her thoughts ran along
the lines of, "Wow—that's cool." Like many children, she dreamed of becoming an astronaut, but
she never thought this would actually happen.

After an early career as a helicopter pilot and
captain for the United States Navy, Williams
applied for NASA's astronaut program—and
her dream became a reality. Williams spent 322
days in space over the course of two stays on the
International Space Station—from December
2006 to June 2007, and from July to November
2012—setting a record for the second-longest
amount of time for a female astronaut. During
her first mission on the International Space Station, she broke the record among female astronauts for both the highest number of space walks
and the longest amount of time spent outside of
a spacecraft. Her records were broken by Peggy
Whitson in December 2007, but then Williams
beat Whitson's numbers during her second mission. With her two space station trips combined,
Williams has gone on seven space walks and has
spent fifty hours and forty minutes outside of the
space station.

Astronaut Williams is also an athlete. She
became the first person to run a marathon in
space, completing the Boston Marathon in April
2007 while aboard the International Space Station. She also became the first person to complete a triathlon in space in September 2012.

## EARLY LIFE AND FLIGHT TRAINING
Sunita "Suni" Lyn Williams was born Sunita
Pandya Krishna on September 19, 1965, in Eu-
clid, Ohio, to neuroanatomist Deepak Pandya
and X-ray technician Ursuline "Bonnie" Zalokar
Pandya. The youngest of three children, Williams was raised in Needham, Massachusetts;
the Pandya family moved to Massachusetts in
1966, after Deepak Pandya accepted a position
in Boston. Growing up, Williams was active in
athletics, particularly competitive swimming. After graduating from high school, she considered
studying to become a veterinarian. However,
when her older brother Jay, who attended the US
Naval Academy, suggested she do the same because it would suit her active lifestyle, she chose
instead to take his advice. Williams graduated
from the academy in 1987 with a bachelor's degree in physical science.

After graduation, Williams attended flight
school in Pensacola, Florida, where she trained
to become a helicopter pilot. Williams joined a
helicopter support squadron in Norfolk, Virginia,

AFP/Getty Images

in 1989, and the following year was deployed to the Middle East during the Gulf War to take part in Operation Desert Shield and then Operation Provide Comfort in 1991. After serving in the Gulf War, Williams continued to fly as a captain for the Navy. In September 1992, for example, she led H-46 helicopters to Miami, Florida, as part of the Navy's Hurricane Andrew relief operations.

In 1993, Williams graduated from US Naval Test Pilot School in Patuxent, Maryland, enabling her to perform test flights of military helicopters. Williams was not finished with school yet, however. She next attended the Florida Institute of Technology in Melbourne, earning a master's degree in engineering management in 1995.

## BECOMING AN ASTRONAUT

A career as an astronaut had never crossed the adult Williams's mind—until she visited the Johnson Space Center in Houston, Texas, during a field trip with her test pilot school classmates. There, she met several astronauts, including John Young, who had walked on the moon for the Apollo 16 space mission in April 1972. Being introduced to these astronauts made Williams realize that she already had many of the skills one needs to pilot spacecraft, and she decided to apply for the NASA (National Aeronautics and Space Administration) astronaut program. "I remember him [Young] talking about learning how to fly a helicopter to land the lunar lander," Williams recalled during a NASA preflight interview (9 Aug. 2006). "Something just clicked in my head, and I said, 'wow,' you know, maybe there's a use for helicopter pilots, if we're going to go back to the moon." She added, "So, I sort of said to myself,

the only one who's telling me I'm not going to be an astronaut is me. I did the research on what was required, and I got my master's degree and applied, and, lo and behold, the second application, I got an interview." NASA accepted Williams's second application in June 1998; she began her astronaut training that August.

Williams's training at NASA covered a variety of areas, from piloting NASA's supersonic T-38 training jet, to operating robotic arms, to wilderness and underwater survival techniques. She then worked with the Russian Space Agency in Moscow, helping with the Russian contribution to the International Space Station (ISS)—launched into space in November 1998—and the ISS's Expedition 1, the first long-duration human stay on board the station, begun when the crew docked on November 2, 2000. During her time in Moscow, Williams learned to speak Russian, which would later help her communicate with Russian cosmonauts while on board the ISS. After Expedition 1 returned to Earth in March 2001, Williams focused her work on ISS robotic technology.

## LIVING UNDERWATER

While NASA is generally associated with missions in space, the administration has also conducted other "extreme environment" missions. In May 2002, Williams spent nine days living in the NASA Aquarius Laboratory, an underwater habitat located off the coast of Florida, near Key Largo. Owned by the National Oceanic and Atmospheric Administration (NOAA), Aquarius is the research station for NEEMO (NASA Extreme Environment Mission Operations), a NASA analog mission of astronauts, scientists, and engineers, who can live up to three weeks in the station underwater. The idea behind NEEMO is that, like space, the underwater world is a hostile and alien environment for humans; by living underwater, NEEMO "aquanauts" experience some of the same challenges that they might face in outer space. For example, aquanauts learn to live in the confined environment of a spacecraft and are able to test spacewalking techniques. The underwater pressure also helps NASA members simulate living in different levels of gravity.

Williams was a member of NEEMO 2, the second crew to live in Aquarius. The four-member crew "officially became aquanauts" on the second day of their mission, according to trainer Marc Reagan's mission journal (14 May 2002), posted on NASA's website. "Not 'certified trained as aquanauts,' not 'wannabe aquanauts,' but real aquanauts. Welcome to a pretty exclusive club. In case you were wondering, there is no door prize, but the job benefits are outstanding. Technically, the term aquanaut is limited to those who stay underwater for 24 hours or more."

## FROM THE *DISCOVERY* TO THE ISS

Williams's first trip into space began on December 9, 2006, as a member of NASA's STS-116 mission: the launch of the space shuttle *Discovery* from Florida, bound for the ISS. The STS-116 crew worked on construction of the ISS over the course of four space walks, adding a part (the P5 spacer truss segment), rewiring the station's power system, and taking down solar arrays that had folded the wrong way. The crew also provided the ISS with more than two tons of equipment and supplies, as well as a new flight engineer for the ISS's fourteenth expedition: Sunita Williams.

The arrival of Williams meant the departure of German flight engineer Thomas Reiter, who had been on board the space station since July 2006, as part of the Expedition 13 crew and then Expedition 14. Reiter explained the reason for crew switchover overlap during a NASA pre-flight interview (23 Feb. 2006), posted on NASA's website. "The crew that has been on station needs to explain to the newcomers how all the on board systems are configured, where things are stowed and so forth. Once they are gone the only, only place they can ask is the control center." Three- or four-member crews have become the norm for long-duration stays on board the ISS; visiting crew arrives periodically to add parts to the station, provide supplies, and make repairs.

## EXPEDITIONS 14 AND 15

Williams would become a member of Expedition 15 after Expedition 14's commander, Michael Lopez-Alegria, and flight engineer Mikhail Tyurin left in April 2007. They were replaced by Expedition 15 commander Fyodor Yurchikhin and flight engineer Oleg Kotov, two Russian cosmonauts who arrived in April aboard the Soyuz TMA-10 mission. "I think it's going to be pretty busy. But, it's going to be a lot of fun, and I'm absolutely lucky to be in this place at this time," Williams told reporters during her NASA pre-flight interview, posted on NASA's website (9 Aug. 2006).

In addition to making repairs in her capacity as a flight engineer, Williams also acted as the NASA ISS science officer on board, researching how people can safely live and work in the weightlessness of space. For example, the astronauts recorded how well exercise mitigates the otherwise inevitable bone and muscle mass loss that occurs while living in space. They also recorded what they ate and how this food affected bone and muscle mass, as well as how food is metabolized in a body living in a weightless environment. Williams returned to Earth with the NASA STS-117 mission, on board the space shuttle *Atlantis*, which landed on June 22, 2007 at Edwards Air Force Base in California.

## A RECORD-SETTER IN SPACE

During her first stay on the International Space Station, Williams broke the world record for the longest amount of Extravehicular Activity (EVA) performed by a woman—EVA is time spent outside spacecraft, commonly referred to as spacewalking. Her four space walks, which totaled a cumulative twenty-nine hours and seventeen minutes, broke the record for the number of space walks completed by a female astronaut. Williams's 195 days in space also broke the record for the longest amount of time a woman has spent in space.

Once Williams arrived on board the ISS in December 2006, she had her long hair cut by fellow astronaut Joan Higginbotham. Her ponytail of cut hair was brought back to Earth with the STS-116 crew and donated to Locks of Love, a nonprofit organization that gives hairpieces to children who lose their hair due to medical conditions. Williams's hair, which sometimes floated above her head while she lived in the station, would become somewhat iconic for fans of the astronaut, particularly after the release of a twenty-five minute video tour of the ISS that Williams made during her second stay on the station. As Robert Krulwich wrote in a story for NPR about the video tour (3 Jan. 2013): "If I had a thick, rich mane of hair like International Space Station commander Sunita Williams, I wouldn't need a comb, because combs are for getting hair to stay in place. But up there, hair doesn't have a place, it just floats—like you do."

## FROM DEEP-SEA PHONE CALLS TO THE BOSTON MARATHON

On January 26, 2007, Williams participated in the first-ever phone call between a deep-ocean submersible and a spacecraft. A phone call had been conducted between the ISS and Aquarius on June 30, 2003, but the call that Williams participated in was the first of its kind. She spoke for approximately thirty minutes with Tim Shank, a biologist of the Woods Hole Oceanographic Institution (WHOI), who was diving to the floor of the Pacific Ocean in a submersible called *Alvin*. The conversation, guided by more than four hundred questions that children from across the world had submitted for the event, was broadcast on NASA TV, as well as the WHOI and NASA websites.

Williams completed the Boston Marathon on April 16, 2007, while in space—the first person ever to do so. She ran the 26.2-mile Massachusetts marathon on an ISS treadmill while her crewmates cheered her on, finishing in four hours, twenty-three minutes, and ten seconds. At the same time, she received updates about the runners in Boston, including her sister Dina, fellow astronaut Karen L. Nyberg, and friend Ronnie Harris. The ISS circled Earth at least twice during her run. Williams ran the marathon to "encourage kids to start making physical fitness part of their daily lives," she stated in a NASA interview (16 Apr. 2007). In addition, astronauts need to exercise regularly in order to maintain their bone density while in space. "In microgravity . . . we don't use our legs to walk around and don't need the bones and muscles to hold us up under the force of gravity," Williams explained during her interview. Williams ran the Boston Marathon again in 2008, though this time on Earth. "Anything regarding Boston makes Suni light up. Her running passion is manifested in the best marathon in the world, which happens to be her home town," Harris stated in the NASA interview. "You need to experience the Boston Marathon to understand why she is gonna do it in orbit."

## ISS EXPEDITIONS 32 AND 33

In 2008, Williams became a deputy chief of NASA's Astronaut Office, one of the most senior leadership positions an active astronaut can take. She worked with chief Steve W. Lindsey until he handed the position to Peggy Whitson in October 2009, then continued to work on various aspects of the ISS until preparing for a second trip into space in 2012.

Williams once again launched into space on July 14, 2012, this time from the Baikonur Cosmodrome in Kazakhstan. She traveled to the International Space Station with Russian Soyuz commander Yuri Malenchenko and Japanese flight engineer Akihiko Hoshide. As part of Expedition 32 and then Expedition 33, Williams spent four months on board the ISS, where she conducted research and made repairs. She worked as a flight engineer for Expedition 32, but for Expedition 33, she was appointed commander.

Peggy Whitson had broken Williams's space walk records in December 2007, with six space walks and thirty-nine hours and forty-six minutes of EVA during Expedition 16, but Williams once again held both records after her second time aboard the ISS. She and Hoshide went on three space walks to replace a power component of the station—using such improvised tools as a spare toothbrush—and to fix an ammonia leak. These space walks increased Williams's total number to seven and her cumulative amount of EVA to fifty hours and forty minutes. Williams spent 127 days in space for her second mission, which ranked her at number six for the all-time US astronaut endurance list and at number two for a female astronaut. Her total of 322 days spent in space was just fifty-five days shy of Whitson's 377-day total.

## TRIATHLONS IN SPACE

Becoming the first person to complete a triathlon in space—or the equivalent of one—was another achievement for Williams during her 2012 stay on the ISS. On September 16, 2012, during the Nautica Malibu Triathlon held in southern California, she used a resistance machine to simulate swimming for half a mile, a stationary bicycle to bike for eighteen miles, and treadmill to run for four miles; she completed the triathlon in one hour, forty-eight minutes, and thirty-three seconds.

Exercise equipment on board the ISS has harnesses and straps to make sure astronauts do not float away. For "swimming" during the triathlon, Williams used a strength-training machine called the Advanced Resistive Exercise Device (ARED), which allows a person to do weightlifting and resistance exercises that simulate the activity in microgravity. "It's critically important to understand human physiology and how to keep you strong on orbit," NASA's Mission Control flight director stated upon Williams's completion of the triathlon, as reported by Clara Moskowitz for the Associated Press (18 Sept. 2012). "I'm happy to be done," Williams stated. "It wasn't easy, and I'm sure everybody in California's very happy to be done too."

Williams landed back in Kazakhstan on November 18, 2012. Shortly before leaving, she wrote in her blog for NASA (19 Nov. 2012): "I love the fact that we are all up here together from such different places . . . What a diverse group of people and somehow we all find a common ground and find humor in our daily lives together. Both crews, this one and Expedition 32, have shown that folks from such different lives, perspectives, cultures, religions can easily be really productive when working together." She added: "Where we will be in 10, 25, 50 or 100 years from now . . . it is hard to imagine, but I can't wait to find out."

## PERSONAL LIFE

Williams is married to police officer Michael J. Williams. They have two dogs, a Jack Russell terrier named Gorby and a Labrador retriever named Bailey. Williams spends her free time performing sports such as snowboarding, windsurfing, running, bicycling, swimming, and competing in triathlons. Williams is also a big fan of Cesar Millan's *Dog Whisperer* show on the National Geographic Channel. She appeared with Gorby on an episode of the show in November 2010.

## SUGGESTED READING

Krulwich, Robert. "Big Hair, No Sitting, Velcroed to Your Pillow: What It's Like to Live Weightlessly." *NPR*. National Public Radio, 3 Jan. 2013. Web. 11 Jan. 2013.

"Preflight Interview: Suni Williams." *NASA International Space Station, Expedition 14*. National Aeronautics and Space Administration, 9 Aug. 2006. Web. 11 Jan. 2013.

"Preflight Interview: Suni Williams." *NASA: International Space Station, Expedition 32*. National Aeronautics and Space Administration, 4 June. 2012. Web. 11 Jan. 2013.

"Race from Space Coincides with Race on Earth." *NASA: International Space Station, Expedition 14*. National Aeronautics and Space Administration, 16 Apr. 2007. Web. 11 Jan. 2013.

Williams, Suni. *Space to Run. NASA Blogs*. National Aeronautics and Space Administration, 13 July 2012–19 Nov. 2012. Web. 11 Jan. 2013.

—*Julia Gilstein*

# Tim Wise

**Born:** October 4, 1968
**Occupation:** Antiracist writer and educator

AP Photo

Tim Wise is a prominent antiracist educator, activist, and author who has written seven books on the topic of racism in the United States. He has spoken in all fifty states, at more than eight hundred colleges, universities, and high schools across the United States. He has also trained schoolteachers, physicians, and law enforcement officials to recognize and resist the effects of institutional racism in their lines of work, and has provided antiracism seminars and workshops to a number of corporations and government agencies, including the Ford Motor Company, Lockheed-Martin, and the Federal Highway Administration. Molefi Kete Asante, professor of African American studies at Temple University and the author of dozens of books on race and racism, has called Wise "one of the most brilliant voices of our time." Wise's speeches and essays blend his own personal experiences with the hard facts concerning racism in the United States, from the country's early history to the present day.

One of the primary issues that Wise explores in his work is how discussions of racism in the United States are never complete if the focus remains solely on the effects that racism has on Americans of color. Wise, who is white, assesses the impact of race and racism in his life and encourages other white Americans to consider the ways in which they have been affected by and benefitted from a historical legacy of disparate privilege and opportunity, such that the average white family in the United States today has twenty-two times the wealth of the average African American family. In a speech given at Mt. Holyoke College in Massachusetts in 2008, Wise commented, "Just because we acknowledge racism and discrimination, doesn't mean that we'll necessarily acknowledge the flipside of that—doesn't mean that we will acknowledge that for everyone who is targeted by that discrimination, which we're willing to admit does exist, there is somebody else *not* being targeted. . . . We like to talk about those who are down as if there

is no up." One theme Wise often touches upon in many of his speeches is that although white Americans should not feel guilty for the history of discrimination and oppression in the United States, they should feel responsible for addressing it today. He encourages white Americans to make an honest assessment of how racism has benefitted them and their families historically, but he ultimately stresses how racism damages and undermines all Americans, particularly the poor.

## EARLY LIFE

Timothy Jacob Wise was born to Michael Julius Wise and LuCinda Anne (McLean) Wise on October 4, 1968, in Nashville, Tennessee. His parents were both young, under twenty-two years old, when their son was born, and his maternal grandparents had not initially approved of their son-in-law. "My mom's folks never took well to my dad, in part because of the large cultural gap between the two families." Wise explained in his first book, *White Like Me*, "The Wises were Jews, a bit too cosmopolitan and, well, *Jewish*, for the liking of the McLeans" (5).

Though white racial privilege is a topic that Wise often explores, he did not grow up particularly well off. His father worked as a stand-up comedian and actor, and often travelled to perform various shows. Soon after Wise's birth, his parents moved the family into the Royal Arms apartment complex in the Green Hills community of Nashville. When it became time to enroll Wise in a preschool program, Wise's mother chose not to enroll her son at any preschool in the predominantly white neighborhood of Green Hills. Instead, she decided her son would attend the early childhood education program at Tennessee State University (TSU), Nashville's historically black university. Wise was one of only three white students in a class of twenty or more, yet this early experience of being in the minority was extremely formative for Wise. As he wrote in *White Like Me*, Wise's education at TSU "meant that I would be socialized in a non-dominant setting, my peers mostly African American children. Because I had bonded with black kids early on, once I entered elementary school it would be hard not to notice the way that we were so often separated in the classroom" (34).

In 1974, Wise began attending Burton Elementary in Nashville. Although the Supreme Court had outlawed school segregation in 1954, ongoing resistance to integration efforts had prevented busing policies from being implemented at the high school level until 1971 Wise notes, "It would be 1974, the year I began first grade, before busing would filter down to the elementary level. This means that the class of 1986, *my* graduating class, was the first that had been truly desegregated throughout its entire educational experience" (*White Like Me* 22). Wise states that he was never a strong student and had difficulty applying himself to topics he did not immediately find interesting; nevertheless, he consistently found himself tracked higher than his black friends and peers, regardless of their ability. Wise attended the Stokes School for fifth and sixth grade, where he began taking theater classes as an elective.

## GROWING POLITICAL CONSCIOUSNESS

Wise attended junior high school at John Trotwood Moore School in Nashville. During this time, Wise's home life grew increasingly unstable as his father's alcoholism worsened and his parents' relationship became strained. Also during this time, Wise began to lose touch with many of his closest friends from childhood. Wise explains how, as they grew up, he and his black friends found that their experiences and interests were beginning to diverge. "Our experiences had been so different, our treatment so disparate, that by junior high, we just didn't have much in common anymore" (59). One of the things that sustained Wise during this period was his participation with the school's forensics team, through which he competed in speechwriting and debate tournaments throughout the state of Tennessee. Wise took on an afterschool job bagging groceries at a local market in order to cover for the travel expenses incurred by the forensics competitions. At his first forensics competition, Wise panicked and left the presentation room and did not return until well after his time to present had passed. "Thankfully," he writes, "my coach made me go back in for the second and third rounds, and I've been speaking ever since" (68).

While attending Hillsboro High School in Nashville, Wise became interested in punk music, which fed into his growing political awareness. He was particularly concerned about the

ways in which the United States supported the contra rebels in Central America and the apartheid government in South Africa. In the summer following his junior year in high school, Wise attended a debate camp at the American University in Washington, DC, which helped to improve his debate and public-speaking skills.

## INCREASING ACTIVISM

In his senior year of high school, Wise was accepted to Tulane University in New Orleans. He failed to secure enough scholarship funds and financial aid to cover the costs of his first year at Tulane, so his mother took out at $10,000 loan using her mother's home as collateral. As Wise later acknowledged, his family's ability to secure this loan was largely attributable to their race. Though his grandparents were not rich, they were able to afford the house in a nice, entirely white neighborhood by securing a loan through the Federal Housing Association—loans that through the 1960s went almost exclusively to white homebuyers. Regardless of their qualifications or creditworthiness, black Americans were routinely denied these loans through the FHA's explicit redlining policies. Wise has claimed, "My very presence at Tulane had been related to whiteness. During my time there I would come to learn that the same school that ultimately traveled 540 miles to pluck me out of Nashville had not been recruiting for several years at Fortier High, the basically all-black high school located about five hundred yards from the entrance to campus" (96).

At Tulane, Wise became increasingly involved in political work, initially working with the Movement for Peace in Central America (MPCA), where he performed his earliest activism work by organizing protests and teach-ins. In his freshman year, he wrote a term paper on Guatemalan civilian deaths caused by US military action in Central America; after turning in his paper, Wise received his first death threat, which was phoned into his dorm room by someone claiming to have ties to the US military. Undeterred, Wise remained committed to his activism work. Nevertheless, by sophomore year, his involvement with MPCA began to wane as he became increasingly involved in a student-led movement at Tulane to convince the university to divest its stockholdings in companies that continued to support the apartheid government of South Africa.

## DIVESTMENT EFFORTS AT TULANE

In March 1988, Wise became one of the founding members of the Tulane Alliance Against Apartheid. Administrators at Tulane later insisted that the group change its name to Tulane Students Against Apartheid, to avoid implying that the university endorsed the group's efforts in any way. In addition to demanding that Tulane divest certain stock holdings, the group also fought for the creation of an African American studies program and condemned the university's weak enforcement of affirmative-action policies in student and faculty recruitment.

The group had one of its most visible successes after Tulane extended an honorary degree to the antiapartheid activist Desmond Tutu, who had won the Nobel Peace Prize in 1984 for his antiracism work in South Africa. The group sent Tutu a packet of materials outlining Tulane's investments in South Africa and requesting that Tutu condemn the university's stockholdings. Soon after, Tutu announced that he would not accept the honorary degree from Tulane, or any university that continued to invest in companies supporting the South African apartheid government.

Wise continued to work with Tulane Students Against Apartheid in senior year, though by that time, many black members of the group had left as the group's focus narrowed from its original demands to just focus on antiapartheid efforts. Wise realized how racism can be reinforced even by efforts aimed at resisting it. Wise claimed he later had a "light bulb moment" following a debate class, where the topic had been divestment in South Africa. After Wise presented, a black classmate raised her hand to ask him, "What one thing have you done to address apartheid in this city?" (*White Like Me* 121). Wise was caught off guard and deeply embarrassed, responding after a pause, "Um, we all pick our battles" (122). Wise remembers "so shaken was I by her question and my answer, not because I had been in possession of a better answer that I had simply forgotten to offer, but because I had no answer at all. That had been it. I had told the truth, and now had to confront what such disturbing honesty suggested" (122). This instance would later be the primary reason Wise decided to remain in New Orleans following his graduation. Wise completed his honor's thesis on the civil rights movement in Mississippi and graduated in 1990.

## ANTIRACISM WORK IN NEW ORLEANS

Wise's decision to remain in New Orleans after graduation in order to do something to address racism in the city eventually led him to join the Louisiana Coalition Against Racism and Nazism. There, he was involved in efforts to defeat the ex-Klansman and white supremacist David Duke in his 1990 campaign for the US Senate. Wise was placed in charge of coordinating the group's efforts with Louisiana college campuses. Though Duke lost the election in 1990, the following year Duke announced his campaign for governor of Louisiana, prompting Wise to rejoin the Louisiana Coalition. While his work with the coalition led Wise to decide that he did not want to pursue a career in politics, he nevertheless

gained valuable experience in coordinating various groups and mounting an effective public relations campaign. His work at the coalition also solidified his decision to devote his career to racial equity. In 1992, Wise appeared on the *Jane Whitney Show* to participate in a discussion on racism and white supremacy in the United States. His appearance on the show prompted a football coach named Jimmy Jackson to contact Wise, asking him to serve as an expert witness on his racial discrimination lawsuit against the World League of American Football. Though Jackson ultimately lost his case, Wise recalled in *White Like Me* that "my involvement with Jimmy would ultimately serve as the best education I could have received about how racism works, specifically at the institutional level" (160). Wise would go on to serve as an expert witness and consultant on several other racial-bias cases in the future.

In 1995 Wise landed a job as a researcher and community organizer for the Agenda for Children, a child advocacy group with an antiracist philosophy. Agenda required all of its employees to complete antiracism training at the People's Institute for Survival and Beyond in New Orleans. With Agenda, Wise worked in some of the most impoverished areas of New Orleans. Around this time, Wise applied to a progressive speaker's bureau known as Speak Out. The bureau added Wise to its catalog and in early 1995 Wise secured his first speaking engagements. As his speaking engagements began to demand more and more of his time, he decided to leave the Agenda for Children and relocate to Nashville.

## REACHING A WIDER AUDIENCE

Requests for Wise to speak at various colleges and universities began to increase so that, within five years, Wise had spoken to an estimated sixty thousand people at more than two hundred school campuses around the country. In 1995, a short book Wise had written called *Little White Lies: The Truth about Affirmative Action and "Reverse Discrimination"* was published by the Twomey Center for Peace through Justice at Loyola University. In 1999, Wise began writing essays for an online commentary service known as Z *Magazine*. From 1999 to 2003, Wise served as an advisor to the Fisk University Race Relations Institute, an organization that promotes racial equity through expanding the national dialogue and research efforts on racism in the United States. Wise was also featured in the book *White Men Challenging Racism*, published by Duke University Press in 2003.

In early 2004, Wise decided to act upon "an admonition from people of color I knew in New Orleans to 'take inventory' of my life, to get clear on why I cared so much about racism, to understand my own motivation for challenging it" (*White Like Me* viii). Soon after, Wise began writing a book that would be published in 2005 as *White Like Me: Reflections on Race from a Privileged Son*, a highly acclaimed memoir in which Wise examines the way race and racism have shaped his life and his commitment to antiracist activism.

As Wise became more prominent, he was repeatedly asked to appear on CNN, MSNBC, and other news stations to offer commentary on race-based current events and issues, such as affirmative action policies, media-generated racial stereotypes, and hate crimes. Following the election of President Barack Obama, the first African American president of the United States, Wise's media appearances became more frequent and he began work on two books that critically examine popular claims that the United States had become a postracial nation following President Obama's election. Wise also maintains a website, which he regularly updates with critical essays and commentary.

Wise is one of the most impassioned and well-known speakers on the legacy of racism in the United States. Michael Eric Dyson, a renowned scholar on race and professor of sociology at Georgetown University, has commented, "Tim Wise is one of the most brilliant, articulate, and courageous critics of white privilege in the nation. His considerable rhetorical skills, his fluid literary gifts, and his relentless search for the truth make him a critical ally in the fight against racism." In his writings and speeches, Wise has taken an uncommon approach to the discussion of racism by critically examining the ways in which white Americans are distorted and damaged by racism as well as black and brown Americans. One of the primary arguments Wise emphasizes is how racism undermines the economic interests of working-class Americans, both white and black, because it obscures their commonality of interests in securing better economic conditions for themselves. For his efforts, the progressive magazine *Utne Reader* recognized Wise as one of twenty-five visionaries who were changing the world in 2010.

Wise currently lives in Nashville with his wife, Kristy Cason, and their two daughters, Ashton and Rachel.

## SUGGESTED READING

"By the Color of their Skin: Tim Wise on the Myth of a Postracial America." Interview by David Cook. *Sun.* Sun Magazine, July 2009. Web. 14 Nov. 2012.
Hart, Joe. "Tim Wise: The Confrontationalist." *Utne Reader*. Ogden Publications, Nov. 2010. Web. 12 Nov. 2012.
Wise, Tim. *Colorblind: The Rise of Post-Racial Politics and the Retreat from Racial Equity*. Cambridge: City Lights, 2010. Print.
---. *White Like Me: Reflections on Race from a Privileged Son*. 3d ed. Berkeley: Soft Skull, 2011. Print.

## SELECTED WORKS

*White Like Me: Reflections on Race from a Privileged Son*, 2005; *Colorblind: The Rise of Post-Racial Politics and the Retreat from Racial Equity*, 2010; *Speaking Treason Fluently: Anti-Racist Reflections from an Angry White Male*, 2009.

—Mary Woodbury

# Susan Wojcicki

**Born:** 1968
**Occupation:** Businesswoman and Google executive

Susan Wojcicki is often called the most important Google employee most people have not heard of. While this title accurately describes her crucial role in the company, it seems that Wojcicki's era of relative obscurity is coming to an end. In 2012 she was ranked the twenty-fifth most powerful woman in the world by *Forbes* and the eighteenth most powerful woman in business by *Fortune*, and Google's financial reports revealed that her department was responsible for more than 90 percent of Google's revenue for the previous year—a total of more than thirty billion dollars. As Google's senior vice president of advertising, Wojcicki is responsible for managing such products as AdWords, AdSense, and more recent acquisitions such as AdMob and DoubleClick.

After renting out the garage of her California home to Google founders Larry Page and Sergey Brin in 1998 and witnessing the company's early success firsthand, Wojcicki joined Google the following year as head of the company's marketing department. As Google grew, the scope of her role there expanded, and she was eventually named vice president of product management. In that role, she participated in the acquisition of video-sharing website YouTube. Much of her focus, however, has been on leading the development of Google's advertising products. "The question is," she told Caroline Howard for *Forbes* (6 May 2011), "how do we deliver the most perfect ad for every query? It has to be user-driven and it has to be useful and relevant."

## EARLY LIFE AND EDUCATION

Susan Diane Wojcicki was born in 1968 to Stanley Wojcicki, a physics professor who taught at Stanford University, and Esther Wojcicki, a journalism teacher. Wojcicki and her two younger sisters grew up on the Stanford campus in Palo

Wirelmage

Alto, California. Stanley and Esther valued education and placed particular emphasis on independent learning, to great success. Wojcicki's sister Janet became a professor of pediatrics, while her sister Anne, who married Google co-founder Brin, founded the genetic analysis company 23andMe.

After graduating from Gunn High School, Wojcicki attended Harvard University, from which she earned a bachelor's degree in history and literature in 1990. She returned to California to attend the University of California, Santa Cruz, receiving a master's degree in economics from the university in 1993. She went on to attend the Anderson School of Management at the University of California, Los Angeles (UCLA), and earned a master of business administration degree in 1998. During the 1990s, Wojcicki worked for the management consulting firms Bain & Company and R. B. Webber Company as well as the technology company Intel.

## CAREER

In 1998, while working in Intel's marketing department, Wojcicki made a decision that would shape the rest of her career. "I had just got out of business school and bought a house," she told Emma Barnett for the London *Sunday Telegraph* (5 Dec. 2010). "So I needed to get some renters in order to help pay the mortgage." She decided to rent out the garage of her house in Menlo Park, California, to two graduate students from Stanford, Sergey Brin and Larry Page. Beginning

in September 1998, Brin and Page paid $1,700 per month to use the garage as a headquarters for their newly formed company, Google. The company later purchased the property in September of 2006.

Although Wojcicki witnessed Google's development and early success firsthand, she did not join the company immediately. In a talk delivered to students at UCLA's Anderson School of Management, Wojcicki described the moment in which she recognized that she wanted to be part of it. "Google search went down . . . and I couldn't access it for this one moment in time," she explained. "At that moment, I realized, 'I can't get my work done. I can't find anything.' This made me realize how important the service was." Wojcicki joined Google in 1999 as head and sole member of the marketing department, becoming the company's sixteenth hire.

## GOOGLE

Originally known as BackRub, the Google search engine was the product of several years of work on the part of Brin and Page. In August of 1998, the company received its first major loan, and Brin and Page filed for incorporation soon after. In February of 1999, Google moved out of Wojcicki's garage and into office space in Palo Alto. The company moved again later that year, establishing its first office in Mountain View, California, which would later become the home of Google's headquarters, known as the Googleplex.

In her role as head of marketing, Wojcicki was responsible for managing Google's early marketing efforts. She designed several of Google's early "doodles," the variant logos that appear on the search engine's main page on holidays and special occasions. As her role there developed, however, one of her key tasks became determining how to generate revenue for the company. As a free-to-use search engine, Google was difficult to monetize. Wojcicki initially focused on securing licensing agreements in which companies paid to use customized versions of Google's search tool on their websites. Google gained significant visibility in mid-2000 when the company entered into an agreement to become the search provider for the website Yahoo!, which at that time provided a directory of websites but did not yet have a search engine of its own.

Google's strategy for generating revenue changed in late 2000 with the introduction of advertisements. Initially, Google allowed businesses to purchase text-only advertisements that appeared on pages of search results. This product, known as AdWords, is based on the concept of keywords. For example, an online electronics store can pay for a keyword such as the name of a specific brand and model of television. When a Google user searches for that television, they will see a targeted advertisement for that business and potentially choose to purchase a new television from that store. This allows businesses to target only users who are likely interested in a product or service rather than waste money showing advertisements to uninterested viewers.

## ADSENSE

While Google was able to offer advertisers the chance to reach new audiences, the effectiveness of these advertisements was limited by the fact that they only appeared on Google search pages. In addition, the company sought to offer individual companies and website owners the opportunity to host advertisements on their sites and earn revenue. Wojcicki took the lead in supervising the development of a contextual advertising system that would place advertisements on sites other than Google. Google announced the launch of this system in March of 2003 and only a month later purchased the company Applied Semantics, adopting its contextual search system, AdSense.

Website owners enrolled in AdSense are able to designate areas on their websites in which advertisements will appear. Unlike advertisements based on simple keywords, AdSense ads placed on a website are based on the content of the website itself. When a user clicks on an advertisement, the website's owner receives a portion of the money that the original advertiser paid to Google. In recognition of her work with AdSense, Wojcicki was awarded the Google Founders' Award. When asked about her contributions, former Google CEO Eric Schmidt told Jefferson Graham for *USA Today* (5 July 2007), "There are no sets of words that can be used to describe Susan's contribution to the company." He added, "She's historic, in terms of our company's founding."

As AdSense became increasingly popular, Wojcicki continued to manage Google's advertising efforts, supervising the company's move into such areas as mobile advertising and display advertising. "We used to have a one-size fits-all approach," Wojcicki told Howard. "We're starting to think about how we can make ads richer, really creative and make sure we're always giving the best information to users." These efforts have been extraordinarily successful; by 2011, her department was responsible for more than 90 percent of Google's revenue. Wojcicki herself has benefited professionally from her success, serving as vice president of product management before rising to the position of senior vice president of advertising in late 2010.

## ACQUISITION AND INNOVATION

As Google expanded, Wojcicki's role in the company expanded as well. She supervised a number of projects that both broadened the vision of the company and tied in to its existing initiatives.

"We're a search company, and we'll always be a search company," she told Antony Bruno for *Billboard* (22 July 2006). "Our mission is to enable users to connect to the right information when they want it."

One such project was Google Video, which launched in 2005. The site allowed users to search for videos online as well as to upload videos that could then be viewed by the public and even embedded in other sites. While the site initially attracted users, the immediate success of rival video site YouTube stymied Google Video's development. "We quickly realized that YouTube was generating a lot more traffic and it was more popular," Wojcicki told Howard. In response, Google purchased YouTube in late 2006. Wojcicki played a key role in the acquisition. "It's very hard when you build a product to admit that there's this other product that's better—and you're going to pay $1.65 billion for it," she admitted. "The lesson that I learned was that when you make a mistake, admit it as soon as possible."

Wojcicki was also an essential contributor to Google's acquisition of the digital marketing company DoubleClick. Acquired in early 2008 for more than three billion dollars, DoubleClick specializes in creating display advertisements that feature images, videos, or animations in addition to text. As part of Google's stable of advertising initiatives, DoubleClick allows a variety of businesses and other advertisers to create and manage complex advertising campaigns and provides website owners with an additional potential source of revenue.

Mobil advertising represents the next major challenge for Wojcicki and her department. "Mobile is an incredibly fast-growing market, and will continue to be," she told Howard. "Think about how fast users are adopting mobile phones." She has noted that the first step will be optimizing both advertisers' websites and the advertisements themselves for mobile viewing. Google's efforts to develop and improve mobile advertising, she wrote in an official blog post announcing the acquisition of the mobile advertising company AdMob (21 May 2010), will benefit "mobile developers and publishers who will get better advertising solutions, marketers who will find new ways to reach consumers, and users who will get better ads and more free content."

## ADVANCING WOMEN IN TECHNOLOGY

Many profiles of Wojcicki have focused on the fact that she was both the first woman to work for Google and the first to give birth while employed there. Wojcicki herself tends to deemphasize these points, focusing instead on her accomplishments. "What's important is that I do my job really well, that I build great products and that I'm a great leader," she explained to Howard. "All those things matter independent of gender."

Nevertheless, Wojcicki recognizes that her status as a woman and an executive at one of the world's best-known technology companies makes her unusual. "I do think there's a responsibility for me to support other women at Google," she told Howard. As the first woman to give birth while at Google, Wojcicki was responsible for convincing the company's leadership to establish on-site childcare services. She regularly appears at events focused on women in technology, has participated in mentorship programs organized by *Fortune* magazine and the US State Department, and was included in the *Forbes* list of the world's most powerful women in 2011 and 2012.

In an article in *Time* magazine (2 Nov. 2011), Wojcicki offered advice to woman seeking to enter the technology field. "I always like to remind women that you don't *need* to have science or technology degrees to build a career in tech," she wrote. "All tech companies need sales, business development, marketing or finance." She continued, "The possibilities are endless. . . . If you come up with the next best thing in a fast and growing global market, it doesn't matter what gender or background you are."

## PERSONAL LIFE

Wojcicki married Dennis Troper on August 23, 1998. Troper joined Google as well, eventually becoming the project management director responsible for the company's social networking site, Google+. The couple has four children. When not working to improve Google's advertising and other services, Wojcicki enjoys raising chickens in her backyard, an activity that she described to Howard as "a universal language." She explained, "With technology, some people are more into than others. But everyone cares about growing things and animals."

## SUGGESTED READING

Graham, Jefferson. "The House That Helped Build Google." *USA Today*. USA Today, 5 July 2007. Web. 18 Dec. 2012.

Howard, Caroline. "Google's Susan Wojcicki Takes Lead of Engineering and Ads." *Forbes*. Forbes, 6 May 2011. Web. 18 Dec. 2012.

Miller, Claire Cain. "Google Promotes Susan Wojcicki, Advertising Executive." *Bits*. New York Times Co., 25 Oct. 2010. Web. 18 Dec. 2012.

"Susan Wojcicki ('98): Responsible for 96% of Google Revenue." *Media Relations*. UCLA Anderson School of Management, 27 Apr. 2012. Web. 18 Dec. 2012.

Wojcicki, Susan. "Good News about Women in Tech." *Time*. Time, 2 Nov. 2011. Web. 18 Dec. 2012.

—*Joy Crelin*

# Shinya Yamanaka

**Born:** September 4, 1962
**Occupation:** Japanese physician and researcher

In 2006, Japanese physician and researcher Shinya Yamanaka revolutionized stem cell research when he discovered a novel way to generate stem cells from existing cells in the human body. He adopted this approach after visiting a friend's fertility clinic during the late 1990s. "Watching the embryos, I felt that if there was a way to find cures for human diseases without destroying [the embryos], then that's what I should pursue," he recalled to Prashant Nair for the *Proceedings of the National Academy of Sciences* (12 June 2012). By 2006, Yamanaka was able to generate mouse skin cells into induced pluripotent stem (iPS) cells, embryonic-like stem cells that are derived from adult tissue and can differentiate into any other type of cell. A year later, he was able to produce the same result with adult human skin cells.

Yamanaka's efforts garnered him recognition within the scientific community. In 2011, he was named a co-recipient of the Wolf Prize, which is regarded as one of the most prestigious awards in medicine. The following year the Nobel Committee awarded him the 2012 Nobel Prize in Physiology or Medicine.

## AN EARLY INTEREST IN MEDICINE

Yamanaka was born on September 4, 1962, in Osaka, the largest city in western Japan. He lived there with his parents and older sister before moving to Nara at the age of ten. Growing up, Yamanaka was a naturally curious child, often playing with the various machines at his father's small factory, which was adjacent to the family home. While attending Tennoji Junior High School and High School, he developed an interest in math and science. He also practiced judo, a sport that inspired his decision to study medicine. "I suffered from bone fractures more than 10 times from playing judo in school," he told Nair. "I went to orthopedic clinics so often, it was natural for me to be interested in orthopedic surgery."

Yamanaka also credited his parents as early influences. "My father and my mother encouraged me to do whatever I wanted to do," he said in an interview posted at the Academy of Achievement website (6 July 2008). "I didn't have any physicians in my family, but since my father told me I can do whatever I want, that was why I decided . . . to be a doctor."

In 1981, upon completing high school, Yamanaka studied medicine at Kobe University, where he also played rugby. He first developed a passion for laboratory work while helping to perform autopsies and conducting research into alcoholism. After obtaining his medical degree in

Scanpix Sweden/Reuters/Landov

1987, he embarked on a residency in orthopedic surgery at National Osaka Hospital but seriously began to reconsider his choice two years later, when he operated on a patient for the first time, removing a benign tumor. "An ordinary orthopedic surgeon would take only ten minutes to finish, but to the utter amazement of my supervisor and nurses, it took me a total of two hours," he said during his acceptance speech at the 2010 Kyoto Prize. "I thought I was useless as a surgeon and began thinking of ways that I could be of some help."

## A SWITCH IN FOCUS

Yamanaka decided to shift his focus to laboratory research. In 1989, he pursued doctoral studies in pharmacology at Osaka City University's Graduate School of Medicine, under the guidance of professors Kenjiro Yamamoto and Katsuyuki Miura. Yamanaka conducted experiments involving a blood protein known as platelet-activating factor (PAF) and sought to prove that PAF played a part in reducing blood pressure in dogs. What he discovered was that administering an inhibitor of a lipid found in PAF had an unexpected result. Rather than keeping the dogs' blood pressure from going down, as had been originally predicted, it had the opposite effect. This surprising finding was published in the May 1992 issue of *Circulation Research*, the official journal of the American Heart Association; it further sparked Yamanaka's interest in research.

## "KNOCKOUT" MICE

While attending graduate school, Yamanaka also became fascinated with biomedical research after coming across a paper about genetically engineered, or "knockout," mice that detailed how researchers could select any gene and produce a mouse that lacked that gene. "I was astonished by mouse transgenesis and gene targeting, which specifically induce or delete a gene of interest, because no pharmacological agents could perform such miracles," Yamanaka wrote for *Nature Medicine* (Oct. 2009). In 1992, upon completing his PhD, he applied for postdoctoral positions at several research labs in the United States, since no research institutions in Japan were working with transgenic technology. By November of that year, he had accepted a fellowship from Thomas Innerarity, a senior investigator at the San Francisco, California-based Gladstone Institute of Cardiovascular Diseases, a nonprofit company focused on research into cardiovascular, viral, and neurological diseases.

Yamanaka's assignment at Gladstone involved performing experiments on transgenetic, or genetically engineered, mice to uncover new methods of reducing low-density lipoprotein, or "bad cholesterol," a leading cause of atherosclerosis, or heart disease. (The chief component of bad cholesterol is apolipoprotein B [apoB] protein, which is normally found in the liver and in the intestines.) Yamanaka was able to locate APOBEC1, an enzyme that shortens the apoB protein and makes it less harmful. Since this enzyme is present in the small intestines but inactive in the liver, Yamanaka and his Gladstone colleagues believed that by triggering this enzyme in the liver, they could create the version of the apoB protein that could lower bad cholesterol. "To our surprise, however, the transgenic mice developed liver tumors," Yamanaka explained in *Nature Medicine*. "Naturally, we were disappointed, but at the same time we became very interested in the molecular mechanisms of this totally unexpected finding. We identified a novel target of Apobec1, Nat1, which was aberrantly edited in the transgenic mouse livers."

## NAT1 GENE STUDIES

Next, Yamanaka began studying the function of the newly discovered NAT1 gene, which was responsible for the tumor growth in the livers. He also wanted to figure out whether cancer would develop in mice that did not contain the NAT1 gene. In order to create genetically engineered mice without NAT1, Yamanaka would have to use mouse embryonic stem (ES) cells, since they have a high proliferation rate and are also pluripotent, or capable of developing into many types of individual cells, including skin, muscle, and blood. With the help of Gladstone assistant investigator Robert V. Farese and his research associate Heather Myers, Yamanaka learned how to create embryonic stem cells. "At the time, the Farese lab was the only lab at Gladstone with the tools to develop embryonic stem cell cultures, and a lot of scientists would come asking us for help," Myers recalled in a profile of Yamanaka that is posted on the Gladstone Institutes website. "But Dr. Yamanaka was one of the few who wanted to take part in every step. He kept saying he wanted to learn it all himself so he wouldn't have to keep asking me for help all the time."

Yamanaka's tenure at Gladstone ended in 1996, when he returned to his native Japan because of family issues. In addition to accepting an assistant professorship in the pharmacology department at his alma mater, Osaka City University, he continued to perform research on the NAT1 gene, experimenting on knockout mice that he had brought back from Gladstone. What Yamanaka discovered was that the NAT1 gene is essential for early development in mice. He made another discovery: Although the ES cells in the NAT1 gene reproduce at a normal rate, they lack the ability to properly differentiate. As a result of this discovery, he decided to switch the focus of his research. "This unexpected finding changed the meaning of mouse ES cells to me from research tool to research subject," he recounted in *Nature Medicine*. "I became interested in how ES cells maintain their differentiation ability while rapidly proliferating."

### EMBRYONIC STEM CELL RESEARCH

However, Yamanaka's work with the NAT1 gene failed to generate sufficient interest from fellow researchers at Osaka City University's medical school and from medical journals. Yamanaka was equally frustrated by the lack of significant funding, as well as by the inordinate amount of time he spent every week cleaning out mice cages by himself. "I grew so depressed from the lack of support that I considered quitting," he said to Martin Fackler for the *New York Times* (11 Dec. 2007). "No one understood me." Yamanaka found renewed purpose following two landmark nuclear transplantation cases: British embryologist Sir Ian Wilmut's 1997 cloning of a sheep, Dolly, using a single adult sheep cell, and the 1998 announcement by James A. Thomson, a University of Wisconsin–Madison professor, that he successfully generated the first human embryonic stem cells from human embryos. The idea of cellular, or nuclear, reprogramming was initially established in 1962 by Sir John Gurdon, who created a tadpole by using the intestinal cell of an adult frog.

A year later, Yamanaka accepted a position as an associate professor at the Nara Institute of Science and Technology (NAIST), where he was also given the opportunity to oversee a knockout mouse research facility. Sparked by Wilmut's and Thomson's landmark achievements, as well

as his own personal interest in ES cells, Yamanaka decided to make embryonic stem cells the long-term focus for his laboratory. At the time, stem cell research was coming under fire from the international medical community for its ethical implications, which arose from opposition to harvesting cells from human embryos discarded by fertility clinics.

Following a 1999 visit to his friend's fertility clinic, Yamanaka became determined to come up with another option to circumvent the moral issues involved with human stem cell research. "When I saw the embryo, I suddenly realized there was such a small difference between it and my daughters," he told Fackler. "I thought, we can't keep destroying embryos for our research."

### A NEW VISION

For his lab's long-term mission, Yamanaka envisioned generating cells that function like embryonic stem cells from adult somatic cells (i.e. skin or blood cells), instead of using human stem cells. Yamanaka sought to prove that the same genetic factors that sustain pluripotency of mouse ES cells could also be capable of reprogramming adult somatic cells back to an embryonic state.

Backed by three talented graduate students, an assistant, and generous funding from NAIST, Yamanaka painstakingly researched the findings from evolving embryonic stem cell studies and identified about one hundred transcription factors that are responsible for instructing mouse ES cells to develop, or turn into, other types of cells. From 2000 to 2004, he assembled a catalog of the twenty-four most promising combination of genes that may be able to cause pluripotency in adult mouse cells, with the hope of eventually replicating this in human cells.

### LANDMARK STEM CELL FINDINGS

However, Yamanaka knew that he would eventually encounter difficulty obtaining human ES cells, since NAIST did not have a medical school or hospital. With that in mind, he left NAIST in 2004—with his lab researchers and knockout mice in tow—and accepted a professorial position at Kyoto University's Institute for Frontier Medical Sciences. The recipient of a 2004 research grant from the Inamori Foundation, Yamanaka tested the twenty-four candidate genes in knockout mice and identified four genes—Oct-3/4, Sox2, Klf4, and c-Myc—that could turn mouse skin cells into ES-like cells. He and his research team combined those four genes with a retrovirus. They then inserted this mixture into the nucleus of mouse fibroblast (connective tissue) cells, successfully transforming the skin cells into ES-like cells, which they called induced pluripotent stem cells.

Yamanaka published his landmark finding in the August 2006 issue of the medical journal *Cell*. He made headlines again a year later, when he succeeded in generating iPS cells from adult human skin cells, or fibroblasts. The latter finding proved significant, since it provided an alternative method of obtaining human stem cells without the controversial use of human embryos. In 2008, Yamanaka made two important contributions to stem cell research: the successful generation of iPS cells without the c-Myc gene, making the cells noncancerous, and the creation of iPS cells from mouse liver and stomach cells. Yamanaka is working toward using iPS cell technology to develop new drugs to treat illnesses such as Parkinson's disease, diabetes, and blood diseases. He hopes to be able to conduct clinical trials on human patients eventually.

## RECOGNITION OF STEM CELL RESEARCH ACHIEVEMENTS

Yamanaka's accomplishments in stem cell biology have earned him numerous accolades, most notably the Robert Koch Prize (2008), the Albert Lasker Basic Medical Research Award (2009) from the Lasker Foundation, the Kyoto Prize in Advanced Technology (2010), the Wolf Prize in Medicine (2011), and the Millennium Technology Award (2012). He received his highest honor in 2012, when he was awarded the Nobel Prize in Physiology or Medicine—an award he shared with Gurdon. With his Nobel win, Yamanaka also became the seventh scientist to capture both the Kyoto Prize and the Nobel Prize. He is also a member of the US National Academy of Sciences.

Since 2007, Yamanaka has served as a senior investigator at Gladstone Institutes and as a professor of anatomy at University of California, San Francisco. He divides his time between the United States and Japan, where he works as director at Kyoto University's Center for iPS Cell Research and Application.

Yamanaka and his wife, Chika, a dermatologist, are parents to two daughters, both medical students. He is also an avid marathon runner, participating in the 2011 Osaka Marathon, as well as the 2012 Tokyo Marathon and the 2012 Kyoto Marathon.

## SUGGESTED READING

Fackler, Martin. "Risk Taking Is in His Genes." *New York Times*. New York Times Co., 11 Dec. 2007. Web. 14 Apr. 2013.

Geddes, Linda. "Japan's Yamanaka Wins Nobel for Stem Cell Breakthrough." *New Scientist*. Reed Business Information, 15 Dec. 2007. Web. 14 Apr. 2013.

Nair, Prashant. "Profile of Shinya Yamanaka." *The Proceedings of the National Academy of Sciences* 109.24 (2012): n.pag. Web. 14 Apr. 2012.

"The Nobel at Gladstone: The Postdoc Years." *Gladstone Institutes*. Gladstone Institutes, n.d. Web. 14 Apr. 2013.

"Shinya Yamanaka Biography: Embryonic Stem Cell Research." Achievement.org. Academy of Achievement, 18 Jan. 2013. Web. 14 Apr. 2013.

Yamanaka, Shinya. "Ekiden to iPS Cells." *Nature Medicine* 15.10 (2009): n.pag. Web. 14 Apr. 2012.

—*Bertha Muteba*

# Samar Yazbek

**Born:** August 18, 1970
**Occupation:** Journalist and author

Samar Yazbek is an award-winning Syrian journalist and novelist who received the PEN Pinter Prize for her book *A Woman in the Crossfire: Diaries of the Syrian Revolution* (2012). She shared the award with British poet Carol Ann Duffy, who personally selected Yazbek for the award as an international writer of courage. Yazbek's book, which was translated into English by Max Weiss, is her account of the first one hundred days of the bloody Syrian revolution that began in March 2011.

Yazbek was a well-known writer from a powerful family that enjoyed some amount of political security, but her attempts to report the events of the uprising were met with chilling intimidation tactics from the government and opposition from her own family, who later disowned her. A published novelist, Yazbek presents her own struggle in her diaries in the lyrical prose of fiction: "I would pretend I was a character on paper, not made of flesh and blood, or that I was reading about a blindfolded woman forcibly taken to an unknown location, to be insulted and spat upon because she had the gall to write something true that displeased the tyrant. At this point in my fantasy I would feel strong and forget all about how weak my body was, about the vile smells and the impending unknown."

Yazbek fled Syria with her teenage daughter in July 2011. She has said that she feared for her daughter's life. The two women now live in exile in Paris. Despite the protests of her closest friends, Yazbek has visited Syria in secret several times to assuage the guilt she felt for leaving the country.

## BORN INTO THE ALAWITE CLAN

Yazbek was born in Jableh, a city on the Mediterranean coast of Syria, on August 18, 1970, the same year Hafez al-Assad came to power and established a dictatorship under the Ba'ath Party. Yazbek was the daughter of a wealthy family in the small but powerful Alawite clan, the same clan as Syria's ruling family and most of the country's elites, though they account for only

© Rikard Stadler/Demotix/Corbis

about 12 percent of Syria's population. Hafez al-Assad's presidency, captured by force in a coup, brought the minority Alawites, who follow a branch of Shia Islam, to power over the Sunni majority. The iron rule of Bashar al-Assad, his son, has perpetuated that power.

The current uprising against the Assad regime has been called a sectarian war—a characterization Yazbek vehemently disagrees with—and threatens to oust the Alawites from their advantageous position. Despite this, a number of Alawites, like Yazbek, have publicly joined the revolution. She told Aida Edemariam for the *Guardian* (12 Oct. 2012), "It's a revolution of the poor against the rich. . . . It's a problem of conscience. It's not a problem of Sunni, Shiite, or anything else."

Yazbek has five brothers and two sisters; she refuses to share more information about her family for fear of putting them in more danger from the regime. She told Edemariam that prior to the uprising, her family disapproved of her racy and politically provocative novels. Since then, she has been declared a traitor to the government, and her family has disowned her. Supporters of the regime refuse to speak to her family now, she told Edemariam, explaining, "They think my brothers are not men because they didn't kill me."

## BREAKING OUT ON HER OWN

Yazbek was rebellious from an early age. Even though women in Syria enjoy a better status than women in other Middle Eastern countries, Yazbek was frustrated that the life she could reasonably expect for herself was far different from the lives available to her brothers. At age sixteen, she ran away from home. "I wanted to be liberated,

I always felt caught . . . like all teenagers, you know?" she told Edemariam. "But I actually did it. And it's horrible in our society—it's a shame for the family, for the girl—many people want to kill their daughters. Everyone thought I wanted to be with a man, but it's not true—I wanted to be alone, I wanted to make my own future, I wanted to be a writer."

Yazbek returned home, only to run away again at the age of nineteen. She lived alone and then married a man in a civil ceremony. The couple moved to the Mediterranean island country of Cyprus, where Yazbek gave birth to a baby girl. She left her husband after four years of marriage and moved to Damascus, Syria's capital, with her daughter. There, they lived in one room outside of the city, while Yazbek worked an administrative job twelve hours a day. Though she barely kept herself and her daughter out of utter poverty, she refused to accept help from her family.

Yazbek, who cites tenth-century intellectual Abū Hayyān Al-Tawhīdī and Virginia Woolf as literary influences, went on to earn a degree in Arabic literature and gain recognition as a journalist, author, and writer for Syrian television and films. She received an award from UNICEF for a television script she wrote about child brides and edited a feminist e-zine called *Nesa Syria* (Women of Syria).

## *CINNAMON* AND OTHER NOVELS

According to Neil MacFarquhar for the *New York Times* (23 Nov. 2012), Yazbek has written "nearly a dozen books" in Arabic, including five novels. Her first novel was called *Tiflat as-sama* (Heavenly Girl, 2002). Her second, *Silsal* (Clay, 2005), tells the story of two military officers within the Assad regime. One officer approves of the elder Assad's coup in 1970, while the other does not. Though the two Alawite men are friends and share religious views, their political views come between them. "I tried to describe how the regime has destroyed all human relationships, all values," she told Frederic Joignot for the French newspaper *Le Monde* (7 Jan. 2012).

Her 2008 novel, *Ra'ihat al-qirfah*, was translated into English by Emily Danby and published as *Cinnamon* in 2012. It is the story of two unhappy women living in Damascus. Hanan is a wealthy woman who hates her husband; Aliyah, who comes from a violent, poor neighborhood, is a maid in Hanan's house. The two women pursue an erotic relationship to find solace from oppression. In addition to its exploration of lesbian relationships, *Cinnamon* also tackles themes of gender and class inequality against the backdrop of the pre-revolution Assad regime. On some level, all of Yazbek's novels address the biggest taboos in Arab culture: politics, sex, and religion. Some of her books were banned, but prior to the uprising, the Assad regime largely chose to look the other way in terms of her political subject matter.

Her most recent novel, *Laha maraya* (In her mirrors, 2010), is a *Romeo and Juliet*–style love story initially set in 2000, after the death of Hafez al-Assad and on the cusp of his son's rise to power. Laila, an Alawite, and her lover, Said, relive their story of passion and painful separation through the ages. It is based on the traditional Alawite belief in reincarnation.

## FROM UPRISING TO ARMED REBELLION

Bashar al-Assad assumed power in Syria in 2000, after his father's death, and initiated a series of economic reforms that benefited the country's wealthiest citizens, including Yazbek's family and other Alawites, but devastated the rest of the population. Amid terrible poverty, starvation, and an overbearing regime, a few Syrians called for a revolution after witnessing the uprisings in Tunisia and Egypt, but at least initially, only a small number committed themselves to the cause. This could probably be attributed to the far-reaching power of what Joe Sterling for CNN.com (1 Mar. 2012) called "the Goliath-sized, all-seeing and all-knowing security and spying apparatus" of the Assad regime.

Then in February, several teenage boys were arrested for scrawling anti-regime graffiti on a wall in the small town of Daraa, near the Jordanian border. Reports that the boys were being beaten and tortured in prison spread, and several peaceful protests were held across the country demanding their release. The protestors were met with brute force—at a demonstration in Daraa on March 18, 2011, police opened fire, killing four people—but the regime's powerful tactics only strengthened the resistance. According to Yazbek, the Syrian people had reached a point of no return. "When the repression became more violent and wild, it changed our relationship to fear," she told Joignot.

## *A WOMAN IN THE CROSSFIRE*

Yazbek participated in a demonstration in Damascus in February, thus beginning her involvement in the uprising, but her diary, which she later published as *A Woman in the Crossfire*, begins in March. During the whole of Yazbek's participation, which is chronicled in her book, the uprising was brutally violent yet still bore traits of a civilian resistance. The Free Syrian Army was created at the end of July, made up of military defectors. As the rebels and other opposition groups took up arms, the resistance became increasingly military.

Yazbek began sharing her opposition to the regime, as well as written accounts of the violence she had witnessed and heard from others, on Facebook and rebel websites. Each update, made from a hacked computer in a bugged apartment, triggered a threat from the regime. According to Yazbek, the regime was (and, to some extent, still is) focused on painting the revolution as sectarian violence between the Alawites and Sunni fundamentalists; Yazbek's activism did not fit Assad's narrative of a united, pro-government Alawite community. Fortunately for Yazbek, the regime seemed reluctant to kill her, but it did not shy away from harassment and intimidation. She was arrested five times, and in her hometown, people distributed leaflets that called for her death. In her book, Yazbek describes being briefly blindfolded after an interrogation and then led through a series of torture cells where the dead and still-living bodies of young men hung suspended from metal clamps. When one man tried to raise his head, she saw that he did not have a face.

The first entry in her diary is a piece that appeared on the Internet in April 2011, a month after her tour of Assad's torture chambers. She wrote, "I curl up into myself: I am an infiltrator now among my family. An infiltrator in my bed. An infiltrator in a silent and impossible love. . . . I slip into the sadness of every Syrian who passes before my gaze. I listen to the sounds of bullets and the shouts and the prayers. I am a piece of flesh that walks in the morning from house to house, that tries to find a last piece of paper for salvation and to claim that it is doing anything at all."

## PUBLICATION AND CRITICAL RECEPTION

After its publication in English in 2012, Yazbek's *A Woman in the Crossfire* was praised for its raw reportage from inside a revolution that was continuing to unfold. The book combines Yazbek's own observations with the testimonies of others. It also includes several interview transcripts. The book, Edemariam wrote, "is drenched in fear and grief. [Yazbek] chain-smokes, weeps and screams through it, and cannot sleep without tranquilisers." Throughout the arrests, the intimidation, and the falling out with her family, her daughter begs her to stop her activities. In the end, it was fear for her daughter's safety that spurred Yazbek to leave in July 2011; this is where her diary ends.

Yazbek has been praised for her nuanced and often poetic approach. She imbued her nonfiction account with the detail of a novelist. Hadani Ditmars wrote of the book for the *Globe and Mail* (16 Nov. 2012), "The only relief amid the litany of despair—and the verbatim transcripts of interviews with young men and women of all creeds who have been tortured, raped and stomped on by sadistic regime security agents—comes in the form of Yazbek's often lyrical reflections on her city and her homeland."

In 2012, Yazbek was awarded the PEN Pinter Prize. Established by the British playwright Harold Pinter, it is awarded each year to a British writer, who in turn chooses an international writer who has been persecuted for his or her work to share the prize. Yazbek was chosen by, and shares the prize with, the poet Carol Ann Duffy. She dedicated the award to the men and women of the Syrian resistance. Yazbek was also featured in the 2012 documentary *Comme si nous attrapions un cobra* (*As If We Were Catching a Cobra*), directed by Hala Alabdalla.

### ACTIVISM IN EXILE

Yazbek has continued her activism from her exile in Paris and has traveled to other countries to speak out about the necessity of Western intervention in Syria—a tactic she did not always support. She has criticized the United States and other Western countries for their silence. "There is a complicity with Assad in the West, even if it's not official, or said, or clear," she told Edemariam. "But they are helping him to stay. And that is very dangerous for the Syrian people." Yazbek has high hopes for democracy in a post-Assad Syria, and as a committed secular feminist, she is currently working to strengthen rights for women in the country.

### SUGGESTED READING

Edemariam, Aida. "Syrian Writer Samar Yazbek: 'A Woman Like Me Makes Life Difficult.'" *Guardian*. Guardian News and Media, 12 Oct. 2012. Web. 11 June 2013.

Joignot, Frederic. "Yazbek in *Le Monde*: Syria Is Defying Fear." *RAYA*. RAYA, 11 Jan. 2012. Web. 11 June 2013.

MacFarquhar, Neil. "Branded a Betrayer for Embracing Syria's Rebels." *New York Times*. New York Times Co., 23 Nov. 2012. Web. 11 June 2013.

Perriman, Grace. "Non-Fiction Heroine." Rev. of *A Woman in the Crossfire: Diaries of the Syrian Revolution*, by Samar Yazbek. *Majalla*. Al Majalla, 8 Jan. 2013. Web. 11 June 2013.

Sterling, Joe. "Daraa: The Spark That Lit the Syrian Flame." *CNN.com*. Cable News Network, 1 Mar. 2012. Web. 11 June 2013.

—Molly Hagan

# Jennifer Yuh Nelson

**Born:** May 7, 1972
**Occupation:** Director and artist

"When people think of a movie director, they likely would not think of someone like me," Jennifer Yuh Nelson wrote for the Women Worth Watching website (18 Apr. 2011). "I don't chomp cigars, make virtual movie screen shapes with my hands or hang out at hot spots with even hotter celebrities. In fact, very few directors fit such

© Mark Savage/Corbis

stereotypes. . . . They are all varied and unique. I for example am a soft-spoken, Korean American woman who lives a very tame and settled life. But the one thing that binds us all is a love of film."

Filmgoers undeniably love Yuh Nelson's work. Her feature-film directorial debut, the animated 2011 film *Kung Fu Panda 2*, earned more than $660 million at the global box office, making her the highest-grossing female director in the world to date. As John Young wrote for *Entertainment Weekly* (29 Aug. 2011), it was "one small step for giant panda, one giant leap for female filmmakers."

### EARLY YEARS

Jennifer Yuh Nelson was born Jennifer Yuh in South Korea on May 7, 1972, and immigrated to the United States with her family when she was four years old. She had started drawing even before then, along with her two older sisters, who were also artistically inclined. Yuh Nelson told David Poland on his talk show *DP/30: Conversations about Movies* (13 Dec. 2011), hosted by the website Movie City News, that when she was growing up, "if there [was] a blank piece of paper around [in the house], it would get covered with pictures." Although her mother never pursued a professional career in the visual arts, she was highly skilled, and Yuh Nelson has told reporters that she spent many hours of her childhood watching her mother sketch and draw at the kitchen table. "I have a memory from age three, when I was still living in Korea, sitting at a table and watching my mother draw," she told an interviewer for *Variety* (3 Jan. 2012). "I was fascinated to see someone with so much control over a line, and I could only make a murky circle."

Upon their arrival in the United States, Yuh Nelson's family settled in Lakewood, a planned community in Los Angeles County, California, that was built after World War II. Yuh Nelson and her sisters often collaborated on creating elaborate scenarios that they would then sketch out on paper. "I have been . . . making movies in my head for almost as long [as I have been drawing]. In fact, drawing for me was a way to express those films when I had no other means of doing so," she wrote in her piece for the Women Worth Watching website. "I had no idea what career could use such a weird skill as drawing movies. But I did it because it brought me joy."

Yuh Nelson also enjoyed watching Disney films and science-fiction epics such as *Blade Runner* (1982) and *The Terminator* (1984), as well as martial-arts films. She particularly loved Hong Kong action films, which are known for their Hollywood-style exploits combined with Chinese storytelling and aesthetics. One particular subset of Hong Kong cinema is *wuxia*, a historical genre that commonly features fantastic elements such as mysticism and emphasizes the chivalric code of honor to which certain martial artists adhere, and *Kung Fu Panda* 2 was heavily influenced by Yuh Nelson's love of the form. "We based all the animal fighting forms on the traditional techniques of kung fu," Yuh Nelson said at a June 2013 global forum sponsored by *Fortune* magazine. "And [we] sought to instill the characters . . . with [the] nobility of true martial arts masters." She explained to Andrew Penn Romine for *Fantasy Magazine* (June 2011), "A lot of martial arts films have a sweet emotional core to them. The characters are motivated to do good."

## EDUCATION

Yuh Nelson's older sisters studied illustration at California State University, Long Beach, and when Yuh Nelson finished high school, she did the same. In a public service announcement that she made for the university system in 2011, she asserted that she had received a superlative education there, "worth far more than people are asked to pay [in tuition]." Among the school's other famed graduates are filmmaker Steven Spielberg and actor and comedian Steve Martin.

While at California State University, Yuh Nelson heard a talk given by a professional storyboard artist who had worked with Spielberg. The job of a storyboard artist is to sketch scenes from screenplays into comic book–style illustrations that help directors convey their vision to the actors and crew, particularly when complex scenes involving battles or chases need to be carefully plotted out ahead of time. Because Yuh Nelson had never heard of the profession, the lecture was revelatory. "My mind exploded," she wrote for Women Worth Watching. Although she had always loved the idea of being involved in filmmaking, she had never considered pursuing it

professionally. After that lecture, her attitude changed. In 1994 she graduated with a bachelor of fine arts degree in illustration and embarked on a search for work in the film industry.

## EARLY CAREER

Yuh Nelson quickly found work at Jetlag Productions, an animation studio that also employed one of her sisters. Jetlag created straight-to-video pictures, many of which were based on fairy tales or classic literature. Yuh Nelson began her career as a cleanup animator, refining the initial rough drafts that are prepared for the director of an animated film. She is credited as an assistant designer on several Jetlag productions, including *Happy, the Littlest Bunny* (1994), *Leo the Lion: King of the Jungle* (1994), *Cinderella* (1994), *A Christmas Carol* (1994), *Magic Gift of the Snowman* (1995), *Alice in Wonderland* (1995), *Jungle Book* (1995), and *Heidi* (1995).

In 1996 she joined Hanna-Barbera Productions, a venerable company whose shows had dominated the Saturday-morning airwaves from the late 1950s to the early 1990s. Yuh Nelson was hired to work on *The Real Adventures of Jonny Quest*, which was shown on the Cartoon Network and other Ted Turner–owned stations from 1996 to 1999. The program, a revival of the 1960s science-fiction/adventure cartoon *Jonny Quest*, follows the adventures of the titular hero, a teenage computer whiz who battles evildoers in a cyberspace realm known as Questworld. Yuh Nelson is credited as a character designer, background artist, or storyboard artist on several 1996 episodes.

Yuh Nelson also worked as a production illustrator and storyboard artist on the live-action science-fiction film *Dark City* (1998), work that took her to Australia for an extended period. Previously she had worked for a time in South Korea and Japan.

## HBO

After her stint at Hanna-Barbera, Yuh Nelson was hired as a visual-effects creator for the short-lived animated show *Spicy City*, which ran for only six episodes in 1997. The adult-oriented science-fiction series was set in a seedy, futuristic city and aired on HBO. Actor and singer Michelle Phillips provided the voice of the female lead, and the iconoclastic animator Ralph Bakshi—famed for the risqué cartoon comedy *Fritz the Cat* (1972), the first feature-length animated film to receive an X rating—served as executive producer and directed some of the episodes, in addition to voicing one of the characters.

Yuh Nelson remained at HBO for her next effort, the animated series *Spawn*, based on the popular comic book by Todd McFarlane. The series, for which she served at various times as director, storyboard artist, and character designer, aired from 1997 to 1999. Its antihero is a former Vietnam commando and CIA operative named Al Simmons who was burned to death by a man he believed to be his friend. By making a pact with an overlord of hell, Simmons is allowed to return to earth to seek revenge and to see his wife, Wanda, in exchange for serving in the overlord's army. Yuh Nelson directed all six episodes of the second season and two episodes of the third. The darkly atmospheric show resonated with audiences and critics alike, winning an Emmy Award in the category of outstanding animated program. Yuh Nelson enjoyed working on *Spawn*, she told Poland, because the show was "pushing what animation can do." She added, "In other parts of the world, it's not just a children's medium. It's just a medium."

## DREAMWORKS

In 1998 Yuh Nelson began working at Dream-Works Studios. At the time, her sister Catherine Yuh Rader was working as an artist at Pacific Data Images (PDI), a subsidiary of DreamWorks. The company was founded in 1994 by Steven Spielberg, former Walt Disney Company executive Jeffrey Katzenberg, and music mogul David Geffen. The same year Yuh Nelson signed on, the studio released its first two animated features, *Antz* and *The Prince of Egypt*. In the fall of 2004, the animation division of the studio was spun off into a publicly traded company, Dream-Works Animation, with Katzenberg as CEO.

Yuh Nelson's first DreamWorks project was *Spirit: Stallion of the Cimarron* (2002), for which she served as story artist; in fact, she had first applied to work at DreamWorks because she knew the company was producing *Spirit*, and she enjoyed drawing horses. The film, about a wild stallion who travels across the western frontier, befriending a young Lakota man and helping save an American Indian village, received mixed reviews. When the film was released, Mick LaSalle, expressing sentiments echoed by many other reviewers, wrote for the *San Francisco Chronicle* (24 May 2002), "The animation is . . . hit-and-miss. *Spirit* is excellent at duplicating kinetic camera movement. For example, the opening sequence, of a herd of horses galloping over the American plains of 125 years ago, is presented as if shot from a crane in one unbroken take. It's exhilarating. . . . Yet the drawing of the horses and the humans lacks the sort of detail we've come to expect. The faces and bodies are somewhat blocky and undefined." Dave Kehr wrote even more bluntly for the *New York Times* (24 May 2002), "The horses and the humans . . . look like refugees from a dull children's book."

Yuh Nelson next served as story artist on the 2005 film *Madagascar*, working directly under Yuh Rader, who was lead story artist. The animation won some praise: Roger Ebert described it in the *Chicago Sun-Times* (27 May 2005) as "good-looking in a retro cartoon way,"

and Michael Atkinson wrote for the *Village Voice* (17 May 2005), "Even as the references fall flat and the story plods, it's obvious the animation crew for the supporting creatures—including an unlucky duckling and a Mogwai bush baby—had the most fun."

## KUNG FU PANDA

In 2008 Yuh Nelson was credited as the head of story for *Kung Fu Panda*, a computer-animated martial-arts comedy about a bumbling panda bear, Po, who becomes a kung fu master and brings peace to his land, a *wuxia*-inspired version of ancient China. Although Yuh Nelson, who also directed the film's opening sequence, had previously waited for assignments from the DreamWorks higher-ups, when she heard about the concept for *Kung Fu Panda*, she approached them and asked to be allowed to work on the picture.

Many reviews specifically mention the opening sequence Yuh Nelson created. In an assessment for the *New York Times* (6 June 2008), for example, Manohla Dargis praised the "lovingly created animation, both computer generated and hand drawn," and wrote, "What charms the most about *Kung Fu Panda* is that it doesn't feel as if it's trying to be a live-action film. It's an animation through and through, starting with the stunningly beautiful opening dream sequence, a graphically bold hand-drawn interlude . . . that looks like an animated woodblock print with slashes of black and swaths of oxblood red. This opener is so striking and so visually different from most mainstream American animations that it takes a while [for the viewer] to settle into the more visually familiar look of the rest of the movie." For her storyboarding work on the movie, Yuh Nelson won an Annie Award, the United States' premier award for excellence in animation.

## TAKING OVER THE FRANCHISE

In 2011 DreamWorks released *Kung Fu Panda 2*, which pits Po against even more formidable enemies and explores his backstory further. This time, Yuh Nelson directed the entire feature-length film. "I was on the first movie for four and a half years, a very long time, and being familiar with the story, characters, nuances . . . when the option came up for the second film, they came to me about it and I said sure, I just wanted to keep going with it, keep working on the story and the characters because I liked them so much," she explained to Stan Robinson for the website Examiner (24 Feb. 2012). "I really didn't care [in] what capacity."

Yuh Nelson was joining a select group; in 2012, only about 14 percent of the director members of the Directors Guild of America were female. "I don't think about the gender thing very much," Yuh Nelson told Pamela McClintock for the *Hollywood Reporter* (8 Dec. 2011). "But when I speak at schools, I've had female students say to me afterwards, 'I never envisioned myself being a director, since I've never seen women do it.' But after seeing me, they can picture themselves directing, so maybe we'll see more female directors. And half of these kids in art and animation schools are girls."

*Kung Fu Panda 2* earned more than $660 million worldwide, including almost $100 million in China alone, signaling, as many financial reporters pointed out, a phenomenal growth in that country's film market. That $660 million figure made Yuh Nelson the highest-grossing female director in the world, breaking a record set by Phyllida Lloyd with 2008's *Mamma Mia!*, a live-action musical that earned almost $610 million globally. *Kung Fu Panda 2* was nominated for an Academy Award for best animated film, making Yuh Nelson the first female director ever to receive that particular honor. She also won an Annie Award for her directing. The *Kung Fu Panda* franchise has had a cultural effect beyond its box-office receipts: baseball star Pablo Sandoval was nicknamed Kung Fu Panda for his fierce but appealing demeanor, and in February 2011, Zoo Atlanta named its three-month-old baby panda Po in tribute to the then-upcoming sequel.

In 2012, Yuh Nelson began working on *Kung Fu Panda 3*, scheduled for release in December 2015. Of the several years it takes to create a single animated feature, she told an interviewer for the *Hollywood Reporter* (7 Dec. 2011), "A lot of the time in animation is spent getting the story right—that's something you can't rush."

When she is not working, Yuh Nelson enjoys spending time with her husband, Tom Nelson, whom she met while at HBO, and her nephews. She is a self-described video-game geek and is an avid supporter of the Burbank Animal Shelter.

## SUGGESTED READING

Kilday, Gregg. "DreamWorks Scores Two for the Home Team." *Hollywood Reporter* 17 Feb. 2012: 93. Print.

Sperling, Nicole. "Tough Enough." *Los Angeles Times*. Los Angeles Times, 25 May 2011. Web. 9 Sept. 2013.

Yuh Nelson, Jennifer. "Feature Interview: Jennifer Yuh Nelson, Director of *Kung Fu Panda 2*." Interview by Andrew Penn Romine. *Fantasy Magazine*. Fantasy Magazine, June 2011. Web. 9 Sept. 2013.

Yuh Nelson, Jennifer. "Jennifer Yuh Nelson, Dreamworks." *Women Worth Watching*. Diversity Journal, 18 Apr. 2011. Web. 9 Sept. 2013.

Yuh Nelson, Jennifer, and Angelina Jolie. "Angelina Jolie and Jennifer Yuh Nelson: Newest Members of a Very Small Club." Interview by Pamela McClintock. *Hollywood Reporter*. Hollywood Reporter, 8 Dec. 2011. Web. 9 Sept. 2013.

## SELECTED WORKS

*Spirit: Stallion of the Cimarron*, 2002; *Madagascar*, 2005; *Kung Fu Panda*, 2008; *Kung Fu Panda 2*, 2011

—*Mari Rich*

# OBITUARIES

## Chinua Achebe

**Born:** Ogidi, Nigeria; November 16, 1930
**Died:** Boston, Massachusetts; March 21, 2013
**Occupation:** Nigerian novelist

Chinua Achebe was a Nigerian novelist whose first novel, *Things Fall Apart* (1958), earned him international recognition. The novel was translated into forty-five languages and sold more than eight million copies, and it established themes that Achebe would explore throughout his literary career, including anticolonialism and the clash between Western civilization and Africa. In a 1965 interview, he referred to this confrontation between the two cultures as the main concern to most Africans. In his fiction, he attempted to unravel this conflict and expose the religious, social, and political underpinnings of the African people.

Achebe was born on November 16, 1930, in Ogidi, a small Igbo village in Nigeria that was then under British colonial rule. During his childhood, Achebe experienced the racism of British colonial rule and violence from various ethnic groups in Nigeria. These experiences would form the foundation for his best-selling novel, *Things Fall Apart*, which tells the story of Okonkwo, the protagonist who was caught in the crossroads between the two cultures. The novel illustrates how the Igbo culture was self-sustaining and prosperous on its own, but things began to "fall apart" with the arrival of the British. Ultimately, British colonial rule and the subsequent oppression resulted in turmoil and Okonkwo's suicide. His second novel, *No Longer at Ease* (1960), continues the story with Okonkwo's grandson, Obi, who learns to adapt to life under British colonial rule.

Achebe would later write about the Nigerian Civil War (1967–70), which resulted in the massacre of approximately thirty thousand Igbo people. A prominent example is his book of poetry, *Beware Soul Brother* (1971), which was inspired by the civil war and won the Commonwealth Poetry Prize. After the war, Achebe lived in Nigeria briefly before accepting teaching positions at the University of Connecticut and the University of Massachusetts. Achebe also taught at Bard College in New York, Brown University, and the University of Nigeria.

Achebe studied Western Literature at the University College of Ibadan, where he learned from mainly European teachers. He received numerous literary awards, including the prestigious Man Booker International Prize for lifetime achievement in 2007. In addition to his literary success, Achebe also worked in broadcasting at the Nigerian Broadcasting Cooperation in Lagos, Nigeria.

Achebe died in Boston, Massachusetts, on March 21, 2013. He was eighty-two years old. His survivors include his wife, Christie Chinwe Okoli; his two daughters, Chinelo and Nwando; and his two sons, Ikechukwu and Chidi.

*See Current Biography Illustrated 1992.*

## Giulio Andreotti

**Born:** Rome, Italy, January 14, 1919
**Died:** Rome, Italy, May 6, 2013
**Occupation:** Italian prime minister

An enigmatic leader who represented both Italy's post–World War II reconstruction, and the corruption that would eventually plague its government, Giulio Andreotti was the prime minister of Italy seven times overall. Ferociously loyal to the papacy, Andreotti struck a peculiar balance between devout moralist and political opportunist. He reportedly met his first pope—Pius XI—when he was a young boy. During his political career, Andreotti provided advice and was a close confidant to several popes. His ties to the Vatican were so deep, that Pope John XXIII informed him of the calling of the historic Second Vatican Council three days before its official announcement. Andreotti attended Mass every day. But his piety did not find its match in his propriety—Andreotti was an often harsh leader whose career was plagued by scandal, including allegations of conspiracy to murder and collusion with the Mafia. Andreotti's Christian Democratic Party—which he helped to resurrect alongside Alcide De Gasperi after the fall of Fascist Italy—became the dominant force in the country's postwar political world. But the party's power was built on a model of cronyism and corruption that spurred numerous government investigations over the years, and eventually led to its end in 1994.

Perhaps the most devastating and controversial incident to occur during his time as prime minister was the 1978 kidnapping and subsequent murder of former Prime Minister Aldo Moro at the hands of the Red Brigades—a Marxist-Leninist paramilitary group. A leader of the Christian Democratic Party, and Andreotti's longtime friend and sometime rival, Moro pleaded in letters to be freed by prisoner exchange. But Andreotti stuck to his resolution to not negotiate with terrorists, and weeks later, Moro's body was found in an old car in Rome. Near the end of his career, Andreotti was twice put on trial. In one case, he was accused of covertly working with the Mafia to obtain electoral support, ensuring his continued power. In the other, he was accused of having arranged for the murder of journalist Carmine Pecorelli in 1979. The editor of a small newspaper, Pecorelli was reported to have possessed evidence of Andreotti's involvement in the Moro murder. The case stayed in the courts for over twenty years, resulting in a conviction in 2002, and a subsequent overturning by Italy's court of cassation the following year.

Giulio Andreotti was born in Rome on January 14, 1919. His father was a teacher, but died when Andreotti was only one year old (some sources say he was two). He earned a law degree from the University of Rome in 1940, and served as the head of the Italian Catholic University federation from 1942 to 1945. It was during this time—when Andreotti was conducting research at the Vatican—that he met De Gasperi. Following the fall of Communism, Andreotti was president of the European Community in 1990. In this role, he worked to improve diplomatic ties with former Soviet bloc nations and to establish the European Central Bank. Andreotti died on May 6, 2013, in Rome. He was ninety-four. Andreotti is survived by his wife, Livia Danese, and four children.

*See Current Biography 1977.*

# Richard Artschwager

**Born:** Washington, DC; December 26, 1923
**Died:** Albany, New York; February 9, 2013
**Occupation:** Painter and sculptor

Richard Artschwager was an American artist known for his paintings, sculptures, installations, and conceptual art. Some of his best-known works include his sculpture, *Table with Pink Tablecloth* (1964), and his breakthrough piece, *Handle* (1962), a three-dimensional, wooden object that was hung on the wall like a painting. Artschwager's work has appeared in a number of art exhibitions, including the Centre Pompidou, Paris (1989), and two retrospectives for the Whitney Museum of American Art, New York (1988, 2012–13).

Born on December 26, 1923, Artschwager was the son of immigrants; his father was a German-born botanist and his mother, an artist, was Ukrainian. Artschwager followed in his father's footsteps and went to Cornell University, but his studies were interrupted when he was

drafted by the Army in 1944 to serve in Europe during World War II. He saw combat and was wounded in the Battle of the Bulge, a German counteroffensive that lasted from December 16, 1944, to January 28, 1945. After the war, he met and married Elfriede Wejmelka, his first of four wives (three of which ended in divorce), in 1946 while working in Vienna, Austria, where he was assigned to counterintelligence.

In 1947 he was discharged from the army and completed his undergraduate degree at Cornell. But soon thereafter, he decided to pursue art and studied at the Studio School in New York City. In order to support his family, he built and sold furniture in the 1950s, but he returned to art after his wood workshop was severely damaged by a fire in 1958. One of his first notable works was *Handle* (1962), and his first solo exhibit debuted in 1965 at the Leo Castelli Gallery in New York City. In the 1960s, he also created an art installation known as "Blps," (pronounced "blips") which are essentially black, abstract forms that are relatively small in size. They were made of black wood or vinyl.

Artschwager's work appears in the permanent collections of a number of art museums, including the Museum of Modern Art (MOMA) in New York City; the Art Institute of Chicago; and the Museum Ludwig in Cologne, Germany. The Whitney Museum of American Art produced its first retrospective exhibition of Artschwager's work in 1988. His second Whitney retrospective (titled "Richard Artschwager!") began in 2012 and will travel to the Hammer Museum in Los Angeles, California, and the Haus der Kunst in Munich, Germany, in 2013.

Artschwager died on February 9, 2013, in Albany, New York. He was eighty-nine years old. Artschwager is survived by his wife, Ann; his sister, Margarita Kay; his daughters, Eva and Clara; his son, Augustus; and his grandson.

*See Current Biography 1990.*

# Gae Aulenti

**Born:** Palazzolo dello Stella, Italy; December 4, 1927
**Died:** Milan, Italy; October 31, 2012
**Occupation:** Italian artist, designer, and architect

Gae Aulenti was a celebrated artist and architect known for her elaborate renovations, most notably the Gare d'Orsay in Paris, a former railroad station that she converted into a world-class art museum, the Musée d'Orsay. Her other significant renovations include the Palazzo Grassi, an art and historical museum in Venice, Italy; the Beaux Art Library that she converted into the San Francisco Art Museum; and the Museu Nacional d'Art de Catalunya, an exhibition hall in Barcelona.

After going against her parents' wishes and studying architecture at the Milan Polytechnic Institute, Aulenti became one of the few women architects working in post-World War II Italy. Her design aesthetic was part of the Neo-Liberty movement, which rejected modernism in favor of individual expression and an emphasis on preserving local buildings and architecture. Her career took off after designing showrooms for Gianni Agnelli, a prominent Italian businessman and head of the Italian car company, Fiat.

Aulenti's success culminated in her daring and radical design of the Musée d'Orsay in Paris, France. Her design for the museum received mixed reactions and harsh criticism, but the popularity of the museum was ultimately a huge success and attracted thousands of visitors every day after its completion in 1986. Also in Paris, Aulenti designed the contemporary art gallery in the Georges Pompidou Center. Her considerable success in architecture earned her the prestigious Praemium Imperiale award in 1991.

In addition to architecture, Aulenti was also a renowned furniture maker and designed for Knoll, Zanotta, Kartell, and other esteemed design houses. One of her more famous furniture pieces is a coffee table made of thick glass, which can be seen today in the Museum of Modern Art in New York City. Aulenti also dabbled in stage design for Luca Ronconi's productions, including *Samstag aus Licht* (1984).

Gae Aulenti died at her home in Milan on October 31, 2012, from a chronic illness. She was eighty-four years old. Twice divorced, Aulenti is survived by her daughter, Giovanna Buzzi, a notable costume designer, and one granddaughter.

*See Current Biography 1999.*

## Letitia Baldrige

**Born:** Miami, Florida; February 9, 1926
**Died:** Bethesda, Maryland; October 29, 2012
**Occupation:** American etiquette expert and public relations executive

Letitia "Tish" Baldrige was best-known as Jacqueline Kennedy's social secretary and chief of staff. As the social secretary in the White House, Baldrige would coordinate social events—dinner parties, ballets, musicals, concerts—and oversee administrative tasks, such as handling the First Lady's mail. But Baldrige was also valuable to President Kennedy, who claimed she helped him through many social situations, including reminding him to toast at events. Baldrige, in other words, was an important social presence in the White House and a well-known expert in etiquette.

Letitia Baldrige was born in Miami, Florida on February 9, 1926, but she grew up in Omaha, Nebraska. Her family was politically active: her father, Howard Malcolm Baldrige, was a lawyer and served two terms as a Republican congressman; her brother, Malcolm Baldrige, was the Commerce secretary for the Reagan administration. Baldrige met Jacqueline Onassis while attending Miss Porter's School in Connecticut. After graduating from Vassar College with the future First Lady, she served briefly as the social secretary to David K. E. Bruce, the US ambassador to France. Afterwards, she became the first female executive at Tiffany and Company, a jewelry company in New York City.

Baldrige joined the Kennedy White House in 1961, but she resigned several months before President Kennedy's assassination on November 22, 1963. Her legacy as social secretary, however, lived on. She brought an unaccustomed air of elegance and grace to the social scene in Washington, introducing events such as theatre and opera.

After leaving the White House, Baldrige started her own public relations and marketing business, Letitia Baldrige Enterprises, which had offices in New York City, Washington, and Chicago. She was also the author of over twenty books, including *Letitia Baldrige's Complete Guide to Executive Manners* (1985), *Public Affairs, Private Relations* (1990), and *In the Kennedy Style: Magical Evenings in the Kennedy White House* (1997). Moreover, she worked on revising *The Amy Vanderbilt Complete Book of Etiquette: A Guide to Contemporary Living* (1978).

Baldrige died on October 29, 2012, at a nursing facility in Maryland. She was eighty-six years old. She is survived by her husband, Robert Hollensteiner; daughter, Claire Smyth; son, Malcolm Baldrige Hollensteiner; and seven grandchildren.

*See Current Biography 1988.*

## Will Barnet

**Born:** Beverly, Massachusetts; May 25, 1911
**Died:** New York City, New York; November 13, 2012
**Occupation:** American artist

Will Barnet was an American artist known for his watercolor paintings, prints, drawings, and masterful depictions of the human body and animals. He is most famous, however, for his portraits of women, children, and the family. He was both a social realist, depicting ordinary scenes of life and people in their natural environment, and a modernist, drawing inspiration from Picasso and producing abstract works of art. His ambidextrous artistic ability and mastery of realism and abstraction earned him numerous awards, including the Artists' Lifetime Achievement Award Medal by the National Academy of Design, and the Childe Hassam Prize by the American Academy and Institute of Art.

After studying at the School of the Museum of Fine Arts in Boston, he studied under the famous modernist American painter, Stuart Davis, at the Art Students League of New York. In 1936, Barnet became the printer for the Arts Students League and taught classes on graphic design at the school. He would also go on to teach at Yale University, the Pennsylvania Academy of Fine Arts, and the Cooper Union.

Barnet's first solo exhibit as an artist was in 1935 at the Eighth Street Playhouse in Manhattan. His first gallery show debuted in 1938 at the Hudson Walker Gallery, also in Manhattan. Barnet began his career focusing on realism; however, by 1940, his work became primarily abstract. He became a part of the art movement known as Indian Space Painting, which focused on complex abstract painting inspired by Native American and modern European art. Barnet's painting, *Singular Image*, for example, is an abstract painting composed of four quadrangles and is famous for its tension of motion that was indicative of the abstract movement.

Barnet returned to realism in the 1960s and produced a number of figurative paintings. During this time, he is best-known for his *Silent Seasons* series and his portraits of family. Over the course of his career, Barnet's work was showcased in many of the major art collections in the United States, including the Museum of Fine Arts in Boston, the Museum of Modern Art, New York, and the Metropolitan Museum of Art. In 2012, President Barack Obama awarded him with the 2011 National Medal of Arts.

Will Barnet died in New York City on November 13, 2012. He was 101 years old. Barnet is survived by his wife, Elena Barnet; his three sons, Peter, Richard, and Todd; his daughter, Ona; nine grandchildren; and three great-grandchildren.

*See Current Biography 1985.*

## Jacques Barzun

**Born:** Créteil, France; November 30, 1907
**Died:** San Antonio, Texas; October 25, 2012
**Occupation:** Historian, philosopher of education

Jacques Barzun was a prominent French-born American historian and academic best known for establishing the field of cultural history. He was one of the first historians to blend the study of history, war, and government with the disciplines of art, science, fashion, and other aspects of culture.

Barzun taught at Columbia University for over fifty years. He published numerous articles, essays, and books—most notably *From Dawn to Decadence* (2000), a best seller that chronicles Western civilization and culture from 1500 to the present. His other critically acclaimed books include *The Culture We Deserve* (1989), *The House of Intellect* (1959), and *Teacher in America* (1945), a classic that concerns the analysis of education and culture. In addition to writing over forty books, Barzun also helped found the Readers' Subsection Book Club in 1950 (later to be succeeded by the Mid-Century Book Society), an organization devoted to spreading the awareness of scholarship and literature.

After World War I, Barzun moved to the United States at the age of twelve and attended preparatory school. He later received his bachelor's and master's degrees and his PhD from Columbia University, where he would teach history from 1928 to 1955. After his extensive career as a college professor, Barzun became the dean of the graduate school in 1955 and was named an Extraordinary Fellow of Churchill College at the University of Cambridge.

In 2003, President George W. Bush awarded Barzun the highest civilian honor: the Presidential Medal of Freedom. This prestigious award is given to civilians that have made a significant contribution to the national interest, security, or culture of the United States. Barzun, however, was not only passionate about history and academia; he was also a well-known baseball lover. His famous quote from his essay on baseball, "Whoever wants to know the heart and mind of America had better learn baseball," can be seen today in the Baseball Hall of Fame.

On October 25, 2012, Jacques Barzun died in his home in San Antonio from natural causes. He was 104 years old. Barzun is survived by his second wife, Marguerite Davenport, his three children, ten grandchildren, and eight great-grandchildren.

*See Current Biography 1964.*

## Berthold Beitz

**Born:** Zemmin, Germany; September 26, 1913
**Died:** Sylt, Germany; July 30, 2013
**Occupation:** German industrialist

Berthold Beitz was a German industrialist who played a pivotal role in restoring Germany's crippled economy and industry in the wake of World War II. During the war, Beitz was appointed the head of an oil company in Boryslav, Poland, where he purposely created jobs for Poles and Jews, thus saving them from being sent to Nazi concentration camps. He also hid Jews in the basement of his home, which placed his own life in danger. His efforts to save the lives of Jews led the Holocaust memorial in Israel (the Yad Vashem) to appoint him "Righteous Among the Nations" in 1973, its most prestigious honor for non-Jews who helped save Jews during the war.

Beitz was born in Zemmin, Germany, on September 26, 1913. In 1938, he joined the Shell Oil Company and began his career in the oil industry. His experience in the oil industry resulted in his appointment to supervise the Boryslav oilfields in Poland during the war. After the war, he became the head of Iduna, a German insurance company, which grew into one of the largest in the industry. In 1952, his success with Iduna caught the attention of the owner of the Krupp Steel company, Alfried Krupp, who made Beitz the chairman of the company. Krupp, who had served part of a twelve-year sentence in prison for war crimes, chose Beitz in part because he needed someone with an unspoiled reputation to lead the company.

After Krupp's death in 1967, Beitz made the company a publicly traded corporation and established the Alfried Krupp von Bohlen and Halbach Foundation. He was also made executor of Krupp's will, and he used Krupp's fortune to fuel his philanthropic endeavors, including establishing a foundation to restore the Ruhr Valley into a center of art and culture. In addition to his success in business, Beitz was also instrumental in repairing Germany's fractured relations with countries in Europe. For example, in the 1960s, Chancellor Konrad Adenauer sent him to Poland to help renew diplomatic ties.

Beitz died on July 30, 2013, on the German island of Sylt. He was ninety-nine years old. Beitz is survived by his wife of more than seventy years, Else, and his three daughters, Barbara Ziff, Susanne Henle, and Bettina Poullain. Upon the news of his death, German Chancellor Angela Merkel remarked that Germany "has lost one of its most eminent and successful corporate personalities, who helped shape the country in important ways."

*See Current Biography 1973.*

# Richard Rodney Bennett

**Born:** Kent, United Kingdom; March 29, 1936
**Died:** New York City, New York; December 24, 2012
**Occupation:** British composer

Richard Rodney Bennett was an Oscar-nominated British composer known for his classical works, jazz performances, and film scores. Throughout the course of his career, he composed three symphonies, seventeen concertos, five operas, and a number of chamber works. He received Oscar nominations for three of his film scores: *Far from the Madding Crowd* (1967),

*Nicholas and Alexandra* (1974), and *Murder on the Orient Express* (1974). He never won an Oscar, but his score for *Murder on the Orient Express* won a Bafta award in 1975.

Bennett began playing the piano at the age of three or so, according to a statement that his sister, Meg Peacocke, made in an interview. He had written string quartets by the age of eighteen, and he completed his first film score at the age of nineteen. His first published piece, however, was his *Sonata for Piano* (1954).

In 1953, he began his studies at the Royal Academy of Music in London. Soon thereafter, he received a scholarship (1957–59) to study in Paris under the composer Pierre Boulez, where he explored his skills with serial composition techniques.

In addition to his more than fifty film scores and three Oscar-nominations, Bennett's notable works include his opera *The Mines of Sulphur* (1965); his *Piano Concerto* (1968); and his *Guitar Concerto* (1970). Bennett also experimented with jazz and cabaret, performing with musicians such as Eartha Kitt; Clare Martin, a British jazz singer; and Marian Montgomery, a singer from Mississippi. One of his best-known jazz works was *Jazz Calendar* (1963–64), which was choreographed by the famous dancer and choreographer, Frederick Ashton. Bennett's *Jazz Calendar* was performed at the Royal Ballet in London.

On December 24, 2012, Bennett died in New York at the age of seventy-nine. He is survived by his sister, Meg Peacocke, a poet who writes under the name M. R. Peacocke.

*See Current Biography Illustrated 1992.*

# Boris A. Berezovsky

**Born:** Moscow, Russia; January 23, 1946
**Died:** London, United Kingdom; March 23, 2013
**Occupation:** Russian financier and government official

Boris A. Berezovsky was one of the wealthiest and most politically active of the Russian oligarchs, a small and elite group of individuals who controlled the majority of Russia's wealth and industry. A mathematician by training, Berezovsky initially acquired his wealth through an automobile business he started with Aleksandr Voloshin. He then expanded to a number of other industries, including the media, the Russian airline, and oil. But soon after Vladimir Putin won the presidential election in 2000, Berezovsky exiled himself to London, United Kingdom, where he was granted political asylum.

Berezovsky was born on January 23, 1946, in Moscow, Russia. He attended the Moscow Forestry Engineering Institute and earned his doctorate in mathematics from the Russian Academy of Sciences in 1975. He then worked as an engineer and researcher until the Soviet government began to implement new reforms in the 1980s that allowed for the creation of privately owned companies, which opened the door for Berezovsky to pursue his business ventures.

In 1994, Berezovsky survived an assassination attempt: a bomb exploded in his car and decapitated his driver. Nevertheless, Berezovsky persevered and used his wealth to help finance President Boris Yeltsin's reelection campaign in 1996. He also gave Yeltsin considerable coverage through the media outlets he owned. After winning the election, Yeltsin appointed Berezovsky the vice secretary of the Kremlin security council.

Putin won the presidential election in 2000, and, unlike Yeltsin, he resisted Berezovsky and the other oligarchs who he believed threatened Russia's free market economy. Putin began to file tax claims against Berezovsky, who then exiled himself to London and was granted political asylum. While in London, he attempted to sue the Russian oligarch, Roman Abramovich, for approximately $5 billion. Berezovsky lost the case, and the judge, Elizabeth Gloster, called him an "unimpressive and inherently unreliable witness."

Berezovsky had reportedly been depressed in the months after losing the lawsuit against Abramovich, which hurt him financially (the legal and other costs associated reached an estimated $250 million). On March 23, 2013, Berezovsky was found dead on his bathroom floor. He was sixty-seven years old. Post-mortem exams revealed that the cause of death was "consistent with hanging."

See *Current Biography International Yearbook 2002.*

# Karen Black

**Born:** Park Ridge, Illinois; July 1, 1939
**Died:** Los Angeles, California; August 8, 2013
**Occupation:** American actor

A character actor known for her memorable portrayals of unabashedly rough-hewn women, Karen Black played opposite some of Hollywood's biggest leading men in the 1970s, before lending her unique presence to smaller, independent films later in her career. Black caught her break playing an LSD-tripping prostitute companion to Peter Fonda and Dennis Hopper's motorcycle rebels in the 1969 counterculture landmark, *Easy Rider*. She garnered second-billing and a best supporting actress Academy Award nomination for her turn as an unhappy waitress devoted to Jack Nicholson's talented but aimless pianist in *Five Easy Pieces* (1970). The success

of *Easy Rider* and *Five Easy Pieces* made Black an "it" girl of sorts among critics who admired her raw and free-spirited performances. She appeared in Nicholson's directorial debut, *Drive, He Said*, in 1971, playing a college professor's wife who has an affair with one of the school's basketball stars. Black played the girlfriend of Richard Benjamin's young Jewish lawyer in the 1972 take on Philip Roth's *Portnoy's Complaint*, and played Myrtle Wilson—Tom Buchanan's lover—in the Robert Redford's adaptation of F. Scott Fitzgerald's *The Great Gatsby* (1974). In 1976, Black played a kidnapper in the comedy/murder mystery *Family Plot*—legendary director Alfred Hitchcock's final film.

Black was born Karen Blanche Ziegler on July 1, 1939, in Park Ridge, Illinois. She got her start acting in local theater productions, before dropping out of high school and marrying a man named Charles Black. By the late 1950s, the couple had divorced, and Black was eager to get her acting career back off the ground. She enrolled in Northwestern University's drama program, where she studied for two years before moving to New York City, where she won roles off and on Broadway. While Black's film career never again reached the heights of her 1970s success, she continued acting up until her death from complications of cancer on August 8, 2013. She was seventy-four. Black is survived by her fourth husband—Stephen Eckelberry, whom she married in 1987; two siblings; three children; four grandchildren; and two great-grandchildren.

See *Current Biography 1976.*

# Bobby "Blue" Bland

**Born:** Rosemark, Tennessee; January 27, 1930
**Died:** Germantown, Tennessee; June 23, 2013
**Occupation:** American blues singer

A blues pioneer who brought romantic formality to a genre known for its gruff minimalism, Bobby "Blue" Bland was a fixture on the American rhythm and blues scene for over half a century. While Bland never garnered the widespread popularity of contemporaries like B. B. King—for whom Bland worked as a driver early in his career—his trademark style influenced countless blues and rock musicians, from Eric Clapton to Otis Redding. Bland began recording music in the early 1950s, but arrived at his signature, tearful sound on 1958's "Little Boy Blue." Over the next decade, Bland had more than thirty songs break into the top twenty rhythm and blues charts. Bland's struggle with alcoholism adversely affected his live performances, and eventually led to the breakup of his band in 1968. In the 1970s, Bland quit

drinking and released two of his most successful albums—*His California Album* (1973) and
*Dreamer* (1974). *Together for the First Time*, also
released in 1974, was Bland's first collaborative album with longtime friend B. B. King. The
pair's second collaboration, *Together Again*, followed in 1976.

Robert Calvin Brooks was born on January
27, 1930, in Rosemark, Tennessee, eventually
moving to Memphis with his mother in 1947.
When Bland dropped out of school in the third
grade, he had already begun singing gospel music as part of the Miniatures. Once in Memphis,
Bland got in with the Beale Streeters—a group
of blues musicians that featured a young B. B.
King as well as other stars-to-be like Johnny Ace
and Rosco Gordon. Bland was drafted in 1952,
serving a portion of his tour in Japan before being discharged in 1954.

He was inducted into the Blues Foundation Hall of fame in 1981, as well as the Rock
and Roll Hall of Fame in 1991. He was given
a Grammy Award for lifetime achievement in
1997, and received a similar honor from the
Blues Foundation in 1998. Bland died at his
home in Germantown, Tennessee, on June 23,
2013. He was eighty-three. Bland is survived by
his fourth wife, Willie Mae, two children, and
four grandchildren.

*See Current Biography 2001.*

growing HIV/AIDS epidemic, Bowen highlighted the danger the disease posed, even to those
in the heterosexual community. If more action
were not taken to fight HIV/AIDS, Bowen said
in 1987, the disease would prove more deadly
than past epidemics like the Black Death and
smallpox.

The son of a schoolteacher, Otis Ray Bow-
en was born on February 26, 1918, in Richland
Center, Indiana. He received his medical degree from Indiana University Medical School
in 1942, and served in the Army Medical Corps
during World War II. After the war he practiced
family medicine in Bremen, Indiana. Bowen's
political career began in 1952 when he was
elected coroner of Marshall County. Four years
later, he was elected to the Indiana legislature,
becoming its speaker in 1967. After an unsuccessful bid for governor of Indiana in 1968,
Bowen was elected to the post in 1972. He became Indiana's first governor to be elected to
a second term in more than a century. During
that time, Bowen revised Indiana state tax policy, reducing reliance on property taxes. Bowen
died on May 4, 2013, in Donaldson, Indiana,
of unspecified causes. He was ninety-five. Predeceased by his first two wives, Bowen is survived by his third wife, Carol Hahn Mikesell;
four children from his first marriage; and six
stepchildren.

*See Current Biography 1986.*

# Otis R. Bowen

**Born:** Richland Center, Indiana; February 26, 1918
**Died:** Donaldson, Indiana; May 4, 2013
**Occupation:** American governor and secretary
of health and human services

In 1985, Otis R. Bowen became the first physician to be appointed secretary of the US
Department of Health and Human Services
(HHS). Chosen by President Ronald Reagan to
replace Margaret M. Heckler, Secretary Bowen
was an independent political mind and a key
voice in the HIV/AIDS debate. Though he was
a Republican and had been recommended for
the post by Senator Dan Quayle, he maintained
a certain independence during his time in
Washington, and got along well with legislators
on both sides of the aisle. When Bowen and
his chief of staff, Thomas R. Burke, proposed
a bill that would extend Medicare coverage,
the historic expansion plan—formulated under
an administration known for its small government views—received bipartisan support and
praise. The law, which extended Medicare benefits to cover illnesses of extraordinary length
or severity, was repealed in 1989 after benefi-
ciaries complained of its effect on premiums
and some conservatives criticized it. Amid the

# Jack Brooks

**Born:** Crowley, Louisiana; December 18, 1922
**Died:** Beaumont, Texas; December 4, 2012
**Occupation:** American politician

Jack Brooks was an American politician and
member of the Democratic Party. He represented Southeast Texas in the United States House
of Representatives for forty-two years until he
lost the general election to Republican Steve
Stockman in 1994. Throughout his career in
Congress, Brooks was one of the few liberal
Southern politicians and a strong supporter of
civil rights. He refused, for example, to sign
the Southern Manifesto of 1956, which was
designed to oppose racial integration. But he
remained conservative on certain issues such
as the death penalty and gun control. Brooks
is also known for being in the motorcade when
President John F. Kennedy was assassinated in
Dallas, Texas on November 22, 1963.

During World War II, Brooks, a Marine
private, fought in the Pacific theater. In 1946,
he was elected to the Texas Legislature as the
representative from Jefferson County. As a state
representative, he graduated from the University of Texas Law School in 1949 and drafted a

bill that made Lamar College (his alma mater) a four-year-institution.

Brooks was elected to the US House of Representatives in 1952 and served there until 1995, after being voted out of office in the 1994 election that gave Republicans control over the House. Brooks's many accomplishments in Congress include sponsoring the 1965 Brooks Act, a bill for government information technology that is credited for facilitating the spread of technology in the twentieth century by opening government technology procurement to competitive bidding when it became law in 1972. He also helped write a number of important documents, including the Civil Rights Act of 1964 that banned racial segregation, the Voting Rights Act of 1965 that outlawed discriminatory voting practices, and the 1974 articles of impeachment against President Richard Nixon during the Watergate scandal.

Brooks held various leadership roles in the House of Representatives. He was the head of the House Government Operations Committee (1975–88), where he helped pass the Inspector General Act of 1978. He also served on the Judiciary Committee from 1955 to 1995 and was the committee's chair during the last six years of his tenure. Brooks received a number of awards for his service in Congress, including NASA's Distinguished Service Medal on April 23, 2001. A federal courthouse and a park in Beaumont, Texas, are named in his honor.

Brooks died on December 4, 2012, in Beaumont. He was eighty-nine years old. He is survived by his wife, Charlotte; his two daughters, Kate and Kim; his son, Jeb; and his two grandchildren.

*See Current Biography 1992.*

# Joyce Brothers

**Born:** New York, New York; October 20, 1927
**Died:** Fort Lee, New Jersey; May 13, 2013
**Occupation:** American psychologist and media personality

Dr. Joyce Brothers was an American psychologist whose advice was heard by millions of Americans across the country through mass media: the radio, television, film, newspaper, and in her books such as *The Brothers System for Liberated Love and Marriage* (1972). Brothers was best-known for hosting a number of nationally syndicated television shows, including *The Dr. Joyce Brothers Show* (1958–63), *Ask Dr. Brothers* (1965–75), and *Living Easy with Dr. Joyce Brothers* (1973). She was the self-proclaimed mother of mass-media psychology, which she declared

in an interview with the *Washington Post*: "I invented media psychology. I was the first. The founding mother."

Brothers was born Joyce Diane Bauer on October 20, 1927, in New York City. After earning her bachelor's degree in economics and psychology from Cornell University in 1947, Brothers attended Columbia University, where she earned her master's degree in 1949. Soon thereafter, she married medical student Milton Brothers. She received her doctorate from Columbia in 1953 and taught psychology at both Hunter College and Columbia University. By the mid 1950s, however, she had left her career in academia to take care of her newborn daughter.

Brothers' fame initially came from her appearance on *The $64,000 Challenge*, a popular game show on CBS where contestants were quizzed on a chosen area of expertise. Brothers' expertise for the show was the sport of boxing (the show was known for quizzing contestants on a subject that seemed infelicitous with their profession). After weeks of intense study on the history and nature of boxing, an effort that she compared to preparing to write a dissertation, Brothers stunned viewers by answering question after difficult question. On December 6, 1955, she shocked America when she answered the capstone question worth $64,000. She was only the second person to win the grand prize.

Her success on the show launched a long and lucrative career that spanned across multiple media platforms. She first appeared as a commentator on the television show *Sports Showcase* in 1956, which lead to a number of television appearances on variety shows such as *The Merv Griffin Show*, *The Mike Douglas Show*, *The Sonny and Cher Comedy Hour*, and *The Tonight Show*. In the late 1950s, she began hosting her first of many television shows, the *Dr. Joyce Brothers Show*. Later in her career, she appeared in a number of films, including *Lover's Knot* (1996), *Beethoven's 4th* (2001), and *Analyze That* (2002).

In addition to film and television, Brothers had a call-in radio show, a nationally syndicated newspaper column, and a long-running column in *Good Housekeeping*. She authored fifteen books, most notably *Widowed* (1990), which concerned how she overcame her grief following the death of her husband on January 9, 1989. He was sixty-two years old.

On May 13, 2013, Brothers died at her home in Fort Lee, New Jersey, from respiratory failure. She was eighty-five years old. She is survived by her sister, Elaine Goldsmith; her daughter, Lisa Brothers Arbisser, an ophthalmic surgeon; four grandchildren; and two great-grandchildren.

*See Current Biography 1971.*

# Dave Brubeck

**Born:** Concord, California; December 6, 1920
**Died:** Norwalk, Connecticut; December 5, 2012
**Occupation:** American jazz pianist and composer

Dave Brubeck was a leading figure in progressive jazz (also known as cool jazz), a style of modern jazz that incorporates a relaxed tempo and elements of classical music. Brubeck was celebrated for his jazz standards, including "In Your Own Sweet Way" (1955), and for his work with the Dave Brubeck Quartet. But Brubeck is best known for the album *Time Out* (1959), which included the hit songs "Take Five" and "Blue Rondo à la Turk." The album went platinum and became the first jazz album to sell one million copies.

After graduating from the College of the Pacific in Stockton, California, Brubeck enlisted in the US Army during World War II and met his long term musical partner, Paul Desmond, who played the alto saxophone. In 1951, Brubeck and Desmond established the Dave Brubeck Quartet. That same year, Brubeck had an accident and damaged his vertebrae, resulting in nerve pain in his hands. It is believed that this accident influenced his musical style. As a result of the nerve pain in his hands, he was no longer able to play high speed tempos adequately. Therefore, he adapted a slower style that made use of complex chords and classical elements.

The Dave Brubeck Quartet recorded a number of albums, including *Jazz at the College of the Pacific* (1954) and *Jazz Goes to College* (1954), the band's debut album with Columbia Records. They recorded their record-breaking album, *Time Out*, in 1959. The following year, the quartet was at the height of their success and began to produce a few albums every year. Other notable achievements include recording a live album at Carnegie Hall in 1963. They also wrote the theme song for the CBS television show *Mr. Broadway* (1964), featuring Craig Stevens.

The Dave Brubeck Quarter parted ways in 1967. Brubeck took a break from jazz and focused on longer orchestral and choral work—including a cantata, *The Gates of Justice* (1969) and an oratorio, *The Light in the Wilderness* (1968). Much of his work at this time focused on themes of religion and social justice.

Brubeck was the second jazz musician to be featured on the cover of *Time* magazine. He was also the recipient of many prestigious awards, such as the Benjamin Franklin Award for Public Diplomacy (2008). On December 10, 2008, he was inducted into the California Hall of Fame. A year later, he became a Kennedy Center Honoree.

On Father's Day in 2011, Dave Brubeck gave his last performance in Chicago. He died of heart failure the following year in Norwalk, Connecticut, the day before his ninety-second birthday. Brubeck is survived by his wife, four sons, daughter, ten grandchildren, and four great-grandchildren.

See *Current Biography Illustrated 1956, 1993.*

# Héctor Camacho

**Born:** Bayamón, Puerto Rico; May 24, 1962
**Died:** San Juan, Puerto Rico; November 24, 2012
**Occupation:** Professional boxer

Héctor Luís Camacho Matías, more commonly known by the nickname, "Macho Camacho," was a professional boxer from Puerto Rico. He won several boxing championships, including the World Boxing Council (WBC) super featherweight (1983), WBC lightweight (1985), and World Boxing Organization (WBO) junior welterweight (1989 and 1991). After winning major titles in seven different weight classes, Camacho became the first boxer to earn the prestigious distinction of septuple champion.

Camacho was born in Bayamón, Puerto Rico, but he later moved to Spanish Harlem in New York City, where he grew up. After studying boxing and karate as a teenager, Camacho, with the help of his high school English teacher, Patrick Flannery, entered into the Golden Glove Competition. He proved himself as a talented boxer and won three Golden Glove Championships.

Camacho continued his career as a professional boxer and added numerous victories to his name. A notable win occurred in 1985, when Camacho defeated Roque Montoya to clench the championship for the United States Boxing Association. Soon thereafter, he would defeat José Luis Ramírez, the previous world champion, in the WBC Lightweight Championships in Las Vegas. After moving up in weight class to the light welterweight division, he defeated Ray Mancini in 1989 and became the World Boxing Association (WBA) light welterweight champion, thus making him one of the few boxers to win three weight divisions.

In addition to his successful career as a professional boxer, Camacho made appearances on television shows—*Super Sábados, El Show del Mediodía, The Wayans Bros*—and created his own dating show, *It's Macho Time* (2012). Camacho's criminal activity also made frequent headlines. He was known for frequent drug abuse, car theft, a 2005 burglary attempt in Gulfport, Mississippi, and an alleged child abuse scandal in November 2011. That same year, he was shot three times in a housing project in San Juan.

On November 20, 2012, Camacho was shot in the face in Bayamón, Puerto Rico. The bullet penetrated his left mandible and damaged his carotid artery. Four days later, he died in the hospital from cardiac arrest after being taken off life support. He was fifty years old. Camacho is survived by his mother, father, three sisters, a brother, four sons, and two grandsons.

*See Current Biography 2001.*

# Scott Carpenter

**Born:** Boulder, Colorado; May 1, 1925
**Died:** Denver, Colorado; October 10, 2013
**Occupation:** American astronaut

Scott Carpenter was launched into space on May 24, 1962, making him the second US astronaut to orbit the earth. He made three orbits during his five-hour flight aboard the *Aurora 7* capsule. The mission, however, was compromised when equipment aboard the capsule malfunctioned, forcing Carpenter to manually take over the landing. He survived the landing, which he described as "a dicey time" in his memoir *For Spacious Skies* (2002), but he was approximately 250 nautical miles from his intended landing point.

Malcolm Scott Carpenter was born in Boulder, Colorado, on May 1, 1925. He attended the University of Colorado for one semester, but left to join the US Navy during World War II. After the war, he resumed his studies at the University of Colorado, but he never graduated. However, after he orbited the earth, the university awarded him a bachelor's degree in aeronautical engineering in 1962. He rejoined the US Navy in 1949, where he began flight training and later entered the Fleet Airborne Electronics Training School in San Diego, California. During the Korean War, he served as a member of a patrol squadron based in Barbers Point, Hawaii. He also underwent training at the Navy Test Pilot School at Patuxent River, Maryland, in 1954.

His experience as a test pilot with the US Navy and his engineering skills caught the attention of the National Aeronautics and Space Administration (NASA), which selected him as a member of Project Mercury, America's original space program. It was in this capacity that Carpenter issued his famous send-off to his fellow astronaut John Glenn as he became the first US astronaut to be launched into space on February 20, 1962: "Godspeed, John Glenn." Three months later, Carpenter embarked on his own mission to orbit the earth, which he described as "the nicest thing that ever happened to me. The zero-gravity sensation and visual sensation

of spaceflight are transcending experiences and I wish everybody could enjoy them."

In addition to his well-known space mission aboard *Aurora 7*, Carpenter also helped develop the *Apollo* lunar lander for NASA in the 1960s. Carpenter died on October 10, 2013, in Denver, Colorado. He was eighty-eight years old and, with Glenn, one of the last two surviving Project Mercury astronauts, also known as the Mercury Seven. His first three marriages ended in divorce. Predeceased by two sons, Carpenter is survived by his fourth wife, Patty Barrett Carpenter; two daughters, Kristen Stoever and Candace Carpenter; four sons, Jay, Nicholas, Matthew, and Zachary; his granddaughter; and five step-grandchildren.

*See Current Biography 1962.*

# Elliott Carter

**Born:** Manhattan, New York; December 11, 1908
**Died:** Manhattan, New York; November 5, 2012
**Occupation:** American composer

Elliott Carter was an American composer whose music won numerous awards, including two Pulitzer Prizes. Carter's musical works were considered to be primarily neoclassical in aesthetic, and they were so structurally complex that, in 2002, the *New York Times* called them "the most difficult music ever conceived." Carter wrote an impressive number of compositions that were played by major orchestras and professional musicians internationally. Among his most famous works include his Variations for Orchestra (1954–55), his Piano Concerto (1964–65), and his Concerto for Orchestra (1969). His Second String Quartet (1959) and Third String Quartet (1971) won him two Pulitzer Prizes for Music, in 1960 and 1973, respectively.

After graduating from Harvard University with an English degree, Carter focused on musical composition and received a graduate degree in music, also from Harvard. He earned his doctorate in music from the École Normale de Musique in Paris, France. Early in his career, he followed in the footsteps of famous composers such as Stravinsky and Copeland (specifically Stravinsky, who he dedicated his Piano Concerto to as a present for his eighty-fifth birthday).

It was not until after 1950 that Elliott's music became increasingly complex—establishing his signature style and earning him international recognition as a contemporary composer. In his Pulitzer Prize–winning Second String Quartet, for example, each instrument is assigned its own distinct rhythms, thus creating an atonal and purposely stratified composition that was unique in classical music. Likewise, the instruments in his Double Concerto (1961) also have their own rhythms and therefore produce a complex, broken, and atonal sound.

His complex and unique compositions were criticized for their lack of color and emotion, but Carter did not care about popularity. Instead, he wrote for himself and created innovative music that went against the mainstream. His goal was to make people really listen to his music and, unlike conventional classical composers, he wanted to give the audience something that was challenging to comprehend.

Carter was a prolific composer and was particularly productive later in life, composing more than fifty-four pieces after the age of ninety. He completed his final work, "Twelve Short Epigrams" for piano trio, on August 13, 2012. On November 5, 2012, Elliott Carter died in Manhattan at the age of 103 and is survived by his son, David, and a grandson. He will be remembered as one of the most influential voices in contemporary music.

*See Current Biography Illustrated 1960.*

# Hugo Chávez

**Born:** Sabaneta, Venezuela; July 28, 1954
**Died:** Caracas, Venezuela; March 5, 2013
**Occupation:** Venezuelan president

Hugo Chávez was the president of Venezuela from February 2, 1999, until his death on March 5, 2013. During his fourteen years in office, he implemented a number of reforms in Venezuela, including free health care, extension of the president's term by one year, and a series of socialist programs to benefit the poor. He also changed the name of the country to the Bolivarian Republic of Venezuela. Chávez was greatly admired by the poor, and he was credited with helping to improve the economic conditions of Venezuela's poor population. When he took office in 1999, for example, 23.4 percent of the population was significantly impoverished, but by 2011, this number had decreased to 8.5 percent.

Chávez made a number of controversial political decisions that sparked tension with the United States, including allying himself with that nation's enemies, such as Libya and Iran. Moreover, he blamed the Central Intelligence Agency (CIA) and George W. Bush's administration for facilitating a coup in 2002 that ousted him from power for two days. He also objected to the Iraq War and supported the government of former Cuban leader Fidel Castro.

Chávez was born on July 28, 1954, in Sabaneta, Venezuela. In 1975, he earned a degree in military science and engineering from the Venezuelan Academy of Military Sciences. After completing his education, he served as an officer in the military before joining the Revolutionary Bolivarian Movement, which, in 1992, attempted to oust President Carlos Andrés Pérez from power. The coup failed, however, and Chávez spent two years in prison.

After he was pardoned and released from prison, Chávez left his career in the military and became a politician with the Movement of the Fifth Republic, a left-wing political party. He ran for president and was elected in 1998. He officially took office on February 2, 1999. During his presidency, Chávez was a dogmatic leader who not only publicly blamed the United States for the 2002 coup, but also referred to President George W. Bush as "the devil" during a controversial speech at the United Nations in September 2006. During his speech he also proclaimed that the United States would be "finished in the near future, for the good of all mankind."

Despite Chávez's disagreements with the United States, Venezuela remained its fourth-largest supplier of foreign oil. In 2011, Venezuela's net oil export was approximately $60 billion (according to OPEC, the Organization of Petroleum Exporting Countries), a drastic increase from the $14.4 billion when Chávez came to power in 1999. Under his leadership, unemployment was nearly cut in half over the course of a decade, from 14.5 percent in 1999 to 7.6 percent in 2009. Violence and crime, however, increased significantly during his fourteen years as president, and inflation rates increased to an estimated 31.6 percent by 2012.

In June 2011, Chávez was diagnosed with cancer. The government did not share many details about his condition with the public. Despite his illness, he was reelected in October 2012 to a term that would have lasted until 2019. After two years of undergoing chemotherapy, radiation, and a number of operations, Chávez died on March 5, 2013, in Caracas, Venezuela. He was fifty-eight years old.

*See Current Biography Illustrated 2000.*

# Patrice Chéreau

**Born:** Lézigné, France; November 2, 1944
**Died:** Paris, France; October 7, 2013
**Occupation:** French theatrical, opera, and film director

Patrice Chéreau was a French theatrical, opera, and film director best known for his provocative opera productions. In his 1976 production of Wagner's *Der Ring des Nibelungen* (*The Ring of the Nibelung*) he took a risk and replaced the traditional mythological scenery with industrial age machinery. Consequently, his work helped to redefine the way directors interpret operas by replacing traditional sets with settings from their own artistic vision.

Chéreau was born on November 2, 1944, in Lézigné, Maine-et-Loire, in western France. Chéreau's parents, Jean-Baptiste and Marguerite Chéreau, were both painters, and he grew up in an artistic environment. He had a passion for theater from a young age, and in a 1977 interview with *Le Monde* he explained how his parents had a profound impact on the way he perceives theater: "They told stories through painting, and what I do is basically the same."

Chéreau attended Lycée Louis-le-Grand, and he managed a theater group at the age of fifteen. His passion for theater continued at the University of Paris (the Sorbonne), where he directed his first production, *L'intervention*, by Victor Hugo. He then left the Sorbonne to start his own theater company, the Théâtre de Sartrouville, in a northwestern suburb of Paris. During this time, he was mentored by the esteemed stage directors Giorgio Strehler and Roger Planchon.

In addition to *Der Ring des Nibelungen*, Chéreau's best-known opera productions include Berg's *Wozzeck*, Mozart's *Don Giovanni*, and Wagner's *Tristan und Isolde*. He was also a prolific film director and produced such provocative films as *L'homme blessé* (*The Wounded Man*, 1983), which depicts the affair between a teenage boy and an older man. *Intimacy* (2001), his only film in English, concerns the sexual relationship between a divorced father and a housewife; it won the Berlin Film Festival Golden Bear award in 2001. His other notable films include *Persécution* (2009), *Son frère* (2003), and *The Flesh of the Orchid* (1975). Chéreau also taught film classes at a number of universities, including the School of Visual Arts in 2003.

Chéreau died on October 7, 2013, in Paris, France. He was sixty-eight years old. He is survived by his brother.

*See Current Biography 1990.*

# Yash Chopra

**Born:** Lahore, Punjab; September 27, 2012
**Died:** Mumbai, Maharashtra; October 21, 2012
**Occupation:** Indian film director, script writer, and producer

Yash Chopra was a prolific Indian filmmaker who directed and produced many of the highest grossing and critically acclaimed films in the history of India's film industry (also known as Bollywood). Chopra, often called the "King of Romance," directed over twenty films and produced more than forty. Among the most notable in his filmography are the action thriller *Deewar* (1975), the romantic drama *Khabie, Khabie* (1976), and the cult classic *Lamhe* (1991).

After completing his education at Doaba College, Jalandhar, Chopra moved to Mumbai and worked under director I. S. Johar. Chopra directed his first film, *Dhool Ka Phool*, in 1959, which was well received by film critics and became one of the highest grossing films of that year. But it wasn't until his 1962 film *Dharupta*—the first Indian film to portray the partition of India—that Chopra received widespread recognition and the National Award for Best Feature Film in Hindi.

Chopra founded his own film company, Yash Raj Films, with his brother in 1971. This allowed Yash the creative freedom to direct and produce the films of his choosing. Many Indian film stars emerged from his films, most notably Amitabh Bachchan, who starred in *Deewar* and *Trishul*. Arguably the most successful of Yash's films was the 1989 cult classic, *Chandri*, which established his signature romantic style that was heroine-oriented and contained melodic-music. This film was celebrated for ending the trend of violence in Bollywood films, replacing it with music and dance. *Chandri* won the National Film Award for Best Popular Film for that year.

In addition to his award winning films, Chopra himself was the recipient of many awards—including the Padma Bhushan (one of India's highest civilian honors), the Lifetime Achievement Award at the 2006 International film festival, and the Outstanding Achievement in Cinema award at the Asian Awards.

Yash's last film, *Jab Tak hai Jaan*, premiered on November 12, 2012, less than a month after his death. The film was honored and celebrated by India's film industry and the people of India. The Prime Minister of India, Manmohan Singh, publicly announced that Chopra was an "icon of India cinema."

Yash Chopra died on Sunday, October 21, 2012, in Mumbai's Lilavati hospital from complications with his liver. He was eighty years old. Chopra is survived by his wife, Pamela, and their two sons, Aditya and Uday.

*See Current Biography 2006.*

# Chinwe Chukwuogo-Roy

**Born:** Awka, Nigeria; May 2, 1952
**Died:** Hacheston, United Kingdom; December 17, 2012
**Occupation:** Nigerian painter

Chinwe Chukwuogo-Roy was a Nigerian artist best known for her acclaimed Golden Jubilee portrait of the United Kingdom's Queen Elizabeth II, which marked the fiftieth anniversary of the monarch's accession to the throne. Some of her other celebrated portraits include Emeka Anyaoku, Commonwealth secretary general; Geoffrey Watling, the president of Norwich City FC; and

Kriss Akabusi, an Olympic track-and-field athlete from the United Kingdom.

Chukwuogo-Roy was born in Awka, Nigeria, on May 2, 1952. A survivor of the Nigerian Civil War (also known as the Biafran war, 1967–70), she completed her secondary education at the Igwebuike Grammar School in Awka, Nigeria, in 1973. She relocated to the United Kingdom in 1975 to study graphic design at the Hornsey College of Art (now known as Middlesex University), where she graduated with her bachelor's degree in graphic design in 1979. She started to focus on painting in 1988, and her work was soon being displayed in a number of exhibitions in Suffolk, including the Boundary Gallery in 1991, the Butley Gallery in 1992 and 1995, and the Yoxford Gallery in 1995.

After painting a portrait of Kriss Akabusi in 1966, he commissioned her to paint a series of works about the African Diaspora, which were subsequently exhibited at Whiteley's Atrium Gallery and the Westbourne Gallery. Chukwuogo-Roy further explored her African heritage in works such as *Africa: Past, Present and Future*, *The African Slave Trade*, and *Masks and Masquerades*.

Her most famous work is her portrait of Queen Elizabeth II, a six-by-four-foot canvas of the queen in a royal blue blouse and skirt, standing in front of the window in Buckingham Palace. It was revealed in 1999 and now hangs in the Marlborough House, a mansion in the City of Westminster, central London. In 2009, Chinwe Chukwuogo-Roy was appointed a Member of the British Empire (MBE), a prestigious honor for her contributions to art.

Chinwe Chukwuogo-Roy died on December 17, 2012, in Hacheston, United Kingdom, after a three-year battle with breast cancer. She was sixty years old. Chukwuogo-Roy is survived by her husband, Roderick, whom she married in 1980; her mother; six siblings; two sons, Rogan and Alasdai; a daughter, Nwiru; and her grandson.

*See Current Biography 2007.*

## Tom Clancy

**Born:** April 12, 1947; Baltimore, Maryland
**Died:** October 1, 2013; Baltimore, Maryland
**Occupation:** American novelist

Tom Clancy was a best-selling American novelist known for his action-packed military novels such as *Patriot Games* (1987) and *Clear and Present Danger* (1989). He sold more than one hundred million copies of his novels throughout his career, and seventeen reached number one on the New York Times Best Sellers list. His last novel to reach number one was *Threat Vector*, which was released in December 2012. Many of Clancy's novels were adapted to film, including

*Sum of All Fears* (1991), which debuted in theatres in 2002.

Thomas Leo Clancy Jr. was born in Baltimore, Maryland, on April 12, 1947. He graduated from Loyola College with an English degree in 1969. His first novel, *The Hunt for Red October* (1984), was a huge success—selling more than two million copies during the first two years of its publication. Its commercial success was boosted by then President Ronald Reagan, who called the novel "my kind of yarn" and said he couldn't put it down; Secretary of Defense Caspar W. Weinberger praised the novel for its vast and accurate technical detail. Soon after releasing *The Hunt for Red October*, Clancy published a *Red Storm Rising* (1986, with Larry Bond), *Patriot Games* (1987), *The Cardinal of the Kremlin* (1988), and *Clear and Present Danger* (1989).

In addition to the publishing world, the main protagonist of his novels, Jack Ryan, has been turned into video games such as *Rainbow Six*, a tactical shooter game developed by the company Red Storm Entertainment, which Clancy founded. His books also inspired the video game series *Ghost Recon* and *Splinter Cell*. A number of Hollywood stars played Jack Ryan in films adapted from his novels, including Harrison Ford in *Patriot Games* (1992) and *Clear and Present Danger* (1994), and Ben Affleck in *The Sum of All Fears*.

Clancy died on October 1, 2013, in Baltimore, Maryland. He was sixty-six years old. Clancy and his first wife, Wanda Thomas King, divorced in 1999. He is survived by his second wife, Alexandra Llewellyn Clancy, and their daughter, Alexis Clancy, as well as four children from his first marriage, Michelle Bandy, Christine Blocksidge, Thomas L. Clancy III, and Kathleen Clancy.

*See Current Biography Illustrated 1988.*

## William Patrick Clark Jr.

**Born:** Oxnard, California; October 23, 1931
**Died:** Shandon, California; August 10, 2013
**Occupation:** American lawyer, judge, and government official

During President Ronald Reagan's first term, fellow Californian William Patrick Clark Jr. served as deputy secretary of state, national security adviser, and secretary of the interior. He was one of Reagan's most trusted advisors, possessing an intimacy with the notoriously reserved president—and a level of influence that came with such closeness—that in 1983, led *Time* magazine to declare him the second most powerful man in the White House. Clark first worked for Reagan as Ventura County chairman of the future-president's first gubernatorial campaign in 1966. He became Reagan's chief of staff in the governor's office, and was subsequently appointed state judge, eventually working his way up to the California Supreme Court. As national security advisor in the Reagan administration, Clark was a major proponent of the domino theory of Communism, particularly as it applied to Central America. He pushed for higher military spending, and took a firm stance against Soviet interests.

William Patrick Clark Jr. was born in Oxnard, California, on October 23, 1931, to William Pettit and Bernice Clark. He was a member of the fifth generation of the Clark family in California, where his father was a cattle rancher and police chief, and his grandfather a sheriff. A youth spent working on the ranch gave way to an unsuccessful attempt at collegiate life. After trying his hand at Stanford and the University of Santa Clara, Clark was admitted to Loyola Law School despite never having earned a degree. His studies were interrupted by the draft in 1953, when he joined the Army as a counterintelligence agent in Germany. Clark never finished his courses at Loyola, but nonetheless passed the California bar examination in 1958 on his second try.

Clark—a Democrat for much of his young life—became actively involved in the American conservative movement after hearing Ronald Reagan speak on behalf of presidential candidate Barry M. Goldwater in 1964. One year later, Clark hosted a party for Reagan, thus beginning a partnership that would endure through 1985, when he returned to California to practice law. Clark died of complications of Parkinson's disease on August 10, 2013, at his ranch outside Shandon, California. He was eighty-one. He is survived by his two sisters; three sons and two daughters; nine grandchildren; and one great-grandchild. His wife, Joan, whom he married while serving in Germany, died in 2009.

*See Current Biography 1982.*

# Van Cliburn

**Born:** Shreveport, Louisiana; July 12, 1934
**Died:** Fort Worth, Texas; February 27, 2013
**Occupation:** American pianist

Van Cliburn was an American pianist who rose to international fame after winning first place at the 1958 International Tchaikovsky Competition in Moscow. Cliburn's victory was not only a personal achievement—many in the United States considered it a victory over the Soviet Union during the height of the Cold War, only about six months after the Russians launched the world's first artificial satellite, Sputnik, on October 4, 1957. The recording of Cliburn's Tchaikovsky First Piano Concerto, which helped clench his victory in 1958, was the first classical album to go platinum, selling more than three million copies.

Cliburn was born on July 12, 1934, in Shreveport, Louisiana. His mother, Rildia Bee O'Bryan Cliburn, was a classical trained musician and Cliburn's first piano teacher. When he was thirteen, he won a competition to play with the Houston Symphony, where he performed his Tchaikovsky Concerto, which would become his signature piece. In 1951, at the age of seventeen, Cliburn received a scholarship to the Julliard School of Music in New York City. In 1954, he graduated from Julliard, and, that same year, he earned the prestigious Leventritt Foundation award, which provided him the opportunity to play with major orchestras such as the New York Philharmonic.

After receiving a grant from the Martha Baird Rockefeller Aid to Music, he was able to afford the trip to Moscow and compete in the first International Tchaikovsky Competition. He was twenty-three years old when he clenched first place at the competition in April 1958, receiving standing ovations for his performances of Tchaikovsky's First Piano Concerto and Rachmaninoff's Third Concerto. The celebration continued when he returned to New York City, where he was honored with a ticker-tape parade in Lower Manhattan.

His victory in Moscow launched a lucrative and successful career. From 1958 to 1959, for example, the income he received during the concert season was approximately $150,000. His performances, however, decreased in the 1960s, and he retired from the stage in 1978. Although he returned to the stage in 1989, he did not continue to perform regularly.

Cliburn received a number of honors and awards, including the Presidential Medal of Freedom, the National Medal of Arts, and the Russian Order of Friendship, which was given by Russian president Vladimir Putin. Cliburn died on February 27, 2013, at his home in Fort Worth, Texas. He was seventy-eight years old. Cliburn is survived by Thomas L. Smith, with whom he had lived for many years.

*See Current Biography Illustrated 1958.*

# Cardiss Collins

**Born:** St. Louis, Missouri; September 24, 1931
**Died:** Alexandria, Virginia; February 3, 2013
**Occupation:** American congresswoman

Cardiss Collins was the first African American woman to represent Illinois in Congress, and the fourth African American woman to serve in the US House of Representatives when she took office in 1973. During her more than twenty-four-year tenure in the House, she held a number of leadership positions, including the chair of the Congressional Black Caucus (1979–81). She was an advocate for issues such as gender equity in college sports, affirmative action, minority employment, and women's health.

Collins was born on September 24, 1931, in St. Louis, Missouri. She attended college at Northwestern University in Chicago, where she graduated in 1967 from the business school. After college, she worked briefly as stenographer for the Illinois Department of Labor. She married George W. Collins in 1958 and subsequently helped him campaign for the office of alderman. He won the office and served from 1964 to 1970, when he was elected to the US House of Representatives after the death of Representative Daniel J. Ronan.

Not long after he was elected to a second congressional term, George W. Collins was one of the forty-five people killed when United Airlines Flight 553 crashed on December 8, 1972. At the time, Collins was an auditor for the Illinois Revenue Department. Despite having doubts about fulfilling her husband's seat in the House, she was encouraged by Democrats to run, and, in June 1973, she won the special election with 92 percent of the vote.

In 1979, Collins became the chair of the Congressional Black Caucus (CBC), where she served until 1981. She was a champion for African American rights and women's health, and she had many notable achievements in Congress, including helping to pass a 1990 law that expanded Medicare coverage for mammography screenings for elderly and disabled women. In 1993, she initiated the Equity in Athletics Disclosure Act, which required colleges and universities that received federal aid to disclose information regarding their number of men's and women's athletics teams, as well the amount of scholarship money and other expenses used by these teams.

Collins retired from the House in 1996 and was succeeded by Danny K. Davis. On February 3, 2013, Collins died in Alexandria, Virginia, at Inova Alexandria Hospital. She was eighty-one years old. Collins is survived by her son, Kevin, and her granddaughter.

*See Current Biography 1997.*

# Emilio Colombo

**Born:** Potenza, Italy; April 11, 1920
**Died:** Rome, Italy; June 24, 2013
**Occupation:** Italian politician

Emilio Colombo was an Italian politician who served as the prime minister of Italy for eighteen months from August 1970 to February 1972. In addition to prime minster, Colombo held a number of other high-ranking positions in Italy's government, including the minister of foreign trade (1958–59), agriculture (1955–58), finance (1959–63), and foreign affairs (1980–83 and 1992–93). Colombo had many accomplishments during his prolific career in politics, but he is perhaps best-known for helping author the Treaty of Rome (1957) and facilitating Italy's economic recovery in the wake of World War II.

Colombo was born on April 11, 1920, in Potenza, Italy, the capital of Basilicata, a region in the south. After earning his law degree from the University of Rome, Colombo joined the Catholic Action Youth, a political organization, and worked his way up to vice president, which opened the door to his election to parliament in 1948. He entered his first major leadership post in 1955 as minister of agriculture. In 1957, he was involved in drafting the Treaty of Rome, which helped break down the barriers dividing Europe after World War II and open economic ties between the countries. Signed into law on March 25, 1957, the Treaty of Rome (also known as the Treaty of the European Community) established the European Economic Community, which was a precursor to the European Union (EU).

Colombo served as the minister of agriculture and minister of foreign affairs before becoming prime minister in August 1970. During his eighteen-month term in office, Colombo made a number of important contributions, including financing a project to save the city of Venice from subsidence. Colombo also passed a highly controversial law that legalized divorce in Italy; however, it was this contentious law that contributed to his party's downfall. In February of 1972, the Republican Party withdrew its support and he was subsequently succeeded by Giulio Andreotti. Colombo then returned to the treasury and went on to hold a number of other government positions, including the minister of foreign affairs (1980–83 and 1992–93).

Colombo was appointed a senator for life in 2003, a significant accomplishment for his professional career. His private life, however, was criticized after he disclosed, not long after his prestigious appointment, two controversial secrets—he had been using cocaine for more than a year, and he was gay. He was known for saying that politics was, in his opinion, a "kind of priesthood," and he therefore never married. There were, however, constant rumors about his sexuality throughout his career.

Colombo died on June 24, 2013, in Rome. He was ninety-three years old. Information about his survivors is not available.

*See Current Biography 1971.*

# Alex Colville

**Born:** Toronto, Canada; August 24, 1920
**Died:** Wolfville, Canada; July 16, 2013
**Occupation:** Canadian painter

Alex Colville was a Canadian painter and modern artist whose works have appeared in many internationally renowned art collections, including New York's Museum of Modern Art and the Centre Pompidou in Paris. Colville was perhaps best-known for the 1954 painting *Horse and Train*, which depicts a dark horse galloping towards an oncoming train, an image evoked by lines from a poem by Roy Campbell: "Against a regiment I oppose a brain / And a dark horse against an armoured train." Some of his other notable works include *Child and Dog* (1952), *To Prince Edward Island* (1965), and *Nude and Dummy* (1950).

Colville was born on August 24, 1920, in Toronto, Ontario, Canada. After receiving his bachelor's degree in fine arts from Mount Allison University in 1942, he enlisted in the Canadian Army to serve during World War II and was deployed to Europe. Here, he famously illustrated a gruesome scene from a Nazi concentration camp, where thousands of bodies lay in an open grave. This work is now featured in the Canadian war museum in Ottawa.

After the war, Colville became a faculty-member at Mount Ellison University in 1946, where he remained until he retired in 1963 to focus on his painting full time. In 1966, he represented Canada at the Venice biennale, a major contemporary art festival that takes place in Venice, Italy. In addition to painting, Colville was asked in 1965 to design coins for Canada's centennial; he also designed the Governor's General's Medal in 1978. In 1982, he became a Companion of the Order of Canada.

Colville died on July 16, 2013, in Wolfville, Nova Scotia, Canada. He was ninety-two years old. Colville's wife, Rhoda Wright, who appeared as a nude model in many of his paintings, died in December 2012. His son, John, also died in 2012. Colville is survived by his sons, Graham and Charles; his daughter, Ann Kitz; and his eight grandchildren and three great-grandchildren.

*See Current Biography 1985.*

# Barnaby Conrad

**Born:** San Francisco, California; March 27, 1922
**Died:** Carpinteria, California; February 12, 2013
**Occupation:** American author and painter

Barnaby Conrad was an American author, painter, and an amateur matador who took part in a number of bullfights in Spain, Mexico, and Peru. He wrote numerous books about bullfighting, including *In La Fiesta Brava: The Art of the Bull Ring* (1953), which covered the history of bullfighting and analyzed the sport; and *The Death of Manolete* (1958), a biography of his friend and fellow bullfighter, Manuel Laureano Rodríguez Sánchez (also known as Manolete). His best-known work, however, was his fictional novel, *Matador* (1952), which sold more than two million copies and was translated into twenty-eight languages.

Conrad was born on March 27, 1922, in San Francisco, California, but he was raised in the nearby suburb of Hillsborough. After studying at the University of North Carolina in 1940, Conrad left for Mexico in 1941 to study art at the University of Mexico. While in Mexico, Conrad was exposed to bullfighting and developed an interest in the sport.

Conrad returned to the United States to study art at Yale University. He then served in Spain as the United States vice-consul (1943–46). While in Spain, his interest in bullfighting was reawakened and he returned to the sport. He was severely wounded during a fight in El Escorial, Spain, in 1958, when a horn pierced his left thigh. Conrad used his experience fighting bulls in Spain to write his first novel, *Innocent Villa* (1948), and his best seller, *Matador*.

In 1947, Conrad was the personal secretary for Sinclair Lewis, an American novelist and winner of the 1930 Nobel Prize in Literature. Conrad and Sinclair made a tentative agreement to coauthor a book on John Wilkes Booth, but they never completed it together. Conrad eventually worked on the project on his own and published *The Second Life of John Wilkes Booth* in 2010. It was his final work of fiction. His last work of nonfiction was *101 Best Sex Scenes Ever Written: An Erotic Romp through Literature for Writers and Readers* (2011).

In addition to his career as an author, Conrad was also a successful painter. The portraits he painted of his famous literary friends—Truman Capote, Alex Haley, and James Michener—are displayed in the National Portrait Gallery in Washington, DC.

At the age of ninety, Conrad died on February 12, 2013, in Carpinteria, California. In addition to his wife of fifty years, Mary, Conrad is survived by his four children, two stepsons, eight grandchildren, and five step-grandchildren.

*See Current Biography 1959.*

# Jayne Cortez

**Born:** Fort Huachuca, Arizona; May 10, 1934
**Died:** New York City, New York; December 28, 2012
**Occupation:** African American poet

Jayne Cortez was an African American Poet and a performer who played a role in the Black Arts

Movement of the 1960s and 1970s. She published numerous volumes of poetry, including *Festivals and Funerals* (1971), *Jazz Fan Looks Back* (2002), and *Coagulations* (1984). She was also known for her public performances such as *Unsubmissive Blues* (1979) and *There It Is* (1982), which were recorded and set to music. Her works often took on themes such as race and gender issues, and she was heavily devoted to political protest and social change.

Cortez was born at Fort Huachuca, an army base in Arizona, but was raised mainly in Los Angeles, California, where here she relocated at the age of seven. She later became involved with the civil rights movement and worked in Mississippi at the Student Nonviolent Coordinating Committee in the summers of 1963 and 1964.

After founding the Watts Repertory Theatre Company in 1964, she gave her first poetry reading. She also founded Bola Press, where she published the majority of her books. Cortez blended both the oral and written arts. When she performed, for example, the words in her poetry took on musical qualities such as tempo, tone, and repetition. She performed in a number of well-known theatres, including Carnegie Hall. In 1954, she married the famous jazz musician Ornette Coleman with whom she had one son, Denardo. Cortez was also part of the Firespitters, a jazz band that included her son.

Cortez and Coleman divorced in 1964, and Cortez married the famous artist and sculptor, Melvin Edwards, in 1975. She taught at a number of universities—Rutgers, for example—and was a founder of the Organization for Women Writers of Africa in 1991.

Jayne Cortez died on December 28, 2012, in New York City from heart failure. She was seventy-eight years old. Cortez is survived by her son and second husband; her sister, Shawn Smith; three stepdaughters; and one grandson.

*See Current Biography 2001.*

# Colin Davis

**Born:** Weybridge, England; September 25, 1927
**Died:** London, England; April 14, 2013
**Occupation:** British conductor

A conductor noted for both dynamic exuberance and quiet confidence, Sir Colin Davis was the president of the London Symphony Orchestra, as well as its longest-serving principal conductor. Though Davis spent much of his career in London, he had international influence and appeal. In the United States, Davis served as the principal guest conductor for both the Boston Symphony (1972–84), and the New York Philharmonic (1998–2003). He was best known for his interpretations of Berlioz and the composers of the Romantic period—many performances of which were recorded, winning Davis ten Grammys over the course of his career. He became the principal conductor of the London Symphony in 1995 before becoming the orchestra's president in 2007.

Colin Rex Davis was born on September 25, 1927, in Weybridge—a town just southeast of London—the fifth of seven children. In his school-age years he excelled in the sciences, but Davis was determined to make music his life. He was admitted to the Royal College of Music in London on a clarinet scholarship, but having never learned piano, was barred from the school's conducting courses. Following a stint in the military from 1946 to 1948—during which he played in the band of the Life Guards at Windsor Castle—Davis began conducting the Kalmar Orchestra in 1949. That same year, he married his first wife, April Cantelo.

He garnered critical acclaim ten years later when, in October 1959, he substituted for Germany's Otto Klemperer at a performance with the London Philharmonic, conducting Mozart's *Don Giovanni*. Over the next year, Davis made an international name for himself. His ascension through the ranks of the professional music world was at times turbulent, as his temper and stubbornness sometimes led to clashes with musicians, organizations, and audiences alike.

Davis had two children with his first wife before the couple divorced. He married Ashraf Naini in 1964, and the couple had five children. Naini died in 2010. Davis was knighted in 1980, appointed Companion of Honour in 2001, and awarded the Queen's Medal for Music in 2009. He died on April 14, 2013, of unspecified causes. He was eighty-five.

*See Current Biography 1968.*

# Lisa Della Casa

**Born:** Burgdorf, Switzerland; February 2, 1919
**Died:** Münsterlingen, Switzerland; December 10, 2012
**Occupation:** Swiss opera singer

Lisa Della Casa was a Swiss soprano who was often referred to as the most beautiful woman on the operatic stage. She is best known for her natural and effortless singing ability and her portrayal of female heroines in operas such as Countess Almaviva in *The Marriage of Figaro* and Donna Elvira in *Don Giovanni*. Since her opera debut as the title role in Puccini's *Madama Butterfly* in 1941 at Solothurn-Biel Municipal Theater, Della Casa has appeared in hundreds of opera performances. At the Metropolitan Opera House in New York City, for example, she appeared in 147 performances.

At the age of fifteen, Della Casa started her professional vocal training at the Zurich Conservatory. After completing her training, she joined the Zurich Municipal Opera House in 1943, where she sang in Mozart's *The Magic Flute* and in *Così fan Tutte* as Dorabella. It wasn't until 1951, however, that she found her signature role as Strauss's Arabella and gained widespread recognition.

After Della Casa performed the secondary soprano role of Zdenka in *Arabella* in 1947, Strauss was so taken with her rendition that he said that she would one day have the title role. Della Casa's performance also caught the attention of the Vienna State Opera House, where she would spend the majority of her career. Some of her more notable performances include Arabella at the Covent Garden in Bavaria, Cleopatra in Handel's *Julius Caesar* at Munich in 1955, and her debut at the Metropolitan Opera House in New York City in the role of the Countess Almaviva in *The Marriage of Figaro*. She would return to the Metropolitan for eleven seasons, performing the role of the Countess Almaviva a total of forty-seven times.

In 1970, Della Casa's daughter, Vesna, had an aneurysm. In order to assist her husband and manager, Dragan Debeljevic, with their daughter's recovery, Della Casa cut back her performance schedule. She gave her last performance at the Vienna State Opera on October 25, 1973. A year later, despite being at the height of her career, she officially announced her retirement at the age of fifty-five. In her retirement, Della Casa lived with her family, splitting time between their Swiss castle and a seaside villa in Spain. Della Casa received a number of awards, including the Golden Opera Medal, the Gold Medal of the City of Vienna, and a Hans Reinhart Ring.

Lisa Della Casa died on December 10, 2012, in Münsterlingen, Switzerland. She was ninety-three years old. The city of Salzburg raised a black flag upon the news of her death.

*See Current Biography 1956.*

# Deanna Durbin

**Born:** December 4, 1921; Winnipeg, Canada
**Died:** April 20, 2013; Neauphle-le-Château, France
**Occupation:** Canadian singer and actor

Deanna Durbin was a Canadian singer and actress who starred in twenty-one feature films during her Hollywood career, including *Three Smart Girls* (1936), *One Hundred Men and a Girl* (1937), and *Lady on a Train* (1945). In 1939

Durbin was presented a special Academy Award for "bringing to the screen the spirit and personification of youth." Despite her fame and financial success, Durbin ended her acting career early in 1949 when she was twenty-eight years old and relocated to Neauphle-le-Château, France, with her husband, Charles David, a French film director. One of her most famous quotes about Hollywood sheds light on her decision to end her acting career at a young age: "I hated being stuck in a goldfish bowl."

Durbin was born on December 4, 1921, in Winnipeg, Manitoba, but she was raised in Southern California. After being discovered by MGM studios, she costarred with Judy Garland in the short film *Every Sunday* (1936). But Durbin's fame came after starring in her first feature-length film, *Three Smart Girls* (1936), which she made with Universal Studios (her career with MGM ended after they dropped her contract). The film's success catapulted Durbin's career and she landed lead roles in ten popular Universal films before she was twenty years old, including *First Love* (1939) and *Spring Parade* (1940). Consequently, she became one of the highest paid actors of the time with a salary surpassing $320,000 in 1946.

Similar to many young stars, however, Durbin had difficulty making the transition from child star to adult actress. In the 1944 film *Christmas Holiday*, for instance, she was criticized for her attempt to portray an adult role—a prostitute in love with a murderer—that critics believed was incongruous with her child-star persona. On top of her poor reviews, her first two marriages ended in divorce.

While filming *Lady on a Train* (1945), Durbin met her third husband, Charles David, the film's director. They were married in 1950. Both their marriage and the film were a success: David and Durbin were together for nearly fifty years, and the film received good reviews. Durbin's twenty-first and last film was *For the Love of Mary* (1948), after which she retired with her husband to a farmhouse in Neauphle-le-Château, France, and withdrew from the public eye. In a 1982 interview with the *Times* David revealed that Durbin had "retired from the film world when we were married. When she was a star she behaved like a star, and played ball with the publicity boys. But she never enjoyed that part of her life. As soon as she could, she gave it up."

On April 20, 2013, Durbin died at her home in Neauphle-le-Château, France. She was ninety-one years old. Her husband, David, died in 1999 just prior to their fiftieth wedding anniversary. In addition to her daughter from her second marriage, Jesse Jackson, Durbin is survived by her son, Peter H. David.

*See Current Biography 1941.*

# Charles Durning

**Born:** Highland Falls, New York; February 28, 1923
**Died:** New York City, New York; December 24, 2012
**Occupation:** American actor

Charles Durning was an American actor whose career spanned the stage, television, and film. Some of his notable film appearances include *The Sting* (1973), *True Confessions* (1981), and *Tootsie* (1982), in which he played the role of Dustin Hoffman's would-be suitor. He also portrayed a small town mayor in the play *That Championship Season* (1972), which won the Pulitzer Prize, the Tony Award, and the New York Drama Critics Circle Award. But he is perhaps known best for his performances as a corrupt governor in *The Best Little Whorehouse in Texas* (1982), and a Nazi colonel in *To Be or Not to Be* (1983), each of which earned him a best supporting actor Oscar nomination.

Durning was born on February 28, 1923, in Highland Falls, New York. He was one of ten children and was born into poverty. He served in World War II and was in the first wave of US soldiers that landed on Omaha Beach during the D-Day invasion of Normandy. Durning survived wounds he sustained from being shot and stabbed, and he escaped a massacre of US soldiers after being captured by German soldiers during the Battle of the Bulge. He was awarded the Silver Star for valor and three Purple Hearts for his service in World War II. In 2008, France awarded him the National Order of the Legion of Honor.

After the war, he became an acting student at the American Academy of Dramatic Arts in New York. In 1962, Joseph Papp, founder of the New York Shakespeare Festival, asked Durning to audition and gave him his first big break as an actor. He subsequently appeared in a number of plays, including *The Happiness Cage* (1970) and *The Wars of the Roses* (1970). He also saw success in television and was Emmy-nominated for his performances in *Captains and the Kings* (1976), *Attica* (1980), and a CBS production of *Death of a Salesman* (1985).

In addition to his Oscar-nominated performances in *The Best Little Whorehouse in Texas* (1982) and *To Be or Not to Be* (1983), he also played notable roles as Chief Brandon in *Dick Tracey* (1990) and a Southern governor in *O Brother, Where Art Thou?* (2000). His last film appearance was in *Scavenger Killers*, which, at the time of his death, was scheduled to release in 2013.

Durning died at his home in Manhattan on December 24, 2012. He was eighty-nine years old. He had three children with his first wife, Carole Doughty, whom he divorced in 1972.

He married Mary Ann Amelio in 1974, but the couple was separated at the time of his death. Durning is survived by his two daughters, Michele and Jeanine, and his son, Douglas.

*See Current Biography 1997.*

# Ronald Myles Dworkin

**Born:** Worcester, Massachusetts
December 11, 1931
**Died:** London, United Kingdom; February 14, 2013
**Occupation:** American law professor

Ronald Myles Dworkin was an American law professor and legal philosopher. He taught law at a number of universities, including Yale University, New York University, and University College, London. Dworkin was the author of books such as *Life's Dominion* (1993), on the controversial issues of abortion and euthanasia; and *Law's Empire* (1986), which explained the workings of the Anglo-American legal system and the nature of adjudication, the formal judgment or legal process in a court of law. According to his colleague, the legal philosopher Tomas Nagel, Dworkin had the ability to "explain difficult moral issues about law, politics and society in lucid terms to a general nonacademic audience."

On December 11, 1931, Dworkin was born in Worcester, Massachusetts. After graduating from Harvard University in 1953, he became a Rhodes Scholar at Oxford University, where he graduated with a BA in 1955. He then returned to Cambridge, Massachusetts, and earned his LLB from Harvard Law School in 1957. After leaving Harvard and working briefly as a law clerk for Judge Learned Hand, Dworkin worked as an associate for Sullivan & Cromwell, a law firm based in New York, from 1958 to 1962.

Dworkin's career in academia began in 1962, when Yale University invited him to join their faculty as an assistant professor of law. He was promoted to full professor of law in 1965 and soon attracted the attention of other universities. In 1969 he became the professor of jurisprudence at Oxford University. He continued to teach at Oxford, but also joined New York University's law school in 1975 with a joint appointment as a professor of law. He therefore became conversant with the legal systems of both the United States and the United Kingdom.

Dworkin published numerous articles on law, including "Is the Law a System of Rules?" (1967), which was known for its critique of legal positivism. Dworkin's first book, *Taking Rights Seriously* (1977), was a collection of essays that analyzed and offered arguments against both legal positivism and utilitarianism. Another notable book was *Freedom's Law: The Moral Reading of the American Constitution* (1996), which helped establish Dworkin's theory about the United States Constitution's plasticity and ability to adapt to changing times.

In addition to his successful career in academia, Dworkin's liberal views on issues such as abortion, civil liberties, and affirmative action caught the attention of the Democratic Party. He was, therefore, selected as a delegate to the Democratic National Convention in 1972 and 1976. He was also the chairman of Democrats Abroad (1972–74).

On February 14, 2013, Dworkin died in London from leukemia. He was eighty-one years old. His first wife, Betsy, died in 2000. Dworkin is survived by his second wife, Irene Brendel Dworkin; his son, Anthony; his daughter, Jennifer; and his two grandchildren.

*See Current Biography Illustrated 2000.*

# Roger Ebert

**Born:** Urbana, Illinois; June 18, 1942
**Died:** Chicago, Illinois; April 4, 2013
**Occupation:** American film critic

Roger Ebert was one of the best-known American film critics whose trademark thumbs-up-or-thumbs-down approach could make or break a movie. In 1975, he became the first film critic to win a Pulitzer Prize for the movie reviews he wrote for the *Chicago Sun-Times*, where he had worked for more than forty years. Ebert was known for his sarcastic and often humorous reviews, such as his review of the 1996 film *Mad Dog Time*: "Watching *Mad Dog Time* is like waiting for the bus in a city where you're not sure they have a bus line." However, according to a statement released by President Obama, when Ebert liked a film, "he was effusive—capturing the unique power of the movies to take us somewhere magical."

Roger Ebert was born on June 18, 1942, in Urbana, Illinois. He showed an interest in journalism at a young age, writing and self-publishing a newspaper, the *Washington Street News*, in his home and distributing it to houses in his neighborhood. Ebert graduated from the University of Illinois at Urbana-Champaign in 1964 with a degree in journalism. He was also a doctoral candidate at the University of Chicago, but he left before earning his PhD in English to accept a full-time position at the *Chicago Sun-Times*. In 1967, he became the paper's film critic at the age of twenty-four.

By the 1970s, Ebert's film reviews for the *Sun-Times* were being syndicated to approximately one hundred newspapers across the country. After winning the Pulitzer in 1975, he was asked to cohost a movie review program, *Opening Soon at a Theater Near You*, in Chicago with Gene Siskel, a film critic for the *Chicago Tribune*. The show was an instant success and, by 1978, the Public Broadcasting Service (PBS) was broadcasting the show nationwide. (The show's name changed a number of times, but it was perhaps best known as *Siskel and Ebert at the Movies*.) The criticism of Ebert and Siskel could help lift a film to the top of the charts, or destroy its reputation, as expressed by Eddie Murphy in a 1987 interview: "Siskel and Ebert go, 'Horrible picture,' and I'm telling you, [they] can definitely kill a movie." After Siskel died from a brain tumor in 1999, the show became *Roger Ebert and the Movies*, and then *Ebert and Roeper*, after Richard Roeper joined as the permanent cohost in 2000.

In addition to his criticism of Hollywood blockbusters, Ebert was also credited for bringing independent and artistic films to the public's attention. He launched a film festival, eventually called Ebertfest, which featured mainly independent films that were not on the public's radar.

Ebert's struggle with cancer and related health problems began in 2002. Consequently, he had a number of operations on his chin and thyroid that left him unable to speak. But he continued to write reviews and utilized social media to maintain his public presence. At the time of his death, for example, he had more than 800,000 followers on Twitter.

Ebert died on April 4, 2013, in Chicago, Illinois. The last film Ebert wrote a review for was *To the Wonder* (2012), and it was published posthumously in the *Chicago Sun-Times*. Ebert gave the film 3.5 stars. Ebert is survived by his wife, Chaz Hammelsmith.

*See Current Biography 1997.*

# Dennis Farina

**Born:** Chicago, Illinois; February 29, 1944
**Died:** Scottsdale, Arizona; July 22, 2013
**Occupation:** American actor

Dennis Farina was an American actor best-known for his detective roles in the television series *Law and Order* and *Crime Story*. Prior to his acting career, Farina was a police officer in Chicago for approximately twenty years. It was partly his experience in law enforcement that caught the attention of director Michael Mann, who sought Farina's consultation for the film *Thief* (1981) and cast him in a minor role as a crime boss's enforcer. Farina appeared in a number of other films, most notably *Manhunter* (1986), *Get Shorty* (1995), and *Saving Private Ryan* (1998), which won five Academy Awards.

Farina was born in Chicago, Illinois, on February 29, 1944. After serving in the US Army (1962–65), he returned to Chicago and took a job in law enforcement. Farina's plans to become a detective were diverted when his friend and retired police officer, Charlie Adamson, introduced him to director Michael Mann. Farina landed a small role in Mann's film *Thief*, which opened the door to other acting opportunities. In 1984, he appeared in hit television shows, including *The Killing Floor* and *Miami Vice*. During this time, Farina juggled his career as a police officer with acting, but by 1986 he had retired from the police force altogether to pursue a full-time career in Hollywood.

Farina's first major film role was the mobster Ray "Bones" Barboni in the 1995 hit film *Get Shorty*. The film grossed more than $70 million in the United States. This was soon followed by roles in Spielberg's *Saving Private Ryan* (1998) and Soderbergh's *Out of Sight* (1998). Despite the success of these films, the quality of Farina's roles declined slightly; for example, his television series, *Buddy Faro* (1998), was canceled after only eight episodes. His luck improved, however, in 2004 when he landed the role of Joe Fontana in *Law & Order*, one of the most successful and longest-running shows on television.

Farina died on July 22, 2013, in Scottsdale, Arizona, from a blood clot in his lungs, according to his publicist, Lori De Waal. He was sixty-nine years old. His first marriage to Patricia Farina ended in divorce in 1980. He is survived by his partner of more than thirty years Marianna Cahill; his three sons, Dennis Jr., Michael, and Joseph; and his six grandchildren.

*See Current Biography 2001.*

# Martin Fay

**Born:** Dublin, Ireland; September 19, 1936
**Died:** Dublin, Ireland; November 14, 2012
**Occupation:** Irish fiddler and member of the Chieftains

Martin Fay was an Irish fiddler and one of the founding members of the Chieftains, a traditional Irish band from Dublin. In 1962, Fay joined Chieftain's founder, Paddy Maloney, along with Sean Potts, a whistle player, and Michael Tubridy, who played the tin whistle, Irish flute, and the concertina. Over the course of his career, the Chieftains have received eighteen Grammy nominations and won six times. In addition to the Grammy awards, they have won an Emmy and a Genie award.

Fay's passion for music began after watching a film on Niccolò Paganini, a famous Italian violinist, which inspired him to take up the violin. He was a classically trained violinist, and this training provided him with an excellent foundation for his mastery of the fiddle. Fay received a full scholarship to the Municipal School of Music in Dublin and played briefly for Ireland's Abbey Theater, where he was a member of the orchestra.

The Chieftains were celebrated for reviving traditional Irish music. The success of their traditional approach to music led not only to recording contracts, but also work in television and film. Their song, "Women of Ireland," for example, was featured in *Barry Lyndon* (1975), a film by Stanley Kubrick. Another milestone in their career was the 1979 concert for Pope John Paul II, where they played before more than one million people in Phoenix Park, Dublin. Due to their international success, The Chieftains were made the official musical ambassadors for the Republic of Ireland in 1989.

When Martin Fay stopped touring in 2001, he had contributed to more than thirty albums with the Chieftains. A year later, they received the Lifetime Achievement Award by the BBC in the United Kingdom. Fay will be remembered not only for his musicianship, but for his vivacious personality, his wonderful sense of humor, and his captivating stage presence.

On November 14, 2012, Martin Fay died in his home in Dublin, Ireland. He was seventy-six years old. Fay is survived by his sister; his wife, Grainne; his daughter, Dearbhla Fay; his son Fergal; and a grandson.

*See Current Biography 2004.*

# Thomas Foley

**Born:** Spokane, Washington; March 6, 1929
**Died:** Washington, DC; October 18, 2013
**Occupation:** American Speaker of the House

Thomas Foley was best known for serving as the Speaker of the US House of Representatives from June 6, 1989, to January 3, 1995. During his tenure as Speaker, Foley was successful in influencing President George Bush to increase taxes in a 1990 deficit-reduction deal, and he helped pass President Clinton's 1993 budget plan in the House. Foley was also commended for his ability to cooperate with both political parties, which former House Speaker Nancy Pelosi called his "unrivaled ability to build consensus and find common ground."

Foley was born on March 6, 1929, in Spokane, Washington. After graduating from the University of Washington in 1951 with this bachelor's degree and his law degree in 1957, he became the deputy prosecutor of Spokane County in 1958. He then became the assistant state attorney general in 1960, and from there he was hired by Senator Henry M. Jackson of Washington and became a staff member of the Senate

Committee on the Interior. In 1964, Senator Jackson encouraged Foley to run against Walt Horan, the Republican incumbent. Despite his apprehension to run for office in a conservative district in eastern Washington State, he entered the race, defeated Horan, and was elected to the US House of Representatives.

In addition to Speaker of the House, Foley held a number of leadership positions in Congress, including the chairman of the agricultural committee (1975–80), Democratic whip (1981–87), and the House majority leader (1987–89). On June 6, 1989, he replaced the incumbent Jim Wright, a Democrat from Texas, as Speaker of the House. He served as Speaker until he was defeated in his bid for reelection in 1994. That year, Republicans gained the majority in the House; then Representative Newt Gingrich of Georgia became the new Speaker. After his defeat, Foley left Congress and became the chairman of President Clinton's Foreign Intelligence Advisory Board from 1995 to 1997. He then was appointed by Clinton to serve as the United States ambassador to Japan from 1997 to 2001.

Foley died on October 18, 2013, in Washington, DC. He was eighty-four years old. He is survived by his wife, Heather Strachan, whom he married in 1968, and his sister, Maureen Latimer.

*See Current Biography 1989.*

# Frederic Franklin

**Born:** Liverpool, United Kingdom; June 13, 1914
**Died:** New York, New York; May 4, 2013
**Occupation:** British ballet dancer and choreographer

Frederic Franklin was a British-born ballet dancer and choreographer best known for his renowned performances with his dance partner Alexandra Danilova, a famous Russian ballerina, in ballets such as *Swan Lake* and *Coppélia*. Known as Freddie in the dance world, Franklin enjoyed a prolific career and continued to perform characters roles in *Swan Lake* and *Romeo and Juliet* into his nineties, long after most ballet dancers retire from the stage. His extensive experience coupled with his impressive memory of the ballets he appeared in made him a sought after and well-respected teacher to a new generation of ballet dancers. Franklin was also an inspiration to many notable choreographers, including George Balanchine, one of the most famous contemporary choreographers of ballet.

Franklin was born on June 13, 1914, in Liverpool, United Kingdom. When he was six years old, his mother signed him up for dance lessons at Mrs. Kelly's Dance School in Liverpool. In 2009, he told the *Guardian* that he was "the only

boy in my dancing class, but it never bothered me. I danced in competitions and the next day, when I went into school and said I'd won a medal, the other children were all very interested. There was no teasing. None." But he was raised during a time when ballet roles for male dancers were scarce, and he was unable to find one when he moved to London at the age of seventeen. Instead, he joined the Lancashire Lads, a tap-dancing group. The group performed as the Jackson Boys in a Parisian cabaret-style show starring Josephine Baker. It wasn't until 1935 that Franklin joined the Markova-Dolin Ballet and was able to pursue his passion. Here, he caught the attention of Léonide Massine, a well-known Russian choreographer, who urged Franklin to join the Ballet Russe de Monte Carlo in 1938.

Franklin performed with the Ballet Russe for more than fifteen years, touring throughout Europe and the United States. He also teamed up with Alexandra Danilova while with the Ballet Russe, and the pair danced together in a number of productions, most notably as the Prince and Odette in *Swan Lake*.

In addition to performing on the stage, Franklin choreographed his own ballets such as *Tribute* in 1961 for the Ballet Russe and *Creole Giselle*, a restaged version of *Giselle* for the Dance Theatre Harlem in 1984. He also teamed up with Jean M. Riddel in 1962 to establish the National Ballet of Washington. After the company was dissolved in 1974, he worked as an advisor to a number of dance companies such as Dance Theater of Harlem and the Oakland Ballet. Among many awards and honors, Franklin was named a Commander of the British Empire in 2004. In 2011 he received the New York Dance and Performance Award—also known as a Bessie—for Outstanding Service to the Field of Dance, one of the highest honors in the world of dance.

Franklin died on May, 4, 2013, in New York City. He was ninety-eight years old. His last performance was in 2010 with the American Ballet Theatre as the friar in *Romeo and Juliet*. Franklin is survived by his partner of forty-eight years, William Haywood Ausman; his brother, John; his niece, Pamela Hayes Brookfield; and four nephews.

*See Current Biography 1943.*

# Antonio Frasconi

**Born:** Buenos Aires, Argentina; April 28, 1919
**Died:** Norwalk, Connecticut; January 8, 2013
**Occupation:** Uruguayan painter and wood engraver

Antonio Frasconi was an artist best-known for his woodcuts. His work has appeared in art museums and art festivals throughout the world, including the Metropolitan Museum of Art and the Museum of Modern Art in New York City; the National Gallery of Art and the Smithsonian American Art Museum in Washington, DC; and the Venice Biennale, a contemporary arts festival in Venice, Italy, that occurs every two years. His art often dealt with themes such as war and racism. Some of his best-known works, for example, were two series of woodcuts entitled *The Disappeared* (1981) and *In Memoriam* (1981–88), respectively, which portrayed the torture and incarceration of the victims of the rightist military dictatorship in Uruguay that lasted from 1973 to 1985. He also illustrated more than one-hundred books, including *12 Fables of Aesop* (1967).

The son of Italian immigrants, Frasconi and his family moved to Uruguay a few weeks after he was born in Buenos Aires, Argentina, on April 28, 1919. He dropped out of art school at a young age, but would later receive a one-year scholarship in 1945 to study at the Arts Students League in New York. In 1962, he won a Horn Book Fanfare award for the bilingual children's book *The Snow and the Sun/La Nieve y el Sol* (1961). In addition to books, Frasconi also illustrated poems by Langston Hughes, such as *Let America Be America Again* (2005) and Pablo Neruda's *Bestiary/Bestiario* (1965).

Frasconi received the great honor of representing his home country of Uruguay at the prestigious Venice Biennale art festival in Venice, Italy in 1968, where he showcased over twenty years' worth of artwork. He was also celebrated for his illustrations of children's books, including the bilingual book, *The House That Jack Built/La Maison que Jacques a Bâtie* (1958) that was awarded the Caldecott honor in 1971 by the American Library Association.

Frasconi died at his home in Norwalk, Connecticut on January 8, 2013. He was ninety-three years old. His second wife, Leona Pierce, died in 2002. He is survived by his two sons, Miguel and Pablo, and his granddaughter.

*See Current Illustrated Biography 1972.*

# William Clyde Friday

**Born:** Raphine, Virginia; July 13, 1920
**Died:** Chapel Hill, North Carolina; October 12, 2012
**Occupation:** American educator and television host

William Clyde "Bill" Friday was a prominent American educator and head of the University of North Carolina System from 1956 to 1986. He is credited with overseeing substantial growth for the North Carolina education system—increasing the student body by more than eight times its original size, from an estimated 15,000 to over 125,500 students. The budget also saw considerable improvement and increased to $1.5

billion from $40.7 million. Friday's most significant accomplishment, however, was guiding North Carolina though a federal order (*Brown vs. Board of Education*) to desegregate public schools, which he referred to as, "the greatest social issue we have faced in generations."

Despite controversy and pressure from Washington that Friday was not fully complying with the desegregation law, he introduced moderate segregation in order to avoid conflict in a state with a long and deep-rooted history of racial tension. Friday was determined to implement the law as he saw fit, disregarding criticism from the NAACP and the plan established by the US Department of Health, Education, and Welfare.

Friday, who held a bachelor's degree in textile manufacturing from UNC and a law degree from the University of North Carolina at Chapel Hill, overcame competition from academics with extensive experience and PhDs and was elected president of the North Carolina Education System in 1956. He was also the cofounder of the Knight Foundation Commissions on Intercollegiate Athletics, a program dedicated to improving athletic programs in universities and establishing academic standards for college athletes. In addition to his career in higher education, Friday was also the popular host of a North Carolina television show, *North Carolina People with William Friday*.

On October 12, 2012, William Clyde Friday died from natural causes in his home in Chapel Hill, North Carolina. He was ninety-two years old. Friday is survived by his wife, Ida, and his two daughters, Frances and Mary. After his death, the governor of North Carolina, Bev Perdue, publicly honored Friday's achievements in education: "There has been no person in North Carolina's history who more fully exemplified how one individual can, year after year, make a tremendous difference."

*See Current Biography 1958.*

# David Frost

**Born:** Tenterden, England; April 7, 1939
**Died:** August 31, 2013
**Occupation:** English broadcaster

David Frost was a broadcast journalist best known for his interviews of famous figures such as John Lennon, George Clooney, and every US president from Richard M. Nixon to George W. Bush. Frost's most memorable interview, however, was with Nixon in 1977, about three years after the Watergate scandal.

After President Nixon resigned on August 9, 1974, he was eager to salvage his reputation. The series of interviews with Frost ended

Nixon's silence on Watergate and prompted his much-anticipated apology and famous statement of regret: "I let the American people down and I have to carry that burden with me for the rest of my life." Frost also elicited a number of widely quoted and controversial remarks from Nixon concerning the abuse of presidential power, including, "Well, when the president does it, that means that it is not illegal." The interview was broadcast around the world and became the most-watched television interview at the time; consequently, Frost became an internationally known broadcast journalist.

Frost was born on April 7, 1939, in Tenterden, England. After graduating from Cambridge University, he became the host of the BBC television show *That Was the Week That Was* in 1962. Frost then continued his career in television and appeared on a number of shows, including *David Frost's Night Out in London* and *The Frost Report*, a sketch show that became popular in the United States.

In addition to his world-famous interviews and television career, Frost was also the author of more than a dozen books, including *The Americans* (1970), *Billy Graham Talks with David Frost* (1987), and *I Gave Them a Sword: Behind the Scenes of the Nixon interviews* (1978). His interviews with Nixon became the premise for the 2007 Oscar-nominated film *Frost/Nixon*.

Frost died on August 31, 2013, from a heart attack while aboard the ocean liner Queen Elizabeth. He was seventy-four years old. Frost is survived by his wife, Carina, and his three sons.

*See Current Biography 1969.*

---

# Annette Funicello

**Born:** Utica, New York; October 22, 1942
**Died:** Bakersfield, California; April 8, 2013
**Occupation:** American actress and singer

Annette Funicello began her career on the children's television show *The Mickey Mouse Club* in 1955, where she was cast as one of the twenty four original Mouseketeers. Funicello would later transition to film with her debut in *The Shaggy Dog* (1959). She was also a recording artist and released albums such as *Dance Annette* (1961) and had two top ten singles: "O Dio Mio" (1960) and "Tall Paul" (1959). Her other notable film appearances include *Babes in Toyland* (1961), *The Monkey's Uncle* (1965), and a number of so-called beach movies in the 1960s, such as *Muscle Beach Party* (1964).

Funicello was born on October 22, 1942, in Utica, New York. She was twelve years old when Walt Disney, head of the Disney film studio, discovered her during a performance of *Swan Lake* at her high school. Disney personally invited

Funicello to audition for *The Mickey Mouse Club*, and she was cast in 1955. After the show ended in 1959, she was the only original Mouseketeer to be offered a studio contract from Disney. In the first year of her contract, Funicello released her hit single "Tall Paul," (1959), and she began to record a number of albums with the company, such as *Italiannette* (1960) and *Hawaiiannette* (1960).

In the 1960s, Funicello starred in a number of beach-themed movies with Frankie Avalon, including *Beach Party* (1963) and *Bikini Beach* (1964). She married Jack Gilardi, her agent, in 1965 (the couple divorced in 1981). Funicello reunited with Avalon in the 1987 film *Back to the Beach*, which playfully parodied their beach party films of the 1960s. In 1987, Funicello was also diagnosed with multiple sclerosis (MS), a chronic autoimmune disease.

Funicello kept her diagnosis a secret for five years, but she disclosed her illness after physical symptoms became visible. She became a spokesperson for the disease and started the Annette Funicello Research Fund for Neurological Diseases, which funds research aimed at developing treatments and cures for multiple sclerosis and other neurological diseases. She published an autobiography about her career and her struggle with MS, *A Dream Is a Wish Your Heart Makes* (1994) and, in 1995, appeared in a television film based on the book.

Funicello died on April 8, 2013, in Bakersfield, California, from complications associated with multiple sclerosis. She was seventy years old. In 1986, she married Glen Holt, who survives her, along with her three children, four step-children, twelve grandchildren, and four great-grandchildren.

*See Current Biography 2002.*

---

# James Gandolfini

**Born:** Westwood, New Jersey; September 18, 1961
**Died:** Rome, Italy; June 19, 2013
**Occupation:** American actor

James Gandolfini was best known for his portrayal of Tony Soprano, a tough-talking and anxiety-ridden New Jersey mafia boss on HBO's hit television series, *The Sopranos*. The show, which aired from 1999 to 2007, not only made HBO one of the most popular programs for scripted television series, but also earned Gandolfini three Emmy Awards for outstanding actor in a lead drama (he was nominated six times). *The Sopranos* also won two Emmys for outstanding drama series. The show centered on the complicated character of Tony Soprano, whose dark and violent exterior life as a mob boss was juxtaposed with a vulnerable and caring family life that elicited sympathy and understanding from the audience.

James Gandolfini was born in Westwood, New Jersey, on September 18, 1961. He attended Rutgers University and graduated in 1983 with a degree in communications. He started taking acting classes not long after graduating college, and his professional acting career began in the horror film *Shock! Shock! Shock!* (1987). It wasn't until the mid-1990s, however, that Gandolfini found his niche in mob roles in films such as *True Romance* (1993) and *The Juror* (1996). In 1999, David Chase, the creator of *The Sopranos*, casted Gandolfini as Tony Soprano, a role that earned him super-star status. According to Chase, Gandolfini was "one of the greatest actors of this or any time…I remember telling him many times: 'You don't get it. You're like Mozart."

Before accepting the title role on *The Sopranos*, Gandolfini studied the Meisner acting technique, which emphasizes instinctual and emotional reactions that express genuine emotion in a performance. For example, in an interview with *Inside the Actor's Studio*, Gandolfini recalled how he used the Meisner technique to evoke believable anger by not sleeping or walking around with a rock in his shoe.

After *The Sopranos* ended in 2007, Gandolfini appeared in a number of film roles, including *The Taking of Pelham 123* (2009), *Welcome to the Rileys* (2010), and *Zero Dark Thirty* (2012). He also won a Tony Award in 2009 for his role in the Broadway production of *God of Carnage*. In addition to film and theatre, Gandolfini produced two documentaries, *Alive Day Memories: Home from Iraq* (2007) and *Wartorn: 1861–2010* (2010), about the impact of war on US soldiers returning from battle.

James Gandolfini died from a heart attack on June 19, 2013, while vacationing in Rome, Italy. He was fifty-one years old. Gandolfini's first marriage to Marcella Wudarski ended in divorce in 2002. He is survived by his second wife, Deborah Lin Gandolfini; his sisters, Leta Gandolfini and Johanna Antonacci; his son, Michael; and his daughter, Liliana.

*See Current Biography 2000.*

## John J. Gilligan

**Born:** Cincinnati, Ohio; March 22, 1921
**Died:** Cincinnati, Ohio; August 26, 2013
**Occupation:** American governor and congressman

John J. Gilligan was best known as the governor of Ohio (1971–74) who implemented the state's controversial income tax in 1971. Also as governor, Gilligan helped create the Ohio Environmental Protection Agency and pass the strip-mine-reclamation laws, and he increased state funding

for schools. Despite his accomplishments, the hefty income tax he enacted was not well received by voters, and Gilligan lost the 1974 gubernatorial election to James A. Rhodes.

Gilligan was born on March 22, 1921, in Cincinnati, Ohio. After graduating from Notre Dame University in 1943, Gilligan was a US Navy gunnery officer during World War II. He received a number of honors for his military service, including three Area Campaign Ribbons, five Battle Stars, and a Silver Star for saving crew members during a battle in Okinawa. After the war, he attended the University of Cincinnati and earned his master's degree in literature in 1947. He then taught English literature at Xavier University in Cincinnati until 1953, when he made a transition into politics and was elected to the Cincinnati's City Council. He was elected to the US House of Representatives in 1964, but lost reelection in 1966. He was defeated again in the 1968 election for US Senate by William B. Saxbe.

Gilligan successfully campaigned for the Democratic nomination for governor and won the general election on November 3, 1970. When he took office he faced a significant crisis in which twenty-four school districts closed due to a lack of necessary funds. The primary goal of the income tax he implemented was to raise money to deal with the failing school districts and to prevent others from closing down. The income tax, however, was unpopular with the public, and his opponent in the 1974 gubernatorial election, James A. Rhodes, used this to his advantage to defeat Gilligan by a slim margin of eleven thousand votes. After losing the election, Gilligan became a fellow at the Woodrow Wilson International Center for scholars in Washington, DC. He returned to the University of Cincinnati in 1992 to direct the College of Law's Civic Forum.

Gilligan died on August 26, 2013, at his home in Cincinnati, Ohio. He was ninety-two years old. His first wife, Mary Katharine Dixon, died in 1996. Gilligan's daughter, Kathleen Sebelius, served as the governor of Kansas and is the Obama administration's health and human services secretary. In addition to Sebelius, Gilligan is survived by his second wife, Susan Fremont; another daughter, Ellen Gilligan; and his two sons, Donald and John.

*See Current Biography 1972.*

## Donald Arthur Glaser

**Born:** Cleveland, Ohio; September 21, 1926
**Died:** Berkeley, California; February 28, 2013
**Occupation:** American physicist

Donald Arthur Glaser was an American physicist and winner of the Nobel Prize in Physics (1960) for his invention of the bubble chamber. The bubble chamber, which Glaser described as a "pressure cooker with windows," allowed physicists to observe residual gas bubbles left in the wake of a subatomic particle that passed through a superheated liquid. This device enhanced the study and visualization of subatomic particles and lead to the discovery of other subatomic particles. For example, the bubble chamber allowed scientists to discover that, similar to how neutrons and protons compose an atom's nucleus, neutrons and protons are composed of subatomic particles called quarks.

On September 21, 1926, Glaser was born in Cleveland, Ohio. He was a graduate of the Case School of Applied Science (now part of Case Western Reserve University) and received his PhD from the California Institute of Technology. In 1949, he joined the faculty of the University of Michigan, where he began his research on his Nobel Prize–winning invention, the bubble chamber. He would later teach at the University of California, Berkeley starting in 1959.

Glaser was twenty-five years old when he invented the bubble-chamber in 1952. The device he created substituted a superheated liquid for gas—which was used in a cloud chamber, then the main device for studying subatomic particles. He found that liquid was superior to gas because it showed a particle's trajectory in more detail via a trail of bubbles that could be photographed and studied. After winning the Nobel in 1960, Glaser moved on to research microbiology and later neurobiology. For example, he experimented with and developed mathematical models that simulated how the human brain perceived motion. In 1971, he helped found Cetus Corporation, a biotech company that focused on developing cancer treatments.

Glaser died on February 28, 2013, at his home in Berkeley, California. He was eighty-six years old. Glaser's marriage to Ruth Thompson Glaser ended in divorce. His survivors include his second wife, Lynn Bercovitz Glaser; his daughter, Louise; his son, William; and his four grandchildren.

*See Current Biography Illustrated 1961.*

# Jozef Glemp

**Born:** Inowroclaw, Poland; December 18, 1929
**Died:** Warsaw, Poland; January 23, 2013
**Occupation:** Polish cardinal of the Roman Catholic Church

Jozef Glemp was the cardinal of Poland and the religious leader of its approximately thirty-four million Catholics. His leadership was tested in the 1980s when Poland's Communist regime clashed with the Solidarity worker's movement, an independent labor union. He was accused a number of times of anti-Semitism, including an incident in 1989 when he defended the location of a Carmelite convent (a community of Catholic nuns) at the former site of Auschwitz, where the Nazis operated their largest concentration camp and extermination camp during World War II.

Glemp was born in Inowroclaw, Poland, on December 18, 1929. After his ordination as a priest in 1956, he went to Rome and earned doctorates in civil and canon law. After completing his studies in Rome at the Pontifical Gregorian University in the Vatican, Glemp returned to Poland and became the legal advisor to Poland's Cardinal, Stefan Wyszynski, in 1967.

Pope John Paul II appointed Glemp the Bishop of Warmia in 1979, where he served more than one million Catholics in the diocese. After the death of Cardinal Wyszynski in 1981, the pope named Glemp the eightieth metropolitan archbishop of Warsaw and the fifty-sixth primate of Poland. He became a cardinal in 1983.

During his leadership of Poland's Roman Catholic Church, Glemp played an important role in promoting peace when martial law was implemented in 1981 and tensions between the Communist regime and the Solidarity worker's movement intensified. In 1989, Glemp saw the first semifree elections in Poland and the election of Tadeusz Mazowiecki, a non-Communist, as prime minister.

In 2006, Cardinal Glemp left his position as archbishop of Warsaw and was replaced by Stanislaw Wielgus, who resigned after being in office a mere two days over allegations that he had been a spy for the Communist authorities. Glemp retired as primate of Poland in 2009, but he continued to be a religious presence in Poland until his death on January 23, 2013, in Warsaw. He was eighty-three years old and has no survivors.

*See Current Biography 1982.*

# Eydie Gorme

**Born:** New York, New York; August 16, 1928
**Died:** Las Vegas, Nevada; August 10, 2013
**Occupation:** American singer

Hailed for her lively stage presence and wide vocal range, Eydie Gorme charmed audiences as a solo artist and as part of a duo with her husband Steve Lawrence. As Steve and Eydie, Gorme and Lawrence churned out pop standards at a time when rock and roll was taking off in America. The couple's popular stage show was rife with banter about their married life that sometimes bordered on risqué by the day's standards. In 1960, Steve and Eydie won a Grammy Award for best pop duo, and the pair went on to win a 1979

Emmy Award for outstanding comedy-variety or music program for their television special *Steve & Eydie Celebrate Irving Berlin*. As a solo artist, Gorme—who spoke Spanish fluently—had a major hit in Spanish-speaking countries with the single "Amor," and garnered a Grammy nomination of her own in 1963 for "Blame It on the Bossa Nova."

Edith Gormezano was born in the Bronx, on August 16, 1928 to an Italian father and a Turkish mother. Both were Sephardic Jews and spoke Ladino, a variant of Old Spanish, and English at home. After graduating from high school, Gorme worked as a translator for the United Nations while trying to get her singing career off the ground. Gorme caught her break on Steve Allen's local New York show in 1953, when she was hired to perform for two weeks, but ended up staying on for years, following the show through its transformation into *Tonight*. It was during her time with Steve Allen that Gorme met Lawrence, a fellow cast member. The couple married in Las Vegas, Nevada, in December 1957. Gorme died on August 10, 2013, in Las Vegas. She was eighty-four. Gorme is survived by Lawrence; their son, David Lawrence; and a grandchild. The couple's older son, Michael Lawrence, died in 1986.

*See Current Biography 1965.*

# William H. Gray III

**Born:** Baton Rouge, Louisiana; August 20, 1941
**Died:** London, United Kingdom; July 1, 2013
**Occupation:** American congressman and college fund administrator

William H. Gray III was an American congressman best known as the chairman of the Budget Committee, one of the most prestigious positions in the US House of Representatives. He was also elected the majority whip in 1989, which is the third highest-ranking job in the House leadership. At the time, this was the highest position held by an African American in Congress. Gray overcame considerable racial boundaries to acquire his leadership positions in Congress, which he explained in a 1985 interview with the *New York Times*: "People see your skin before they see anything else, and sometimes that's all they see. . . . If I do an effective job as chairman, I will break down a barrier and demonstrate that race is not an obstacle to heading a major financial committee or winning a leadership post."

On August 20, 1941, Gray was born in Baton Rouge, Louisiana, to Dr. William H. Gray Jr., a clergyman and an educator, and Hazel Gray, a teacher. In 1925, Gray's father succeeded his grandfather as pastor of Philadelphia's Bright Hope Baptist Church. Gray would continue his family's legacy and become the church's pastor

in 1972 after his father's death, serving for thirty-five years, even during his time in Congress.

In 1978, Gray, a Democrat, defeated incumbent representative Robert N. C. Nix Sr. in the race for Pennsylvania's Second Congressional District seat. He became the first African American chairman of the Budget Committee in 1985. In this leadership position, Gray guided the congressional budget throughout the 1980s. Despite his success in Congress, Gray abruptly resigned in 1991 to head the United Negro College Fund. Rumors that his resignation was influenced by threats of federal investigations of a financial nature were never proven, and he was never charged. According to the fund's website, Gray raised an excess of $2.3 billion as head of the United Negro College Fund before his retirement in 2004.

On July 1, 2013, Gray collapsed and died while attending the Wimbledon tennis tournament in London. He was seventy-one years old. Gray is survived by his mother, Hazel; his wife of forty-two years, Andrea; his three sons, William IV, Justin, and Andrew; and his two grandchildren.

*See Current Biography 1988.*

# Andrew M. Greeley

**Born:** Oak Park, Illinois; February 5, 1928
**Died:** Chicago, Illinois; May 30, 2013
**Occupation:** American sociologist, priest, and novelist

Andrew M. Greeley was many things—a sociologist, a novelist, an embattled academic. But his work as a priest in the Roman Catholic Church is what ultimately defined his life and informed his manifold other pursuits. Greeley published fifty novels and over one hundred nonfiction works in his career. The novels—often steamy tales of intrigue and priestly bad behavior—were best-selling critical duds that drew both a devoted readership among laymen and the ire of church officials. As a sociologist, Greeley was a prominent and often controversial voice on the place of the Catholic Church in America during a time when values regarding issues like education, sex, and divorce were rapidly shifting. In the early 1960s, Greeley worked with sociologist Peter H. Rossi on research demonstrating the strength of parochial schools at a time when secular education was considered by many to have eclipsed Catholic school education in quality. Greeley conducted additional research focused on the dichotomy between what Catholics believed about issues like marriage and sexual health—the average churchgoer's generally permissive stance on artificial birth control, for example—and the stricter, traditional views of the church.

Greeley saw himself as a misunderstood outsider within the church. He had a documented problem with authority, and often took outspoken, contrarian stances against church leaders. As early as 1989, Greeley began advocating on behalf of victims of clergy abuse, writing columns for various Chicago newspapers publicly discussing and condemning abuse at the hands of pedophile priests and imploring the church to take action, angering the archdiocese in the process.

Andrew Moran Greeley was born on February 5, 1928, in Oak Park, Illinois, to Andrew Thomas and Grace Greeley. He aspired to the priesthood from an early age, attending Chicago's Quigley Preparatory Seminary—from which he graduated in 1947—before entering St. Mary of the Lake Seminary, where he earned a BA degree, a bachelor of sacred theology degree, and a lector of sacred theology degree, before being ordained in May 1954. Greeley earned an MA in sociology from the University of Chicago in 1961, and a PhD in 1962. He joined the faculty at University of Chicago, working with the National Opinion Research Center to survey American attitudes regarding religion and other cultural issues. Greeley was up for tenure at the university in 1973, but was ultimately denied—a rejection he attributed to prejudice against his being a Catholic priest. Greeley died on May 30, 2013, at his home in Chicago. He was 85.

*See Current Biography Illustrated 1972.*

## Inder K. Gujral

**Born:** Jhelum, Punjab, British India;
December 4, 1919
**Died:** Gurgaon, Harayana, India; November 30, 2012
**Occupation:** Indian politician and prime minister

Inder Kumar Gujral served as the twelfth prime minister of India from April 21, 1997 to March 19, 1998. Despite his brief stay in office, he succeeded in implementing his Gujral Doctrine, which established a set of principles to relieve tension with India's neighbors, Pakistan and Bangladesh. The Gujral Doctrine was successful in promoting peace and respect for territorial sovereignty in a region that has been riddled with violence in the wake of the partition of British India in 1947.

Gujral's political career began in Jhelum (at the time a province of India), where he was heavily involved in the freedom movement against British rule. After the partition of India and the creation of Pakistan, Gujral left the now Pakistani state of Jhelum and relocated to Delhi, India. The partition of India resulted in one of the largest mass migrations in human history and the loss of approximately one million lives.

Consequently, this event created deep-rooted hostility between India and the newly created Islamic country of Pakistan.

In Delhi, Gujral met the politician Indira Gandhi, who would later become the prime minster of India and serve three back-to-back terms from 1966 to 1977 and a fourth term from 1980 until her assassination in 1984. With her help, Gujral joined the Upper House of Parliament. He held many leadership positions throughout his political career; among other roles, he was information and broadcasting minister in 1975 and the foreign minister for two nonconsecutive terms (1989–90, 1996–97). He became prime minister in 1997, replacing former Prime Minister H. D. Deve Gowda.

Gujral was prime minster of India briefly, from April 1997 to March 1998, but the Gujral Doctrine he implemented while in office is celebrated for being the first serious effort to reach out to Pakistan. One of his achievements was a meeting with Pakistan's prime minister at the time, Nawaz Sharif, which resulted in talks of peace and continued open communication between the two countries. The Bujral Doctrine also settled a long-standing dispute with Bangladesh over the rights to the Ganges River.

On November 30, 2012, Inder Gujral died in Gurgaon, India. He was ninety-two years old. Predeceased by his wife, Sheila, in 2011, he is survived by his two sons, Naresh and Vishal, and his brother, Satish, a notable Indian architect and painter.

*See Current Biography 1999.*

## Larry Hagman

**Born:** Fort Worth, Texas; September 21, 1931
**Died:** Dallas, Texas; November 23, 2012
**Occupation:** Actor, director, and producer

Larry Hagman was a prominent film and television actor, director, and producer. His notable acting roles include the famous villain J. R. Ewing in the prime time soap opera, *Dallas* (1978–91), and Major Anthony Nelson in *I Dream of Jeannie* (1965–70). He also appeared in the short-lived 1970s sitcoms, *Here We Go Again* and *The Good Life*.

Hagman's stage career began at Dallas's Margo Jones Theatre-in-the-Round. In 1951, after a role in a New York City production of *Taming of the Shrew* and a stint in regional theater, his mother, the actor Mary Martin, asked him to take a small role in the London production of the Broadway musical *South Pacific*, in which she starred as Ensign Nellie Forbush. Hagman stayed with the London cast for five years. During the late 1950s and early 1960s, he would take his acting career to New York City, where he appeared in the Off-Broadway productions *Once around the Block* and James Lee's *Career*. He also acted in five Broadway plays—*Comes a Day*, *The Nervous Set* (1959), *The Warm Peninsula*, *God and Kate Murphy*, and *The Beauty Part*.

In 1964, Hagman moved to Hollywood and landed his film debut in *Ensign Pulver*. Also in 1964, he played a small yet memorable role as the interpreter for the president, played by Henry Fonda, in the film *Fail Safe*. But it wasn't until *I Dream of Genie* that Hagman received his breakthrough part as Major Anthony Nelson. His most famous role, however, came a few years later in 1977, when he was offered the role of J. R. Ewing in *Dallas*. The show became an international success, and Hagman became one of the highest-paid and most celebrated television stars of the 1970s and 1980s.

Hagman received two Emmy nominations in 1980 and 1981 and a Golden Globe nomination for his role as J. R. Ewing. He was a five-time recipient of the Soap Opera Digest Award. In addition to his work in film and television, Hagman, who was a habitual cigarette smoker, became an antismoking advocate after quitting permanently.

Later in his career, Hagman made numerous appearances on hit television shows such as *Nip/Tuck* (2003–2010) and the *Desperate Housewives* (2004–2012). He also appeared in the films *Nixon* (1995) and *Primary Colors* (1998). Most recently, he was working on a renewal of his famous role as the villain J. R. Ewing in the 2012 revival of *Dallas* on TNT.

Larry Hagman publicly announced his cancer diagnosis in 2011. On November 23, 2012, Hagman died from throat cancer in Dallas, Texas. He was eighty-one years old. Hagman is survived by his wife of more than fifty years, Maj (née Axelsson); his son, Preston; his daughter, Kristina; his half-sister, Hellar Halliday; five granddaughters; a niece; and three nephews. Larry Hagman will be remembered as one of the most famous villains in the history of television.

*See Current Biography 1980.*

# Han Suyin

**Born:** Xinyang, Henan, China
**Died:** Lausanne, Switzerland; November 2, 2012
**Occupation:** Author and physician

Han Suyin was the pen name of Elizabeth Comber, a physician and author of novels, autobiographical memoirs, and books on modern China. She is perhaps best known for her 1952 novel *A Many-Splendored Thing*, which was adapted to a 1955 Academy Award–winning film, *Love is a Many-Splendored Thing*. Suyin published thirty books, including the notable novel *The Mountain Is Young* (1958), and the autobiographies *A Mortal Flower* (1966) and *My House Has Two Doors* (1980).

The exact date of Han Suyin's birth is uncertain, but it is believed to be September 12, 1916 or 1917. Suyin was born Rosalie Matilda Kuanghu Chow and grew up in Beijing, China, to parents of different ethnic backgrounds—her dad was a Chinese engineer and her mother was from Belgium. She attended medical school in Brussels and worked briefly as a doctor, but she abandoned a career in medicine to pursue writing. Some of the major themes in her writing are women, exploitation, class and peasants, and the divide between town and country. The cultural conflicts between Eastern countries and the West and the liberation of Southeast Asia were also prominent themes. Han Suyin wrote primarily in English and French, and she is celebrated for introducing Asian characters that were not based on preconceived notions and stereotypes to America and the Western world.

Han Suyin was deeply invested in China's history and growth. She was an outspoken supporter of the Chinese Cultural Revolution—a major theme in her book *China in the Year 2001* (1967)—and was criticized for being slow to acknowledge the Chinese government's violent crimes against its people. Her books about Mao Zedong, the *Morning Deluge* (1972) and *Wind in the Tower* (1976), contained a detailed history of China. In addition to writing, Suyin helped establish the National Rainbow Award for Best Literary Translation, and the Han Suyin Award for Young Translators.

On November 2, 2012, Han Suyin died in Lausanne, Switzerland, at the age of ninety-five. Her third husband, Vincent Ratnaswamy, from whom she was separated, died in 2003. She is survived by her sister, two daughters, a granddaughter, and three great-grandchildren.

*See Current Biography 1957.*

# Julie Harris

**Born:** Grosse Pointe Park, Michigan; December 2, 1925
**Died:** Chatham, Massachusetts; August 24, 2013
**Occupation:** American actor

An actor praised for her astounding range and unwavering consistency, Julie Harris was one of the most prolific performers of her time. Ever the dramatic chameleon, Harris played such disparate roles as the clairvoyant Nell Lance in the 1963 horror movie *The Haunting*, and the romantically torn Abra in *East of Eden* (1955)—a role that put her alongside the legendary James Dean in one of his three credited film appearances. Harris was well known among television viewers for her nearly eight-year stint on the *Dallas* spinoff *Knots Landing*, and her frequent appearances in Hallmark Hall of Fame productions, and a variety of popular comedies, dramas, and romances. Despite her formidable television and film résumé, it was Harris's on-stage legacy that defined her career. Nominated for an unparalleled ten Tony Awards—winning a record six—Harris made her first Broadway appearance in 1945 while still a college student, and graced the stage for the last time in the 1997 revival of D. L. Coburn's *The Gin Game*. Her breakout role came in 1950, when, at the age of twenty-four, Harris played twelve-year-old Frankie Addams, the lonely tomboy lead in the stage adaptation of Carson McCullers's *The Member of the Wedding*. Critics lauded her performance, and Harris went on to star in the 1952 film adaptation of the play, for which she received an Academy Award nomination.

Julie Ann Harris was born in Grosse Pointe Park, Michigan, on December 2, 1925. She had her first taste of the stage in local school performances, and before long had enrolled in Miss Hewitt's Classes, a Manhattan prep school that offered drama courses. At the age of twenty, Harris—then a student in the Yale School of Drama—landed her first Broadway role, playing a professor's daughter caught in a moral bind in the comedy *It's a Gift*. Her theater career was marked by a penchant for touring and short-run shows. Harris had a fondness for historical roles, playing such famous figures as Mary Todd Lincoln in *The Last of Mrs. Lincoln* (1972), and Emily Dickinson in *The Belle of Amherst* (1976)—a role which *New York Times* theater critic Walter Kerr declared the peak of her career up to that point.

In 2001, Harris suffered a stroke while in Chicago for her part in a production of Claudia Allen's *Fossils*. After that, her theater, television, and film appearances became less frequent. In 2002, she won a Tony for lifetime achievement, and in 2005, she was a Kennedy Center honoree. Harris died of congestive heart failure on August 24, 2013, at her home in Chatham, Massachusetts. She was eighty-seven. Her three marriages ended in divorce. She is survived by her son, Peter Gurian.

*See Current Biography 1977.*

# Ray Harryhausen

**Born:** Los Angeles, California; June 29, 1920
**Died:** London, United Kingdom; May 7, 2013
**Occupation:** American special effects technician and animator

Ray Harryhausen was an American film animator best-known as a master of stop-motion animation, a difficult and tedious technique where small, three-dimensional figures are photographed one frame at a time. The illusion of movement is achieved by incremental adjustments made in the figure's motion after each frame. Before the innovation of computer-animation techniques, stop-motion was the primary method used to breathe life into fantastic creatures on the screen, including Harryhausen's dinosaurs in *The Beast from 20,000 Fathoms* (1953), his skeleton warriors in *Jason and the Argonauts* (1963), and his gigantic octopus in *It Came from Beneath the Sea* (1955). Harryhausen is credited for inspiring a generation of animators and paving the way for the development of new computer techniques seen in films such as *Jurassic Park*, *Star Wars*, and the *Lord of the Rings* trilogy. He received a career Academy Award for technical achievement at the 1992 Oscar ceremony.

Harryhausen was born on June 29, 1920, in Los Angeles, California. After seeing *The Lost World* (1925) and *King Kong* (1933), he became fascinated with both dinosaurs and stop-motion animation and began creating stop-motion films at home in his garage. In order to refine his craft, he took classes in anatomy at Los Angeles City College and studied drama at the University of Southern California (USC). His perseverance paid off in 1942, when he was hired by Paramount as a technician to work on stop-motion puppet shorts called "Puppetoons."

The first feature-film he worked on was *Mighty Joe Young* (1949), which won an Academy Award for special effects. The film's special effects were a result of the collaboration between Harryhausen and the man who inspired him to become an animator, Willis O'Brien, the stop-motion animator of *King Kong*. In his autobiography, *Ray Harryhausen: An Animated Life* (2003), Harryhausen expressed the profound influence Willis and *King Kong* had on his career: "My work, and therefore to a large extent my life, have been tied to a specific film and the man responsible for it."

*The Beast from 20,000 Fathoms* (1953) was the first feature-length film for which Harryhausen created the special effects on his own. He used a new split-screen technique he developed called Dynamation. This technique helped breathe life into the film's gigantic dinosaur as it rampaged through New York City.

He proceeded to successfully experiment with other prehistoric animals in films such as *Mysterious Island* (1961), and *The Valley of Gwangi* (1969). By the 1980s, however, computer animated techniques were beginning to take precedence over stop-motion, and Harryhausen's work load gradually slowed; his last feature film was *Clash of the Titans* (1981). He did not have any interest in new animation techniques and believed they compromised the magic of a film's fantasy: "If you make things too real, sometimes you bring it down to the mundane," he said in 2006. Harryhausen believed that stop-motion animation added a surreal quality that did not diminish a film's fantasy, but enhanced it.

Harryhausen died on May 7, 2013, in London. He was ninety-two years old. He is survived by his wife, Diana Livingston, and his daughter, Vanessa.

*See Current Biography 2001.*

# Hans Hass

**Born:** Vienna, Austria; January 23, 1919
**Died:** Vienna, Austria; June 16, 2013
**Occupation:** Austrian marine biologist, diver, and activist

Hans Hass was an Austrian marine biologist and diver best known for the more than one-hundred films he made exploring the underwater world of coral reefs and deep-sea creatures, including clouds of fish, stingrays, jelly-fish, and barracudas. But the main features of his films were sharks, and his close encounters with these dangerous predators (he carried a spear with him for protection) served as the climax for his films and stunned audiences. In his memoir, *Diving to Adventure* (1951; originally published in German as *Drei Jäger auf dem Meeresgrund*, 1947), Hass explained his technique for coaxing sharks into filming range: "I pretended to flee as conspicuously as possible, thus awakening the instinct in every beast of prey to chase what tries to escape. And I actually succeeded thus in luring sharks after me." Hass claimed to have suffered five nonlethal shark attacks throughout his filming career.

Hass was born on January 23, 1919, in Vienna, Austria. He first became interested in the sport of diving after meeting Guy Gilpatric, an American writer and diver, who introduced the young Hass to the sport while on vacation in the French Rivera. Hass studied law at the universities of Vienna and Berlin, but he later switched his field to zoology and immersed himself in the study of the underwater world. He released *Jagd unter Wasser mit Harpune und Kamera* (Hunt under water with harpoon and camera), his first book of underwater photographs, in 1939. *Pirsch unter Wasser* (*Stalking under Water*), his first underwater film, was finished in 1940. During this time, Hass also worked on his doctoral thesis in marine biology at Berlin University, which he completed in 1943.

Hass's first marriage to Hannelore Schroth, a German film actor, ended in divorce. He married his second wife, Lotte Baierl, in 1950, and she appeared in the majority of his films. Together, they created the BBC television series *Diving to Adventure* (based on his book) in 1956, and later *The Undersea World of Adventure* in 1958. In 1961, however, Hass abandoned his filmmaking career to focus on his academic pursuits and writing books. He wrote twenty-eight books in his career, including *The Human Animal: The Mystery of Man's Behavior* (1970), *Men beneath the Sea: Man's Conquest of the Underwater World* (1975), and *Der Hai* (1977; The shark).

Hass died on June 16, 2013, in Vienna, Austria, at the age of ninety-four. In addition to his wife, Lotte, Hass is survived by his son from his first marriage, Hans Hass Jr.

*See Current Biography 1955.*

# David Hayes

**Born:** Hartford, Connecticut; March 15, 1931
**Died:** Coventry, Connecticut; April 9, 2013
**Occupation:** American sculptor

David Hayes was an American sculptor whose work was featured in a number of prestigious art museums and exhibits in the United States and abroad, including the Museum of Modern Art (MoMA), the Guggenheim Museum in New York, and the Forma Viva sculpture symposium in Portoroz, Yugoslavia. According to James Johnson Sweeny, the former director of the Guggenheim Museum, "A work by Hayes is never a 'Large Beast,' a 'Chimera,' a 'Women with Sheep,' nor a bare assemblage of sheet steel, but something brought to life by the artist's sensibility to the relationship between an idea and the forms his material proposes to him."

Hayes was born on March 15, 1931, in Hartford, Connecticut. He attended the University of Notre Dame, where he was initially a premedical student but switched his major to fine art. He earned his bachelor's degree in June 1953, and then enrolled at Indiana University. Here, he studied under David Smith, who was credited with introducing metal sculpture to the United States. Smith had a significant influence on Hayes's aesthetic, and he adopted metal as his medium of choice. Hayes gradated with his MFA in June 1955.

After serving two years in the US Navy, he relocated to Coventry, Connecticut, and began working in Hartford's Fuller Welding Company. Soon thereafter, his work was exhibited in a solo show at Wesleyan University in Middletown, Connecticut, in 1958, and the Guggenheim Museum put several of his sculptures on exhibit that same year, acquiring one of them, *Animal and Young*, for its permanent collection. But his true entrée into the New York City art scene occurred in 1959 after his solo New Talent show at the Museum of Modern Art. From here, his work began to attract more attention and appeared in numerous exhibitions, including the New Haven Arts Festival, where he won best in show. In addition to a Fulbright award and a Guggenheim fellowship, Hayes received the Logan Prize for Sculpture and an award from the National Institute of Arts and Letters.

On April 9, 2013, Hayes died at his home in Coventry, Connecticut, from leukemia. He was eighty-two years old. He is survived by his wife, Julia Moriarty, whom he married in 1957; two of his three siblings, Cathy and Richard; four children, David, Brian, Mary, and John; and his granddaughter, Alexandra.

*See Current Biography 1996.*

# Seamus Heaney

**Born:** County Derry, Northern Ireland; April 13, 1939
**Died:** Dublin, Ireland; August 30, 2013
**Occupation:** Irish poet

Seamus Heaney was considered the most celebrated Irish poet since William Butler Yeats. Heaney referred to words as "bearers of history and mystery," and he used his poetry to capture historical events in Ireland, including the more than three decades of violence during the conflict in Northern Ireland, also known as the Troubles. But according to Carál Ní Chuilín, Northern Ireland's culture, arts, and leisure minister, his poetry also, "captured the character of this land and its people, and conveyed it in words which will echo for generations." Heaney's most notable poetry collections include *Death of a Naturalist* (1966), *Wintering Out* (1972), and *The Spirit Level* (1996). In 1995, Heaney was awarded the Nobel Prize in Literature. The Nobel committee praised Heaney's poetry for its "lyrical beauty and ethical depth, which exalt everyday miracles and the living past." He was the fourth Irish writer to win the honor.

Heaney was born on April 13, 1939, in County Derry, Northern Ireland He attended Queen's University in Belfast, where he graduated with a bachelor's degree in English language and literature. His first collection of poetry, *Death of a Naturalist*, was published in 1966 and depicted country life and rural settings with poems such as "Digging" and "A Drink of Water." This collection was soon followed by *Door into the Dark* (1969) and *Wintering Out* (1972), which established him as not only a powerful poetic voice in Ireland, but an international figure in literature.

In addition to writing poetry, Heaney was a professor at Oxford University (1989–94), and, starting in 1985, he taught at Harvard, where he was an assistant professor and poet in residence. He also taught at the University of California, Berkeley.

Heaney died on August 30, 2013, in Dublin, Ireland. He was seventy-four years old. His last collection of poetry, *Human Chain*, was published in 2010. Upon news of his death, former US president Bill Clinton hailed him as "our finest poet of the rhythms of ordinary lives" and a "powerful voice for peace." Heaney is survived by his wife, Marie Devlin; his two sons, Christopher and Michael; and his daughter, Catherine.

*See Current Biography 1982.*

# Hans Werner Henze

**Born:** Gütersloh, Westphalia; July 1, 1926
**Died:** Dresden, Germany; October 27, 2012
**Occupation:** German composer

Hans Werner Henze was a prolific German composer whose work spanned many musical genres, including symphonies, chamber works, concertos, stage works, operas, and a requiem. Known for his passionate and romantic music, Werner gained international recognition in the 1960s with his Fifth Symphony, which was played by the New York Philharmonic. But he is perhaps best known for composing more than two dozen operas—both adapted works and original compositions—such as *A Country Doctor* (1951), *Kong Hirsh* (1953), and his last opera, *Phaedra* (2010).

Henze studied music at the Braunshcweig music school, where he developed skills in piano performance, composition, and music theory. In 1946, after serving in World War II as a radio officer, Henze's talent caught the attention of Schotts, a music publisher, which would later call him, "one of the most important and influential composers of our time."

Hezne was a prodigal musician that blended an array of musical and artistic styles—jazz, surrealism, twelve-tone technique, neoclassicism, and rock and popular music. The themes of his works were also eclectic: they were political, romantic, adapted from novels and fairly tales, dealt explicitly with social issues, and were conventional and modern. His Ninth Symphony, for example, concerned German Anti-Fascism, and his 2003 opera, *L'Upupa und der Triumph der Sohnesliebe* (The hoopoe and the triumph of filial love), was adapted from a Syrian fairy tale.

In addition to composing musical works, he established the music school Cantiere Internazionale d'Arte in Montepulciano, and music festivals such as the Munich Biennale and the Deutschlandsberg Youth Music Festival. He was also a teacher at Mozarteum in Salzburg and a visiting professor at Dartmouth College. He served as the composer in residence at Tanglewood in Massachusetts.

Henze was recognized for his contributions to music in 1995, when he received the prestigious Westphalian Music Prize. And in 2004, he received an honorary doctorate in musicology from the University for Music and Performing Arts in Munich.

Henze died from natural causes in Dresden, Germany, on October 27, 2012. He was eighty-six years old. His life partner, Fasuto Moroni, passed away in 2007.

*See Current Biography Illustrated 1966.*

# John B. Hightower

**Born:** Atlanta, Georgia; May 23, 1933
**Died:** Newport News, Virginia; July 6, 2013
**Occupation:** American art museum director

John B. Hightower was an American art museum director best known as the director of the Museum of Modern Art (MoMa) in Manhattan starting in 1970. His leadership of the museum, however, was short-lived: he was fired less than two years after his appointment. The reason for his termination was attributed to the turbulence of the times, which precipitated protests of the museum's exhibits and tension among the museum's board members.

Hightower was born on May 23, 1933, in Atlanta, Georgia. After graduating from Yale with an English degree in 1955, he served in the US Marines for two years. In 1963, he began his career in the art world when he joined the state arts council as an assistant to the director. By 1964, he was named the head of the agency, a position he would hold until his appointment as the director of the Museum of Modern Art in 1970.

Hightower was only thirty-seven when he became director of MoMa, and, according to his 1996 interview for the museum's oral history archive, his young age worked against him: "So with all of my thirty-something hubris, lack of experience and naïveté, I walked into the director's office . . . It was really a nightmare." A series of unfortunate events followed soon after his appointment—employees unionized, artists and demonstrators protested, and tensions escalated between board members. Consequently, Hightower, who had held the position for less than two years, was asked to resign. He was succeeded by Richard Oldenburg.

Hightower went on to head the South Street Seaport Museum in 1977, and later the Mariners' Museum in Newport News, which he directed from 1993 to 2007. Hightower died on July 6, 2013, in Newport News, Virginia, at the age of eighty. He is survived by his second wife, Marty; his son Matthew; his daughter Amanda; and his four grandchildren.

*See Current Biography 1970.*

# James D. Hodgson

**Born:** Dawson, Minnesota; December 3, 1915
**Died:** Malibu, California; November 28, 2012
**Occupation:** American politician

James Day Hodgson was an American politician who served as President Richard Nixon's secretary of labor and as the ambassador to Japan during the Ford administration. He is perhaps best known for facilitating efforts to promote employment opportunities for minority workers. Hodgson also helped establish the Occupational Safety and Health Act of 1970, which required employers to provide safe and sanitary working conditions that are free from toxic chemicals and other potential health hazards.

After graduating from the University of Minnesota in 1938 with a degree in sociology and anthropology, Hodgson worked briefly as a supervisor for a state youth employment program. In 1941, he joined Lockheed Martin, one of the largest worldwide providers of military weapons and aircraft, and remained here for the majority of his career. In 1943, he temporarily left Lockheed to join the US Navy during World War II. He worked his way up to the rank of lieutenant and became an intelligence officer. After his discharge in 1946, he returned to Lockheed, where he became the vice president of industrial relations in 1968. Under his leadership, Lockheed became one of the first large American corporations to actively recruit minority workers.

On July 2, 1970, Hodgson left Lockheed again to become President Nixon's secretary of labor. His best-known accomplishment in this role (1970–73) was helping to pass the Occupational Safety and Health Act of 1970. He also helped pass the Emergency Employment Act of 1971, which increased employment training programs and job opportunities to combat the recession following the Vietnam War.

After the Watergate scandal and Nixon's subsequent resignation, Hodgson became ambassador to Japan under President Gerald R. Ford. While serving as ambassador (1974–77), Hodgson wrote two books: *American Senryu* (1992), a collection of haiku-inspired short poems, and *Doing Business with the New Japan* (2000). From 1977 to 1982, he served as the chairman for a uranium mining company called the Pathfinder Mines Corporation.

James Hodgson died at his home in Malibu, California, on November 28, 2012. He was ninety-six years old. Hodgson is survived by his wife, Maria; his son, Frederic; and his daughter, Nancy.

*See Current Biography 1970.*

# John Hollander

**Born:** New York, New York; October 28, 1929
**Died:** Branford, Connecticut; August 17, 2013
**Occupation:** American poet

John Hollander was an American poet who published twenty collections of poetry in his career, most notably *Spectral Emanations* (1978), *Tales Told of the Fathers* (1975), and *Powers of Thirteen* (1983), which won Yale's Bollingen poetry prize. Praised for its wit and versatility, his poetry ranged from accessible poems dealing with his childhood to more lengthy and complex poems, such as "The Head of the Bed," that dealt with philosophical and metaphysical intricacies. According to the poet Richard Howard, Hollander's poetry possessed "a technical prowess probably without equal in American verse today."

Hollander was born on October 28, 1929, in New York, New York. He attended Columbia University, where he met the poet Allen Ginsberg, who became his friend and mentor. Despite their different literary styles, both Hollander and Ginsberg shared a belief and an interest in the "mythological weight" of poetic form and the "realms of imagination." Moreover, their experience selling blood at St. Luke's Hospital in Manhattan was the inspiration for one of Hollander's best-known poems, "Helicon," from his 1965 collection *Visions from a Ramble*.

Hollander received his bachelor's degree from Columbia in 1950 and his master's degree in 1952. He left his doctoral studies at Indiana University in 1954 to join the Society of Fellows at Harvard University, but would later complete his PhD in 1959 at Indiana. Hollander taught at Connecticut College in New London, was an instructor at Yale University, and joined the faculty at Hunter College in New York City before accepting a full time position in 1977 at Yale, where he was a professor until his retirement in 2002.

Hollander's first collection of poetry, *A Crackling of Thorns* (1958), was selected by W. H. Auden for the Yale Younger Poets series, thus establishing him as an emerging poetic voice. His second collection of poetry, *Movie-Going and Other Poems* (1962), contained accessible poems about experiences in his youth in New York City. Hollander would later describe his early works as "verse essay" or "epigram literature," and his later works became increasingly complex and intellectually demanding. For example, regarding his 1979 collection *Blue Wine and Other Poems*, the American poet Richmond Lattimore remarked that Hollander's poetry "does not become easier as he goes. . . . He is always on the point of being fully comprehensible and never quite arrives at that point."

Hollander died on August 17, 2013, in Branford, Connecticut, from pulmonary congestion. He was eighty-three years old. Survivors include his second wife, Natalie Charkow Hollander; his brother, Michael; his daughters, Elizabeth and Martha; and three grandchildren.

*See Current Biography 1991.*

# D. Brainerd Holmes

**Born:** Brooklyn, New York; May 24, 1921
**Died:** Memphis, Tennessee; January 11, 2013
**Occupation:** Aerospace industry executive and NASA official

Dyer Brainerd Holmes was best known as the head of NASA's manned space flight program from September 1961 to August 1963. During his leadership position at NASA, Holmes helped develop Project Mercury, NASA's first human spaceflight program, which resulted in John Glenn becoming the first US astronaut to orbit Earth on February 20, 1962. Holmes was also involved in developing NASA's Gemini and Apollo manned flight programs.

After receiving his degree in electrical engineering from Cornell University in 1943, Holmes served in the US Navy during World War II. After the war, he worked at Bell Telephone Labs (1945–53), and RCA (1953–61), where he was involved in developing a number of innovative defense technologies—including the Air Force's Ballistic Missile Early Warning System (BMEWS).

When Holmes joined NASA in 1961 he was under pressure from the Kennedy Administration, whose ambitions for the US space program included putting a man on the moon before 1970. President Kennedy was determined to compete with the Soviet Union which had successfully launched the first satellite, Sputnik, in 1957. Despite resigning from his position after two years, NASA saw progress under his leadership: John Glenn became the first man to enter Earth's orbit; financing increased for NASA's programs; and the Gemini and Apollo manned flight programs were developed.

Holmes resigned from NASA in 1963. On July 20, 1969, the Apollo program he helped develop put Neil Armstrong and Edwin E. "Buzz" Aldrin on the moon. After his tenure at NASA, Holmes became an executive at Raytheon and later the president of the company. During his time as president of Raytheon in the 1970s, Raytheon developed the Patriot missile, a tracking missile that uses a radar system to target enemy aircraft and missiles.

Holmes died on January 11, 2013, in Memphis, Tennessee, from pneumonia complications. He was ninety-one years old. Holmes is survived by his wife, Mary; two daughters; a stepson; two stepdaughters; six grandchildren; five-step-grandchildren; and seven great-grandchildren.

*See Current Biography 1963.*

# Donald F. Hornig

**Born:** Milwaukee, Wisconsin; March 17, 1920
**Died:** Providence, Rhode Island; January 21, 2013
**Occupation:** Chemist, university president, and presidential advisor

Donald F. Hornig was a Harvard-educated chemist who served as the president of Brown University and as the science and technology advisor to Presidents John F. Kennedy and Lyndon. B. Johnson. He was also known for being involved with the Manhattan Project (1942–45), a US government project that developed and tested the first atomic bomb, thus introducing the world to the nuclear age.

Hornig graduated from Harvard University with his undergraduate degree in chemistry in 1940 and completed his doctorate in physical chemistry there in 1943. The following year, Hornig, then twenty-five years old, was asked to join the top-secret Manhattan Project. He and his wife, Lilli Schwenk, who also had a doctorate in chemistry from Harvard, relocated to Los Alamos, New Mexico. Here, they joined J. Robert Oppenheimer, the director of the Manhattan Project, and a number of other scientists in the development of the first atomic bomb, which was first tested on July 16, 1945. Hornig was specifically involved with developing the firing mechanism for the bomb, a device called the "X-unit." He also climbed the Trinity tower and guarded the atomic bomb per the request of Oppenheimer, who was afraid of leaving the bomb alone on the day of the test.

In 1946, Hornig joined the faculty at Brown University until 1957, when he took a position at Princeton University. Hornig would later return to Brown as its president from 1970 to 1976. As the university's president, he helped reduce its debt from approximately $4 million to $636,000. He also merged Brown's Pembroke College for women with the university's all-male undergraduate college.

While he was at Princeton, Hornig served on President Dwight Eisenhower's scientific advisory committee. On November 7, 1963, President John F. Kennedy appointed Hornig his science and technology advisor. Fifteen days later, however, President Kennedy was assassinated. After Kennedy's vice president, Lyndon B. Johnson, was sworn into the presidency he upheld Hornig's position.

On January 21, 2013, Hornig died in Providence, Rhode Island, from compilations resulting from Alzheimer's disease. He was ninety-two years old. His daughter Leslie died in 2012. In addition to his wife, Hornig is survived by his three children, Joanna, Ellen, and Christopher; his brother, Arthur; his sister, Arlene; nine grandchildren; and ten great-grandchildren.

*See Current Biography 1964.*

# Ada Louise Huxtable

**Born:** New York City, New York; March 14, 1921
**Died:** New York City, New York; January 7, 2013
**Occupation:** American architecture critic

Ada Louise Huxtable was the first architecture critic to write full-time for the *New York Times*. Described as having a fiery and powerful critical voice, she championed historic preservation and influenced the development of the New York skyline during the 1960s and 70s. In 1970, her criticism won a Pulitzer Prize. She also wrote a number of books about architecture, including *Kicked a Building Lately* (1976) and *Goodbye History, Hello Hamburger* (1986).

Huxtable (née Landman) was born in New York City on March 14, 1921. After graduating from Hunter College in 1941 with a degree in art and architectural history, she pursued further studies at New York University's Institute of Fine Arts. From 1946 to 1950, she worked as an assistant curator at the Museum of Modern Art. She was also a Fulbright fellow (1950–52) and studied Italian architecture and design in Italy.

She was invited by Clifton Daniel, the assisting managing editor, to join the *New York Times* as a full-time daily architecture critic in 1963. In this capacity, she wrote about a number of architectural projects and buildings in New York City, including the Gallery of Modern Art at Two Columbus Circle, which she famously referred to as a "die-cut Venetian Palazzo on lollipops" in 1964.

In 1973, Huxtable gave up her position as the architecture critic and joined the *New York Times* editorial board. She would remain in this position until receiving a MacArthur Fellowship in 1981, which awarded her the opportunity to leave her full-time job and write books such as *The Tall Building Artistically Reconsidered: The Search for a Skyscraper Style* (1984). In 1997, she accepted a position at the *Wall Street Journal*.

Huxtable's last book, *On Architecture: Collected Reflections on a Century of Change*, was published in 2008. Her last article, "Undertaking Its Destruction," appeared in the *Wall Street Journal* on December 3, 2012, and criticized the plans to reconstruct the New York Public Library.

Huxtable died on January 7, 2013, at Memorial Sloan-Kettering Cancer Center in New York.

She was ninety-one years old. Her husband, L. Garth Huxtable, died in 1989. She has no immediate survivors.

*See Current Biography 1973.*

# Daniel K. Inouye

**Born:** Honolulu, Hawaii; September 7, 1924
**Died:** Bethesda, Maryland; December 17, 2012
**Occupation:** United States senator

Daniel Ken Inouye was a United States senator from Hawaii and a member of the Democratic Party. In June 2010, he became the president pro tempore, the second-highest-ranking official in the US Senate after the vice president, and third in line to presidential succession. He was, therefore, the highest-ranking Asian American politician in US history. Inouye also received the Medal of Honor for his heroic military service during World War II.

In 1943, Inouye enlisted in the US Army's all–Japanese American 442nd Regimental Combat Team. Even though the ban on Japanese Americans in the US Army was lifted in 1943, he enlisted during a time when Japanese Americans faced widespread discrimination and were being forced into relocation camps. Inouye, however, was determined to serve his country and combat the negative image of Japanese Americans that resulted from the Japanese attack on Pearl Harbor on December 7, 1941. He fulfilled this goal when he earned the Distinguished Service Cross for his heroism during a battle near Terenzo, Italy, on April 21, 1945, in which he lost his arm. In 2000, more than fifty years later, President Clinton awarded Inouye the Medal of Honor, along with other Japanese American soldiers who had been denied this honor because of their race.

After the war, Inouye attended the University of Hawaii for his undergraduate degree (1950) and earned a law degree from the George Washington University Law School in 1952. Inouye was elected to Hawaii's territorial legislature twice, in 1954 and 1956, and was majority leader there for four years. Upon Hawaii's statehood in 1959, Inouye became Hawaii's first full member in the US House of Representatives. In 1962, he was elected to the Senate, where he would serve for forty-nine years, making him the second-longest-serving senator after Robert C. Byrd, who served fifty-one years. Inouye held many leadership roles in the Senate. In addition to his role as president pro tempore, he chaired two influential committees, the Senate Committee on Intelligence and the Senate Committee on Appropriations.

Daniel Inouye died on December 17, 2012, in Bethesda, Maryland. He was eighty-eight years old. Inouye is survived by his wife, Irene; his son, Daniel; his granddaughter, Maggie; and his stepdaughter, Jennifer. He received the rare and great honor of lying in state in the United States Capitol rotunda on December 20, 2012. Only thirty-one people have received this honor. Upon news of his death, President Obama released a statement saying that America had lost "a true American hero."

*See Current Biography 1960, 1987.*

# Thomas Penfield Jackson

**Born:** Washington, DC; January 10, 1937
**Died:** Compton, Maryland; June 15, 2013
**Occupation:** American judge

A United States District Court judge since 1982, Thomas Penfield Jackson presided over such high-profile cases as the Microsoft antitrust suit and the trial of Washington, DC, Mayor Marion Barry on charges of cocaine possession. Jackson—a lifelong Republican—was President Ronald Reagan's first nominee to the US District Court. In 1988, Jackson made his first headline-grabbing ruling, when he found Michael K. Deaver, a former Reagan aide, guilty of lying under oath about improper lobbying practices and imposed a fine of $100,000. Jackson's June 2000 ruling that Microsoft—which he had designated a monopoly that April—must be split into two companies was later vacated by the Court of Appeals in Washington due to comments Jackson had made to journalists that the court said indicated bias.

Thomas Penfield Jackson was born on January 10, 1937, in Washington, DC. As a young man, Jackson served in the US Navy aboard the destroyer *Charles S. Sperry*. While serving, he attended the Navy School of Military Justice, allowing him to serve as the ship's prosecutor. Jackson then attended Harvard Law School, graduating in 1964. He worked as an associate—and eventually made partner—at Jackson & Campbell, a Washington, DC, firm founded by his father. Jackson was admitted to practice before the US Supreme Court in 1970. In 1972, the infamous Committee to Reelect the President—the group tasked with putting Nixon back in the White House—hired Jackson as a junior lawyer. In 1980, Jackson was briefly considered as a potential candidate for the DC Superior Court and the DC Court of Appeals. At the time, many in the legal world suspected that Jackson failed to garner the nomination due to his membership in the Chevy Chase Club—a social organization that did not allow black members. Jackson retired in 2004, returning to private practice at Jackson & Campbell. He died on June 15, 2013, at his home in Compton,

Maryland. He was seventy-six. Jackson is survived by his wife and two daughters.

See Current Biography 2001.

## François Jacob

**Born:** Nancy, France; June 17, 1920
**Died:** Paris, France; April 19, 2013
**Occupation:** French biologist

Dr. François Jacob was a French biologist who won the 1965 Nobel Prize in Physiology or Medicine for his discovery of cellular genetic function (he shared the Nobel with two colleagues, Dr. Jacques Monod and Dr. André Lwoff). Jacob and his colleague's work helped uncover the mechanism for gene regulation, which is essentially how a gene's distinct characteristics and functions can be switched on and off. According to Sven Gard, a member of the Nobel Committee in Physiology or Medicine, Jacob's discovery had "given a strong impetus to research in all domains of biology with far-reaching effects spreading out like ripples in the water." This includes shedding light on how genetic traits are inherited in humans, and helping to unravel the mystery of human growth and development.

Jacob was born in Nancy, France, on June 17, 1920. He showed an interest in becoming a doctor from an early age, but his medical studies were interrupted during World War II and Hitler's occupation of France in 1940. Jacob joined the Free French Army, where he served as a medical officer in France and North Africa. While fighting alongside Allied forces in Normandy, he was severely wounded during a German attack and subsequently hospitalized.

After the war, Jacob completed his medical studies in 1947, and he earned his bachelor's degree in biology (1951) and doctoral degree (1954) from the Sorbonne. The injuries he suffered to his hands during the war prevented him from pursuing a career as a surgeon; therefore, he concentrated on research and became involved with the Pasteur Institute in 1950. At the institute, he teamed up with Dr. Jacques Monod in the lab of Dr. André Lwoff and began experimenting with genetic traits in bacteria. Their research resulted in the groundbreaking discovery of regularity genes, which earned them the Nobel in 1965.

Jacob expanded his research to a number of other medical issues, including cancer growth and how bacteria can mutate and develop resistance to antibiotics. In addition to the Nobel Prize, Jacob received awards and honors for his military service in World War II, including the Legion of Honor and the Croix de Guerre.

On April 19, 2013, Jacob died in Paris, France, at the age of ninety-two. He married his first wife, the pianist Lysiane Bloch, in 1947. After her death in 1983, he married Genevieve Barrier in 1999.

See Current Biography Illustrated 1966.

## Arthur Robert Jensen

**Born:** San Diego, California; August 24, 1923
**Died:** Kelseyville, California; October 22, 2012
**Occupation:** Professor of educational psychology

Arthur Robert Jensen was a notable professor of education psychology, and he is considered one of the most important psychologists of the twentieth century. He is best known for his work with differential psychology, the study of how individuals differ in behavior, and psychometrics, which includes the study of knowledge, personality traits, and educational measurement. Jensen is also a prominent advocate for the role of genetics in the nature versus nurture debate. He believed intelligence and personality, for example, are not determined by one's environment, but are hereditary and passed down genetically.

After earning his PhD from Columbia University in 1956 and performing postdoctoral research at the University of London, Institute of Psychology, Jensen joined the faculty of the University of California, Berkeley, as a professor and researcher. During his time at Berkeley, Jensen focused on the link between genes and intelligence and the role culture and development play in the formation of an individual's personality and intelligence. His work as a hereditarian (an advocate for the theory that human characteristics are based on genetics) earned him the prestigious Kistler Prize in 2003.

Jensen was involved in testing school children, which lead him to distinguish between different levels of learning abilities. He believed so-called Level I learning concerned the simple memorization of facts, and Level II concerned the ability to solve problems and conceptualize information. A highly controversial aspect of his research however, was race-based difference in intelligence: he believed Level II learning occurred more among whites and Asian Americans than African Americans and Latino Americans. Jensen was criticized extensively for his theories on race-based intelligence.

Jensen was the author of over four hundred scientific papers published in various journals, including his most controversial research, "How Much Can We Boost I.Q. and Scholastic Achievement," which was published in 1969 in the *Harvard Education Review*. This work was criticized for its assertion that educational programs had failed to increase the intelligence quotient of

African Americans, thus reinforcing his theory that IQ is genetically determined.

Jensen was also the author of the notable book, *The g Factor: The Science of Mental Ability* (1998), and, most recently, *Clocking the Mind: Mental Chronometry and Individual Differences* (2006). Jensen was honored for his work in educational psychology with the Lifetime Achievement Award in 2006 by the International Society for Intelligence Research.

On October 22, 2012, Jensen died in his home in Kelseyville, California. He was eighty-nine years old. He is survived by his daughter, Roberta Morey, and his grandson.

*See Current Biography 1973.*

# Ruth Prawer Jhabvala

**Born:** Cologne, Germany; May 7, 1927
**Died:** New York, New York; April 3, 2013
**Occupation:** German-born screenwriter and novelist

Ruth Prawer Jhabvala was a German-born screenwriter and novelist who won two Academy Awards for best-adapted screenplay for *A Room with a View* (1986) and *Howards End* (1992), both film adaptations of E. M. Foster novels. Her screenplay for *Remains of the Day* (1993) also won her an Oscar nomination. Jhabvala, however, was a well-known novelist before she began writing screenplays, and her 1975 novel, *Heat and Dust*, won the Booker Prize, the highest literary honor in the United Kingdom. She also wrote a number of short story collections, including her first collection, *Like Birds, Like Fishes* (Murray, 1962; Norton, 1964).

Jhabvala was born in Cologne, Germany, on May 7, 1927. When she was twelve years old, she and her family fled to the United Kingdom as refugees after Hitler came to power. She would later attend Queen Mary College, University of London, where she studied English and earned her master's degree in 1951. She also married her husband, Cyrus S. H. Jhabvala, in 1951, and the couple relocated to New Delhi, India.

*To Whom She Will* (1955) was Jhabvala's first published book (it was published as *Amrita* in 1956 in the United States). But it was her novel *The Householder* (1960) that caught the attention of Ismail Merchant and James Ivory, who approached Jhabvala about adapting the book to film. The film was released in the United States in 1963, thus beginning her long and successful relationship with the Merchant Ivory filmmaking team, which resulted in more than twenty films. In addition to the two films that won Academy Awards, other notable films include *The Europeans* (1979), *The Golden Bowl* (2000), and *Le*

*Divorce* (2003), which was the last film the trio collaborated on.

Jhabvala continued to write novels and short stories in conjunction with her film career. Her twelfth novel, *My Nine Lives*, was published in 2004, and her last short story collection, *A Lovesong for India*, in 2012. At the time of her death, her last published short story, "The Judge's Will," appeared in the March 25 issue of the *New Yorker*.

On April 3, 2013, Jhabvala died at her home in New York City. She was eighty-five years old. Her husband survives her, as well as her three daughters, Renana, Firoza, and Ava; and her six grandchildren.

*See Current Biography 1977.*

# Virginia E. Johnson

**Born:** Springfield, Missouri; February 11, 1925
**Died:** St. Louis, Missouri; July 24, 2013
**Occupation:** American psychologist and sexologist

Virginia E. Johnson was a psychologist and sexologist who was a pioneer in openly discussing the nature and physiology of sex in American society. In collaboration with Dr. William H. Masters, her business partner and husband (the couple divorced in 1993), she wrote a number of groundbreaking books that brought sex into the public eye, including *Human Sexual Response* (1966), *The Pleasure Bond: A New Look at Sexuality and Commitment* (1974, with Robert J. Levin), and *Masters and Johnson on Sex and Human Loving* (1982, with Robert C. Kolodny).

Johnson was born Mary Virginia Eshelman on February 11, 1925, in Springfield, Missouri. She studied briefly at Drury College in Springfield, but took a job at an insurance company and never graduated. She then studied music at the Kansas City Conservatory of Music, and later sociology at Washington University. It was at Washington University where she met Dr. William H. Masters, who was researching sexuality at a time when it was not considered a legitimate area of scientific study. It was even more of a taboo for women to talk about sex during this time, but Johnson joined Masters in 1957 and would continue to work with him for more than three decades. They made a good team at the Masters and Johnson Institute (formerly the Reproductive Biology Foundation), with the sociable Johnson responsible for administrative tasks and publicity while Masters oversaw the research and science.

Together Johnson and Masters helped dispel many misconceptions about human sexuality: They asserted that the length of man's sexual organ does not influence his ability to satisfy his partner, and that sex for the elderly was in fact possible and not out of the ordinary. They also helped many men and women overcome a variety of sexual issues—men with impotence problems and premature ejaculation, and women with the inability to achieve orgasm—and, therefore, paved the way for a new generation of sex therapists.

One of Johnson and Master's best-known studies included some 694 volunteers who were hooked up to instruments that recorded heart rate and brain activity while they engaged in sexual activity. Moreover, a camera inside an artificial phallus was able to uncover, for the first time, what happens inside the female genitalia during sexual intercourse.

Johnson died on July 24, 2013, in St. Louis, Missouri. She was eighty-eight years old. She was married four times, all of which ended in divorce. Johnson is survived by her son, Scott; her daughter, Lisa; and her two grandchildren.

*See Current Biography 1976.*

# David C. Jones

**Born:** Aberdeen, South Dakota; July 9, 1921
**Died:** Potomac Falls, Virginia; August 10, 2013
**Occupation:** US government official and Air Force officer

David C. Jones was best known as the chairman of the Joint Chiefs of Staff (1978–82) during the Carter and Reagan administrations. During his tenure as chairman, Jones enacted a number of reforms to the nation's military command, including giving more power to the Joint Chiefs. Many of his suggestions were implemented into the Goldwater-Nichols Act (1986) that reworked the command structure of the military. Also under Jones's leadership, eight military service members died when their helicopter crashed during an attempt to rescue fifty-three US hostages in Iran. The cause of the crash was attributed to a sandstorm. Nevertheless, Jones was the chief planner of the rescue mission and, therefore, he was criticized by military officials and members of Congress for its failure.

Jones was born on July 9, 1921, in Aberdeen, South Dakota. Jones attended the University of South Dakota and Minot State College, but he left college after earning his pilot's license and joined the US Army Air Corps in 1942. He trained pilots during World War II, but he didn't see combat action until the Korean War, where he flew B-29 bombers on missions over North Korea. He would later climb the ranks and become the vice commander of the Seventh Air Force in Vietnam and then the US Air Force chief of staff in 1974. He presided over the Air Force during the Cold War and a period of

growing tension between the Soviet Union and United States in their competition for the world's top military power. Under his recommendation, President Carter approved the development of a "medium-sized, highly accurate missile capable of being moved from launch point to launch point," which would augment the power of the Air Force.

President Carter named Jones the chairman of the Joint Chiefs of Staff after the former chairman, General George S. Brown, became terminally ill. During his tenure as chairman, Jones was a key player in supporting the second phase of Carter's Strategic Limitation Treaty (SALT II) and negotiations with the Soviet Union. He also played a role in advocating for the removal of the US embargo on Turkey. These accomplishments, however, were overshadowed by the failed rescue mission of hostages in Iran. Despite this failure, Ronald Reagan retained Jones in his position as chairman after Reagan took office in 1981.

Jones stepped down from chairman on June 18, 1982, after eight years of service. Jones was the recipient of a number of awards, including the Distinguished Service Medal with Oak Leaf Cluster, the Distinguished Flying Cross, the Bronze Star Medal, and the French Legion of Honor.

Jones died of Parkinson's disease on August 10, 2013, in Potomac Falls, Virginia. He was ninety-two years old. His wife, Lois Tarbell Jones, died in 2009. Jones is survived by his sister, Jean Brown; his two daughters, Kathy Franklin and Susan Coffin; his son, David Curtis Jones; four grandchildren; and two great-grandchildren.

*See Current Biography 1982.*

# George Jones

**Born:** Saratoga, Texas; September 12, 1931
**Died:** Nashville, Tennessee; April 26, 2013
**Occupation:** American country singer

George Jones was an American country singer and the recipient of two Grammy Awards for his songs "Choices" in 1999 and "He Stopped Loving Her Today" in 1981. He also received a lifetime achievement Grammy Award in 2012. Jones was best known for his golden voice that many consider to be the best in the history of country music: "The greatest voice to ever grace country music will never die," said Garth Brooks, an American country singer, upon the news of his death. Likewise, Travis Tritt remarked that, "his voice will be influencing singers one hundred years from now and beyond." But despite his acclaimed vocals and number-one hits on the country music charts, Jones battled a drug and alcohol addiction throughout the majority of his career. His struggles with alcoholism inspired songs such as "If Drinking Don't Kill Me (Her Memory Will)" (1980) and were immortalized in the lyrics of his song "Choices": "By an early age I found I liked drinkin'/ Oh, and I never turned it down."

Jones was born in Saratoga, Texas, on September 12, 1931. He began playing the guitar at the age of nine, and as a teenager he performed in church and on the streets, placing a plastic cup on the pavement to collect tips. He released his first single, "No Money in This Deal," in 1954, but his first hit came in 1955 with "Why Baby Why," which made it to the top ten on the country-music charts. His first album, *George Jones Sings*, was released in 1956.

"White Lightning" (1959) was his first single to reach number one on the country-music charts. The song's lyrics revealed his fondness for "white lighting," also known as moonshine whiskey: "We brewed white lightnin' 'til the sun went down/ Then he'd fill him a jug and he'd pass it around/ Mighty, mighty pleasin, pappy's corn squeezin'." He had a number of other number-one hits, including "Walk through This World with Me," (1967) "He Stopped Loving Her Today," (1980), and "I Always Get Lucky with You" (1983).

Jones married, Tammy Wynette, a country singer, in 1969. The couple wrote and performed duets, three of which—"We're Gonna Hold On" (1973), "Golden Ring" (1976), and "Near You" (1977)—reached number one on the country-music charts. The couple's divorce in 1975 inspired Jones to write two albums that were released in 1976: *The Battle* and *Alone Again*. The pair reunited in the 1980s and released the album *Together Again* (1980). They reunited a second time in the 1990s and released the album *One* (1995). Wynette died in 1998.

Jones was inducted into the Country Music Hall of Fame in 1992. He was also one of the artists honored at the Kennedy Center in 2008. Jones died on April 26, 2013, in Nashville, Tennessee. He was eighty-one years old. Jones is survived by his fourth wife, and his sister, children, and grandchildren.

*See Current Biography 1995.*

---

# Ed Koch

**Born:** New York City, New York; December 12, 1924
**Died:** New York City, New York; February 1, 2013
**Occupation:** American politician

From January 1, 1978, to December 31, 1989, Edward Irving Koch served as the mayor of New York City. During his three terms in office, Koch helped pull the city out of a budget deficit that was officially $249 million, but which other sources estimate to have been about $400 million. Not only did he balance the budget, but he also established housing programs; restored neighborhoods that had been neglected and riddled by crime; rebuilt damaged bridges and roads; and improved education and employment conditions, thus helping to restore the city's economy.

On December 12, 1924, Koch was born in New York City, but was raised primarily in Newark, New Jersey, where he graduated from South Side High School in 1941. He studied at the College of the City of New York, but left after he was drafted by the United States Army during World War II. As a combat infantryman, he fought in France and Germany, earned two battle stars, and eventually became a sergeant. After the war, Koch attended New York University's law school and earned his LLB degree in 1948. He began practicing law in Manhattan in 1949. In 1963 he helped start the Wall Street law practice of Koch, Lankenau, Schwartz & Kovener and became the firm's senior partner.

Koch ran for a state assembly seat in 1962, but his first campaign for public office was not successful. In 1963, however, he defeated Tammany boss Carmine De Sapio and became the Democratic district leader from Greenwich Village. This victory helped launch his political career and opened the door for a number of other successful political campaigns. In 1966, he was elected to a seat in the New York City Council. Two years later, he was elected to the United States House of Representatives, where he represented Manhattan's Seventeenth Congressional District through December 31, 1977, when he resigned after being elected mayor of New York City that fall.

In the 1977 New York mayoral race, Koch defeated both the incumbent, Abraham D. Beame, and Mario M. Cuomo, who received 42 percent of the vote. Koch was inaugurated on January 1, 1978. He was reelected again in 1981 and in 1985, making him, at the time, the third person to serve a third term as mayor of New York City (Fiorello H. LaGuardia and Robert F. Wagner Jr. also served three terms). During his third term, Koch was criticized for his faulty efforts to address the AIDS crisis in the city, as well as other problems such as crime and homelessness. In 1982, Mario M. Cuomo defeated Koch in the gubernatorial primary. During the race for mayor in 1989, he was defeated in the Democratic primary by David N. Dinkins, who became the first African American mayor of New York City.

In addition to his career in politics, Koch was an adjunct professor at a number of universities, including New York University and Brandeis University. He was also the author of seventeen books, including *Mayor* (1984), *His Eminence and Hizzoner* (1989), and *Buzz: How to Create It and Win with It* (2007).

On February 1, 2013, Koch died of heart failure at New York-Presbyterian/Columbia Hospital in New York City. He was eighty-eight years old. Koch is survived by his sister, Pat Koch Thaler. His brother, Harold M. Koch, died in 1995.

*See Current Biography Illustrated 1978.*

## C. Everett Koop

**Born:** New York, New York; October 14, 1916
**Died:** Hanover, New Hampshire; February 25, 2013
**Occupation:** United States surgeon general

Charles Everett Koop was a pediatric surgeon and served as the surgeon general of the United States under the Reagan administration from 1982 to 1989. He initially caught the attention of conservative politicians with his antiabortion views. However, while in office, he did not let moral issues take precedence over scientific facts. For example, when President Ronald Reagan asked Koop to issue a report on the psychological effects of having an abortion, Koop refused to release the report because he found there was a lack of scientific evidence to conclude whether or not abortions were psychologically damaging. In the early 1980s, he was one of the few high-ranking government officials to speak out against the AIDS crisis (then considered a homosexual disease) and he educated the public on methods of preventing HIV infection. He also played a role in educating Americans about the health dangers of smoking cigarettes.

Dr. Koop was born on October 14, 1916, in New York City. After graduating from Dartmouth College in 1937 with a degree in zoology, Koop entered medical school at Cornell University. He graduated from Cornell in 1941 and started his residency at the University of Pennsylvania Hospital, where he began his surgical training. He was a skilled surgeon, and, after completing his residency, his professor, Dr. I. S. Ravdin, presented him with the position of surgeon-in-chief at Children's Hospital in Philadelphia in 1948.

During his lengthy career as surgeon-in-chief (1948–81), Koop pioneered a number of pediatric surgeries and procedures, including a successful procedure for esophageal atresia, a previously fatal congenital defect in which the esophagus and stomach are not connected. After thirty-five years at Children's Hospital, Koop was nominated by President Ronald Reagan to become the surgeon general of the United States.

After being confirmed by the Senate on November 16, 1981, Koop was officially sworn in as surgeon general on January 21, 1982. His accomplishments during his tenure as surgeon general included increasing AIDS awareness—mailing brochures with information about the disease to more than one hundred million households—and initiating antismoking campaigns. By the time he left office in 1989, the number of cigarette smokers in the United States had dropped (from 33 percent to 26 percent); forty states had restricted smoking in public places; and smoking was restricted in thousands of federal buildings. The restriction of smoking in public places and buildings was due, in part, to Koop's 1986 report on secondhand smoke's proven role as a carcinogen. Koop's message on cigarettes also helped to initiate a number of antismoking campaigns by organizations such as the American Heart Association.

Koop died on February 25, 2013, at his home in Hanover, New Hampshire. He was ninety-six years old. Koop's first wife, Elizabeth Flanagan, died in 2007. Koop and Flanagan published a book, *Sometimes Mountains Move* (1979), which told of the death of their son, David, who died in 1968. Koop is survived by his second wife, Cora Hogue; three children, Allen, Norman, and Elizabeth; and eight grandchildren.

*See Current Biography 1983.*

## Hilary Koprowski

**Born:** Warsaw, Poland; December 5, 1916
**Died:** Philadelphia, Pennsylvania; April 11, 2013
**Occupation:** Polish-born virologist

Hilary Koprowski was a virologist and immunologist who in 1948 developed the world's first oral vaccine for polio, a crippling and potentially fatal disease of the nervous system. His vaccine was never approved for use in the United States and was overshadowed by Albert Sabin's oral vaccine, which was approved by the United States Public Health Service. Nevertheless, it is believed that Koprowski's work paved the way for the Sabin oral vaccine. Koprowski was also known for helping to develop a more effective vaccine for rabies and for his research with monoclonal antibodies used to fight cancer.

Koprowksi was born on December 5, 1916, in Warsaw, Poland. He studied music at the Warsaw Conservatory and medicine at the University of Warsaw, where he received his MD in 1939. After working with the Yellow Fever Research Service in Rio de Janiero, Brazil, where he worked on developing a vaccine for the yellow fever virus, Koprowski accepted a position at Lederle Laboratories, a pharmaceutical company in Pearl River, New York. Here, he began his research on rabies and polio, but focused on the latter, which was a more serious and widespread threat at the time. Koprowski developed a vaccine that contained live cultures of the polio virus that were weakened to the point that the body's immune system could defeat it and develop antibodies, thus preventing the contraction of the disease and its debilitating effects.

In 1958, Koprowski administered the vaccine on approximately 250,000 people in the Belgian Congo and Ruanda-Urandi areas of Africa, and it was, "completely safe, almost 100 percent effective," according to a report released by *Time* magazine. However, the US Surgeon General, Leroy E. Burney, announced that the Sabin vaccine was approved in the United States, not Koprowski's. This was due, in part, to the live cultures used in Koprowski's vaccine, which were believed to carry more of a risk.

For more than thirty years, Koprowski was the director of a biomedical research center in Philadelphia, the Wistar Institute. He was also a faculty member at the University of Pennsylvania. He received a number of awards for his work, including the French Legion of Honor.

Koprowski died on April 11, 2013, at his home in Philadelphia, Pennsylvania. He was ninety-six years old. His wife, Irene, whom he met at the University of Warsaw, died in 2012. He is survived by his two sons, Christopher and Claude.

*See Current Biography 1968.*

# Bert Lance

**Born:** Gainesville, Georgia; June 3, 1931
**Died:** Calhoun, Georgia; August 15, 2013
**Occupation:** American banker and presidential adviser

Bert Lance was an American banker who became an adviser to President Jimmy Carter and the director of the Office of Management and Budget. He succeeded the former director, James T. Lynn, on January 23, 1977. His tenure as budget director, however, was cut short after less than one year due to a high-profile investigation of his alleged illegal banking practices, including personally issuing loans to the president, and he subsequently resigned in 1977. He was later acquitted of all charges.

Lance was born on June 3, 1931, in Gainesville, Georgia. He dropped out of Emory University in 1951 to support his family as a teller at the Calhoun First National Bank, and worked his way up to become the bank's chief executive in 1963. This experience leading the bank qualified him to take graduate courses at Louisiana State University in 1956 and at Rutgers University in 1963. The bank grew considerably under his leadership—mainly from doing business with carpet companies that were attracted to the bank's easy financing—and his success and wealth opened doors to the social circle of Georgia's elite, including Jimmy Carter. When Carter became governor of Georgia in 1970, he

appointed Lance commissioner of the Georgia Department of Transportation.

After an unsuccessful attempt to succeed Carter as governor of Georgia, Lance became the head of the National Bank of Georgia. He would later follow Carter to Washington after he won the presidential election in 1976. Upon being accused of lending money to friends and relatives, Lance resigned in 1977. Though eventually acquitted, he was indicted again in 1991, this time for alleged crimes involving the Bank of Credit and Commerce International (BCCI). He was later acquitted again. Overall, he was investigated by at least eight federal agencies (including the US Senate and the Internal Revenue Service), but he was never convicted of a crime.

Despite his indictments, Lance remained a reputable figure in Georgia and remained involved in politics. He chaired the Georgia Democratic Party in 1982 and Walter Mondale's presidential campaign in 1984, and also advised the Reverend Jesse Jackson during his 1988 presidential nomination bid. In 2000 a stretch of highway on Interstate 75 in Resaca, Georgia, was named Bert Lance Highway in his honor.

Lance died on August 15, 2013, at his home in Calhoun, Georgia. He was eighty-two years old. Lance is survived by his wife, LaBelle (David), and his three sons, David Lance (the president and CEO of Greater Rome Bank), Stuart, and Thomas; his fourteen grandchildren; and ten great-grandchildren.

*See Current Biography 1977.*

# Frank Lautenberg

**Born:** Paterson, New Jersey; January 23, 1924
**Died:** New York, New York; June 3, 2013
**Occupation:** United States senator

Frank Lautenberg served nearly three decades as a United States senator from New Jersey. Lautenberg helped author and pass a number of bills during his career in the senate, but he is perhaps best known for passing legislation concerning public health and safety. In 1989, for example, he helped draft and pass a provision that banned smoking cigarettes on commercial aircrafts. In 1984, he pushed through a provision that established twenty-one as the national legal drinking age, which helped reduce the number of drunk drivers under the age of twenty-one, and, therefore, the number of deaths resulting from underage drunk driving. Jay A. Winsten, the associate dean of the Harvard School of Public Health, estimates that more than twenty-five thousand lives have been saved as a result of this bill.

Lautenberg was born on January 23, 1924, in Paterson, New Jersey. After he was discharged from the US Army Signal Corps in 1946, Lautenberg took advantage of the GI Bill and attended Columbia University, graduating in 1949 with a degree in economics. In 1952, Lautenberg and his two childhood friends founded Automatic Data Processing (ADP), a payroll service company. ADP made Lautenberg a wealthy businessman, and by the time he retired as CEO in 1982 the company had grown to approximately fifteen thousand employees, making it one of the largest computer service companies in the world.

Lautenberg was first elected to the Senate after defeating the incumbent Millicent Fenwick in 1982. He retired from the senate in 2000 after eighteen years in office; however, after Senator Robert G. Torricelli decided not to seek reelection in 2002, Lautenberg entered the race and won the seat. He was reelected in 2008.

In addition to passing public health and safety legislation, Lautenberg was also a proponent of mass transit projects and significantly increased the National Railroad Passenger Corporation's (doing business as Amtrak) funding with legislation in 2008. He also helped draft and pass legislation that protected citizens from gun violence, granted refugee status to previously persecuted groups, including people of Jewish heritage, and secured funds to clean up toxic waste.

Lautenberg died on June 3, 2013, in New York, New York, from complications of viral pneumonia. At the time of his death, he was the oldest serving Senate member at eighty-nine years of age. Lautenberg divorced his first wife, Lois Levenson, in 1988. He is survived by his second wife, Bonnie; four children; two stepchildren; and thirteen grandchildren.

*See Current Biography 1991.*

# George Michael Leader

**Born:** York County, Pennsylvania; January 17, 1918
**Died:** Hershey, Pennsylvania; May 9, 2013
**Occupation:** American politician

George Michael Leader was best known as the Democratic governor of Pennsylvania from 1955 to 1959. Leader was thirty-seven years old when he was inaugurated on January 18, 1955, making him the second-youngest governor in Pennsylvania's history. (Robert E. Pattison, who was first elected in 1883, was the youngest at thirty-two years old.) Some of Leader's most notable accomplishments while in office include improving the quality of life for people with disabilities and mental illness. He poured funds into mental health clinics in the community, thus contributing to patients' rehabilitation back into society and reducing the population in mental hospitals

from 39,000 to 11,000. He also required schools in Pennsylvania to offer special education for children with disabilities.

Leader was born on January 17, 1918, in York County, Pennsylvania, and grew up on his family's poultry farm. With ambitions to become a teacher, he attended York Collegiate Institute and Gettysburg College, but later transferred to the University of Pennsylvania, where he received his bachelor's degree in education in 1939. In 1942, Leader attended graduate school at the Wharton School of Finance, but left after one semester to join the United States Naval Reserve during World War II, where he served on the USS *Randolph*, an aircraft carrier stationed in the Pacific Ocean.

After the war, Leader used a GI loan to purchase a farm in York County, Pennsylvania, and became involved in local politics. When his father, Guy Leader, retired as a state senator representing the Twenty-Eighth District, Leader was elected to his father's seat in 1950 and served until 1954. He lost the election for state treasurer in 1952, but in the process of his campaign he increased his public presence in the state. He decided to run in the 1954 gubernatorial election. Leader was considered an underdog to his opponent, Lieutenant Governor Lloyd Wood, but he used television advertisements to his advantage and won the election by a landslide of 280,000 votes. During his four-year term (this was the maximum term-limit allowed by law at the time), Leader implemented a number of reforms that contributed to human welfare and social progress, including mental health, education, industrial development, and expanding rights for people with disabilities. He was also the first governor in Pennsylvania's history to seat an African American on his cabinet.

In 1958, Leader lost the US Senate race to Congressman Hugh Scott, and he never ran for public office again. Instead, he focused on issues such as prison reform and established an assisted-living business, launching Country Meadows Retirement Communities throughout Pennsylvania and Maryland. In his eighth decade, he established another assisted-living company called Providence Place. Leader also served as the National Crusade Chairman of the American Cancer Society and on the board of the Philadelphia Home Loan Bank.

Leader died on May 9, 2013, in an assisted-living center in Hershey, Pennsylvania. He was ninety-five years old. His wife of over seventy years, Mary Jane (Strickler), died in 2011, and his son, Fred, died in 2003. Leader is survived by his sons, George Michael and David; his daughter, Jane; twelve grandchildren; and two great-grandsons.

*See Current Biography 1956.*

# Elmore Leonard

**Born:** New Orleans, Louisiana; October 11, 1925
**Died:** Bloomfield Township, Michigan;
August 20, 2013
**Occupation:** American author

A prolific author in a genre populated by pro-lific authors, Elmore Leonard—praised for his succinct but literary prose and bitingly crisp dialogue—lent the crime novel a certain liter-ary legitimacy. Leonard filled his forty-five books with bad guys that were often more interesting and relatable than the good guys. His 1985 novel *Glitz*—a cat and mouse tale about a serial rap-ist and the cop who put him away—was a na-tional bestseller, and landed him on the cover of *Newsweek*. Later in Leonard's career, film and television adaptations of his stories introduced the writer to a broader audience. The 1995 ad-aptation of Leonard's *Get Shorty* (1990), star-ring John Travolta, opened at number one at the weekend box office and renewed mainstream interest in his work. Director Quentin Tarantino chose to adapt Leonard's *Rum Punch* (1992) for his third film. Tarantino took some liberties with the source material, resulting in a blaxploitation send-up titled *Jackie Brown* (1997). Leonard expressed fondness for the adaptation in inter-views, pointing to stylistic similarities between his and Tarantino's storytelling. In 2010, *Justi-fied*, a television series based on Leonard's short story "Fire in the Hole" premiered on FX. The success of the show prompted Leonard to re-visit Raylan Givens—the story's hero—in *Raylan* (2012), the last novel Leonard published before his death.

Elmore John Leonard Jr. was born in New Orleans, Louisiana, on October 11, 1925. In 1935, his father, who worked as an executive with General Motors, moved the family to De-troit, Michigan—the city that Leonard would later immortalize in so many of his novels. Af-ter graduating from the University of Detroit in 1950, Leonard worked as a copywriter for a Detroit advertising agency, working on writing Westerns in the hours before he left for his day job. His first novel, *The Bounty Hunters*, was published in 1953. Leonard suffered a stroke in early August 2013, and died at his home in Bloomfield Township, Michigan, on August 20, 2013. He was eighty-seven. Married three times and divorced twice, Leonard was predeceased by his second wife, Joan Shepard, in 1993. His survivors include five children, thirteen grand-children, and five great-grandchildren.

*See Current Biography 1985.*

# Gerda Lerner

**Born:** Vienna, Austria; April 30, 1920
**Died:** Madison, Wisconsin; January 2, 2013
**Occupation:** American historian

Gerda Lerner was an American historian best known for creating what many historians con-sider to be the first US graduate program for the study of women's history, which she estab-lished in 1972 at Sarah Lawrence College. She was the author of many books on women's his-tory, including *The Woman in American History* (1971); *The Creation of Patriarchy* (1986); and *The Creation of Feminist Consciousness* (1993). Her efforts to collect and publish women's dia-ries, letters, and other primary sources were in-strumental in making such materials available to historians for study. Lerner also established a doctoral program in women's history at the Uni-versity of Wisconsin-Madison, where she taught for many years.

On April 30, 1920, Lerner was born in Vi-enna, Austria, to a Jewish couple named Robert and Ilona (Neumann) Kronstein. When she was in her late teens, Lerner spent six weeks in pris-on during the Nazi occupation of Austria. In her autobiography, *Fireweed: a Political Autobiogra-phy* (2002), she stated, "Everything I needed to get through the rest of my life I learned in jail in those six weeks." She was released from prison after her father forfeited his assets in Austria in return for her freedom.

In 1941, she married Carl Lerner, a theater director and film editor. The Lerners lived in Hollywood, but when it became hard for him to secure work due to his political affiliation, they returned to New York City in 1949. Carl Lerner was soon in demand as a film editor for *Twelve Angry Men* and other films; Gerda Lerner con-tinued her education at the New School and earned a bachelor's degree in history in 1963. She then enrolled at Columbia University, where she completed her master's degree in 1965 and her doctorate in 1966.

In 1968, Lerner began teaching history at Sarah Lawrence College, where, in 1972, she helped implement what is considered to be the United States' first graduate program with a fo-cus on women's history. In 1980, she joined the faculty at the University of Wisconsin-Madison and established a doctoral program in women's history. A year later, she was elected president of the Organization of American Historians, one of the largest professional societies for the study of history.

Since 1992, an award named in her honor, the Lerner-Scott Prize, is given annually to the student with the best doctoral dissertation in US women's history. (This award is also named after the historian Anne Firor Scott.) Lerner was the recipient of many awards and honors, including the Austrian Cross of Honor for Science and Art, and the Lifetime Achievement Award for Scholarly Distinction of the American Historical Association.

On January 2, 2013, Lerner died in Madison, Wisconsin, at the age of ninety-two. Her husband died in 1973. She is survived by her two children, Dan and Stephanie; her sister, Nora Kronstein; and her four grandchildren.

*See Current Biography 1998.*

# Rita Levi-Montalcini

**Born:** Turin, Italy; April 22, 1909
**Died:** Rome, Italy; December 30, 2012
**Occupation:** Italian neurologist

Rita Levi-Montalcini was an Italian neurologist and a recipient of the 1986 Nobel Prize in Physiology or Medicine. She is best known for discovering a protein called the nerve growth-promoting factor (NGF), which plays a role in cell development. Her discovery has provided doctors and scientists with the tools to understand and develop potential treatments for health conditions such as cancer and Alzheimer's disease.

Against her father's wishes, Levi-Montalcini attended the University of Turin medical school, where she graduated summa cum laude in 1936. After graduating, she began studying under the histologist Giuseppe Levi, from whom she learned how to isolate nerve cells using a technique called silver-staining. Her professional career, however, was interrupted when Mussolini imposed a law that prevented persons of non-Aryan race from working in medicine and academia. Nevertheless, she set up a lab in her home and began to study chicken embryos with the intent on finding the mechanism behind the development of nerve growth.

During World War II, Levi-Montalcini and her Jewish Italian family fled Turin, Italy for the countryside and then Florence. They did not return to Turin until the end of the war in 1945. Levi-Montalcini left Turin again in 1947 to join Viktor Hamburger at Washington University in St. Louis for a research position. She would later become a professor of neurobiology at the university in 1958.

During her time at Washington University, she and one of her students, the biochemist Stanley Cohen, isolated a protein that played a role in nerve growth—a protein they named the nerve growth-promoting factor (NGF). In 1971, almost twenty years after their initial discovery,

Levi-Montalcini and Cohen published the structure of the NGF protein. In 1986, they both awarded the Nobel Prize in Physiology or Medicine for their discovery. Levi-Montalcini was also the recipient of the National Medal of Science and many other honors and awards.

Rita Levi-Montalcini died at her home in Rome, Italy, on December 30, 2012. She was 103 years old. She never married and has no children.

*See Current Biography 1989.*

# Joseph Anthony Lewis

**Born:** New York, New York; March 27, 1927
**Died:** Cambridge, Massachusetts; March 25, 2013
**Occupation:** American journalist

Anthony Joseph Lewis was an American journalist best known as a Supreme Court reporter for the *New York Times*. In 1955, he won his first Pulitzer Prize while working at the *Washington Daily Post* for his reporting on Abraham Chasanow, who was targeted during the McCarthy Era as a security risk. In 1963, while writing for the *New York Times*, he received his second Pulitzer for his Supreme Court coverage. In addition to his award-winning work as a journalist, Lewis was also the author of a number of books, including *Gideon's Trumpet* (1964), an account of the 1963 *Gideon v. Wainright* decision, and *Make No Law: The Sullivan Case and the First Amendment* (1991), which concerned the *New York Times v. Sullivan* case in 1964.

On March 27, 1927, Lewis was born in New York City. He attended the Horace Mann School in New York City. During World War II, he served in the Navy, but was discharged shortly after joining due to an eye condition. After his discharge, he went to Harvard University and graduated with an English degree in 1948.

Lewis accepted his first position at the *New York Times* in 1948, where he wrote for the News of the Week in Review section. Lewis then worked briefly for Adlai Stevenson's 1952 presidential campaign, before returning to his career in journalism, this time at the *Washington Daily Post*. Lewis's banner year at the *Post* was 1955, when he won the Pulitzer Prize as well as the Broun Award of the American Newspaper. Lewis returned to the *New York Times* that year, where he would establish himself as an authority on the Supreme Court.

In order to prepare himself to write about law, Lewis attended Harvard Law School on a Nieman Fellowship (1956–57). He wrote a number of critically acclaimed articles on the Supreme Court, including his coverage of *Baker v. Carr*, a landmark case in 1962 that established that federal courts have the authority to determine whether or not a state's voting districts are constitutional. His coverage of this particular case was singled out by the 1963 Pulitzer citation.

Lewis published his final book, *Freedom for the Thought That We Hate: A Biography of the First Amendment*, in 2008. On March 25, 2013, Lewis died at his home in Cambridge, Massachusetts. He was eighty-five years old. His marriage to Linda Rannels ended in divorce in 1982. Rannels died in 1995. Lewis married Margaret Marshall in 1984. Lewis is survived by Marshall; his children, Eliza, David, and Mia; and seven grandchildren.

*See Current Biography Illustrated 1955.*

# Lotfi Mansouri

**Born:** Tehran, Iran; June 15, 1929
**Died:** San Francisco, California; August 30, 2013
**Occupation:** Iranian American opera director

Lotfi Mansouri was an Iranian-born opera director best known for running the Canadian Opera Company (1976–88) and the San Francisco Opera (1988–2001). During his tenure with the San Francisco Opera, Mansouri was responsible for ambitious productions such as Steward Wallace's *Harvey Milk* in 1996, and Mikhail Glinka's *Ruslan and Lyudmila* in 1995. He was also credited with leading the renovation of the War Memorial Opera House, the home of the San Francisco Opera, which was damaged by the Loma Preita earthquake in 1989.

Mansouri was born in Tehran, Iran, on June 15, 1929. He studied at the University of California at Los Angeles (UCLA), where he graduated with his bachelor's degree in psychology in 1953. He continued to take classes at UCLA for nine years so he could maintain his student visa and remain in the United States. Seeing Puccini's *Madame Butterfly* at the Hollywood Bowl inspired Mansouri to take classes at UCLA's opera workshop. In 1957, he became an associate professor of music at UCLA. He directed his first opera performance, Mozart's *Così fan tutte*, at Los Angeles City College in 1959.

After studying voice at the Santa Barbara's Music Academy of the West, he was appointed artistic director of the Zurich Opera, and, in 1960, he became the resident stage director. In 1975, Mansouri began his twelve-year tenure as director of the Canadian Opera Company in Toronto, Canada. In addition to introducing thirty new productions with the company, and making it internationally known, Mansouri introduced an innovative system of synchronous translations called supertitles during a 1983 production of *Elektra*. The supertitles provided audience

members who did not speak German with an English translation of the libretto on the frame above the stage. Mansouri's innovation inspired other opera houses to follow suit with supertitles or similar simultaneous translation systems. In 1988, Mansouri made his transition to the San Francisco Opera, where he oversaw celebrated productions such as *Dead Man Walking* and *A Street Car Named Desire*. He was the recipient of many awards and honors, including the title of Chevalier of France's Order des Arts et des Lettres and a 2009 lifetime achievement award from the National Endowment of the Arts Opera Honors.

Mansouri died from complications of pancreatic cancer on August 30, 2013, in San Francisco, California. He was eighty-four years old. His wife, Marjorie, survives him, along with his daughter, Dr. Shireen Mansouri.

*See Current Biography 1990.*

# Wilfried Martens

**Born:** Sleidinge, Belgium; April 19, 1936
**Died:** October 9, 2013
**Occupation:** Belgian prime minister

Wilfried Martens served as the prime minister of Belgium from April 3, 1979, to March 31, 1981, and again from December 17, 1981, to March 7, 1992. During his tenure as prime minister, he helped bring stability to a country known for its arduous language barriers and mercurial factions. In 1976, he helped found the European People's Party (EPP), the major European political party of the center-right. He served as president of the European People's Party from 1990 until his death. According to Martin Schulz, the president of the European parliament, Martens was "a great statesman of Belgium, Europe and an outstanding leader in the European Parliament."

Martens was born in Sleidinge, Belgium, on April 19, 1936. He had a difficult, impoverished childhood, which was compounded by the early death of his father. After graduating from the college of Eeklo and completing his secondary school education, Martens enrolled in the Catholic University of Louvain in 1954. Here, he received a doctorate of law in 1958, as well as degrees in notarial studies and philosophy. During his time at Louvain, he was the chairman of the Flemish association of Catholic university students.

In 1962, Martens became a member of the Christian People's Party (CVP), where he would later serve as chairman (1972–79). In 1974 he was elected to the house of representatives, the lower branch of the bicameral Belgian parliament, where he proved to be a skilled negotiator and a savvy politician. Consequently, he was nominated by Belgium's King Baudouin to form a government, and, in 1979, Martens became prime minister. His appointment ended a six-month crisis during which Belgium had been ruled by a caretaker government led by former CVP Prime Minister Paul Van Den Boeynants.

Martens had a number of accomplishments during his tenure as prime minister, including his attempt to assuage a tense situation in 1986 when a French-speaking mayor, Jose Happart, refused to speak Flemish in a Flemish-speaking province, which resulted in angry protests. Martens ended the conflict by threatening to resign. Martens was succeeded by Jean-Luc Dehaene as prime minister in 1992. He then pursued a career in the European Parliament, becoming chairman of the European People's Party in 1994.

Martens died on October 9, 2013, although information about the location and cause of death has not been released. He was seventy-seven years old. Martens married his third wife, Miet Smet, in 2008. Smet survives him, as well as his five children.

*See Current Biography 1987.*

# Pierre Mauroy

**Born:** Cartignies, France; July 5, 1928
**Died:** Paris, France; June 7, 2013
**Occupation:** French politician

Pierre Mauroy was France's first Socialist prime minister since the outset of the Fifth Republic in 1958. Along with François Mitterrand—who appointed him prime minister upon becoming president of France in 1981—Mauroy lead a particularly effective Socialist government that instituted such major changes to French society as the lowering of the retirement age, an expansion of welfare benefits, the addition of a fifth week of paid vacation for French workers, and the abolition of the death penalty. But the Mitterand-Mauroy government's radical reforms came at a price. A growing budget deficit coupled with a rising rate of inflation forced Mauroy to institute austerity measures and make cuts to state-run industry. A weak showing from the Left in subsequent local elections reflected the French citizenry's growing distaste for the party's policies. Mitterrand replaced Mauroy with then Minister of Industry Laurent Fabius in 1984.

Pierre Mauroy was born into a working-class Roman Catholic family on July 5, 1928, in Cartignies, France. Mauroy became politically active at a young age, joining the Young Socialists when he was seventeen. By 1966, he was general secretary of what was then known as the French Section of the Workers' International—a

political party founded in 1905 that became the Socialist Party in 1969. In 1971, Mauroy began his career in government service, becoming a councilman and the deputy mayor of the city of Lille. In 1973, he was elected mayor of Lille—a post which he held until 2001. In his lifetime, Mauroy served in the European Parliament, as well as both houses of the French legislature, leaving the senate in 2011 due to failing health. Mauroy died on June 7, 2013, near Paris. He was eighty-four. Mauroy is survived by his wife, Gilberte, and their son, Fabien.

*See Current Biography 1982.*

# Duke K. McCall

**Born:** Meridian, Mississippi; September 1, 1914
**Died:** Delray Beach, Florida; April 2, 2013
**Occupation:** American religious leader

Duke K. McCall was an American religious leader best-known as the former president of the Southern Baptist Theological Seminary in Louisville, Kentucky, from 1951 to 1982, making him the longest-serving president of the seminary. He also served as the president of the New Orleans Baptist Theological Seminary (1943–46) and the executive secretary of the Executive Committee of the Southern Baptist Convention (1946–51), which was one of the largest Baptists groups in the United States at the time. He had many accomplishments during his leadership of the Southern Baptist Theological Seminary, including increasing endowment and enrollment, and supporting the civil rights of African Americans. According to R. Albert Mohler Jr., the current president of Southern Seminary, "Dr. McCall was a giant among Southern Baptists. He belongs to that great generation of Southern Baptist leaders who shaped the convention as the twentieth century brought new opportunities and new challenges. He, along with Drs. W. A. Criswell and Herschel H. Hobbs, brought the Southern Baptist Convention into the modern age."

McCall was born on September 1, 1914, in Meridian, Mississippi. He was an English major at Furman University in Greenville, South Carolina, where he graduated as valedictorian of his class in 1935. After receiving his master's degree in theology (1938) and PhD (1942) from the Southern Baptist Theological Seminary, he became the pastor of the Broadway Baptist Church in Louisville, Kentucky. From here, he continued to assume leadership positions. He became the president of the New Orleans Baptist Theological Seminary in 1943, and, in 1946, the executive secretary of the Executive Committee of the Southern Baptist Convention in Nashville, Tennessee.

McCall was only twenty-eight years old when he became the president of the Southern Baptist Theological Seminary, making him the youngest person to acquire this prestigious position. He held the presidency for approximately three decades. Before he assumed the presidency, McCall travelled to countries around the world to visit Southern Baptist mission fields, where he supported the spread of new churches.

McCall died on April 2, 2013. He was ninety-eight years old. His first wife, Marguerite, died in 1983. He is survived by his second wife, Winona, as well as four sons, twelve grandchildren, and fourteen great-grandchildren.

*See Current Biography 1959.*

# Marian McPartland

**Born:** Windsor, England; March 20, 1918
**Died:** Port Washington, New York;
August 20, 2013
**Occupation:** American jazz pianist

Marian McPartland was an American jazz pianist and the host of the popular National Public Radio (NPR) show *Marian McPartland's Piano Jazz* (commonly known as *Piano Jazz*). She overcame gender boundaries in the 1940s and early 1950s to become one of the most recognized figures in the male-dominated American jazz scene. The jazz critic, Leonard Feather, for example, stated that "she'll never make it: she's English, white and a woman." By 1958, however, McPartland was famous enough to be one of the fifty-seven jazz musicians included in Art Kane's famous *Esquire* magazine group photograph titled *A Great Day in Harlem*. Some of her best-known compositions include "Ambiance" (1970), "With You in Mind" (1957), and "Twilight World" (2008).

Marian McPartland was born Margaret Marian Turner on March 20, 1918, in Windsor, United Kingdom. She was a piano prodigy from the age of three, and by the age of seventeen she was accepted into the prestigious Guildhall School of Music in London. She left Guildhall in 1943, however, to perform with a piano vaudeville act.

McPartland moved to New York City in 1949, where she met and befriended the notable jazz pianist Mary Lou Williams. By 1952, she began performing regularly at the Hickory House, a famous jazz room in New York City, thereby establishing her name in the jazz scene playing with Bill Crow on bass and Joe Morello on drums. The trio recorded their first song, "The Marian McPartland Trio," with Capitol records in 1954. McPartland formed her own jazz label, Halcyon, in 1969. Under her leadership, the label produced eighteen albums until 1979, when she left to sign a recording contract with Concord Jazz.

During the second half of her career, McPartland was known for her radio show, *Piano Jazz*, which premiered on NPR in 1978. The show consisted of performances and interviews with some of the most celebrated jazz musicians, including Eubie Blake, Cecil Taylor, and Steely Dan. The show won a Peabody award in 1983. In addition to the Peabody, McPartland was the recipient of a number of awards and honors, including a lifetime achievement Grammy Award in 2004 and induction into the National Radio Hall of Fame in 2007. McPartland's last *Piano Jazz* show was recorded in 2010.

McPartland died on August 20, 2013, in Port Washington, New York. She was ninety-five years old. After over twenty years of marriage, McPartland divorced her husband, American jazz cornetist Jimmy McPartland, in 1970. The two remained friends and collaborators, however, and eventually remarried shortly before Jimmy died in 1991. McPartland is survived by her nieces and nephews, and by her husband's grandchildren.

*See Current Biography 1976.*

# Russell Means

**Born:** Pine Ridge Indian Reservation, South Dakota; November 10, 1939
**Died:** Porcupine, South Dakota; October 22, 2012
**Occupation:** American Indian activist

Russell Means was one of the most prominent American Indian activists of the century. Means was a pioneer of the American Indian Movement (AIM), and a leader in the battle to recover stolen land from the US government, improve the plight of tribes and reservations, and preserve the culture and freedom of American Indians.

Means received national attention during the Wounded Knee incident in South Dakota: a seventy-one-day armed occupation of the town during which occupiers impeached Richard Wilson, the tribe president, and protested the failure of the US government to honor treaties with American Indians. Despite the death of three people during the conflict, Wounded Knee received widespread support and sympathy from the American people—raising national awareness for the rights of American Indians. Public figures, such as Marlon Brando and Jane Fonda, also voiced their support in the wake of the conflict.

Russell Means was born Oglala Lakota on the Pine Ridge Indian Reservation in South Dakota. Growing up on the impoverished and problematic Indian Reservation influenced Means to fight for improving the condition of American Indians—a cause to which he would devote the rest of his life. His activism began by protesting the use of American Indian mascots in college sports, which he believed were degrading to his people. In 1971, he became the American Indian Movement's first national coordinator. He was arrested numerous times, however, due to his sometimes extreme protest—including Wounded Knee and the seven-day occupation of the Bureau of Indian Affairs in Washington, DC.

Means asserted his most important accomplishment was his proposal for the Republic of Lakotah, an independent American Indian nation in the United States. His proposal was based off of the 1851 Treaty of Fort Laramie between the US government and the Lakotah, which guaranteed Lakotah the ownership of the Black Hills and regions in South Dakota, Montana, and Wyoming.

In addition to activism, Means was also a Hollywood actor and appeared in many films, most notably *The Last of the Mohicans* (1999) and *Natural Born Killers* (1994). He also ran for president in 1988 under the Libertarian Party, but was unsuccessful. He is the author of *Where White Men Fear to Tread,* an autobiography.

On October 22, 2012, Russell Means died in his home in Porcupine, South Dakota, from esophageal cancer. He was seventy-two years old.

*See Current Biography 1978.*

# Thomas M. Messer

**Born:** Bratislava, Czechoslovakia; February 9, 1920
**Died:** New York, New York; May 15, 2013
**Occupation:** Museum director and art historian

Thomas M. Messer was best known as the director of the Solomon R. Guggenheim Museum in New York City from 1961 to 1988. Messer was also the head of the Solomon R. Guggenheim Foundation from 1980 to 1988. During his leadership, the Guggenheim expanded its exhibitions and added to its collection, most notably with the acquisition of two substantial private collections: one from Peggy Guggenheim, the other from Justin K. Thannhauser. These collections added works by a number of renowned artists, including Picasso, Kandinsky, and Pollock. This addition, coupled with Messer's aesthetic sensibility and leadership, helped transform the Guggenheim into one of the most celebrated museums of modern art in the world.

Messer was born on February 9, 1920, in Bratislava, Czechoslovakia. He studied chemistry in Prague and at Thiel College in Pennsylvania, and modern languages at Boston University, where he graduated in 1942. On September 3, 1939, Messer was on a ship, the *Athenia,* from Liverpool to Montreal when it was sunk by a German U-boat. Messer survived the attack, and went on to serve as an Army interrogator

for military intelligence in Europe during World War II. After the war, Messer studied art at the Sorbonne in Paris, graduating with a degree in 1947, and then earned his master's degree in art history from Harvard University in 1951.

Messer assumed his leadership position at the Guggenheim only five years after its relocation to the iconic Frank Lloyd Wright building on Fifth Avenue. The building's unique, spiraling architecture posed an aesthetic challenge for Messer, who referred to it as "the circular geography of hell." In order for vertical pieces of art to not appear off balance in the curving shape of the gallery, he placed them on plinths situated at an angle. He "showed the possibilities of using the Frank Lloyd Wright space and the rotunda in remarkable ways," said Lisa Dennison, a former Guggenheim curator and director.

In addition to his ingenuity, Messer's success as director of the museum was a testament to his skills in diplomacy. For example, he succeeded in acquiring the massive art collection of Peggy Guggenheim, whose uncle had founded the Guggenheim museum in New York City. (Sir Norman Reid, the director of the Tate, also pursued Guggenheim's collection, but was not successful.) The acquisition included pieces from a number of artists such as Picasso, Braque, and de Chirico, as well as Guggenheim's former home, the Palazzo Venier dei Leoni, in Venice, which is now a museum called the Peggy Guggenheim Collection.

Messer died on May 15, 2013, in New York City. He was ninety-three years old. Since his leadership of the Guggenheim, it has spread to not only Venice, but locations in Bilbao and Berlin, and has plans to open a location in Abu Dhabi. According to Peter Lawson-Johnston, a grandson of Solomon R. Guggenheim and president of the Guggenheim during Messer's tenure, "The foundation for all this was laid by Tom Messer. And I can tell you, he laid that foundation under budget." Messer's wife, Remedios Garcia Villa, died in 2002. He has no immediate survivors.

*See Current Biography 1961.*

# Marvin Miller

**Born:** Bronx, New York; April 14, 1917
**Died:** Manhattan, New York; November 27, 2012
**Occupation:** Executive director of the Major League Baseball Players Association

Marvin Miller is one of the most important figures in the history of baseball. He was the executive director of the Major League Baseball Players Association (MLBPA), which became one of the largest and most powerful unions in the United States under his direction. Miller ultimately transformed the structure and business of baseball, but his involvement with the MLB-PA also revolutionized other professional sports, including football, basketball, and hockey.

Miller earned a degree in economics from New York University. Before taking control of the MLBPA, he worked for the National War Labor Board, where he worked on labor-management issues. When Miller took control of the MLBPA in 1966, the owners of baseball teams had all the power—they controlled the player's salaries (which averaged $19,000) and prevented them from switching to other teams. Miller, however, took power away from the club owners and gave it to the players. As a result, their salaries increased significantly, they received fair pension plans, and they gained the ability to hire agents and have bargaining power with other teams. Because of the changes Miller implemented, professional baseball players and athletes have become pop culture stars in today's society, and they can demand celebrity status salaries. For example, the highest paying player in baseball, Alex Rodriguez, commands $30 million per season.

Marvin Miller was well-respected by baseball players for standing up for their rights. In his 1991 memoir, *A Whole Different Ball Game*, Miller stated that "baseball players were among the most exploited workers in America." His efforts, however, were met with considerable challenges, including the thirteen-day strike in 1972 and a fifty-day strike during the middle of the 1981 season.

Miller, despite considerable support from venerable players and baseball executives, was never inducted into the Baseball Hall of Fame; however, he will be eligible again in 2014. But Miller did receive numerous distinctions, including the MLB's creation of the Marvin Miller Man of the Year Award in 1997, and his 2009 induction into the National Jewish Sports Hall of Fame.

On November 27, 2012, Miller died from liver cancer in his Manhattan home. He was ninety-five years old. Miller is survived by sister, Thelma Berenson; his daughter, Susan; his son, Peter; and a grandson.

*See Current Biography 1973.*

# Patrick Moore

**Born:** Pinner, United Kingdom; March 4, 1923
**Died:** Selsey, United Kingdom; December 9, 2012
**Occupation:** British amateur astronomer and television presenter

Sir Patrick Moore was a British astronomer acclaimed for his research and writing, but he is perhaps best known as the host of the BBC television series, *The Sky at Night*. His knowledge of space

and his quirky, amiable personality made him an irresistible television personality. Moore also published sixty books on astronomy with a main focus on the moon. His first book, for example, was *Patrick Moore on the Moon* (1952). Moore also published fiction books, including *The Master of the Moon* (1952) and the Scott Saunders Space Adventure series (1977–80) for young adults.

Patrick Moore's fascination with space began at an early age, and he joined the British Astronomical Society at the age of eleven. His main focus throughout his career as an astronomer was the moon—particularly the far side of the moon, which is not visible from Earth. In 1946, he claimed to have discovered the Mare Orientale (the Eastern Sea) of the Moon, but he later retracted this claim. He coined the term "transient lunar phenomenon" in 1968 to describe the glowing surface of the moon.

Patrick Moore became a public figure thanks to his talk show, *The Sky at Night*, which has been on the air since 1957 and is the longest-running television series with the same host. In addition to educating the public on space, Moore's talk show also provided entertainment, including spoofs on April Fools Days. In addition to *The Sky at Night*, Moore made a number of appearances on other television shows, including *Just a Minute* (1976) and *GamesMaster* (1992–98).

Moore was responsible for compiling the *Caldwell Catalogue*, a collection of 109 astronomical objects first published in *Sky and Telescope* in December 1995 and subsequently republished in book form in 1999. His honors and awards include being elected a fellow of the Royal Astronomical Society (1945) and an honorary fellow of the Royal Society (2001); a Jackson-Gwilt Medal (1977); and the British Academy of Film and Television Arts Award (2002) for his long career in television. In 1982 the International Astronomical Union named a minor planet in his honor. He was knighted in 2001. The Royal Astronomical Society created the Patrick Moore Medal in 2012, given to outstanding teachers of secondary school astronomy or geophysics.

Patrick Moore died in his home in Sesley, United Kingdom, on December 9, 2012. He was eighty-nine years old. Roger Mosey, the acting director of television for the BBC, released a statement saying Moore will be remembered as "one of the great educators of modern television."

*See Current Biography Illustrated 2003.*

# Butch Morris

**Born:** Long Beach, California; February 10, 1947
**Died:** New York City; New York; January 29, 2013
**Occupation:** American cornet player and composer

Lawrence Douglas "Butch" Morris was an American cornet player, composer, and a conductor who created his own improvisational style. Morris referred to his conducting method as "conduction," which he defined as, "an improvised duet for ensemble and conductor." His conduction method was essentially a language of gestures that he used to direct the ensemble. If he wanted his ensemble to repeat something they played, for example, he would use his thumb and forefinger to form a "U Shape." His conductions encompassed a variety of musical styles and instruments—jazz, folk, classical, saxophones, harps, Eastern instruments, and, of course, elements of improvisation. His ten-disc album, *Testament: A Conduction Collection* (1995), is one of his best-known works and includes his first fifty conductions, performed from 1985 to 1995.

Morris was born in Long Beach, California, on February 10, 1947, and he grew up in the Watts neighborhood of Los Angeles, California. He was very involved in his high school's music program—he played in the marching band and the orchestra, and he studied music theory and composition. After graduating, he performed locally with jazz bands and musicians such as the bassist George Morrow. In 1966, however, he left California and served in the US armed forces as a medic during the Vietnam War.

After the war, Morris returned to California and became involved with the free-jazz scene. He moved to Oakland, California, in 1971, where he took up the cornet and began studying music at Grove Street College. In 1976, he moved to New York City, but he left the city that same year to tour Europe with Frank Lowe, a musician he had met in California during the 1970s. While in Europe with Lowe, Morris contributed his first recorded musical performance to Lowe's album, *The Other Side*. In addition to performing, he also taught improvisation in Holland, Belgium, and France. His return to New York City in 1981 was followed by a number of performances and albums. His first recorded conduction, *Current Trends in Racism in Modern America (A Work in Progress)*, debuted in 1985 in New York City. The recording of the performance was published by Sound Aspects in 1986. In addition to *Testament: A Conduction Collection* (1995), his other notable albums include *Burning Cloud* (1996), and *Nine Below Zero* (1988), the latter a collaboration with the musicians Wayne Horvitz and Robert Previte.

Morris received a number of awards and honors for his career in music. He was nominated at the 1999 Bell Atlantic Jazz Awards for creative musician of the year and composer of the year. The National Endowment of the Arts awarded him a grant, and he was a composer in residence for more than twenty universities, including Tufts University in Medford, Massachusetts, and Bilgi University in Istanbul, Turkey.

Morris died from cancer on January 29, 2013, in New York City. He was sixty-five years old. His survivors include a brother, Michael; and a sister, Marceline; and a son, Alexandre. His brother, Wilber Morris, died in 2002.

*See Current Biography 2005.*

# Albert Murray

**Born:** Nokomis, Alabama; May 12, 1916
**Died:** New York, New York; August 18, 2013
**Occupation:** American novelist, essayist, and music historian

Albert Murray was an American novelist, essayist, and music historian best known for writing about race in American society. He was an important figure during the civil rights movement, and was often compared to famous African American writers and activists such as James Baldwin, Ralph Ellison, and Richard Wright. Murray emphasized the integration of the black experience into American culture, which he believed was as much a part of America's history as white culture. Murray's writing style was influenced by blues and jazz, and he explored the theme or race and American identity in books such as *Stomping the Blues* (1976), *Train Whistle Guitar* (1974), and *South to a Very Old Place* (1971).

Murray was born in Nokomis, Alabama, on May 12, 1916. He was adopted soon after birth by Mattie and Hugh Murray. He attended the Tuskegee Institute in Tuskegee, Alabama, where he was exposed to the works of Hemingway, Faulkner, and Joyce. He graduated from Tuskegee in 1939 with a bachelor's of science degree in education. Murray began graduate work at the University of Michigan, but he left to accept a teaching position at Tuskegee, where he taught literature and composition.

In 1943, Murray joined the US Army Air Corps during World War II. He attended New York University after the war with help from the GI Bill and earned his master's of arts degree in 1948. He served again in 1951 and joined the US Air Force until his retirement in 1962. Murray did not publish until he was in his fifties; his first book, *The Omni-Americans*, was released in 1970. But this was soon followed by nine books published from 1970 to the mid-1990s, including *South to a Very Old Place* (1971) and *The Hero of the Blues* (1973). Murray published *The Spyglass Tree*, the first in a series of fiction novels that dealt with his experience as a college student at Tuskegee, in 1991. The fourth and last novel in the series, *The Magic Keys*, was published in 2005.

The most distinct feature of Murray's writing was the incorporation of the rhythms and vibe of jazz and the blues into his aesthetic. He once referred to the blues as "not the creation of a crushed-spirited people. . . . It is the product of a forward-looking, upward-striving people." This message was captured in the book *Stomping Blues* (1976), which explored how jazz and the blues can be viewed as a positive reaction to hardships in the past. In addition to his aesthetic, Murray also included in *Stomping Ground* portrayals of famous African American jazz and blues musicians such as Ella Fitzgerald, Lester Young, and Duke Ellington.

Murray died on August 18, 2013, in Harlem. He was ninety-two years old. Murray is survived by his wife of over seventy years, Mozelle Menefee, and his daughter, the dancer Michéle Murray.

*See Current Biography 1994.*

## Stan Musial

**Born:** Donora, Pennsylvania; November 21, 1920
**Died:** Ladue, Missouri; January 19, 2013
**Occupation:** American baseball player

Occasionally overlooked, but never forgotten by those in the know, Stan "The Man" Musial was a baseball player of uncommon reputation and ability. As a St. Louis Cardinal, Musial rode his signature corkscrew stance to a .331 career batting average, placing him among the best hitters the game has ever seen. Musial made 475 home runs and 3,630 hits—1,815 at home and 1,815 on the road—in his twenty-two seasons of major league play. He won seven National League batting titles and was named MVP three times during his career.

A player of startling consistency, Musial is remembered equally for his attitude as for his athletic skill. Musial was known for his friendly, humble, everyman demeanor—a quiet hard worker who lacked the eccentricity and glamorous off-field life that many of his contemporaries became famous for. When black players first took the field for major league ball teams in 1947, Musial didn't taunt them or threaten to strike like many other white players did. He was known for carrying a harmonica on which he'd play "Take Me Out to the Ball Game" and "Happy Birthday" to the patrons who frequented Stan Musial and Biggie's—the restaurant he owned later in life. Not one, but two statues dedicated to Musial stand outside the Cardinals' Busch Stadium, one of which features words delivered by former commissioner Ford Frick at a ceremony on the day of Musial's final game in 1963: "Here stands baseball's perfect warrior. Here stands baseball's perfect knight."

Stanley Frank Musial was born to a family of Polish immigrants in Donora, Pennsylvania,

on November 21, 1920. His father worked in the town's steel mills and never saw much use for baseball. Though his high school didn't have a baseball team, Musial found field time with American Legion teams, and was eventually signed to a minor-league contract with the Cardinals in 1938. In 1941, he joined the Cardinals' major league team. He played various fielding positions throughout his career, but his legend was written from home plate. As of 2013, Musial had the fourth most career hits in Major League Baseball history.

Musial died at his home in Ladue, Missouri, on January 19, 2013. He was ninety-two. In May 2012 Lillian, Musial's wife of more than sixty years, died. He is survived by the couple's son and three daughters, as well as many grandchildren.

*See Current Biography 1948.*

## Allen Neuharth

**Born:** Eureka, South Dakota; March 22, 1924
**Died:** Cocoa Beach, Florida; April 19, 2013
**Occupation:** American newspaper publisher

Allen Neuharth was an American newspaper publisher and businessman who headed the Gannett Company, a publicly traded media-holding company, and created *USA Today*. When Neuharth released the first issue of *USA Today* on September 15, 1982, he was competing not only with established newspapers—*The New York Times* and *The Washington Post*, for example—but with another popular medium, television, as well. Neuharth, therefore, attempted to simulate the experience of television by adding bright colors and bold graphics to the newspaper. According to Bill Kovach, the former editor of the *Atlanta Journal*, this innovative approach had a pervasive impact: "Virtually no newspaper in the country, nor many around the world, have not been deeply affected by *USA Today* in terms of look, color, graphics and brevity." Others, however, criticized the paper, calling it "junk-food journalism" and claiming that it placed the reader's demands before informative and authentic journalism.

On March 22, 1924, Neuharth was born in Eureka, South Dakota. After serving in the military during World War II, he went to the University of South Dakota on the GI Bill and graduated cum laude in 1950 with a journalism degree and a minor in political science. In 1954, he became a reporter for *The Miami Herald*, where he worked his way up from copy editor to assistant managing editor. He was promoted to assistant executive editor of the *Detroit Free Press* in 1960, became the general manager of two Gannett newspapers in 1963, and by 1973 he had worked his way up to chief executive. While at Gannett, Neuharth contributed to the company's growth and revenue, which exceeded $3 billion from the roughly $390 million when he first started his tenure as chief executive.

Neuharth took a risk in 1982 when he launched *USA Today*, which nearly failed and was not profitable until 1993. Readers, however, were buying the paper from its inception, but it was slow to attract advertisers. Today, *USA Today* is one of the largest newspapers in the country.

In addition to his financial success, Neuharth also made a significant contribution to employment equality by making an effort to hire women and minorities at a time when the industry was predominately run by men. Neuharth was the recipient of numerous awards, including the Ida Wells Award for his commitment to providing job opportunities for minorities.

Neuharth died on April 19, 2013, at his home in Cocoa Beach, Florida. He was eighty-nine years old. He is survived by his third wife, Dr. Rachel Fornes; two children from his first marriage to Loretta Helgeland; six children he adopted with Fornes; and two grandchildren.

*See Current Biography 1986.*

## Oscar Niemeyer

**Born:** Rio de Janeiro, Brazil; December 15, 1907
**Died:** Rio de Janeiro, Brazil; December 5, 2012
**Occupation:** Brazilian architect

Oscar Niemeyer was a prolific Brazilian architect who designed more than six hundred projects in his career. He is best known for designing civic buildings for Brasília, the capital of Brazil. He was also involved in the design of the United Nations Headquarters in New York City. Although initially influenced by the Swiss architect and designer Le Corbusier, Niemeyer's design aesthetic rejected straight lines and angles and incorporated abstract, free-flowing curves that he modeled after Brazil's mountainous landscape and rivers. His use of abstract forms and curves pushed the limit of architectural capabilities and made him an influential figure in the modern architectural movement.

Niemeyer completed his education in 1934, graduating with a degree in architecture from the Escola Nacional de Belas Artes in Rio de Janeiro. He embarked on his first major architectural endeavor with the design of buildings for Pampulha, a suburb of Belo Horizonte. As part of this project, he designed the Church of Saint Francis of Assisi, for which Niemeyer received international acclaim. Consequently, he became one of the most well-known Brazilian architects of the twentieth century.

Niemeyer's career took off in the 1940s and 1950s. He designed buildings in Brazil and throughout the world, including the National Congress of Brazil; the Cathedral of Brasília; the Museum of Modern Art in Caracas, Venezuela; Algeria's University of Science and Technology, Houari Boumediene; and the United Nations Headquarters in New York City.

Niemeyer's architecture earned him numerous awards, including the prestigious Pritzker Architecture Prize in 1988, the Royal Institute of British Architects gold medal (1998), and the ALBA Arts Award in 2008. He became an honorary member of the American Academy of Arts and Sciences (1949), the US National Institute of Arts and Letters (1964), and the Academy of Arts USSR (1983).

Niemeyer continued to design in the twenty-first century. At the age of ninety-four, for example, he designed one of his last major projects, the Oscar Niemeyer Museum, which was completed in 2002. Niemeyer died in Rio de Janeiro on December 5, 2012, only ten days before his 105th birthday. He was predeceased by his first wife, Annita Baldo, and their daughter, Anna Maria. He is survived by his second wife, Vera; four grandchildren; thirteen great-grandchildren; and six great-great grandchildren.

*See Current Biography 1960.*

## Milo O'Shea

**Born:** Dublin, Ireland; June 2, 1926
**Died:** New York, New York; April 2, 2013
**Occupation:** Irish American actor

A character actor of impish charm and formidable versatility, Milo O'Shea endeared himself to audiences over a decades-long career spanning countless roles and media. O'Shea began his career in the United Kingdom as a stage and television actor. He first gained recognition for his starring role as swinging executive Bunjy Kennefick in the sitcom *Me Mammy* (1968–71). On the silver screen, O'Shea caught his big break playing Leopold Bloom in Joseph Strick's 1967 adaptation of James Joyce's *Ulysses*. His role as the devious mad scientist Durand Durand in Roger Vadim's *Barbarella* (1968) inspired the name of internationally acclaimed New Wave act Duran Duran; O'Shea even reprised the role in the band's 1984 concert video, *Arena*. O'Shea moved to the United States in 1976 and eventually became a citizen. American audiences knew O'Shea best for his bit parts on any number of classic sitcoms—a drunken priest on *Cheers*, a couples therapist on *Frasier*, a con man on *The Golden Girls*, the chief justice of the Supreme Court on Aaron Sorkin's *The West Wing*—and his supporting role alongside Paul Newman in Sidney Lumet's *The Verdict* (1982).

O'Shea was born in Dublin on June 2, 1926, to a professional singer and a ballet dancer. In his formative years, he performed at Dublin's famed Gate Theatre, appearing in a production of George Bernard Shaw's *Caesar and Cleopatra* at age twelve. After graduating from the Guildhall School in London with a degree in music and drama, he made his London stage debut in 1949, portraying a pantry boy in John Gielgud's production of *Treasure Hunt*, a jewelry theft caper. O'Shea made his Broadway debut in 1967 in *Staircase* and received a 1968 Tony Award best actor nomination for his performance. He received a second Tony nomination in 1982 for his role as a jaded, comfort-loving priest in Bill C. Davis's *Mass Appeal* (1981). He worked well into his later years, appearing on *The West Wing* in 2004 at the age of seventy-seven. O'Shea died on April 2, 2013, in Manhattan. He was eighty-six. O'Shea is survived by his second wife Kitty, two sons from his first marriage to Maureen Toal, and three grandchildren.

*See Current Biography 1982.*

# Patti Page

**Born:** Claremore, Oklahoma; November 8, 1927
**Died:** Encinitas, California; January 1, 2013
**Occupation:** American singer

Patti Page—the silken-voiced singer who in 1952 asked America, "(How Much Is) That Doggie in the Window?"—was one of the most successful pop performers of the twentieth century. On the cusp of rock and roll, and born of big band swing, Page blended country croon with string-laden glamour for a subdued, but potent pop cocktail that led presenters to call her "the singing rage, Miss Patti Page." While critics considered her music sterile and safe to a fault, Page's catalog represented a post–World War II pop landscape in which comfort and familiarity were valued over the edge and rebellion that would characterize the rock and roll of the late 1950s. Page's biggest hit—1950's "Tennessee Waltz"—sold 10 million copies and is considered to be popular music's first crossover hit, spending months on the country, pop, and rhythm-and-blues charts.

Born Clara Ann Fowler, in Claremore, Oklahoma, on November 8, 1927, Page began her show business career in radio, where she hosted a country-music show called "Meet Patti Page" on Tulsa's KTUL. She kept the name of the fictional host she portrayed on the show and parlayed the show's success into a budding music career that included gigs with "The King of Swing," Benny Goodman, and bandleader Jimmy Joy. Page was signed to Mercury Records,

and began recording hits as a solo performer in 1950 with songs like "With My Eyes Wide Open, I'm Dreaming," "Mockin' Bird Hill," and "Cross over the Bridge." Following a short-lived movie career in the early 1960s, Page's career began to thin out. Page continued to perform live in her seventies. She won a Grammy in 1999 for "Live at Carnegie Hall," a recording of her 1997 performance commemorating fifty years on stage, and between 2002 and 2003, Page released a children's album, a best of collection, and a Christmas album.

Page died of unnamed causes on January 1, 2013, in Encinitas, California. She was eighty-five. Page is survived by her son, daughter, and grandchildren.

*See Current Biography 1965.*

# Pauline Phillips

**Born:** Sioux City, Iowa; July 4, 1918
**Died:** Minneapolis, Minnesota; January 16, 2013
**Occupation:** Advice columnist

Her name was Pauline Phillips, but the periodical readers of America and the letter writers who sought her advice knew her as Abigail Van Buren—Abby, for short. As the pen behind the wildly popular Dear Abby advice column, Phillips delivered her two cents with rapier wit and a dash of sass. She fielded questions on any number of subjects, and her answers—which struck a balance between sassy and sympathetic—heralded an era of advice columns attune to the changing mores of the modern world. In life and work, Phillips was always competing against her twin sister Esther Pauline "Eppie" Lederer, author of another widely read advice column, Ask Ann Landers.

Phillips was born seventeen minutes after Lederer in Sioux City, Iowa, on July 4, 1918, to Russian immigrants Abraham and Rebecca Friedman. The twins' intense sibling rivalry began young, and would follow them throughout their lives, eventually going public as the two achieved national fame. Phillips and Lederer both attended Morningside College in Sioux City, where they wrote a gossip column together for the school newspaper. Phillips—Pauline Esther "Popo" Friedman, at the time—dropped out in 1939 to marry Morton Phillips, businessman and heir to the Ed Phillips and Sons liquor fortune. When Lederer first started writing the Ask Ann Landers column for the *Chicago Sun-Times* in 1955, she would solicit Phillips' help responding to the piles of mail she received daily. Eventually, the *Sun-Times* made Lederer stop sending letters out of the office, and Phillips decided to make her own way in the advice business. Dear Abby first appeared in the *San Francisco*

*Chronicle* in 1956. Her daughter, Jeanne Phillips, began contributing to the column in 1987. By 2000—when Phillips retired and Jeanne became the sole author of the column—the column had appeared in 1,400 newspapers, with a readership of over 110 million.

Phillips suffered from Alzheimer's disease later in life, and died on January 16, 2013, in Minneapolis. She was ninety-four. She was predeceased by Esther Lederer, who died in 2002 at the age of eighty-three; her two other sisters, Helen Brodkey and Dorothy Rubin; as well as her son, Eddie Phillips. Phillips is survived by her husband Morton, daughter Jeanne, four grandchildren, and two great-granddaughters.

*See Current Biography 1960.*

# Steuart L. Pittman

**Born:** Albany, New York; June 6, 1919
**Died:** Davidsonville, Maryland; February 10, 2013
**Occupation:** United States government official; lawyer

Steuart L. Pittman was a lawyer based in Washington, DC, and he served as the assistant secretary of defense (1961–64) under President John F. Kennedy. He was appointed to this position in 1961 during the Cold War and the constant threat of a nuclear attack from the Soviet Union. Pittman was, therefore, given the task of creating fallout shelters that would offer all United States citizens protection in the event of a nuclear strike. The exact number of shelters he helped establish is not known, and estimates vary, but Pittman did release a statement that declared there were enough shelters to protect approximately two-thirds of the population.

Pittman was born in Albany, New York, on June 6, 1919, but he grew up primarily on Manhattan's East Side. After graduating from Yale University in 1941, he worked briefly for a Pan American World Airways subsidiary in Asia before joining the United States Marine Corps in 1943. Towards the end of World War II, the Japanese attacked the Chinese-American unit Pittman was commanding on two Chinese junks in the East China Sea. His unit killed forty-three enemy soldiers and captured thirty-nine; consequently, Pittman was awarded the Silver Star for valor.

After the war, Pittman returned to Yale and earned his law degree in 1948. He worked for Cravath, Swaine & Moore, a law firm in New York City, for about two years before moving to Washington, DC, in 1950. Here, he helped establish a law firm, Shaw, Pittman, Potts & Trowbridge, in 1954. He worked for the firm until his retirement in the 1980s, but took a temporary leave when President John F. Kennedy nominated him for the position of assistant secretary of defense on August 30, 1961. The Senate confirmed Pittman's nomination on September 15, 1961.

As the new head of the fallout-shelter program, Pittman began a nation-wide search to seek out space to establish community shelters. The threat of a possible nuclear attack from the Soviet Union precipitated the need for this program, and Pittman managed to stock approximately one-hundred thousand model shelters in fourteen cities. However, the cost of implementing enough fallout-shelters to protect all United States citizens was estimated to be between five and six billion dollars, and the high cost sparked significant controversy in Congress. Pittman resigned in March 1964 after Congress rejected a budget allocation of $190 million for the fallout-shelter program.

On February 10, 2013, Pittman died at his home in Davidsonville, Maryland. According to his wife, Barbara, the apparent cause of death was a stroke. He was ninety-three years old. In addition to his wife, Pittman is survived by his seven children and fifteen grandchildren.

*See Current Biography 1963.*

# Lou Reed

**Born:** New York, New York; March 2, 1942
**Died:** Amagansett, New York; October 27, 2013
**Occupation:** American singer

Lou Reed was an American singer, songwriter, and guitarist best known as the lead singer of Velvet Underground, an American rock band during the late 1960s and early 1970s. During his time with Velvet Underground, Reed helped write and produce classic rock songs such as "Heroin," released on their 1967 debut album, *The Velvet Underground and Nico*, and "Sweet Jane," which was included on the band's 1970 album, *Loaded*. After leaving the Velvet Underground in 1970, Reed embarked on a successful career as a solo artist, producing such notable albums as *Transformer* (1972), *Metal Machine Music* (1975), and *New York* (1989).

Reed was born in Brooklyn on March 2, 1942. He attended Syracuse University, where he majored in English and met the poet Delmore Schwartz, his college professor at the time, who significantly influenced Reed's literary style and eventually his songwriting and lyrics. After graduating from Syracuse in 1964, Reed relocated to New York City and worked as a songwriter at Pickwick International, a record label. In 1965, Reed joined Sterling Morrison, a guitarist, John Cale, a viola, keyboard, and electric bass player, and Maureen Tucker, a drummer, to form the band the Velvet Underground, which they named after the book *The Velvet Underground* (1963) by Michael Leigh.

The newly formed Velvet Underground began playing in Café Bizarre in Greenwich Village, a neighborhood in the lower west side of Manhattan, where they caught the attention of Andy Warhol, an iconic American artist, in 1966. The band subsequently became a part of Warhol's Exploding Plastic Inevitable, a touring multimedia performance-art act. With Warhol's help, the band was able to secure a record deal with MGM/Verve. The band's first album, *The Velvet Underground and Nico*, was released in 1967 and produced by Warhol, who designed the album's now iconic cover: a banana painted on a white ground. *Rolling Stone* ranked their debut album as the thirteenth greatest of all time.

The Velvets' other albums included *White Light/White Heat* (1968), *The Velvet Underground* (1969), and *Loaded* (1970). After leaving the band in 1970, Reed worked briefly at his father's accounting firm before teaming up with David Bowie, who helped him produce the album *Transformer* (1972), which reached number 29 on Billboard's Top 200. The album also contained the hit song "Walk on the Wild Side," which was Reed's only Top 40 hit.

A number of now famous musicians and bands have credited Reed's music as an inspiration, including David Bowie, U2, and R.E.M. But according to Brian Eno, an English musician and composer, Reed was an inspiration to a generation of musicians: "The first Velvet Underground record sold 30,000 copies in the first five years. I think everyone who bought one of those 30,000 copies started a band!" He was also credited for giving a voice to gay and transgender people. The profound impact his music had on people can be attributed to how Reed was not just seeking to create music, but to create something that would, as he told the *New York Times* in 1982, "speak to people the way Shakespeare speaks to me, the way Joyce speaks to me. Something with that kind of power; something with bite to it."

Reed died on October 27, 2013, in Amagansett, New York, from liver disease. He was seventy-one years old. Reed is survived by his mother, Toby Reed; his sister, Merrill Weiner; and his wife, the singer/performance artist Laurie Anderson.

*See Current Biography Illustrated 1989.*

# Regina Resnik

**Born:** New York, New York; August 30, 1922
**Died:** New York, New York; August 8, 2013
**Occupation:** American opera singer

Regina Resnik was an American opera singer best known for playing leading roles such as George Bizet's Carmen and Richard Strauss's Klytemnestra. Resnik sang in more than three-hundred performances with the Metropolitan Opera since making her debut there in 1944 at the age of twenty-two. Resnik was known for her versatility when she made the daring switch from soprano to mezzo-soprano after noticing her range was decreasing in the mid-1950s. The move, which she referred to as the "biggest gamble of my life," proved to be fortuitous and offered her more leading roles such as the Countess in *Queen of Spades* and Mistress Quickly in *Falstaff*.

Resnik was born in the Bronx on August 30, 1922. After graduating from James Monroe High School, she attended Hunter College, from which she graduated in 1942 with a bachelor's degree in music education. When she was twenty years old, Fritz Busch, the founder of the New Opera Company, recruited her and made her the understudy to Florence Kirk for the lead role of Lady Macbeth. Kirk became ill before the last performance, which provided Resnik with the opportunity to sing the role at New York's Broadway Theatre in 1942. Her performance was celebrated by critics, and she was subsequently offered the opportunity to be a guest artist with the Opera Nacional in Mexico City, where she sang the roles of Leonore in *Fidelio* and Micaela in *Carmen* under the direction of Erich Kleiber.

In 1944, Resnik was Zinka Milanov's understudy for the role of Leonora in *Il trovatore* at the Metropolitan Opera when Milanov came down with laryngitis and was unable to perform. Resnik, therefore, was called in on twenty-four hours notice to replace Milanov. Despite not being well-prepared for the role, which she had not practiced in more than two years, what turned out to be Resnik's debut performance for the Met was celebrated by critics.

With the help of her friend, the baritone Giuseppe Danise, Resnik managed to make the difficult transition from soprano to mezzo-soprano. After the switch, which she completed after a year-long period of study, Resnik remarked that her range was "exactly the same," but that she was "happier in the depth of her voice than in its height." Consequently, Resnik landed some of the most notable roles of her career as a mezzo-soprano, including Klytemnestra in *Elektra*. In addition to performing opera, Resnik also directed productions such as *Carmen* and *Falstaff* in the 1970s, and she sang on Broadway in *Cabaret*, which earned her a 1988 Tony Award nomination.

Resnik died in Manhattan on August 8, 2013, from complications of a stroke. She was ninety years old. Her first marriage to Harry W. Davis ended in divorce, and her second husband and collaborator, Arbit Blatas, died in 1999. Resnik is survived by her brother, Jack, and her son from her first marriage, Michael.

*See Current Biography Illustrated 1956.*

# Paul Rogers

**Born:** Plympton, England; March 22, 1917
**Died:** London, England; October 6, 2013
**Occupation:** British actor

Paul Rogers was a British actor best known for playing Shakespearean roles such as Macbeth, Falstaff in *Henry IV*, Nick Bottom in *Midsummer Night's Dream*, Shylock in *The Merchant of Venice*, and Mercutio in *Romeo and Juliet*. Rogers made a number of appearances on Broadway, including his Tony Award–winning performance as Max in *The Homecoming*. Rogers also appeared on Broadway in Anthony Shaffer's *Sleuth* in the early 1970s.

Rogers was born in Plympton, England, on March 22, 1917. While still a student at the Newton Abbot Grammar School, where his father was the headmaster, he was approached by the West Regional Broadcasting Company to perform as a professional actor. After graduating, he was mentored by Michael Chekhov, a Russian American actor and director (and Anton Chekhov's nephew), and studied at the Chekhov Theatre Studio in Dartington, Devon. He made his debut at the Scala Theatre in 1938 as Charles Dickens in *Bird's Eye of Valour*. His acting pursuits, however, were interrupted when he joined the Royal Navy during World War II.

After the war, Rogers continued working with the Colchester Repertory Company, where he was given the opportunity to perform in *Romeo and Juliet*, *The Apple Cart*, and other dramas. But his big break came in September 1947 at the Theatre Royal in King Street, Bristol, when he joined the Bristol Old Vic Company; consequently, Rogers started playing roles such as Roderigo in *Othello* and Polonius in *Hamlet*. In 1956, Rogers joined Old Vic on a tour of the United States and performed the title role in *Macbeth*; John of Gaunt in *Richard II*; Mercutio in *Romeo and Juliet*; and Pandarus in *Troilus and Cressida*.

Rogers later joined the Royal Shakespeare Company. In 1965, he became the first actor to play the role of Max, head of a dysfunctional family, in Harold Pinter's drama *The Homecoming*. The company brought its production of the play to Broadway in 1967. Rogers, continuing in the role of Max, won the Tony Award that year for best actor; the production itself won the Tony for best play. In addition to his career on stage, Rogers also appeared in films such as *Beau Brummell* (1954), *Our Man in Havana* (1959), *The Beachcomber* (1954), and *The Trials of Oscar Wilde* (1960).

Rogers died on October 6, 2013, in London. He was ninety-six years old. A complete list of his survivors was not available.

*See Current Biography 1960.*

# Warren B. Rudman

**Born:** Boston, Massachusetts; May 18, 1930
**Died:** Washington, DC; November 19, 2012
**Occupation:** United States senator

Known as a combative, resolute voice of centrism in American politics, Warren B. Rudman was a Republican senator from New Hampshire from 1980 to 1993. During his time in the Senate, Rudman established himself as a steadfast champion of centrist principle, a voice of reasoned conviction who spoke truth to power and abhorred petty politics. As vice chairman of the Senate contingent of the Congressional investigation into the Iran-Contra affair, Rudman defiantly broke rank with House Republicans, joining the majority report concluding that Reagan administration officials had willfully broken the law by selling arms to Iran and using the profits to aid Nicaraguan rebels.

Rudman's aversion to partisan sparring and legislative inefficiency made his Senate career a frustrating one. In the mid-80s, he cosponsored two bills that would have forced the government to reign in deficits by instituting automatic spending cuts should Congress and the president not reach compromise on balancing the budget. The two bills were enacted and became known as Gramm-Rudman, but Democrats' reluctance to limit social programs, and Republicans' refusal to raise taxes meant the bills were amended and repealed before they could force drastic spending cuts. Rudman cited the failure of these bills at the hands of ideological stubbornness as one of the reasons for his retirement from the Senate. As chairman and then vice chairman of the Senate Ethics Committee, Rudman oversaw the Keating Five hearings, firmly admonishing Senator Alan Cranston (D-CA) for saying he had done favors for savings-and-loan executive Charles H. Keating because everyone else had done so as well.

A middle-of-the-road conservative, Rudman distrusted the religious right, supported abortion rights, and acknowledged tax hikes as an effective means of balancing the budget. He has cited his role in the selection of Supreme Court Justice David H. Souter as his proudest political achievement. Souter served as Rudman's deputy when he was attorney general of New Hampshire in the 1970s. Though Souter leaned liberal on social issues, Rudman considered his views to be ahead-of-their-time, saying in a 2010 interview that Souter's views "will become majority opinions and will become law of the land."

Rudman was born in Boston, Massachusetts, the child of second-generation Jewish-Americans. The Rudman family soon moved to New Hampshire—the state where Rudman would spend the rest of his life—settling in Nashua. In his memoirs, Rudman wrote that, as a child, he experienced anti-Semitism at school. This often led to the young Rudman engaging the offending students in fist fights, foretelling of his years spent as an amateur boxer in the 1950s.

He died in Washington, DC, from complications of lymphoma. He was eighty-two. Rudman's wife of fifty-seven years, Shirley, died in 2010, and his son Alan died in 2004. He is survived by his second wife, Margaret Shea Rudman; two sisters, Jean Gale and Carol Rudman; two daughters, Laura Rudman Robie and Debra Gilmore; and three grandchildren.

*See Current Biography 1989.*

# H. Norman Schwarzkopf

**Born:** Trenton, New Jersey; August 22, 1934
**Died:** Tampa, Florida; December 27, 2012
**Occupation:** American general

Described by Defense Secretary Leon Panetta as "one of the great military giants of the twentieth century" (qtd. by CNN 28 Dec. 2012) and popularly known as "Stormin' Norman," General H. Norman Schwarzkopf commanded the American-led international forces that decimated Iraqi infrastructure and liberated Kuwait in 1991's Operation Desert Storm. Combat led by Schwarzkopf was brief, lasting only six weeks, and the victory was decisive, if not a foregone certainty. Coalition forces comprised of 765,000 troops, hundreds of ships, and thousands of aircraft overwhelmed Saddam Hussein's Republican Guard, freeing the small, oil-rich country of Kuwait from Iraqi occupation. It was the world's first widely televised war, and Schwarzkopf emerged as a highly visible figurehead, garnering public adoration and a ticker-tape parade up Broadway.

Despite a decorated military career, Schwarzkopf was largely unknown to most Americans prior to the Gulf War. Herbert Norman Schwarzkopf Jr. was born on August 22, 1934, in Trenton, New Jersey. He was named after his father, a graduate of West Point and veteran of both world wars, who brought young Schwarzkopf to live with him in Germany, Iran, Italy, and Switzerland. Schwarzkopf attended Valley Forge Military Academy as a teenager, and was fluent in French and German at seventeen. He attended West Point, graduating in the top 10 percent of his class in 1956. As a captain, he saw combat in Vietnam in 1965, and was promoted to major in 1966. He returned to Vietnam as a battalion commander from 1969–70. During this second tour he was wounded twice and won three Silver Stars for bravery.

In 1988, Schwarzkopf became commander of the United States Central Command at MacDill Air Force Base and was responsible for supervising military activities in the Persian Gulf region. When Iraqi forces occupied Kuwait in August 1990, Schwarzkopf set up command headquarters in Riyadh, Saudi Arabia. Despite the widespread support for Schwarzkopf's campaign in the Persian Gulf at the time, his legacy has since been questioned. Some critics see the campaign as a lopsided conflict that ended without removing Saddam Hussein from power, and published first-hand accounts have shed negative light on Schwarzkopf's handling of his field commanders.

Even so, Schwarzkopf received a hero's welcome, earning the Presidential Medal of Freedom and even an honorary knighthood from Queen Elizabeth II, among other honors both in the United States and abroad. He retired in August 1991, and he spent his last years giving lectures, supporting charities, and avoiding persistent calls to run for public office. Schwarzkopf died of complications caused by pneumonia on December 27, 2012, in Tampa, Florida. He was seventy-eight. He is survived by his wife, Brenda; two daughters; and a son.

*See Current Biography Illustrated 1991.*

# William Warren Scranton

**Born:** Madison, Connecticut; July 19, 1917
**Died:** Montecito, California; July 28, 2013
**Occupation:** American governor

William Warren Scranton was best known as the Republican governor of Pennsylvania from 1963 to 1967. In addition to governor, Scranton had a prolific career in government: He served five presidents, was a member of the Eighty-Seventh US Congress (1963–67), and was the United States ambassador to the United Nations (1976–77). He also served on the board of a number of major companies, including American Express, New York Life Insurance Co., and IBM Corp.

Scranton was born on July 19, 1917, in Madison, Connecticut. He came from an affluent family, and he was a direct descendent of George W. Scranton, the founder of Scranton, Pennsylvania. Scranton graduated from Yale University in 1933 with a degree in history. He then enrolled in Yale Law School, but left soon thereafter to join the US Army Air Corps during World War II. After the war, he returned to Yale and earned his law degree in 1946. He then returned to Scranton, Pennsylvania, to work in his family's business.

Scranton first became involved in politics when he caught the attention of President Dwight D. Eisenhower, who invited him to Washington to be the special assistant to

Secretary of State John Foster. In 1962, with the backing of Eisenhower, Scranton defeated Mayor Richardson Dilworth in the gubernatorial race. During his tenure as governor, Scranton created a community college system in the state, lowered the unemployment rate, and promoted the state's economic growth. He made a bid to be the 1964 GOP presidential candidate, but lost his party's nomination to Barry M. Goldwater and remained in the governor's office until 1967. He was unable to run for reelection because the state constitution at the time limited the governorship to a single term.

After serving as governor, Scranton was employed by a number of presidents: Nixon sent him to the Middle East in 1969 and named him chairman of a Commission on Campus Unrest in 1970; and President Ford appointed him a United States representative to the United Nations in 1976 (he retired from the position in 1977). Overall, Scranton served on ten presidential commissions, including President Johnson's Commission on Insurance for Riot Torn Areas, and the General Advisory Committee on Arms Control and Disarmament for Presidents Nixon and Ford.

Scranton died on July 28, 2013, in Montecito, California. He was ninety-six years old. Scranton is survived by his wife, Mary; his daughter, Susan; his three sons, William, Joseph, and Peter; and his three grandchildren.

*See Current Biography 1964.*

Shankar performed at musical festivals including Woodstock in 1969 and the Monterey International Pop Festival in 1967. He also helped organize the Concert for Bangladesh to raise international awareness and funds for the victims of the violent war between Pakistan and Bangladesh in 1971. The concert sold out Madison Square Garden in New York City and showcased, in addition to Shankar, performers such as Bob Dylan, Eric Clapton, and Ringo Starr. The concert and its subsequent album and film raised millions of dollars for UNICEF.

In addition to winning three Grammy awards, Shankar received a number of honors from countries throughout the world. In 1999, India designated him a Bharat Ratna, or "Jewel of India," a prestigious civilian honor. In 2000, France awarded him the Commandeur de La Légion d'Honneur. Shankar was also an honorary member of the American Academy of Arts and Letters.

Shankar died at a hospital in San Diego, California, on December 11, 2012. He was ninety-two years old. His son from his first marriage to Annapurna Devi, Shubhendra Shankar, died in 1992. Shankar is survived by his second wife, Sukanya; his daughters, Anoushka Shankar and Norah Jones; three grandchildren; and four great-grandchildren. In the weeks before his death, Shankar was told that he would receive the lifetime achievement Grammy Award in February 2013.

*See Current Biography 1968.*

## Ravi Shankar

**Born:** Varanasi, India; April 7, 1920
**Died:** San Diego, California; December 11, 2012
**Occupation:** Indian musician and composer

The music of renowned Indian sitarist and composer Ravi Shankar was celebrated for transcending cultural and racial boundaries and introducing Indian rhythms and sound to the Western world. In the 1950s, Shankar began touring Europe and the United States, playing with celebrated musicians such as the Beatles, Philip Glass, and George Harrison, who called Shankar "the godfather of world music."

At the age of eighteen, Shankar became the apprentice of Allauddin Khan, a famous Indian musician, who helped Shankar develop his skills with a plucked string instrument called the sitar. He gave his debut concert in 1939, and soon thereafter he began composing music for films such as *Dharti ke Lal* (1946) directed by Khwaja Ahmad Abbas. His success as a musician earned him the title of music director for All India Radio in 1949, where he formed the National Orchestra that consisted of both Indian and Western instruments and sound.

## Shenouda

**Born:** Asyut, Egypt; August 3, 1923
**Died:** Cairo, Egypt; March 17, 2012
**Occupation:** Pope and patriarch of the Church of Alexandria

His Holiness Pope Shenouda III was the 177th Pope of the Church of Alexandria in Egypt, one of the original four Apostolic Sees of Christianity. Shenouda held this position for over forty years, and during his reign, the Coptic Church experienced significant growth. Shenouda, for example, appointed the first bishops in North America, Europe, Australia, and South America. He is also respected for his commitment to ecumenism—Christian unity and cooperation between diverse religions—and fostering a shared spirituality. He preached the importance of peace and understanding in his teaching and writings, and gained the respect of the Muslim community in Egypt and the Middle East, which has a long history of tension with Christianity.

Pope Shenouda was born Nazeer Gayed Roufail in Aysut, Egypt. Upon graduating from the University of Cairo with a BA in history, he spent many years as a high school teacher of history and social sciences in Cairo. After working as a journalist, he became a monk at the Syrian Monastery in 1954 and entered the priesthood in 1958. Pope Cyril VI appointed him as General Bishop for Christian Education in 1962, whereupon he adopted the name of a Coptic saint, Shenouda. He was elected as the new Pope after the death of Pope Cyril VI in 1971.

During his papacy, Shenouda overcame considerable political obstacles and contributed significantly to the Coptic Church. In 1981, after years of tension with Egypt's president, Anwar Sadat—stemming from the growth of Islamic extremism and an increase in violence against Christians—Shenouda spent three years in exile. He returned to Egypt, however, in 1985 after President Hosni Mubarak overturned Sadat's decree.

Upon his return to the church of Alexandria, Shenouda expanded the Coptic Church and played a significant role as a leader of Egypt and its growing Christian population. He was celebrated for his wisdom and preaching against violence and promoted peaceful relations among all religions—especially Muslims and Christians in the Middle East.

On March 17, 2012, Shenouda died from cancer. He was eighty-eight years old. Millions of supporters gathered to mourn his loss, and Sheikh Ahmed el-Tayib, Egypt's highest Islamic authority, publicly honored his life and legacy: "Egypt has lost one of its rare men at a sensitive moment when it most needs the wisest of its wise—their expertise and their purity of minds."

*See Current Biography 2003.*

# Muriel Siebert

**Born:** Cleveland, Ohio; September 12, 1928
**Died:** New York, New York; August 24, 2013
**Occupation:** American financier

As the first woman to hold a seat on the New York Stock Exchange (NYSE), Muriel "Mickie" Siebert represented a determined vanguard in the male-dominated world of finance. Siebert spent her early career toiling away at various finance firms for significantly less money than her male counterparts, but eventually struck out on her own, seeking to buy a seat on the NYSE. She was turned down nine times before she finally secured a sponsor for her bid. The exchange then informed Siebert that her seat would cost $445,000, and that she would have to get a bank to lend her $300,000 of it before her candidacy would be considered—a condition never before demanded of an applicant. Siebert's request for a loan was met with numerous refusals, as each

bank she approached refused to lend her the money until the exchanged had admitted her. It took months, but Siebert eventually got the loan from Chase Manhattan, and on December 28, 1967, she was elected to the NYSE. She would remain the only woman on the exchange for ten years.

Muriel Siebert was born in Cleveland, Ohio, on September 12, 1928, though throughout her career she gave her birth year as 1932. In 1949, she went to Western Reserve University—now Case Western Reserve University—to study accounting, but left in 1952 before earning a degree in order to care for her cancer-stricken father. She moved to New York in 1954, and after struggling to find a job without a degree, she fibbed her way into a trainee research analyst position at Bache & Company, claiming that she had, in fact, completed school.

After her election to the NYSE, Siebert founded Muriel Siebert & Company in 1969, a NYSE member brokerage firm. In 1977, Siebert put her company in a blind trust in order to accept an appointment to the position of New York state superintendent of banking, a position she held for five years. After a failed bid for the US Senate in 1982, Siebert returned to her firm in 1983, merged it with the J. Michaels furniture store chain, and took the resulting holding company, Siebert Financial Corporation, public in 1996.

Siebert died of complications of cancer in Manhattan, on August 24, 2013. She was eighty-four. Her sister, Elaine Siebert, survives her.

*See Current Biography 1997.*

# Paolo Soleri

**Born:** Turin, Italy; June 21, 1919
**Died:** Paradise Valley, Arizona; April 9, 2013
**Occupation:** Italian-born architect

An architect ahead of his time in vision and environmental awareness, Paolo Soleri was best known for his livable masterpiece, Arcosanti—an off-the-grid experimental settlement built in the Arizona desert and the embodiment of a philosophy that he called "arcology," the unification of architecture and ecology. Soleri's life's work has garnered praise and attention as a symbol of the society-bucking idealism that defined the hippie era, even though the full potential of Soleri's lifestyle experiment has not yet been realized. Designed to hold a community of five thousand, Arcosanti's present capacity is limited to several hundred people at a time; fewer than sixty residents live there currently. The settlement continues Arcosanti's construction and programs, however, and hosts about 35,000 visitors each year.

Paolo Soleri was born on June 21, 1919, in Turin, Italy. After serving in World War II as part of an Italian building construction and maintenance unit, Soleri earned a PhD in architecture from the Polytechnic University of Turin in 1946. After completing his doctorate, Soleri spent nearly two years working with architect Frank Lloyd Wright at Taliesin West, a residence and schooling facility outside Scottsdale, Arizona. In 1949, he designed the Dome House—a cast concrete and natural stone building not unlike the structures that would eventually make up Arcosanti. The building, located in Cave Creek, Arizona, was commissioned by Leonora Woods, a Philadelphia heiress. Soleri married Woods' daughter Corolyn, known as Colly, in 1950. After several years working in Italy, Soleri returned to Arizona with his wife in 1956. He designed a foundry, studio, and gallery for a site he called Cosanti, in Scottsdale, before buying 860 acres of land north of Phoenix in the late 1960s and beginning work on Arcosanti in 1970. His 1969 book, *The City in the Image of Man*, resonated with environmentally conscious students, who attended lectures by Soleri in flocks and even paid for the privilege of working at the settlement in its early days.

Soleri died on April 9, 2013 at his home in Paradise Valley, Arizona. He was ninety-three. Predeceased by Colly, who died in 1982, Soleri is survived by his two daughters and two grandchildren.

*See Current Biography 1972.*

## Jean Stapleton

**Born:** New York, New York; January 19, 1923
**Died:** New York, New York; May 31, 2013
**Occupation:** American actor

As the none-too-bright, but endlessly endearing wife of Archie Bunker on the trail-blazing television series *All in the Family* (1971–79), Jean Stapleton represented an emerging feminist voice in mainstream American entertainment. While known to most as Edith Bunker—the open-hearted counterpart to Carroll O'Connor's hard-headed bigot, Archie Bunker—Stapleton's career spanned decades and media, from her work on Broadway and Off Broadway, to bit parts in feature films like 1998's *You've Got Mail*. Stapleton got her start on stage in the late 1940s, appearing in touring companies, summer stock shows, and Broadway productions for more than twenty years before *All in the Family* premiered on CBS. Her work on the sitcom—known for its taboo-shattering frankness regarding racism, sexism, and other prejudices—earned her three Emmys.

Jean Stapleton was born Jeanne Murray on January 19, 1923, in New York City, to Joseph Murray and Marie Stapleton Murray—an advertising salesman and a professional singer, respectively. After graduating from high school, Stapleton worked as a secretary while taking acting classes at the American Apprentice Theater and the American Actors' Company. After several years performing with touring productions, Stapleton landed her first Broadway role in the 1953 Playhouse Theater production of Jane Bowles's *In the Summer House*. In 1957, Stapleton married the producer and director William Putch, operator of the Totem Pole Playhouse in Pennsylvania, where she often spent summers performing. A spattering of character parts on both television and the big screen preceded Stapleton's run as Edith on *All in the Family* and the subsequent spinoff *Archie Bunker's Place* (1979–83), in which she appeared for a few episodes of the first season. After playing Edith, she pursued other work, including guest appearances on several television series, roles in Off Broadway productions, and a starring role as Eleanor Roosevelt in the television movie *Eleanor: First Lady of the World* (1982). Stapleton died at her home in New York City on May 31, 2013. She was ninety years old. Stapleton is survived by the two children she had with Putch, who died in 1983.

*See Current Biography 1972.*

## János Starker

**Born:** Budapest, Hungary; July 5, 1924
**Died:** Bloomington, Indiana; April 28, 2013
**Occupation:** Hungarian American cellist

János Starker was a Hungarian American cellist who played with some of the world's most prestigious orchestras, including the Metropolitan Opera Orchestra and the Chicago Symphony Orchestra. Known for his interpretations of Bach, Starker won a Grammy Award in 1997 for his recording of Bach's six suites for solo cello. In addition to Bach, his discography of more than 150 recordings features notable works by Bartók, Brahms, Beethoven, Dvořák, Kodály, and Schumann. In a 2006 interview for *Strings*, Starker stated that his most important accomplishment was not his prolific recording or performance career, but the more than fifty years he dedicated to teaching music at Indiana University: "The most important thing for me is teaching. . . . No matter how great the ovation is after a concert, the people eventually sit down and stop applauding. But if you teach, you may affect generations."

Starker was born to a Jewish family on July 5, 1924, in Budapest, Hungary. A child prodigy,

Starker studied at the Franz Liszt Academy of Music and was a teenager when he gave his first professional orchestral performance of Dvořák's Cello Concerto in 1938. During World War II he was sent to a Nazi concentration camp on an island in the Danube outside of Budapest. Starker survived the Holocaust, but many members of his family—including his older brothers, Tibor and Ede, both violinists—did not live to see the end of the war. In the biography *Janos Starker: "King of Cellists"* (2008), Joyce Greeting wrote that after surviving life in the concentration camp Starker was, "unafraid of anyone because he concluded that nothing worse could possibly happen to him."

After the war, Starker first gained international recognition when he won France's most prestigious honor for recorded music, the Grand Prix du Disque, for his 1947 recording of Hungarian composer Zoltán Kodály's solo Sonata. In 1948 he immigrated to the United States to join the Dallas Symphony Orchestra as the principal cellist. He was later the principal cellist for the Metropolitan Opera Orchestra. At the height of his performance career, Starker performed in approximately one hundred concerts per year.

Starker left the Chicago Symphony Orchestra in 1958 to accept a teaching position at Indiana University, where he taught for more than fifty years. He continued to pursue his solo performance career in conjunction with teaching, which, in a 1993 interview with the *Chicago Tribune*, he stated went hand-in-hand: "I personally cannot perform without teaching, and I cannot teach without performing. When you have to explain what you are doing, you discover what you are really doing." Starker continued to teach into his late eighties, leaving the classroom nine months before his death.

Starker died on April 28, 2013, in Bloomington, Indiana. He was eighty-eight years old. Starker's first marriage to Eva Uranyi ended in divorce. He is survived by his second wife of fifty-two years, Rae (née Busch); his daughter, Gabriella Starker-Saxe; his stepdaughter, Gwen Starker Preucil; and his three grandchildren.

*See Current Biography 1963.*

# Richard G. Stern

**Born:** New York, New York; February 25, 1928
**Died:** Tybee Island, Georgia; January 24, 2013
**Occupation:** American novelist and short story writer

To the chagrin of his contemporaries, who regarded him highly, writer Richard G. Stern never achieved much mainstream success. The author of twenty books and a storied professor of literature and creative writing at the University of Chicago, Stern's academic and social circle was a roster of the day's most celebrated authors. Stern sat on a faculty that claimed Philip Roth and Saul Bellow among its ranks, and his classroom lectures featured visits from Norman Mailer, John Berryman, Kingsley Amis, Ralph Ellison, Flannery O'Connor, and Robert Lowell.

Stern was the author of more than twenty books, most of them novels and short story collections, ranging from his first novel, *Golk* (1960) to *Almonds to Zhoof: Collected Stories* (2005). His last published book *Still on Call*, a collection of essays, lectures, and other prose pieces, came out in 2010. Perhaps his most widely read novel was 1973's *Other Men's Daughters*, a tale of heated romance between professor and student that, like much of his work, dealt with matters of family, passion, and intellect. In 1973, Stern won a Guggenheim Fellowship. He was awarded the Medal of Merit for the Novel by the Academy of Arts and Letters in 1985, placing him among past winners such as Ernest Hemingway and Vladimir Nabokov.

Born on February 25, 1928, in New York City, Stern began writing stories at age twelve, and went on to earn his BA from the University of North Carolina (1947), his master's degree from Harvard (1949), and his PhD from the University of Iowa (1954). His first published short story appeared in *The Kenyon Review*, and in 1954 he won an O. Henry award for "The Sorrows of Captain Schreiber," another early short story. Stern taught for a year at Connecticut College in New London, Connecticut, before he began teaching at the University of Chicago in 1955, where he remained until his retirement in 2001.

Stern died of cancer at his home in Tybee Island, Georgia, on January 24, 2013. He was eighty-four. Stern is survived by his second wife, the poet Alane Rollings; four children from his first marriage to Gay Clark; and five grandchildren.

*See Current Biography 1994.*

# Risë Stevens

**Born:** New York City, New York; June 11, 1913
**Died:** New York City, New York; March 20, 2013
**Occupation:** American opera singer

Risë Stevens was an American opera singer best known for her role as Carmen in Georges Bizet's opera *Carmen*, which she performed a total of 124 times with the Metropolitan Opera Company. She was also celebrated for performing the role of Octavian in Strauss's *Der*

*Rosenkavalier,* as well as Dalila in Camille Saint-Saën's *Samson et Dalila.* In addition to her more than twenty-year career with the Metropolitan Opera in New York City, Stevens performed with La Scala in Milan, Italy, and many other prestigious opera houses around the world. Her career, however, was not limited to opera, but spanned across television, radio, Broadway, and film. For example, she was the voice of Glinda the Good Witch in the animated film *Journey Back to Oz* (1974), and she performed alongside Bing Crosby in the Hollywood film *Going My Way* (1944), which won the Academy Award for best picture.

Stevens was born in New York City on June 11, 1913. Her vocal talent was apparent at a young age, and, after graduating from Newtown High School in Long Island, she began performing with the Little Theater Opera Company in New York City. It was here that the eighteen-year-old Stevens caught the attention of Anna Schoen-René, a voice teacher at the Julliard School, who became her vocal coach. This arrangement resulted in Stevens receiving a scholarship to study at Julliard beginning in 1933.

On December 17, 1938, Steven's gave her first opera performance on the Metropolitan stage in Ambroise Thomas's *Mignon.* From here, she began her long and successful career with the Metropolitan, most notably in the role of Carmen, which was, appropriately, her last performance with the company on April 12, 1961.

After Stevens formally retired from opera performance, she was a general manager of the Metropolitan Opera National Company and an executive director for the Metropolitan Opera National Council Regional Auditions. In 1975 she became the president of the Mannes College of Music in New York City. Stevens received a number of honors and awards—she was a Kennedy Center honoree in 1990, and she was honored by the National Endowment for the Arts in 2011.

Stevens died on March 20, 2013, at her home in New York City. She was ninety-nine years old. Her husband, Walter Surovy, died in 2001. She is survived by her son, Nicolas Surovy, and her granddaughter.

*See Current Biography Illustrated 1941.*

# Frank Stranahan

**Born:** Toledo, Ohio; August 5, 1922
**Died:** West Palm Beach, Florida; June 23, 2013
**Occupation:** American golfer

Frank Stranahan was an American golfer who won more than fifty amateur tournaments and six PGA Tour events, including the 1958 Los Angeles Open, which was considered his most notable win on the PGA Tour. In addition to golfing, Stranahan was also a bodybuilder (something that golfers of his era shunned because they feared it would limit their flexibility and performance) and he won a number of bodybuilding championships in the 1970s.

Frank Richard Stranahan was born on August 5, 1922, in Toledo, Ohio. He was one of seven children in the well-to-do family of Page Ellyson (Lewis) Stranahan and Robert Allen Stranahan, head of the Champion Spark Plug Company. As a teenager, Stranahan took golfing lessons with Byron Nelson, an American PGA Tour golfer, at the Inverness course in Toledo. He would later tie his former teacher for second place in the 1947 Masters Tournament. After being sent to a private school in Arizona in 1941, Stranahan won the Arizona State Amateur golfing tournament, which was followed by victories at the Ohio Amateur and the Trans-Mississippi match. He put his golfing career on hold, however, to serve as a pilot in the US Army Air Force during World War II.

Stranahan returned to golf after the war and won a number of tournaments, including the Western Amateur in 1946 (he also won in 1949 and 1950); the Canadian Amateur Championship in 1947 and 1948; and the 1948 and 1950 British Amateur Championship. Stranahan also tied with three others for second at the 1953 British Open. He officially turned pro in 1954, and in 1955 he clenched first place at the Eastern Open.

Despite his success, Stranahan was considered a controversial and sometimes temperamental figure in the golf world. For example, he once fired his caddie for giving him the wrong line to the pin during the middle of the 1946 Amateur Championship. His wealth was also criticized by his fellow players (he was on his father's payroll while touring), but he tried to explain his situation: "Between tournaments I hit the road for the company and I have work to do like any other employee. I wish people would understand that I have to work to stay on the payroll."

Stranahan retired from golf in 1964 and attended the Wharton School at the University of Pennsylvania, where he earned his master's degree in business. He then established Stranahan Investments and pursued a career as an investment banker.

Stranahan died on June 23, 2013, in West Palm Beach, Florida, at the age of ninety. He was predeceased by his wife, the amateur golfer Ann Williams, and by two sons, Frank Jr. and James. Stranahan's remaining son, Lance, is his only survivor.

*See Current Biography 1951.*

# Curtis W. Tarr

**Born:** Stockton, California; September 18, 1924
**Died:** Walnut Creek, California; June 21, 2013
**Occupation:** American educator and government official

Curtis W. Tarr was an American educator and government official best known as the former head of the Selective Service System, the US government agency that oversees military conscription. President Richard Nixon selected Tarr to direct the Selective Service System in 1970 when the draft for the Vietnam War was becoming increasingly controversial and sparking widespread protests. During his time as the director from 1970 to 1972, Tarr made the draft fairer by making the pool more random in its selection of draftees and increasing its size by cutting back on the number of deferments.

Tarr was born in Stockton, California, on September 18, 1924. After serving in Europe during World War II and earning three battle stars, Tarr attended Stanford University, where he graduated in 1948 with a degree in economics. He went on to earn his master of business administration degree from Harvard University in 1950. From 1958 to 1963, Tarr was an instructor of American business history at Stanford University, where he earned his doctoral degree in 1962.

Tarr joined Lawrence College in Appleton, Wisconsin, as the college's president in 1963, but he left in 1969 to accept a position as assistant secretary of the US Air Force, his first of three government appointments during the Nixon administration. In 1970, Nixon appointed him the president of the Selective Service System, replacing General Lewis B. Hershey. Tarr was responsible for implementing vital changes to the lottery system that was introduced towards the end of the war (before Tarr's lottery, the selection of draftees was left to the discretion of local boards). Dick Flahavan, spokesman for the Selective Service, said that Tarr, "took the local personalities out of the system," thereby making it fairer and less subjective.

According to Tarr's daughter, Pam, her father would say that his role as the president of the Selective Service System was "one of his greatest responsibilities," and that he was "a very principled man, and in every position he had, he wanted to do what was right." Tarr left his position at the Selective Service in May 1972, and was appointed the undersecretary of state for security assistance, which he held for one year. In 1973 he left government service and held a number of leadership roles. From 1985 to 1989 he served as dean of Cornell University's Samuel Curtis Johnson Graduate School of Management.

Tarr died on June 21, 2013, in Walnut Creek, California. He was eighty-eight years old. He is survived by his wife, Mary; his sisters, Muriel Kurtz and Marian Schreiter; his daughters, Cynthia and Pam; and his grandson, Ace.

*See Current Biography 1970.*

# Margaret Thatcher

**Born:** Grantham, United Kingdom; October 13, 1925
**Died:** London, United Kingdom; April 8, 2013
**Occupation:** British prime minister

Margaret Thatcher was the first woman to serve as prime minister of Britain and, therefore, the first woman to lead a Western power in modern times. Known as the "Iron Lady," a sobriquet given to her by a Soviet military newspaper, the *Red Star*, Thatcher was in office for eleven years (1979–90), the longest of any twentieth-century prime minister in Britain. While in office, she defeated Argentina in the battle over the Falkland Islands, negotiated the terms under which Hong Kong would return to China after more than a century of British control, and joined US president Ronald Reagan in the fight against communism and the Soviet Union during the height of the Cold War.

Thatcher was born on October 13, 1925, in Grantham, Lincolnshire. Her father, Alfred Roberts, owned a grocery store, above which the family lived in an apartment with no running hot water. Coming from this humble background, Thatcher lacked advantages such as access to upper-class wealth and connections in a country historically divided by firm class boundaries. Roberts, however, instilled in his daughter a strong worth ethic, traditional moral values, and a fierce independence. On the day she took office as prime minister, she said these characteristics and her upbringing were "just the things that I believe have won the election." Thatcher's father was also a local politician—serving as councilman, alderman, and mayor of Grantham—and she was surrounded by politics from a young age. "Politics was in my bloodstream," she said.

In 1947 Thatcher graduated from Oxford University, where she was the first female president of the Oxford University Conservative Association, with a degree in chemistry. She later earned a master's degree in the same subject. She then made her transition into law and politics, and, after two failed attempts to enter Parliament (1950 and 1951) and passing the bar in 1953, she was elected to the House of Commons in 1959.

Thatcher was elected prime minister on May 3, 1979, and she was reelected in 1983 and again in 1987. While in office, she implemented conservative economic and social reforms, including curbing the power of the labor unions and reducing taxes on income. During her first term in office, she showed her perseverance and willpower when she ordered a Royal Navy fleet to defeat Argentine forces that had invaded the Falkland Islands in April 1982, despite the advice of allies, including the United States, who urged her to employ diplomatic measures instead of force. In 1984, Thatcher narrowly escaped an assassination attempt when the Irish Republican Army detonated a bomb in her hotel room. Thatcher showed her iron tenacity again and said, "All attempts to destroy democracy by terrorism will fail."

After stepping down as prime minister on November 28, 1990, Thatcher continued to be a voice on the international stage, supporting President George W. Bush's mission to dispel Saddam Hussein from power following the September 11 terrorist attacks. Later in life, Thatcher suffered from dementia, which was portrayed by Meryl Streep in the Oscar-winning film, *The Iron Lady* (2011).

Thatcher died on April 8, 2013, in London from a stroke. She was eighty-seven years old. Her husband, Dennis Thatcher, died in 2003. Thatcher is survived by her two children, Mark and Carol, and her grandchildren.

*See Current Biography 1975, 1989.*

# Helen Thomas

**Born:** Winchester, Kentucky; August 4, 1920
**Died:** Washington, DC; July 20, 2013
**Occupation:** American journalist

Helen Thomas was an American journalist best known as a long-time White House correspondent who covered every president from John F. Kennedy to Barack Obama. She entered the press corps during a time when men dominated the industry, but Thomas overcame gender boundaries and became a pioneer for women in journalism. She continued to work into her eighth decade, long after most journalists retire, and her stamina earned her both the admiration and respect of her colleagues and many presidents. President Obama, for example, brought her cupcakes on her eighty-ninth birthday. Thomas was considered the so-called dean of the White House press corps who, on behalf of her colleagues, ended every presidential press conference with, "Thank you, Mr. President."

Thomas was born on August 4, 1920, in Winchester, Kentucky, but she was raised in Detroit, Michigan. She graduated from Wayne State University in Detroit in 1942 with an English degree, and then moved to Washington, DC, where she found a job as a waitress. She was eventually hired by United Press International

(UPI) in 1943. By 1956, she was a member of the UPI team that covered federal agencies. In 1960, she became a reporter for John F. Kennedy's presidential campaign, thus beginning what turned out to be more than five decades of presidential coverage.

Upon news of her death, President Obama said in a statement that Thomas, "never failed to keep presidents—myself included—on their toes." Indeed, she was known for her often frank questions that held presidents accountable. For example, during a press conference she famously grilled President George W. Bush on the war in Iraq: "Your decision to invade Iraq has caused the deaths of thousands of Americans and Iraqis, wounds of Americans and Iraqis for a lifetime. Every reason given, publicly at least, has turned out not to be true. My question is: Why did you really want to go to war?" Thomas was also involved in the Nixon Watergate scandal, and her interviews with Martha Mitchell, the wife of Attorney General John Mitchell, helped to shed light on hidden details of the scandal.

During her career Thomas held many positions of importance, including that of senior White House Correspondent position for UPI, officer and president of the White House Correspondents Association, and member of the Gridiron Club. Thomas was also the author of a number of books, most notably *Front Row at the White House: My Life and Times* (2000), and *Watchdogs of Democracy? The Waning Washington Press Corps and How It Has Failed the Public* (2006).

In 2010, Thomas announced her retirement in the middle of a scandal over a comment she had made at a White House event in which she had said that Jews should "get the hell out of Palestine." She later apologized for her remark and asserted her belief that peace could only come to the Middle East when all parties treated each other with "mutual respect and tolerance."

Thomas died on July 20, 2013, in Washington, DC. She was ninety-two years old. Her husband, Douglas Cornell, died in 1982. She had no children and information about her survivors is not available.

*See Current Biography 1993.*

# John Thomas

**Born:** Boston, Massachusetts; March 3, 1941
**Died:** Brockton, Massachusetts; January 15, 2013
**Occupation:** American high jumper

On January 31, 1959, John Thomas—then just seventeen years old—became the first person to clear seven feet in the indoor high jump. That year's Millrose Games at Madison Square Garden saw many victories, but it was Thomas's record-setting leap that would be remembered as the most thrilling moment in the annual competition's history. Thomas would go on to clear the seven feet mark 190 more times in his athletic career. His rivalry with Russian high jumper Valery Brumel is considered one of the greatest in the sport's history—the tensions and competition of the Cold War embodied in sport. Thomas was a favorite to win gold at the 1960 Olympics in Rome and the 1964 Olympics in Tokyo, but suffered what sports commentators considered to be disappointing losses both times at the hands of Brumel—even though he won a bronze and a silver medal, respectively. Thomas only ever beat Brumel (who died in 2003) once in his career, but the two became close friends.

Thomas spent most of his life in Massachusetts and attended Boston University (BU), where he was the National Collegiate Athletic Association (NCAA) high jump champion during each of his four years there. In March 1959, Thomas's foot was crushed in an elevator accident, almost ending his career. But Thomas recovered in time to continue competing by January 1960. The college inducted Thomas into the BU Hall of Fame in 1968. He made the USA Track and Field Hall of Fame in 1985. In later life, Thomas served as the athletic director at Roxbury Community College in Boston.

Thomas died in Brockton, Massachusetts, on January 15, 2013, while undergoing surgery. He was seventy-one. Thomas is survived by his three daughters and two sons; twelve grandchildren; and one great-grandchild.

*See Current Biography 1960.*

# Jack Hood Vaughn

**Born:** Lame Deer, Montana; August 18, 1920
**Died:** Tucson, Arizona; October 29, 2012
**Occupation:** American diplomat and government official

Best known as the second director of the United States Peace Corps, Jack Hood Vaughn cemented the organization's reputation for international service and bolstered its ranks, ushering in an era of record volunteer enrollment. Vaughn was appointed to the position of director by President Lyndon B. Johnson in 1966. During the Kennedy administration, the Peace Corps' founding director, R. Sargent Shriver, built the framework for the organization and began the process of recruiting volunteers. Under Vaughn, the number of volunteers rose from around 12,000 to more than 15,500. The program was initially met with hostility from politicians who feared that the corps would be an easy out for draft dodgers during the Vietnam War. But Vaughn was an uncompromising champion of the corps, fighting for the autonomy of the organization and its volunteers.

While serving as Peace Corps director, Vaughn held a number of other influential foreign affairs positions. From 1964 through 1965, Vaughn was the ambassador to Panama. He then worked as the assistant secretary of state for inter-American affairs from 1965 to 1966. Following his departure from the Peace Corps in 1969, Vaughn took another diplomatic post in Latin America, this time serving as ambassador to Colombia. Vaughn officially resigned from the Foreign Service in 1970, citing the Nixon administration's preoccupation with the Vietnam War and apparent disregard for Latin American affairs as one of his reasons for leaving. In his nongovernment work, Vaughn showed a passion for a wide array of pursuits. He was president of the Planned Parenthood Federation for a time, and even served as director of international programs for the Children's Television Workshop, producing foreign versions of *Sesame Street*. Professionally and personally, Vaughn was an avid environmentalist. In the late 1980s he was chairman of Conservation International before becoming the founding chairman of Ecotrust in the early 1990s.

Born in Lame Deer, Montana, Vaughn came from a family of five children. After enlisting in the Marine Corps and serving in the Pacific during World War II, Vaughn earned a master's in economics from his undergrad alma mater, the University of Michigan. While there, he coached the university's boxing team, and spent time competing as a professional featherweight boxer. After earning his master's Vaughn, who was fluent in Spanish, joined the United States Information Agency, which tasked him with running a cultural center in Bolivia. He eventually became program director for the United States Agency for International Development in Panama, Mali, Bolivia, Senegal, and Mauritania.

Vaughn died of cancer on October 29, 2012 at his home in Tucson, Arizona. He was 92. Vaughn is survived by his second wife, Margaret; three daughters; a son; and two grandchildren.

*See Current Biography 1966.*

# Ken Venturi

**Born:** San Francisco, California; May 15, 1931
**Died:** Rancho Mirage, California; May 17, 2013
**Occupation:** American golfer and sportscaster

Ken Venturi was an American professional golfer and a sportscaster for CBS Sports. He won fourteen professional golf tournaments from 1957 to 1966, including the 1964 United States Open Championship, one of the four major championships in golf. He was also named the Professional Golfers' Association (PGA) player of the year in 1964. However, not long after winning the US Open, carpal tunnel syndrome and surgery on his hands brought a premature end to his professional golfing career. Venturi, however, remained a presence in the golf world as the lead golf analyst for CBS from 1968 until his retirement in 2002.

Venturi was born in San Francisco, California, on May 15, 1931. He suffered from a severe stutter as a child, and his doctor told his mother that, "your son will never be able to speak. He's an incurable stammerer." It was this stutter that initially inspired Venturi to take up golf, which he referred to as "the loneliest sport I know." He started playing golf at a public golf course called Harding Park, where his parents ran the pro shop.

Venturi first gained widespread attention after leading the 1956 Masters by four shots in the final round. However, he ended up losing the tournament to Jack Burke Jr. by one stroke. Venturi's claim to fame came on June 20, 1964, in the US Open. The temperature was upwards of one hundred degrees, and a doctor advised him to stop playing after he experienced heat exhaustion and dehydration. But he persevered and clenched the victory, exclaiming after his final put, "My God, I've won the Open!"

Soon after the victory, carpal tunnel syndrome brought an early end to his professional golfing career. But Venturi overcame his "uncurable stammer" and proved his childhood doctor's diagnosis false, becoming the lead sports analyst and commentator for CBS Sports in 1968 and his voice was heard by millions of viewers. He retired from CBS in 2002, making him one of the longest-running lead analysts in sport's history. He "was not only one of golf's greatest champions but also the signature voice of golf for almost two generations of fans and viewers," said Sean McManus, chairman of CBS Sports.

Venrturi died on May 17, 2013, in Rancho Mirage, California, from complications resulting from pneumonia, a spinal infection, and an intestinal infection. He was eighty-two years old. Just days before his death, Venturi was inducted into the World Golf Hall of Fame. Though unable to attend the ceremony himself due to health issues, his two sons, Tim and Matthew, accepted the honor for him. "He had a twinkle in his eye," his son, Tim Venturi, said on the night of his induction. Venturi is survived by his sons, and his third wife, Kathleen Venturi.

*See Current Biography 1966.*

# Jacques Vergès

**Born:** Udon, Kingdom of Siam (present-day Thailand); March 5, 1925
**Died:** Paris, France; August 15, 2013
**Occupation:** French lawyer

A career spent defending dictators, terrorists, and war criminals earned French attorney Jacques Vergès a sobriquet of which he was particularly proud—"The Devil's Advocate." Vergès was considered a legal thinker of unique intelligence by some, and a publicity-hungry egotist by others. His list of clients ranged from small-time prostitutes, to internationally reviled figures like Nazi war criminal Klaus Barbie, and Venezuelan terrorist Carlos the Jackal. In the late 1950s Vergès began defending members of the FLN—Algeria's militant National Liberation Front—accused of bombing cafes and bars in their struggle against French colonialism. Though most of his clients were convicted and jailed—including Djamila Bouhired, whom Vergès married after her release from prison—the trials were a showcase for what would become his trademark strategy of "disruption" defense, in which the legitimacy of the courts and law as a whole is called into question. Challenging the legal and moral validity of a colonial court system prosecuting self-professed liberation fighters, earned Vergès the approval of the Algerian public, but a temporary suspension from the Paris bar. He would go on to use a similar strategy in the 1987 trial of Gestapo member Klaus Barbie, called "the Butcher of Lyon" for his role in the torture and execution of thousands of French citizens. As he did in the FLN trials, Vergès largely ignored the charges against Barbie, opting to attack France and other nations for committing crimes against humanity that he called "more serious" than those of which Barbie was accused.

Jacques Vergès and his twin brother, Paul, were born in Udon, in the Kingdom of Siam (now Thailand), on March 5, 1925, to a French father and a Vietnamese mother, who died when Vergès was three years old. Vergès's father raised the brothers on the French-controlled, Indian Ocean island of Réunion, where Paul would found the Réunion Communist Party, and eventually become a member of the European Parliament. After joining Charles de Gaulle's Free French Forces in the early 1940s, Vergès studied law at the University of Paris, where he joined the Communist Party, and became friends with Saloth Sar, better known as Pol Pot. Vergès disappeared for a period of eight years in 1970, and, as of his death, had never revealed where he spent that time. He reappeared in Paris in 1978, where he resumed his law career. He volunteered to represent former Iraqi dictator Saddam Hussein after his capture in 2003—though the offer was turned down—and once said that he would have defended Adolf Hitler in court. Vergès died August 15, 2013, of a heart attack in a Parisian home where the Enlightenment philosopher Voltaire once lived. He was eighty-eight.

*See Current Biography 2004.*

# Jorge Rafael Videla

**Born:** Mercedes, Argentina; August 2, 1925
**Died:** Buenos Aires, Argentina; May 17, 2013
**Occupation:** Argentine general and president

Jorge Rafael Videla was an Argentine military dictator who led the so-called Dirty War in Argentina during the mid-1970s. It is estimated that at least fifteen thousand people were killed under Videla's rule, and many others were tortured and separated from their families. Thousands, in fact, were "disappeared," or thrown out of military aircrafts into the Atlantic Ocean and the River Plate. In 1975, Videla declared his reasoning behind these murders: "As many people as is necessary will die in Argentina to protect the hemisphere from the international communist conspiracy." Videla was later charged with crimes against humanity and sentenced to life in prison.

Videla was born on August 2, 1925, in Mercedes, Argentina. Raised in a military family—his father was a colonel—he continued his family's military legacy and attended the National Military College in 1944. He climbed up the military ranks and was eventually appointed commander in chief of the armed forces by President Isabel Martínez de Perón (the widow of Juan Domingo Perón, who died on July 1, 1974) in 1975. At the time of his appointment, Argentina was under a state of emergency that had been declared by Perón in November 1974 in response to an increase in attacks by leftist radical groups.

Videla became president after a nonviolent coup that ousted President Perón in 1976. Thus began Vildela's military rule and the violent campaign he launched against leftist guerillas that were battling the government. Leftist guerillas were not Videla's only targets, however; he also tortured and killed journalists, trade unionists, lawyers, and students who he claimed were involved with leftists groups. According to Frederico Finchelstein, a historian at the New School University, Videla, "viewed his mission as sacred, and those who disagreed with it as sinful enemies." Human rights officials estimate that the death toll may be as high as thirty thousand.

In 1981, Videla stepped down and was succeeded by General Roberto Viola. But eight months later, Viola stepped down due to illness and General Leopoldo Galtieri assumed power.

It was under Galtieri's rule that Argentina had started and lost its 1982 battle with the United Kingdom over the Falkland Islands. Consequently, military rule ended in Argentina.

Raúl Alfonsín was elected to the presidency after democracy was restored in 1983. In 1985, Videla was tried and sentenced to life in prison for crimes against humanity. However, he was released in 1990 by President Carlos Menem, who overturned the court's decision. Videla returned to trial in 2010 and received another life sentence in prison for human rights abuses.

Videla died on May 17, 2013, in his prison cell at the Marcos Paz Prison in Buenos Aires, Argentina. He was eighty-seven years old.

*See Current Biography 1978.*

# Galina Vishnevskaya

**Born:** Leningrad, Soviet Union; October 25, 1926
**Died:** Moscow, Russia; December 11, 2012
**Occupation:** Russian opera singer

Legendary Russian soprano Galina Vishnevskaya was known for her bold interpretations of heroines such as Tatyana in Tchaikovsky's opera *Eugene Onegin* and Natasha Rostova in Prokofiev's *War and Peace*. The Soviet Union prevented her from regularly performing in the West, but she did make infrequent appearances at the Metropolitan Opera in New York City, including her performance of the lead role in *Tosca* in 1975. As a high-profile political dissident, she was sent into exile by the Soviet Union between 1978 and 1990.

Vishnevskaya was born in Leningrad (today the city of St. Petersburg) and began singing at a very young age. After surviving the violent siege of Leningrad by the Germans that lasted for more than two years and killed approximately one million people, Vishnevskaya joined the Leningrad Operetta Theatre in 1944. She began training under the renowned voice teacher, Vera Garina, in 1951, and joined the preeminent Bolshoi Theatre of Russia in 1952. Here, she performed more than thirty roles in her twenty-three years with the company, including one of her most famous roles as Tatyana in Tchaikovsky's *Eugene Onegin*.

Vishnevskaya received a number of awards for her achievements as an opera singer. In 1971, she received the Order of Lenin, a prestigious prize in the Soviet Union. A few months after she received the award, however, the Soviet government imposed a media blackout on Vishnevskaya and she was censored from print and television. In 1978, she and her husband Mstislav Rostropovich, the famous violinist and conductor, were abroad when the Kremlin revoked their citizenship on grounds that they had criticized the government's censorship of artists. The couple were not allowed to return to the Soviet Union until their citizenship was restored in 1990 by President Mikhail S. Gorbachev.

Vishnevskaya was a born survivor and overcame death many times: she survived the Stalinist purge of the 1930s; the siege of Leningrad by the Germans during World War II; a postpartum infection that killed her ten-week-old child; and she overcame tuberculosis despite doctors telling her it would end her life without surgery.

In addition to her successful career as an opera singer, Vishnevskaya was also the author of a memoir, *Galina: A Russian Story* (1984), which told of her experience in exile. In 2002, she established the Galina Vishnevskaya Opera Center to train young Russian singers. At the age of eighty, she gave a celebrated performance in Aleksandr Sokurov's film *Alexandra* (2007).

Vishnevskaya died in Moscow on December 11, 2012. She was eighty-six years old. Predeceased by Rostropovich, who died in 2007, she is survived by her two daughters, Elena and Olga, and six grandchildren.

*See Current Biography Illustrated 1966.*

# Robert Ward

**Born:** Cleveland, Ohio; September 13, 1917
**Died:** Durham, North Carolina; April 3, 2013
**Occupation:** American composer

Robert Ward was an American composer best known for his opera *The Crucible* (1961), which won the 1962 Pulitzer Prize for music. The opera was an adaptation of Arthur Miller's 1953 stage play, an allegory of the political blacklisting that took place during the McCarthy era of the late 1940s and 1950s. In addition to the Pulitzer, *The Crucible* received the New York Critics Circle citation (1962). Ward wrote seven other operas, including *Pantaloon* (1956), *The Lady From Colorado* (1964), and *Claudia Legare* (1978). He also composed seven symphonies, choral and chamber works, and orchestral works.

Ward was born on September 13, 1917, in Cleveland, Ohio. After earning his bachelor's degree in music in 1939 from the Eastman School of Music of the University of Rochester, he enrolled at the Julliard Graduate School on a fellowship that same year. At Julliard he studied music and composition under Frederick Jacobi and conducting under Edgar Schenkman. He also wrote his first symphony in 1941, *Symphony No. 1*, which won a Julliard publications award. In the summer of that year he studied with composer Aaron Copeland at the Berkshire Music Center (now known as Tanglewood Music Center).

In 1942, Ward left Julliard to serve in the United States Army as a private during World War II. He attended the United States Army music school at Fort Myer, Virginia, where he wrote an orchestral piece, *Adagio and Allegro* (1943). He was then deployed to the Pacific where he became the conductor of the Seventh Infantry Division band. Ward received a Bronze Star for his service during World War II.

Ward returned to Julliard after the war, and he earned his postgraduate certificate in May 1946. He then became a faculty member at the school. He also taught at Columbia University, Queen's College, and Duke University. In addition to teaching, Ward was the executive vice-president and managing editor of Galaxy Music, a publisher of classical music.

Ward's first opera, *Pantaloon*, was put on by the Columbia University Opera Workshop and debuted on May 17, 1956, at Julliard. This was followed by his second opera, *The Crucible*, which debuted in New York City with the New York Opera Company on October 26, 1961. In addition to the Pulitzer, Ward received a number of other honors and awards, including the Cleveland Arts Prize in 1972 and the National Endowment for the Arts Opera Honors award in 2011.

Ward died on April 3, 2013, in Durham, North Carolina. He was ninety-five years old. His wife, Mary, died in 2006. Ward is survived by his two daughters, Melinda and Johanna; three sons, Mark, Jonathon, and Timothy; eleven grandchildren; and three great grandchildren.

*See Current Biography Illustrated 1963.*

# David S. Ware

**Born:** Plainfield, New Jersey; November 7, 1949
**Died:** New Brunswick, New Jersey; October 18, 2012
**Occupation:** American jazz saxophonist and composer

David S. Ware was a notable figure in jazz music, an industry that produces few stars. By the end of his career, he established himself not only as a master of the saxophone, but a respected musician and composer.

Known for his big, distinctive sound and improvisational talent, Ware was associated with major music labels—Columbia, Fidelity, DIW—and produced over twenty-five albums. He is also celebrated for reviving the culture of "free jazz," an approach to jazz that replaces conventional chord changes and tempos with experimental and avant-garde improvisation, in New York City. Ware's band, the David S. Ware Quartet, was considered by Gary Giddins, a notable jazz critic, to be "the best small jazz band."

Ware first picked up an alto saxophone at the age of nine and would later transition to tenor sax, his instrument of choice. He would continue to develop his skills on the tenor saxophone and go on to study, albeit briefly, at Berklee College of Music in Boston, Massachusetts. During his time at Berklee, Ware met the pianist Cooper-Moore, with whom he would later play in Apogee, a free jazz-group in the 1970s. By the 1980s, Ware was a prominent figure within small circles of jazz musicians, but he did not become a widely recognizable figure in the music world until twenty years after the start of his career. Throughout the 1980s and most of the 1990s, for instance, he was a cab driver in New York City to support himself.

But after recording for DIW, a Japanese record label, in 1997, Ware was signed with Columbia records. During this time, his performances in New York City were becoming more regular and attracting a larger audience. As his popularity increased, he recorded ten albums for Fidelity Records from 2001 onward.

Ware was diagnosed with kidney failure in 1999, and, after living on dialysis for many years, his health began to decline. He received a kidney transplant on May 12, 2009. After the surgery, he made a successful return to the music scene and performed many solo concerts in the New York City area. He continued to suffer from health complications, however, and eventually developed a severe blood infection

On October 18, 2012, Ware died at Robert Wood Johnson University Hospital in New Brunswick, New Jersey, from complications stemming from his kidney. He was sixty-two years old. Ware is survived by his wife, Setsuko, and his sister, Corliss Olivia Farrar.

*See Current Biography 2003.*

# Earl Weaver

**Born:** St. Louis, Missouri; August 14, 1930
**Died:** Caribbean Sea; January 19, 2013
**Occupation:** American baseball manager

A chain-smoking firebrand known for his chess-like approach to the game, Earl Weaver was the manager of the Baltimore Orioles from 1968–82, and again from 1985–86. He had a lifetime winning percentage of .583, the ninth highest of any manager to ever field a team. A man of diminutive stature, the prone-to-outburst Weaver was often called "the little genius." His strategic mind for baseball was legendary—almost as legendary as his tantrums. By the end of his career, Weaver had been ejected by officials ninety-eight times. The Hall of Famer's first retirement came in 1982, marked by a "Thanks, Earl Day" celebration, complete with a telegram

of congratulations from President Ronald Reagan. But two and a half years later, Orioles manager Joe Altobelli was fired, and owner Edward Bennett Williams entreated Weaver to return. His second and final retirement came at the end of the 1986 season, which saw the club finish with a record of 73–89—the only losing season in Weaver's career with the Orioles.

Born in St. Louis, Missouri, on August 14, 1930, Earl Sidney Weaver was the son of a dry cleaner who counted the Browns—now the Baltimore Orioles—and the Cardinals among his customers. Weaver became enthralled with baseball at an early age and eventually drew contract offers from both the local major league teams. But Weaver wasn't the strongest player, and ended up spending two decades in the minor leagues starting in 1948 when he signed with the Cardinals. He began to play less often and started taking on more managerial responsibilities. In 1957 he was hired by the Orioles as their Fitzgerald, Georgia, rookie player-manager; he stopped playing altogether in 1960. He was promoted to the majors as a first base coach in April 1968, and replaced Hank Bauer as manager that July. In all, he won 1,480 games as manager of the Orioles.

Weaver died on a baseball-themed cruise in the Caribbean. His death was confirmed on January 19, 2013. He was eighty-two. He leaves behind his second wife, as well as a son, two daughters and one stepdaughter, seven grandchildren, and three great-grandchildren.

*See Current Biography Illustrated 1983.*

# Joe Weider

**Born:** Montreal, Quebec; November 29, 1919
**Died:** Los Angeles, California; March 23, 2013
**Occupation:** Canadian bodybuilder and publisher

Joe Weider was a Canadian bodybuilder and entrepreneur who helped found Weider Publications, which publishes some of the world's most popular bodybuilding and fitness magazines, including *Muscle and Fitness*, *Shape*, and *Flex*. Weider served as the publisher's president and CEO. He also established, along with his brother, Ben, the International Federation of Body Builders (IFBB), one of the largest bodybuilding organizations in the world today. The IFBB sponsors celebrated bodybuilding competitions such as Mr. Olympia, Mr. Universe, and Ms. Olympia. In addition to his successful business ventures, Weider also promoted the careers of Hollywood stars such as Sylvester Stallone, Arnold Schwarzenegger, and Lou Ferrigno, who played the Incredible Hulk.

Weider was born in Montreal, Canada, on November 29, but the exact year of his birth is not known as all of his records were lost in a fire (the year of his birth is believed to be in the range of 1919 to 1923). In his autobiography, *Brothers of Iron* (2006), which was co-authored with his brother, Ben, and Mike Steere, Weider recalled how he was a small, scrawny teenager who was bullied by the kids in his neighborhood. He also described how his determination to become a bodybuilder was fueled by his experience of being bullied: "I got sick and tired of putting my head down and walking away to avoid trouble . . . I needed some muscle." He turned his passion for bodybuilding into a lucrative career, and by the young age of nineteen his fitness newsletter, *Your Physique*, was being sold throughout the United States and Canada.

By the 1950s, Weider was publishing sixteen magazines, and he began to sell fitness equipment and dietary supplements through a mail-order business. By the 1990s, his products were being sold in more than sixty countries and his company's annual gross was reported to be hundreds of millions dollars. His success, however, was not only financial—he helped make bodybuilding a celebrated sport and promoted health and fitness worldwide by means of his magazines and products. Weider was the recipient of many awards, including the United States Sports Academy's Dwight D. Eisenhower Fitness Award (1992), and the Publisher of the Year Award, from the Periodical Book Association (1983).

On March 23, 2013, Weider died at his home in Los Angeles, California, from heart failure. He was ninety-three years old. Weider divorced his first wife, Vicky Uzra, in 1960 and married the former Betty Brosmer in 1961. He is survived by Betty; his daughter, Lydia Ross; and his three grandchildren.

*See Current Biography 1998.*

few dramatic roles—*The Hoodlum Saint* (1946), *The Unguarded Moment* (1956)—were ill-received by audiences and critics alike.

Esther Jane Williams was born on August 8, 1921 in Inglewood, California. She was the youngest of five siblings. Her older brother Stanton was a silent movie star whose income accounted for much of the family's funds. Williams learned to swim at the age of eight, taking a job counting wet towels at the neighborhood pool to pay for swimming time. The Los Angeles Athletic Club asked Williams to join its swim team at the age of fifteen, and in 1939, she won her first round of competitive titles including three gold medals at the national championships, which secured her a spot on the 1940 United States Olympic team. Williams's chance at Olympic stardom was dashed, however, when the 1940 games were cancelled due to the outbreak of World War II.

A brief stint in Billy Rose's Aquacade at the Golden Gate International Exposition in San Francisco marked Williams's first foray into professional show business, and in 1941, Louis B. Mayer of MGM approached her about taking up acting. For her first role, she was cast in 1942's *Andy Hardy's Double Life*. Audiences loved her and her acting career took off. By the early 1960s, however, Williams's acting career was on the decline and she retired from the screen, though she went on to endorse a swimwear collection as well as a line of aboveground pools.

Williams died in her sleep on June 6, 2013, in Beverly Hills, California. She was ninety-one. Williams is survived by her fourth husband, Edward Bell; two children from a previous marriage; three stepsons, including the actor Lorenzo Lamas; three grandchildren; and eight step-grandchildren.

*See Current Biography 1955.*

## Esther Williams

**Born:** Inglewood, California; August 8, 1921
**Died:** Beverly Hills, California; June 6, 2013
**Occupation:** American swimmer and actor

A one-time Olympic swimming hopeful who found greater success in Hollywood, Esther Williams was Metro-Goldwyn-Mayer's leading lady in a streak of aquatic-themed films during the 1940s and '50s. Known more for her athletic, swimsuit-clad build than her acting prowess, Williams's films were often flighty comedies of error, carried by elaborate swimming sequences set to music. She starred alongside MGM's top male stars in such movies as 1945's *Thrill of a Romance*, playing opposite Van Johnson, and 1952's *Million Dollar Mermaid*, with Victor Mature. In a career defined by light fare, Williams's

## Kenneth Geddes Wilson

**Born:** Waltham, Massachusetts; June 8, 1936
**Died:** Saco, Maine; June 15, 2013
**Occupation:** American physicist

Kenneth Geddes Wilson was awarded a Nobel Prize in physics (1982) for developing a general theory to explain and calculate the behavior of substances on a particle level as they undergo phase transitions. Wilson's work revealed the universal applicability of an existent calculation method called the renormalization group. He applied his methods to quantum field theory, significantly advancing the understanding of the elementary particles that make up everything.

On June 8, 1936, Kenneth Geddes Wilson was born in Waltham, Massachusetts. His father was a National Medal of Science–winning professor of chemistry at Harvard and his maternal grandfather was a professor of mechanical engineering at Massachusetts Institute of Technology. At the age of sixteen, Wilson enrolled in Harvard's mathematics program and took physics courses outside his major. He graduated from the university with a bachelor's degree in 1956, and subsequently began working on his doctorate at the California Institute of Technology, where he studied physics with Nobel laureate Murray Gell-Mann until 1960.

In 1963, Wilson began his tenure at Cornell University in Ithaca, New York, accepting a position in the physics department. Wilson conducted his Nobel-winning work at Cornell, and met his wife, Alison Brown, there as well when they both attended one of Ithaca's famed folk dances. In the late 1980s, Wilson and Brown moved to Ohio State University. She became the assistant director of a new supercomputer center there, and he was instrumental in founding the school's Physics Education Research Group.

The couple moved to Maine in 1995, but Wilson remained associated with Ohio State until his retirement in 2008. Wilson died on June 15, 2013, at his home in Saco, Maine. He was seventy-seven. His survivors include Brown; his stepmother, Thérèse Wilson; and his siblings, David Wilson, Nina Cornell, Anne Goldizen, Paul Wilson, and Steven Wilson.

*See Current Biography 1983.*

# Jonathan Winters

**Born:** Dayton, Ohio; November 11, 1925
**Died:** Montecito, California; April 11, 2013
**Occupation:** American comedian

Jonathan Winters was an American comedian known for his improvisational comedy and impressions of various colorful characters. In addition to stand-up comedy, he appeared in films such as *The Russians Are Coming, the Russians Are Coming* (1966) and *It's a Mad, Mad, Mad, Mad World* (1963). Winters was also a regular on late-night television programs—*The Tonight Show* and *The Steve Allen Show*—and had his own television shows, including *The Jonathan Winters Show* (1956–57). Winters was an inspiration for celebrities and comedians such as Steve Martin and Jim Carrey, and he was a mentor to Robin Williams, who said in an interview for *60 Minutes* that Winters taught him that, "the world is open for play, that everything and everybody is mockable, in a wonderful way."

Winters was born in Dayton, Ohio on November 11, 1925. He was seventeen years old when he left high school in 1943 to join the US Marine Corps during World War II. After the war, he studied art at Kenyon College and

the Dayton Art Institute, where he met Eileen Schauder. Winters and Schauder were married in 1948.

Winters, with his wife's encouragement, abandoned his career in art and entered a talent contest in Dayton, which he won (the grand prize was a wrist watch) and was subsequently hired at a Dayton radio station. After moving to New York in 1953, he began appearing in commercials and television shows, as well as performing stand-up comedy in nightclubs. In his comedy shows, he did impressions of various characters such as B. B. Bindlestiff, a small-town tycoon, and perhaps his most memorable: Maude Frickert, a cranky grandmother who would later be featured in commercials for Hefty garbage bags. One of his best-known television roles was the character Mearth in the sci-fi sitcom *Mork and Mindy* (1978–82), which starred Robin Williams and Pam Dawber.

Winters died on April 11, 2013, at his home in Montecito, California. He was eighty-seven years old. His wife, Eileen, died in 2009. Winters is survived by his son, Jonathan Winters IV; his daughter, Lucinda; and his grandchildren.

*See Current Biography 1965.*

# Carl R. Woese

**Born:** Syracuse, New York; July 15, 1928
**Died:** Urbana, Illinois; December 30, 2012
**Occupation:** American microbiologist

Carl R. Woese rewrote the book on evolutionary biology. In two papers published in 1977, Woese and his colleagues introduced a "third domain" of life called archaea—dismissing the long held notion that all life on Earth could be lumped into the categories of bacteria and everything else. Woese's work focused largely on comparing genetic sequences in protein-building ribosomes.

Carl Richard Woese was born in Syracuse, New York. He attended Amherst College and graduated in 1950 with dual undergraduate degrees in physics and math. In 1953, Woese earned his PhD in biophysics from Yale. For his postdoctoral education, he spent two years studying medicine at the University of Rochester and several years working as a biophysics researcher at Yale. He accepted a position at the General Electric Research Laboratory in Schenectady, New York, as biophysicist in 1960. In 1964, Woese became a professor of microbiology at the University of Illinois at Urbana-Champaign where he would continue to teach for the balance of his career.

Woese was the recipient of many distinguished honors, including a MacArthur Foundation grant (1984), the Leeuwenhoek Medal

(1992), and the National Medal of Science (2000). The Royal Swedish Academy of Sciences presented Woese with the Crafoord Prize in Biosciences in 2003 for his discovery of archaea.

Woese died at his home in Urbana, Illinois, on December 30, 2012. He was eighty-four. He is survived by his wife, Gabriella; a sister, Donna Daniels; and two children, Robert and Gabriella.

*See Current Biography 2003.*

# Jane Cooke Wright

**Born:** New York, New York; November 30, 1919
**Died:** Guttenberg, New Jersey; February 19, 2013
**Occupation:** American oncologist

Dr. Jane Cooke Wright was an American oncologist and a pioneer of chemotherapy techniques and treatments for cancer patients. She was the director of the Harlem Hospital Cancer Research Foundation and a faculty member at the New York University Medical Center. In 1967, she became a professor of surgery and associate dean of the cancer chemotherapy department at New York Medical College, which at the time was the highest-ranking position held by an African American woman at a medical institution in the United States.

Wright was born on November 30, 1919, in New York City. She came from a family of doctors: Her father, Dr. Louis T. Wright, was one of the first African Americans to graduate from Harvard Medical School; her grandfather was a graduate of Nashville's Meharry Medical College, the first medical institution to train African American doctors in the South. After graduating from Smith College in North Hampton, Massachusetts, in 1942, Wright attended the New York Medical College on a full scholarship. She graduated from medical school in 1945 and began her career in cancer research at the Harlem Hospital Cancer Research Foundation, which was established by her father. Here, she researched a variety of anticancer drugs, including triethylene melamine, a drug used in chemotherapy. Wright became the director of the center after her father's death in 1952.

Wright joined the faculty of the New York University Medical Center in 1955, where she was the director of cancer chemotherapy research. One of her accomplishments at NYU was working with a team that developed a non-surgical method to administer anticancer drugs to areas of certain organs, such as the spleen, that were hard to treat with previous methods. She was also an assistant professor at NYU and, starting in 1961, an adjunct associate professor of research surgery. In 1967, Wright became a professor of surgery and associate dean at her alma mater, New York Medical College. In addition to her administrative duties as associate dean, she also directed a new cancer research laboratory at the school that studied anticancer drugs.

Wright was among the seven doctors who founded the American Society of Clinical Oncology (ASCO), where she served as secretary-treasurer from 1964 to 1967. She was also appointed by President Lyndon B. Johnson to the President's Commission on Heart Disease, Cancer, and Stroke. In 2011, The ASCO and the Conquer Cancer Foundation honored Dr. Wright's contribution to the field of oncology by establishing the Jane C. Wright, MD, Young Investigator Award.

Wright died on February 19, 2013, at her home in Guttenberg, New Jersey. She was ninety-three years old. Her husband, David D. Jones, died in 1976. Wright is survived by her two daughters, Jane and Alison, and her sister, Dr. Barbara Wright Pierce.

*See Current Biography 1968.*

# Zao Wou-ki

**Born:** Beijing, China; February 13, 1921
**Died:** Nyon, Switzerland; April 9, 2013
**Occupation:** Chinese French painter

As an expatriate in France, artist Zao Wou-ki brought an Eastern aesthetic to Western abstraction, and was one of the most commercially successful and highly regarded Chinese painters of his time. Known for abstract works that seemed to craft barely there landscapes from explosions of color and light, Zao drew inspiration from painters like Paul Klee, Jackson Pollock, and Franz Kline. His paintings—which in 2011, totaled $90 million in sales—can be found in private collections across Asia, and in museums like New York's Museum of Modern Art, the Guggenheim, and the Tate Modern.

Born in Beijing on February 13, 1921, to a wealthy family, Zao, with the encouragement of his father, began to study art at an early age, attending the Hangzhou School of Fine Arts. After studying under Lin Fengmian—a figurehead of modern Chinese painting who was imprisoned during the Cultural Revolution—he began to work as a teacher at the Hangzhou School, leaving for Paris in the late 1940s, just before the Communists came to power in China. In Paris, Zao flourished and was welcomed by the art community. He became close friends with the likes of artists Joan Miró, and Alberto Giacometti, and the painter and poet Henri Michaux. Early in his career, Zao struggled to define himself as a painter bound by two traditions, Chinese and French. He stated in interviews that he fought to find his own identity on every canvas he painted. But private collectors in Taiwan and Hong Kong began to buy up Zao's paintings in the 1970s, and throughout the next two decades, much of his existing work was sold on the Asian market. By the 2000s, the demand for his paintings from newly moneyed Chinese buyers caused prices to skyrocket. A Zao piece painted in 1968 sold at auction to Chinese buyers for $8.8 million in October 2011.

Zao, who became a French citizen in 1964, was first appointed to the Legion of Honor in 1984. He was designated a Grand Officer of the Legion of Honor in 2006 by then president Jacques Chirac. He was also honored by the imperial family of Japan in 1994 with the Praemium Imperiale. Zao died on April 9, 2013, in Nyon, Switzerland from complications of Alzheimer's disease. Zao was married three times, and is survived by his third wife, Françoise Marquet, and a son from a previous marriage.

*See Current Biography 2001.*

# CLASSIFICATION BY PROFESSION

## ACTIVISM
Carter, Majora
Karman, Tawakkol
Khan, Daisy
Walla, Kah
Wise, Tim

## AGRICULTURE
Allen, Will

## ARCHITECTURE
Arad, Michael

## ART
Euclide, Gregory
Harris, Jonathan
Hirst, Damien
Kapoor, Anish
Liu Bolin
Marchetto, Marisa Acocella
Sacco, Joe
Yuh Nelson, Jennifer

## ASTRONAUTICS
Williams, Sunita

## BUSINESS
Amoruso, Sophia
Bianchini, Gina
Blakely, Sara
Bremmer, Ian
Burke, Brian
Calagione, Sam
Carter, Majora
Frankel, Bethenny
Kaspersky, Eugene
Le, Tan
Milner, Yuri
Naegle, Sue
Ohlsson, Mikael
O'Neill, Jim
Pincus, Mark
Ransom, Victoria
Ruhle, Stephanie
Smolyansky, Julie
Von Tobel, Alexa
Wojcicki, Susan

## COMEDY
Ansari, Aziz
Armisen, Fred
Black, Michael Ian
Dujardin, Jean

## ECONOMICS
O'Neill, Jim

## EDUCATION
Filippenko, Alex
Grotzinger, John
Khan, Salman
Klawe, Maria
Kobilka, Brian
Koller, Daphne
Loeb, Abraham (Avi)
Penrose, Roger
Plantinga, Alvin
Rushkoff, Douglas
Sáenz Ryan, Maritza

## FASHION
Amoruso, Sophia
McNairy, Mark
Raassi, Tala

## FILM
Akhtar, Ayad
Ansari, Aziz
Armisen, Fred
Black, Michael Ian
Campbell, Bruce
Dinklage, Peter
Dujardin, Jean
Evans, Chris
Faith, Paloma
Freeman, Martin
Hamm, Jon
Hemsworth, Chris
Jones, Rashida
Labaki, Nadine
Lavant, Denis
Lawrence, Jennifer
Moss, Elisabeth
Mulligan, Carey
Nolan, Jonathan
Peli, Oren
Spurlock, Morgan
Stone, Emma
Wiig, Kristen
Yuh Nelson, Jennifer

## GASTRONOMY
Andrés, José
Bernstein, Michelle
Calagione, Sam
Colicchio, Tom
De Laurentiis, Giada
Feniger, Susan
Hamilton, Gabrielle
Ripert, Eric

## GOVERNMENT & POLITICS, FOREIGN
Banda, Joyce
Hollande, François
McGuinty, Dalton
Mulcair, Thomas
Persad-Bissessar, Kamla
Walla, Kah

## GOVERNMENT & POLITICS, U.S.
Bremmer, Ian
Castro, Julián
Cruz, Ted
Gabbard, Tulsi
Gillibrand, Kirsten
Heitkamp, Heidi
King, Angus
Martinez, Susana
Messina, Jim
Ryan, Paul
Verveer, Melanne

## JOURNALISM
Addario, Lynsey
Andrews, Erin
Chang, Juju
Ganim, Sara
Gessen, Masha
Karman, Tawakkol
Navarro Bello, Adela
Nelson, Soraya Sarhaddi
Phillips, Kyra
Ruhle, Stephanie
Sacco, Joe
Silver, Nate
Suskind, Ron
Uygur, Cenk
Yazbek, Samar

## LITERATURE
Akhtar, Ayad
Carle, Eric
de Botton, Alain
Donoghue, Emma
Flynn, Gillian
Hosseini, Khaled
Ives, David
James, E. L.
Marchetto, Marisa Acocella
Sacco, Joe

## MATHEMATICS
Silver, Nate

## MEDICINE
Mukherjee, Siddhartha

## MILITARY
Sáenz Ryan, Maritza

## MUSIC
Beam, Sam (Iron and Wine)
Black Keys, The
Bonamassa, Joe
Case, Neko
Epworth, Paul
Faith, Paloma
Goulding, Ellie
Higdon, Jennifer
Jepsen, Carly Rae
Keb' Mo'
Koz, Dave
LaMontagne, Ray
Levine, Adam
Luger, Lex (Lexus Arnel Lewis)
Meyers, Anne Akiko
Minaj, Nicki
Miranda, Lin-Manuel
Monáe, Janelle
Núñez, Francisco J.
O'Connor, Mark
Weilerstein, Alisa

## NONFICTION
Andrés, José
Bell, Rob
Bremmer, Ian
de Botton, Alain
De Laurentiis, Giada
Feniger, Susan
Gessen, Masha
Hamilton, Gabrielle
Isaacson, Walter
Keen, Andrew
McGonigal, Jane
Mukherjee, Siddhartha
Plantinga, Alvin
Rushkoff, Douglas
Silver, Nate
Wise, Tim
Yazbek, Samar

## ORGANIZATIONS
Isaacson, Walter
Karumba, Christine
Kerger, Paula
Khan, Daisy
Khan, Salman
Novogratz, Jacqueline
Verveer, Melanne

## PHILOSOPHY
Plantinga, Alvin

## PHOTOGRAPHY
Addario, Lynsey
Steinmetz, George

**RADIO**
Uygur, Cenk

**RELIGION**
Bell, Rob
Francis
Khan, Daisy

**SCIENCE**
Filippenko, Alex
Grotzinger, John
Keasling, Jay
Kish, Daniel
Klawe, Maria
Kobilka, Brian
Koller, Daphne
Loeb, Abraham (Avi)
Mukherjee, Siddhartha
Penrose, Roger
Yamanaka, Shinya

**SPORTS**
Allen, Will
Aymar, Luciana
Azarenka, Victoria
Bloom, Jeremy
Burke, Brian
Carlsen, Magnus
Catchings, Tamika
Dickey, R. A.
Eto'o, Samuel
Fanning, Mick
Griner, Brittney
Harper, Bryce
Hunter, Billy
Jones, Jon
Lin, Jeremy
Love, Kevin
May-Treanor, Misty
McCutchen, Andrew
Mutai, Geoffrey
Newton, Cam
O'Brien, Bill
O'Sullivan, Ronnie
Pastrana, Lyn-Z Adams
Soni, Rebecca
Stamkos, Steven
Suh, Ndamukong
Taylor, Katie
Trout, Mike
Walsh Jennings, Kerri
Watson, Bubba
Wiggins, Bradley

**TECHNOLOGY**
Bianchini, Gina
Bloom, Jeremy
Ezarik, Justine
Harris, Jonathan
Ive, Jonathan
Kaspersky, Eugene
Keen, Andrew
Le, Tan
McGonigal, Jane
Mullenweg, Matt
Persson, Markus
Pincus, Mark
Ransom, Victoria
Rossy, Yves
Von Tobel, Alexa

**TELEVISION**
Andrews, Erin
Ansari, Aziz
Armisen, Fred
Black, Michael Ian
Chang, Juju
Colicchio, Tom
De Laurentiis, Giada
Dinklage, Peter
Ezarik, Justine
Feniger, Susan
Frankel, Bethenny
Freeman, Martin
Hamm, Jon
Jones, Rashida
Moss, Elisabeth
Parsons, Jim
Phillips, Kyra
Ruhle, Stephanie
Vergara, Sofía
Wiig, Kristen

**THEATER**
Akhtar, Ayad